REUTTER'S

THE LAW OF PUBLIC EDUCATION

SIXTH EDITION

By

CHARLES J. RUSSO
Panzer Chair in Education and Adjunct Professor of Law
University of Dayton

FOUNDATION PRESS

2006

THOMSON
—————
WEST

© 1970, 1976, 1985, 1994, 2004 FOUNDATION PRESS
© 2006 By FOUNDATION PRESS
        395 Hudson Street
        New York, NY 10014
        Phone Toll Free 1–877–888–1330
        Fax (212) 367–6799
        foundation-press.com
Printed in the United States of America

ISBN–13: 978–1–59941–058–6
ISBN–10: 1–59941–058–3

 TEXT IS PRINTED ON 10% POST CONSUMER RECYCLED PAPER

To Debbie:

With all of my love, now, always, and forever.

*

PREFACE

As with past editions, the Sixth Edition of *Reutter's The Law of Public Education* is designed to provide basic knowledge of the law affecting public education in the United States. The textual material covers principles and patterns of law that apply to a variety of aspects of public education. This edition incorporates important recent developments into the conceptual framework that has been present since the First Edition in 1970.

In addition to including citations to about 400 cases from 2004 and 2005 and substantive discussions of many of these disputes, this Sixth Edition includes two noteworthy substantive modifications. First, material from chapter 4, which focused on local school boards, was removed and joined to text that was moved from chapter 13's treatment of student rights; these sections were combined to form a new chapter 12, Compulsory Attendance, Curriculum, and Other Instructional Issues. Second, chapter 5, which covered board procedures, was joined to the remaining part of chapter 4 to form a chapter on school boards. Chapters 5 through 11 were then renumbered to reflect these changes. Of course, citations throughout continue to include references to West's *Education Law Reporter*, thereby making it easier for instructors, students, and other readers to locate cases.

The cases cited in the more than 3,500 footnotes as well as in the notes-on-cases were selected as the most authoritative and representative illustrations of applicable law. This screening should enhance the book's usefulness as a reference volume and starting point for further research. Moreover, while recognizing that they are of extremely limited precedential value, this edition includes a very limited number of citations to cases from WESTLAW and the Federal Appendix, referring to these disputes typically for the underlying issues involved rather than their holdings as substantive points of law. Except for chapter 1, which is designed for those who are unfamiliar with the general operation of the law and American legal system, each chapter focuses on the legal aspects of an area in education. As there is some necessary overlapping between and among the chapters, the Table of Contents and the Index should help users to locate the information that they need.

The principal cases at the end of the chapters provide opportunities to examine judicial reasoning on major issues. The cases were edited to improve readability by deleting material unimportant to themes of education law, yet to preserve flavor as well as continuity. Omissions, except for citations, are marked. Cases were selected for their precedential value based on the substantive questions that they addressed and collectively to illustrate judicial thinking in a manner intended to enhance readers' understanding of the issues and principles that they examined. Where possible, the text continues to rely on cases from the United States Supreme

Court. Except for chapter 2, which presents cases chronologically, since doing so provides a better sense of the development of the Supreme Court's Establishment Clause jurisprudence, generally appear in the same order as they are discussed in the text.

The Sixth Edition strives to analyze and synthesize judicial interpretations of constitutions, statutes, regulations, and the common law in an objective manner while avoiding personal value judgments. I have continued the approach of Professors Reutter and Hamilton in hoping that readers will concern themselves ultimately not only with what the law is, but with what it should be. Insofar as making intelligent legal decisions depends on knowledge of the law itself, I hope that this book will provide students and practitioners of education law with the information that will help them to make the best judgments possible.

ACKNOWLEDGMENTS

As with any book of this magnitude, there are many people to be thanked. I would like to thank individuals in five different groups. First, I would like to thank Professor E. Edmund Reutter for the confidence that he displayed in offering me the opportunity to work on a book that meant so much to him and his good friend Professor Hamilton. I greatly appreciate the chance to keep the book current and hope that I have "made him proud."

Second, I would like to thank the professionals at Foundation Press, led by its Publisher, Mr. John Bloomquist, in Eagan, Minnesota, for his support through the process of writing and editing. I would also like to thank John's predecessor, Mr. Steve Errick. Thanks, too, to Mr. James D. Coates, Principal Attorney Editor and Ms. Sharon Pizzi, Principal Editor, at Foundation's headquarters in Minnesota for their invaluable assistance in preparing the manuscript for publication. It has been a pleasure working with all of these professionals. Needless to say, I look forward to continuing to work together on future editions.

Third, I would like to express my gratitude to colleagues who served as reviewers of the text: Dr. Ralph Sharp at East Central University, Ada, Oklahoma; Dr. Georges Fouron of the State University of New York at Stony Brook; Dr. Allan G. Osborne, Jr., Principal of Snug Harbor Elementary School in Quincy, Massachusetts (especially for his generous assistance on the law of special education); Dr. Jerry Horgen, Adjunct Professor, Capella University, in Minneapolis, Minnesota; Mr. William E. Thro, Solicitor General of the Commonwealth of Virginia (especially for his generous assistance on the Eleventh Amendment); and Dr. Jack P. Lipton, Partner and Chair of the Education Law Practice Group at Burke, Williams & Sorensen, LLP in California, and Adjunct Professor at Southwestern University School of Law. I greatly appreciate all of the assistance that these dedicated professionals provided in making useful suggestions and comments on the content of the chapters that they read as their efforts helped me to focus on these chapters. I would like to extend a special note of thanks to Dr. Ralph Sharp who went above and beyond the call of duty, virtually from the moment that I started planning for the Sixth Edition, shortly after the publication of the Fifth Edition, for his constant support as he read, and we discussed, a variety of issues pertaining to topics in the book.

Fourth, at the University of Dayton, I would like to thank Dr. Thomas J. Lasley, Dean, and Dr. Dan Raisch, Associate Dean, of the School of Education and Allied Professions, and Dean Lisa Kloppenberg in our School of Law. In addition, I would be remiss if I did not offer special thanks to Rev. Joseph D. Massucci, my Chair in the Department of Educational Leadership. The friendship and support of these friends helped to make the writing process easier. I would also like to thank Ms. Marianne E. Graham, University of Dayton School of Law, class of 2007, for her assistance in cite-checking the many footnotes and other references throughout the book. Thanks, too, to Ms. Jody Thornburg of the Education Law Association, housed here at the University of Dayton, for her editing of the text. Further, I would like to thank Ms. Colleen Wildenhaus and Ms. Cheryl Marcus, both at the University of Dayton, for their assistance in proofreading the text. A special thanks is in order for my assistant, Ms. Elizabeth Pearn at the University of Dayton for her help proofreading and preparing the manuscript for publication.

Last, and certainly not least, keeping in mind the often-cited maxim of Supreme Court Justice Joseph Story, that the law " ... is a jealous mistress and requires a long and constant courtship ... , " I would like to take this opportunity to express my undying love and devotion to my wife, Debbie, and our children, David and Emily, for allowing me to take the time away from our family life to work on this book. I would also like to thank Debbie for her loving, and generous, assistance in helping to locate the *Education Law Reporter* cites for all of the cases in the book. I am truly blessed to have such a wonderful, loving family.

April 2006

SUMMARY OF CONTENTS

*

TABLE OF CONTENTS

TABLE OF CONTENTS

TABLE OF CONTENTS

*

TABLE OF LEGAL TOPICS ILLUSTRATED BY CASES

Case Number

*

TABLE OF CASES

Principal cases are in bold type. Non-principal cases are in roman type. References are to Pages.

TABLE OF CASES

c

Reutter's

THE LAW OF PUBLIC EDUCATION

*

Chapter 1

LEGAL FRAMEWORK FOR PUBLIC EDUCATION

Introduction

Public schooling in the United States is an arm of the state that is charged with the duty of preparing children to become productive members of society.[1] As a prelude to a discussion of legal issues that arise in public elementary and secondary schools, it is important to acknowledge that a large and ever-growing body of law regulates the actions of educational officials. At the same time, it is worth noting that Education (or School) Law, as this area of study is known, is but one part of a much larger collection of laws dealing with governmental operations that affect the daily responsibilities of educators. To this end, this chapter examines the sources and types of laws in the American legal system and discusses how these laws impact the daily operations of public schools.

The Common Law

In medieval England, legal scholars and practitioners devoted a great deal of time and attention to the "discovery" of law, based on their belief that the laws of nature were available to deal with problems if only they could be found.[2] As the modern study of law emerged, lawyers and scholars focused a great deal of effort analyzing judicial decisions from all parts of the realm in order to uncover the widely held view of the natural law. Contemporaneously, professional communities in London, the Inns of Court, which Churchill described as "half colleges, half law schools ... produced annual law reports or Year Books"[3] that judges began to recognize as authoritative. In this way, common law, also referred to as judge made law, the basis for precedent, was "discovered" as a result of litigation. The "discovered" common law stood in contrast to the enacted laws of constitutions and statutes.

The legal system in the United States, sometimes referred to as the Anglo–American system of jurisprudence, evolved out of English common law. As customs became accepted bases of conduct, they were

---

1. For a history of urban education, with a focus on the "one best system" for educating all children, *see* DAVID B. TAYAK, THE ONE BEST SYSTEM: A HISTORY OF URBAN AMERICAN EDUCATION (1974).

2. BLACKSTONE'S COMMENTARIES (circa 1760) embraced this belief; the Declaration of Independence shares this approach. To-

day a concept such as "widespread agreement" would be more likely to be invoked as a basis for the values underlying the law.

3. 1 WINSTON S. CHURCHILL, HISTORY OF THE ENGLISH SPEAKING PEOPLES 176–177 (1956).

distilled into principles that courts enunciated in specific cases. These judicial pronouncements formed English and, later, American common law. As the courts tended to follow their earlier decisions, the doctrine of *stare decisis*, literally, "to abide by," also referred to as precedent or *res judicata*, literally, "a matter judged," emerged. *Stare decisis* stands for the proposition that once a court has resolved an issue, the question is ordinarily not revisited. However, as a flexible principle, *stare decisis* permits the judiciary to revisit issues such as where the Supreme Court's opinion in *Brown v. Board of Education (Brown)*[4] repudiated the pernicious doctrine of "separate but equal" that it enunciated in *Plessy v. Ferguson.*[5] Even so, by relying on precedent, judges instilled a degree of certainty and predictability in legal proceedings. Moreover, by basing their judgments on the collected wisdom of earlier cases, judges did not have to "re-invent the wheel" whenever a new, or seemingly new, legal issue arose. Rather, judges could rely on these older judicial opinions in resolving disputes.

The greater part of American law remains heavily indebted to the common law. Among the many areas that evolved from common law are the rights and responsibilities of parents in caring for their minor children; the authority of school officials to act *in loco parentis*, literally, "in place of the parents," when dealing with students; the elements of contracts; the essentials of torts; the principles of land ownership; and a myriad of other legal concepts. Accordingly, the fundamental principles governing many aspects relating to the daily operation of public schools are not the result of statutory or constitutional provisions but exist by virtue of the common law.

The Federal Constitution

Simply stated, the Constitution of the United States is the law of the land. Put another way, all federal statutes and regulations, state constitutions, state laws and regulations, ordinances of local governmental units, and school board rules are subject to the Constitution as interpreted by the Supreme Court. In addition to serving as the source of American law, the Constitution creates three co-equal branches of the federal government, each of which is discussed further in the following sections. Article I of the Constitution delineates the power of Congress, the legislative body that is charged with the responsibility of "making" law. Article II explains the role of the President, the chief executive, who exercises the authority to enforce the laws passed by Congress, chiefly through regulations promulgated by various federal departments and agencies. Article III sets forth the power of the courts, which are responsible for interpreting the law. As a democratic republic, state constitutions in the United States, which are supreme in their own jurisdictions as long as they do not vary from or contradict the Federal Constitution, create governmental systems that reflect the structure of

---

4. 347 U.S. 483, 74 S.Ct. 686, 98 L.Ed. 873 (1954) [Case No. 123].

5. 163 U.S. 537, 16 S.Ct. 1138, 41 L.Ed. 256 (1896).

the federal government and operate in essentially the same manner as their federal counterparts.

In setting forth the duties of the federal government, and distinguishing its role from that of state governments, four types of powers emerge in the United States Constitution. Article I, Section 8, contains the enumerated powers that only the federal government can exercise;[6] among these powers are "to provide for the common Defence and general welfare of the United States ... [t]o regulate Commerce with foreign Nations, and among the several States ... [t]o coin Money, and regulate the value thereof ... [t]o promote Post Offices ..., [and] [t]o constitute Tribunals inferior to the Supreme Court."

Over time, the second set of powers, implied powers, those that are reasonably needed to effectuate the express authority of the federal government, emerged. For example, in providing for minting of coins and other currency, the federal government has the implied authority to create the Department of Treasury and such bureaucracies as it deems necessary to exercise this responsibility.

As discussed below under the Tenth Amendment, the third set of powers, reserved, are those not delegated to the United States by the Constitution nor prohibited by it to the States or to the people. From the perspective of the study of Education Law, the most important reserved power is education because despite its coverage of a wide area of powers, duties, and limitations, the Constitution is silent with regard to education. The absence of any mention of education in the Constitution notwithstanding, it is worth noting that the earliest federal enactment addressing schooling is the Northwest Ordinance of 1787, which encourages the creation of schools and the means of education.[7]

The final type of power, concurrent, is shared by both the federal and state governments. The most noteworthy example of a concurrent power is taxation, in that both levels of government can impose on and collect tax from their residents.

School-related litigation generally involves relatively few sections of the Constitution. The amendments protecting individual rights are the sections of the Constitution that impact most dramatically on schools. The restrictions on Congressional power and the States that most frequently come before the courts are Article I, Sections 8 and 10, as well as the First, Fourth, Fifth, and Fourteenth Amendments.

One key provision of Article I, Section 8, is the Commerce Clause, which the Supreme Court has applied with interesting results. For example, in *Katzenbach v. McClung*,[8] a non-school case, the Court

---

6. *See* THE FEDERALIST No. 45, at 292 (James Madison) (Clinton Rossiter ed., 1961). "The powers delegated by the proposed Constitution to the federal government are few and defined."

7. According to Article 3 on the Northwest Ordinance, "Religion, morality, and knowledge, being necessary to good govern- ment and the happiness of mankind, schools and the means of education shall forever be encouraged." SOUL OF AMERICA: DOCUMENTING OUR PAST, VOL. I: 1492–1870 86 (Robert C. Baron ed., 1994).

8. 379 U.S. 294, 85 S.Ct. 377, 13 L.Ed.2d 290 (1964).

broadly interpreted Congressional authority under the Civil Rights Act of 1964 in helping to eliminate racial discrimination in restaurants. After generally deferring to Congressional authority pursuant to the Commerce Clause since 1937,[9] for the first time in almost sixty years, in *United States v. Lopez*,[10] the Court struck down federal legislation, the Gun–Free School Zones Act, on the basis that Congress exceeded its authority in relying on the Commerce Clause in attempting to limit the flow of guns into public schools. Five years later, in *United States v. Morrison*,[11] albeit set in higher education, the Court again struck down a federal statute, the Violence Against Women Act, after a student was viciously raped by three members of her university's football team, on the basis that it did not involve interstate commerce. In a telling comment on the relationship between the Court and Congress that reflects part of the difference between members of the Court who are strict constructionists and those who are activists, a topic that is discussed a bit more below, Chief Justice Rehnquist's majority opinion observed that "[d]ue respect for the decisions of a coordinate branch of Government demands that we invalidate a congressional enactment only upon a plain showing that Congress has exceeded its constitutional bounds."[12] Of course, the majority thought that Congress clearly exceeded its power.

Contracts Clause

Early in American history, political leaders recognized that the need to preserve the integrity of contracts was of paramount importance. The Framers of the Constitution acknowledged that unless contractual agreements between parties could be relied on without possible subsequent modifications or abrogation by state laws, the national economy could neither progress nor develop. To this end, Article I, Section 10, provides in part that "no State shall ... pass any ... law impairing the obligation of contracts." This provision is involved when state legislatures seek to change teachers' tenure rights, salaries, or retirement benefits to the possible detriment of individuals who acquired vested status under the law. In analyzing legal disputes of this type, one of the important considerations that courts must consider is whether relationships between public school officials and educators are contractual. If relationships are contractual, such as under collective bargaining agreements, then school boards or state officials may not make changes without the risk of having violated Article I, Section 10, of the Constitution.

---

9. Starting with *NLRB v. Jones & Laughlin Steel Corp.*, 301 U.S. 1, 57 S.Ct. 615, 81 L.Ed. 893 (1937), the Court afforded Congress considerably greater latitude in regulating conduct and transactions under the Commerce Clause than under its earlier case law.

10. 514 U.S. 549, 115 S.Ct. 1624, 131 L.Ed.2d 626 [99 Educ. L. Rep. 24] (1995).

11. 529 U.S. 598, 613, 607, 120 S.Ct. 1740, 146 L.Ed.2d 658 [144 Educ. L. Rep. 28] (2000). The Court went on to explain that that "[g]ender-motivated crimes of violence are not, in any sense of the phrase, economic activity.... We accordingly reject the argument that Congress may regulate noneconomic, violent criminal conduct...."*Id.* at 598.

12. *Id.* at 607.

The Bill of Rights

Once the Constitution took effect, it became apparent to political leaders that they may have created a federal government that, unless its powers were restricted, might have ignored the civil rights of individual citizens. In order to offer a counterbalance to the authority of the federal government, the Framers of the Constitution proposed ten amendments, comprising the so-called Bill of Rights, to guarantee personal rights. Article V delineates the process for amending the constitution. The Bill of Rights was ratified and added to the Constitution in 1791. The following discussion highlights the amendments that are most relevant for education.

First Amendment

The First Amendment was designed to insure certain basic personal freedoms or civil rights in declaring that:

> Congress shall make no law respecting an establishment of religion, or prohibiting the free exercise thereof; or abridging the freedom of speech, or of the press; or the right of the people peaceably to assemble, and to petition the Government for a redress of grievances.

The initial clause of the First Amendment, which reads that "Congress shall make no law respecting an establishment of religion, or prohibiting the free exercise thereof," has been subject to vast amounts of litigation in the context of public, and non-public, education. Under the second part of this clause, every individual has the fundamental right to worship according to the dictates of personal conscience, free from government intervention. Although the First Amendment's restrictions concerning religion relate solely to the power of Congress, the Supreme Court extended this protection to the States through its interpretation of the Fourteenth Amendment.[13] As discussed primarily in Chapter 2, the Religion Clauses of the First Amendment have been involved in two categories of cases involving schools: those overseeing the use of public funds to aid students in religiously affiliated non-public schools and those involving a wide array of prayer and/or religious activities in public schools.

Litigants in educational settings have regularly invoked the First Amendment's freedom of speech clause since the 1960's. Most of the case law over the free speech rights of students and teachers substantively involved expression, whether spoken, written, or symbolic. The amount of attention devoted to the rights of assembly and petition and the derivative right of association in connection with employee organizations such as unions to engage in concerted actions designed to influence

---

13. *Cantwell v. State of Conn.*, 310 U.S. 296, 303, 60 S.Ct. 900, 903, 84 L.Ed. 1213 (1940). *But see Barron v. Mayor and City Council of Baltimore*, 32 U.S. 243, 8 L.Ed. 672 (1833) (holding that the Bill of Rights was inapplicable to the States because its history indicated that it was limited in force to the federal government).

educational policies, especially those affecting working conditions, has decreased in recent years. Consequently, this remains a fruitful area of litigation.

Fourth Amendment

The Fourth Amendment forbids unreasonable searches and seizures, asserting that warrants "describing the place to be searched, and the persons or things to be seized" can be issued only "upon probable cause," a high standard that ordinarily applies in criminal, rather than civil, cases. The Fourth Amendment has been contested in more than two hundred school cases since the Court first applied it in an educational setting in *New Jersey v. T.L.O.*[14] Additionally, the Fourth Amendment is sometimes mentioned in connection with the right of privacy, a concept that is also associated with the notion of liberty in the Fourteenth Amendment.

Fifth Amendment

The Fifth Amendment provides protection for persons who are accused of crimes:

> No person ... shall be compelled in any criminal case to be a witness against himself, nor be deprived of life, liberty, or property, without due process of law; nor shall private property be taken for public use, without just compensation.

The final clause in the Fifth Amendment is relevant in cases where state officials or local school boards attempt to acquire property for school building sites. The next to the last clause provides due process with regard to the acts of the federal government. The remainder of this section is implicated in matters encompassing possible crimes such as illegal dealings involving school funds or property. Even so, it is worth noting that school operations typically involve civil, rather than criminal, matters.

Tenth Amendment

Insofar as education is not mentioned in the Constitution, it is a function of the States under the Tenth Amendment:

> The powers not delegated to the United States by the Constitution, nor prohibited by it to the States, are reserved to the States respectively, or to the people.

The Constitution's silence with regard to education should not be interpreted as meaning that it does not affect schooling. Beginning largely with *Brown v. Board of Education*, the Supreme Court, soon to be followed by lower federal courts, recognized that constitutional rights,

---

14. 469 U.S. 325, 105 S.Ct. 733, 83 L.Ed.2d 720 [21 Educ. L. Rep. 1122] (1985) [Case No. 108]

such as equal protection under the Fourteenth Amendment, have a major impact on schooling. Consequently, as the courts and Congress have taken a more active role in education, the number of cases involving federal Constitutional and statutory questions increased dramatically since *Brown*.

Eleventh Amendment

According to the Eleventh Amendment:

The Judicial power of the United States shall not be construed to extend to any suit in law or equity, commenced or prosecuted against one of the United States by Citizens of another State, or by Citizens or Subjects of any Foreign State.

The adoption of the Constitution "did not disturb States' immunity from private suits, thus firmly enshrining this principle in our constitutional framework."[15] The widespread acceptance of the proposition "that the Constitution would not strip the States of sovereign immunity"[16] can be seen in the reaction to *Chisholm v. Georgia (Chisholm)*,[17] wherein the Supreme Court held that private citizens from one State could sue another State.[18] Almost immediately, Congress passed and the States ratified the Eleventh Amendment, effectively overturning *Chisholm* and restoring a concept that derived in part from the common-law tradition coupled with constitutional design.

The Eleventh Amendment's being facially limited to the "provisions of the Constitution that raised concerns during the ratification debates and ... *Chisholm* ..."[19] aside, it confirms the broader notion that States are immune from suit. Further, the Eleventh Amendment bars suits against a variety of entities, including corporations created by the federal government,[20] and applies in such important venues for education as state courts[21] and federal administrative proceedings.[22]

As broad as sovereign immunity is, it is not absolute since it permits five exceptions. First, under extraordinary circumstances, Congress may abrogate the sovereign immunity of States[23] but must do so explicitly.[24]

---

15. *Federal Maritime Comm'n v. South Carolina State Ports Auth.*, 535 U.S. 743, 752, 122 S.Ct. 1864, 152 L.Ed.2d 962 (2002).

16. *Alden v. Maine*, 527 U.S. 706, 716, 119 S.Ct. 2240, 144 L.Ed.2d 636 (1999).

17. 2 U.S. 419, 2 Dall. 419, 1 L.Ed. 440 (1793).

18. The Court explicitly acknowledged that *Chisholm* was wrong. *See Federal Maritime Comm'n*, 535 U.S. at 752–53; *Alden*, 527 U.S. at 721–22.

19. *Alden v. Maine*, 527 U.S. 706, 723, 119 S.Ct. 2240, 144 L.Ed.2d 636 (1999).

20. *Smith v. Reeves*, 178 U.S. 436, 20 S.Ct. 919, 44 L.Ed. 1140 (1900).

21. *Alden v. Maine*, 527 U.S. 706, 712, 119 S.Ct. 2240, 144 L.Ed.2d 636 (1999).

22. *Federal Maritime Comm'n v. South Carolina State Ports Auth.*, 535 U.S. 743, 760, 122 S.Ct. 1864, 152 L.Ed.2d 962 (2002).

23. *Fitzpatrick v. Bitzer*, 427 U.S. 445, 96 S.Ct. 2666, 49 L.Ed.2d 614 (1976). *But see Seminole Tribe of Fla. v. Florida*, 517 U.S. 44, 116 S.Ct. 1114, 134 L.Ed.2d 252 (1996) (affirming that Congress lacked authority under the Indian Commerce Clause to abrogate the States' Eleventh Amendment immunity).

24. *Dellmuth v. Muth*, 491 U.S. 223, 109 S.Ct. 2397, 105 L.Ed.2d 181 [53 Educ. L. Rep. 792] (1989) (noting that since Con-

Second, States may waive their sovereign immunity.[25] Third, by invoking the jurisdiction of the federal courts, States expose themselves to the equivalent of compulsory counterclaims that do not exceed the amounts or differ in kind from the relief they seek.[26] Fourth, federal courts generally may order state officials, in their official capacities, to conform their conduct to federal law.[27] Finally, "States, in ratifying the Constitution, did surrender a portion of their inherent immunity by consenting to suits brought by sister States or by the Federal Government."[28]

Fourteenth and Fifth Amendments

Section 1 of the Fourteenth Amendment defines citizenship, specifying privileges that citizens of the United States and other persons share:

> All persons born or naturalized in the United States, and subject to the jurisdiction thereof, are citizens of the United States and of the State wherein they reside. No State shall make or enforce any law which shall abridge the privileges or immunities of citizens of the United States; nor shall any State deprive any person of life, liberty, or property, without due process of law; nor deny to any person within its jurisdiction the equal protection of the laws.

The last two clauses of the Fourteenth Amendment have widespread applicability to public education. The Fourteenth Amendment's next-to-last clause, the Due Process Clause, has perhaps been construed more frequently than any other provision of the Constitution with regard to schooling. The final clause, the Equal Protection Clause, has also received wide attention in educational disputes.

The Fourteenth Amendment's Due Process Clause, enacted in 1868, applies to the States. Conversely, the Fifth Amendment's Due Process Clause, according to which "[n]o person shall ... be deprived of life, liberty, or property, without due process of law ..." applies to the federal government. The Supreme Court recognized the difference between the Fifth and Fourteenth Amendment when, on the same day that it struck down segregated schooling in *Brown* based on the Equal Protection Clause, it relied on the Fifth Amendment's Due Process Clause in vitiating the practice in *Bolling v. Sharpe* (*Bolling*),[29] a dispute which originated in the Nation's capital. The Court applied the Fifth,

gress can abrogate States' immunity only by making its intention unmistakably clear in a statute's language, it did not do so under the then Education for All Handicapped Children's Act, now the Individuals with Disabilities Education Act). However, Congress essentially overturned this decision in the stature. *See* 20 U.S.C.A. § 1403(a) "A State shall not be immune under the 11th amendment to the Constitution of the United States from suit in Federal court for a violation of this chapter."

25. *College Sav. Bank v. Florida Prepaid Postsecondary Educ. Expense Bd.*, 527 U.S. 666, 119 S.Ct. 2219, 144 L.Ed.2d 605 [135 Educ. L. Rep. 362] (1999).

26. *See, e.g., Oklahoma Tax Comm'n v. Citizen Band Potawatomi Indian Tribe of Okla.*, 498 U.S. 505, 111 S.Ct. 905, 112 L.Ed.2d 1112 (1991).

27. *Ex parte Young*, 209 U.S. 123, 28 S.Ct. 441, 52 L.Ed. 714 (1908); *Frew ex rel. Frew v. Hawkins*, 540 U.S. 431, 124 S.Ct. 899, 157 L.Ed.2d 855 (2004).

28. *Federal Maritime Comm'n v. South Carolina State Ports Auth.*, 535 U.S. 743, 752, 122 S.Ct. 1864, 152 L.Ed.2d 962 (2002).

29. 347 U.S. 497, 74 S.Ct. 693, 98 L.Ed. 884 (1954).

rather than the Fourteenth, Amendment in *Bolling* because public schools in Washington, D.C., are under the control of Congress and hence the federal government.

Due process includes a pair of distinct aspects that may be viewed as the two sides of a coin. Substantive due process pertains to the rights that Americans have whether under the constitution or specific legislative (or regulatory) enactments. Under this concept, a law must both have a purpose within the legitimate power of government and be rationally related to the accomplishment of that goal. Put another way, as reflected in the ensuing discussion of equal protection, substantive due process protects individuals against grossly unfair acts of government. On the other hand, procedural due process pertains to the decision-making process followed in evaluating whether a law has been violated. Pursuant to this provision, those purporting to implement a law must apply basic fairness. More specifically, individuals who may suffer deprivations must be informed of what they are accused of and must be offered the opportunity to defend their actions before a fair and impartial third-party decision-maker.

Individuals who have substantive due process rights, such as tenured teachers, are automatically entitled to procedural due process. Conversely, individuals, such as non-tenured teachers, who do not enjoy substantive due process rights are not entitled to procedural due process unless it is conferred on them by collective bargaining contracts or state law.

At the heart of equal protection is the notion that individuals or groups that "are similarly situated should be treated alike."[30] In other words, all within a classification must be accorded the same rights and privileges while being subjected to the same duties. Per se classifications are also subject to closer examination. They must be based on differences relevant to the subject and not prohibited by law. The government's failure to follow these principles can result in unlawful discrimination.

Under equal protection analysis, the general constitutional test for acceptability of a criterion for classification is whether it is rationally related to a legitimate governmental purpose.[31] There is very strong, but rebuttable, presumption that a criterion established through the legislative process is constitutional.[32] At the other end of the continuum, when legislation or an act of a governmental official or body allegedly infringes on a fundamental constitutional right (such as one that is mentioned explicitly in the Constitution including freedom of religion or speech or

30. *Cleburne v. Cleburne Living Ctr.*, 473 U.S. 432, 439, 105 S.Ct. 3249, 87 L.Ed.2d 313 (1995).

31. The Supreme Court declared that "... if a law neither burdens a fundamental right nor targets a suspect class, we will uphold the legislative classification so long as it bears a rational relation to some legitimate end." *Romer v. Evans*, 517 U.S. 620, 632, 116 S.Ct. 1620, 134 L.Ed.2d 855 [109 Educ. L. Rep. 539] (1996).

32. *See Hazelwood School Dist. v. Kuhlmeier*, 484 U.S. 260, 273, 108 S.Ct. 562, 98 L.Ed.2d 592, 43 Educ. L. Rep. 515 (1988) [Case No. 113] "... [w]e hold that educators do not offend the First Amendment by exercising editorial control over the style and content of student speech in school-sponsored expressive activities so long as their actions are reasonably related to legitimate pedagogical concerns."

that is implicitly there as declared by the Supreme Court), or disadvantages a suspect class by categorizing individuals based on a constitutionally "suspect" factor (such as race), a legislatively protected category (such as age in some situations), the courts apply the "strict scrutiny" test and are unlikely to uphold such a classification unless it is based on compelling justification.[33] Suspect classes are clearly defined groups that require extraordinary protection from the majoritarian political process because they have been subjected purposefully to unequal treatment or are relegated to a position of virtual political powerlessness. More specifically, under strict scrutiny analysis, the burden shifts to the government to demonstrate that there is a compelling need for such a classification. Further, even if a restriction is permissible, it must be as narrowly drawn as possible. If a court applies the so-called compelling interest test, a governmental classification, or action, is likely to fail.

Some classifications, such as illegitimacy and gender, fall into a third, in-between, category and continue to be subject to heightened judicial scrutiny. In limited circumstances, the Court has adopted an intermediate standard of review that is not as difficult for the government to meet as the compelling interest test but which involves less deference to legislation than does the rational relations test. Under this test, the Court will not uphold a classification unless it has a "substantial relationship" to an "important" government interest.[34]

As noted earlier, the Supreme Court interpreted the First Amendment as applying to the States through the Fourteenth Amendment.[35] Consequently, restrictions under the First and Fourteenth Amendments must be considered along with limits on state constitutions when examining the validity of state statutes or local school board rules. As to funding non-public schools, for example, courts must take both the First and Fourteenth Amendments into consideration. In *Everson v. Board of Education*,[36] the plaintiff unsuccessfully raised the Fourteenth Amendment's prohibition against using public funds for private purposes. The Court pointed out that the First Amendment's relevant bar is against using public funds for religious purposes, a subcategory of private purposes.[37] The Fourteenth Amendment has been applied in a wide variety of educational disputes such as those dealing with the rights of parents to direct the education of their children,[38] teachers who are

33. For a notorious example of a case wherein the Court allowed a race-based classification to survive strict scrutiny, *see Korematsu v. United States*, 323 U.S. 214, 65 S.Ct. 193, 89 L.Ed. 194 (1944) (upholding the interment of Japanese–Americans during World war II based on their ancestry).

34. The case that comes closest to applying this standard in a school setting was *Plyler v. Doe*, 457 U.S. 202, 102 S.Ct. 2382, 72 L.Ed.2d 786 [4 Educ. L. Rep. 953] (1982), *reh'g denied*, 458 U.S. 1131, 103 S.Ct. 14, 73 L.Ed.2d 1401 (1982), even though the majority did not clearly indicate

that it was applying this test. [Case No. 102]

35. *See Cantwell v. State of Conn.*, 310 U.S. 296, 303, 60 S.Ct. 900, 903, 84 L.Ed. 1213 (1940).

36. *Everson v. Board of Educ.*, 330 U.S. 1, 67 S.Ct. 504, 91 L.Ed. 711 (1947), *reh'g denied*, 330 U.S. 855, 67 S.Ct. 962, 91 L.Ed. 1297 (1947). [Case No. 1]

37. *See* the discussion of *Lemon v. Kurtzman*, 403 U.S. 602, 91 S.Ct. 2105, 29 L.Ed.2d 745 (1971) and its progeny in Chapter 2. [Case No. 6]

38. *See, e.g., Meyer v. Nebraska*, 262 U.S. 390, 43 S.Ct. 625, 67 L.Ed. 1042 (1923).

subject to dismissal,[39] student discipline,[40] and challenges to racial segregation.[41]

Federal Statutes and Regulations

Pursuant to the Tenth Amendment, education is a constitutional power reserved to the States.[42] Even so, Congress retains the authority to enact laws under the general welfare clause of Article I, Section 8,[43] by offering funds for purposes that it deems to serve the public good. Beginning in the 1960's, Congress enacted a series of statutes, such as the Civil Rights Act of 1964,[44] which subjects public school systems to its anti-discrimination in employment provisions that have had a profound effect on public education.[45]

Many of the federal statutes that directly and substantially impact public education make federal funds available to state and local governments conditioned on their observing specified prescriptions for the use of the money. By way of illustration, in order to receive funding for special education under the Individuals with Disabilities Education Act,[46] states, in and through state and local educational agencies, have had to develop detailed procedures to identify children with disabilities and offer each qualified child a free appropriate public education in the least restrictive environment.

In another example of federal involvement in education, in 2002, Congress enacted the No Child Left Behind Act (NCLB), as one of the

39. *See, e.g., Cleveland Board of Education v. Loudermill*, 470 U.S. 532, 105 S.Ct. 1487, 84 L.Ed.2d 494 [23 Educ. L. Rep. 473] (1985). *On remand*, 763 F.2d 202 [25 Educ. L. Rep. 158] (6th Cir.1985), *on remand*, 651 F.Supp. 92 [37 Educ. L. Rep. 502] (N.D.Ohio 1986), *aff'd*, 844 F.2d 304 [46 Educ. L. Rep. 523] (6th Cir.1988), *cert. denied*, 488 U.S. 941, 109 S.Ct. 363, 102 L.Ed.2d 353 (1988), *cert. denied*, 488 U.S. 946, 109 S.Ct. 377, 102 L.Ed.2d 365 [50 Educ. L. Rep. 15] (1988). [Case No. 85]

40. *See, e.g., Goss v. Lopez*, 419 U.S. 565, 95 S.Ct. 729, 42 L.Ed.2d 725 (1975). [Case No. 107]

41. *See, e.g., Brown v. Board of Educ.*, 347 U.S. 483, 74 S.Ct. 686, 98 L.Ed. 873 (1954) [Case No. 123].

42. *Epperson v. State of Ark.*, 393 U.S. 97, 104, 89 S.Ct. 266, 21 L.Ed.2d 228 (1968) [Case No. 6] ("By and large, public education in our Nation is committed to the control of state and local authorities. Courts do not and cannot intervene in the resolution of conflicts which arise in the daily operation of school systems and which do not directly and sharply implicate basic constitutional values. On the other hand, '[t]he vigilant protection of constitutional freedoms is nowhere more vital than in the community of American schools,' (internal citations omitted))."

43. According to this section: "The Congress shall have Power to ... provide for ... [the] general welfare of the United States."

44. 42 U.S.C.A. § 2000e–2a [popularly known as "Title VII," its designation in the Civil Rights Act of 1964, made applicable to public schools in 1972].

45. Federal statutes, which consist of fifty titles, are published in the United States Code, abbreviated U.S.C. The unofficial version., the United States Code Annotated, published by Thomson–West, abbreviated U.S.C.A., included useful annotations, or brief summaries of all cases that have cited federal statutes. In addition to WESTLAW and LEXIS, both of which are available by subscription, federal statutes can be found in a variety of on-line websites. *See, e.g.,* http://www.gpoaccess.gov/uscode/ (official website of the Government Printing Office); http://thomas.loc.gov/home/bills_res.html (official website of the Library of Congress).

46. 20 U.S.C.A.§§ 1400 *et seq.* See Chapter 14 for a full discussion of this far-reaching statute.

most controversial of federal education statutes.[47] According to the NCLB's far-ranging provisions, states that receive federal financial assistance must take steps to improve academic achievement among students who are economically disadvantaged; assist in preparing, training, and recruiting "highly qualified" teachers (and principals); provide improved language instruction for children of limited English proficiency; make school systems accountable for student achievement, particularly by imposing standards for annual yearly progress for students and districts; require school systems to rely on teaching methods that are research based and that have been proven effective; and afford parents better choices while creating innovative educational programs, especially if local school systems are unresponsive to their needs.[48]

If a state accepts federal funds, educational officials are bound by whatever conditions Congress has attached to the legislation. If challenged, a federal court must be satisfied that a condition passes constitutional muster. In 1987, Congress expanded its authority by defining a "program or activity" as encompassing "all of the operations of [an entity] any part of which is extended Federal financial assistance."[49] This broad general prohibition covers "race, color or national origin,"[50] "sex,"[51] and "otherwise qualified handicapped individuals,"[52] categories that have become increasingly important in school settings.

Regulations promulgated by the Federal Department of Education and other administrative agencies afford the executive branch the opportunity to enforce statutes by carrying out their full effect.[53] In other words, while statutes set broad legislative parameters with regard to, for example, compulsory attendance, regulations permit administrative agencies to fill in necessary details such as the amount of time that children must be in class and the subject matter that they need to study in order to satisfy the law. Within their ambits, regulations are presumptively valid and are truly laws as are acts of Congress.

State Constitutions

Subject to the supremacy of the United States Constitution and federal statutes, state constitutions form the basic law of individual

---

47. 20 U.S.C.A. §§ 6301 *et seq.*

48. Two federal trial courts rejected claims that the NCLB creates private rights of actions in parents and private service providers, respectively, who opposed its provisions. *See Association of Community Org. v. New York*, 269 F.Supp.2d 338 [179 Educ. L. Rep. 661] (S.D.N.Y. 2003); *Fresh Start Academy v. Toledo Bd. of Educ.*, 363 F.Supp.2d 910 [197 Educ. L. Rep. 275] (N.D. Ohio 2005) while a third dismissed a suit alleging that it was an unfunded federal mandate. *See School Dist. of the City of Pontiac v. Spellings*, 2005 WL 3149545 (E.D. Mich. 2005).

49. Civil Rights Restoration Act, 20 U.S.C.A. § 1687.

50. 42 U.S.C.A. § 2000d [known as Title VI, its designation in the Civil Rights Act of 1964].

51. 20 U.S.C.A. § 1681 [known as Title IX, its designation in the Education Amendments of 1972].

52. 29 U.S.C.A. § 794 [known as Section 504, its designation in the Rehabilitation Act of 1973].

53. Federal regulations are published in the Code of Federal Regulations, abbreviated C.F.R. In addition to Westlaw and Lexis, both of which are available by subscription, federal statutes can be found in a variety of on-line websites. *See, e.g.,* http://www.gpo-access.gov/cfr/index.html (official website of the Government Printing Office).

states. The primary function of state constitutions is to restrict the powers of state legislatures, which have complete legislative authority except as restricted by federal law or state constitutions. State constitutions may require legislatures to perform certain acts, most notably for the purpose of this book such as establishing public educational systems, and may forbid certain acts such as using a state's credit to support private ventures.

State constitutions typically deal with many of the same matters as their federal counterpart, particularly in the areas of church-state relations and individual freedoms. Consistent with equal protection analysis, states may, for example, provide more, but not fewer, bars to governmental relations with religious bodies than are mandated by the Federal Constitution. Further, states may also provide more, but not fewer, rights to teachers and students than are required by the Federal Constitution.

To the extent that a state constitution is a direct product of the people, no legislature, as is also the case with Congress, has sole authority to amend a state constitution. Indeed, a legislature itself is a creature of the constitution. To this end, it follows that a legislature has no authority to amend the document that gives it existence. Procedures for amending state constitutions are found within those documents. Normally, amending a constitution is a slow process because of the importance of deliberation before changes can be made in such a fundamental legal document.

State Statutes and Regulations

The most abundant source of law affecting public schools is statutes enacted by state legislatures.[54] The courts consistently describe the power of state legislatures over their public school systems as plenary. This, of course, is true only in a relative sense. As discussed above, state legislatures are subject to the limitations of federal law and of state constitutions in their actions as they apply to education, just as is the case with legislation applying to other agencies and segments of society.

Public school systems, along with many other governmental agencies, have become so complex that it is impossible, perhaps even undesirable, to attempt to control their administration in detail by specific legislative enactments. In light of this fact, the law is well settled that state and local boards of education, administrators, and teachers have the authority to adopt and enforce reasonable rules and regulations to ensure the smooth operation and management of schools. As such, rules and regulations are subject to the same constitutional limitations as specific statutes passed by duly constituted legislative bodies. Moreover, it is possible for teachers, through the promulgation of rules or regulations, and in some jurisdictions through opinions of state attorneys general, for classroom management, to violate the civil rights of stu-

54. State statutes and regulations are published in state publications and on-line websites that appear under a variety of titles.

dents. For example, if it is unconstitutional for Congress or state legislatures to enact laws violating the free speech rights of children, it is equally impermissible for teachers to do so by creating rules that apply only in their classrooms. At the same time, it is important to observe that legislation or rule-making on any level, whether federal or state, cannot conflict with higher authority. For instance, a local school board cannot require parents and/or students to pay fees if state law prohibits the practice.

The Courts

In General

Constitutional provisions, statutes, and regulations are not self-executing. Rather, they merely permit or require respective government agencies, including educational systems, to engage in or avoid specific actions. If individuals or bodies affected by a particular provision think that it is being improperly implemented, they may turn to the courts to settle the controversy. Insofar as the judiciary cannot act on its own initiative, the courts can intervene only when parties initiate litigation.

The duty of the courts is to interpret the law. If there is no codified law, or a statute or regulation is unclear, courts apply common law. Insofar as common law is a judicial creation, the courts may adjust it to changing circumstances. Where legislation is at issue, the task of the courts is to uncover, as far as possible, the intent of the legislative body that enacted a law. In many cases, it is almost impossible to escape the conclusion that courts are obliged to impute to a legislature the intent that they believe that the lawmakers would have had if the matter had been called specifically to their attention. In reaching their judgments, the courts cannot avoid taking economic, political, social, educational, and perhaps other implications of the cases before them into consideration.

There is a great deal of disagreement between and among legal scholars and the courts as to whether judges should engage in judicial restraint, seeking to interpret constitutional provisions, laws, or regulations as closely as possible to their "original intent" or whether they are free to interpret them more broadly, often according to their own points of view, and so engage in judicial activism.[55] This debate plays itself out frequently in legal battles involving education.

As with the rest of the legal system, the complex American judiciary operates at both the federal and state levels. The most common feature of these systems is a three-tiered system with trial courts, intermediate appellate courts, and courts of last resort, most commonly named supreme courts.

---

55. The first section in Chapter 2 includes a brief discussion of original intent, at least with regard to religion.

Federal Courts

According to Article III, Section 1, of the United States Constitution, "The judicial Power of the United States, shall be vested in one supreme Court, and in such inferior Courts as the Congress may from time to time ordain and establish." Federal litigation typically begins in trial courts, properly known as United States district courts, before possibly proceeding to circuit courts of appeal and the Supreme Court.

Federal jurisdiction is created by acts of Congress. A plaintiff ordinarily has recourse to the federal courts when there is a disagreement over a provision in the Federal Constitution, a federal statute, a federal regulation, or when there is diversity of state residence between litigants.[56] Since the 1960's one provision has perhaps most profoundly affected public education, and other governmental functions, by serving as a basis for suits in federal courts. The statute goes back to the Civil Rights Act of 1871 but was revitalized and utilized as a vehicle for federal court scrutiny of many rules of school authorities pertaining to students or teachers. The law, 42 U.S.C.A. section 1983, is commonly referred to as section 1983:

> Every person who, under color of any statute, ordinance, regulation, custom, or usage, of any State or Territory, subjects, or causes to be subjected, any citizen of the United States or other person within the jurisdiction thereof to the deprivation of any rights, privileges, or immunities secured by the Constitution and laws, shall be liable to the party injured in an action at law, suit in equity, or other proper proceeding for redress.

By invoking section 1983, students or educators who claim the deprivation of a federal constitutional or statutory right, by an act of a school official or by operation of a law or regulation, can often invoke federal jurisdiction. In effect, such plaintiffs can have federal courts address the validity of laws or regulations while adjudicating complaints where federal jurisdiction might otherwise have been difficult to establish. Even so, section 1983 does not require federal courts to resolve all suits in which parties allege that they suffered from unconstitutional deprivations since federal constitutional or statutory questions must exist in substance, not in mere assertions. On the whole, the federal courts have become very receptive to such suits in recent years.

Federal District Courts

Federal trial courts of general jurisdiction, which generally have few limits on the types of cases that they may hear, are named United States

---

56. In suits based on diversity,

"(a) ... district courts shall have original jurisdiction of all civil actions where the matter in controversy exceeds the sum or value of $75,000, exclusive of interest and costs, and is between—

(1) citizens of different States;

(2) citizens of a State and citizens or subjects of a foreign state;

(3) citizens of different States and in which citizens or subjects of a foreign state are additional parties; and

(4) a foreign state, defined in section 1603(a) of this title, as plaintiff and citizens of a State or of different States." 28 U.S.C.A. § 1332.

district courts.[57] Each state contains at least one or more federal trial courts for a total of eighty-nine federal districts in the fifty states; including courts in Puerto Rico, the Virgin Islands, the District of Columbia, Guam, and the Northern Mariana Islands, there are ninety-four United States district courts.[58] From 1910 to 1976, if a party sought to enjoin the enforcement of a state statute on the ground that it violated the Federal Constitution, the dispute was resolved by a special panel composed of three federal district court judges.[59] Appeals from such courts went directly to the Supreme Court. In 1976, Congress sharply curtailed the types of cases that were to be handled in this manner.

Federal Circuit Courts

For most appeals in the federal judicial system, the country is divided into eleven numbered federal circuit courts of appeal, commonly referred to as circuit courts, plus the District of Columbia Circuit.[60] A thirteenth court, the Federal Circuit, has appellate jurisdiction over patents, federal government contracts, federal merit system protection, trademarks, and international trade. (See map on page 17.) Rulings of each circuit are binding on federal trial courts in the states within their ambit and persuasive on other courts.[61] Cases in the circuit courts are usually resolved by three-judge panels. Under special circumstances, all judges in a circuit will review a case in an en banc hearing.[62] Appeals from circuit courts go to the Supreme Court of the United States.[63]

The Supreme Court

As noted, pursuant to Article III, Section 1, of the United States Constitution, "The judicial Power of the United States, shall be vested in one supreme Court...."[64] Even so, it was not until *Marbury v. Madi*

---

57. Published opinions of federal district courts can be found in the Federal Supplement, abbreviated F.Supp., now in its second series, F.Supp.2d. In addition to Westlaw and Lexis, federal cases can be found in a variety of on-line websites. *See, e.g.*, www.uscourts.gov (official website of the federal judiciary); http://www.supreme courtus.gov (official website of the Supreme Court).

58. The list of federal district courts is located at 28 U.S.C.A. §§ 81–131.

59. Such a three member panel was involved in *Goss v. Lopez*, 419 U.S. 565, 95 S.Ct. 729, 42 L.Ed.2d 725 (1975). [Case No. 107]

60. Published opinions of federal circuit courts can be found in the Federal Reporter, abbreviated F., now in its third series, F.3d. Further, cases that are not selected for publication in F.3d are included in the Federal Appendix, abbreviated Fed. Appx. Cases in the Fed.Appx. are of limited precedential value.

61. A list of the states composing each circuit is set forth in 28 U.S.C § 41.

62. *See, e.g., Newdow v. U.S. Congress*, 328 F.3d 466 [176 Educ. L. Rep. 44] (9th Cir. 2003), where the Ninth Circuit refused a request for an en banc panel to reconsider a ruling over the constitutionality of the "the words 'under God' in" Pledge of Allegiance.

63. Chief Justice John Roberts' *2005 Year–End Report on the Federal Judiciary* revealed that [during 2005] [f]ilings in the regional courts of appeal rose 9 percent to an all-time high of 68,473, marking the 10th consecutive record-breaking year and the 11th consecutive year of growth. This increase stemmed from upswings in criminal appeals, original proceedings, and prisoner petitions.... As large as the increase is, it would have been higher had not the Court of Appeals for the Fifth Circuit's operations been affected by Hurricane Katrina. ... http://www.supremecourtus.gov/publicinfo/year-end/2005year-endreport.pdf at 8, n.2.

64. Published opinions of Supreme Court can be found in the United States Reports, abbreviated U.S., published by the Supreme Court; the Supreme Court Report

Federal Judicial Center 1991

son[65] that the Court asserted the authority to review decisions of the other branches of government. This nine-member body is primarily an appellate court.[66] The Court can summarily affirm lower court rulings or dismiss appeals for want of a substantial federal question, rather than decide cases with full opinions after examining the complete record of lower court proceedings, reviewing written briefs that have been submitted by the litigants and other interested parties and hearing oral arguments.

The Supreme Court has discretion to review rulings of lower federal courts and state high courts[67] that involve federal constitutional, statutory, or regulatory issues. When the Court agrees to hear an appeal, it issues a writ of *certiorari*, "to be informed of." In order for the Court to grant *certiorari*, a minimum of four justices must agree to hear an appeal. When a case is resolved, the Court's opinion authoritatively enunciates federal law on the matter while explaining the rationale for its judgment.[68]

State Courts

Each state has its own judicial system established by its constitution and legislature; these systems vary in organization and degree of complexity.[69] State judicial systems generally include a number of inferior courts such as small claims and county courts; these courts exercise limited jurisdiction that is expressly indicated in the laws creating them. Each state has a trial court of general jurisdiction and at least one level of appellate review. However, there is little consistency in the names that states apply to their various levels of court. Most states have two levels of appellate courts. As in the federal system, the first level of

er, abbreviated S.Ct., published by West; and Lawyer's Edition, abbreviated L.Ed, published by Lawyer's Cooperative Publishing Company, now in its second series.

65. 5 U.S. (1 Cranch) 137, 2 L. Ed. 60 (1803).

66. The Court has original jurisdiction, meaning that a case can begin there in limited circumstances. Among the areas over which Article III, Section 2, identifies as being in the Court's original jurisdiction are "Cases affecting Ambassadors ... other public Ministers and Consuls ... to Controversies between two or mote States...."

67. 469 U.S. 325, 105 S.Ct. 733, 83 L.Ed.2d 720 [21 Educ. L. Rep. 1122] (1985), for example, was an appeal from the Supreme Court of New Jersey. [Case No. 108]

68. Chief Justice John Roberts' *2005 Year–End Report on the Federal Judiciary* revealed that

The annual number of case filings in the Supreme Court decreased from 7,814 in the 2003 Term to 7,496 in the 2004 Term—a decrease of 4.1 percent. Filings

in the Court's *in forma pauperis* [literally "in the manner of a pauper," meaning that individuals filed without the ability to pay fees or costs] docket decreased from 6,092 to 5,755—a 5.5% decrease. The Court's paid docket increased by 19 cases, from 1,722 to 1,741—a 1.1 percent increase. During the 2004 Term, 87 cases were argued and 85 were disposed of in 74 signed opinions, compared to 91 cases argued and 89 disposed of in 73 signed opinions in the 2003 Term. No cases from the 2004 Term were scheduled for reargument in the 2005 Term.

http://www.supremecourtus.gov/publicinfo/ year-end/2005year-endreport.pdf at 7.

69. Published opinions of state courts can be found in a variety of sources both in print and on-line. The most widely available source is West's National Reporter System which divides the United States into seven regions: Atlantic, North Eastern, North Western, Pacific, South Eastern, Southern, and South Western; each is in at least its second series.

review, generically referred to as intermediate appellate courts, is typically before a panel of three judges. The highest court in any state is generically referred to as a court of last resort. In states with two levels of appeal, the absolute right of appeal for some cases is only to the intermediate appellate court; most other appeals are by the leave of the court.

State courts are, of course, bound by the United States Constitution and are obliged to apply it in their decisions, which, under limited circumstances, are subject to review by the Supreme Court. On matters of state law, state courts are parallel to their federal counterparts. State courts' interpretations of federal law are subject to review only by the Supreme Court.

Insofar as education is a state function and federal courts exist for federal matters, most educational controversies are handled by state courts. Unless there is a substantial federal question, a case must be tried in a state court. If a substantial federal question is involved with a state question, a case may be heard in either a state or federal court. The increased emphasis on civil rights and liberties, coupled with the use of section 1983, has led to increasing numbers of education cases being decided in federal courts. When federal courts examine cases involving both state and federal law, they must follow interpretations of state law made by the state courts within which they sit.

Judicial Procedures

The procedures of federal and state courts are a complex amalgam of statutes, rules, and common law. Yet, since some basic principles are generally consistent, an overview of these procedures can help one to have a better understanding of education law.

A suit starts when a plaintiff, the party initiating the litigation, files a summons and complaint or, as it is called in some states, a petition, which alleges the facts that are in dispute. The facts are designed to allege that some harm has occurred, that a law is being or has been violated, or that some official or agency is not performing or has not performed a specified legal duty. The party that initiates an action requests a court to grant relief, whether legal (or monetary) damages, equitable (ordering a party to do or not do something), or a combination of the two. A plaintiff may, for example, ask a court to find that a board of education broke a contract and that the aggrieved employee may receive monetary damages for the loss of salary and an order returning the individual to the job. Alternatively, if parents challenge a board of education's actions in not providing educational programming for their child, they may seek an order to obtain such services. If a plaintiff seeks to require a public officer or agency to perform a nondiscretionary duty, the action is to seek a writ of mandamus. If an agency or an individual allegedly is indulging in illegal activity, a plaintiff may ask a court to grant an injunction ordering the party to discontinue the illegal act.

A party may also seek an injunction to maintain the legal status quo by preventing an action that is being contemplated. A permanent injunction is issued after a trial on the merits, meaning the substance of the controversy. A court may grant a preliminary or temporary injunction, pending a matter's full adjudication. A temporary injunction is typically issued when a plaintiff can show that he or she will suffer irreparable harm if relief is not granted at once, that there is a reasonable probability or substantial likelihood of prevailing on the merits, that the threatened injury outweighs the potential harm an injunction would do to the defendant, and that the public interest will not suffer. While a court's rationale on a motion for a preliminary injunction is instructive on the law, it cannot ultimately apply the law to the facts until they are fully set forth at a trial.

Insofar as Article 3 of the Constitution requires courts to resolve real cases or controversies, the judiciary does not ordinarily decide hypothetical cases or provide advisory opinions.[70] Not only must there be a genuine controversy, but a plaintiff must have an individualized legal interest, or standing, in the resolution of a disputed point.[71] Common law precedents grant taxpayers who wish to sue standing when they challenge local school board expenditures. Merely being a taxpayer under common law generally does not grant one standing to sue state-level agencies; further, taxpayer status definitely does not give standing to sue federal agencies. Absent statutory authorization, an individual bringing suit solely to contest a state or federal expenditure must allege some individualized harm, not simply an injury that would be suffered by all citizens or taxpayers.

When a plaintiff challenges a statute or a regulation, it may be questioned either on its face or as applied. A facial challenge involves a claim that a provision is completely invalid and incapable of any legal application. In such a situation, a court is not required to examine the facts of any actual instances of alleged unlawfulness. Conversely, when an attack is on a statute as applied, a court must consider its impact in a specific situation.

As a dispute heads to trial, it passes through several stages. Once the parties have informed each other of what the dispute is over, the case proceeds to discovery. During discovery, the parties seek to narrow the disputed issues for trial. In this way, if the parties agree that a teacher's contract was terminated on a specific date, then the parties can so stipulate and focus on other issues such as the reason for the school board's action. Attorneys ordinarily rely on two tools in discovery:

70. *See, e.g., State v. Self*, 155 S.W.3d 756, 761 [195 Educ. L. Rep. 1019] (Mo. 2005) ("... a constitutional controversy cannot be manufactured in the trial court or on appeal in order to obtain an advisory opinion") (reversing a mother's conviction for knowingly or purposely failing to cause her daughter to attend school regularly). *But see Advisory Opinion to the Attorney Gen.*, 824 So.2d 161 [169 Educ. L. Rep. 449] (Fla. 2002) (offering an advisory opinion upholding the constitutionality of a ballot initiative amending the state constitution to require funding of universal pre-kindergarten programs).

71. *See, e.g., Elk Grove School Dist. v. Newdow*, 542 U.S. 1, 124 S.Ct. 2301 [188 Educ. L. Rep. 17] 159 L.Ed.2d 98 (2004), *reh'g denied*, 542 U.S. 961, 125 S.Ct. 21, 159 L.Ed.2d 851 (2004) (holding that a father's challenge to the words "under God" in the Pledge of Allegiance could not proceed because he lacked standing). [Case No. 15] interrogatories and depositions. An interrogatory consists of a series of written questions prepared by the respective attorneys of both sides that each party must answer. On the other hand, a deposition is an oral statement made in the presence of the attorneys. A deposition can allow a party to refresh his or her memory of events before trial since a fair amount of time may pass between the time that a suit is filed and when it finally makes its way to court. A deposition can also serve as the basis by which to challenge the accuracy of a witness's testimony or to introduce the evidence if a witness is unavailable to appear either due to death or because the person is unable, or unwilling, to attend and the court lacks the authority to compel the individual to appear.

Once a dispute goes to trial, the plaintiff bears the ultimate burden of proof. In civil cases, the general standard of proof is preponderance of the evidence, meaning that the plaintiff must provide evidence that is accorded greater weight than that presented by the defendant. Although discussions of these matters are beyond the scope of this text, in criminal cases, the burden of proof is the much higher "beyond a reasonable doubt" standard. Further, in some civil cases, where experience demonstrates the need for greater certainty, courts may rely on the intermediate standard of "clear and convincing evidence," which is more than a preponderance but less than beyond a reasonable doubt; this applies in such admittedly non-education types of disputes as those involving having individuals declared as mentally incompetent and patent law.

At trial, after a plaintiff has established an initial point, the burden may shift to the defendant to counter inferences by proving another point. For example, if a teacher who is contesting the nonrenewal of an employment contract can prove that an activity protected by the First Amendment was a substantial factor in a school board's decision, it must bear the burden of demonstrating that the teacher's contract would not have been renewed even if the protected activity had not occurred.

A complaint may be dismissed before trial if a judge determines that allegations, should they be eventually proven, would not have legally entitled the plaintiff to the relief requested. Also, a judge may terminate a trial if, after the plaintiff's side has presented its evidence, the court is convinced that even if the evidence were accepted as true, it did not prove the case. If a plaintiff passes these two hurdles, the defense has the opportunity to present its version of the case.

The two key "players" at a trial are the jury and judge.[72] A jury, often referred to as the trier of fact, makes findings of fact in evaluating what occurred and applies them to the law as interpreted by the judge, sometimes called the trier of law, reaching conclusions that culminate in a judgment and a decree specifying the outcome of the litigation. Federal trial courts and some state trial courts hand down written opinions explaining their rationales. Although technically only the parties to a

---

72. According to Article II, Section II of the Constitution, the President "shall nominate and by and with the Advice and Consent of the Senate, shall appoint ... Judges of the supreme Court, and all other officers of the United States...." Depending on state and local law, some judges are elected while others are appointed.

particular case are bound by a trial court's ruling,[73] an opinion becomes part of the common law, indicating what the outcome of a similar case is likely to be unless there are material differences between disputes.

At least one level of appeal is generally available for all civil cases. The party bringing an appeal is generally known as the appellant or petitioner; the opposing party is typically referred to as the appellee or respondent. An appellant attempts to demonstrate that a lower court erred either in its findings of fact, conclusions of law, or both. As to facts, a party may claim that a judge improperly admitted evidence, misinterpreted testimony and exhibits, and/or otherwise incorrectly conducted a trial. As to law, a party may claim that a judge applied the wrong law or misconstrued the law in some fashion in reaching a judgment.

Appellate courts neither hear witnesses nor consider issues that were not raised at trial. Rather, they review the written record of lower court proceedings, including the testimony of the witnesses, examine briefs, and usually hear oral arguments of both parties. As part of the appellate process, both parties submit written arguments known as briefs to the judges in support of their positions. In addition, in many cases, most notably at the Supreme Court, parties that are interested in the outcome of a case can submit so-called *amicus curiae*, "friend of the court," briefs that seek to sway the judges in favor of their positions.

As a result of its deliberations, appellate courts can affirm, reverse, vacate, modify and/or remand earlier judgments. In remanding, or sending cases back to lower courts for further action, appellate panels can direct lower courts to modify their previous decisions or, in cases involving remands to trial courts, can order them to re-try disputes in their entirety. On questions of fact, appellate courts must accept the findings of trial courts unless they are clearly erroneous. Appellate panels must accept the evidence from trial courts because the latter were "on the scene" to observe the parties and witnesses, while appellate courts are limited to evidence in the written records that they review. Yet, as to conclusions of law, appellate courts owe no deference to the reasoning of trial courts and may disagree on the meaning of laws.

The opinion of the majority of judges becomes precedent, the law of the case that is controlling within a jurisdiction. Judges who agree with the ultimate outcome but who do not support all of the reasoning in the majority opinion may file concurring opinions. Judges may also file dissenting opinions that explain their reasons for disagreeing with the majority of the court. Once a majority of judges agrees on an opinion, regardless of the margin of a vote, it becomes precedent in a given jurisdiction. For example, a ruling of the United States Supreme Court is

---

73. A class action involves one or more representatives of a "class" bringing suit on behalf of all members of the group. If a court permits a case to proceed as a class action, the outcome is binding on all members of the class. In order to maintain a class action, the plaintiff class must assert claims that are typical of the class, the question(s) of law must be common to all members of the class, getting all members of the class into the suit individually must be impracticable, and the plaintiff class must adequately protect the interests of all members of the class.

binding on all lower courts while a decision of a state supreme court is binding only in that state.

On occasion, judges include gratuitous statements in their opinions that address rules of law or legal principles that are not directly involved in the resolution of cases. Insofar as these comments, known as *obiter dictum*, "a remark by the way," or *dictum* (*dicta*, in plural) are of no precedential value, judges, lawyers, and students of the law must be careful to distinguish between such voluntary, non-binding comments and a case's holding or rule of law.

The opinions of appellate courts indicate the point or points of law on which they agree, or disagree, with lower courts. The higher a court is in the judicial hierarchy, the more authoritative its opinions. Lower courts are bound by the orders and opinions of higher courts in their jurisdiction. At common law, opinions of courts in one jurisdiction, although not binding precedent on courts in another jurisdiction, are persuasive or non-binding on points that are not treated by their legislatures. Decisions of federal circuit courts are binding on federal trial courts within their jurisdictions and persuasive elsewhere. As there is ultimately only one answer to a question of federal law, the Supreme Court usually grants *certiorari* to resolve disagreements between and among the circuits.[74] Each time a court cites an opinion approvingly, the weight of that case on the matter increases. In the uncommon situation of a plurality, where less than a majority of justices agrees on the same rationale for a decision, the earlier judgment remains in place for the parties but is not binding on other litigants or in other jurisdictions.[75]

Once the highest court in a jurisdiction renders its judgment, its opinion becomes *res judicata*, literally, "a matter judged," such that a party cannot return the matter to court for further litigation. This is true not only for a specific court system, but also between state and federal courts when one system has addressed an issue. Further, *res judicata* bars any attempt to relitigate the same claim under a different theory of recovery.

Postscript

To the extent that this, and all legal textbooks, rely on the legal

74. *Compare, e.g., Sherman v. Community Consol. School Dist. 21 of Wheeling Township*, 980 F.2d 437 [79 Educ. L. Rep. 396] (7th Cir.1992), *cert. denied*, 508 U.S. 950, 113 S.Ct. 2439, 124 L.Ed.2d 658 (1993) (upholding the constitutionality of the Pledge of Allegiance) with *Elk Grove School Dist. v. Newdow*, 542 U.S. 1, 124 S.Ct. 2301 [188 Educ. L. Rep. 17] 159 L.Ed.2d 98 (2004), *reh'g denied*, 542 U.S. 961, 125 S.Ct. 21, 159 L.Ed.2d 851 (2004) (initially striking down the words "under God" in the Pledge as psychologically coercive). [Case No. 15]

75. For plurality decisions, *see, e.g., Regents of the Univ. of Cal. v. Bakke*, 438 U.S. 265, 98 S.Ct. 2733, 57 L.Ed.2d 750 (1978) (permitting a medical school admissions policy that was designed to increase minority enrollment to remain in place); *Mitchell v. Helms*, 530 U.S. 793, 120 S.Ct. 2530, 147 L.Ed.2d 660 [145 Educ. L. Rep. 44] (2000) (upholding the constitutionality of Chapter 2 of Title I, now Title VI, of the Elementary and Secondary Education Act, a far-reaching federal law permitting the loan of instructional materials including library books, computers, television sets, tape recorders, and maps, to non-public schools).

system of citation, this brief postscript is intended for students who are taking their first law course.

As imposing as they may appear, legal citations are actually easy to read. The first number in a citation indicates the volume number where the case, statute, or regulation can be located; the following abbreviation refers to the book or series in which the material may be found; the second number refers to the page on which a case begins or the section number of a statute or regulation; the last part of a citation typically includes the name of the court,[76] and the year in which a dispute was resolved.

The following brief illustrations of how to read citations for cases, statutes, and regulations should help to clarify this material. The citation for *Brown v. Board of Education*, the Supreme Court's monumental ruling that called for equal educational opportunities for all children by ending segregation based on race, 347 U.S. 483, 74 S.Ct. 686, 98 L.Ed. 873 (1954), reveals that it can be found in volume 347 of the United States Reports, the Court's official version, starting at page 483. *Brown* can also be located in volume 74 of West's Supreme Court Reporter, beginning on page 686, and volume 98 of the Lawyer's Edition, published by Lawyers Cooperative Publishing Company, starting on page 873. Of course, *Brown* was decided in 1954.

The advantage of the unofficial versions is that in addition to the entire text of the Court's opinions, the publishers provide valuable research tools and assistance, in the forms of headnotes that make it easier to engage in legal research, for attorneys, educational practitioners, and students of the law.

Turning to a statute, the Individuals with Disabilities Education Act (IDEA), 20 U.S.C.A. §§ 1400 *et seq.*, can be found in title 20 of the United States Code starting at section 1400. Further, the IDEA's regulations are located at 300 C.F.R. §§ 300.1 *et seq.*, meaning that they are in title 300 of the Code of Federal Regulations, starting at section 300.1.

---

76. An exception applies to the Supreme Court as the name of the reporter suffices in this regard.

Chapter 2

CHURCH–STATE RELATIONS
IN EDUCATION

Introduction

The First Amendment became part of the United States Constitution when it was ratified in 1791 as part of the Bill of Rights. Yet, the Supreme Court did not address a case involving religion and public education on the merits of a First Amendment claim until 1947 in *Everson v. Board of Education (Everson)*.[1] In the years since *Everson*, the Court has resolved more cases dealing with the religion clauses of the First Amendment than any other subject. Further, the Court refused to review or affirmed without opinion many lower court cases and resolved disputes in other realms of church-state relations that have implications for public education.[2]

According to the religion clauses of the First Amendment, "Congress shall make no law respecting an establishment of religion, or prohibiting the free exercise thereof." Insofar as the First Amendment explicitly prohibits only Congress from making laws establishing religion, in 1940, the Court applied the provisions of the First Amendment to the states through the Fourteenth Amendment.[3] To this end, individuals are afforded the same rights in suits against the federal or state governments with regard to the establishment of religion.

In addressing First Amendment religion cases, the Court created confusion over the appropriate judicial standard. Initially, the Court created a two-part test in *School District of Abington Township v. Schempp* and *Murray v. Curlett*[4] to review the constitutionality of prayer and Bible reading in public schools. The Court subsequently expanded this two-part test into the tripartite Establishment Clause standard in

---

1. 330 U.S. 1, 67 S.Ct. 504, 91 L.Ed. 711 (1947), *reh'g denied*, 330 U.S. 855, 67 S.Ct. 962, 91 L.Ed. 1297 (1947). [Case No. 1]

2. *See, e.g., Employment Div., Dep't of Human Resources of Or. v. Smith (Smith)*, 494 U.S. 872, 886, 110 S.Ct. 1595, 1600, 108 L.Ed.2d 876 (1990) (in upholding the dismissal of drug counselors who ingested peyote as part of a sacramental ritual in the Native American Church, a legally organized religious movement that was recognized by the federal government, declaring that "generally applicable, religion-neutral laws that have the effect of burdening a particular religious practice need not be justified by a compelling government interest);" *City of Boerne v. Flores*, 521 U.S. 507, 117 S.Ct. 2157, 138 L.Ed.2d 624 (1997)

(striking down the Religious Freedom Restoration Act because, in creating a statutory remedy that was essentially eliminated in *Smith*, Congress exceeded the enforcement provision of section 5 of the Fourteenth Amendment).

3. *Cantwell v. Connecticut*, 310 U.S. 296, 60 S.Ct. 900, 84 L.Ed. 1213 (1940). Previously, in *Barron v. Mayor and City Council of Baltimore*, 32 U.S. 243, 8 L.Ed. 672 (1833) the Court held that the Bill of Rights was inapplicable to the states because its history revealed that it was limited to the federal government.

4. 374 U.S. 203, 83 S.Ct. 1560, 10 L.Ed.2d 844 (1963). [Case No. 4]

Lemon v. Kurtzman (*Lemon*),[5] a dispute involving government aid to religiously affiliated non-public schools.

When the Court applied the *Lemon* test in cases involving aid and religious activity, its failure to explain how, or why, this test had become a kind of "one-size fits all" measure left lower courts, commentators, and school officials seeking clarity. This confusion is exacerbated because as membership on the Supreme Court changes, its jurisprudence on the status of state aid to non-public schools and religious activity in public schools, however broadly these terms are construed, is also subject to modification. For example, in *Agostini v. Felton*,[6] the Court modified the *Lemon* test by reviewing only its first two parts, purpose and effect, while recasting entanglement as one criterion in evaluating a statute's effect. Moreover, in *Lee v. Weisman*,[7] the Court enunciated the so-called psychological coercion test when addressing prayer in schools while in *Lynch v. Donnelly*,[8] a non-school case, the Court discussed what one justice described as the endorsement test when dealing with religious activity in the public marketplace of ideas.

Appeals to history over the original intent of the Establishment Clause fail to provide clear answers, stemming largely from the fact that close ties between religion and government began during the colonial period.[9] Rather than engage in a lengthy discussion of the different approaches to the Establishment Clause, suffice it to say that two major camps emerged at the Supreme Court and elsewhere in the federal judiciary: separationists and accommodationists. On the one hand are supporters of the Jeffersonian[10] metaphor that calls for maintaining a "wall of separation" between church and state,[11] language that does not appear in the constitution; this is the perspective most often associated

---

5. 403 U.S. 602, 91 S.Ct. 2105, 29 L.Ed.2d 745 (1971). [Case No. 7]

6. 521 U.S. 203, 117 S.Ct. 1997, 138 L.Ed.2d 391 [119 Educ. L. Rep. 29] (1997). [Case No. 11]

7. 505 U.S. 577, 112 S.Ct. 2649, 120 L.Ed.2d 467 [75 Educ. L. Rep. 43] (1992). [Case No. 10]

8. 465 U.S. 668, 687ff, 104 S.Ct. 1355, 1366ff, 79 L.Ed.2d 604 (1984).

9. Up until the time of the Revolutionary War, there "... were established churches in at least eight of the thirteen former colonies and established religions in at least four of the other five." *Engel v. Vitale*, 370 U.S. 421, 428 n. 5, 82 S.Ct. 1261, 8 L.Ed.2d 601 (1962).

10. The metaphor of the "wall of separation" comes from Thomas Jefferson's letter of January 1, 1802 to Nehemiah Dodge, Ephraim Robbins, and Stephen S. Nelson, A Committee of the Danbury Baptist Association. 16 WRITINGS OF THOMAS JEFFERSON 281 (Andrew A., ed. 1903). Jefferson wrote:

Believing with you that religion is a matter which lies solely between man and his

God ... I contemplate with sovereign reverence that act of the whole American people which declared that their legislature should "make no law respecting an establishment of religion, or prohibiting the free exercise thereof," thus building a wall of separation between church and state.

The Supreme Court first used the term in *Reynolds v. United States*, 98 U.S. 145, 164, 25 L.Ed. 244 (1878) (rejecting a Free Exercise Clause challenge to a federal polygamy statute).

11. The metaphor of the "wall of separation" traces its origins to Roger Williams who coined the term more than 150 years before Thomas Jefferson first employed it. *See* Roger Williams, Mr. Cotton's Letter Lately Printed, Examined and Answered (1644), reprinted in 1 THE COMPLETE WRITINGS OF ROGER WILLIAMS 392 (Russell & Russell 1963) ("and when they have opened a gap in the hedge or wall of Separation between the Garden of the Church and the Wilderness of the world....").

with the Supreme Court over the past fifty plus years.[12] On the other hand, accommodationists maintain that the government is not prohibited from permitting some aid or accommodating the needs of children under the so-called "Child Benefit" test or from accommodating the religious preferences of parents who send their children to public schools.

This book focuses on federal, rather than state, law. Even so, it is important to recognize that developments at both levels often overlap. In other words, while many cases arise under state law, such as vouchers in Cleveland, Ohio,[13] they are often ultimately resolved on the basis of the Federal Constitution. It is thus worth noting that the Federal Constitution is more open to some forms of aid to religious schools than its state counterparts, a distinction that emerged during the latter part of the Nineteenth Century.

The push for separation between Church and State received a boost on December 7, 1875, when President Grant, in his final "State of the Union" address to Congress, called for a constitutional amendment "forbidding the teaching [of religion in public schools] . . . and prohibiting the granting of any school funds, or school taxes or any part thereof, either by legislative, municipal, or other authority, for the benefit or in aid, directly or indirectly, of any religious sect or denomination. . . ."[14]

Following the lead of President Grant, Senator James K. Blaine of Maine unsuccessfully introduced a constitutional amendment in 1875 that would have prevented aid from going to schools "under the control of any religious sect,"[15] code for Roman Catholic schools. While the Amendment failed to win passage in 1876, most states adopted Blaine-type constitutional provisions that place substantial limits on the relationship between religious institutions and state governments.[16] Despite

---

12. Members of the Court have adopted widely different perspectives on the "wall." *See, e.g.*, Chief Justice Rehnquist's dissent in *Wallace v. Jaffree*, 472 U.S. 38, 107, 105 S.Ct. 2479, 86 L.Ed.2d 29 [25 Educ. L. Rep. 39] (1985) soundly criticized the wall in writing that it was ". . . a metaphor based on bad history, a metaphor which has proved useless as a guide to judging. It should be frankly and explicitly abandoned." *But see Lynch v. Donnelly*, 465 U.S. 668, 673, 104 S.Ct. 1355, 79 L.Ed.2d 604 (1984) (upholding the display of a creche among secular symbols) (Brennan, J., concurring) at 673: "The concept of a 'wall' of separation is a useful figure of speech. . . ."

13. *See Zelman v. Simmons–Harris* 536 U.S. 639, 649, 122 S.Ct. 2460, 153 L.Ed.2d 604 [166 Educ. L. Rep. 30] (2002). [Case No. 15]

14. 4 Cong. Rec. 175 (1875) (annual message of the President of the United States). Near the end of his address he reiterated that "[n]o sectarian tenets shall ever be taught in any school supported in whole or in part by the State, nation, or by the

proceeds of any tax levied upon any community." *Id.* at 181.

15. The entire proposed Amendment read:

No State shall make any law respecting an establishment of religion or prohibiting the free exercise thereof; and no money raised by taxation in any State for the support of public schools, or derived from any public fund therefore, nor any public lands devoted thereto, shall ever be under the control of any religious sect, nor shall any money so raised or lands so devoted be divided between religious sects or denominations.

See 4 Cong. Rec. 205 (1875) (Blaine's statement submitting a proposed constitutional amendment to Congress).

16. Thirty six states, plus the Commonwealth of Puerto Rico, have Blaine-type language in their constitutions. *See, e.g.*, Alaska Constit. art. VII, § 1; Cal. Constit. art. XVI, § 5; Colo. Constit. art. IX, § 7; Fla.

this early concern over the interplay between religion and education, another half-century would pass before the Court addressed its first case in this contentious arena, initially reviewing disputes under the Fourteenth Amendment, and did not accept a case on the merits of such a claim until *Everson* in 1947.

Pre-History

Prior to the emergence of its modern Establishment Clause jurisprudence in *Everson*, the Supreme Court examined two cases that significantly impacted religiously affiliated non-public schools and their students. In both instances, the Court relied on the Due Process Clause of the Fourteenth Amendment rather than the Establishment Clause.

Pierce v. Society of Sisters of the Holy Names of Jesus and Mary

The first, and arguably more far-reaching, of the Court's two early cases involving religion and education was *Pierce v. Society of Sisters of the Holy Names of Jesus and Mary (Pierce).*[17] In *Pierce*, the proprietors of a Roman Catholic school and a secular school, the Hill Military Academy, challenged a voter-approved initiative in Oregon that led to the creation of a new compulsory attendance law. The law required all "normal" students, meaning those who did not need what would today be described as special education, between the ages of eight and sixteen who had not completed the eighth grade, to attend public schools. After a federal trial court enjoined enforcement of the statute, the Supreme Court affirmed in favor of the schools.

In its unanimous opinion, the Court ruled that enforcement of the statute would have seriously impaired, if not destroyed, the profitable features of the schools' businesses and greatly diminished the value of their property. Although recognizing the power of the state "reasonably to regulate all schools, to inspect, supervise, and examine them, their teachers and pupils ...,"[18] the Court focused on the schools' property rights under the Fourteenth Amendment. The Court grounded its judgment on the realization that the schools sought protection from unreasonable interference with their students and the destruction of their business and property. The Court also decided that while states may oversee such important features as health, safety, and teacher qualifications relating to the operation of non-public schools, they could not do so to an extent greater than they did for public schools.

Constit. art. I, § 3; Haw. Constit. art. X, § 1; Mich. Constit. art. I, § 4; Mo. Constit. art. IX, § 8; Neb. Constit. art. VII, § 11; N.Y. Constit. art. XI, § 3; Okla. Constit. art. II, § 5; Pa. Constit. art. III, § 29; Tex. Constit. art. I, § 7; Va. Constit. art. IV, § 16; Wis. Constit. art. I, § 18. For a discussion of the Blaine Amendment, *see Mitchell v. Helms*, 530 U.S. 793, 828–29, 120 S.Ct. 2530, 2551–52, 147 L.Ed.2d 660 [145 Educ. L. Rep. 44, 65–66] (2000), *reh'g denied*, 530 U.S. 1296, 121 S.Ct. 15, 147 L.Ed.2d 1039 (2000), *on remand sub nom. Helms v. Picard*, 229 F.3d 467 [148 Educ. L. Rep. 32] (5th Cir. 2000).

17. 268 U.S. 510, 45 S.Ct. 571, 69 L.Ed. 1070 (1925). [Case No. 91]

18. *Id.* at 534.

Along with serving as a kind of Magna Carta that protected the right of non-public schools to operate, the Court included important language about parental rights, acknowledging that "[t]he child is not the mere creature of the state; those who nurture him and direct his destiny have the right, coupled with the high duty, to recognize and prepare him for additional obligations."[19] The Court thus affirmed that Oregon's compulsory attendance law was unconstitutional because it "unreasonably interfere[d] with the liberty of parents and guardians to direct the upbringing and education of children under their control."[20]

Cochran v. Louisiana State Board of Education

Cochran v. Louisiana State Board of Education (Cochran)[21] involved a statute from Louisiana that provided free textbooks for all students in the state, regardless of where they attended school. A taxpayer unsuccessfully challenged the law on the ground that it violated the Fourteenth Amendment by taking private property through taxation for a non-public purpose. As in *Pierce*, the Court resolved the dispute based on the Due Process Clause of the Fourteenth Amendment rather than the First Amendment's Establishment Clause.

In unanimously affirming the judgment of the Supreme Court of Louisiana that since the students, rather than their schools, were the beneficiaries of the law, the Court was satisfied that the statute served a valid secular purpose. In so doing, the Court presaged the Child Benefit Test that would emerge in *Everson v. Board of Education*.[22] As discussed below, while the Supreme Court has consistently upheld similar textbook provisions, state courts have struck them down under their own constitutions.[23]

The Court's Modern Establishment Clause Jurisprudence: State Aid to Students who Attend Religiously Affiliated Non–Public Schools

The Court's modern Establishment Clause jurisprudence with regard to state aid in the context of K–12 education, sometimes referred to as parochiaid, evolved through three phases. During the first stage, which began in 1947 with *Everson v. Board of Education*,[24] and ended in

---

19. *Id.* at 535.

20. *Id.* at 534–535.

21. 281 U.S. 370, 50 S.Ct. 335, 74 L.Ed. 913 (1930).

22. 330 U.S. 1, 67 S.Ct. 504, 91 L.Ed. 711 (1947), *reh'g denied*, 330 U.S. 855, 67 S.Ct. 962, 91 L.Ed. 1297 (1947). [Case No. 1]

23. *See, e.g., People ex rel. Klinger v. Howlett,* 305 N.E.2d 129 (Ill.1973); *Gaffney v. State Dep't of Educ.,* 220 N.W.2d 550 (Neb.1974); *Paster v. Tussey,* 512 S.W.2d 97 (Mo.1974), *cert. denied,* 419 U.S. 1111, 95 S.Ct. 785, 42 L.Ed.2d 807 (1975); *Bloom v. School Comm. of Springfield,* 379 N.E.2d 578 (Mass.1978); *California Teachers Ass'n v. Riles,* 632 P.2d 953 (Cal. 1981); *In re Advisory Opinion,* 228 N.W.2d 772 (Mich. 1975); *Fannin v. Williams,* 655 S.W.2d 480 (Ky.1983); *Matter of Certification of a Question of Law from U.S. Dist. Ct., Dist. of S.D.,* 372 N.W.2d 113 [26 Educ. L. Rep. 1232] (S.D.1985).

24. 330 U.S. 1, 67 S.Ct. 504, 91 L.Ed. 711 (1947).

1968 with *Board of Education v. Allen*,[25] the Court enunciated the Child Benefit Test, a legal construct that permits an array of publicly funded aid on the ground that it assists children rather than their religiously affiliated non-public schools. The years between the Court's 1971 judgment in *Lemon v. Kurtzman*[26] and *Aguilar v. Felton*[27] in 1985 were static with regard to the Child Benefit Test as the Court largely refused to move beyond the limits it created in *Everson* and *Allen*. However, with its 1993 ruling in *Zobrest v. Catalina Foothills School District*,[28] the Court breathed new life into the Child Benefit Test that extends through the present day. The following sections examine the many topics and cases involving state aid to religiously affiliated non-public schools and their students.

Transportation

Everson[29] stands out as the first Supreme Court case on the merits of the Establishment Clause and education. At issue in *Everson* was a statute from New Jersey that permitted local school boards to make rules and contracts for student transportation. After a local board, acting pursuant to the statute, authorized reimbursement to parents for the money they spent on bus fares sending their children to Catholic schools, a taxpayer filed suit claiming that the law was unconstitutional in two respects: first, in an approach not unlike the plaintiff's unsuccessful argument in *Cochran*, he alleged that the law authorized the state to take the money of some citizens by taxation and bestow it on others for the private purpose of supporting non-public schools in contravention of the Fourteenth Amendment; second, he charged that the statute was one "respecting an establishment of religion" since it forced him to contribute to support church schools in violation of the First Amendment.

A closely divided Court affirmed the statute's constitutionality. The Court flatly rejected the plaintiff's Fourteenth Amendment argument since it found that facilitating secular education is clearly a public purpose. As to the First Amendment, the Court declared that neither a state nor the federal government could aid one religion, all religions, or prefer one religion over another. The Court added that no tax, large or small, could be levied to support any religious activity or institution. Yet, in permitting the statute to remain in effect, the Court reasoned that the First Amendment did not prohibit a state from extending general benefits to all of its citizens without regard to their religious beliefs as it placed student transportation in the same category of other public services such as police, fire, and health protection. The Court also introduced the Jeffersonian metaphor into the lexicon of its First Amendment jurisprudence, writing that: "[t]he First Amendment has

25. 392 U.S. 236, 88 S.Ct. 1923, 20 L.Ed.2d 1060 (1968). [Case. No. 5]

26. 403 U.S. 602, 91 S.Ct. 2105, 29 L.Ed.2d 745 (1971). [Case No. 7]

27. 473 U.S. 402, 105 S.Ct. 3232, 87 L.Ed.2d 290 [25 Educ. L. Rep. 1022] (1985).

28. 509 U.S. 1, 113 S.Ct. 2462, 125 L.Ed.2d 1 [83 Educ. L. Rep. 930] (1993).

29. 330 U.S. 1, 67 S.Ct. 504, 91 L.Ed. 711 (1947), *reh'g denied*, 330 U.S. 855, 67 S.Ct. 962, 91 L.Ed. 1297 (1947). [Case No. 1]

erected a wall between church and state. That wall must be kept high and impregnable. We could not approve the slightest breach."[30]

Following *Everson*, each state must choose whether to provide publicly funded transportation to students who attend religiously affiliated non-public schools. As might have been anticipated, lower courts, relying on state constitutional provisions, reached mixed results on this issue. Consequently, some cases prohibited states from providing transportation to students in religious schools in determining that doing so violated their constitutions.[31] For instance, a federal trial court in Iowa,[32] relying on the state constitution, prohibited a board of education from offering transportation to a student who attended a religious school outside of its boundaries. Conversely, the federal trial court in Connecticut[33] and the First Circuit,[34] both of which explicitly rejected the case from Iowa, and the Supreme Court of Pennsylvania,[35] permitted students from religiously affiliated schools to be transported beyond district lines.

In *Wolman v. Walter (Wolman)*,[36] the Supreme Court addressed the related question of field trips. At issue was a statute from Ohio that permitted public funds to be used to provide transportation for field trips for children who attended religiously affiliated non-public schools. The Court maintained that such a practice was unconstitutional because insofar as field trips were oriented to the curriculum, they were in the category of instruction rather than that of non-ideological secular services such as transportation to and from school.

Textbooks

Following the lead of *Cochran*, albeit on the basis of the First, rather than the Fourteenth, Amendment, in *Board of Education v. Allen (Allen)*,[37] the Supreme Court affirmed the constitutionality of a statute from New York that required local school boards to loan books to children in grades 7 to 12 who attended non-public schools.[38] The law did

30. *Id.* at 18.

31. *See, e,g, Visser v. Nooksack Valley School Dist. No. 506*, 207 P.2d 198 (Wash. 1949). *McVey v. Hawkins*, 258 S.W.2d 927 (Mo.1953); *Matthews v. Quinton*, 362 P.2d 932 (Alaska 1961), *cert. denied*, 368 U.S. 517, 82 S.Ct. 530, 7 L.Ed.2d 522 (1962); *Board of Educ. for Indep. School Dist. No. 52 v. Antone*, 384 P.2d 911 (Okla. 1963); *Epeldi v. Engelking*, 488 P.2d 860 (Idaho 1971), *cert. denied*, 406 U.S. 957, 92 S.Ct. 2058, 32 L.Ed.2d 343 (1972); *Luetkemeyer v. Kaufmann*, 364 F.Supp. 376 (W.D.Mo. 1973), *aff'd*, 419 U.S. 888, 95 S.Ct. 167, 42 L.Ed.2d 134 (1974).

32. *Americans United for Separation of Church and State v. Benton*, 413 F.Supp. 955 (S.D. Iowa 1975).

33. *Cromwell Property Owners Ass'n v. Toffolon*, 495 F.Supp. 915 (D.Conn.1979).

34. *Members of Jamestown School Comm. v. Schmidt*, 699 F.2d 1 [9 Educ. L. Rep. 70] (1st Cir.1983), *cert. denied*, 464 U.S. 851, 104 S.Ct. 162, 78 L.Ed.2d 148 (1983).

35. *Pequea Valley School Dist. v. Commonwealth of Pa. Dep't of Educ.*, 397 A.2d 1154 (Pa. 1979), *appeal dismissed for want of a substantial federal question*, 443 U.S. 901, 99 S.Ct. 3091, 61 L.Ed.2d 869 (1979).

36. 433 U.S. 229, 97 S.Ct. 2593, 53 L.Ed.2d 714 (1977).

37. 392 U.S. 236, 88 S.Ct. 1923, 20 L.Ed.2d 1060 (1968). [Case No. 5]

38. *Board of Educ. of Cent. School Dist. No. 1, Towns of East Greenbush v. Allen*, 273 N.Y.S.2d 239 (N.Y.Sup.1966), *rev'd*, 276 N.Y.S.2d 234 (N.Y.App.Div.1966), *aff'd*, 281 N.Y.S.2d 799 (N.Y.1967), *probable jurisdic-*

not mandate that the books had to be the same as those used in the public schools but did require that titles be approved by local boards before they could be adopted. Relying largely on the Child Benefit Test, the Court observed that the statute's purpose was not to aid religion or non-public schools and that its primary effect was to improve the quality of education for all children.

Allen represented the outer limit of the Child Benefit Test prior to the Court's ruling in *Agostini v. Felton*,[39] discussed below. The Court upheld similar textbook provisions in *Meek v. Pittenger*[40] and *Wolman*, both of which are also discussed in more detail below.

Secular Services and Salary Supplements

In its most significant case involving the Establishment Clause and education, *Lemon v. Kurtzman (Lemon)*,[41] the Court struck down a statute from Pennsylvania that called for the purchase of secular services and a law from Rhode Island that provided salary supplements for teachers in non-public schools. More specifically, the Pennsylvania statute authorized the commonwealth's superintendent of education to purchase specified secular educational services from non-public schools. Officials then directly reimbursed the non-public schools for their actual expenditures for teacher salaries, textbooks, and instructional materials. The superintendent had to approve the textbooks and materials, which were restricted to the areas of mathematics, modern foreign languages, physical science, and physical education. In Rhode Island, officials were authorized to supplement the salaries of certificated teachers of secular subjects in non-public elementary schools by directly paying them amounts not in excess of 15 percent of their current annual salaries; their salaries could not then exceed the maximum paid to public school teachers. The supplements were available to teachers in non-public schools where average per pupil expenditures on secular education were less than in public schools. In addition, the teachers had to use the same materials as were used in public schools.

Invalidating both statutes, the Court enunciated a tripartite standard destined to become known as the *Lemon* test. In creating this measure, the Court added a third prong, dealing with excessive entanglement, from *Walz v. Tax Commission of New York City*,[42] to the two-part test it created in *Abington v. Schempp*. The Court wrote that:

> Every analysis in this area must begin with consideration of the cumulative criteria developed by the Court over many years. Three such tests may be gleaned from our cases. First, the statute must have a secular legislative purpose; second, its principal or primary

tion noted, 389 U.S. 1031, 88 S.Ct. 767, 19 L.Ed.2d 819 (1968).

39. 521 U.S. 203, 117 S.Ct. 1997, 138 L.Ed.2d 391 [119 Educ. L. Rep. 29] (1997). [Case No. 11]

40. 421 U.S. 349, 95 S.Ct. 1753, 44 L.Ed.2d 217 (1975).

41. 403 U.S. 602, 91 S.Ct. 2105, 29 L.Ed.2d 745 (1971). [Case No. 7]

42. 397 U.S. 664, 90 S.Ct. 1409, 25 L.Ed.2d 697 (1970) (upholding New York State's practice of providing state property tax exemptions for church property that is used in worship services).

effect must be one that neither advances nor inhibits religion; finally, the statute must not foster "an excessive government entanglement with religion."[43]

In addressing entanglement and state aid to religiously affiliated institutions, the Court noted that three additional factors came into consideration: "we must examine the character and purposes of the institutions that are benefitted, the nature of the aid that the State provides, and the resulting relationship between the government and religious authority."[44]

As part of its analysis, the Court reviewed its prior cases on the relationship between church and state in education, concluding that total separation was unnecessary. However, the Court posited that the relationship in *Lemon* was too close since the religious schools, which constituted an integral part of the mission of the Catholic Church, involved substantial religious activities. Moreover, Catholic schools were the sole beneficiaries in Rhode Island and were virtually so in Pennsylvania.

The *Lemon* Court distinguished aid for teachers' salaries from secular, neutral, or non-ideological services, facilities, or materials. Recalling *Allen*, the Court remarked that teachers have a substantially different ideological character than books. In terms of potential for involving some aspect of faith or morals in secular subjects, the Court was of the view that while the content of a textbook is ascertainable, a teacher's handling of a subject matter is not. The Court also took notice of the inherent conflict when teachers who work under the direction of religious officials are faced with separating religious and secular aspects of K–12 education. The Court was concerned that the restrictions and surveillance necessary to ensure that teachers play non-ideological roles give rise to the kind of entanglement that the Constitution prohibits. The Court contended that an ongoing history of government grants to non-public schools suggests that these programs were almost always accompanied by varying measures of control. According to the Court, weighing which expenditures of church-related schools were religious and which were secular created an impermissible intimate and continuing relationship between church and state. The Court went on to discuss the divisive political potential of such programs, asserting that although political debate and division generally are normal and healthy manifestations of the American government, protection against political division along religious lines was one of the principal purposes of the religion clauses of the First Amendment.

In what has developed into a kind of "catch–22" situation, programs typically passed *Lemon's* first two prongs only to have had excessive entanglement serve as the basis for invalidating various forms of aid to students in religiously affiliated non-public schools. The difficulty was exacerbated due to the realization that even though the first two parts of

---

43. *Lemon v. Kurtzman*, 403 U.S. 602, 612–613, 91 S.Ct. 2105, 29 L.Ed.2d 745 (1971). [Case No. 7]

44. *Id.* at 615.

the *Lemon* test were developed in the context of prayer cases, the Court applied it widely in disputes involving aid to non-public schools and their students.

Tuition Reimbursements to Parents

Two months after *Lemon*, the Pennsylvania legislature enacted a statute that permitted parents whose children attended non-public schools to request tuition reimbursement. The same parent as in *Lemon* challenged the new law as having the primary effect of advancing religion.[45] In *Sloan v. Lemon (Sloan)*,[46] the Supreme Court affirmed that the law impermissibly singled out a class of citizens for a special economic benefit. The Court thought that it was plain that this was unlike the sort of "indirect" and "incidental" benefits that flowed to religious schools from programs that aided all parents by supplying bus transportation and secular textbooks for their children. The Court was persuaded that such benefits as transportation and books were carefully restricted to the purely secular side of church-affiliated schools and did not provide special aid to their students.

The Court expanded *Sloan's* rationale in a companion case from New York, *Committee for Public Education and Religious Liberty v. Nyquist (Nyquist)*.[47] The Court decreed that even though the grants went to parents rather than to school officials, this did not compel a different result. The Court commented that since parents would have used the money to pay for tuition and the law failed to separate secular from religious uses, the aid's effect unmistakably would have provided the desired financial support for non-public schools. As such, the Court rejected the state's argument that parents were not simply conduits because they were free to spend the money in any manner they chose since they paid the tuition and the law merely provided for reimbursements. The Court decided that even if the grants were offered as incentives to have parents send their children to religious schools, the law violated the Establishment Clause regardless of whether the money made its way into the coffers of the religious institutions.

Income Tax Benefits

Another section of the same New York statute in *Nyquist* aided parents via income tax benefits. Under the law, parents of children who attended non-public schools were entitled to income tax deductions as long as they did not receive tuition reimbursements under the other part of the statute. The Court invalidated this provision in pointing out that in practical terms there was little difference, for purposes of evaluating whether such aid had the effect of advancing religion, between a tax benefit and a tuition grant. The Court based its judgment on the notion

---

45. *Lemon v. Sloan*, 340 F.Supp. 1356 (E.D.Pa.1972).

46. 413 U.S. 825, 93 S.Ct. 2982, 37 L.Ed.2d 939 (1973).

47. 413 U.S. 756, 93 S.Ct. 2955, 37 L.Ed.2d 948 (1973).

that under both programs qualifying parents received the same form of encouragement and reward for sending their children to non-public schools.

Ten years later, in *Mueller v. Allen (Mueller)*,[48] the Court upheld the constitutionality of a statute from Minnesota that granted all parents state income tax deductions for the actual costs of tuition, textbooks, and transportation associated with sending their children to elementary or secondary schools. The statute afforded parents deductions of $500 for children in grades K–6 and $700 for those in grades 7–12. The Court distinguished *Mueller* from *Nyquist* primarily on the grounds that the tax benefit at issue was available to all parents, not only those whose children were in non-public schools, and that the deduction was one among many rather than a single, favored type of taxpayer expenditure. In acknowledging the legislature's broad latitude to create classifications and distinctions in tax statutes, and that the state could have been considered to benefit from the scheme since it promoted an educated citizenry while reducing the costs of public education, the Court was convinced that the law satisfied all three of *Lemon's* prongs. Interestingly, the Court did not pay much attention to the fact that since the state's public schools were essentially free, the expenses of parents with children in them were at most minimal and that about 96 percent of the taxpayers who benefitted had children who were enrolled in religious schools.

In a more recent version of this issue, the federal trial court in Arizona dismissed a challenge to the statute that authorized a tuition tax credit which allowed state income taxpayers who voluntarily contributed money to a "student tuition organization" to receive dollar-for-dollar tax credits of up to $500 of their annual tax liability.[49] In dismissing the claim that the tax credit violated the Establishment Clause, the court held that the credit, which neither mentioned religion nor provided aid directly to religious schools, was part of a secular state policy designed to maximize parental choices as to where they sent their children to school. The court also found that the tax credit was a program of "true private choice" since its benefits were available to a broad spectrum of groups and had multiple layers of private choice. Previously, in a case that did not reach the merits of the tax credit, *Hibbs v. Winn*,[50] the Supreme Court affirmed that the Tax Injunction Act did not prevent taxpayers from challenging it on the basis that it violated the Establishment Clause by subsidizing religion.

Reimbursements to Religiously Affiliated Non–Public Schools

In yet another aspect of *Nyquist*, the Court vitiated the statute's maintenance and repair provision for non-public schools since it placed

48. 463 U.S. 388, 103 S.Ct. 3062, 77 L.Ed.2d 721 [11 Educ. L. Rep. 763] (1983). [Case No. 8]

49. *Winn v. Hibbs*, 361 F.Supp.2d 1117 [197 Educ. L. Rep. 103] (D. Ariz. 2005).

50. *Hibbs v. Winn*, 542 U.S. 88, 124 S.Ct. 2276, 159 L.Ed.2d 172 (2004).

almost no restrictions on how funds were used.[51] The Court wrote that since it was clear that the government is forbidden from erecting buildings in which religious activities are conducted, it may not pay to renovate them when they fall into disrepair.

On the same day as it handed down *Nyquist*, in another case from New York, the Court applied essentially the same rationale in *Levitt v. Committee for Public Education and Religious Liberty (Levitt),*[52] invalidating a statute that permitted the state to reimburse non-public schools for expenses incurred while complying with requirements for the administration and reporting test results and other records. Insofar as there were no restrictions on the use of the funds, such that apparently teacher-prepared tests on religious subject matter were seemingly reimbursable, the Court discerned that the aid had the primary effect of advancing religious education because there were insufficient safeguards in place to regulate how the monies were spent.

Four years later in *Wolman v. Walter*,[53] the Court upheld a law from Ohio that allowed reimbursement for religious schools that used standardized tests and scoring services. The Court distinguished these tests from the ones in *Levitt* because the latter were neither drafted nor scored by non-public school personnel. The Court also reasoned that the law from Ohio did not authorize payments to church-sponsored schools for costs associated with administering the tests.

The Court revisited *Levitt* in *Committee for Public Education and Religious Liberty v. Regan*[54] after the New York State legislature modified the law. Under its new provisions, the statute provided for reimbursements to non-public schools for the actual costs of complying with state requirements for reporting on students and for administering both mandatory and optional state-prepared examinations. Unlike the testing procedure in Ohio, this law provided that the tests were to be graded by personnel in the non-public schools that were, in turn, reimbursed for these services. In addition, the law created accounting procedures to monitor reimbursements. The Court recognized that the differences between the statutes were permissible since scoring of essentially objective tests and recording their results along with attendance data offered no significant opportunity for religious indoctrination while serving secular state educational purposes. The Court added that the accounting method did not create excessive entanglement since the reimbursements were equal to the actual costs.

Instructional Materials and Equipment

In *Meek v. Pittenger (Meek)*,[55] the Supreme Court reviewed the constitutionality of loans of instructional materials, including textbooks

51. 413 U.S. 756, 93 S.Ct. 2955, 37 L.Ed.2d 948 (1973).

52. 413 U.S. 472, 93 S.Ct. 2814, 37 L.Ed.2d 736 (1973).

53. 433 U.S. 229, 97 S.Ct. 2593, 53 L.Ed.2d 714 (1977).

54. 444 U.S. 646, 100 S.Ct. 840, 63 L.Ed.2d 94 (1980).

55. 421 U.S. 349, 95 S.Ct. 1753, 44 L.Ed.2d 217 (1975).

and equipment, to religiously affiliated non-public schools in Pennsylvania. Although the Court upheld Pennsylvania's loan of textbooks, it struck down provisions dealing with periodicals, films, recordings, and laboratory equipment as well as equipment for recording and projecting on the basis that the statute had the primary effect of advancing religion because of the predominantly religious character of participating schools. The Court was troubled by the fact that the only statutory requirement imposed on the schools to qualify for the loans was that they provide for the subjects and activities prescribed by the state board of education. The Court stated that the church-related schools were the primary beneficiaries and that the massive aid to their educational function necessarily resulted in aid to their sectarian enterprises as a whole.

Two years later, the Court reached similar results in *Wolman v. Walter (Wolman)*[56] in upholding a statute from Ohio which specified that textbook loans were to be made to students or their parents, rather than directly to their non-public schools. The Court struck down a provision that would have allowed loans of instructional equipment including projectors, tape recorders, record players, maps and globes, and science kits. Echoing the words of *Meek*, the Court invalidated the statute's authorizing the loans in light of its fear that since it would be impossible to separate the secular and sectarian functions for which these items were being used, the aid inevitably provided support for the religious roles of the schools.

Mitchell v. Helms,[57] a case from Louisiana, saw the Court further expand the boundaries of permissible aid to religiously affiliated non-public schools. A plurality upheld the constitutionality of Chapter 2 of Title I, now Title VI, of the Elementary and Secondary Education Act (Chapter 2),[58] a federal law that permits the loans of instructional materials including library books, computers, television sets, tape recorders, and maps to non-public schools. The Court grounded its judgment in the fact that *Agostini v. Felton,* discussed below, modified the *Lemon* test by reviewing only its first two parts while recasting entanglement as one criterion in determining a statute's effect. Insofar as the purpose part of the test was not challenged, the plurality believed it necessary only to consider Chapter 2's effect, concluding that Chapter 2 did not foster impermissible religious indoctrination because aid was allocated on the basis of neutral secular criteria that neither favored nor disfavored religion and was available to all schools based on secular, nondiscriminatory grounds. At the same time, the plurality explicitly reversed those parts of *Meek* and *Wolman* that were inconsistent with its analysis on loans of instructional materials.

56. 433 U.S. 229, 97 S.Ct. 2593, 53 L.Ed.2d 714 (1977).

57. 530 U.S. 793, 120 S.Ct. 2530, 147 L.Ed.2d 660 [145 Educ. L. Rep. 44] (2000), *reh'g denied*, 530 U.S. 1296, 121 S.Ct. 15, 147 L.Ed.2d 1039 (2000), *on remand sub nom. Helms v. Picard*, 229 F.3d 467 [148 Educ. L. Rep. 32] (5th Cir. 2000).

58. 20 U.S.C.A. §§ 7301–73.

Auxiliary Services

In *Meek v. Pittenger*,[59] the Supreme Court struck down a statute that allowed public school personnel to provide auxiliary services on-site in religiously affiliated non-public schools. The Court also banned the delivery of remedial and accelerated instructional programs, guidance counseling and testing, and services to aid children who were educationally disadvantaged. The Court asserted that it was immaterial that the students would have received remedial, rather than advanced, work since the required surveillance to ensure the absence of ideology would have given rise to excessive entanglement between church and state.

Two years later, in *Wolman v. Walter*,[60] the Court reached a variety of results. In addition to upholding the textbook loan program, the Court permitted the state to supply non-public schools with state mandated tests, and allowed public school employees to go on-site to perform diagnostic tests to evaluate whether students needed speech, hearing, and psychological services. Further, the Court permitted public funds to be spent in providing therapeutic services to students from non-public schools as long as they were delivered off-site. However, the Court prohibited the state from loaning instructional materials and equipment to schools or from using funds to pay for field trips for students in non-public schools.

Zobrest v. Catalina Foothills School District[61] signaled a dramatic shift in the Court's Establishment Clause jurisprudence. At issue was a school board's refusal to provide a sign-language interpreter, under the Individuals with Disabilities Education Act,[62] for a deaf student in Arizona who transferred to a Catholic high school. After the Ninth Circuit affirmed that such an arrangement would have violated the Establishment Clause,[63] the Court disagreed. The Court determined that an interpreter provided neutral aid to the student without offering financial benefits to his parents or school, and there was no governmental participation in the instruction because the interpreter was only a conduit to effectuate the child's communications. The Court relied in part on *Witters v. Washington Department of Services for the Blind*,[64] wherein it upheld the constitutionality of extending a general vocational assistance program to a blind man who was studying to become a clergyman at a religious college.[65] The Supreme Court of Washington subsequently ruled that the state constitution forbade such use of public funds, and the Supreme Court refused to hear an appeal.[66]

59. 421 U.S. 349, 95 S.Ct. 1753, 44 L.Ed.2d 217 (1975).

60. 433 U.S. 229, 97 S.Ct. 2593, 53 L.Ed.2d 714 (1977).

61. 509 U.S. 1, 113 S.Ct. 2462, 125 L.Ed.2d 1 [83 Educ. L. Rep. 930] (1993).

62. 20 U.S.C.A. §§ 1400 *et seq.*

63. 963 F.2d 1190 [75 Educ. L. Rep. 178] (9th Cir.1992).

64. 474 U.S. 481, 106 S.Ct. 748, 88 L.Ed.2d 846 [29 Educ. L. Rep. 496] (1986).

65. *But see Locke v. Davey,* 540 U.S. 712, 124 S.Ct. 1307, 158 L.Ed.2d 1 [185 Educ. L. Rep. 30] (2004) (vitiating a program from Washington that would have provided a scholarship for a student who pursued a degree in pastoral theology because program rules prohibited the release of funds to pay for individuals who wished to study for the ministry).

66. *Witters v. State Comm'n for the Blind,* 771 P.2d 1119 [53 Educ. L. Rep. 278] (Wash.1989), *cert. denied,* 493 U.S. 850, 110 S.Ct. 147, 107 L.Ed.2d 106 (1989).

A year later, the Court considered a case where the New York State legislature created a school district which had the same boundaries as those of a religious community. The legislature created the special district in an attempt to accommodate the needs of parents of children with disabilities who wished to send them to a nearby school that would have honored their religious practices. After all three levels of the state courts struck the statute down as violating the Establishment Clause, the Supreme Court, in *Board of Education of Kiryas Joel Village School District v. Grumet*,[67] affirmed that the law was unconstitutional. The Court agreed that the case-specific creation of the district deprived it of a means to review such state action for the purpose of safeguarding the principle that government should not prefer one religion to another or religion to no religion. The Court explained that while a state may accommodate a group's religious needs by alleviating special burdens, it stepped over the line, especially since the board could have offered an appropriate program at one of its public schools or at a neutral site near one of the village's religious schools.

Days after the Supreme Court struck down the statute, the New York state legislature amended the statute in an attempt to eliminate the Establishment Clause problem. Even so, the Court of Appeals of New York struck down the revised statute on the basis that it violated the Establishment Clause because it had the effect of advancing one religion.[68]

Four years later, the Eighth Circuit, in a case from Minnesota, reached an interesting result in accommodating the religious beliefs of parents who objected to the use of technology in public education. The court permitted what was essentially a special public school to operate without the use of technology because it was satisfied that the local board did not improperly endorse religion.[69]

Shared Facilities and Shared Time

Conflicts have arisen when officials in public and non-public schools entered into cooperative arrangements. The extent to which such arrangements are permissible is an open question since not all jurisdictions agree on whether public and non-public schools can share facilities, engage in shared time, and/or operate dual enrollment programs. Key issues in these disputes involve whether public funds are used for religious purposes and whether religious influences are present in public schools.

When dealing with the use of public funds in religious schools, disputes can occur when school boards lease part or all of church-owned

---

67. 512 U.S. 687, 114 S.Ct. 2481, 129 L.Ed.2d 546 [91 Educ. L. Rep. 810] (1994).

68. *Grumet v. Cuomo*, 659 N.Y.S.2d 173 [119 Educ. L. Rep. 603] (N.Y.1997); *Grumet v. Pataki*, 697 N.Y.S.2d 846 [139 Educ. L. Rep. 986] (N.Y.1999), *cert. denied*, 528 U.S. 946, 120 S.Ct. 363, 145 L.Ed.2d 284 (1999).

69. *Stark v. Independent School Dist., No. 640*, 123 F.3d 1068 [121 Educ. L. Rep. 41] (8th Cir.1997), *reh'g and suggestion for reh'g en banc denied* (1997), *cert. denied*, 523 U.S. 1094, 118 S.Ct. 1560, 140 L.Ed.2d 792 (1998).

buildings. In a pair of cases separated by forty years, the Supreme Court of Nebraska initially invalidated a leasing program since the part of a building used by a religious school, emphasizing that the garb and devotional attitude of the sisters who taught there, the instructions and services that the local priest offered the chapel and classrooms, and the insignia around the building created an environment that reflected Catholic beliefs.[70] In the second case, the court observed that a public school board may use or lease classrooms in a church or other building affiliated with a religious organization for public school purposes if the property is under the control of public school officials and the instruction is secular.[71] In citing the latter case from Nebraska, the Supreme Court of Georgia recently affirmed that an arms-length commercial agreement pursuant to which a public school system leased classroom space from a church did not violate the Establishment Clause of the State Constitution.[72] The court pointed out that since the purpose of the lease was to permit the public school system to establish and operate a kindergarten in a nonsectarian environment, the lease payments did not constitute an unconstitutional form of monetary aid to the church.

Questions involving shared time or dual enrollment depend, to a large extent, on the wording of a jurisdiction's compulsory education statute relating to religion and education. In an early case, the Supreme Court of Pennsylvania posited that a student who attended a religious school could not be denied the opportunity to enroll in a manual training course in a local public school.[73] More than fifty years later, an appellate court in Illinois upheld an experimental program which allowed students who otherwise would have been eligible for full-time enrollment in public high schools to attend classes there on a part-time basis and take other courses in a religious school.[74] Rather than rely on the First Amendment, the court rooted its judgment in the fact that the local board had the power to experiment in an educational program that applied to all non-public schools, not specifically ones that were religiously affiliated. The court was of the opinion that the state's compulsory education law did not specify that all classes had to take place in one location. Shortly thereafter, the Supreme Court of Missouri adopted a contrary position with regard to the state's compulsory education law.[75] In its order, the court questioned procedures whereby public funds were used to send speech teachers into religious schools to provide speech therapy and under which some of these students went to public schools to receive speech therapy during the regular class day. The court prohibited both

---

70. *State ex rel. Pub. School Dist. No. 6, Cedar County v. Taylor*, 240 N.W. 573 (Neb. 1932). The Supreme Court of New Mexico reached a similar result where many direct and indirect religious influences were present in a school in *Zellers v. Huff*, 236 P.2d 949 (N.M.1951).

71. *State ex rel. School Dist. of Hartington v. Nebraska State Bd. of Educ.*, 195 N.W.2d 161 (Neb.1972), *cert. denied*, 409 U.S. 921, 93 S.Ct. 220, 34 L.Ed.2d 182 (1972).

72. *Taetle v. Atlanta Indep. School Sys.*, 625 S.E.2d 770 (Ga. 2006).

73. *Commonwealth ex rel. Wehrle v. School Dist.*, 88 A. 481 (Pa.1913).

74. *Morton v. Board of Educ.*, 216 N.E.2d 305 (Ill.Ct.App.1966).

75. *Special Dist. for Educ. and Training of Handicapped Children v. Wheeler*, 408 S.W.2d 60 (Mo.1966).

public school personnel from going into religious schools and invalidated the practice of permitting children from the religious schools to travel to public schools. The court interpreted the state's compulsory education law as stipulating that the school day had to be of a given length and that it had to be spent entirely in one type of school.

The Supreme Court of Michigan discussed shared time in relation to a state constitutional amendment prohibiting financial aid to students or their non-public schools. The court upheld the program in clarifying that if teaching took place on leased premises or in non-public schools, services had to be provided only under conditions appropriate for public schools.[76] The court maintained that ultimate and immediate control of subject matter, personnel, and premises had to be under the control of public school officials, and the courses had to be open to all eligible students. Yet, federal trial courts in New Hampshire[77] and Kentucky[78] struck down dual-enrollment plans that essentially would have permitted boards to lease space in religious schools and have teachers selected by public school officials teach secular subjects in non-public schools.

More than a decade after the Supreme Court of Michigan upheld the state constitutional amendment on shared time, officials in Grand Rapids created an extensive program. The program increased to the point where publicly paid teachers conducted 10 percent of classes in religious schools and a substantial number of them had worked in the religious schools. The Sixth Circuit held that the plan violated the Establishment Clause.[79] On further review, in *School District of City of Grand Rapids v. Ball (Ball)*,[80] the Supreme Court affirmed that the released time program failed all three prongs of the *Lemon* test. The Court also invalidated a community education after-school program in which teachers from religious schools worked part-time for the local public school board, instructing participating students in their own buildings.

On the same day that it resolved *Ball*, the Court addressed a companion case from New York City over the constitutionality of permitting public school teachers to provide remedial instruction under Title I of the Elementary and Secondary Education Act of 1965 (Title I)[81] for specifically targeted children, who were educationally disadvantaged, on-site in their religiously affiliated schools. Title I funds also paid for all of the materials used in the program. After a federal trial court refused to enjoin the program and the Second Circuit vitiated the program, a

76. *In re Proposal C.*, 185 N.W.2d 9 (Mich.1971).

77. *Americans United for Separation of Church and State v. Paire*, 359 F.Supp. 505 (D.N.H. 1973).

78. *Americans United for Separation of Church and State v. Board of Educ.*, 369 F.Supp. 1059 (E.D.Ky.1974).

79. *Americans United for Separation of Church and State v. School Dist. of City of Grand Rapids*, 718 F.2d 1389 [14 Educ. L. Rep. 40] (6th Cir.1983).

80. 473 U.S. 373, 105 S.Ct. 3216, 87 L.Ed.2d 267 [25 Educ. L. Rep. 1006] (1985).

81. In an earlier case involving the Elementary Secondary Education Act, the Supreme Court concluded that federal funds provided under the Act for educationally deprived children in public and non-public schools could not be used to supply publicly employed teachers to give remedial instruction on-site in the non-public schools. *Wheeler v. Barrera*, 417 U.S. 402, 94 S.Ct. 2274, 41 L.Ed.2d 159 (1974).

divided Supreme Court, in *Aguilar v. Felton (Aguilar)*,[82] affirmed that the program was unconstitutional. Even though the New York City Board of Education (NYCBOE) developed safeguards to insure that public funds were not spent for religious purposes, the Court struck it down based on the fear that a monitoring system might have created excessive entanglement of church and state.

Twelve years later, in *Agostini v. Felton (Agostini)*,[83] the Supreme Court took the unusual step of dissolving the injunction that it upheld in *Aguilar*. In a major shift in its jurisprudence, the Court reasoned that the Title I program did not violate any of the three standards that it used to consider whether state aid advanced religion since there was no governmental indoctrination, there were no distinctions between recipients based on religion, and there was no excessive entanglement. To this end, the majority ruled that a federally funded program that provides supplemental, remedial instruction and counseling services to disadvantaged children on a neutral basis is not invalid under the Establishment Clause when the assistance is provided on-site in religiously affiliated non-public schools pursuant to a program containing safeguards such as those that the NYCBOE implemented. Perhaps the most significant development in *Agostini* was that the Court modified the *Lemon* test by reviewing only its first two parts, purpose and effect, while recasting entanglement as one criterion in evaluating a statute's effect.

In a case with broad similarities to *Agostini*, the Circuit Court for the District of Columbia was of the view that the federally chartered AmeriCorps Education Awards Program (EAP), a nationwide community service program, did not violate the Establishment Clause even though some participants taught religion along with secular subjects in religious schools.[84] The court reasoned that the EAP was permissible because it was a government program that was neutral toward religion, providing aid directly to a broad class of citizens who, in turn, directed government assistance to religious schools entirely on their own genuine and independent private choices. The court added that the program was constitutional because no objective observer who was familiar with the full history and context of the EAP would have thought that the aid that went to the religious institutions carried the imprimatur of governmental endorsement.

Vouchers

Considerable controversy has arisen over the use of vouchers with courts reaching mixed results in disputes over their constitutionality. The Supreme Court of Wisconsin[85] and an appellate court in Florida[86] initially upheld vouchers for students who attended religious schools. However, in the aftermath of *Zelman*, an intermediate appellate court in

82. 473 U.S. 402, 105 S.Ct. 3232, 87 L.Ed.2d 290 [25 Educ. L. Rep. 1022] (1985).

83. 521 U.S. 203, 117 S.Ct. 1997, 138 L.Ed.2d 391 [119 Educ. L. Rep. 29] (1997). [Case No. 11]

84. *American Jewish Congress v. Corporation for Nat'l and Community Serv.*, 399 F.3d 351 [195 Educ. L. Rep. 733] (D.C.Cir. 2005), *cert. denied*, ___ U.S. ___, 126 S.Ct. 1132, ___ L.Ed.2d ___ (2006).

85. *Jackson v. Benson*, 578 N.W.2d 602 [126 Educ. L. Rep. 399] (Wis.1998), *cert. denied*, 525 U.S. 997, 119 S.Ct. 466, 142 L.Ed.2d 419 (1998). *See also Thomas More*

Florida decided that the no-aid provision of the state constitution prohibited the state from providing indirect benefits to "sectarian" schools due to their having received tax dollars through the voucher program.[87] On further review, the Supreme Court of Florida affirmed that the voucher system violated the state constitution's requirement of a uniform system of free public schools.[88]

Conversely, state[89] and federal[90] appellate courts upheld a law from Maine that included non-sectarian schools but specifically excluded religiously affiliated non-public schools from participating in a tuition voucher program. In a similar vein, the Supreme Court of Vermont affirmed the unconstitutionality of a state law that would have permitted taxpayer support to reimburse parents for tuition for religiously affiliated non-public schools.[91] Yet, it was not until a dispute from Ohio made its way to the Supreme Court that vouchers assumed center stage.

The Ohio General Assembly, acting pursuant to a desegregation order, enacted the Ohio Pilot Project Scholarship Program (OPPSP) to assist children in Cleveland's failing public schools.[92] The main goal of the OPPSP, which contains significant anti-discrimination provisions, was to permit an equal number of students to receive vouchers and receive tutorial assistance grants while still attending regular public schools. Another part of the law provided greater choices to parents and children via the creation of community (known as charter schools elsewhere) and magnet schools while a third section featured tutorial assistance for children.

In an initial challenge, the Supreme Court of Ohio upheld the OPPSP[93] but severed the part of the law affording priority to parents who belonged to a religious group supporting a sectarian institution. In deciding that the OPPSP violated the state constitutional requirement that every statute have only one subject, the court struck it down. The court stayed enforcement of its order to avoid disrupting the then current school year. The General Assembly of Ohio quickly re-enacted a revised statute.

A federal trial court in Ohio, relying largely on *Nyquist*,[94] enjoined the operation of the revised statute as violative of the Establishment

High School v. Burmaster, 704 N.W.2d 349 [202 Educ. L. Rep. 793] (Wis. Ct. App. 2005), *review denied* (2005) (affirming that the program applied only to non-public schools in Milwaukee).

86. *Bush v. Holmes*, 767 So.2d 668 [147 Educ. L. Rep. 1125] (Fla.Dist.Ct.App.2000), *review denied*, 790 So.2d 1104 (Fla.2001).

87. *Bush v. Holmes*, 886 So.2d 340 [193 Educ. L. Rep. 938] (Fla Dist. Ct. App. 2004).

88. *Bush v. Holmes*, 919 So.2d 392 (Fla. 2006).

89. *Bagley v. Raymond School Dep't*, 728 A.2d 127 [134 Educ. L. Rep. 226] (Me. 1999), *cert. denied*, 528 U.S. 947, 120 S.Ct. 364, 145 L.Ed.2d 285 (1999).

90. *Strout v. Albanese*, 178 F.3d 57 [135 Educ. L. Rep. 398] (1st Cir.1999), *cert. denied*, 528 U.S. 931, 120 S.Ct. 329, 145 L.Ed.2d 256 (1999).

91. *Chittenden Town School Dist. v. Department of Educ.*, 738 A.2d 539 [138 Educ. L. Rep. 858] (Vt.1999).

92. OHIO REV. CODE ANN. §§ 3313.974 *et seq.*

93. *Simmons–Harris v. Goff*, 711 N.E.2d 203 [135 Educ. L. Rep. 596] (Ohio 1999).

94. 413 U.S. 756, 93 S.Ct. 2955, 37 L.Ed.2d 948 (1973).

Clause.[95] A divided Sixth Circuit, also applying *Nyquist,* affirmed that the OPPSP had the impermissible effect of advancing religion.[96]

In *Zelman v. Simmons–Harris (Zelman),* the Court reversed the judgment of the Sixth Circuit and upheld the constitutionality of the OPPSP. Relying on *Agostini,* the Court began by considering "whether the government acted with the purpose of advancing or inhibiting religions [and] whether the aid has the 'effect' of advancing or inhibiting religion."[97] Recognizing the lack of a dispute over the program's valid secular purpose in providing programming for poor children in a failing school system, the Court examined whether the program had the forbidden "effect" of advancing or inhibiting religion. The Court was satisfied that the voucher program was constitutional because, as part of the state's far-reaching attempt to provide greater educational opportunities in a failing school system, it allocated aid on the basis of neutral secular criteria that neither favored nor disfavored religion, was made available to both religious and secular beneficiaries on a nondiscriminatory basis, and offered assistance directly to a broad class of citizens who directed the aid to religious schools based entirely on their own genuine and independent private choices. The Court was not troubled by the fact that most of the participating schools were religiously affiliated insofar as this situation arose because surrounding public schools refused to take part in the program. The majority also indicated that since the Ohio program differed greatly from the one in *Nyquist,* the lower courts misplaced their reliance on it. The Court concluded that since it was following an unbroken line of cases supporting true private choice that provided benefits directly to a wide range of needy private individuals, its only choice was to uphold the voucher program.

Post-*Zelman* litigation challenging vouchers has focused largely on state constitutional grounds since they are typically more stringent than under the Federal Constitution. For example, the Supreme Court of Colorado affirmed that a program that required school boards to pay a portion of locally raised tax revenues to parents with children who were performing at an unsatisfactory level in public schools, which in turn required the parents to pay those funds to non-public schools with special programs designed for those children, violated the local control provisions of the state constitution.[98] At the same time, the First Circuit affirmed that a law in Maine, which stipulated that only non-sectarian non-public schools were eligible to participate in a program that permitted students to receive public funds to attend schooling from kindergarten through eighth grade, did not violate equal protection rights because rational relationship existed between the statute and the state's legitimate interests.[99] The court also rejected the parental claim that such a

---

95. *Simmons-Harris v. Zelman,* 72 F.Supp.2d 834 [140 Educ. L. Rep. 243] (N.D.Ohio 1999).

96. *Simmons-Harris v. Zelman,* 234 F.3d 945 [149 Educ. L. Rep. 691] (6th Cir. 2000).

97. 536 U.S. 639, 649, 122 S.Ct. 2460, 153 L.Ed.2d 604 [166 Educ. L. Rep. 30] (2002). [Case No. 15]

98. *Owens v. Colorado Congress of Parents, Teachers and Students,* 92 P.3d 933 [189 Educ. L. Rep. 395] (Colo. 2004).

99. *Eulitt ex rel. Eulitt v. Maine, Dep't of Educ.,* 386 F.3d 344 [192 Educ. L. Rep. 651] (1st Cir. 2004).

judgment would have infringed on their free exercise of religion because the limitation on funds did not impermissibly interfere with their fundamental right to choose religious education for their children. Similarly, the Eleventh Circuit affirmed that under a voucher program that was available only to children who attended failing schools, the state of Florida had no duty to pay for students to attend non-public schools.[100]

The Court's Modern Establishment Clause Jurisprudence: Religious Activities and Public Schools

Unlike its evolving jurisprudence with regard to aid to students and their religiously affiliated non-public schools, the Supreme Court's attitude toward school-sponsored prayer and religious activity in public education has remained constant. After striking down, then upholding, different types of released-time programs for religious instruction, starting with *Engel v. Vitale*,[101] the Court has had an essentially unbroken line of cases prohibiting school-sponsored prayer and religious activity in public schools.

Released Time

The practice of permitting public school officials to release children during the class day so that they could receive religious instruction reached the Supreme Court in two different cases. The first challenge arose in Champaign, Illinois, where members of the Jewish, Roman Catholic, and Protestant faiths formed a voluntary association and obtained approval from the local school board for a cooperative plan to offer religion classes to children whose parents agreed to have them take part in the program. The students had to be released from their public schools while their religion instructors notified their regular teachers if they were absent. The classes were taught in regular classrooms, in three separate groups, by Protestant teachers, Catholic priests, and a Jewish rabbi. Students who did not attend religious instruction had to go to some other place in their schools to pursue their secular studies.

In *People of State of Illinois ex rel. McCollum v. Board of Education of School District No. 71, Champaign County (McCollum)*,[102] the Court invalidated the program. The Court pointed out not only that tax-supported public school buildings were being used to disseminate religious doctrine but also that public school officials gave religious groups an invaluable, albeit impermissible, aid in helping them by providing students for their classes via the state's compulsory education machinery.

Four years later, the Supreme Court considered the constitutionality of a different type of released-time program. A statute from New York

---

100. *Children A & B ex rel. Cooper v. Florida*, 355 F.Supp.2d 1298 [195 Educ. L. Rep. 889] (N.D. Fla. 2004), *aff'd sub nom.; Cooper v. Florida*, 140 Fed.Appx. 845 [201 Educ. L. Rep. 111] (11th Cir. 2005).

101. 370 U.S. 421, 82 S.Ct. 1261, 8 L.Ed.2d 601 (1962).

102. 333 U.S. 203, 68 S.Ct. 461, 92 L.Ed. 649 (1948). [Case No. 2]

permitted officials to release students from their public schools so that they could attend religious classes at other locations. Opponents of the program claimed that this plan was not basically different from the one in *McCollum,* arguing that the weight and influence of public schools was used to support a program of religious instruction because records were kept with regard to which children were released while the remaining students had to stay in school even though regular classes were halted so that their peers could attend released time classes.

In *Zorach v. Clauson*,[103] the Court affirmed that the program was constitutional, agreeing that state officials can accommodate the religious wishes of parents by releasing their children at their request. Unlike *McCollum*, the Court was satisfied that the practice was permissible since public school buildings were not used for religious instruction. The Court commented that this disagreement, like many in constitutional law, was one of the degrees of separation of Church and State. The Court also analogized that released-time was similar to acceptable arrangements and excuses for students who were absent for religious reasons.

More than fifty years later, the Second Circuit rejected a challenge to another released-time program from New York that a mother filed on behalf of her children, neither of whom participated in the activity. Under the program, parents who wished to have their children take part in its activities were released from classes early so that they could receive instruction at nearby religious schools. Students who did not take part in the program remained in school classrooms but did not engage in organized activities until the participants returned. Affirming a grant of summary judgment in favor of the school board, the court determined that the program passed Establishment Clause analysis because it did not use public funds or on-site religious instruction, was purely voluntary, and educators did not bring any specific coercion or pressure to bear on non-participants.[104]

Use of the Bible

Long a staple resource in the education of American children,[105] the landscape with regard to the use of the Bible in public schools shifted dramatically in light of the companion cases of *School District of Abington Township v. Schempp* and *Murray v. Curlett (Abington)*.[106] In *Abington*, the Supreme Court found that prayer and Bible reading, as part of the opening of a school day, violated the Establishment Clause. In its analysis, the Court extensively documented its point that in prohibiting Bible reading, it was not deviating from its established precedents. The

---

103. 343 U.S. 306, 72 S.Ct. 679, 96 L.Ed. 954 (1952). [Case No. 3]

104. *Pierce ex rel. Pierce v. Sullivan West Cent. School Dist.*, 379 F.3d 56 [191 Educ. L. Rep. 36] (2d Cir. 2004).

105. For apparently the first case involving the Bible in public schools, *see*

Board of Educ. v. Minor, 23 Ohio St. 211 (Ohio 1872) (upholding a school board's vote to stop Bible reading in public schools).

106. 374 U.S. 203, 83 S.Ct. 1560, 10 L.Ed.2d 844 (1963). [Case No. 4]

Court indicated that since the Bible was a sectarian document, the First Amendment dictated governmental neutrality with regard to religious matters based on the premises that the state could not aid any or all religions and that every person has a right to choose a personal course with reference to religion, free of any compulsion from the state. The Court postulated that it consistently recognized that the First Amendment withdrew from the government all legislative power respecting religious belief or its expression.

In creating a measure to evaluate the constitutionality of prayer and Bible reading in public schools, the Court declared that "[t]he test may be stated as follows: what are the purpose and the primary effect of the [legislative] enactment? . . . [T]o withstand the strictures of the Establishment Clause there must be a secular legislative purpose and a primary effect that neither advances nor inhibits religion."[107] Perhaps in an attempt to allay concerns that it was anti-religious, the Court added in dicta that nothing in its opinion excluded the secular study of the Bible in public schools in an appropriate context such as literature or history.[108]

Following *Abington*, controversies continue over the place, if any, of the Bible in the public school curriculum.[109] For instance, the Fifth Circuit disapproved a "Bible as Literature" course because it was taught essentially from a Christian religious perspective as part of fundamentalist and/or evangelical doctrine.[110] The court also noted that the state-approved textbook did not contain a discussion of the Bible's literary qualities. Other courts suggested guidelines under which the Bible could have been studied, including using fully certificated teachers who are employed in the same manner as other staff, vesting complete control of course content and materials in school boards, supervising courses to assure objectivity in teaching, and requiring that no part of courses be mandatory for students.[111]

The Eighth Circuit affirmed the unconstitutionality of a program in Arkansas that permitted students to leave their regular classrooms to learn about the Bible in voluntary sessions that took place during regular school hours.[112] The classes were taught by volunteers who did

---

107. *Id.* at 222.

108. The Court wrote that:

"It certainly may be said that the Bible is worthy of study for its literary and historic qualities. Nothing we have said here indicates that such study of the Bible or of religion, when presented objectively as part of a secular program of education, may not be effected consistently with the First Amendment." *Id.* at 225.

"Justice Brennan's concurrence added that [t]he holding of the Court today plainly does not foreclose teaching about the Holy Scriptures or about the differences between religious sects in classes in literature or history . . . ," *Id.* at 300 (Brennan J., concurring).

109. *See, e.g., Roberts v. Madigan,* 921 F.2d 1047 [64 Educ. L. Rep. 1038] (10th Cir.1990), *cert. denied,* 505 U.S. 1218, 112 S.Ct. 3025, 120 L.Ed.2d 896 (1992) (preventing a teacher from silently reading a Bible during class time).

110. *Hall v. Board of School Comm'rs of Conecuh County,* 656 F.2d 999 [11 Educ. L. Rep. 445] (5th Cir.1981).

111. *Wiley v. Franklin,* 497 F.Supp. 390 (E.D.Tenn.1980); *Crockett v. Sorenson,* 568 F.Supp. 1422 [13 Educ. L. Rep. 290] (W.D.Va.1983).

112. *Doe v. Human,* 725 F.Supp. 1503 [57 Educ. L. Rep. 888] (W.D.Ark.1989), *aff'd,* 923 F.2d 857 [65 Educ. L. Rep.714]

not act on behalf of any church, and students did not receive course credit for participating. In sidestepping whether the classes were primarily religious or secular, the court contended that the program had the principal effect of advancing Christianity. Five years later, a federal trial court in Mississippi forbade a school board from offering a Bible-study class that was taught in a rotation with music, physical education, and library classes or one that purported to teach the history of the Middle East as violating the Establishment Clause.[113] Similarly, opponents challenged a school board's adoption of a two-semester Bible history course, with time equally divided between the Old and New Testaments, even though it already had a comparative religion class. A federal trial court in Florida permitted the Old Testament class to proceed but enjoined the one on the New Testament based on its belief that the plaintiffs were likely to prevail on the merits of their claim that it violated the Establishment Clause.[114] More recently, the Sixth Circuit affirmed that a school board in Tennessee's fifty-one year practice of permitting students from a local Christian college to teach weekly religion classes that presented the Christian Bible as religious truth during the regular school day for students in grades K–5 violated the Establishment Clause because it failed all three parts of the *Lemon* test.[115] The court was convinced that permitting religious instruction in public schools was an unconstitutional establishment of religion.

Prayer in School

In *Engel v. Vitale*,[116] the Supreme Court accepted its first case involving school prayer. At issue was a prayer composed by the New York State Board of Regents for suggested use in public schools to inculcate moral and spiritual values in students. When a local school board adopted the prayer as part of a policy that required its daily recitation in class, parents challenged its doing so even though it included a provision that permitted them to request that their children be exempted from taking part as long as they did so in writing. The prayer was:

> Almighty God, we acknowledge our dependence upon Thee, and we beg Thy blessings upon us, our parents, our teachers and our country.[117]

The Supreme Court reversed earlier judgments in favor of the school board, ruling that the daily recitation of prayer was a religious activity inconsistent with the Establishment Clause. The Court devoted a significant portion of its opinion to a review of the history of state-sponsored

---

(8th Cir.1990), *cert. denied*, 499 U.S. 922, 111 S.Ct. 1315, 113 L.Ed.2d 248 (1991).

113. *Herdahl v. Pontotoc County School Dist.*, 933 F.Supp. 582 [112 Educ. L. Rep. 131] (N.D. Miss.1996).

114. *Gibson v. Lee County School Bd.*, 1 F.Supp.2d 1426 [127 Educ. L. Rep. 85] (M.D. Fla. 1998).

115. *Doe v. Porter*, 370 F.3d 558 [188 Educ. L. Rep. 100] (6th Cir. 2004).

116. 370 U.S. 421, 82 S.Ct. 1261, 8 L.Ed.2d 601 (1962).

117. *Id.* at 422.

prayer in the Anglo–American system of government from Sixteenth Century England through the Colonial Period, asserting that "[t]here can be no doubt that New York State's prayer program officially establishes the religious beliefs embodied in the Regents' prayer."[118]

In its rationale, the Court observed that the First Amendment's Establishment and Free Exercise Clauses forbid different types of governmental encroachment against religion. It maintained that since the Establishment Clause, unlike the Free Exercise Clause, does not depend on any direct government compulsion, public officials violate it by enacting laws that establish an official religion regardless of whether their action coerces non-believers. The Court voiced its fear that even absent overt pressure, placing the power, privilege, and support of the government behind a particular religious belief ran the risk of asserting indirect coercion on others, especially minorities, to conform to the officially approved religion. The Court posited that since the Founders of the Constitution considered religion to be "too personal, too sacred, too holy, to permit its 'unhallowed perversion' by a civil magistrate," state-sponsored prayer was contrary to their original intent in drafting the First Amendment.

A year later, the Court barred the use of prayer as part of opening exercises in public schools in *Abington,* discussed in the previous section. Subsequently, almost twenty years would pass before the Court returned to the question of prayer in public schools on the merits.

In the interim, lower courts addressed prayer in a variety of circumstances. In an illustrative dispute, the Second Circuit upheld a principal's prohibiting students from reciting prayers before eating a mid-morning snack.[119] The Seventh Circuit barred the use of a prayer that did not include the word "God"[120] even though school assemblies were voluntary and leaders of the student council had requested permission to begin them with a prayer. In addition, the Supreme Court of New Jersey invalidated a local board policy that would have allowed students, immediately prior to the formal opening of school, to join in a voluntary religious exercise in a gymnasium, where a student volunteer would select, and read, the remarks of the chaplain of the Congressional Record to the gathered assembly.[121] The court feared that this procedure was no different from reading prayers directly from a religious source.

The question of voluntary school prayer emerged in several forms. The Supreme Judicial Court of Massachusetts ordered an end to a local board's plan for voluntary prayer that it instituted in accord with a statute permitting students to participate in such activities before the beginning of the school day if their parents approved.[122] During that

---

118. *Id.* at 430.

119. *Stein v. Oshinsky,* 348 F.2d 999 (2d Cir.1965), *cert. denied,* 382 U.S. 957, 86 S.Ct. 435, 15 L.Ed.2d 361 (1965).

120. *DeSpain v. DeKalb County Community School Dist.,* 384 F.2d 836 (7th Cir. 1967), *cert. denied,* 390 U.S. 906, 88 S.Ct. 815, 19 L.Ed.2d 873 (1968).

121. *State Bd. of Educ. v. Board of Educ. of Netcong,* 270 A.2d 412 (N.J.1970), *cert. denied,* 401 U.S. 1013, 91 S.Ct. 1253, 28 L.Ed.2d 550 (1971).

122. *Commissioner of Educ. v. School Comm. of Leyden,* 267 N.E.2d 226 (Mass. 1971), *cert. denied,* 404 U.S. 849, 92 S.Ct. 85, 30 L.Ed.2d 88 (1971). *See also Kent v.*

same year, the Third Circuit also struck down a program, adopted at the urging of students and parents in Pennsylvania, to permit voluntary nondenominational mass prayer and Bible reading on the basis that it was state action.[123] A decade later, the Fifth Circuit struck down a similar statute from Louisiana[124] while the Eleventh Circuit argued that it was unconstitutional for teachers in Alabama to engage in prayer if there was no board policy or state statute that motivated their activities.[125] The court wrote that since the school board was aware of the activities and took no steps to stop them, it, in effect, ratified the teachers' conduct.

When a board knowingly permitted a band teacher to conduct prayer and religious activities at school functions, the Eighth Circuit held it liable for attorney fees incurred in obtaining an injunction to stop the practice.[126] In a case from Georgia, the Eleventh Circuit barred a plan that would have not only allowed representatives of the student government to make a random selection of invocation speakers from non-clergy volunteers but which would also have permitted ministers to offer invocations prior to the start of high school football games.[127] In like manner, the Fifth Circuit affirmed that school employees in Texas could neither initiate nor lead students in prayer before and after athletic practices and competitions.[128]

After not addressing such a case in almost twenty years, the Supreme Court examined school-sponsored prayers in public schools in a dispute from Providence, Rhode Island. At issue was whether a religious leader, here a rabbi, could offer prayers as part of official school graduation ceremony incident to a board policy that permitted principals to invite members of the clergy to offer non-sectarian prayers. The principals also gave speakers guidelines for prayers on civic occasions prepared by an interfaith organization. Students were not required to attend the graduation ceremony in order to receive their diplomas.

In *Lee v. Weisman* (*Lee*),[129] a typically divided Supreme Court affirmed earlier judgments that the school-sponsored graduation prayer at issue was unconstitutional. Sidestepping the *Lemon* test, the Court based its judgment on two major points. First, the Court thought that prayer was unacceptable because the state, through school officials, played a pervasive role in the process not only by selecting who would

Commissioner of Educ., 402 N.E.2d 1340 (Mass.1980).

123. *Mangold v. Albert Gallatin Area School Dist.*, 438 F.2d 1194 (3d Cir.1971).

124. *Karen B. v. Treen*, 653 F.2d 897 (5th Cir.1981), *aff'd without written opinion*, 455 U.S. 913, 102 S.Ct. 1267, 71 L.Ed.2d 455 (1982).

125. *Jaffree v. Wallace*, 705 F.2d 1526 [11 Educ. L. Rep. 51] (11th Cir.1983), *aff'd as to this issue*, 466 U.S. 924, 104 S.Ct. 1704, 80 L.Ed.2d 178 (1984).

126. *Steele v. Van Buren Pub. School Dist.*, 845 F.2d 1492 [46 Educ. L. Rep. 572] (8th Cir. 1988).

127. *Jager v. Douglas County School Dist.*, 862 F.2d 824 [50 Educ. L. Rep. 694] (11th Cir. 1989), *cert. denied*, 490 U.S. 1090, 109 S.Ct. 2431, 104 L.Ed.2d 988 (1989).

128. *Doe v. Duncanville Indep. School Dist.*, 70 F.3d 402 [104 Educ. L. Rep. 1032] (5th Cir. 1995).

129. 505 U.S. 577, 112 S.Ct. 2649, 120 L.Ed.2d 467 [75 Educ. L. Rep. 43] (1992). [Case No. 10]

pray but also by directing the content of prayer. Second, the Court feared that such governmental activity could result in psychological coercion of students. The Court was of the opinion that since students were a captive audience who may have been forced, against their own wishes, to participate in ceremonies, they were not genuinely free to be excused from attending.

On the same day that the Court struck down *Lee*, it vacated and remanded without comment a case from the Fifth Circuit with a similar set of facts.[130] The major difference between the suits was that in this case members of a high school's senior class, Texas rather than school officials, selected volunteers to deliver non-sectarian, non-proselytizing prayers at their graduation. On remand, the Fifth Circuit followed the dissent in *Lee* and narrowly interpreted it as precluding only school-sponsored prayers.[131] This time, the Court refused to hear a further appeal, thereby leaving the door open to further controversy.

Following *Lee*, the circuit courts remain divided over the question of student-sponsored prayer at graduation ceremonies. Both the Third and Ninth Circuits struck down student-sponsored prayer while the Fifth, as noted, and Eleventh Circuits have upheld the use of prayer. The Ninth Circuit initially invalidated student-sponsored prayer in Idaho on the ground that since school officials still ultimately controlled the ceremony, they could not permit students to choose whether to have prayer at graduation.[132] The Supreme Court avoided the controversy by vacating the judgment as moot and remanding with instructions to dismiss, apparently since the students had graduated.[133] Shortly thereafter, the Fifth Circuit allowed part of a statute from Mississippi that permitted student-sponsored prayer at graduation to remain in effect but struck down those portions of the law that allowed students to initiate non-sectarian, non-proselytizing prayer at various compulsory and non-compulsory events.[134] The same court also invalidated a law from Louisiana that permitted school officials to allow an opportunity, at the start of each day, for those students and teachers desiring to do so to observe a brief time in prayer or meditation as a violation of the Establishment Clause.[135]

The Third Circuit affirmed that a policy of permitting student-led prayer at a public high school graduation ceremony in New Jersey

130. *Jones v. Clear Creek Indep. School Dist.*, 930 F.2d 416 [67 Educ. L. Rep. 89] (5th Cir. 1991), *cert. granted, vacated, and remanded*, 505 U.S. 1215, 112 S.Ct. 3020, 120 L.Ed.2d 892 [75 Educ. L. Rep. 108] (1992).

131. *Jones v. Clear Creek Indep. School Dist.*, 977 F.2d 963 [78 Educ. L. Rep. 42] (5th Cir. 1992), *reh'g denied*, 983 F.2d 234 (5th Cir.1992), *cert. denied*, 508 U.S. 967, 113 S.Ct. 2950, 124 L.Ed.2d 697 (1993).

132. *Harris v. Joint School Dist. No. 241*, 41 F.3d 447 [95 Educ. L. Rep. 892] (9th Cir.1994).

133. *Cert. granted, judgment vacated with directions to dismiss as moot*, 515 U.S. 1154, 115 S.Ct. 2604, 132 L.Ed.2d 849 [102 Educ. L. Rep. 34] (1995).

134. *Ingebretsen v. Jackson Pub. School Dist.*, 83 F.3d 274 [110 Educ. L. Rep. 942] (5th Cir. 1996), *cert. denied sub nom. Moore v. Ingebretsen*, 519 U.S. 965, 117 S.Ct. 388, 136 L.Ed.2d 304 (1996).

135. The Fifth Circuit affirmed that a statute permitting verbal prayer in school was unconstitutional. *Doe v. School Bd. of Ouachita Parish*, 274 F.3d 289 [160 Educ. L. Rep. 17] (5th Cir.2001).

violated the Establishment Clause since the board's having retained significant authority over the ceremony meant that prayer could not have been treated as promoting the free speech rights of students.[136] After first upholding a board policy from Idaho that would have allowed a minimum of four graduating students to offer an address, poem, reading, song, musical presentation, prayer, or any other presentation at their commencement based on neutral secular criteria,[137] the Ninth Circuit vacated its earlier judgment in decreeing that a parent lacked standing to challenge the policy since the plaintiff graduated.[138]

In two separate cases from California, the Ninth Circuit affirmed that school officials could refuse to allow students to deliver sectarian prayers or proselytizing valedictory addresses. In the first, the court added that the prohibition did not violate the students' free speech rights.[139] In the second, the court agreed that when school officials denied a student's request to include religious proselytizing comments in his salutatorian commencement address, they did not violate his rights to freedom of religion, speech, or equal protection.[140]

The issue of prayers at high school football games re-emerged in Texas where parents and students challenged two board policies that permitted student volunteers to pray at graduations and football games. A federal trial court upheld both policies as long as the prayers were non-sectarian and non-proselytizing. Subsequently, the Fifth Circuit affirmed that prayer at graduation had to be non-sectarian and non-proselytizing but reversed in striking down the policy permitting prayers at football games.[141] Even though the board appealed on both forms of prayer, at graduation and prior to football games, the Supreme Court opted to address only the latter,[142] thereby leaving the split between the circuits over student-led graduation prayer in place.

In *Santa Fe Independent School District v. Doe (Santa Fe)*,[143] a typically closely divided Supreme Court affirmed that the policy permitting student-led prayers prior to the start of high school football games violated the Establishment Clause. In *Santa Fe*, the Court primarily relied on the endorsement test[144] rather than the psychological coercion

---

136. *American Civil Liberties Union of N.J. v. Black Horse Pike Reg'l Bd. of Educ.*, 84 F.3d 1471 [109 Educ. L. Rep. 1118] (3d Cir.1996).

137. *Doe v. Madison School Dist. No. 321*, 147 F.3d 832 [127 Educ. L. Rep. 607] (9th Cir. 1998).

138. *Doe v. Madison School Dist. No. 321*, *reh'g granted, opinion withdrawn*, 165 F.3d 1265 [132 Educ. L. Rep. 67] (9th Cir. 1999), *vacated*, 177 F.3d 789 [135 Educ. L. Rep. 387] (9th Cir.1999).

139. *Cole v. Oroville Union High School Dist.*, 228 F.3d 1092 [147 Educ. L. Rep. 878] (9th Cir. 2000), *cert. denied sub nom. Niemeyer v. Oroville Union High School Dist.*, 532 U.S. 905, 121 S.Ct. 1228, 149 L.Ed.2d 138 (2001).

140. *Lassonde v. Pleasanton Unified School Dist.*, 320 F.3d 979 [173 Educ. L. Rep. 778] (9th Cir.2003), *cert. denied*, 540 U.S. 817, 124 S.Ct. 78, 157 L.Ed.2d 34 (2003).

141. *Doe v. Santa Fe Indep. School Dist.*, 168 F.3d 806 [132 Educ. L. Rep. 687] (5th Cir.1999).

142. 528 U.S. 1002, 120 S.Ct. 494, 145 L.Ed.2d 381 [140 Educ. L. Rep. 21] (1999).

143. 530 U.S. 290, 120 S.Ct. 2266, 147 L.Ed.2d 295 [145 Educ. L. Rep. 21] (2000). [Case No. 12]

144. The endorsement test, which asks whether the purpose of a governmental action is to endorse or approve of a religion or religious activity, first arose in *Lynch v.*

test enunciated in *Lee*. Put another way, the Court reviewed the status of prayer from the perspective of whether its being permitted at football games was an impermissible governmental approval or endorsement of religion rather than as a form of psychological coercion that subjected fans to values and/or beliefs other than their own. In striking down the prayer policy, the Court rejected the board's three main arguments. First, it rejected the board's contention that the policy furthered the free speech rights of students. Second, the Court disagreed with the board's stance that the policy was neutral on its face. Third, the majority rebuffed the board's defense that a legal challenge was premature since prayer had not been offered at a football game under the policy. In a related dispute, the Fifth Circuit ultimately affirmed that a high school student and her parents lacked standing to challenge the constitutionality of a board policy prohibiting religious references in public address system messages broadcast prior to football games because they could not demonstrate any adverse effect from the judgment.[145]

Controversy remains after *Santa Fe*. In two separate cases, the Eleventh Circuit upheld student-initiated prayer in school settings. In Alabama, parents challenged a state statute permitting non-sectarian, non-proselytizing student-initiated prayer at school-related assemblies, sporting events, graduation ceremonies, and other school events. According to the court, the board's permitting genuinely student-initiated religious speech in school and at school-related events did not violate the Establishment Clause and was required under the Free Speech and Freedom of Expression Clauses. The court also acknowledged that while the students' religious speech could not be supervised by the state, it was subject to time, manner, and place restrictions.[146] On remand, the Eleventh Circuit responded that the injunction, which prevented the board from permitting any prayer in a public context at school functions, was over-broad to the extent that it equated all student religious speech in any public context at school with state-supported speech.[147] The court was of the opinion that the school officials may not prohibit genuinely student-initiated religious speech nor apply restrictions, on the time, place, and manner of that speech, which exceed those placed on students' secular speech. The Supreme Court again refused to hear an appeal.[148]

In Florida, a superintendent of schools issued a memorandum for high school graduation ceremonies in response to a request from students who wanted to have some type of brief opening and/or closing

Donnelly, 465 U.S. 668, 687ff, 104 S.Ct. 1355, 1366ff, 79 L.Ed.2d 604 (1984) (O'Connor, J., concurring) (a non-school case upholding a display including a creche among secular symbols).

145. *Ward v. Santa Fe Indep. School Dist.*, 393 F.3d 599 [194 Educ. L. Rep. 488] (5th Cir. 2004).

146. *Chandler v. James*, 180 F.3d 1254 [136 Educ. L. Rep. 201] (11th Cir.1999), *request for en banc reh'g denied*, 198 F.3d 265 (11th Cir.1999), *cert. granted, judgment vacated and remanded sub nom. Chandler v. Siegelman*, 530 U.S. 1256, 120 S.Ct. 2714, 147 L.Ed.2d 979 [146 Educ. L. Rep. 622] (2000).

147. *Chandler v. Siegelman*, 230 F.3d 1313 [148 Educ. L. Rep. 138] (11th Cir. 2000), *suggestion for reh'g en banc denied*, *Chandler v. Siegelman*, 248 F.3d 1032 [153 Educ. L. Rep. 528] (11th Cir.2001).

148. *Cert. denied sub nom. Chandler ex rel. Chandler v. Siegelman*, 533 U.S. 916, 121 S.Ct. 2521, 150 L.Ed.2d 694 (2001).

message by a classmate. The guidelines afforded students the chance to direct their own graduation messages without being monitored or reviewed by school officials. When speakers at ten of seventeen high school graduation ceremonies delivered some form of religious message, other students unsuccessfully challenged the practice as an establishment of religion and an infringement on their free exercise of religion. A federal trial court entered a judgment in favor of the board. On appeal, the Eleventh Circuit initially reversed in favor of the students[149] but was overruled by an en banc panel.[150] The Supreme Court vacated and remanded[151] for further consideration in light of *Santa Fe*. The Eleventh Circuit reinstated its original judgment since it was satisfied that the policy of permitting a graduating student, elected by members of the class, to deliver an unrestricted message did not facially violate the Establishment Clause insofar as it had the secular purposes of not only affording graduating students the opportunity to direct their graduation ceremony but also of permitting student freedom of expression.[152] In addition, the Ninth Circuit affirmed that school officials did not violate a student's right to the free exercise of religion in requiring him to delete religious proselytizing comments from a commencement address.[153]

A novel question arose in Nebraska where a school board member recited the Lord's Prayer at a commencement ceremony. Under the threat of litigation, the board dropped a proposed invocation and benediction from the ceremony. Even so, the board member, acting on his own initiative, included the prayer as part of his remarks. A divided Eighth Circuit affirmed that the board was not liable since the individual who recited the prayer did so privately in opposition to the board's collectively choosing not to include it in the ceremony.[154]

The question of prayer at a school board meeting arose in Ohio where a teacher sued his board for opening its sessions in such a manner. The Sixth Circuit vitiated the practice as unconstitutional since students were often involved in the meetings and hearings in a variety of settings.[155] At the same time, the court rejected the notion that meetings qualified under the legislative prayer exception because they were an integral component of the public school system. In a similar dispute from California, the Ninth Circuit found that teachers had standing to sue and that their school board violated the Establishment Clause by allowing prayers "in the name of Jesus" at its meetings.[156] Further, a federal

---

149. *Adler v. Duval County School Bd.*, 174 F.3d 1236 [134 Educ. L. Rep. 790] (11th Cir.1999).

150. *Adler v. Duval County School Bd.*, 206 F.3d 1070 [142 Educ. L. Rep. 773] (11th Cir.2000).

151. *Adler v. Duval County School Bd.*, 531 U.S. 801, 121 S.Ct. 31, 148 L.Ed.2d 3 [148 Educ. L. Rep. 31] (2000).

152. *On remand, opinion reinstated, Adler v. Duval County School Bd.*, 250 F.3d 1330 [154 Educ. L. Rep. 80], *cert. denied*, 534 U.S. 1065, 122 S.Ct. 664, 151 L.Ed.2d 579 (2001).

153. *Lassonde v. Pleasanton Unified School Dist.*, 320 F.3d 979 [173 Educ. L Rep. 778] (9th Cir.2003).

154. *Doe ex rel. Doe v. School. Dist. of the City of Norfolk*, 340 F.3d 605 [180 Educ. L. Rep. 39] (8th Cir. 2003).

155. *Coles ex rel. Coles v. Cleveland Bd. of Educ.*, 171 F.3d 369 [133 Educ. L. Rep. 392] (6th Cir.1999), *petition for reh'g en banc denied*, 183 F.3d 538 (6th Cir.1999).

156. *Bacus v. Palo Verde Unified School Dist. Bd. of Educ.*, 52 Fed.Appx. 355 [172 Educ. L. Rep. 24] (9th Cir.2002).

trial court in Louisiana enjoined a school board from starting its meetings with prayer in explaining that doing so violated the *Lemon* test.[157] Conversely, in a case with an interesting twist, the federal trial court in Delaware decided that prayer at a school board meeting was constitutional.[158] Unlike the previous three cases, the court relied on the legislative prayer exception that the Supreme Court enunciated in *Marsh v. Chambers*.[159]

In a similar vein, a case from Arkansas involved a dispute over whether school officials could start mandatory in-service training sessions and faculty meetings with prayer. In the face of a challenge by a teacher and part-time bus driver who objected to conducting prayers at mandatory meetings, the Eighth Circuit affirmed that the practice violated the Establishment Clause since it constituted government endorsement of religion.[160]

Periods of Silence

The lower federal courts have not agreed on whether a brief period of silence before the start of a school day involves religion. For example, the federal trial court in Massachusetts dismissed a challenge to a law in deciding that it did not violate the First Amendment or the students' right of free exercise of religion and did not prohibit or inhibit parental right to guide and instruct their children with regard to religion.[161] Moreover, after a federal trial court in Tennessee struck down such a statute, the Sixth Circuit vacated and remanded its judgment.[162] However, shortly thereafter, a federal trial court in New Mexico vitiated such a law for lacking a secular purpose.[163]

In its first case on the merits of such a dispute, the Supreme Court reviewed a law from Alabama that authorized a period of silence at the start of the school day for "meditation or voluntary prayer." In *Wallace v. Jaffree*,[164] the Court examined the bill's legislative history, including the purpose of the sponsors to return voluntary prayer to the public schools and its preamble, concluding that it lacked a secular purpose. Subsequently, after lower federal courts struck a statute from New Jersey down as unconstitutional, the Supreme Court dismissed an appeal

157. *See also Doe v. Tangipahoa Parish School Bd.*, 2005 WL 517341 (E.D. La. 2005).

158. *Dobrich v. Walls*, 380 F.Supp.2d 366 [201 Educ. L. Rep. 163] (D. Del. 2005).

159. *Marsh v. Chambers*, 463 U.S. 783, 103 S.Ct. 3330, 77 L.Ed.2d 1019 (1983) (permitting prayer at the start of legislative sessions in Nebraska).

160. *Warnock v. Archer*, 380 F.3d 1076 [191 Educ. L. Rep. 620] (8th Cir. 2004), *reh'g and reh'g en banc denied, on remand*, 397 F.3d 1024 (8th Cir. 2005).

161. *Gaines v. Anderson*, 421 F.Supp. 337 (D.Mass.1976). *See also Opinion of the Justices*, 108 N.H. 97, 228 A.2d 161 (1967) (holding that a law requiring a period of silence for meditation would not have violated the First Amendment).

162. *Beck v. McElrath*, 548 F.Supp. 1161 [7 Educ. L. Rep. 156] (M.D.Tenn. 1982), *judgment vacated, appeal dismissed sub nom. Beck v. Alexander*, 718 F.2d 1098 (6th Cir.1983).

163. *Duffy v. Las Cruces Pub. Schools*, 557 F.Supp. 1013 [9 Educ. L. Rep. 1206] (D.N.M. 1983).

164. 472 U.S. 38, 105 S.Ct. 2479, 86 L.Ed.2d 29 [25 Educ. L. Rep. 39] (1985).

without reaching the issue on the merits.[165] The Court ruled that the former speaker of the state general assembly and former president of the state senate who intervened in and participated in the litigation to uphold the law's constitutionality could no longer participate in the suit since they lacked standing by virtue of having lost their leadership positions.

More recently, two circuit courts upheld statutes permitting silence in school. The Eleventh Circuit affirmed that a state statute from Georgia that permitted a moment of silent reflection in school was constitutional since it passed all three prongs of the *Lemon* test.[166] Similarly, the Fourth Circuit upheld a law from Virginia, mandating a minute of silence in schools that included the word pray in listing an unlimited range of mental activities that it authorized.[167] The court affirmed that the statute did not violate the Establishment Clause because even though it had two purposes, one clearly secular and the other an accommodation of religion, it did not run afoul of the *Lemon* test's requirement of only a secular purpose. The court reasoned that the statute neither advanced nor hindered religion and did not result in the government's becoming excessively entangled with religion.

Student-Initiated Religious Activity

In an early dispute, the Supreme Court chose not to review a case that upheld a school board's refusal to allow students to conduct voluntary communal prayer meetings in school immediately before the start of the academic day.[168] Previously, the Second Circuit noted that the prohibition did not infringe the students' rights to the free exercise of religion, freedom of speech, or equal protection since educational officials had a compelling interest to remove any indication that they sponsored religious activity in public schools.

A week before it refused to hear an appeal in the preceding case, in *Widmar v. Vincent (Widmar)*,[169] the Court determined that a state university in Missouri that made its facilities generally available for activities of registered student groups could not close them to other such groups based on the religious content of their speech. Relying on the framework of freedom of speech, the Court recognized that since over 100 registered student groups used the facilities, officials created a forum for exchange of ideas and so could not bar access to it solely because of content of the speech. The Court expressly distinguished the case from those involving religious activities in public grade schools by

---

165. *Jurisdiction dismissed sub nom. Karcher v. May*, 479 U.S. 1062, 107 S.Ct. 946, 93 L.Ed.2d 995 [38 Educ. L. Rep. 416] (1987), *appeal dismissed*, 484 U.S. 72, 108 S.Ct. 388, 98 L.Ed.2d 327 [42 Educ. L. Rep. 1062] (1987).

166. *Bown v. Gwinnett County School Dist.*, 112 F.3d 1464 [118 Educ. L. Rep. 28] (11th Cir. 1997).

167. *Brown v. Gilmore*, 258 F.3d 265 [155 Educ. L. Rep. 1031] (4th Cir.2001), *cert. denied*, 533 U.S. 1301, 122 S.Ct. 1, 150 L.Ed.2d 782 (2001).

168. *Brandon v. Board of Educ. of Guilderland Cent. School Dist.*, 635 F.2d 971 (2d Cir.1980), *cert. denied*, 454 U.S. 1123, 102 S.Ct. 970, 71 L.Ed.2d 109 (1981).

169. 454 U.S. 263, 102 S.Ct. 269, 70 L.Ed.2d 440 [1 Educ. L. Rep. 13] (1981).

observing that facilities in these settings are not generally used as open forums and that university students are less impressionable than younger students.

Two years later, the Supreme Court refused to review a case from Texas wherein the Fifth Circuit held that a board policy of permitting students to gather at a school with supervision for voluntary religious meetings close to the beginning or end of the day was unconstitutional.[170] The court wrote that the policy implied recognition of religious activities and meetings as an integral part of a school's extracurricular program along with implicit approval of educational officials.

Spurred on in large part in response to *Widmar*, Congress enacted the Equal Access Act,[171] which provides that any public secondary school that receives federal financial assistance and permits one or more non-curriculum related student groups to meet on school premises during noninstructional time must not withhold such privilege on the basis of the religious, political, philosophical, or other content of the speech at such meetings.

The Supreme Court upheld the Equal Access Act in *Board of Education of Westside Community Schools v. Mergens (Mergens)*.[172] Relying on statutory interpretation rather than reaching the constitutional question, the Court was of the view that Congress maintained that most high school students could recognize that allowing a religious club to function in school does not imply endorsement of religion. However, insofar as Congress did not define "non-curriculum related," the Court thought it necessary to do so in order to ascertain the status of some student groups. The Court asserted that since several existing clubs failed to satisfy the criteria, the religious group was entitled to meet in school. Insofar as only four Justices agreed that the Equal Access Act passed Establishment Clause muster, but upheld it on the basis of statutory interpretation, the Court left the door open to further litigation in a line of cases that treat religious expression as a hybrid that protect the rights of religious groups to express their opinions as a form of free speech.[173]

Following *Mergens*, it was clear that the Equal Access Act expressly does not protect speech that is otherwise unlawful. In such a case, the Ninth Circuit held that the Equal Access Act did not protect a violation of a state constitutional church-state restriction greater than that in the Establishment Clause.[174] The panel emphasized the Court's determina-

---

170. *Lubbock Civil Liberties Union v. Lubbock Indep. School Dist.*, 669 F.2d 1038 [2 Educ. L. Rep. 961] (5th Cir.1982), *cert. denied*, 459 U.S. 1155, 103 S.Ct. 800, 74 L.Ed.2d 1003 (1983).

171. 20 U.S.C.A. §§ 4071 *et seq.* This statute is in the appendix.

172. 496 U.S. 226, 110 S.Ct. 2356, 110 L.Ed.2d 191 [60 Educ. L. Rep. 320] (1990). [Case No. 9]

173. *See, e.g., Rosenberger v. Rector and Visitors of Univ. of Va.*, 515 U.S. 819, 115 S.Ct. 2510, 132 L.Ed.2d 700 [101 Educ. L. Rep. 552] (1995).

174. *Garnett v. Renton School Dist. No. 403*, 987 F.2d 641 [81 Educ. L. Rep. 704] (9th Cir. 1993), *cert. denied*, 510 U.S. 819, 114 S.Ct. 72, 126 L.Ed.2d 41 (1993), *appeal after remand*, 21 F.3d 1113 [91 Educ. L. Rep. 31] (9th Cir.1994), *on remand*, 1994 WL 555397 (W.D.Wash. 1994) (granting a declaratory judgment and awarding attorney fees to the plaintiffs).

tion that the Equal Access Act had to be read as effectuating a broad Congressional purpose and so remained in effect, thereby preempting state law.

Circuit courts have since extended the scope of the Equal Access Act to allow students to select leaders who comply with a club's religious standards,[175] to meet during lunch time[176] and a school's morning "activity period" at which attendance was taken,[177] and to have access to funding and fund-raising activities, a school yearbook, public address system, bulletin board, school supplies, school vehicles, and audio-visual equipment.[178] Yet, at least one court rejected the claim that a school board created a limited open forum that would have permitted members of a religious club to make announcements involving prayers and Bible readings before classes on a school's public address system; the court did permit voluntary student prayer before school to continue.[179] Further, in a novel application of the statute, federal courts in California[180] and Utah[181] ruled that clubs sponsored by gay and lesbian students could not be denied use of school facilities under the Equal Access Act. At the same time, federal trial courts in Texas[182] and Colorado[183] reached the opposite result. Insofar as these cases did not involve religion, they are discussed in Chapter 13.

Access to School Facilities by Non–School Religious Groups

A dispute in New York arose when a school board, acting pursuant to a state statute, enacted a policy that permitted it to make its facilities available to an array of social and civic groups. When the board refused to rent a facility to a religious group which sought to show a film series on child-rearing, lower courts ruled in favor of the board.[184]

The Supreme Court, in a rare unanimous judgment in *Lamb's Chapel v. Center Moriches Union Free School District (Lamb's Chapel)*,[185]

---

175. *Hsu v. Roslyn Union Free School Dist.*, 85 F.3d 839 [109 Educ. L. Rep. 1145] (2d Cir. 1996), *cert. denied*, 519 U.S. 1040, 117 S.Ct. 608, 136 L.Ed.2d 534 (1996).

176. *Ceniceros v. Board of Trustees of the San Diego Unified School Dist.*, 106 F.3d 878 [116 Educ. L. Rep. 82] (9th Cir. 1997).

177. *Donovan ex rel. Donovan v. Punxsutawney Area School Bd.*, 336 F.3d 211 [179 Educ. L. Rep. 48] (3d Cir. 2003).

178. *Prince v. Jacoby*, 303 F.3d 1074 [169 Educ. L. Rep. 85] (9th Cir.2002), *cert. denied*, 540 U.S. 813, 124 S.Ct. 62, 157 L.Ed.2d 27 (2003).

179. *Herdahl v. Pontotoc County School Dist.*, 933 F.Supp. 582 [112 Educ. L. Rep. 131] (N.D.Miss.1996).

180. *Colin ex rel. Colin v. Orange Unified School Dist.*, 83 F.Supp.2d 1135 [142 Educ. L. Rep. 138] (C.D.Cal.2000).

181. *East High Gay/Straight Alliance v. Board of Educ.*, 81 F.Supp.2d 1166 [141 Educ. L. Rep. 776] (D.Utah 1999), 81 F.Supp.2d 1199 [141 Educ. L. Rep. 809] (D.Utah 1999); *East High School Prism Club v. Seidel*, 95 F.Supp.2d 1239 [144 Educ. L. Rep. 260] (D.Utah 2000).

182. *Caudillo v. Lubbock Indep. School Dist.*, 311 F.Supp.2d 550 [187 Educ. L. Rep. 564] (N.D. Tex. 2004).

183. *Palmer High School Gay/Straight Alliance v. Colorado Springs School Dist. No. 11*, 2005 WL 3244049 (D. Colo. 2005).

184. *Lamb's Chapel v. Center Moriches Union Free School Dist.*, 770 F.Supp. 91 [69 Educ. L. Rep. 787] (E.D.N.Y.1991), *aff'd*, 959 F.2d 381 [73 Educ. L. Rep. 915] (2d Cir.1992).

185. 508 U.S. 384, 113 S.Ct. 2141, 124 L.Ed.2d 352 [83 Educ. L. Rep. 30] (1993) [Case No. 44], *on remand*, 17 F.3d 1425 [89 Educ. L. Rep. 783] (2d Cir.1994).

reversed in favor of the religious group. In a hybrid situation wherein it treated religious speech as a form of free speech, the Court essentially extended *Mergens'* rationale. The Court indicated that since the board created a limited open forum, it violated the free speech rights of the group by engaging in viewpoint discrimination.

Eight years later, a dispute arose when officials in another school system in New York refused to permit a non-school-sponsored club to meet during non-class hours so that members and moderators could discuss child-rearing along with character and moral development from a religious perspective. Even though the school system prevented the religious club from meeting, officials allowed three other groups to gather because although they addressed similar topics, they did so from a secular perspective. On further review of rulings in favor of the board,[186] the Supreme Court agreed to hear an appeal to resolve a split in the lower courts since the Eighth Circuit[187] had upheld the right of the same kind of club in Missouri to use school facilities for its meeting.[188]

In *Good News Club v. Milford Central School (Milford)*,[189] the Supreme Court reversed in favor of the club. The Court reasoned not only that the board violated the club's rights to free speech by engaging in impermissible viewpoint discrimination when it refused to permit it to use school facilities for its meetings, which were not worship services, but also that such a restriction was not justified by fears of violating the Establishment Clause.

The Second Circuit, in a long-running case in New York City,[190] in light of *Milford*, acknowledged that a school board did not have a valid Establishment Clause concern in preventing a religious group from using school premises to meet on a weekend.[191] In the latest iteration of the dispute, a federal trial court enjoined enforcement of a policy that would have refused to allow the outside religious group to use school facilities on Sundays for religious services and worship. The court decreed that the policy violated the First Amendment as a form of religious viewpoint discrimination.[192] The court was also persuaded that permitting the church to meet at school neither advanced nor inhibited religion and

---

186. 21 F.Supp.2d 147 [130 Educ. L. Rep. 678] (N.D.N.Y.1998), *aff'd*, 202 F.3d 502 [141 Educ. L. Rep. 475] (2d Cir.2000).

187. *Good News/Good Sports Club v. School Dist. of the City of Ladue*, 28 F.3d 1501 [92 Educ. L. Rep. 1148] (8th Cir.1994), *cert. denied*, 515 U.S. 1173, 115 S.Ct. 2640, 132 L.Ed.2d 878 (1995).

188. *See also Daugherty v. Vanguard Charter School Academy*, 116 F.Supp.2d 897 [148 Educ. L. Rep. 208] (W.D. 2000) (permitting a ''Moms' Prayer Group'' to use a Parents' Room for ninety minutes once a week since other groups were allowed to do so).

189. 533 U.S. 98, 121 S.Ct. 2093, 150 L.Ed.2d 151 [154 Educ. L. Rep. 45] (2001). [Case No. 13]

190. *See, e.g., Bronx Household of Faith v. Community School Dist. No. 10*, 127 F.3d 207 [121 Educ. L. Rep. 892] (2d Cir. 1997), *cert. denied sub nom. Bronx Household of Faith v. Board of Educ. of City of N.Y.*, 523 U.S. 1074, 118 S.Ct. 1517, 140 L.Ed.2d 670 (1998), *leave to file for reh'g denied*, 524 U.S. 934, 118 S.Ct. 2337, 141 L.Ed.2d 708 (1998).

191. *Bronx Household of Faith v. Board of Educ. of the City of N.Y.*, 331 F.3d 342 [177 Educ. L. Rep. 108] (2d Cir. 2003).

192. *Bronx Household of Faith v. Board of Edu. of the City of N.Y.*, 400 F.Supp.2d 581 [205 Educ. L. Rep. 229] (S.D.N.Y. 2005).

that the policy would not have fostered excessive government entanglement with religion to the extent that school officials would have had to attempt to distinguish between "religious services and religious worship services" from permissible conduct of teaching of character and morals from a religious viewpoint.

On a related topic dealing with access, courts agreed that if school boards permit their facilities to be made available to a variety of non-profit organizations, they may not charge higher fees to religious groups. In such a case, the Fourth Circuit posited that a board regulation in Virginia, which allowed officials to charge churches an escalating rate for the use of school facilities, discriminated both against religious speech and interfered with or burdened the church's right to speak and practice its religion.[193]

Other Religious Influences

Flag Salute

Amid controversy over the constitutionality of requiring students to salute the American flag and repeat the Oath of Allegiance, the Supreme Court initially chose not to address the question on its merits, summarily affirming a ruling that refused to enjoin a state statute that required students to recite the pledge.[194] A year later, in *Minersville School District v. Gobitis* (*Gobitis*),[195] the Court rejected the claim of Jehovah's Witnesses who argued that requiring their children to salute the flag while in school was equivalent to forcing them to worship an image contrary to a fundamental of their religious beliefs. The Court pointed out that the students were not free to excuse themselves from participating in the pledge.

In the face of significant criticism of *Gobitis*, the Court revisited the question of the pledge salute when Jehovah's Witnesses and others challenged the constitutionality of a state regulation that required students to participate or risk being charged with insubordination and expelled from school. As in *Gobitis*, the Jehovah's Witnesses argued that the pledge violated their rights to religious freedom. In *West Virginia State Board of Education v. Barnette*,[196] the Court, torn between the conflict over the limits of state power and individual rights, ruled that children could not be compelled to salute the flag. The Court was

193. *Fairfax Covenant Church v. Fairfax County School Bd.*, 17 F.3d 703 [89 Educ. L. Rep. 763] (4th Cir. 1994), *cert. denied*, 511 U.S. 1143, 114 S.Ct. 2166, 128 L.Ed.2d 888 (1994). For an earlier case with a similar result, *see Shumway v. Albany County School Dist. No. One Bd. of Educ.*, 826 F.Supp. 1320 [84 Educ. L. Rep. 989] (D. Wyo. 1993);

194. *See, e.g., Johnson v. Town of Deerfield*, 25 F.Supp. 918 (D.Mass.1939) (refusing to enjoin a state statute requiring students to recite the pledge), *aff'd*, 306 U.S. 621, 59 S.Ct. 791, 83 L.Ed. 1027 (1939),

reh'g denied, 307 U.S. 650, 59 S.Ct. 832, 83 L.Ed. 1529 (1939). *See also Leoles v. Landers* 192 S.E. 218 (Ga. 1937), *appeal dismissed*, 302 U.S. 656, 58 S.Ct. 364, 82 L.Ed. 507 (1937); *Gabrielli v. Knickerbocker*, 82 P.2d 391 (Cal. 1938), *appeal dismissed, cert. denied*, 306 U.S. 621, 59 S.Ct. 786, 83 L.Ed. 1026 (1939).

195. 310 U.S. 586, 60 S.Ct. 1010, 84 L.Ed. 1375 (1940).

196. 319 U.S. 624, 63 S.Ct. 1178, 87 L.Ed. 1628 (1943).

convinced that requiring children to salute the flag exceeded constitutional limits on governmental power because it invaded the individual's sphere of intellect and spirit that is protected by the First Amendment.

Almost a quarter-century later, the Supreme Court of New Jersey faced the issue of whether Black Muslim children who refused to pledge allegiance to the flag could be excluded from public school when they claimed that the ceremony violated their religious beliefs.[197] School officials excluded the students based on their contention that their beliefs were motivated as much by politics as by religion, rejecting their claim of "conscientious scruples" since the two were closely intertwined with their racial aspirations. Although not resolving whether the students' refusal to salute the flag was religious or political, the court ordered their reinstatement in noting that they stood respectfully at attention during the pledge and were not disruptive.

Maryland's highest court[198] and the Fifth Circuit[199] struck down requirements that would have had students who objected to the flag salute stand while their classmates recited the pledge. In neither of these cases had school officials offered students the option of leaving their rooms. However, even where students had the option of either leaving a room or standing silently during the pledge, the Second Circuit held that school officials could not discipline a child who remained quietly seated.[200] The court declared that forcing students to stand could no more be required than the pledge and that having individuals leave rooms during its recitation might have been viewed as a punishment for not participating. The court emphasized that there was no evidence that the student was disruptive or interfered with the rights of others.

A dispute from New York involved the rights of a nine-year-old student with a disability who refused to stand during the pledge. While not reaching the merits of the claim, a federal trial court refused to grant the school board's motion for summary judgment in a disagreement over whether the child was punished for refusing to participate in the pledge.[201] Further, a former high school student in Alabama sued his school principal and others for violating his rights to free speech for punishing him because he raised his fist during the recitation of the pledge. The student was given a choice of paddling or a detention, which would have delayed his receiving his diploma at graduation. On further review of a grant of summary judgment in favor of school officials, the Eleventh Circuit reversed and remanded.[202] The court was of the opinion that since genuine issues of material fact remained over whether the student was punished for failing to say the pledge, in violation of his

197. *Holden v. Board of Educ., Elizabeth*, 216 A.2d 387 (N.J.1966).

198. *State v. Lundquist*, 278 A.2d 263 (Md.1971).

199. *Banks v. Board of Pub. Instruction of Dade County*, 314 F.Supp. 285 (S.D.Fla. 1970), *aff'd*, 450 F.2d 1103 (5th Cir.1971).

200. *Goetz v. Ansell*, 477 F.2d 636 (2d Cir.1973).

201. *Rabideau v. Beekmantown Cent. School Dist.*, 89 F.Supp.2d 263 [143 Educ. L. Rep. 202] (N.D.N.Y. 2000).

202. *Holloman ex rel. Holloman v. Harland*, 370 F.3d 1252 [188 Educ. L. Rep. 620] (11th Cir. 2004).

clearly established right to be free from compelled speech, his case should not have been dismissed.

Returning to controversies over the inclusion of the words "under God" in the pledge, the Seventh Circuit affirmed that school officials in Illinois could lead the pledge, including the contested phrase, as long as students were free not to participate.[203] The court interpreted the use of the phrase in the context of the secular vow of allegiance as patriotic or ceremonial expression rather than religious speech. Conversely, after the Ninth Circuit affirmed that a school board in California violated the Establishment Clause by having students recite the words "under God" in the pledge,[204] the Supreme Court intervened. In *Elk Grove School District v. Newdow* (*Newdow*),[205] the Court sidestepped the merits of the constitutionality of the words "under God," resolving the dispute on the ground that the non-custodial father lacked standing to challenge the policy, thereby leaving the door open for future litigation.

In the first post-*Newdow* appellate case involving the pledge, the Third Circuit affirmed that a statute from Pennsylvania, that required school officials to provide for its recitation or the singing of the national anthem each morning and to notify the parents of students who declined or refrained from doing so, constituted viewpoint discrimination in violation of the First Amendment.[206] The court also ascertained that requiring private schools to provide for the recitation of the pledge or national anthem at the beginning of each school day violated their First Amendment right to freedom of expressive association.

The Fourth Circuit, in a case from Virginia that was put on hold in light of *Newdow*, rejected the argument of a father who claimed that the daily recital of the pledge forced his children to worship a secular state. In affirming, the court was satisfied that the voluntary daily recitation of the pledge did not violate the Establishment Clause because it did not have a religious purpose or effect and did not create excessive government entanglement with religion insofar as even though it was a religious statement, it is largely a patriotic expression.[207] The court also ruled that the non-attorney father of the minor students could not litigate their pro se claim. Yet, less than a month later, a federal trial court in California, relying on the case from the Ninth Circuit that the Supreme Court vacated as moot in *Newdow*, granted the plaintiffs'

203. *Sherman v. Community Consol. School Dist. 21 of Wheeling Township*, 980 F.2d 437 [79 Educ. L. Rep. 396] (7th Cir. 1992), *cert. denied*, 508 U.S. 950, 113 S.Ct. 2439, 124 L.Ed.2d 658 (1993).

204. *Newdow v. U.S. Congress*, 292 F.3d 597 [166 Educ. L. Rep. 108] (9th Cir. 2002), 328 F.3d 466 [176 Educ. L. Rep. 44] (9th Cir. 2003), *cert. granted sub nom. Elk Grove Unified School Dist. v. Newdow*, 540 U.S. 945, 124 S.Ct. 384, 157 L.Ed.2d 274, 182 Educ. L. Rep. 34 (2003).

205. 542 U.S. 1, 124 S.Ct. 2301 [188 Educ. L. Rep. 17] 159 L.Ed.2d 98 (2004), [Case No. 15], *reh'g denied*, 542 U.S. 961, 125 S.Ct. 21, 159 L.Ed.2d 851 (2004) (resolving the dispute on the ground that the non-custodial father lacked standing to challenge the policy, thereby leaving the door open for future litigation).

206. *Circle Schools v. Pappert*, 381 F.3d 172 [191 Educ. L. Rep. 629] (3d Cir. 2004).

207. *Myers v. Loudoun County Pub. Schools*, 418 F.3d 395 [200 Educ. L. Rep. 581] (4th Cir. 2005).

request to prevent students from reciting the words "under God" in the pledge as violative of the Establishment Clause.[208]

Student Beliefs

In the nexus between student beliefs and curricular control, the courts have generally upheld the judgments of school officials as long as they were able to demonstrate that they relied on legitimate pedagogical reasons when acting. For example, the Sixth Circuit affirmed that a student in Tennessee could not write a biography about Jesus as a historical figure since she failed to follow her teacher's directions in completing the assignment.[209] Previously, the same court agreed that school officials in Michigan did not violate a second-grade student's First Amendment rights to freedom of religion in preventing her from showing a videotape of herself singing a proselytizing religious song to classmates during show-and-tell.[210] The court maintained that school officials had the legitimate pedagogical purpose of avoiding a situation where other children or their parents would have been offended by the song's religious content.

The Eleventh Circuit affirmed that a high school principal in Florida did not violate a student's First Amendment rights to free speech or free exercise of religion by requiring her to remove religious messages from a mural she painted as part of a school-wide beautification project.[211] The court ruled that since the project was under the direction of a teacher, and officials had no intention of creating a public forum, they could regulate the content of the student's speech because it was part of a school-sponsored activity.

In a dispute from Michigan, a student sued school officials after they refused to permit her to participate in a panel discussion involving clergy and religious leaders on homosexuality and religion because they disagreed with her message and sought to insure that only one point-of-view was presented. The court found that officials violated the student's rights because their actions violated all three parts of the *Lemon* test.[212] The court thought that the panel lacked a secular purpose because it had an overtly religious character by virtue of its being made up of clergy and religious leaders, some of whom wore religious garb. Next, the court wrote that since the panel was created to communicate a religious

208. *Newdow v. Congress of U.S.*, 383 F.Supp.2d 1229 [201 Educ. L. Rep. 915] (E.D. Cal. 2005).

209. *Settle v. Dickson County School Bd.*, 53 F.3d 152 [100 Educ. L. Rep. 32] (6th Cir.1995), *cert. denied*, 516 U.S. 989, 116 S.Ct. 518, 133 L.Ed.2d 426 (1995).

210. *DeNooyer v. Livonia Pub. Schools*, 799 F.Supp. 744 [77 Educ. L. Rep. 1182] (E.D. Mich. 1992), *aff'd sub nom. Denooyer v. Merinelli*, 1 F.3d 1240 [85 Educ. L. Rep. 39] (6th Cir.1993), *reh'g denied, opinion superseded without published opinion*, 12

F.3d 211 [88 Educ. L. Rep. 551] (6th Cir. 1993), *cert. denied*, 511 U.S. 1031, 114 S.Ct. 1540, 128 L.Ed.2d 193 (1994).

211. *Bannon v. School Dist. of Palm Beach County*, 387 F.3d 1208 [193 Educ. L. Rep. 78] (11th Cir. 2004), *reh'g and reh'g en banc denied*, 125 Fed.Appx. 984 (11th Cir. 2004), *cert. denied*, ___ U.S. ___, 126 S.Ct. 330, 163 L.Ed.2d 43 [202 Educ. L. Rep. 26] (2005).

212. *Hansen v. Ann Arbor Pub. Schools*, 293 F.Supp.2d 780 [183 Educ. L. Rep. 825] (E.D. Mich. 2003).

perspective on homosexuality, it had the primary effect of advancing religion. The court concluded that the panel violated the Establishment Clause because school officials became excessively entangled with religion since they selected the clergy participants, vetted their views, afforded them the use of school facilities and a captive student audience, and censored the plaintiff's speech based on her religious beliefs.

Two federal appellate courts reached similar results involving the expressions of younger students. The Third Circuit affirmed that school officials in New Jersey could prohibit a first-grade student from reading a religious story to classmates and from placing a religious poster on a school wall.[213] Yet, the court permitted the plaintiffs to amend their complaint about the poster. In the second case, parents of a kindergarten child in New York filed suit after a teacher refused to display their son's entire poster. When directed to illustrate "simple ways to save the environment," the child selected and cut out pictures from a magazine with the help of his mother, arranging them on a poster. In response to the teacher's question about who the man with outstretched arms was, he responded that it was Jesus, "the only way to save the world." On being told that the poster was unacceptable due to "religious" reasons, the child and his mother composed a second poster. The second poster also depicted a robed man but included people picking up and recycling trash along with children holding hands encircling the world. After a federal trial court granted the educators' motions for summary judgment, the Second Circuit reversed in favor of the parents on the free speech claim.[214] The court held that since the assignment was curriculum related, the teacher could reject the child's work as not responsive to the assignment. Even so, the court reversed in favor of the parents on the free speech claim because genuine issues of fact remained as to whether the reasons that educators proffered for censoring the poster constituted viewpoint discrimination since they may not have excluded secular images that were equally non-responsive. However, the court affirmed that when officials folded the child's unresponsive poster before displaying it so that the robed religious figure was not visible, they did not violate the Establishment Clause.

As to extracurricular activities such as sports practices[215] and graduation ceremonies,[216] the few courts that addressed the issue agreed that school officials did not have to reschedule events in order to accommodate the religious beliefs of students. Further, in what can only be described as an interesting case involving religion and extracurricular activities, the Sixth Circuit rejected a claim by parents that the use of the "Blue Devil" as a mascot in the schools that their children attended

213. *C.H. ex rel. Z.H. v. Oliva*, 226 F.3d 198 [148 Educ. L. Rep. 585] (3d Cir.2000), *cert. denied sub nom. Hood v. Medford Township Bd. of Educ.*, 533 U.S. 915, 121 S.Ct. 2519, 150 L.Ed.2d 692 (2001).

214. *Peck ex rel. Peck v. Baldwinsville Cent. School Dist.*, 426 F.3d 617 [202 Educ. L. Rep. 512] (2d Cir. 2005).

215. *Keller v. Gardner Community Consol. Grade School Dist. 72C*, 552 F.Supp. 512 [8 Educ. L. Rep. 271] (N.D.Ill.1982).

216. *Smith by Smith v. Board of Educ., North Babylon Union Free School Dist.*, 844 F.2d 90 [46 Educ. L. Rep. 518] (2d Cir. 1988).

violated the Establishment Clause.[217] The court affirmed that the claim was without merit since no reasonable observer would have believed that the "Blue Devil's" principal or primary effect was to advance or inhibit religion or that the use of devil was meant to endorse or disapprove any religious choice.

Religious Garb

Students

The courts seem to agree that educators must come up with less restrictive alternatives to placing an explicit ban on students who wish to wear religious garb to school.[218] In such a case, the Ninth Circuit affirmed that school officials violated the rights of Sikh students by trying to prevent them from wearing ceremonial daggers under their clothes.[219] The court decided that school officials overstepped their authority because they made no showing that a total ban on weapons was the least restrictive alternative available to promote campus safety. Further, in a case that overlaps with issues of dress, when students wore rosaries to school as necklaces, a federal trial court in Texas ruled that educators violated their First Amendment right to pure speech because rosaries were a form of religious expression.[220]

Teachers

Many older cases dealt with the issue of whether teachers in public schools could wear distinctive religious garb. The disputes often arose over whether Roman Catholic nuns could wear their habits while teaching in public schools.[221] Turning to an early case, the Supreme Court of Pennsylvania affirmed the authority of a local school board to hire Catholic nuns as teachers and to permit them to teach in their habits.[222] Shortly thereafter, the state legislature enacted a statute specifically designed to prevent teachers from wearing any dress or insignia indicating membership in any religious order while at work. Subsequently, deferring to legislative authority, the same court upheld the law that banned nuns from teaching in their habits.[223]

217. *Kunselman v. Western Reserve Local School Dist.*, 70 F.3d 931 [105 Educ. L. Rep. 43] (6th Cir. 1995).

218. In a similar kind of dispute, a federal trial court granted a school board's motion for summary judgment when a student relied on the First Amendment right to free speech to wear a head wrap to school to celebrate her cultural heritage. *Isaacs v. Board of Educ. of Howard County, Md.*, 40 F.Supp.2d 335 [134 Educ. L. Rep. 166] (D.Md.1999).

219. *Cheema v. Thompson*, 67 F.3d 883 [104 Educ. L. Rep. 57] (9th Cir.1995).

220. *Chalifoux v. New Caney Indep. School Dist.*, 976 F.Supp. 659 [121 Educ. L. Rep. 751] (S.D.Tex.1997).

221. In a related matter, at least one court indicated that simply because nuns turned their earnings over to their religious superiors was not a justification for barring them from serving as public school teachers. *See Gerhardt v. Heid*, 267 N.W. 127 (N.D.1936).

222. *Hysong v. School Dist. of Gallitzin Borough*, 30 A. 482 (Pa.1894). For a similar case, *see Rawlings v. Butler*, 290 S.W.2d 801 (Ky.1956).

223. *Commonwealth v. Herr*, 78 A. 68 (Pa.1910). For a similar result, *see O'Connor v. Hendrick*, 77 N.E. 612 (N.Y.1906); *Zellers v. Huff*, 236 P.2d 949 (N.M.1951).

The Supreme Court of Oregon, in a case involving a teacher who became a Sikh and wore white clothes and a white turban while teaching, posited that she was subject to a state legislative ban on religious dress while performing her teaching duties.[224] In dicta the court acknowledged that such a prohibition would not have applied to incidental elements such as a cross or Star of David or to ethnic or cultural dress.

Two other cases reached mixed results. The Supreme Court of Mississippi ascertained that school officials could not dismiss a teacher who was a member of the African Hebrew Israelites out of Ethiopia faith for insubordination when she wore a religious head wrap to school.[225] Yet, the Third Circuit, relying on the statute discussed two paragraphs earlier, rejected the claim of a female Muslim teacher in Pennsylvania who adhered to the religious conviction that she should, when in public, cover her entire body except face and hands.[226]

In two recent cases, it appears that whether educators could wear religious symbolism depended largely on their obviousness and size. The federal trial court in Connecticut granted a school board's motion for summary judgment in a dispute where officials directed a substitute teacher either to cover a tee-shirt with the message "Jesus 2000" on it or to go home and change into other clothes.[227] The court was of the opinion that administrators did not violate the teacher's First Amendment rights to the free exercise of religion or free speech. On the other hand, a federal trial court in Pennsylvania granted an instructional assistant's motion for a preliminary injunction after she was suspended for refusing to remove or conceal a small cross that she regularly wore on a necklace, as required by her school board's religious affiliations policy.[228] In granting the assistant's motion, the court agreed that the policy violated the Free Exercise Clause since its being directed only at religious exercise and symbolic expression made it impermissibly content and viewpoint based.

Distribution of Proselytizing Materials/Religious Literature in Schools

In an early case, the Supreme Court of New Jersey was of the view that where school officials enacted a generally applicable policy for all student groups, educators could impose reasonable time, manner, and place restrictions on the ability of students to distribute religious literature such as the Gideons[229] or proselytize in schools. More recently, amid

224. *Cooper v. Eugene School Dist. No. 4J*, 723 P.2d 298 [34 Educ. L. Rep. 614] (Or.1986), *appeal dismissed*, 480 U.S. 942, 107 S.Ct. 1597, 94 L.Ed.2d 784 (1987).

225. *Mississippi Employment Securities Comm'n v. McGlothin*, 556 So.2d 324 [58 Educ. L. Rep. 859] (Miss.1990), *cert. denied*, 498 U.S. 879, 111 S.Ct. 211, 112 L.Ed.2d 171 (1990).

226. *United States v. Board of Educ. for School Dist. of Philadelphia*, 911 F.2d 882 [62 Educ. L. Rep. 460] (3d Cir.1990).

227. *Downing v. West Haven Bd. of Educ.*, 162 F.Supp.2d 19 [157 Educ. L. Rep. 112] (D. Conn.2001).

228. *Nichol v. ARIN Intermediate Unit 28*, 268 F.Supp.2d 536 [179 Educ. L. Rep. 315] (W.D. Pa. 2003).

229. *Tudor v. Board of Educ. of Borough of Rutherford*, 100 A.2d 857 (N.J.

considerable controversy over the distribution of religious materials and literature in schools, the courts have reached mixed results.

On the one hand, the Fifth[230] and Seventh[231] Circuits, along with a variety of federal trial courts,[232] agreed that students cannot distribute religious materials in school or invitations to such events as alternatives to Halloween parties where the activities were motivated by religious objections[233] or religious meetings.[234] On remand from the Fourth Circuit, which would have permitted the distribution of religious material in school,[235] the federal trial court in Maryland declared that a religious organization's claim about its ability to participate in the district's back-to-school nights, open houses, and bulletin boards was rendered moot due to a change in board policy.[236] The court added that the board's flyer-distribution policy, which limited submitting groups to only a few, each of which had a connection to traditional educational activities, was permissible under the First Amendment. In an interesting twist that might presage developments elsewhere, the court determined that since the district's internal mail facility, when utilized as a vehicle for distribution of flyers to students, was a non-public forum, the group did not have access to it to disseminate its information.

On the other hand, the Third,[237] Fourth,[238] Sixth,[239] and Ninth[240] Circuits permitted groups to distribute religious materials in schools on

1953), cert. denied, 348 U.S. 816, 75 S.Ct. 25, 99 L.Ed. 644 (1954).

230. *Meltzer v. Board of Pub. Instruction of Orange County, Fla.*, 577 F.2d 311 (5th Cir.1978), *cert. denied*, 439 U.S. 1089, 99 S.Ct. 872, 59 L.Ed.2d 56 (1979).

231. *Berger v. Rensselaer Cent. School Corp.*, 982 F.2d 1160 [80 Educ. L. Rep. 68] (7th Cir. 1993), *cert. denied*, 508 U.S. 911, 113 S.Ct. 2344, 124 L.Ed.2d 254 (1993); *Muller by Muller v. Jefferson Lighthouse School*, 98 F.3d 1530 [113 Educ. L. Rep. 1085] (7th Cir.1996), *cert. denied*, 520 U.S. 1156, 117 S.Ct. 1335, 137 L.Ed.2d 495 (1997). *But see Sherman v. Community Consol. School Dist. 21*, 8 F.3d 1160 [87 Educ. L. Rep. 57] (7th Cir.1993), *cert. denied*, 511 U.S. 1110, 114 S.Ct. 2109, 128 L.Ed.2d 669 (1994) (affirming that the distribution of Boy Scout materials did not violate the Establishment Clause); *Doe v. Duncanville Indep. School Dist.*, 70 F.3d 402 [104 Educ. L. Rep. 1032] (5th Cir.1995) (ruling that a student and her father lacked standing to challenge the practice of distributing Bibles in school since she was not in a class where they were given out and the board did not expend any funds in the process).

232. *See, e.g, Hemry v. School Bd. of Colorado Springs School Dist. No. 11*, 760 F.Supp. 856 [67 Educ. L. Rep. 142] (D.Colo. 1991) *But see Rivera v. East Otero School Dist. R–1*, 721 F.Supp. 1189 [56 Educ. L. Rep. 861] (D.Colo.1989) (wherein the same

court permitted a student to distribute a religious newsletter); *Thompson v. Waynesboro Area School Dist.*, 673 F.Supp. 1379 [43 Educ. L. Rep. 138] (M.D.Pa.1987); *Walz ex rel. Walz v. Egg Harbor Township Bd. of Educ.*, 342 F.3d 271 [180 Educ. L. Rep. 115] (3d Cir. 2003), *cert. denied*, 541 U.S. 936, 124 S.Ct. 1658, 158 L.Ed.2d 356 (2004).

233. *See, e.g., Guyer v. School Bd. of Alachua County*, 634 So.2d 806 [90 Educ. L. Rep. 961] (Fla.Dist.Ct.App.1994), *review denied without published opinion*, 641 So.2d 1345 (Fla.1994), *cert. denied*, 513 U.S. 1044, 115 S.Ct. 638, 130 L.Ed.2d 544 (1994); *Johnston–Loehner v. O'Brien*, 859 F.Supp. 575 [94 Educ. L. Rep. 167] (M.D.Fla.1994).

234. *Muller by Muller v. Jefferson Lighthouse School*, 98 F.3d 1530 [113 Educ. L. Rep. 1085] (7th Cir.1996), *cert. denied*, 520 U.S. 1156, 117 S.Ct. 1335, 137 L.Ed.2d 495 (1997).

235. *Child Evangelism Fellowship of Md. v. Montgomery County Pub. Schools*, 373 F.3d 589 [189 Educ. L. Rep. 42] (4th Cir. 2004).

236. *Child Evangelism Fellowship of Md. v. Montgomery County Pub. Schools*, 368 F.Supp.2d 416 [198 Educ. L. Rep. 570] (D. Md. 2005).

237. *Child Evangelism Fellowship of N.J. v. Stafford Township School Dist.*, 386 F.3d 514 [192 Educ. L. Rep. 670] (3d Cir. 2004).

the ground that doing so did not violate the Establishment Clause. These courts generally recognized that there were safeguards in place such as educators reviewing material to ensure that they were not proselytizing and brochures were sent home to parents who then had to choose whether their children would participate in the activities.[241]

School (or State) Sponsored Religious Displays on School Grounds

In its only case directly involving schools, *Stone v. Graham*,[242] the Supreme Court noted that posting the Ten Commandments in classrooms, even if they were purchased with private funds, violated the Establishment Clause. The Court's brief per curiam opinion ascertained that the Kentucky statute requiring the posting lacked a secular purpose, emphasizing that the Ten Commandments were not integrated into the school curriculum. The Court was unpersuaded by a notation "in small print" to the effect that the Commandments were part of the fundamental legal code of Western Civilization and the common law of the United States.

Debate continues to rage over the Ten Commandments in school settings. A federal trial court in Kentucky granted a student's request for an injunction to prevent school officials from displaying the Ten Commandments and other religious documents, pointing out that she had a strong likelihood of success on the merits of her claim.[243] Two cases from the Sixth Circuit reached results that were consistent with non-school cases on point.[244] In the first, the court affirmed an injunction against a board in Ohio's displaying stone monuments inscribed with the Ten Commandments at a high school on the ground that the plaintiffs

---

238. *Peck v. Upshur County Bd. of Educ.*, 155 F.3d 274 [129 Educ. L. Rep. 77] (4th Cir.1998) (while finding that a neutral board policy permitting non-students to disseminate Bibles and other religious materials in school during class during hours did not violate the Establishment Clause, the court struck the policy down as it applied to children in elementary schools).

239. *Rusk v. Crestview Local School Dist.*, 379 F.3d 418 [191 Educ. L. Rep. 84] (6th Cir.2004).

240. *Hills v. Scottsdale Unified School Dist. No. 48*, 329 F.3d 1044 [176 Educ. L. Rep. 557] (9th Cir. 2003), *cert. denied*, 540 U.S. 1149, 124 S.Ct. 1146, 157 L.Ed.2d 1042, 184 Educ. L. Rep. 23 (2004). *But see Culbertson v. Oakridge School Dist.*, 258 F.3d 1061 [155 Educ. L. Rep. 1085] (9th Cir.2001) (holding that distribution of Good News Club permission slips would have violated the Establishment Clause).

241. *See also Daugherty v. Vanguard Charter School Acad.*, 116 F.Supp.2d 897 [148 Educ. L. Rep. 208] (W.D. Mich.2000).

242. 449 U.S. 39, 101 S.Ct. 192, 66 L.Ed.2d 199 (1980), *reh'g denied*, 449 U.S. 1104, 101 S.Ct. 904, 66 L.Ed.2d 832 (1981), *on remand*, 612 S.W.2d 133 (Ky.1981).

243. *Doe v. Harlan County School Dist.*, 96 F.Supp.2d 667 [144 Educ. L. Rep. 503] (E.D. Ky. 2000).

244. *See, e.g., Indiana Civil Liberties Union v. O'Bannon*, 259 F.3d 766 (7th Cir. 2001), *cert. denied*, 532 U.S. 1058, 121 S.Ct. 2209, 149 L.Ed.2d 1036 (2001) (prohibiting a monument on the grounds of the statehouse including the Ten Commandments); *Books v. City of Elkhart*, 235 F.3d 292 (7th Cir.2000), *cert. denied*, 532 U.S. 1058, 121 S.Ct. 2209, 149 L.Ed.2d 1036 (2001) (forbidding a monument on the lawn of a city's municipal building that was inscribed with the Ten Commandment); *Suhre v. Haywood County*, 131 F.3d 1083 (4th Cir.1997) (banning a display of the Ten Commandments in a county courtroom); *Glassroth v. Moore*, 229 F.Supp.2d 1290 (N.D.Ala.2002) (proscribing a monument engraved with the Ten Commandments in a courthouse).

had standing to file suit and that the board failed to establish a secular purpose for the display.[245] In the second case, the Sixth Circuit rejected modifications to displays in a county courthouse and public school in Kentucky that included a variety of documents along with the Ten Commandments such as the full text of the Magna Carta, the Declaration of Independence, and a Biblical citation. The court decided that the display violated the Establishment Clause because it had the effect of advancing religion.[246] This latter case ultimately made its way to the Supreme Court but was limited to a review of the dispute involving the courthouse.

In two non-school related cases, the Supreme Court reached mixed results. In the first, *McCreary County, Kentucky v. American Civil Liberties Union of Kentucky*,[247] the Court, focusing on the fact that officials erected, and modified, the display at the county courthouse three times since erecting it in 1999, affirmed that it violated the Establishment Clause largely because it failed *Lemon's* secular purpose test. Conversely, in *Van Orden v. Perry*,[248] a plurality of the Court affirmed that a display of the Ten Commandments that included seventeen monuments and twenty-one historical markers commemorating the state's history that were spread out over the twenty-two acres of the Texas State Capitol was constitutional. In eschewing the *Lemon* test, the plurality essentially decided that including the Ten Commandments in the display was constitutional because even though they continue to have religious significance, the fact that the monument was a far more passive display than in *Stone*, it was constitutional. Shortly after these cases were resolved, the Eighth Circuit rejected a challenge to a long-standing granite monument in a city park that was donated by a civic organization and had been displayed without objection for decades.[249] In explaining that the words on the monument faced away from the park and that the Ten Commandments had undeniable historic meaning in addition to their religious significance, the court ruled that its simply having religious content or promoting a message consistent with a religious doctrine did not run afoul of the Establishment Clause.

When dealing with other kinds of displays, courts also reached mixed results.[250] In a case involving the school from the tragic shootings in Columbine, Colorado, the Tenth Circuit held that a tile painting and an installation project that the board created as part of the building's

---

245. *Baker v. Adams County/Ohio Valley School*, 86 Fed.Appx. 104 [184 Educ. L. Rep. 745] (6th Cir. 2004).

246. *American Civil Lib. Union v. McCreary County, Kentucky*, 354 F.3d 438 [184 Educ. L. Rep. 67] (6th Cir. 2003), *cert. granted*, 543 U.S. 924, 125 S.Ct. 310, 160 L.Ed.2d 221 [192 Educ. L. Rep. 631] (2004) (also forbidding the posting of the Ten Commandments in a county court house).

247. __ U.S. __, 125 S.Ct. 2722, 162 L.Ed.2d 729 (2005).

248. __ U.S. __, 125 S.Ct. 2854, 162 L.Ed.2d 607 (2005).

249. *ACLU Neb. Found. v. City of Plattsmouth*, 419 F.3d 772 (8th Cir. 2005).

250. *Washegesic v. Bloomingdale Pub. Schools*, 33 F.3d 679 [94 Educ. L. Rep. 32] (6th Cir. 1994), *reh'g and suggestion for reh'g en banc denied* (1994), *cert. denied*, 514 U.S. 1095, 115 S.Ct. 1822, 131 L.Ed.2d 744 (1995) (directing officials to remove a portrait of Jesus that was painted by a graduate of a school which hung in a school hall on the ground that it violated the Establishment Clause).

reconstruction was school-sponsored speech.[251] As such, the court wrote that school officials could exercise editorial control under the First Amendment because their actions were reasonably related to legitimate pedagogical concerns. The court also posited that officials could exclude bricks from a walkway in front of the school on the basis that the inscriptions on the bricks contained Christian messages and/or referred to Jesus.[252] Conversely, a federal trial court in Virginia granted parents' request for summary judgment where a school board removed bricks decorated with Latin crosses, while allowing bricks decorated with secular symbols to remain in place in a school's walkway of fame.[253] The court thought that the actions of school officials who removed only bricks with religious symbols constituted viewpoint discrimination.[254]

Curricular Elements

Consistent with dicta in *Abington v. Schempp* that "[t]he holding of the Court today plainly does not foreclose teaching about the Holy Scriptures or about the differences between religious sects in classes in literature or history . . . ,"[255] the judiciary has reached mixed results with regard to the place of religion in the public school curriculum. The challenge for the courts is to discover the appropriate balance between teaching about religion and the teaching of religion in public schools.

In an early case, the Supreme Court of New Hampshire upheld the practice of displaying plaques, which contained the words "In God we Trust,"[256] that were visible in each classroom. According to the court, the display was acceptable because it was the national motto that appeared on coins and currency,[257] on public buildings,[258] and in the national anthem.

251. *Fleming v. Jefferson County School Dist. R–1*, 298 F.3d 918 [167 Educ. L. Rep. 649] (10th Cir. 2002), *as amended on denial of reh'g and reh'g en banc* (2002), *cert. denied*, 537 U.S. 1110, 123 S.Ct. 893, 154 L.Ed.2d 783 (2003).

252. *See also Seidman v. Paradise Valley Unified School Dist. No. 69*, 327 F.Supp.2d 1098 [191 Educ. L. Rep. 175] (D. Ariz. 2004) (rejecting parents' motion for summary judgment in a suit against a board for violations of their First and Fourteenth Amendment rights, arising from imposition of requirement that they remove word "God" from proposed inscription "God Bless Quinn We Love You Mom and Dad," and similar inscription for daughter that would have appeared on wall tiles which would have been displayed on an interior school wall).

253. *Demmon v. Loudon County Pub. Schools*, 342 F.Supp.2d 474 [193 Educ. L. Rep. 497] (E.D. Va. 2004).

254. *See also Anderson v. Mexico Academy and Cent. School*, 186 F.Supp.2d 193 [162 Educ. L. Rep. 262] (N.D.N.Y. 2002), *remanded sub nom. Kiesinger v. Mexico Academy & Cent. School*, 56 Fed.Appx. 549 [173 Educ. L. Rep. 709] (2d Cir. 2003) (remanding for a review on the entire record where the trial court decided that a board's exclusion of plaintiffs' bricks from the brick walkway in front of school on the basis that the inscriptions on them contained Christian messages and/or referred to "Jesus" violated the plaintiffs' right to free speech by engaging in viewpoint discrimination but not the Establishment Clause).

255. *School District of Abington Township v. Schempp and Murray v. Curlett*, 374 U.S. 203, 300, 83 S.Ct. 1560, 10 L.Ed.2d 844 (1963). [Case No. 4]

256. *Opinion of the Justices*, 228 A.2d 161 (N.H.1967).

257. *See also Aronow v. United States*, 432 F.2d 242 (9th Cir. 1970) (affirming that the phrase "In God we Trust" on American currency and coins as well as in the national anthem has nothing to do with the establishment of religion). *See also O'Hair v. Murray*, 588 F.2d 1144 (5th Cir. 1979), *cert.*

The Third Circuit enjoined the teaching of the "Science of Creative Intelligence," also known as Transcendental Meditation or TM, in public schools.[259] The course was an elective taught at five high schools in different districts using the same textbook and techniques of instruction with special teachers paid by an organization which sought to disseminate the experience throughout the United States. The panel relied on the trial court's detailed analysis of the ceremony of receiving one's mantra, a sound aid essential to practicing TM, in concluding that this violated the Establishment Clause insofar as this was a religious activity.

As to religious celebrations in schools, the Eighth Circuit affirmed the constitutionality of a set of guidelines that a school board in South Dakota developed for use with regard to religious observances, most notably Christmas, and holidays in public schools.[260] The guidelines permitted objective discussion of holidays with both religious and secular bases. The court observed that explanations of historical and contemporary values relating to a holiday; short-term use of religious symbols as examples of religious heritage; and integration of music, art, literature, and drama with religious themes could be integrated into the curriculum as long as they were presented objectively as a traditional part of a holiday's cultural and religious heritage. In a later case wherein it affirmed that material in a curriculum which asked children to discuss witches or create poetic chants and pretend that they were witches or sorcerers did not require students to "practice the religion" of witchcraft in violation of the Establishment Clause or the California Constitution, the Ninth Circuit went so far in dicta as to suggest that "a reenactment of the Last Supper or a Passover dinner might be permissible if presented for historical or cultural purposes."[261]

In another case with regard to commemorating holidays, a federal trial court in Pennsylvania addressed a situation where school officials permitted a "Winter Holiday" display that included information on Chanukah and Kwanza, but nothing on Christmas.[262] The court rejected a challenge from a youth minister, responding that the display did not offend the Establishment Clause by favoring one religion over another.

On another issue, courts are reluctant to allow teachers to use supplemental classroom materials with religious content. In such a case,

denied sub nom. O'Hair v. Blumenthal, 442 U.S. 930, 99 S.Ct. 2862, 61 L.Ed.2d 298 (1979) (affirming the dismissal of a similar challenge).

258. *See also Lambeth v. Board of Comm'rs of Davidson County*, 407 F.3d 266 (4th Cir. 2005), *cert. denied*, ___ U.S. ___, 126 S.Ct. 647, 163 L.Ed.2d 525 (2005) (affirming that the inscription "In God we Trust" on a county government center did not violate the Establishment Clause).

259. *Malnak v. Yogi*, 592 F.2d 197 (3d Cir.1979).

260. *Florey v. Sioux Falls School Dist. 49–5*, 619 F.2d 1311 (8th Cir.1980), *cert.*

denied, 449 U.S. 987, 101 S.Ct. 409, 66 L.Ed.2d 251 (1980).

261. *Brown v. Woodland Joint Unified School Dist.*, 27 F.3d 1373, 1380, n.6 [92 Educ. L. Rep. 828] (9th Cir. 1994).

262. *Sechler v. State College Area School Dist.*, 121 F.Supp.2d 439 [149 Educ. L. Rep. 141] (M.D.Pa.2000). For a similar result in a non-school setting, *see Spohn v. West*, 2000 WL 1459981 (S.D.N.Y.2000) (dismissing the claim of a Christian worker in a public hospital that a display of Jewish, but not Christian, religious symbols during the December holiday season violated his First Amendment rights under the Establishment Clause).

a federal trial court in California largely rejected the claims of an elementary school teacher that officials violated his rights by prohibiting him from using religious materials in class and talking about religion with his students.[263] The court asserted that if the plaintiff could prove that officials permitted other similarly situated teachers to include religious expression in their lessons and supplemental handouts but prevented him from doing so, then he would have had evidence to present a case that they violated his right to equal protection. On the flip side of this issue, the federal trial court in Maine denied a school board's motion for summary judgment where a history teacher filed suit claiming that officials forbade him from teaching about non-Christian religions and to include only references to Christianity.[264] The court was convinced that since material issues of fact remained as to whether officials buckled to pressure from parents who did not want the teacher to provide information about religions other than Christianity, the case should have proceeded to trial.

Evolution

Judicial controversy over the origins of humankind in public schools first arose in the so-called "Scopes Monkey Trial." At issue was a challenge to a state law that forbade the teaching of evolution since doing so contradicted the literalist Biblical interpretation of creation found in Genesis. After a substitute science teacher agreed to confess to having violated the law even though post-trial evidence suggests that he did not do so, he was fined $100 as part of a plan to get the case to a higher court. While leaving the anti-evolution statute that made teaching evolution a crime in place, in *Scopes v. State*,[265] the Supreme Court of Tennessee reversed the teacher's conviction on the ground that the judge improperly assessed a fine that could only have been imposed by a jury. Further, officials followed the court's advice and did not take any further action in light of its comment that there was "nothing to be gained by prolonging the life of this bizarre case."[266]

The Supreme Court considered its first challenge to a 1928 law from Arkansas that forbade the teaching of evolution in state-supported schools in *Epperson v. Arkansas*.[267] The Court reasoned that the statute failed to comply with the recently created judicial test from *Abington*, which not only required the state to avoid any practice that "aids or opposes" any religion but which also cautions it to avoid any enactment that has a purpose and primary effect that neither advances nor inhibits religion. More specifically, the Court held that the statute was unconstitutional since it attempted to blot out a particular theory because of its supposed conflict with the literal biblical account of creation. Subse-

---

263. *Williams v. Vidmar*, 367 F.Supp.2d 1265 [198 Educ. L. Rep. 292] (N.D. Cal. 2005).

264. *Cole v. Maine School Admin. Dist. No. 1*, 350 F.Supp.2d 143 [195 Educ. L. Rep. 130] (D. Me. 2004).

265. *Scopes v. State*, 289 S.W. 363 (Tenn. 1927).

266. *Id.* at 367.

267. 393 U.S. 97, 89 S.Ct. 266, 21 L.Ed.2d 228 (1968). [Case No. 6]

quently, a federal trial court struck down another law from Arkansas that would have required providing balanced treatment for instruction on Biblical notions of creation if evolution was included in the curriculum.[268]

A second Supreme Court case on evolution arose in Louisiana where a statute prohibited the teaching of "evolution-science" in public elementary and secondary schools unless accompanied by instruction on "creation-science." In *Edwards v. Aguillard*,[269] the Court found that the law was unconstitutional because it violated the first prong of the *Lemon* test insofar as it lacked a secular purpose. The Court added that the legislation affected the science curriculum in a way that reflected a religion-based view, namely, either the banishment of the theory of evolution from the classroom or the presentation of a religious viewpoint that rejects evolution in its entirety.

Most recently, in Louisiana, a school board adopted a resolution disclaiming the endorsement of evolution after it failed to introduce creation science into its district curriculum as a legitimate scientific alternative to evolution. Parents successfully challenged the disclaimer under the Establishment Clause in both the federal and state constitutions.[270] The Fifth Circuit affirmed that the disclaimer did not advance the articulated objective of encouraging informed freedom of belief or critical thinking by students and that it furthered the purposes of disclaiming orthodoxy of belief and of reducing offense to the sensibilities of any student or parent. Further, a federal trial court in Georgia held that a board's ordering officials to place stickers on biology textbooks, proclaiming that evolution was a theory, not fact, and inviting students to approach material in their books with open minds, study it carefully, and give it critical consideration, violated the Establishment Clause by impermissibly favoring religion.[271]

As the newest battleground in disputes over the origins of mankind, a federal trial court in Pennsylvania invalidated a school board policy on the teaching of intelligent design in a high school biology class. The policy would have required students to hear a statement mentioning intelligent design as an alternative to Darwin's theory of evolution. The court decreed that the policy was unconstitutional since it not only amounted to an endorsement of religion in violation of the Establishment Clause but also since it violated the *Lemon* test insofar as the policy's primary purpose was to change the district's biology curriculum to advance religion and it had the primary effect of imposing a religious view of biological origins into the biology course.[272]

268. *McLean v. Arkansas Bd. of Educ.*, 529 F.Supp. 1255 [2 Educ. L. Rep. 685] (E.D. Ark.1982).

269. 482 U.S. 578, 107 S.Ct. 2573, 96 L.Ed.2d 510 [39 Educ. L. Rep. 958] (1987).

270. *Freiler v. Tangipahoa Parish Bd. of Educ.*, 185 F.3d 337 [137 Educ. L. Rep. 195] (5th Cir. 1999), *reh'g en banc denied*, 201 F.3d 602 [141 Educ. L. Rep. 458] (5th Cir. 2000), *cert. denied*, 530 U.S. 1251, 120 S.Ct. 2706, 147 L.Ed.2d 974 (2000).

271. *See Selman v. Cobb County School Dist.* 390 F.Supp.2d 1286 [203 Educ. L. Rep. 637] (N.D. Ga. 2005).

272. *Kitzmiller v. Dover Area School Dist.*, 400 F.Supp.2d 707 [205 Educ. L. Rep. 250] (M.D. Pa. 2005).

Religious disputes have also arisen over whether teachers can be required to teach about evolution. In such a case, an appellate court in California rejected the claim of a teacher who alleged that officials violated his rights to free speech when they directed him not to talk about religion during the school day because he refused to teach about evolution.[273] At the same time, an appellate court in Minnesota upheld a board's reassigning a teacher to teach a different biology course after he refused to teach about evolution.[274]

[Case No. 1] Constitutionality of Providing Transportation to Students who Attend Non–Public Schools

EVERSON v. BOARD OF EDUCATION OF EWING TOWNSHIP

Supreme Court of the United States, 1947.
330 U.S. 1, 67 S.Ct. 504, 91 L.Ed. 711.

Mr. Justice Black delivered the opinion of the Court.

A New Jersey statute authorizes its local school districts to make rules and contracts for the transportation of children to and from schools. The appellee, a township board of education, acting pursuant to this statute authorized reimbursement to parents of money expended by them for the bus transportation of their children on regular busses operated by the public transportation system. Part of this money was for the payment of transportation of some children in the community to Catholic parochial schools. These church schools give their students, in addition to secular education, regular religious instruction conforming to the religious tenets and modes of worship of the Catholic Faith. The superintendent of these schools is a Catholic priest.

· · ·

The only contention here is that the State statute and the resolution, in so far as they authorized reimbursement to parents of children attending parochial schools, violate the Federal Constitution in these two respects, which to some extent, overlap. First. They authorize the State to take by taxation the private property of some and bestow it upon others, to be used for their own private purposes. This, it is alleged, violates the due process clause of the Fourteenth Amendment. Second. The statute and the resolution forced inhabitants to pay taxes to help support and maintain schools which are dedicated to, and which regularly teach, the Catholic Faith. This is alleged to be a use of State power to support church schools contrary to the prohibition of the First Amendment which the Fourteenth Amendment made applicable to the states.

First. The due process argument that the State law taxes some people to help others carry out their private purposes is framed in two

273. *Peloza v. Capistrano Unified School Dist.*, 37 F.3d 517 [94 Educ. L. Rep. 1159] (9th Cir. 1994), *cert. denied*, 515 U.S. 1173, 115 S.Ct. 2640, 132 L.Ed.2d 878 (1995).

274. *LeVake v. Independent School Dist. No. 656*, 625 N.W.2d 502 [153 Educ. L. Rep. 356] (Minn. Ct. App. 2001), *review denied* (2001), *cert. denied*, 534 U.S. 1081, 122 S.Ct. 814, 151 L.Ed.2d 698 (2002).

phases. The first phase is that a state cannot tax A to reimburse B for the cost of transporting his children to church schools. This is said to violate the due process clause because the children are sent to these church schools to satisfy the personal desires of their parents, rather than the public's interest in the general education of all children. This argument, if valid, would apply equally to prohibit state payment for the transportation of children to any non-public school, whether operated by a church, or any other non-government individual or group. But, the New Jersey legislature has decided that a public purpose will be served by using tax-raised funds to pay the bus fares of all school children, including those who attend parochial schools. The New Jersey Court of Errors and Appeals has reached the same conclusion. The fact that a state law, passed to satisfy a public need, coincides with the personal desires of the individuals most directly affected is certainly an inadequate reason for us to say that a legislature has erroneously appraised the public need.

. . .

It is much too late to argue that legislation intended to facilitate the opportunity of children to get a secular education serves no public purpose. The same thing is no less true of legislation to reimburse needy parents, or all parents, for payment of the fares of their children so that they can ride in public busses to and from schools rather than run the risk of traffic and other hazards incident to walking or "hitchhiking." Nor does it follow that a law has a private rather than a public purpose because it provides that tax-raised funds will be paid to reimburse individuals on account of money spent by them in a way which furthers a public program. Subsidies and loans to individuals such as farmers and home owners, and to privately owned transportation systems, as well as many other kinds of businesses, have been commonplace practices in our state and national history.

. . .

Second. The New Jersey statute is challenged as a "law respecting an establishment of religion." The First Amendment, as made applicable to the states by the Fourteenth, commands that a state "shall make no law respecting an establishment of religion, or prohibiting the free exercise thereof." These words of the First Amendment reflected in the minds of early Americans a vivid mental picture of conditions and practices which they fervently wished to stamp out in order to preserve liberty for themselves and for their posterity. Doubtless their goal has not been entirely reached; but so far has the Nation moved toward it that the expression "law respecting an establishment of religion," probably does not so vividly remind present-day Americans of the evils, fears, and political problems that caused that expression to be written into our Bill of Rights. Whether this New Jersey law is one respecting the "establishment of religion" requires an understanding of the meaning of that language, particularly with respect to the imposition of taxes. Once again, therefore, it is not inappropriate briefly to review the background and environment of the period in which that constitutional language was fashioned and adopted.

. . .

The "establishment of religion" clause of the First Amendment means at least this: Neither a state nor the Federal Government can set up a church. Neither can pass laws which aid one religion, aid all religions, or prefer one religion over another. Neither can force nor influence a person to go to or to remain away from church against his will or force him to profess a belief or disbelief in any religion. No person can be punished for entertaining or professing religious beliefs or disbeliefs, for church attendance or non-attendance. No tax in any amount, large or small, can be levied to support any religious activities or institutions, whatever they may be called, or whatever form they may adopt to teach or practice religion. Neither a state nor the Federal Government can, openly or secretly, participate in the affairs of any religious organizations or groups and vice versa. In the words of Jefferson, the clause against establishment of religion by law was intended to erect "a wall of separation between Church and State."

. . . New Jersey cannot consistently with the "establishment of religion" clause of the First Amendment contribute tax-raised funds to the support of an institution which teaches the tenets and faith of any church. On the other hand, other language of the amendment commands that New Jersey cannot hamper its citizens in the free exercise of their own religion. Consequently, it cannot exclude individual Catholics, Lutherans, Mohammedans, Baptists, Jews, Methodists, Nonbelievers, Presbyterians, or the members of any other faith, *because of their faith, or lack of it,* from receiving the benefits of public welfare legislation. While we do not mean to intimate that a state could not provide transportation only to children attending public schools, we must be careful, in protecting the citizens of New Jersey against state-established churches, to be sure that we do not inadvertently prohibit New Jersey from extending its general State law benefits to all its citizens without regard to their religious belief.

Measured by these standards, we cannot say that the First Amendment prohibits New Jersey from spending tax-raised funds to pay the bus fares of parochial school pupils as a part of a general program under which it pays the fares of pupils attending public and other schools. It is undoubtedly true that children are helped to get to church schools. There is even a possibility that some of the children might not be sent to the church schools if the parents were compelled to pay their children's bus fares out of their own pockets when transportation to a public school would have been paid for by the State. . . . Similarly, parents might be reluctant to permit their children to attend schools which the state had cut off from such general government services as ordinary police and fire protection, connections for sewage disposal, public highways and sidewalks. Of course, cutting off church schools from these services, so separate and so indisputably marked off from the religious function, would make it far more difficult for the schools to operate. But such is obviously not the purpose of the First Amendment. That Amendment requires the state to be a neutral in its relations with groups of religious believers and non-believers; it does not require the state to be their adversary. State power is no more to be used so as to handicap religions, than it is to favor them.

This Court has said that parents may, in the discharge of their duty under state compulsory education laws, send their children to a religious rather than a public school if the school meets the secular educational requirements which the state has power to impose. It appears that these parochial schools meet New Jersey's requirements. The State contributes no money to the schools. It does not support them. Its legislation, as applied, does no more than provide a general program to help parents get their children, regardless of their religion, safely and expeditiously to and from accredited schools.

The First Amendment has erected a wall between church and state. That wall must be kept high and impregnable. We could not approve the slightest breach. New Jersey has not breached it here.

Affirmed.

Notes

1.   The dissent argued that it was impossible to select the cost of transportation from among other expenses associated with education and characterize it as not aiding non-public schools because, where needed, it is "as essential to education as any other element" of the total cost burden. Did the majority respond to this point? If so, how?

2.   In concurring opinions in *Engel v. Vitale* and *School District of Abington Township v. Schempp*, Justice Douglas wrote that in retrospect he agreed with the dissenters. Had he initially voted with the dissent, how might this have changed the face of Church–State relations?

3.   In *Neal v. Fiscal Court, Jefferson County*, 986 S.W.2d 907 [133 Educ. L. Rep. 624] (Ky.1999), the Supreme Court of Kentucky affirmed the constitutionality of a statute that allocated funding for students who attended non-public elementary schools. The court ruled that the plan did not unconstitutionally aid religiously-affiliated and other non-public schools.

[Case No. 2]   Constitutionality of Voluntary Religious Instruction in Public Schools

PEOPLE OF THE STATE OF ILLINOIS EX REL. McCOLLUM v. BOARD OF EDUCATION OF SCHOOL DISTRICT 71, CHAMPAIGN COUNTY

Supreme Court of the United States, 1948.
333 U.S. 203, 68 S.Ct. 461, 92 L.Ed. 649.

MR. JUSTICE BLACK delivered the opinion of the Court.

. . .

... In 1940 interested members of the Jewish, Roman Catholic, and a few of the Protestant faiths formed a voluntary association called the

Champaign Council on Religious Education. They obtained permission from the Board of Education to offer classes in religious instruction to public school pupils in grades four to nine inclusive. Classes were made up of pupils whose parents signed printed cards requesting that their children be permitted to attend; they were held weekly, thirty minutes for the lower grades, forty-five minutes for the higher. The council employed the religious teachers at no expense to the school authorities, but the instructors were subject to the approval and supervision of the superintendent of schools. The classes were taught in three separate religious groups by Protestant teachers, Catholic priests, and a Jewish rabbi, although for the past several years there have apparently been no classes instructed in the Jewish religion. Classes were conducted in the regular classrooms of the school building. Students who did not choose to take the religious instruction were not released from public school duties; they were required to leave their classrooms and go to some other place in the school building for pursuit of their secular studies. On the other hand, students who were released from secular study for the religious instructions were required to be present at the religious classes. Reports of their presence or absence were to be made to their secular teachers.

The foregoing facts, without reference to others that appear in the record, show the use of tax-supported property for religious instruction and the close cooperation between the school authorities and the religious council in promoting religious education. The operation of the state's compulsory education system thus assists and is integrated with the program of religious instruction carried on by separate religious sects. Pupils compelled by law to go to school for secular education are released in part from their legal duty upon the condition that they attend the religious classes. This is beyond all question a utilization of the tax-established and tax-supported public school system to aid religious groups to spread their faith. And it falls squarely under the ban of the First Amendment (made applicable to the States by the Fourteenth) as we interpreted it in *Everson v. Board of Education*. There we said: "Neither a state nor the Federal Government can set up a church. Neither can pass laws which aid one religion, aid all religions, or prefer one religion over another. Neither can force or influence a person to go to or to remain away from church against his will or force him to profess a belief or disbelief in any religion. No person can be punished for entertaining or professing religious beliefs or disbeliefs, for church attendance or nonattendance. No tax in any amount, large or small, can be levied to support any religious activities or institutions, whatever they may be called, or whatever form they may adopt to teach or practice religion. Neither a state nor the Federal Government can, openly or secretly, participate in the affairs of any religious organizations or groups, and vice versa. In the words of Jefferson, the clause against establishment of religion by law was intended to erect 'a wall of separation between Church and State.' " The majority in the *Everson* case, and the minority as shown by quotations from the dissenting views, . . . agreed that the First Amendment's language, properly interpreted, had erected a wall of separation between Church and State. They disagreed as to the facts shown by the record and as to the proper application of the First Amendment's language to those facts. . . .

To hold that a state cannot consistently with the First and Fourteenth Amendments utilize its public school system to aid any or all religious faiths or sects in the dissemination of their doctrines and ideals does not, as counsel urge, manifest a governmental hostility to religion or religious teachings. A manifestation of such hostility would be at war with our national tradition as embodied in the First Amendment's guaranty of the free exercise of religion. For the First Amendment rests upon the premise that both religion and government can best work to achieve their lofty aims if each is left free from the other within its respective sphere. Or, as we said in the *Everson* case, the First Amendment has erected a wall between Church and State which must be kept high and impregnable.

Here not only are the state's tax-supported public school buildings used for the dissemination of religious doctrines. The State also affords sectarian groups an invaluable aid in that it helps to provide pupils for their religious classes through use of the state's compulsory public school machinery. This is not separation of Church and State.

Notes

1. Note that the Court quoted with approval from *Everson* on the point of the unconstitutionality of government aid to all religions.

2. Do you think the Court would have reached the same result if the children who attended religion classes were dismissed from school?

3. On remand from the Fifth Circuit's having vitiated a volunteer school counseling program that involved the use of clergy because it violated the Establishment Clause by advancing religion and by creating excessive entanglement, a federal trial court in Texas agreed that the program failed the neutrality test of *Lemon v. Kurtzman*. *Oxford v. Beaumont Indep. School Dist.*, 224 F.Supp.2d 1099 [171 Educ. L. Rep. 182] (E.D. Tex. 2002).

[Case No. 3]   Constitutionality of "Released Time" Program for Religious Instruction

ZORACH v. CLAUSON

Supreme Court of the United States, 1952.
343 U.S. 306, 72 S.Ct. 679, 96 L.Ed. 954.

MR. JUSTICE DOUGLAS delivered the opinion of the Court.

New York City has a program which permits its public schools to release students during the school day so that they may leave the school buildings and school grounds and go to religious centers for religious instruction or devotional exercises. A student is released on written request of his parents. Those not released stay in the classrooms. The churches make weekly reports to the schools, sending a list of children who have been released from public school but who have not reported for religious instruction.

This "released time" program involves neither religious instruction in public school classrooms nor the expenditure of public funds. All costs, including the application blanks, are paid by the religious organizations. The case is therefore unlike *McCollum v. Board of Education*....

It takes obtuse reasoning to inject any issue of the "free exercise" of religion into the present case. No one is forced to go to the religious classroom and no religious exercise or instruction is brought to the classrooms of the public schools. A student need not take religious instruction. He is left to his own desires as to the manner or time of his religious devotions, if any.

There is a suggestion that the system involves the use of coercion to get public school students into religious classrooms. There is no evidence in the record before us that supports that conclusion. The present record indeed tells us that the school authorities are neutral in this regard and do no more than release students whose parents so request. If in fact coercion were used, if it were established that any one or more teachers were using their office to persuade or force students to take the religious instruction, a wholly different case would be presented....

Moreover, apart from that claim of coercion, we do not see how New York by this type of "released time" program has made a law respecting an establishment of religion within the meaning of the First Amendment. There is much talk of the separation of Church and State in the history of the Bill of Rights and in the decisions clustering around the First Amendment. There cannot be the slightest doubt that the First Amendment reflects the philosophy that Church and State should be separated. And so far as interference with the "free exercise" of religion and an "establishment" of religion are concerned, the separation must be complete and unequivocal. The First Amendment within the scope of its coverage permits no exception; the prohibition is absolute. The First Amendment, however, does not say that in every and all respects there shall be a separation of Church and State. Rather, it studiously defines the manner, the specific ways, in which there shall be no concert or union or dependency one on the other. That is the common sense of the matter. Otherwise the state and religion would be aliens to each other— hostile, suspicious, and even unfriendly. Churches could not be required to pay even property taxes. Municipalities would not be permitted to render police or fire protection to religious groups....

We would have to press the concept of separation of Church and State to these extremes to condemn the present law on constitutional grounds. The nullification of this law would have wide and profound effects. A Catholic student applies to his teacher for permission to leave the school during hours on a Holy Day of Obligation to attend a mass. A Jewish student asks his teacher for permission to be excused for Yom Kippur. A Protestant wants the afternoon off for a family baptismal ceremony. In each case the teacher requires parental consent in writing. In each case the teacher, in order to make sure the student is not a truant, goes further and requires a report from the priest, rabbi, or the minister. The teacher in other words cooperates in a religious program to the extent of making it possible for her students to participate in it. Whether she does it occasionally for a few students, regularly for one, or pursuant to a systematized program designed to further the religious needs of all the students does not alter the character of the act.

We are a religious people whose institutions presuppose a Supreme Being. We guarantee the freedom to worship as one chooses. We make room for as wide a variety of beliefs and creeds as the spiritual needs of man deem necessary. We sponsor an attitude on the part of government that shows no partiality to any one group and that lets each flourish according to the zeal of its adherents and the appeal of its dogma. When the state encourages religious instruction or cooperates with religious authorities by adjusting the schedule of public events to sectarian needs, it follows the best of our traditions. For it then respects the religious nature of our people and accommodates the public service to their spiritual needs. To hold that it may not would be to find in the Constitution a requirement that the government show a callous indifference to religious groups. That would be preferring those who believe in no religion over those who do believe. Government may not finance religious groups nor undertake religious instruction nor blend secular and sectarian education nor use secular institutions to force one or some religion on any person. But we find no constitutional requirement which makes it necessary for government to be hostile to religion and to throw its weight against efforts to widen the effective scope of religious influence. The government must be neutral when it comes to competition between sects. It may not thrust any sect on any person. It may not make a religious observance compulsory. It may not coerce anyone to attend church, to observe a religious holiday, or to take religious instruction. But it can close its doors or suspend its operations as to those who want to repair to their religious sanctuary for worship or instruction. No more than that is undertaken here.

This program may be unwise and improvident from an educational or a community viewpoint. That appeal is made to us on a theory, previously advanced, that each case must be decided on the basis of "our own prepossessions." Our individual preferences, however, are not the constitutional standard. The constitutional standard is the separation of Church and State. The problem, like many problems in constitutional law, is one of degree.

In the *McCollum* case the classrooms were used for religious instruction and the force of the public school was used to promote that instruction. Here, as we have said, the public schools do no more than accommodate their schedules to a program of outside religious instruction. We follow the *McCollum* case. But we cannot expand it to cover the present released program unless separation of Church and State means that public institutions can make no adjustments of their schedules to accommodate the religious needs of the people. We cannot read into the Bill of Rights such a philosophy of hostility to religion....

Notes

1.   This is the only case in the realm of Church-State relations in education in which Justices Black and Douglas disagreed. In his dissent, Justice Black saw "no significant difference" between the invalid plan in *McCollum* and the one in New York since in both "school authorities release some of the children on the condition that they attend the religious classes, get reports on whether they attend, and hold the other children in the school building until the religious hour is over." *Zorach v. Clauson*, 343 U.S. 306, 316, 72 S.Ct. 679, 96 L.Ed. 954 (1952). (Black, J., dissenting).

2.   Justice Douglas, writing for the Court, commented that "released time" may be unwise from an educational viewpoint. What do you think?

3.   The Supreme Court of Wisconsin, in a case involving an amendment to the state constitution that permitted released time, rejected a claim that *Zorach* was superseded by later Supreme Court cases. *See State ex rel. Holt v. Thompson*, 225 N.W.2d 678 (Wis.1975). The Fourth, *Smith v. Smith*, 523 F.2d 121 (4th Cir.1975), *cert. denied*, 423 U.S. 1073, 96 S.Ct. 856, 47 L.Ed.2d 83 (1976), and Ninth, *Lanner v. Wimmer*, 662 F.2d 1349 [1 Educ. L. Rep. 138] (10th Cir.1981), Circuits rebuffed similar challenges to *Zorach's* viability.

[Case No. 4]   Constitutionality of the Bible and the Lord's Prayer in Public Schools

SCHOOL DISTRICT OF ABINGTON TOWNSHIP v. SCHEMPP, MURRAY v. CURLETT

Supreme Court of the United States, 1963.
374 U.S. 203, 83 S.Ct. 1560, 10 L.Ed.2d 844.

MR. JUSTICE CLARK delivered the opinion of the Court.

. . . These companion cases present the issues in the context of state action requiring that schools begin each day with readings from the Bible. While raising the basic questions under slightly different factual situations, the cases permit of joint treatment. In light of the history of the First Amendment and of our cases interpreting and applying its requirements, we hold that the practices at issue and the laws requiring them are unconstitutional under the Establishment Clause, as applied to the States through the Fourteenth Amendment.

. . . The Commonwealth of Pennsylvania by law, . . . requires that "At least ten verses from the Holy Bible shall be read, without comment, at the opening of each public school on each school day. Any child shall be excused from such Bible reading, or attending such Bible reading, upon the written request of his parent or guardian." The Schempp family, husband and wife and two of their three children, brought suit to enjoin enforcement of the statute. . . .

The appellees Edward Lewis Schempp, his wife Sidney, and their children, Roger and Donna, are of the Unitarian faith and are members of the Unitarian Church in Germantown, Philadelphia, Pennsylvania, where they . . . regularly attend religious services. . . .

On each school day at the Abington Senior High School between 8:15 and 8:30 a.m., while the pupils are attending their home rooms or advisory sections, opening exercises are conducted pursuant to the statute. The exercises are broadcast into each room in the school building through an intercommunications system and are conducted under the supervision of a teacher by students attending the school's radio and television workshop. Selected students from this course gather each morning in the school's workshop studio for the exercises, which include readings by one of the students of 10 verses of the Holy Bible, broadcast to each room in the building. This is followed by the recitation of the Lord's Prayer, likewise over the intercommunications system, but also by the students in the various classrooms, who are asked to stand and join in repeating the prayer in unison. The exercises are closed with the flag salute and such pertinent announcements as are of interest to the students. Participation in the opening exercises, as directed by the statute, is voluntary. The student reading the verses from the Bible may select the passages and read from any version he chooses, although the only copies furnished by the school are the King James version, copies of which were circulated to each teacher by the school district. During the period in which the exercises have been conducted the King James, the Douay and the Revised Standard versions of the Bible have been used, as well as the Jewish Holy Scriptures. There are no prefatory statements, no questions asked or solicited, no comments or explanations made and no interpretations given at or during the exercises. The students and parents are advised that the student may absent himself from the classroom or, should he elect to remain, not participate in the exercises . . . .

At the first trial Edward Schempp and the children testified as to specific religious doctrines purveyed by a literal reading of the Bible "which were contrary to the religious beliefs which they held and to their familial teaching." The children testified that all of the doctrines to which they referred were read to them at various times as part of the exercises. Edward Schempp testified at the second trial that he had considered having Roger and Donna excused from attendance at the exercises but decided against it for several reasons, including his belief that the children's relationships with their teachers and classmates would be adversely affected . . . .

. . . [In Murray the] petition particularized the petitioners' atheistic beliefs and stated that the rule, as practiced, violated their rights

> "in that it threatens their religious liberty by placing a premium on belief as against non-belief and subjects their freedom of conscience to the rule of the majority; it pronounces belief in God as the source of all moral and spiritual values, equating these values with religious values, and thereby renders sinister, alien and suspect the beliefs and ideals of your Petitioners, promoting doubt and question of their morality, good citizenship and good faith."

. . .

The wholesome "neutrality" of which this Court's cases speak . . . stems from a recognition of the teachings of history that powerful sects or groups might bring about a fusion of governmental and religious functions or a concert or dependency of one upon the other to the end that official support of the State or Federal Government would be placed behind the tenets of one or of all orthodoxies. This the Establishment Clause prohibits. And a further reason for neutrality is found in the Free Exercise Clause, which recognizes the value of religious training, teaching and observance and, more particularly, the right of every person to freely choose his own course with reference thereto, free of any compulsion from the state. This the Free Exercise Clause guarantees. Thus, as we have seen, the two clauses may overlap. As we have indicated, the Establishment Clause has been directly considered by this Court eight times in the past score of years and, with only one Justice dissenting on the point, it has consistently held that the clause withdrew all legislative power respecting religious belief or the expression thereof. The test may be stated as follows: what are the purpose and the primary effect of the enactment? If either is the advancement or inhibition of religion then the enactment exceeds the scope of legislative power as circumscribed by the Constitution. That is to say that to withstand the strictures of the Establishment Clause there must be a secular legislative purpose and a primary effect that neither advances nor inhibits religion. . . .

Applying the Establishment Clause principles to the cases at bar we find that the States are requiring the selection and reading at the opening of the school day of verses from the Holy Bible and the recitation of the Lord's Prayer by the students in unison. These exercises are prescribed as part of the curricular activities of students who are required by law to attend school. They are held in the school buildings under the supervision and with the participation of teachers employed in those schools. . . .

. . . Nor are these required exercises mitigated by the fact that individual students may absent themselves upon parental request, for that fact furnishes no defense to a claim of unconstitutionality under the Establishment Clause. Further, it is no defense to urge that the religious practices here may be relatively minor encroachments on the First Amendment. . . .

It is insisted that unless these religious exercises are permitted a "religion of secularism" is established in the schools. We agree of course that the State may not establish a "religion of secularism" in the sense of affirmatively opposing or showing hostility to religion, thus "preferring those who believe in no religion over those who do believe." We do not agree, however, that this decision in any sense has that effect. In addition, it might well be said that one's education is not complete without a study of comparative religion or the history of religion and its relationship to the advancement of civilization. It certainly may be said that the Bible is worthy of study for its literary and historic qualities. Nothing we have said here indicates that such study of the Bible or of religion, when presented objectively as part of a secular program of education, may not be effected consistent with the First Amendment. But the exercises here do not fall into those categories. They are religious exercises, required by the States in violation of the command of the First Amendment that the Government maintain strict neutrality, neither aiding nor opposing religion. . . .

The place of religion in our society is an exalted one, achieved through a long tradition of reliance on the home, the church and the inviolable citadel of the individual heart and mind. We have come to recognize through bitter experience that it is not within the power of government to invade that citadel, whether its purpose or effect be to aid or oppose, to advance or retard. In the relationship between man and religion, the State is firmly committed to a position of neutrality. Though the application of that rule requires interpretation of a delicate sort, the rule itself is clearly and concisely stated in the words of the First Amendment. . . .

Notes

1. In the trial court, the father of the *Schempp* family testified that he declined to request that his children be excused from the morning exercises because he thought they would have been labeled "odd." Was the father's concern justified?

2. In *Engel v. Vitale*, the Supreme Court struck down a policy that called for the recitation of a "non-denominational" at the beginning of each school day. Is there a different constitutional issue raised when a prayer is formulated by school officials rather than their requiring the Lord's Prayer?

[Case No. 5]   Constitutionality of Providing Textbooks to Students in Non–Public Schools

BOARD OF EDUCATION OF CENTRAL SCHOOL DISTRICT NO. 1 v. ALLEN

Supreme Court of the United States, 1968.
392 U.S. 236, 88 S.Ct. 1923, 20 L.Ed.2d 1060.

MR. JUSTICE WHITE delivered the opinion of the Court.

A law of the State of New York requires local public school authorities to lend textbooks free of charge to all students in grades seven through 12; students attending private schools are included. This case presents the question whether this statute is a "law respecting the establishment of religion or prohibiting the free exercise thereof," and so in conflict with the First and Fourteenth Amendments to the Constitution, because it authorizes the loan of textbooks to students attending parochial schools. We hold that the law is not in violation of the Constitution.

Until 1965, § 701 of the Education Law of the State of New York, McKinney's Consol. Laws, c. 16, authorized public school boards to designate textbooks for use in the public schools, to purchase such books with public funds, and to rent or sell the books to public school students. In 1965 the Legislature amended § 701, basing the amendments on findings that the "public welfare and safety require that the state and local communities give assistance to educational programs which are important to our national defense and the general welfare of the state." Beginning with the 1966–1967 school year, local school boards were required to purchase textbooks and lend them without charge "to all children residing in such district who are enrolled in grades seven to twelve of a public or private school which complies with the compulsory education law." The books now loaned are "textbooks which are designated for use in any public, elementary or secondary schools of the state or are approved by any boards of education," and which—according to a 1966 amendment—"a pupil is required to use as a text for a semester or more in a particular class in the school he legally attends." . . .

Everson v. Board of Education is the case decided by this Court that is most nearly in point for today's problem. . . .

Of course books are different from buses. Most bus rides have no inherent religious significance, while religious books are common. However, the language of § 701 does not authorize the loan of religious books, and the State claims no right to distribute religious literature. Although the books loaned are those required by the parochial school for use in specific courses, each book loaned must be approved by the public school authorities; only secular books may receive approval. The law was construed by the Court of Appeals of New York as "merely making available secular textbooks at the request of the individual student," supra, and the record contains no suggestion that religious books have been loaned. Absent evidence we cannot assume that school authorities, who constantly face the same problem in selecting textbooks for use in the public schools, are unable to distinguish between secular and religious books or that they will not honestly discharge their duties under the law. In judging the validity of the statute on this record we must proceed on the assumption that books loaned to students are books that are not unsuitable for use in the public schools because of religious content.

The major reason offered by appellants for distinguishing free textbooks from free bus fares is that books, but not buses, are critical to the teaching process, and in a sectarian school that process is employed to teach religion. However, this Court has long recognized that religious schools pursue two goals, religious instruction and secular education. In the leading case of *Pierce v. Society of Sisters*, the Court held that although it would not question Oregon's power to compel school attendance or require that the attendance be at an institution meeting State-imposed requirements as to quality and nature of curriculum, Oregon had not shown that its interest in secular education required that all children attend publicly operated schools. A premise of this holding was the view that the State's interest in education would be served sufficiently by reliance on the secular teaching that accompanied religious training in the schools maintained by the Society of Sisters. Since *Pierce,* a substantial body of case law has confirmed the power of the States to insist that attendance at private schools, if it is to satisfy state compulsory-attendance laws, be at institutions which provide minimum hours of instruction, employ teachers of specified training, and cover prescribed subjects of instruction. Indeed, the State's interest in assuring that these standards are being met has been considered a sufficient reason for refusing to accept instruction at home as compliance with compulsory education statutes. . . .

Underlying these cases, and underlying also the legislative judgments that have preceded the court decisions, has been a recognition that private education has played and is playing a significant and valuable role in raising national levels of knowledge, competence, and experience. Americans care about the quality of the secular education available to their children. They have considered high quality education to be an indispensable ingredient for achieving the kind of nation, and the kind of citizenry, that they have desired to create. Considering this attitude, the continued willingness to rely on private school systems, including parochial systems, strongly suggests that a wide segment of informed opinion, legislative and otherwise, has found that those schools do an acceptable job of providing secular education to their students. This judgment is further evidence that parochial schools are performing, in addition to their sectarian function, the task of secular education.

Against this background of judgment and experience, unchallenged in the meager record before us in this case, we cannot agree with appellants either that all teaching in a sectarian school is religious or that the processes of secular and religious training are so intertwined that secular textbooks furnished to students by the public are in fact instrumental in the teaching of religion. This case comes to us after summary judgment entered on the pleadings. Nothing in this record supports the proposition that all textbooks, whether they deal with mathematics, physics, foreign languages, history, or literature, are used by the parochial schools to teach religion. No evidence has been offered about particular schools, particular courses, particular teachers, or particular books. We are unable to hold, based solely on judicial notice, that this statute results in unconstitutional involvement of the State with religious instruction or that § 701, for this or the other reasons urged, is a law respecting the establishment of religion within the meaning of the First Amendment. . . .

The judgment is affirmed.

Notes

1. Justice Douglas' dissent declared that there is nothing ideological about a bus, school lunch, public nurse, or scholarship. However, he thought that textbooks go to the very heart of education in non-public schools. Is this a valid distinction?

2. The Supreme Court struck down a program that would have furnished textbooks to students who attended non-public schools that had racially discriminatory policies. *Norwood v. Harrison*, 413 U.S. 455, 93 S.Ct. 2804, 37 L.Ed.2d 723 (1973).

3. The Court affirmed, without a written opinion, a case from New Jersey invalidating a plan which allowed parents whose children attended non-public schools to be reimbursed for purchasing secular textbooks. *Public Funds for Pub. School v. Marburger*, 358 F.Supp. 29 (D.N.J.1973), *aff'd*, 417 U.S. 961, 94 S.Ct.

3163, 41 L.Ed.2d 1134 (1974). The Court maintained that reimbursement was unconstitutional since it applied exclusively to parents whose children were enrolled in non-public, primarily religious, schools. Previously, the Court refused to hear an appeal wherein the Supreme Court of Oregon held that a state law that authorized free textbooks for students who were enrolled in a religiously affiliated non-public school violated the state constitution. *Dickman v. School Dist. No. 62C, Oregon City, Clackamas County*, 366 P.2d 533 (Or. 1961), *cert. denied sub nom. Carlson v. Dickman*, 371 U.S. 823, 83 S.Ct. 41, 9 L.Ed.2d 62 (1962).

[Case No. 6] Constitutionality of Statute Forbidding Teaching of Evolution

EPPERSON v. STATE OF ARKANSAS

Supreme Court of the United States, 1968.
393 U.S. 97, 89 S.Ct. 266, 21 L.Ed.2d 228.

MR. JUSTICE FORTAS delivered the opinion of the Court.

I

This appeal challenges the constitutionality of the "anti-evolution" statute which the State of Arkansas adopted in 1928 to prohibit the teaching in its public schools and universities of the theory that man evolved from other species of life. . . .

The Arkansas law makes it unlawful for a teacher in any state-supported school or university "to teach the theory or doctrine that mankind ascended or descended from a lower order of animals," or "to adopt or use in any such institution a textbook that teaches" this theory. Violation is a misdemeanor and subjects the violator to dismissal from his position.

The present case concerns the teaching of biology in a high school in Little Rock. According to the testimony, until the events here in litigation, the official textbook furnished for the high school biology course "did not have a section on the Darwinian Theory." Then, for the academic year 1965–1966, the school administration, on recommendation of the teachers of biology in the school system, adopted and prescribed a textbook which contained a chapter setting forth "the theory about the origin . . . of man from a lower form of animal."

Susan Epperson, a young woman who graduated from Arkansas' school system and then obtained her master's degree in zoology at the University of Illinois, was employed by the Little Rock school system in the fall of 1964 to teach 10th grade biology at Central High School. At the start of the next academic year, 1965, she was confronted by the new textbook (which one surmises from the record was not unwelcome to her). She faced at least a literal dilemma because she was supposed to use the new textbook for classroom instruction and presumably to teach the statutorily condemned chapter; but to do so would be a criminal offense and subject her to dismissal. . . .

... Only Arkansas, Mississippi, and Tennessee have such "anti-evolution" or "monkey" laws on their books. There is no record of any prosecutions in Arkansas under its statute. It is possible that the statute is presently more of a curiosity than a vital fact of life in these States. Nevertheless, the present case was brought, the appeal as of right is properly here, and it is our duty to decide the issues presented.

II

At the outset, it is urged upon us that the challenged statute is vague and uncertain and therefore within the condemnation of the Due Process Clause of the Fourteenth Amendment. The contention that the Act is vague and uncertain is supported by language in the brief opinion of Arkansas' Supreme Court. That court, perhaps reflecting the discomfort which the statute's quixotic prohibition necessarily engenders in the modern mind, stated that it "expresses no opinion" as to whether the Act prohibits "explanation" of the theory of evolution or merely forbids "teaching that the theory is true." Regardless of this uncertainty, the court held that the statute is constitutional.

On the other hand, counsel for the State, in oral argument in this Court, candidly stated that, despite the State Supreme Court's equivocation, Arkansas would interpret the statute "to mean that to make a student aware of the theory ... just to teach that there was such a theory" would be grounds for dismissal and for prosecution under the statute; and he said "that the Supreme Court of Arkansas' opinion should be interpreted in that manner." He said "If Mrs. Epperson would tell her students that 'Here is Darwin's theory, that man ascended or descended from a lower form of being,' then I think she would be under this statute liable for prosecution."

In any event, we do not rest our decision upon the asserted vagueness of the statute. On either interpretation of its language, Arkansas' statute cannot stand. It is of no moment whether the law is deemed to prohibit mention of Darwin's theory, or to forbid any or all of the infinite varieties of communication embraced within the term "teaching." Under either interpretation, the law must be stricken because of its conflict with the constitutional prohibition of state laws respecting an establishment of religion or prohibiting the free exercise thereof. The overriding fact is that Arkansas' law selects from the body of knowledge a particular segment which it proscribes for the sole reason that it is deemed to conflict with a particular religious doctrine; that is, with a particular interpretation of the Book of Genesis by a particular religious group. . . .

Judicial interposition in the operation of the public school system of the Nation raises problems requiring care and restraint. Our courts, however, have not failed to apply the First Amendment's mandate in our educational system where essential to safeguard the fundamental values of freedom of speech and inquiry and of belief. By and large, public education in our Nation is committed to the control of state and local authorities. Courts do not and cannot intervene in the resolution of conflicts which arise in the daily operation of school systems and which

do not directly and sharply implicate basic constitutional values. On the other hand, "The vigilant protection of constitutional freedoms is nowhere more vital than in the community of American schools," and "This Court will be alert against invasions of academic freedom...." As this Court said in *Keyishian v. Board of Regents*, the First Amendment "does not tolerate laws that cast a pall of orthodoxy over the classroom."
...

There is and can be no doubt that the First Amendment does not permit the State to require that teaching and learning must be tailored to the principles or prohibitions of any religious sect or dogma. In *Everson v. Board of Education*, this Court, in upholding a state law to provide free bus service to school children, including those attending parochial schools, said: "Neither [a State nor the Federal Government] can pass laws which aid one religion, aid all religions, or prefer one religion over another." ...

In the present case, there can be no doubt that Arkansas has sought to prevent its teachers from discussing the theory of evolution because it is contrary to the belief of some that the Book of Genesis must be the exclusive source of doctrine as to the origin of man. No suggestion has been made that Arkansas' law may be justified by considerations of state policy other than the religious views of some of its citizens. It is clear that fundamentalist sectarian conviction was and is the law's reason for existence. Its antecedent, Tennessee's "monkey law," candidly stated its purpose: to make it unlawful "to teach any theory that denies the story of the Divine Creation of man, as taught in the Bible, and to teach instead, that man has descended from a lower order of animals." Perhaps the sensational publicity attendant upon the *Scopes* trial induced Arkansas to adopt less explicit language. It eliminated Tennessee's reference to "the story of the Divine Creation of man" as taught in the Bible, but there is no doubt that the motivation for the law was the same: to suppress the teaching of a theory which, it was thought, "denied" the divine creation of man....

The judgment of the Supreme Court of Arkansas is reversed.

Notes

1. The Supreme Court of Mississippi struck down the last anti-evolution statute in *Smith v. State, 242 So.2d 692* (Miss.1970). Subsequently, Tennessee enacted a statute prohibiting the use of any textbook that discussed evolution unless there were a disclaimer that the doctrine was only a theory and not scientific fact as to the origin of man. The statute required the inclusion of the Genesis version of creation, if any version at all was included, while permitting it alone to be printed without the disclaimer. Also the statute declared "the Holy Bible shall not be defined as a textbook, but is hereby declared to be a reference work, and shall not be required to carry the disclaimer." The Sixth Circuit declared the statute unconstitutional because it gave a preferential position to the Biblical version of creation. *Daniel v. Waters*, 515 F.2d 485, 487 (6th Cir.1975).

2. Several state legislatures have discussed including intelligent design in public school curricula. What do you think about this approach?

[Case No. 7]   Constitutionality of Reimbursements to Non–Public Schools

LEMON v. KURTZMAN
EARLEY v. DICENSO

Supreme Court of the United States, 1971.
403 U.S. 602, 91 S.Ct. 2105, 29 L.Ed.2d 745.

MR. CHIEF JUSTICE BURGER delivered the opinion of the Court.

These two appeals raise questions as to Pennsylvania and Rhode Island statutes providing state aid to church-related elementary and secondary schools. Both statutes are challenged as violative of the Establishment and Free Exercise Clauses of the First Amendment and the Due Process Clause of the Fourteenth Amendment.

Pennsylvania has adopted a statutory program that provides financial support to non-public elementary and secondary schools by way of reimbursement for the cost of teachers' salaries, textbooks, and instructional materials in specified secular subjects. Rhode Island has adopted a statute under which the State pays directly to teachers in non-public elementary schools a supplement of 15% of their annual salary. Under each statute state aid has been given to church-related educational institutions as well as other private schools. We hold that both statutes are unconstitutional.

I

The Rhode Island Statute

The Rhode Island Salary Supplement Act was enacted in 1969. It rests on the legislative finding that the quality of education available in non-public elementary schools has been jeopardized by the rapidly rising salaries needed to attract competent and dedicated teachers. The Act authorizes state officials to supplement the salaries of teachers of secular subjects in non-public elementary schools by paying directly to a teacher an amount not in excess of 15% of his current annual salary. As supplemented, however, a non-public school teacher's salary cannot exceed the maximum paid to teachers in the State's public schools, and the recipient must be certified by the state board of education in substantially the same manner as public school teachers.

In order to be eligible for the Rhode Island salary supplement, the recipient must teach in a non-public school at which the average per-pupil expenditure on secular education is less than the average in the State's public schools during a specified period. Appellant state Commissioner of Education also requires eligible schools to submit financial data. If this information indicates a per-pupil expenditure in excess of the statutory limitation, the records of the school in question must be examined in order to assess how much of the expenditure is attributable to secular education and how much to religious activity.

The Act also requires that teachers eligible for salary supplement must teach only those subjects that are offered in the State's public schools. They must use "only teaching materials which are used in the public schools." Finally, any teacher applying for a salary supplement must first agree in writing "not to teach a course in religion for so long as or during such time as he or she receives any salary supplements" under the Act. . . .

The District Court concluded that the Act violated the Establishment Clause, holding that it fostered "excessive entanglement" between government and religion. In addition two judges thought that the Act had the impermissible effect of giving "significant aid to a religious enterprise." We affirm.

The Pennsylvania Statute

. . .

The statute authorizes appellee state Superintendent of Public Instruction to "purchase" specified "secular educational services" from non-public schools. Under the "contracts" authorized by the statute, the State directly reimburses non-public schools solely for their actual expenditures for teachers' salaries, textbooks, and instructional materials. A school seeking reimbursement must maintain prescribed accounting procedures that identify the "separate" cost of the "secular educational service." These accounts are subject to state audit. The funds for this program were originally derived from a new tax on horse and harness racing, but the Act is now financed by a portion of the state tax on cigarettes.

There are several significant statutory restrictions on state aid. Reimbursement is limited to courses "presented in the curricula of the public schools." It is further limited "solely" to courses in the following "secular" subjects: mathematics, modern foreign languages, physical science, and physical education. Textbooks and instructional materials included in the program must be approved by the state Superintendent of Public Instruction. Finally, the statute prohibits reimbursement for any course that contains "any subject matter expressing religious teaching, or the morals or forms of worship of any sect."

. . .

The court granted [Pennsylvania's] motion to dismiss the complaint for failure to state a claim for relief. It held that the Act violated neither the Establishment nor the Free Exercise Clauses, Chief Judge Hastie dissenting. We reverse.

II

In *Everson v. Board of Education* this Court upheld a state statute which reimbursed the parents of parochial school children for bus transportation expenses. There Mr. Justice Black, writing for the majority, suggested that the decision carried to "the verge" of forbidden territory under the Religion Clauses. Candor compels acknowledgement, moreover, that we can only dimly perceive the lines of demarcation in this extraordinarily sensitive area of constitutional law.

The language of the Religion Clauses of the First Amendment is at best opaque, particularly when compared with other portions of the Amendment. Its authors did not simply prohibit the establishment of a state church or a state religion, an area history shows they regarded as very important and fraught with great dangers. Instead they commanded that there should be "no law *respecting* an establishment of religion." A law may be one "respecting" the forbidden objective while falling short of its total realization. A law "respecting" the proscribed result, that is, the establishment of religion, is not always easily identifiable as one violative of the Clause. A given law might not *establish* a state religion but nevertheless be one "respecting" that end in the sense of being a step that could lead to such establishment and hence offend the First Amendment.

In the absence of precisely stated constitutional prohibitions, we must draw lines with reference to the three main evils against which the Establishment Clause was intended to afford protection: "sponsorship, financial support, and active involvement of the sovereign in religious activity." *Walz v. Tax Commission*.

Every analysis in this area must begin with consideration of the cumulative criteria developed by the Court over many years. Three such tests may be gleaned from our cases. First, the statute must have a secular legislative purpose; second, its principal or primary effect must be one that neither advances nor inhibits religion, *Board of Education v. Allen*; finally, the statute must not foster "an excessive government entanglement with religion." *Walz.....*

III

. . .

Our prior holdings do not call for total separation between church and state; total separation is not possible in an absolute sense. Some relationship between government and religious organizations is inevitable. Fire inspections, building and zoning regulations, and state requirements under compulsory school attendance laws are examples of necessary and permissible contacts....

In order to determine whether the government entanglement with religion is excessive, we must examine the character and purposes of the institutions which are benefited, the nature of the aid that the State provides, and the resulting relationship between the government and the religious authority.... Here we find that both statutes foster an impermissible degree of entanglement.

(a) Rhode Island program

. . .

The church schools involved in the program are located close to parish churches. This understandably permits convenient access for religious exercises since instruction in faith and morals is part of the total educational process. The school buildings contain identifying religious symbols such as crosses on the exterior and crucifixes, religious paintings and statues either in the classrooms or hallways. Although only approximately 30 minutes a day are devoted to direct religious instruction, there are religiously oriented extracurricular activities. Approximately two-thirds of the teachers in these schools are nuns of various religious orders. Their dedicated efforts provide an atmosphere in which religious instruction and religious vocations are natural and proper parts of life in such schools. Indeed, as the District Court found, the role of teaching nuns in enhancing the religious atmosphere has led the parochial school authorities to attempt to maintain a one-to-one ratio between nuns and lay teachers in all schools rather than permitting some to be staffed almost entirely by lay teachers.

On the basis of these findings the District Court concluded that the parochial schools constituted "an integral part of the religious mission of the Catholic Church." The various characteristics of the schools make them "a powerful vehicle for transmitting the Catholic faith to the next generation." This process of inculcating religious doctrine is, of course, enhanced by the impressionable age of the pupils, in primary schools particularly. In short, parochial schools involve substantial religious activity and purpose.

The substantial religious character of these church-related schools gives rise to entangling church-state relationships of the kind the Religion Clauses sought to avoid. Although the District Court found that concern for religious values did not inevitably or necessarily intrude into the content of secular subjects, the considerable religious activities of these schools led the legislature to provide for careful governmental controls and surveillance by state authorities in order to ensure that state aid supports only secular education.

The dangers and corresponding entanglements are enhanced by the particular form of aid that the Rhode Island Act provides. Our decisions from *Everson* to *Allen* have permitted the States to provide church-related schools with secular, neutral, or non-ideological services, facilities, or materials. But transportation, school lunches, public health services, and secular textbooks supplied in common to all students were not thought to offend the Establishment Clause. We note that the dissenters in *Allen* seemed chiefly concerned with the pragmatic difficulties involved in ensuring the truly secular content of the textbooks provided at state expense.

In *Allen* the Court refused to make assumptions, on a meager record, about the religious content of the textbooks that the State would be asked to provide. We cannot, however, refuse here to recognize that teachers have a substantially different ideological character than books. In terms of potential for involving some aspect of faith or morals in secular subjects, a textbook's content is ascertainable, but a teacher's handling of a subject is not. We cannot ignore the dangers that a teacher under religious control and discipline poses to the separation of the religious from the purely secular aspects of precollege education. The conflict of functions inheres in the situation. . . .

We do not assume, however, that parochial school teachers will be unsuccessful in their attempts to segregate their religious beliefs from their secular educational responsibilities. But the potential for impermissible fostering of religion is present. The Rhode Island Legislature has not, and could not, provide state aid on the basis of a mere assumption that secular teachers under religious discipline can avoid conflicts. The State must be certain, given the Religion Clauses, that subsidized teachers do not inculcate religion—indeed the State here has undertaken to do so. To ensure that no trespass occurs, the State has therefore carefully conditioned its aid with pervasive restrictions. An eligible recipient must teach only those courses that are offered in the public schools and use only those texts and materials that are found in the public schools. In addition the teacher must not engage in teaching any course in religion.

A comprehensive, discriminating, and continuing state surveillance will inevitably be required to ensure that these restrictions are obeyed and the First Amendment otherwise respected. Unlike a book, a teacher cannot be inspected once so as to determine the extent and intent of his or her personal beliefs and subjective acceptance of the limitations imposed by the First Amendment. These prophylactic contacts will involve excessive and enduring entanglement between state and church.

.   .   .

(b) Pennsylvania program

The Pennsylvania statute also provides state aid to church-related schools for teachers' salaries. The complaint describes an educational system that is very similar to the one existing in Rhode Island. According to the allegations, the church-related elementary and secondary schools are controlled by religious organizations, have the purpose of propagating and promoting a particular religious faith, and conduct their operations to fulfill that purpose. Since this complaint was dismissed for failure to state a claim for relief, we must accept these allegations as true for purposes of our review.

As we noted earlier, the very restrictions and surveillance necessary to ensure that teachers play a strictly non-ideological role give rise to entanglements between church and state. The Pennsylvania statute, like that of Rhode Island, fosters this kind of relationship. Reimbursement is not only limited to courses offered in the public schools and materials approved by state officials, but the statute excludes "any subject matter expressing religious teaching, or the morals or forms of worship of any sect." In addition schools seeking reimbursement must maintain accounting procedures that require the State to establish the cost of the secular as distinguished from the religious instruction.

The Pennsylvania statute, moreover, has the further defect of providing state financial aid directly to the church-related schools. This factor distinguishes both *Everson* and *Allen,* for in both those cases the

Court was careful to point out that state aid was provided to the student and his parents—not to the church-related school. ... The history of government grants of a continuing cash subsidy indicates that such programs have almost always been accompanied by varying measures of control and surveillance. The government cash grants before us now provide no basis for predicting that comprehensive measures of surveillance and controls will not follow. In particular the government's post-audit power to inspect and evaluate a church-related school's financial records and to determine which expenditures are religious and which are secular creates an intimate and continuing relationship between church and state.

IV

A broader base of entanglement of yet a different character is presented by the divisive political potential of these state programs. In a community where such a large number of pupils are served by church-related schools, it can be assumed that state assistance will entail considerable political activity. Partisans of parochial schools, understandably concerned with rising costs and sincerely dedicated to both the religious and secular educational missions of their schools, will inevitably champion this cause and promote political action to achieve their goals. Those who oppose state aid, whether for constitutional, religious, or fiscal reasons, will inevitably respond and employ all of the usual political campaign techniques to prevail. Candidates will be forced to declare and voters to choose. It would be unrealistic to ignore the fact that many people confronted with issues of this kind will find their votes aligned with their faith.

Ordinarily political debate and division, however vigorous or even partisan, are normal and healthy manifestations of our democratic system of government, but political division along religious lines was one of the principal evils against which the First Amendment was intended to protect. The potential divisiveness of such conflict is a threat to the normal political process. To have States or communities divide on the issues presented by state aid to parochial schools would tend to confuse and obscure other issues of great urgency. We have an expanding array of vexing issues, local and national, domestic and international, to debate and divide on. It conflicts with our whole history and tradition to permit questions of the Religion Clauses to assume such importance in our legislatures and in our elections that they could divert attention from the myriad issues and problems which confront every level of government. The highways of church and state relationships are not likely to be one-way streets, and the Constitution's authors sought to protect religious worship from the pervasive power of government. The history of many countries attests to the hazards of religion intruding into the political arena or of political power intruding into the legitimate and free exercise of religious belief. ...

The potential for political divisiveness related to religious belief and practice is aggravated in these two statutory programs by the need for continuing annual appropriations and the likelihood of larger and larger demands as costs and populations grow. . . .

V

. . .

Finally, nothing we have said can be construed to disparage the role of church-related elementary and secondary schools in our national life. Their contribution has been and is enormous. Nor do we ignore their economic plight in a period of rising costs and expanding need. Taxpayers generally have been spared vast sums by the maintenance of these educational institutions by religious organizations, largely by the gifts of faithful adherents.

The merit and benefits of these schools, however, are not the issue before us in these cases. The sole question is whether state aid to these schools can be squared with the dictates of the Religion Clauses. Under our system the choice has been made that government is to be entirely excluded from the area of religious instruction and churches excluded from the affairs of government. The Constitution decrees that religion must be a private matter for the individual, the family, and the institutions of private choice, and that while some involvement and entanglement is inevitable, lines must be drawn. . . .

Notes

1.   On the same day that it ruled in *Lemon*, the Supreme Court upheld the constitutionality of the Higher Education Facilities Act of 1963. This law made construction grants available to institutions of higher education, including church related colleges and universities, to erect academic facilities. In *Tilton v. Richardson (Tilton)*, 403 U.S. 672, 91 S.Ct. 2091, 29 L.Ed.2d 790 (1971), the Court reasoned that while the section of the law that limited recipients' obligation not to use federally-financed facilities for sectarian instruction or religious worship to twenty years unconstitutionally allowed a contribution of property of substantial value to religious bodies, that section was severable. However, the Court was satisfied that the remainder of the statute did not violate the First Amendment. In upholding the remainder of the law, the Court distinguished *Tilton* from *Lemon* insofar as in *Tilton*, indoctrination was not a substantial purpose or activity of church-related colleges since the student body was not composed of impressionable children, the aid was non-ideological, and there was no excessive entanglement where the grants were one-time and single-purpose. Two years later, in *Hunt v. McNair*, 413 U.S. 734, 93 S.Ct. 2868, 37 L.Ed.2d 923 (1973), the Court decided that since religion was not pervasive in the institution, the State of South Carolina was free to issue revenue bonds to benefit the church-related college because it did not guarantee them with public funds.

2.   In his concurrence in *Lamb's Chapel v. Center Moriches Union Free School District*, 508 U.S. 384, 398, 113 S.Ct. 2141, 124 L.Ed.2d 352 [83 Educ. L. Rep. 30] (1993) [Case No. 44], *on remand*, 17 F.3d 1425 [89 Educ. L. Rep. 783] (2d Cir.1994) [Case No. 53], Justice Scalia employed a caustic description of the *Lemon* test: "Like some ghoul in a late-night horror movie that repeatedly sits up in its grave and shuffles abroad, after being repeatedly killed and buried, *Lemon* stalks our Establishment Clause jurisprudence once again, frightening

the little children and school attorneys of Center Moriches Union Free School District.'' What do you think of this characterization?

[Case No. 8] Constitutionality of Income Tax Deduction for Certain Educational Expenses in Public or Non–Public Schools

MUELLER v. ALLEN

Supreme Court of the United States, 1983
463 U.S. 388, 103 S.Ct. 3062, 77 L.Ed.2d 721 [11 Educ. L. Rep. 763].

JUSTICE REHNQUIST delivered the opinion of the Court.

. . .

Minnesota, by a law originally enacted in 1955 and revised in 1976 and again in 1978, permits state taxpayers to claim a deduction from gross income for certain expenses incurred in educating their children. The deduction is limited to actual expenses incurred for the "tuition, textbooks and transportation" of dependents attending elementary or secondary schools. A deduction may not exceed $500 per dependent in grades K through six and $700 per dependent in grades seven through twelve. Minn. Stat. § 290.09. . . .

Today's case is no exception to our oft-repeated statement that the Establishment Clause presents especially difficult questions of interpretation and application. . . .

One fixed principle in this field is our consistent rejection of the argument that "any program which in some manner aids an institution with a religious affiliation" violates the Establishment Clause. For example, it is now well-established that a state may reimburse parents for expenses incurred in transporting their children to school, *Everson v. Board of Education*, and that it may loan secular textbooks to all schoolchildren within the state, *Board of Education v. Allen*.

Notwithstanding the repeated approval given programs such as those in *Allen* and *Everson*, our decisions also have struck down arrangements resembling, in many respects, these forms of assistance. *See, e.g., Lemon v. Kurtzman; Levitt v. Committee for Public Education; Meek v. Pittenger; Wolman v. Walter.* In this case we are asked to decide whether Minnesota's tax deduction bears greater resemblance to those types of assistance to parochial schools we have approved, or to those we have struck down. Petitioners place particular reliance on our decision in *Committee for Public Education v. Nyquist*, where we held invalid a New York statute providing public funds for the maintenance and repair of the physical facilities of private schools and granting thinly disguised "tax benefits," actually amounting to tuition grants, to the parents of children attending private schools. As explained below, we conclude that § 290.09(22) bears less resemblance to the arrangement struck down in *Nyquist* than it does to assistance programs upheld in our prior decisions and those discussed with approval in *Nyquist*.

The general nature of our inquiry in this area has been guided, since the decision in *Lemon v. Kurtzman*, by the "three-part" test laid down in that case:

"First, the statute must have a secular legislative purpose; second, its principle or primary effect must be one that neither advances nor inhibits religion ... ; finally, the statute must not foster 'an excessive government entanglement with religion.' "

While this principle is well settled, our cases have also emphasized that it provides "no more than [a] helpful signpost" in dealing with Establishment Clause challenges. With this *caveat* in mind, we turn to the specific challenges raised against § 290.09(22) under the *Lemon* framework.

Little time need be spent on the question of whether the Minnesota tax deduction has a secular purpose. Under our prior decisions, governmental assistance programs have consistently survived this inquiry even when they have run afoul of other aspects of the *Lemon* framework. This reflects, at least in part, our reluctance to attribute unconstitutional motives to the states, particularly when a plausible secular purpose for the state's program may be discerned from the face of the statute.

A state's decision to defray the cost of educational expenses incurred by parents-regardless of the type of schools their children attend-evidences a purpose that is both secular and understandable. An educated populace is essential to the political and economic health of any community, and a state's efforts to assist parents in meeting the rising cost of educational expenses plainly serves this secular purpose of ensuring that the state's citizenry is well-educated. Similarly, Minnesota, like other states, could conclude that there is a strong public interest in assuring the continued financial health of private schools, both sectarian and non-sectarian. By educating a substantial number of students such schools relieve public schools of a correspondingly great burden-to the benefit of all taxpayers. ... All these justifications are readily available to support § 290.09(22), and each is sufficient to satisfy the secular purpose inquiry of *Lemon*.

We turn therefore to the more difficult but related question whether the Minnesota statute has "the primary effect of advancing the sectarian aims of the non-public schools." In concluding that it does not, we find several features of the Minnesota tax deduction particularly significant. First, an essential feature of Minnesota's arrangement is the fact that § 290.09(22) is only one among many deductions-such as those for medical expenses and charitable contributions-available under the Minnesota tax laws. Our decisions consistently have recognized that traditionally "[l]egislatures have especially broad latitude in creating classifications and distinctions in tax statutes," in part because the "familiarity with local conditions" enjoyed by legislators especially enables them to "achieve an equitable distribution of the tax burden." Under our prior decisions, the Minnesota legislature's judgment that a deduction for educational expenses fairly equalizes the tax burden of its citizens and encourages desirable expenditures for educational purposes is entitled to substantial deference.

Other characteristics of § 290.09(22) argue equally strongly for the provision's constitutionality. Most importantly, the deduction is available for educational expenses incurred by *all* parents, including those whose children attend public schools and those whose children attend non-sectarian private schools or sectarian private schools. ... "[T]he provision of benefits to so broad a spectrum of groups is an important index of secular effect."

In this respect, as well as others, this case is vitally different from the scheme struck down in *Nyquist.* There, public assistance amounting to tuition grants, was provided only to parents of children in *non-public* schools. This fact had considerable bearing on our decision striking down the New York statute at issue; we explicitly distinguished both *Allen* and *Everson* on the grounds that "In both cases the class of beneficiaries included *all* schoolchildren, those in public as well as those in private schools." Moreover, we intimated that "public assistance (*e.g.,* scholarships) made available generally without regard to the sectarian-nonsectarian or public-non-public nature of the institution benefited," might not offend the Establishment Clause. We think the tax deduction adopted by Minnesota is more similar to this latter type of program than it is to the arrangement struck down in *Nyquist.* Unlike the assistance at issue in *Nyquist,* § 290.09(22) permits *all* parents—whether their children attend public school or private—to deduct their children's educational expenses.... [A] program, like § 290.09(22), that neutrally provides state assistance to a broad spectrum of citizens is not readily subject to challenge under the Establishment Clause.

We also agree with the Court of Appeals that, by channeling whatever assistance it may provide to parochial schools through individual parents, Minnesota has reduced the Establishment Clause objections to which its action is subject. It is true, of course, that financial assistance provided to parents ultimately has an economic effect comparable to that of aid given directly to the schools attended by their children. It is also true, however, that under Minnesota's arrangement public funds become available only as a result of numerous, private choices of individual parents of school-age children. For these reasons, we recognized in *Nyquist* that the means by which state assistance flows to private schools is of some importance: we said that "the fact that aid is disbursed to parents rather than to ... schools" is a material consideration in Establishment Clause analysis, albeit "only one among many to be considered." It is noteworthy that all but one of our recent cases invalidating state aid to parochial schools have involved the direct transmission of assistance from the state to the schools themselves. The exception, of course, was *Nyquist,* which, as discussed previously, is distinguishable from this case on other grounds. Where, as here, aid to parochial schools is available only as a result of decisions of individual parents no "imprimatur of State approval" can be deemed to have been conferred on any particular religion, or on religion generally.

... The Establishment Clause of course extends beyond prohibition of a state church or payment of state funds to one or more churches. We do not think, however, that its prohibition extends to the type of tax deduction established by Minnesota. The historic purposes of the clause simply do not encompass the sort of attenuated financial benefit, ultimately controlled by the private choices of individual parents, that eventually flows to parochial schools from the neutrally available tax benefit at issue in this case.

Petitioners argue that, notwithstanding the facial neutrality of § 290.09(22), in application the statute primarily benefits religious institutions. Petitioners rely ... on a statistical analysis of the type of persons claiming the tax deduction. They contend that most parents of public school children incur no tuition expenses, and that other expenses deductible under § 290.09(22) are negligible in value; moreover, they claim that 96% of the children in private schools in 1978–1979 attended religiously-affiliated institutions. Because of all this, they reason, the bulk of deductions taken under § 290.09(22) will be claimed by parents of children in sectarian schools. Respondents reply that petitioners have failed to consider the impact of deductions for items such as transportation, summer school tuition, tuition paid by parents whose children attended schools outside the school districts in which they resided, rental or purchase costs for a variety of equipment, and tuition for certain types of instruction not ordinarily provided in public schools.

We need not consider these contentions in detail. We would be loath to adopt a rule grounding the constitutionality of a facially neutral law on annual reports reciting the extent to which various classes of private citizens claimed benefits under the law. Such an approach would scarcely provide the certainty that this field stands in need of, nor can we perceive principled standards by which such statistical evidence might be evaluated. . . .

Thus, we hold that the Minnesota tax deduction for educational expenses satisfies the primary effect inquiry of our Establishment Clause cases.

Turning to the third part of the *Lemon* inquiry, we have no difficulty in concluding that the Minnesota statute does not "excessively entangle" the state in religion. The only plausible source of the "comprehensive, discriminating, and continuing state surveillance" necessary to run afoul of this standard would lie in the fact that state officials must determine whether particular textbooks qualify for a deduction. Making decisions such as this does not differ substantially from making the types of decisions approved in earlier opinions of this Court. In *Board of Education v. Allen*, for example, the Court upheld the loan of secular textbooks to parents or children attending non-public schools; though state officials were required to determine whether particular books were or were not secular, the system was held not to violate the Establishment Clause. . . .

For the foregoing reasons, the judgment of the Court of Appeals is

Affirmed.

Notes

1.   Should it have mattered that 96 percent of the children in non-public schools in Minnesota attended religious schools?

2.   What do you think about the tax deduction from the points of view of public policy, economics, and fairness to all taxpayers.

3.   An appellate court in Illinois upheld a tax credit of up to $500 for educational expenses incurred on behalf of a qualifying pupil in grades K–12 at any state public or non-public school that complies with various state laws. The court rejected arguments that the credit had the effect of advancing religion not only because the majority of non-public schools are religiously affiliated but also because eighty-two out of the state's 102 counties do not have any non-sectarian schools. Should these two facts have made a difference? *Griffith v. Bower*, 747 N.E.2d 423 [153 Educ. L. Rep. 938] (Ill.Ct.App.2001), *appeal denied*, 755 N.E.2d 477 (Ill.2001).

[Case No. 9]   Interpretation of Federal Equal Access Act

BOARD OF EDUCATION OF WESTSIDE COMMUNITY SCHOOLS v. MERGENS

Supreme Court of the United States, 1990.
496 U.S. 226, 110 S.Ct. 2356, 110 L.Ed.2d 191 [60 Educ. L. Rep. 320].

JUSTICE O'CONNOR delivered the opinion of the Court, except as to Part III.

This case requires us to decide whether the Equal Access Act, 20 U.S.C.[A.] §§ 4071–4074, prohibits Westside High School from denying a student religious group permission to meet on school premises during noninstructional time, and if so, whether the Act, so construed, violates the Establishment Clause of the First Amendment.

I

. . .

Students at Westside High School are permitted to join various student groups and clubs, all of which meet after school hours on school premises. The students may choose from approximately 30 recognized groups on a voluntary basis. . . .

There is no written school board policy concerning the formation of student clubs. Rather, students wishing to form a club present their request to a school official who determines whether the proposed club's goals and objectives are consistent with school board policies and with the school district's "Mission and Goals"—a broadly worded "blueprint" that expresses the district's commitment to teaching academic, physical, civic, and personal skills and values.

In January 1985, respondent Bridget Mergens . . . requested permission to form a Christian club at the school. The proposed club would have the same privileges and meet on the same terms and conditions as other Westside student groups, except that the proposed club would not have a faculty sponsor. According to the students' testimony at trial, the club's purpose would have been, among other things, to permit the students to read and discuss the Bible, to have fellowship, and to pray together. Membership would have been voluntary and open to all students regardless of religious affiliation.

... The school officials explained that school policy required all student clubs to have a faculty sponsor, which the proposed religious club would not or could not have, and that a religious club at the school would violate the Establishment Clause. In March 1985, Mergens appealed the denial of her request to the Board of Education, but the Board voted to uphold the denial....

II

A

In *Widmar v. Vincent,* we invalidated, on free speech grounds, a state university regulation that prohibited student use of school facilities " 'for purposes of religious worship or religious teaching.' " In doing so, we held that an "equal access" policy would not violate the Establishment Clause under our decision in *Lemon v. Kurtzman.* In particular, we held that such a policy would have a secular purpose, would not have the primary effect of advancing religion, and would not result in excessive entanglement between government and religion. We noted, however, that "[u]niversity students are, of course, young adults. They are less impressionable than younger students and should be able to appreciate that the University's policy is one of neutrality toward religion."

In 1984, Congress extended the reasoning of *Widmar* to public secondary schools. Under the Equal Access Act, a public secondary school with a "limited open forum" is prohibited from discriminating against students who wish to conduct a meeting within that forum on the basis of the "religious, political, philosophical, or other content of the speech at such meetings." Specifically, the Act provides:

> "It shall be unlawful for any public secondary school which receives Federal financial assistance and which has a limited open forum to deny equal access or a fair opportunity to, or discriminate against, any students who wish to conduct a meeting within that limited open forum on the basis of the religious, political, philosophical, or other content of the speech at such meetings."

A "limited open forum" exists whenever a public secondary school "grants an offering to or opportunity for one or more non-curriculum related student groups to meet on school premises during non-instructional time." "Meeting" is defined to include "those activities of student groups which are permitted under a school's limited open forum and are not directly related to the school curriculum." "Non-instructional time" is defined to mean "time set aside by the school before actual classroom instruction begins or after actual classroom instruction ends." Thus, even if a public secondary school allows only one "non-curriculum related student group" to meet, the Act's obligations are triggered and the school may not deny other clubs, on the basis of the content of their speech, equal access to meet on school premises during non-instructional time.

The Act further specifies that "[s]chools shall be deemed to offer a fair opportunity to students who wish to conduct a meeting within its limited open forum" if the school uniformly provides that the meetings are voluntary and student-initiated; are not sponsored by the school, the government, or its agents or employees; do not materially and substantially interfere with the orderly conduct of educational activities within the school; and are not directed, controlled, conducted, or regularly attended by "non-school persons." "Sponsorship" is defined to mean "the act of promoting, leading, or participating in a meeting. The assignment of a teacher, administrator, or other school employee to a meeting for custodial purposes does not constitute sponsorship of the meeting." If the meetings are religious, employees or agents of the school or government may attend only in a "non-participatory capacity." Moreover, a State may not influence the form of any religious activity, require any person to participate in such activity, or compel any school agent or employee to attend a meeting if the content of the speech at the meeting is contrary to that person's beliefs.

Finally, the Act does not "authorize the United States to deny or withhold Federal financial assistance to any school" or "limit the authority of the school, its agents or employees, to maintain order and discipline on school premises, to protect the well-being of students and faculty, and to assure that attendance of students at the meetings is voluntary".

B

The parties agree that Westside High School receives federal financial assistance and is a public secondary school within the meaning of the Act. The Act's obligation to grant equal access to student groups is therefore triggered if Westside maintains a "limited open forum"—*i.e.,* if it permits one or more "non-curriculum related student groups" to meet on campus before or after classes.

Unfortunately, the Act does not define the crucial phrase "non-curriculum related student group." Our immediate task is therefore one of statutory interpretation. We begin, of course, with the language of the statute. The common meaning of the term "curriculum" is "the whole body of courses offered by an educational institution or one of its branches.".... Any sensible interpretation of "non-curriculum related student group" must therefore be anchored in the notion that such student groups are those that are not related to the body of courses offered by the school. The difficult question is the degree of "unrelatedness to the curriculum" required for a group to be considered "non-curriculum related."

The Act's definition of the sort of "meeting[s]" that must be accommodated under the statute sheds some light on this question. "[T]he term 'meeting' includes those activities of student groups which are ... not *directly related* to the school curriculum." (emphasis added).

Congress' use of the phrase "directly related" implies that student groups directly related to the subject matter of courses offered by the school do not fall within the "non-curriculum related" category and would therefore be considered "curriculum related."

The logic of the Act also supports this view, namely, that a curriculum-related student group is one that has more than just a tangential or attenuated relationship to courses offered by the school. Because the purpose of granting equal access is to prohibit discrimination between religious or political clubs on the one hand and other non-curriculum-related student groups on the other, the Act is premised on the notion that a religious or political club is itself likely to be a non-curriculum-related student group. It follows, then, that a student group that is "curriculum related" must at least have a more direct relationship to the curriculum than a religious or political club would have.

Although the phrase "non-curriculum related student group" nevertheless remains sufficiently ambiguous that we might normally resort to legislative history, we find the legislative history on this issue less than helpful. Because the bill that led to the Act was extensively rewritten in a series of multilateral negotiations after it was passed by the House and reported out of committee by the Senate, the committee reports shed no light on the language actually adopted. During congressional debate on the subject, legislators referred to a number of different definitions, and thus both petitioners and respondents can cite to legislative history favoring their interpretation of the phrase. . . .

We think it significant, however, that the Act, which was passed by wide, bipartisan majorities in both the House and the Senate, reflects at least some consensus on a broad legislative purpose. The committee reports indicate that the Act was intended to address perceived widespread discrimination against religious speech in public schools, and, as the language of the Act indicates, its sponsors contemplated that the Act would do more than merely validate the status quo. The committee reports also show that the Act was enacted in part in response to two federal appellate court decisions holding that student religious groups could not, consistent with the Establishment Clause, meet on school premises during noninstructional time. A broad reading of the Act would be consistent with the views of those who sought to end discrimination by allowing students to meet and discuss religion before and after classes.

In light of this legislative purpose, we think that the term "non-curriculum related student group" is best interpreted broadly to mean any student group that does not *directly* relate to the body of courses offered by the school. In our view, a student group directly relates to a school's curriculum if the subject matter of the group is actually taught, or will soon be taught, in a regularly offered course; if the subject matter of the group concerns the body of courses as a whole; if participation in the group is required for a particular course; or if participation in the group results in academic credit. We think this limited definition of groups that directly relate to the curriculum is a commonsense interpretation of the Act that is consistent with Congress' intent to provide a low threshold for triggering the Act's requirements.

For example, a French club would directly relate to the curriculum if a school taught French in a regularly offered course or planned to teach the subject in the near future. A school's student government would generally relate directly to the curriculum to the extent that it addresses concerns, solicits opinions, and formulates proposals pertaining to the body of courses offered by the school. If participation in a school's band or orchestra were required for the band or orchestra classes, or resulted in academic credit, then those groups would also directly relate to the curriculum. The existence of such groups at a school would not trigger the Act's obligations.

On the other hand, unless a school could show that groups such as a chess club, a stamp collecting club, or a community service club fell within our description of groups that directly relate to the curriculum, such groups would be "non-curriculum related student groups" for purposes of the Act. The existence of such groups would create a "limited open forum" under the Act and would prohibit the school from denying equal access to any other student group on the basis of the content of that group's speech. Whether a specific student group is a "non-curriculum related student group" will therefore depend on a particular school's curriculum, but such determinations would be subject to factual findings well within the competence of trial courts to make.

Petitioners contend that our reading of the Act unduly hinders local control over schools and school activities, but we think that schools and school districts nevertheless retain a significant measure of authority over the type of officially recognized activities in which their students participate. First, schools and school districts maintain their traditional latitude to determine appropriate subjects of instruction. To the extent that a school chooses to structure its course offerings and existing student groups to avoid the Act's obligations, that result is not prohibited by the Act. On matters of statutory interpretation, "[o]ur task is to apply the text, not to improve on it." Second, the Act expressly does not limit a school's authority to prohibit meetings that would "materially and substantially interfere with the orderly conduct of educational activities within the school." The Act also preserves "the authority of the school, its agents or employees, to maintain order and discipline on school premises, to protect the well-being of students and faculty, and to assure that attendance of students at meetings is voluntary." Finally, because the Act applies only to public secondary schools that receive federal financial assistance, a school district seeking to escape the statute's obligations could simply forego federal funding. Although we do not doubt that in some cases this may be an unrealistic option, Congress clearly sought to prohibit schools from discriminating on the basis of the content of a student group's speech, and that obligation is the price a federally funded school must pay if it opens its facilities to non-curriculum-related student groups. . . .

C

... Petitioners contend that all of these student activities [cited as being non-curriculum-related] are curriculum-related because they further the goals of particular aspects of the school's curriculum.... Subsurfers [scuba diving] furthers "one of the essential goals of the Physical Education Department—enabling students to develop lifelong recreational interests." Chess "supplement[s] math and science courses because it enhances students' ability to engage in critical thought processes." ...

To the extent that petitioners contend that "curriculum related" means anything remotely related to abstract educational goals, however, we reject that argument. To define "curriculum related" in a way that results in almost no schools having limited open fora, or in a way that permits schools to evade the Act by strategically describing existing student groups, would render the Act merely hortatory....

Rather, we think it clear that Westside's existing student groups include one or more "non-curriculum related student groups." Although Westside's physical education classes apparently include swimming, counsel stated at oral argument that scuba diving is not taught in any regularly offered course at the school. Based on Westside's own description of the group, Subsurfers does not directly relate to the curriculum as a whole in the same way that a student government or similar group might. Moreover, participation in Subsurfers is not required by any course at the school and does not result in extra academic credit. Thus, Subsurfers is a "non-curriculum related student group" for purposes of the Act. Similarly, although math teachers at Westside have encouraged their students to play chess, chess is not taught in any regularly offered course at the school, and participation in the chess club is not required for any class and does not result in extra credit for any class. The chess club is therefore another "non-curriculum related student group" at Westside.... The record therefore supports a finding that Westside has maintained a limited open forum under the Act....

The remaining statutory question is whether petitioners' denial of respondents' request to form a religious group constitutes a denial of "equal access" to the school's limited open forum. Although the school apparently permits respondents to meet informally after school, respondents seek equal access in the form of official recognition by the school. Official recognition allows student clubs to be part of the student activities program and carries with it access to the school newspaper, bulletin boards, the public address system, and the annual Club Fair. Given that the Act explicitly prohibits denial of "equal access ... to ... any students who wish to conduct a meeting within [the school's] limited open forum" on the basis of the religious content of the speech at such meetings, we hold that Westside's denial of respondents' request to form a Christian club denies them "equal access" under the Act.

Because we rest our conclusion on statutory grounds, we need not decide—and therefore express no opinion on—whether the First Amendment requires the same result.

III

Petitioners contend that even if Westside has created a limited open forum within the meaning of the Act, its denial of official recognition to the proposed Christian club must nevertheless stand because the Act violates the Establishment Clause of the First Amendment, as applied to the States through the Fourteenth Amendment. Specifically, petitioners maintain that because the school's recognized student activities are an integral part of its educational mission, official recognition of respondents' proposed club would effectively incorporate religious activities into the school's official program, endorse participation in the religious club, and provide the club with an official platform to proselytize other students.

We disagree. . . .

Notes

1.   Eight Justices concluded that the Equal Access Act did not violate the Establishment Clause. Even so, the plurality could not reach an agreement on this point.

2.   In the plurality opinion upholding the constitutionality of the Equal Access Act, four Justices agreed that it was rational for Congress to make the determination left open by the Court in *Widmar v. Vincent*: secondary school students are capable of distinguishing between State-initiated, school-sponsored, or teacher-led religious speech and student-initiated and led religious speech. What do you think?

3.   If the Equal Access Act were to be repealed, could a school board reestablish a bar to a Christian club? Would it be obliged to do so?

[Case No. 10]   Constitutionality of Invocation and Benediction at Graduation Ceremony

LEE v. WEISMAN

Supreme Court of the United States, 1992.
505 U.S. 577, 112 S.Ct. 2649, 120 L.Ed.2d 467 [75 Educ. L. Rep. 43].

JUSTICE KENNEDY delivered the opinion of the Court.

School principals in the public school system of the city of Providence, Rhode Island, are permitted to invite members of the clergy to offer invocation and benediction prayers as part of the formal graduation ceremonies for middle schools and for high schools. The question before us is whether including clerical members who offer prayers as part of the official school graduation ceremony is consistent with the Religion Clauses of the First Amendment, provisions the Fourteenth Amendment makes applicable with full force to the States and their school districts.

I

A

Deborah Weisman graduated from Nathan Bishop Middle School, a public school in Providence, at a formal ceremony in June 1989. She was about 14 years old. . . . Acting for himself and his daughter, Deborah's father, Daniel Weisman, objected to any prayers at Deborah's middle school graduation, but to no avail. The school principal, petitioner Robert E. Lee, invited a rabbi to deliver prayers at the graduation exercises for Deborah's class. . . .

It has been the custom of Providence school officials to provide invited clergy with a pamphlet entitled "Guidelines for Civic Occasions," prepared by the National Conference of Christians and Jews. The Guidelines recommend that public prayers at non-sectarian civic ceremonies be composed with "inclusiveness and sensitivity," though they acknowledge that "[p]rayer of any kind may be inappropriate on some civic occasions." The principal gave Rabbi Gutterman the pamphlet before the graduation and advised him the invocation and benediction should be non-sectarian.

.   .   .

The school board (and the United States, which supports it as *amicus curiae*) argued that these short prayers and others like them at graduation exercises are of profound meaning to many students and parents throughout this country who consider that due respect and acknowledgment for divine guidance and for the deepest spiritual aspirations of our people ought to be expressed at an event as important in life as a graduation. We assume this to be so in addressing the difficult case now before us, for the significance of the prayers lies also at the heart of Daniel and Deborah Weisman's case. . . .

II

These dominant facts mark and control the confines of our decision: State officials direct the performance of a formal religious exercise at promotional and graduation ceremonies for secondary schools. Even for those students who object to the religious exercise, their attendance and participation in the state-sponsored religious activity are in a fair and real sense obligatory, though the school district does not require attendance as a condition for receipt of the diploma.

This case does not require us to revisit the difficult questions dividing us in recent cases, questions of the definition and full scope of the principles governing the extent of permitted accommodation by the State for the religious beliefs and practices of many of its citizens. For without reference to those principles in other contexts, the controlling precedents as they relate to prayer and religious exercise in primary and secondary public schools compel the holding here that the policy of the city of Providence is an unconstitutional one. We can decide the case without reconsidering the general constitutional framework by which public schools' efforts to accommodate religion are measured. Thus we do not accept the invitation of petitioners and *amicus* the United States to reconsider our decision in *Lemon v. Kurtzman*. The government involvement with religious activity in this case is pervasive, to the point of creating a state-sponsored and state-directed religious exercise in a public school. Conducting this formal religious observance conflicts with settled rules pertaining to prayer exercises for students, and that suffices to determine the question before us.

The principle that government may accommodate the free exercise of religion does not supersede the fundamental limitations imposed by the Establishment Clause. It is beyond dispute that, at a minimum, the Constitution guarantees that government may not coerce anyone to support or participate in religion or its exercise, or otherwise act in a way which "establishes a [state] religion or religious faith, or tends to do so." The State's involvement in the school prayers challenged today violates these central principles.

That involvement is as troubling as it is undenied. A school official, the principal, decided that an invocation and a benediction should be given; this is a choice attributable to the State, and from a constitutional perspective it is as if a state statute decreed that the prayers must occur. The principal chose the religious participant, here a rabbi, and that choice is also attributable to the State. The reason for the choice of a rabbi is not disclosed by the record, but the potential for divisiveness over the choice of a particular member of the clergy to conduct the ceremony is apparent.

Divisiveness, of course, can attend any state decision respecting religions, and neither its existence nor its potential necessarily invalidates the State's attempts to accommodate religion in all cases. The potential for divisiveness is of particular relevance here though, because it centers around an overt religious exercise in a secondary school environment where, as we discuss below, subtle coercive pressures exist and where the student had no real alternative which would have allowed her to avoid the fact or appearance of participation.

The State's role did not end with the decision to include a prayer and with the choice of clergyman. Principal Lee provided Rabbi Gutterman with a copy of the "Guidelines for Civic Occasions," and advised him that his prayers should be non-sectarian. Through these means the principal directed and controlled the content of the prayer. Even if the only sanction for ignoring the instructions were that the rabbi would not be invited back, we think no religious representative who valued his or her continued reputation and effectiveness in the community would incur the State's displeasure in this regard. It is a cornerstone principle of our Establishment Clause jurisprudence that "it is no part of the business of government to compose official prayers for any group of the American people to recite as a part of a religious program carried on by government," *Engel v. Vitale,* and that is what the school officials attempted to do.

Petitioners argue, and we find nothing in the case to refute it, that the directions for the content of the prayers were a good-faith attempt by the school to ensure that the sectarianism which is so often the flashpoint for religious animosity be removed from the graduation ceremony. The concern is understandable, as a prayer which uses ideas or images identified with a particular religion may foster a different sort of sectarian rivalry than an invocation or benediction in terms more neutral. The school's explanation, however, does not resolve the dilemma caused by its participation. The question is not the good faith of the school in attempting to make the prayer acceptable to most persons, but the legitimacy of its undertaking that enterprise at all when the object is to produce a prayer to be used in a formal religious exercise which students, for all practical purposes, are obliged to attend. . . .

The First Amendment's Religion Clauses mean that religious beliefs and religious expression are too precious to be either proscribed or prescribed by the State. The design of the Constitution is that preservation and transmission of religious beliefs and worship is a responsibility and a choice committed to the private sphere, which itself is promised freedom to pursue that mission. . . .

These concerns have particular application in the case of school officials, whose effort to monitor prayer will be perceived by the students as inducing a participation they might otherwise reject. Though the efforts of the school officials in this case to find common ground appear to have been a good-faith attempt to recognize the common aspects of religions and not the divisive ones, our precedents do not permit school officials to assist in composing prayers as an incident to a formal exercise for their students. *Engel v. Vitale.* And these same precedents caution us to measure the idea of a civic religion against the central meaning of the Religion Clauses of the First Amendment, which is that all creeds must be tolerated and none favored. The suggestion that government may establish an official or civic religion as a means of avoiding the establishment of a religion with more specific creeds strikes us as a contradiction that cannot be accepted.

The degree of school involvement here made it clear that the graduation prayers bore the imprint of the State and thus put school-age children who objected in an untenable position. We turn our attention now to consider the position of the students, both those who desired the prayer and she who did not.

To endure the speech of false ideas or offensive content and then to counter it is part of learning how to live in a pluralistic society, a society which insists upon open discourse towards the end of a tolerant citizenry. And tolerance presupposes some mutuality of obligation. It is argued that our constitutional vision of a free society requires confidence in our own ability to accept or reject ideas of which we do not approve, and that prayer at a high school graduation does nothing more than offer a choice. . . . This argument cannot prevail, however. It overlooks a fundamental dynamic of the Constitution.

The First Amendment protects speech and religion by quite different mechanisms. Speech is protected by insuring its full expression even when the government participates, for the very object of some of our most important speech is to persuade the government to adopt an idea as its own. The method for protecting freedom of worship and freedom of conscience in religious matters is quite the reverse. In religious debate or expression the government is not a prime participant, for the Framers deemed religious establishment antithetical to the freedom of all. The

Free Exercise Clause embraces a freedom of conscience and worship that has close parallels in the speech provisions of the First Amendment, but the Establishment Clause is a specific prohibition on forms of state intervention in religious affairs with no precise counterpart in the speech provisions. The explanation lies in the lesson of history that was and is the inspiration for the Establishment Clause, the lesson that in the hands of government what might begin as a tolerant expression of religious views may end in a policy to indoctrinate and coerce. A state-created orthodoxy puts at grave risk that freedom of belief and conscience which are the sole assurance that religious faith is real, not imposed.

.   .   .

As we have observed before, there are heightened concerns with protecting freedom of conscience from subtle coercive pressure in the elementary and secondary public schools. Our decisions in *Engel v. Vitale* and *School District of Abington Tp. v. Schempp* recognize, among other things, that prayer exercises in public schools carry a particular risk of indirect coercion. . . . What to most believers may seem nothing more than a reasonable request that the nonbeliever respect their religious practices, in a school context may appear to the nonbeliever or dissenter to be an attempt to employ the machinery of the State to enforce a religious orthodoxy. . . .

. . . Research in psychology supports the common assumption that adolescents are often susceptible to pressure from their peers towards conformity, and that the influence is strongest in matters of social convention. . . . [T]he government may no more use social pressure to enforce orthodoxy than it may use more direct means. . . .

There was a stipulation in the District Court that attendance at graduation and promotional ceremonies is voluntary. Petitioners and the United States, as *amicus,* made this a center point of the case, arguing that the option of not attending the graduation excuses any inducement or coercion in the ceremony itself. The argument lacks all persuasion. Law reaches past formalism. And to say a teenage student has a real choice not to attend her high school graduation is formalistic in the extreme. True, Deborah could elect not to attend commencement without renouncing her diploma; but we shall not allow the case to turn on this point. Everyone knows that in our society and in our culture high school graduation is one of life's most significant occasions. A school rule which excuses attendance is beside the point. Attendance may not be required by official decree, yet it is apparent that a student is not free to absent herself from the graduation exercise in any real sense of the term "voluntary," for absence would require forfeiture of those intangible benefits which have motivated the student through youth and all her high school years. Graduation is a time for family and those closest to the student to celebrate success and express mutual wishes of gratitude and respect, all to the end of impressing upon the young person the role that it is his or her right and duty to assume in the community and all of its diverse parts.

The importance of the event is the point the school district and the United States rely upon to argue that a formal prayer ought to be permitted, but it becomes one of the principal reasons why their argument must fail. Their contention, one of considerable force were it not for the constitutional constraints applied to state action, is that the prayers are an essential part of these ceremonies because for many persons an occasion of this significance lacks meaning if there is no recognition, however brief, that human achievements cannot be understood apart from their spiritual essence. We think the Government's position that this interest suffices to force students to choose between compliance or forfeiture demonstrates fundamental inconsistency in its argumentation. It fails to acknowledge that what for many of Deborah's classmates and their parents was a spiritual imperative was for Daniel and Deborah Weisman religious conformance compelled by the State. While in some societies the wishes of the majority might prevail, the Establishment Clause of the First Amendment is addressed to this contingency and rejects the balance urged upon us. The Constitution forbids the State to exact religious conformity from a student as the price of attending her own high school graduation. This is the calculus the Constitution commands.

The Government's argument gives insufficient recognition to the real conflict of conscience faced by the young student. The essence of the Government's position is that with regard to a civic, social occasion of this importance it is the objector, not the majority, who must take unilateral and private action to avoid compromising religious scruples, here by electing to miss the graduation exercise. This turns conventional First Amendment analysis on its head. It is a tenet of the First Amendment that the State cannot require one of its citizens to forfeit his or her rights and benefits as the price of resisting conformance to state-sponsored religious practice. To say that a student must remain apart from the ceremony at the opening invocation and closing benediction is to risk compelling conformity in an environment analogous to the classroom setting, where we have said the risk of compulsion is especially high. Just as in *Engel v. Vitale* and *School District of Abington Township v. Schempp,* we found that provisions within the challenged legislation permitting a student to be voluntarily excused from attendance or participation in the daily prayers did not shield those practices from invalidation, the fact that attendance at the graduation ceremonies is voluntary in a legal sense does not save the religious exercise....

We do not hold that every state action implicating religion is invalid if one or a few citizens find it offensive. People may take offense at all manner of religious as well as nonreligious messages, but offense alone does not in every case show a violation. We know too that sometimes to endure social isolation or even anger may be the price of conscience or non-conformity. But, by any reading of our cases, the conformity required of the student in this case was too high an exaction to withstand the test of the Establishment Clause. The prayer exercises in this case are especially improper because the State has in every practical sense compelled attendance and participation in an explicit religious exercise at an event of singular importance to every student, one the objecting student had no real alternative to avoid. . . .

For the reasons we have stated, the judgment of the Court of Appeals is

Affirmed.

Notes

1.   In *Lee*, for the first time since 1971 in a K–12 Establishment Clause case, the Court did not apply *Lemon*.

2.   Rabbi Gutterman's prayers were:

INVOCATION: "God of the Free, Hope of the Brave: For the legacy of America where diversity is celebrated and the rights of minorities are protected, we thank You. May these young men and women grow up to enrich it. For the liberty of America, we thank You. May these new graduates grow up to guard it. For the political process of America in which all its citizens may participate, for its court system where all may seek justice we thank You. May those we honor this morning always turn to it in trust. For the destiny of America we thank You. May the graduates of Nathan Bishop Middle School so live that they might help to share it. May our aspirations for our country and for these young people, who are our hope for the future, be richly fulfilled. AMEN."

BENEDICTION: "O God, we are grateful to You for having endowed us with the capacity for learning which we have celebrated on this joyous commencement. Happy families give thanks for seeing their children achieve an important milestone. Send Your blessings upon the teachers and administrators who helped prepare them. The graduates now need strength and guidance for the future, help them to understand that we are not complete with academic knowledge alone. We must each strive to fulfill what You require of us all: To do justly, to love mercy, to walk humbly. We give thanks to You, Lord, for keeping us alive, sustaining us and allowing us to reach this special, happy occasion. AMEN." *Lee* at 581–582.

"God" appears twice and "lord" once in the 252 words of prayer. Justice Blackmun's concurrence noted that the phrase in the Benediction, "We must each strive to fulfill what you require of us all, to do justly, to love mercy, to walk humbly" conveys a Judeo–Christian message that was clearly borrowed from the Prophet Micah at Chapter 6, verse 8. (Blackmun, J., concurring), at 604, note 5. Similarly, Justice Souter's concurrence feared that the reference from Micah "embodies a straightforwardly theistic premise" (Souter, J., concurring), at 617.

What do you think about these prayers?

3.   In a caustic dissent, Justice Scalia, joined by Chief Justice Rehnquist and Justices White and Thomas, wrote:

I find it a sufficient embarrassment that our Establishment Clause jurisprudence regarding holiday displays has come to "requir[e] scrutiny more commonly associated with interior decorators than with the judiciary." But interior decorating is a rock-hard science compared to psychology practiced by amateurs. A few citations of "[r]esearch in psychology" that have no particular bearing upon the precise issue here, cannot disguise the fact that the Court has gone beyond the realm where judges know what they are doing. The Court's argument that state officials have "coerced" students to take part in the invocation and benediction at graduation ceremonies is, not to put too fine a point on it, incoherent. *Lee v. Weisman*, 505 U.S. 577, 636, 112 S.Ct. 2649, 120 L.Ed.2d 467, 75 Educ. L. Rep. 43, (Scalia, J., dissenting).

4. The Sixth and Seventh Circuits, in cases involving public universities in Tennessee and Indiana, respectively, upheld prayer at graduation ceremonies. The courts essentially decided that the prayers did not violate the Establishment Clause because they did not involve young students and attendance in higher education is voluntary. *Tanford v. Brand*, 104 F.3d 982 [115 Educ. L. Rep. 339] (7th Cir. 1997), *cert. denied*, 522 U.S. 814, 118 S.Ct. 60, 139 L.Ed.2d 23 (1997); *Chaudhuri v. State of Tenn.*, 130 F.3d 232 [122 Educ. L. Rep. 573] (6th Cir. 1997), *cert. denied*, 523 U.S. 1024, 118 S.Ct. 1308, 140 L.Ed.2d 473 (1998). Are these fair distinctions?

5. In light of Justice Kennedy's opinion, what place should research from the social sciences, including psychology, especially with regard to peer pressure, occupy in resolving such cases?

[Case No. 11]   Constitutionality of the Use of Federal Funds for Educationally Deprived Children in Religiously Affiliated Non–Public Schools

AGOSTINI v. FELTON

Supreme Court of the United States, 1997.
521 U.S. 203, 117 S.Ct. 1997, 138 L.Ed.2d 391 [119 Educ. L. Rep. 29].

JUSTICE O'CONNOR delivered the opinion of the Court.

In *Aguilar v. Felton* this Court held that the Establishment Clause of the First Amendment barred the city of New York from sending public school teachers into parochial schools to provide remedial education to disadvantaged children pursuant to a congressionally mandated program. On remand, the District Court for the Eastern District of New York entered a permanent injunction reflecting our ruling. Twelve years later, petitioners—the parties bound by that injunction—seek relief from its operation. Petitioners maintain that *Aguilar* cannot be squared with our intervening Establishment Clause jurisprudence and ask that we explicitly recognize what our more recent cases already dictate: *Aguilar* is no longer good law. We agree with petitioners that *Aguilar* is not consistent with our subsequent Establishment Clause decisions and further conclude that, on the facts presented here, petitioners are entitled under Federal Rule of Civil Procedure 60(b)(5) to relief from the operation of the District Court's prospective injunction.

I

In 1965, Congress enacted Title I of the Elementary and Secondary Education Act of 1965 to "provid[e] full educational opportunity to every child regardless of economic background" (hereinafter Title I). Toward that end, Title I channels federal funds, through the States, to "local educational agencies" (LEA's). The LEA's spend these funds to provide remedial education, guidance, and job counseling to eligible students. An eligible student is one (i) who resides within the attendance boundaries of a public school located in a low-income area and (ii) who is failing, or is at risk of failing, the State's student performance standards. Title I funds must be made available to all eligible children, regardless of whether they attend public schools, and the services provided to children attending private schools must be "equitable in comparison to services and other benefits for public school children."

An LEA providing services to children enrolled in private schools is subject to a number of constraints that are not imposed when it provides aid to public schools. Title I services may be provided only to those private school students eligible for aid, and cannot be used to provide services on a "school-wide" basis. In addition, the LEA must retain complete control over Title I funds; retain title to all materials used to provide Title I services; and provide those services through public employees or other persons independent of the private school and any religious institution. The Title I services themselves must be "secular, neutral, and non-ideological" and must "supplement, and in no case supplant, the level of services" already provided by the private school.

Petitioner Board of Education of the City of New York (hereinafter Board), an LEA, first applied for Title I funds in 1966 and has grappled ever since with how to provide Title I services to the private school students within its jurisdiction. Approximately 10% of the total number of students eligible for Title I services are private school students. Recognizing that more than 90% of the private schools within the Board's jurisdiction are sectarian, the Board initially arranged to transport children to public schools for after-school Title I instruction. But this enterprise was largely unsuccessful. Attendance was poor, teachers and children were tired, and parents were concerned for the safety of their children. The Board then moved the after-school instruction onto private school campuses, as Congress had contemplated when it enacted Title I. After this program also yielded mixed results, the Board implemented the plan we evaluated in *Aguilar v. Felton.*

That plan called for the provision of Title I services on private school premises during school hours. Under the plan, only public employees could serve as Title I instructors and counselors. Assignments to private schools were made on a voluntary basis and without regard to the religious affiliation of the employee or the wishes of the private school. As the Court of Appeals in *Aguilar* observed, a large majority of Title I teachers worked in non-public schools with religious affiliations different from their own. The vast majority of Title I teachers also moved among the private schools, spending fewer than five days a week at the same school.

Before any public employee could provide Title I instruction at a private school, she would be given a detailed set of written and oral instructions emphasizing the secular purpose of Title I and setting out the rules to be followed to ensure that this purpose was not compromised. Specifically, employees would be told that (i) they were employees of the Board and accountable only to their public school supervisors; (ii) they had exclusive responsibility for selecting students for the Title I program and could teach only those children who met the eligibility criteria for Title I; (iii) their materials and equipment would be used only in the Title I program; (iv) they could not engage in team teaching or other cooperative instructional activities with private school teachers; and (v) they could not introduce any religious matter into their teaching or become involved in any way with the religious activities of the private schools. All religious symbols were to be removed from classrooms used for Title I services. The rules acknowledged that it might be necessary for Title I teachers to consult with a student's regular classroom teacher to assess the student's particular needs and progress, but admonished instructors to limit those consultations to mutual professional concerns regarding the student's education. To ensure compliance with these rules, a publicly employed field supervisor was to attempt to make at least one unannounced visit to each teacher's classroom every month.

In 1978, six federal taxpayers-respondents here-sued the Board in the District Court for the Eastern District of New York. Respondents sought declaratory and injunctive relief, claiming that the Board's Title I program violated the Establishment Clause. The District Court permitted the parents of a number of parochial school students who were receiving Title I services to intervene as codefendants. The District Court granted summary judgment for the Board, but the Court of Appeals for the Second Circuit reversed.... In a 5–to–4 decision, this Court affirmed on the ground that the Board's Title I program necessitated an "excessive entanglement of church and state in the administration of [Title I] benefits." On remand, the District Court permanently enjoined the Board "from using public funds for any plan or program under [Title I] to the extent that it requires, authorizes or permits public school teachers and guidance counselors to provide teaching and counseling services on the premises of sectarian schools within New York City."

The Board, like other LEA's across the United States, modified its Title I program so it could continue serving those students who attended private religious schools. Rather than offer Title I instruction to parochial school students at their schools, the Board reverted to its prior practice of providing instruction at public school sites, at leased sites, and in mobile instructional units (essentially vans converted into classrooms) parked near the sectarian school. The Board also offered computer-aided instruction, which could be provided "on premises" because it did not require public employees to be physically present on the premises of a religious school.

It is not disputed that the additional costs of complying with *Aguilar's* mandate are significant. Since the 1986–1987 school year, the Board has spent over $100 million providing computer-aided instruction, leasing sites and mobile instructional units, and transporting students to those sites. Under the Secretary of Education's regulations, those costs "incurred as a result of implementing alternative delivery systems to comply with the requirements of *Aguilar v. Felton*" and not paid for with other state or federal funds are to be deducted from the federal grant before the Title I funds are distributed to any student. These "*Aguilar* costs" thus reduce the amount of Title I money an LEA has available for remedial education, and LEA's have had to cut back on the number of students who receive Title I benefits. From Title I funds available for New York City children between the 1986–1987 and the 1993–1994 school years, the Board had to deduct $7.9 million "off-the-top" for compliance with *Aguilar*. When *Aguilar* was handed down, it was estimated that some 20,000 economically disadvantaged children in the city of New York and some 183,000 children nationwide would experience a decline in Title I services.

In October and December of 1995, petitioners-the Board and a new group of parents of parochial school students entitled to Title I services-filed motions in the District Court seeking relief under Federal Rule of Civil Procedure 60(b) from the permanent injunction entered by the District Court on remand from our decision in *Aguilar*. Petitioners argued that relief was proper ... because the "decisional law [had] changed to make legal what the [injunction] was designed to prevent." Specifically, petitioners pointed to the statements of five Justices in *Board of Education of Kiryas Joel Village School District v. Grumet* calling for the overruling of *Aguilar*. The District Court denied the motion.... The Court of Appeals for the Second Circuit affirmed.... We granted certiorari and now reverse.

II

The question we must answer is a simple one: Are petitioners entitled to relief from the District Court's permanent injunction under Rule 60(b)? Rule 60(b)(5), the subsection under which petitioners proceeded below, states:

> "On motion and upon such terms as are just, the court may relieve a party ... from a final judgment [or] order ... [when] it is no longer equitable that the judgment should have prospective application."

In *Rufo v. Inmates of Suffolk County Jail*, we held that it is appropriate to grant a Rule 60(b)(5) motion when the party seeking relief from an injunction or consent decree can show "a significant change either in factual conditions or in law." A court may recognize subsequent changes in either statutory or decisional law. A court errs when it refuses to modify an injunction or consent decree in light of such changes.

Petitioners point to three changes in the factual and legal landscape that they believe justify their claim for relief under Rule 60(b)(5). They first contend that the exorbitant costs of complying with the District Court's injunction constitute a significant factual development warranting modification of the injunction. Petitioners also argue that there have been two significant legal developments since *Aguilar* was decided: a majority of Justices have expressed their views that *Aguilar* should be reconsidered or overruled; and *Aguilar* has in any event been undermined by subsequent Establishment Clause decisions....

Respondents counter that, because the costs of providing Title I services off site were known at the time *Aguilar* was decided, and because the relevant case law has not changed, the District Court did not err in denying petitioners' motions. Obviously, if neither the law supporting our original decision in this litigation nor the facts have changed, there would be no need to decide the propriety of a Rule 60(b)(5) motion. Accordingly, we turn to the threshold issue whether the factual or legal landscape has changed since we decided *Aguilar*.

We agree with respondents that petitioners have failed to establish the significant change in factual conditions required by *Rufo*. Both petitioners and this Court were, at the time *Aguilar* was decided, aware that additional costs would be incurred if Title I services could not be provided in parochial school classrooms. . . .

We also agree with respondents that the statements made by five Justices in *Kiryas Joel* do not, in themselves, furnish a basis for concluding that our Establishment Clause jurisprudence has changed. . . . The views of five Justices that the case should be reconsidered or overruled cannot be said to have effected a change in Establishment Clause law.

In light of these conclusions, petitioners' ability to satisfy the prerequisites of Rule 60(b)(5) hinges on whether our later Establishment Clause cases have so undermined *Aguilar* that it is no longer good law. We now turn to that inquiry.

III

A

In order to evaluate whether *Aguilar* has been eroded by our subsequent Establishment Clause cases, it is necessary to understand the rationale upon which *Aguilar*, as well as its companion case, *School District of Grand Rapids v. Ball* rested.

In *Ball*, the Court evaluated two programs implemented by the School District of Grand Rapids, Michigan. The district's Shared Time program, the one most analogous to Title I, provided remedial and "enrichment" classes, at public expense, to students attending non-public schools. The classes were taught during regular school hours by publicly employed teachers, using materials purchased with public funds, on the premises of non-public schools. The Shared Time courses were in subjects designed to supplement the "core curriculum" of the non-public schools. Of the 41 non-public schools eligible for the program, 40 were " 'pervasively sectarian' " in character-that is, " 'the purpos[e] of [those] schools [was] to advance their particular religions.' "

The Court conducted its analysis by applying the three-part test set forth in *Lemon*. . . . The Court acknowledged that the Shared Time program served a purely secular purpose, thereby satisfying the first part of the so-called *Lemon* test. Nevertheless, it ultimately concluded that the program had the impermissible effect of advancing religion.

The Court found that the program violated the Establishment Clause's prohibition against "government-financed or government-sponsored indoctrination into the beliefs of a particular religious faith" in at least three ways. First, drawing upon the analysis in *Meek v. Pittenger*, the Court observed that "the teachers participating in the programs may become involved in intentionally or inadvertently inculcating particular religious tenets or beliefs."....

The presence of public teachers on parochial school grounds had a second, related impermissible effect: It created a "graphic symbol of the 'concert or union or dependency' of church and state," especially when perceived by "children in their formative years." ...

Third, the Court found that the Shared Time program impermissibly financed religious indoctrination by subsidizing "the primary religious mission of the institutions affected." ...

The New York City Title I program challenged in *Aguilar* closely resembled the Shared Time program struck down in *Ball*, but the Court found fault with an aspect of the Title I program not present in *Ball*: The Board had "adopted a system for monitoring the religious content of publicly funded Title I classes in the religious schools." Even though this monitoring system might prevent the Title I program from being used to inculcate religion, the Court concluded, as it had in *Lemon* and *Meek*, that the level of monitoring necessary to be "certain" that the program had an exclusively secular effect would "inevitably resul[t] in the excessive entanglement of church and state," thereby running afoul of *Lemon's* third prong. In the majority's view, New York City's Title I program suffered from the "same critical elements of entanglement" present in *Lemon* and *Meek*: the aid was provided "in a pervasively sectarian environment ... in the form of teachers," requiring "ongoing inspection ... to ensure the absence of a religious message." Such "pervasive monitoring by public authorities in the sectarian schools infringes precisely those Establishment Clause values at the root of the prohibition of excessive entanglement." The Court noted two further forms of entanglement inherent in New York City's Title I program: the "administrative cooperation" required to implement Title I services and the "dangers of political divisiveness" that might grow out of the day-to-day decisions public officials would have to make in order to provide Title I services.

Distilled to essentials, the Court's conclusion that the Shared Time program in *Ball* had the impermissible effect of advancing religion rested on three assumptions: (i) any public employee who works on the premises of a religious school is presumed to inculcate religion in her work; (ii) the presence of public employees on private school premises creates a symbolic union between church and state; and (iii) any and all public aid that directly aids the educational function of religious schools impermissibly finances religious indoctrination, even if the aid reaches such schools as a consequence of private decisionmaking. Additionally, in *Aguilar* there was a fourth assumption: that New York City's Title I program necessitated an excessive government entanglement with religion because public employees who teach on the premises of religious schools must be closely monitored to ensure that they do not inculcate religion.

B

Our more recent cases have undermined the assumptions upon which *Ball* and *Aguilar* relied. To be sure, the general principles we use to evaluate whether government aid violates the Establishment Clause have not changed since *Aguilar* was decided. For example, we continue to ask whether the government acted with the purpose of advancing or inhibiting religion, and the nature of that inquiry has remained largely unchanged. Likewise, we continue to explore whether the aid has the "effect" of advancing or inhibiting religion. What has changed since we decided *Ball* and *Aguilar* is our understanding of the criteria used to assess whether aid to religion has an impermissible effect.

1

As we have repeatedly recognized, government inculcation of religious beliefs has the impermissible effect of advancing religion. Our cases subsequent to *Aguilar* have, however, modified in two significant respects the approach we use to assess indoctrination. First, we have abandoned the presumption erected in *Meek* and *Ball* that the placement of public employees on parochial school grounds inevitably results in the impermissible effect of state-sponsored indoctrination or constitutes a symbolic union between government and religion. . . .

Second, we have departed from the rule relied on in *Ball* that all government aid that directly assists the educational function of religious schools is invalid. . . .

. . . [U]nder current law, the Shared Time program in *Ball* and New York City's Title I program in *Aguilar* will not, as a matter of law, be deemed to have the effect of advancing religion through indoctrination. Indeed, each of the premises upon which we relied in *Ball* to reach a contrary conclusion is no longer valid. First, there is no reason to presume that, simply because she enters a parochial school classroom, a full-time public employee such as a Title I teacher will depart from her assigned duties and instructions and embark on religious indoctrination, any more than there was a reason in *Zobrest* to think an interpreter would inculcate religion by altering her translation of classroom lectures. Certainly, no evidence has ever shown that any New York City Title I instructor teaching on parochial school premises attempted to inculcate religion in students. . . .

As discussed above, *Zobrest* also repudiates *Ball's* assumption that the presence of Title I teachers in parochial school classrooms will, without more, create the impression of a "symbolic union" between church and state. . . . We do not see any perceptible (let alone dispositive) difference in the degree of symbolic union between a student receiving remedial instruction in a classroom on his sectarian school's campus and one receiving instruction in a van parked just at the school's curbside. To draw this line based solely on the location of the public employee is neither "sensible" nor "sound" and the Court in *Zobrest* rejected it.

Nor under current law can we conclude that a program placing full-time public employees on parochial campuses to provide Title I instruction would impermissibly finance religious indoctrination. In all relevant respects, the provision of instructional services under Title I is indistinguishable from the provision of sign-language interpreters under the IDEA. Both programs make aid available only to eligible recipients. That aid is provided to students at whatever school they choose to attend. Although Title I instruction is provided to several students at once, whereas an interpreter provides translation to a single student, this distinction is not constitutionally significant. Moreover, as in *Zobrest*, Title I services are by law supplemental to the regular curricula. These services do not, therefore, "reliev[e] sectarian schools of costs they otherwise would have borne in educating their students."

. . .

We are also not persuaded that Title I services supplant the remedial instruction and guidance counseling already provided in New York City's sectarian schools. Although Justice SOUTER maintains that the sectarian schools provide such services and that those schools reduce those services once their students begin to receive Title I instruction, his claims rest on speculation about the impossibility of drawing any line between supplemental and general education, and not on any evidence in the record that the Board is in fact violating Title I regulations by providing services that supplant those offered in the sectarian schools. We are unwilling to speculate that all sectarian schools provide remedial instruction and guidance counseling to their students, and are unwilling to presume that the Board would violate Title I regulations by continuing to provide Title I services to students who attend a sectarian school that has curtailed its remedial instruction program in response to Title I. Nor are we willing to conclude that the constitutionality of an aid program depends on the number of sectarian school students who happen to receive the otherwise neutral aid. *Zobrest* did not turn on the fact that James Zobrest had, at the time of litigation, been the only child using a publicly funded sign-language interpreter to attend a parochial school.

What is most fatal to the argument that New York City's Title I program directly subsidizes religion is that it applies with equal force when those services are provided off campus, and *Aguilar* implied that providing the services off campus is entirely consistent with the Establishment Clause. . . .

2

Although we examined in *Witters* and *Zobrest* the criteria by which an aid program identifies its beneficiaries, we did so solely to assess whether any use of that aid to indoctrinate religion could be attributed to the State. A number of our Establishment Clause cases have found that the criteria used for identifying beneficiaries are relevant in a second respect, apart from enabling a court to evaluate whether the program subsidizes religion. Specifically, the criteria might themselves have the effect of advancing religion by creating a financial incentive to undertake religious indoctrination. This incentive is not present, however, where the aid is allocated on the basis of neutral, secular criteria that neither favor nor disfavor religion, and is made available to both religious and secular beneficiaries on a nondiscriminatory basis. Under such circumstances, the aid is less likely to have the effect of advancing religion.

In *Ball* and *Aguilar*, the Court gave this consideration no weight. Before and since those decisions, we have sustained programs that provided aid to all eligible children regardless of where they attended school. . . .

Applying this reasoning to New York City's Title I program, it is clear that Title I services are allocated on the basis of criteria that neither favor nor disfavor religion. The services are available to all children who meet the Act's eligibility requirements, no matter what their religious beliefs or where they go to school. The Board's program does not, therefore, give aid recipients any incentive to modify their religious beliefs or practices in order to obtain those services.

3

We turn now to *Aguilar's* conclusion that New York City's Title I program resulted in an excessive entanglement between church and state. Whether a government aid program results in such an entanglement has consistently been an aspect of our Establishment Clause analysis. We have considered entanglement both in the course of assessing whether an aid program has an impermissible effect of advancing religion and as a factor separate and apart from "effect." Regardless of how we have characterized the issue, however, the factors we use to assess whether an entanglement is "excessive" are similar to the factors we use to examine "effect." That is, to assess entanglement, we have looked to "the character and purposes of the institutions that are benefited, the nature of the aid that the State provides, and the resulting relationship between the government and religious authority." Similarly, we have assessed a law's "effect" by examining the character of the institutions benefited and the nature of the aid that the State provided. Indeed, in *Lemon* itself, the entanglement that the Court found "independently" to necessitate the program's invalidation also was found to have the effect of inhibiting religion. Thus, it is simplest to recognize why entanglement is significant and treat it—as we did in *Walz*—as an aspect of the inquiry into a statute's effect.

Not all entanglements, of course, have the effect of advancing or inhibiting religion. Interaction between church and state is inevitable and we have always tolerated some level of involvement between the two. Entanglement must be "excessive" before it runs afoul of the Establishment Clause. . . .

The pre-*Aguilar* Title I program does not result in an "excessive" entanglement that advances or inhibits religion. As discussed previously, the Court's finding of "excessive" entanglement in *Aguilar* rested on three grounds: (i) the program would require "pervasive monitoring by public authorities" to ensure that Title I employees did not inculcate religion; (ii) the program required "administrative cooperation" between the Board and parochial schools; and (iii) the program might increase the dangers of "political divisiveness." Under our current understanding of the Establishment Clause, the last two considerations are insufficient by themselves to create an "excessive" entanglement. They are present no matter where Title I services are offered, and no court has held that Title I services cannot be offered off campus. Further, the assumption underlying the first consideration has been undermined. In *Aguilar*, the Court presumed that full-time public employees on parochial school grounds would be tempted to inculcate religion, despite the ethical standards they were required to uphold. Because of this risk pervasive monitoring would be required. But after *Zobrest* we no longer presume that public employees will inculcate religion simply because they happen to be in a sectarian environment. Since we have abandoned the assumption that properly instructed public employees will fail to discharge their duties faithfully, we must also discard the assumption that pervasive monitoring of Title I teachers is required. There is no suggestion in the record before us that unannounced monthly visits of public supervisors are insufficient to prevent or to detect inculcation of religion by public employees. Moreover, we have not found excessive entanglement in cases in which States imposed far more onerous burdens on religious institutions than the monitoring system at issue here.

To summarize, New York City's Title I program does not run afoul of any of three primary criteria we currently use to evaluate whether government aid has the effect of advancing religion: It does not result in governmental indoctrination; define its recipients by reference to religion; or create an excessive entanglement. We therefore hold that a federally funded program providing supplemental, remedial instruction to disadvantaged children on a neutral basis is not invalid under the Establishment Clause when such instruction is given on the premises of sectarian schools by government employees pursuant to a program containing safeguards such as those present here. The same considerations that justify this holding require us to conclude that this carefully constrained program also cannot reasonably be viewed as an endorsement of religion. Accordingly, we must acknowledge that *Aguilar*, as well as the portion of *Ball* addressing Grand Rapids' Shared Time program, are no longer good law.

C

The doctrine of stare decisis does not preclude us from recognizing the change in our law and overruling *Aguilar* and those portions of *Ball* inconsistent with our more recent decisions.... As discussed above, our Establishment Clause jurisprudence has changed significantly since we decided *Ball* and *Aguilar*, so our decision to overturn those cases rests on far more than "a present doctrinal disposition to come out differently from the Court of [1985]." We therefore overrule *Ball* and *Aguilar* to the extent those decisions are inconsistent with our current understanding of the Establishment Clause.

Nor does the "law of the case" doctrine place any additional constraints on our ability to overturn *Aguilar*. Under this doctrine, a court should not reopen issues decided in earlier stages of the same litigation. The doctrine does not apply if the court is "convinced that [its prior decision] is clearly erroneous and would work a manifest injustice." In light of our conclusion that *Aguilar* would be decided differently under our current Establishment Clause law, we think adherence to that decision would undoubtedly work a "manifest injustice," such that the law of the case doctrine does not apply.

IV

We therefore conclude that our Establishment Clause law has "significant[ly] change[d]" since we decided *Aguilar*. We are only left to decide whether this change in law entitles petitioners to relief under Rule 60(b)(5). We conclude that it does. Our general practice is to apply the rule of law we announce in a case to the parties before us. We adhere to this practice even when we overrule a case. . . .

. . . we see no reason to wait for a "better vehicle" in which to evaluate the impact of subsequent cases on *Aguilar's* continued vitality. To evaluate the Rule 60(b)(5) motion properly before us today in no way undermines "integrity in the interpretation of procedural rules" or signals any departure from "the responsive, non-agenda-setting character of this Court." Indeed, under these circumstances, it would be particularly inequitable for us to bide our time waiting for another case to arise while the city of New York labors under a continuing injunction forcing it to spend millions of dollars on mobile instructional units and leased sites when it could instead be spending that money to give economically disadvantaged children a better chance at success in life by means of a program that is perfectly consistent with the Establishment Clause.

For these reasons, we reverse the judgment of the Court of Appeals and remand the cases to the District Court with instructions to vacate its September 26, 1985, order.

It is so ordered.

Notes

1.   Note how the composition of the Court can affect the outcome of a case. In *Aguliar*, Justice O'Connor authored a scathing dissent that would have permitted the on-site delivery of aid. In *Agostini* she authored the majority opinion.

2.   In *Agostini* the Court modified the *Lemon* test, at least as it applies to state-aid to students in religiously affiliated non-public schools test by reviewing only its first two parts, purpose and effect, while recasting entanglement as one criterion in evaluating a statute's effect. Does this modification make sense?

[Case No. 12] Constitutionality of Prayer at Public School Sporting Events

SANTA FE INDEPENDENT SCHOOL DISTRICT v. DOE

Supreme Court of the United States, 2000.
530 U.S. 290, 120 S.Ct. 2266, 147 L.Ed.2d 295 [145 Educ. L. Rep. 21].

JUSTICE STEVENS delivered the opinion of the Court.

Prior to 1995, the Santa Fe High School student who occupied the school's elective office of student council chaplain delivered a prayer over the public address system before each varsity football game for the entire season. This practice, along with others, was challenged in District Court as a violation of the Establishment Clause of the First Amendment. While these proceedings were pending in the District Court, the school district adopted a different policy that permits, but does not require, prayer initiated and led by a student at all home games. The District Court entered an order modifying that policy to permit only non-sectarian, non-proselytizing prayer. The Court of Appeals held that, even as modified that ... the football prayer policy was invalid. We granted the school district's petition for certiorari to review that holding.

I

The Santa Fe Independent School District (District) is a political subdivision of the State of Texas, responsible for the education of more than 4,000 students.... The District includes the Santa Fe High School, two primary schools, an intermediate school and the junior high school. Respondents are two sets of current or former students and their respective mothers. One family is Mormon and the other is Catholic. The District Court permitted respondents (Does) to litigate anonymously to protect them from intimidation or harassment.

Respondents commenced this action in April 1995 and moved for a temporary restraining order to prevent the District from violating the Establishment Clause at the imminent graduation exercises. In their complaint the Does alleged that the District had engaged in several proselytizing practices, such as promoting attendance at a Baptist revival meeting, encouraging membership in religious clubs, chastising children who held minority religious beliefs, and distributing Gideon Bibles on school premises. They also alleged that the District allowed students to read Christian invocations and benedictions from the stage at graduation ceremonies, and to deliver overtly Christian prayers over the public address system at home football games.

On May 10, 1995, the District Court entered an interim order addressing a number of different issues. With respect to the impending graduation, the order provided that "non-denominational prayer" consisting of "an invocation and/or benediction" could be presented by a senior student or students selected by members of the graduating class. The text of the prayer was to be determined by the students, without scrutiny or preapproval by school officials. References to particular religious figures "such as Mohammed, Jesus, Buddha, or the like" would be permitted "as long as the general thrust of the prayer is non-proselytizing."

In response to that portion of the order, the District adopted a series of policies over several months dealing with prayer at school functions. The policies enacted in May and July for graduation ceremonies provided the format for the August and October policies for football games. The May policy provided: " 'The board has chosen to permit the graduating senior class, with the advice and counsel of the senior class principal or designee, to elect by secret ballot to choose whether an invocation and benediction shall be part of the graduation exercise. If so chosen the class shall elect by secret ballot, from a list of student volunteers, students to deliver non-sectarian, non-proselytizing invocations and benedictions for the purpose of solemnizing their graduation ceremonies.' " The parties stipulated that after this policy was adopted, "the senior class held an election to determine whether to have an invocation and benediction at the commencement [and] the class voted, by secret ballot, to include prayer at the high school graduation." In a second vote the class elected two seniors to deliver the invocation and benediction.

In July, the District enacted another policy eliminating the requirement that invocations and benedictions be "non-sectarian and non-proselytising," but also providing that if the District were to be enjoined from enforcing that policy, the May policy would automatically become effective. The August policy, which was titled "Prayer at Football Games," was similar to the July policy for graduations. It also authorized two student elections, the first to determine whether "invocations" should be delivered, and the second to select the spokesperson to deliver them. Like the July policy, it contained two parts, an initial statement that omitted any requirement that the content of the invocation be "non-sectarian and non-proselytising," and a fallback provision that automatically added that limitation if the preferred policy should be enjoined. On August 31, 1995, according to the parties' stipulation, "the district's high school students voted to determine whether a student would deliver prayer at varsity football games. . . . The students chose to allow a student to say a prayer at football games." A week later, in a separate election, they selected a student "to deliver the prayer at varsity football games."

The final policy (October policy) is essentially the same as the August policy, though it omits the word "prayer" from its title, and refers to "messages" and "statements" as well as "invocations." It is the validity of that policy that is before us.

The District Court did enter an order precluding enforcement of the first, open-ended policy. . . . Both parties appealed. . . . The Court of Appeals majority agreed with the Does.

We granted the District's petition for certiorari, limited to the following question: "Whether petitioner's policy permitting student-led, student-initiated prayer at football games violates the Establishment Clause." We conclude, as did the Court of Appeals, that it does.

II

The first Clause in the First Amendment to the Federal Constitution provides that "Congress shall make no law respecting an establishment of religion, or prohibiting the free exercise thereof." The Fourteenth Amendment imposes those substantive limitations on the legislative power of the States and their political subdivisions. In *Lee v. Weisman* we held that a prayer delivered by a rabbi at a middle school graduation ceremony violated that Clause. Although this case involves student prayer at a different type of school function, our analysis is properly guided by the principles that we endorsed in *Lee*. . . .

In this case the District first argues that this principle is inapplicable to its October policy because the messages are private student speech, not public speech. It reminds us that "there is a crucial difference between government speech endorsing religion, which the Establishment Clause forbids, and private speech endorsing religion, which the Free Speech and Free Exercise Clauses protect." We certainly agree with that distinction, but we are not persuaded that the pregame invocations should be regarded as "private speech."

These invocations are authorized by a government policy and take place on government property at government-sponsored school-related events. Of course, not every message delivered under such circumstances is the government's own. We have held, for example, that an individual's contribution to a government-created forum was not government speech. Although the District relies heavily on *Rosenberger* and similar cases involving such forums, it is clear that the pregame ceremony is not the type of forum discussed in those cases. The Santa Fe school officials simply do not "evince either 'by policy or by practice,' any intent to open the [pregame ceremony] to 'indiscriminate use,' . . . by the student body generally." Rather, the school allows only one student, the same student for the entire season, to give the invocation. The statement or invocation, moreover, is subject to particular regulations that confine the content and topic of the student's message. . . .

Granting only one student access to the stage at a time does not, of course, necessarily preclude a finding that a school has created a limited public forum. Here, however, Santa Fe's student election system ensures that only those messages deemed "appropriate" under the District's policy may be delivered. That is, the majoritarian process implemented by the District guarantees, by definition, that minority candidates will never prevail and that their views will be effectively silenced.

Recently, in *Board of Regents of University of Wisconsin System v. Southworth*, we explained why student elections that determine, by majority vote, which expressive activities shall receive or not receive school benefits are constitutionally problematic: "To the extent the referendum substitutes majority determinations for viewpoint neutrality it would undermine the constitutional protection the program requires. The whole theory of viewpoint neutrality is that minority views are treated with the same respect as are majority views. Access to a public forum, for instance, does not depend upon majoritarian consent. That principle is controlling here." Like the student referendum for funding in *Southworth*, this student election does nothing to protect minority views but rather places the students who hold such views at the mercy of the majority. Because "fundamental rights may not be submitted to vote; they depend on the outcome of no elections," the District's elections are insufficient safeguards of diverse student speech.

In Lee, the school district made the related argument that its policy of endorsing only "civic or non-sectarian" prayer was acceptable because it minimized the intrusion on the audience as a whole. We rejected that claim by explaining that such a majoritarian policy "does not lessen the offense or isolation to the objectors. At best it narrows their number, at worst increases their sense of isolation and affront." Similarly, while Santa Fe's majoritarian election might ensure that most of the students are represented, it does nothing to protect the minority; indeed, it likely serves to intensify their offense. Moreover, the District has failed to divorce itself from the religious content in the invocations. It has not succeeded in doing so, either by claiming that its policy is " 'one of neutrality rather than endorsement' " or by characterizing the individual student as the "circuit-breaker" in the process. Contrary to the District's repeated assertions that it has adopted a "hands-off" approach to the pregame invocation, the realities of the situation plainly reveal that its policy involves both perceived and actual endorsement of religion. In this case, as we found in Lee, the "degree of school involvement" makes it clear that the pregame prayers bear "the imprint of the State and thus put school-age children who objected in an untenable position."

The District has attempted to disentangle itself from the religious messages by developing the two-step student election process. The text of the October policy, however, exposes the extent of the school's entanglement. The elections take place at all only because the school "board has chosen to permit students to deliver a brief invocation and/or message." The elections thus "shall" be conducted "by the high school student council" and "[u]pon advice and direction of the high school principal." The decision whether to deliver a message is first made by majority vote of the entire student body, followed by a choice of the speaker in a separate, similar majority election. Even though the particular words used by the speaker are not determined by those votes, the policy mandates that the "statement or invocation" be "consistent with the goals and purposes of this policy," which are "to solemnize the event, to promote good sportsmanship and student safety, and to establish the appropriate environment for the competition."

In addition to involving the school in the selection of the speaker, the policy, by its terms, invites and encourages religious messages. The policy itself states that the purpose of the message is "to solemnize the event." A religious message is the most obvious method of solemnizing an event. Moreover, the requirements that the message "promote good citizenship" and "establish the appropriate environment for competition" further narrow the types of message deemed appropriate, suggesting that a solemn, yet nonreligious, message, such as commentary on

United States foreign policy, would be prohibited. Indeed, the only type of message that is expressly endorsed in the text is an "invocation"—a term that primarily describes an appeal for divine assistance. In fact, as used in the past at Santa Fe High School, an "invocation" has always entailed a focused religious message. Thus, the expressed purposes of the policy encourage the selection of a religious message, and that is precisely how the students understand the policy. The results of the elections described in the parties' stipulation make it clear that the students understood that the central question before them was whether prayer should be a part of the pregame ceremony. We recognize the important role that public worship plays in many communities, as well as the sincere desire to include public prayer as a part of various occasions so as to mark those occasions' significance. But such religious activity in public schools, as elsewhere, must comport with the First Amendment.

The actual or perceived endorsement of the message, moreover, is established by factors beyond just the text of the policy. Once the student speaker is selected and the message composed, the invocation is then delivered to a large audience assembled as part of a regularly scheduled, school-sponsored function conducted on school property. The message is broadcast over the school's public address system, which remains subject to the control of school officials. It is fair to assume that the pregame ceremony is clothed in the traditional indicia of school sporting events, which generally include not just the team, but also cheerleaders and band members dressed in uniforms sporting the school name and mascot. The school's name is likely written in large print across the field and on banners and flags. The crowd will certainly include many who display the school colors and insignia on their school T-shirts, jackets, or hats and who may also be waving signs displaying the school name. It is in a setting such as this that "[t]he board has chosen to permit" the elected student to rise and give the "statement or invocation."

In this context the members of the listening audience must perceive the pregame message as a public expression of the views of the majority of the student body delivered with the approval of the school administration. In cases involving state participation in a religious activity, one of the relevant questions is "whether an objective observer, acquainted with the text, legislative history, and implementation of the statute, would perceive it as a state endorsement of prayer in public schools." Regardless of the listener's support for, or objection to, the message, an objective Santa Fe High School student will unquestionably perceive the inevitable pregame prayer as stamped with her school's seal of approval.

The text and history of this policy, moreover, reinforce our objective student's perception that the prayer is, in actuality, encouraged by the school. When a governmental entity professes a secular purpose for an arguably religious policy, the government's characterization is, of course, entitled to some deference. But it is nonetheless the duty of the courts to "distinguis[h] a sham secular purpose from a sincere one."

According to the District, the secular purposes of the policy are to "foste[r] free expression of private persons . . . as well [as to] solemniz[e] sporting events, promot[e] good sportsmanship and student safety, and establis[h] an appropriate environment for competition." We note, however, that the District's approval of only one specific kind of message, an "invocation," is not necessary to further any of these purposes. Additionally, the fact that only one student is permitted to give a content-limited message suggests that this policy does little to "foste[r] free expression." Furthermore, regardless of whether one considers a sporting event an appropriate occasion for solemnity, the use of an invocation to foster such solemnity is impermissible when, in actuality, it constitutes prayer sponsored by the school. And it is unclear what type of message would be both appropriately "solemnizing" under the District's policy and yet non-religious.

Most striking to us is the evolution of the current policy from the long-sanctioned office of "Student Chaplain" to the candidly titled "Prayer at Football Games" regulation. This history indicates that the District intended to preserve the practice of prayer before football games. The conclusion that the District viewed the October policy simply as a continuation of the previous policies is dramatically illustrated by the fact that the school did not conduct a new election, pursuant to the current policy, to replace the results of the previous election, which occurred under the former policy. Given these observations, and in light of the school's history of regular delivery of a student-led prayer at athletic events, it is reasonable to infer that the specific purpose of the policy was to preserve a popular "state-sponsored religious practice."

School sponsorship of a religious message is impermissible because it sends the ancillary message to members of the audience who are non-adherents "that they are outsiders, not full members of the political community, and an accompanying message to adherents that they are insiders, favored members of the political community." The delivery of such a message—over the school's public address system, by a speaker representing the student body, under the supervision of school faculty, and pursuant to a school policy that explicitly and implicitly encourages public prayer—is not properly characterized as "private" speech.

III

The District next argues that its football policy is distinguishable from the graduation prayer in Lee because it does not coerce students to participate in religious observances. Its argument has two parts: first, that there is no impermissible government coercion because the pregame messages are the product of student choices; and second, that there is really no coercion at all because attendance at an extracurricular event, unlike a graduation ceremony, is voluntary.

The reasons just discussed explaining why the alleged "circuit-breaker" mechanism of the dual elections and student speaker do not turn public speech into private speech also demonstrate why these mechanisms do not insulate the school from the coercive element of the final message. In fact, this aspect of the District's argument exposes anew the concerns that are created by the majoritarian election system. The parties' stipulation clearly states that the issue resolved in the first election was "whether a student would deliver prayer at varsity football games," and the controversy in this case demonstrates that the views of the students are not unanimous on that issue.

One of the purposes served by the Establishment Clause is to remove debate over this kind of issue from governmental supervision or control. We explained in *Lee* that the "preservation and transmission of religious beliefs and worship is a responsibility and a choice committed to the private sphere." The two student elections authorized by the policy, coupled with the debates that presumably must precede each, impermissibly invade that private sphere. The election mechanism, when considered in light of the history in which the policy in question evolved, reflects a device the District put in place that determines whether religious messages will be delivered at home football games. The mechanism encourages divisiveness along religious lines in a public school setting, a result at odds with the Establishment Clause. Although it is true that the ultimate choice of student speaker is "attributable to the students," the District's decision to hold the constitutionally problematic election is clearly "a choice attributable to the State."

The District further argues that attendance at the commencement ceremonies at issue in *Lee* "differs dramatically" from attendance at high school football games, which it contends "are of no more than passing interest to many students" and are "decidedly extracurricular," thus dissipating any coercion. Attendance at a high school football game, unlike showing up for class, is certainly not required in order to receive a diploma. Moreover, we may assume that the District is correct in arguing that the informal pressure to attend an athletic event is not as strong as a senior's desire to attend her own graduation ceremony.

There are some students, however, such as cheerleaders, members of the band, and, of course, the team members themselves, for whom seasonal commitments mandate their attendance, sometimes for class credit. The District also minimizes the importance to many students of attending and participating in extracurricular activities as part of a complete educational experience. As we noted in *Lee*, "[l]aw reaches past formalism." To assert that high school students do not feel immense social pressure, or have a truly genuine desire, to be involved in the extracurricular event that is American high school football is "formalistic in the extreme." We stressed in *Lee* the obvious observation that "adolescents are often susceptible to pressure from their peers towards conformity, and that the influence is strongest in matters of social convention." High school home football games are traditional gatherings of a school community; they bring together students and faculty as well as friends and family from years present and past to root for a common cause. Undoubtedly, the games are not important to some students, and they voluntarily choose not to attend. For many others, however, the choice between whether to attend these games or to risk facing a personally offensive religious ritual is in no practical sense an easy one. The Constitution, moreover, demands that the school may not force this difficult choice upon these students for "[i]t is a tenet of the First Amendment that the State cannot require one of its citizens to forfeit his or her rights and benefits as the price of resisting conformance to state-sponsored religious practice."

Even if we regard every high school student's decision to attend a home football game as purely voluntary, we are nevertheless persuaded that the delivery of a pregame prayer has the improper effect of coercing those present to participate in an act of religious worship. For "the government may no more use social pressure to enforce orthodoxy than it may use more direct means." As in *Lee*, "[w]hat to most believers may seem nothing more than a reasonable request that the nonbeliever respect their religious practices, in a school context may appear to the nonbeliever or dissenter to be an attempt to employ the machinery of the State to enforce a religious orthodoxy." The constitutional command will not permit the District "to exact religious conformity from a student as the price" of joining her classmates at a varsity football game.

The Religion Clauses of the First Amendment prevent the government from making any law respecting the establishment of religion or prohibiting the free exercise thereof. By no means do these commands impose a prohibition on all religious activity in our public schools. Indeed, the common purpose of the Religion Clauses "is to secure religious liberty." Thus, nothing in the Constitution as interpreted by this Court prohibits any public school student from voluntarily praying at any time before, during, or after the school day. But the religious liberty protected by the Constitution is abridged when the State affirmatively sponsors the particular religious practice of prayer.

IV

Finally, the District argues repeatedly that the Does have made a premature facial challenge to the October policy that necessarily must fail. The District emphasizes, quite correctly, that until a student actually delivers a solemnizing message under the latest version of the policy, there can be no certainty that any of the statements or invocations will be religious. Thus, it concludes, the October policy necessarily survives a facial challenge.

This argument, however, assumes that we are concerned only with the serious constitutional injury that occurs when a student is forced to participate in an act of religious worship because she chooses to attend a school event. But the Constitution also requires that we keep in mind "the myriad, subtle ways in which Establishment Clause values can be eroded," *Lynch*, and that we guard against other different, yet equally important, constitutional injuries. One is the mere passage by the District of a policy that has the purpose and perception of government establishment of religion. Another is the implementation of a governmental electoral process that subjects the issue of prayer to a majoritarian vote.

The District argues that the facial challenge must fail because "Santa Fe's Football Policy cannot be invalidated on the basis of some 'possibility or even likelihood' of an unconstitutional application." Our Establishment Clause cases involving facial challenges, however, have not focused solely on the possible applications of the statute, but rather have considered whether the statute has an unconstitutional purpose. Writing for the Court in *Bowen*, the Chief Justice concluded that "[a]s in previous cases involving facial challenges on Establishment Clause grounds, we assess the constitutionality of an enactment by reference to the three factors first articulated in *Lemon v. Kurtzman* . . . . which guides '[t]he general nature of our inquiry in this area.' Under the Lemon standard, a court must invalidate a statute if it lacks 'a secular legislative purpose.' " It is therefore proper, as part of this facial challenge, for us to examine the purpose of the October policy.

. . . [T]he text of the October policy alone reveals that it has an unconstitutional purpose. The plain language of the policy clearly spells out the extent of school involvement in both the election of the speaker and the content of the message. Additionally, the text of the October policy specifies only one, clearly preferred message—that of Santa Fe's traditional religious "invocation." Finally, the extremely selective access of the policy and other content restrictions confirm that it is not a content-neutral regulation that creates a limited public forum for the expression of student speech. Our examination, however, need not stop at an analysis of the text of the policy.

This case comes to us as the latest step in developing litigation brought as a challenge to institutional practices that unquestionably violated the Establishment Clause. One of those practices was the District's long-established tradition of sanctioning student-led prayer at varsity football games. The narrow question before us is whether implementation of the October policy insulates the continuation of such prayers from constitutional scrutiny. It does not. Our inquiry into this question not only can, but must, include an examination of the circumstances surrounding its enactment. Whether a government activity violates the Establishment Clause is "in large part a legal question to be answered on the basis of judicial interpretation of social facts. . . . Every government practice must be judged in its unique circumstances. . . ." Our discussion in the previous sections demonstrates that in this case the District's direct involvement with school prayer exceeds constitutional limits.

The District, nevertheless, asks us to pretend that we do not recognize what every Santa Fe High School student understands clearly—that this policy is about prayer. The District further asks us to accept what is obviously untrue: that these messages are necessary to "solemnize" a football game and that this single-student, year-long position is essential to the protection of student speech. We refuse to turn a blind eye to the context in which this policy arose, and that context quells any doubt that this policy was implemented with the purpose of endorsing school prayer.

Therefore, the simple enactment of this policy, with the purpose and perception of school endorsement of student prayer, was a constitutional violation. We need not wait for the inevitable to confirm and magnify the constitutional injury. In Wallace, for example, we invalidated Alabama's as yet unimplemented and voluntary "moment of silence" statute based on our conclusion that it was enacted "for the sole purpose of expressing the State's endorsement of prayer activities for one minute at the beginning of each school day." Therefore, even if no Santa Fe High School student were ever to offer a religious message, the October policy fails a facial challenge because the attempt by the District to encourage prayer is also at issue. Government efforts to endorse religion cannot evade constitutional reproach based solely on the remote possibility that those attempts may fail.

This policy likewise does not survive a facial challenge because it impermissibly imposes upon the student body a majoritarian election on the issue of prayer. Through its election scheme, the District has established a governmental electoral mechanism that turns the school into a forum for religious debate. It further empowers the student body majority with the authority to subject students of minority views to constitutionally improper messages. The award of that power alone, regardless of the students' ultimate use of it, is not acceptable. Like the referendum in *Board of Regents of University of Wisconsin System v. Southworth*, the election mechanism established by the District undermines the essential protection of minority viewpoints. Such a system encourages divisiveness along religious lines and threatens the imposition of coercion upon those students not desiring to participate in a religious exercise. Simply by establishing this school-related procedure, which entrusts the inherently nongovernmental subject of religion to a majoritarian vote, a constitutional violation has occurred. No further injury is required for the policy to fail a facial challenge.

... To properly examine this policy on its face, we "must be deemed aware of the history and context of the community and forum." Our examination of those circumstances above leads to the conclusion that this policy does not provide the District with the constitutional safe harbor it sought. The policy is invalid on its face because it establishes an improper majoritarian election on religion, and unquestionably has the purpose and creates the perception of encouraging the delivery of prayer at a series of important school events.

The judgment of the Court of Appeals is, accordingly, affirmed.

It is so ordered.

Notes

1. In granting *certiorari* in this case, the Court side-stepped the key question of prayer at public school graduation ceremonies. Should the Court have accepted this question in light of all of the conflicting results in the circuit courts?

2. In a scathing dissent, in *Santa Fe* at 318, Chief Justice Rehnquist, joined by Justice Scalia and Thomas, accused the Court of "bristl[ing] with hostility to all things religious in public life." The dissent viewed the issue in *Santa Fe* as

student, not government, speech where, unlike *Lee's* having a prayer delivered by a rabbi under the direction of a school official, the policy allowed students to select or create prayers. The dissent added that if a student had been selected on wholly secular criteria, such as public speaking skills or social popularity, he or she could have delivered a religious message that would likely have passed constitutional muster. What do you think?

3. In *Bauchman v. West High School*, 132 F.3d 542 [122 Educ. L. Rep. 1133] (10th Cir.1997), *cert. denied*, 524 U.S. 953, 118 S.Ct. 2370, 141 L.Ed.2d 738 (1998), the Tenth Circuit affirmed the dismissal of a student's complaint that officials violated her rights under the Establishment and Free Exercise Clauses by permitting the school choir to sing Christian religious music, including the song, "The Lord Bless You and Keep you." Earlier, in *Doe v. Duncanville Indep. School Dist.*, 70 F.3d 402 [104 Educ. L. Rep. 1032] (5th Cir.1995), the Fifth Circuit ruled that permitting a school choir to adopt the same song as its theme song did not violate the Establishment Clause. Is this different from prayer at school sponsored events such as a football game?

[Case No. 13]   Access Rights of Religious Groups to Use Public School Facilities

GOOD NEWS CLUB v. MILFORD CENTRAL SCHOOL

Supreme Court of the United States, 2001.
533 U.S. 98, 121 S.Ct. 2093, 150 L.Ed.2d 151 [154 Educ. L. Rep. 45].

JUSTICE THOMAS delivered the opinion of the Court.

This case presents two questions. The first question is whether Milford Central School violated the free speech rights of the Good News Club when it excluded the Club from meeting after hours at the school. The second question is whether any such violation is justified by Milford's concern that permitting the Club's activities would violate the Establishment Clause. We conclude that Milford's restriction violates the Club's free speech rights and that no Establishment Clause concern justifies that violation.

I

The State of New York authorizes local school boards to adopt regulations governing the use of their school facilities. In particular, N.Y. Educ. Law § 414 enumerates several purposes for which local boards may open their schools to public use. In 1992, respondent Milford Central School (Milford) enacted a community use policy adopting seven of § 414's purposes for which its building could be used after school. Two of the stated purposes are relevant here. First, district residents may use the school for "instruction in any branch of education, learning or the arts." Second, the school is available for "social, civic and recreational meetings and entertainment events, and other uses pertaining to the welfare of the community, provided that such uses shall be nonexclusive and shall be opened to the general public." Stephen and Darleen Fournier reside within Milford's district and therefore are eligible to use the school's facilities as long as their proposed use is approved by the school. Together they are sponsors of the local Good News Club, a private Christian organization for children ages 6 to 12.

Pursuant to Milford's policy, in September 1996 the Fourniers submitted a request to Dr. Robert McGruder, interim superintendent of the district.... The next month, McGruder formally denied the Fourniers' request on the ground that the proposed use—to have "a fun time of singing songs, hearing a Bible lesson and memorizing scripture,"—was "the equivalent of religious worship." According to McGruder, the community use policy, which prohibits use "by any individual or organization for religious purposes," foreclosed the Club's activities. In response to a letter submitted by the Club's counsel, Milford's attorney requested information to clarify the nature of the Club's activities. The Club sent a set of materials used or distributed at the meetings and the following description of its meeting: "The Club opens its session with Ms. Fournier taking attendance. As she calls a child's name, if the child recites a Bible verse the child receives a treat. After attendance, the Club sings songs. Next Club members engage in games that involve, inter alia, learning Bible verses. Ms. Fournier then relates a Bible story and explains how it applies to Club members' lives. The Club closes with prayer. Finally, Ms. Fournier distributes treats and the Bible verses for memorization." McGruder and Milford's attorney reviewed the materials and concluded that "the kinds of activities proposed to be engaged in by the Good News Club were not a discussion of secular subjects such as child rearing, development of character and development of morals from a religious perspective, but were in fact the equivalent of religious instruction itself." In February 1997, the Milford Board of Education adopted a resolution rejecting the Club's request to use Milford's facilities "for the purpose of conducting religious instruction and Bible study." In March 1997, petitioners, the Good News Club, Ms. Fournier, and her daughter Andrea Fournier (collectively, the Club), filed an action under 42 U.S.C.[A.] § 1983 against Milford ..... The Club alleged that Milford's denial of its application violated its fr$TBee speech rights under the First and Fourteenth Amendments, its right to equal protection under the Fourteenth Amendment, and its right to religious freedom under the Religious Freedom Restoration Act of 1993.

The Club moved for a preliminary injunction to prevent the school from enforcing its religious exclusion policy against the Club and thereby to permit the Club's use of the school facilities. On April 14, 1997, the District Court granted the injunction. The Club then held its weekly after school meetings from April 1997 until June 1998 in a high school resource and middle school special education room. In August 1998, the District Court vacated the preliminary injunction and granted Milford's motion for summary judgment.... The Club appealed, and a divided panel of the ... Second Circuit affirmed.... There is a conflict among the Courts of Appeals on the question whether speech can be excluded from a limited public forum on the basis of the religious nature of the speech.... We granted certiorari to resolve this conflict.

II

The standards that we apply to determine whether a State has unconstitutionally excluded a private speaker from use of a public forum depend on the nature of the forum. If the forum is a traditional or open public forum, the State's restrictions on speech are subject to stricter scrutiny than are restrictions in a limited public forum. We have previously declined to decide whether a school district's opening of its facilities pursuant to N.Y. Educ. Law § 414 creates a limited or a traditional public forum. Because the parties have agreed that Milford created a limited public forum when it opened its facilities in 1992 we need not resolve the issue here. Instead, we simply will assume that Milford operates a limited public forum.

When the State establishes a limited public forum, the State is not required to and does not allow persons to engage in every type of speech. The State may be justified "in reserving [its forum] for certain groups or for the discussion of certain topics." The State's power to restrict speech, however, is not without limits. The restriction must not discriminate against speech on the basis of viewpoint, and the restriction must be "reasonable in light of the purpose served by the forum."

III

Applying this test, we first address whether the exclusion constituted viewpoint discrimination. We are guided in our analysis by two of our prior opinions, *Lamb's Chapel* and *Rosenberger*. In *Lamb's Chapel*, we held that a school district violated the Free Speech Clause of the First Amendment when it excluded a private group from presenting films at the school based solely on the films' discussions of family values from a religious perspective. Likewise, in *Rosenberger*, we held that a university's refusal to fund a student publication because the publication addressed issues from a religious perspective violated the Free Speech Clause. Concluding that Milford's exclusion of the Good News Club based on its religious nature is indistinguishable from the exclusions in these cases, we hold that the exclusion constitutes viewpoint discrimination. Because the restriction is viewpoint discriminatory, we need not decide whether it is unreasonable in light of the purposes served by the forum....

Milford has opened its limited public forum to activities that serve a variety of purposes, including events "pertaining to the welfare of the community." Milford interprets its policy to permit discussions of subjects such as child rearing, and of "the development of character and morals from a religious perspective." For example, this policy would allow someone to use Aesop's Fables to teach children moral values. Additionally, a group could sponsor a debate on whether there should be a constitutional amendment to permit prayer in public schools, id., at N6, and the Boy Scouts could meet "to influence a boy's character, development and spiritual growth." In short, any group that "promote[s] the moral and character development of children" is eligible to use the school building. Just as there is no question that teaching morals and character development to children is a permissible purpose under Milford's policy, it is clear that the Club teaches morals and character development to children. For example, no one disputes that the Club instructs children to overcome feelings of jealousy, to treat others well regardless of how they treat the children, and to be obedient, even if it does so in a non-secular way. Nonetheless, because Milford found the Club's activities to be religious in nature—"the equivalent of religious instruction itself," it excluded the Club from use of its facilities. Applying *Lamb's Chapel*, we find it quite clear that Milford engaged in viewpoint discrimination when it excluded the Club from the after school forum. In *Lamb's Chapel*, the local New York school district similarly had adopted § 414's "social, civic or recreational use" category as a permitted use in its limited public forum. The district also prohibited use "by any group for religious purposes...."

Like the church in *Lamb's Chapel*, the Club seeks to address a subject otherwise permitted under the rule, the teaching of morals and character, from a religious standpoint. Certainly, one could have characterized the film presentations in Lamb's Chapel as a religious use, as the Court of Appeals did. And one easily could conclude that the films' purpose to instruct that " 'society's slide toward humanism ... can only be counterbalanced by a loving home where Christian values are instilled from an early age' " was "quintessentially religious." The only apparent difference between the activity of *Lamb's Chapel* and the activities of the Good News Club is that the Club chooses to teach moral lessons from a Christian perspective through live storytelling and prayer, whereas *Lamb's Chapel* taught lessons through films. This distinction is inconsequential. Both modes of speech use a religious viewpoint. Thus, the exclusion of the Good News Club's activities, like the exclusion of Lamb's Chapel's films, constitutes unconstitutional viewpoint discrimination. Our opinion in *Rosenberger* also is dispositive. In Rosenberger, a student organization at the University of Virginia was denied funding for printing expenses because its publication, Wide Awake, offered a Christian viewpoint. Just as the Club emphasizes the role of Christianity in students' morals and character, Wide Awake " 'challenge[d] Christians to live, in word and deed, according to the faith they proclaim and ... encourage[d] students to consider what a personal relationship with Jesus Christ means.' " Because the university "select[ed] for disfavored treatment those student journalistic efforts with religious editorial viewpoints," we held that the denial of funding was unconstitutional.... Despite our holdings in *Lamb's Chapel* and *Rosenberger*, the Court of Appeals, like Milford, believed that its characterization of the Club's activities as religious in nature warranted treating the Club's activities as different in kind from the other activities permitted by the school. The "Christian viewpoint" is unique, according to the court, because it contains an "additional layer" that other kinds of viewpoints do not. That is, the Club "is focused on teaching children how to cultivate their relationship with God through Jesus Christ," which it characterized as "quintessentially religious." With these observations, the court concluded that, because the Club's activities "fall outside the bounds of pure 'moral and character development,' " the exclusion did not constitute viewpoint discrimination.

We disagree that something that is "quintessentially religious" or "decidedly religious in nature" cannot also be characterized properly as the teaching of morals and character development from a particular viewpoint. What matters for purposes of the Free Speech Clause is that we can see no logical difference in kind between the invocation of Christianity by the Club and the invocation of teamwork, loyalty, or patriotism by other associations to provide a foundation for their lessons. It is apparent that the unstated principle of the Court of Appeals' reasoning is its conclusion that any time religious instruction and prayer are used to discuss morals and character, the discussion is simply not a "pure" discussion of those issues. According to the Court of Appeals, reliance on Christian principles taints moral and character instruction in a way that other foundations for thought or viewpoints do not. We, however, have never reached such a conclusion. Instead, we reaffirm our holdings in *Lamb's Chapel* and *Rosenberger* that speech discussing otherwise permissible subjects cannot be excluded from a limited public forum on the ground that the subject is discussed from a religious viewpoint. Thus, we conclude that Milford's exclusion of the Club from use of the school, pursuant to its community use policy, constitutes impermissible viewpoint discrimination.

Justice SOUTER recitation of the Club's activities is accurate. But in our view, religion is used by the Club in the same fashion that it was used by Lamb's Chapel and by the students in *Rosenberger*: religion is the viewpoint from which ideas are conveyed. We did not find the *Rosenberger* students' attempt to cultivate a personal relationship with Christ to bar their claim that religion was a viewpoint. And we see no reason to treat the Club's use of religion as something other than a viewpoint merely because of any evangelical message it conveys. According to Justice SOUTER, the Club's activities constitute "an evangelical service of worship." Regardless of the label Justice SOUTER wishes to use, what matters is the substance of the Club's activities, which we conclude are materially indistinguishable from the activities in *Lamb's Chapel* and *Rosenberger*.

IV

Milford argues that, even if its restriction constitutes viewpoint discrimination, its interest in not violating the Establishment Clause outweighs the Club's interest in gaining equal access to the school's facilities. In other words, according to Milford, its restriction was required to avoid violating the Establishment Clause. We disagree. We have said that a state interest in avoiding an Establishment Clause violation "may be characterized as compelling," and therefore may justify content-based discrimination. However, it is not clear whether a State's interest in avoiding an Establishment Clause violation would justify viewpoint discrimination. We need not, however, confront the issue in this case, because we conclude that the school has no valid Establishment Clause interest.

We rejected Establishment Clause defenses similar to Milford's in two previous free speech cases, *Lamb's Chapel* and *Widmar*. In particular, in *Lamb's Chapel*, we explained that "[t]he showing of th[e] film series would not have been during school hours, would not have been sponsored by the school, and would have been open to the public, not just to church members." Accordingly, we found that "there would have been no realistic danger that the community would think that the District was endorsing religion or any particular creed." Likewise, in *Widmar*, where the university's forum was already available to other groups, this Court concluded that there was no Establishment Clause problem. The Establishment Clause defense fares no better in this case. As in *Lamb's Chapel*, the Club's meetings were held after school hours, not sponsored by the school, and open to any student who obtained parental consent, not just to Club members. As in *Widmar*, Milford made its forum available to other organizations. The Club's activities are materially indistinguishable from those in *Lamb's Chapel* and *Widmar*. Thus, Milford's reliance on the Establishment Clause is unavailing. Milford attempts to distinguish *Lamb's Chapel* and *Widmar* by emphasizing that Milford's policy involves elementary school children. According to Milford, children will perceive that the school is endorsing the Club and will feel coercive pressure to participate, because the Club's activities take place on school grounds, even though they occur during non-school hours. This argument is unpersuasive.

First, we have held that "a significant factor in upholding governmental programs in the face of Establishment Clause attack is their neutrality towards religion." Milford's implication that granting access to the Club would do damage to the neutrality principle defies logic. For the "guarantee of neutrality is respected, not offended, when the government, following neutral criteria and evenhanded policies, extends benefits to recipients whose ideologies and viewpoints, including religious ones, are broad and diverse." The Good News Club seeks nothing more than to be treated neutrally and given access to speak about the same topics as are other groups. Because allowing the Club to speak on school grounds would ensure neutrality, not threaten it, Milford faces an uphill battle in arguing that the Establishment Clause compels it to exclude the Good News Club.

Second, to the extent we consider whether the community would feel coercive pressure to engage in the Club's activities, the relevant community would be the parents, not the elementary school children. It is the parents who choose whether their children will attend the Good News Club meetings. Because the children cannot attend without their parents' permission, they cannot be coerced into engaging in the Good News Club's religious activities. Milford does not suggest that the parents of elementary school children would be confused about whether the school was endorsing religion. Nor do we believe that such an argument could be reasonably advanced.

Third, whatever significance we may have assigned in the Establishment Clause context to the suggestion that elementary school children are more impressionable than adults, we have never extended our Establishment Clause jurisprudence to foreclose private religious conduct during non-school hours merely because it takes place on school premises where elementary school children may be present. None of the cases discussed by Milford persuades us that our Establishment Clause jurisprudence has gone this far . . . .

Fourth, even if we were to consider the possible misperceptions by schoolchildren in deciding whether Milford's permitting the Club's activities would violate the Establishment Clause, the facts of this case simply do not support Milford's conclusion. There is no evidence that young children are permitted to loiter outside classrooms after the school day has ended. Surely even young children are aware of events for which their parents must sign permission forms. The meetings were held in a combined high school resource room and middle school special education room, not in an elementary school classroom. The instructors are not schoolteachers. And the children in the group are not all the same age as in the normal classroom setting; their ages range from 6 to 12. In sum, these circumstances simply do not support the theory that small children would perceive endorsement here.

Finally, even if we were to inquire into the minds of schoolchildren in this case, we cannot say the danger that children would misperceive the endorsement of religion is any greater than the danger that they would perceive a hostility toward the religious viewpoint if the Club were excluded from the public forum. This concern is particularly acute given the reality that Milford's building is not used only for elementary school children. Students, from kindergarten through the 12th grade, all attend school in the same building. There may be as many, if not more, upperclassmen than elementary school children who occupy the school after hours . . . .

We cannot operate, as Milford would have us do, under the assumption that any risk that small children would perceive endorsement should counsel in favor of excluding the Club's religious activity. We decline to employ Establishment Clause jurisprudence using a modified heckler's veto, in which a group's religious activity can be proscribed on the basis of what the youngest members of the audience might misperceive. . . . There are countervailing constitutional concerns related to rights of other individuals in the community. In this case, those countervailing concerns are the free speech rights of the Club and its members. . . . And, we have already found that those rights have been violated, not merely perceived to have been violated, by the school's actions toward the Club.

We are not convinced that there is any significance in this case to the possibility that elementary school children may witness the Good News Club's activities on school premises, and therefore we can find no reason to depart from our holdings in *Lamb's Chapel* and *Widmar*. Accordingly, we conclude that permitting the Club to meet on the school's premises would not have violated the Establishment Clause.

V

When Milford denied the Good News Club access to the school's limited public forum on the ground that the Club was religious in nature, it discriminated against the Club because of its religious viewpoint in violation of the Free Speech Clause of the First Amendment. Because Milford has not raised a valid Establishment Clause claim, we do not address the question whether such a claim could excuse Milford's viewpoint discrimination.

The judgment of the Court of Appeals is reversed, and the case is remanded for further proceedings consistent with this opinion.

Notes

1.   In a similar case from Louisiana, wherein the Supreme Court vacated and remanded the Fifth Circuit's judgment in light of *Milford*, *Campbell v. St. Tammany's School Bd.*, 533 U.S. 913, 121 S.Ct. 2518, 150 L.Ed.2d 691 [154 Educ. L. Rep. 73] (2001), *on remand*, 300 F.3d 526 [168 Educ. L. Rep. 128] (5th Cir.2002), a federal trial court granted the group's request that it be permitted to use school facilities. *Campbell v. St. Tammany Parish School Bd.*, 2003 WL 21783317 (E.D. La. 2003).

[Case No. 14]   Public Funds for Vouchers to Religiously Affiliated Non–Public Schools

ZELMAN v. SIMMONS–HARRIS

Supreme Court of the United States, 2002.
536 U.S. 639, 122 S.Ct. 2460, 153 L.Ed.2d 604 [166 Educ. L. Rep. 30].

CHIEF JUSTICE REHNQUIST delivered the opinion of the Court.

The State of Ohio has established a pilot program designed to provide educational choices to families with children who reside in the Cleveland City School District. The question presented is whether this program offends the Establishment Clause of the United States Constitution. We hold that it does not.

There are more than 75,000 children enrolled in the Cleveland City School District. The majority of these children are from low-income and minority families. Few of these families enjoy the means to send their children to any school other than an inner-city public school. For more than a generation, however, Cleveland's public schools have been among the worst performing public schools in the Nation. In 1995, a Federal District Court declared a "crisis of magnitude" and placed the entire Cleveland school district under state control. Shortly thereafter, the state auditor found that Cleveland's public schools were in the midst of a "crisis that is perhaps unprecedented in the history of American education." The district had failed to meet any of the 18 state standards for minimal acceptable performance. Only 1 in 10 ninth graders could pass a basic proficiency examination, and students at all levels performed at a dismal rate compared with students in other Ohio public schools. More than two-thirds of high school students either dropped or failed out before graduation. Of those students who managed to reach their senior year, one of every four still failed to graduate. Of those students who did graduate, few could read, write, or compute at levels comparable to their counterparts in other cities.

It is against this backdrop that Ohio enacted, among other initiatives, its Pilot Project Scholarship Program. The program provides financial assistance to families in any Ohio school district that is or has been "under federal court order requiring supervision and operational management of the district by the state superintendent." Cleveland is the only Ohio school district to fall within that category.

The program provides two basic kinds of assistance to parents of children in a covered district. First, the program provides tuition aid for students in kindergarten through third grade, expanding each year through eighth grade, to attend a participating public or private school of their parent's choosing. Second, the program provides tutorial aid for students who choose to remain enrolled in public school.

The tuition aid portion of the program is designed to provide educational choices to parents who reside in a covered district. Any private school, whether religious or nonreligious, may participate in the program and accept program students so long as the school is located within the boundaries of a covered district and meets statewide educational standards. Participating private schools must agree not to discriminate on the basis of race, religion, or ethnic background, or to "advocate or foster unlawful behavior or teach hatred of any person or group on the basis of race, ethnicity, national origin, or religion." Any public school located in a school district adjacent to the covered district may also participate in the program. Adjacent public schools are eligible to receive a $2,250 tuition grant for each program student accepted in addition to the full amount of per-pupil state funding attributable to each additional student. All participating schools, whether public or private, are required to accept students in accordance with rules and procedures established by the state superintendent.

Tuition aid is distributed to parents according to financial need. Families with incomes below 200% of the poverty line are given priority and are eligible to receive 90% of private school tuition up to $2,250. For these lowest-income families, participating private schools may not charge a parental co-payment greater than $250. For all other families, the program pays 75% of tuition costs, up to $1,875, with no co-payment cap. These families receive tuition aid only if the number of available scholarships exceeds the number of low-income children who choose to participate. Where tuition aid is spent depends solely upon where parents who receive tuition aid choose to enroll their child. If parents choose a private school, checks are made payable to the parents who then endorse the checks over to the chosen school.

The tutorial aid portion of the program provides tutorial assistance through grants to any student in a covered district who chooses to remain in public school ... The number of tutorial assistance grants offered to students in a covered district must equal the number of tuition aid scholarships provided to students enrolled at participating private or adjacent public schools.

The program has been in operation within the Cleveland City School District since the 1996–1997 school year. In the 1999–2000 school year,

56 private schools participated in the program, 46 (or 82%) of which had a religious affiliation. None of the public schools in districts adjacent to Cleveland have elected to participate. More than 3,700 students participated in the scholarship program, most of whom (96%) enrolled in religiously affiliated schools. Sixty percent of these students were from families at or below the poverty line. In the 1998–1999 school year, approximately 1,400 Cleveland public school students received tutorial aid. This number was expected to double during the 1999–2000 school year.

The program is part of a broader undertaking by the State to enhance the educational options of Cleveland's schoolchildren in response to the 1995 takeover [t]hat includes programs governing community and magnet schools. Community schools are funded under state law but are run by their own school boards, not by local school districts. These schools enjoy academic independence to hire their own teachers and to determine their own curriculum. They can have no religious affiliation and are required to accept students by lottery. During the 1999–2000 school year, there were 10 start-up community schools in the Cleveland City School District with more than 1,900 students enrolled. For each child enrolled in a community school, the school receives state funding of $4,518, twice the funding a participating program school may receive.

Magnet schools are public schools operated by a local school board that emphasize a particular subject area, teaching method, or service to students. For each student enrolled in a magnet school, the school district receives $7,746, including state funding of $4,167, the same amount received per student enrolled at a traditional public school. As of 1999, parents in Cleveland were able to choose from among 23 magnet schools, which together enrolled more than 13,000 students in kindergarten through eighth grade. . . .

In 1996, respondents, a group of Ohio taxpayers, challenged the Ohio program. . . . The Ohio Supreme Court rejected respondents' federal claims, but held that the enactment of the program violated certain procedural requirements of the Ohio Constitution. The state legislature immediately cured this defect, leaving the basic provisions discussed above intact.

In July 1999, respondents filed this action . . . seeking to enjoin the reenacted program on the ground that it violated the Establishment Clause. . . . In August 1999, the District Court issued a preliminary injunction barring further implementation of the program, which we stayed pending review by the Court of Appeals. In December 1999, the District Court granted summary judgment for respondents. In December 2000, a divided panel of the Court of Appeals affirmed . . . finding that the program had the "primary effect" of advancing religion in violation of the Establishment Clause. The Court of Appeals stayed its mandate pending disposition in this Court. We granted certiorari, and now reverse the Court of Appeals.

The Establishment Clause of the First Amendment ... prevents a State from enacting laws that have the "purpose" or "effect" of advancing or inhibiting religion.... There is no dispute that the program challenged here was enacted for the valid secular purpose of providing educational assistance to poor children in a demonstrably failing public school system. Thus, the question presented is whether the Ohio program nonetheless has the forbidden "effect" of advancing or inhibiting religion.

To answer that question, our decisions have drawn a consistent distinction between government programs that provide aid directly to religious schools and programs of true private choice, in which government aid reaches religious schools only as a result of the genuine and independent choices of private individuals. While our jurisprudence with respect to the constitutionality of direct aid programs has "changed significantly" over the past two decades, our jurisprudence with respect to true private choice programs has remained consistent and unbroken. Three times we have confronted Establishment Clause challenges to neutral government programs that provide aid directly to a broad class of individuals, who, in turn, direct the aid to religious schools or institutions of their own choosing. Three times we have rejected such challenges.

In *Mueller,* we rejected an Establishment Clause challenge to a Minnesota program authorizing tax deductions for various educational expenses, including private school tuition costs, even though the great majority of the program's beneficiaries (96%) were parents of children in religious schools. We began by focusing on the class of beneficiaries, finding that because the class included "all parents," including parents with "children [who] attend non-sectarian private schools or sectarian private schools," the program was "not readily subject to challenge under the Establishment Clause." Then, viewing the program as a whole, we emphasized the principle of private choice, noting that public funds were made available to religious schools "only as a result of numerous, private choices of individual parents of school-age children." This, we said, ensured that " 'no imprimatur of state approval' can be deemed to have been conferred on any particular religion, or on religion generally." We thus found it irrelevant to the constitutional inquiry that the vast majority of beneficiaries were parents of children in religious schools....

In *Witters,* we used identical reasoning to reject an Establishment Clause challenge to a vocational scholarship program that provided tuition aid to a student studying at a religious institution to become a pastor. Looking at the program as a whole, we observed that "[a]ny aid ... that ultimately flows to religious institutions does so only as a result of the genuinely independent and private choices of aid recipients...."

Five Members of the Court, in separate opinions, emphasized the general rule from *Mueller* that the amount of government aid channeled to religious institutions by individual aid recipients was not relevant to the constitutional inquiry. Our holding thus rested not on whether few or many recipients chose to expend government aid at a religious school but, rather, on whether recipients generally were empowered to direct the aid to schools or institutions of their own choosing.

Finally, in *Zobrest,* we applied *Mueller* and *Witters* to reject an Establishment Clause challenge to a federal program that permitted sign-language interpreters to assist deaf children enrolled in religious schools ... we stated that "government programs that neutrally provide benefits to a broad class of citizens defined without reference to religion are not readily subject to an Establishment Clause challenge...." we observed that the program "distributes benefits neutrally to any child qualifying as 'disabled.'" Its "primary beneficiaries," we said, were "disabled children, not sectarian schools."

We further observed that "[b]y according parents freedom to select a school of their choice, the statute ensures that a government-paid interpreter will be present in a sectarian school only as a result of the private decision of individual parents." Our focus again was on neutrality and the principle of private choice, not on the number of program beneficiaries attending religious schools....

Mueller, Witters, and *Zobrest* thus make clear that where a government aid program is neutral with respect to religion, and provides assistance directly to a broad class of citizens who, in turn, direct government aid to religious schools wholly as a result of their own genuine and independent private choice, the program is not readily subject to challenge under the Establishment Clause. A program that shares these features permits government aid to reach religious institutions only by way of the deliberate choices of numerous individual recipients. The incidental advancement of a religious mission, or the perceived endorsement of a religious message, is reasonably attributable to the individual recipient, not to the government....

We believe that the program challenged here is a program of true private choice, consistent with *Mueller, Witters,* and *Zobrest,* and thus constitutional. As was true in those cases, the Ohio program is neutral in all respects toward religion. It is part of a general and multifaceted undertaking by the State of Ohio to provide educational opportunities to the children of a failed school district. It confers educational assistance directly to a broad class of individuals defined without reference to religion, *i.e.,* any parent of a school-age child who resides in the Cleveland City School District. The program permits the participation of all schools within the district, religious or nonreligious. Adjacent public schools also may participate and have a financial incentive to do so. Program benefits are available to participating families on neutral terms, with no reference to religion. The only ... preference [is] for low-income families, who receive greater assistance and are given priority for admission....

There are no "financial incentive[s]" that "ske[w]" the program toward religious schools. Such incentives "[are] not present ... where the aid is allocated on the basis of neutral, secular criteria that neither favor nor disfavor religion, and is made available to both religious and secular beneficiaries on a nondiscriminatory basis." The program here in fact creates financial disincentives for religious schools, with private schools receiving only half the government assistance given to community schools and one-third the assistance given to magnet schools. Adjacent public schools, should any choose to accept program students, are also eligible to receive two to three times the state funding of a private religious school. Families too have a financial disincentive to choose a private religious school over other schools. Parents that choose to participate in the scholarship program and then to enroll their children in a private school (religious or nonreligious) must copay a portion of the school's tuition. Families that choose a community school, magnet school, or traditional public school pay nothing. . . .

Respondents suggest that even without a financial incentive for parents to choose a religious school, the program creates a "public perception that the State is endorsing religious practices and beliefs." But we have repeatedly recognized that no reasonable observer would think a neutral program of private choice, where state aid reaches religious schools solely as a result of the numerous independent decisions of private individuals, carries with it the *imprimatur* of government endorsement. The argument is particularly misplaced here since "the reasonable observer in the endorsement inquiry must be deemed aware" of the "history and context" underlying a challenged program. Any objective observer familiar with the full history and context of the Ohio program would reasonably view it as one aspect of a broader undertaking to assist poor children in failed schools, not as an endorsement of religious schooling in general.

There also is no evidence that the program fails to provide genuine opportunities for Cleveland parents to select secular educational options for their school-age children. Cleveland schoolchildren enjoy a range of educational choices: They may remain in public school as before, remain in public school with publicly funded tutoring aid, obtain a scholarship and choose a religious school, obtain a scholarship and choose a nonreligious private school, enroll in a community school, or enroll in a magnet school. That 46 of the 56 private schools now participating in the program are religious schools does not condemn it as a violation of the Establishment Clause. The Establishment Clause question is whether Ohio is coercing parents into sending their children to religious schools, and that question must be answered by evaluating all options Ohio provides Cleveland schoolchildren, only one of which is to obtain a program scholarship and then choose a religious school.

Justice SOUTER speculates that because more private religious schools currently participate in the program, the program itself must somehow discourage the participation of private nonreligious schools. But Cleveland's preponderance of religiously affiliated private schools certainly did not arise as a result of the program; it is a phenomenon common to many American cities. Indeed, by all accounts the program has captured a remarkable cross-section of private schools, religious and nonreligious. It is true that 82% of Cleveland's participating private schools are religious schools, but it is also true that 81% of private schools in Ohio are religious schools. To attribute constitutional significance to this figure, moreover, would lead to the absurd result that a neutral school-choice program might be permissible in some parts of Ohio, such as Columbus, where a lower percentage of private schools are religious schools, but not in inner-city Cleveland, where Ohio has deemed such programs most sorely needed, but where the preponderance of religious schools happens to be greater. Likewise, an identical private choice program might be constitutional in some States, such as Maine or Utah, where less than 45% of private schools are religious schools, but not in other States, such as Nebraska or Kansas, where over 90% of private schools are religious schools.

Respondents and Justice SOUTER claim that even if we do not focus on the number of participating schools that are religious schools, we should attach constitutional significance to the fact that 96% of scholarship recipients have enrolled in religious schools. They claim that this alone proves parents lack genuine choice, even if no parent has ever said so. We need not consider this argument in detail, since it was flatly rejected in *Mueller,* where we found it irrelevant that 96% of parents taking deductions for tuition expenses paid tuition at religious schools. Indeed, we have recently found it irrelevant even to the constitutionality of a direct aid program that a vast majority of program benefits went to religious schools. The constitutionality of a neutral educational aid program simply does not turn on whether and why, in a particular area, at a particular time, most private schools are run by religious organizations, or most recipients choose to use the aid at a religious school....

This point is aptly illustrated here. The 96% figure upon which respondents and Justice SOUTER rely discounts entirely (1) the more than 1,900 Cleveland children enrolled in alternative community schools, (2) the more than 13,000 children enrolled in alternative magnet schools, and (3) the more than 1,400 children enrolled in traditional public schools with tutorial assistance. Including some or all of these children in the denominator of children enrolled in nontraditional schools during the 1999–2000 school year drops the percentage enrolled in religious schools from 96% to under 20%. The 96% figure also represents but a snapshot of one particular school year. In the 1997–1998 school year, by contrast, only 78% of scholarship recipients attended religious schools. The difference was attributable to two private nonreligious schools that had accepted 15% of all scholarship students electing instead to register as community schools, in light of larger per-pupil funding for community schools and the uncertain future of the scholarship program generated by this litigation. Many of the students enrolled in these schools as scholarship students remained enrolled as community school students, thus demonstrating the arbitrariness of counting one type of school but not the other to assess primary effect....

Respondents finally claim that we should look to *Committee for Public Ed. & Religious Liberty v. Nyquist* to decide these cases. We disagree for two reasons. First, the program in *Nyquist* was quite different from the program challenged here. *Nyquist* involved a New York program that gave a package of benefits exclusively to private schools and the parents of private school enrollees. Although the program was enacted for ostensibly secular purposes, we found that its "function" was "unmistakably to provide desired financial support for non-public, sectarian institutions. . . ." The program thus provided direct money grants to religious schools. It provided tax benefits "unrelated to the amount of money actually expended by any parent on tuition," ensuring a windfall to parents of children in religious schools. It similarly provided tuition reimbursements designed explicitly to "offe[r] . . . an incentive to parents to send their children to sectarian schools." Indeed, the program flatly prohibited the participation of any public school, or parent of any public school enrollee. Ohio's program shares none of these features.

Second, were there any doubt that the program challenged in *Nyquist* is far removed from the program challenged here, we expressly reserved judgment with respect to "a case involving some form of public assistance (*e.g.*, scholarships) made available generally without regard to the sectarian-non-sectarian, or public-non-public nature of the institution benefited." That, of course, is the very question now before us, and it has since been answered, first in *Mueller*, then in *Witters*, and again in *Zobrest*. To the extent the scope of *Nyquist* has remained an open question in light of these later decisions, we now hold that *Nyquist* does not govern neutral educational assistance programs that, like the program here, offer aid directly to a broad class of individual recipients defined without regard to religion.

In sum, the Ohio program is entirely neutral with respect to religion. It provides benefits directly to a wide spectrum of individuals, defined only by financial need and residence in a particular school district. It permits such individuals to exercise genuine choice among options public and private, secular and religious. The program is therefore a program of true private choice. In keeping with an unbroken line of decisions rejecting challenges to similar programs, we hold that the program does not offend the Establishment Clause.

The judgment of the Court of Appeals is reversed.

It is so ordered.

Notes

1. The dissenters, led by Justice Stevens' raising the specters of "the Balkans, Northern Ireland, and the Middle East," *Zelman v. Simmons–Harris*, 536 U.S. 639, 686, 122 S.Ct. 2460, 153 L.Ed.2d 604 [166 Educ. L. Rep. 30] (2002) (Stevens, J., dissenting), all voiced concerns about divisiveness and religious strife based on the majority's upholding the voucher program. Is Justice Stevens' fear, in particular, well-founded? Can you distinguish the situation in the United States and those three locations?

2. Given the narrowness of the vouchers statute at issue, insofar as it was developed exclusively for Cleveland as part of a school desegregation suit, are similar programs likely to withstand constitutional challenges? Are constitutional challenges more likely to succeed in federal or state courts?

[Case No. 15]   The Constitutionality of the Words "Under God" in the Pledge

ELK GROVE UNIFIED SCHOOL DISTRICT v. NEWDOW

Supreme Court of the United States, 2004.
542 U.S. 1, 124 S.Ct. 2301, 159 L.Ed.2d 98, [188 Educ. L. Rep. 17].

JUSTICE STEVENS delivered the opinion of the Court.

Each day elementary school teachers in the Elk Grove Unified School District (School District) lead their classes in a group recitation of the Pledge of Allegiance. Respondent, Michael A. Newdow, is an atheist whose daughter participates in that daily exercise. Because the Pledge contains the words "under God," he views the School District's policy as a religious indoctrination of his child that violates the First Amendment. A divided panel of the Court of Appeals for the Ninth Circuit agreed with Newdow. In light of the obvious importance of that decision, we granted certiorari to review the First Amendment issue and, preliminarily, the question whether Newdow has standing to invoke the jurisdiction of the federal courts. We conclude that Newdow lacks standing and therefore reverse the Court of Appeals' decision.

I

"The very purpose of a national flag is to serve as a symbol of our country," and of its proud traditions "of freedom, of equal opportunity, of religious tolerance, and of good will for other peoples who share our aspirations." As its history illustrates, the Pledge of Allegiance evolved as a common public acknowledgement of the ideals that our flag symbolizes. Its recitation is a patriotic exercise designed to foster national unity and pride in those principles.

The Pledge of Allegiance was initially conceived more than a century ago. As part of the nationwide interest in commemorating the 400th anniversary of Christopher Columbus' discovery of America, a widely circulated national magazine for youth proposed in 1892 that pupils recite the following affirmation: "I pledge allegiance to my Flag and the Republic for which it stands: one Nation indivisible, with Liberty and Justice for all." In the 1920's, the National Flag Conferences replaced the phrase "my Flag" with "the flag of the United States of America."

In 1942, in the midst of World War II, Congress adopted, and the President signed, a Joint Resolution codifying a detailed set of "rules and customs pertaining to the display and use of the flag of the United States of America." ... This resolution, which marked the first appearance of the Pledge of Allegiance in positive law, confirmed the importance of the flag as a symbol of our Nation's indivisibility and commitment to the concept of liberty.

Congress revisited the Pledge of Allegiance 12 years later when it amended the text to add the words "under God." The House Report that accompanied the [1954] legislation observed that, "[f]rom the time of our earliest history our peoples and our institutions have reflected the traditional concept that our Nation was founded on a fundamental belief in God." The resulting text is the Pledge as we know it today: "I pledge allegiance to the Flag of the United States of America, and to the Republic for which it stands, one Nation under God, indivisible, with liberty and justice for all."

II

Under California law, "every public elementary school" must begin each day with "appropriate patriotic exercises." The statute provides that "[t]he giving of the Pledge of Allegiance to the Flag of the United States of America shall satisfy" this requirement. The Elk Grove Unified School District has implemented the state law by requiring that "[e]ach elementary school class recite the pledge of allegiance to the flag once each day." Consistent with our case law, the School District permits students who object on religious grounds to abstain from the recitation.

In March 2000, Newdow filed suit in the United States District Court for the Eastern District of California against the United States Congress, the President of the United States, the State of California, and the Elk Grove Unified School District and its superintendent. At the time of filing, Newdow's daughter was enrolled in kindergarten in the Elk Grove Unified School District and participated in the daily recitation of the Pledge. Styled as a mandamus action, the complaint explains that Newdow is an atheist who was ordained more than 20 years ago in a ministry that "espouses the religious philosophy that the true and eternal bonds of righteousness and virtue stem from reason rather than mythology." The complaint seeks a declaration that the 1954 Act's addition of the words "under God" violated the Establishment and Free Exercise Clauses of the United States Constitution, as well as an injunction against the School District's policy requiring daily recitation of the Pledge. It alleges that Newdow has standing to sue on his own behalf and on behalf of his daughter as "next friend."

The case was referred to a Magistrate Judge, whose brief findings and recommendation concluded, "the Pledge does not violate the Establishment Clause." The District Court adopted that recommendation and dismissed the complaint on July 21, 2000. The Court of Appeals reversed and issued three separate decisions discussing the merits and Newdow's standing.

In its first opinion the appeals court unanimously held that Newdow has standing "as a parent to challenge a practice that interferes with his right to direct the religious education of his daughter." ... On the merits, over the dissent of one judge, the court held that both the 1954 Act and the School District's policy violate the Establishment Clause of the First Amendment.

After the Court of Appeals' initial opinion was announced, Sandra Banning, the mother of Newdow's daughter, filed a motion for leave to intervene, or alternatively to dismiss the complaint. She declared that although she and Newdow shared "physical custody" of their daughter, a state-court order granted her "exclusive legal custody" of the child, "including the sole right to represent [the daughter's] legal interests and make all decision[s] about her education" and welfare. Banning further stated that her daughter is a Christian who believes in God and has no objection either to reciting or hearing others recite the Pledge of Allegiance, or to its reference to God. Banning expressed the belief that her daughter would be harmed if the litigation were permitted to proceed, because others might incorrectly perceive the child as sharing her father's atheist views. Banning accordingly concluded, as her daughter's sole legal custodian, that it was not in the child's interest to be a party to Newdow's lawsuit. On September 25, 2002, the California Superior Court entered an order enjoining Newdow from including his daughter as an unnamed party or suing as her "next friend." That order did not purport to answer the question of Newdow's Article III standing.

In a second published opinion, the Court of Appeals reconsidered Newdow's standing.... The court noted that Newdow no longer claimed to represent his daughter, but unanimously concluded that "the grant of sole legal custody to Banning" did not deprive Newdow, "as a non-custodial parent, of Article III standing to object to unconstitutional government action affecting his child." The court held that under California law Newdow retains the right to expose his child to his particular religious views even if those views contradict the mother's, and that Banning's objections as sole legal custodian do not defeat Newdow's right to seek redress for an alleged injury to his own parental interests.

On February 28, 2003, the Court of Appeals issued an order amending its first opinion and denying rehearing en banc. The amended opinion omitted the initial opinion's discussion of Newdow's standing to challenge the 1954 Act and declined to determine whether Newdow was entitled to declaratory relief regarding the constitutionality of that Act. Nine judges dissented.... We granted the School District's petition for a writ of certiorari to consider two questions: (1) whether Newdow has standing as a non-custodial parent to challenge the School District's policy, and (2) if so, whether the policy offends the First Amendment.

III

In every federal case, the party bringing the suit must establish standing to prosecute the action. "In essence the question of standing is whether the litigant is entitled to have the court decide the merits of the dispute or of particular issues." The standing requirement is born partly of " 'an idea, which is more than an intuition but less than a rigorous and explicit theory, about the constitutional and prudential limits to the powers of an unelected, unrepresentative judiciary in our kind of government.' "

The command to guard jealously and exercise rarely our power to make constitutional pronouncements requires strictest adherence when matters of great national significance are at stake. Even in cases concededly within our jurisdiction under Article III, we abide by "a series of rules under which [we have] avoided passing upon a large part of all the constitutional questions pressed upon [us] for decision." Always we must balance "the heavy obligation to exercise jurisdiction," against the "deeply rooted" commitment "not to pass on questions of constitutionality" unless adjudication of the constitutional issue is necessary.

Consistent with these principles, our standing jurisprudence contains two strands: Article III standing, which enforces the Constitution's case or controversy requirement; and prudential standing, which embodies "judicially self-imposed limits on the exercise of federal jurisdiction." The Article III limitations are familiar: The plaintiff must show that the conduct of which he complains has caused him to suffer an "injury in fact" that a favorable judgment will redress. Although we have not exhaustively defined the prudential dimensions of the standing doctrine, we have explained that prudential standing encompasses "the general prohibition on a litigant's raising another person's legal rights, the rule barring adjudication of generalized grievances more appropriately addressed in the representative branches, and the requirement that a plaintiff's complaint fall within the zone of interests protected by the law invoked." . . .

One of the principal areas in which this Court has customarily declined to intervene is the realm of domestic relations. Long ago we observed that "[t]he whole subject of the domestic relations of husband and wife, parent and child, belongs to the laws of the States and not to the laws of the United States." So strong is our deference to state law in this area that we have recognized a "domestic relations exception" that "divests the federal courts of power to issue divorce, alimony, and child custody decrees." We have also acknowledged that it might be appropriate for the federal courts to decline to hear a case involving "elements of the domestic relationship," even when divorce, alimony, or child custody is not strictly at issue . . . Thus, while rare instances arise in which it is necessary to answer a substantial federal question that transcends or exists apart from the family law issue, in general it is appropriate for the federal courts to leave delicate issues of domestic relations to the state courts.

As explained briefly above, the extent of the standing problem raised by the domestic relations issues in this case was not apparent until August 5, 2002, when Banning filed her motion for leave to intervene or dismiss the complaint following the Court of Appeals' initial decision. At that time, the child's custody was governed by a February 6, 2002, order of the California Superior Court. That order provided that Banning had " 'sole legal custody as to the rights and responsibilities to make decisions relating to the health, education and welfare of' " her daughter. The order stated that the two parents should " 'consult with one another on substantial decisions relating to' " the child's " 'psychological and educational needs,' " but it authorized Banning to " 'exercise legal control' " if the parents could not reach " 'mutual agreement.' "

That family court order was the controlling document at the time of the Court of Appeals' standing decision. After the Court of Appeals ruled, however, the Superior Court held another conference regarding the child's custody. At a hearing on September 11, 2003, the Superior

Court announced that the parents have "joint legal custody," but that Banning "makes the final decisions if the two . . . disagree."

Newdow contends that despite Banning's final authority, he retains "an unrestricted right to inculcate in his daughter—free from governmental interference—the atheistic beliefs he finds persuasive." The difficulty with that argument is that Newdow's rights, as in many cases touching upon family relations, cannot be viewed in isolation. This case concerns not merely Newdow's interest in inculcating his child with his views on religion, but also the rights of the child's mother as a parent generally and under the Superior Court orders specifically. And most important, it implicates the interests of a young child who finds herself at the center of a highly public debate over her custody, the propriety of a widespread national ritual, and the meaning of our Constitution.

The interests of the affected persons in this case are in many respects antagonistic. Of course, legal disharmony in family relations is not uncommon, and in many instances that disharmony poses no bar to federal-court adjudication of proper federal questions. What makes this case different is that Newdow's standing derives entirely from his relationship with his daughter, but he lacks the right to litigate as her next friend. . . .

Newdow's parental status is defined by California's domestic relations law. Our custom on questions of state law ordinarily is to defer to the interpretation of the Court of Appeals for the Circuit in which the State is located. In this case, the Court of Appeals, which possesses greater familiarity with California law, concluded that state law vests in Newdow a cognizable right to influence his daughter's religious upbringing. The court based its ruling on two intermediate state appellate cases holding that "while the custodial parent undoubtedly has the right to make ultimate decisions concerning the child's religious upbringing, a court will not enjoin the non-custodial parent from discussing religion with the child or involving the child in his or her religious activities in the absence of a showing that the child will be thereby harmed." Animated by a conception of "family privacy" that includes "not simply a policy of minimum state intervention but also a presumption of parental autonomy," the state cases create a zone of private authority within which each parent, whether custodial or non-custodial, remains free to impart to the child his or her religious perspective.

Nothing that either Banning or the School Board has done, however, impairs Newdow's right to instruct his daughter in his religious views. Instead, Newdow . . . wishes to forestall his daughter's exposure to religious ideas that her mother, who wields a form of veto power, endorses, and to use his parental status to challenge the influences to which his daughter may be exposed in school when he and Banning disagree. The California cases simply do not stand for the proposition that Newdow has a right to dictate to others what they may and may not say to his child respecting religion. [The California cases] . . . are concerned with protecting " 'the fragile, complex interpersonal bonds between child and parent,' " and with permitting divorced parents to expose their children to the " 'diversity of religious experiences [that] is itself a sound stimulant for a child.' " The cases speak not at all to the problem of a parent seeking to reach outside the private parent-child sphere to restrain the acts of a third party. A next friend surely could exercise such a right, but the Superior Court's order has deprived Newdow of that status.

In our view, it is improper for the federal courts to entertain a claim by a plaintiff whose standing to sue is founded on family law rights that are in dispute when prosecution of the lawsuit may have an adverse effect on the person who is the source of the plaintiff's claimed standing. When hard questions of domestic relations are sure to affect the outcome, the prudent course is for the federal court to stay its hand rather than reach out to resolve a weighty question of federal constitutional law. There is a vast difference between Newdow's right to communicate with his child—which both California law and the First Amendment recognize—and his claimed right to shield his daughter from influences to which she is exposed in school despite the terms of the custody order. We conclude that, having been deprived under California law of the right to sue as next friend, Newdow lacks prudential standing to bring this suit in federal court.

The judgment of the Court of Appeals is reversed.

It is so ordered.

Notes

1. Justices Kennedy, Souter, Ginsburg, and Breyer joined Justice Stevens' opinion with regard to standing. Three members of the Court concurred separately. Chief Justice Rehnquist's concurrence was joined by Justice O'Connor and in part by Justice Thomas. Justice O'Connor and Justice Thomas wrote separate concurrences. All of these Justices would have granted the father standing and would have upheld the Pledge on its face. In light of critical comments that he made about this case as it was pending, Justice Scalia did not take part in its consideration or decision.

2. In limiting its decision to standing, the Court avoided the issue of whether the words "under God" are ceremonial (or civic) deism, representing the place that religion has played in American history or a form of impermissible establishment of religion. What do you think?

3. At the start of section III of its opinion, the Court reiterated the general rule that it would not address questions of constitutionality unless it is absolutely necessary to do so. Instead, the Court prefers to address statutory, or procedural, concerns if possible. What do you think about this approach?

Chapter 3

STATE–LEVEL ENTITIES

Introduction

Under the Tenth Amendment to the United States Constitution, education is a function of the state, rather than the federal, government. Thus, absent federal restrictions on their authority, state legislatures have plenary, or full, power over education subject only to the limits present in state constitutions, typically through their departments of education. As reflected in this chapter, courts typically uphold legislative control to distribute duties and responsibilities between and among state, intermediate, and local educational agencies. To the extent that their authority over public education is plenary, legislatures may change their state educational systems in any manner they deem necessary.

Establishment and Alteration of School Districts

In General

School districts and their governing bodies, typically called school boards, boards of education, or in a limited number of jurisdictions, school committees, are agencies of the state[1] that act independently of local governments and municipalities.[2] Local boards are thus "creatures of the state" that are designed by legislatures to carry out their state constitutional mandates to educate the children entrusted to their care.[3] As "creatures of the state" that "can only be formed, dissolved, or altered in accordance with ..."[4] state law, school boards have only the power and authority that they are granted by their state legislatures.[5]

Acting pursuant to their plenary power, state legislatures have the authority to set district boundaries,[6] abolish all local school units, and/or redistrict states regardless of pre-existing boundaries[7] by means of

---

1. *Department of Fin. v. Commission on State Mandates*, 134 Cal.Rptr.2d 237 [176 Educ. L. Rep. 894] (Cal. 2003).

2. *City of Manchester School Dist. v. City of Manchester*, 843 A.2d 966 [186 Educ. L. Rep. 449] (N.H. 2004).

3. *See, e.g., State ex rel. School Dist. of City of Independence v. Jones*, 653 S.W.2d 178 [12 Educ. L. Rep. 582] (Mo.1983); *Plum Borough School Dist. v. Schlegel*, 855 A.2d 939 [191 Educ. L. Rep. 416] (Pa. Commw. Ct. 2004).

4. *Pocantico Home & Land Co. v. Union Free School Dist. of Tarrytowns*, 799 N.Y.S.2d 235, 239 [200 Educ. L. Rep. 300]

(N.Y. App. Div. 2005), *appeal dismissed*, 806 N.Y.S.2d 167 (N.Y. 2005).

5. *See, e.g., National Educ. Ass'n-Wichita v. Unified School Dist. No. 259, Sedgwick County*, 674 P.2d 478 [15 Educ. L. Rep. 948] (Kan.1983); *Academy of Charter Schools v. Adams County School Dist. No. 12*, 32 P.3d 456 [157 Educ. L. Rep. 896] (Colo.2001), *reh'g denied*.

6. *See, e.g., Sherwood School Dist. 88J v. Washington County Educ. Serv. Dist.*, 6 P.3d 518 [146 Educ. L. Rep. 879] (Or.Ct. App.2000).

7. *Moore v. Board of Educ. of Iredell County*, 193 S.E. 732 (N.C.1937); *Opinion of*

157

detachment, annexation, dissolution, consolidation (sometimes also referred to as regionalization[8] or mergers[9]) or a combination of methods.[10] States can also set specific procedures that landowners must comply with when challenging reorganizations to combine school districts.[11] In addition, as illustrated by a case from the Supreme Court of South Dakota, when homeowners petition to move from one district to another, school officials are free to combine requests that cover essentially the same tract of land as long as their actions are not arbitrary and capricious.[12]

In a detachment and annexation case, the Supreme Court of Illinois followed the general rule in cautioning that such a petition should only be granted when there is an overall benefit to the annexing system and a detachment outweighs the detriment to the detaching district and its surrounding community.[13] More than a decade later, the same court permitted an annexation on the ground that there was no substantial detriment to either district and the educational benefit to the family involved would have been considerable since the mother taught in the annexing system and most of the friends of the children lived there.[14] Similarly, in deferring to the discretion of the state board of education, in one case the Supreme Court of North Dakota affirmed an annexation because the transfer of a smaller parcel of territory than was originally at issue would have had a less significant overall impact on the budgets of two local school boards.[15] In another case, the same court affirmed that economic factors may be valid considerations for a school board to take into account when reviewing petitions for minor boundary changes.[16]

An appellate court in California considered whether state law required a school board to admit children who lived on a property that was situated partly within its geographic boundaries. Where a family's property straddled the boundary line between two school systems, and only 26 percent was located in the receiving district, the court affirmed that the family's home was within that system, thereby rejecting the board's claim that "in" the district should have been interpreted as meaning

---

the Justices, 246 A.2d 90 (Del.1968); Rose v. Council for Better Educ., 790 S.W.2d 186 [60 Educ. L.Rep. 1289] (Ky.1989).

8. Board of Educ. of Borough of Englewood Cliffs v. Board of Educ. of Borough of Tenafly, 788 A.2d 729 [161 Educ. L. Rep. 542] (N.J.2002).

9. Kings Mountain Bd. of Educ. v. North Carolina State Bd. of Educ., 583 S.E.2d 629 [179 Educ. L. Rep. 499] (N.C. Ct. App. 2003), writ denied, review denied, 588 S.E.2d 476 (N.C. 2003).

10. Charleston School Dist. No. 9 v. Sebastian County Bd. of Educ., 778 S.W.2d 614 [56 Educ. L. Rep. 1340] (Ark.1989).

11. Nicholson v. Red Willow County School Dist. No. 0170, 699 N.W.2d 25 [199 Educ. L. Rep. 934] (Neb. 2005).

12. Pruchniak v. School Bd. of Elk Point–Jefferson School Dist. #61–7, 691 N.W.2d 298 [194 Educ. L. Rep. 946] (S.D. 2004).

13. Carver v. Bond/Fayette/Effingham Reg'l Bd. of School Trustees, 586 N.E.2d 1273 [72 Educ. L. Rep. 967] (Ill.1992).

14. Dukett v. Regional Bd. of School Trustees, 795 N.E.2d 945 [180 Educ. L. Rep. 859] (Ill. App. Ct. 2003).

15. New Town Public School Dist. No. 1 v. State Bd. of Pub. Educ., 650 N.W.2d 813 [169 Educ. L. Rep. 412] (N.D.2002). See also Johnson v. Lennox School Dist. No. 41–4, 649 N.W.2d 617 [168 Educ. L. Rep. 491] (S.D.2002).

16. Kirby v. Hoven School District No. 53–2, 686 N.W.2d 905 [192 Educ. L. Rep. 252] (S.D. 2004).

that the property was entirely within the boundaries of the receiving system.[17]

Unless required by a state constitution[18] or statute,[19] state and local officials do not need consent from district residents before redistricting. Indeed, even if residents vote against a boundary alteration, a legislature can still proceed with a consolidation.[20] A more recent dispute over the input of district residents involved the attempt of two towns to withdraw from regional school systems. When the towns sought to withdraw from their school administrative units after obtaining the required public input, the state commissioner of education refused to set a date for the municipal vote without revisions to the withdrawal agreement. Town officials unsuccessfully argued that since they only had to prepare a withdrawal agreement for voters, negotiations over remaining matters could follow, rather than precede, voter approval. In deferring to the authority of the commissioner, the Supreme Judicial Court of Maine declared that state officials did not have to set a date for the vote on the withdrawal agreement until town and district officials completed an acceptable withdrawal agreement.[21]

If a legislature authorizes a local board to petition for a boundary change, it may do so despite the wishes of local voters.[22] Even so, legislatures may not change boundaries in ways that would violate the Federal Constitution as, for example, when modifications deliberately impacted adversely on the racial balance of students,[23] impeded a remedy for de jure segregation,[24] or intentionally helped a religious group.[25] Where statutes provide for alterations of districts by means of elections, courts strictly enforce procedural matters before voters can go to the polls. Once elections are over, courts intervene only on showings of fraud or that alleged procedural violations prevented electors from giving full expression of their wills.[26]

The Supreme Court of Kansas, in a dispute over a school board's challenge to orders of the state superintendent of public instruction to transfer part of its territory to other districts, affirmed that even though a district is a legal body that may sue or be sued, it lacked the authority to file suit questioning the boundaries or the validity of the organization

---

17. *Katz v. Los Gatos–Saratoga Joint Union High School Dist.*, 11 Cal.Rptr.3d 546 [186 Educ. L. Rep. 916] (Cal. Ct. App. 2004).

18. *Fisher v. Fay*, 122 N.E. 811 (Ill. 1919).

19. *Petition of 2,952 Registered Voters of Wayne County, In Opposition to Reorganization of Wayne County School Dist.*, 574 So.2d 619 [65 Educ. L. Rep. 991] (Miss. 1990).

20. *Fruit v. Metropolitan School Dist. of Winchester*, 172 N.E.2d 864 (Ind.1961).

21. *Town of Eagle Lake v. Commissioner, Dept. of Educ.*, 818 A.2d 1034 [174 Educ. L. Rep. 1017] (Me. 2003).

22. *Kosmicki v. Kowalski*, 171 N.W.2d 172 (Neb.1969).

23. *Akron Bd. of Educ. v. State Bd. of Educ. of Ohio*, 490 F.2d 1285 (6th Cir. 1974).

24. *Wright v. Council of City of Emporia*, 407 U.S. 451, 92 S.Ct. 2196, 33 L.Ed.2d 51 (1972).

25. *Grumet v. Board of Educ. of Kiryas Joel Village School Dist.*, 601 N.Y.S.2d 61 [85 Educ. L. Rep. 209] (N.Y.1993).

26. *Eriksen v. Ray*, 321 N.W.2d 59 (Neb. 1982).

of another district.[27] The court explained that such a suit can be brought only in the state's name by duly authorized state officers. In like fashion, the Supreme Court of Minnesota affirmed that the state school boards association lacked standing to contest the constitutionality of a consolidation statute because its interests were those of its members who could not bring such a suit.[28] The Supreme Court of Nebraska also affirmed the dismissal of an action by local school board members who attempted to sue as individuals rather than members of a board in order to avoid precedent with regard to a transfer of parcels of property.[29] The court characterized the board's efforts as a facade.

To the extent that states create political subdivisions, such as municipal corporations[30] and school boards,[31] in order to better facilitate governmental action, these entities lack substantive rights under the Federal Constitution that they may invoke against their creators. Yet, a court may consider a challenge by a local board if there is a substantial allegation that a legislature used unconstitutional means to effect a boundary change.[32] Insofar as such an unusual claim would not be questioning the basic power of legislatures to create, alter, or abolish school districts courts could address the merits of the contention.

Charter Schools

In addition to creating school districts, state legislatures have the authority to fund innovative forms of schooling.[33] Accordingly, charter schools are discussed here, as an innovative approach that must be approved initially at the state level, rather than in Chapter 4 even though these schools and local boards interact significantly.

The charter school movement began in 1991 when Minnesota passed the first such statute.[34] To date, forty states plus the District of Columbia and Puerto Rico have enacted laws permitting the creation of charter schools.[35] Charter schools, which have survived challenges to their constitutionality,[36] are public schools of choice, meaning that parents can opt, but may not be required, to send their children to such schools.

---

27. *Unified School Dist. No. 335 v. State Bd. of Educ.*, 478 P.2d 201 (Kan.1970).

28. *Minnesota Ass'n of Pub. Schools v. Hanson*, 178 N.W.2d 846 (Minn.1970).

29. *In re Plummer Freeholder Petition*, 428 N.W.2d 163 [48 Educ. L. Rep. 973] (Neb.1988).

30. *Williams v. Mayor and City Council of Baltimore*, 289 U.S. 36, 53 S.Ct. 431, 77 L.Ed. 1015 (1933).

31. *Triplett v. Tiemann*, 302 F.Supp. 1239 (D.Neb.1969).

32. *Hall v. City of Taft*, 302 P.2d 574 (Cal.1956).

33. See *Moreau v. Avoyelles Parish School Bd.*, 897 So.2d 875 [197 Educ. L. Rep. 463] (La. Ct. App. 2005), *writs denied*, 904 So.2d 704, 705 (La. 2005) (declaring

that no statute requires local boards to fund charter schools since doing so is a responsibility of the state).

34. MINN. STAT. ANN. § 124D.10

35. http://www.uscharterschools.org (overview).

36. *See, e.g., Council of Organizations and Others for Educ. About Parochiaid v. Governor*, 566 N.W.2d 208 [120 Educ. L. Rep. 265] (Mich.1997); *In re Grant of Charter School Application of Englewood on Palisades Charter School*, 753 A.2d 687 [145 Educ. L. Rep. 431] (N.J.2000). *See also State ex rel. Ohio Congress of Parents and Teachers v. State Bd. of Educ.*, 822 N.E.2d 809 (Ohio 2005) (accepting a challenge to the constitutionality of Ohio's charter, or community, school program).

Charter schools, the number of which is typically specified or limited by state law,[37] operate under contracts, or charters, usually granted by local and/or state boards of education.[38] Applicants for charters may have limited rights of appeal if their applications are denied.[39]

Depending on state legislation, groups of parents or for-profit entities[40] may form charter schools anew or can convert them from existing public schools.[41] Either way, faculty and staff at charter schools are public employees who typically cannot be assigned to charter schools without their consent. In addition, faculty and staff at charter schools are ordinarily covered by operative collective bargaining agreements.

Prior to receiving charters, organizers must submit detailed plans about how schools will function.[42] In a manner similar to non-public schools, the goal of charter schools is to permit officials to operate schools free of many of the regulations that apply to traditional public schools. In this way, organizers and parents are free to develop the missions, programs, and goals of their schools, all of which are aimed at enhancing student achievement.

Litigation is beginning to emerge over the denial of applications to operate charter schools. Of course, if a local school board has the authority to approve or deny an application to form a charter school, it must do so in good faith. In such a case, an appellate court in Florida affirmed that where a local board denied an application based on unsupported assumptions about the quality of the education that it might have provided and its concerns about the applicants' lack of capital funding or use of operational dollars, the state board of education had the authority to overrule its action.[43] The court decided that in denying the charter application, the local board failed to act in good faith because it did not provide a legally sufficient reason for doing so. However, where a charter school applicant's proposal failed to comply with state law, the Supreme Court of Illinois refused to disturb an earlier judicial order rejecting it since the trial court's action was not clearly erroneous.[44]

---

37. *See, e.g., Taos Mun. Schools Charter School v. Davis,* 102 P.3d 102 [194 Educ. L. Rep. 415] (N.M. Ct. App. 2004), *cert. denied* (2004) (noting that according to state law, there can be no more than fifteen charter schools).

38. *See, e.g., Board of Educ. of School Dist. No. 1 in City and County of Denver v. Booth,* 984 P.2d 639 [137 Educ. L. Rep. 1109] (Colo.1999) (holding that the State Board of Education did not unconstitutionally infringe on a local school board's control of instruction in ordering approval of charter application).

39. *Berkley Elementary School Advisory Council v. School Bd. of Polk County,* 826 So.2d 364 [170 Educ. L. Rep. 405] (Fla.Dist.Ct.App.2002).

40. *West Chester Area School Dist. v. Collegium Charter School,* 812 A.2d 1172 [172 Educ. L. Rep. 855] (Pa. 2002).

41. *See, e.g.,* OHIO REV. CODE ANN. § 3314.02. In Ohio, charter schools are referred to as community schools.

42. *Shelby School v. Arizona State Bd. of Educ.,* 962 P.2d 230 [128 Educ. L. Rep. 1254] (Ariz.Ct.App.1998) (holding that organizers do not have a constitutional right to open charter schools).

43. *School Bd. of Osceola County v. UCP of Cent. Fla.,* 905 So.2d 909 [200 Educ. L. Rep. 421] (Fla. Dist. Ct. App. 2005), *review denied,* 914 So.2d 954 (Fla. 2005).

44. *Comprehensive Community Solutions v. Rockford School Dist. No. 205,* 837 N.E.2d 1 [203 Educ. L. Rep. 318] (Ill. 2005).

In the first of three other cases involving denials of charter applications, the Supreme Court of Wyoming addressed a dispute where the issue was whether the applicants sought to operate a school in violation of a provision in the statute that forbade charter schools from opening if their sole purpose was to avoid school closures or consolidations. In remanding, the court held that since the local board's initial denial was not supported by a finding that the applicants intended to avoid compliance with the statute, it had to act anew on the application.[45] Further, the Supreme Court of Oklahoma affirmed a grant of summary judgment in favor of a rejected applicant who sought to compel a local board to agree to binding arbitration pursuant to the state's Dispute Resolution Act.[46] The court ruled that the state statute was inapplicable since it did not authorize the school's organizers to compel the board to proceed to binding arbitration. Conversely, officials in Pennsylvania successfully challenged a local board's denial of their application to create a charter school.[47] An appellate court affirmed that local school board authorities failed to demonstrate that the organizers were unable to comply with state law in light of the fact that the charter school's officials created a proposed governance structure, identified the proposed location of the facility, provided a detailed curriculum and objectives, and submitted an adequate faculty and professional development plan.

Charter schools remain subject to federal and state anti-discrimination laws and must be open, without cost, to all children, including those with disabilities. In Pennsylvania, an appellate court rejected a local board's claim that a charter school that was designed for mentally gifted students impermissibly discriminated on intellectual ability.[48] The court affirmed not only that a charter school may limit admission by specialty areas but also that officials demonstrated sustainable parental support, the presence of an adequate financial plan, and appropriate physical facilities.

On the other hand, in New Jersey, a dispute arose when officials at two charter schools transferred students with special needs to private schools without consulting their local school boards and then sought reimbursement for their expenses. The federal trial court granted the charter schools' motion for summary judgment on the basis that the Individuals with Disabilities Education Act does not grant school boards a private right of action to dispute the placement of students from charter schools unless the parties first exhaust administrative remedies by means of a due process hearing.[49] In another case from New Jersey, an appellate court remanded a suit for a hearing over whether a charter school's practices, such as a lottery, a waiting list, a sibling preference

45. *Laramie County School Dist. No. 2 v. Albin Cats Charter School*, 109 P.3d 552 [196 Educ. L. Rep. 971] (Wyo. 2005).

46. *Pentagon Academy v. Independent School Dist. No. 1*, 82 P.3d 587 [184 Educ. L. Rep. 589] (Okla. 2003).

47. *Carbondale Area School Dist. v. Fell Charter School*, 829 A.2d 400 [179 Educ. L. Rep. 833] (Pa. Commw. Ct. 2003).

48. *Central Dauphin School Dist. v. Founding Coalition of Infinity Charter School*, 847 A.2d 195 [187 Educ. L. Rep. 665] (Pa. Commw. Ct. 2004), *appeal denied*, 860 A.2d 491 (Pa. 2004).

49. *Asbury Park Bd. of Educ. v. Hope Academy Charter School*, 278 F.Supp.2d 417 [181 Educ. L. Rep. 494] (D. N.J. 2003).

list, and its withdrawal policy, all of which were designed to increase its enrollments, exacerbated a local district's racial imbalance.[50]

Depending on state law, a local board may be required to provide transportation for children to and from their charter schools.[51] However, the Seventh Circuit affirmed that since students at an independent public charter school were not similarly situated to those who attended other schools within a local district, officials did not violate the rights of the children in the charter school to equal protection.[52] The court reasoned that since the charter school operated wholly independently of the board, it was more similar to an autonomous school district than an individual school, thereby permitting officials to exclude the students from their statutory busing duty.

In return for being exempted from many state regulations, charter schools are accountable for the academic achievement of their students. While charters vary in length, they typically range from three to five years.[53] When contracts expire, again depending on state law, the entities granting charters can renew or terminate agreements.

Delegation of Legislative Power

As noted, state legislatures can use their discretion to create or abolish school districts. Yet, since legislatures are seldom able to make the necessary state surveys to evaluate the most effective plan for forming districts, they ordinarily enact general legislation setting forth policies for creating districts and delegating authority to lower officials or bodies to execute their directives as long as they do not do so "understandingly or advantageously."[54] Thus, a county board of education may act as an agent of the legislature with power circumscribed by an enabling statute. Accordingly, interpretation of the statute under which the agency acts is a judicial question over whether an agency exceeds or misinterprets its authority.[55] Even so, courts typically do not consider whether an agency's action is in the best interests of an area since this is a legislative prerogative.[56] Delegation aside, legislatures cannot avoid their constitutional responsibilities by delegating their authority to local authorities. In such a case, the Supreme Court of California ordered state officials to prevent a local school board from ending its school year six weeks early because of financial difficulties on

50. *In re Red Bank Charter School*, 843 A.2d 365 [186 Educ. L. Rep. 405] (N.J. Super. Ct. App. Div. 2004), *certification denied*, 852 A.2d 193 (N.J. 2004).

51. *Moreau v. Avoyelles Parish School Bd.*, 897 So.2d 875 [197 Educ. L. Rep. 463] (La. Ct. App. 2005), *writs denied*, 904 So.2d 704, 705 (La. 2005); *Mosaica Acad. Charter School v. Commonwealth Dep't of Educ.*, 813 A.2d 813 (Pa.2002).

52. *Racine Charter One v. Racine Unified School Dist.*, 424 F.3d 677 [202 Educ. L. Rep. 40] (7th Cir. 2005).

53. *Missouri v. Williamson*, 141 S.W.3d 418 [191 Educ. L. Rep. 899] (Mo. Ct. App. 2004), *reh'g denied* (2004) (noting that a charter was good for five years as a matter of law and that officials were not entitled to judicial review of a school board's refusal to renew a charter).

54. *Hill v. Relyea*, 216 N.E.2d 795, 797 (Ill.1966).

55. *Brandon Valley Indep. School Dist. No. 150 v. Minnehaha County Bd. of Educ.*, 181 N.W.2d 96 (S.D.1970).

56. *Thorland v. Independent Consol. School Dist.*, 74 N.W.2d 410 (Minn.1956).

the basis that they had the duty of furthering the state's policy of insuring uniform education for all children.[57]

A fundamental principle of American government is the separation of powers between and among the executive, legislative, and judicial branches. Put another way, one branch of the government cannot encroach on the prerogatives of another. Insofar as each branch is charged with the specific powers, one may not divest itself of these or delegate them to any other branch of government. To this end, an unconstitutional delegation of power occurs "when the Legislature confers upon an administrative agency the unrestricted authority to make fundamental policy determinations."[58] This division of powers between and among the branches of state government does not present a question of federal constitutional law.[59]

The courts purportedly adhere to the principle of separation of powers, but differ by degree on how far legislatures can go in delegating authority to subordinate agencies or officials over the formation and alteration of districts. The basic inquiry is how much detail legislatures have placed in statutes guiding administrative actions.

State courts vary in the amount of attention to guidelines and standards that they require legislation to include in order for it to be upheld as a constitutional delegation of authority. In following the general rule, the Supreme Court of Pennsylvania advised its legislature to provide "adequate standards which will guide and restrain the exercise of the delegated administrative functions"[60] in reorganizing school districts. In like fashion, the Supreme Court of Kansas interpreted its state constitution as permitting the legislature to go so far as to authorize the state superintendent to establish unified school districts and disorganize others if either an election has been conducted approving such an establishment or local school boards petitioned for such an action.[61] Conversely, the Supreme Court of Illinois struck down a statute as an unconstitutional delegation of authority where the legislature left the formation of high school districts up to county superintendents without providing any guidelines for their formation and efficient operations on such matters as area, assessed valuation, number of students, and size.[62] The court found that the law was not uniformly applicable in similar situations and territories in the state because it was subject to different opinions of county superintendents and to variations within a county if a superintendent left office. More recently, another appellate court in Illinois upheld the state board of education's granting a waiver to Chicago's board of education with regard to the physical education requirement in the state curriculum in order to make room for increased

57. *Butt v. State*, 842 P.2d 1240 [79 Educ. L. Rep. 1039] (Cal.1992).

58. *Clean Air Constituency v. California State Air Resources Bd.*, 523 P.2d 617, 626 (Cal. 1974).

59. *Highland Farms Dairy v. Agnew*, 300 U.S. 608, 57 S.Ct. 549, 81 L.Ed. 835 (1937).

60. *Chartiers Valley Joint Schools v. County Bd. of School Directors*, 211 A.2d 487, 493 (Pa. 1965).

61. *Tecumseh School Dist. v. Throckmorton*, 403 P.2d 102 (Kan.1965).

62. *Kenyon v. Moore*, 122 N.E. 548 (Ill. 1919).

requirements in mathematics, science, and foreign languages. The court affirmed that the waiver was not an unconstitutional delegation of legislative authority since it simply excused the board from compliance with a portion of the law for a period of time.[63]

Uniformity does not necessarily mean sameness. Rather, uniformity means that the bases of classification should be clear and reasonable in relation to a statute's subject matter and purposes. In one case, the Supreme Court of Iowa addressed the constitutionality of a statute that provided for the reorganization of school districts based on whether there was a resident average daily attendance of at least 300. In upholding the classification, the court observed that if there were a reasonable ground for a classification and if it operated equally on all within the same class, it achieved constitutional uniformity.[64]

Impairment of Obligations of Contracts

The universally acknowledged legislative right to create, alter, or abolish districts is subject to the limitation that such an action must not conflict with Article I, Section 10, of the Federal Constitution, which provides that no state shall enact any law that impairs the obligation of contracts. At the same time, it must also be recalled that state subdivisions do not have any contracts between them and the legislature that can be impaired by boundary adjustments. The Supreme Court reiterated this point in a case involving school redistricting.[65] Insofar as the law passed muster under the state constitution, the Court was satisfied that it did not violate the Federal Constitution.

A second case from Michigan illustrates the way in which the Federal Constitution's bar against obligation of contract impairment can be raised.[66] A statute provided that where school district territory was annexed to another system, the remaining portion remained liable for bonds issued for lands and buildings located in the remaining portion. Due to a boundary change, the amount of property on which a tax could have been levied to meet bond obligations was lessened. The state supreme court struck the law down as an unconstitutional impairment on the obligations of a contract of the bondholders since it relieved a considerable part of the territory, which was in the district when the bonds were issued, from payment without making any provision for payment from any other source. Further, Maine's highest court vitiated a law that provided that towns detached from a school district which had outstanding bonds would be liable only if the reorganized district could not pay after a levy on all its assets.[67]

---

63. *Reece v. Board of Educ. of City of Chicago*, 767 N.E.2d 395 [166 Educ. L. Rep. 283] (Ill. App. Ct. 2002).

64. *Becker v. Board of Educ.*, 138 N.W.2d 909 (Iowa 1965).

65. *Attorney General of State of Mich. ex rel. Kies v. Lowrey*, 199 U.S. 233, 26 S.Ct. 27, 50 L.Ed. 167 (1905). [Case No. 16]

66. *Board of Educ. of City of Lincoln Park v. Board of Educ. of City of Detroit*, 222 N.W. 763 (Mich.1929).

67. *Canal Nat. Bank v. School Admin. Dist. No. 3*, 203 A.2d 734 (Me.1964).

Pre-existing Assets and Debts

When school districts are reorganized or dissolved, legislatures can distribute assets and liabilities in any manner that does not affect existing contracts. Absent statutory provisions for the disposition of property, most courts agree that property belongs to the district in which it is located once a change is made. In one such case, the Supreme Court of New Hampshire determined that the undisposed of property of the dissolved school district vested in the cooperative system that assumed the functions of the original board.[68] In so doing, the court rejected the argument of officials from the local town that the municipality should have been awarded the disputed property.

As discussed earlier, school property is not that of a school board in the sense that it may not be transferred to other districts by legislative or judicial action. Rather, any property belongs to the state that maintains it in trust for a board to use in providing education for the children who live within its boundaries. The fact that property is located in another district after a boundary change does not relieve the original system of its liability to pay for indebtedness incurred in connection with it since the original district remains an entity regardless of how its size may have changed.[69] This doctrine is based on the theory that no school board owns property in the true sense of the word by binding itself to pay for such property because it incurs liability for state, not local, purposes. Instead, district residents are legally bound to know that legislatures may change their school systems' boundaries and that school buildings or other facilities may be located in other systems.

The Supreme Court dismissed an appeal from the Supreme Court of Washington for want of a substantial federal question in a case over the constitutionality of a statute that transferred property financed by bonds issued by local school boards to the state board that dealt with community colleges.[70] In leaving the statute in place, the Court noted that the legislature expressly reaffirmed all contracts between local school boards and their bondholders.

Approaching the issue from another perspective, although legislatures may provide for the division of school board property and the apportionment of debts when a part of their territory and property are transferred to other districts, legislative failure to do so does not invalidate a reorganization statute. Absent such a provision, most courts follow the common law rule which leaves property where it is found and a debt on the original debtor.[71] As illustrated by a case from the Supreme Court of Illinois, this approach can create hardships.[72] The court was of

---

68. *In re Beauregard*, 859 A.2d 1153 [193 Educ. L. Rep. 266] (N.H. 2004).

69. *People ex rel. Raymond Community High School Dist. v. Bartlett*, 136 N.E. 654 (Ill.1922).

70. *Moses Lake School Dist. No. 161 v. Big Bend Community College*, 503 P.2d 86

(Wash. 1972), *appeal dismissed*, 412 U.S. 934, 93 S.Ct. 2776, 37 L.Ed.2d 393 (1973).

71. *Pass School Dist. v. Hollywood City School Dist.*, 105 P. 122 (Cal.1909).

72. *People ex rel. Raymond Community High School Dist. v. Bartlett*, 136 N.E. 654 (Ill.1922).

the opinion that a county clerk could not have been required to extend a tax for the payment of bonded indebtedness that was incurred before a district was divided against detached territory. Thus, the remaining board incurred a much larger tax burden than contemplated when the debts were incurred.

Most states have statutes that address financial difficulties that arise when changes are made in district boundaries as legislatures have attempted to provide for an equitable division of debts. Although these laws are frequently attacked on a variety of grounds, a case from the Supreme Court of Michigan reveals how such statutes are uniformly sustained.[73] The court maintained that a statute, which required a receiving district to pay the debts of the sending district in proportion to the value of the property detached, did not violate the constitutional inhibition against taking property without due process.

On the other hand, a state constitution may prohibit indebtedness from being imposed on a district absent a vote of electors. In such a case, a legislature may not require one board to pay any portion of bonded or other indebtedness of another system or part of a district attached to it.[74] If a portion of a district is detached, such a provision is not violated by the original district's being allocated a proportionate share of bond indebtedness that arose before detachment.[75]

Absent controlling constitutional provisions, legislatures have almost unlimited authority to provide for the payment of debts in old districts. Statutes typically provide that designated agencies such as county school boards must make equitable distributions of an old district's assets and debts. While the issue of what constitutes an equitable distribution is a question of fact, these statutes have survived constitutional challenges.[76] The Supreme Court of Wyoming rejected such a challenge to a state law that provided that in a reorganization of districts, a county committee had the power to allocate equitably the assets and debts affected by its plan. In brushing aside a claim that the statute violated a state constitutional provision that no new debts could be created without a vote of the people who were to be affected, the court upheld the law in agreeing that it concerned the division of existing debts rather than the creation of new ones.[77] The court interpreted the statute as meaning that there must be a bona fide allocation of debts to any area according to the benefits it received from additional assets accrued in the reorganization.

Various other aspects of the distribution of financial assets and liabilities have faced judicial scrutiny. For example, the Supreme Court of Missouri affirmed that the failure of state officials to consult with

73. *School Dist. No. 3 of Bloomfield Township v. School Dist. of City of Pontiac*, 246 N.W. 145 (Mich.1933).

74. *Protest of Missouri–Kansas–Texas Railroad Co.*, 73 P.2d 173 (Okla.1937).

75. *Fullerton Joint Union High School Dist. v. State Bd. of Educ.*, 654 P.2d 168 (Cal.1982).

76. *Rapp v. Bethel–Tate Consol. School Dist.*, 16 N.E.2d 224 (Ohio App.1937).

77. *Lund v. Schrader*, 492 P.2d 202 (Wyo.1971).

voters in a district that had a surplus in its treasury before it was consolidated did not violate the state or federal constitutions.[78] In addition, the Supreme Court of Ohio upheld an arrangement whereby taxpayers of a receiving district in a consolidation plan were taxed on their property for payment of the indebtedness of the old school system.[79]

Exercise of Discretion

The agency designated to pass on the alteration or consolidation of districts must exercise discretion that is neither arbitrary nor unreasonable. In such a situation, the Supreme Court of South Dakota reviewed the refusal of a legislatively designated committee to allow property owners to have their land detached from an independent district and added to a common school district.[80] The plaintiffs alleged that the taxes in the independent district were so great that they had difficulty paying them. In considering the adverse effects that this change would have had on the independent district, the court pointed out that the property needed to remain in the independent district as a source of revenue, thereby justifying the committee's refusal to detach the property. The same court later recognized that taxpayers could seek judicial review of an order of the state agency that had the power to alter school district boundaries.[81] The court asserted that since the committee exceeded its statutory authority, the territorial change it ordered had to be annulled.

Judicial authority to invalidate administrative acts that are arbitrary or unreasonable does not include the power to direct specific courses of action. The Supreme Court of Minnesota thus affirmed the annulment of the chief state school officer's rejection of an application to consolidate school districts.[82] The court also affirmed that the trial court lacked the authority to approve the proposed consolidation plan.

Legislatures must designate bodies to examine district boundaries and cannot leave the matter completely to the desires of individual residents. In such a case, the Supreme Court of Kansas decreed that the state statute, which permitted landowners to exclude their property from a school district by exercising their own will, was unconstitutional as an impermissible delegation of legislative power.[83] However, in concluding that "all things being equal," the desires of the residents may be considered, an appellate court in Illinois was of the view that petitions may be given weight as long as officials comply with statutory and constitutional safeguards.[84]

78. *State ex rel. Bilby v. Brooks*, 249 S.W. 73 (Mo.1923).

79. *Rapp v. Bethel–Tate Consol. School Dist.*, 16 N.E.2d 224 (Ohio Ct. App.1937).

80. *Snow v. South Shore Indep. School Dist.*, 283 N.W. 530 (S.D.1939).

81. *Elk Point Indep. School Dist. No. 3 v. State Comm'n on Elementary and Secondary Educ.*, 187 N.W.2d 666 (S.D.1971).

82. *Granada Indep. School Dist. No. 455 v. Mattheis*, 170 N.W.2d 88 (Minn. 1969).

83. *State ex rel. Jackson v. School Dist. No. 2*, 34 P.2d 102 (Kan.1934).

84. *Burnidge v. County Bd. of School Trustees of Kane County*, 167 N.E.2d 21 (Ill. App. Ct. 1960).

The Supreme Court of Nebraska invalidated a statute, which conferred the authority to change district boundaries without notice or opportunity for hearing, from property owners to county superintendents of schools, clerks, and boards of education. The court posited that this arrangement violated the Fourteenth Amendment's Due Process Clause.[85] While some statutes mandate hearings before districts can be altered, decision-making agencies are not bound to follow the results of these hearings. In these situations, courts typically examine the results of hearings to assure that basic facts were presented and that viewpoints were not suppressed.

Even though courts may be inclined to overlook procedural irregularities in reorganization proceedings, a case from the Supreme Court of Illinois demonstrates that proposals must be presented adequately.[86] State law dictated that prior to a hearing on a proposed reorganization, a map depicting the districts involved had to be submitted to a county board along with information on the probable effects of the changes. The court invalidated a proceeding at which a board secretary's map consisted merely of a drawing of rectangles while his financial report only showed assessed valuations, amounts levied and expended, and the amount of state aid claims. In invalidating the proposed plan as inadequate, the court indicated that the secretary did not offer information on tax rates or indebtedness, that there was no testimony to supplement the scanty information in his report, and that there was unsatisfactory testimony on educational conditions in one of the districts.

Where the state legislature enacted a scheme for the decentralization of the New York City public school system, it established general criteria including one that each subdistrict should have 20,000 students. When the city board of education issued a tentative decentralization plan for Manhattan that contained six districts, some of them had far less than the statutorily prescribed number of students. Following the prescribed hearing on the plan, the board developed a scheme to have five districts in Manhattan. On further review of a challenge to the plan, the state's highest court vitiated it as substantially different from the one on which the hearing was conducted and ordered further hearings.[87] The court added that the districts proposed at the hearing did not meet the legislative mandate for the number of students.

According to the Supreme Court of Iowa, even where a proposed merger of districts met statutory requirements, the state education agency was not obligated to grant its approval.[88] The court affirmed that the agency could reject the proposed merger if its action was supported by legally sufficient reasons.

85. *Ruwe v. School Dist. No. 85 of Dodge County,* 234 N.W. 789 (Neb.1931).

86. *Crainville School Dist. v. County Bd. of School Trustees,* 177 N.E.2d 248 (Ill. App. Ct. 1961).

87. *Tinsley v. Monserrat,* 308 N.Y.S.2d 843 (N.Y.1970).

88. *Armstrong-Ringsted Community School Dist. v. Lakeland Area Educ. Agency,* 597 N.W.2d 776 [136 Educ. L. Rep. 1048] (Iowa 1999).

Powers of a State Education Agency

In General

Each state has a central education agency, the limits and authority of which are delineated in its constitutions and statutes. Other than Minnesota and Wisconsin,[89] all jurisdictions have state boards of education which have general authority over public schools. Each state has a chief state school officer, usually called the state superintendent of schools or state commissioner of education, who has authority to implement the board's directives.[90] State agencies also have staff members who actually perform these functions. In general, state boards are charged with policy making one level below the legislature, the execution of which is under the direction of the chief state school officer.[91] In most states, intermediate educational agencies, typically at the county level, operate between state and local boards. While the duties and powers of intermediate units vary widely, they are generally assigned specific responsibilities for operation within their geographical boundaries.

The most common methods of selecting members of state boards of education are appointments by the governor and popular elections. At least one state, Ohio, applies a hybrid approach as it has eleven elected and eight appointed (by the governor) members.[92] A few state board members get their posts ex officio by being placed on them because they have been elected to some other post in the state government.[93] The method of selecting members of state boards of education generally is not critical in relation to their legal powers.

Chief state school officers are typically appointed by state boards of education, popularly elected, or appointed by governors. Where chief state school officers are elected, statutes, or occasionally constitutional provisions, usually assign specified powers to that office. Problems arise in the general area of responsibility and authority when chief administrators are selected by voters rather than by state boards of education or governors.

Where the state constitution authorized the legislature to provide for the election of a state superintendent of public instruction, it enacted a law directing the state board to elect this official to serve both as its head and as chief executive of the state department of education. When challenged, the Supreme Court of Oregon invalidated the law as unconstitutional.[94] The court rejected the argument that the state board's having selected a professional was a more desirable method of identifying the superintendent than a popular election. The court interpreted the constitutional provision calling for an election to mean one by state voters rather than the state board. The court thought that while the

---

89. http://www.nasbe.org/Organization _Information/Association.html.

90. *Bailey v. Truby,* 321 S.E.2d 302 [20 Educ. L. Rep. 980] (W.Va.1984); *Abbott by Abbott v. Burke,* 575 A.2d 359 [60 Educ. L. Rep. 1175] (N.J.1990).

91. *See, e.g., New Haven v. State Bd. of Educ.,* 638 A.2d 589 [90 Educ. L. Rep. 236] (Conn. 1994).

92. Ohio Rev. Code Ann. §§ 3301.01–02.

93. Again, in Ohio, as an illustration, the Chair of the state Senate and House Committees dealing primarily with education are non-voting ex officio members of the state board.

94. *State ex rel. Musa v. Minear,* 401 P.2d 36 (Or.1965).

statute providing for election of superintendent by the state board was unconstitutional, the present superintendent, who was in office prior to being appointed by the governor, did not have to vacate the office.

In a second case from Oregon, a dispute arose about the powers of the state superintendent in relation to those of the state board of education over a rule on the minimum standard for average class load per teacher. While the state board wished to raise the class load per teacher, the superintendent contended that since his office was mentioned in the constitution, the legislature could delegate this authority only to him and not to the appointed board. The Supreme Court of Oregon disagreed, contending that since the constitutional creation of the title of superintendent of public instruction was neither a limitation nor a prohibition on the legislative power to create the board, it had the authority to adopt and enforce rules as it saw fit.[95]

The Constitution of Idaho directs the legislature to create a state board of education with general supervisory power over the state's public schools. In the face of a challenge, the state supreme court struck down an act that would have divided jurisdiction among three bodies: a council governing higher education, a council governing public schools, and a board comprised of both councils to oversee public educational endeavors not falling directly under either of the councils.[96] The court wrote that since the state constitution plainly required a single board, the legislature and governor were powerless to change that basic structure. Similarly, the Supreme Court of Wyoming specified that where a statute empowered the state board to adopt rules and exceptions governing the certification of teachers and administrators, it, rather than the chief state school officer, had final say in a disagreement over the rules.[97] Further, the Supreme Court of New Jersey emphasized that the commissioner and the state board did not share equal status as administrative decision-makers since the latter had ultimate authority in this area.[98]

Conflicts frequently develop due to a lack of clarity or specificity in constitutional or statutory language. In such a case, the Third Circuit affirmed that the power to formulate a school calendar resided in a territorial board of education rather than the department of education even though the latter was designated as the collective bargaining agent for the territory.[99] The court relied on the board's more expansive general powers in resolving the matter while suggesting that a legislative response would have been desirable.

Delegation of Legislative Power to the State Education Agency

The general principle of separation of powers is frequently invoked in challenges to rules and regulations of state agencies and officials. As

---

95. *State Bd. of Educ. v. Fasold*, 445 P.2d 489 (Or.1968).

96. *Evans v. Andrus*, 855 P.2d 467 [84 Educ. L. Rep. 522] (Idaho 1993).

97. *Wyoming State Dep't of Educ. v. Barber*, 649 P.2d 681 [5 Educ. L. Rep. 1272] (Wyo.1982).

98. *Probst v. Board of Educ. of Borough of Haddonfield, Camden County*, 606 A.2d 345 [74 Educ. L. Rep. 137] (N.J.1992).

99. *Virgin Islands Joint Bd. of Educ. v. Farrelly*, 984 F.2d 97 (3d Cir.1993).

long as legislatures provide reasonably adequate standards governing such delegations, the courts are generally content not to interfere.[100] In such a case, the Court of Appeals of Maryland upheld a contract that the state board of education entered into with a private company to operate schools that failed to meet student performance standards.[101] The court explained that in light of the concept of legislative ratification, which permits a governmental entity to engage in an action that it may not be expressly authorized to perform, the legislators ratified the board's action in agreeing that a private company can be the employer of a teacher in a failing school.

On the other hand, where a legislative power cannot be delegated, the issue of an administrative regulation's reasonableness is usually not addressed. The Supreme Court of Nebraska considered the principle of separation of powers in a dispute over a statute that expressly granted the state superintendent the authority to formulate rules and regulations for high schools to collect free high school tuition money.[102] The court struck the statute down as an unconstitutional delegation of authority in violation of the principle of separation of powers since the legislature failed to provide the superintendent with a sufficiently definite policy framework within which to act.

At the same time, the courts recognize that the increasing complexity of schools requires that guidelines not be too specific. Insofar as the separation of powers doctrine was not intended to confine legislatures to the alternatives of virtual inaction or the imposition of rigidly inflexible laws that would have distorted rather than promoted their objectives, broad guidelines consistent with legislative plans generally meet constitutional standards.[103] Yet, laws delegating power must not be so vague that their operational meaning is almost totally dependent on the subjective discretion of administrative boards or officers. In an illustrative case, the Supreme Court of Connecticut affirmed the invalidity of granting local boards the power to expel students for conduct that was inimical to the best interests of schools.[104]

The issue of delegation of authority to a state superintendent of education developed in an unusual way in Illinois at the time when it did not have a state board. Where the state superintendent of public instruction followed legislative directives in preparing regulations specifying minimum requirements for the health and safety of students, including school construction, a local board contested the necessity of complying with them. The local board alleged that the directives amounted to an unconstitutional delegation of legislative power. Acknowledging that judicial yardsticks measuring the delegation of powers must vary according to the nature of a given issue, the state's highest court generally

100. *Ward v. Scott*, 93 A.2d 385 (N.J. 1952).

101. *Baltimore Teachers Union v. Maryland State Bd. of Educ.*, 840 A.2d 728 [184 Educ. L. Rep. 910] (Md. 2004). [Case No. 17]

102. *School Dist. No. 39 of Washington County v. Decker*, 68 N.W.2d 354 (Neb. 1955). [Case No. 18]

103. *Schreiber v. County Bd. of School Trustees*, 198 N.E.2d 848 (Ill.1964).

104. *Mitchell v. King*, 363 A.2d 68 (Conn.1975).

upheld the legislature's ability to delegate authority to the superintendent.[105] The court also examined the limits set by the superintendent, declaring that he exceeded the legislative intent to establish minimum standards. In conceding that the legislature had not given the superintendent unfettered power to set his own standards of excellence, the court decided that the ones he created were invalid because they were considerably more stringent than other well-recognized norms for school construction.

Ramifications of the delegation of authority to a state board of education constitute less of a problem than to a state superintendent of education. In Ohio, for example, a local board that was warned that a high school failed to meet several minimum standards challenged the state board's authority to revoke the school's charter. An appellate court, although stating that its sympathies were with the local board, believed that the state board had the power to enforce the law requiring high schools to meet minimum state requirements.[106] The court rejected the local board's raising the issue of the improper delegation of authority on the basis that it was not the "real question" because the legislature had almost unlimited power which it could delegate to any agency it created as long as it retained the ability to withdraw that power.

The issue of whether the state legislature delegated authority to its state board of education arose in a suit in connection with rules promulgated to enforce, ultimately through fund cut-offs, a statute requiring boards to eliminate de facto segregation in local districts. The Supreme Court of Illinois held that the rules exceeded the authority of state education officials since a statute specifically treating the matter placed responsibility in the hands of local boards and directed the state attorney general to provide for their enforcement.[107] The court remarked that the legislative provision empowering the state board to promulgate rules for establishing and maintaining free schools was limited by the specific legislation pertaining to de facto segregation and means to correct the problem. Shortly thereafter, another dispute arose in Illinois over the state board's ability to withhold funds for a program for gifted students due to alleged racial segregation in a district. The state's highest court ascertained that the state board lacked the authority to withhold funds and that no federal law gave it the power to do so.[108]

A dispute in North Carolina involved a charge that the state board of education exercised powers regarding teacher certification without legislative standards or guidelines. In rejecting this claim, the state's highest court noted that the state constitution conferred this power on

105. *Board of Educ. of City of Rockford v. Page*, 211 N.E.2d 361 (Ill.1965).

106. *Board of Educ. of Aberdeen–Huntington Local School Dist. v. State Bd. of Educ.*, 189 N.E.2d 81 (Ohio Ct. App.1962).

107. *Aurora East Pub. School Dist. No. 131 v. Cronin*, 442 N.E.2d 511 [8 Educ. L. Rep. 85] (Ill.1982).

108. *Board of Educ. of City of Peoria, School Dist. No. 150 v. Sanders*, 502 N.E.2d 730 [36 Educ. L. Rep. 835] (Ill.Ct.App. 1986), *appeal denied*, 508 N.E.2d 208 [39 Educ. L. Rep. 1183] (Ill.1987), *cert. denied*, 484 U.S. 926, 108 S.Ct. 290, 98 L.Ed.2d 250 [42 Educ. L. Rep. 1060] (1987).

the state board subject to legislative limitation and revision.[109] The court was thus convinced that since the legislature had not acted, the board retained the broad power to regulate teacher qualifications. In addition, the court commented that delegation of powers comes into play in relation to legislative, not constitutional, powers. The same court later heard a case involving the effect of legislation on a state board rule that sought to prevent local boards from contracting with a private company to provide daily twelve-minute television news programs containing two minutes of commercial advertising. The state board long had the statutory power to adopt textbooks while other laws directed local boards to adopt written procedures used in selecting supplementary materials that were consistent with the textbooks. Shortly after the state board enacted the new rule, the legislature amended the supplementary materials statute to give local boards complete control over these matters. In concluding that the legislature abrogated the rule of the state board, the court observed that since public policy was in the province of the legislature, it did not violate the constitutional rights of students or any one else.[110]

As illustrated by a case from Iowa, the separation principle is not restricted to the powers of agencies exercising state-wide authority. Where state law gave county boards the ability to fix the boundaries of reorganized school districts, the state's highest court rejected the charge that the legislature reposed absolute, unregulated, and undefined discretionary powers of a legislative nature in the county boards.[111] In the opinion of the court, the fact that standards for the action of county boards were statutorily prescribed, namely that educational conditions in the areas should be studied and that hearings were to be conducted on petitions for district reorganization, was a sufficient statement of the legislative policy under which the boards were authorized to act. The court emphasized that life has become so complex that for the legislature to enact laws in detail covering many governmental services would not only have been impractical, but impossible. As such, the court ruled that many matters must be left to administrative agencies.

Legislatures may confer powers of local regulation on municipal corporations without violating the separation-of-powers principle. Under this theory, since local boards are recognized as quasi-municipal corporations, state officials may properly grant them the powers of local self-governance.[112] Even so, a delegated power must not conflict with overarching state legislation. In such a case, an appellate court in California invalidated a provision in the city charter of San Francisco relating to tenure for school administrators and supervisors because it conflicted with state statutes.[113] The court observed that the fact that the charter was enacted prior to the conflicting statutes was of no consequence.

109. *Guthrie v. Taylor*, 185 S.E.2d 193 (N.C.1971).

110. *State v. Whittle Communications*, 402 S.E.2d 556 [66 Educ. L. Rep. 1299] (N.C.1991), *reh'g denied*, 404 S.E.2d 878 (N.C.1991).

111. *Wall v. County Bd. of Educ.*, 86 N.W.2d 231 (Iowa 1957).

112. *American Fed'n of Teachers v. Yakima School Dist. No. 7*, 447 P.2d 593 (Wash.1968).

113. *Whisman v. San Francisco Unified School Dist.*, 150 Cal.Rptr. 548 (Cal.Ct.App. 1978).

The different legal effects of a legislature's enacting a policy and a state board's doing so under legislatively delegated powers is well illustrated in connection with modifying teacher certification requirements. It is well settled that individuals who possess certificates do not have contracts and that requirements for retention or renewal are subject to change. When the state board of education attempted to reduce the length of existing five-year certificates, the Supreme Court of Rhode Island enjoined it from doing so.[114] The court distinguished the case at bar from one resolved a short while earlier in Connecticut[115] since the source of the changes was the state board rather than the legislature.

Administrative Powers

The generality of many statutes related to the powers of state education agencies has given rise to a great deal of litigation over the extent of their authority. Statutes commonly provide that state superintendents, state boards, or both have general supervision and control over state school systems. Whether a general statute confers a specific power is subject to judicial review. Additionally, although state educational officials can enact reasonable rules directing the operation of public schools, whether a specific rule or action is reasonable is subject to judicial review.[116]

A case from the Supreme Court of Illinois reflects the general rule with regard to the administrative authority of state educational officials. A statute gave the chief state school official the authority to act as the legal adviser of all school officers with the ability to offer his opinion on any question arising under the state's school laws. The court was satisfied that the law neither encroached on the judiciary's power to regulate the practice of law nor removed the common law powers of the attorney general which did not extend beyond acting as adviser to executive officers, boards, and departments of the state government.[117]

The Court of Appeals of New York upheld the state commissioner of education's invalidating a local school board regulation on the ground that it was unsound educational policy.[118] The provision required teachers who had been members of the Communist Party to identify colleagues whom they knew were party members in order to show that they withdrew from it in good faith. The court agreed that since such a regulation would have been upsetting to school systems, the commissioner's action was reasonable.

Maryland's highest court considered the extent of a general grant of power when a local school board passed a resolution requiring that

114.　*Reback v. Rhode Island Bd. of Regents for Elementary and Secondary Educ.*, 560 A.2d 357 [54 Educ. L. Rep. 1213] (R.I. 1989).

115.　*Connecticut Educ. Ass'n v. Tirozzi*, 554 A.2d 1065 [52 Educ. L. Rep. 604] (Conn.1989).

116.　*Board of Educ. of Plainfield v. Cooperman*, 523 A.2d 655 [38 Educ. L. Rep. 607] (N.J. 1987).

117.　*Board of Educ., School Dist. No. 142, Cook County v. Bakalis*, 299 N.E.2d 737 (Ill.1973).

118.　*Board of Educ. of City of N.Y. v. Allen*, 188 N.Y.S.2d 515 (N.Y.1959).

fingerprint cards of its employees be sent to the local police for review.[119] In upholding the state board's power in the face of a challenge by a local board, the court relied on the general statutes that gave the former control and supervision on the basis that this mandate afforded it the final word on matters concerning educational policy or administration. The court maintained that since screening employees was an administrative concern, it lay within the power of the state board.[120] Subsequently, in a suit over a busing contract, the same court affirmed that the state board has the authority to set educational policies for public schools and to adopt by-laws by which its dictates are carried out.[121]

The Supreme Court of Washington examined a dispute over whether the state board of education could deny accreditation to a proposed high school even though the local board responsible for its operation met all of the state's requirements. In upholding the state board's denial of accreditation in part because there was no need for the school since adequate facilities existed in a neighboring district, the court asserted that the legislature did not intend for accreditation to be granted automatically to every school that met the state board's minimum standards.[122] Put another way, the court reasoned that accreditation was not a purely ministerial duty. Later, when the board applied essentially the same rationale in denying accreditation to another new school, a different local board claimed that it did not properly consider a report and recommendations from the state superintendent.[123] The court disagreed with the local board, arguing that the recommendations were advisory only and that a review of the board's minutes revealed that it did not ignore the report which contained caveats along with serious, unanswered questions about fiscal responsibility. In noting that accreditation was a qualification for participation in activities receiving state funds in addition to a recognition of academic proficiency, the court emphasized that the state board exercised its fiscal and academic responsibility.

In a case from New York, a state law provided that funds for construction of school buildings would not be paid to any board that was scheduled for reorganization unless the commissioner of education certified that an allocation would not have impeded reorganization. When voters in two districts which were to be merged under a state master plan rejected the proposal by decisive margins, one of the boards unsuccessfully applied for a certificate of non-impedance and for an apportionment of state aid for the construction of a new music room. In its suit against the commissioner, an appellate court rejected the local board's claim that the funds could have been used after the commissioner

119. *Wilson v. Board of Educ. of Montgomery County*, 200 A.2d 67 (Md.1964).

120. For a similar result, *see Henry v. Earhart*, 553 A.2d 124 [51 Educ. L. Rep. 959] (R.I.1989).

121. *Chesapeake Charter v. Anne Arundel County Bd. of Educ.*, 747 A.2d 625 [142 Educ. L. Rep. 994] (Md.2000).

122. *State ex rel. DuPont–Fort Lewis School Dist. No. 7 v. Bruno*, 384 P.2d 608 (Wash.1963).

123. *DuPont–Fort Lewis School Dist. No. 7 v. Bruno*, 489 P.2d 171 (Wash.1971).

approved the reorganization.[124] Instead, the court was persuaded that the issue was whether the use of state funds to improve existing facilities that were slated to become part of a reorganized district would have impeded reorganization. The court upheld the statute, which left the decision on whether such aid would impede reorganization to the discretion of the commissioner, on the ground that this was a valid delegation of authority and that he had not abused his discretion.

Where a statute provided for a state subsidy to school boards for capital outlays, one purchased land to develop into an athletic facility. When the commissioner of education refused to grant the aid on the ground that the project was not covered by the statute, it filed suit. In directing the commissioner to fund the project, the Supreme Judicial Court of Maine posited that since the law invited a broad interpretation, it would exercise the traditional liberal policy of an expansive interpretation of the concept of educational purposes and needs.[125]

In a case where the state constitution granted general supervisory powers over education to the state board, the Supreme Court of Kansas found that this provision empowered it to require local boards to adopt policies, which were to be reviewed by a local attorney and filed with it, regulating student and employee conduct.[126] Conversely, as to a school district organization, the same court decreed that the state board's failure to follow legislative guidelines meant that its action was arbitrary as a matter of law.[127]

Interpreting provisions in its constitution as they related to powers of the boards of the commonwealth and local school systems, the Supreme Court of Virginia pointed out that the former lacked the authority to require the latter to submit disputes between themselves and non-supervisory employees to binding arbitration.[128] The court distinguished the power of general supervision vested in the state board from the supervision of schools vested in local boards. The court determined that giving the commonwealth's board the authority it claimed would have rendered the constitutional grant of power to local boards for supervision of schools meaningless.

The Supreme Court of Pennsylvania upheld the right of the commonwealth's board of education to promulgate mandatory system-wide regulations covering a wide range of aspects of student discipline.[129] In rejecting a claim that the board exceeded its power, the court thought that the legislature's granting the board the authority to make regulations carrying out its duties was an essential element of the educational process included in its mandate to set standards governing school programs.

---

124. *Siegel v. Allen*, 255 N.Y.S.2d 336 (N.Y.App.Div.1965).

125. *City of Westbrook v. Logan*, 227 A.2d 793 (Me.1967).

126. *State ex rel. Miller v. Board of Educ. of Unified School Dist. No. 398, Marion County (Peabody)*, 511 P.2d 705 (Kan. 1973).

127. *State ex rel. Dix v. Board of Educ.*, 578 P.2d 692 (Kan.1978).

128. *School Bd. of City of Richmond v. Parham*, 243 S.E.2d 468 (Va.1978).

129. *Girard School Dist. v. Pittenger*, 392 A.2d 261 (Pa.1978).

If legislation is specific, a state board is not empowered to deviate from its prescriptions. Thus, where a state statute provided for a minimum of 175 days each school year, the Supreme Court of Wyoming indicated that the state board lacked the authority to approve an experimental four-day week for a local district that would have resulted in a 144 day school year.[130] The court added that the alternative schedule, which had been in operation for about seven months, may have jeopardized state-aid entitlements since the number of days required was fixed.

Where state educational officials adopted policies to promote better racial balances in schools, the courts have sustained their actions. New York went further than perhaps any other state in this regard in establishing a system-wide policy to eliminate de facto segregation. The policy's rationale was that de facto segregation resulted in a poorer quality of education than in places where the races are better balanced. A formidable number of cases arose wherein citizens or local boards challenged aspects of state implementation of this policy. In one dispute, the Court of Appeals of New York upheld the commissioner of education's order directing a local board to implement a specific plan to effectuate a better racial balance.[131] The court judged that since the legislature made the commissioner the head of the state system of education and the final authority on questions of its administration, the judiciary would not interfere except in cases of pure arbitrariness. The court stated that since the commissioner's action rested squarely on his finding of educational inadequacy in de facto segregated schools, and he had the authority to substitute his judgment for that of local school boards, it lacked the ability to overturn his determination.

The increasing complexity of legal matters in education has prompted courts to construe broadly the powers of state administrative officers. The Supreme Court of New Jersey, for example, held that since the powers of its state commissioner of education are more extensive than in other states, he or she may have to act on matters that some commissioners apparently preferred not to consider on their own initiatives. The court explained that the commissioner was responsible for making an independent judgment over the non-retention of an administrator, not merely considering whether a local school board's actions were arbitrary, capricious, or the result of prejudice.[132] The court was of the view that its order did not interfere with the commissioner's policy of allowing local boards to select their own solutions in the first instance but that on appeal, he would have had to substitute his judgment in certain circumstances rather than simply disapprove a local board's action and remand the matter for further action. The court reaffirmed, extending this notion in a case involving de facto segregation, expressly directing the

130. *Johnston v. Board of Trustees, School Dist. No. 1 West, Sheridan County,* 661 P.2d 1045 [10 Educ. L. Rep. 832] (Wyo. 1983).

131. *Vetere v. Allen,* 258 N.Y.S.2d 77 (N.Y.1965).

132. *In re Masiello,* 138 A.2d 393 (N.J. 1958).

commissioner to take whatever steps appeared appropriate to correct a problem that a local board was not alleviating.[133]

In another case involving racial balances in New Jersey, at issue was the commissioner's quasi-judicial finding that the proposed establishment of a new high school in a virtually all-white community, which had been sending its students to a school in a district with a mixed racial population, would have resulted in an increased racial imbalance in the one school and the creation of a virtually all-white school in the neighboring community.[134] The one district completely encircled the other, and the two were closely interrelated by commercial and transportation patterns since there was considerable interdependency in municipal public services. Although the commissioner wrote that he lacked the authority to intervene, the Supreme Court of New Jersey adopted a contrary view. Citing the previous cases, the court contended that since the legislature granted the commissioner broad powers, it would not permit him the administrative narrowing of duties that resulted in a disavowal of both power and responsibility. The court commented that the commissioner had the power to direct the continuance of the sending-receiving relationship between the districts after the expiration of the present contract, to order the boards to proceed with suitable steps toward regionalization, and to order a merger if he was convinced that doing so was necessary to fulfill the state's educational and school desegregation policies.[135]

As far-reaching as their powers may be, state officials and agencies cannot retrospectively approve local board actions that involve individual rights. Such a case arose where state law did not specify the teaching areas within which one could have earned tenure. Over the years, the courts recognized administrative rules of the commissioner and state department that provided for "horizontal" tenure (such as for kindergarten, elementary, and secondary schools as well as for some specified special subjects) rather than "vertical" tenure (such as in English, social studies, mathematics, and the like). In the face of a challenge to one of the commissioner's unreviewed pronouncements, which declared that tenure areas could be created by administrative action at the district level, subject only to his ad hoc retrospective approval, the Court of Appeals of New York acknowledged that such a view was erroneous.[136] The court stated that since the commissioner failed to furnish standards for local boards, he undermined the purposes of the tenure statute because boards could easily have manipulated the standard in withholding or withdrawing tenure from teachers. According to the court, while the statute did not prohibit vertical tenure, the legislature or board of regents had to clarify the extent to which this could be done before such rules could be put into effect.

---

133. *Booker v. Board of Educ., Plainfield*, 212 A.2d 1 (N.J.1965).

134. *Jenkins v. Township of Morris School Dist.*, 279 A.2d 619 (N.J.1971).

135. For a case with a similar result, *see Board of Educ. of Borough of Englewood*

Cliffs v. Board of Educ. of Borough of Tenafly, 788 A.2d 729 [161 Educ. L. Rep. 542] (N.J. 2002).

136. *Baer v. Nyquist*, 357 N.Y.S.2d 442 (N.Y.1974).

A more recent case reflects the discretion that a system-wide board exercises over teacher licenses. The Supreme Judicial Court of Massachusetts affirmed that the commonwealth's board of education had the authority to promulgate regulations that required mathematics teachers in under-performing schools to pass an assessment test prior to licensure.[137] The court remarked that since the regulations were rationally related to the commonwealth's interest in having high-quality mathematics teachers in schools where student performances in the state-wide student mathematics assessment were low, they did not violate the educators' rights to equal protection rights under either the federal or commonwealth constitutions.

Enforcement of Administrative Powers

The enforcement of administrative powers and the penalties that state-level agencies may invoke against non-compliance frequently leads to litigation. Among the penalties that state officials can impose for non-compliance are the denial of accreditation, revocation of teaching certificates, and the removal of local board members from office in the face of substantial proof of dereliction. The need for evidence is particularly true where, as in the overwhelming majority of districts, board members are popularly elected. This principle was illustrated in a case where the Supreme Court of Kentucky upheld the removal of members of a local county board for misconduct in office.[138] The board members violated state law by awarding a construction contract without the prior approval of the chief state school officer, by voting to purchase storage tanks for more than $10,000 without seeking competitive bids and for purchasing more than $10,000 worth of equipment from one member's brother. The same court later declared that the legislature did not exceed its authority by enacting a law that empowered the commonwealth's board to remove individuals for causes not enumerated in the Constitution of Kentucky since it vested it with authority to consider who is eligible to serve as school board members.[139] The court refused to uphold the removal of board members for perceived inadequacy with regard to their efforts to apprise themselves of their district's financial condition.

When dealing with the removal of local school board members, a state legislature is not under the same restrictions as are subordinate agencies such as a state board of education. This issue arose in a challenge to the constitutionality of a state law abolishing the incumbent board in New York City and ordering the mayor to appoint a new one under a different system. The state's highest court sustained the new law on the basis that the legislature had the power to abolish an office it created or modify its term even if doing so curtailed an incumbent's

137. *Massachusetts Fed'n of Teachers v. Board of Educ.*, 767 N.E.2d 549 [164 Educ. L. Rep. 393] (Mass.2002).

138. *State Bd. for Elementary and Secondary Educ. v. Ball*, 847 S.W.2d 743 [81 Educ. L Rep. 633] (Ky.1993).

139. *Hale v. Combs*, 30 S.W.3d 146 [148 Educ. L. Rep. 1084] (Ky.2000).

unexpired term.[140] In a second case from New York, an appellate court affirmed that the commissioner of education had the statutory authority to remove local school board members for violations of law or neglect of duty.[141] The court cautioned that this express power did not impose an overseer invested with veto power to substitute his or her opinions for those of local board members.

If a school system falls into chaos, state education officials have the implied power to intervene. In such a case, the Supreme Court of New Jersey affirmed the appointment of a monitor general to supervise activities in a school district that was "in an abysmal state due almost entirely to the mismanagement and incompetence of the members of the local board of education."[142] In a later dispute related to the state takeover of another school system in New Jersey due to poor management, an appellate court affirmed that while officials violated the rights of administrators and an auditor in extinguishing their contractual rights, the plaintiffs were not entitled to compensation for vacation time.[143] Similarly, the Supreme Court of California ruled that state officials had the duty to intervene when a school board planned to close a district due to financial problems.[144] While interpreting state law as not requiring a takeover of operations, the court agreed that even if state officials resisted acting, they could not avoid the state's ultimate responsibility.

As reflected by a case from the Supreme Court of Pennsylvania, if a legislature enacts a takeover law, it must be clear that it is not aimed at a particular district.[145] The court upheld a takeover statute that allowed mayors in specified cities to assume control over failing school systems because it was satisfied that the law violated neither equal protection nor a statute against special laws and did not interfere with any branch of the mayor-council optional form of government.

Challenges to the authority of state officials and boards also arise from their attempts to control the actions of local boards by withholding state funds. In general, courts are reluctant to approve the cutting off of funds as a means of ensuring compliance with state policies. This is particularly true if state-level authorities do not afford offending boards opportunities to be heard and/or to correct objectionable practices before denying state aid. If officials are clearly violating a financing statute, a court may order the withholding of public funds until there is compliance. In a case where a statute concerning teacher salaries was unambiguous, the Supreme Court of Arkansas ordered the state department of

---

140. *Lanza v. Wagner*, 229 N.Y.S.2d 380 (N.Y.1962), *cert. denied*, 371 U.S. 901, 83 S.Ct. 205, 9 L.Ed.2d 164 (1962).

141. *Verbanic v. Nyquist*, 344 N.Y.S.2d 406 (N.Y.App.Div.1973).

142. *Matter of Board of Educ. of Trenton*, 431 A.2d 808, 809 (N.J.1981).

143. *Caponegro v. State Operated School Dist. of City of Newark, Essex Coun-*ty, 748 A.2d 1208 [143 Educ. L. Rep. 562] (N.J.Super.App.Div.2000).

144. *Butt v. State*, 842 P.2d 1240 [79 Educ. L. Rep. 1039] (Cal.1992).

145. *Harrisburg School Dist. v. Zogby*, 828 A.2d 1079 [179 Educ. L. Rep. 412] (Pa. 2003).

education to withhold funds from a school board that it had permitted not to comply with the law.[146]

In an early case, the Supreme Court of Wisconsin resolved a dispute over whether the state superintendent could withhold funds in order to enforce state regulations in a dispute over his attempt to require a local board to abandon an antiquated school building and replace it with one that was satisfactory.[147] Where state law called for the appointment of a building inspector and permitted the withholding of state funds to enforce the superintendent's orders, the local board succeeded in forcing him to allot it the district's share of state funds despite its failure to comply with the building inspector's order. The court emphasized that since other sections of the law placed the power to build schools in the hands of local boards, the state superintendent could not assume this responsibility by attempting to withhold funds to enforce state regulations. Another early case supporting the withholding of state aid by a chief state school officer involved a statute that permitted the denial of funds until a board provided suitable facilities with convenient access to its students. The Supreme Court of New Jersey interpreted the law as requiring local boards to provide transportation to students who lived more than two miles from school.[148]

Conversely, a dispute arose in Texas where state law provided that a county superintendent's salary and expenses were to be paid from local district funds. The law also made the state superintendent responsible for the general superintendency of business relating to the state's public schools. A controversy arose when one board refused to contribute its share to a county superintendent and the state superintendent sought to impound part of its allocated funds to cover this expense. An appellate court granted the local board's request for mandamus in ascertaining that the state superintendent lacked the power to interfere with the legally prescribed course of state funds that were allocated to its treasury.[149]

In later cases, the Supreme Court of Illinois[150] and an appellate panel in Ohio[151] approved the withholding of funds from boards that did not comply with state transportation laws. However, the Supreme Court of Ohio subsequently ordered the state superintendent to grant a one-day waiver of required instruction to a school system when not doing so would have cost it $750,000 due to a midwinter closure due to a strike by school personnel.[152]

146. *Junction City School Dist. v. Alphin*, 855 S.W.2d 316 [83 Educ. L. Rep. 1193] (Ark.1993).

147. *State ex rel. School Dist. No. 8, Town of Wauwatosa v. Cary*, 163 N.W. 645 (Wis.1917).

148. *Board of Educ. of West Amwell Township v. State Bd. of Educ.*, 135 A. 664 (N.J.1927).

149. *Austin Indep. School Dist. v. Marrs*, 41 S.W.2d 9 (Tex. Comm'n App. 1931).

150. *Board of Educ., School Dist. No. 142, Cook County v. Bakalis*, 299 N.E.2d 737 (Ill.1973).

151. *In re Resolution*, 385 N.E.2d 295 (Ohio Ct. App.1978).

152. *State ex rel. Cleveland Bd. of Educ. v. State Bd. of Educ. of Ohio*, 464 N.E.2d 137 [17 Educ. L. Rep. 932] (Ohio 1984). [Case No. 19]

Quasi-Judicial Powers

Ordinarily, courts resolve disputes involving the rights of individuals or organizations. Yet, in many jurisdictions some controversies may, or must, be resolved by administrative agencies acting in quasi-judicial fashion. At the state level, quasi-judicial authority may rest in the hands of a state superintendent, state board, or some other legislatively approved authority such as a local superintendent.[153] Adjudications of administrative agencies are binding on the parties. Absent state constitutional, statutory, or regulatory provisions to the contrary, the courts usually permit state agencies and officers latitude in developing procedures such as the form of hearings and over the admissibility of evidence.

Even in states where administrative review is available, agencies may not hear all cases. As such, it is important to consider what disputes may, or must, be referred for review before a petitioner has recourse to the courts. A question also remains over the nature of judicial review and whether it must be a trial de novo or a review on the record and, if the latter, what standard applies. Illustrations of quasi-judicial functioning within state education agencies follow.

In New York, a party can appeal an educational dispute to the state commissioner or directly to the courts. Appeals to the commissioner are final subject to judicial review on the limited question of whether, on the record, his or her action was arbitrary or lacked a rational basis.[154] Courts in New York agreed that the commissioner's judgment can substitute for that of other education authorities, including local school boards and hearing panels.[155] If, on the other hand, a matter primarily involves the meaning of constitutional or statutory provisions, the courts are likely to examine the commissioner's action more closely.[156] If an issue of educational policy is linked with a constitutional question such as academic freedom, the scope of judicial review remains limited.[157] Further, reflecting the general rule that the judiciary defers to administrative agencies, courts in New York agreed that where the regulations governing appeals to the commissioner provide for the review of affidavits and exhibits rather than evidentiary hearings, this approach did not violate due process.[158]

On the other hand, in Rhode Island the state commissioner of education conducts evidentiary hearings on complaints and must render

153. *Strother v. Board of Educ. of Howard County,* 623 A.2d 717 [82 Educ. L. Rep. 557] (Md. Ct.Spec.App.1993).

154. *Gundrum v. Ambach,* 448 N.Y.S.2d 466 [3 Educ. L. Rep. 1075] (N.Y.1982).

155. *Board of Educ. of City of N.Y. v. Allen,* 188 N.Y.S.2d 515 (N.Y.1959); *Conley v. Ambach,* 472 N.Y.S.2d 598 [16 Educ. L. Rep. 576] (N.Y.1984). [Case No. 20]

156. *Ross v. Wilson,* 127 N.E.2d 697 (N.Y.1955).

157. *Malverne Union Free School Dist. v. Sobol,* 586 N.Y.S.2d 673 [76 Educ. L. Rep. 1124] (N.Y.App.Div.1992), *appeal withdrawn,* 591 N.Y.S.2d 141 (N.Y.1992).

158. *Forrest v. Ambach,* 463 N.Y.S.2d 84 [11 Educ. L. Rep. 590] (N.Y.App.Div.1983), *appeal dismissed,* 468 N.Y.S.2d 1028 (N.Y. 1983); *Akshar v. Mills,* 671 N.Y.S.2d 856 [125 Educ. L. Rep. 802] (N.Y.App.Div.1998), *leave to appeal dismissed,* 683 N.Y.S.2d 172 (N.Y.1998).

decisions de novo.[159] Also, unlike New York, Rhode Island provides for appeals of most of the commissioner's actions to the state board before the courts can assume jurisdiction. In such instances, the courts review cases based on the facts as provided by the commissioner and affirmed by the board, unless they are unsupported by evidence in the record.[160] The fact that a record may contain additional evidence to support contrary conclusions is irrelevant.[161] For instance, the Supreme Court of Rhode Island maintained that where a statute expressly vested a power in a local board, the commissioner could not substitute his judgment for its.[162]

In New Jersey, the state commissioner is empowered with decision-making power in educational disputes with further review possible by the state board of education. While state law calls for evidentiary hearings, exhaustion of statutory remedies prior to seeking judicial review is not absolute since, in a far-ranging opinion, the state's highest court declared that the requirement is a policy of convenience and discretion rather than of law.[163] In addition, the court was satisfied that while the judiciary may intervene without waiting for other tribunals to act, it generally leaves educational matters to the disposition of state education officials.[164]

The legislature of Texas provides for review of school disputes through appeals to the state commissioner and the state board of education. The courts in Texas appear to agree that parties must exhaust administrative remedies before resorting to judicial review[165]but make a major exception regarding tax matters which can be taken directly to court without recourse to the central agency.[166] Moreover, Texas law permits an initial resort to the courts where there are undisputed facts and the only issue is a pure question of law.[167] In reviewing an adjudication of the state board, courts in Texas not only apply the common rule that an action must be upheld if it is supported by substantial evidence but also do not consider whether they would have reached the same result.[168] This rule is applied to an order of the state board, not to one of a local board or the commissioner since the latter are subordinate administratively.[169] Less common in Texas is the

---

159. *Slattery v. Cranston School Comm.*, 354 A.2d 741 (R.I.1976).

160. *Campbell v. School Comm. of Coventry*, 21 A.2d 727 (R.I.1941).

161. *Brown v. Elston*, 445 A.2d 279 [4 Educ. L. Rep. 211] (R.I.1982).

162. *Exeter–West Greenwich Reg'l School Dist. v. Pontarelli*, 460 A.2d 934 [11 Educ. L. Rep. 559] (R.I.1983).

163. *Redcay v. State Bd. of Educ.*, 25 A.2d 632 (N.J.1942).

164. For similar results, *see Laba v. Board of Educ. of Newark*, 129 A.2d 273 (N.J.1957); *In re Massiello*, 138 A.2d 393 (N.J.1958).

165. *Ball v. Kerrville Indep. School Dist.*, 504 S.W.2d 791 (Tex. Civ.App.1973);

see also Sanchez v. Huntsville Indep. School Dist., 844 S.W.2d 286 [80 Educ. L. Rep. 736] (Tex.Civ. App.1992).

166. *City of Dallas v. Mosely*, 286 S.W. 497 (Tex.Civ.App.1926). [Case No. 21]

167. *Alvin Indep. School Dist. v. Cooper*, 404 S.W.2d 76 (Tex.Civ.App.1966); *Calvin V. Koltermann, Inc. v. Underream Piling Co.*, 563 S.W.2d 950 (Tex.Civ.App.1977).

168. *Board of Trustees of Crystal City Indep. School Dist. v. Briggs*, 486 S.W.2d 829 (Tex.Civ. App.1972).

169. *Temple Indep. School Dist. v. State Bd. of Educ.*, 493 S.W.2d 543 (Tex.Civ.App. 1973).

requirement that a trial court accept testimony from the parties along with examining the record of state-level administrative bodies.[170]

At issue in Maryland was whether the state board of education was required to hear appeals from county boards since the chief state school officer lacked a quasi-judicial role. Even though a statute provided for such a route, the state board claimed that it did not have to accept all requests for review. In rejecting the state board's interpretation of the statute, the court suggested that the board's argument over the fiscal implications that such a workload would have imposed on it had to be addressed by the legislature.[171]

Judicial Review of Actions of State–Level Agencies

In General

As a general rule, the courts are inclined to allow state education officials discretion in creating and enforcing rules,[172] going so far as to note that a state commissioner has primary jurisdiction to hear and resolve all controversies arising under state school laws.[173] To this end, an appellate court in Maryland recognized that since the visitorial power conferred on the state board gave it the authority to have the last word on disputes over the administration of public schools, the judiciary had limited power to interfere.[174] As noted earlier, courts ordinarily do not intervene in disagreements involving state agencies unless allegations include, for example, claims that their actions implicated a constitutional claim;[175] violated a specific law;[176] exceeded their general powers;[177] acted arbitrarily, capriciously, or unreasonably;[178] or were not based on substantial evidence.[179]

---

170. *Wylie Indep. School Dist. v. Central Educ. Agency*, 488 S.W.2d 166 (Tex.Civ. App.1972).

171. *Board of Educ. of Garrett County v. Lendo*, 453 A.2d 1185 [8 Educ. L. Rep. 686] (Md. 1982).

172. *See, e.g., Ware v. Valley Stream High School Dist.*, 551 N.Y.S.2d 167 [58 Educ. L. Rep. 1242] (N.Y.1989); *Kletzkin v. Board of Educ. of Borough of Spotswood, Middlesex County*, 642 A.2d 993 [91 Educ. L. Rep. 1025] (N.J.1994); *Morton Community Unit School Dist. No. 709 v. J.M.*, 152 F.3d 583 [128 Educ. L. Rep. 972] (7th Cir. 1998), *cert. denied*, 526 U.S. 1004, 119 S.Ct. 1140, 143 L.Ed.2d 208 (1999).

173. *Bower v. Board of Educ. of City of East Orange*, 694 A.2d 543 [119 Educ. L. Rep. 176] (N.J.1997).

174. *Hurl v. Board of Educ. of Howard County*, 667 A.2d 970 [105 Educ. L. Rep. 565] (Md.Ct. Spec.App.1995).

175. *Pinckney v. Board of Educ. of Westbury Union Free School Dist.*, 920 F.Supp. 393 [108 Educ. L. Rep. 664] (E.D.N.Y.1996); *Brownsville Area School Dist. v. Student X*, 729 A.2d 198 [134 Educ. L. Rep. 534] (Pa.Cmwlth.Ct.1999), *appeal denied*, 745 A.2d 1225 (Pa.1999).

176. *Yaw v. Walla Walla School Dist. No. 140*, 722 P.2d 803 [34 Educ. L. Rep. 296] (Wash. 1986); *Fairbanks North Star Borough School Dist. v. NEA–Alaska*, 817 P.2d 923 [70 Educ. L. Rep. 223] (Alaska 1991).

177. *Petition of Dunlap*, 604 A.2d 945 [73 Educ. L. Rep. 993] (N.H.1991).

178. *Petition of Dunlap*, 604 A.2d 945 [73 Educ. L. Rep. 993] (N.H.1991); *Dennery v. Board of Educ. of Passaic County Reg'l High School Dist. No. 1, Passaic County*, 622 A.2d 858 [81 Educ. L. Rep. 945] (N.J. 1993).

179. *Pushay v. Walter*, 481 N.E.2d 575 [26 Educ. L. Rep. 1194] (Ohio 1985); *Brownsville Area School Dist. v. Student X*, 729 A.2d 198 [134 Educ. L. Rep. 534] (Pa. Cmwlth.Ct.1999), *appeal denied*, 745 A.2d 1225 (Pa.1999).

The courts are more likely to examine quasi-judicial rather than administrative actions. In *Board of Education of Hendrick Hudson Central School District v. Rowley*, the Supreme Court, admitting that the judiciary is ill-equipped to act as a kind of "super" school board in evaluating complex factors affecting education, cautioned judges not to substitute their views of proper educational methodology for that of competent school officials. More specifically, the Court observed that "[w]e previously have cautioned that courts lack the 'specialized knowledge and experience' necessary to resolve 'persistent and difficult questions of educational policy. . . .' Therefore, once a court determines that the requirements of the Act have been met, questions of methodology are for resolution by the States [through school officials]."[180] On the other hand, the Supreme Court of Wyoming reasoned that "the courts are always open to correct arbitrary, capricious, or fraudulent action taken by an administrative official or board."[181] The one condition to this rule is that as long as important rights are not extinguished, a legislature can provide for review of different decisions by different paths to the courts.[182]

Rules and Their Enforcement

The extent of rule-making authority of administrative agencies under general grants of power has been the subject of a great deal of litigation. While generalizations are difficult, at least two courts have addressed this issue. The Supreme Court of Montana presented two criteria for considering whether administrative regulations are inconsistent with legislative intent. The court held that regulations are unauthorized if they "engraft additional and contradictory requirements on the statute" or if they "engraft additional, noncontradictory requirements on the statute which were not envisioned by the legislature."[183] The Supreme Court of Washington, albeit in a case from higher education, posited that rules may fill in gaps in legislation if they are "necessary to the effectuation of a general statutory scheme," adding that administrative rules adopted pursuant to legislative grants of authority should be upheld if they are "reasonably consistent with the statute[s] being implemented."[184]

Courts generally agree that state agencies can resolve matters that fall within their jurisdiction. Even so, considerable difficulty ensues if a power that is exercised is based on a generalized statute. When reviewing the authority of state officials, the courts often maintain that the powers of their offices extend only to educational, rather than legal, matters. Yet, constitutional rights as to person and property, not to

---

180. 458 U.S. 176, 208, 102 S.Ct. 3034, 73 L.Ed.2d 690 [5 Educ. L. Rep. 34] (1982) (internal citations omitted). [Case No. 118]

181. *School Dists. Nos. 2, 3, 6, 9, and 10 v. Cook*, 424 P.2d 751, 755 (Wyo.1967).

182. *Board of Educ. of Armstrong High School Dist. No. 225 v. Ellis*, 328 N.E.2d 294 (Ill.1975).

183. *Bell v. Department of Licensing*, 594 P.2d 331, 333 (Mont.1979).

184. *Green River Community College, Dist. No. 10 v. Higher Educ. Personnel Bd.*, 622 P.2d 826, 828 (Wash.1980).

mention statutory interpretations, are often inextricably intertwined with educational considerations. The more cases one reads on the distinction between legal and educational matters, the more involved the differentiation becomes. Insofar as the courts have the final word as to whether a matter is educational or legal, their judgments often influence the course of education on substantive issues.

To the extent that there is a presumption that an administrative officer or body has exercised its power properly, the burden of proof is generally on the party challenging an administrative action.[185] As reflected throughout, the courts typically do not pass on the wisdom of a discretionary act of state (or local[186]) officials, limiting themselves to legal considerations. At most, if courts invalidate orders, they can require further administrative actions consistent with their decrees.

Another pertinent generalization is that if a statute outlines procedures for solving a problem or securing redress within the executive branch, the courts usually require parties to exhaust administrative remedies before assuming jurisdiction. However, if a federal constitutional or statutory right is involved, the Supreme Court decided that section 1983 is available to provide "immediate access to the federal courts notwithstanding any provision of state law to the contrary."[187]

Occasionally, state boards or chief state school officers fail to carry out their duties. If a duty is ministerial, or mandatory, such as dealing with apportioning state funds, a party can seek a writ of mandamus to require performance.[188] Where a duty involves elements of discretion, it is up to the judiciary to set liabilities for harm flowing from nonperformance. In an example of the latter, the Sixth Circuit affirmed that where Ohio's State Board of Education did not discharge its responsibilities to halt intentionally segregative practices in Cleveland, it could be required to share in the costs of desegregating its schools.[189]

A more recent example of judicial review of state-level activity involved the Tennessee Secondary School Athletic Association (TSSAA), a not-for-profit membership corporation funded largely through gate receipts from interscholastic sports events, organized to regulate interscholastic high school sports in public and private schools. Even though no school was forced to join, about eighty-four percent of the state's public high schools and fifty-five private schools were members. Under the TSSAA's bylaws, member schools were represented by their principal or a faculty member who had a vote in selecting members of its

185. *Steubenville v. Culp*, 38 Ohio St. 18 (1882).

186. *See, e.g., Board of Educ. of Indep. School Dist. No. 92 of Pottawatomie v. Earls*, 536 U.S. 822, 838, 122 S.Ct. 2559, 153 L.Ed.2d 735 [166 Educ. L. Rep. 79] (2002), *on remand*, 300 F.3d 1222 [168 Educ. L. Rep. 581] (10th Cir.2002). [Case No. 112] ("In upholding the constitutionality of the [random drug testing] Policy [at issue], we express no opinion as to its wisdom. Rather, we hold only that Tecumseh's Policy is a reasonable means of furthering the School District's important interest in preventing and deterring drug use among its schoolchildren.")

187. *Patsy v. Board of Regents of the State of Fla.*, 457 U.S. 496, 504, 102 S.Ct. 2557, 73 L.Ed.2d 172 (1982).

188. *Board of Educ. of Iron Mt. v. Voelker*, 259 N.W. 891 (Mich.1935).

189. *Reed v. Rhodes*, 662 F.2d 1219 [1 Educ. L. Rep. 120] (6th Cir.1981).

governing bodies. The TSSAA sets membership standards and student eligibility rules and has the power to penalize any member school that violates those rules. Half of the TSSAA's meetings took place during official hours at public schools.

When the TSSAA penalized a private school for violating a recruiting rule, the school sued it and its executive director under section 1983, claiming that it engaged in a state action in violation of the First and Fourteenth Amendments. In *Brentwood Academy v. Tennessee Secondary School Athletic Association*,[190] the Supreme Court ruled in favor of the private school. Rejecting the TSSAA's arguments to the contrary, the Court found that its regulatory activity was state action due to its pervasive interaction with public school officials. The Court added that insofar as the TSSAA would virtually not have existed but for the support it received from the public schools and their officials, it had to be viewed as a public institution.

Hearings

Where statutes require administrative bodies to convene hearings before acting, courts typically examine the manner in which they are conducted in order to ensure that they complied with due process. As such, it is vital to distinguish two basic types of hearings: legislative or rule-making and quasi-judicial or adversarial.

The purpose of a legislative hearing is to convey information and opinions to a decision-making body. Even though there is no constitutional requirement that a rule-making agency conduct hearings before acting, statutes frequently grant them discretion as to whether a hearing is necessary to clarify the positions of the parties.[191] In addition, there is typically no legal compulsion for such a body to do any more than listen to the views expressed because it has the power to act as it sees fit.

Quasi-judicial hearings are required where a precise determination of fact and law is needed. This type of hearing implicates constitutional due process because liberty or property rights are involved. The most common cases in these categories, as reflected in the appropriate chapters later in this book, pertain to the dismissals of teachers and student discipline. In these situations, the courts require certain minimal procedures, but do not expect administrative bodies to comply with the same procedural strictness as in judicial settings.

State boards may employ hearing officers to conduct quasi-judicial hearings and offer recommendations. While state bodies can reject hearing officers' findings or conclusions, they still must review the transcripts of hearings before doing so.[192] Once officials review the evidence,

190. 531 U.S. 288, 121 S.Ct. 924, 148 L.Ed.2d 807 [151 Educ. L. Rep. 18] (2001), *on remand*, 262 F.3d 543 [157 Educ. L. Rep. 467] (6th Cir. 2001), *reh'g en banc denied, cert. denied*, 535 U.S. 971, 122 S.Ct. 1439, 152 L.Ed.2d 382 (2002), *on remand*, 304 F.Supp.2d 981 [186 Educ. L. Rep. 180] (M.D.Tenn. 2003). [Case No. 22]

191. *State of Cal., Dep't of Educ. v. Bennett*, 843 F.2d 333 [46 Educ. L. Rep. 52] (9th Cir.1988).

192. *Board of Educ. of Melrose Mun. Schools v. New Mexico State Bd. of Educ.*, they will have satisfied due process. In rejecting a contention to the contrary, the Supreme Court, in a non-school case, declared that it is not necessary for officials who are responsible for reaching an ultimate decision be present when evidence is received.[193]

Absent statutory specifications as how a hearing is to be conducted, and if the subject matter is essentially one of policy formulation or application, rather than individual rights, the presumption is in favor of a legislative-type hearing.[194] By way of illustration, the Supreme Court of Oregon pointed out that a judicial-type hearing was not necessary where a legislatively created district boundary board conducted a hearing on proposed changes once it provided the requisite notice.[195] The chairman of the hearing board reviewed the stipulations governing its ability to act on petitions for annexation, after which members of the audience were invited to express their opinions about the proposed change, all of which were recorded in the board's minutes. Once the hearing was completed, the board made the requested boundary changes. The court rejected a challenge to the board's vote on the ground that it did not make formal findings on such issues as the effect that the proposed changes would have had on the ability of districts to provide mandated educational programs since the statute did not require it to do so.

The Supreme Court of Wisconsin affirmed that for a non-judicial hearing, the only issues subject to judicial review are whether a board acted within its jurisdiction and whether its order was arbitrary and/or capricious.[196] The court noted that a board action is arbitrary and capricious when it lacks a rational base, is unreasonable when all facts and opinions are considered, or when it is the result of an unconsidered, wilful and irrational choice of conduct rather than the result of a winnowing and sifting process. The court also determined that the board was not limited to considering facts within the record since it was free to utilize other information within its knowledge. The court concluded that even though a board member had expressed a general view on a controversial matter such as a school district reorganization plan, this did not bar the individual from participating in the board's action.

[Case No. 16] Power of State Legislature to Change District Boundaries

ATTORNEY GENERAL OF MICHIGAN EX REL. KIES v. LOWREY

Supreme Court of the United States, 1905.
199 U.S. 233, 26 S.Ct. 27, 50 L.Ed. 167.

MR. JUSTICE MCKENNA delivered the opinion of the court: The Constitution of the state of Michigan requires the legislature to establish and

740 P.2d 123 [40 Educ. L. Rep. 1279] (N.M.Ct.App.1987).

193. *Morgan v. United States*, 298 U.S. 468, 56 S.Ct. 906, 80 L.Ed. 1288 (1936).

194. *Johnson v. Schrader*, 507 P.2d 814 (Wyo.1973).

195. *School Dist. No. 7 of Wallowa County v. Weissenfluh*, 387 P.2d 567 (Or. 1963).

196. *Joint School Dist. No. 2 v. State Appeal Bd.*, 266 N.W.2d 374 (Wis.1978).

provide a system of public schools, whereby a school shall be kept open at least three months in each year in every school district in the state. In fulfillment of this requirement legislation was enacted from time to time providing for the formation of school districts. Under this legislation (1881) four school districts were organized in the townships of Somerset and Moscow, county of Hillsdale. In 1901 the legislature passed an act.... By this act one of the districts formed in the townships of Somerset and Moscow in which the village of Jerome is situated, and portions of other districts, were set off and incorporated in one school district to be known as "the public schools of the village of Jerome." The act appointed defendants in error trustees of the new district, to continue in office until their successors should be elected, as provided in the act. The act gave to the new district the property within its limits which had belonged to the districts from which it was created, and required the new district to assume and pay the debts and obligations of the old districts. The new district did not include all of the lands of the old districts....

The grounds of attack upon the validity of the act creating the new district in the supreme court of the state were as follows:

First. It deprives this school district or municipality of the right of local self-government, guaranteed to all municipalities by the Constitution....

Fourth. The act as passed impairs the obligation of contracts, within the meaning of the Constitution of the United States and the Constitution of the state of Michigan.

With the first three grounds we have no concern. They present strictly local questions. We are concerned with the fourth ground only in so far as it invokes the Constitution of the United States. The supreme court disposed of this ground as follows: "We have already shown that the obligation of contracts is not impaired. The districts did not hold this property under any contract with the state, but as a public agency." In other words, the nonexistence of a contract was rested on the construction of the Constitution and the laws of the state, and hence defendant in error contends that the decision of the court did not involve a Federal question. This, however, overlooks the power and duty of this court to determine for itself the existence or nonexistence of a contract. Other grounds in support of the motion to dismiss are urged which, we think, are also untenable. The motion is therefore denied.

Plaintiff in error broadened in this court his objection to the act, based on the Constitution of the United States. He urges, besides the contract clause of the Constitution, that provision of the 14th Amendment which protects private property from deprivation without due process of law, and section 4, article 4, which provides: "The United States shall guarantee to every state in this Union a republican form of government." But the grounds all depend ultimately upon the same arguments. If the legislature of the state has the power to create and alter school districts, and divide and apportion the property of such district, no contract can arise, no property of a district can be said to be taken, and the action of the legislature is compatible with a republican form of government even if it be admitted that section 4, article 4, of the Constitution, applies to the creation of, or the powers or rights of property of, the subordinate municipalities of the state. We may omit, therefore, that section and article from further consideration. The decision of the other grounds urged we may rest upon the opinion of the supreme court of the state and the case of *Laramie County v. Albany County*. It is there said in many ways, with citation of many supporting cases, that the legislature of the state has absolute power to make and change subordinate municipalities. The following quotation meets exactly the contentions of plaintiff in error:

> "Institutions of the kind, whether called counties or towns, are the auxiliaries of the state in the important business of municipal rule and cannot have the least pretension to sustain their privileges or their existence upon anything like a contract between them and the legislature of the state, because there is not, and cannot be, any reciprocity of stipulation, and their objects and duties are utterly incompatible with everything of the nature of compact. Instead of that, the constant practice is to divide large counties and towns, and to consolidate small ones, to meet the wishes of the residents, or to promote the public interests as understood by those who control the action of the legislature. Opposition is sometimes manifested, but it is everywhere acknowledged that the legislature possesses the power to divide counties and towns at their pleasure, and to apportion the common property and the common burdens in such manner as to them may seem reasonable and equitable." . . .

Notes

1.　Consider this case both in terms of consolidating small districts and of breaking up large districts. How should a state organize school districts for the present and future? Should state constitutions include limitations on the redistricting powers of legislatures?

2.　"There is no contract relation existing between the state and the school districts provided for by the Legislature. Such a relation, however, does exist between the plaintiff district and the purchasers of the bonds issued by it." Citing the main case, the Supreme Court of Michigan held that although the legislature possessed the power to detach a part of the territory from one school district and attach it to another, "it may not impair the obligation in the bondholders' contract by taking such action without making provision for the payment thereof." *Board of Educ. of City of Lincoln Park v. Board of Educ. of Detroit*, 222 N.W. 763, 764 (Mich.1929).

[Case No. 17]   Authority of A State Board To Contract with a Private, For–Profit Corporation to Operate a School

BALTIMORE TEACHERS UNION, AMERICAN FEDERATION OF TEACHERS, LOCAL 340, AFL–CIO v. MARYLAND STATE BOARD OF EDUCATION

Court of Appeals of Maryland, 2004.
840 A.2d 728 [184 Educ. L. Rep. 910].

ELDRIDGE, J.

Baltimore Teachers Union, American Federation of Teachers, Local 340, AFL–CIO, filed in the Circuit Court for Baltimore City a complaint for a declaratory judgment and injunctive relief, alleging that the Maryland State Board of Education lacked statutory authority to enter into a contract with Edison Schools, Inc. for the operation and management of three Baltimore City public elementary schools. The Circuit Court held that the State Board acted within its statutory authority conferred by the General Assembly. Before argument in the Court of Special Appeals, the Union filed in this Court a petition for a writ of certiorari. We granted the petition and shall affirm.

I

Governance of the Maryland public school system is two-tiered. The Maryland State Board of Education is the head of the State Department of Education.... Twenty-three county boards of education and the New Baltimore City Board of School Commissioners (the "New Board") operate as the statutory heads of the twenty-four local public school systems. The State Board is charged with the general supervision of the Maryland public schools, including the development and implementation of educational policies. The State Board is authorized to adopt rules and regulations for the administration and enforcement of the education law. In 1993, the Board promulgated regulations establishing public school performance standards that were adopted and codified in the Code of Maryland Regulations (COMAR). Regulation .01 establishes the scope of the regulations and regulation .02 is the definition section. The student performance areas tracked by the State are set forth in regulation .03. Regulation .04 establishes the standards that apply to the student performance areas. Regulation .05 sets out the reporting requirements, and the mandate that each public school develop a school improvement plan is set forth in regulation .06.

The regulations further set forth a two-phased process for public schools that fail to meet the prescribed student performance standards. Regulations .07 and .08 describe "local reconstitution" where, if a school fails to meet all standards at a level of satisfactory or better in the student performance areas, the State Board may require the overall program and management of a school to be placed under the direct control of the local school board. By February 2000, the State Board had ordered 97 schools throughout Maryland to be placed under local reconstitution. Of these, 83 schools were in Baltimore City.

If a school under local reconstitution fails to show sufficient improvement, regulation .10 provides for "state reconstitution" by which the State Board determines the overall program and management of the school. In 1999, the State Board reconstituted three of the lowest performing public elementary schools in Baltimore City.... Student performance remained stagnant at these elementary schools despite being under local reconstitution for at least three years. No more than 10% of the students at the schools had met the State's standard in all student performance areas in any year since 1993 when the school performance regulations were adopted.

The State Board examined the feasibility of closing one or more of the underperforming elementary schools. The Board determined that any closure would result in increased transportation costs and the transfer of students to other low performing public schools already under local reconstitution. The Board concluded that the most viable option was to contract out the operation and management of the three schools to a third party. Following a request for proposals in accordance with the State procurement procedure, the State Board and the New Board entered into a "Contract for the Operation and Management of Schools Under State Reconstitution in Baltimore City" with Edison Schools, Inc., for a term of five years. The contract with Edison was approved by the Maryland Board of Public Works on March 22, 2000.

Edison is a private company specializing in the management of public schools. It operates under contracts with local school districts and boards of charter schools. Pursuant to its contract with the State Board, Edison is required to provide the three public elementary schools with curriculum and curriculum development, instructional services, instructional and support personnel, teaching tools, special education and related services, educational services with limited or no English proficiency, and other services which may be necessary. Edison serves as the employer of all employees hired for the elementary schools and is responsible for providing management and professional development for all personnel working in the three schools. Edison has the power to hire, assign, discipline, and dismiss all personnel hired at the schools.

The Baltimore Teachers Union initiated the present action in the Circuit Court for Baltimore City against the State Board and the New Board....

The State Board and the New Board filed motions to dismiss the complaint for lack of standing. Alternatively, the State Board moved for summary judgment, maintaining that the Board acted within the scope of its statutory authority by promulgating the challenged regulations and contracting with a private vendor for the operation of the three elementary schools. The Union filed a cross-motion for summary judgment. Edison filed a motion to intervene which was unopposed. Following a hearing, the Circuit Court issued an order declaring that the Union had standing, that the challenged regulations were within the State Board's statutory authority, and that the two Boards were statutorily authorized to enter into the contract.

The Union filed a notice of appeal to the Court of Special Appeals, and the State Board filed a cross-appeal on the standing issue. Prior to argument in the intermediate appellate court, the Union filed in this Court a petition for a writ of certiorari which we granted. The petition presented the single question of whether the challenged regulations and contract were authorized by the General Assembly.

II

As a threshold matter, we must first consider whether the Baltimore Teachers Union had standing to challenge the reconstitution regulations and the Edison contract. . . .

. . . we hold that the Union has demonstrated that, as the designated collective bargaining representative of Baltimore City Public School employees, it has standing to maintain the present judicial action.

III

Turning to the merits of the case, Baltimore Teachers Union argues that COMAR exceed[s] the statutory authority of the Maryland State Board of Education, and that the State Board's contractual delegation of the operation and management of the reconstituted schools illegally grants powers to Edison which are vested exclusively in the New Board. While the State Board exercises general supervisory authority, the Union argues that the State Board lacks statutory authority to take over the basic functions of the local boards. The Union contends that there exists "no statute which directly and without equivocation authorizes the State Board" to turn over a public school to a third party and place it under the sole control of a private business.

We need not and shall not decide whether the State Board was statutorily authorized to adopt the reconstitution regulations in 1993. Even if the State Board lacked the statutory authority to promulgate the reconstitution regulations in 1993, subsequent enactments by the General Assembly remove any doubt as to the statutory authorization for the State Board's actions. The General Assembly has passed legislation which confirms and ratifies the State Board's power to issue the reconstitution regulations and to enter into third party contracts pursuant to those regulations. The legislation makes clear that the General Assembly knew of and approved of the State Board's exercise of its statutory authority to contract with Edison for the operation and management of the three public elementary schools.

The principle of legislative ratification is well-established in the law. In the situation where a governmental entity takes action which may or may not be statutorily authorized, but where the appropriate legislative body later ratifies that action, the ratification clearly validates the action prospectively and, in the absence of constitutional limitations, may validate the action retroactively. As Justice Harlan stated for the Supreme Court long ago, "it is not perceived why subsequent legislative ratification is not, in the absence of constitutional restrictions upon such legislation, equivalent to original authority." This Court has also recognized "that whatever a legislative body 'may authorize in prospect, it may adopt and validate in retrospect, so long as there is no interference with vested rights.' "

In 1997, the General Assembly directed the New Board to take actions necessary to "[i]mprove the status of schools that are subject to a State reconstitution notice." In 1999 the General Assembly passed legislation regarding stipends for classroom teachers and, in doing so, distinguished between a local school board as an employer and a private employer of a teacher in a reconstituted school. Section 6–306(b)(4) mandates that a classroom teacher holding an advanced professional certificate, who teaches in a public school identified by the State Board "as a reconstitution school, a reconstitution-eligible school, or a challenge school, shall receive a stipend from the State in the amount of $2,000 for each year that the teacher performs satisfactorily in the classroom." This language is in contrast to subsection (b)(2) that authorizes a stipend from the State for a classroom teacher "who is employed by a [local] board and who holds a certificate issued by the National Board for Professional Teaching Standards."

The General Assembly enacted legislation in 2000 protecting the pension rights of teachers previously employed by the local boards, working for a third party contractor operating a school under the reconstitution regulations. The statutory provisions specifically reference "an employee of the New Baltimore City Board of School Commissioners or another county board of education" who is "hired by a third-party contractor to work in a school that is reconstituted by order of the Maryland State Board of Education." The statute authorizes public school employees, whether vested or not in the retirement system, who are hired by a private contractor operating a school under state reconstitution, to withdraw their accumulated retirement or pension benefits without penalty, to receive service credit for the time employed with the private contractor, and to purchase up to five years of service credit at the employee rate for the period of employment with a third party contractor in a reconstituted school.

The 1997, 1999 and 2000 legislation demonstrates the General Assembly's awareness and approval that the State Board would be entering into contracts with private vendors in accordance with the reconstitution regulations. The statutory language directly references schools "subject to a State reconstitution notice" in addition to those schools "identified by the State Board as a reconstitution school, reconstitution-eligible school, or a challenge school." The language distinguishes between teachers "employed by a [local] board" and those who teach "in a public school identified by the State Board as a reconstitution school" for purposes of stipends and bonuses. The legislation affirmatively makes provisions to protect the pension rights of school teachers employed by third party contractors.

Given the language incorporating the reconstitution regulations and protecting the retirement benefits of those working in reconstituted schools, it is clear that the General Assembly recognized that the employer of a teacher in a public school under State reconstitution may be a private employer, and, thus, it is reasonable to infer legislative ratification of the regulations. As the Circuit Court correctly observed, "the General Assembly has considered and ... countenanced and condoned the [Board's] authority to enter into a third party contract." The General Assembly has clearly ratified the reconstitution regulations.

IV

The Union in its brief before this Court, for the first time in this case, argues that the challenged regulations and the Edison contract violate Article VIII, § 1, of the Maryland Constitution.

As earlier mentioned, the Union in its Circuit Court complaint emphasized that the "claims in this action are solely a matter of statutory law." In its complaint, cross-motion for summary judgment, and memoranda filed in the Circuit Court, the Union never raised a constitutional issue. The Circuit Court's memorandum and its declaratory judgment made no mention of a constitutional issue, as the Union had raised no such issue. The Union's certiorari petition did not present a constitutional issue....

Since the constitutional issue raised in the Union's brief was not raised in the trial court, we shall decline to address it. It is particularly important not to address a constitutional issue not raised in the trial court in light of the principle that a court will not unnecessarily decide a constitutional question.

.... The challenged action in the case at bar was ratified and authorized by the General Assembly.

JUDGMENT AFFIRMED, WITH COSTS.

Notes

1. One member of the court concurred that the union had standing to proceed, but disagreed with the outcome. The judge argued that the majority did not answer whether the Maryland State Board of Education had the authority to compel a local board to privatize a public school, permitting a private, for-profit corporation to control the school's staff and curriculum.

2. Should a state board have the authority to permit the privatization of under-performing public schools?

[Case No. 18] Delegation of Legislative Powers to Chief State School Officer

SCHOOL DISTRICT NO. 39 OF WASHINGTON COUNTY v. DECKER
Supreme Court of Nebraska, 1955.
68 N.W.2d 354.

CHAPPELL, JUSTICE. Plaintiff, School District No. 39 of Washington County, generally known as Rose Hill School District, is a rural Class II school district conducting both elementary and ninth and tenth high school grades in Washington County. It brought this action in equity to enjoin the enforcement of Rule III–3 of Section B, "Criteria for Approved Schools" promulgated as of July 1, 1952, by defendant Freeman Decker, then Superintendent of Public Instruction, under purported authority granted him by the last sentence of section 79–307, R.R.S.1943. Such section provides: "The Superintendent of Public Instruction shall prescribe forms for making all reports and regulations for all proceedings under the general school laws of the state. *He shall also formulate rules and regulations for the approval of all high schools for the collection of free high school tuition money.*" (Italics supplied.)

Rule III–3 also provides: "The teacher-pupil ratio for high school (grades 9–12) shall not be less than 1–5."

On May 12, 1953, defendant had removed plaintiff's high school from the list of approved schools for the school year 1953–1954 because its teacher-pupil ratio was "1–4 which is less than the minimum standards" required by Rule III–3. Concededly, such removal made plaintiff ineligible for collection of free high school tuition for nonresident pupils, deprived it of exemption from the free high school tax levy together with the right to be considered for accreditation status, and, as stated by defendant, "so far as our records are concerned, there is no high school in Rose Hill."

Insofar as important here, plaintiff sought injunctive relief primarily upon the ground that the last sentence of section 79–307, R.R.S.1943, was an unconstitutional and invalid delegation of legislative authority and power to an executive or administrative officer of the state. In other words, plaintiff contended that Rule III–3 was invalid and unenforceable because such statute granted defendant authority to "formulate rules and regulations for the approval of all high schools for the collection of free high school tuition money" without therein or otherwise in any statute in pari materia therewith providing any legislative numerical limitations, standards, rules, or criteria for the guidance of defendant in so doing. . . .

As disclosed by the record, defendant admitted that there is no magic in the ratio of 1–5 required by Rule III–3, and that it could as well have been higher or lower, but should be higher. As a matter of fact, defendant also admitted that there are only eight ninth and tenth grade high schools left in Nebraska, but that in the recent past he had waived the ratio of 1–5 for two or three other like high schools in Washington County because they had prospects for more students in the future, or had suggested the possibility of reorganization.

Thus the Superintendent of Public Instruction has been delegated a free hand without legislative limitations or standards to make or change at will any numerical ratio or standard required for approval of high schools for the collection of free high school tuition money when it would have been a simple matter for the Legislature, which had the power and authority, to have incorporated limits and standards in the statute. As a consequence, without questioning the motives or ability of the Superintendent of Public Instruction, there might well be approval of some high schools upon one standard and a withholding of approval from others by a qualification of such standard or by virtue of another. Thus, defendant had arbitrary power over the life or death of all high schools in this state and the preservation or destruction of their property and the grant or denial of free high school revenue, dependent upon the granting or refusal of approval.

Article II, section 1, Constitution of Nebraska provides: "The powers of the government of this state are divided into three distinct departments, the legislative, executive and judicial, and no person or collection of persons being one of these departments, shall exercise any power properly belonging to either of the others, except as hereinafter expressly directed or permitted." . . .

As said in 42 Am.Jur., Public Administrative Law, § 45, p. 342, citing authorities from many states: "It is a fundamental principle of our system of government that the rights of men are to be determined by the law itself, and not by the let or leave of administrative officers or bureaus. This principle ought not to be surrendered for convenience, or in effect nullified for the sake of expediency. However, it is impossible for the legislature to deal directly with the host of details in the complex conditions on which it legislates, and when the legislature states the purpose of the law and sets up standards to guide the agency which is to administer it, there is no constitutional objection to vesting discretion as to its execution in the administrators. . . . A statute which in effect reposes an absolute, unregulated, and undefined discretion in an administrative body bestows arbitrary powers and is an unlawful delegation of legislative powers. The presumption that an officer will not act arbitrarily but will exercise sound judgment and good faith cannot sustain a delegation of unregulated discretion." . . .

. . . We have considered the question of constitutionality in the light of the presumption of validity to which a legislative act is entitled. Nevertheless, we conclude that the last sentence of section 79–307, R.R.S. 1943, . . . [unconstitutionally] delegates legislative authority to the Superintendent of Public Instruction. . . .

Notes

1. The line of demarcation between the ability of chief state school officers to legislate, which is unconstitutional, and their authority to formulate reasonable rules and regulations is unclear. Do you agree with the court's placing the power to classify districts on the legislative side of the line?

2. From an educational view, was the regulation that the superintendent promulgated a sound one?

3. Do you think it likely the regulation that precipitated this case would have withstood judicial scrutiny if the legislature had indicated that one of the items that the superintendent could have taken into account was the student-teacher ratio?

[Case No. 19]   Mandamus against Chief State School Officer

STATE EX REL. CLEVELAND BOARD OF EDUCATION
v. STATE BOARD OF EDUCATION OF OHIO

Supreme Court of Ohio, 1984.
464 N.E.2d 137 [17 Educ. L. Rep. 932].

PER CURIAM.

This action in mandamus was brought by the Cleveland Board of Education to compel respondent, the State Board of Education of Ohio and its superintendent, Dr. Franklin B. Walter, to waive one day of required instruction in the Cleveland Public School System for the 1983–1984 school year.

On January 11, 1984 and January 12, 1984, members of the Unity Unions employed by the Cleveland Board of Education engaged in a work stoppage. These were primarily custodial employees whose duties included operating the boilers in the schools and other maintenance functions. On the days in question, the temperature in Cleveland ranged from 5° F to 18° F. Considering the lack of personnel to operate the heating systems and maintain the buildings, relator's superintendent closed the schools for those two days.

As a result of the closing of school on these two days, the Cleveland Public Schools will have been open for instruction one day less than required by R.C. 3313.48 if the regularly scheduled school year is not extended. The make-up day of instruction is currently scheduled for June 19, 1984, which Relator alleges will cost $750,000.

Relator initially sought a waiver of two days of instruction from respondent which was denied. Relator's request for an adjudication hearing pursuant to R.C. 119.07 and 119.09 was granted. A hearing was held and on May 24, 1984, the state superintendent issued his final order denying the requested waiver.

On May 25, 1984, this action in mandamus was filed seeking the issuance of a writ to compel respondent to waive the one day of instruction. (It is conceded that relator has available an appeal to the court of common pleas from its R.C. Chapter 119 appeal. However, in view of the fact that this dispute concerns whether the schools will be open on June 19, 1984, it would be impossible for relator to obtain the relief requested through that appeal process.) . . .

PER CURIAM. The sole issue presented is whether relator is entitled to the waiver of one day of required instruction as requested. The waiver of the minimum school year requirements is governed by R.C. 3317.01(B) which provides in relevant part:

   . . . This requirement shall be waived by the superintendent of public instruction if it had been necessary for a school to be closed because of disease epidemic, hazardous weather conditions, damage to a school building, or other temporary circumstances due to utility failure rendering the school building unfit for school use, ...

For the reasons that follow, we conclude that relator is entitled to the waiver of one day of instruction due to "other temporary circumstances due to utility failure rendering the school building unfit for school use" under R.C. 3317.01(B). We note first that no argument was made nor evidence presented to suggest that relator's superintendent acted imprudently in closing the schools. The utilities were inoperable, creating a genuine concern for the welfare of the students if classes were held. We sympathize with respondent's concern that too lenient enforcement of minimum school year requirements will erode the protections they afford to Ohio's public school students. However, the purpose of the minimum school year is to provide guidelines to insure that public schools offer quality education. We cannot conclude that one day of instruction will improve the quality of education offered in the Cleveland Public Schools this year, particularly when the one day will cost relator $750,000.

In so holding, we expressly reject relator's contention that the reason for the utility failure is irrelevant in determining whether a waiver is appropriate under R.C. 3317.01(B). We find simply that the reasons for the utility failure herein do not justify requiring relator to schedule a make-up day of instruction at a cost of $750,000. This expenditure can only adversely affect relator's students in the long run, with no practical benefit in return.

Accordingly, the writ is allowed.

Notes

1.   The common-law writ of mandamus is designed to compel performance of a non-discretionary duty. Did the superintendent's decision not to grant the waiver clearly fit in that category?

2.   Why was this case decided by the state's highest court without its having gone through the lower courts first?

3.   With whom do you agree, the superintendent or the court?

[Case No. 20]   Judicial Review of Decision of Chief State School Officer

CONLEY v. AMBACH

Court of Appeals of New York, 1984.
472 N.Y.S.2d 598 [16 Educ. L. Rep. 576].

MEMORANDUM.

The authority of the Commissioner of Education to review the findings of a hearing panel ... [in connection with charges against a tenure teacher] includes the right to annul the decision of the panel on the ground of bias or partiality of the panel chairman. The standard by which the determination of the commissioner in the exercise of such authority is to be judged on judicial review is whether his determination "was made in violation of lawful procedure, was affected by an error of law or was arbitrary and capricious or an abuse of discretion". The operative test in this instance is whether the commissioner's determination to annul the decision of the hearing panel was arbitrary and capricious.

His determination was made on the ground that, during the course of the proceedings before the panel, its chairman accepted a remunerative position with the New York State United Teachers (NYSUT) as one of eight arbitrators available to hear disputes between NYSUT and its professional employees, without disclosure thereof to the board of education until subsequent to the close of the hearings. This employment, coupled with the circumstance that counsel for NYSUT represented the teacher at the hearings, was found to raise a sufficient question as to the impartiality of the chairman (or the appearance thereof) as to warrant vacatur of the decision of the panel. Although no direct relationship between the chairman and one of the parties to the proceeding was revealed, there was shown to have been an undisclosed connection between the chairman and counsel for the teacher. This connection alone, without any showing of actual partiality or impropriety on the part of the chairman (of neither of which is there any suggestion in this record), constituted a rational basis for the commissioner's action. Accordingly, his determination of annulment was not arbitrary or capricious and must be sustained.

The commissioner had no authority, however, to impose the prescriptions that he did on the further conduct of the hearings. Specifically, he had no authority to direct the selection of the new chairman of the panel by the parties; the statute mandates that the third member of the panel shall be chosen by mutual agreement of the other two panel members.

Additionally, inasmuch as portions of the evidence at the hearings consisted of conflicting testimony of live witnesses, the credibility and persuasive force of which testimony might not be susceptible to adequate evaluation on the basis of a reading of the transcript only, it was an abuse of discretion, in view of the key role played by the chairman of the hearing panel as its only impartial member, to order the determination of the reconstituted panel to be based only "upon the record already established". This is not to say that portions or all of the transcript of the first hearings cannot be employed by the new panel in making its determination; it is to say only that, absent agreement of the parties and the new chairman, the commissioner cannot order that the consideration of the new panel be confined to the record already established. . . .

Notes

1. The hearing panel found the teacher guilty of two of thirteen charged specifications and recommended a $300 fine. When the board appealed, the commissioner annulled the panel's decision, but the trial court overturned the commissioner's action. The appellate court reinstated the commissioner's order, writing that as chief educational officer of the state, he had the authority to adopt higher ethical standards for disclosure than might have existed in commercial or other arbitration situations.

2. A unanimous appellate court rejected any notion suggesting that the appearance of bias did not exist where a board's appointee to a hearing panel sought and obtained from it an additional $100 per-diem fee, an arrangement unknown to the teacher, her attorney, or other panel members. The court thus upheld the annulment of the panel's split decision recommending the teacher's dismissal and the board's acceptance thereof. The panel had conducted forty-six days of hearings, after which the chair and, the board's appointee, voted for dismissal, with the teacher's appointee disagreeing on the major charges and recommending only a letter of reprimand and caution. The court concluded that an entirely new hearing panel would have to consider the charges. *Syquia v. Board of Educ. of Harpursville Cent. School Dist.*, 591 N.Y.S.2d 996 [80 Educ. L. Rep. 182] (N.Y.1992).

[Case No. 21]   Necessity of Appeal to Chief State School Officer—Power of Local Board to Maintain a Department of Health

CITY OF DALLAS v. MOSELY

Court of Civil Appeals of Texas, 1926.
286 S.W. 497.

JONES, C.J. Appellees prevailed in the trial of an injunction suit in the district court of Dallas County, Tex., and a judgment was entered restraining the board of education of the city of Dallas, and each individual member thereof, from maintaining in the public free schools of the city of Dallas the department of health in connection with said schools, and restraining the city of Dallas, its auditor and treasurer, from the payment of any money for such purpose. . . .

The allegations of the petition for injunction charge that said health department is being maintained in said public schools without lawful authority and by the illegal expenditure of large sums of money thus diverted from the legitimate purpose for which it was collected by the levy of taxes for the support of public free schools in the city of Dallas. The answer of appellant challenged the jurisdiction of the court to entertain said suit, because of the failure of appellees to seek relief by an appeal to the superintendent of public instruction, and, if necessary, to the state board of education, before filing the suit. Appellants also contend that the establishment and maintenance of said health department in the public free schools of said city in the manner and for the purpose same was maintained is legal and clearly within the discretionary powers of the board of education; that such health department is necessary for the proper discharge of the duty resting on said board to establish and maintain an efficient system of public free schools. These respective contentions present the controlling issues on this appeal. . . .

After a careful investigation of the working of health departments in other cities by the school authorities of the city of Dallas, and believing that the efficiency of the city's free schools would thereby be increased, the board of education, by resolution duly adopted, established this department, and it was in force for the school year 1925–26. An appropriation of $30,000, or so much thereof as necessary, was duly made from the funds derived from the special taxes levied by the city of Dallas for maintaining its public schools, for the establishment and maintenance of said health department. A competent physician was employed as superintendent of this department at a salary of $4,000 per year, and such physician is required to devote his entire time to the work. Six women nurses were employed for the school year of nine months, each at a salary of $125 per month. During a portion of the year a dentist was employed at a salary of $2,000....

Appellants have duly assigned error on the action of the trial court in overruling their plea in abatement. The specific ground on which the plea in abatement was urged is that, as the petition of appellees discloses that no appeal was prosecuted by them from the action of the board of education in overruling their protest to the establishment of said department of health and in making the appropriation of school money for that purpose, to the state superintendent of public instruction, and, if necessary, to the state board of education, this suit cannot be maintained. This contention is based on a provision in article 2656, which reads as follows:

> "The state superintendent shall be charged with the administration of the school laws and a general superintendency of the business relating to the public schools of the state, and he shall have printed for general distribution such number of copies of school laws as the state board of education may determine. He shall hear and determine all appeals from the rulings and decisions of subordinate school officers, and all such officers and teachers shall conform to his decisions. Appeal shall always be from his rulings to the state board...."

If the allegations in appellees' petition are susceptible to the construction that the board of education only abused its discretion either in establishing the said health department or in the manner in which it is maintained, then we think appellants' position would be well taken. We cannot agree with appellees that, because section 1 of article 5 of the charter of the city of Dallas provides that the board of education created by said section "shall have exclusive control of the public schools of the city of Dallas," that the state superintendent is thereby divested by this special legislative act of all power of supervision of the public free schools within said city. Such has not been the construction of our higher courts in reference to similar provisions in city charters.

The petition in the instant case does not charge an abuse of discretion that could be legally exercised by the board of education, but charges the doing of acts beyond its power and concerning which it had no discretion, and that, in furtherance of such unlawful acts, it is diverting public money, coming into its possession for a special purpose. We do not believe it was the intention of the Legislature in the above-quoted enactment to close the door of the courts to taxpayers in cases of misapplication of public school money by public officers, charged with its proper expenditure, until the slow processes of appeal have been perfected to the state superintendent of public instruction and the state board of education, who are not vested with judicial powers. We think the appeal authorized by the said statute is from purely administrative matters in the conduct of the schools by boards of education....

... We therefore hold that the court did not err in overruling appellants' plea in abatement....

It is apparent, therefore, that the correct solution of the question under inquiry is dependent largely on whether the said health department, as it is maintained by the said board of education, has for its primary purpose improving the efficiency of the system of public schools for the city of Dallas. As shown by the rules governing said department, by means of the records made of the physical examination made of the pupils, the teachers are informed of the physical condition of the children under their instruction and said teachers are thereby enabled intelligently to diagnose the mental aptitude and powers of such pupils and to direct their teaching in the light of such knowledge. The parents are informed of the physical defects, in many instances curable, that may hinder the mental process of their children, and thereby given opportunity to have such defects as will yield to treatment corrected. Those in charge of the health department are also required to instruct the teachers and pupils in reference to the laws of health and hygiene, and the children are thereby enabled to pursue their education under more favorable conditions than would otherwise obtain. The directors of the playground activities, where the children are given the necessary healthful exercise, are enabled to judge the amount of exercise and character of play in which those children who are physically deficient can engage without endangering their health.

As shown by this record, the work of the health department in the public free schools of the city of Dallas is within itself educational and instructive on matters directly related to the efficiency of such schools, and tends to their betterment. This being true, its establishment and maintenance as a part of the public free school system of Dallas are within the lawful discretion of the board of education....

Notes

1. The rule that emerged in this case, that it is not necessary to appeal "legal" matters to the state superintendent of public instruction as a condition precedent to having recourse to the courts, represents the weight of authority.

2. Note the breadth of the language used in the statute in the case. The statute gives the state superintendent general authority over "business" relating to public schools. Should spending money here have been considered "business?"

3. Examine the statutes in your state to evaluate the rights of aggrieved persons in educational disputes. How, if at all, are the chief state school officer and the state board of education involved?

[Case No. 22] "Judicial Review of the Authority of a State Athletic Association."

BRENTWOOD ACADEMY v. TENNESSEE SECONDARY SCHOOLS ATHLETIC ASSOCIATION

Supreme Court of the United States, 2001.
531 U.S. 288, 121 S.Ct. 924, 148 L.Ed.2d 807 [151 Educ. L. Rep. 18].

JUSTICE SOUTER delivered the opinion of the Court.

The issue is whether a statewide association incorporated to regulate interscholastic athletic competition among public and private secondary schools may be regarded as engaging in state action when it enforces a rule against a member school. The association in question here includes most public schools located within the State, acts through their representatives, draws its officers from them, is largely funded by their dues and income received in their stead, and has historically been seen to regulate in lieu of the State Board of Education's exercise of its own authority. We hold that the association's regulatory activity may and should be treated as state action owing to the pervasive entwinement of state school officials in the structure of the association, there being no offsetting reason to see the association's acts in any other way.

I

Respondent Tennessee Secondary School Athletic Association (Association) is a not-for-profit membership corporation organized to regulate interscholastic sport among the public and private high schools in Tennessee that belong to it. No school is forced to join, but without any other authority actually regulating interscholastic athletics, it enjoys the memberships of almost all the State's public high schools (some 290 of them or 84% of the Association's voting membership), far outnumbering the 55 private schools that belong. A member school's team may play or scrimmage only against the team of another member, absent a dispensation.

The Association's rulemaking arm is its legislative council, while its board of control tends to administration. The voting membership of each of these nine-person committees is limited under the Association's bylaws to high school principals, assistant principals, and superintendents elected by the member schools, and the public school administrators who so serve typically attend meetings during regulars school hours. Although the Association's staff members are not paid by the State, they are eligible to join the State's public retirement system for its employees. Member schools pay dues to the Association, though the bulk of its revenue is gate receipts at member teams' football and basketball tournaments, many of them held in public arenas rented by the Association.

The constitution, bylaws, and rules of the Association set standards of school membership and the eligibility of students to play in interscholastic games. Each school, for example, is regulated in awarding financial aid, most coaches must have a Tennessee state teaching license, and players must meet minimum academic standards and hew to limits on student employment. Under the bylaws, "in all matters pertaining to the athletic relations of his school," the principal is responsible to the Association, which has the power "to suspend, to fine, or otherwise penalize any member school for the violation of any of the rules of the Association or for other just cause."

Ever since the Association was incorporated in 1925, Tennessee's State Board of Education (State Board) has (to use its own words) acknowledged the corporation's functions "in providing standards, rules and regulations for interscholastic competition in the public schools of Tennessee." More recently, the State Board cited its statutory authority when it adopted language expressing the relationship between the Association and the State Board. Specifically, in 1972, it went so far as to adopt a rule expressly "designat[ing]" the Association as "the organization to supervise and regulate the athletic activities in which the public junior and senior high schools in Tennessee participate on an interscholastic basis." The Rule provided that "the authority granted herein shall remain in effect until revoked" and instructed the State Board's chairman to "designate a person or persons to serve in an ex-officio capacity on the [Association's governing bodies]." That same year, the State Board specifically approved the Association's rules and regulations, while reserving the right to review future changes. Thus, on several occasions over the next 20 years, the State Board reviewed, approved, or reaffirmed its approval of the recruiting Rule at issue in this case. In 1996, however, the State Board dropped the original Rule expressly designating the Association as regulator; it substituted a statement "recogniz[ing] the value of participation in interscholastic athletics and the role of [the Association] in coordinating interscholastic athletic competition," while "authoriz[ing] the public schools of the state to voluntarily maintain membership in [the Association]."

The action before us responds to a 1997 regulatory enforcement proceeding brought against petitioner, Brentwood Academy, a private parochial high school. . . . The Association's board of control found that Brentwood violated a rule prohibiting "undue influence" in recruiting athletes when it wrote to incoming students and their parents about spring football practice. The Association accordingly placed Brentwood's athletic program on probation for four years, declared its football and boys' basketball teams ineligible to compete in playoffs for two years, and imposed a $3,000 fine. When these penalties were imposed, all the voting members of the board of control and legislative council were public school administrators.

Brentwood sued the Association and its executive director in federal court under Section 1983, claiming that enforcement of the Rule was state action and a violation of the First and Fourteenth Amendments. The District Court entered summary judgment for Brentwood and enjoined the Association from enforcing the Rule. . . . [the court] found that the State had delegated authority over high school athletics to the Association, characterized the relationship between the Association and its public school members as symbiotic, and emphasized the predominantly public character of the Association's membership and leadership. The court relied on language in *National Collegiate Athletic Ass'n v. Tarkanian* suggesting that statewide interscholastic athletic associations are state actors, and on other federal cases in which such organizations had uniformly been held to be acting under color of state law.

The . . . Sixth Circuit reversed. It recognized that there is no single test to identify state actions and state actors but applied three criteria derived from *Blum v. Yaretsky*, *Lugar v. Edmondson Oil Co.*, and *Rendell–Baker v. Kohn*, and found no state action under any of them. It said the District Court was mistaken in seeing a symbiotic relationship between the State and the Association, it emphasized that the Association was neither engaging in a traditional and exclusive public function nor responding to state compulsion, and it gave short shrift to the language from *Tarkanian* on which the District Court relied. Rehearing en banc was later denied over the dissent of two judges, who criticized the panel decision for creating a conflict among state and federal courts, for being inconsistent with *Tarkanian*, and for lacking support in the "functional" analysis of private activity . . . for assessing the significance of cooperation between public officials and a private actor.

We granted certiorari to resolve the conflict and now reverse.

A

Our cases try to plot a line between state action subject to Fourteenth Amendment scrutiny and private conduct (however exceptionable) that is not. The judicial obligation is not only to " 'preserv[e] an area of individual freedom by limiting the reach of federal law' and avoi[d] the imposition of responsibility on a State for conduct it could not control," but also to assure that constitutional standards are invoked "when it can be said that the State is responsible for the specific conduct of which the plaintiff complains." If the Fourteenth Amendment is not to be displaced, therefore, its ambit cannot be a simple line between States and people operating outside formally governmental organizations, and the deed of an ostensibly private organization or individual is to be treated sometimes as if a State had caused it to be performed. Thus, we say that state action may be found if, though only if, there is such a "close nexus between the State and the challenged action" that seemingly private behavior "may be fairly treated as that of the State itself."

What is fairly attributable is a matter of normative judgment, and the criteria lack rigid simplicity. From the range of circumstances that could point toward the State behind an individual face, no one fact can function as a necessary condition across the board for finding state action; nor is any set of circumstances absolutely sufficient, for there may be some countervailing reason against attributing activity to the government.

Our cases have identified a host of facts that can bear on the fairness of such an attribution. We have, for example, held that a challenged activity may be state action when it results from the State's exercise of "coercive power," when the State provides "significant encouragement, either overt or covert," or when a private actor operates as a "willful participant in joint activity with the State or its agents." We have treated a nominally private entity as a state actor when it is controlled by an "agency of the State" when it has been delegated a public function by the State, when it is "entwined with governmental policies," or when government is "entwined in [its] management or control."

Amidst such variety, examples may be the best teachers, and examples from our cases are unequivocal in showing that the character of a legal entity is determined neither by its expressly private characterization in statutory law, nor by the failure of the law to acknowledge the entity's inseparability from recognized government officials or agencies . . . . .

These examples of public entwinement in the management and control of ostensibly separate trusts or corporations foreshadow this case, as this Court itself anticipated in *Tarkanian*. *Tarkanian* arose when an undoubtedly state actor, the University of Nevada, suspended its basketball coach, *Tarkanian*, in order to comply with rules and recommendations of the National Collegiate Athletic Association (NCAA). The coach charged the NCAA with state action, arguing that the state university had delegated its own functions to the NCAA, clothing the latter with authority to make and apply the university's rules, the result being joint action making the NCAA a state actor.

To be sure, it is not the strict holding in *Tarkanian* that points to our view of this case, for we found no state action on the part of the NCAA. We could see, on the one hand, that the university had some part in setting the NCAA's rules, and the Supreme Court of Nevada had gone so far as to hold that the NCAA had been delegated the university's traditionally exclusive public authority over personnel. But on the other side, the NCAA's policies were shaped not by the University of Nevada alone, but by several hundred member institutions, most of them having no connection with Nevada, and exhibiting no color of Nevada law. Since it was difficult to see the NCAA, not as a collective membership, but as surrogate for the one State, we held the organization's connection with Nevada too insubstantial to ground a state-action claim.

But dictum in *Tarkanian* pointed to a contrary result on facts like ours, with an organization whose member public schools are all within a single State. "The situation would, of course, be different if the [Association's] membership consisted entirely of institutions located within the same State, many of them public institutions created by the same sovereign." To support our surmise, we approvingly cited two cases: *Clark v. Arizona Interscholastic Ass'n*, a challenge to a state high school athletic association that kept boys from playing on girls' interscholastic volleyball teams in Arizona; and *Louisiana High School Athletic Ass'n v. St. Augustine High School*, a parochial school's attack on the racially segregated system of interscholastic high school athletics maintained by the athletic association. In each instance, the Court of Appeals treated the athletic association as a state actor.

B

Just as we foresaw in *Tarkanian*, the "necessarily fact-bound inquiry" leads to the conclusion of state action here. The nominally private character of the Association is overborne by the pervasive entwinement of public institutions and public officials in its composition and workings, and there is no substantial reason to claim unfairness in applying constitutional standards to it.

The Association is not an organization of natural persons acting on their own, but of schools, and of public schools to the extent of 84% of the total. . . .

Although the findings and prior opinions in this case include no express conclusion of law that public school officials act within the scope of their duties when they represent their institutions, no other view would be rational, the official nature of their involvement being shown in any number of ways. Interscholastic athletics obviously play an integral part in the public education of Tennessee, where nearly every public high school spends money on competitions among schools. Since a pickup system of interscholastic games would not do, these public teams need some mechanism to produce rules and regulate competition. The mechanism is an organization overwhelmingly composed of public school officials who select representatives (all of them public officials at the time in question here), who in turn adopt and enforce the rules that make the system work. Thus, by giving these jobs to the Association, the 290 public schools of Tennessee belonging to it can sensibly be seen as exercising their own authority to meet their own responsibilities. Unsurprisingly, then, the record indicates that half the council or board meetings documented here were held during official school hours, and that public schools have largely provided for the Association's financial support. A small portion of the Association's revenue comes from membership dues paid by the schools, and the principal part from gate receipts at tournaments among the member schools. Unlike mere public buyers of contract services, whose payments for services rendered do not convert the service providers into public actors, the schools here obtain membership in the service organization and give up sources of their own income to their collective association. The Association thus exercises the authority of the predominantly public schools to charge for admission to their games; the Association does not receive this money from the schools, but enjoys the schools' moneymaking capacity as its own.

In sum, to the extent of 84% of its membership, the Association is an organization of public schools represented by their officials acting in their official capacity to provide an integral element of secondary public schooling. There would be no recognizable Association, legal or tangible, without the public school officials, who do not merely control but overwhelmingly perform all but the purely ministerial acts by which the Association exists and functions in practical terms. Only the 16% minority of private school memberships prevents this entwinement of the

Association and the public school system from being total and their identities totally indistinguishable.

To complement the entwinement of public school officials with the Association from the bottom up, the State of Tennessee has provided for entwinement from top down. State Board members are assigned ex officio to serve as members of the board of control and legislative council, and the Association's ministerial employees are treated as state employees to the extent of being eligible for membership in the state retirement system. . . .

But the removal of the designation language from [the] Rule [at issue] affected nothing but words. Today the State Board's member-designees continue to sit on the Association's committees as nonvoting members, and the State continues to welcome Association employees in its retirement scheme. The close relationship is confirmed by the Association's enforcement of the same pre-amendment rules and regulations reviewed and approved by the State Board (including the recruiting Rule challenged by Brentwood), and by the State Board's continued willingness to allow students to satisfy its physical education requirement by taking part in interscholastic athletics sponsored by the Association. The most one can say on the evidence is that the State Board once freely acknowledged the Association's official character but now does it by winks and nods. The amendment to the Rule in 1996 affected candor but not the "momentum" of the Association's prior involvement with the State Board. The District Court spoke to this point in finding that because of "custom and practice," "the conduct of the parties has not materially changed" since 1996, "the connections between TSSAA and the State [being] still pervasive and entwined."

The entwinement down from the State Board is therefore unmistakable, just as the entwinement up from the member public schools is overwhelming. Entwinement will support a conclusion that an ostensibly private organization ought to be charged with a public character and judged by constitutional standards; entwinement to the degree shown here requires it.

C

Entwinement is also the answer to the Association's several arguments offered to persuade us that the facts would not support a finding of state action under various criteria applied in other cases. These arguments are beside the point, simply because the facts justify a conclusion of state action under the criterion of entwinement, a conclusion in no sense unsettled merely because other criteria of state action may not be satisfied by the same facts.

The Association places great stress, for example, on the application of a public function test, as exemplified in *Rendell–Baker v. Kohn*. There, an apparently private school provided education for students whose special needs made it difficult for them to finish high school. The record, however, failed to show any tradition of providing public special education to students unable to cope with a regular school, who had historically been cared for (or ignored) according to private choice. It was true that various public school districts had adopted the practice of referring students to the school and paying their tuition, and no one disputed that providing the instruction aimed at a proper public objective and conferred a public benefit. But we held that the performance of such a public function did not permit a finding of state action on the part of the school unless the function performed was exclusively and traditionally public, as it was not in that case. The Association argues that application of the public function criterion would produce the same result here, and we will assume, arguendo, that it would. But this case does not turn on a public function test, any more than *Rendell–Baker* had anything to do with entwinement of public officials in the special school.

For the same reason, it avails the Association nothing to stress that the State neither coerced nor encouraged the actions complained of. "Coercion" and "encouragement" are like "entwinement" in referring to kinds of facts that can justify characterizing an ostensibly private action as public instead. Facts that address any of these criteria are significant, but no one criterion must necessarily be applied. When, therefore, the relevant facts show pervasive entwinement to the point of largely overlapping identity, the implication of state action is not affected by pointing out that the facts might not loom large under a different test.

D

This is not to say that all of the Association's arguments are rendered beside the point by the public officials' involvement in the Association, for after application of the entwinement criterion, or any other, there is a further potential issue, and the Association raises it. Even facts that suffice to show public action ... may be outweighed in the name of some value at odds with finding public accountability in the circumstances. In Polk County, a defense lawyer's actions were deemed private even though she was employed by the county and was acting within the scope of her duty as a public defender. Full-time public employment would be conclusive of state action for some purposes, but not when the employee is doing a defense lawyer's primary job; then, the public defender does "not ac[t] on behalf of the State; he is the State's adversary." The state-action doctrine does not convert opponents into virtual agents.

The assertion of such a countervailing value is the nub of each of the Association's two remaining arguments, neither of which, however, persuades us. The Association suggests, first, that reversing the judgment here will somehow trigger an epidemic of unprecedented federal litigation. Even if that might be counted as a good reason for a Polk County decision to call the Association's action private, the record raises no reason for alarm here. Save for the Sixth Circuit, every Court of Appeals to consider a statewide athletic association like the one here has found it a state actor.... No one, however, has pointed to any explosion of § 1983 cases against interscholastic athletic associations in the affected jurisdictions. Not to put too fine a point on it, two District Courts in Tennessee have previously held the Association itself to be a state actor; but there is no evident wave of litigation working its way across the State. A reversal of the judgment here portends nothing more than the harmony of an outlying Circuit with precedent otherwise uniform.

Nor do we think there is anything to be said for the Association's contention that there is no need to treat it as a state actor since any public school applying the Association's rules is itself subject to suit under § 1983 or Title IX. . . . If Brentwood's claim were pushing at the edge of the class of possible defendant state actors, an argument about the social utility of expanding that class would at least be on point, but because we are nowhere near the margin in this case, the Association is really asking for nothing less than a dispensation for itself. Its position boils down to saying that the Association should not be dressed in state clothes because other, concededly public actors are; that Brentwood should be kept out of court because a different plaintiff raising a different claim in a different case may find the courthouse open. Pleas for special treatment are hard to sell, although saying that does not, of course, imply anything about the merits of Brentwood's complaint; the issue here is merely whether Brentwood properly names the Association as a § 1983 defendant, not whether it should win on its claim.

The judgment of the Court of Appeals for the Sixth Circuit is reversed, and the case is remanded for further proceedings consistent with this opinion.

It is so ordered.

Notes

1. Do you agree with the Court? Put another way, what should the relationship between a state board of education and a state athletic association be?

2. Have interscholastic sports taken on a life of their own that conflicts with academic programming in schools? What can or should school officials and/or parents do about this?

Chapter 4

LOCAL SCHOOL BOARDS: POWERS AND PROCEDURES

Introduction

Education was a primary concern in America from the earliest days of colonial New England. In fact, in 1642, a Massachusetts law directed "certain chosen men of each town to ascertain from time to time, if parents and masters were attending to, their educational duties; if the children were being trained in learning and labor and other employments."[1] After five years, the law was abandoned since it did not mandate the establishment of public schools.

A second law, passed in 1647, was more successful. The "ye old deluder" statute, so-called because it was designed to combat Satan's desire to delude people into ignorance of scriptures in order to lead them more easily to damnation, required all towns with more than fifty households to establish and maintain schools.[2] The law also decreed that towns where officials did not follow the law were to be fined. While this law was not strictly complied with only a decade after its enactment, it did introduce the legal principle that education is a function of local government. Officials in Connecticut enacted virtually the same law in 1650.[3] In 1693, local control over education in Connecticut was further solidified when officials enacted another law directing town selectmen to operate schools and to impose taxes to support them if so directed by a vote of residents at a town meeting.[4] Similar laws were soon in effect throughout New England.

In early America, public education was a function of local government, administered via town meetings and later by town selectmen. Yet, since selectmen were responsible for all town agencies, not just education, they often delegated authority for such tasks as choosing a new teacher or supervising the construction of a new school building. When it became necessary for selectmen to delegate more and more of their duties relating to education, in 1721 they appointed the first permanent

---

1. SOUL OF AMERICA: DOCUMENTING OUR PAST, VOL I: 1492–1870 19 (Robert C. Baron ed., 1994).

2. DOCUMENTS OF AMERICAN HISTORY, VOL. I: TO 1898 29. (Henry Steele Commager, ed., 7th ed., 1965). Keeping its original spelling, the statute begins: "It being one chiefe project of ye ould deluder, Satan, to keepe men from the knowledge of ye Scriptures,.... [i]t is therefore ordred, yt evry townshhip ... [with 50 households shall]

forthwith appoint one ... to teach all such children ... to write & reade [and] whose wages shall be paid eithr by ye parents ot mastrs of such children, or by ye inhabitants in genrall...."

3. LAWRENCE A. CREMIN, AMERICAN EDUCATION: THE COLONIAL EXPERIENCE, 1607–1783 181–182 (1970).

4. CHARLES E. REEVES, SCHOOL BOARDS: THEIR STATUS, FUNCTIONS AND ACTIVITIES 19 (1954, reprinted 1969).

school committee in Boston. This action marked the beginning of the process of separating school governing bodies from other local governmental entities.[5]

The first federal document to mention education was the Northwest Ordinance, adopted in 1787. According to Article III of the Ordinance, "religion, morality, and knowledge, being necessary to good government and the happiness of mankind, schools and the means of education shall forever be encouraged."[6] This language greatly influenced state constitutions in the Midwest and is evident today as states grant plenary powers to local school boards.

The colonial practice of local control carried over into the new American nation. In 1789, a Massachusetts law authorized the creation of separate school committees. Later that year, a statute from Boston called for the election of a twelve-member committee to serve as a separate governing body over public schools.[7] In 1798, Massachusetts recognized the committees as separate governing bodies while selectmen or other town officials were sometimes members of the board. In 1826, legislators amended the law to ensure that the committees were independent of other governmental bodies.[8] In this way, the process begun over a century earlier was brought to completion in New England before spreading throughout the country.

Powers in General

The evolution of the American public education is characterized by broad judicial interpretations of implied powers of local school officials. The Supreme Court acknowledged this point in *San Antonio Independent School District v. Rodriguez*[9] in commenting that local school boards have the authority to tailor educational needs to their communities. Judicial deference to local boards, as long as they do not act in "unreasonable, arbitrary, capricious or unlawful manner[s],"[10] has encouraged freedom and experimentation out of proportion to that suggested by the legal structure of public education. Creative boards typically introduce new practices in what may be described as exercises of latent implied powers. If practices are not challenged, or survive judicial scrutiny, they may spread until they become generally accepted. In an overwhelming number of cases involving new educational practices, local boards have prevailed, usually on the basis that an activity is a desirable way of achieving broad legislative and/or educational goals. The earliest, and perhaps most dramatic, example of this process was the extension of a common school system to include high schools when the Supreme Court

---

5. *Id.* at 17.

6. BARON, *supra* note 1 at 86.

7. Raymond E. Callahan. *The American Board of Education, 1789–1960*. In UNDERSTANDING SCHOOL BOARDS 19 (Peter J. Cistone, ed. 1975).

8. REEVES, *supra* note 3 at 20.

9. 411 U.S. 1, 93 S.Ct. 1278, 36 L.Ed.2d 16 (1973).

10. *Sherwood Nat'l Educ. Ass'n v. Sherwood–Cass R–VIII School Dist.*, 168 S.W.3d 456 [201 Educ. L. Rep. 394] (Mo. Ct. App. 2005), *reh'g and/or transfer denied* (Mo. Ct. App. 2005), *transfer denied* (Mo. 2005).

of Michigan's acceptance of this practice meant that similar challenges would not be vigorously pursued in other states.[11]

Insofar as most geographic locations are home to both school boards and local governments, relations between the two are often before the courts. At this point, it is important to stress the basic separateness of the two entities. That is, even where the boundaries of a municipal unit and a school district are coterminous, there is no merger of their affairs.[12] While so-called "home rule" charters, which allow municipalities the exclusive right to enact legislation addressing local needs, do not diminish a state's power to regulate education,[13] such authority must typically yield to municipal home rule provisions governing the same subject matter such as school budgets. In such a case, the Supreme Court of Connecticut held that a municipality and local school board could jointly discharge their responsibilities to ensure that an education budget met general state requirements to address the needs of the town's children.[14] However, as reflected by a decision of the Supreme Court of New Hampshire, municipalities must not exceed the scope of their authority in attempting to turn independent school boards into city departments.[15]

As school boards exercise their legal authority, the three dimensions of their power reflect the tripartite division of authority that is evident in both the federal and state governments. Put another way, local school boards, like their state counterparts, exercise executive, legislative, and quasi-judicial authority. Boards exercise their legislative authority when they set policy by approving rules and regulations, whether involving students, teachers, or other matters, that are necessary to carry out their express dictates. Of course, once boards set policy for themselves, they are bound to follow the rules that they have established.[16] Boards exercise their executive power when they enter into contracts with personnel and/or for services. Boards function in a quasi-judicial manner when they hear appeals over the implementation of their policies such as whether students should be expelled for violating disciplinary rules or whether the contracts of employees should be terminated or not renewed due to poor performance.

Boards exercise the three dimensions of their powers through two distinct types of legal actions, ministerial or mandatory and discretionary or directory duties. While it may be difficult at times to distinguish between these two categories, they are sufficiently different to allow for a delineation of the legal principles involved.

11. *Stuart v. School Dist. No. 1 of Village of Kalamazoo*, 30 Mich. 69 (Mich. 1874).

12. *State ex rel. Harbach v. Mayor of City of Milwaukee*, 206 N.W. 210 (Wis. 1925).

13. *School Comm. of the Town of Winslow v. Inhabitants of the Town of Winslow*, 404 A.2d 988 (Me.1979).

14. *Board of Educ. of the Town and Borough of Naugatuck v. Town and Bor-* *ough of Naugatuck*, 843 A.2d 603 [186 Educ. L. Rep. 420] (Conn. 2004).

15. *City of Manchester School Dist. v. City of Manchester*, 843 A.2d 966 [186 Educ. L. Rep. 449] (N.H. 2004).

16. *See, e.g., Limestone County Educ. Ass'n v. Limestone County Bd. of Educ.*, 880 So.2d 446 [191 Educ. L. Rep. 919] (Ala. Civ. App. 2003), *cert. denied* (2003).

Ministerial or mandatory functions are those that state law requires boards to perform. The failure of boards to exercise their ministerial duties may result in corporate and/or personal liability for them and their members. Moreover, ministerial duties allow for little or no choice concerning whether or how they are to be performed. Laws relating to mandatory board duties typically include such obligations as adopting bylaws and rules to discharge their duties, to hire a superintendent and other school personnel, to purchase sites on which to build schools, to prescribe courses of instruction and textbooks, and to enforce compulsory state education laws.[17]

Boards cannot delegate their authority to act in matters that legislatures specifically assigned to them such as hiring personnel. At the same time, "school boards are limited in their employment decisions in that such decisions must be reasonable, in the best interests of the students, and not arbitrary or capricious."[18] Even so, since it is impractical, if not impossible, for boards to be involved actively in the process of hiring all new teachers, they must rely on their administrative staff to make recommendations about prospective job applicants. As such, even where board approval is a mere formality, they will have carried out their legal mandate by acting on recommendations from school administrators. Further, in light of the emergence of school-based decision-making and new working relationships between school boards and building-level management councils concerning personnel, budgetary, and curricular matters,[19] it will be interesting to observe what changes might transpire in relations between school boards and their professional staffs.

Discretionary powers afford school boards the authority to act should they desire to involve non-mandatory duties that arguably account for the larger part of their actions. Examples of discretionary power include the right to expand the size of a school's professional staff, whether to accept federal aid for school programs, and/or whether to adopt curricular standards that are more stringent than state guidelines. As discussed earlier, as long as boards properly exercise their discretionary power by not acting arbitrarily or capriciously, the courts are reluctant to interfere with their decisions.

As litigation reflects, since the line between mandatory and discretionary duties is a fine one, it is easily blurred. That is, while extracurricular activities are ordinarily discretionary in nature, it is difficult to imagine what schools would be like for students if they were not present.

To the extent that it is not possible to foresee, or legislate on, all of the issues that can arise in schools, the courts agree that in addition to

---

17. *See, e.g.,* Ariz. Rev. Stat. Ann. §§ 15–341 *et seq.,* Colo. Rev. Stat. Ann. §§ 22–32–101 *et seq.,* Fla. Stat. Ann. §§ 1001.42 et seq., 105 Ill. Comp. Stat. Ann. 5/14–6.01, Ky. Rev. Stat. Ann. § 160.290, La. Rev. Stat. Ann. §§ 17.81.01 *et seq.,* Mich. Comp. Laws Ann. §§ 380.1131 *et seq.,* Miss. Code Ann. § 37–7–301, N.M. Stat. Ann. § 22–5–4, Tex. Educ.

Code Ann. § 28–11 App., Utah Code. Ann. § 53A–1a–501.6.

18. *Board of Educ. of County of Randolph v. Scott,* 617 S.E.2d 478, 484 [201 Educ. L. Rep. 365] (W. Va. 2005).

19. For two extensive statutes of this type, *see* 105 Ill. Comp. Stat. Ann. 5/34–2.2 *et seq.,* Ky. Rev. Stat. Ann. § 160.345.

express powers, local boards may exercise their authority "by necessary implication"[20] in ways that enable them to carry out their duties. At this point, it is important to emphasize that while boards have implied powers related only to education, not general governmental concerns, they must be careful not to exceed their implied power. In such a case, the Supreme Court of Pennsylvania found that a local board exceeded its implied power in providing funds to help combat juvenile delinquency since this was not part of a school's program.[21] However, almost thirty years later, a federal trial court in Pennsylvania noted that this earlier judgment was explicitly superseded by statute in a dispute wherein it upheld the legality of a condom distribution program in high schools.[22] More recently, the Supreme Court of South Dakota, although reiterating the general rule that a board has the authority to act when the legislature expressly grants it power that can be necessarily implied by statute, affirmed that a local board exceeded its authority when it reimbursed two private citizens for the legal fees they incurred in their private legal action to overturn a decision of a school election recount board.[23] The court explained that the board was not authorized to reimburse the private legal fees.

When in doubt, the courts, applying common law, are inclined to find against the existence of implied powers since boards have no inherent authority. Case law reveals that while courts typically do not deviate from this principle, they construe implied powers broadly, seeming to have become even more open to this notion in recent years. As reflected by a case from the Supreme Court of Arkansas, a board cannot enlarge its powers if doing so conflicts with state law. Where a state law provided for annual contracts for teachers, the court decided that a local board could not offer an employment agreement to a teacher that exceeded the statutory limit.[24]

The judicial rule that local boards possess not only express, but also implied, powers is essentially one of expedience as a legal basis for sustaining board actions that appear to be educationally sound. If courts apply statutes strictly, they can limit the implied powers of boards but may have the undesired effect of restricting educational experimentation. In these situations, empowering statutes can be changed to bring a power in question within the scope of a board's express authority. By the same token, if legislatures disagree with judicial extensions of the implied powers, they can restrict or withdraw board authority by enacting new statutes.

Clearly, boards must exercise their authority in accord with statutory and common law procedures. A key common law principle in this

20. *D.O.F. v. Lewisburg Area School Dist. Bd. of School Directors,* 868 A.2d 28, 33 [196 Educ. L. Rep. 263] (Pa.Cmwlth. Ct. 2004).

21. *Barth v. School Dist. of Philadelphia,* 143 A.2d 909 (Pa.1958).

22. *Parents United for Better Schools v. School Dist. of Philadelphia Bd. of Educ.,* 978 F.Supp. 197 [122 Educ. L. Rep. 155]

(E.D. Pa. 1997), *aff'd,* 148 F.3d 260 [127 Educ. L. Rep. 670] (3d Cir. 1998).

23. *In re Writ of Certiorari as to Wrongful Payments of Attorney Fees made by Brookings School Dist. School Bd.,* 668 N.W.2d 538 [180 Educ. L. Rep. 301] (S.D. 2003).

24. *Nethercutt v. Pulaski County Special School Dist.,* 475 S.W.2d 517 (Ark.1972).

regard is that a delegated power may not be further delegated by the person or body to whom it was originally delegated. Thus, even if not required to do so, boards may, but are not required to, seek advice from committees, regular employees, consultants, students, and the public. Boards must thus make final decisions since they have no power to diminish their authority even if they wish to do so. In an illustrative dispute, an appellate court in Florida indicated that a hiring committee was merely advisory since the final decision whether to employ an individual rested with the board and superintendent.[25]

It is often unclear whether the power to execute a matter is nondelegable or even whether an act constitutes an improper delegation. The latter problem is similar to that of delegation of legislative power discussed in Chapter 3.[26] Legislatures can substantially clarify the rules of delegation through specific statutes pertaining to board powers while the judiciary can evaluate the boundaries of legislative delegation.

Boards must retain their nondelegable powers even where collective bargaining contracts are enforceable since a board can no more bargain away a power than it can unilaterally impose its will.[27] Where collective bargaining statutes specifically cover matters in relation to other statutes applicable to how boards function, the question of delegability may be answered implicitly, if not explicitly.

Questions of delegation of school board authority to administrators frequently arise when plaintiffs seek to have actions nullified. To this end, where a school board overturned a superintendent's approval of a teacher's transfer in light of its interpretation of its operative bargaining agreement, the Supreme Court of Wyoming ruled that if the provision placed final authority over transfers in the hands of the superintendent, it would have been forced to excise that portion of the contract as invalid since the assignment of teachers was a discretionary, nondelegable board function.[28] Similarly, the Supreme Court of Washington invalidated a board policy authorizing a superintendent to place a teacher on probation and to impose a monetary sanction.[29] The court pointed out that even if a policy is negotiated with a professional organization, the result would have been a nullity because only school boards can set working conditions.

Boards can delegate ministerial functions that execute their decisions or to act on their behalf. Where a statute required school boards to notify teachers in writing of their intent not to renew their employment contracts, the Supreme Court of South Dakota affirmed that a letter conveying this message that was signed only by a superintendent did not

---

25. *Knox v. District School Bd. of Brevard*, 821 So.2d 311 [167 Educ. L. Rep. 971] (Fla.Dist. Ct.App.2002).

26. For such a case, *see Reece v. Board of Educ. of City of Chicago*, 767 N.E.2d 395 [166 Educ. L. Rep. 283] (Ill.Ct.App.2002).

27. *Dayton Classroom Teachers Ass'n v. Dayton Bd. of Educ.*, 323 N.E.2d 714 (Ohio 1975).

28. *Diefenderfer v. Budd*, 563 P.2d 1355 (Wyo.1977).

29. *Noe v. Edmonds School Dist. No. 15 of Snohomish County*, 515 P.2d 977 (Wash. 1973).

violate the law.[30] The court contended that only a strained construction would have suggested that the board could not have permitted the superintendent from transmitting the information. Further, where the Chicago Board of Education had a long-standing practice of sending all summonses naming it as defendant to the receptionist of its law department, who accepted them on its behalf, the Supreme Court of Illinois affirmed that this was a lawful delegation of the authority to accept service.[31]

Giving substantial weight to the principle of nondelegability of school board powers, the Court of Appeals of New York observed that where questions of arbitrability arise in collective bargaining contracts, absent a clear, unequivocal agreement to the contrary, a board did not intend to refer differences to that forum.[32] The same court also posited that a board could not bargain away its right to inspect teacher personnel files.[33]

Boards are generally empowered to adopt policies establishing procedures for exercising their nondelegable powers. These procedures may have the effect of curtailing the exercise of powers for a while, but courts generally do not treat agreeing to procedural parameters as constituting illegal delegation. For example, the highest court in Massachusetts asserted that a board can bind itself for a limited period in time to observe certain criteria in disapproving transfers of personnel approved by the superintendent.[34]

The question of illegal delegation of school board powers has been unsuccessfully raised in cases that sought to invalidate rules of state athletic or activities associations. The Supreme Court of South Dakota, in upholding a statute that expressly permitted boards to join groups that regulate interscholastic activities on an annual basis, emphasized that a school board was not required to join.[35] If the board became a member, the court maintained that it, in effect, ratified the association's rules and made them its own.

In addition, boards may contractually limit selected powers for periods of time. Unless bound by contract or the common law doctrine of promissory estoppel, boards can change policies as they see fit in the interests of carrying out their duties.[36]

---

30. *Cutshaw v. Karim*, 256 N.W.2d 566 (S.D.1977).

31. *Sarkissian v. Chicago Bd. of Educ.*, 776 N.E.2d 195 [170 Educ. L. Rep. 327] (Ill.2002).

32. *Acting Superintendent of Schools of Liverpool Cent. School Dist. v. United Liverpool Faculty Ass'n*, 399 N.Y.S.2d 189 (N.Y. 1977).

33. *Board of Educ., Great Neck Union Free School Dist. v. Areman*, 394 N.Y.S.2d 143 (N.Y. 1977).

34. *Bradley v. School Comm. of Boston*, 364 N.E.2d 1229 (Mass.1977).

35. *Anderson v. South Dakota High School Activities Ass'n*, 247 N.W.2d 481 (S.D.1976).

36. *Michie v. Board of Trustees of Carbon County School Dist. No. 1*, 847 P.2d 1006 [81 Educ. L. Rep. 581] (Wyo.1993). [Case No. 23]

Rules and Regulations in General

Local boards of education have the implied power to make and enforce reasonable rules and regulations designed to ensure efficient school operations. Insofar as the question of reasonableness is often difficult, and board rules pertain to a wide range of subjects, a large number of cases involved discussions of whether boards have acted properly. As the courts have adopted a rule of presumptive validity that boards have acted reasonably, the burden of proof is ordinarily on the party contesting a rule. The judicial presumption in favor of board rules rests on the premise that the role of the courts is not to make policy but to assure that board discretion is not exercised arbitrarily or unreasonably.

A substantial part of the common law of education derives from situations in which courts have been asked to review the actions of local school officials. It is clear that most matters requiring the attention of these officials cannot be dealt with definitively on levels above the local. A statute may thus specify that children are eligible to enter school at age six, but this could mean that on the day they reach six, at the beginning of the school year in which they reach six, or at various other points. The Supreme Court of Montana addressed the reasonableness of entrance cut-off dates where a state law directed that the schools were to be open to all children between the ages of six and twenty-one. In this case, a local board had a rule that only children who reached the age of six prior to November 15 could be admitted to first grade at the beginning of the school year in September. The court upheld the board's authority to prevent a child who was born in November on the basis that it exercised sound judgment in adopting a rule that did not conflict with the purpose of the state law.[37]

As reflected by a case from New Jersey, local rules cannot be contrary to statutes such as where the state supreme court struck down a retirement incentive because of the impact that it would have had on the state system.[38] Regardless, it is not always clear whether a regulation conflicts with legislation. For instance, provisions in board policies that are out of line with state-level prescriptions for teacher tenure are not enforceable. Put another way, local boards cannot bind themselves to re-employ probationary teachers who have received favorable evaluations[39] or to submit to arbitration over the non-renewal of a probationary teacher's contract.[40] Further, the Supreme Court of Illinois declared that a board could not avoid, or alter, a statutory provision with regard to full-time service during a teacher's probationary period even if motivated by a shortage of funds.[41] In a second case from Illinois, an appellate court applied this principle despite the fact that a local board formally ap-

37. *State ex rel. Ronish v. School Dist. No. 1 of Fergus County,* 348 P.2d 797 (Mont.1960).

38. *Fair Lawn Educ. Ass'n v. Fair Lawn Bd. of Educ.,* 401 A.2d 681 (N.J. 1979). [Case No. 24]

39. *Leonard v. Converse County School Dist. No. 2,* 788 P.2d 1119 [59 Educ. L. Rep. 534] (Wyo.1990).

40. *Mindemann v. Independent School Dist. No. 6 of Caddo County,* 771 P.2d 996 [53 Educ. L. Rep. 270] (Okla.1989).

41. *Johnson v. Board of Educ. of Decatur School Dist.,* 423 N.E.2d 903 (Ill.1981).

proved tenure status for some teachers six years before a case involving the issue arose.[42] Moreover, where a state-level system of conducting disciplinary hearings for tenured teachers included a pay scale for the members of the hearing panel, an appellate court was of the opinion that a local board lacked the authority to augment the per diem stipend of its appointee.[43]

In Utah, the state board policy on fees for elements of school-sponsored activities called for waivers to ensure that no students were denied opportunities to participate in activities due to financial inability to pay. An appellate court struck down a local board's implementation of the policy that limited the waiver to families receiving public assistance while also permitting partial waivers.[44] The court vitiated the first provision because it was more restrictive than the state regulation. As to the second, court wrote that since the state regulation did not contemplate such a situation, the local board could abridge, enlarge, extend, or modify it by creating another right or imposing a new duty.

Where state officials have not created prescriptions, school boards may have implied power to act. In such a case, the Supreme Court of Oregon thought that a board had the implied power to require physical examinations whether applicants for teaching positions were afflicted with communicable diseases or were incapable of discharging their duties.[45] Other courts contended that a teacher who was already employed could have been required to submit to an examination to check on his fitness to continue to work when he returned from a medical leave of absence[46] while a teacher who wished to return from medical leave could have been required to present medical records and pass a physical examination.[47] In this connection, of course, a board cannot set up rules regarding physical qualifications that are unrelated to the performance of teaching duties.[48]

School officials must administer board rules with an even hand. As such, the First Circuit determined that if a school committee allowed the use of the internal distribution system of its schools to disseminate notices opposing the use of busing to achieve school integration, it had to permit the same access to opposing groups.[49] In like fashion, an appellate court in Illinois affirmed that if a school board used a mailing list to communicate with parents about a referendum, officials had to make the same list available to others who wished to express their views on the

---

42. *Evans v. Benjamin School Dist. No. 25*, 480 N.E.2d 1380 [26 Educ. L. Rep. 753] (Ill.Ct. App. 1985).

43. *Syquia v. Board of Educ. of Harpursville Cent. School Dist.*, 591 N.Y.S.2d 996 [80 Educ. L. Rep. 182] (N.Y.1992).

44. *Lorenc v. Call*, 789 P.2d 46 [59 Educ. L. Rep. 547] (Utah Ct.App.1990).

45. *School Dist. No. 1, Multnomah County v. Teachers' Retirement Fund Ass'n*, 95 P.2d 720 (Or.1939).

46. *Dusanek v. Hannon*, 677 F.2d 538 [4 Educ. L. Rep. 409] (7th Cir.1982), *cert. de-*

nied, 459 U.S. 1017, 103 S.Ct. 379, 74 L.Ed.2d 512 (1982).

47. *Strong v. Board of Educ. of Uniondale Union Free School Dist.*, 902 F.2d 208 [60 Educ. L. Rep. 379] (2d Cir.1990), *cert. denied*, 498 U.S. 897, 111 S.Ct. 250, 112 L.Ed.2d 208 (1990). [Case No. 25]

48. *Chavich v. Board of Examiners*, 258 N.Y.S.2d 677 (N.Y.App.Div.1965). *See also Sontag v. Bronstein*, 351 N.Y.S.2d 389 (N.Y. 1973).

49. *Bonner–Lyons v. School Comm. of City of Boston*, 480 F.2d 442 (1st Cir.1973).

matter.[50] Further, where a board created a pressroom for members of the media to cover its meetings, a federal trial court in Florida remarked that it had to articulate the existence of a compelling interest before it could deny access to representatives of the teacher union's in-house publication.[51]

School Building Sites and Standards

In carrying out major responsibilities, as long as boards comply with state law, they have implied power to select and purchase sites on which school buildings are to be placed. Under this principle, where procedures for erecting and paying for school buildings are spelled out, local boards have no power to enter agreements to lease buildings with arrangements for future purchases.[52] At the same time, neither may boards discharge all attendance personnel where only these employees are statutorily authorized to enforce compulsory education requirements.[53]

A case from Connecticut illustrates how taxpayer challenges to board actions in selecting sites for buildings are often litigated based on the charge that they abused their discretion.[54] The taxpayers did not claim that the board's action was tainted by fraud or corruption or that it was illegal in the sense that it was procedurally irregular. Rather, the only claim that the taxpayers advanced was that the board should have been enjoined because its action constituted a gross abuse of discretion that should have been subject to re-examination before being implemented. The court refused to consider the arguments that other sites were more desirable, specifying that it is not for the judiciary to say how many alternative methods of accomplishing a desired result must be investigated or considered before authorities embark on a course of action.

A more recent case over whether a board complied with state law included an interesting twist over whether a board could exchange school property for privately-owned land without conducting a public auction. The Supreme Court of Wyoming affirmed that even though the state constitution prohibited the "sale" of school lands without a public auction, it did not forbid an "exchange" of school lands.[55] The court was of the opinion that since there was not a clear constitutional prohibition against the transaction, the legislature properly exercised its power to authorize exchanges of school lands for private lands of equal value.

The Supreme Court of Indiana rejected a claim that board members were unduly influenced by recommendations from experts at a university that they consulted over a building situation.[56] One or more of the board

---

50. *Wood v. School Dist. No. 65*, 309 N.E.2d 408 (Ill.Ct.App.1974).

51. *United Teachers of Dade v. Stierheim*, 213 F.Supp.2d 1368 [168 Educ. L. Rep. 347] (S.D. Fla.2002).

52. *Haschke v. School Dist. of Humphrey in County of Platte*, 167 N.W.2d 79 (Neb.1969).

53. *Geduldig v. Board of Educ. of City of N.Y.*, 351 N.Y.S.2d 167 (N.Y.App.Div. 1974).

54. *McAdam v. Sheldon*, 216 A.2d 193 (Conn.1965).

55. *Director of the Office of State Lands & Investments v. Merbanco*, 70 P.3d 241 [177 Educ. L. Rep. 558] (Wyo. 2003).

56. *Cooper v. Huntington County Community School Corp.*, 232 N.E.2d 887 (Ind.

members who were originally opposed to the establishment of a single senior high school apparently became convinced otherwise after seeing the results of a survey advising such a course of action. In commenting favorably on its seeking the services of the university faculty, the court sustained the board's action.

In New Mexico, where a recall of school board members was constitutionally permitted for malfeasance or misfeasance in office or for violations of the oath of office, the state's highest court halted a recall election based on a choice of site for a new high school.[57] In recognizing that the site had a number of disadvantages that were listed in the petition, the court affirmed that the charge was without merit since malfeasance in connection with a recall had to evince an improper motive.

Administrative agencies that have fiscal relationships with school officials cannot dispute locations of school buildings absent specific authority to do so. In such a case, the Supreme Court of Tennessee explained that the authority invested in non-school bodies for general fiscal approval of school expenditures did not extend to the location of buildings.[58]

In Pennsylvania, an appellate court considered whether city officials could withhold their approval under a zoning code for an addition to a school because they believed that the board was overbuilding.[59] In ascertaining that the board complied with all zoning and building requirements except obtaining conditional-use approval, the court stressed that a municipality may not interfere with a school board's power to locate a school facility in a district. Although acknowledging that building styles and sizes, assignment patterns, and transportation arrangements are beyond a municipality's power to regulate, the court added that the board had to make a properly documented application for permits as required of all other developers. Subsequently, an appellate court in Pennsylvania affirmed that a zoning board could limit the use of a district's athletic fields to school-related activities.[60] The court upheld the rejection since the zoning board had already granted the school board an exception to construct the fields in an area zoned for residential use.[61]

The extent to which school boards must comply with local building and zoning codes varies from one jurisdiction to another. The Supreme

---

1968). *See also Christian v. Geis,* 225 N.W.2d 868 (Neb.1975).

57. *CAPS v. Board Members,* 832 P.2d 790 [75 Educ. L. Rep. 1211] (N.M.1992).

58. *Mosier v. J.C. Thompson,* 393 S.W.2d 734 (Tenn.1965).

59. *School Dist. of Pittsburgh v. City of Pittsburgh,* 352 A.2d 223 (Pa.Cmwlth.Ct. 1976).

60. *Hazleton Area School Dist. v. Zoning Hearing Board of Hazle Township,* 720 A.2d 220 [130 Educ. L. Rep. 839] (Pa. Cmwlth.Ct.1998).

61. *See also Mitchell v. Zoning Hearing Bd. of the Borough of Mount Penn,* 838 A.2d 819 [184 Educ. L. Rep. 420] (Pa. Cmwlth. Ct. 2003), *reargument denied* (2004) (affirming that a trial court properly limited special exceptions regarding the accessory use of a gymnasium and auditorium for elementary school students and that the use of the facilities by all other students in the district was not authorized because it was not incidental to the proposed elementary school).

Court of Washington addressed the crucial considerations in reviewing whether a board was bound by a municipal building code.[62] According to the court, the major point was whether the state, by legislation and delegation to administrative agencies, preempted the field of regulating school construction such as where there were detailed and comprehensive standards for school construction and state governmental machinery for their enforcement by an agency other than the city in which a school district lies. The court found that the state had not deprived the municipality of jurisdiction over certain aspects of school construction, although it could have done so. The court rejected as illusory the claim that making a school conform to the municipal building code would lead ultimately to permitting municipalities to interfere with the operation, management, and control of public schools. In like manner, the Supreme Court of Pennsylvania held that a school board had to comply with a local zoning ordinance which required it to provide off-street parking when a new building was erected.[63] Conversely, the Supreme Court of Michigan examined whether a school construction plan should have been altered to take local ordinance requirements regarding parking, setback, storm water control, and environmental issues into account. The court affirmed that since state law granted the superintendent of public instruction exclusive jurisdiction over school construction and site plans, boards were immunized from local zoning ordinances.[64] Previously, an appellate court in New Jersey believed that a board was not subject to municipal regulations covering such matters as height, setbacks, and parking.[65]

If board selection of a site is subject to voter approval in a referendum, a question can arise as to how much information school officials must voluntarily give to the public. Where board members, an architect, and school building contractor were indicted for allegedly failing to disclose conditions of the subsurface at a building site, an appellate court in New Jersey dismissed the charge of misconduct in office because it was not supported by sufficient evidence insofar as the defendants were not accused of corruption.[66] The court was convinced that in making a policy decision to build the school after it considered the facts, the board had no legal duty to make all of the details available to the public.

School Board Membership

Generally

Regardless of whether legislatures provide for school board members

62. *Edmonds School Dist. No. 15 v. City of Mountlake Terrace,* 465 P.2d 177 (Wash. 1970).

63. *School Dist. of Philadelphia v. Zoning Bd. of Adjustment,* 207 A.2d 864 (Pa. 1965).

64. *Charter Township of Northville v. Northville Pub. School,* 666 N.W.2d 213 [178 Educ. L. Rep. 943] (Mich. 2003).

65. *Murnick v. Board of Educ. of City of Asbury Park,* 561 A.2d 1193 [55 Educ. L. Rep. 189] (N.J.Super.Ct.App.Div.1989).

66. *State v. Lally,* 194 A.2d 252 (N.J.Super.Ct.Law Div.1963).

to be appointed[67] or elected,[68] they are state, not local, officers since education is a statewide responsibility.[69] Once in office, board members remain there under the auspices of, and may have their powers extended or limited by, the discretion of state legislatures since they possess only those powers invested in them by their legislatures.[70]

State legislatures set qualifications for school board membership. Reflective of the rule that a legislature cannot adopt an unconstitutional criterion, the Supreme Court, in *Turner v. Fouche*,[71] rejected ownership of real property in a district as a qualification. In one instance, where state law did not specify a minimum age to become a board member, an appellate court in New Jersey stated that the statute implied that candidates had to be old enough to vote.[72]

Legislatures may not only set eligibility requirements[73] such as district residency,[74] prohibiting teachers from serving on boards in the districts where they work,[75] and/or imposing anti-nepotism requirements for members,[76] but can also change the methods of selecting members even if an incumbent is removed in the process.[77] In a dispute over residency, an appellate court in Louisiana affirmed the rejection of a challenge to a candidate's qualification to run for a board based on the claim that he was not actually domiciled in the parish the preceding year. Reiterating the presumption against a change of domicile unless an individual makes a clear statement to do so, the court agreed that the candidate was qualified since he spent 80 percent of his time at his residence in the parish and otherwise met the criteria to establish a household.[78] In a case with a twist as to membership, an appellate court in Connecticut, in a long-running suit, affirmed that part of an amendment to a town charter that allowed its mayor to serve automatically on its school board.[79] The court noted that since a state statute specifically allowed such an alteration, the mayor could serve on the board.

67. *Ham v. The Mayor, Aldermen and Commonalty of the City of N.Y.*, 70 N.Y. 459 (N.Y. 1877) (holding that even where board members were appointed by a mayor, they were not municipal officials).

68. At least one federal court has ruled that there is no fundamental right to have an elected school board. *Hawkins v. Johanns*, 88 F.Supp.2d 1027 [143 Educ. L. Rep. 169] (D.Neb.2000).

69. *State ex rel. Walsh v. Hine*, 21 A. 1024 (Conn.1890); *Landis v. Ashworth*, 31 A. 1017 (N.J.1895).

70. *Packer v. Board of Educ. of Town of Thomaston*, 717 A.2d 117 [129 Educ. L. Rep. 400] (Conn.1998).

71. 396 U.S. 346, 90 S.Ct. 532, 24 L.Ed.2d 567 (1970).

72. *Vittoria v. West Orange Bd. of Educ.*, 300 A.2d 356 (N.J.Super.Ct.App.Div.1973).

73. *Unified School Dist. No. 501, Shawnee County, Kan. v. Baker*, 6 P.3d 848 [146 Educ. L. Rep. 902] (Kan.2000).

74. *Ben Hill County Bd. of Educ. v. Davis*, 510 S.E.2d 826 [132 Educ. L. Rep. 1017] (Ga. 1999).

75. *State ex rel. Pryor ex rel. Jeffers v. Martin*, 735 So.2d 1156 [136 Educ. L. Rep. 1100] (Ala.1999); *Unified School Dist. No. 501, Shawnee County, Kan. v. Baker*, 6 P.3d 848 [146 Educ. L. Rep. 902] (Kan.2000).

76. *Commonwealth ex rel. Stumbo v. Crutchfield*, 157 S.W.3d 621 [196 Educ. L. Rep. 984] (Ky. 2005).

77. *Lanza v. Wagner*, 229 N.Y.S.2d 380 (N.Y.1962), *appeal dismissed*, 371 U.S. 74, 83 S.Ct. 177, 9 L.Ed.2d 163 (1962).

78. *Knott v. Angelle*, 846 So.2d 825 [177 Educ. L. Rep. 741] (La. Ct. App. 2003).

79. *Board of Educ. of Town and Borough of Naugatuck v. Town and Borough of Naugatuck*, 800 A.2d 517 [166 Educ. L. Rep. 659] (Conn. Ct. App. 2002), *aff'd on other grounds*, 843 A.2d 603 [186 Educ. L. Rep. 420] (Conn. 2004).

A key condition for membership is that if legislatures choose to have elected school boards, they cannot limit the rights of district residents to vote absent compelling reasons for doing so. In *Kramer v. Union Free School District No. 15*,[80] the Supreme Court struck down a statute in New York that limited voting to individuals who were otherwise eligible to cast ballots in state and federal elections based on whether they owned or leased taxable real property within a district or were parents or custodians of children enrolled in the local public schools.

Removal of Board Members

Absent inappropriate considerations such as race, legislatures may delineate the circumstances under which board members can be removed from office pursuant to recall elections[81] or where districts are experiencing financial and academic difficulties.[82] Of course, board members can be removed from office for dereliction of duty[83] or criminal misconduct, even if misbehavior was committed in a state other than where an individual serves.[84]

As reflected in a case from New York, even if it is not as a result of a recall election, a board member may be entitled to a name clearing hearing where allegations that lead to removal may harm an individual's reputation. The Second Circuit ruled that a board member who was removed from office for allegedly sprinkling voodoo dust in front of the door of a school official was entitled to a pre-deprivation hearing before removal to determine whether the chancellor of schools violated her liberty interest under the Fourteenth Amendment.[85]

When recall elections occur, judicial review functions as it does in connection with regular elections,[86] including the requirement of providing a member who is subject to removal with notice,[87] unless provisions specify additional duties such as determining sufficiency or specificity of the grounds that gave rise to the recall election.[88]

---

80. 395 U.S. 621, 89 S.Ct. 1886, 23 L.Ed.2d 583 (1969). *See also Hussey v. City of Portland*, 64 F.3d 1260 (9th Cir.1995), *cert. denied*, 516 U.S. 1112, 116 S.Ct. 911, 133 L.Ed.2d 843 (1996); *Mixon v. State of Ohio*, 193 F.3d 389 [139 Educ. L. Rep. 59] (6th Cir.1999).

81. *See, e.g.*, CAL. GOV'T CODE §§ 1770(b), (f); LA. REV. STAT. ANN. § 42:1411; MD. CODE ANN., EDUC. § 3–108; MICH. STAT. ANN. § 168.316; N.J. STAT. ANN. § 18A:12–3; N. M. STAT. ANN. § 22–7–13; N.Y. EDUC. LAW § 2559; Ohio Rev. Code Ann. § 3.07; OR. REV. STAT. ANN. § 332.030(1)(f).

82. *McKnight v. Hayden*, 65 F.Supp.2d 113 [139 Educ. L. Rep. 333] (E.D.N.Y.1999).

83. *In re Removal of Kuehnle*, 830 N.E.2d 1173 [200 Educ. L. Rep. 310] (Ohio Ct. App. 2005).

84. *Caldwell v. Owens*, 781 So.2d 895 [152 Educ. L. Rep. 891] (La. Ct. App. 2001).

85. *Velez v. Levy*, 401 F.3d 75 [196 Educ. L. Rep. 76] (2d Cir. 2005).

86. *Johnson v. Maehling*, 597 P.2d 1 (Ariz.1979).

87. *State ex rel. Ragozine v. Shaker*, 772 N.E.2d 1192 [167 Educ. L. Rep. 909] (Ohio 2002).

88. *State ex rel. Citizens Against Mandatory Bussing v. Brooks*, 492 P.2d 536 (Wash.1972); *CAPS v. Board Members*, 832 P.2d 790 [75 Educ. L. Rep. 1211] (N.M. 1992).

School Board Procedures

Generally

Insofar as local school boards are legal entities only as a whole, their members have no individual authority to act independently on behalf of their districts.[89] In order for board actions to be binding, they must convene in legal meetings. Even if board members have individually signed a document, it is not valid if a board subsequently repudiates it at a meeting.[90]

Where a collective bargaining agreement provided that if a school committee and its teachers' association agreed to abide by an arbitrator's award, they were to use that method of dispute resolution in resolving their differences. After the committee refused to accede to the arbitrator's award on the ground that its chair lacked the authority to bind it, the Supreme Judicial Court of Massachusetts agreed.[91] The court reasoned that neither the bargaining agreement nor the application that the committee chair signed consenting to arbitration committed it to such a course of action since this could only have been done by a majority vote of the committee as a whole.

Absent a statute to the contrary, school boards have the authority to formulate and adopt mandatory procedural rules for their meetings.[92] If neither a board nor a legislature establishes board procedure, the rules of parliamentary procedure, which flow from general principles of common law, govern board meetings.[93] As illustrated by an early case from Kentucky, some legislatures require boards to adopt rules and bylaws. The court was satisfied that since a law of this sort clothes board rules with the effect and force of the statutory provisions authorizing them, actions to the contrary are void.[94]

The Court of Appeals of New York considered whether a school board could reconsider its dismissal of a probationary employee since the resolution calling for the action did not receive the required majority vote when it was initially introduced but was reintroduced, and adopted, at the next meeting. In rejecting the employee's argument that the initial vote essentially rendered the matter *res judicata*, the court explained that *res judicata* applied to judicial, not administrative, actions.[95]

Notice of Meetings

School boards may take official action only at legal meetings. In order for board meetings to be legal, common law requires that all of their members must be given notice unless a meeting is a regular one

89. *Bender v. Williamsport Area School Dist.*, 475 U.S. 534, 106 S.Ct. 1326, 89 L.Ed.2d 501 [30 Educ. L. Rep. 1024] (1986).

90. *State ex rel. Steinbeck v. Treasurer of Liberty Township*, 22 Ohio St. 144 (1871).

91. *Sheahan v. School Comm. of Worcester*, 270 N.E.2d 912 (Mass.1971).

92. *Ex parte Etowah County Bd. of Educ.*, 584 So.2d 528 [69 Educ. L. Rep. 981]

(Ala.1991); *Iversen v. Wall Bd. of Educ.*, 522 N.W.2d 188 [94 Educ. L. Rep. 499] (S.D. 1994).

93. *McCormick v. Board of Educ.*, 274 P.2d 299 (N.M.1954).

94. *Montenegro–Riehm Music Co. v. Board of Educ.*, 145 S.W. 740 (Ky.1912).

95. *Venes v. Community School Bd. of Dist. 26*, 402 N.Y.S.2d 807 (N.Y.1978).

whose date was set by law.[96] In the case of regular meetings, all members and officials are charged with notice of the dates on which they will take place. The purpose of the notice requirement for special meetings is to insure that all board members have the opportunity to attend. If board meetings could be conducted by part of a board without notice to its remaining members, the public might be deprived of part of its representation at meetings. Of course, the presence of all members is not essential to a meeting's legality because only a quorum is required. Notice is thus designed to afford, as far as possible, each member the opportunity to attend. The public is also ordinarily entitled to notice that a special board meeting is to take place.[97]

Courts construe notice requirements strictly. Not only does the public have a right to have all board members made aware of meetings, but individual members have a right to be notified.[98] Where statutes impose requirements for special meetings, which are typically different from those for regular meetings, they must be followed.[99] Even absent statutory requirements for notice of special meetings, the general rule is that boards have no authority to act in the absence of any members unless all have had reasonable notice and an opportunity to attend. A reasonable time before such notice must be given means that a board member must have sufficient time to prepare and know of a meeting's time and place.[100]

A case from Iowa illustrates the type of circumstances that may render it unnecessary to give notice to all board members. Where a dispute arose over the hiring of a superintendent at a contested meeting, and board membership changed, it sought to annul his contract on the ground that he was hired at an illegal meeting since one member did not receive notice. Evidence revealed that the absent member was in California on the day of the meeting and had been there for months. The court affirmed that since the member would have been unable to attend even if he had notice, the meeting at which the superintendent was hired was legal.[101]

If, despite the lack of notice, all board members attend and participate in a meeting, actions cannot be invalidated for lack of notice.[102] This applies the common sense rule that if all members are present, the purpose of the notice requirement is met. Even if all board members are present at a special meeting that is convened without proper notice, should a member refuse to act, any actions will be of no effect.[103]

96. *Twitchell v. Bowman*, 440 P.2d 513 (Wyo.1968).

97. *Rampello v. East Irondequoit Cent. School Dist.*, 653 N.Y.S.2d 469 (N.Y.App. Div.1997).

98. *Elsemore v. Inhabitants of Town of Hancock*, 18 A.2d 692 (Me.1941).

99. *Katterhenrich v. Federal Hocking Local School Dist. Bd. of Educ.*, 700 N.E.2d 626 [129 Educ. L. Rep. 776] (Ohio Ct.App. 1997), *appeal not allowed*, 684 N.E.2d 707 (Ohio 1997).

100. *Green v. Jones*, 108 S.E.2d 1 (W.Va.1959).

101. *Consolidated School Dist. of Glidden v. Griffin*, 206 N.W. 86 (Iowa 1925).

102. *Hanna v. Wright*, 89 N.W. 1108 (Iowa 1902).

103. *Johnson v. Dye*, 127 S.W. 413 (Mo. Ct.App.1910). *See also Knickerbocker v. Redlands High School Dist.*, 122 P.2d 289 (Cal.Ct.App.1942).

Local board members cannot, by private agreement, waive the right to receive notice. To this end, even if a three-member board agrees that two of its members can act to bind the third in his or her absence, even with providing prior notice, any action at such a meeting is invalid.[104] When a regular meeting is postponed, common law only requires notice be given to those who were absent from the meeting at which the new date was set.[105] If a meeting continues on another day, it is not necessary to send notice of the continuance to any members who were absent.[106]

Voting

In order for a board meeting to be legal, a quorum of members must be present.[107] Under common law, a quorum is a simple majority.[108] For board action to be legal, absent a statute specifying differently, a majority vote of a quorum is required.[109] A legislature may specify different numerical votes to transact specific items of business.[110]

Absent prohibitions to the contrary, board members may vote in any manner they wish, such as raising their hands, secret ballots, or voice votes, subject only to the general proscription that they cannot operate arbitrarily or fraudulently. Boards may even adopt one form of voting on some propositions and another on others at the same meeting. For example, since nothing in common law prohibits one from doing so, a board might vote by secret ballot on some questions and by voice vote on others. Some states dictate that specified board actions can only take place by roll-call votes.[111] This requirement is usually treated as mandatory and an action taken by any other form of voting is not legally binding.[112] In such a case, where state law specified that a board can only act by a roll-call vote, an appellate court in Colorado invalidated a principal's reassignment because the board failed to vote in this manner.[113] Conversely, a year earlier, the Supreme Court of Pennsylvania decided that since the statutory requirement of a recorded roll-call vote for teacher appointments was not mandatory, a board's failure to comply did not automatically invalidate the contracts since doing so would have been unconscionable.[114]

104. *School Dist. No. 22 v. Castell*, 150 S.W. 407 (Ark.1912).

105. *Keyes v. Class "B" School Dist. No. 421 of Valley County*, 261 P.2d 811 (Idaho 1953).

106. *Barnhart Indep. School Dist. v. Mertzon Indep. School Dist.*, 464 S.W.2d 197 (Tex.Civ. App.1971).

107. *Konovalchik v. School Comm. of Salem*, 226 N.E.2d 222 (Mass.1967). [Case No. 26]

108. *East Poinsett County School Dist. No. 14 v. Massey*, 876 S.W.2d 573 [91 Educ. L. Rep. 723] (Ark.1994).

109. *State ex rel. Mason v. Mayor and Aldermen of the City of Paterson*, 35 N.J.L. 190 (1871); *Federal Trade Comm'n v. Flo-* *till Products*, 389 U.S. 179, 88 S.Ct. 401, 19 L.Ed.2d 398 (1967).

110. *Board of School Trustees of South Vermillion School Corp. v. Benetti*, 492 N.E.2d 1098 [32 Educ. L. Rep. 242] (Ind.Ct. App.1986).

111. *See, e.g.,* ALASKA STAT. § 14.20.180 (dismissal or non-retention of teachers); IOWA CODE ANN. § 279.13 (automatic continuation of teacher contracts).

112. *Ready v. Board of Educ.*, 17 N.E.2d 635 (Ill.Ct.App.1938).

113. *Robb v. School Dist. No. RE 50(J)*, 475 P.2d 30 (Colo.Ct.App.1970).

114. *Mullen v. Board of School Directors of DuBois Area School Dist.*, 259 A.2d 877 (Pa.1969).

A case from the Supreme Court of Arkansas is consistent with the rule that even if an illegal voting procedure is well-intentioned and of long standing, it cannot be validated. At issue was a superintendent's practice of getting the approval of three board members over the employment and dismissal of teachers in each of their local schools. Pursuant to this arrangement, the whole board did not consider these actions. The court found that since the board's dismissal of a teacher was a nullity under the circumstances, it had to pay her salary until the end of the contract period.[115]

Questions arise about the legal effects of a member's refraining from voting on an issue that is properly before a board since one who is present when there is a quorum is obligated to vote. A member who thus refrains from voting is regarded as acquiescing in a board's action.[116] Insofar as abstentions are not counted in evaluating whether a majority voted for a motion, if seven members are present, with three voting in favor, two voting against, and two not voting, a resolution is considered passed absent a statutory requirement of an affirmative vote of a majority of all present or of a majority of a board's full membership.[117]

Voting rules for boards are firmly established at common law. Even so, cases frequently arise as to the application of voting rules. A case from Missouri involved the legality of a meeting about an election that two members of a three-person board attended. The third member declined to attend because he opposed calling the election. When the board president, who favored calling the election, presented the petition to the member who was present, and the latter refused to vote, the president cast his vote in favor of the proposition and called the election. In upholding the vote, the court indicated that the fact that only one member of the board actually voted did not render the election invalid because when a member sits silently by during a call for a vote, such a person is regarded as acquiescing in, rather than opposing, the measure.[118]

If a board member who does not wish to vote on a measure actually withdraws from a meeting, thereby leaving no quorum, a board cannot act under normal circumstances as long as the withdrawal is genuine.[119] In such a case, where three trustees stepped away from the part of the room where the rest of the board was in order to take places among the bystanders, the Supreme Court of Indiana affirmed that they could not change from trustees to mere spectators when they still had an opportunity to vote with the others.[120] In agreeing that the trustees could not use such a procedural maneuver to thwart a vote, the court found that the action of the three voting members was valid, in effect, by a vote of three-to-none with three abstentions.

115. *Farris v. Stone County School Dist. No. 1,* 450 S.W.2d 279 (Ark.1970).

116. *Payne v. Petrie,* 419 S.W.2d 761 (Ky.1967).

117. *Bunsen v. County Bd. of School Trustees,* 198 N.E.2d 735 (Ill.Ct.App.1964).

118. *Mullins v. Eveland,* 234 S.W.2d 639 (Mo.Ct.App.1950).

119. *Levisa Oil Corp. v. Quigley,* 234 S.E.2d 257 (Va.1977).

120. *State ex rel. Walden v. Vanosdal,* 31 N.E. 79 (Ind.1892).

In another case involving a three-person board, one member proposed an action that the second opposed and the third supported before becoming incapacitated. The Supreme Court of Minnesota affirmed that since the third member did not fulfill his obligation to vote, the general rule that main motions are voted on in the order in which they are made applied.[121] The first motion, in effect, passed by a vote of one-to-zero with two abstentions. However, some states require an affirmative vote of a fixed percent of all members or of all members present on specified matters. In these situations, a blank ballot or a refusal to vote is not considered an acquiescence to the will of the majority.[122]

Local boards cannot change the common law on basic procedures for voting absent legislative permission. A board's formally adopting rules to this effect are generally invalid as its customary procedure is irrelevant since local bodies cannot make rules in derogation of the law over how ballots are counted and a majority is determined.[123] In such a case, the Supreme Court of Wisconsin declared that a local board lacked the authority to change the common law rule concerning a quorum, even though a statute authorized it to establish its own rules of procedure.[124] The court added that where the legislature conferred a power on a board that it could exercise without the legislature's providing the number of members necessary to act, the common law rule prevailed, and a majority of a board quorum may act lawfully. While recognizing that the legislature could have changed the rule or could have empowered a local board to modify its own rules, the court also wrote that, absent a controlling provision, the common law principle that a majority of a whole body is necessary to constitute a quorum applies.

An appellate court in New Jersey rejected a board's claim that it was bound by a bylaw specifying a two-thirds vote of its full membership to close and sell a school building since state law only required a role-call majority of full membership.[125] The court still forbade the sale because another bylaw required two public meetings for adoption of such a matter.

Occasionally, it turns out that after a board has acted, one of its members was ineligible to serve. Further, during challenges to the elections of members or to one's continued eligibility to continue to serve, boards cannot suspend operations pending judicial resolution. Under such circumstances, questions arise as to the validity of board actions. Board members whose eligibility is subsequently rejected are considered "de facto members" with regard to actions that were taken during the pendency of ultimately successful challenges. A case from Kentucky illustrates such a situation where a board appointed a superin-

---

121. *Edwards v. Mettler*, 129 N.W.2d 805 (Minn.1964).

122. *Forbis v. Fremont County School Dist. No. 38*, 842 P.2d 1063 [79 Educ. L. Rep. 665] (Wyo.1992).

123. *Murdoch v. Strange*, 57 A. 628 (Md.1904).

124. *Endeavor–Oxford Union Free High School Dist. v. Walters*, 72 N.W.2d 535 (Wis. 1955).

125. *Matawan Reg'l Teachers Ass'n v. Matawan–Aberdeen Reg'l School Dist. Bd. of Educ.*, 538 A.2d 1331 [45 Educ. L. Rep. 1123] (N.J.Super.Ct.App.Div.1988). [Case No. 27] tendent to a new term that was to begin seven months later, when his current contract expired, and to the post of board secretary. Insofar as a vote of a de facto member was necessary to approve the second action, an appellate court reiterated the general rule that a contract made by a board pending ouster proceedings against a member would normally not be retroactively invalidated if it depended on the vote of a member who was ultimately removed.[126] Relying on the fact that there was no necessity to act on the contract renewal or appointment as board secretary so far in advance of the expiration of the two contracts, the court reached the opposite result, observing that the vote of the de facto member could not be counted.

Public Nature of Meetings

Courts uniformly uphold statutes that require school board meetings to be open to the public.[127] Open meeting laws typically direct boards to give reasonable advanced publicized notice of the time and place of their sessions in part so that the public may attend and speak.[128] Whether boards have complied with state open meeting laws is not always easy to evaluate since there are two legal issues to consider: that the public is permitted to be present and that records of the meeting are made available to them. This reflects the notion that the term public is relative, rather than absolute, in describing board meetings. A good example of this principle took place in California where a board met briefly in open session, adjourned for about an hour, reconvened in executive session, and met again in open session to terminate the contracts of teachers who challenged the session on the basis that it did not meet the statutory requirement of being public. An appellate court affirmed that the meeting was legal even though the board met in an executive session that excluded the public.[129] The court asserted that the board could convene in executive session to discuss matters affecting teachers' contracts, as long as it took its final action in an open session. In a different situation, an appellate court in New York affirmed that a school board could not exclude teachers, as members of the public, from the open part of the meeting at which it voted to terminate their contracts.[130]

Entire board meetings need not be open to the public. Only those parts of meetings at which boards take final actions must be open to the public.[131] In one such case, the Supreme Court of Minnesota affirmed that it is essential for a board meeting to be conducted in a public place

126. *Board of Educ. of McCreary County v. Nevels*, 551 S.W.2d 15 (Ky.Ct.App. 1977).

127. *See, e.g., Kavanaugh v. West Sonoma County Union High School Dist.*, 62 P.3d 54 [173 Educ. L. Rep. 171] (Cal.2003); *McComas v. Board of Educ. of Fayette County*, 475 S.E.2d 280 (W.Va.1996).

128. *Rauert v. School Dist. 1–R of Hall County*, 555 N.W.2d 763 [114 Educ. L. Rep. 628] (Neb. 1996).

129. *Alva v. Sequoia Union High School Dist.*, 220 P.2d 788 (Cal.Ct.App.1950).

130. *Goetschius v. Board of Educ. of Greenburgh Eleven Union Free School Dist.*, 664 N.Y.S.2d 811 [122 Educ. L. Rep. 764] (N.Y.App.Div.1997).

131. *Jewell v. Board of Educ., Duquoin Community Unit Schools, Dist. No. 300*, 312 N.E.2d 659 (Ill.Ct.App.1974).

located within a school district's territorial confines.[132] The court vitiated a board meeting that convened in a private office at the county seat, twenty miles from the district. In like fashion, an appellate court in Florida pointed out that board members who attended a workshop at the state's semi-annual school boards convention that met more than 100 miles from its headquarters in another county violated state law because it did not give citizens a reasonable opportunity to attend.[133] In another case, even absent a specific statute, the Supreme Court of Utah concluded that "unless matters were of such a delicate nature or of the type where public policy dictates nondissemination, the meeting itself should be open to the public and press."[134]

Boards typically discuss personnel,[135] and other sensitive matters, in executive or closed sessions, reconvening to vote in public. Even so, states typically limit the use of executive sessions since they are exceptions to the rule that government business should be conducted in public.[136] For instance, the Supreme Court of Louisiana forbade a closed board session where there was an advanced call, an agenda, a polling of members' views, and a recording of what occurred.[137] Similarly, the Supreme Court of Colorado barred closed gatherings of board members at which they talked about matters prior to voting on them without engaging in public discussions.[138] The Supreme Court of Minnesota, remarking that "there is a way to illegally circumvent any rule the court might fashion, and therefore it is important that the rule not be so restrictive as to lose the public benefit of personal discussion between public officials while gaining little assurance of openness,"[139] maintained that the state's open meeting law covered gatherings of a quorum or more of board members when they discussed, decided, or received information as a group on issues related to its official business. A state can dispense with the requirement that a board take minutes in executive session as long as a final vote is taken in public.[140]

The Supreme Judicial Court of Massachusetts considered a case where more than ninety individuals applied for a superintendency and a screening committee of a school committee selected sixteen for inter-

---

132. *Quast v. Knutson*, 150 N.W.2d 199 (Minn.1967).

133. *Rhea v. School Bd. of Alachua County*, 636 So.2d 1383 [91 Educ. L. Rep. 780] (Fla.Dist. Ct.App.1994).

134. *Conover v. Board of Educ. of Nebo School Dist.*, 267 P.2d 768, 771 (Utah 1954). [Case No. 28]

135. *See, e.g., Henry v. Anderson*, 827 N.E.2d 522 [197 Educ. L. Rep. 704] (Ill. App. Ct. 2005) (holding that while an executive session based on an "employee matter" and "reclassification of employment" did not violate the state's Open Meetings Act, basing it on potential litigation was impermissible since a suit was not pending and the board failed to find either that one was probable or imminent).

136. *See, e.g.,* KY. REV. STAT. ANN. § 61.800, "Legislative Statement of Poli-

cy:" "The General Assembly finds and declares that the basic policy of KRS 61.805 to 61.850 is that the formation of public policy is public business and shall not be conducted in secret and the exceptions provided for by KRS 61.810 or otherwise provided for by law shall be strictly construed."

137. *Reeves v. Orleans Parish School Bd.*, 281 So.2d 719 (La.1973).

138. *Bagby v. School Dist. No. 1, Denver*, 528 P.2d 1299 (Colo.1974).

139. *Moberg v. Independent School Dist. No. 281*, 336 N.W.2d 510, 518 [12 Educ. L. Rep. 932] (Minn.1983).

140. *Kyle v. Morton High School*, 144 F.3d 448 [126 Educ. L. Rep. 651] (7th Cir. 1998).

views. The committee reviewed candidates at a public meeting, not by name, but by assigned numbers, selecting five finalists. Although the committee released the names of the finalists and interviewed each at a public meeting, it refused to disclose the names of other candidates. The court affirmed that the open meeting statute required the committee to release the names of the sixteen finalists along with the minutes of the meeting where their credentials were discussed.[141] While conceding the possibility that disclosure might have invaded the privacy of candidates, the court decreed that whether doing so reduced the effectiveness of hiring procedures was a question best left for the legislature.

A question arises as to discussions that occur at informal gatherings of board members. The Eighth Circuit affirmed that an informal conversation between a superintendent and board members in Missouri over a construction contract did not violate the state's open meetings law since there was no quorum present, no formal vote was taken or recorded, and the meeting had not been planned to discuss the issue.[142] In like fashion, a federal trial court in Tennessee contended that a gathering at the superintendent's house before the start of a regular board meeting did not violate state law because even though he may have spoken with some members about public business, he did not discuss matters individually or in a group with all of them or even about the same topics.[143] Previously, a federal trial court in Illinois was of the opinion that although board members and other school officials were present at a political rally, their discussion of public policy issues unrelated to schools did not violate the state's open meetings law.[144] Conversely, the Supreme Court of Appeals of West Virginia affirmed that a gathering at which four of five board members were present the day before they voted on school closings and consolidations violated state law.[145] The court determined that the gathering constituted a meeting because even though those present did not follow formalities and had no intent to violate the law, it gave the superintendent the advantage in persuasion and coalition building for proposals that passed with little discussion the following day.

At common law there is no necessity that an agenda be published in advance when all members have proper notice. Generally, any matter that can be considered at a regular meeting may be acted on at a special session.[146] If boards issue agendas in advance, they do not thereby waive their right to amend them at meetings.[147] If state law requires boards to

141. *Attorney General v. School Comm. of Northampton,* 375 N.E.2d 1188 (Mass. 1978).

142. *Hanten v. School Dist. of Riverview Gardens,* 183 F.3d 799 [136 Educ. L. Rep. 761] (8th Cir.1999).

143. *Bundren v. Peters,* 732 F.Supp. 1486 [59 Educ. L. Rep. 733] (E.D.Tenn. 1989).

144. *Nabhani v. Coglianese,* 552 F.Supp. 657 [8 Educ. L. Rep. 276] (N.D.Ill. 1982).

145. *McComas v. Board of Educ. of Fayette County,* 475 S.E.2d 280 (W.Va.1996).

146. *Moore v. City Council of City of Perry,* 93 N.W. 510 (Iowa 1903).

147. *Crifasi v. Governing Body of Oakland,* 383 A.2d 736 (N.J.Super.Ct. App.Div.1978); *Unified School Dist. No. 407 by Boatwright v. Fisk,* 660 P.2d 533 [10 Educ. L. Rep. 392] (Kan.1983).

release agendas prior to meetings, they cannot transact any other business[148] even if members had not contemplated adding a new issue.[149] Once in executive sessions, boards have no authority to act on matters that were not identified in open meetings with proper notice. In such a case, the Supreme Court of Kentucky voided a variety of a board's personnel actions.[150] The court thought that the open meeting law required the board to identify a specific subject of discussion for a closed session and to limit its discussions to that topic.

A dispute involving open meetings that overlapped with board committees arose in Florida where access to hiring interviews was at issue. Where there was a vacancy as principal of a middle school, an area superintendent appointed a committee of five board employees to join her in interviewing eleven candidates; team members were to rank candidates based on their performances in the interviews. A parent alleged that this committee was a governmental board that performed official acts of interviewing and recommending job candidates. An appellate court denied the parent's request for an injunction, positing that the committees served in fact-finding, advisory capacities and that the ultimate hiring decision was made by the district superintendent and board.[151]

Board Records

As with meetings, official board minutes are open to public inspection.[152] Even so, not every board document is subject to a state's open records law. A practical aspect of the issue arose over whether a board clerk's notes were "public writings" subject to disclosure. The Supreme Court of Utah ascertained that while the clerk's notes were not available for public inspection, the final transcribed minutes, awaiting only approval and placement in the board's records, were subject to public inspection.[153]

If boards do not act in executive sessions, there is apparently no need for minutes.[154] If boards do act in executive sessions, the minutes of their regular meetings must record not only that they convened in such sessions but must also include references to the subject matter and a record of their final actions or votes.[155]

Courts have upheld tape recording[156] and videotaping[157] of regular board meetings. In a case from New York, an appellate court was of the

148. *Santa Barbara School Dist. v. Superior Ct.*, 118 Cal.Rptr. 637 (Cal.1975).

149. *Barrett v. Lode*, 603 N.W.2d 766 [140 Educ. L. Rep. 763] (Iowa 1999).

150. *Floyd County Bd. of Educ. v. Ratliff*, 955 S.W.2d 921 [122 Educ. L. Rep. 873] (Ky.1997).

151. *Knox v. District School Bd. of Brevard*, 821 So.2d 311 [167 Educ. L. Rep. 971] (Fla.Dist. Ct.App.2002).

152. *Cloud v. Independent School Dist. No. 38, Red Lake*, 508 N.W.2d 206 [87 Educ. L. Rep. 605] (Minn.Ct.App.1993).

153. *Conover v. Board of Educ. of Nebo School Dist.*, 267 P.2d 768 (Utah 1954). [Case No. 28]

154. *State ex rel. Zinngrabe v. School Dist. of Sevastopol*, 431 N.W.2d 734 [50 Educ. L. Rep. 181] (Wis.Ct.App.1988).

155. *Gersen v. Mills*, 737 N.Y.S.2d 137 [161 Educ. L. Rep. 930] (N.Y.App.Div.2002).

156. *Belcher v. Mansi*, 569 F.Supp. 379 [13 Educ. L. Rep. 318] (D.R.I.1983); *Mitchell v. Board of Educ. of Garden City Union Free School Dist.*, 493 N.Y.S.2d 826 [27 Educ. L. Rep. 1201] (N.Y.App.Div.1985).

view that permitting parents to videotape a meeting was not only consistent with the legislative intent of the state's open meeting laws but also that while a board may reasonably regulate use of cameras to ensure that they do not interfere with meetings, one may not directly prohibit their use.[158] Previously, an appellate court in Louisiana affirmed that a board could prevent one of its members from tape recording an executive session based on the confidential nature of the material that it was to discuss.[159]

School officials often defend attempts to keep records from the public based on privacy concerns even though boards act for the public and spend public money. The common law inquiry, augmented by widespread freedom-of-information statutes, is whether the desired materials would invade someone's privacy and, if so, whether the privacy interest outweighs the public interest served by disclosure. Insofar as presumptions favor disclosure, the courts seem to be in complete agreement that salary data must be disclosed.[160] For example, the highest court of Massachusetts believed that the public records statute required disclosure of absentee records of teachers when they only revealed the dates and generic classifications of their absences.[161]

As reflected by a case from the Supreme Court of Oregon, a school board cannot adopt a policy that conflicts with a state's open records law. Where a board promised confidentiality of names and addresses to teachers it employed during strikes, the court struck its action down on the ground that such a blanket policy thwarted the legislative intent to have records of public bodies open to the public unless there was an individualized reason not to do so.[162] Similarly, the Supreme Court of Georgia, in a case from higher education, affirmed that the records of candidates for the presidency of a state university had to be made public.[163] The court judged that it could not consider the concern of the regents that the law hampered their ability to obtain good candidates because insofar as the law was clear, only the legislature could change the policy of full openness.

The adequacy of board records is another source of litigation as courts are unable to agree whether failure to keep records invalidates actions that should have been recorded. Of course, a great deal depends on the nature of the underlying actions. Courts recognize that it may be unreasonable to require all of a board's actions to be recorded in an

---

157. *Maurice River Township Bd. of Educ. v. Maurice River Township Teachers Ass'n*, 475 A.2d 59 [17 Educ. L. Rep. 537] (N.J.Super.Ct.App.Div. 1984); *Hain v. Board of School Directors of Reading School Dist.*, 641 A.2d 661 [91 Educ. L. Rep. 234] (Pa.Cmwlth.Ct.1994).

158. *Csorny v. Shoreham–Wading River Cent. School Dist.*, 759 N.Y.S.2d 513 [177 Educ. L. Rep. 490] (N.Y. App. Div. 2003).

159. *Dean v. Guste*, 414 So.2d 862 [5 Educ. L. Rep. 1300] (La.Ct.App.1982).

160. *Mans v. Lebanon School Bd.*, 290 A.2d 866 (N.H.1972); *Hastings and Sons Pub. Co. v. City Treasurer of Lynn*, 375 N.E.2d 299 (Mass.1978).

161. *Brogan v. School Comm. of Westport*, 516 N.E.2d 159 [43 Educ. L. Rep. 362] (Mass. 1987).

162. *Guard Pub. Co. v. Lane County School Dist. No. 4J*, 791 P.2d 854 [60 Educ. L. Rep. 973] (Or.1990).

163. *Board of Regents of Univ. Sys. of Ga. v. The Atlanta Journal*, 378 S.E.2d 305 [52 Educ. L. Rep. 1287] (Ga.1989).

official minutes book in order to be legal. The Supreme Court of Iowa thus affirmed that a law requiring an official record of board proceedings in connection with designating students whose tuition should be paid in another district was only directory.[164] The court upheld the board's vote absent a formal record because there was other evidence substantiating its action.

If records must be kept, courts do not always require them to provide all of the details. Even so, "minutes certainly should be prepared promptly and be made available to the public within a reasonable time."[165] The minimum requirement for a record is to show that a board acted. In such a case, where it thought that there was enough information in board records to provide a full understanding of a bond sale, the Supreme Court of Montana refused to invalidate a transaction even though it agreed that more details would have been desirable.[166]

The official record of a school board meeting is prima facie evidence of its action. While oral testimony cannot be used to enlarge or restrict information that is in records,[167] it may be able to fill in omissions or to clarify a record if it is not clear on its face.[168] As occasionally happens, when officials realize that a record is incorrect, boards may amend them to convey events accurately.[169]

Use of Committees

Just as individual members lack authority to act for boards, so also committees have no power to act for whole boards. This aside, it is often necessary, and occasionally desirable, to have a small group complete fact-finding and preliminary work rather than have an entire board do so. When this happens, committees must report back to their boards so that they can act. To the extent that they cannot act independently, it is not surprising that an appellate court in New York affirmed that board subcommittees and ad hoc committees were not subject to the state's open meetings law.[170]

Allegations surface from time to time that boards perfunctorily adopted committee recommendations without proper deliberations. Yet, it is difficult to prove lack of proper consideration where boards approve committee recommendations. The Supreme Court of New Jersey rejected a charge that board members failed to engage in due deliberation in a

164. *School Dist. of Soldier Township v. Moeller*, 73 N.W.2d 43 (Iowa 1955).

165. *In re Removal of Kuehnle*, 830 N.E.2d 1173, 1194 [200 Educ. L. Rep. 310] (Ohio Ct. App. 2005).

166. *Elliot v. School Dist. No. 64–JT*, 425 P.2d 826 (Mont.1967).

167. *Lewis v. Board of Educ. of Johnson County*, 348 S.W.2d 921 (Ky.1961); *Tuscaloosa City Bd. of Educ. v. Roberts*, 440 So.2d 1058 [14 Educ. L. Rep. 857] (Ala.1983); *Cross v. Commonwealth ex rel. Cowan*, 795

S.W.2d 65 [62 Educ. L. Rep. 1246] (Ky.Ct. App.1990).

168. *Spann v. Joint Boards of School Directors*, 113 A.2d 281 (Pa.1955); *Knutsen v. Frushour*, 436 P.2d 521 (Idaho 1968).

169. *State v. Board of Educ. of Bath–Richfield Local School Dist.*, 218 N.E.2d 616 (Ohio 1966).

170. *Jae v. Board of Educ. of Pelham Union Free School Dist.*, 802 N.Y.S.2d 228 [202 Educ. L. Rep. 766] (N.Y. App. Div. 2005).

dispute over a contract to purchase desks.[171] The court held that while the board had to act as a whole, the fact that a committee conducted negotiations and reported back to it was sufficient to render the contract valid.

Boards may delegate the performance of purely ministerial functions such as procuring and recording a deed to property that it purchased to one or more of its members.[172] On the other hand, boards cannot delegate discretionary functions even to their presidents.[173] In addition, boards cannot permit committees to take final actions on matters that they must consider as a whole. To this end, committees cannot be charged with such duties as selecting a building site and contracting to have a school built[174] or rescinding a contract with a consultant.[175]

Whether entire boards must participate in all phases of an activity is not always clear since the failure of all members to be present throughout a session can lead to challenges. Generally, absent statutes to the contrary, quorums may act for whole boards. However, where state law required a "full board" to be present at a hearing for nontenured teachers, the Supreme Court of Rhode Island ruled that all members had to attend.[176] Further, an appellate court in Pennsylvania upheld the commonwealth board of education's use of a panel to hear a case on school district reorganization where the whole board reviewed the record before acting.[177] Four years earlier, the Supreme Court of Minnesota reasoned that a board had implied power to employ a hearing examiner to conduct hearings with no board members present.[178] The court commented that the examiner heard the evidence, summarized the facts, and offered conclusions but did not render a judgment on the merits, did not recommend how the matter should have been resolved, and took no part in the board's decision-making process.

School Elections

Generally

One way in which the public can participate directly in school operations is through elections. Insofar as elections may be on whatever matters legislatures choose, the procedures by which they occur are subject only to restrictions of the federal and state constitutions. In addition, elections for school board members may differ from those on

---

171. *State v. Board of Educ.*, 51 A. 483 (N.J.1902).

172. *Looney v. Consolidated Indep. School Dist.*, 205 N.W. 328 (Iowa 1925).

173. *Maasjo v. McLaughlin School Dist. No. 15–2*, 489 N.W.2d 618 [77 Educ. L. Rep. 496] (S.D.1992).

174. *Kinney v. Howard*, 110 N.W. 282 (Iowa 1907).

175. *School Dist. No. 1 of Silver Bow County v. Driscoll*, 568 P.2d 149 (Mont. 1977).

176. *Jacob v. Board of Regents for Educ.*, 365 A.2d 430 (R.I.1976).

177. *Independent School Dist. Comprised of Western Portions of Hamlin and Sargeant Townships, McKean County v. Commonwealth, State Bd. of Educ.*, 417 A.2d 269 (Pa.Cmwlth. Ct.1980).

178. *Whalen v. Minneapolis Special School Dist. No. 1*, 245 N.W.2d 440 (Minn. 1976).

bond issues or other matters while special elections may be subject to restrictions not placed on regular elections. If elections lack legislative authority, or are contrary to material provisions of the law, they are nullities.

Petitions for Elections

Election procedures are usually set in motion when candidates file petitions in the form provided by law. Statutes usually provide that petitions must contain the signatures of a specified number or a percentage of electors in districts and must be presented to the designated officers or boards that are authorized to call elections. Whether the calling of elections is ministerial or discretionary depends on state law. Even where it is discretionary, a court may order an election to proceed if it thinks that officials abused their discretion.[179]

Officials designated to act on election petitions are responsible for evaluating both whether the signers are legal electors and whether their signatures are genuine since the mere recital in a petition itself that its signers are legal electors is no evidence of that fact.[180] In some states, the officer or agency who is directed to act on a petition may rely on the affidavits of those who circulated them that the signatures are genuine, that the persons who signed are electors, and that they did so before the filing deadline.[181]

State law may require individuals who sign petitions to provide their addresses so that officials can readily determine the identity of registered voters.[182] Absent a statutory requirement that signatures be compared, the failure to do so is no basis for striking names from petitions.[183] The principle saving circumstance that protects boards from having elections invalidated due to inadequate petitions is that the validity of signatures may not be attacked for the first time after an election, or other action specified on it, occurred. The Supreme Court of Nebraska applied this rule where a party sought to enjoin a board from asserting dominion and control over territory.[184] An opponent challenged the board by claiming that since one person who signed the petition was not a qualified voter, if his name were struck from the petition it would not have had the requisite number of signatures. The court dismissed the claim without hearing evidence because the opponent questioned the validity of the petition collaterally insofar as he filed suit for another purpose, namely about the board's taking on new territory.

179. *Gibson v. Winterset Community School Dist.*, 138 N.W.2d 112 (Iowa 1965).

180. *People ex rel. Anderson v. Community Unit School Dist. No. 201*, 129 N.E.2d 28 (Ill.Ct. App.1955).

181. *Burns v. Kurtenbach*, 327 N.W.2d 636 [8 Educ. L. Rep. 434] (S.D.1982).

182. *Board of Educ. of Rich Township High School Dist. No. 227, Cook County v.* *Brown*, 724 N.E.2d 956 [144 Educ. L. Rep. 553] (Ill.Ct.App.1999), *appeal denied*, 731 N.E.2d 762 (Ill.2000), *cert. denied*, 531 U.S. 958, 121 S.Ct. 383, 148 L.Ed.2d 295 (2000).

183. *Johnson v. Maehling*, 597 P.2d 1 (Ariz.1979).

184. *Cacek v. Munson*, 69 N.W.2d 692 (Neb.1955).

Opponents challenged a petition dealing with district consolidations on the grounds that a number of the individuals signed on Sunday, some petitions were not signed in the presence of the circulator, and some persons signed for others. The Supreme Court of Michigan refused to invalidate the election even in acknowledging the general rule that before an election takes place public officials must follow the exact provisions of the state law if a party files suit over their enforcement.[185] The court declared that if an election is contested after it is over, statutory requirements are to be treated as directory unless the law specifies that noncompliance is a fatal defect or renders the result doubtful.

Questions about the legality of one's signing for another occur most frequently with spouses. The question is typically whether the general rule of signature ratification or adoption applies on school petitions. The general rule is that a person who ratifies or adopts a signature placed there by another person is bound by the same. The Supreme Court of Missouri applied this rule where evidence showed that a husband authorized his wife to sign his name to a petition.[186] The court observed that generally no particular mode or form of authorization is necessary to authorize one person to sign another's name to a legal document and that oral permission is sufficient unless a statute requires the authority to be in writing.

Assuming that a petition is signed validly, questions arise as to the right of signers to withdraw their names. Clearly, there must be a cutoff point beyond which signatures may not be withdrawn since the petition procedure could not operate effectively. At common law, a signer of a petition may always withdraw before it is presented to the agency or officer designated by statute to receive and act upon the document.

Courts have agreed that names may not be withdrawn from petitions after they were filed with the proper agencies or officers even if they had not been acted on.[187] For example, the Supreme Court of North Dakota refused to allow the withdrawal of names from a petition about re-opening a school after it was filed.[188] The court pointed out that once the petition was accepted as sufficient, the school board was not empowered to permit withdrawals. According to the court, since there was no statutory provision for a hearing on such petitions, the filing was equivalent to the board's acting because the law required schools to be re-opened. Conversely, other courts have permitted signers to withdraw their names at any time before petitions are acted on. In such a case, the Supreme Court of Nebraska refused to restrict a citizen's ability to withdraw his name from a petition when the statutes had forbidden his doing so and when no consideration seemed to require such a restriction.[189] The court asserted that permitting an individual to withdraw

---

185. *Richey v. Board of Educ. of Monroe County*, 77 N.W.2d 361 (Mich.1956).

186. *State ex rel. Kugler v. Tillatson*, 312 S.W.2d 753 (Mo.1958).

187. *Zilske v. Albers*, 29 N.W.2d 189 (Iowa 1947).

188. *Judson PTO v. New Salem School Bd.*, 262 N.W.2d 502 (N.D.1978).

189. *State ex rel. Larson v. Morrison*, 51 N.W.2d 626 (Neb.1952).

from a petition before it had been acted on was calculated to discourage hasty presentations of a petition without a full disclosure of the merits of the question. Similarly, an appellate court in Illinois indicated that an individual name can be withdrawal from a petition after action on it has begun, but before final disposition, and can lead to a procedure's being terminated if an insufficient number of names remain on it.[190]

In the few jurisdictions with provisions preventing the removal of signatures other than under unusual circumstances, such as having signed due to duress or misrepresentation, state law governs.[191] Additionally, even after a petition is accepted, names may be withdrawn in the face of evidence that signers were induced to do so by fraud, misrepresentation, or misapprehension. Usually, withdrawal under these circumstances may be made only by leave of a court or other body having jurisdiction over the proceedings.[192]

Cases have also arisen on the flip side of the question, namely over adding names. In such a case, the Supreme Court of Nebraska remarked that the rules governing the withdrawal of names from petitions also apply to their being added.[193] The court specified that even though the deadline for signing passed, names could be added before the petition was filed.

The Supreme Court of Ohio reviewed two questions about petitions. In the first, the court was satisfied that adding a name to a petition after a board of elections found that it was valid did not violate the statutory proscription against altering, correcting, or adding to a petition once it had been filed.[194] The court wrote that since the challenge did not involve fraud, deception, or undue influence in the petitioning process, and the purpose of the statutory prohibition was to prevent alterations between a petition's being filed and addressed, there was no reason to render it invalid. The second case considered whether noncompliance with a statute prohibiting the signing of another's name on an election petition with the knowledge and permission of the circulator invalidated only the signature or an entire petition. The court rejected the law's calling for the latter, stating that absent evidence indicating that the word "knowingly" in the statute meant more than its ordinary meaning, it would enforce the common understanding.[195]

Notice of Elections

Notice requirements with regard to school elections vary widely. Among the common specifications are publication of notice for a set

190. *Konald v. Board of Educ. of Community Unit School Dist. 220*, 448 N.E.2d 555 [10 Educ. L. Rep. 1150] (Ill.Ct.App. 1983).

191. *State ex rel. Muter v. Mercer County Bd. of Educ.*, 175 N.E.2d 305 (Ohio Ct. App.1959).

192. *In re Mercerburg Indep. School Dist.*, 85 A. 467 (Pa.1912).

193. *Retzlaff v. Synovec*, 132 N.W.2d 314 (Neb.1965).

194. *State ex rel. Carson v. Jones*, 263 N.E.2d 567 (Ohio 1970).

195. *State ex rel. Dennis v. Miller*, 274 N.E.2d 459 (Ohio 1971).

number of days or weeks prior to the date of an election and posting notices in public places. At the very least, notice must inform voters on such matters as an election's purpose, the date and place at which it is to take place, and when the polls open and close.

The adequacy of notice is often challenged on the ground that it contains omissions or errors. The proper wording of election notices is one of considerable nicety, especially with regard to bond elections. In bond elections, the terminology of notice should be sufficiently detailed to enable voters to understand the nature of a proposition, a brief description of the underlying project,[196] and its cost[197] yet sufficiently broad to avoid unduly restricting a board in the use of bond proceeds.

A case from Ohio illustrates the effect of an error in notice. State law required bond election notices to declare the amount of a proposed issue, its purpose, the maximum term of the bonds, and the estimated additional tax rate, expressed in dollars and cents for each one hundred dollars of valuation and in mills for each dollar of valuation. Due to an error, the notice omitted the amount of the annual tax levy in mills for each dollar of valuation, a portion of the issue's purpose, and the amount of the annual tax levy in cents for each one hundred dollars of valuation was stated as being 3.2 rather than .32, the proper rate. An appellate court rejected the claim that these errors rendered the result invalid since there was no evidence that the election was widely publicized in the district.[198] Acknowledging that newspaper articles described the needs of the schools, the amount of the bond issue, and its proposed uses, the court was satisfied that voters properly received notice through other media. Similarly, the Supreme Court of Missouri rejected a claim of inadequacy of notice in the face of a charge that three of five notices were not in public places because insofar as they were on school property, they were inaccessible to the public. The court rejected the allegation that people who entered school property to read the notice would have been trespassers because there would not have been an unauthorized entry.[199] The court also rejected the argument that having three notices set back from a street rendered them improper as it interpreted state as not requiring a public place to be near a street.

In a case that examines notice from a different perspective, the Supreme Court of Georgia reversed in favor of a board member who challenged the validity of a referendum that purportedly was designed to provide an opportunity for then-current board members to remain in office.[200] The court held that since the referendum, which did not inform voters that their approval would have shortened the terms of some board members by two years, did not comply with the law prohibiting the

196. *Borough of Brentwood v. Department of Community Affairs*, 657 A.2d 1025 [100 Educ. L. Rep. 204] (Pa.Cmwlth.Ct. 1995).

197. *Simonetti v. Commonwealth, Dept. of Community Affairs*, 651 A.2d 626 [96 Educ. L. Rep. 623] (Pa.Cmwlth.Ct.1994).

198. *State ex rel. Bd. of Educ. of the Plain Local School Dist. v. McGlynn*, 135 N.E.2d 632 (Ohio Ct.App.1955).

199. *Montgomery v. Reorganized School Dist. No. 1*, 339 S.W.2d 831 (Mo.1960).

200. *Burton-Callaway v. Carroll County Bd. of Elections*, 619 S.E.2d 634 [202 Educ. L. Rep. 869] (Ga. 2005).

abolition of elective office or shortening or lengthening their terms without the approval of local voters, it was invalid.

As reflected in a case from the Supreme Court of Utah, alleged misadvice to electors through notices can lead to litigation. Where a school board distributed a brochure explaining a bond election and its purpose, parts of it were printed in newspapers in conjunction with, but not as a part of, the statutory notice. After the election, due to underestimates of costs, the board sought to use more money for one project and thus did not allocate the funds for all of the projects specified in the brochure. The court refused to enjoin the re-adjusted building program in declaring that the usual rule was that if a board publishes notice pursuant to law that binds it, collateral statements or explanatory materials do not.[201] Although not basing its judgment on the status of the brochure, the court upheld the board's reasonable power to re-allocate bond money following the election since there was no deceit, fraud, or corruption.

Courts tend to construe election laws to preserve voters' choices.[202] Mere irregularity of notice or failure to give notice for the full time prescribed by statute is generally not fatal to an election's validity if voters knew that it was coming and the matter at issue was generally known in a district, if a comparatively full vote was cast, and if the irregularity did not mislead voters to their disadvantages. Courts ordinarily construe notice requirements as directory unless a law clearly indicates that legislative intent that an election is to be rendered invalid if statutory requirements are not fulfilled or unless there is a gross irregularity.[203] An example of the latter occurred where the resolution calling a bond election stated that a specified sum of money was to be voted for school purposes. The Supreme Court of New Mexico affirmed that the wording was not sufficiently precise so as to advise the electorate of the actual purpose of the proposed bond issue.[204] While conceding that the notice did not have to include details of proposed uses of the funds, the court explained that it had to be less broad than the wording that was used.

Ballots

Assuming that elections are called legally, specified officials are charged with preparing ballots. The usual requirement of secret ballots ordinarily applies to school elections. When, by accident or design, elections are conducted in ways that destroy the secrecy of ballots, they can usually be invalidated.[205]

201. *Ricker v. Board of Educ. of Millard County School Dist.*, 396 P.2d 416 (Utah 1964).

202. *Abts v. Board of Educ. of School Dist. Re–1 Valley in Logan County*, 622 P.2d 518 (Colo.1980).

203. *Eustace v. Speckhart*, 514 P.2d 65 (Or.Ct.App.1973); *Wright v. Board of Trustees of Tatum Indep. School Dist.*, 520 S.W.2d 787 (Tex.Civ.App.1975).

204. *Board of Educ. of City of Aztec v. Hartley*, 394 P.2d 985 (N.M.1964).

205. *Corn v. Blackwell*, 4 S.E.2d 254 (S.C.1939).

The strong public interest in the secrecy of the ballot and the right of voters not to reveal how they voted notwithstanding, there are exceptions to the exercise of this right. If an investigation establishes that an individual was ineligible to vote, and if it appears that the result of the election could have been changed by this vote, an individual may be required to disclose how he or she voted. Insofar as this requirement is designed to purge an election of illegal votes, the right to a secret ballot may, in such a situation, have to give way to the public interest in having all voters qualified.[206]

Requirements that are designed to insure the integrity of the election process are usually treated as mandatory. Thus, an election official's failure to follow provisions covering duplicate ballots when originals are damaged can lead to having ballots invalidated, even if it means disenfranchising voters who cast them. In such a case, an appellate court in Illinois vitiated ballots even though there were no allegations of impropriety and officials claimed that the damaged ballots and duplicates could easily have been matched.[207] The court was of the view that since the provisions of the election code were mandatory, officials had to apply them strictly in order to contribute substantially to the integrity of the election process.

Individuals have challenged elections where ballots were not worded in such a fashion as to provide voters with a clear choice between alternative propositions. In cases involving charges that ballots contained more than one proposition, courts have ruled that the language of ballots must be plain, understandable, and subject to only one interpretation. These cases have led to the creation of what is referred to as the "single proposition" rule. This rule is designed to prevent including two or more unrelated propositions on one ballot, thereby compelling voters to accept an undesirable proposition in order to obtain a desirable one. In order to constitute a single proposition or question, there must be a natural relationship between the objects covered on a ballot so that they form one whole plan.

Turning to examples, the Supreme Court of Montana affirmed that it was unnecessary to have separate petitions to transfer elementary and school territories since a single petition clearly identified the intent to transfer both parcels of land.[208] Earlier, the Supreme Court of Illinois determined that "constructing" and "equipping" schools can be treated as a single purpose since the terms were not so unrelated as to require separate propositions.[209] Similarly, the Supreme Court of Minnesota posited that to constitute duplicity of subject matter in violation of the state constitution's single-proposition requirement, a ballot must embrace "two or more dissimilar and discordant subjects which cannot

206. *Wehrung v. Ideal School Dist. No. 10,* 78 N.W.2d 68 (N.D.1956). [Case No. 29]

207. *Larson v. Board of Educ. of Bement Community School Dist. No. 5, in Piatt and Champaign Counties,* 455 N.E.2d 866 [14 Educ. L. Rep. 561] (Ill.Ct.App. 1983).

208. *McKirdy v. Vielleux,* 19 P.3d 207 [151 Educ. L. Rep. 627] (Mont.2000).

209. *Carstens v. Board of Educ. of East Alton–Wood River Community High School Dist.,* 187 N.E.2d 682 (Ill.1963).

reasonably be said to have any legitimate connection."[210] The court sustained a bond issue that was designed to permit a board to acquire and better its schools on the basis that it satisfied the single-proposition rule. Previously, the same court struck down a proposition that read, "Shall the Independent Consolidated School District No. 1 of Stevens County issue bonds in the sum of $400,000 for the erection of a new schoolhouse and/or expansion, improvement, and equipment of its schoolhouses?"[211] as violating the single-proposition rule. The court maintained that this single question contained three alternative proposals: erect a new school building; improve equipment and expand existing buildings; or a combination of new construction and improvements. The court added that this ballot's vice was that the three-part question made it impossible to evaluate whether a majority of voters agreed to authorize any of the three proposals since they could not have approved their choices without also voting for the alternatives.

When elections are completed, propositions as worded on ballots are binding. Although the full text of a proposition need not be on a ballot, what is printed must clearly identify the matter and its chief features in words of plain meaning.[212] As illustrated by a case from the Supreme Court of Oregon, agreements not part of a resolution are generally not enforceable. At issue was whether an agreement signed by school board members in all of the districts involved in a consolidation was binding on the new board that was being created, with some voters having the understanding that the agreement was to be incorporated into the reorganization plan. Five years after accepting the agreement that no school would have been changed, moved, or consolidated without approval of electors in its attendance area, the voters in the new district passed a bond issue for just one high school. The court affirmed that since the agreement was not incorporated in the plan, the alleged misadvice did not invalidate the election and its binding effect on the district.[213]

Voter Qualifications

One who meets the qualifications for casting a ballot in an election is known as an elector. One who actually casts a ballot is a voter. Although the terms are often used synonymously, the difference can be important. For instance, some statutes require pre-set percentages of "electors" to approve certain items.[214] Absent such express provisions, measures are carried by a majority of those casting ballots.

210. *Buhl v. Joint Indep. Consol. School Dist. No. 11,* 82 N.W.2d 836, 839 (Minn. 1957).

211. *Green v. Independent Consol. School Dist. No. 1,* 68 N.W.2d 493, 494 (Minn.1955).

212. *Wright v. Board of Trustees of Tatum Indep. School Dist.,* 520 S.W.2d 787 (Tex.Civ.App. 1975).

213. *Grant v. School Dist. No. 61, Baker County,* 415 P.2d 165 (Or.1966), *cert. de-*

nied, 385 U.S. 1010, 87 S.Ct. 717, 17 L.Ed.2d 547 (1967). [Case No. 30]

214. *See, e.g.,* ARK. CODE ANN. § 6–13–615(a)(2) ("The petitions calling for such an [electing board members] issue to be placed on the ballot shall be signed by not less than ten percent (10%) of the qualified electors of the district, based upon the total number of registered voters in the district."); FLA. STAT. ANN. § 105.035(3) ("(3) Each candidate for election to . . . the office of school board member shall obtain the

Constitutional and statutory provisions setting forth voter eligibility exist in all states. While the requirements vary slightly, a common element is residence both per se and for a specified minimum period before an election. Whether individuals are residents when seeking to vote or have been district residents for a sufficient period of time is not always a simple matter. The mere fact that persons may be physically present in districts does not necessarily constitute being residents for voting purposes. By the same token, neither is voters' absence from districts, even for substantial periods of time, necessarily determinative of one's ineligibility to vote. Whether one is a resident depends on a wide variety of circumstances since some courts equate residence for voting purposes with "domicile," or permanent place of abode, only one of which a person may have.

A case from the Supreme Court of North Dakota reflects the rule that one does not lose residence for voting purposes merely because a family moves from a district, enrolls its children in schools outside of it, and a parent accepts a position elsewhere. The court decided that where a voter intended to return to the first district, and evidence revealed that he was only living in the second temporarily, he remained a resident of the first for voting purposes.[215]

Statutes requiring persons to reside in districts for set periods of time before becoming eligible to vote are subject to strict scrutiny. In *Dunn v. Blumstein*,[216] the Supreme Court affirmed that bona fide residents could not be required to live in locations for three months prior to voting. The Court suggested that a period of thirty days appeared to be ample to complete administrative tasks related to checking on residence and preventing voter fraud. While some state courts have adopted a thirty-day rule,[217] the Court has upheld a fifty-day requirement.[218]

In setting special qualifications for school elections, their validity depends on whether they constitute inconsistent classifications subject to strict scrutiny. In *Kramer v. Union Free School District No. 15*, the Supreme Court struck down a provision from New York which sought to restrict voting in specified districts essentially to parents of children enrolled in the public schools and owners or lessees of taxable real property and their spouses. The Court was of the opinion that:

> [T]he issue is not whether the legislative judgments are rational. A more exacting standard obtains. The issue is whether the requirements do in fact sufficiently further a compelling state interest to justify denying the franchise to a bachelor living with his parents. The statutory requirements were "not sufficiently tailored to limit-

signature of a number of qualified electors equal to at least 1 percent of the total number of registered electors of the district, circuit, county, or other geographic entity represented by the office. . . .").

215. *Wehrung v. Ideal School Dist. No. 10*, 78 N.W.2d 68 (N.D.1956). [Case No. 29]

216. 405 U.S. 330, 92 S.Ct. 995, 31 L.Ed.2d 274 (1972).

217. *Torres v. Laramie County School Dist. No. 1*, 506 P.2d 817 (Wyo.1973), *cert. denied*, 414 U.S. 990, 94 S.Ct. 342, 38 L.Ed.2d 229 (1973).

218. *Marston v. Lewis*, 410 U.S. 679, 93 S.Ct. 1211, 35 L.Ed.2d 627 (1973).

ing the franchise to those 'primarily interested' in school affairs to justify the denial of the franchise to appellant and members of his class."[219]

On the same day, the Court also invalidated a statute from Louisiana allowing only "property taxpayers" to vote in an election called to approve the issuance of public utility bonds.[220]

One Person–One–Vote Principle

The courts generally apply the one-person, one-vote principle to school board elections. Pursuant to this principle, each qualified voter must be given an equal opportunity to participate in an election.[221] However, courts have examined the principle of one-person, one-vote in connection with other types of situations in school board elections. In *Sailors v. Board of Education of Kent County*,[222] the Supreme Court affirmed that the principle did not apply to county boards that were chosen by delegates from local boards. In not contesting the elections of the latter, opponents challenged the fact that each local board had one delegate, regardless of how many people lived in a district. The Court conceded that the system was basically appointive, rather than elective, and that county boards performed essentially administrative, and not legislative, functions. The Court concluded that insofar as the choice of members of the county board was based on appointment and not election, and since no election was required for nonlegislative officers, the principle of one-person, one-vote was inapplicable.

Emphasizing its rationale in the preceding case with regard to the dichotomy between appointive and elective boards, the Supreme Court, in *Hadley v. Junior College District of Metropolitan Kansas City, Missouri*,[223] found that when members of an elected body are chosen from separate districts, the arrangement must be such that, to the extent practicable, equal numbers of voters can vote for proportionally equal numbers of officials. In so deciding, the Court struck down a statute that permitted component public school boards to create consolidated junior college districts.

States may require more than simple majority votes to pass bond referenda. Although such an arrangement mathematically gives more weight to negative votes, the Supreme Court was satisfied that such a situation did not violate the Fourteenth Amendment. In *Gordon v. Lance*,[224] the Court noted that the Constitution requires more than majority votes on certain matters. The Court contended that as long as provisions do not discriminate against a group of voters who can be

219. 395 U.S. 621, 633, 89 S.Ct. 1886, 23 L.Ed.2d 583 (1969).

220. *Cipriano v. City of Houma*, 395 U.S. 701, 89 S.Ct. 1897, 23 L.Ed.2d 647 (1969).

221. *English v. Board of Educ. of Town of Boonton*, 301 F.3d 69 [168 Educ. L. Rep. 590] (3d Cir. 2002), *cert. denied*, 537 U.S. 1148, 123 S.Ct. 852, 154 L.Ed.2d 851 [173 Educ. L. Rep. 40] (2003).

222. 387 U.S. 105, 87 S.Ct. 1549, 18 L.Ed.2d 650 (1967).

223. 397 U.S. 50, 90 S.Ct. 791, 25 L.Ed.2d 45 (1970).

224. 403 U.S. 1, 91 S.Ct. 1889, 29 L.Ed.2d 273 (1971).

identified by inappropriate criteria such as race or wealth, they do not violate the right to equal protection. Further, the Supreme Court of New Hampshire ruled that a change in the super-majority voting requirement necessary to authorize the issuance of bonds did not violate the state constitutional requirement that called for a referendum to change the charter or form of government.[225] The court ascertained that the change did not violate equal protection because insofar as voters in some districts operated under distinctly different forms of government than others, not all voters and districts were similarly situated.

The Supreme Court of Illinois nullified a decentralization arrangement in the Chicago School Reform Act under which the state legislature created local school councils for each school and granted them substantial governmental powers.[226] According to the law, each council was to consist of ten elected members: six parents chosen by parents, two residents of the school area elected by residents, and two teachers elected by the school staff. The court rejected the notion that parents were to elect six council members based on the claim that they had a greater interest in the school than qualified voters who did not have children in the schools or that parents had any special competence to select council members of quality. In invalidating the law, the court emphasized that each council had broad powers for all members in its attendance zone.

A mother in New York City challenged the method of selecting members of the board of education. The board consists of one appointed member from each of the five borough school boards and two others who are appointed by the mayor. Insofar as the five boroughs have vastly different populations, the mother claimed that the system violated the principle of one-person, one-vote. A federal trial court rejected the mother's claim, holding that this principle only applies to elected, not appointed, representatives such as school board members.[227] In a second case from New York, members of a high school district unsuccessfully complained that a board's appointing members from residents from a larger feeder district meant that they received the same number of appointees as did the other smaller districts. The court granted the board's motion to dismiss, reiterating that the principle of one-person, one-vote applies only when officials are elected, not appointed.[228]

Use of School Funds for Board Elections

At best, election notices can contain only brief statements of their purposes. Insofar as the ability of voters to make informed judgments depends on the completeness of their knowledge and understanding of the propositions before them, local boards have the implied power, if not the duty, to disseminate relevant information about elections. Accordingly, boards can make reasonable expenditures designed to inform voters.

225. *McGraw v. Exeter Region Co-op. School Dist.*, 765 A.2d 710 [150 Educ. L. Rep. 769] (N.H.2001).

226. *Fumarolo v. Chicago Bd. of Educ.*, 566 N.E.2d 1283 [65 Educ. L. Rep. 1181] (Ill.1990).

227. *Cohanim v. New York City Bd. of Educ.*, 204 F.Supp.2d 452 [166 Educ. L. Rep. 158] (E.D.N.Y.2002).

228. *Vernet v. Bellmore–Merrick Cent. High School Dist.*, 343 F.Supp.2d 186 [193 Educ. L. Rep. 726] (E.D.N.Y. 2004), *aff'd without published opinion*, 155 Fed.Appx. 32 (2d Cir. 2005). [Case 31]

A different issue is present when boards seek to use school monies to advocate their views. When boards abandon their functions of providing information on both sides of an issue and use school funds to advocate favorable votes, they exceed their authority. The Supreme Court of New Jersey, in reaching this result in a case involving a brochure that contained an exhortation to "vote yes," thought that it did not mean to imply that the board was restrained from advocating the adoption of its plan in ways other than those involving expenditures of public funds.[229] The court suggested that the board could finance public forums and radio or television broadcasts as long as views on both sides of the issue were freely expressed.

The Supreme Court of California reasoned that since governmental neutrality in election contests is a "fundamental precept of this nation's democratic electoral process,"[230] public funds could not be used to lobby to promote a position. Similarly, the Tenth Circuit affirmed that a city and school board improperly spent money to help defeat a proposed amendment to the Colorado Constitution that would have mandated voter approval of all acts resulting in tax increases.[231] The court was of the view that a statute permitting contributions to campaigns that only involve issues in which the state's political subdivisions have an official concern did not provide the city and board with the authority to spend money on the campaign to oppose the proposed amendment.

Two cases from New York reflect differing judicial attitudes, even within the same state, with regard to how far school officials may go when encouraging voters to support a proposal. The state's highest court affirmed that "vote yes" to "help protect our school facilities and the quality of education in our District" exceeded the boundaries that were reasonably necessary to educate voters about budget and bond-issue proposals.[232] Conversely, an appellate court declared that expressions of opinion in school district publications, including characterizations of a bond issue as a critical initiative that would build the future of the community's children's, was not impermissible advocacy.[233]

[Case No. 23] Power of Board to Change Policy—Promissory Estoppel

MICHIE v. BOARD OF TRUSTEES
Supreme Court of Wyoming, 1993.
847 P.2d 1006 [81 Educ. L. Rep. 581].

Macy, Chief Justice.

. . .

Dr. Michie served as an elected member of the Board of Trustees from 1981 to December 1988. In the fall of 1984, the Board of Trustees

229. *Citizens to Protect Pub. Funds v. Board of Educ. of Parsippany–Troy Hills Township*, 98 A.2d 673 (N.J.1953). [Case No. 32]

230. *Stanson v. Mott*, 551 P.2d 1, 9 (Cal. 1976).

231. *Campbell v. Joint Dist. 28–J*, 704 F.2d 501 [10 Educ. L. Rep. 132] (10th Cir. 1983).

232. *Phillips v. Maurer*, 499 N.Y.S.2d 675, 676 [31 Educ. L. Rep. 200] (N.Y.1986).

233. *Karpoff v. Mills*, 744 N.Y.S.2d 725 (N.Y.App.Div.2002), *leave to appeal denied*, 752 N.Y.S.2d 588 (N.Y.2002).

requested the school superintendent to investigate whether the board members could legally participate in the school district's insurance plan. The superintendent contacted the school attorney for a legal opinion.

At a Board of Trustees meeting held on October 11, 1984, the school attorney opined that the board members could participate in the insurance plan without violating [a Wyoming statute barring compensation for school trustees] as long as each participant paid his own premium. The superintendent also informed the board members that participation in the insurance plan would not be limited to their terms on the Board of Trustees. The minutes reflect that the Board of Trustees took the following action:

> Smith then moved to allow board members to be put on the group insurance program at their own expense. Motion seconded by Michie and carried.

Dr. Michie canceled his family's health insurance policy shortly after the aforestated action was taken and enrolled under the school district's insurance plan effective December 1, 1984. John Smith enrolled sometime later.

Dr. Michie and Mr. Smith did not serve on the Board of Trustees after 1988. On March 23, 1989, the then-elected Board of Trustees voted unanimously to disallow participation by all board members, past or present, in the school district's insurance plan. . . .

The Michies filed a complaint against the Board of Trustees in the United States District Court for the District of Wyoming on April 3, 1991. . . .

The federal district court ruled in its summary judgment order that the Michies could not maintain their 42 U.S.C. § 1983 action because they possessed no property right, under either contract law or equity, to continue to participate in the school district's insurance plan. The court made this ruling upon determining: (1) that the 1989 Board of Trustees effectively voided the alleged contract because the Michies failed to demonstrate that it was either "reasonably necessary or of a definable advantage" to the school district; and (2) that equitable remedies, being discretionary in nature, do not give rise to legal rights cognizable under 42 U.S.C. § 1983. The court accordingly granted a summary judgment in favor of the Board of Trustees on the Michies' breach-of-contract and 42 U.S.C. § 1983 claims. It also dismissed the Michies' promissory estoppel . . . [claim], without prejudice, for lack of subject matter jurisdiction.

The Michies renewed their promissory estoppel claim against the Board of Trustees by filing a complaint in state district court on January 13, 1992. . . .

The Michies concede on appeal that the federal district court determined that they did not have an enforceable contract with the school district because any contract which might have existed was effectively voided by the 1989 Board of Trustees. They contend, however, that the state district court erred as a matter of law by granting a summary judgment on their promissory estoppel claim, apparently on this basis. The Michies argue that an enforceable contractual obligation is not an element of a promissory estoppel claim.

We agree that a claim for promissory estoppel is not dependent upon the existence of a promise which is enforceable under traditional contract principles. By definition, promissory estoppel is an equitable remedy for detrimental reliance upon a promise which does not rise to the level of a formal contract. As explained in Restatement (Second) of Contracts § 90(1) (1981):

> A promise which the promisor should reasonably expect to induce action or forbearance on the part of the promisee or a third person and which does induce such action or forbearance is binding if injustice can be avoided only by enforcement of the promise. The remedy granted for breach may be limited as justice requires.

This Court has recognized that promissory estoppel may be used as an affirmative cause of action. The elements which must be proved in a promissory estoppel action are:

> "(1) a clear and definite agreement; (2) proof that the party urging the doctrine acted to its detriment in reasonable reliance on the agreement; and (3) a finding that the equities support the enforcement of the agreement."

Whether elements one and two exist are questions for the finder of fact. Whether element three is satisfied is decided as a matter of law by the court.

In the instant case, the Michies contend that they presented evidence to satisfy each promissory estoppel element. We agree, however, with the state district court that the Michies failed to demonstrate "the existence of a contract or enforceable promise." ... [W]e understand the court's summary judgment order to be founded upon simple deductive reasoning: If it is against public policy to enforce an extended-term governmental contract, it is also against public policy to enforce an extended-term governmental promise embodied in the contract.

In [a prior case] this Court directly addressed the issue of whether extended-term governmental contracts are voidable as a matter of public policy.... On appeal, this Court stated:

> [A]n agreement extending beyond the term of the contracting authority ... may be voidable by the government or void upon attack by a third party if, under the facts and circumstances, the agreement is not reasonably necessary or of a definable advantage to the

city or governmental body. The issue when raised is decided as a matter of law, and the burden of evidence of the actual facts defining convenience and necessity devolve either upon the nongovernmental contracting party when attacked by the government or upon the third party who separately might attack the validity of the contract. . . .

The public policy underlying the rule . . . is straightforward: A governing body should not be able to deprive its successor in interest of discretion to act for the public good. We believe that this policy applies not only to extended-term governmental contracts but also to extended-term governmental promises which do not constitute formal contracts. Accordingly, both are voidable absent a showing of reasonable necessity or definable advantage. The Michies were not able to satisfy this requirement in federal court and are collaterally estopped from attempting to do so now. The equities of this case do not support the application of the doctrine of promissory estoppel against the Board of Trustees. The Board of Trustees was entitled to a summary judgment as a matter of law.

Affirmed.

Notes

1. Although a board of education, as a corporate body, is not affected by changes in membership, successor boards (with new members or with old members who change their minds) are not powerless to change course. Consider the court's articulation of this common law principle as it relates to contracts.

2. Do you agree with the school board attorney's initial advice that the arrangement would not have violated the statutory provision that board members "shall serve without compensation?"

3. An appellate court in Ohio held that even though a superintendent, based on conversations with individual board members, promised that two nonresident students would be able to attend local schools by paying tuition until they graduated, the arrangement was unenforceable since only the board could enter into a binding contract. The court concluded that the fact that the students attended for four years did not create a basis for promissory estoppel against the board. *Walker v. Lockland City School Dist. Bd. of Educ.*, 429 N.E.2d 1179 [2 Educ. L. Rep. 203] (Ohio App.1980).

[Case No. 24] Power of Board to Offer Retirement Incentive

FAIR LAWN EDUCATION ASSOCIATION v. FAIR LAWN BOARD OF EDUCATION

Supreme Court of New Jersey, 1979.
401 A.2d 681.

PASHMAN, J. In this case we are called upon to assess the validity of an Early Retirement Remuneration Plan (ERR) agreed to by the Fair Lawn Board of Education (Board) and the Fair Lawn Education Association (Association)—the majority representative of the Board's teaching employees. For the reasons to be given below, we conclude that the particular plan here at issue: (1) lacks statutory authorization; (2) contravenes this Court's holdings in [2 cases]; and (3) is preempted by the comprehensive statutory scheme relating to the operation of retirement benefits. Consequently, that plan cannot be implemented.

On July 1, 1976, the Association and the Board entered into a collective agreement covering the 1976–1977 and 1977–1978 school years. Article VI of that agreement set forth the provisions of the ERR plan whose legality is here in dispute. Under the terms of the contract, teachers between the ages of 55 and 64 who retired prior to September 1, 1977 would receive an additional payment in the amount of $6,000 upon leaving the Board's employ. Instructors retiring after the start of the 1977–1978 school year were also entitled to remuneration over and above their normal pension. The value of their benefit, however, was dependent upon age, with those relinquishing their positions at an earlier age receiving a larger bonus. The sums to be paid ranged from $500 for a 64–year-old teacher to $6,000 for retiring instructors aged 55 to 57. Four payment options—including lump sum and various installment alternatives—were provided. The goals underlying the adoption of this plan were twofold: (1) to "reward loyalty and long years of service," and (2) to encourage early retirements in order that tenured teachers could be replaced by younger, less experienced instructors whose salary levels would be much lower. . . .

On June 24, 1977, the Association filed suit in the Chancery Division seeking both a declaration that the ERR plan was valid and specific performance of its terms. The Board—named as sole defendant—joined the Teachers' Pension and Annuity Fund (TPAF) as third-party defendant. The pleadings and arguments below demonstrate that of these parties, the Board and the Association are in fact aligned in interest, and that TPAF is the only opponent of the plan. . . .

I

Local boards of education are creations of the State and, as such, may exercise only those powers granted to them by the Legislature—either expressly or by necessary or fair implication. We must therefore determine whether local boards have been delegated the authority to make payments to employees which are unrelated to services rendered for the sole purpose of inducing early retirement.

The trial court held that authorization for the plan could be found in two statutory provisions: N.J.S.A. 18A:27–4 (a local board may set the "terms and tenure of employment, . . . salaries and time and mode of payment thereof . . .") and N.J.S.A. 34:13A–5.3 (public employers and their employees may negotiate concerning "terms and conditions of employment"). We disagree.

N.J.S.A. 18A:27–4 does not confer upon local boards an unlimited power to negotiate all types of financial benefits for their teaching employees. Rather, the statute's use of the word "salaries" indicates that the Legislature intended to grant boards the power to set the "time and mode of payment" only of compensation which bears some relation to the rendition of past or present services. Under the ERR plan here at issue, payments are geared to age, not service. Moreover, the sums to which instructors are entitled decrease as length of service increases. It is thus clear that the parties to this contract intended to reward early retirement rather than the amount and quality of the work that a particular teacher had performed. As such, these payments are not authorized by N.J.S.A. 18A:27–4.

Nor are the payments called for by the ERR plan authorized by the Employer–Employee Relations Act, N.J.S.A. 34:13A–1 et seq. That statute does not enlarge the areas in which the Board has been delegated the responsibility to act. Rather, it merely recognizes the right of public employee representatives to negotiate with the Board over matters which, in the absence of negotiation, could have been set unilaterally by the Board. As such, the provisions of the Employer–Employee Relations Act do not operate to confer authority upon the Board to agree to compensation schemes which bear no relation to the amount and quality of the services which its teaching employees have rendered.

We therefore conclude that the Board has not been delegated the power to agree to or make the payments called for by the ERR plan here at issue. These payments, being unrelated to service, do not constitute "compensation" or "customary fringe benefits" with respect to which negotiation is permissible. Consequently, Article VI of the parties' collective agreement is *ultra vires* and unenforceable.

II

. . .

[The court reviewed two prior decisions (involving nonschool public employees) in which it had enunciated the principle that "actions taken by a state agency which may substantially affect retirement age and thus the actuarial assumptions of a statutory pension system are impermissible unless clearly and unequivocally authorized by the legislature."]

III

It is axiomatic that a municipality may not act in an area which the Legislature has preempted. In deciding whether a particular municipal activity has been preempted, the Court must determine whether the Legislature intended its action to preclude the exercise of local authority. . . .

In assessing the legislative intent, the primary factor to be considered is whether the municipal action adversely affects the legislative scheme. . . . [ERR's] adverse effect upon the comprehensive legislative scheme has been fully documented. . . . Hence, its existence stands " 'as an obstacle to the accomplishment and execution of the full purposes and objectives' of the Legislature[.]" . . .

. . .

Although we are not unsympathetic to the desire of local boards of education to reduce their expenses, sanction for plans such as the one at issue must come from the Legislature. That branch of government has determined that preservation of the TPAF's fiscal integrity is presently to be accorded paramount concern. We are not at liberty to reassess the policy judgment which it has made. Absent clear and unequivocal statutory authority, ERR plans such as Fair Lawn's may not be established. . . .

Notes

1. From an educational viewpoint, do you think the plan that was struck down had merit?

2. The court lists three bases for invalidating the plan in the first paragraph. Are they independent of each other?

3. Could a local school board pay teachers who retire a lump sum for unused sick leave days? Could the state legislature permit local boards to offer financial incentives for early retirement?

[Case No. 25] Power of Board to Require Physical Examination of Teacher

STRONG v. BOARD OF EDUCATION OF UNIONDALE UNION FREE SCHOOL DISTRICT

United States Court of Appeals, Second Circuit, 1990.
902 F.2d 208 [60 Educ. L. Rep. 379].

IRVING R. KAUFMAN, CIRCUIT JUDGE: The primary issue presented is whether a local school board denied a tenured public school teacher due process by refusing to allow her to return from an extended medical absence before she provided medical records and submitted to a physical examination by the school board doctor. In affirming the grant of summary judgment below, we hold that procedural due process is satisfied when a teacher in such circumstances is provided notice and an opportunity to respond to the adverse action of the school board, and when the state also affords a mechanism for obtaining judicial review of the board's decision on a subsequent petition for reinstatement. In addition, we find no constitutional violation of appellant's interest in privacy.

BACKGROUND

Appellant Marilyn Strong has been employed since 1980 by the Uniondale Union Free School District, in Nassau County, New York (School District). She has taught sixth grade at Northern Parkway Elementary School since 1981, and was awarded tenure in 1984.

From May 17, 1988 through the end of the academic year in late June, Strong was absent from the classroom because of illness. On June 8, after the School District inquired into the condition of its employee's health, it received a terse note from Strong's personal physician describing her as suffering from "severe nosebleed, vertigo, [and] arthritis."

In addition, Strong signed an insurance form (The form was a request by Strong to her insurance company to have certain premiums waived because of her disability.) and forwarded it to the School District in July, indicating she was currently "disabled" and that the date of her return to work was "unknown." Significantly, the form contained an "Authorization to Obtain Information" clause directly above Strong's signature which explicitly authorized any doctor who had treated her to release "any and all information" concerning her medical history to the insurance company.

During the ensuing summer months, the School District sought in vain to communicate with Strong. Registered letters to her home address went unclaimed; repeated efforts to reach her by telephone proved futile. Moreover, Strong's mother purportedly refused to provide the School District with her daughter's current address. Strong explains by alleging that she was under doctor's orders not to contact her employers because it made her ill to do so.

Unsuccessful in its efforts to contact Strong directly, the School District sent a letter dated August 17, 1988 to Strong's counsel, who had been retained pursuant to an unrelated discrimination claim against it. The letter directed Strong to produce an evaluation by her treating physician of her medical condition indicating whether she would be capable of resuming her teaching post. The communication specifically required Strong to provide "the names of all doctors she has seen since the commencement of her illness, along with releases permitting such doctors to provide the District with her medical records."

In response, Strong's lawyers stated that she would be returning to work at the start of the 1988–89 school year, but omitted any discussion of their client's health or medical records. Accordingly, on August 29 the School District asserted that Strong needed to provide "her medical records and history" to the School District's physician and be examined by him before returning to the classroom. Strong did not comply.

When Strong attempted to resume teaching on the first day of the new school year, September 6, 1988, School District Superintendent Alan Hernandez informed her (both orally and in subsequent letters summarizing their conversation) that she could not return until she submitted to a medical examination and produced her records. Strong indicated her willingness to be examined by the School District's doctor, but steadfastly refused to provide her medical records, except for a doctor's note stating that she has been treated "for chest pains, arthritis, palpitations, [and] headaches" and asserting her ability to return to teaching. The School District's doctor, however, maintained that he could not certify a teacher as fit to return from an extended illness without medical reports from that teacher's treating physician and that the conclusory assertions of Strong's personal physician fell far short of the information necessary to render an informed medical opinion.

On November 22, 1988, the Board of Education passed a resolution . . . instructing Strong to appear at the office of the School District's doctor for a physical examination. The resolution directed Strong to bring any and all medical records relating to her absence from school commencing May 16, 1988, to her examination so that the School

District's physician could properly evaluate the status of her health. To date, Strong has neither submitted to an examination nor proffered her medical records. Since she has exhausted her accrued sick leave, Strong no longer receives a salary.

Strong initiated this suit in December 1988, alleging that the School District's actions violated her constitutional rights to privacy and due process. . . .

DISCUSSION

I. *Due Process*

Strong urges that before the School District acted to bar her from the classroom she should have been notified of the "charges" against her, given an explanation of the School District's evidence, and provided an opportunity to present her side of the story.

Strong's procedural due process claim triggers analysis under a familiar framework. The threshold issue is whether Strong asserts a property interest protected by the Constitution. *See Board of Regents v. Roth.* If a protected interest exists, we must then determine whether the School District deprived Strong of that interest without due process. The constitutional contours of due process turn on the specific circumstances of the case, including the governmental and private interests at issue. Due process is a flexible concept requiring only such procedural protection as the particular situation demands.

Strong's position as a tenured teacher is indisputably a property interest protected by the fourteenth amendment. Whether the School District deprived her of that interest without affording adequate procedural safeguards thus depends on what process was due.

Under New York law a tenured teacher may be removed only pursuant to certain substantive and procedural safeguards, including notice and a full-blown adversarial hearing. On the other hand, the New York Court of Appeals has held that a prior hearing is not necessary before placing a tenured teacher on involuntary sick leave, *i.e.,* inactive status without pay due to illness. The *Brown* court's decision rested on the fact that the plaintiff, unlike a teacher who had been suspended or removed, retained all of her rights as a tenured teacher and could apply at anytime to be returned to active status. The court noted, moreover, that an adverse decision on Brown's application for reinstatement could be reviewed . . . in state court.

In the instant appeal, Strong has neither been "removed" from her teaching position, nor has she been involuntarily placed on sick leave. Under New York law, a teacher who is not permitted to return from an extended voluntary sick leave because of a failure to supply medical records is not considered suspended or terminated. Rather, we face the mirror image of the situation confronted in *Brown*. Here, we have a tenured teacher who has been barred against her will from resuming teaching after a hiatus taken on her own initiative. Yet the result is the same. By refusing to automatically reinstate her following her voluntary sick leave, the School District has barred her from working and effectively cut off her salary. As in *Brown,* Strong retains the right to petition for reinstatement and to challenge the denial of that petition in state court.

We recognize that, ordinarily, procedural due process requires notice and an opportunity to be heard. But an important government interest, accompanied by a substantial assurance that the deprivation is not baseless or unwarranted may justify postponing the opportunity to be heard until after the initial deprivation. In cases where a pretermination hearing is required, "an initial check" to determine whether there are reasonable grounds to support the proposed action is sufficient. *Cleveland Bd. of Educ. v. Loudermill.* Accordingly, deciding whether the procedures followed by the School District meet the constitutional minimum requires a balancing of the private and governmental interests at stake.

The private interest affected-the right of a tenured teacher to continue practicing her profession and receiving her salary-is substantial indeed. On the other hand, the School District had a strong interest in safeguarding the health and welfare of the students in the teacher's class and the other children attending the school; also, it had ample reason to question Strong's physical fitness to teach and to require more than conclusory assertions that she had regained her health.

Moreover, Strong received adequate notice in the August letters to her counsel that she was required to provide her medical records to the School District's doctor prior to returning to work. Contrary to Strong's assertions, the letters could not have provided details as to the "charges" against her, since there are no pending charges. The letters were not disciplinary; they merely sought information from which the School District's doctor could make a reasoned professional judgment about her fitness to teach.

Although Strong urges that there should have been some type of hearing before she was barred from the classroom, it is difficult to envision what would have transpired at such a hearing. She was adequately notified that the School District needed her medical records to assess her fitness to teach. The parties were well aware of each other's assertions and any further hearing would have amounted to an empty formality.

Moreover, as we have noted, adequate "post-deprivation" procedures are available to protect Strong's property interest in her tenured teaching position. All the process that was due in this case has been provided.

II. *Right to Privacy*

Strong also contends that even if the procedures for barring her from automatically returning to work were fair, compelling her to disclose her medical records amounts to an unconstitutional invasion of privacy.

Legitimate requests for medical information by those responsible for the health of the community do not rise to an impermissible invasion of privacy. The Sixth Circuit recently upheld a city ordinance requiring employees returning from extended absences to divulge certain medical information. We find persuasive the position of the Sixth Circuit in this similar setting. As we have noted, the School District has a strong interest in protecting the children under its care. Its request for Strong's medical records, limited to the period of her absence from school, was reasonably tailored in scope and does not violate her privacy rights....

Notes

1. *Board of Regents v. Roth* is Case No. 66. *Cleveland Bd. of Educ. v. Loudermill* is Case No. 85.

2. The Second Circuit ruled that a school board's refusal to allow a female teacher to be examined at her own expense by any female physician that it selected, rather than the male school physician, was arbitrary. *Gargiul v. Tompkins*, 704 F.2d 661 [10 Educ. L. Rep. 472] (2d Cir.1983), *vacated on other grounds*, 465 U.S. 1016, 104 S.Ct. 1263, 79 L.Ed.2d 670 (1984).

3. According to the Eighth Circuit, a board had the authority to require a second medical opinion attesting to fitness to return to duty for a driver education teacher. The court did not think that it was necessary to conduct a hearing before imposing this condition. *Scheideman v. West Des Moines Community School Dist.*, 989 F.2d 286 [82 Educ. L. Rep. 39] (8th Cir.1993).

[Case No. 26]   Board Procedures in Contracting

KONOVALCHIK v. SCHOOL COMMITTEE OF SALEM

Supreme Judicial Court of Massachusetts, 1967.
226 N.E.2d 222.

WHITTEMORE, JUSTICE. The issue on this appeal in a proceeding under G.L. c. 231A is whether, as the judge in the Superior Court ruled, certain votes of the defendant school committee on December 13, 1965, and subsequent events resulted in a three year contract with the plaintiff as head coach of football. The evidence is reported.

Most of the facts are not in dispute. We state others as the judge could have found them. The committee has power to make such a contract.

The school committee on December 13, 1965, by a vote of four in favor to three opposed voted to award to the plaintiff a contract as football coach for three years from December 31, 1965, at a salary of $3,000 for the first year and $3,500 for the two succeeding years. Motions to reconsider failed of passage. In another vote the city solicitor was requested to draw up a contract and have it at the December 27, 1965, meeting. The city solicitor was in the hospital from December 21, 1965, to January 15, 1966. Charles Geary, a member of the majority, typed out a contract substantially in the form of the plaintiff's existing contract that was to expire August 31, 1966, except for the term, the compensation, and one omission, and had the plaintiff sign it. The

December 27 meeting was convened at the stated hour with the three dissenters in attendance. They adjourned the meeting at 8:20 P.M. for lack of a quorum with knowledge that at least some of the majority were then in the building but had not responded promptly to the mayor's notice that the meeting was in session. They knew that Geary was there and had the draft contract with him. About 8:20 P.M. the four members of the majority signed the contract form in the secretary's office "where we sign most contracts." One copy of the contract was given to the plaintiff, one went to the office of the superintendent of schools and one to the city hall records. There was newspaper notice of the purported contract "sometime after the meeting of December 27."

We hold that no contract was made. The engagement was dependent upon the drafting and submission to the committee, and its approval, of a formal contract. The December 13 votes were not in themselves an offer which the plaintiff could accept.

Geary and his associates of the December 13 majority were without authority to determine for the committee the contract terms or to submit any document or offer of contract to the plaintiff. It may not be inferred that counsel would have recommended or the committee would have approved Geary's draft, or a contract like the existing contract.

We recognize that parliamentary tactics have operated to defeat the basic intention of the committee, at least as constituted in December, 1965. That circumstance cannot, however, operate to change rules of law.

The final decree is reversed. A decree is to enter in accordance with this opinion.

So ordered.

Notes

1. Did the result in this case serve the cause of education?

2. A written document may be necessary to the validity of a contract or may be only a memorandum of a previously formed contract. Apparently the court considered this case as falling within the first category. Could the court have found that a contract was actually formed at the December 13 meeting?

[Case No. 27]   Voting Procedures of Boards

MATAWAN REGIONAL TEACHERS ASSOCIATION v. MATAWAN–ABERDEEN REGIONAL SCHOOL DISTRICT BOARD OF EDUCATION

Superior Court of New Jersey, Appellate Division, 1988.
538 A.2d 1331 [45 Educ. L. Rep. 1123].

BRODY, J.A.D. The issue in this appeal is whether a local school board may lawfully adopt a plan, which includes the closing and sale of a school building, by a majority vote of its full membership after consideration at a single public meeting even though its bylaws require adoption by a 2/3 vote of its full membership after consideration at two public meetings. We hold that the board is not bound by the bylaw that limits the authority of the majority, but is bound by the bylaw that requires two public meetings for adoption of the plan.

The dispute arose when the nine members of the Matawan–Aberdeen Regional School District Board of Education (the board) voted 5 to 4 to reorganize the school district by adopting "Plan C" (the plan). The cornerstone of the plan is the closing and sale of a school and an administration building in the Borough of Matawan. Closing the school requires relocating students and changing the range of classes in the remaining schools. Adoption of the plan is a matter of substantial local public interest. Petitioners are the union that represents board employees, and 92 resident-taxpayers of the district.

An administrative law judge (ALJ) summarily dismissed the claim that the bylaws barred adoption of the plan. The Commissioner of Education and the State Board of Education affirmed the ALJ's summary dismissal for the reasons he had expressed.

The relevant bylaws provide the following:

No policy shall be adopted by the Board until it has received a vote of the full Board at two public meetings. . . .

Bylaws shall be adopted, amended or repealed by a 2/3 vote of the full Board.

Local boards of education "may exercise only those powers granted to them by the Legislature-either expressly or by necessary or fair implication." *Fair Lawn Educ. Ass'n v. Fair Lawn Bd. of Educ.* Boards derive the authority to adopt bylaws from N.J.S.A. 18A:11–1c, which provides that a local board shall

Make, amend and repeal rules, not inconsistent with this title or with the rules of the state board, for its own government and the transaction of its business and for the government and management of the public schools and public school property of the district and for the employment, regulation of conduct and discharge of its employees. . . .

Boards derive the authority to govern and manage the district from N.J.S.A. 18A:11 d, which provides that a local board shall

Perform all acts and do all things, consistent with law and the rules of the state board, necessary for the lawful and proper conduct, equipment and maintenance of the public schools of the district.

N.J.S.A. 18A:111 is silent with respect to the number of votes necessary to adopt rules and to govern and manage the district. It must be assumed that by its silence the Legislature intended the common-law rule to apply, i.e., a majority vote of the members of the board constituting a quorum shall be sufficient. At common law, a majority of a public body constitutes a quorum. Thus the Legislature has empowered a majority of the majority of a local board to adopt bylaws and conduct the board's business.

We reject the argument that the Legislature has merely established a minimum number of affirmative votes necessary for local board action, which the board may increase in its bylaws to assure a broader consensus. Depriving the majority of its authority and responsibility to govern in favor of a broader consensus carries the risk of inaction where action is warranted. There may be actions which should be taken with the affirmative votes of an enhanced majority because of their overwhelming importance or because they constitute a departure from the norm. The Legislature has provided for such particular instances by requiring the vote of an enhanced majority. A relevant example is the statute that prohibits a local board from selling school lands except "by a recorded roll call majority vote of its full membership." N.J.S.A. 18A:205. That requirement was met here.

We conclude that the Legislature has preempted a local board's authority to strike the balance between requiring a broad consensus for action and the attendant risk of inaction. We arrive at this conclusion because striking that delicate balance is a matter of major governmental importance calling for uniform treatment throughout the State and is a subject on which the Legislature has acted in many specific instances by requiring an enhanced majority.

Our holding conforms to long-standing precedent in this State. In *Barnert v. Paterson*, the court held:

> When the charter of a municipal corporation or a general law of the state does not provide to the contrary, a majority of the board of aldermen constitute a quorum, and the vote of a majority of those present, there being a quorum, is all that is required for the adoption or passage of a motion or the doing of any other act the board has power to do.

> Under the twenty-third section of the charter, the board is given power "to establish its own rules of procedure." But I do not think that under this power it was designed to confer upon this board the adoption of a rule changing either the general law or any special provision in the charter. Power to make such rules and by-laws was inherent in the corporation without this provision. Such by-laws must be in accordance with the charter or the general rules of law. The charter is silent and the general law requires a majority vote. . . .

By contrast, the bylaw requiring that action on non-emergent matters of policy be considered at two public meetings does not conflict directly or indirectly with any statute. Its purpose is not to remove the responsibility and authority to act from those members of a local board who are authorized by state law to act. Rather, its purpose is to assure that those having that responsibility and authority act only upon due deliberation after notice to the public and interested third parties. Our courts have long compelled public bodies to adhere to such bylaws.

In *Eggers v. Newark*, a Board of Street and Water Commissioners adopted an ordinance during the meeting at which it was introduced despite a bylaw that required publication between the first and second readings. The commissioners purported to suspend the bylaw by unanimous consent. The court held that the bylaws had been duly adopted pursuant to statute and therefore "constituted the working regulations governing [the Board's] action so far as not regulated by higher authority of the statute." In upholding the bylaws and setting aside the ordinance the court said,

> [I]t is evident that if they can be rendered nugatory by the suspension of a mere rule of order, the by-laws are little more than a suggestion instead of being, as they should be, a set of regulations for the transaction of public business by a public body, on which regulations the public itself has a right to rely. The more radical proposition is also advanced that, as the vote was unanimous to suspend the by-law and pass the ordinance, no one can be heard to complain. But this likewise loses sight of the right of the public to expect that ordinances, involving as they do the interests of the public, shall be enacted in due form as provided by law, and that part of that law is the regulations adopted and promulgated by the legislative body. The ordinance in question was one in which the public were vitally interested.

In *Hicks v. Long Branch Commission*, the Court set aside a special appropriation because, in violation of the Commission's bylaws, each commissioner's vote was not recorded. The Court said,

> The standing rules, adopted by ordinance under the express authority of the charter, as before stated, provide that "on every vote relating to any special appropriation the yeas and nays shall be taken and recorded." This rule was as binding upon the commission and its members as any statute or other law of the commonwealth. Its importance is manifest. It is designed to secure, in matters relating to the public funds, deliberate action on the part of each commissioner, and immediate as well as permanent public evidence thereof, readily accessible to the voters of the municipality, on which their representatives may be held responsible.

The binding effect of bylaws designed to give the public notice before official action is taken was reaffirmed by the Court in *Erie R.R. Co. v. Paterson* where a Board of Public Works adopted an ordinance at a meeting held on a date not scheduled in its bylaws. In setting aside the ordinance the Court cited the language in *Eggers* with approval.

In the absence of any statute to the contrary, the board's bylaw requiring two public meetings to adopt the plan is binding. We must therefore set aside the resolution that purported to adopt the plan at a single meeting. Our determination renders moot the other issues that have been raised in this appeal.

Reversed.

Notes

1. This case illustrates an important distinction between procedural rules that can be enacted and then must be followed by lower government bodies and those that cannot be enacted absent state legislation. The administrative law

judge, the commissioner of education, and the state board of education erred as to the distinction.

2.   Contemplate the rationale expressed in *Eggers v. Newark* and *Hicks v. Long Branch Commission* (quoted in the case) that served as basis of the opinion. How does it serve the long-range interests of democratic government?

[Case No. 28]   Public Nature of Board Meetings and Records

CONOVER v. BOARD OF EDUCATION OF NEBO SCHOOL DISTRICT

Supreme Court of Utah, 1954.
267 P.2d 768.

HENRIOD, JUSTICE. Appeal from a judgment holding that the minutes of a local board of education meeting, transcribed by its Clerk, were not a public writing subject to inspection under Titles 78–26–1, 2, U.C.A. 1953. Reversed, no costs awarded.

This appears to be a friendly suit to determine applicability of our statutes on public writings to the facts of this case, and there is nothing here indicating any disposition to withhold information on the part of anyone. It is here on the pleadings, which reflect the following circumstances: On Feb. 16, 1953, in answer to the Clerk's inquiry, the State Superintendent of Public Instr., legal adviser to boards under the terms of an unusual statute, where one not an attorney may act in that capacity, advised the Clerk that minutes of local board meetings were not official until approved by the board, which body should determine its own policy with reference to releasing such minutes to persons other than board members. On Feb. 18, the board held a meeting which was open to the public. The Clerk took notes of what transpired, and transcribed them into minutes for board approval and placement in his Journal. On Feb. 19 the plaintiffs asked permission to examine and copy the minutes so transcribed, but the Clerk, partly because of the Superintendent's letter, advised that they would not be available for inspection until the board approved them at its next meeting. The minutes, as transcribed, later were approved by the board unchanged, and were placed in the Journal which, by statute, the Clerk must keep. What was in the minutes, unfortunately, was not presented to us, so we cannot determine what, if any, action was taken that might have been of such public concern as to require immediate publication, or whether it was so inconsequential that immediate publication would serve no useful purpose.

Plaintiffs urge that the notes of the Clerk, or at least the transcribed minutes, prepared for Journal entry, subject only to board approval, were a public writing under our statute and should have been open to inspection immediately after preparation, and that preparation immediately should have followed the meeting. Defendants say this might lead to public misinformation and embarrassment to board members because of possible inaccuracies in what they claim were tentative minutes, unofficial until approved and placed in the Journal.

The statutes and cases relating to public writings are divergent as the shading of the spectrum. There appears to be no formula for determining what is or is not a public writing, except by defining the terms, looking at the facts, and relying on court decisions for determination and settlement. The contentions of opposing counsel, however, point up what frequently is true, that between two extremes, not necessarily midway, there is a point where reason shows brightest, dimming as the point shifts in one direction or the other. To hold that a public writing includes the unexpurgated scribbled notes of a Clerk, legible, perhaps, to him alone, would be unreasonable, we think, and even might deify doodling. It would be unreasonable also to hold that any record made by the Clerk short of approval by a board and placement in a Journal, is not a public writing. Such conclusion might deify dawdling. We hold, therefore, that the Clerk's untranscribed notes reasonably are not classifiable as a public writing under the statute, whereas the transcribed minutes, in final form, but awaiting only approval and placement in the Journal, are a public writing in contemplation of the statute. In so holding, we are aware of those authorities stating that not every memorandum of a public officer is a public record. We believe, however, that the more pertinent cases are found in a long line holding that whenever a written record of a transaction of a public officer in his office is a *convenient* and *appropriate* mode of discharging the duties of his office, and is kept by him as such, whether required by express provision of law or not, such a record is a public record. To hold that the minutes in this case were not, but the Journal was, a public writing, would attach a magic significance to the word "journal," and might repose in boards a power to act on matters of great public moment without opportunity for public scrutiny.

Here the Clerk did everything he intended to do by way of recording the meeting. Under the statute he could have placed the minutes in the Journal as soon as prepared. The board's policy of having him refrain from doing so until approval was had cannot justify circumvention of a statute requiring him to prepare the minutes, nor the withholding of information from the public for an unreasonable length of time. It is no answer to our conclusions to say that the meeting was open to the public. We cannot blind ourselves to the facts that many such meetings go unattended by the public, that no newspaper can have its agents at all of such meetings, and that no country editor can be in two towns or counties at once.

The parties here have requested that we address ourselves also to the matter of when the minutes should be available for public inspection. We cannot determine here when the Clerk reasonably should have had his minutes available to the public, since nobody has told us what was in them. We believe that what is a reasonable time to prepare a record of a public board meeting depends entirely on the facts of each case. If the board action called for the purchase of textbooks advocating communism, the record reasonably should be prepared for public release at once after the meeting, while a resolution to dismiss school on Washington's Birthday perhaps need never be documented, at least so far as one very important segment of the public is concerned, the children. It seems to us that the reasonable time when the record of such meetings should be made available to the public, may vary with the exigencies of the particular case, and the time for preparation and dissemination would be directly proportional to the importance of the action taken.

Both sides concede that the public is entitled to know what happened at school board meetings within a reasonable time. Competent authority supports this proposition. We believe further, that a reasonable time after the meeting for making available the record of actions taken there would be some time before any important action was to take place. If available only after action was taken, such information would have little or no news value, except as it might be the basis for criticism of injudicious action. The people would be precluded from indulging their traditionally democratic practice and privilege of complaining of or approving the actions of their elected servants.

There is the further problem as to when information of what transpired at the meeting should be made available to the public, quite apart from documentation in a public writing. It would seem that, unless matters were of such a delicate nature or of the type where public policy dictates nondissemination, the meeting itself should be open to the public and press, and information concerning what transpired there should be made available, at least in a general way, to both at any time thereafter, by him whose duties require its recordation. There is nothing unreasonable in that under our free and democratic way of life. The truth about the official acts of public servants always should be displayed in the public market place, subject to public appraisal. Any attempt to withhold information after a meeting, itself should be a subject for a wide publicity, irrespective of the fact that withholding it might prevent someone's embarrassment because of inaccuracy. Such inaccuracy may be reason enough to replace him responsible therefor, but most certainly is no reason for withholding information to which the public is entitled; nor to prevent the embarrassment of anyone; nor to perpetuate anyone in public office. We believe and hold that although the Clerk's action in refusing permission to inspect his minutes, was reasonable for the purpose of obtaining an adjudication of correlative rights and duties, it would be unreasonable in preventing the public and press from obtaining information as to what happened at the meeting. . . .

Notes

1.   What problems may arise from having citizens or the press gain information about a meeting through the words of a board clerk before they were approved by the board? Is possible misinformation an appropriate risk in the interest of prompt public access to records?

2.   Board minutes may be amended at any time to conform to what occurred at a meeting. *Jewell v. Board of Educ., Duquoin Community Unit Schools, Dist. No. 300*, 312 N.E.2d 659 (Ill. App.Ct.1974).

[Case No. 29]   Residence for Voting Purposes—Disqualified Voters

WEHRUNG v. IDEAL SCHOOL DISTRICT NO. 10

Supreme Court of North Dakota, 1956.
78 N.W.2d 68.

GRIMSON, JUDGE. On the 14th day of October 1955, the Ideal School District No. 10, of McKenzie County, North Dakota, held an election to determine whether to issue negotiable bonds in the amount not exceeding $120,000. A notice of said election was duly published and at said election 480 votes were cast in favor of issuance of the bonds and 237 were cast against it. The vote in favor was more than the required 66 2/3 percent of the voters who had voted. As a result the proposition of issuing the bonds was declared carried. In due time seven taxpayers of Ideal School District No. 10 commenced a contest of the election alleging that the election had been conducted illegally and that many illegal votes were cast. They prayed that the officers of the district be enjoined from proceeding further and that the election be declared null and void. The contestees deny the illegality of the election. A hearing was duly had in district court and judgment entered sustaining the election. The contestants appealed to this court and ask for a trial de novo.

There are several issues but appellants summarize them under three points as follows:

"1. Permitting, or requiring, an unqualified voter to disclose how he voted.

"2. Permitting people, not qualified voters of the district, to vote.

"3. Permitting the voters of the First Addition to the Wold Addition in the townsite of Watford City to vote claiming that Addition was not legally annexed to the Ideal School District."

As to the first point the contestants and appellants presented 12 witnesses who were examined as to their legal qualifications to vote at that election. When the witnesses were examined as to how they voted at this election the court informed those whom it found to be qualified voters that they did not need to disclose that fact unless they wished to do so. In *Torkelson v. Byrne*, this court held the qualified elector cannot be compelled to disclose for whom he voted. However, this privilege of secrecy is entirely a personal one and the voter himself may waive his privilege and testify for whom he voted.

Two voters were found to be disqualified to vote in this election. As to those two voters the court ruled they would have to disclose how they voted. In *Hanson v. Village of Adrian*, the court held:

"Having proven that the contestees voted without right, it is proper by competent evidence to ascertain how they voted, so as to purge the election of the illegal vote."

The court was clearly right in requiring the disqualified voters to disclose how they voted and to deduct their votes from the total. As it happened one voted for and the other against the bonds so that the result was not changed, and more than 66 2/3rds percent remained in favor of bonds.

On the next point the contestants and appellants object to the ruling of the court holding several of the challenged voters were qualified to vote. They especially question the votes of Earl Quale and his wife. Mr. Quale testified that he had a home in Watford City located in Ideal School District No. 10; that for more than a year while he had no work in Watford City he had been living temporarily in Arnegard, renting his home in Watford City because he needed the income from the rent to save his home from foreclosure; that even though his children went to school at Arnegard during that time he always intended to come back to make Watford City his permanent home; that he now has work there and is waiting until his tenant finds another place to move into, so that he can bring his family back to his home; that he never voted in Arnegard. Other witnesses were cross-examined as to their residence and disclosed that even though they temporarily worked on a farm or other places, they had a home in Watford City and always intended to return there and never voted anywhere else.

Residence is the place where one lives when not called elsewhere for labor or other special purposes and to which on such occasions he returns. There can be only one residence and it cannot be lost until another is gained. It can be changed only by union of act and intent. The testimony of the witnesses whose residence in Watford City was questioned was that they had homes in Watford City and intended to return there and did return when occasion arrived. They had no intent of obtaining a residence anywhere else. Residence is a question of fact in which the intention of the party enters as an important element. Under the testimony those witnesses had a residence in Watford City of sufficient length of time to become qualified electors. The district court so found and the evidence supports such finding. . . .

Notes

1. Do you agree with the rationale for the rule that a qualified voter cannot be compelled to disclose for whom he voted, but a disqualified voter can be so compelled? *See Corn v. Blackwell*, 4 S.E.2d 254 (S.C. 1939), wherein officials inadvertently had ballots printed and numbered consecutively from one up to hundreds. The ballots were then cast in such a manner as to render it easy to determine how each person voted. The court held that since this destroyed the secrecy of the ballot, the election results had to be invalidated.

2. Compare the legal concept of residence for purpose of voting with that of residence for tuition-free attendance in public schools.

[Case No. 30]   Misadvice to Electors in School Election

GRANT v. SCHOOL DISTRICT NO. 61, BAKER COUNTY

Supreme Court of Oregon, 1966.
415 P.2d 165.

DENECKE, JUSTICE. This is a declaratory judgment proceeding brought because of a controversy concerning the formation of an Administrative School District and the acts of such District.

Under the provisions of what is now ORS 330.505 *et seq.*, the Baker County School Reorganization Committee proposed an Administrative School District, in effect consolidating several school districts in the northeastern part of the county. The residents of Eagle Valley, the area of one of the school districts, were apprehensive that the proposed district would cause them to lose their high school and that one high school, to serve the entire district, would be built in the more populous Pine Valley. At a public hearing on the proposed new district, called pursuant to the school reorganization statute, a document was referred to which commenced, "To Whomsoever It May Concern." It was signed by the directors and clerks of all the districts proposed to be in the new Administrative District. It provided, among other things, as follows: "That no school be changed, moved or consolidated without the approval of the patrons in the attendance area which that school serves."

The complaint filed by plaintiffs as representatives of the residents of Eagle Valley alleges that the Eagle Valley residents "were advised that said agreement [the above-quoted statement] would be incorporated in the school district reorganization plan." The "said agreement" was not in fact incorporated in the school reorganization plan. Plaintiffs further allege that because of their belief that they would continue to have their own high school until they approved a change, they voted in favor of the new Administrative District.

About five years after the new Administrative District was formed, a majority of the voters of the new district passed a bond issue for one high school for the entire district, to be built in Pine Valley.

The plaintiffs sought a declaration that the defendant Administrative District had no right to move the school without obtaining the consent of the Eagle Valley voters.

The trial court held against the plaintiffs and we affirm its ruling.

Art. VIII, 3, of the Oregon Constitution, vests the state legislature with the responsibility for public education.

The legislature has provided that a bond issue is passed and binding upon the entire district if it is approved by a majority of the voters in the entire district.

That legislative command is binding upon the new district. The alleged misadvice to the Eagle Valley voters cannot change or limit that legislative command. See [cases] holding that misrepresentations made during a campaign by public officials will not vitiate an election.

Affirmed.

Notes

1. In common business transactions, misrepresentations relied on by others to their detriment are grounds for invalidating the transactions. Should the same rule apply to elections?

2. The Supreme Court of Arizona affirmed that an election to rescind a bond issue that was approved at a prior election was valid as long as officials had not sold any bonds. The court acknowledged that other courts were divided on the question. *Members of Bd. of Educ. of Pearce Union High School Dist. v. Leslie*, 543 P.2d 775 (Ariz.1975).

3. Massachusetts' highest court invalidated an election where, contrary to statute, an unsuccessful candidate for re-election to a school committee was unintentionally not designated as an incumbent while others were properly identified. *Rizzo v. Board of Election Comm'rs of Revere*, 525 N.E.2d 409 [47 Educ. L. Rep. 685] (Mass.1988). Is this reasonable? Fair?

[Case No. 31] One–Person, One–Vote Applies Only to Elected Positions

VERNET v. BELLMORE–MERRICK CENTRAL HIGH SCHOOL DISTRICT

United States District Court, Eastern District of New York, 2004.
343 F.Supp.2d 186 [193 Educ. L. Rep. 726].

PLATT, DISTRICT JUDGE.

Defendant Bellmore–Merrick High School District ("Bellmore–Merrick") moves, prior to serving its answer, to dismiss Plaintiff Stephen P. Vernet's ("Mr.Vernet") complaint pursuant to FED. R. CIV. P. 12(b)(6) on the ground that the exact same claims were decided by this Court thirty years ago in favor of Bellmore–Merrick.

Mr. Vernet brings this action under 42 U.S.C. § 1983, and invokes the jurisdiction of this Court under 28 U.S.C. §§ 1331 and 1343. Jurisdiction is further invoked under 28 U.S.C. §§ 2201 and 2202 as Mr. Vernet is seeking a declaratory judgment.

.   .   .

For the following reasons, Bellmore–Merrick's motion is GRANTED.

Facts

Bellmore–Merrick is organized under New York Education Law § 1901. Bellmore–Merrick oversees the administration of two middle schools and three high schools located in the Town of Hempstead, Nassau County, the State of New York. Bellmore–Merrick is composed of four Union Free School Districts ("UFSD"). The respective populations of the four USFD's vary widely: . . . .

The four districts govern the elementary schools that feed into two middle schools and three high schools which make up the Bellmore–Merrick school district. The UFSD's, i.e. the elementary schools, are each governed by a school board consisting of members elected by the residents of each Union Free School District:. . . .

Each school board, acting separately for their own UFSD's, then appoints two of its members to serve on the Bellmore–Merrick school board which governs the middle and high schools. The residents of the four UFSD's do not vote directly for the individuals who serve on the Bellmore–Merrick school board.

Mr. Vernet claims that the current practice of allowing each UFSD to select two of its members to serve on the Bellmore–Merrick school board despite a disparity in the number of residents within each UFSD, violates the "one man, one vote" principle and the Equal Protection Clause of the 14th Amendment. Mr. Vernet contends the individual votes of residents in each of the UFSD are "diluted" because each UFSD has the same number of members selected to represent their community on the Bellmore–Merrick school board.

Standard

In deciding a motion to dismiss under FED. R. CIV. P. 12(b) the Court is required to accept as true all factual allegations in the complaint and to consider documents attached to and incorporated by reference in the complaint. In a Rule 12(b)(6) motion to dismiss for failure to state claims upon which relief may be granted, Bellmore–Merrick bears the burden of showing that even if Mr. Vernet's allegations are accepted as true, and all reasonable inferences are drawn in Mr. Vernet's favor, Mr. Vernet is still not entitled to relief.

Discussion

I. *Defendant's Argument: The Decision in Rosenthal v. Board of Education Mandates Dismissal of Plaintiff's Action.*

Bellmore–Merrick's sole reason for dismissal of Mr. Vernet's claims is grounded in the *stare decisis* impact of a 1974 decision by this Court involving the same claims and defendant. [In *Rosenthal*] . . . the Court considered whether the process by which board members are chosen to serve on the Bellmore–Merrick school board violated the "one man, one vote" principle and was therefore unconstitutional. The Court held that the two-tiered method of choosing board members was an appointive vice elective process and that the "one man, one vote" principle only applied in cases where "the officials whose election is challenged must have been elected by popular vote."

II. *Plaintiff's Response*

a. *Rosenthal mislabeled the Bellmore–Merrick school board selection process as an appointive governing body.*

Mr. Vernet concedes that "(i)n *Rosenthal,* the Second Circuit properly recognized the 'one man, one vote' principle only applies to elective bodies."

Mr. Vernet argues that although the Second Circuit correctly reaffirmed the Supreme Court's holding that the "one person, one vote" principle does not apply where officials are appointed, the Bellmore–Merrick school board only *appears* to be an appointed governing body. Mr. Vernet alleges that the term appointment is merely a label misapplied to the Bellmore–Merrick school board selection process and argues that discovery should be permitted to substantiate this allegation.

Mr. Vernet, however, fails to allege any facts in his complaint whatsoever to support his contention that the Bellmore–Merrick school board selection process is anything other than appointive in nature. Mr. Vernet challenges whether the *Rosenthal* Court properly defined the Bellmore–Merrick school board's selection process on the grounds that the "plaintiff in *Rosenthal* did not conduct an evidentiary exploration of the issue of elective versus appointive nature of the [Bellmore–Merrick school board]."

The Court of Appeals for the Second Circuit convened the *Rosenthal* three Judge panel specifically for the task of deciding whether the Bellmore–Merrick school board selection process was appointive or elective. The three Judge panel determined that the nature of the Bellmore–Merrick school board selection process was appointive in nature. Included in the Court's analysis was testimony from the then President of the Bellmore–Merrick school board concerning the functions of the school board. The Court also reviewed New York Education Law § 1901. Mr. Vernet provides no reason for this Court to doubt that the *Rosenthal* three Judge panel would have come to a different conclusion today considering the two tier selection process remains—as Mr. Vernet concedes—unchanged.

Mr. Vernet further alleges that he has learned, through his own research, that members of the Bellmore–Merrick school board "are voted upon by motion in open meetings of the Union Free School District Boards of Education." Mr. Vernet does not describe the research he conducted. Moreover, Mr. Vernet's complaint is devoid of any factual allegations related to such research. He further questions whether the names of those selected to be on the Bellmore–Merrick school board are "discussed" and whether "general campaigning" occurs during UFSD meetings. Mr. Vernet asks this Court to permit further discovery in the hopes of substantiating these questions on the grounds that "all of these events and more are indicative of an election."

Naturally board members wishing to be appointed to a position of increased responsibility would not simply sit on their hands and wish for an appointment. Even if it were true that members of the individual UFSD's campaigned amongst their colleagues to be selected to the Bellmore–Merrick school board, that fact would not change the essential appointive nature of the selection process. The key factor in deciding whether the Bellmore–Merrick school board selection process violates the principle of one person, one vote, is whether the board members selected to serve on the Bellmore–Merrick school board are popularly elected: "The emphasis we put on popular election as the test echoes the Supreme Court's recognition that the crucial factor in the application of Fourteenth Amendment considerations to any apportionment scheme is that the officials whose election is challenged must have been elected by popular vote."

b.   *The current structure of the Bellmore–Merrick Central High School District supports a weighted voting system and is therefore unconstitutional.*

Mr. Vernet's other argument is that the current selection process of the Bellmore–Merrick school board supports a weighted voting system. Mr. Vernet contends that his ability to participate in the selection of members to the Bellmore–Merrick school board is diluted because his more populous UFSD has an equal number of members on the Bellmore–Merrick school board as do the smaller UFSD's. Mr. Vernet asks the Court to compare the facts of this case to *Jackson v. Nassau County Board of Supervisors*, in which a group of residents in Nassau County challenged the make-up of the Nassau County Board of Supervisors on the grounds that the more populous Town of Hempstead had more weighted votes than the other, smaller towns, and that such practice was unconstitutional.

At the time the Court in *Jackson* evaluated the political process in Nassau County, the Nassau County Board of Supervisors were elected from each of the five towns within Nassau County using a weighted voting system. This method of voting gave supervisors from more populous towns more voting power when deciding issues before the Board. The Court determined that this process was unconstitutional on the grounds that i) the "one man, one vote" applied to local governmental agencies; ii) the United States Supreme Court had rejected weighted voting; and iii) the formula by which votes were distributed amongst the towns in Nassau County created a standard deviation between the actual population and the weighted votes which was impermissibly large and thereby violated the one person, one vote requirement.

Bellmore–Merrick responds that *Jackson* is distinguishable form the case at bar because representatives on the Nassau County Board of Supervisors were popularly elected. In this case there exists a two-tiered system in which the Bellmore–Merrick school board members are not popularly elected but appointed by school boards which are popularly elected. Bellmore–Merrick asserts that under the holding of *Rosenthal* it does not matter in a two-tiered selection process that the members of the local boards who make the appointments to the second tier were themselves popularly elected.

This Court agrees with Bellmore–Merrick that *Rosenthal* and *Warden* provide the requisite *stare decisis* effect to stave off Mr. Vernet's challenges to the appointive nature of the Bellmore–Merrick school board and his claim that residents' votes within the UFSD's are diluted. *Jackson* is distinguishable because in that case the residents of Nassau County directly elected members to the Board of Supervisors whereas in the case at bar, the Bellmore–Merrick's school board members are appointed.

The result is the same even if this Court applied the holding in *Jackson* to the first tier of the Bellmore–Merrick school board selection process. The individual UFSD's do not meet as a single governing unit unlike the now dismantled Nassau County Board of Supervisors. The weight of one resident's vote is equal to any other vote within the Bellmore, North Bellmore, Merrick or North Merrick school districts when choosing representatives for their applicable UFSD. Neither the first or second tier of the Bellmore–Merrick school board selection process involves the unconstitutional practice of weighted voting as described by the Court in Jackson.

Conclusion

Mr. Vernet seems to suggest that the issue of diluted voting was a new inequity in the American political landscape discovered by the Court in the *Jackson* case: "Until the mid–1990s the courts tolerated an illegal weighted voting system which violated the 'one man, one vote' principle." In fact, the *Rosenthal* Court specifically discussed the issue of weighted voting in its analysis of the Bellmore–Merrick school board selection process: "If plaintiff did in fact vote for the members of the [Bellmore–Merrick school board] representing his union free school district, his vote would be diluted in violation of the one man, one vote principle." The Court instead held that the Bellmore–Merrick school board was appointive in nature and so like Mr. Rosenthal's claims thirty years ago, Mr. Vernet's contention that his vote as a resident within the Bellmore–Merrick school district is diluted has no merit. Despite Mr. Vernet's frustrations with New York Education Law § 1901 and the Bellmore–Merrick school board selection process, nothing presented by Mr. Vernet in his complaint persuades this Court that the holding in *Rosenthal* should be disturbed.

Accordingly, Defendant Bellmore–Merrick's motion pursuant to FED. R. CIV. P. 12(b)(6) to dismiss Plaintiff Mr. Vernet's complaint is hereby GRANTED.

SO ORDERED.

Notes

1. Do you agree with the court?

2. Should local school board members be appointed or elected?

[Case No. 32] Power of Board to Expend Funds to Advocate Favorable Vote

CITIZENS TO PROTECT PUBLIC FUNDS v. BOARD OF EDUCATION OF PARSIPPANY–TROY HILLS TOWNSHIP

Supreme Court of New Jersey, 1953.
98 A.2d 673.

WILLIAM J. BRENNAN, Jr., J. . . . Defendant proposed a program for enlarging several school buildings and to issue bonds in the amount of $560,000 to finance the first half of the program. There being existing debt limitations, approval of the proposal, as required by R.S. 18:5–86 . . . was first obtained from the State Commissioner of Education and the Local Government Board before the proposal was submitted, as is also required by that statute and as was in any event required by R.S. 18:7–73, N.J.S.A., to a referendum vote at an election held December 2, 1952 when the proposal was adopted by a vote of 875 to 542. However, the defendant board did not prior to that election submit the proposed building expansion plans to the local planning board for approval as to "location, character and extent thereof," according to R.S. 40:55–7, as amended. . . .

When the building program was authorized by resolution adopted August 27, 1952, the 1952–1953 school budget included an appropriation captioned "Current expenses, administrative, architecture fees, preliminary." Some $358.85 of this appropriation was spent by defendant for "printing, artist's work and postage" to print and circulate an 18–page booklet entitled "Read the Facts Behind the Parsippany–Troy Hills School Building Program." All but one page of the booklet depicts in graphic form, effectively illustrated to arrest the reader's attention, such facts as the growth of the grade school population (from 1945, doubled, and by 1956 to be tripled), the inadequacies of existing facilities, the proposed immediate additions, with architectural sketches, to two schools, other expansions planned to be deferred until 1955, the aggregate and annual costs, principal and interest, of the immediate program and the effect upon taxes of such cost. However, there also appears on the cover and on two of the pages "Vote Yes," and "Vote Yes–December 2, 1952," and an entire page which, except for an accompanying sketch, we reproduce:

"What Will Happen if You Don't Vote Yes?"

"Double Sessions!!!"

"This will automatically Cheat your child of 1/3 of his education (4 hours instead of 6).

"Yearly school changing and hour long Bus rides will continue for many children.

"Morning Session (8:30–12:30) Children will leave home ½ hour earlier.

"Afternoon Session (12:30–4:30) Children will return home 1 ½ hours later (many after dark).

"Children in some families would be attending different sessions (depending upon grade).

"Transportation costs will increase (could double) with 2 sets of bus routes per day.

"Temporary room rentals will continue ($4,000 per year).

"Double use of equipment will necessitate more rapid replacement.

"Note: Operating expenses will continue to rise as the enrollment increases (more teachers, more supplies and equipment for children. This Will Be So Whether We Build Or Not.)"

On December 1, the day before the referendum election, radio station WMTR broadcast a 15–minute panel discussion of the proposed building program as one of the station's "public interest" programs. The panel was composed of a member of the defendant board of education and two members of a citizens advisory committee which assisted the board in the formulation of the building program. The superintendent of schools, with the approval of the board's president, advised the principals of the several schools equipped with public address systems or radios that school children in grades four to eight might be permitted to hear the broadcast. According to the numerous affidavits of teachers offered to support defendant's motion for dismissal, some turned on the program and others did not, the reception was unsatisfactory in many instances and the broadcast for that reason was not heard, many children paid no attention to it, and the reaction of at least one class was why "do we have to listen to this sort of thing." And it appears without contradiction that the panel discussion was purely informative as to the scope of the building program and that there was no exhortation to vote affirmatively for the proposed bond issue at the referendum election the next day. . . .

The contention that there was error in the denial of a declaratory judgment as to the legality of the expenditures for the printing and distribution of the booklet, and the exposure of school children to the radio broadcast is premised solely upon the assertion that the same things may be done or attempted by the defendant board in connection with the balance of the building program upon its submission to the electorate for adoption. It was conceded on the oral argument that the actions under attack, if improper, would not suffice to invalidate the election already held. But the actions taken, it is admitted, had particular relation only to the proposal before the electorate on December 2, 1952, and for aught that appears they seem to have spent their force. The booklet on its face shows that it is not intended for use in connection with future plans for completing the balance of the expansion program. Plainly, then, any issues as to both the booklet and the radio broadcast are moot and the resolution of new, or even similar, issues as to other actions attempted by the defendant for a similar purpose in the future must await the event. . . .

There is no express statutory provision authorizing the expenditure by boards of education of public funds in the manner done by the defendant board for the printing and distribution of the booklet. The power, however, within the limits hereafter stated, is to be found by necessary or fair implication in the powers expressly conferred by R.S. 18:7–77.1, N.J.S.A., which enumerates the permissible items which may be included in the annual budget, and more particularly as incident to "(b) the building, enlarging, repairing or furnishing of a schoolhouse or schoolhouses."

The power so implicit plainly embraces the making of reasonable expenditures for the purpose of giving voters relevant facts to aid them in reaching an informed judgment when voting upon the proposal. In these days of high costs, projects of this type invariably run into very substantial outlays. This has tended to sharpen the interest of every taxpayer and family man in such projects. Adequate and proper school facilities are an imperative necessity, but the large additional tax burden their cost often entails concerns taxpayers that they be obtained with the maximum economy of cost. At the same time the complexities of today's problems make more difficult the task of every citizen in reaching an intelligent judgment upon the accommodation of endurable financial cost with the acknowledged need for adequate education. The need for full disclosure of all relevant facts is obvious, and the board of education is well qualified to supply the facts. But a fair presentation of the facts will necessarily include all consequences, good and bad, of the proposal, not only the anticipated improvement in educational opportunities, but also the increased tax rate and such other less desirable consequences as may be foreseen. If the presentation is fair in that sense, the power to make reasonable expenditure for the purpose may fairly be implied as within the purview of the power, indeed duty, of the board of education to formulate the construction program in the first instance. And the choice of the media of communication to give such facts, whether by the use of a booklet, as in this case, radio broadcast, newspaper advertising, or other means, is within the discretion, reasonably exercised, of the board of education. The booklet under attack here, in 17 of its 18 pages, fairly presents the facts as to need and the advantages and disadvantages of the program, including the tax effect of its cost, and if it stopped there, none could fairly complain that the reasonable expenditure made for its preparation and distribution was without the scope of the implied power.

But the defendant board was not content simply to present the facts. The exhortation "Vote Yes" is repeated on three pages, and the dire consequences of the failure so to do are over-dramatized on the page reproduced above. In that manner the board made use of public funds to advocate one side only of the controversial question without affording the dissenters the opportunity by means of that financed medium to present their side, and thus imperilled the propriety of the entire expenditure. The public funds entrusted to the board belong equally to the proponents and opponents of the proposition, and the use of the funds to finance not the presentation of facts merely but also arguments to persuade the voters that only one side has merit, gives the dissenters just cause for complaint. The expenditure is then not within the implied power and is not lawful in the absence of express authority from the Legislature. In *Mines v. DelValle*, it was said:

> It must be conceded that the electors of said city opposing said bond issue had an equal right to and interest in the funds in said power fund as those who favored said bonds. To use said public funds to advocate the adoption of a proposition which was opposed by a large number of said electors would be manifestly unfair and unjust to the rights of said last-named electors, and the action of the board of public service commissioners in so doing cannot be sustained, unless the power to do is given to said board in clear and unmistakable language.

And in *Elsenau v. City of Chicago*, appears the following:

> The conduct of a campaign, before an election, for the purpose of exerting an influence upon the voters, is not the exercise of an authorized municipal function and hence is not a corporate purpose of the municipality.

We do not mean that the public body formulating the program is otherwise restrained from advocating and espousing its adoption by the voters. Indeed, as in the instant case, when the program represents the body's judgment of what is required in the effective discharge of its responsibility, it is not only the right but perhaps the duty of the body to endeavor to secure the assent of the voters thereto. The question we are considering is simply the extent to and manner in which the funds may with justice to the rights of dissenters be expended for espousal of the voters' approval of the body's judgment. Even this the body may do within fair limits. The reasonable expense, for example, of the conduct of a public forum at which all may appear and freely express their views pro and con would not be improper. The same may be said of reasonable expenses incurred for radio or television broadcasts taking the form of debates between proponents of the differing sides of the proposition. It is the expenditure of public funds in support of one side only in a manner which gives the dissenters no opportunity to present their side which is outside the pale.

We acknowledge that the limits here pronounced are not suggested in the decision of the former Court of Errors and Appeals in *City Affairs Committee of Jersey City v. Board of Com'rs of Jersey City*. We are persuaded, however, that simple fairness and justice to the rights of dissenters require that the use by public bodies of public funds for advocacy be restrained within those limits in the absence of a legislative grant in express terms of the broader power. . . .

Notes

1. Employees can spend school funds to draw up building plans, and in most jurisdictions, for educational and architectural consultants. Is it logical to prevent these same officials from spending funds to urge the acceptance of their proposed plans?

2. If school officials work diligently with community participation to develop a proposal for school improvement, is strict neutrality as regards to its acceptance clearly in the public interest? How can board members work for its acceptance within the bounds of this decision?

3. The Supreme Court of Mississippi cited this case as unquestionably the most thorough discussion of permissible expenditures by public bodies. The court maintained that board members were personally liable for flagrantly unauthorized expenditures, including paying campaign workers and a fish fry, in support of a school bond referendum. *Smith v. Dorsey*, 599 So.2d 529 [75 Educ. L. Rep. 692] (Miss.1992).

Chapter 5

SCHOOL FINANCE

Introduction

Financing public education is ordinarily a joint enterprise of state and local school boards. While cases concern various aspects of school finance as it relates to local school systems, relatively little litigation impacts state-level concerns. Cases involving states typically address constitutional mandates and legislative limits on how resources to pay for public schools are raised and/or allocated, often resulting in judicial orders calling for the creation of new funding formulas.[1] In the process, school finance cases seem to take on lives of their own, frequently requiring multiple rounds of litigation before returning to legislatures.[2] In light of the issues surrounding how state and local school boards pay for education, this chapter focuses on raising and distributing funds for public education.

The School Tax

Power to Levy

As discussed in Chapter 3, school boards are creatures of the state that are charged with the responsibility of implementing state constitutional mandates dealing with public education. As such, the same legislatures that create school boards not only set tax rates but have the authority to identify which properties are to be taxed and which may be exempt from taxation.[3] Further, boards may exercise only those powers that legislatures confer on them, whether expressly or impliedly, and may be classified and granted fiscal powers in a variety of ways, even in the same state.[4]

The authority of local school boards to establish and operate schools does not include the implied power to levy taxes, which, with the exception of Michigan,[5] is ordinarily based on the value of real property

---

1. *See, e.g., Robinson v. Cahill*, 303 A.2d 273 (N.J.1973), *cert. denied*, 414 U.S. 976, 94 S.Ct. 292, 38 L.Ed.2d 219 (1973); *Edgewood Indep. School Dist. v. Kirby*, 777 S.W.2d 391 [56 Educ. L. Rep. 663] (Tex. 1989); *Rose v. Council for Better Educ.*, 790 S.W.2d 186 [60 Educ. L. Rep. 1289] (Ky. 1989).

2. *See, e.g., DeRolph v. State*, 677 N.E.2d 733 [116 Educ. L. Rep. 1140] (Ohio 1997). This litigation resulted in more than ten reported opinions, with the state supreme court culminating judicial involve-

ment, at least for the time being, *sub nom. State v. Lewis*, 786 N.E.2d 60 [174 Educ. L. Rep. 1073] (Ohio 2003), and returning the dispute to the state legislature.

3. *School Dist. of City of Monessen v. Farnham & Pfile Co.*, 878 A.2d 142 [200 Educ. L. Rep. 250] (Pa. Cmwlth. Ct. 2005).

4. *Pirrone v. City of Boston*, 305 N.E.2d 96 (Mass.1973).

5. MICH. COMP. LAWS ANN. § 388.1620. *See also DeRolph v. State*, 754 N.E.2d 1184, 1212–13 [156 Educ. L. Rep. 1290] (Ohio

---

within a district.[6] Accordingly, school boards have no inherent power to tax.[7] Rather, since taxation is a special power that legislatures must specifically confer on subordinate governmental agencies, even when school boards may levy taxes for specific purposes, they do not have constitutional rights to do so.[8]

In delegating their taxing powers, both as to kinds and rates, legislatures can limit the ability of lower bodies, such as school boards, to tax as long as taxing authorities include elected officials. Insofar as state constitutional tax limits must be observed,[9] the courts do not permit even indirect exceptions.[10] Legislatures cannot delegate their power to levy taxes to appointed bodies unless they set clear limits on the extent of transferred powers.[11] As long as legislative delegations specify the purposes and maximum amounts or rates for taxes, they are likely to be upheld.[12] Under such arrangements, courts are ordinarily satisfied that legislatures have set taxes and are merely granting local administrators discretion in their implementation. Even so, legislatures run the risk of violating the separation of powers doctrine if they permit local legislators to approve tax rate increases imposed by county school boards.[13]

Turning to examples, a dispute arose in Chicago over the school board's authority to prepare its own budget even though it depended on city officials to levy taxes. The Supreme Court of Illinois rejected the claim that the city's levying taxes was an unlawful exercise of power under the state constitution, pointing out that the statutory language authorizing the levy was framed in the conjunctive, joining the board and city.[14] The court reasoned that since the board had to complete all preliminary steps before adopting a budget, and no school taxes would have been forthcoming if the city council had not passed an ordinance levying one, the board did not levy the tax. Previously, the Supreme Court of Tennessee held that where the legislature set the rate by which the amount of tax was deduced from events occurring within a year, this was a direct exercise of taxing power rather than a permissible delegation to school officials.[15] In like manner, the Supreme Court of Delaware upheld a legislative grant of power to the state board of education to

2001) (Douglas, J., concurring) (discussing Michigan's approach).

6. *State v. Campbell County School Dist.*, 32 P.3d 325 [157 Educ. L. Rep. 366] (Wyo.2001).

7. *Marion & McPherson Ry. Co. v. Alexander*, 64 P. 978 (Kan.1901) [Case No. 33]; *Frazier v. State By and Through Pittman*, 504 So.2d 675 [39 Educ. L. Rep. 417] (Miss. 1987); *Unified School Dist. No. 229 v. State*, 885 P.2d 1170 [96 Educ. L. Rep. 258] (Kan. 1994), *cert. denied*, 515 U.S. 1144, 115 S.Ct. 2582, 132 L.Ed.2d 832 (1995).

8. *Edgewood Indep. School Dist. v. Meno*, 917 S.W.2d 717 [108 Educ. L. Rep. 1310] (Tex. 1995).

9. *Hurd v. City of Buffalo*, 355 N.Y.S.2d 369 (N.Y.1974).

10. *Bethlehem Steel Corp. v. Board of Educ. of City School Dist. of Lackawanna*, 406 N.Y.S.2d 752 (N.Y.1978), *appeal dismissed*, 439 U.S. 922, 99 S.Ct. 303, 58 L.Ed.2d 315 (1978).

11. *Wilson v. School Dist. of Philadelphia*, 195 A. 90 (Pa.1937); *Crow v. McAlpine*, 285 S.E.2d 355 [1 Educ. L. Rep. 1004] (S.C.1981).

12. *Minsinger v. Rau*, 84 A. 902 (Pa. 1912); *Village of West Milwaukee v. Area Bd. of Vocational, Technical and Adult Educ.*, 187 N.W.2d 387 (Wis.1971).

13. *Gunter v. Blanton*, 192 S.E.2d 473 (S.C.1972).

14. *Latham v. Board of Educ. of the City of Chicago*, 201 N.E.2d 111 (Ill.1964).

15. *Kee v. Parks*, 283 S.W. 751 (Tenn. 1926).

impose a tax on reorganized districts to cover payments for bonded indebtedness.[16]

Insofar as education is a state rather than a local function, school taxes are state, not local, funds even if they are levied by local boards. As illustrated by a case from Kansas, state officials may compel a local board to establish and maintain schools that operate under specified standards even if district residents do not consent to such arrangements.[17] In like manner, Maryland's highest court agreed that a board may be required to issue bonds to raise funds to erect a school where voters have not consented to the plan.[18] However, other courts have ruled that if taxes are levied for special purposes, the funds must be used only for those purposes.[19] Funds remaining after a goal is achieved may be distributed as legislatures permit.[20]

Absent a statutory or constitutional provision to the contrary, such as where the Constitution of Kentucky permitted a sheriff's commission to do so,[21] when a municipal body collects taxes levied by a school board, it is entitled to the entire proceeds.[22] In a related matter, an appellate court in Pennsylvania affirmed that a tax collector was not entitled to additional compensation for collecting a district's real estate taxes. The tax collector unsuccessfully argued that since the applicable statute only required him to collect taxes passed by an ordinance, not a school district resolution, he was entitled to additional compensation for his efforts. The court noted that while both a resolution and an ordinance are vehicles by which political subdivisions may levy and collect taxes, and school boards were limited to the former, boards had no other means to direct elected officials to collect their taxes.[23] At the same time, a municipality is not permitted to assess a school board's collection fee or retention of accrued interest.[24]

Courts generally permit land developers to be charged impact fees to pay for facilities needed to accommodate changes in civic services occasioned by developments with school boards often being one or the sole beneficiary. For example, the Supreme Court of California decided that the use of a local fee that resulted in a board's being the sole beneficiary did not violate equal protection.[25] Additionally, the Supreme Court of

---

16. *Opinion of the Justices*, 246 A.2d 90 (Del.1968).

17. *State v. Freeman*, 58 P. 959 (Kan. 1899).

18. *Revell v. City of Annapolis*, 31 A. 695 (Md.1895). [Case No. 34]

19. *Thomas v. Board of Educ., County of McDowell*, 261 S.E.2d 66 (W.Va.1979); *Lind v. Rockland School Dist. No. 382*, 821 P.2d [71 Educ. L. Rep. 946] (Idaho 1991) (also holding that board spending is limited to the amount authorized in an election).

20. *Douglas Indep. School Dist. No. 3 of Meade and Pennington Counties v. Bell*, 272 N.W.2d 825 (S.D.1978).

21. *Marshall v. Commissioner ex rel. Hatchett*, 20 S.W.3d 478 [145 Educ. L. Rep. 797] (Ky.Ct. App.2000).

22. *New Orleans v. Fisher*, 180 U.S. 185, 21 S.Ct. 347, 45 L.Ed. 485 (1901).

23. *Plum Borough School Dist. v. Schlegel*, 855 A.2d 939 [191 Educ. L. Rep. 416] (Pa. Cmwlth. Ct. 2004).

24. *State ex rel. School Dist. of Springfield R–12 v. Wickliffe*, 650 S.W.2d 623 [11 Educ. L. Rep. 735] (Mo.1983), *Grand Rapids Pub. Schools v. City of Grand Rapids*, 381 N.W.2d 783 [30 Educ. L. Rep. 888] (Mich.Ct.App.1985).

25. *Candid Enterprises v. Grossmont Union High School Dist.*, 218 Cal.Rptr. 303 [27 Educ. L. Rep. 950] (Cal.1985).

Florida agreed that such an arrangement did not violate the state constitutional mandate for a uniform system of free schools.[26]

Irregular Levies

Where state laws require local agencies and boards to follow set procedures in levying taxes, their failure to do so can give rise to questions over the validity of taxes. A tax's validity in the face of irregularities depends on whether courts construe statutory collection provisions as mandatory or discretionary. If courts believe that legislatures intended statutory steps to be conditions precedent to the validity of taxes, they are treated as mandatory. Courts are confronted with the alternatives of declaring irregularly levied taxes invalid and perhaps crippling schools or treating them as valid and imposing hardships on taxpayers. Additionally, courts generally agree that taxes are valid if irregularities are minor and do not deprive taxpayers of substantial rights.

If it appears that irregularities deprive taxpayers of a voice over whether taxes should be levied, the courts are disposed to treat statutory provisions as mandatory. This situation arises most often in connection with giving notice of elections that address taxes, especially if they are not general elections, the time and place of which are fixed by law, but which are set by local boards. In the former case, the electorate is bound to take note of elections set by law such that local notice is treated as merely a reminder. In the latter situation, since voters have no notice of an election except as provided by a local board, statutory notice is more likely to be treated as mandatory.[27] If evidence reveals that residents knew of elections and had the opportunity to vote, or that providing notice would not have changed the results, the courts do not disturb their outcomes.[28]

Rate of Levy

Once school board officials formulate budgets, they must levy taxes to raise funds. Then, in order to establish tax rates, officials must make estimates of revenues. In this way, boards may raise more funds than anticipated. Generally speaking, school boards cannot use their taxing powers to establish surplus funds. Even so, the Supreme Court of Illinois reached different results in two cases that were, admittedly, separated by sixty-seven years. In the first, the court invalidated a levy by a local board that was designed to accumulate a fund to be used at some time in the future to build a school.[29] Conversely, the court rejected a claim that a tax levy was illegal because it was excessive.[30] The court acknowledged

26. *St. Johns County v. Northeast Florida Builders Ass'n*, 583 So.2d 635 [69 Educ. L. Rep. 636] (Fla.1991).

27. *Roberts v. Murphy*, 86 S.E. 545 (Ga. 1915).

28. *Shelton v. School Bd.*, 142 P. 1034 (Okla.1914).

29. *Cleveland, C., C. & St. L. Ry. Co. v. People*, 69 N.E. 832 (Ill.1904).

30. *People ex rel. Sweet v. Central Ill. Pub. Serv. Co.*, 268 N.E.2d 404 (Ill.1971).

that although boards may not levy taxes beyond their needs, and thereby unnecessarily accumulate funds, they need not wait until money is actually required to pay outstanding obligations before levying a tax. Previously, the Supreme Court of Nebraska upheld a levy that would have generated a small surplus if all of the funds had been collected.[31] The court pointed out that possible fluctuations in the amounts of expenses and revenues made it necessary for the board to estimate the sums that it would need.

When a county school board in Georgia increased the tax rate to almost twice that of the previous year, taxpayers sought to enjoin its action as an abuse of discretion. The board countered that the levy was necessary due to considerable uncertainty over the continued availability of federal funds. The Supreme Court of Georgia, observing that the funds to be raised by the increase in the rate were approximately equivalent to the money ordinarily expected from the federal source, refused to enjoin the board.[32]

A dispute arose between a municipality and a school board when the former sought to compel the latter to spend an accumulated surplus before remitting the taxes that it was required to collect for schools. In directing the municipality to remit the taxes, an appellate court in New Jersey indicated that the board was entitled to maintain a reasonable surplus in order to meet unforeseen contingencies.[33] The court added that since the state commissioner of education created a procedure for reviewing board budgets, a municipality could not impose its own limits.

In a case that had become moot, the Supreme Court of South Dakota determined that although it approved a school board's transfer of one year's surplus general funds to capital outlay funds,[34] there was a substantial difference when it did this for three years.[35] The court prevented the board from acting in the second situation since it feared that it could have circumvented the requirement of obtaining voter approval for funding large building programs.

Remedies of Taxpayer against Illegal Taxation

Ordinarily, individuals who voluntarily pay taxes cannot recover based on the theory that since they are presumed to know the law, and have paid the tax knowing of their invalidity, they not claim ignorance as a ground on which to recover payments.[36] Occasionally, individual taxpayers or group of taxpayers, in class action suits,[37] challenge their

---

31. *C. R. T. Corp. v. Board of Equalization*, 110 N.W.2d 194 (Neb.1961).

32. *Watkins v. Jackson*, 179 S.E.2d 747 (Ga.1971).

33. *Board of Educ. of Borough of Fair Lawn v. Mayor and Council of Borough of Fair Lawn*, 362 A.2d 1270 (N.J. Super.Ct.Law Div.1976), aff'd, 380 A.2d 290 (N.J.Super.Ct.App.Div.1977).

34. *Blumer v. School Bd. of Beresford Indep. School Dist.*, 237 N.W.2d 655 (S.D. 1975).

35. *Anderson v. Kennedy*, 264 N.W.2d 714 (S.D.1978).

36. *Cornell v. Board of Educ. for High School Dist. No. 99*, 3 N.E.2d 717 (Ill.Ct. App. 1936).

37. *Frank v. Barker*, 20 S.W.3d 293 [146 Educ. L. Rep. 933] (Ark.2000).

having paid taxes under laws that were struck down, after their property was improperly assessed, or after they mistakenly made payments. In cases of this sort, questions arise as to taxpayers' rights to recover their funds. For instance, where a school board incorrectly assessed real property, an appellate court in Pennsylvania directed officials to refund the difference to the aggrieved retirement center.[38]

The general rule with regard to the recovery of improperly paid taxes does not apply when payments are made under duress or compulsion such as an imminent threat of seizure of the property. Payments that are made after protests are insufficient to render them involuntary such that a party can claim to have made a payment under duress.[39] Yet, some jurisdictions recognize that payments are made under protest for the purposes of possible recovery.[40] In addition, a court can distinguish between a taxing authority's erroneous and illegal conduct, permitting recovery in the latter situation.[41]

Many cases turn on whether courts believe that the public interest should be protected to the extent of requiring individual taxpayers to bear the losses for mistaken or illegal collections of funds. These courts rely on the notion that since public agencies made commitments on the assumption that funds paid into their treasuries would have remained available, the public could suffer a great hardship if agency funds are depleted by having to make repayments. While there is some conflict in case law, the rule of non-recovery is still widely applied, especially where a taxing authority's failure was due to an error or to exceeding a power that was unclear beforehand.[42] Even so, it seems well settled that the collection of illegal taxes may be enjoined.[43]

As reflected by a case from Texas, while taxpayers can enjoin the collection of an illegal tax, illegality is not necessarily a defense in a suit for delinquent taxes. The case arose when taxpayers, who did not protest a taxing scheme when it was instituted, refused to pay the tax but attempted to defend their behavior by attacking the illegality of the system when they were sued. In dismissing the suit, an appellate court declared that the taxpayers failed to meet their burden of proving that they suffered substantial financial losses due to the city's and board's failure to assess their property legally since it was not enough to show that officials used an illegal system of rendering and assessing taxes.[44]

In a second case from Texas, an appellate court ruled that a school taxing authority's failure to include personal property on a tax roll was

38. *Nottingham Vill. Ret. Ctr. Assoc., LP v. Northumberland County Bd. of Assessments*, 885 A.2d 93 [203 Educ. L. Rep. 303] (Pa.Cmwlth. Ct. 2005).

39. *Wilson v. School Dist. of Philadelphia*, 195 A. 90 (Pa.1937).

40. *McDonough v. Aylward*, 500 S.W.2d 721 (Mo.1973); *Jenkins by Agyei v. State of Mo.*, 967 F.2d 1248 [76 Educ. L. Rep. 42] (8th Cir.1992), *cert. denied*, 506 U.S. 1033, 113 S.Ct. 811, 121 L.Ed.2d 684 (1992).

41. *Niagara Mohawk Power Corp. v. City School Dist. of City of Troy*, 464 N.Y.S.2d 449 [12 Educ. L. Rep. 450] (N.Y. 1983).

42. *Gulesian v. Dade County School Bd.*, 281 So.2d 325 (Fla.1973).

43. *Shaffer v. Carter*, 252 U.S. 37, 40 S.Ct. 221, 64 L.Ed. 445 (1920).

44. *City of Houston v. McCarthy*, 371 S.W.2d 587 (Tex.Civ.App.1963).

not a basis for enjoining an assessment of real property. The court rejected the argument that leaving personal property off tax rolls required officials to levy higher taxes on real property in order to raise the revenue for school operations. The court was of the view both that the omission was simply an unchallenged custom and that the taxpayers failed to show that the new approach would have resulted in substantial changes in taxes.[45] Similarly, the Supreme Court of Wyoming found that the state legislature had the prerogative to limit school funding taxes to property taxes even though nothing prohibited it from imposing other taxes or creating new methods of raising revenues.[46]

Taxpayers cannot claim tax adjustments simply because they allegedly do not receive equal shares of benefits.[47] The Supreme Court of New Hampshire applied this principle in interpreting a century-and-a-half-old statute which permitted town governments to abate the taxes of those who claimed that they were aggrieved by a tax assessment.[48] The court declared that the plaintiff's claim was meritless since he was not personally aggrieved by the statute insofar as the town allowed for a limited real estate tax abatement to those who paid for the education of their high school aged children outside of the school system.

Apportionment of State School Funds

Funds collected by local boards are state monies that may, subject to constitutional restrictions, be spent in any manner that legislatures deem to be in the best interest of their states. Accordingly, statewide taxes to raise money for school purposes are constitutional even if their proceeds are distributed so that less-wealthy districts get more state aid than wealthier ones. Opponents of this approach claim that such legislation deprives some citizens of property without due process of law, that it violates the constitutional prohibition against unequal taxation, and that it constitutes taxation for a private purpose. The courts have consistently rejected these contentions in firmly establishing the validity of laws designed to equalize educational opportunities.[49]

Taxes need not be spent in the districts where they are collected. Yet, the manner of apportioning state funds has caused considerable legal difficulty. Some state constitutions specify distribution plans for funds while others identify only goals or purposes. In a case that addressed such a distinction, the Supreme Court of Illinois upheld the statutory language that "the state has the primary responsibility for financing the system of public education"[50] as a purpose that does not require state officials to supply more than half of needed funds to local boards.

45. *Kirkpatrick v. Parker*, 406 S.W.2d 81 (Tex.Civ.App.1966).

46. *State v. Campbell County School Dist.*, 32 P.3d 325 [157 Educ. L. Rep. 366] (Wyo.2001).

47. *Union Refrigerator Transit Co. v. Kentucky*, 199 U.S. 194, 26 S.Ct. 36, 50 L.Ed. 150 (1905).

48. *Barksdale v. Town of Epsom*, 618 A.2d 814 [80 Educ. L. Rep. 132] (N.H.1992).

49. *Sawyer v. Gilmore*, 83 A. 673 (Me. 1912) [Case No. 35]; *State ex rel. Woodahl v. Straub*, 520 P.2d 776 (Mont.1974).

50. *Blase v. State*, 302 N.E.2d 46, 47 (Ill.1973).

Constitutional apportionment plans address only those funds specified in their provisions. If it is permissible to create a fund that is separate and distinct from the one covered by a state constitution, it may be distributed as a legislature dictates. To this end, Connecticut's highest court asserted that although public funds could not be used to transport children to non-public schools, non-constitutional funds could be used.[51] On the other hand, if all money coming into a state's coffers for school purposes automatically becomes part of the constitutional fund, it cannot be distributed except in accordance with the constitutional plan.

Where the state constitution once provided for distribution based on school population, and the legislature set up a program that focused on a school system's measure of need, the Supreme Court of Michigan invalidated the statute as unconstitutional.[52] In another case from Michigan, where the constitution prevented officials from "reducing the state financed proportion of the necessary costs of any existing activity or service required of units of local government by state law,"[53] the state's highest court held that the provision covered categorical aid for specific courses required by state officials such as driver education and special education but did not cover general aid to schools. The same court subsequently interpreted this provision as not covering a board's share of Social Security payments for school employees.[54]

In a case where county officials planned to impose a levy on all taxable property within the county's boundaries, and the proceeds were to be distributed to schools based on their needs, opponents challenged the proposed tax. The opponents claimed that the tax violated the constitutional provision that taxes had to be uniform on the same class of subjects within the territorial limits of the authority levying the tax. The Supreme Court of Idaho upheld the levy, positing that since it was on all taxable property in the county, there was no lack of uniformity because financial need provided a rational basis for distributing educational funding.[55] The court was satisfied that even though the proceeds were not distributed equally throughout the county, its uniformity was not destroyed as long as receipts were apportioned fairly in an effort to equalize educational standards.

In Georgia, a state law permitted specified types of school districts to receive financial aid based on calculations of property values that were one-third higher than they actually were. The record reflected that the law had the effect of reducing state contributions to these systems while proportionately increasing aid to less-wealthy districts. The state's highest court upheld the statute in maintaining that since its key feature was that it sought to help all schools, it required each board to do its best

51. *Snyder v. Town of Newtown*, 161 A.2d 770 (Conn.1960).

52. *Board of Educ. of City of Detroit v. Fuller*, 218 N.W. 764 (Mich.1928).

53. *Durant v. State Bd. of Educ.*, 381 N.W.2d 662, 666 [30 Educ. L. Rep. 870] (Mich.1985).

54. *Schmidt v. Department of Educ.*, 490 N.W.2d 584 [78 Educ. L. Rep. 517] (Mich.1992).

55. *Board of Trustees of Joint Class A School Dist. No. 151 v. Board of County Comm'rs of Cassia County*, 359 P.2d 635 (Idaho 1961).

before receiving a state supplement to secure the minimum level of funding. The court commented that although the system was imperfect, since the idea was commendable, it could not be "shackled by legalistic theories and hair splitting."[56]

The 1970's ushered in a wave of litigation challenging school financing systems that tolerated markedly uneven per-pupil expenditures in local districts. Over the past forty plus years, litigation is almost evenly split as challenges have succeeded in about half of the states where plaintiffs questioned systems of funding public education.[57]

In *Serrano v. Priest (Serrano I)*,[58] the opinion of the Supreme Court of California generated more reaction than any other state court case on school finance. At the core of *Serrano I* was the court's perspective that a funding scheme, which rendered the quality of a child's education dependent on a school district's wealth, invidiously discriminated against the poor in violation of the Equal Protection Clause of the Fourteenth Amendment and the state constitution. More specifically, the court believed that the wealth of districts was the basis for substantially different per-pupil expenditures as reflected by examples of systems with high property values which, with low tax rates, spent much more per child than others with high tax rates and lower property valuations. The court was also troubled by the fact that the state's financial aid program fell far short of equalizing discrepancies such that of the $355 per child state guarantee for students in elementary schools, $125 was distributed on a flat basis regardless of a district's wealth, thereby actually widening the gap in some instances between rich and poor school systems. In discussing education as a fundamental interest to both individuals and society, the court applied strict scrutiny in striking down the state's system of financing education for failing to serve a compelling state interest. Although the United States Supreme Court essentially repudiated *Serrano I's* analysis under the Federal Constitution a year and one-half later, the Supreme Court of California ultimately reaffirmed its initial judgment on the basis of the state constitution.[59]

Shortly after *Serrano I*, a federal trial court embraced its analysis in striking down Texas' system of financing schools under the Equal Protection Clause of the Fourteenth Amendment. The court directed officials to change the taxing and financing system but stayed its order for two years to give the legislature time to act so that the educational opportunities were not made "a function of wealth other than the wealth of the State as a whole."[60]

On further review in *San Antonio Independent School District v. Rodriguez (San Antonio)*,[61] its only case on school finance, the Supreme

---

56. *Rice v. Cook*, 150 S.E.2d 822, 824 (Ga.1966).

57. For a list of cases from courts of last resort addressing school funding, *see* note 6 following *San Antonio Indep. School Dist. v. Rodriguez [Case No. 36]*.

58. 487 P.2d 1241 (Cal.1971).

59. *Serrano v. Priest (II)*, 557 P.2d 929 (Cal.1976), *cert. denied*, 432 U.S. 907, 97 S.Ct. 2951, 53 L.Ed.2d 1079 (1977).

60. *Rodriguez v. San Antonio Indep. School Dist.*, 337 F.Supp. 280, 284 (W.D.Tex.1971).

61. 411 U.S. 1, 93 S.Ct. 1278, 36 L.Ed.2d 16 (1973). [Case No. 36]

Court reversed in favor of Texas. At the outset, even though it conceded that the wealth discrimination before it was unlike any of the forms of wealth discrimination it previously reviewed, the Court ruled that the proper Fourteenth Amendment standard was the rational basis test rather than strict scrutiny. The Court decreed that its prior cases in which it invalidated wealth classifications, individuals or groups constituting a class who suffered from discrimination had two distinguishing characteristics: "because of their impecunity they were completely unable to pay for some desired benefit, and as a consequence, they sustained an absolute deprivation of a meaningful opportunity to enjoy that benefit."[62] By contrast, in *San Antonio*, the Court did not think that anyone was completely deprived of educational opportunities based on the statewide minimum foundation program that was financed by state and local revenues. If anything, the Court offered that the amount that local boards contributed to the program reflected their relative taxpaying ability measured by assessable property. The Court further recognized that local boards could supplement the foundation program by levying additional property taxes.

In *San Antonio*, the Court rejected the plaintiffs' claim that the system was discriminatory since per-child expenditures revealed an inverse variation with the wealth of a student's family. According to the Court, the data did not support the allegation that the poorest families were clustered in the poorest-property districts. Importantly, the Court rejected the notion that education is a fundamental right, writing that the key to "fundamental" is not in "comparisons of the relative societal significance of education as opposed to subsistence or housing" or "by weighing whether education is as important as the right to travel" since the answer lies "in assessing whether there is a right to education explicitly or implicitly guaranteed by the Constitution."[63] As such, in a far-reaching phrase, the Court emphasized that "[e]ducation, of course, is not among the rights afforded explicit protection under our Federal Constitution. Nor do we find any basis for saying it is implicitly so protected."[64]

The *San Antonio* Court ascertained that the state's desire to retain a degree of local educational autonomy met the rational basis test. Although admitting that reliance on local property taxation for school revenues provided less freedom of choice with respect to expenditures for some districts, the Court remarked that the existence of inequalities in the manner in which a state achieves its goal is not alone a sufficient basis for vitiating an entire system. In a "cautionary postscript" the Court referred to the need for expertise and deliberation in resolving matters of educational finance, expressing its concern about the consequences of a judicially imposed change. In concluding, the Court reiterated that while its action should not have been viewed as approval of the

---

62. *Id.* at 20.   **64.** *Id.* at 35.
63. *Id.* at 33.

status quo, "ultimate solutions must come from the lawmakers and from the democratic pressures of those who elect them."[65]

Following *San Antonio*, school finance remains the province of state courts, ordinarily under the equal protection clauses of state constitutions. State supreme courts have ordered changes to financing systems when discrepancies vary greatly between and among districts, where a lower end is very low, where a plan for distributing financial aid does little to help poor districts or increases the variations between richer and poorer districts, and/or where state mandates impede local boards from providing education of reasonable quality. The courts typically grant legislatures a period of time in which to redesign their plans.

Turning to a brief historical review of state litigation, the Supreme Court of New Jersey eschewed the influence of *Rodriguez*, striking down the state's method of financing schools as violating the state constitutional provision calling for a thorough and efficient system of free public schools on the basis of discrepancies in dollar input per pupil.[66] In this initial round of litigation, the court was not satisfied by the fact that state aid covered only 28 percent of operating expenses, some of which was distributed regardless of local taxpaying ability. Connecticut's highest court invalidated a similar state aid plan in applying strict scrutiny under general state constitutional provisions.[67]

The Supreme Court of Washington, focusing on the unique words "paramount duty" and "ample provision" in its state constitutional mandate for education, interpreted these terms as necessitating the legislature's making regular tax sources available for a basic program of schooling.[68] The Supreme Court of Arkansas vitiated the state's system of distributing funds as completely irrational because it actually increased inequities among districts.[69] The same court has since reached the same outcome.[70] On the other hand, as one of the courts that sustained financing systems, the Supreme Court of Oregon,[71] relying on *Rodriguez*, agreed that the state's interest in local control, the fact that a minimum educational program was available in all districts, and that several important services other than education relied largely on local property taxes, provided sufficient justification to leave the system in tact.

Mandating that the test for a fundamental right under the Federal Constitution was inappropriate under a state constitution, the Supreme Court of Ohio upheld the state's financing system as a rational way of meeting the constitutional mandate for a "thorough and efficient system

---

65. *Id.* at 59.

66. *Robinson v. Cahill*, 303 A.2d 273 (N.J.1973), *cert. denied*, 414 U.S. 976, 94 S.Ct. 292, 38 L.Ed.2d 219 (1973).

67. *Horton v. Meskill*, 376 A.2d 359 (Conn.1977).

68. *Seattle School Dist. No. 1 of King County v. State*, 585 P.2d 71 (Wash.1978).

69. *Dupree v. Alma School Dist. No. 30 of Crawford County*, 651 S.W.2d 90 [11 Educ. L. Rep. 1091] (Ark.1983).

70. *Lake View School Dist. No. 25 of Phillips County v. Huckabee*, 91 S.W.3d 472 [173 Educ. L. Rep. 248] (Ark.2002).

71. *Olsen v. State*, 554 P.2d 139 (Or. 1976).

of common schools.''[72] This court, in later litigation discussed below, reached a different result. Maryland's highest court reached the same outcome as the original case from Ohio under a similarly worded constitutional education provision.[73] In dicta, the court suggested that the state's school finance plan would have been constitutional even under heightened scrutiny.

One aspect of a case from New York presented a new challenge to the state's system of finance: the plan discriminated against large city school districts for an array of reasons including special non-education demands on the property, diminished purchasing power of municipal education dollars, and larger concentrations of pupils with special needs. In upholding the system, the Court of Appeals of New York stipulated that the state was long regarded as a leader in public education, that it was third in the nation in per-pupil expenditures, and that it was a legislative function to allocate funds among services, certainly in the absence of gross and glaring inadequacy, which had not been shown to exist due to the financing system.[74] As with Ohio, more recent litigation, discussed below, reached the opposite result. Other states that rejected challenges to their systems of financing schools included Georgia[75] and Illinois.[76]

In a novel approach, Wisconsin tried to remove property wealth as a factor in school funding. The plan embodied the notion of establishing a ratio for each district between equalized value of real estate per student within a system and a statewide amount. Under the plan, districts were to be equalized in power to finance education. The new formula purported to provide equal tax dollars for educational purposes from equal tax effort regardless of disparities in tax bases with some property-wealthy districts receiving no state aid due to their using tax rates to raise more than the state-guaranteed amount. The overage was to go into the general state fund to be distributed to property-poor districts. The Supreme Court of Wisconsin invalidated the plan in holding that the legislature could not compel a board to tax its residents for the direct benefit of another or for the sole benefit of the state.[77] The same court later upheld the state's funding system as adequate.[78] The Supreme Court of Texas applied a similar rationale in disapproving a legislative plan that was created to comply with its mandate to change the state's method of financing public schools.[79] The court noted that local property tax revenues for education were not subject to state redistribution.

72. *Board of Educ. of City School Dist. of Cincinnati v. Walter*, 390 N.E.2d 813 (Ohio 1979).

73. *Hornbeck v. Somerset County Bd. of Educ.*, 458 A.2d 758 [10 Educ. L. Rep. 592] (Md. 1983).

74. *Board of Educ., Levittown Union Free School Dist. v. Nyquist*, 453 N.Y.S.2d 643 [6 Educ. L. Rep. 147] (N.Y.1982), *appeal dismissed*, 459 U.S. 1139, 103 S.Ct. 775, 74 L.Ed.2d 986 (1983).

75. *McDaniel v. Thomas*, 285 S.E.2d 156 [1 Educ. L. Rep. 982] (Ga.1981).

76. *Blase v. State*, 302 N.E.2d 46 (Ill. 1973).

77. *Buse v. Smith*, 247 N.W.2d 141 (Wis.1976).

78. *Kukor v. Grover*, 436 N.W.2d 568 [52 Educ. L. Rep. 241] (Wis.1989), *reconsideration denied*, 443 N.W.2d 314 (Wis.1989).

79. *Edgewood Indep. School Dist. v. Kirby*, 804 S.W.2d 491 [66 Educ. L. Rep. 496] (Tex. 1991).

However, the court suggested that the state could redistrict and thereby alter the local tax bases of school districts. The court later decided that the state's system of taxation for funding public schools violated the state constitution's prohibition against state-wide ad valorem taxes.[80] Although it conceded that it was a close question, the court was convinced that the state provided sufficient money to fund schools within the meaning of the state constitution's requirements for an adequate, efficient, and suitable public school system, remanding the issue to the state legislature.

The Supreme Court of New Jersey re-entered the school finance arena seventeen years after its original case, reasoning that the legislative response that it originally upheld on its face[81] was unconstitutional as applied to poorer urban school districts.[82] The court thus called for a revamping of the state's financing system to assure that educational funding in poorer urban districts would be substantially equal to that of property-rich districts. The court also specified that the level of funding had to be adequate to provide for the special educational needs of the disadvantaged districts. As that litigation continued, the court issued a series of judgments clarifying its initial order.[83]

The Supreme Court of Kentucky, in a far-reaching opinion, emphasized the quality of education along with calling for more parity in access to funds by local boards. The court bluntly stated that "Kentucky's entire system of common schools is unconstitutional.... This decision applies to the statutes creating, implementing and financing the *system* and to all regulations, etc., pertaining thereto."[84] Subsequently, the Supreme Judicial Court of Massachusetts applied Kentucky's goals in broadly outlining that commonwealth's constitutional duty toward education. The provision, first adopted while a colony, in 1780, directed the legislature to "cherish ... public schools and grammar schools in the towns."[85] More recently, the highest courts of Arkansas,[86] New Hampshire,[87] Kansas,[88] Montana,[89] Ohio,[90] Tennessee,[91] New York,[92] and Ver-

80. *Neeley v. West Orange–Cove Consol. Indep. School Dist.*, 176 S.W.3d 746 [204 Educ. L. Rep. 793] (Tex. 2005).

81. *Robinson v. Cahill*, 303 A.2d 273 (N.J.1973), *cert. denied*, 414 U.S. 976, 94 S.Ct. 292, 38 L.Ed.2d 219 (1973).

82. *Abbott by Abbott v. Burke*, 575 A.2d 359 [60 Educ. L. Rep. 1175] (N.J.1990).

83. *See, e.g.*, *Abbott by Abbott v. Burke*, 643 A.2d 575 [92 Educ. L. Rep. 545] (N.J. 1994); 693 A.2d 417 [118 Educ. L. Rep. 371] (N.J.1997), *appeal after remand*, 710 A.2d 450 [126 Educ. L. Rep. 258] (N.J.1998); *opinion clarified*, 751 A.2d 1032 [145 Educ. L. Rep. 427] (N.J.2000); 748 A.2d 82 (N.J. 2000), *order clarified*, 790 A.2d 842 [162 Educ. L. Rep. 407] (N.J.2002).

84. *Rose v. Council for Better Educ.*, 790 S.W.2d 186, 215 [60 Educ. L. Rep. 1289] (Ky.1989).

85. *McDuffy v. Secretary of Executive Office of Educ.*, 615 N.E.2d 516, 557 [83 Educ. L. Rep. 657] (Mass.1993).

86. *Lake View School Dist. No. 25 of Phillips County v. Huckabee*, 91 S.W.3d 472 [173 Educ. L. Rep. 248] (Ark.2002). Based on allegations that the state failed to satisfy an earlier order to provide an adequate and substantially equal education for all students, the court reopened the litigation. The court rejected the state's argument that its earlier release of jurisdiction required the parties to file a new case. *Lake View School Dist. No. 25 of Phillips County, Arkansas v. Huckabee*, ___ S.W.3d ___, 2005 WL 1358308 (Ark. 2005).

87. *Claremont School Dist. v. Governor*, 703 A.2d 1353 [123 Educ. L. Rep. 233] (N.H.1997), *reh'g denied, motion to vacate stay denied*, 725 A.2d 648 [133 Educ. L. Rep. 161] (N.H.1998).

88.–92. See notes 88–92 on page 293.

mont[93] struck down their systems of funding. On the other hand, the highest courts in Alabama,[94] Alaska,[95] South Carolina,[96] and Wisconsin,[97] upheld their state systems of funding.

Courts also continue to address school finance litigation that has yet to reach the final merits of claims. For example, in a long-running suit, the Supreme Court of Connecticut affirmed that taxpayers who sought a declaratory judgment that the state's funding statute, which required each town to contribute to a district's educational expenses based on per pupil cost of education, lacked standing.[98] The court indicated that since the plaintiffs failed to demonstrate that they would have suffered an actual injury, they could not participate in the suit. Similarly, the Supreme Court of Nebraska affirmed that a local school board could not intervene in a challenge to the constitutionality of the state's school funding system on the basis that its speculative allegation that it would have been harmed due to any loss of funding was insufficient to present a direct legal right permitting it to take part in the suit.[99]

School Bonds

In General

Absent express statutory authority, school boards operate on cash bases, meaning that they meet current expenses out of tax proceeds of former years or other funds.[100] Other boards operate on deficit bases, referring to the fact that they have insufficient cash reserves and rely on

88. *Montoy v. State*, 102 P.3d 1160 [194 Educ. L. Rep. 439] (Kan. 2005), *republished with concurring opinion*, 120 P.3d 306 [202 Educ. L. Rep. 319] (Kan. 2005), *opinion supplemented*, 112 P.3d 923 [198 Educ. L. Rep. 703] (Kan. 2005).

89. *Columbia Falls Elementary School Dist. No. 6 v. State*, 109 P.3d 257 [196 Educ. L. Rep. 958] (Mont. 2005). Previously, the same court vitiated its state's system of funding as violating the state constitutional guarantee of equal educational opportunities for all children. *Helena Elementary School Dist. No. 1 v. State*, 769 P.2d 684 [52 Educ. L. Rep. 342] (Mont. 1989), *opinion amended*, 784 P.2d 412 [57 Educ. L. Rep. 1374] (Mont.1990) (postponing the effect of the initial judgment to allow the legislature and governor's office time to implement a satisfactory system of funding).

90. *DeRolph v. State*, 677 N.E.2d 733 [116 Educ. L. Rep. 1140] (Ohio 1997). *See also State v. Lewis*, 786 N.E.2d 60 [174 Educ. L. Rep. 1073] (Ohio 2003).

91. *Tennessee Small School Systems v. McWherter*, 91 S.W.3d 232 [172 Educ. L. Rep. 1044] (Tenn.2002).

92. *Campaign for Fiscal Equity v. State of N.Y.*, 769 N.Y.S.2d 106 [183 Educ. L. Rep. 970] (N.Y.2003). For an unsuccessful companion case involving the city of Roch-

ester, *see Paynter v. State of N.Y.*, 765 N.Y.S.2d 819 [181 Educ. L. Rep. 757] (N.Y. 2003).

93. *Brigham v. State*, 692 A.2d 384 [117 Educ. L. Rep. 667] (Vt.1997).

94. *Alabama, Ex parte James*, 836 So.2d 813 [174 Educ. L. Rep. 487] (Ala.2002).

95. *Matanuska–Susitna Borough School Dist. v. State*, 931 P.2d 391 [116 Educ. L. Rep. 401] (Alaska 1997).

96. *Abbeville County School Dist. v. State*, 515 S.E.2d 535 [135 Educ. L. Rep. 833] (S.C.1999).

97. *Vincent v. Voight*, 614 N.W.2d 388 [146 Educ. L. Rep. 422] (Wis.2000).

98. *Seymour v. Region One Bd. of Educ.*, 874 A.2d 742 [198 Educ. L. Rep. 645] (Conn. 2005).

99. *Douglas County School Dist. 0001 v. Johanns*, 694 N.W.2d 668 [196 Educ. L. Rep. 949] (Neb. 2005).

100. *Conn v. Middlebury Union High School Dist. No. 3*, 648 A.2d 1385 [95 Educ. L. Rep. 300] (Vt.1994); *Clay v. Independent School Dist. No. 1 of Tulsa County*, 935 P.2d 294 [117 Educ. L. Rep. 756] (Okla. 1997).

levies from current years to meet their expenses.[101] Either way, the duties of state officials include ensuring that local schools boards manage educational appropriations wisely while encouraging them to avoid having deficits and directing them to pay-off those that can be promptly eliminated.[102] At this point, it is important to recall that boards have no implied authority to borrow money, whether by issuing bonds or other negotiable instruments.[103] Even when legislatures permit boards to borrow funds, this right is strictly construed. For instance, if a legislature grants a board the power to borrow money or issue bonds for a specific purpose, those funds can be applied only to that purpose.[104]

Statutes authorizing boards to issue bonds typically include detailed procedures and prerequisites including time periods within which challenges must be filed.[105] When challenged, a usual question arises as to a bond's validity if the exact procedure has not been followed. The general rule is that if it appears that the legislative intent was for the prescribed procedure to be a condition precedent to an issue's validity, failure to comply renders bonds invalid. On the other hand, there is a strong judicial disposition to uphold a bond issue if it appears that irregularities did not deprive taxpayers of a substantial right that they would have enjoyed had they not transpired[106] or did not affect the outcome of an election.[107] If a school board complies with procedural requirements to secure bond funding to pay for construction, it is likely to be upheld in the face of a challenge.[108] In such a case, when a legislature enacted new procedural requirements for bonds after an earlier version was declared unconstitutional, taxpayers unsuccessfully challenged the use of bond funds that were secured under old standards. The Supreme Court of Wyoming pointed out that insofar as the bonds were approved while the previous regulations were still in place, the amended statutes governing the new bonding procedures did not apply retroactively.[109]

Problems often arise in connection with the requirement that notice of an election must be published a set number of days before one takes place. If electors have adequate notice, signified by a majority's having appeared and cast ballots, and the result could not have been affected by the shorter notice, an election is likely to be sustained.[110] In an illustrative case, the Supreme Court of New Hampshire upheld the validity of a

---

101. *In re County Collector of Du Page County for Judgment for Taxes for Year 1993*, 718 N.E.2d 164 [144 Educ. L. Rep. 364] (Ill.1999).

102. *Maryland State Bd. of Educ. v. Bradford*, 875 A.2d 703 [199 Educ. L. Rep. 298] (Md. 2005).

103. *Hewitt v. Board of Educ.*, 94 Ill. 528 (1880).

104. *State ex rel. Howard v. Crawford*, 16 P.3d 473 [150 Educ. L. Rep. 496] (Okla. Civ.App. 2000).

105. *Snell v. Johnson County School Dist. No. 1*, 86 P.3d 248 [185 Educ. L. Rep. 1063] (Wyo. 2004); *de Konig v. Mallema*,

534 N.W.2d 391 [101 Educ. L. Rep. 1106] (Iowa 1995).

106. *Ganske v. Independent School Dist. No. 84*, 136 N.W.2d 405 (Minn.1965).

107. *Abts v. Board of Educ. of School Dist. Re–1 Valley in Logan County*, 622 P.2d 518 (Colo. 1980).

108. *See, e.g., Nicholson v. Red Willow County School Dist. No. 0170*, 699 N.W.2d 25 [199 Educ. L. Rep. 934] (Neb. 2005).

109. *Snell v. Johnson County School Dist. No. 1*, 86 P.3d 248 [185 Educ. L. Rep. 1063] (Wyo. 2004).

110. *State ex rel. School Dist. No. 2 v. March*, 189 N.W. 283 (Neb.1922).

bond issue against the charge that there were defects in the report that school officials had to submit to the state.[111] The court acknowledged that the acts of town meetings should be liberally construed and, if they fell within the authorized power of town officials, minor distinctions would not be allowed to defeat the voters' intent. Insofar as the information required in the report received wide publicity otherwise, and was discussed in public meetings, the court concluded that officials substantially complied with the statute. More recently, the First Circuit affirmed that a state law from New Hampshire, which required a lower voter percentage in districts using an official ballot system for bond approvals, as opposed to those that relied on town meetings to gain acceptance, did not violate equal protection.[112] The court found this approach to be acceptable because it was rationally related to the legitimate governmental interest of ensuring that residents could vote.

Problems can arise when school boards publish information about bond elections but later wish to deviate from their initial statements. The Supreme Court of Utah discussed this issue in a case where taxpayers sought to prevent a board from proceeding with a building plan after it published a notice of a bond election and printed an explanatory brochure, copies of which were distributed to the public, and parts published in newspapers in connection with, but not as part of, the statutory notice. The brochure explained that the funds were to be spent under the two main categories of elementary and secondary schools. The bond issue passed, but when the projected costs in the preliminary estimate for the high school proved to be too low, the board proposed to use a much greater proportion of the fund for its construction, leaving a relatively small amount for the elementary school. The court rejected the claim that the board's revised proposal was a breach of faith in recognizing that it had latitude carrying out its goal of providing the best school system in the most efficient and economic way.[113]

Where a state statute raised the maximum rate of interest that could be paid on school bonds, a question emerged as to whether the higher rate applied to bonds that were authorized by an election that took place prior to the law's passage. The Supreme Court of Kansas affirmed that the higher rate applied since bonds are not considered as issued until they are actually delivered or put into circulation.[114] In ruling that the law in effect at the time of the issuance became part of the bond contract, the court decided that the statute was not rendered retroactive when applied to bonds which were not issued as of its effective date.

111. *Hecker v. McKernan*, 196 A.2d 38 (N.H.1963).

112. *Walker v. Exeter Region Co-op. School Dist.*, 284 F.3d 42 [162 Educ. L. Rep. 701] (1st Cir.2002); *See also Opinion of the Justices*, 765 A.2d 706 [150 Educ. L. Rep. 765] (N.H.2001); *McGraw v. Exeter Region Co-op. School Dist.*, 765 A.2d 710 [150 Educ. L. Rep. 769] (N.H. 2001).

113. *Ricker v. Board of Educ. of Millard County School Dist.*, 396 P.2d 416 (Utah 1964). [Case No. 37]

114. *Baker v. Unified School Dist. No. 346, County of Linn*, 480 P.2d 409 (Kan. 1971).

Liability on Illegal Bonds

Insofar as bonds that are issued contrary to law are void, investors cannot recover their losses. Even so, since illegality is often not discovered until after boards have received and spent the funds derived from bond sales, an issue arises as to whether bondholders must bear the losses or may recover their investments.

Some courts permit recovery in quasi-contract for the value of the benefit conferred on boards subject to the exception that they must have had authority to issue valid bonds in the first place.[115] In other words, if bonds are invalid due to boards' lack of power to issue them, bondholders cannot recover any expected benefits but may be able to reclaim unspent funds that boards retain or can try to recover property purchased with their investments if they can trace it to specific property and recovery does not seriously injure other board property or disrupt orderly school management. If boards lack authority to issue bonds, the courts usually do not find that there were implied contracts in favor of bondholders since doing so would deprive boards of the very protection that statutes were designed to afford.

School District Warrants

School warrants are orders drawn against board funds, or, if a statute specifically permits, against funds to be collected within the period defined by statute. Unlike bonds, warrants are not designed to run for a number of years since they are not negotiable instruments in the sense that an innocent purchaser may be protected against a board if it appears that it had a defense when they were issued.

To the extent that investors are charged with notice of any illegality in the issuance of instruments, they purchase them at their own risk.[116] The reason is clear: if innocent purchasers were not afforded protection, boards would be able to spend district funds illegally by issuing negotiable warrants, and taxpayers would have no recourse. Public policy requires individuals who deal with boards to assume responsibility for the legality of warrants rather than open the way to possible depletion of school funds through the issuance of illegal warrants.

In an operational illustration, the Supreme Court of New Hampshire reviewed a case on the content of a warrant. The court affirmed that state laws granting governing bodies or school boards broad discretion to determine the number, format, and content of articles that they place on warrants do not afford them unfettered discretion to do so if another statute places restrictions on the format of warrant articles.[117]

---

115. *Geer v. School Dist. No. 11*, 111 F. 682 (8th Cir.1901).

116. *Kellogg v. School Dist. No. 10*, 74 P. 110 (Okla.1903).

117. *In re Inter Lakes School Bd.*, 780 A.2d 1275 [157 Educ. L. Rep. 747] (N.H. 2001).

Limitations on District Indebtedness

In General

States typically impose constitutional or statutory limits on the amount of debt that school boards can incur. The question of what constitutes indebtedness has generated judicial conflict. According to the majority position, net, not gross, indebtedness is the appropriate measure in evaluating whether a board can incur additional debt.[118] Net indebtedness is that which remains after deducting board assets that are available for the payment of existing debts from the total of all outstanding debts, including cash on hand, taxes levied, and other available assets. Assets do not actually have to be applied to pay for debts but only need to be available. Further, contracts for current expenses are not considered indebtedness while funds on hand to meet them are not treated as assets. In other words, even though boards may have reached their legal debt limits, they may still levy taxes for current operating expenses.[119]

A minority of courts refuse to apply the net indebtedness test, maintaining that even though assets may be on hand to pay debts, they remain until they are paid.[120] This view may appear more logical and more nearly in accord with the commonly accepted understanding of what constitutes a debt, but would greatly restrict boards from financing their operations.

Borrowed money is not considered a debt if the funding is through revenue, rather than general obligation, bonds. Individuals who own revenue bonds must depend entirely on income produced by the venture that their money finances. Generally, while school boards may not issue revenue bonds, states may. The Supreme Court of Michigan rejected a plan that sought to apply the state constitutional debt limit to bonds that the state sought to issue to generate funds to loan to boards with large operating deficits.[121] Under the plan, the payments of principal and interest would have been made by local boards, and, if they defaulted, by the state from its aid payments due the boards. The court conceded that regardless of how the plan was presented, the state was the borrower despite the fact that repayment would have been made primarily by residents of school districts and that the bonds were, in effect, general obligation bonds subject to the constitutional debt limit.

If it appears to be to a board's advantage to enter into contracts for a period of years for supplies or services, most courts agree that such agreements are legal even if the funds extend board indebtedness beyond the legal limit. In such cases, contracts usually provide that payment is

118. *Rettinger v. School Bd. of City of Pittsburgh*, 109 A. 782 (Pa.1920).

119. *Grant v. City of Davenport*, 36 Iowa 396 (1873).

120. *Angola Brick & Tile Co. v. Millgrove School Township*, 127 N.E. 855 (Ind. Ct.App.1920).

121. *In re Advisory Opinion Constitutionality of P.A. 1 and 2*, 211 N.W.2d 28 (Mich.1973).

to be made on an annual basis from accrued funds such that the amount falling due each year should equal the indebtedness incurred, not the total identified in the contract.[122] While this rule is ordinarily restricted to contracts for goods or services and is not extended to those for construction, the Supreme Court of Indiana applied it to a lease agreement between a board and a public corporation set up for school construction.[123]

At issue in another case was whether a contested bond issue would have exceeded constitutional debt limits. At the time of the bond vote, a school board had the cash on hand to pay the principal of the outstanding debt. The Supreme Court of New Hampshire posited that the sum on hand could have been subtracted from the outstanding authorized indebtedness, thereby bringing the amount of the bond issue within the legal debt limit.[124]

In a third case dealing with limits on bond indebtedness, the Supreme Court of New Jersey interpreted the school funding provision of the state constitution as authorizing state-backed school bonds without reference to its debt limitation clause.[125] The court affirmed that in allowing the state to guarantee local debt, the school fund language advanced the constitutional guarantee of providing each student with a thorough and efficient education.

As reflected by a case from the Supreme Court of South Carolina, special problems can occur when districts are reorganized. The court evaluated the validity of bonds issued by the board in a consolidated district that succeeded to the property, rights, and obligations of the systems it was formed out of when they ceased to exist as separate entities. The court was of the view that the consolidated board's debt was limited to the constitutional maximum of 8 percent of the property value that had been placed on each of the constituent districts.[126]

Where district boundaries and counties or cities are coterminous, and each has a debt limit, an issue can arise as to the relationship of the debt limit. In such a situation, a school board was only able to raise about $300,000 out of the needed $800,000 due to its constitutional debt limit. Pursuant to a provision in the state constitution which permitted a county to sell bonds for a corporate purpose, it sold $500,000 worth of bonds and turned the proceeds over to the board. Opponents argued both that the bond sale was not for a corporate purpose since the duty of operating a school system devolved on its board rather than the county and that since the district and county had a coterminous boundary, the effect of turning over the proceeds indirectly permitted the board to incur a debt beyond its constitutional debt limitation. However, under

122. *La Porte v. Gamewell Fire–Alarm Telegraph Co.*, 45 N.E. 588 (Ind.1896).

123. *Teperich v. North Judson–San Pierre High School Bldg. Corp.*, 275 N.E.2d 814 (Ind. 1971), *cert. denied*, 407 U.S. 921, 92 S.Ct. 2462, 32 L.Ed.2d 806 (1972).

124. *Hecker v. McKernan*, 196 A.2d 38 (N.H.1963).

125. *Lonegan v. State*, 809 A.2d 91 [171 Educ. L. Rep. 266] (N.J.2002), *clarification denied*, 807 A.2d 189 (N.J.2002).

126. *Boatwright v. McElmurray*, 146 S.E.2d 716 (S.C.1966).

the provisions of the state constitution, the legislature did not have the power to authorize any county to levy a tax or issue bonds except for specified purposes, one of which was education. In construing the latter provision as express constitutional authority for the authorization, the Supreme Court of South Carolina was satisfied that the arrangement did not exceed the debt limit because even though the boundary of the county and board were coterminous, they were separate and distinct corporate entities subject to different constitutional debt limitations.[127]

Short-Term Borrowing

Short-term borrowing is usually necessary due to emergencies, a board's failure to collect anticipated revenues, and/or a board's desire to carry out programs deemed immediately necessary or desirable for the welfare of the schools for which funds are not presently available. As with individuals or businesses, situations may arise in which it is advisable to borrow money for short periods rather than operate strictly on cash bases. Aware of this reality, statutes generally permit short-term borrowing subject to various restrictions. Yet, in most situations, short-term borrowing is not considered an implied board power.[128]

Constitutional or statutory debt limits apply equally to short and long-term borrowing. Anticipation of revenues is limited since it would be poor business and educational practice to permit boards to commit district revenues for an unreasonable time in advance. It is conceivable that absent such limitations, future school operations could be rendered difficult, if not impossible. The most common restriction is that boards cannot anticipate revenues in excess of those of the fiscal year in which anticipations are made. The purpose of this restriction is to prevent boards from continuing to pile up non-bonded indebtedness.

When legislatures grant boards authority to borrow money, state laws usually specify procedures that they must strictly follow. While the authority to borrow does not ordinarily include the ability to issue negotiable instruments of indebtedness, there are cases to the contrary. For example, the Supreme Court of Florida maintained that when a statute permits borrowing but does not specify the procedure to be followed, a board has implied authority to execute its evidence of indebtedness in accord with standard business practices.[129]

In operating schools, boards may sometimes accumulate such a degree of indebtedness that attempting to pay off the entire amount in a single year would put too great a strain on budgets. This leads to a consideration of whether boards can fund indebtedness and arrange for their payments over relatively short periods of time. Some statutes permit boards to issue bonds under such circumstances, but only after votes of district residents at potentially considerable expense. If boards

127. *Grey v. Vaigneur,* 135 S.E.2d 229 (S.C.1964).

128. For an exception *see Logan v. Board of Pub. Instruction for Polk County,* 158 So. 720 (Fla. 1935).

129. *Board of Pub. Instruction for Bay County v. Barefoot,* 193 So. 823 (Fla.1939).

can fund existing debt by short-term loans, they can avoid a great deal of expense and inconvenience. Consequently, state laws often authorize boards to fund their obligations in this way.

The question that boards most frequently face in connection with funding obligations is whether doing so constitutes the creation of new indebtedness, which extends their total indebtedness beyond statutory or constitutional limits or beyond that which they can incur during a single year. Insofar as courts typically agree that funding present obligations does not create new debt, an obligation's validity must be viewed in light of a board's financial status when the original debt was incurred, not as of the date of the funding.[130]

Budgetary Procedures

In order for school officials to plan more carefully, state laws require them to prepare budgets of proposed expenditures. Detailed provisions vary but include such requirements as having budgets itemized and published as well as being subject to public hearings, reviewing agencies, and procedures for transferring funds from some budgetary items to others.

When a reviewing agency seeks to exert a measure of control over school expenditures or when taxpayers challenge a budget, these disputes are subject to judicial review. In general, attempts by reviewing agencies or taxpayers to modify board expenditures are generally unsuccessful unless they can demonstrate that pertinent statutes are clear that they can do so. The judicial attitude is ordinarily that since boards are responsible for school operations, they must be free to consider how and where expenditures are made, subject only to constitutional limitations on their total amount. The major exception seems to arise when schools are fiscally dependent on municipal governments. In these cases, with courts liberally construing board powers, they present total budgets to municipal authorities who may reduce the totals or eliminate items not required by state law and not placed in their province.[131] Under this form of organization, boards are not restricted to adherence to particular items in a budget as long as they do not attempt to spend more than the total amount appropriated for the support of schools.[132]

Where voters rejected an item in a proposed school budget that would have provided for four teacher aides, the board rehired the one aide it previously employed and paid her under an appropriation for the salaries of school district officials. In upholding the board's action, the Supreme Court of New Hampshire asserted that the board had the power to transfer funds that had voter approval and that the action of

---

130. *Citizens Bank v. Rowan County Bd. of Educ.*, 118 S.W.2d 704 (Ky.1938).

131. *Ring v. Woburn*, 43 N.E.2d 8 (Mass.1942); *Carroll v. City of Malden*, 320 N.E.2d 843 (Mass. Ct. App.1974).

132. *Leonard v. School Comm. of Springfield*, 135 N.E. 459 (Mass.1922). *See also Lynch v. City of Fall River*, 147 N.E.2d 152 (Mass.1958); *Warwick School Comm. v. Gibbons*, 410 A.2d 1354 (R.I.1980).

the voters could not be interpreted as a retroactive disapproval of the aide's employment.[133]

The Supreme Court of Georgia, in upholding a board's entering into a contract for a field house, construed the requirement that no funds shall be disbursed by a local board except in accordance with a budget filed with the state board of education.[134] In recognizing that not every expenditure had to be a line item in the budget, the court affirmed that since the board had a balance of unobligated funds in excess of the proposed expenditure, it acted within its power.

As illustrated by a case from the Supreme Court of Utah, claims that school officials have not provided sufficient itemization in budgets are generally unsuccessful. Where state law required school budgets to be itemized, a taxpayer challenged a published budget consisting of ten classifications of accounts, each of which was further subdivided into sixty items. After the budget was approved, officials further divided it into more than 1,500 accounts, leading the court to affirm its validity as sufficiently itemized in compliance with state law.[135]

In a dispute over whether broad classifications constituted adequate itemization to the state as to the purposes for which expenditures were to be made, the Supreme Court of Arizona observed that a total of forty-one sub-items in six categories was sufficient.[136] In another aspect of the case, the court commented that while a school board could transfer funds among sub-items in each of the six general categories, it could not transfer funds among the general categories.

Courts adhere to the rule that funds raised by taxation for one purpose cannot be diverted to another.[137] In an illustrative case, where a school board made a budgetary transfer from its general to its capital outlay fund, the Supreme Court of South Dakota upheld the transfer on the grounds that there was no evidence that the transferred money was raised by local tax levies and the amount was less than that derived from sources other than local taxes.[138] Similarly, the Supreme Court of Idaho determined that setting monies aside from a fund designed to purchase notes to pay for defaulted school bonds did not violate the state constitution since they were part of a common scheme to increase the flexibility of the management of the state's school endowment fund.[139]

On another matter, current tax revenues cannot be used to pay obligations that accrued during previous school years. Moreover, unless a budget permits a board to use current funds for old debts, such pay-

133. *Ashley v. Rye School Dist.*, 274 A.2d 795 (N.H.1971).

134. *Concerned School Patrons & Taxpayers v. Ware County Bd. of Educ.*, 263 S.E.2d 925 (Ga. 1980). [Case No. 38]

135. *Tuttle v. Board of Educ. of Salt Lake City*, 294 P. 294 (Utah 1930).

136. *Isley v. School Dist.*, 305 P.2d 432 (Ariz.1956).

137. *School Dist. No. 2 v. Jackson–Wilson High School Dist.*, 52 P.2d 673 (Wyo. 1935).

138. *Stene v. School Bd. of Beresford Indep. School Dist., No. 68*, 206 N.W.2d 69 (S.D.1973).

139. *Idaho Endowment Fund Investment Bd. v. Crane*, 23 P.3d 129 [153 Educ. L. Rep. 973] (Idaho 2001).

ments can be enjoined.[140] However, at least one court thought that if a past debt was paid, a request for an injunction would be rendered moot.[141]

School Finance and Municipal Authorities

As boards seek sufficient funds to operate schools, they often encounter difficulties with local government agencies such as city councils. Insofar as state legislatures grant powers both to boards and municipalities, they may establish methods of finance which either keep the two operations completely separate or have them intertwined.

A state legislature's power to require city authorities to issue bonds to raise money to build schools was at the heart of a leading, albeit older, case from Maryland. The state's highest court reasoned that the legislature had the power to direct city authorities to create a debt for a school building.[142] Similarly, a legislature can set a minimum sum that city officials must raise for school purposes and can require them to do so without discretion.[143] Further, a legislature can require city officials to allocate a specified percent of a total budget to a fiscally dependent school board.[144]

Where a city sought to enjoin construction of a high school until the board received approval from a referendum, the Supreme Court of Pennsylvania was of the opinion that granting one governmental unit standing to sue due to a hypothetical threat to property tax revenues would have meant that neither could have effectively functioned since each could have challenged the other's actions.[145] The court also rejected the city's argument that it could sue on behalf of its taxpayers who lacked standing.

The Supreme Court of Alaska addressed a different aspect of municipal and school board power where a home rule borough sought to require a coterminous school system to participate in centralized accounting without the statutorily required board approval. At issue was the validity of an ordinance from a home rule borough that conflicted with a state statute. The court ascertained that it previously adopted a local activity rule as a method of resolving impasses between state statutes, which was designed to further specific policies and municipal ordinances that directly or collaterally impeded such implementation, depending on whether the matter was of statewide or local concern. The court concluded that since the state constitutional provision, which vested power in the legislature to establish and maintain a system of public schools, was decisive, insofar as state control was not diminished

---

140. *Warren v. Sanger Indep. School Dist.*, 288 S.W. 159 (Tex.Com.App.1926).

141. *Rawson v. Brownsboro Indep. School Dist.*, 263 S.W.2d 578 (Tex.Civ.App. 1953).

142. *Revell v. City of Annapolis*, 31 A. 695 (Md.1895). [Case No. 34]

143. *City of Louisville v. Commonwealth*, 121 S.W. 411 (Ky.1909).

144. *Board of Educ. of City School Dist. of City of N.Y. v. City of N.Y.*, 394 N.Y.S.2d 148 (N.Y. 1977).

145. *City of Hazleton v. Hazleton Area School Dist.*, 276 A.2d 545 (Pa.1971).

by the legislature's having delegated selected functions to local boards, the board could not be required to take part in centralized accounting.[146] The same court later remarked that a state law that conferred authority on municipal assemblies to appropriate school budgets did not pre-empt a home rule municipality charter which granted a mayor veto power over a school budget even though the law was silent as to the mayor's role in the appropriations process.[147]

The preceding cases should not be viewed as meaning that statutes absolutely prohibit municipalities from approving appropriations for educational purposes. Even so, absent laws clearly granting this power to municipalities, courts generally agree that school boards have independent authority to calculate the amount of money needed for schools while municipalities must levy, collect, and turn over tax proceeds without question.[148] Moreover, municipal or county units that collect taxes ordinarily can retain a share for administrative expenses unless statutorily permitted to do so[149] or keep accrued interest on collected school taxes.[150] If municipal bodies violate this rule and improperly retain expenses for collecting taxes, boards can recover the funds even if the former spent them.[151]

Occasionally, municipal or county tax collectors take in more money than school boards request due to difficulties in accurately predicting the exact amount of money a tax is likely to produce. In one such case, Maryland's highest court was persuaded that a board was entitled to the funds.[152] The court was of the view that since state law required county boards to submit proposed budgets to county officials, their obligation was to levy taxes and distribute the proceeds to boards.

Where a school committee included a provision in the collective bargaining agreement with its teachers that created a procedure to fund payments to a health and welfare fund, a city whose boundaries was coterminus with those of the district claimed that the committee's power to set compensation for its employees did not include making payments to third persons for their benefit. The Supreme Judicial Court of Massachusetts disagreed, believing that the payments to the fund were acceptable because they were modest in amount and intelligent in purpose while having no different impact on the city than direct payments to teachers.[153]

Courts may occasionally require municipal governing bodies and/or school boards to expend funds to implement their orders. For instance,

146. *Macauley v. Hildebrand*, 491 P.2d 120 (Alaska 1971).

147. *Municipality of Anchorage v. Repasky*, 34 P.3d 302 [158 Educ. L. Rep. 822] (Alaska 2001).

148. *Board of Educ. of Town of Stamford v. Board of Finance of Town of Stamford*, 16 A.2d 601 (Conn.1940).

149. *Coleman v. Kiley*, 225 S.E.2d 273 (Ga.1976).

150. *State ex rel. School Dist. of Springfield R–12 v. Wickliffe*, 650 S.W.2d 623 [11 Educ. L. Rep. 735] (Mo.1983).

151. *Venhaus v. Board of Educ. of Pulaski County*, 659 S.W.2d 179 [14 Educ. L. Rep. 598] (Ark.1983).

152. *Board of Educ. of Montgomery County v. Montgomery County*, 205 A.2d 202 (Md.1964).

153. *Kerrigan v. City of Boston*, 278 N.E.2d 387 (Mass.1972).

the Second Circuit, although conceding that it would have been a better practice to direct a fiscally dependent school board under a desegregation decree to supply details regarding expenditures of additional funds that it claimed to have needed from a city, nevertheless upheld an order that a city council add a specific sum to the school board's budget.[154] More recently, a dispute arose over a town's proposed amendment to its home rule charter in relation to budgeting for education. The Supreme Court of Connecticut acknowledged that even though providing education is a statewide concern, since the procedure pursuant to which the town adopted its budget was not a statewide concern, its funding board and the local school board could work together to pass a budget that would have satisfied the state's general state requirements with regard to educating the town's children.[155]

Alimentation of School Funds

State statutes create a variety of procedures addressing the manner of distribution and amounts of funds to be received by different types of districts, depending on which agencies distribute monies to local school boards. In some states, since boards within specific classes are entitled to set amounts of funds, public officials lack discretion as they exercise purely ministerial duties. In other states that grant discretion for distributing funds subject to only broad restrictions, courts typically do not intervene absent charges that officials acted in bad faith or unreasonably.[156]

Difficulties arise when state officials either fail, or refuse, to make payments to boards or questions arise as to how the amounts of funds are calculated. Where state law required the superintendent of public instruction to apportion equalization funds to boards by a set date, the Supreme Court of Michigan upheld a city school board's request for a mandamus order compelling him to do so.[157]

Another aspect of alimentation, or meeting a school system's needs, arises when state officials err by disbursing funds to boards that they are not entitled to receive. Situations of this type can be exacerbated insofar as errors typically do not appear until after funds are spent. Under these circumstances, since a writ of mandamus is of little value because the funds are no longer in the hands of state officials who cannot disburse them to the proper board, the only remedy available to an aggrieved board is to seek to recover the amount from the system that received the funds inappropriately.[158]

154. *Arthur v. Nyquist*, 712 F.2d 809 [12 Educ. L. Rep. 656] (2d Cir.1983), *cert. denied*, 466 U.S. 936, 104 S.Ct. 1907, 80 L.Ed.2d 456 (1984).

155. *Board of Educ. of the Town and Borough of Naugatuck v. Town and Borough of Naugatuck*, 843 A.2d 603 [186 Educ. L. Rep. 420] (Conn. 2004).

156. *State ex rel. King v. Board of Educ. of Russell County*, 108 So. 588 (Ala.1926).

157. *Board of Educ. of Iron Mountain v. Voelker*, 259 N.W. 891 (Mich.1935).

158. *Independent School Dist. No. 1 v. Common School Dist. No. 1*, 55 P.2d 144 (Idaho 1936).

State laws typically provide that proceeds from fines, forfeitures, and other specified sources become part of school funds. The Constitution of North Carolina stipulates that "[c]lear proceeds of all penalties and forfeitures and all fines collected in the several counties for any breach of penal or military laws of the state shall be faithfully appropriated for establishing and maintaining the free public schools in the several counties of the state."[159] The state's highest court invalidated a statute that permitted judicial clerks to earn 5 percent commissions on all such funds in deciding that since the term "clear proceeds" meant "total sums collected," no subtractions were permitted.

In disputes over alimentation, courts clearly insist that there should be no interference with the way in which spending agencies disburse funds as they typically reject administrative attempts to hinder such distributions absent express authority. The courts recognize that school operations could be rendered impossible if funds can be tied up pending the resolution of every question raised by officials who are part of the alimentation process. To this end, the Supreme Court of Wisconsin found that the disbursement of school aid is a ministerial function once officials ascertained specified facts and were satisfied that boards met standards.[160] The court explained that the initial discretionary authority of state-level officials did not transform the mandatory aid payments into departmental funds that were incurred in the execution or administration of a programmatic responsibility subject to reductions by the state's chief fiscal officer.

It is important to distinguish between legislative authorizations and appropriations of funds. Appropriations allocate funds for authorized programs. If there is only an authorization, the Supreme Court of Michigan ruled that a school board could not pursue funds through a mandamus action against the state.[161] Three years later, when state officials appropriated insufficient funds to pay intermediate school boards the amounts to which they were entitled, the same court upheld the state's board's having reduced each system's allocation by the percentage needed to conform to the appropriation.[162]

Where a statutory definition of exceptional children included those who were gifted and talented, a statute required commonwealth officials to reimburse boards for costs of special education. When a board refused to establish a program for the gifted until it received such money, the Supreme Court of Pennsylvania noted that since the receipt of public funds was not a condition precedent, the board had to establish the program on its own, after which time it could seek a writ of mandamus if officials failed to meet their ministerial duty of allocating funds.[163]

159. *Board of Educ. of Guilford County v. City of High Point*, 197 S.E. 191, 192 (N.C.1938), citing art. 9, § 5 of the state constitution.

160. *School Dist. of LaFarge v. Lindner*, 301 N.W.2d 196 (Wis.1981).

161. *Board of Educ. of Oakland Schools v. Porter*, 221 N.W.2d 345 (Mich.1974).

162. *Board of Educ. of Oakland Schools v. Superintendent of Pub. Instruction*, 257 N.W.2d 73 (Mich.1977).

163. *Central York School Dist. v. Commonwealth, Dep't of Educ.*, 399 A.2d 167 (Pa. Cmwlth. Ct.1979).

Similarly, the Supreme Judicial Court of Massachusetts pointed out that a local school committee could not refuse to provide special education services for qualified children on the basis that it refused to comply with an unfunded mandate.[164] The court decided that even if the statutes and regulations pertaining to special education were unfunded local mandates, the committee was only entitled to a declaration that they were ineffective, not to reimbursement of the monies it spent.

In a case involving a novel, albeit unsuccessful, defense, when Chicago's board operated schools for fewer than the state-mandated minimum number of days due to a teacher strike and a shortage of funds, it challenged the state's adjusting the amount of its financial aid. The Supreme Court of Illinois rejected the board's argument that the strike was "an act of God" that rendered its compliance with state law impossible.[165] Rather, the court suggested that the board should have directed its plea for forgiveness to the legislature. In like manner, the Supreme Court of Pennsylvania upheld reductions in aid to districts that were open for fewer than the required number of days due to teacher strikes.[166] Conversely, the Supreme Court of Montana reasoned that state statutes were so vague and uncertain that penalizing a board that did not offer classes on a specified number of days due to a teacher strike was impermissible.[167]

The power of governors to reduce state aid to education is partly a statutory question and partly a constitutional one involving the separation of powers. Massachusetts' highest court indicated that statutes authorizing the governor to make reductions did not cover education aid because the funds were not administered by an agency under the control of the governor or one of the governor's secretaries.[168] The court added that constitutional issues of significance would have been worthy of attention had it been unable to resolve the case on the basis of the statutory wording.

Federal Funds

The Supreme Court has interpreted the general welfare clause in the Constitution as authorizing Congress to spend money for the educational benefit of the people of the United States as long as the primary purpose is regulation or control.[169] To this end, if Congress offers aid to states primarily for educational purposes, such as with regard to educat-

164. *City of Worcester v. The Governor*, 625 N.E.2d 1337 [88 Educ. L. Rep. 227] (Mass.1994).

165. *Cronin v. Lindberg*, 360 N.E.2d 360 (Ill.1976).

166. *School Dist. of Pittsburgh v. Commonwealth, Dep't of Educ.*, 422 A.2d 1054 (Pa.1980).

167. *Missoula High School Legal Defense Ass'n v. Superintendent of Pub. Instruction*, 637 P.2d 1188 [1 Educ. L. Rep. 1293] (Mont.1981).

168. *Town of Brookline v. Governor*, 553 N.E.2d 1277 [60 Educ. L. Rep. 181] (Mass. 1990).

169. According to this provision, "The Congress shall have Power To . . . . provide for the . . . general Welfare of the United States;" U.S. CONST. ART. I, § 8. *See United States v. Butler*, 297 U.S. 1, 56 S.Ct. 312, 80 L.Ed. 477 (1936), *Helvering v. Davis*, 301 U.S. 619, 57 S.Ct. 904, 81 L.Ed. 1307 (1937).

ing children with disabilities, it may attach conditions that become contractual when state officials accept the money.[170] In addition, Congress can require states that accept federal funds to submit assurances of compliance forms[171] and may recover monies that officials misspend.[172] However, before these states are bound to comply with conditions, there must be clear Congressional intent that such conditions are present so that officials can knowingly choose whether to accept the funds.[173]

Conditions that are attached to federal funds must not be unconstitutional. Further, if conditions are imposed as administrative regulations, they must not exceed an agency's authority. For example, the Court of Appeals for the District of Columbia Circuit declared that the Secretary of Agriculture exceeded his rule making authority by barring the sale of foods in schools that competed with those provided in the federally subsidized school breakfast and lunch until after the last service of the day.[174] Yet, the court upheld restrictions on the sale of "junk foods" in schools on the basis that they were authorized by Congress for the purpose of promoting consumption of nutritious foods.

Under an act of Congress, impacted school areas, meaning those with populations that are substantially enlarged by the attendance of children of federal employees, but which lose school tax revenues due to the federal government's being exempt from property taxes, receive funds according to a formula. When officials deducted a substantial amount of impact aid that a local board would have received from the state, a federal trial court in New Mexico decreed that this violated the supremacy clause of the Constitution,[175] because federal financial relief did not reach local taxpayers to the extent Congress contemplated.[176] The court invalidated the plan in explaining that the purpose of the federal law was to aid local boards, not provide compensation for the state. A more recent case from New Mexico dealing with impact aid involved an unsuccessful challenge by two school boards to an order of the United States Secretary of Education certifying that the state's aid program equalized expenditures for local districts. This order permitted the state to factor in the receipt of impact aid payments when making its own aid distributions to those boards. In rejecting the boards' claim that state officials erred in making their aid calculations, the Tenth Circuit maintained that since the Department of Education's construction of the

170. *See, e.g.,* The Individuals with Disabilities Act, 20 U.S.C.A. §§ 1400 *et seq.*

171. *Grove City College v. Bell,* 465 U.S. 555, 104 S.Ct. 1211, 79 L.Ed.2d 516 [15 Educ. L. Rep. 1079] (1984).

172. *Bell v. New Jersey and Pa.,* 461 U.S. 773, 103 S.Ct. 2187, 76 L.Ed.2d 312 [11 Educ. L. Rep. 30] (1983).

173. *Pennhurst State School and Hosp. v. Halderman,* 451 U.S. 1, 101 S.Ct. 1531, 67 L.Ed.2d 694 (1981).

174. *National Soft Drink Ass'n v. Block,* 721 F.2d 1348 [15 Educ. L. Rep. 32] (D.C.Cir.1983).

175. This Clauses reads that "This Constitution, and the Laws of the United States which shall be made in Pursuance thereof; and all Treaties made, or which shall be made, under the Authority of the United States, shall be the supreme Law of the Land; and the Judges in every State shall be bound thereby, any Thing in the Constitution or Laws of any State to the Contrary notwithstanding." U.S. Const. art. VI, § 2.

176. *Shepheard v. Godwin,* 280 F.Supp. 869 (E.D.Va.1968). [Case No. 39]

disparity standard was permissible, its interpretation was entitled to judicial deference.[177]

Courts do not necessarily presume that the supremacy clause permits federal legislation to supersede state power absent Congressional intent to do so. Applying this rule, the Tenth Circuit upheld a finance plan from New Mexico that treated one district differently from others as long as it received special federal funds connected with the community's having been established as a federally owned and managed installation for atomic research and development.[178] The record reflected the fact that the government transferred ownership of schools it built to a newly created board and continued to provide it with financial grants. The court distinguished this situation from that in impact aid cases where the aid was supplementary, discerning that there was no such intent in the atomic-energy-community legislation, remarking that when the plan to finance the community originated, there was nothing to supplement.

In another case, substantial cutbacks in federal impact aid prompted a school board in North Carolina that enrolled large numbers of children whose parents were connected with the federal government, whether in or out of the military, to charge tuition for non-domiciliary enrollees. The Fourth Circuit invalidated the plan on contractual and constitutional grounds.[179] The court premised its contractual rationale on the board's having accepted federal aid for school construction that was available both to systems that experienced substantial enrollments of children whose parents were connected with the federal government and which promised to make the facilities which were still in service equally available to these students as well as children of local families. The court anchored its constitutional analysis on the supremacy clause, concluding that the tuition charges were in effect a tax that discriminated against individuals who were connected with the federal government and, by extension, against the federal government.

The Supreme Court applied the supremacy clause to invalidate a statute from South Dakota that would have required local governments to distribute federal payments in lieu of taxes to compensate for the loss of tax revenues from federally administered national parks and wilderness areas in the same way that they distributed general tax revenues.[180] The Court interpreted Congressional intent as wishing to permit units of local government to choose how to use the money unfettered by state intervention.

177. *Zuni Pub. School Dist. No. 89 v. United States Dep't of Educ.*, 393 F.3d 1158 [194 Educ. L. Rep. 515] (10th Cir. 2004).

178. *Los Alamos School Bd. v. Wugalter*, 557 F.2d 709 (10th Cir.1977), *cert. denied*, 434 U.S. 968, 98 S.Ct. 512, 54 L.Ed.2d 455 (1977).

179. *United States v. Onslow County Bd. of Educ.*, 728 F.2d 628 [16 Educ. L. Rep. 717] (4th Cir.1984).

180. *Lawrence County v. Lead–Deadwood School Dist. No. 40–1*, 469 U.S. 256, 105 S.Ct. 695, 83 L.Ed.2d 635 [21 Educ. L. Rep. 1111] (1985).

[Case No. 33]   Power of Board to Levy Taxes

MARION & McPHERSON RAILWAY CO. v. ALEXANDER

Supreme Court of Kansas, 1901.
64 P. 978.

CUNNINGHAM, J. The plaintiff in error in this action seeks to enjoin the collection of all taxes levied for school purposes in school district No. 79, Marion county, Kan., in excess of 2 per cent on the taxable property owned by it in said district. A graded school district, No. 79, had been organized, identical in boundaries and inhabitants with school district No. 79; such organization being authorized by article 7, c. 92, of the General Statutes of 1889. That article generally provided for the organization of union or graded schools, its principal sections being as follows: Section 107 provides for the selection of a board of directors by the graded school district, and that such board shall consist of a director, clerk, and treasurer. Section 108 directs that such board of directors shall, in all matters relating to the graded school, possess all the powers and discharge all the like duties of boards of directors in other districts. Section 109 provides that the union districts thus formed shall be entitled to an equitable share of the school funds, to be drawn from the treasurer of each district so uniting, in proportion to the number of children attending the said graded school for each district. Section 110: "The said union district may levy taxes for the purpose of purchasing a building or furnishing proper buildings for the accommodation of the school or for the purpose of defraying necessary expenses and paying teachers, but shall be governed in all respects by the law herein provided for levying and collecting district taxes." Section 111 provides certain duties for the clerk of the union district in relation to reports, and that the district treasurer shall apportion the amount of school moneys due the union district, and pay the same over to the treasurer of the union district on order of the clerk and director thereof. Section 112, that the clerk of the union district shall make report to the county superintendent, and discharge all the duties of clerk in like manner as the clerk of the district. Section 113, that the treasurer of the district shall perform all the duties of treasurer as prescribed in the act in like manner as the district treasurer. Section 115, that any single district shall possess power to establish graded schools in like manner and subject to the same provisions as two or more districts united. Section 28 of the same chapter (being the section which gives the general power for levying district taxes) provides: "The inhabitants qualified to vote at a school meeting, lawfully assembled, shall have power: ... To vote a tax annually not exceeding two per cent on the taxable property in the district, as the meeting shall deem sufficient for the various school purposes, and distribute the amount as the meeting shall deem proper in the payment of teachers' wages, and to purchase or lease a site."

These are all the sections which afford light for the solution of the question involved. From these, it is contended by plaintiff in error that while the inhabitants of one or more school districts may form a union or graded district, and create machinery to run the same and to maintain any and all schools therein, the total levy "for the various school purposes" cannot exceed 2 per cent on the taxable property in any one district annually. It is contended by the defendants in error that the various sections quoted, conferring as they do upon the various members of the graded school district board all the powers of like officers of ordinary district boards, and erecting a separate entity for the purpose of managing a separate school, and conferring upon that entity the power to levy taxes as found in section 110, give the power to such graded school district to make within its bounds an additional levy not to exceed 2 per cent; that is, that it may levy as much as the original school district may, and this in addition to what the original district levies, and not that the total of both levies must be the limit fixed in section 28. The court below took this view of the question. In this we do not agree. We think that by section 28 the entire levy may not exceed 2 per cent; and we are strengthened in this conclusion by the language of section 109, which says that a union district shall be entitled to "an equitable share of the school funds," and also by that in section 111, "the district treasurer shall apportion the amount of school money due the union district and pay the same over to the union district." The law fixes the time for holding the annual meetings of the union or graded districts in June, while the annual meetings of school districts occur in July. All these provisions, taken together, indicate that it was the purpose of the legislature that, while the first meeting that of the graded district could suggest the levy desired for graded school purposes, the last one only possessed the power to vote the tax which for "the various school purposes" could not in any one year exceed 2 per cent. Or, at least, there must be such harmony in the action of both bodies that the aggregate levy may not exceed the limit found in section 28. We may say that the question is not one entirely free from doubt, but can hardly believe that the legislature would have left it in that condition, had its purpose been to confer the right to so largely increase the burden of taxation. The authority to levy taxes is an extraordinary one. It is never left to implication, unless it is a necessary implication. Its warrant must be clearly found in the act of the legislature. Any other rule might lead to great wrong and oppression, and when there is a reasonable doubt as to its existence the right must be denied. Therefore to say that the right is in doubt is to deny its existence.

The levies sought to be enjoined are those for the years 1894 and 1895, and our conclusion is that the judgment of the district court must be reversed, and it be directed to make the injunction perpetual, enjoining all of the defendants from collecting all of said school taxes in excess of 2 per cent All the justices concurring.

Notes

1. "The power of the board of education of a non-high school district to levy taxes is statutory. The language granting that power is to be strictly construed and will not be extended beyond the plain import of the words used." *People ex rel. Smith, County Collector v. Wabash Railway Co.*, 28 N.E.2d 119, 122 (Ill.1940).

2. How can one account for such tax limitations? How are they justified?

3.   Generally, school boards may not levy taxes to build up surpluses beyond a fixed percent, set by legislatures, of current expenses. The Supreme Court of Nebraska found that although a reasonable contingency was permissible, a tax levy creating a surplus of 50 percent of a budget was excessive. *Kissinger v. School Dist. No. 49 of Clay County*, 77 N.W.2d 767 (Neb. 1956).

[Case No. 34]   Power of State to Require Local Issue of Bonds

REVELL v. MAYOR, ETC., OF ANNAPOLIS

Court of Appeals of Maryland, 1895.
31 A. 695.

ROBINSON, C.J. The act of 1894, c. 620, provides for the erection of a public school building in the city of Annapolis, and, to pay for the same, it authorizes and directs the school commissioners of Anne Arundel county to borrow money, not exceeding the sum of $20,000, on bonds to be indorsed by the county commissioners; and for the same purpose it directs that the city of Annapolis shall issue bonds to the amount of $10,000, and that said bonds shall be issued without submitting the question of their issue to the voters of said city. The city of Annapolis has refused to issue the bonds as thus directed by the act, and the question is whether the legislature has the power to direct that the city authorities shall issue bonds to raise money to be applied to the erection of a public school building in said city. This power is denied, on the broad ground that it is not competent for the legislature to compel a municipal corporation to create a debt or levy a tax for a local purpose, in which the state has no concern, or to assume a debt not within the corporate powers of a municipal government. If the correctness of this general proposition be conceded for the purposes of this case, we do not see how it affects in any manner the validity of the act now in question. We cannot agree that the erection of buildings necessary for the public schools is a matter of merely local concern, in which the state has no interest. In this country the people are not only in theory, but in practice, the source of all governmental power, and the stability of free institutions mainly rests upon an enlightened public opinion. Fully recognizing this, the constitution declares that it shall be the duty of the legislature "to establish throughout the state a thorough and efficient system of free public schools, and to provide, by taxation or otherwise," for their maintenance and support.... And the legislature has accordingly established a public school system, and has provided for its support by state and local taxation. It cannot be said, therefore, that the erection of buildings for public school purposes is a matter in which the state has no concern; nor can we agree that the creation of a debt for such purposes is not within the ordinary functions of municipal government. What is a municipal corporation? It is but a subordinate part of the state government, incorporated for public purposes, and clothed with special and limited powers of legislation in regard to its own local affairs. It has no inherent legislative power, and can exercise such powers only as have been expressly or by fair implication delegated to it by the legislature.... The legislature may, at its pleasure, alter, amend, and enlarge its powers. It may authorize the city authorities to establish public schools within the corporate limits, and direct that bonds shall be issued to raise money for their support, payable at intervals during a series of years. There is no difference in principle between issuing bonds and the levying of a tax in one year sufficient to meet the necessary expenditure. It would be less burdensome to the taxpayers to issue bonds payable at intervals than to levy a tax to raise $10,000 in any one year. This, however, is a matter of detail, within the discretion of the legislature, and over which the courts have no control.

If the legislature has the power to direct the city authorities to create a debt for a public school building, the exercise of this power in no manner depends upon their consent or upon the consent of the qualified voters of the city. We recognize the force of the argument that the question whether a municipal debt is to be created ought to be left to the discretion and judgment of the people who are to bear the burden. We recognize the fact that the exercise of this power by the legislature may be liable to abuse. But this abuse of a power is no argument against its exercise. The remedy, however, in such cases, is with the people to whom the members of the legislature are responsible for the discharge of the trust committed to them. It is a matter over which the courts have no control. . . .

Notes

1. When a school board fails to carry out its duties to a community's satisfaction, are residents justified in seeking legislative action to accomplish their wishes?

2. To what extent is special legislation justified to cope with problems not generally present in a state?

3. This case is cited in opinions involving legislative powers, the status of local political entities, and the role of the judiciary. Is it appropriate to continue to do so?

[Case No. 35] Power of State to Raise and Distribute School Funds

SAWYER v. GILMORE

Supreme Judicial Court of Maine, 1912.
83 A. 673.

CORNISH, J. This bill in equity is brought to enjoin the Treasurer of State and his successors in office from collecting a tax assessed under the provisions of chapter 177 of the Public Laws of 1909. . . .

The case comes up on report, and by stipulation the only question raised and to be considered is the constitutionality of the chapter above referred to under the state and federal Constitutions.

Chapter 177 of the Public Laws of 1909, the statute in question, reads as follows:

"Section 1. A tax of one and a half mills on a dollar shall annually be assessed upon all of the property in the state according to the valuation thereof and shall be known as the tax for the support of common schools. . . .

"Sec. 3. One-third of this fund shall be distributed by the Treasurer of State on the first day of January, annually, to the several cities, towns and plantations according to the number of scholars therein, as the same shall appear from the official returns made to the state superintendent of public schools for the preceding year, and the remaining two-thirds of said fund shall be distributed by the Treasurer of State on the first day of January, annually, to the several cities, towns and plantations, according to the valuation thereof as the same shall be fixed by the state assessors for the preceding year." . . .

Objections . . . are raised to the manner of distribution. . . .

The first objection is that this act imposes an unequal burden of taxation upon the unorganized townships of the state, because, while the fund is created by the taxation of all the property in such townships as well as upon the property in the cities, towns, and plantations, no provision is made for the distribution of any part thereof to such townships, but it is all apportioned among the cities, towns, and plantations. The townships are omitted. In other words, while four subdivisions of the state are made to contribute to the fund, only three are permitted to share in the financial benefits.

This objection, however, is without legal foundation. The Legislature has the right under the Constitution to impose an equal rate of taxation upon all the property in the state, including the property in unorganized townships, for the purpose of distributing the proceeds thereof among the cities, towns, and plantations for common school purposes, and the mere fact that the tax is assessed upon the property in four municipal subdivisions and distributed among three is not in itself fatal. . . .

. . . The fundamental question is this: Is the purpose for which the tax is assessed a public purpose, not whether any portion of it may find its way back again to the pocket of the taxpayer or to the direct advantage of himself or family. Were the latter the test, the childless man would be exempt from the support of schools and the sane and well from the support of hospitals. In order that taxation may be equal and uniform in the constitutional sense, it is not necessary that the benefits arising therefrom should be enjoyed by all the people in equal degree, nor that each one of the people should participate in each particular benefit. Laws must be general in their character, and the benefits must affect different people differently. This is due to difference in situation. . . . In a Republic like ours each must contribute for the common good, and the benefits are received not directly in dollars and cents, but indirectly in a wider diffusion of knowledge, in better homes, saner laws, more efficient administration of justice, higher social order, and deeper civic righteousness. . . .

But the plaintiff further attacks the method of distribution as unconstitutional because it is made, not according to the number of scholars, as is the school mill fund, but one-third according to the number of scholars and two-thirds according to valuation, thus benefiting the cities, and richer towns more than the poorer.

But that result is not the test of constitutionality. Inequality of assessment is necessarily fatal, inequality of distribution is not, provided the purpose be the public welfare. The method of distributing the proceeds of such a tax rests in the wise discretion and sound judgment of the Legislature. If this discretion is unwisely exercised, the remedy is with the people, and not with the court. Such distribution might be according to population, or according to the number of scholars of school age, or according to school attendance, or according to valuation, or partly on one basis and partly on another. The Constitution prescribes no regulation in regard to this matter, and it is not for the court to say that one method should be adopted in preference to another. We are not to substitute our judgment for that of a co-ordinate branch of the government working within its constitutional limits. The distribution of the school mill fund of 1872 has resulted in inequality. That distribution has been, and continues to be, based on the number of scholars, thereby benefiting the poorer towns more than the richer, because they receive more than they pay, and in the opinion of the justices before cited that method is deemed constitutional. The act under consideration apportions the newly created common school fund one-third according to the number of scholars and two-thirds according to the valuation as fixed by the state assessors, thereby benefiting the richer towns more than the poorer, producing inequality in the other direction, but we are unable to see why this method is not equally constitutional with the other. Both taxes are assessed for the same admittedly public purpose, both promote the common welfare, and the fact that the Legislature has seen fit to distribute the two on different bases is not fatal to the validity of either. It may be that the two methods taken together produce a more equal distribution than either operating alone. In any event, the Legislature has adopted both methods, and both must stand or fall together. . . .

Our conclusion therefore is that chapter 177 of the Public Laws of 1909 violates neither the state nor the federal Constitution. . . .

Notes

1. This same court previously upheld the School Mill Act of 1872 which was the first in the state to impose a tax on property devoted to the maintenance of common schools. *Opinion of the Justices*, 68 Me. 582 (Me.1878).

2. Is the court's appraisal of the benefits of public education sound? To what extent, if at all, should public services be supported by its users? Does the answer depend on a particular service?

[Case No. 36] Constitutionality of State Finance Plan in Relation to Equality of Educational Opportunity

SAN ANTONIO INDEPENDENT SCHOOL DISTRICT v. RODRIGUEZ

Supreme Court of the United States, 1973.
411 U.S. 1, 93 S.Ct. 1278, 36 L.Ed.2d 16.

MR. JUSTICE POWELL delivered the opinion of the Court.

This suit attacking the Texas system of financing public education was initiated by Mexican–American parents whose children attend the elementary and secondary schools in the Edgewood Independent School District, an urban school district in San Antonio, Texas. They brought a class action on behalf of schoolchildren throughout the State who are members of minority groups or who are poor and reside in school districts having a low property tax base.... The complaint was filed in the summer of 1968 and a three-judge court was impaneled in January 1969. In December 1971 the panel rendered its judgment in a per curiam opinion holding the Texas school finance system unconstitutional under the Equal Protection Clause of the Fourteenth Amendment.... For the reasons stated in this opinion, we reverse the decision of the District Court.

I

The first Texas State Constitution, promulgated upon Texas' entry into the Union in 1845, provided for the establishment of a system of free schools. Early in its history, Texas adopted a dual approach to the financing of its schools, relying on mutual participation by the local school districts and the State....

Recognizing the need for increased state funding to help offset disparities in local spending and to meet Texas' changing educational requirements, the state legislature in the late 1940's undertook a thorough evaluation of public education with an eye toward major reform. In 1947, an 18–member committee, composed of educators and legislators, was appointed to explore alternative systems in other States and to propose a funding scheme that would guarantee a minimum or basic educational offering to each child and that would help overcome interdistrict disparities in taxable resources. The Committee's efforts led to ... establishing the Texas Minimum Foundation School Program. Today, this Program accounts for approximately half of the total educational expenditures in Texas.

The Program calls for state and local contributions to a fund earmarked specifically for teacher salaries, operating expenses, and transportation costs. The State, supplying funds from its general revenues, finances approximately 80% of the Program, and the school districts are responsible-as a unit-for providing the remaining 20%. The districts' share, known as the Local Fund Assignment, is apportioned among the school districts under a formula designed to reflect each district's relative taxpaying ability. The Assignment is first divided among Texas' 254 counties pursuant to a complicated economic index that takes into account the relative value of each county's contribution to the State's total income from manufacturing, mining, and agricultural activities. It also considers each county's relative share of all payrolls paid within the State and, to a lesser extent, considers each county's share of all property in the State. Each county's assignment is then divided among its school districts on the basis of each district's share of assessable property within the county. The district, in turn, finances its share of the Assignment out of revenues from local property taxation.

The design of this complex system was twofold. First, it was an attempt to assure that the Foundation Program would have an equalizing influence on expenditure levels between school districts by placing the heaviest burden on the school districts most capable of paying. Second, the Program's architects sought to establish a Local Fund Assignment that would force every school district to contribute to the education of its children but that would not by itself exhaust any district's resources. Today every school district does impose a property tax from which it derives locally expendable funds in excess of the amount necessary to satisfy its Local Fund Assignment under the Foundation Program. . . .

The school district in which appellees reside, the Edgewood Independent School District, has been compared throughout this litigation with the Alamo Heights Independent School District. This comparison between the least and most affluent districts in the San Antonio area serves to illustrate the manner in which the dual system of finance operates and to indicate the extent to which substantial disparities exist despite the State's impressive progress in recent years. Edgewood is one of seven public school districts in the metropolitan area. Approximately 22,000 students are enrolled in its 25 elementary and secondary schools. The district is situated in the core-city sector of San Antonio in a residential neighborhood that has little commercial or industrial property. The residents are predominantly of Mexican–American descent: approximately 90% of the student population is Mexican–American and over 6% is Negro. The average assessed property value per pupil is $5,960—the lowest in the metropolitan area-and the median family income ($4,686) is also the lowest. At an equalized tax rate of $1.05 per $100 of assessed property-the highest in the metropolitan area-the district contributed $26 to the education of each child for the 1967–1968 school year above its Local Fund Assignment for the Minimum Foundation Program. The Foundation Program contributed $222 per pupil for a state-local total of $248. Federal funds added another $108 for a total of $356 per pupil.

Alamo Heights is the most affluent school district in San Antonio. Its six schools, housing approximately 5,000 students, are situated in a residential community quite unlike the Edgewood District. The school population is predominantly "Anglo," having only 18% Mexican–Americans and less than 1% Negroes. The assessed property value per pupil exceeds $49,000, and the median family income is $8,001. In 1967–1968 the local tax rate of $.85 per $100 of valuation yielded $333 per pupil over and above its contribution to the Foundation Program. Coupled with the $225 provided from that Program, the district was able to supply $558 per student. Supplemented by a $36 per-pupil grant from federal sources, Alamo Heights spent $594 per pupil.

Although the 1967–1968 school year figures provide the only complete statistical breakdown for each category of aid, more recent partial statistics indicate that the previously noted trend of increasing state aid has been significant. For the 1970–1971 school year, the Foundation School Program allotment for Edgewood was $356 per pupil, a 62% increase over the 1967–68 school year. Indeed, state aid alone in 1970–1971 equaled Edgewood's entire 1967–1968 school budget from local, state, and federal sources. Alamo Heights enjoyed a similar increase under the Foundation Program, netting $491 per pupil in 1970–1971. These recent figures also reveal the extent to which these two districts' allotments were funded from their own required contributions to the Local Fund Assignment. Alamo Heights, because of its relative wealth, was required to contribute out of its local property tax collections approximately $100 per pupil, or about 20% of its Foundation grant. Edgewood, on the other hand, paid only $8.46 per pupil, which is about 2.4% of its grant. It appears then that, at least as to these two districts, the Local Fund Assignment does reflect a rough approximation of the relative taxpaying potential of each.

Despite these recent increases, substantial interdistrict disparities in school expenditures found by the District Court to prevail in San Antonio and in varying degrees throughout the State still exist. And it was these disparities, largely attributable to differences in the amounts of money collected through local property taxation, that led the District Court to conclude that Texas' dual system of public school financing violated the Equal Protection Clause. The District Court held that the Texas system discriminates on the basis of wealth in the manner in which education is provided for its people. Finding that wealth is a "suspect" classification and that education is a "fundamental" interest, the District Court held that the Texas system could be sustained only if the State could show that it was premised upon some compelling state interest. On this issue the court concluded that "[n]ot only are defendants unable to demonstrate compelling state interests ... they fail even to establish a reasonable basis for these classifications." ...

This, then, establishes the framework for our analysis. We must decide, first, whether the Texas system of financing public education operates to the disadvantage of some suspect class or impinges upon a fundamental right explicitly or implicitly protected by the Constitution, thereby requiring strict judicial scrutiny. If so, the judgment of the District Court should be affirmed. If not, the Texas scheme must still be examined to determine whether it rationally furthers some legitimate, articulated state purpose and therefore does not constitute an invidious discrimination in violation of the Equal Protection Clause of the Fourteenth Amendment.

II

A

The wealth discrimination discovered by the District Court in this case, and by several other courts that have recently struck down school-financing laws in other States, is quite unlike any of the forms of wealth discrimination heretofore reviewed by this Court. Rather than focusing on the unique features of the alleged discrimination, the courts in these cases have virtually assumed their findings of a suspect classification through a simplistic process of analysis: since, under the traditional systems of financing public schools, some poorer people receive less expensive educations than other more affluent people, these systems discriminate on the basis of wealth. This approach largely ignores the hard threshold questions, including whether it makes a difference for purposes of consideration under the Constitution that the class of disadvantaged "poor" cannot be identified or defined in customary equal protection terms, and whether the relative-rather than absolute-nature of the asserted deprivation is of significant consequence. Before a State's laws and the justifications for the classifications they create are subjected to strict judicial scrutiny, we think these threshold considerations must be analyzed more closely than they were in the court below.

The case comes to us with no definitive description of the classifying facts or delineation of the disfavored class. Examination of the District Court's opinion and of appellees' complaint, briefs and contentions at oral argument suggests, however, at least three ways in which the discrimination claimed here might be described. The Texas system of school financing might be regarded as discriminating (1) against "poor" persons whose incomes fall below some identifiable level of poverty or who might be characterized as functionally "indigent," or (2) against those who are relatively poorer than others, or (3) against all those who, irrespective of their personal incomes, happen to reside in relatively poorer school districts. Our task must be to ascertain whether, in fact, the Texas system has been shown to discriminate on any of these possible bases and, if so, whether the resulting classification may be regarded as suspect.

The precedents of this Court provide the proper starting point. The individuals, or groups of individuals, who constituted the class discriminated against in our prior cases shared two distinguishing characteristics: because of their impecunity they were completely unable to pay for some desired benefit, and as a consequence, they sustained an absolute deprivation of a meaningful opportunity to enjoy that benefit. In *Griffin v. Illinois* and its progeny, the Court invalidated state laws that prevented an indigent criminal defendant from acquiring a transcript, or an adequate substitute for a transcript, for use at several stages of the trial and appeal process. The payment requirements in each case were found to occasion de facto discrimination against those who, because of their indigency, were totally unable to pay for transcripts. And the Court in each case emphasized that no constitutional violation would have been shown if the State had provided some "adequate substitute" for a full stenographic transcript.

Likewise, in *Douglas v. California*, a decision establishing an indigent defendant's right to court-appointed counsel on direct appeal, the Court dealt only with defendants who could not pay for counsel from their own resources and who had no other way of gaining representation. Douglas provides no relief for those on whom the burdens of paying for a criminal defense are relatively speaking, great but not insurmountable. Nor does it deal with relative differences in the quality of counsel acquired by the less wealthy. . . .

Only appellees' first possible basis for describing the class disadvantaged by the Texas school-financing system—discrimination against a class of definably "poor" persons—might arguably meet the criteria established in these prior cases. Even a cursory examination, however, demonstrates that neither of the two distinguishing characteristics of wealth classifications can be found here. First, in support of their charge that the system discriminates against the "poor," appellees have made no effort to demonstrate that it operates to the peculiar disadvantage of any class fairly definable as indigent, or as composed of persons whose incomes are beneath any designated poverty level. Indeed, there is reason to believe that the poorest families are not necessarily clustered in the poorest property districts. A recent and exhaustive study of school districts in Connecticut concluded that "[i]t is clearly incorrect . . . to contend that the 'poor' live in 'poor' districts. . . . Thus, the major factual assumption of *Serrano*—that the educational financing system discriminates against the 'poor'—is simply false in Connecticut." Defining "poor" families as those below the Bureau of the Census "poverty level," the Connecticut study found, not surprisingly, that the poor were clustered around commercial and industrial areas-those same areas that provide the most attractive sources of property tax income for school districts. Whether a similar pattern would be discovered in Texas is not known, but there is no basis on the record in this case for assuming that the poorest people—defined by reference to any level of absolute impecunity—are concentrated in the poorest districts.

Second, neither appellees nor the District Court addressed the fact that, unlike each of the foregoing cases, lack of personal resources has not occasioned an absolute deprivation of the desired benefit. The argument here is not that the children in districts having relatively low assessable property values are receiving no public education; rather, it is that they are receiving a poorer quality education than that available to children in districts having more assessable wealth. Apart from the unsettled and disputed question whether the quality of education may be determined by the amount of money expended for it, a sufficient answer to appellees' argument is that, at least where wealth is involved, the Equal Protection Clause does not require absolute equality or precisely equal advantages. Nor indeed, in view of the infinite variables affecting the educational process, can any system assure equal quality of education except in the most relative sense. . . .

For these two reasons-the absence of any evidence that the financing system discriminates against any definable category of "poor" people or that it results in the absolute deprivation of education-the disadvantaged class is not susceptible of identification in traditional terms.

As suggested above, appellees and the District Court may have embraced a second or third approach, the second of which might be characterized as a theory of relative or comparative discrimination based on family income. Appellees sought to prove that a direct correlation exists between the wealth of families within each district and the expenditures therein for education. That is, along a continuum, the poorer the family the lower the dollar amount of education received by the family's children.

The principal evidence adduced in support of this comparative-discrimination claim is an affidavit submitted by Professor Joel S. Berke of Syracuse University's Educational Finance Policy Institute....

Professor Berke's affidavit is based on a survey of approximately 10% of the school districts in Texas. His findings ... show only that the wealthiest few districts in the sample have the highest median family incomes and spend the most on education, and that the several poorest districts have the lowest family incomes and devote the least amount of money to education. For the remainder of the districts—96 districts composing almost 90% of the sample-the correlation is inverted, i.e., the districts that spend next to the most money on education are populated by families having next to the lowest median family incomes while the districts spending the least have the highest median family incomes. It is evident that, even if the conceptual questions were answered favorably to appellees, no factual basis exists upon which to found a claim of comparative wealth discrimination.

This brings us, then, to the third way in which the classification scheme might be defined-district wealth discrimination. Since the only correlation indicated by the evidence is between district property wealth and expenditures, it may be argued that discrimination might be found without regard to the individual income characteristics of district residents. Assuming a perfect correlation between district property wealth and expenditures from top to bottom, the disadvantaged class might be viewed as encompassing every child in every district except the district that has the most assessable wealth and spends the most on education. Alternatively ... the class might be defined more restrictively to include children in districts with assessable property which falls below the statewide average, or median, or below some other artificially defined level.

However described, it is clear that appellees' suit asks this Court to extend its most exacting scrutiny to review a system that allegedly discriminates against a large, diverse, and amorphous class, unified only by the common factor of residence in districts that happen to have less taxable wealth than other districts. The system of alleged discrimination and the class it defines have none of the traditional indicia of suspectness: the class is not saddled with such disabilities, or subjected to such a history of purposeful unequal treatment, or relegated to such a position of political powerlessness as to command extraordinary protection from the majoritarian political process.

We thus conclude that the Texas system does not operate to the peculiar disadvantage of any suspect class. But in recognition of the fact that this Court has never heretofore held that wealth discrimination alone provides an adequate basis for invoking strict scrutiny, appellees have not relied solely on this contention. They also assert that the State's system impermissible interferes with the exercise of a "fundamental" right and that accordingly the prior decisions of this Court require the application of the strict standard of judicial review. It is this question-whether education is a fundamental right, in the sense that it is among the rights and liberties protected by the Constitution-which has so consumed the attention of courts and commentators in recent years.

B

In *Brown v. Board of Education*, a unanimous Court recognized that "education is perhaps the most important function of state and local governments." What was said there in the context of racial discrimination has lost none of its vitality with the passage of time.... This theme, expressing an abiding respect for the vital role of education in a free society, may be found in numerous opinions of Justices of this Court writing both before and after Brown was decided.

Nothing this Court holds today in any way detracts from our historic dedication to public education. We are in complete agreement with the conclusion of the three-judge panel below that "the grave significance of education both to the individual and to our society" cannot be doubted. But the importance of a service performed by the State does not determine whether it must be regarded as fundamental for purposes of examination under the Equal Protection Clause....

... It is not the province of this Court to create substantive constitutional rights in the name of guaranteeing equal protection of the laws. Thus, the key to discovering whether education is "fundamental" is not to be found in comparisons of the relative societal significance of education as opposed to subsistence or housing. Nor is it to be found by weighing whether education is as important as the right to travel. Rather, the answer lies in assessing whether there is a right to education explicitly or implicitly guaranteed by the Constitution.

Education, of course, is not among the rights afforded explicit protection under our Federal Constitution. Nor do we find any basis for saying it is implicitly so protected. As we have said, the undisputed importance of education will not alone cause this Court to depart from the usual standard for reviewing a State's social and economic legislation. It is appellees' contention, however, that education is distinguishable from other services and benefits provided by the State because it bears a peculiarly close relationship to other rights and liberties accorded protection under the Constitution. Specifically, they insist that education is itself a fundamental personal right because it is essential to the effective exercise of First Amendment freedoms and to intelligent utilization of the right to vote. . . .

We need not dispute any of these propositions. The Court has long afforded zealous protection against unjustifiable governmental interference with the individual's rights to speak and to vote. Yet we have never presumed to possess either the ability or the authority to guarantee to the citizenry the most effective speech or the most informed electoral choice. That these may be desirable goals of a system of freedom of expression and of a representative form of government is not to be doubted. These are indeed goals to be pursued by a people whose thoughts and beliefs are freed from governmental interference. But they are not values to be implemented by judicial intrusion into otherwise legitimate state activities.

Even if it were conceded that some identifiable quantum of education is a constitutionally protected prerequisite to the meaningful exercise of either right, we have no indication that the present levels of educational expenditures in Texas provide an education that falls short. Whatever merit appellees' argument might have if a State's financing system occasioned an absolute denial of educational opportunities to any of its children, that argument provides no basis for finding an interference with fundamental rights where only relative differences in spending levels are involved and where-as is true in the present case-no charge fairly could be made that the system fails to provide each child with an opportunity to acquire the basic minimal skills necessary for the enjoyment of the rights of speech and of full participation in the political process.

Furthermore, the logical limitations on appellees' nexus theory are difficult to perceive. How, for instance, is education to be distinguished from the significant personal interests in the basics of decent food and shelter? Empirical examination might well buttress an assumption that the ill-fed, ill-clothed and ill-housed are among the most ineffective participants in the political process, and that they derive the least enjoyment from the benefits of the First Amendment. . . .

C

It should be clear, for the reasons stated above and in accord with the prior decisions of this Court, that this is not a case in which the challenged state action must be subjected to the searching judicial scrutiny reserved for laws that create suspect classifications or impinge upon constitutionally protected rights.

We need not rest our decision, however, solely on the inappropriateness of the strict-scrutiny test. A century of Supreme Court adjudication under the Equal Protection Clause affirmatively supports the application of the traditional standard of review, which requires only that the State's system be shown to bear some rational relationship to legitimate state purposes. This case represents far more than a challenge to the manner in which Texas provides for the education of its children. We have here nothing less than a direct attack on the way in which Texas has chosen to raise and disburse state and local tax revenues. We are asked to condemn the State's judgment in conferring on political subdivisions the power to tax local property to supply revenues for local interests. In so doing, appellees would have the Court intrude in an area in which it has traditionally deferred to state legislatures. . . .

Thus, we stand on familiar grounds when we continue to acknowledge that the Justices of this Court lack both the expertise and the familiarity with local problems so necessary to the making of wise decisions with respect to the raising and disposition of public revenues. . . .

In addition to matters of fiscal policy, this case also involves the most persistent and difficult questions of educational policy, another area in which this Court's lack of specialized knowledge and experience counsels against premature interference with the informed judgments made at the state and local levels. . . . On even the most basic questions in this area the scholars and educational experts are divided. Indeed, one of the major sources of controversy concerns the extent to which there is a demonstrable correlation between educational expenditures and the quality of education-an assumed correlation underlying virtually every legal conclusion drawn by the District Court in this case. Related to the questioned relationship between cost and quality is the equally unsettled controversy as to the proper goals of a system of public education. And the question regarding the most effective relationship between state boards of education and local school boards, in terms of their respective responsibilities and degrees of control, is now undergoing searching re-examination. The ultimate wisdom as to these and related problems of education is not likely to be divined for all time even by the scholars who now so earnestly debate the issues. In such circumstances, the judiciary is well advised to refrain from imposing on the States inflexible constitutional restraints that could circumscribe or handicap the continued research and experimentation so vital to finding even partial solutions to educational problems and to keeping abreast of ever-changing conditions. . . .

III

. . .

In its reliance on state as well as local resources, the Texas system is comparable to the systems employed in virtually every other State. . . .

. . . While assuring a basic education for every child in the State, it permits and encourages a large measure of participation in and control of each district's schools at the local level. In an era that has witnessed a consistent trend toward centralization of the functions of government, local sharing of responsibility for public education has survived. . . .

The persistence of attachment to government at the lowest level where education is concerned reflects the depth of commitment of its supporters. . . .

Appellees do not question the propriety of Texas' dedication to local control of education. To the contrary, they attack the school-financing system precisely because, in their view, it does not provide the same level of local control and fiscal flexibility in all districts. Appellees suggest that local control could be preserved and promoted under other financing systems that resulted in more equality in educational expenditures. While it is no doubt true that reliance on local property taxation for school revenues provides less freedom of choice with respect to expenditures for some districts than for others, the existence of "some inequality" in the manner in which the State's rationale is achieved is not alone a sufficient basis for striking down the entire system. It may not be condemned simply because it imperfectly effectuates the State's goals. Nor must the financing system fail because, as appellees suggest, other methods of satisfying the State's interest, which occasion "less drastic" disparities in expenditures, might be conceived. Only where state action impinges on the exercise of fundamental constitutional rights or liberties must it be found to have chosen the least restrictive alternative....

IV

In light of the considerable attention that has focused on the District Court opinion in this case and on its California predecessor, *Serrano v. Priest*, a cautionary postscript seems appropriate. It cannot be questioned that the constitutional judgment reached by the District Court and approved by our dissenting Brothers today would occasion in Texas and elsewhere an unprecedented upheaval in public education. Some commentators have concluded that, whatever the contours of the alternative financing programs that might be devised and approved, the result could not avoid being a beneficial one. But, just as there is nothing simple about the constitutional issues involved in these cases, there is nothing simple or certain about predicting the consequences of massive change in the financing and control of public education. Those who have devoted the most thoughtful attention to the practical ramifications of these cases have found no clear or dependable answers and their scholarship reflects no such unqualified confidence in the desirability of completely uprooting the existing system.

The complexity of these problems is demonstrated by the lack of consensus with respect to whether it may be said with any assurance that the poor, the racial minorities, or the children in overburdened core-city school districts would be benefitted by abrogation of traditional modes of financing education....

... We hardly need add that this Court's action today is not to be viewed as placing its judicial imprimatur on the status quo. The need is apparent for reform in tax systems which may well have relied too long and too heavily on the local property tax. And certainly innovative thinking as to public education, its methods, and its funding is necessary to assure both a higher level of quality and greater uniformity of opportunity. These matters merit the continued attention of the scholars who already have contributed much by their challenges. But the ultimate solutions must come from the lawmakers and from the democratic pressures of those who elect them.

Reversed.

Notes

1. To what extent is *San Antonio* an attempt to use the judiciary to accomplish essentially a legislative function? What are the ramifications of this question in terms of education, politics, and social policy?

2. What does, or should, "fundamental" mean when used in connection with rights. Why is the designation of a right as fundamental so important?

3. What does "equality of educational opportunity" mean? Is, or can, it be measured by expenditures? Are there judicially manageable standards by which it can be assessed? Must states endeavor to provide "equality of educational opportunities?"

4. Since *Serrano I*, school finance litigation has produced almost equal results as to the constitutionality of state funding formulas. Insofar as several of these cases resulted in multiple rounds of litigation, this list generally includes only the initial cases where the courts reached consistent later results.

Upholding Finance Plans

Alabama, *Ex parte James*, 836 So.2d 813 [174 Educ. L. Rep. 487] (Ala.2002); Alaska, *Matanuska–Susitna Borough School Dist. v. State*, 931 P.2d 391 [116 Educ. L. Rep. 401] (Alaska 1997); Colorado, *Lujan v. Colorado State Bd. of Educ.*, 649 P.2d 1005 [6 Educ. L. Rep. 191] (Colo.1982); Florida, *Coalition for Adequacy and Fairness in School Funding v. Chiles*, 680 So.2d 400 (Fla. 1996), *reh'g denied* (1996); Georgia, *McDaniel v. Thomas*, 285 S.E.2d 156 [1 Educ. L. Rep. 982] (Ga.1981); Idaho, *Idaho Schools for Equal Educational Opportunity v. Evans*, 850 P.2d 724 [82 Educ. L. Rep. 660] (Idaho 1993); Illinois, *Blase v. State*, 302 N.E.2d 46 (Ill.1973); Louisiana, *Louisiana Ass'n of Educators v. Edwards*, 521 So.2d 390 [45 Educ. L. Rep. 905] (La. 1988), *superseded by constitution amendment as stated in Charlet v. Legislature of State of La.*, 713 So.2d 1199 [128 Educ. L. Rep. 510] (La. Ct. App. 1 Cir. 1998), *writ denied*, 730 So.2d 934 (La. 1998), *reconsideration not considered*, 734 So.2d 1221 [136 Educ. L. Rep. 635] (La. 1999) (upholding the system of funding); Maine, *School Admin. Dist. No. 1 v. Commissioner*, 659 A.2d 854 [101 Educ. L. Rep. 289] (Me.1995); Maryland, *Hornbeck v. Somerset County Bd. of Educ.*, 458 A.2d 758 [10 Educ. L. Rep. 592] (Md.1983); Massachusetts, *Hancock v. Commissioner of Educ.*, 822 N.E.2d 1134 [195 Educ. L. Rep. 591] (Mass. 2005) (refusing to adopt the recommendation of a specially assigned superior court judge that the system of funding failed to satisfy its duty under the Massachusetts Constitution to educate the state's children adequately); Nebraska, *Gould v. Orr*, 506 N.W.2d 349 [86 Educ. L. Rep. 414] (Neb. 1993) (dismissing a challenge for lack of a cause of action); Michigan, *Milliken v. Green*, 212 N.W.2d 711 (Mich.1973); Minnesota, *Skeen v. State*, 505 N.W.2d 299 (Minn.1993); Oklahoma, *Fair School Finance Council of Okla. v. State*, 746 P.2d 1135 [43 Educ. L. Rep. 805] (Okla.1987); Oregon, *Coalition for Equitable School Funding v. State*, 811 P.2d 116 [67 Educ. L. Rep. 1311] (Or.1991); Pennsylvania, *Danson v. Casey*, 399 A.2d 360 (Pa.1979); Rhode Island, *City of Pawtucket v. Sundlun*, 662

A.2d 40 [102 Educ. L. Rep. 235] (R.I.1995); South Carolina, *Abbeville County School Dist. v. State*, 515 S.E.2d 535 [135 Educ. L. Rep. 833] (S.C.1999); Virginia, *Scott v. Commonwealth*, 443 S.E.2d 138 [91 Educ. L. Rep. 396] (Va.1994); Wisconsin, *Vincent v. Voight*, 614 N.W.2d 388 [146 Educ. L. Rep. 422] (Wis.2000).

Invalidating Finance Plans

Arizona, *Roosevelt Elementary School Dist. No. 66 v. Bishop*, 877 P.2d 806 [93 Educ. L. Rep. 330] (Ariz.1994); Arkansas, *Lake View School Dist. No. 25 of Phillips County v. Huckabee*, 91 S.W.3d 472 [173 Educ. L. Rep. 248] (Ark.2002); California, *Serrano v. Priest*, 96 Cal.Rptr. 601 (Cal.1971); Connecticut, *Horton v. Meskill*, 376 A.2d 359 (Conn.1977); Kansas, *Montoy v. State*, 102 P.3d 1160 [194 Educ. L. Rep. 439] (Kan. 2005), *republished with concurring opinion*, 120 P.3d 306 [202 Educ. L. Rep. 319] (Kan. 2005), *opinion supplemented*, 112 P.3d 923 [198 Educ. L. Rep. 703] (Kan. 2005); Kentucky, *Rose v. Council for Better Educ.*, 790 S.W.2d 186 [60 Educ. L. Rep. 1289] (Ky.1989); Massachusetts, *McDuffy v. Secretary of Executive Office of Educ.*, 615 N.E.2d 516 [83 Educ. L. Rep. 657] (Mass.1993); Missouri, *Committee for Educ. Equality v. State*, 878 S.W.2d 446 [92 Educ. L. Rep. 1020] (Mo. 1994) (dismissing appeal since judgment was not final); Montana, *Columbia Falls Elementary School Dist. No. 6 v. State*, 109 P.3d 257 [196 Educ. L. Rep. 958] (Mont. 2005); New Hampshire, *Claremont School Dist. v. Governor*, 703 A.2d 1353 [123 Educ. L. Rep. 233] (N.H.1997); New Jersey, *Robinson v. Cahill*, 303 A.2d 273 (N.J.1973), *cert. denied*, 414 U.S. 976, 94 S.Ct. 292, 38 L.Ed.2d 219 (1973); New York, *Campaign for Fiscal Equity v. State of N.Y.*, 769 N.Y.S.2d 106 [183 Educ. L. Rep. 970] (N.Y.2003); North Carolina, *Hoke County Bd. of Educ. v. State of N.C.*, 599 S.E.2d 365 [190 Educ. L. Rep. 661] (N.C. 2004); North Dakota, *Bismarck Pub. School Dist. No. 1 v. State By and Through N.D. Legislative Assembly*, 511 N.W.2d 247 [88 Educ. L. Rep. 1184] (N.D.1994) (while the court ruled that the funding statute was unconstitutional, it lacked the super majority needed to vitiate the law); Ohio, *DeRolph v. State*, 677 N.E.2d 733 [116 Educ. L. Rep. 1140] (Ohio 1997); Tennessee, *Tennessee Small School Systems v. McWherter*, 91 S.W.3d 232 [172 Educ. L. Rep. 1044] (Tenn.2002); Texas, *Edgewood Indep. School Dist. v. Kirby*, 777 S.W.2d 391 [56 Educ. L. Rep. 663] (Tex. 1989); *see also Neeley v. West Orange–Cove Consol. Indep. School Dist.*, 176 S.W.3d 746 [204 Educ. L. Rep. 793] (Tex. 2005); Vermont, *Brigham v. State*, 692 A.2d 384 [117 Educ. L. Rep. 667] (Vt.1997); Washington, *Seattle School Dist. No. 1 of King County v. State*, 585 P.2d 71 (Wash.1978); West Virginia, *Pauley v. Kelly*, 255 S.E.2d 859 (W. Va.1979); Wyoming, *Campbell County School Dist. v. State*, 907 P.2d 1238 [105 Educ. L. Rep. 771] (Wyo.1995).

[Case No. 37]   Power of Board to Change Building Plans after Approval of Bonds

RICKER v. BOARD OF EDUCATION OF MILLARD COUNTY SCHOOL DISTRICT

Supreme Court of Utah, 1964.
396 P.2d 416.

CROCKETT, JUSTICE: Plaintiffs as taxpayers sued to prevent the Board of Education of Millard County School District from going forward with a planned school-building program, particularly from proceeding with a new junior and senior high school at Delta projected to cost about $1,786,000.

Acting pursuant to Section 53–10–7, U.C.A.1953, the defendant Board published in two local newspapers notice of a school bond election and a copy of the official ballot. It also had printed an explanatory brochure concerning the election and its purpose. Copies were distributed to the public and parts of it were published in the newspapers "in conjunction with," but not as a part of, the statutory notice. The explanation included the purpose of the bonding program, the amount of money to be raised and the effect on the tax levy. It indicated generally that the funds would be spent under two main categories: high schools and elementary schools; that the main item in high schools would be a new combined junior and senior high school at Delta at a cost of about $1,250,000; that about $75,000 would be spent in building a new farm shop at the Millard High School at Fillmore; and at the latter school about $80,000 would be spent on a remodeling project. It also mentioned several proposals under consideration for construction and remodeling of grade schools in the district, for which no cost estimates were given.

The bond election carried, and the Board then proceeded to get a definite estimate from an architect as to the cost of the junior-senior high school at Delta. As is not uncommon in regard to building costs, particularly in recent years, it was found that the preliminary estimate of $1,250,000 for that project was too low; that its actual cost would be between $1,645,000 and $1,786,000. This increase is the main cause of the instant difficulty. Based on the 1964 assessed valuation, the maximum amount of bonds that could be issued is $1,935,000. Consequently, if the Board proceeds with its expressed intention to construct the junior-senior high school at Delta and carries out the project of building the farm shop and remodeling program at the Millard High School at Fillmore, only a comparatively small amount of money will be left for elementary school needs mentioned in the brochure.

Plaintiffs contend that the defendant Board should not be allowed to use substantially all of the money for the high-school projects, but should allocate a proper portion to the elementary school needs as was represented in the brochure. They insist that to do otherwise is a violation of the condition upon which the public voted for the bonds and a breach of faith by defendants in the performance of their duties....

... [F]or the purposes of meeting the principal issue in this case forthrightly, we proceed upon the assumption that plaintiffs are correct in asserting that the public reasonably could and did regard the statements as to the various school needs as part of the notice of the election.

It is undoubted that Sections 53–10–9 and 7, relating to the purpose and requiring publication of the notice of the school bond election, are designed to give notice of the essential facts to the public. But it will be noted that the requirement concerning the use of funds refers only to the general purpose. . . .

... The duties of the board include that of purchasing schoolhouse sites and erecting and remodeling school buildings. Also in harmony with the import of the statutes ... is the fact that it is inherent in the nature of the board's function in managing school district business that it have a broad latitude of discretion in order to carry out its objective of providing the best possible school system in the most efficient and economical way. Indeed it should be said that the board not only has this prerogative, but it could not divest itself of this duty. It is the policy of the law not to favor limitations on the powers of the administrative body, but rather to give it a free hand to function within the sphere of its responsibilities. For that reason, it is to be assumed that the board has and retains its prerogative of using its best judgment as to what course will prove to be of greatest advantage in serving the interests of the district in the long run. And any representations made by it or its members should not be regarded as restricting that prerogative unless it clearly and unequivocally appears that the Board has made a binding commitment or so acted that justice and equity would require it to follow some predetermined course of action. There is no basis to compel any such conclusion here.

As is the case in other areas in our system of government, it is the citizen's right to vote for and elect officials he thinks best qualified to represent his interests. Having so elected the school board, he then must trust them to administer the school program. But it is not his privilege to intrude directly into the management of school affairs. This principle carries over into the bond election. The taxpayers may give or withhold their consent to the issuance of bonds and the creation of the indebtedness. But if the consent is given, the disposition of the money raised then becomes the responsibility of the board. This is not to say that the voters are entirely without remedy. If they believe an unwise course is being followed, there is nothing to prevent them from petitioning the board for further hearings on the matter and bringing to bear whatever force of argument or persuasion is available. Moreover, the power of the future ballot always exists which may influence policies of the board. It is also true that if it were shown that there existed some actual deceit, fraud or corruption; or if the board was acting outside the scope of its authority, or was so completely failing to follow the course of its duties that its actions could be classified as capricious and arbitrary, redress might be had in the courts. But under the facts shown here, the conduct of the Board cannot be so classified. Accordingly, the proposed building program, involving its judgment and discretion, cannot properly be interfered with.

Finally, the conclusion we have arrived at here is in conformity with what we regard as the sound and well-advised policy of reluctance of courts to intrude into the functions of other branches of government. . . .

Notes

1. Is there any substantial danger of fraud or misrepresentation by bond proponents under this case? Aside from the duty of boards to act in good faith, should there be other limitations on their authority to change building programs after bond approval?

2. The court referred to judicial reluctance to intrude into the functions of other branches of government. How consistent are the courts in adhering to such a policy?

3. The Supreme Court of South Carolina held that the failure of school officials to issue bonds for several years after they were authorized did not render them void. "The only limitation which should affect the right to issue bonds under these circumstances is where the purposes for which the bonds were originally voted have ceased to be necessary, or where the conditions have so changed that it would be inequitable to allow the bonds to be issued, and, unless one of these conditions clearly appears to the satisfaction of the court, the exercise of their discretion by the trustees should not be interfered with." *Covington v. McInnis*, 142 S.E. 650, 651 (S.C.1928).

[Case No. 38]   Power of Board to Use Unobligated Funds

CONCERNED SCHOOL PATRONS AND TAXPAYERS v. WARE COUNTY BOARD OF EDUCATION

Supreme Court of Georgia, 1980.
263 S.E.2d 925.

BOWLES, JUSTICE. This controversy arose when the Board of Education of Ware County adopted a resolution authorizing a contract to construct a field house/physical education/athletic facility for a school. Plaintiffs, as taxpayers and patrons of the school system, brought a suit in the superior court of that county seeking to enjoin the action of the board. . . .

. . . A permanent injunction was denied. Plaintiffs appeal to this court. We affirm.

. . .

Art. VII, Sec. I, Par. I of the State Constitution (Code Ann. 2–4901) provides for a system of common schools in the state. Art. VIII, Sec. VII, Par. I (Code Ann. 2–5501) providing for local taxation for education reads in part as follows: "The fiscal authority of each county shall annually levy a school tax for the support and maintenance of education, not greater than twenty mills per dollar as certified to it by the county board of education, upon the assessed value of all taxable property within the county located outside any independent school system or area school district therein.... School tax funds shall be expended only for the support and maintenance of public schools, public education, and activities necessary or incidental thereto, including school lunch purposes...." The legislature in keeping with constitutional provisions adopted an Act known as "Adequate Program for Education in Georgia Act." The Act specifically recognizes the development of good physical and mental health as a part of the educational process. Additionally, [a section] provides for a course in health and physical education. [Another section] provides: "The county boards of education shall have the power to purchase, lease, or rent school sites, build, repair or rent schoolhouses, purchase maps, globes, and school furniture and make all arrangements necessary to the efficient operation of the school.... In respect to the building of schoolhouses, the said board of education may provide for the same by a tax on all property located in the county and outside the territorial limits of any independent school system." Plaintiffs have made no constitutional attack on any pertinent statute.

We conclude that boards of education do have lawful authority to provide for and construct physical education facilities which may incidentally include a field house or related athletic facility.

Although no funds of a county board of education can be disbursed except in accordance with a budget filed with the State Board of Education, this does not mean that every expenditure must be a line item in the budget submitted. With respect to the year in question, the Ware County Board of Education had a beginning balance of unobligated or uncommitted funds in excess of the amount of the proposed expenditure for the athletic facility. Unobligated funds included in the budget may be used by a board of education for any purpose provided by statute, within the constitutional parameters of our state educational system. The unobligated funds on hand may have been accumulated as a result of thrift practiced by the board with respect to any prior year's budget. There is no contention on the part of the plaintiffs that any millage has been determined or levied by county authorities with respect to any year in excess of the 20 mills limitation included in the Georgia Constitution (Code Ann. § 25501)....

Plaintiffs' petition was filed after the millage for the year had been determined and assessed. (And we suspect by December largely paid.) The issue involved is one of authority by the board of education to spend tax money already collected, not the power to levy a tax for a designated purpose.

The obligation incurred by the board of education regarding the expenditure of accumulated funds on hand at the time of the execution of the contract, which were sufficient for the purpose, was not an attempt to bind a succeeding board of education to a future obligation. A board of education may incur a lawful obligation to pay for the purchase or construction of a facility where sufficient funds are on hand for that purpose, even though the construction contract may not be fully completed before the end of the term of some or all of the members of that body.

The trial court did not err in finding in favor of the defendants.

Judgment affirmed.

Notes

1. What was the major reason this case was brought? The building of athletic facilities, as an implied power of local boards, seemed well settled a half century earlier. *See, e.g., McNair v. School Dist. No. 1*, 288 P. 188 (Mont.1930).

2. Note the issue of board authority that the court identified in the next to last full paragraph of its opinion. What is the difference in theory? in practice?

3. Should the board have been allowed to spend unobligated funds with fewer restraints than those imposed on other monies?

[Case No. 39] Relation between Congress and the States Regarding Financial Aid to Local School Districts

SHEPHEARD v. GODWIN

United States District Court, Eastern District of Virginia, 1968.
280 F.Supp. 869.

ALBERT V. BRYAN, CIRCUIT JUDGE: "Impacted" school areas are those whose school populations have been substantially enlarged by the attendance of Federal employees' children, but at the same time are losing school tax revenues because of the United States government's immunity from land taxes, both factors arising from increased Federal activities in the area. These conditions prompted Congress to provide financial aid for operation of the local educational facilities, P.L. 874.

In applying a State formula for State assistance to local school districts, Virginia has deducted from the share otherwise allocable to the district a sum equal to a substantial percentage of any Federal "impact" funds receivable by the district.

Residents, real estate owners and taxpayers of the City of Norfolk, later joined by those of the County of Fairfax, Virginia, in behalf of themselves and others similarly situated, here attack this deduction and an alternative provision as violative of the purpose and intent of the act of Congress and as transgressing the Fourteenth Amendment. We uphold their contention. . . .

Commencing at the 1948–49 school term Virginia established the Minimum Education Program. As the title indicates, it represents a program which was determined necessary to provide each child in the State a minimum education. To take care of the program's cost a Basic State School Aid Fund was created. It fixed a minimum program cost for every political subdivision of the State, i.e. counties and cities. . . .

A contribution to be made by the State to the cost in every political subdivision is spelled out also. It is comprised of (1) a basic State share and (2) a supplementary State share. The basic State share amounts to

60% of the instructional salaries. The supplementary State share is reached by subtracting from the minimum program cost (the gross instructional salaries plus the total of the $100 per pupil ADA) the following items: (1) the basic State share; (2) an amount equivalent to a uniform tax levy of 60 cents per $100 of true values of local taxable real estate and public service corporation property in the subdivision; and (3) 50% (in 1966–68) of the impact funds receivable by the subdivision from the Federal government for operating costs. A maximum is fixed for the supplementary State share. Administration of this allocation of State money is put in the hands of the State Board of Education. . . .

The grievance of the plaintiffs is obvious: any deduction whatsoever of the Federal supplement in apportioning State aid, pro tanto burdens them as taxpayers, for they and the other property owners in Norfolk and Fairfax have to make up the unindemnified portion of the impact costs. They contend that any deduction is prohibited by the purpose and plan of the Federal act.

The rejoinder of the defendant officials is, first, that the impact pupils are counted by the State in computing the minimum program cost in the district, and in accounting with the district for the State's supplementary aid it is not inequitable to insist upon a deduction of a commensurate amount of the impact moneys. At first appealing, this argument ignores the fact that the Federal children are to a large extent paying their own way so far as the State is concerned. Quite soundly, the Congressional Committee on Education and Labor in recommending passage of P.L. 874, observed that the influx of Federal employees, and the withdrawal of real estate from taxes, did not diminish the tax sources of the State or otherwise burden the State. Its revenues are obtained from taxation to which the additional Federal employees are subject along with the other residents of the area. . . .

Secondly, say the defendant State officials, the calculation of the district's share-the equivalent of 60–cent tax-in computing the supplementary aid, omits consideration of the value of the Federal occupied property and hence, in place of this omitted deduction, it is only fair to subtract the amount of the impact funds which are intended to substitute for the Federal-occupied land taxes. But this argument is based on misconception of the Federal aid as substituting for rather than supplementing local revenues. As will appear when we later scrutinize the act, this is a mistaken understanding of the Federal act.

Our conclusion is that the State formula wrenches from the impacted localities the very benefaction the act was intended to bestow. The State plan must fall as violative of the supremacy clause of the Constitution. Our decision rests entirely on the terms, pattern and policy of the act.

The act makes these propositions clear: (1) the Federal funds are exclusively for supplementation of the local sources of revenues for school purposes; and (2) the act was not intended to lessen the efforts of the State. Those postulates are manifested in the statute by these provisions, especially: that the Federal contribution be paid directly to the local school agency on reports of the local agency, and that the contribution be computed by reference to the expenditures "made from revenues derived from local sources" in comparable school districts.

But the State formula at once sets these precepts at naught. It uses the impact funds to account in part for fulfillment of the State's pledge of supplementary aid to the community; and the State moneys thus saved are available for State retention or such use as Virginia determines. Without the inclusion of the Federal sums the State's annual payments towards supplementary aid would be increased, it is estimated, by more than $10,000,000.

This commandeering of credit for the Federal moneys severely injures both the community and the pupil. First and foremost, it does not relieve the local taxpayers to the extent Congress contemplated. Next, without the exclusive application of the funds to the areas where the need arose and remains, the result may be to lower the standard of education provided in an impacted district. Instead of maintaining the previous standards for the additional pupils, the impact money when thinned by the State would obviously be inadequate to continue that level for the increased school attendance, a result certainly thwarting the aim of the Federal law.

The construction and the implications we put upon the act find confirmation in its legislative history....

... Necessarily, then, the upshot is that the defendants must be enjoined from hereafter in any way denying to the impacted area the exclusive use and enjoyment of the impact funds....

The Norfolk plaintiffs have also prayed for an order directing the defendants to restore to the Norfolk schools the amounts of State aid which in prior years have been withheld by the State on account of the Federal impact funds. To accomplish this restitution would require an appropriation by the legislature of Virginia. A decree to that effect would be an order to the State to take affirmative political action, and would convert this into a suit against the Commonwealth of Virginia, prohibited by the Eleventh Amendment....

Notes

1. Within a year, two other federal trial courts cited this opinion in reaching the same outcome with regard to congressional intent, thereby invalidating funding formulas which provided for diminutions in state aid where federal aid was granted to "impacted" districts. *Douglas Indep. School Dist. No. 3 v. Jorgenson*, 293 F.Supp. 849 (D.S.D.1968); *Hergenreter v. Hayden*, 295 F.Supp. 251 (D. Kan.1968).

2. Consider the last paragraph of the opinion in light of the federal system of government and the federal courts. How should these interact?

Chapter 6

USE OF SCHOOL FUNDS AND PROPERTY

Introduction

State constitutions and statutes cannot cover all uses of school funds. Accordingly, courts are often asked to construe general grants of power and apply them in cases over the implied spending ability of local boards. How cases are resolved often depends on what courts consider desirable public policy. What may be a proper use of school funds or property in one state may be improper in another. Further, since what may be improper at one time may be acceptable later, courts are increasingly liberal in interpreting board powers over use of school property.

Transportation of Students

Absent express legislative authority, such as under the Individuals with Disabilities Education Act,[1] or state law, some courts have not permitted school boards to allocate funds to transport children.[2] In addition, courts tend to interpret transportation statutes narrowly, adopting the view that the basic responsibility for getting children to and from school lies with their parents. This judicial attitude may also be affected by the realization that paying for transportation is a relatively expensive venture that does not contribute directly to education per se. For example, the Supreme Court of Michigan, in an older case, held that even under a statute which granted school boards the power "to do all things needful and necessary for the maintenance, prosperity and success of the schools of the district and the promotion of the thorough education of the children thereof,"[3] a board lacked the authority to allocate funds for transportation.

In its only case involving transportation of students that did not involve religion[4] or race,[5] *Kadrmas v. Dickinson Public Schools*,[6] the Supreme Court upheld the constitutionality of a statute from North Dakota that authorized non-reorganized school boards to charge a user fee that did not exceed the actual cost of transporting children to school.

1. 20 U.S.C. § 1401(26)(A).

2. *See, e.g., Harwood v. Dysart Consol. School Dist.*, 21 N.W.2d 334 (Iowa 1946); *Ex parte Perry County Bd. of Educ.*, 180 So.2d 246 (Ala. 1965).

3. *Township School Dist. of Bates v. Elliott*, 268 N.W. 744, 744 (Mich. 1936).

4. *See, e.g., Everson v. Board of Educ.*, 330 U.S. 1, 67 S.Ct. 504, 91 L.Ed. 711 (1947), *reh'g denied*, 330 U.S. 855, 67 S.Ct. 962, 91 L.Ed. 1297 (1947). [Case No. 1]

5. *Swann v. Charlotte–Mecklenburg Bd. of Educ.*, 402 U.S. 1, 91 S.Ct. 1267, 28 L.Ed.2d 554 (1971). [Case No. 125]

6. 487 U.S. 450, 108 S.Ct. 2481, 101 L.Ed.2d 399 [47 Educ. L. Rep. 383] (1988).

The Court acknowledged that since the state constitution did not require boards to transport all students, education officials had no duty to provide it free of charge. The Court rejected an equal protection challenge against charging only parents of children in non-reorganized districts in positing that social and economic legislation can be overturned only if it is completely irrational. In recognizing that the legislature acted out of its desire to encourage voters to adopt plans for reorganization, the court was satisfied that since a suspect class was not discriminated against and no fundamental right was infringed, the law was not subject to strict scrutiny. Four years later, the Supreme Court of California affirmed that a law permitting boards to charge similar fees did not violate the equal protection clause of the state constitution.[7]

Where legislation does not require a board to transport students, officials may discontinue service at any time. In such a case, where boards lacked funds to provide transportation, two appellate courts in Michigan agreed that they were not required to continue to make it available.[8]

In a related issue, the Third Circuit upheld a school board in Pennsylvania's offering only one-way transportation for kindergarten children. The court found that since the commonwealth's law did not require boards to provide kindergarten or transportation for students in public schools, and its action was rationally based on not wishing to employ drivers or engage buses at midday, officials did not violate the Federal Constitution.[9] Following remand, the Third Circuit again rejected a federal trial court's attempt to exercise pendent jurisdiction based on its argument that since the board had power to transport children to and from school, the general purposes of transportation would not have been served by providing it only one way.[10] In a more recent case from Pennsylvania, parents of children who attended a private, half-day kindergarten unsuccessfully sued their school board for offering full-day kindergarten while discontinuing midday busing.[11] The court pointed out that since bus service was discretionary, officials only had to provide it during regular school hours.

Other legislatures permitted or required transportation for students, regardless of whether they attend public, or religiously affiliated non-public, schools. Even so, as reflected by an early case from Iowa, when a legislature grants a board such authority, it is typically strictly con-

7. *Arcadia Unified School Dist. v. State Dep't. of Educ.*, 825 P.2d 438 [72 Educ. L. Rep. 1137] (Cal. 1992).

8. *Sutton v. Cadillac Area Pub. Schools*, 323 N.W.2d 582 [6 Educ. L. Rep. 187] (1982); *Lintz v. Alpena Pub. Schools of Alpena and Presque Isle Counties*, 325 N.W.2d 803 [7 Educ. L. Rep. 411] (Mich. Ct. App. 1982).

9. *Shaffer v. Board of School Directors of Albert Gallatin Area School Dist.*, 687 F.2d 718 [6 Educ. L. Rep. 487] (3d Cir.

1982), *cert. denied*, 459 U.S. 1212, 103 S.Ct. 1209, 75 L.Ed.2d 449 (1983).

10. *on remand, Shaffer v. Board of School Directors of Albert Gallatin Area School Dist.*, 570 F.Supp. 698 [13 Educ. L. Rep. 731] (W.D. Pa. 1983), *rev'd*, 730 F.2d 910 [17 Educ. L. Rep. 9] (3d Cir.1984).

11. *Crowe v. School Dist. of Pittsburgh*, 805 A.2d 691 [169 Educ. L. Rep. 314] (Pa. Commw. Ct. 2002), *appeal granted without opinion*, 815 A.2d 1043 [173 Educ. L. Rep. 897] (Pa. 2003).

strued.[12] At issue was a law that directed boards to transport certain pupils to and from school. In the face of a challenge to a board's practice of transporting students to school-sponsored events outside of the district, the court determined that the statute did not give the board the discretion to expand its power in this way. Conversely, the Supreme Court of Utah ruled that a board was required to transport students at district expense if their presence was required at after school activities.[13] Distinguishing between students who participated in the extracurricular activities and those who were spectators, and whose attendance was not required, the court added that the board could not offer the latter free transportation. Similarly, the Supreme Court of North Carolina decided that school boards could contract for transportation to bring athletic teams and bands to and from scheduled events.[14]

Courts reached mixed results over the duty of boards to provide transportation to children who attend religiously affiliated non-public schools. In *Everson v. Board of Education*,[15] the Supreme Court upheld a statute from New Jersey which permitted local boards to make rules and contracts for the transportation of children to and from their religiously affiliated non-public schools as passing Establishment Clause scrutiny. Moreover, the Supreme Court of North Dakota, without reaching the constitutional question, wrote that state law did not entitle local boards to reimbursement for transporting "pupils" to non-public schools.[16] Based on state law, the court interpreted "pupil" as a "public school enrollee" and "school" as a "public school." On the other hand, the Supreme Court of Kentucky reasoned that allocating funds to transport students to non-public elementary schools, including institutions that were religiously affiliated, was not an unconstitutional form of aid.[17]

Instead of transporting students, some states permit boards to reimburse parents for the cost of bringing their children to school. The Supreme Court of Kansas upheld a board's paying a mileage rate to parents who lived in out-of-the-way locations rather than providing bus transportation.[18] The court was persuaded that this complied with the statutory requirement of providing or furnishing transportation. Where a mileage rate was reasonable, the Supreme Court of Washington asserted that parents were not entitled to compensation for their time, vehicle depreciation, and actual fuel costs.[19]

Generally, courts do not disturb the discretion of school boards to furnish transportation for purposes within their powers unless school

---

12. *Schmidt v. Blair*, 213 N.W. 593 (Iowa 1927).

13. *Beard v. Board of Educ. of N. Summit School Dist.*, 16 P.2d 900 (Utah 1932).

14. *State ex rel. N.C. Utilities Comm. v. McKinnon*, 118 S.E.2d 134 (N.C. 1961).

15. 330 U.S. 1, 67 S.Ct. 504, 91 L.Ed. 711 (1947), *reh'g denied*, 330 U.S. 855, 67 S.Ct. 962, 91 L.Ed. 1297 (1947). [Case No. 1]

16. *Dickinson Pub. School Dist. No. 1 v. Scott*, 252 N.W.2d 216 (N.D.1977).

17. *Neal v. Fiscal Ct., Jefferson County*, 986 S.W.2d 907 [133 Educ. L. Rep. 624] (Ky. 1999).

18. *State ex rel. Stephan v. Board of Educ. of Unified School Dist. 428, Barton County, Ks.*, 647 P.2d 329 [5 Educ. L. Rep. 251] (Kan. 1982).

19. *State ex rel. Rosenberg v. Grand Coulee Dam School Dist.*, 536 P.2d 614 (Wash. 1975).

officials acted arbitrarily. For instance, the Supreme Court of Tennessee rejected a parental argument that their child should have been transported to a school nearer to their home since the board offered him transportation to a more distant school.[20] The court upheld the board's willingness to send the child to the closer school, without transportation, as a valid exercise of its discretion.

Difficulties often arise where laws authorizing transportation do not specify how far students must be transported. In such a situation, the Supreme Court of Connecticut reviewed a law that required local boards to transport children as long as it was "reasonable and desirable"[21] to do so. When a board denied parental transportation requests due to the presence of traffic hazards between their homes and school, the court upheld an order of the state board directing its local counterpart to offer transportation. The court explained that the children were entitled to transportation since their safety had to be taken into consideration. More than two decades later, the Supreme Court of Rhode Island reached a similar result where state law required school boards to provide transportation for students who lived far enough away from school as to make regular attendance impractical.[22] Earlier, the same court was of the opinion that laws requiring boards to transport public school students "to and from school" applied to children who attended non-public schools. The court also noted that the law did not obligate boards to transport children to their out-of-district religious schools since it viewed legislative intent as contemplating that children be transported to schools, regardless of whether they were public or non-public, located within district boundaries.[23] In like fashion, where a state law required boards to transport students from non-public schools up to ten miles beyond district boundaries as long as children in public schools were transported to district schools, the Supreme Court of Pennsylvania declared that a board did not have to transport resident children who attended public schools in other districts on a tuition basis.[24]

The Supreme Court of California indicated that a school board's refusal to provide transportation to children in an inaccessible part of the district was an abuse of discretion.[25] The court rejected the board's claim that doing so would have been too costly, that it would have led to requests from families in other areas, and that the bus would have had trouble operating on the narrow roads in the area. The court concluded that since the students who were from a poor family would have been unable to get to school without transportation, and the board had the financial resources available, it could have purchased a new, smaller bus to bring the children to school. In addition, on three occasions, the

20. *Davis v. Fentress County Bd. of Educ.*, 402 S.W.2d 873 (Tenn. 1966).

21. *Town of Waterford v. Connecticut State Bd. of Educ.*, 169 A.2d 891, 894 (Conn. 1961).

22. *Brown v. Elston*, 445 A.2d 279 [4 Educ. L. Rep. 211] (R.I.1982).

23. *Chaves v. School Comm. of Town of Middletown*, 211 A.2d 639 (R.I. 1965).

24. *Babcock School Dist. v. Potocki*, 466 A.2d 616 [14 Educ. L. Rep. 117] (Pa. 1983).

25. *Manjares v. Newton*, 411 P.2d 901 (Cal. 1966).

Supreme Court of Appeals of West Virginia agreed that transportation must be provided to all children.[26]

In a related concern, boards may set routes, times, and places for bus stops. As long as a bus stop is not located in an unreasonable or dangerous location, a board is unlikely to be liable for injuries to children that occur there.[27] In fact, as long as the distance from home is reasonable, children can be required to walk to bus stops.[28] However, an appellate court in Illinois remarked that students cannot be required to walk to pickup points that are a distance from their homes that is equal to the one beyond which transportation must be furnished.[29]

Insurance

As demonstrated by a case from the Supreme Court of Alabama, the implied power of local boards to insure school property appears to be settled.[30] The court affirmed that a state law requiring school trustees to care for the property and look after the general interests of schools granted them such power. Other states have since extended board duties to include insurance for all of the vehicles they own or permit employees to operate.[31] In an illustrative case, the Supreme Court of Kentucky, overruling a statute and case law to the contrary, decreed that a statute authorizing boards of education to provide for liability and indemnity insurance against negligence of drivers or operators of school buses or other vehicles that they own or operate did not waive their governmental immunity from suit.[32]

Difficulties arise when boards seek to insure school property as part of mutual benefit associations that are based on reciprocal contracts and provide members benefits as a matter of right. This type of insurance does not call for the payment of set premiums and prorates losses among members in such a way that a board may be subject to a heavy loss, the amount of which is uncertain. Where a board's contingent insurance liability was unlimited, the Supreme Court of Idaho invalidated its purchase.[33] Yet, where the amount of contingent liability was set at a

---

26. *Shrewsbury v. Board of Educ., County of Wyo.*, 265 S.E.2d 767 (W. Va. 1980); *Pauley v. Bailey*, 324 S.E.2d 128 (W. Va. 1984); *Collins v. Ritchie*, 351 S.E.2d 416 [36 Educ. L. Rep. 1002] (W. Va. 1986).

27. *See, e.g., Hackler By and Through Hackler v. Unified School Dist. No. 500, of Kansas City*, 777 P.2d 839 [55 Educ. Law Rep. 311] (Kan. 1989); *Moshier v. Phoenix Cent. School Dist.*, 605 N.Y.S.2d 581 [88 Educ. L. Rep. 200] (N.Y. App. Div. 1993).

28. *Flowers v. Independent School Dist. of Tama*, 16 N.W.2d 570 (Iowa 1944).

29. *People ex rel. Schuldt v. Schimanski*, 266 N.E.2d 409 (Ill. App. Ct. 1971).

30. *American Ins. Co. v. Newberry*, 112 So. 195 (Ala. 1927).

31. *See, e.g., Mizen v. Utica Nat'l Ins. Group*, 770 N.E.2d 97 (Ohio Ct. App. 2002); *Mortara v. Cigna Property & Cas. Ins. Co.*, 811 A.2d 458 (N.J. Super. Ct. App. Div. 2001).

32. *Grayson County Bd. of Educ. v. Casey*, 157 S.W.3d 201 [196 Educ. L. Rep. 975] (Ky. 2005) (invalidating *Taylor v. Knox County Board of Educ.*, 167 S.W.2d 700 (Ky. 1942) and *Board of Educ. of Rockcastle County v. Kirby*, 926 S.W.2d 455 [111 Educ. L. Rep. 1046] (Ky. 1996) and Ky. Rev. Stat. § 160.310).

33. *School Dist. No. 8 v. Twin Falls County Mutual Fire Ins. Co.*, 164 P. 1174 (Idaho 1917).

stated maximum, the Supreme Court of Wyoming sustained its validity.[34] The court commented that the board's liability was not absolutely determinative of the policy's constitutionality since it depended on the ultimate liability in relation to the premium charged by ordinary fire insurance companies. The related practice of self-insurance, whether covering property or employees, remains common in many states.[35]

Local boards can also purchase group life, health, and disability insurance for their employees. Insofar as state statutes and collective bargaining contracts typically obligate school boards to do so, it is unlikely that the judiciary would disagree with the Supreme Court of New Mexico's decree that "securing of group insurance for the teachers enables the board of education to procure a better class of teachers, and prevents frequent changes in the teaching force."[36]

When a school board provides group health insurance benefits for staff, some employees are likely to receive more valuable benefits than others. In such a case, a state law in California authorized a board to purchase insurance while another required equal pay for men and women with equivalent certificates who performed like duties. An appellate court contended that a board did not have to provide insurance coverage in a way that would have required it to revise its salary schedules to give the same monetary equivalent to similarly situated employees.[37] The court cited administrative difficulties of calculating cash equivalents for everyone, observing that whether family benefits were to be included was within a board's discretion.

Conflicts with Business

Disputes have arisen over school enterprises, most notably cafeterias and the sale of books and school materials[38] which may conflict with business interests in local communities. The fact that a private enterprise may suffer as a result of a board's conducting a similar operation is not dispositive of whether public funds or property may be used. Rather, in evaluating whether boards can permit activities to proceed, the courts seek to determine a venture's primary purpose. As witnessed by the dearth of litigation in this area, the law is well settled that as long as the purpose of a school enterprise is to serve student needs rather than earn a profit, or to destroy someone's business,[39] board activity in this regard is legal.

34. *Burton v. School Dist. No. 19*, 38 P.2d 610 (Wyo. 1934).

35. *See, e.g., Christensen v. Milbank Ins. Co.*, 658 N.W.2d 580 [174 Educ. L. Rep. 1087] (Minn. 2003) (noting that Minnesota Stat. § 471.981, subd. 1 (2002) authorized a self-insurance pool); *Bass v. New Hanover County Bd. of Educ.*, 580 S.E.2d 431 (Table) (N.C. Ct. App. 2003) (citing N.C. Gen. Stat. § 160A–462 (2001) permitting local boards to establish a joint agencies to administer self-insurance programs to pay claims and judgments).

36. *Nohl v. Board of Educ.*, 199 P. 373, 374 (N.M. 1921).

37. *Sheehan v. Eldredge*, 84 Cal.Rptr. 894 (Cal. Ct. App. 1970).

38. For a more detailed discussion relating to textbooks and course materials, *see* Chapter 12.

39. *Hailey v. Brooks*, 191 S.W. 781 (Tex. Civ. App.1916).

Where boards created school cafeterias to serve student welfare and provide convenience, with prices being set simply to cover the cost of operations, the courts have uniformly upheld their authority to act as a valid public purpose.[40] In the leading case, the Tenth Circuit affirmed that since a board in Colorado operated a cafeteria that was a form of public welfare for the benefit of the student body, and did not serve a private mercantile purpose, it acted lawfully.[41] Similarly, the Supreme Court of Washington agreed that a board could allow students to operate a cafeteria and use the profits to finance extracurricular activities.[42]

As to the sale of school supplies, the Supreme Court of Wisconsin affirmed that a board could sell them to students at cost since doing so aided efficient and successful school operations.[43] Earlier, the same court ascertained that if a dealer could prove that a board permitted principals to conduct stores in their buildings, which sold school books, stationery, and supplies to students at a profit, it would enjoin them from doing so.[44] Conversely, a year earlier, the Supreme Court of Michigan enjoined a board from purchasing and selling books to students even though doing so was more convenient and economical than through local dealers.[45] Subsequently, an appellate court in Illinois affirmed that a school board exceeded its authority in imposing a 15 percent handling charge on books that it sold to students.[46]

Special Equipment and Services

Special Items

The implied power of local boards to purchase materials and equipment that are reasonably necessary to conduct curricular activities now seems beyond genuine dispute.[47] Even so, as illustrated by the different approaches taken by the courts in Massachusetts and Pennsylvania, the judiciary has not always agreed on purchases of special items for small numbers of students that are made without express statutory authority.

In an early case, the Supreme Judicial Court of Massachusetts vitiated a school committee's purchase of special clothing to be worn by a basketball team as beyond its power since the uniforms were not supplies under a commonwealth statute.[48] The court posited that when subjects such as manual arts and cooking were added to the curriculum, the legislature expressly permitted the purchase and loaning to students

40. *Krueger v. Board of Educ.,* 274 S.W. 811 (Mo. 1925).

41. *Goodman v. School Dist. No. 1, City and County of Denver,* 32 F.2d 586 (8th Cir.1929).

42. *Hempel v. School Dist. No. 329 of Snohomish County,* 59 P.2d 729 (Wash. 1936).

43. *Cook v. Chamberlain,* 225 N.W. 141 (Wis. 1929).

44. *Tyre v. Krug,* 149 N.W. 718 (Wis. 1914).

45. *Kuhn v. Board of Educ. of Detroit,* 141 N.W. 574 (Mich. 1913).

46. *Hamer v. Board of Educ. of Township High School Dist. No. 113, County of Lake,* 367 N.E.2d 739 (Ill. App. Ct. 1977).

47. *Commercial State Bank of Shepherd v. School Dist. No. 3 of Coe Township, Isabella County,* 196 N.W. 373 (Mich. 1923).

48. *Brine v. City of Cambridge,* 164 N.E. 619 (Mass. 1929).

of necessary equipment but that it had not done so for physical education.

On the other hand, where a statute authorized boards to purchase necessary furniture, equipment, textbooks, school supplies, and other appliances for school use, it did not refer to athletic supplies and equipment. The Supreme Court of Pennsylvania affirmed that this statute, together with one authorizing school boards to provide gymnasiums and playgrounds, was broad enough to cover athletic supplies and equipment even though they were not specifically mentioned. The court did not grant the board unlimited authority to purchase special athletic paraphernalia "for use merely by school teams playing in competitive sports [since this] is a question to be answered by school boards in the exercise of a cautious discretion, with special reference to the proportionate number of those who will receive the benefit of such supplies."[49]

In a related matter, the Supreme Court of Oklahoma interpreted a state law as permitting a school board to purchase band uniforms. The court specified that since the law granted the board the ability to incur those legal expenses that were necessary to carry out its express authority, and had already organized a complete course in instrumental music, the purchase was appropriate.[50] Using a similar rationale, fifty years earlier, the Supreme Court of Michigan was of the view that since a school board had the authority to include music in a school's curriculum, it could purchase a piano for use in such classes.[51]

As to other items, an appellate court in Michigan affirmed that a board could use its funds to require students and staff to carry identification cards for use in school. The court observed that the board could also use competitive bidding to select one company to take the photographs and could grant it the exclusive right to take and sell pictures to students on school premises.[52] Subsequently, the Fourth Circuit agreed that a board in Virginia could select an "official photographer" for a school yearbook even though it received a portion of the profits from the sale of portraits because students were not required to make any purchases.[53] Similarly, the Supreme Court of Georgia thought that a board could select one instrument company to conduct its band recruitment program since students were not required to buy or rent instruments from that firm.[54] At the same time, an appellate court in Louisiana upheld a board's practice allowing a salesperson of a jewelry company selected by a committee of faculty and students to sell class rings on school premises since no one was required to make a purchase.[55]

49. *Galloway v. School Dist. of Borough of Prospect Park*, 200 A. 99, 101 (1938).

50. *Excise Bd. of Kay County v. Atchison, T. and S.F. Ry. Co.*, 91 P.2d 1087 (Okla. 1939).

51. *Knabe v. Board of Educ. of West Bay City*, 34 N.W. 568 (Mich. 1887).

52. *LaPorte v. Escanaba Area Pub. Schools*, 214 N.W.2d 840 (Mich. Ct. App. 1974).

53. *Stephen Jay Photography v. Olan Mills*, 903 F.2d 988 [60 Educ. L. Rep. 748] (4th Cir. 1990).

54. *Ken Stanton Music v. Board of Educ.*, 181 S.E.2d 67 (Ga. 1971).

55. *Givens Jewelers of Bossier v. Rich*, 313 So.2d 913 (La. Ct. App. 1975).

Legal Services

Absent a state statute to the contrary that requires one to use the services of a specified government counsel,[56] courts have generally upheld a board's implied power to pay for legal services of its own choosing for itself and its members.[57] As demonstrated by a case from New Jersey, a board's legal counsel must engage only in activities in its interest. A dispute arose when a superintendent sued a board president, and individual members, over an allegedly libelous letter that she addressed to him and sent to a local newspaper. An appellate court stated that a board resolution, purportedly approving the president's letter, was ineffective to convert her personal action into a board matter that would have entitled her to have the board pay for her defense. The court also discerned that since the board members who voted for the resolution did so in the course of performing their duties, they were entitled to reimbursement.[58] Even so, insofar as the courts have recognized that it is not in the public interest to inhibit board members as they perform their duties, they liberally permit reimbursements for civil,[59] but not criminal,[60] litigation. On a related matter, an appellate court in Arizona held that a board could not use public funds to protect a board member's right to remain in office after he moved out of the district.[61]

Boards generally do not have the implied power to pay attorney fees for employees who are sued in their individual, rather than in their official, capacities. To this end, a board's paying attorney fees would constitute an impermissible gift of public funds for a private purpose. Reiterating this principle, an appellate court in New York refused to order a board to pay the legal fees of a teacher who was exonerated on a criminal charge of sexual abuse of one of his students.[62] In like fashion, an appellate panel in Maryland decided that a statute requiring a board to furnish counsel for teachers who acted in authorized capacities was not triggered in a sex abuse case since a court or jury could not have concluded that a school board authorized educators to engage in sexual abuse or harassment of their students.[63] Further, as with school board members, the Supreme Court of Rhode Island interpreted an indemnification statute that covered any claim, demand, or suit arising from

56. *Denman v. Webster,* 73 P. 139 (Cal. 1903).

57. *Arrington v. Jones,* 191 S.W. 361 (Tex. Civ. App.1917).

58. *Errington v. Mansfield Township Bd. of Educ.,* 241 A.2d 271 (N.J. Super. Ct. App. Div. 1968).

59. *See, e.g., Miller v. Board of Trustees,* 970 P.2d 512 [131 Educ. L. Rep. 1114] (Idaho 1998); *Dunn v. Jurupa Unified School Dist.,* 94 Cal.Rptr.2d 529 [145 Educ. L. Rep. 1089] (Cal. Ct. App. 2000); *Brade-*

mas v. South Bend Community School Corp., 783 N.E.2d 745 (Ind. App. Ct. 2003).

60. *Powers v. Union City Bd. of Educ.,* 308 A.2d 71 (N.J. Super. Ct. App. Div. 1973).

61. *Campbell v. Harris,* 638 P.2d 1355 [2 Educ. L. Rep. 277] (Ariz. Ct. App.1981).

62. *Lamb v. Westmoreland Cent. School Dist.,* 533 N.Y.S.2d 157 [49 Educ. L. Rep. 952] (N.Y. App. Div. 1988).

63. *Matta v. Board of Educ. of Prince George's County,* 552 A.2d 1340 [51 Educ. L. Rep. 953] (Md. Ct. Spec. App. 1989).

employment as applying only to civil proceedings.[64]

Miscellaneous Uses of Funds

A myriad of cases address whether school boards have the implied power to spend money for particular purposes. The general rule is that boards can make expenditures to carry out their express powers and those reasonably implied to carry out their duties. If boards exceed their authority, the legal remedy for aggrieved parties is ordinarily to seek injunctions. While the courts typically do not order the recovery of expenditures that were based on reasonable assumptions, board members or administrators may be liable for expenditures that were clearly unauthorized[65] even if they did not act with improper motives.[66] The following cases illustrate the types of issues that arise.

The Supreme Courts of Ohio[67] and Pennsylvania[68] agreed that school boards had the authority to build parking facilities under their general powers. On a different matter, two courts disagreed over whether boards had implied authority to purchase camp sites for children.[69] Still other courts ruled that boards could not build residences for staff[70] or purchase land for use in teaching agriculture under a statute authorizing it to acquire land for school buildings and playgrounds.[71] On the other hand, an appellate court in New York acknowledged that a board could hire architects to devise plans for the construction of school buildings.[72] Similarly, an appellate court in Illinois affirmed that a board had the implied power to employ a public relations consultant to serve as a liaison between the press and community.[73]

In a dispute from Massachusetts, the commonwealth's highest court permitted a school committee to reimburse board members for expenses they incurred attending a national convention for school boards.[74] According to the court, the members' attendance at the convention met the parameters of a broad statute since they could have secured information of value that would have improved service in the district. Previously, an appellate court in Kentucky upheld a board's implied power to pay for membership in the commonwealth's association for school boards.[75]

64. *Monti v. Warwick School Comm.*, 554 A.2d 638 [52 Educ. L. Rep. 153] (R.I. 1989).

65. *McGuire v. Hammond*, 405 S.W.2d 191 (Ky.1966); *Smith v. Dorsey*, 599 So.2d 529 [75 Educ. L. Rep. 692] (Miss.1992).

66. *Campbell v. Joint Dist. 28–J*, 704 F.2d 501 (10th Cir.1983).

67. *Wayman v. Board of Educ.*, 215 N.E.2d 394 (Ohio 1966).

68. *In re School Dist. of Pittsburgh*, 244 A.2d 42 (Pa. 1968). [Case No. 40]

69. *Compare Wilson v. Graves County Board of Educ.*, 210 S.W.2d 350 (Ky. 1948) (denying such authority) with *In re Board of Pub. Instruction of Alachua County*, 35 So.2d 579 (Fla. 1948) (recognizing such power).

70. *Cf. Taylor v. Board of Pub. Instruction*, 26 So.2d 180 (Fla.1946).

71. *Board of Educ. of City of Nickerson v. Davis*, 135 P. 604 (Kan. 1913).

72. *People ex rel. Kiehm v. Board of Educ.*, 190 N.Y.S. 798 (N.Y. App. Div. 1921).

73. *Ryan v. Warren Township High School Dist. No. 121*, 510 N.E.2d 911 [40 Educ. L. Rep. 896] (Ill. App. Ct. 1987). [Case No. 41]

74. *Day v. City of Newton*, 174 N.E.2d 426 (Mass. 1961).

75. *Schuerman v. State Bd. of Educ.*, 145 S.W.2d 42 (Ky. Ct. App. 1940).

Paying employees sums of money and/or providing other benefits in order to settle contract claims seems to be spreading. Clearly, abuses can occur when employees are offered money in exchange for resigning and/or not contesting adverse personnel actions. Conversely, with the expense of litigation and the turmoil it can cause, a settlement may be economically and educationally prudent. In any event, boards cannot make payments and, if questioned, simply claim that they exercised their discretion.[76]

Income from School Bond Issues

As discussed in Chapter 5, school boards cannot issue bonds or borrow money unless they are expressly authorized to do so by statute. As the power to issue bonds is an extraordinary one, it may be exercised only for the express purposes set forth in an authorizing statute. The strictness with which bonding authority is construed is understandable in light of the fact that since bonds are issued prospectively, they can obligate district taxpayers for long periods of time. The strict construction given to the language of bonding statutes and the propositions that are placed before voters assures, as far as possible, that the contemplated use of bonding power and bond proceeds will be for the designated purposes.

Where a state auditor refused to register bonds, a school board unsuccessfully challenged his refusal to do so. The Supreme Court of Kansas found that since the bonds were to be used for a new roof and to replace the heating and electrical systems, but there were no structural changes to the building, they were voted on illegally because they were for repairs rather than erecting and equipping a school.[77] Conversely, the Supreme Court of Wisconsin maintained that a statute, which authorized bonding to erect or purchase a school building, was sufficiently broad to cover borrowing for remodeling because such work involved more than repairing or making minor changes to the structure.[78] In like manner, the Supreme Court of North Carolina affirmed that additions to physical facilities necessarily implied acquisition of additional land for a school.[79]

When a board issues construction bonds, questions can arise as to what legally constitutes a part of a building. The Supreme Court of Wyoming considered whether the term "building" included its equipment. In upholding the validity of a bond issue, the court noted that certain types of equipment may properly be considered parts of a building that can be purchased with their proceeds.[80] The court wrote that such equipment was limited to that which, when installed, became

---

76. *Ingram v. Boone*, 458 N.Y.S.2d 671 [8 Educ. L. Rep. 1076] (N.Y. App. Div. 1983). [Case No. 42]

77. *School Dist. No. 6, Chase County v. Robb*, 93 P.2d 905 (Kan. 1939).

78. *Cotter v. Joint School Dist. No. 3 of Village of Plum City*, 158 N.W. 80 (Wis. 1916).

79. *Lutz v. Gaston County Bd. of Educ.*, 192 S.E.2d 463 (N.C. 1972).

80. *Jewett v. School Dist. No. 25 in Fremont County*, 54 P.2d 546 (Wyo. 1936).

part of the building, such as the heating system, light fixtures, and laboratory desks, which are firmly attached to the floor. The court added that even so-called permanent equipment, which is akin to a fixture, should be placed in a building at the time of construction in order to fall within the provision of the bonding statute. Further, an appellate court in New York rejected a suit filed by taxpayers who claimed that a bond proposal's inclusion of computers as equipment in renovated buildings violated constitutional provisions restricting indebtedness of local subdivisions.[81] The court affirmed that state laws prescribing a ten-year period of probable usefulness for computer systems did not prohibit the board from including computers as equipment within the bond proposal.

Occasionally, as school boards seek to utilize bond funds, they must do so in ways that deviate from the wording of bonding propositions. In the first of two cases from Tennessee, the state supreme court affirmed that bond money spent constructing a high school gymnasium that elementary school children used on a regular basis, especially during inclement weather, did not render the board's action illegal.[82] The court deemed that the use of the facility did not change its essential character as a gymnasium. Additionally, when a board realized that its cost estimates for a project were too low, and used the funds for only part of the proposed improvements, an appellate court in Tennessee upheld its action.[83] The court indicated that the board had the authority to spend funds as it judged best under the circumstances. An appellate court in Oklahoma agreed that a school board did not have to spend bond proceeds in the precise amounts allocated to each specific project.[84] The court asserted that the board could use the funds on projects that were outlined in bond issue statements as long as the funds were spent in a manner consistent with the bond issue.

Income from School Activities

Based on their general authority to direct school activities, boards have the power and responsibility to control the income that these activities generate. Insofar as the courts treat such income as school funds, a court in Pennsylvania reiterated the general rule that these monies should be deposited, dispersed, and audited in the same manner as funds derived from taxation or other sources.[85] In a second case from Pennsylvania, an appellate court upheld the validity of a law subjecting school activity funds to an audit.[86] The court recognized that if, as here, funds arise from the use of school property and the services of board personnel, they are district funds that must be deposited in the board's official account and are subject to audit.

81. *Friedman v. Board of Educ. of East Ramapo Cent. School Dist.*, 686 N.Y.S.2d 84 [133 Educ. L. Rep. 565] (N.Y. App. Div. 1999).

82. *Moody v. Williamson County*, 371 S.W.2d 454 (Tenn.1963).

83. *State v. Peacock*, 405 S.W.2d 478 (Tenn. Ct. App. 1965).

84. *State ex rel. Howard v. Crawford*, 16 P.3d 473 [150 Educ. L. Rep. 496] (Okla. Civ. App. 2000), *cert. denied* (2000).

85. *In re German Township School Directors*, 46 Pa. D. & C. 562 (Com. Pl.1943). [Case No. 43]

86. *Petition of Auditors of Hatfield Township School Dist.*, 54 A.2d 833 (Pa. Super. Ct. 1947).

In a dispute primarily over an ousted board member's possible illegal use of funds that were raised via the use of vending machines, the Supreme Court of Kentucky addressed the nature of school activities funds.[87] The court rejected the former board member's arguments that the monies raised by the machines were not school funds because they were raised by children for various projects, that they belonged to various classes or school-related organizations, and that they were kept separate from tax money. In ordering the board member's removal, the court declared that the money from the vending machines was school funds subject to the board's full control.

A more recent case from Texas illustrates how school activity funds still generate litigation. The Fifth Circuit determined that since a principal who resigned in the face of an accusation that she mismanaged school activities funds had not presented a matter of public concern in her letter to the board, she could not file suit for defamation.[88] The important point to be gleaned from this case is that although not directly discussing the matter, the court did not question the principle that the funds were public monies.

Insofar as school activity funds are school property, educators have no authority to administer or dispose of these monies in a manner not specified by law. To this end, questions can arise as to whether administrators can maintain funds that are not under board control and, if so, what accounting is necessary. In a complex case, taxpayers sought to have a principal account for monies that students and high school teachers voluntarily raised, with no input from the board, over four years to pay for items such as athletic equipment and choir robes. The principal exercised sole control over the unaudited funds. When the case first reached the Supreme Court of South Carolina, it remanded for a consideration of whether the principal made a proper accounting and whether there was, in fact, a shortage.[89] The court avoided the question of the legal status of the fund since the board neither raised nor administered it directly or indirectly. Later, the same court affirmed that the taxpayers did not present any issues entitling them to relief.[90] Although conceding that the principal's system of record keeping left much to be desired, the court was of the opinion that nothing in the record suggested that he personally profited from the funds entrusted to his care and no one was financially damaged as a result of his manner of handling the monies.

Income from Gifts

School boards can generally accept gifts for any purposes within their power. When gifts are conveyed by wills, boards may not receive funds or property for designated purposes that they are barred from

87. *Commonwealth ex rel. Breckinridge v. Collins*, 379 S.W.2d 436 (Ky.1964).

88. *Bradshaw v. Pittsburg Indep. School Dist.*, 207 F.3d 814 [143 Educ. L. Rep. 65] (5th Cir. 2000).

89. *Betterson v. Stewart*, 121 S.E.2d 102 (S.C. 1961).

90. *Betterson v. Stewart*, 140 S.E.2d 482 (S.C. 1965).

carrying out by impracticality, impossibility, or illegality. If a situation is one of pure impossibility, such as an award for the highest grade in a subject that is no longer taught, the common law of testamentary charitable trusts, also known as the doctrine of *cy pres*, permits a court to designate another use for the funds as long as it is close to the one specified by the testator.

If a gift would result in a board's being engaged in an illegality, such as where a trust discriminated based on gender and religion,[91] a court may be able to reform it by eliminating the offending restriction. Of prime judicial concern is to execute a testator's general charitable intent. If this can be carried out simply by naming another administrator for a will, a court can apply the doctrine of deviation to effect a change in the administrative terms of the trust. Such a situation would arise not only if a board was legally unable to serve as trustee but also if it were unwilling to do so for policy reasons.[92]

Uses of School Property

Uses in General

School buildings are state property that do not belong to local boards even if they are paid for solely by local funds.[93] This is a point that taxpayers may have difficulty understanding since they are typically inclined to treat schools as "theirs" insofar as they were financed with "their" money. Even though buildings are built for educational purposes, groups often use them for a variety of non-school activities. As might have been anticipated, whether and the extent to which school buildings may be used for non-school purposes has been widely litigated. Placing constitutional considerations aside for a moment, since legislative oversight for use of local school buildings is fairly scarce, "the care, custody, and control of all school property is the responsibility"[94] of local boards.

Permissible Uses and Conditions of Use

School buildings can be used for activities open to parents and the general public, even if officials charge fees for shows.[95] While uncertainty arises when activities are not school-connected, if boards allow their facilities to be used in such a manner, they must be careful to ensure

91. *In re Certain Scholarship Funds*, 575 A.2d 1325 [61 Educ. L. Rep. 149] (N.H. 1990).

92. *Matter of Estate of Wilson*, 465 N.Y.S.2d 900 [13 Educ. L. Rep. 110] (N.Y. 1983).

93. *See, e.g., Pritchett v. County Bd. of School Trustees*, 125 N.E.2d 476 (Ill. 1955); *Bellevue School Dist. No. 405 v. Brazier Const. Co.*, 675 P.2d 232 [15 Educ. L. Rep. 995] (Wash. 1984), *reconsideration granted*, 680 P.2d 40 [17 Educ. L. Rep. 413] (Wash. 1984), *and adhered to on reh'g*, 691 P.2d 178 [21 Educ. L. Rep. 734] (Wash. 1984).

94. *Goldes v. City of N.Y.*, 797 N.Y.S.2d 102, 103 [199 Educ. L. Rep. 371] (N.Y. App. Div. 2005) (rejecting a claim of liability against a city in a personal injury action). *See also Lloyd v. Grella*, 611 N.Y.S.2d 799 [90 Educ. L. Rep. 1202] (N.Y. 1994).

95. *Beard v. Board of Educ. of N. Summit School Dist.*, 16 P.2d 900 (Utah 1932).

that activities neither interfere with school programs nor damage buildings.[96]

Other than their use as polling places, statutes rarely interfere with board discretion relating to the use of school buildings for non-school purposes. In one case dealing with a school's use as a polling place, the Eighth Circuit affirmed that officials did not violate the First Amendment rights of individuals who sought to collect signatures on an initiative petition drive as voting took place at a school in Missouri.[97] The court agreed that the response of school officials in calling the police, who arrested the plaintiffs for refusing to leave, was reasonable and not content-based in light of their safety concerns and disruption coupled with the fact that the petition circulators made no effort to seek or receive permission to be on school property.

California has long gone further than other states in providing statutory guidance for non-school use of buildings. State law created civic centers, as designated public fora, at all public school facilities and grounds that permit community groups to meet to discuss subjects that appeal to their educational, political, economic, artistic, and moral interests.[98] Pursuant to this statute, local boards must adopt reasonable rules dealing with the use of facilities, as long as such use does not interfere with regular school purposes.

In apparently the earliest case under this statute, an appellate court in California upheld a board's authority to permit a social dance in a school auditorium.[99] Other cases before the Supreme Court of California permitted boards to exclude a speaker who created a disturbance in other locations[100] and prospective users who refused to abide by a rule that required them to stipulate that they did not intend to put the property to an illegal use.[101] Conversely, where a speaker wished to address the question of peace, the court rejected a board's claim that doing so would have violated its prohibited use of school buildings for sectarian, political, or partisan purposes.[102] The same court later struck down the statutory requirement that those who applied for permission to use school buildings had to submit statements that they did not advocate the violent overthrow of the government and their groups were neither Communists nor Communist-front organizations.[103]

Courts are reluctant to permit private plaintiffs with similar interests to interfere with school uses. For example, the Supreme Court of Kentucky rejected the claim of the owner of a private music hall that a

96. *Merryman v. School Dist. No. 16*, 5 P.2d 267 (Wyo. 1931).

97. *Embry v. Lewis*, 215 F.3d 884 [145 Educ. L. Rep. 227] (8th Cir. 2000), *reh'g and reh'g en banc denied* (2000).

98. CAL. EDUC. CODE § 38131. *See also* 76 Op. Atty. Gen. 52, 4–20–93.

99. *McClure v. Board of Educ. of City of Visalia*, 176 P. 711 (Cal. Ct. App. 1918).

100. *Payroll Guarantee Ass'n v. Board of Educ.*, 163 P.2d 433 (Cal. 1945).

101. *American Civil Liberties Union of S. Cal. v. Board of Educ. of City of Los Angeles*, 379 P.2d 4 (Cal. 1963).

102. *Goodman v. Board of Educ. of San Francisco*, 120 P.2d 665 (Cal.App. 1941).

103. *American Civil Liberties Union of S. Cal. v. Board of Educ. of City of Los Angeles*, 359 P.2d 45 (Cal. 1961), *cert. denied*, 368 U.S. 819, 82 S.Ct. 34, 7 L.Ed.2d 25 (1961).

board policy, which permitted a local civic organization to rent its gymnasium when not being used for school purposes, had an adverse impact on his business.[104] The court affirmed that the policy was constitutional insofar as it was adopted pursuant to a statute. In addition, the Supreme Court of North Carolina affirmed that a suit by private day care providers, where a board opened an after-school program of its own for children who were left without supervision at the end of the school day and lasted until their parents came home, was without merit. In reasoning that the board charged parents a nominal fee but covered the costs of the school's use and volunteers conducted the program, the court agreed that the program met the constitutional requirement that all expenditures of tax dollars be for public purposes since the program's intent was to further educational achievement of students.[105]

In the first of two cases from the Eighth Circuit that involved dancing, parents sought to have a board in Arkansas sponsor more than the two dances a year that it permitted. The court rejected the parents' claim that dancing should have been treated as a form of expression entitled to First Amendment protection.[106] In refusing to interpret the First Amendment as covering social or recreational dancing, as opposed to dance before an audience as an art form, the court explained that the board had the discretion to permit its facilities to be used as it saw fit. In the second case, the court was unwilling to disturb a long-standing board rule in Missouri that prohibited schools from being used for dances.[107] Even though the board acted in response to a large segment of the community, which opposed social dancing on religious grounds, the court affirmed that the policy did not violate the Establishment Clause since officials were free to use the facilities as they deemed appropriate.

As much discretion as boards have to establish use policies, school employees have no corresponding right to conduct unapproved meetings or use facilities without getting permission from boards. Insofar as disputes in this regard, which typically involve constitutional questions, tend to overlap with litigation that deals with differentiating among users, the final cases in this section serve as a segue to the next part of this chapter.

The Seventh Circuit, in a case from Indiana, affirmed that pursuant to a board policy that officials consistently applied to prohibit the use of school facilities for religious activity, teachers did not have a right to conduct regularly scheduled prayer meetings for themselves before students arrived for class.[108] The court remarked that its rationale was not related to costs of electricity and maintenance or to the content of the

104. *Hall v. Shelby County Bd. of Educ.*, 472 S.W.2d 489 (Ky. 1971).

105. *Kiddie Korner Day Schools v. Charlotte–Mecklenburg Bd. of Educ.*, 285 S.E.2d 110 [1 Educ. L. Rep. 972] (N.C.App. 1981).

106. *Jarman v. Williams*, 753 F.2d 76 [22 Educ. L. Rep. 737] (8th Cir.1985).

107. *Clayton by Clayton v. Place*, 884 F.2d 376 [55 Educ. L. Rep. 920] (8th Cir. 1989), *reh'g denied*, 889 F.2d 192 (8th Cir. 1989), *cert. denied*, 494 U.S. 1081, 110 S.Ct. 1811, 108 L.Ed.2d 942 (1990).

108. *May v. Evansville–Vanderburgh School Corp.*, 787 F.2d 1105 [31 Educ. L. Rep. 727] (7th Cir.1986).

meetings. Rather, the court emphasized the board's concern that permitting such meetings to take place could have caused controversies that were not related to work. The court concluded that if some groups were permitted to meet, the board could not bar others under the freedom of speech clause.

In the first of four cases involving unions, *Perry Education Association v. Perry Local Educators' Association*,[109] the Supreme Court decreed that a board can grant access to its intra-school system mail facilities to the exclusive bargaining representative of teachers while barring use by a rival union. In a like dispute, the Seventh Circuit rejected a challenge from school board candidates in Illinois who claimed that a board violated their rights by permitting the union representing its teachers to use its internal mail system to communicate with members about a board election.[110] The court affirmed that since the policy of allowing the union to use the mail system was viewpoint neutral and reasonable, it did not violate the First Amendment.[111] Also, the Supreme Court of Kansas affirmed that a school board's denial of access to its mail system to an alternative teachers' association-union to distribute brochures through the system's internal mail system did not violate the First Amendment. Previously, where a statute in Maryland permitted boards to deny access to school property to those lacking lawful business there, the Fourth Circuit affirmed that a union representative could be barred from a school parking lot.[112] The court agreed that even though his presence was not disruptive, the board was free to exclude the representative since officials deemed that his solicitations were not related to the education of students and the parking lot had not become a public forum.

Differentiating Among Uses and Users

Pursuant to judicial interpretation of the Free Speech Clause of the First Amendment, there are three different fora where speech occurs.[113] Under the first category, governmental power to regulate expression is most restricted on public properties that are traditional public forums such as parks, streets, and sidewalks. In such fora, a content-based exclusion can be enforced only if it is narrowly drawn to effectuate a compelling state interest. Narrowly tailored content-neutral regulations as to time, place, and manner of expression can be enforced, but only if the governmental interest is significant and alternative channels of communication are open.

109. 460 U.S. 37, 103 S.Ct. 948, 74 L.Ed.2d 794 [9 Educ. L. Rep. 23] (1983).

110. *Davidson v. Community Consol. School Dist. 181*, 130 F.3d 265 [122 Educ. L. Rep. 583] (7th Cir. 1997).

111. *Unified School Dist. No. 233 Johnson County v. Kansas Ass'n of Am. Educators*, 64 P.3d 372 [174 Educ. L. Rep. 419] (Kan. 2003).

112. *Grattan v. Board of School Commr's of Baltimore City*, 805 F.2d 1160 [36 Educ. L. Rep. 56] (4th Cir. 1986).

113. For a discussion of forum analysis, see *Perry Educ. Ass'n v. Perry Local Educators' Ass'n*, 460 U.S. 37, 103 S.Ct. 948, 74 L.Ed.2d 794 [9 Educ. L. Rep. 23] (1983); *Hazelwood School Dist. v. Kuhlmeier*, 484 U.S. 260, 108 S.Ct. 562, 98 L.Ed.2d 592 [43 Educ. L. Rep. 515] (1988). [Case No 113]

The second category of public property is that which the state has opened for public use as a place for expressive activity. A subcategory of such a designated public forum is the limited public forum that a governmental unit opens for discussion of certain subjects or to certain classes of speakers either by express policy or by substantial practice. If there is a limited public forum, First Amendment protections provided to traditional public forums apply, but only to entities of a character similar to those the government admits to the forum. The government is not indefinitely bound to retain the open nature of a limited forum.

A non-public forum, the third category of public property, is a place that is not ordinarily set aside for public communication such as a classroom.[114] In this setting the government can enforce regulations to reserve the forum for its intended purposes, communicative or otherwise, as long as the rules are reasonable and not intended to suppress expression since public officials oppose a viewpoint.[115] During the class day, a school is generally a non-public forum. Once the class day is over, the type of forum that a school becomes depends on board policy and practice.

Given the place of religion in American life, it is not surprising that many suits have been litigated when speech is religious in nature. In *Heffron v. International Society for Krishna Consciousness*, the Supreme Court refused to accord religious organizations "rights to communicate . . . superior to those of other organizations having social, political, or other ideological messages to proselytize."[116] The court thus rejected the religious group's challenge to a regulation of a state fair in Minnesota, which required all solicitations, sales, and/or distributions of material to be from fixed locations.

Six months later, the Court reached a different result after religious speech received less protection than other forms of speech. In *Widmar v. Vincent*,[117] (*Widmar*) the Court posited that officials at the University of Missouri essentially created a forum for student use by making facilities available to over one hundred registered student organizations. The Court was of the view that officials could not bar a student organization that wished to conduct religious meetings. As discussed more fully in Chapter 2, the Court distinguished *Widmar* from cases involving public schools on the bases that this was a forum available to many diverse groups and that university students are less impressionable than young children.

Many pre-*Widmar* cases involving access to school property by outside groups upheld prohibitions against religious use. Whether cases remain valid is cloudy because judicial opinions often did not record all

---

114. *See, e.g., Walz ex rel. Walz v. Egg Harbor Township Bd. of Educ.*, 342 F.3d 271 [180 Educ. L. Rep. 115] (3d Cir. 2003), *cert. denied*, 541 U.S. 936, 124 S.Ct. 1658, 158 L.Ed.2d 356 (2004).

115. *See, e.g., Cornelius v. NAACP Legal Defense and Educ. Fund*, 473 U.S. 788, 105 S.Ct. 3439, 87 L.Ed.2d 567 (1985).

116. 452 U.S. 640, 652–53, 101 S.Ct. 2559, 69 L.Ed.2d 298 (1981).

117. 454 U.S. 263, 102 S.Ct. 269, 70 L.Ed.2d 440 [1 Educ. L. Rep. 13] (1981).

of the facts or respond to some arguments that were important for the disposition of future cases. For instance, the Supreme Court of Pennsylvania upheld a rule that facilities could not be used for any religious or sectarian purpose.[118] The court rejected a claim that a board violated equal protection by permitting nonreligious uses and that its discretionary power to allow use of school facilities had to be exercised in full or not at all.

In the first post-*Widmar* case, the federal trial court in Kansas entered a judgment in favor of a church that was denied occasional use of school facilities for religious services. The board's policy was that facilities were available for recognized community organizations whose activities were of general interest to the community and who used the building for community purposes. Where the facilities were used by an array of groups, and there were no guidelines to distinguish between religious and non-religious meetings, the court concluded that "[h]aving created a public forum, [the board] cannot exclude [the church group] from the forum because of the religious content of [the church group's] intended speech unless such exclusion is justified under applicable constitutional case law."[119]

Acting in large part in response to *Widmar*, Congress enacted the Equal Access Act (EAA).[120] According to the EAA, any public secondary school that receives federal financial assistance, and that permits one or more noncurriculum-related student groups to meet on school premises during noninstructional time, cannot withhold such a privilege on the basis of the religious, political, philosophical, or other content of the speech at such meetings.

In *Board of Education of Westside Community Schools v. Mergens,*[121] a case from Nebraska, the Court upheld the EAA. Relying on statutory interpretation rather than reaching the constitutional question, the Court was convinced that Congress thought that most high school students could recognize that allowing a religious club to function in school does not imply endorsement of religion. The Court's failure to address the constitutional dimensions of the EAA has led to a line of cases that treat religious expression as a kind of hybrid wherein it protects a religious group's right to express its opinion as a form of free speech.[122]

Even after *Mergens*, it is clear that the EAA does not protect speech that is otherwise unlawful. In such a case, the Ninth Circuit held that

118. *McKnight v. Board of Pub. Educ.*, 76 A.2d 207 (Pa.1950), *appeal dismissed*, 341 U.S. 913, 71 S.Ct. 737, 95 L.Ed. 1349 (1951).

119. *Country Hills Christian Church v. Unified School Dist. No. 512, Johnson County, State of Ks.*, 560 F.Supp. 1207, 1219 [10 Educ. L. Rep. 1006] (D. Kan.1983). For a similar result, *see Grace Bible Fellowship v. Maine School Admin. Dist. No. 5*, 941 F.2d 45 [69 Educ. L. Rep. 210] (1st Cir.1991).

120. 20 U.S.C.A. §§ 4071 *et seq.* This statute is in the appendix.

121. 496 U.S. 226, 110 S.Ct. 2356, 110 L.Ed.2d 191 [60 Educ. L. Rep. 320] (1990). [Case No. 9]

122. *See, e.g., Rosenberger v. Rectors and Visitors of Univ. of Va.*, 515 U.S. 819, 115 S.Ct. 2510, 132 L.Ed.2d 700 [101 Educ. L. Rep. 552] (1995).

the Act did not encompass a violation of a state constitutional church-state restriction greater than that in the Establishment Clause.[123] The panel emphasized the Supreme Court's determination that the EAA had to be read as effectuating a broad Congressional purpose and so remained in effect, thereby preempting state law. Other courts have also looked beyond written policies to conduct and actions in evaluating whether a forum is limited and, if so, to what subjects and/or classes of participants. Thus, when a school auditorium was used for some fund-raising activities and for at least one Christmas program, the Second Circuit required access for another religious activity.[124]

The Supreme Court, in a rare unanimous judgment in *Lamb's Chapel v. Center Moriches Union Free School District,*[125] reversed in favor of a religious group in New York. In a hybrid situation wherein it treated religious speech as a form of free speech, the Court essentially extended *Mergens'* rationale albeit not under the EAA. The Court ascertained that since the board created a limited open forum, it violated the group's free speech rights by engaging in viewpoint discrimination. In rejecting so-called viewpoint discrimination, the Court pointed out that a board, which had a policy of allowing its facilities to be used for social, civic, and recreational meetings and entertainment when school was not in session, could not bar a church group from using them to show a six-part film series on family values from the Christian point of view. In relying on the Free Speech Clause, the Court observed that school officials misapplied a board rule, based on a state statute, which prohibited religious use of the property. The Court added that absent a restriction on the subject matter of the films, the board could not erect a bar based on the viewpoint to be expressed about that subject matter.[126]

Eight years later, a dispute arose when officials in another school system in New York refused to permit a non-school sponsored club to meet during non-class hours so that members and moderators could discuss child-rearing along with character and moral development from a religious perspective. School officials permitted other youth groups to meet because even though they addressed similar topics, they did so from secular perspectives. The Supreme Court agreed to hear an appeal to resolve a split in the lower courts since the Eighth Circuit[127] had upheld the right of the same kind of club in Missouri to use school facilities for its meetings.

---

123. *Garnett v. Renton School Dist. No. 403*, 987 F.2d 641 [81 Educ. L. Rep. 704] (9th Cir. 1993), *cert. denied*, 510 U.S. 819, 114 S.Ct. 72, 126 L.Ed.2d 41 (1993), *appeal after remand*, 21 F.3d 1113 [91 Educ. L. Rep. 31] (9th Cir. 1994), *on remand*, 1994 WL 555397 (W.D. Wash. 1994) (granting a declaratory judgment and awarding attorney fees to the plaintiffs).

124. *Travis v. Owego–Apalachin School Dist.*, 927 F.2d 688 [66 Educ. L. Rep. 75] (2d Cir.1991).

125. 508 U.S. 384, 113 S.Ct. 2141, 124 L.Ed.2d 352 [83 Educ. L. Rep. 30] (1993),

on remand, 17 F.3d 1425 [89 Educ. L. Rep. 783] (2d Cir. 1994). [Case No. 44]

126. See also *Rosenberger v. Rector and Visitors of Univ. of Va.*, 515 U.S. 819, 115 S.Ct. 2510, 132 L.Ed.2d 700 [101 Educ. L. Rep. 552] (1995) (treating religious expression as a kind of hybrid, protecting a religious group's right to express its opinion as a form of free speech).

127. *Good News/Good Sports Club v. School Dist. of the City of Ladue*, 28 F.3d 1501 [92 Educ. L. Rep. 1148] (8th Cir.1994), *cert. denied*, 515 U.S. 1173, 115 S.Ct. 2640, 132 L.Ed.2d 878 (1995).

In *Good News Club v. Milford Central School*,[128] the Supreme Court reversed in favor of the club.[129] The Court decided not only that the board violated the club's rights to free speech by engaging in impermissible viewpoint discrimination in refusing to permit it to use school facilities for its meetings, which were not worship services, but also that such a restriction was not justified by fears of violating the Establishment Clause.[130] A year later, in a long-running suit, the Second Circuit affirmed an order that enjoined a board from enforcing a policy which excluded community groups from renting school buildings for religious worship and religious instruction.[131] The court agreed that the plaintiffs demonstrated the clear or substantial likelihood of success on the merits of their claim that the denial of their request to use the facilities would have violated both their First Amendment free speech and religious rights.[132]

A recent case arose in Michigan where an appellate court affirmed the rejection of a challenge filed by an atheist father and his son who objected to a board's permitting the Boy Scouts to use a school's facilities.[133] The court ruled that the board's allowing the Boy Scouts to distribute their literature and collect their communications during school hours, and to hang posters in school hallways, did not implicate the state constitution's Establishment Clause since a wide array of organizations were allowed to display posters and to distribute literature to students as long as those organizations satisfied neutral-qualifying criteria. The court asserted that the board's actions did not denote the group's religious aspect and neither school officials nor the board compelled students to take literature or incorporated it into the curriculum. Chapter 2 explores issues surrounding access to school facilities by religious groups in greater detail while Chapter 13 examines other questions that have arisen under the EAA.

Moving away from religious uses, while school officials can close the door to all outside organizations, based on equal protection, once they make facilities available, they must treat all similar groups similarly. To this end, a board can deny a group, or individual,[134] access to its facilities in the face of evidence of a clear and present danger and/or that public

128. 533 U.S. 98, 121 S.Ct. 2093, 150 L.Ed.2d 151 [154 Educ. L. Rep. 45] (2001). [Case No 13]

129. For an earlier, similar ruling involving the Boy Scouts, *see Sherman v. Community Consol. School Dist. 21 of Wheeling Township*, 8 F.3d 1160 [87 Educ. L. Rep. 57] (7th Cir.1993), *cert. denied*, 511 U.S. 1110, 114 S.Ct. 2109, 128 L.Ed.2d 669 (1994).

130. For a similar result in a long-ranging dispute, *see Bronx Household of Faith v. Board of Educ. of the City of N.Y.*, 226 F.Supp. 401 [171 Educ. L. Rep. 479] (S.D.N.Y. 2002).

131. *Bronx Household of Faith v. Board of Educ. of City of N.Y.*, 331 F.3d 342 [177 Educ. L. Rep. 108] (2d Cir. 2003).

132. *See also Culbertson v. Oakridge School Dist. No. 76*, 258 F.3d 1061 [155 Educ. L. Rep. 1085] (9th Cir. 2001); *Prince v. Jacoby*, 303 F.3d 1074 [169 Educ. L. Rep. 85] (9th Cir. 2002), *cert. denied*, 540 U.S. 813, 124 S.Ct. 62, 157 L.Ed.2d 27 (2003).

133. *Scalise v. Boy Scouts of Am.*, 692 N.W.2d 858 [195 Educ. L. Rep. 961] (Mich. Ct. App. 2005), *appeal denied*, 700 N.W.2d 360 (Mich. 2005).

134. *See, e.g., In re Joseph F.*, 102 Cal. Rptr.2d 641 [149 Educ. L. Rep. 835] (Cal. Ct. App. 2000) (denying a hostile and belligerent student access to school).

disorder[135] and damage to the building would have resulted from a proposed use. However, a board cannot bar an organization simply because it, or a part of the public, might be hostile to a group's opinions as long as a program is not unlawful per se.[136] In an older case that remains relevant, the Court of Appeals of New York applied these principles when a school board sought to bar one of a series of concerts from taking place at its facilities since it was to feature a controversial performer who was critical of American foreign policy.[137] Even though the scheduled date for the concert had passed, the court held that the board impermissibly cancelled it because officials could not prohibit the singer from appearing due to their having disagreed with his views.

Statutes or ordinances preventing loitering on school grounds or in the vicinity of school buildings are increasingly common. Rules of this type are ordinarily acceptable as long as they are not overly vague or restrictive. In one such case, parents and their son sued school officials in Illinois, claiming that their disciplining him for breaking an anti-loitering rule violated his rights to free speech, assembly, and due process and that it was unconstitutionally vague.[138] The Seventh Circuit affirmed a dismissal in favor of school officials in acknowledging both that the use of the term "loitering" in the rule did not render it unconstitutionally vague and that it did not violate his First Amendment guarantees of free speech and free assembly.

As important as parental input in the education of their children is, parents must observe limits when at school facilities. One such dispute involved a non-custodial father in Virginia who was barred from school facilities based on his pattern of verbal abuse and threatening behavior toward officials after his son was not selected for a high school basketball team. The Fourth Circuit affirmed that the father's suit was properly dismissed as insubstantial and frivolous.[139] In another case, a federal trial court in Texas granted a board's motion for summary judgment where a mother sought unauthorized access to monitor her son's class.[140] The court contended that officials did not deny the mother the right to voice her complaints about how her son was being treated when they asked her to leave the building since her presence was disruptive in her child's classroom. Moreover, the Seventh Circuit affirmed that part of a

---

135. *See, e.g., Local Organizing Comm., Denver Chapter, Million Man March v. Cook,* 922 F.Supp. 1494 [109 Educ. L. Rep. 223] (D. Colo. 1996); *Reeves v. Rocklin Unified School Dist.,* 135 Cal.Rptr.2d 213 [177 Educ. L. Rep. 414] (Cal. Ct. App. 2003).

136. *See, e.g., East High Gay/Straight Alliance v. Board of Educ.,* 81 F.Supp.2d 1166 [141 Educ. L. Rep. 776] (D.Utah 1999), 81 F.Supp.2d 1199 [141 Educ. L. Rep. 809] (D.Utah 1999); *East High School Prism Club v. Seidel,* 95 F.Supp.2d 1239 [144 Educ. L. Rep. 260] (D.Utah 2000); *Colin ex rel. Colin v. Orange Unified School Dist.,* 83 F.Supp.2d 1135 [142 Educ. L. Rep. 138] (C.D.Cal.2000) (agreeing that school

officials could not deny clubs sponsored by gay and lesbian students the use of school facilities under the EAA).

137. *East Meadow Community Concerts Ass'n v. Board of Educ.,* 272 N.Y.S.2d 341 (1966). [Case No. 45].

138. *Wiemerslage Through Wiemerslage v. Maine Township High School Dist. 207,* 29 F.3d 1149 [93 Educ. L. Rep. 64] (7th Cir. 1994).

139. *Lovern v. Edwards,* 190 F.3d 648 [138 Educ. L. Rep. 118] (4th Cir. 1999).

140. *Ryans v. Gresham,* 6 F.Supp.2d 595 [127 Educ. L. Rep. 862] (E.D. Tex. 1998).

judgment that a divorced non-custodial father in Illinois did not have a constitutional right to be present on school grounds to monitor the school's protection of his children from bullies.[141] The court specified that the father's interests were outweighed by those of the state, including the need of school officials to have autonomy. At the same time, the court reinstated that part of the father's claim which alleged that officials discriminated against him and other non-custodial parents.

Disposal of Property

Insofar as a board's implied power to use property does not extend to its disposal, this subject is typically covered by statute.[142] Even so, disputes arise where statutory language over the disposal of unneeded school buildings is unclear.[143] If a statute does not address property disposal, courts do not interfere with board discretion unless it is manifestly abused[144] and they are satisfied that officials acted in a school system's best interest.[145] At least one court agreed that a board could even sell unwanted property on an installment, rather than a cash, basis in thinking that it would have been unrealistic to expect developers to mortgage vacant lands while borrowing money for construction.[146] Moreover, a board's authority to manage and control its schools does not imply the power to sell or give away property. To this end, boards cannot, in effect, give away real estate by leasing it for a nominal sum, even for a worthy cause such as leasing property to a community hospital for one dollar a year.[147]

Not all states agree on the role of district residents when a board seeks to dispose of real property. On the one hand, the Supreme Court of Iowa emphasized the mandatory nature of statutes covering disposal of school property when it voided an attempted sale that was not in strict compliance with a statute that permitted boards to dispose of property valued up to a set amount without a vote of the residents.[148] On the other hand, the Supreme Court of Virginia struck down a statute that required boards which wished to sell property to obtain a majority of votes from residents in a referendum, as an unlawful delegation of power to the electorate.[149]

141. *Crowley v. McKinney*, 400 F.3d 965 [196 Educ. L. Rep. 50] (7th Cir. 2005).

142. *See, e.g., Whiteside v. Cherokee County School Dist. No. One*, 428 S.E.2d 886 [82 Educ. L. Rep. 270] (S.C. 1993); *Western Area Business and Civic Club v. Duluth School Bd. Indep. Dist. No. 709*, 324 N.W.2d 361 [6 Educ. L. Rep. 808] (Minn. 1982).

143. *Ross v. Wilson*, 308 N.Y. 605 (N.Y. 1955). [Case No. 46]

144. Merely filing a suit seeking to enjoin a school closing does not prevent a board from selling the physical plant. *See Laurales v. Desha County School Dist. No. 4 of Snowlake*, 632 F.2d 72 (8th Cir.1980).

145. *Veal v. Smith*, 146 S.E.2d 751 (Ga. 1966).

146. *Singer Architectural Servs. Co. v. Doyle*, 254 N.W.2d 587 (Mich. Ct. App. 1977).

147. *Prescott Community Hosp. Comm'n v. Prescott School Dist.*, 115 P.2d 160 (Ariz. 1941).

148. *Unification Church v. Clay Cent. Sch. Dist.*, 253 N.W.2d 579 (Iowa 1977). *See also Davis v. Board of Educ. of Hewlett–Woodmere Union Free School Dist.*, 509 N.Y.S.2d 612 [36 Educ. L. Rep. 854] (N.Y. App. Div. 1986).

149. *Howard v. School Bd. of Alleghany County*, 122 S.E.2d 891 (Va. 1961).

Courts also disagree on when a building is no longer used for school purposes. For example, the Supreme Court of North Dakota indicated that a building where classes were no longer conducted still served school purposes and was not subject to reverter to the original grantor since it was used to store equipment and supplies.[150] Similarly, an appellate court in Illinois affirmed that a former school campus was still district property subject to state school, rather than county, building codes even though the board rented it out to private entities which ran before and after-school programs there.[151] Insofar as schools also used the gymnasium about twice per month and officials stored property there, the court noted that these actions kept the building under the state standards. Conversely, an appellate court in Texas contended that a building was no longer reserved "for school purposes only" when a board leased it to a city to use as a recreation center.[152] In returning the property to the original grantor, the court rejected the board's argument that it leased the building to prevent vandalism and keep it in good repair for eventual reopening as a school by focusing on language in the operative deed that required it to be used "for school purposes only."

[Case No. 40] Power of Board to Acquire Land for Off–Street Parking

IN RE SCHOOL DISTRICT OF PITTSBURGH

Supreme Court of Pennsylvania, 1968.
244 A.2d 42.

EAGEN, JUSTICE.

On June 21, 1966, the Board of Public Education of the School District of Pittsburgh [hereinafter Board] passed a resolution authorizing the filing of declarations of taking for the involved properties [primarily to provide parking facilities at the School Administration Building].... The lower court sustained the preliminary objections solely because it concluded that the Board's condemnation power does not extend to the acquisition of land for parking facilities for administrative employees.

The Board's condemnation power flows from the Act of March 10, 1949, P.L. 30, Art. VII, 24 P.S. § 7–701 *et seq*. Section 703, 24 P.S. § 7–703 provides:

> In order to comply with the provisions of this act, and subject to the conditions thereof, the board of school directors of each district is hereby vested with the necessary power and authority to acquire, in the name of the district, by purchase, lease, gift, devise, agreement, condemnation, or otherwise, any and all such real estate ... as the

---

150. *Ballantyne v. Nedrose Pub. School Dist. No. 4, Ward County*, 177 N.W.2d 551 (N.D. 1970).

151. *County of Lake v. Board of Educ. of Lake Bluff School Dist. No. 65*, 761

N.E.2d 163 [161 Educ. L. Rep. 574] (Ill. App. Ct. 2001).

152. *Sewell v. Dallas Indep. School Dist.*, 727 S.W.2d 586, 587 [38 Educ. L. Rep. 1300] (Tex. App. Ct.1987).

board of school directors may deem necessary to furnish suitable sites for proper school purposes for said district . . .

Section 721, 24 P.S. § 7–721 provides:

> Whenever the board of school directors of any district cannot agree on the terms of its purchase with the owner or owners of any real estate that the board has selected for school purposes, such board of school directors, after having decided upon the amount and location thereof may enter upon, take possession of, and occupy such land as it may have selected for school purposes, whether vacant or occupied, and designate and mark the boundary lines thereof, and thereafter may use the same for school purposes according to the provisions of this act. . . .

The precise issue presented here is whether the lower court correctly determined that the acquisition of land for parking facilities for employees and visitors to the School Administration Building is not a "proper school purpose" within the meaning of the Act of March 10, 1949, supra.

In interpreting the statute we must, of course, bear in mind that provisions conferring the power of eminent domain must be strictly construed. Strict construction does not require, however, that a statute be construed as narrowly as possible, or that it be construed so literally and without common sense that its obvious intent is frustrated.

A close examination of Section 703 of March 10, 1949, supra, indicates that the power and authority of the Board to acquire real estate is limited to acquisition "for proper school purposes" not only when the acquisition is by condemnation, but also when it is by "purchase, lease, gift, devise, agreement . . . or otherwise." Thus, if the Board cannot condemn real estate for the purpose of using it as a parking lot, it apparently cannot lease, purchase or otherwise acquire real estate for parking purposes. To deny the Board this power is serious not only because off street parking usually is desirable for buildings located in congested urban areas, but also because this Court has held that a school board may be compelled to comply with a zoning ordinance requiring provision for off street parking in the erection of a new building.

In approaching the question of whether or not the legislature intended to deny the Board this power, it is significant that the phrase "proper school purposes" in Section 703 of the Act of March 10, 1949, supra, replaced the phrase "school buildings and playgrounds" in Section 602 of the Act of May 18, 1911, P.L. 309. This substitution, fairly read, not only left the Board's power less precisely defined, but also broadened it somewhat. Thus the acquisition of a building to be used solely for administration undoubtedly is for a proper school purpose although an administration building may not be unquestionably within the term "schoolbuilding," which could be read to imply a school house where classes are held.

We think that the acquisition of land for off street parking for school district facilities, including an administration building, is for a "proper school purpose." With particular reference to an administration building, there are two obvious reasons why numerous automobiles are incident to its operation. First, superintendents and supervisors that have central offices in an administration building must have occasion when duty requires their presence in scattered parts of the school district. The availability and effectiveness of these professionals no doubt is greatly enhanced by their use of automobile transportation. Second, teachers, principals and other staff scattered throughout the school system must have occasion when they are required to attend meetings together in the central administration building. To do so without an excessive investment in time, they frequently will have to use automobile transportation. With reference to any school district facility, automobiles will be incident to its operation for other reasons. For instance, professionals, as well as secretarial, clerical and maintenance staff, may not accept employment unless they can commute to and from work by automobile. This might be common in areas where public transportation does not serve either the employee's home or the school district's facility. Even where public transportation is available, we must recognize that today a great part of the public is unwilling to use it because they are almost addicted to the convenience and independence provided by the automobile. Since automobiles are a necessary incident to the operation of school district facilities, off street parking is a practical necessity. The streets simply are not adequate and sometimes are not available for parking. Consequently, the acquisition of land for off street parking, which is a practical necessity to the effective and efficient operation of a school system, is certainly a "proper school purpose." To interpret the statute any more narrowly would be to frustrate its obvious intent to delegate to the Board authority to discharge the legislature's constitutional obligation to provide for an efficient public school system.

.   .   .

Reversed.

Notes

1.   The court recognized that school employees are almost "addicted to the convenience" provided by cars. Does this "addiction" also apply to students? If so, would purchasing land to build a parking lot for students be "for a proper school purpose?"

2.   Under a statute granting the power of eminent domain to school boards for school purposes, the Supreme Court of Alabama upheld its use to construct an administration building for the superintendent and staff. *Smith v. City Bd. of Educ. of Birmingham*, 130 So.2d 29 (Ala. 1961). Do you agree with this outcome?

[Case No. 41]   Power of Board to Employ Consultant—Contract Formulation

RYAN v. WARREN TOWNSHIP HIGH SCHOOL DISTRICT NO. 121

Appellate Court of Illinois, 1987.
510 N.E.2d 911.

JUSTICE WOODWARD delivered the opinion of the court. Defendant, Warren Township High School District No. 121 (hereinafter school district), appeals from a judgment entered for the plaintiff, Keith Ryan and against the school district in the amount of $1,975. On appeal, the school district contends that it lacked the authority under the School Code to contract for plaintiff's services, and that the contract was unenforceable because it violated the Election Interference Prohibition Act.

Plaintiff, the only witness in the case, testified that in September 1985, he was working as a public relations manager for Clausing and Company. He was contacted by Dr. Paul Rundio, the superintendent of the school district, who requested a cost estimate of plaintiff's services. At that time, the school district had decided to raze Warren High School, which had been damaged by fire, and build a new school. However, community members who opposed the school district's plan instituted a lawsuit to block the destruction of the school. Dr. Rundio hired plaintiff to act as a liaison with members of the press and the community, to issue press releases, and to hold public meetings. The term of plaintiff's employment was from September to November 1985, prior to the school board elections.

Plaintiff submitted an itemized proposal and cost estimate totaling $5,000 to Dr. Rundio. Plaintiff was unaware of any public school board meeting adopting his oral contract negotiated with Dr. Rundio. The school district paid an interim bill for plaintiff's services in the amount of $3,200. On November 1, 1985, plaintiff submitted a second bill on the amount of $1,975 to the school district. When the school district refused payment, plaintiff filed this lawsuit.

. . .

The school district contends first that it did not have the authority to contract with plaintiff, so the contract is null and void.

Contracts entered into by a public body which are prohibited by an express provision of the law, or which under no circumstances could be legally entered into, are uniformly held to be *ultra vires* and void. While statutes granting powers to school boards must be strictly construed, a school board has the power expressly conferred and such powers as may be necessary to carry into effect those expressly granted. We conclude that the contract was not prohibited by an express provision of the School Code, and our interpretation of the School Code permits entering into the contract.

Implicit in the school district's power to hold regular and special meetings open to the public is the need to disseminate information to the public and receive feedback from the community. The School Code specifies that the school district should hold meetings where the members of the public are afforded an opportunity to question the board or to comment. Hiring a public relations consultant would enhance the school district's communication with the public especially where the parties described relations between them as "explosive" and "turbulent." Plaintiff arranged public meetings and tours of the old school and generally assisted the board in communicating with the public. Section 10–20.21 of the School Code contemplates the hiring of professionals and highly skilled individuals for their services, although a public relations consultant is not specifically listed. While we express no opinion regarding the board's judgment in hiring a public relations consultant, we conclude that the School Code does not prohibit entering into a contract with the plaintiff.

Defendant's reliance on *Evans v. Benjamin School District No. 25* for the proposition that the school district's actions are limited to the express provisions of the School Code is misplaced. The facts in *Evans* are distinguishable from the case at bar. At issue in *Evans* was the school board's power to grant tenure to a teacher. The teacher had not met the standards set out in section 24–11 of the Illinois School Code. The school district could not ignore the provision and grant tenure based on its own discretion. In this case, the legislature had not sought to provide specifications governing the hiring of consultants.

While the school district's actions were not void and *ultra vires,* no evidence exists establishing that the school district had voted to authorize an expenditure for plaintiff's fees. Section 10–7 of the School Code provides in relevant part:

> "On all questions involving the expenditure of money, the yeas and nays shall be taken and entered on the records of the proceedings of the board . . . .

Plaintiff testified that, to his knowledge, no meeting of the board occurred for the purpose of hiring him or approving the expenditure of his fees. By failing to call a meeting in order to authorize an expenditure for plaintiff's services, the school district irregularly contracted with the plaintiff. The parties do not dispute the trial court's finding that the board irregularly exercised its power in hiring the plaintiff.

Courts have distinguished between cases where the school district was utterly without the power to make a contract and cases in which it had the power, but exercised it in an irregular fashion. In the latter case, it is well settled that the conduct is merely voidable, and plaintiff may recover in *quantum meruit.* The rationale is as follows:

> Contracts entered into by a municipality which are expressly prohibited by law, and which under no circumstances can be entered into, are void and ultra vires. They may not be rendered valid thereafter

by estoppel or ratification of the municipality. However, there is another class of municipality contracts, distinct from the void type heretofore referred to, wherein the municipality has the power to enter into the contract, but where a portion thereof may be beyond its power, or its power may have been irregularly exercised. As to this class of contracts, a municipality may not assert its want of authority, or power, or the irregular exercise thereof, where to do so would give it an unconscionable advantage over the other party. Municipal corporations, as well as private corporations and individuals, are bound by principles of common honesty and fair dealing.

Therefore, although the contract was irregularly entered into, plaintiff is entitled to be reimbursed for his services where the school district ratified the contract by accepting the services and by making the partial payment.

... [P]laintiff's services continued for several months with the board's full knowledge as all the members knew of the public meetings scheduled by the plaintiff, his helping them with interviews, and his discussion with them of ideas for various committees. In this case also, both parties agree that the hiring was done in an irregular fashion.

Defendant's final contention is that the contract is void since it violates the Election Interference Prohibition Act. Section 103 of that Act states as follows:

No public funds shall be used to urge any elector to vote for or against any candidate or proposition, or be appropriated for political or campaign purposes to any candidate or political organization. This provision shall not prohibit the use of public funds for dissemination of factual information relative to any proposition appearing on an election ballot....

The school district alleges that the school board hired the plaintiff as a propagandist to market its decision within days of an election involving the very board members who hired the public relations consultant. Defendants, however, do not support their allegations with any specific facts. Further, even if the allegations were true, the plaintiff was only promoting the board's idea which was to build a new school rather that promoting the candidates themselves.

. . .

Affirmed.

Notes

1. Procedures for employing professionals not engaged in educational functions directly, such as architects, physicians, and lawyers, are generally not covered by competitive bidding statutes. Should they be?

[Case No. 42] Power of Board to Pay Superintendent to Resign

INGRAM v. BOONE

Supreme Court, Appellate Division [New York], 1983.
458 N.Y.S.2d 671.

MEMORANDUM BY THE COURT. . . .

Petitioners are taxpaying residents of the Union Free School District #1 of the Town of Hempstead. . . . They have commenced the instant proceeding to review an agreement entered into between the board of education of the school district and the district superintendent, alleging it was violative of the statutory and constitutional law of this State.

In August, 1980 Dr. Oliver Lancaster contracted with the board of education to serve as superintendent of schools for a period of four years commencing July 1, 1980. Approximately one year later, in the fall of 1981, a dispute allegedly arose between the board of education and Dr. Lancaster concerning his performance as superintendent. The board entered into negotiations with Lancaster in an effort to obtain his resignation which negotiations culminated in a resolution proposed at a public meeting of the board held on December 17, 1981 whereby Dr. Lancaster would resign effective December 31, 1981, the school district would pay him a lump sum of $65,000 and the board would continue Dr. Lancaster's insurance under several policies until the termination date of his employment contract or until he received insurance coverage from another source, whichever date occurred first. The resolution was approved by a vote of four to zero with one abstention. Thereafter, a formal stipulation was executed and general releases were signed. By order to show cause dated December 31, 1981 petitioners instituted the instant proceeding in which they challenge the lawfulness of the subject agreement.

Petitioners had standing to commence this proceeding by virtue of section 1 of article VIII of the State Constitution which forbids gifts of public funds. However, the payment of public funds as damages for breach of a contractual obligation or in settlement of a contested claim is not prohibited by this constitutional provision. On the record before us, it is impossible to determine whether the payment to Dr. Lancaster can be construed as a settlement of a legitimate claim or whether it is, in fact, a gift of public moneys. A mere claim of exercise of discretion and judgment is not enough, in the absence of competent proof, to validate the payment. Accordingly, [the trial court] properly directed that a hearing on this question be held.

Notes

1. The Supreme Court of New Mexico held that a board was not required to conduct a hearing before it suspended its superintendent with full salary for the three months remaining in his contract. The court wrote that this did not amount to a discharge for which a hearing would have been required. *Black v. Board of Educ. of Jemez Mountain School Dist. No. 53*, 529 P.2d 271 (N.M. 1974). What do you think?

2. The Supreme Court of Wyoming, in invalidating the purchase of the remainder of a superintendent's contract on the ground that the special board meeting was not properly called, commented that there was grave doubt about the matter. *Twitchell v. Bowman*, 440 P.2d 513 (Wyo.1968).

[Case No. 43]   Control of School Activities and Funds by Committee of Board

IN RE GERMAN TOWNSHIP SCHOOL DIRECTORS

District and County Court of Pennsylvania, 1943.
46 Pa. D. & C. 562.

[Suit was brought to remove members of the board of directors for failure to perform certain mandatory duties. A number of derelictions were charged against the board members but only that portion of the decision dealing with the delegation of control of school activities and funds to a committee of the board will be reported here.]

DUMBAULD, P.J. . . . Here we find a very interesting and somewhat controversial question for consideration. Respondents, as members of the school board, have proceeded upon the theory that athletic activities, high school band organizations, and other extra-curricular activities may be entirely segregated from the supervision and control of the board as a board. They contend that they may delegate to an appointive athletic control board all jurisdiction over the activities mentioned, and the handling of the finances incident to such management. They insist that the purchase of equipment for athletic teams and uniforms for the high school band and the expenditure of the proceeds arising from these activities are entirely a matter for the athletic board of control without any supervisory action over the conduct of this committee by the board as a whole. The members of the board who are not members of the athletic board of control seek to absolve themselves from their failure to exercise supervision by testifying that they are completely without knowledge of the financial transactions involved in the equipment of the athletic teams and the furnishing of uniforms for the band. Accepting this theory, the board of control deposited the proceeds of the athletic games in a bank, not a depository, and checked out the fund in payment of bills for these departments without any attempt to comply with the provisions of the code as to the manner of authorizing and making payments by the school board. In short, the funds arising from this form of extra-curricular activities never reach the treasury of the school board, nor is the account audited by the township auditors.

Thus we find that, on February 12, 1940, the board, as a board, authorized and drew a voucher in payment of a bill of Dice–Spalding Company, amounting to $965.30, on account of the bill of that company for athletic supplies and equipment, for use in games taken part in or played by pupils as members of the football team of the high school of the German Township School District. This bill was paid without advertisement for bids, receipt of such bids, or letting of a contract. It was paid simply because the athletic board of control or persons authorized by it had purchased equipment for the football team for the payment of which there appears not to have been sufficient money in the account of the athletic board of control at its bank.

During the school year of 1940–1941, the athletic board of control bought from D. Klein & Bros., Inc., through its agent, John Trump, uniforms for the high school band, costing $1,531.40. The check in payment of this item was drawn by the athletic board of control by O.R. Younkin, treasurer, on the Second National Bank of Masontown.

The members of the school board, not members of the athletic board of control, divorce themselves entirely from any act or responsibility in connection with this item of equipment.

. . .

. . . The members of the band, who received instructions in playing the various instruments used in such an organization, and who take part in the varied exercises that take place on the football field, particularly between the halves of the game, are as much a part of the student body as are those who specialize in intellectual achievements.

The comparatively small number of athletically inclined boys who survive the rigors of the training period and carry the colors of the school on the football field are not to be regarded as separate from the great body of pupils in the public schools who are not able, or do not choose, to participate in this line of endeavor.

If this selected few acquiring such special skill in the playing of the game of football, and the relatively small number of pupils who comprise the high school band, by their combined efforts are able to attract large crowds of spectators who are willing to pay substantial admission prices for the entertainment furnished, such students and such activities may not be regarded as a separate institution, subject only to the supervision of the athletic board of control. They constitute a unit or department of the entire school system. They receive no part of the prices of admission. They do not perform for the athletic board of control. They carry on for alma mater. The proceeds of these activities belong to the board of school directors and must be accounted for in the same manner that other funds of the school district are accounted for.

The legal status of these activities and the duty of the board of school directors with reference thereto have been clearly stated by Mr. Justice Stern. . . .:

> . . . Physical education is as much a part of the school curriculum as are subjects of intellectual study, and athletic supplies, therefore, are as 'necessary for school use' as maps, globes, and similar objects. It is not the spirit of our public school system that only children with financial means to purchase their own supplies should have the opportunity of participating in school games and athletic sports. Of course, the extent to which athletic paraphernalia should be purchased for use merely by school teams playing in competitive sports is a question to be answered by school boards in the exercise of a cautious discretion, with special reference to the proportionate number of those who will receive the benefit of such supplies.

This cautious discretion cannot be exercised by an attempt, in the form of a resolution, to delegate to an athletic board of control the entire subject of extra-curricular activities. The requirement that supplies exceeding in cost a certain amount shall be advertised for, and the contract for their furnishing let to the lowest bidder applies to all such supplies as those furnished for the football team and the band uniforms.

The provision of section 403 of the code that requires the names of the directors and the manner in which they voted to be recorded in the letting of contracts for such supplies is also applicable to the transactions mentioned. When a director testifies that he knows nothing about the transactions delegated to the athletic board of control, he admits himself negligent in the performance of his statutory duty. It is a mandatory duty that the board shall supervise, control, and comply with the statutory provisions, as to all receipts and expenditures undertaken by the athletic board of control.

. . .

The school board may hereafter continue to permit the athletic board of control to manage and direct extra-curricular activities, but all moneys received therefrom and all expenditures for equipment to be used therein, must be reported to and approved by the board of directors as a board. The board of athletic control must be considered merely as a committee, with like powers and duties as the teachers' committee, the committee on supplies, or the building committee.

. . .

Notes

1. If the "entire subject of extracurricular activities" cannot be delegated to a board committee, what can, or should, be subject to delegation?

2. What do you think about this case from an educational point of view?

3. What do you think about the court's statement that when school board members testify that they know nothing about transactions delegated to committees, they essentially admit to negligence in the performance of their statutory duties? Should this be a sufficient basis on which to recall board members?

[Case No. 44]   Use of School Building for Social or Civic Purpose by Religious Group

LAMB'S CHAPEL v. CENTER MORICHES UNION FREE SCHOOL DISTRICT

Supreme Court of the United States, 1993.
508 U.S. 384, 113 S.Ct. 2141, 124 L.Ed.2d 352 [83 Educ. L. Rep. 30].

JUSTICE WHITE delivered the opinion of the Court.

Section 414 of the New York Education Law authorizes local school boards to adopt reasonable regulations for the use of school property for 10 specified purposes when the property is not in use for school purposes. Among the permitted uses is the holding of "social, civic and recreational meetings and entertainments, and other uses pertaining to the welfare of the community; but such meetings, entertainment and uses shall be non-exclusive and open to the general public." The list of permitted uses does not include meetings for religious purposes. . . .

Pursuant to § 414's empowerment of local school districts, the Board of Center Moriches Union Free School District (District) has issued rules and regulations with respect to the use of school property when not in use for school purposes. The rules allow only 2 of the 10 purposes authorized by § 414: social, civic, or recreational uses (Rule 10) and use by political organizations if secured in compliance with § 414 (Rule 8). Rule 7, however, consistent with the judicial interpretation of state law, provides that "[t]he school premises shall not be used by any group for religious purposes."

The issue in this case is whether, against this background of state law, it violates the Free Speech Clause of the First Amendment, made applicable to the States by the Fourteenth Amendment, to deny a church access to school premises to exhibit for public viewing and for assertedly religious purposes, a film dealing with family and child-rearing issues faced by parents today.

I

Petitioners (Church) are Lamb's Chapel, an evangelical church in the community of Center Moriches, and its pastor John Steigerwald. Twice the Church applied to the District for permission to use school facilities to show a six-part film series. . . . A brochure provided on request of the District . . . stated that the film series would discuss [a commentator's] views on the undermining influences of the media that could only be counterbalanced by returning to traditional, Christian family values instilled at an early stage. The brochure went on to describe the contents of each of the six parts of the series. The District denied the first application, saying that "[t]his film does appear to be church related and therefore your request must be refused." The second application for permission to use school premises for showing the film, which described it as a "Family oriented movie—from the Christian perspective," was denied using identical language.

[The District Court and the Court of Appeals held for the school district.]

.   .   .

II

There is no question that the District, like the private owner of property, may legally preserve the property under its control for the use to which it is dedicated. It is also common ground that the District need not have permitted after-hours use of its property for any of the uses permitted by § 414 of the state education law. The District, however, did open its property for 2 of the 10 uses permitted by § 414. The Church argued below that because under Rule 10 of the rules issued by the District, school property could be used for "social, civic, and recreational" purposes, the District had opened its property for such a wide variety of communicative purposes that restrictions on communicative uses of the property were subject to the same constitutional limitations as restrictions in traditional public fora such as parks and sidewalks. Hence, its view was that subject-matter or speaker exclusions on District property were required to be justified by a compelling state interest and to be narrowly drawn to achieve that end. Both the District Court and the Court of Appeals rejected this submission, which is also presented to this Court. The argument has considerable force, for the District's property is heavily used by a wide variety of private organizations, including some that presented a "close question," which the Court of Appeals resolved in the District's favor, as to whether the District had in fact already opened its property for religious uses. We need not rule on this issue, however, for even if the courts below were correct in this respect—and we shall assume for present purposes that they were—the judgment below must be reversed.

With respect to public property that is not a designated public forum open for indiscriminate public use for communicative purposes, we have said that "[c]ontrol over access to a nonpublic forum can be based on subject matter and speaker identity so long as the distinctions drawn are reasonable in light of the purpose served by the forum and are viewpoint neutral." The Court of Appeals appeared to recognize that the total ban on using District property for religious purposes could survive First Amendment challenge only if excluding this category of speech was reasonable and viewpoint neutral. The court's conclusion in this case was that Rule 7 met this test. We cannot agree with this holding, for Rule 7 was unconstitutionally applied in this case. (Although the Court of Appeals apparently held that Rule 7 was reasonable as well as viewpoint neutral, the court uttered not a word in support of its reasonableness holding. If Rule 7 were to be held unreasonable, it could be held facially invalid, that is, it might be held that the rule could in no circumstances be applied to religious speech or religious communicative conduct. In view of our disposition of this case, we need not pursue this issue.)

The Court of Appeals thought that the application of Rule 7 in this case was viewpoint neutral because it had been and would be applied in the same way to all uses of school property for religious purposes. That all religions and all uses for religious purposes are treated alike under Rule 7, however, does not answer the critical question whether it discriminates on the basis of viewpoint to permit school property to be used for the presentation of all views about family issues and child-rearing except those dealing with the subject matter from a religious standpoint.

There is no suggestion from the courts below or from the District or the State that a lecture or film about child-rearing and family values would not be a use for social or civic purposes otherwise permitted by Rule 10. That subject matter is not one that the District has placed off limits to any and all speakers. Nor is there any indication in the record before us that the application to exhibit the particular film involved here was or would have been denied for any reason other than the fact that the presentation would have been from a religious perspective. In our view, denial on that basis was plainly invalid . . . [in] that

> [a]lthough a speaker may be excluded from a non-public forum if he wishes to address a topic not encompassed within the purpose of the forum . . . or if he is not a member of the class of speakers for whose special benefit the forum was created . . . the government violates the First Amendment when it denies access to a speaker solely to suppress the point of view he espouses on an otherwise includible subject.

The film involved here no doubt dealt with a subject otherwise permissible under Rule 10, and its exhibition was denied solely because the film dealt with the subject from a religious standpoint. The principle that has emerged from our cases "is that the First Amendment forbids the government to regulate speech in ways that favor some viewpoints or ideas at the expense of others." . . .

The District, as a respondent, would save its judgment below on the ground that to permit its property to be used for religious purposes would be an establishment of religion forbidden by the First Amendment. This Court suggested in *Widmar v. Vincent* that the interest of the State in avoiding an Establishment Clause violation "may be [a] compelling" one justifying an abridgment of free speech otherwise protected by the First Amendment; but the Court went on to hold that permitting use of University property for religious purposes under the open access policy involved there would not be incompatible with the Court's Establishment Clause cases.

We have no more trouble than did the *Widmar* Court in disposing of the claimed defense on the ground that the posited fears of an Establishment Clause violation are unfounded. The showing of this film would not have been during school hours, would not have been sponsored by the school, and would have been open to the public, not just to church members. The District property had repeatedly been used by a wide variety of private organizations. Under these circumstances, as in *Widmar,* there would have been no realistic danger that the community would think that the District was endorsing religion or any particular creed, and any benefit to religion or to the Church would have been no more than incidental. As in *Widmar,* permitting District property to be used to exhibit the film involved in this case would not have been an establishment of religion under the three-part test articulated in *Lemon v. Kurtzman.* The challenged governmental action has a secular purpose, does not have the principal or primary effect of advancing or inhibiting religion, and does not foster an excessive entanglement with religion.

The District also submits that it justifiably denied use of its property to a "radical" church for the purpose of proselytizing, since to do so would lead to threats of public unrest and even violence. There is nothing in the record to support such a justification, which in any event would be difficult to defend as a reason to deny the presentation of a religious point of view about a subject the District otherwise makes open to discussion on District property.

. . .

The Attorney General also argues that there is no express finding below that the Church's application would have been granted absent the religious connection. This fact is beside the point for the purposes of this opinion, which is concerned with the validity of the stated reason for denying the Church's application, namely, that the film sought to be shown "appeared to be church related."

. . . Reversed.

Notes

1. If the church had wanted to conduct a prayer meeting or a religious service, should the board have permitted one to occur?

2. Consider how the lower courts erred in interpreting viewpoint neutrality. Can you distinguish between viewpoint and subject matter neutrality and/or discrimination?

[Case No. 45]   Use of School Building for Performance by Controversial Singer

EAST MEADOWS COMMUNITY CONCERTS ASSOCIATION v. BOARD OF EDUCATION OF UNION FREE SCHOOL DISTRICT NO. 3, COUNTY OF NASSAU

Court of Appeals of New York, 1966.
272 N.Y.S.2d 341.

FULD, JUDGE. Involved in this litigation—which questions the right of the defendant school board to bar the folk singer, Pete Seeger, from giving a concert in one of its school buildings—are important issues of jurisdiction and constitutional law.

The plaintiff, a nonprofit educational and cultural association, has for its purpose the presentation of an annual series of musical concerts, and during the past 10 years it has been permitted by the defendant school board to present these concerts in the auditorium of a high school in East Meadow on Long Island. In June of 1965, following prior procedure, the defendant gave the plaintiff such permission for the 1965–1966 series, including a concert scheduled for March 12, 1966, which was to feature Pete Seeger as the performing artist. The concert was publicized and tickets for the series of three were sold. However, in December of 1965, the defendant withdrew the previously granted permission for the March 12 concert on the ground that, because he had given a concert in Moscow and because some of the songs he sings are critical of American policy in Viet Nam, Seeger is a "highly controversial figure" whose presence might provoke a disturbance with consequent damage to school property. Some time later that same month, the plaintiff instituted the present action in which it sought a judgment, in effect (1) declaring the defendant's action to be unconstitutional and (2) enjoining the defendant from interfering with the presentation of the scheduled concert in the school auditorium.

. . .

That the constitutional issues posed by this case are substantial and, indeed, of high public importance, there can be no doubt. The State is not under a duty to make school buildings available for public gatherings but, if it elects to do so, it is required, by constitutional provision, to grant the use of such facilities "in a reasonable and nondiscriminatory manner, equally applicable to all and administered with equality to all." The defendant has concededly allowed a number of organizations, including the very plaintiff before us, to use the school auditorium for nonacademic purposes for many years. It follows, therefore, that, in deciding who is to be permitted to use its school, the board must not unconstitutionally discriminate against the plaintiff.

Of course, this does not mean that the defendant board is prevented from barring the use of the school auditorium for an unlawful purpose, but in the case before us the justification asserted for canceling the permit is the unpopularity of Seeger's views rather than the unlawfulness of the plaintiff's concert. The expression of controversial and unpopular views, it is hardly necessary to observe, is precisely what is protected by both the Federal and State Constitutions.... Consequently, if there were no danger of immediate and irreparable injury to the public weal, the defendant's refusal to permit Seeger to appear at the March 12 concert would be an unlawful restriction of the constitutional right of free speech and expression.

. . .

Notes

1.   What kind of evidence should a board rely on in order to prevent a group from using its facilities?

2.   The date of an event often passes before the question of the right of the sponsors to use a public facility is litigated fully. As happened here, courts can order officials to set another date for a performance.

[Case No. 46]   Power of Board to Dispose of School Property

ROSS v. WILSON

Court of Appeals of New York, 1955.
308 N.Y. 605.

VAN VOORHIS, JUDGE. The controversy in this proceeding concerns the sale of the schoolhouse which served common school district No. 1 of the Towns of Ellicott and Gerry, in Chautauqua County, before it was superseded by a central school district. This district had been known as the Ross Mills District. In February, 1953, the board of education of the recently formed central school district called a special meeting of the qualified voters of the former common school district to vote upon whether to close the school and sell the school property. Such procedure is required by subdivision 6 of section 1804 of the Education Law, which also provides that if the common school district schoolhouse is sold, the net proceeds be apportioned among the taxpayers of the common school district.

At the special meeting of the common school district called by the board of education in 1953, four propositions were submitted: (1) Should the school of the former common school district be closed? (2) Should the school property be sold to Ross Mills Church of God for $2,000? (3) Should the property be sold to Ross Grange No. 305 for $3,000? (4) Should the property be sold by public auction to the highest bidder? The notice stated that proposition number 1 would be voted upon, "and as many of the succeeding propositions as is necessary to dispose of the property". At the meeting, the proposal to close the school was carried. A motion was then made but declared out of order that the meeting should next ballot upon whether to sell the school property at public auction to the highest bidder. Then proposition number 2 was presented to the meeting to sell the school property to Ross Mills Church of God for $2,000. It was carried by a vote of 32 to 24. That ended the meeting.

The Commissioner of Education on appeal taken to him pursuant to section 310 of the Education Law sustained this action of the board of education. Thereupon this article 78 proceeding was instituted to review his determination, which was annulled by Special Term but reinstated by the Appellate Division upon the ground that decisions by the Commissioner of Education are final unless purely arbitrary, and that his decision could not thus be characterized in this instance inasmuch as subdivision 6 of section 1804 of the Education Law, pursuant to which this schoolhouse was sold, does not expressly state that it must be sold to the highest bidder upon the organization of a central school district. . . .

No question was raised that Ross Grange was financially able to pay $3,000 in cash for the property. In his opinion upholding the action of the school district, the Commissioner of Education placed his decision upon the following ground: "The type and character of the purchaser of such property after centralization is often a matter of vital import to the rural communities of this State. It is my opinion that the legislature fully intended to give the voters of component districts a choice as to the type of person or organization whom they wished to have literally in their midst. If the sale were to be mandated to be made to the highest bidder, it may well be that a 'saloon', filling station or other enterprise undesirable to a specific community might be forced upon it. . . ." . . .

In the conduct of private affairs, the problem sometimes arises whether a better price can be obtained upon the sale of property at private sale or at auction. In the case of a public body, such as a school district, the object to be achieved is likewise to realize the best price for the property, although the judgment of the Legislature must be followed concerning whether that purpose is more likely to be accomplished by public auction. But if the Legislature does not require a schoolhouse to be sold at public auction, it by no means follows from that circumstance that the Legislature intended to authorize the public officials charged with the administration of school property, or even the majority of qualified electors voting at a school district meeting, to sell the property for a smaller amount than has been offered with due formality by a proper purchaser for a lawful use.... If, as was intimated by the Commissioner of Education, a former school site might be used for a filling station, bar and grill or other enterprise undesirable to a specific community, zoning ordinances or other lawful regulatory measures should be adopted....

The amount of money involved is small, but the principle is important; the offer which was rejected was to pay 50% more for this schoolhouse than the one which was accepted. Bogert, writing on Trusts and Trustees, says (§ 745): "Whether the trustee should endeavor to sell by negotiation with possible buyers, or should put the property up at auction, depends upon the circumstances of the individual case. He should use the method which will, considering the place of sale and the type of property for sale, be apt to bring the best price." In the present situation, the Legislature has determined that it was not necessary to sell this property at auction, although that procedure would have been permissible, but the latitude allowed in the method of sale was designed to enable these public fiduciaries to adopt the method which in their judgment would bring the best price, and it was their duty to sell at the best price which it brought, not deliberately to select and to favor a buyer at a lower price than was otherwise obtainable. In the same section of Bogert it is also said: "A power to sell is not equivalent to a power to give away. If the trustee transfers for a merely nominal price or a wholly inadequate price, the sale may be set aside"....

... The direct result of what occurred is, in effect, to approve a contribution of $1,000 by the school district to the church....

This contribution by a common school district to a particular church is not made in aid of any educational activity conducted by the church, but operates as an outright gift of public funds to a church for its general church purposes. Even if the facts of the case did not present the special situation of the use of public money for the support of a religious establishment, neither a common school district meeting nor the district trustees are empowered to expend the resources of the school district for other than educational objects....

There is no power in either the board or the voters at a district meeting to pick and choose arbitrarily between purchasers, each desiring to use the property for lawful and proper purposes, or to transfer the funds or other property of the district in aid of one or to the disadvantage of another. In this instance, there is lack of power to use public funds to aid a church by discriminating against the grange....

For the reasons mentioned, we think that there was a total lack of power in the school district to accept an offer of $2,000 from the Church of God of Ross Mills and at the same time to reject an equally bona fide offer of $3,000 from the grange. Although we respect the desire of the commissioner to uphold, if possible, the action taken by the district meeting, since the meeting lacked power to do what it did, the commissioner's confirmation was thus, in a legal sense, purely arbitrary, and thus reviewable in court. . . .

Notes

1.   At each of the three appellate steps there was a reversal.

2.   The state commissioner of education sustained the board's action. Is this type of question an appropriate one for a chief state school officer?

Chapter 7

TORT LIABILITY OF SCHOOL BOARDS, OFFICERS, AND EMPLOYEES

Introduction

Torts, civil wrongs other than disputes involving contracts, apply to a variety of situations where individuals suffer harm or loss due to the improper conduct of others. The major types of torts that affect schools are negligence, where conduct unintentionally fails to meet an acceptable standard of care, thereby resulting in injury; intentional torts such as assault, battery, and defamation; and strict liability, where injury results from the creation of an unusual hazard and liability is imposed without fault. While the most frequent common law tort, negligence, has generated a significant body of case law, violations of civil rights constitute an expanding area of liability under 42 U.S.C.A. section 1983 (section 1983).[1]

Doctrine of Board Non–Liability

At common law, school boards are not liable for torts committed by their members, agents, or employees. Insofar as there has been increasing dissatisfaction with this principle, many states have modified this doctrine legislatively and/or judicially.

Non-liability, or immunity, based on the common law principle that the state is sovereign and cannot be sued without its consent, has since been supplemented by statute, as discussed below. In a dispute wherein it upheld the aggregate cap in the state's Governmental Immunity Act after two students were killed and three others were seriously injured in a car accident while returning from an out-of-state extracurricular debate tournament, the Supreme Court of Utah reiterated this rule. The court declared that "[t]he right to sue in tort a school district or any other governmental entity engaging in a governmental function does not qualify as such a fundamental right."[2]

The doctrine of board non-liability applies to subordinate state agencies such as school boards under the theory that they are arms of the state carrying out governmental functions. Board immunity for tort liability is historically derived from the concept of sovereignty. Even so, many courts and states have assigned grounds other than that "the sovereign can do no wrong" to support immunity. One basis for avoiding liability is that the law does not provide funds to pay for damages

---

1. This statute is in the appendix.

2. *Tindley v. Salt Lake City School Dist.*, 116 P.3d 295 [200 Educ. L. Rep. 406] (Utah 2005).

against boards since money raised for education may not be diverted to cover the costs of tort claims because such payments are not expenditures for school purposes. Another rationale is that when torts occur, boards cannot be liable since those who acted on their behalf exceeded the scope of their lawful authority. Board immunity for acts of their employees is grounded in the concept that no master-servant relationship is present that would render boards liable for the acts of their employees even if they act within the scope of their employment.

Exceptions to Doctrine of Non–Liability

In General

Insofar as immunity is a common law concept, it is subject to statutory and judicial exceptions and modifications. Not surprisingly, statutory exceptions vary markedly from one jurisdiction to another. There is a great deal of controversy as to whether the legislative or judicial branches should make such changes. Insofar as immunity has existed for so long in the United States and has many ramifications, courts are reluctant to abandon it entirely. As such, courts that are unwilling to accept the concept of immunity in its entirety have recognized exceptions to the doctrine.

Proprietary Acts

A major exception to immunity occurs when courts impose liability on school boards and their employees for torts connected with their proprietary, but not their governmental, functions.[3] This distinction is based on the notion that governmental agencies serve dual capacities. In their governmental capacities, boards exercise rights springing from sovereignty. While performing their officials duties, board acts are treated as political and governmental, thereby giving rise to immunity,[4] even if it is limited statutorily.[5] On the other hand, when boards or their employees perform functions that can be carried out by private persons, and that do not serve "the single and noble purpose ... [of] ... educating the children,"[6] they may be liable for their actions.

Even courts that recognize the dichotomy between governmental and proprietary functions[7] do little more than classify acts in one category or the other. In light of this lack of clarity, it is often difficult to evaluate under which category an act appears until courts have resolved

---

3. *But see Morningstar Water Users Ass'n v. Farmington Mun. School Dist. No. 5,* 901 P.2d 725, 729–30 [103 Educ. L. Rep. 443] (N.M.1995) (citing critiques from Justices Cardozo and Holmes about the advisability of continuing this distinction).

4. *See, e.g., Ledfors v. Emery County School Dist.,* 849 P.2d 1162 [82 Educ. L. Rep. 250] (Utah 1993); *Berler v. City of N.Y.,* 584 N.Y.S.2d 709 [75 Educ. L. Rep. 1166] (N.Y.Sup.Ct. App.Term 1992).

5. *Anderson v. Blankenship,* 790 F.Supp. 695 [75 Educ. L. Rep. 300] (E.D. Tex.1992).

6. *Allen v. Salina Broadcasting,* 630 S.W.2d 225, 227 [3 Educ. L. Rep. 779] (Mo. Ct.App. 1982).

7. *Boyd By and Through Boyd v. Gulfport Mun. Separate School Dist.,* 821 F.2d 308 [40 Educ. L. Rep. 112] (5th Cir.1987).

disputes. In fact, legislative action may require the judiciary to differentiate between governmental and proprietary functions. For example, after the legislature enacted a law providing immunity where a state agency was engaged in the exercise or discharge of a governmental function, the Supreme Court of Michigan reasoned that the concept of "governmental functions," undefined in the statute, is a "term of art" used to describe "those activities of government which due to their public nature should not give rise to liability at common law."[8] The following illustrations of the proprietary-governmental distinction highlight the challenge facing courts as they seek to distinguish between the two.

Claims often arise when individuals are injured while attending events at school facilities. The Supreme Court of Arizona intervened in a dispute where a spectator who was seriously injured due to a faulty railing at a football game sued two school boards that rented a stadium from a third system. The court found that since the third district charged a rental fee for the use of the stadium, thereby abandoning its governmental role and embarking on a proprietary activity, it was liable for the spectator's injuries.[9] Conversely, where a spectator was injured when bleacher seats collapsed during a football game, the Supreme Court of Michigan expressly refused to follow the case from Arizona in denying the plaintiff's claim.[10] The court affirmed that since the spectator was injured in a stadium owned by the home team, which did not intend to make a profit from its admission fee, it was merely promoting an educational activity that entitled it to immunity. Similarly, the Supreme Court of Virginia affirmed that where a board was statutorily authorized to lease school property, including the renting of its auditorium for concerts, it was not liable for injuries that a spectator sustained when she slipped and fell in an aisle since the board never abandoned its governmental capacity.[11] In defining the governmental-proprietary test as whether a function tended to promote the cause of education, the court was satisfied that leasing the auditorium for the concert was permissible since it stimulated and fostered student interest.[12] Further, the Supreme Court of Kansas affirmed that a board engaged in a governmental function when it allowed its community room to be used for a county agricultural extension program.[13] In denying relief to a participant who fell and was injured in an unlighted stairway, the court decided that since the use of the building was governmental, the only duty that the board owed users was to refrain from wilfully and wantonly causing them to be injured.

8. *Thomas v. State Highway Dep't,* 247 N.W.2d 530, 532 (Mich.1976).

9. *Sawaya v. Tucson High School Dist.,* 281 P.2d 105 (Ariz.1955).

10. *Richards v. School Dist. of City of Birmingham,* 83 N.W.2d 643 (Mich.1957).

11. *Kellam v. School Bd. of the City of Norfolk,* 117 S.E.2d 96 (Va.1960).

12. *See also Smith v. Board of Educ. of City of Marietta,* 167 S.E.2d 615 (Ga.App.

1969) (affirming that the operation of a public school auditorium, primarily for the use and benefit of the public, was a governmental function even though the board may have received some incidental revenue from the rentals).

13. *Smith v. Board of Educ. of Caney School Dist. No. 34,* 464 P.2d 571 (Kan. 1970).

On the other hand, the Supreme Court of Pennsylvania determined that when a school board conducted a summer recreation program that was open to the general public, it took on a proprietary function.[14] The court noted that since the board charged a fee for a program that it was not statutorily required to offer, and which could have been provided by a private company, it was liable for injuries that a child sustained while participating in its activities. Fifteen years later, the same court abolished the common law immunity of school boards.[15] More recently, an appellate court in North Carolina ruled that officials were not liable for head injuries that a child sustained while participating in a voluntary after-school enrichment program for which there was a weekly fee.[16] The court explained that since the program was an undertaking traditionally provided by local government, staff members who were sued in their official capacities were entitled to immunity.

Nuisances

Individuals who are injured due to the alleged failures of educators to keep school premises in safe conditions may file suit under an exception, recognized in some jurisdictions, which permits recoveries against boards for maintaining nuisances. While there is a lack of judicial clarity over the meaning of nuisance, courts have extended it to forms of annoyance or inconvenience that interfere with common public rights. A nuisance, in the words of the Supreme Court of Errors of Connecticut, "involves as an essential element that it can be the natural tendency of the act or thing complained of to create dangers and inflict injury upon person or property."[17] Insofar as they may have their origins in negligence, it is sometimes difficult to decide which acts constitute nuisances.

Even though the responsibility for maintaining nuisances seems to be recognized as an exception to the general rule of non-liability, the basis for the exception is not clear. Some courts believe that if officials of public agencies, such as school boards, mismanage an agency's property, they are liable for damages to another person's property or person. Other courts have written that one explanation for the difference between liability for nuisance and non-liability for negligence is that in most situations boards may, by judicial decree, be required to abate nuisances without undue hardship on their part. Of course, if a party sues a board for damages, the usual arguments in favor of immunity apply. To this end, an appellate court in Georgia affirmed that the same immunity that protected school boards and their officials applied equally to claims in negligence and nuisance.[18]

---

14. *Morris v. School Dist. of Township of Mount Lebanon*, 144 A.2d 737 (Pa.1958).

15. *Ayala v. Philadelphia Bd. of Pub. Educ.*, 305 A.2d 877 (Pa.1973).

16. *Schmidt v. Breeden*, 517 S.E.2d 171 [136 Educ. L. Rep. 1063] (N.C.Ct.App. 1999).

17. *Laspino v. City of New Haven*, 67 A.2d 557, 558 (Conn.1949).

18. *Dollar v. Dalton Pub. Schools*, 505 S.E.2d 789 [130 Educ. L. Rep. 330] (Ga. App. 1998).

Another possible factor that renders boards liable is that nuisances usually affect property rights that the courts carefully guard. In older cases, courts agreed that both the discharge of sewage into a stream[19] and the maintenance of a defective privy well on school property were nuisances.[20] On the other hand, more recently, courts refused to find that boards were liable for creating nuisances where a student was injured in a woodworking class,[21] where piles of snow remained in a school playground after a parking lot was plowed,[22] or where a baseball field was constructed at an elementary school.[23]

Liability Insurance and Immunity

Courts have not agreed on whether school boards waive their governmental immunity from tort liability by purchasing insurance. Some courts do not consider purchasing insurance a waiver of district immunity for a variety of reasons.[24] On the flip side, although preserving district funds is the basic modern justification for retaining immunity, since this reason is at least weakened, if not obviated, when boards purchase insurance policies to protect their funds, other courts permit recovery up to the maximum of their coverage.[25]

In states where immunity has not been limited, there appears to be no reason to purchase liability insurance to protect boards except, perhaps, in anticipation of judicial abrogation of the doctrine if it exists solely in common law. Absent a law permitting a board to purchase insurance, such an action could constitute an illegal expenditure of funds. In such a case, the highest court of West Virginia permitted a successor school board to recover premiums from an insurance company.[26] Where state law granted boards the authority to furnish transportation for children but did not authorize them to carry liability insurance on school buses, the court held that the original board made an improper expenditure since there was nothing against which the policy of indemni-

19. *Watson v. New Milford*, 45 A. 167 (Conn.1900).

20. *Briegel v. City of Philadelphia*, 19 A. 1038 (Pa.1890).

21. *Burke v. Austin Indep. School Dist.*, 709 F.Supp. 120 [52 Educ. L. Rep. 1046] (W.D.Tex. 1987).

22. *Hendricks v. Southfield Pub. Schools*, 444 N.W.2d 143 [55 Educ. L. Rep. 729] (Mich.App.1989).

23. *Paredes v. City of North Bay Village*, 693 So.2d 1153 [118 Educ. L. Rep. 796] (Fla.Dist.Ct. App.1997).

24. *See, e.g., Grayson County Bd. of Educ. v. Casey*, 157 S.W.3d 201 [196 Educ. L. Rep. 975] (Ky. 2005); *Smith v. Board of Educ. of Caney School Dist. No. 34*, 464 P.2d 571 (Kan.1970); *Barr v. Bernhard*, 562 S.W.2d 844 (Tex.1978); *Crisp County School*

Sys. v. Brown, 487 S.E.2d 512 [119 Educ. L. Rep. 722] (Ga.Ct.App.1997); *Angel v. Harlan County Bd. of Educ.*, 14 S.W.3d 559 (Ky.Ct.App.2000); *Herring ex rel. Marshall v. Winston–Salem/Forsyth County Bd. of Educ.*, 529 S.E.2d 458 [144 Educ. L. Rep. 1062] (N.C.Ct.App.2000).

25. *See, e.g., Brown v. Egan Consol. School Dist. No. 50–2*, 449 N.W.2d 259 [57 Educ. L. Rep. 1017] (S.D.1989); *Crowell v. School Dist. No. 7 of Gallatin County*, 805 P.2d 522 [65 Educ. L. Rep. 919] (Mont. 1991); *Brewer By and Through Brewer v. Independent School Dist. No. 1*, 848 P.2d 566 [81 Educ. L. Rep. 1093] (Okla.1993).

26. *Board of Educ. of Raleigh County v. Commercial Cas. Ins. Co.*, 182 S.E. 87 (W.Va. 1935). *See also Davis v. Board of County Commr's of Carbon County*, 495 P.2d 21 (Wyo.1972); *Awe v. University of Wyo.*, 534 P.2d 97 (Wyo.1975).

fication could operate, the insurance company had to return the premiums.

Abrogation of the Doctrine of Non–Liability

Judicially

Courts have indicated that since the rule of governmental immunity from tort was created judicially, they can abrogate it if legislatures remain silent. The Supreme Court of Illinois was the first to repudiate the doctrine in a personal injury suit filed on behalf of a student who was hurt due to the negligence of a school bus driver.[27] Having considered the history of immunity and the bases on which it rested, the court concluded that the doctrine was no longer appropriate. In so doing, the court placed school boards in the same legal situation as private corporations that can be sued for injuries caused by the negligence of their officers, agents, or employees. However, the same court subsequently observed that the state legislature repudiated this opinion and set a maximum amount for such recoveries.[28]

Conversely, even after maintaining that the doctrine of governmental immunity was unacceptable, the Supreme Judicial Court of Massachusetts refused to abrogate it based on its stance that "the Legislature should be afforded an opportunity to do this by a comprehensive statute."[29] When the legislature refused to act, the court expressed its intent to abrogate the doctrine in the first appropriate case it addressed following the end of the next legislative session unless that body "acted definitively as to the doctrine"[30] and planned to make the abrogation retroactive to the date of the case in which it first criticized the doctrine. Not surprisingly, the legislature enacted a law permitting some tort claims, excluding those involving the exercise of discretionary functions.[31]

Legislatively

Legislatures have adopted a variety of approaches in modifying the doctrine of non-liability as some imposed liability for selected activities. To this end, "safe place" laws require owners of public buildings to construct and maintain them in a manner that they are safe for employees and others.[32] As reflected in some of the cases reviewed in this chapter, legislatures have completely abrogated the common-law doc-

---

27. *Molitor v. Kaneland Community Unit Dist. No. 302*, 163 N.E.2d 89 (Ill.1959), *cert. denied*, 362 U.S. 968, 80 S.Ct. 955, 4 L.Ed.2d 900 (1960).

28. *See Woodfield Lanes v. Village of Schaumburg*, 523 N.E.2d 36, 40 (Ill.Ct.App. 1988) (citing to the creation of the Illinois Tort Immunity Act).

29. *Morash and Sons v. Commonwealth*, 296 N.E.2d 461, 468 (Mass.1973).

30. *Whitney v. City of Worcester*, 366 N.E.2d 1210, 1211 (Mass.1977).

31. *See Cady v. Plymouth–Carver Reg'l School Dist.*, 457 N.E.2d 294 [14 Educ. L. Rep. 1091] (Mass.Ct.App.1983).

32. *See, e.g.,* Ohio Rev. Code. Ann. § 4167.09; Wisc. Stat. Ann. § 101.11.

trine and placed boards on the same plane as individuals and private corporations. In one such case, the Supreme Court of Ohio was of the opinion that pursuant to a former exception to sovereign immunity that expressly imposed liability, a school board may be liable when the failure of one of its officials to report a teacher's sexual abuse of a minor, in violation of the state's reporting statute, proximately results in that teacher's sexually abusing another minor student.[33] Other courts have abolished the general doctrine but made exceptions precluding liability in specific activities such as those involving high degrees of discretion.

Other legislatures have modified immunity by indirection through the operation of "save harmless" statutes.[34] These laws require school boards to defend, at their own expense, charges against staff arising out of damage claims for their allegedly tortious acts. Under such statutes, boards must pay judgments that may be recovered against employees who act within the scope of their duties. At the same time, boards and/or their employees may be covered by general legislation modifying governmental tort immunity.

By the Supreme Court for Section 1983 Cases

The Supreme Court handed down a series of judgments on the limits of immunity, liability of school board members, and, by extension, other educational officials for constitutional torts under the extensive reach of section 1983. Section 1983, which became law as part of the Civil Rights Act of 1871,[35] was designed to provide a remedy for those whose federally protected civil rights, most notably freed slaves during Reconstruction, were violated. Insofar as plaintiffs can recover monetary awards and attorney fees[36] pursuant to section 1983, it offers protection to those whose civil rights have been violated by school officials.

In *Wood v. Strickland (Wood)*, a case of first impression considering the procedural due process rights of students in Arkansas who were subjected to long-term suspensions, the Supreme Court found that school board members may be sued under section 1983. The Court reasoned that granting board members absolute immunity from damages claims would have vitiated much of section 1983's promise. The Court also considered the need for board members to exercise their "judgment independently, forcefully, and in a manner best serving the long-term interest of the school and the students."[37] Asserting that state courts permit damages claims for bad faith or malicious acts to proceed, the

---

33. *Yates v. Mansfield Bd. of Educ.*, 808 N.E.2d 861 [187 Educ. L. Rep. 1005] (Ohio 2004).

34. *See, e.g.,* CONN. GEN. STAT. ANN. § 10–236a; 14 DEL. CODE ANN. § 1095; 9; FLA. STAT. ANN. § 1012.85; 105 ILL. COMP. STAT. ANN. 5/34A–602; N.J. STAT. ANN. § 18A:12–20; MCKINNEY'S EDUC. LAW § 2561; 24 PA. STAT. ANN. § 24–2451; 16 VA. STAT. ANN. § 1756.

35. The statute was originally known as section 1983 of the Klu Klux Klan Act of

April 20, 1871, "An Act to Enforce the Provisions of the Fourteenth Amendment to the Constitution of the United States, and for other Purposes."

36. 42 U.S.C.A. § 1988.

37. 420 U.S. 308, 320, 95 S.Ct. 992, 43 L.Ed.2d 214 (1975); *on remand, sub nom. Strickland v. Inlow*, 519 F.2d 744 (8th Cir. 1975). [Case No.47]

Court recognized a federal cause of action against board members who act out with "ignorance or disregard of settled, indisputable law."[38] In softening the impact of its judgment, the Court added that board members could be liable to pay damages only if they "acted with such an impermissible motivation or with such disregard of the student's clearly established constitutional rights that his action cannot reasonably be characterized as being in good faith."[39] The Court applied similar language in *Gebser v. Lago Vista Independent School District*,[40] pointing out that school officials can be liable for sexual harassment in schools only if they acted with deliberate indifference to allegations of which they were aware.

In *Carey v. Piphus*,[41] another controversy over student suspensions, this one from Illinois, at issue was whether board members could have been liable for damages for violating procedural due process. The Court unanimously posited that although a violation of procedural due process could trigger a suit without proof of actual damages, an alleged victim must prove damages in order to collect more than a nominal award if the behavior of school officials is ultimately justified. Although conceding that the common law concept of compensatory damages for violations of legal rights applied to section 1983 cases, the Court specified that they could not be presumed in all circumstances solely on violations of due process.

The Court expanded the reach of section 1983 in *Monell v. Department of Social Services of City of New York (Monell)*,[42] a case challenging policies that required pregnant employees to take unpaid leaves of absence before being required to do so for medical reasons. The Court decreed that since local governments, including school boards, are "persons" under section 1983, they may be sued directly under its provision. Insofar as inconsistencies developed over the years, particularly in disputes involving school boards, the Court re-examined the legislative history of section 1983, remarking that Congress did not intend to grant absolute immunity to local governmental bodies. The Court declined to treat the question of whether local governments could be afforded some degree of immunity short of absolute immunity. Even so, the Court expressly stated that a local government may not be sued for an injury that was inflicted solely by one of its employees or agents. Instead, echoing the language of section 1983, the Court was of the view that a public body can be liable only when one of its policies or customs inflicts the injury of deprivation of any rights, privileges, or immunities secured by the Constitution and laws.

Two years later, the Court answered *Monell's* open question. Where a former police chief alleged that he was discharged in violation of his substantive and procedural due process rights, in *Owen v. City of*

38. *Id.* at 321.
39. *Id.* at 322.
40. 524 U.S. 274, 118 S.Ct. 1989, 141 L.Ed.2d 277 [125 Educ. L. Rep. 1055] (1998). [Case No. 115]

41. 435 U.S. 247, 98 S.Ct. 1042, 55 L.Ed.2d 252 (1978). [Case No. 48]

42. 436 U.S. 658, 98 S.Ct. 2018, 56 L.Ed.2d 611 (1978).

Independence, Missouri,[43] the Court ascertained that local government officials were not entitled to qualified immunity based on good faith. The Court asserted that if constitutional violations committed in good faith were not subject to damages claims, public officials could have thwarted section 1983's purposes. According to the Court, it was fairer to allocate any financial burden to the costs of government borne by all taxpayers than to allow the impact to fall solely on those whose rights were violated. The Court contended that since doctrines of tort law changed significantly over the past century, views of governmental responsibility should reflect this evolution.

One result of the Court's reliance on the subjective "impermissible motivation" limit on qualified immunity in *Wood* was that it called for trials with the effect that since section 1983 suits against school, and other public, officials could not be disposed of by summary judgment, the judiciary was becoming unduly burdened by insubstantial claims. Acknowledging the problem in *Harlow v. Fitzgerald*, a case from the District of Columbia over an official's allegedly unlawful discharge from the Air Force, the Court eliminated the subjective standard. The Court left the objective standard in place, which requires defendants to prove that they did not "violate clearly established constitutional or statutory rights of which a reasonable person would have known."[44] The Court was persuaded that officials who violate this objective standard are not entitled to immunity.

In a case that may have a significant impact on the application of section 1983, the Sixth Circuit affirmed that the Michigan athletic association's use of differential scheduling of girls high school sports seasons, when compared to their male counterparts, violated equal protection.[45] On further review, the Supreme Court vacated the Sixth Circuit's judgment[46] in light of *Rancho Palos Verdes v. Abrams* (*Abrams*).[47] In *Abrams*, the Court wrote that a petitioner could not file suit under section 1983 since the telecommunications statute at issue provided a remedy. To the extent that school boards are often sued under section 1983, even though other federal laws provide statutory remedies, if other courts follow *Abrams'* apparent suggestion that plaintiffs cannot rely on section 1983 to file constitutional claims, then it could have a major impact on school-related claims.

Reestablishment of Non–Liability by State Statute

After an initial wave of litigation abrogating immunity, state legislatures re-established at least portions of it for officials who act within the

---

43. 445 U.S. 622, 100 S.Ct. 1398, 63 L.Ed.2d 673 (1980). *See also Maine v. Thiboutot*, 448 U.S. 1, 100 S.Ct. 2502, 65 L.Ed.2d 555 (1980) (holding that officials who acted under color of state law violated the rights of parents in denying them aid to families with dependent children).

44. 457 U.S. 800, 818, 102 S.Ct. 2727, 73 L.Ed.2d 396 (1982).

45. *Committees for Equity v. Michigan High School Athletic Ass'n*, 377 F.3d 504 [190 Educ. L. Rep. 67] (6th Cir. 2004).

46. *Michigan High School Athletic Ass'n v. Communities for Equity*, ___ U.S. ___, 125 S.Ct. 1973, 161 L.Ed.2d 845 (2005).

47. *City of Rancho Palos Verdes, Cal. v. Abrams*, 544 U.S. 113, 125 S.Ct. 1453, 161 L.Ed.2d 316 (2005), *on remand*, 406 F.3d 1094 (9th Cir. 2005).

scope of their authority.[48] Yet, since the courts have the power to review legislative actions, a tension can arise between the two branches of government. While legislation ordinarily treats immunity directly, the Supreme Court of Alabama, conceding that the legislature is the appropriate body to make policy in the field of governmental immunity, ruled that it was conferred by a statute that empowered school boards to file suit but that did not mention that they were immune from liability if sued.[49]

The common law doctrine of non-liability of governmental bodies does not extend to employees.[50] However, it appears that legislatures can grant at least a measure of immunity to employees[51] and, even if they do not prevent suits against employees, can provide indemnification for monetary judgments if they are liable.[52]

On three occasions, the Supreme Court of Illinois interpreted legislation that placed teachers squarely *in loco parentis* with regard to students and provided that boards were not liable for acts of employees unless the individuals were also at fault. Insofar as parents are liable to their children only in the case of wilful and wanton misconduct, the statute makes this the standard that plaintiffs must meet to establish teacher liability.[53] In later cases, the court declared that boards may be liable even if no *in loco parentis* relationship existed at the site of an injury such as where a person with a free pass to a football game was hurt when knocked to the ground by one of a large number of boisterous young people who were milling around[54] and where school officials allegedly provided a player with an inadequate and defective football helmet.[55]

Negligence

In General

Negligence is a common law tort involving fault when one's unintentional conduct breaches a duty of care and injures another person or persons. In school settings, boards and their employees have the duty to protect students from reasonably foreseeable risks of harm. The duty of educators to supervise students aside, they are not insurers of student safety since most injuries in schools derive from what the law calls unavoidable, or pure, accidents, meaning those for which no legal fault

---

48. *See, e.g., Brown v. Wichita State Univ.*, 547 P.2d 1015 (Kan.1976); *English v. Newark Housing Auth.*, 351 A.2d 368 (N.J.Super.Ct.App.Div.1976).

49. *Enterprise City Bd. of Educ. v. Miller*, 348 So.2d 782 (Ala.1977).

50. *Baird v. Hosmer*, 347 N.E.2d 533 (Ohio 1976); *Sansone v. Bechtel*, 429 A.2d 820 (Conn. 1980).

51. *Kobylanski v. Chicago Bd. of Educ.*, 347 N.E.2d 705 (Ill.1976); *Barr v. Bernhard*, 562 S.W.2d 844 (Tex.1978).

52. *Talmadge v. District School Bd. of Lake County*, 355 So.2d 502 (Fla.Dist.Ct. App.1978).

53. *Kobylanski v. Chicago Bd. of Educ.*, 347 N.E.2d 705 (Ill.1976).

54. *Tanari v. School Directors of Dist. No. 502, County of Bureau*, 373 N.E.2d 5 (Ill.1977).

55. *Gerrity v. Beatty*, 373 N.E.2d 1323 (Ill.1978).

lies,[56] and they cannot reasonably be expected to supervise and control students continuously.[57]

In order for school officials to be liable for negligence, injured parties must prove that educators failed to meet the elements of negligence: duty and the related concept of foreseeability, breach, injury, and causation. Moreover, school officials must not have been able to assert a defense such as immunity, assumption of risk, and/or contributory/comparative negligence that can help to reduce, or even eliminate, liability. In reviewing the elements of negligence it is important to realize that since they are not mutually exclusive, many of the cases discussed in this chapter can be used to demonstrate multiple points of law. Insofar as the facts are essential in evaluating whether a party has breached its duty of care[58] and is negligent, the following discussion and use of exemplary cases help to illustrate some of the wide array of issues that arise in school settings.

Duty

In the law of negligence, absent a legal relationship, a person has no duty to act. To this end, it is important to recognize that educators who act within the scope of their duties whether in classrooms, at other schools in a district, or as part of a co-curricular or extracurricular activities whether on campus or off, have a duty to assist all students in a group even if they do not know an individual child or group of students personally. This duty arises based on educators' legal relationships with their school boards as a whole and is not limited to children (or others) from the buildings where they work. Given the significance of the element of duty, it is safe to say that most negligence cases can be viewed in the broad context of adequacy of supervision. Theoretically, since adequate supervision should prevent students from being injured as a result of reasonably foreseeable dangers, all activities must be supervised depending on such factors as their nature and the ages of the children involved.

The Supreme Court of California addressed the question of legally sufficient supervision when a student who was injured at school died.[59] Where two students "slapboxed" during lunch period, one fell backward, fractured his skull, and died that night. Even though responsibility for supervising that area was assigned to members of the physical education department, the head left supervision to whomever was in the gymnasium office rather than create a formal schedule. The court observed that the teacher on duty was eating lunch and preparing for classes at a desk that faced away from the windows, and a wall obscured his view of the

---

56. *See, e.g., Schultz v. Cheney School Dist. No. 360*, 371 P.2d 59 (Wash.1962) (imposing no liability for a bus accident).

57. *Mirand v. City of N.Y.*, 614 N.Y.S.2d 372 [92 Educ. L. Rep. 957] (N.Y.1994).

58. *See Travis v. Bohannon*, 115 P.3d 342 [199 Educ. L. Rep. 942] (Wash. Ct. App.

2005) (reiterating the general rule that whether school officials satisfied the four element of negligence was a question of fact for a jury).

59. *Dailey v. Los Angeles Unified School Dist.*, 470 P.2d 360 (Cal.1970).

area where the slapboxing took place. In explaining that there was evidence from which a jury could have uncovered negligence, the court noted that the mere fact a student's misconduct was the immediate precipitating cause of injury did not necessarily mean that the teacher did not engage in negligent supervision.[60] On the other hand, an appellate court in Pennsylvania affirmed that where a student severely injured his hand during a woodshop class, and the school board characterized the teacher's conduct as negligent supervision, he was entitled to monetary damages.[61]

Once the law recognizes the existence of a legal relationship, educators have the duty to anticipate reasonably foreseeable injuries or risks to students and take reasonable steps to try to protect them from harm. Insofar as foreseeability is a highly flexible concept that varies based on a student's age and physical condition as well as the degree of danger inherent in a situation, the law does not expect educators to foresee all harm that might befall children. Rather, educators are responsible for only those mishaps that can reasonably be anticipated or of which they are actually aware. In Florida, an appellate court illustrated this point in affirming that a school board was liable where a kindergarten student was sexually assaulted in the class bathroom.[62] The court agreed that school officials breached their duty when they failed to warn a substitute teacher that the assaulting child had a history of developmental problems and sexually aggressive behavior or to instruct the substitute about pass procedures used to restrict more than one student at a time from occupying the bathroom.

Whether an act is foreseeable cannot be based on speculation. If school officials take reasonable precautions, and an intervening act that could not have been foreseen occurs, they are not likely to be liable. For example, where teachers could not have anticipated that students were going to pull chairs out from under peers as they attempted to sit down, courts have refused to impose liability.[63] Other courts refused to impose liability on school boards for events that were not foreseeable, such as where a student slipped and was injured during a classroom skit;[64] where a high school student was injured when he ran, or was pushed, into another participant during a "frisbee relay race" in a physical education class;[65] where students engaged in a spontaneous fighting;[66] where a

60. For a similar outcome, *see Sheehan v. St. Peter's Catholic School*, 188 N.W.2d 868 (Minn.1971).

61. *Wells v. Harrisburg Area School Dist.*, 884 A.2d 946 [203 Educ. L. Rep. 288] (Pa.Cmwlth. Ct. 2005).

62. *Miami-Dade County School Bd. v. A.N., Sr.*, 905 So.2d 203 [199 Educ. L. Rep. 1003] (Fla. Dist. Ct. App. 2005), *review denied*, 915 So.2d 1196 (Fla. 2005).

63. *Boyer v. Jablonski*, 435 N.E.2d 436 [4 Educ. L. Rep. 596] (Ohio Ct.App.1980); *Tomlinson v. Board of Educ. of Elmira*, 583 N.Y.S.2d 664 [74 Educ. L. Rep. 1262] (N.Y.App.Div.1992).

64. *Jones v. Jackson Pub. Schools*, 760 So.2d 730 [145 Educ. L. Rep. 845] (Miss. 2000).

65. *Siegell v. Herricks Union Free School Dist.*, 777 N.Y.S.2d 148 [187 Educ. L. Rep. 983] (N.Y. App. Div. 2004).

66. *Hernandez v. Christopher Robin Academy*, 714 N.Y.S.2d 518 [147 Educ. L. Rep. 1057] (N.Y.App.Div.2000); *Johnsen v. Carmel Cent. School Dist.*, 716 N.Y.S.2d 403 [149 Educ. L. Rep. 592] (N.Y.App.Div.2000); *Dadich v. Syosset High School*, 717 N.Y.S.2d 634 [150 Educ. L. Rep. 234] (N.Y.App.Div.2000).

child who was not a member of a group threw rocks at and injured a student who was a participant in an after-school program that was gathered at a playground;[67] where a child suddenly and spontaneously kicked a friend while the two were on a school playground;[68] and where one child struck another after they exited a school bus[69] unless one child was clearly the aggressor and school officials failed to intervene.[70] At the same time, depending on the facts, not all courts agree on whether boards should be liable if children are injured while using playground equipment.[71]

While the requisite level of supervision may decrease before the opening of a school day and after students are dismissed, once officials know, or reasonably should know, that children are present, they must take precautions to ensure their safety. In an older case, the Supreme Court of Washington affirmed that a board was liable for injuries that a nine-year-old sustained where an upright piano fell on her when she was in school after the class day ended.[72] The court recognized that since the sixty-year-old piano was in a position that it could easily have tipped over, and it was foreseeable that small children would try to move it, the board was liable. Similarly, where a board operated a breakfast program but provided only one teacher for the first half hour from the start of breakfast, an appellate court in Louisiana decided that it was responsible for the injuries that a child sustained when she fell in the school's playground prior to the start of classes.[73] Further, where a principal was aware that students were playing football before classes began because he directed them to play in the specific location where a child was injured, the Supreme Court of Idaho found that a trial was necessary to consider whether he breached his duty to supervise the students.[74]

Conversely, where a student was struck by a car after being chased off of school grounds by a peer before classes started, he and his mother unsuccessfully sued the board for negligence.[75] The Supreme Court of Kansas affirmed that the student could not recover for negligence absent evidence that officials affirmatively assumed a duty to render services to,

67. *Rinehart ex rel. Combs v. Boys & Girls Club of Chula Vista*, 34 Cal.Rptr.3d 677 [202 Educ. L. Rep. 246] (Cal. Ct. App. 2005).

68. *Van Leuvan v. Rondout Valley Cent. School Dist.*, 798 N.Y.S.2d 770 [200 Educ. L. Rep. 295] (N.Y. App. Div. 2005).

69. *Murnyack v. Rebon*, 801 N.Y.S.2d 658 [202 Educ. L. Rep. 275] (N.Y. App. Div. 2005).

70. *Shoemaker v. Whitney Point Cent. School Dist.*, 750 N.Y.S.2d 355 [171 Educ. L. Rep. 903] (N.Y.App.Div.2002), *leave to appeal dismissed*, 757 N.Y.S.2d 820 [175 Educ. L. Rep. 662] (N.Y. 2003).

71. For cases rejecting board liability see, *e.g.*, *Navarra v. Lynbrook Pub. Schools*, 733 N.Y.S.2d 730 [159 Educ. L. Rep. 717] (N.Y.App.Div.2001); *Sinto v. City of Long

Beach*, 736 N.Y.S.2d 700 [161 Educ. L. Rep. 594] (N.Y.App.Div.2002). For a case rejecting a board's motion for summary judgment, *see Lemos v. City of Poughkeepsie School Dist.*, 749 N.Y.S.2d 88 [171 Educ. L. Rep. 332] (N.Y.App.Div.2002).

72. *Kidwell v. School Dist. No. 300, Whitman County*, 335 P.2d 805 (Wash. 1959).

73. *Laneheart v. Orleans Parish School Bd.*, 524 So.2d 138 [46 Educ. L. Rep. 1266] (La.Ct. App. 1988).

74. *Bauer v. Minidoka School Dist. No. 331*, 778 P.2d 336 [55 Educ. L. Rep. 748] (Idaho 1989).

75. *Glaser ex rel. Glaser v. Emporia Unified School Dist. No. 253*, 21 P.3d 573 [152 Educ. L. Rep. 795] (Kan.2001).

protect, or supervise him before classes began since he was not in their custody or control.

Litigation often arises when students throw, or propel, various objects around schools and school grounds. As such, where a child was struck in the eye by a paper clip that another student shot from a rubber band, the Supreme Court of New Jersey reasoned that the principal was liable for his injuries.[76] The court maintained that since the principal was present at school but had not set rules for students as they gathered before entering classes, had not assigned teachers or others to assist him in supervising children at that time, and was engaged in activities other than overseeing the children when the accident took place, he was liable.

On the other hand, the Supreme Court of Wyoming was of the opinion that a school board and a teacher's aid were not liable where a seven-year-old was partially blinded by a small rock, which was thrown by a fellow student and bounced off a larger rock, while the children were at recess.[77] The court observed that since the aid who was supervising the playground where the accident occurred walked by the students approximately thirty seconds before the accident took place but did not see anything out of the ordinary, and the injury was not foreseeable, neither she nor the board could be liable. In like fashion, an appellate court in Ohio affirmed that a board was not liable for a first grader's injuries after he was struck in the eye by a dirt-ball thrown by a fourth grader since the older child's action was not foreseeable.[78]

As reflected by two cases from New York, snowballs can create unique controversies. In the first, the Court of Appeals of New York held that school officials were not liable for the injury that a child sustained when he was struck by a snowball that was thrown on school property while he was returning from lunch recess.[79] The court acknowledged that since there was a school rule against throwing snowballs and the injured child's teacher warned students not to throw snowballs, the board was not liable because officials were unaware of any special danger and there was no proof that the teacher was aware of other snowball throwing on the day of the incident. The court went so far as to comment that since no one grows up in New York without throwing, or being hit by, snowballs, it would have required educators to engage in intensive policing, almost child by child, to take all snowball throwing out of play activity. On the other hand, two years later, an appellate court in New York upheld a jury verdict of negligence in another snowball case.[80] In distinguishing its factual setting from the previous case, the court posited that educators knew, or should have known, of hard frozen snow or ice in the school yard that caused the child's injury. Moreover, the court pointed out that there was evidence of inadequate

76. *Titus v. Lindberg*, 228 A.2d 65 (N.J. 1967). [Case No. 49]

77. *Fagan v. Summers*, 498 P.2d 1227 (Wyo.1972).

78. *Allison v. Field Local School Dist.*, 553 N.E.2d 1383 [60 Educ. L. Rep. 191] (Ohio Ct. App.1988).

79. *Lawes v. Board of Educ. of City of N.Y.*, 266 N.Y.S.2d 364 (N.Y.1965). [Case No. 50]

80. *Cioffi v. Board of Educ. of City of N.Y.*, 278 N.Y.S.2d 249 (N.Y.App.Div.1967). *See also Thorne v. Burr*, 340 N.Y.S.2d 677 (N.Y.App.Div.1973).

supervision of the school yard when the child was injured by an iceball after becoming the target for a large number of students who gathered there.

In a case that overlaps with the section on sports and dangerous activities, where a sixteen-year-old female high school football player suffered serious internal injuries after being tackled cleanly by a player from the other team, she and her mother sued their school board for negligent supervision.[81] Even though it voiced its concern over the seriousness of the student's injuries, an appellate court in Maryland affirmed that the board did not have a duty to warn her or her mother of the obvious risks posed by her voluntary participation in interscholastic football because the foreseeable risk of injury was normal and obvious.

As violence continues to rear its ugly head in and around school activities, parties increasingly file suit in attempts to render school officials liable for harm to students. For instance, the tragic shootings at Columbine High School in April 1999 that left fifteen people dead including a teacher and the two students who undertook the rampage, and injured others, gave rise to a series of unsuccessful lawsuits against the board and other public officials.[82]

Two other cases illustrate the types of issues that educators face with regard to violence in and around schools. In Louisiana, the mother of a student who was shot and killed in a parking lot after a school-sponsored fund-raising dance sued the board and the club where the event occurred over an alleged lack of security. An appellate court was satisfied that the board had not breached its duty of care since officials lacked the requisite degree of foreseeability that would have imposed a duty on them to provide additional security in the parking lot.[83] The court added that the club owner was not liable for the student's death since there was only slight foreseeability and gravity of harm from the criminal acts of a third party in the parking lot. Similarly, where a student was shot by an unknown assailant while leaving a dance at his high school cafeteria, an appellate court in New York affirmed a grant of summary judgment in favor of a board in his suit that sought to recover for his injuries.[84] The court agreed that the student's claim of inadequate supervision lacked merit since officials could not reasonably have foreseen that the shooting would take place.

81. *Hammond v. Board of Educ. of Carroll County,* 639 A.2d 223 [90 Educ. L. Rep. 256] (Md.Ct.Spec.App.1994).

82. *See, e.g., Ruegsegger v. Jefferson County School Dist. R–1,* 187 F.Supp.2d 1284 [162 Educ. L. Rep. 796] (D.Colo.2001); *Rohrbough v. Stone,* 189 F.Supp.2d 1088 [163 Educ. L. Rep. 292] (D.Colo.2001), *reconsideration denied,* 189 F.Supp.2d 1144 (D.Colo.2002); *Schnurr v. Board of County Commr's,* 189 F.Supp.2d 1105 [163 Educ. L. Rep. 309] (D.Colo.2001).

83. *Lee v. B & B Ventures,* 793 So.2d 215 [157 Educ. L. Rep. 428] (La.Ct.App.

2001), *writ denied,* 807 So.2d 236 (La. 2002).

84. *Jimenez v. City of N.Y.,* 738 N.Y.S.2d 380 [162 Educ. L. Rep. 500] (N.Y.App.Div.2002). For other cases where school officials were not liable for the off-campus shooting deaths of students *see, e.g., Hill v. Safford Unified School Dist.,* 952 P.2d 754 [124 Educ. L. Rep. 721] (Ariz. Ct.App.1997); *Kindred v. Board of Educ. of Memphis City Schools,* 946 S.W.2d 47 [118 Educ. L. Rep. 1227] (Tenn.Ct.App.1996).

Breach

Two important items must be taken into account when evaluating whether educators have breached their duty of care. The first relates to how educators performed, or did not perform, their duties. More specifically, educators can breach their duties in one of two ways.[85] First, educators can breach their duty by not acting when there is a duty to act; this is referred to as nonfeasance. Second, educators can breach their duty by failing to act properly when there is a duty to act; this is known as misfeasance. In addition, where educators act improperly, or with evil intent, they commit malfeasance, more properly an intentional tort, as in cases involving sexual misconduct with students.[86] Additionally, if school officials are aware that employees are failing to meet their responsibilities, whether due to nonfeasance, misfeasance, or malfeasance, then they, and their boards, may be liable for the tortious conduct of staff members.

The second major consideration under breach is the appropriate standard of care that educators must follow. In evaluating whether individuals have met the appropriate level of care, courts have adopted a common law standard of reasonableness. Another flexible standard,[87] courts typically instruct juries to consider educators' behavior in light of the legal construct known as the reasonable person, also known as the reasonably prudent person. Although stopping short of establishing a clear hierarchy, based on education and years of experience working with children, a reasonable teacher is likely to be expected to provide a higher standard of care than a reasonable person but not to the same level of care as a reasonable parent. That is, courts have tried to create an objective standard that requires teachers to provide the same level of care as reasonably prudent professionals of similar education and background. This degree of care is ordinarily based on equivalent age, training, education, experience, maturity, and other relevant characteristics.

Disputes involving sports illustrate the significance of applying the proper standard of care in negligence cases. When a high school football player who was being considered for an athletic scholarship to college broke his neck while correctly executing a block, the Court of Appeals of New York asserted that the coach should not have been judged under the same standard of care as a reasonably prudent parent.[88] Instead, the

---

85. See *Lindberg ex rel. Conservator for Backlund v. United States*, 368 F.Supp.2d 1028, 1032 [198 Educ. L. Rep. 595] (D.S.D. 2005) ("negligence may be active or passive; it may consist of either doing something negligently or negligently failing to act.").

86. For a discussion of sexual harassment and misconduct, *see* Chapter 13.

87. *See Simmons ex rel. Simmons v. Columbus County Bd. of Educ.*, 615 S.E.2d 69, 74 [199 Educ. L. Rep. 955] (N.C. Ct. App. 2005) (" 'The standard of due care is

always the conduct of a reasonably prudent person under the circumstances. Although the standard remains constant, the proper degree of care varies with the circumstances.' "), citing *Bolkhir v. North Carolina State Univ.*, 365 S.E.2d 898, 900 [45 Educ. L. Rep. 393] (N.C.1988).

88. *Benitez v. New York City Bd. of Educ.*, 543 N.Y.S.2d 29 [54 Educ. L. Rep. 933] (N.Y. 1989). [Case No. 51] court indicated that since the student voluntarily participated in the game, the coach met the less demanding standard of ordinary reasonable care. In addition, the court discussed the defense of assumption of risk, concluding that since the student-athlete voluntarily participated in the game and was aware of the possible risks involved, the coach was not liable. Similarly, a high school football player sued his school board after his coaches, both of whom had teaching certificates and coaching endorsements, allowed him to return to a game in which he had suffered a concussion. The Supreme Court of Nebraska was of the view that the proper standard of care for the coaches was that of a reasonably prudent person with a teaching certificate and coaching endorsement rather than the lower standard of the reasonable person who did not possess such credentials.[89] The court remarked that since coaches with coaching endorsements received specialized training in athletic injuries, including head injuries, they should have met the heightened standard of care. Following remand, the court ascertained that the coaches acted in accord with this higher standard since they evaluated the player several times before permitting him to return to the game and were familiar with the symptoms of a concussion.[90]

A second case from Nebraska involved a first-grade student who was injured while playing a game that his teacher had just taught his class. The state supreme court affirmed that the teacher failed to act in a way that a reasonably prudent person in her position should have because she did not provide direct supervision, even in the early portions of a game that the children were playing for the first time.[91]

Injury

Before an aggrieved party can prevail in a negligence action, an injury must be one for which compensation can be awarded. For example, if a student who was running through a school hallway slipped and fell on water that leaked from a drinking fountain that had been accumulating on the floor for at least an hour, three factors need to be examined. The first question is whether school officials had a duty to keep the floor safe and clean. Assuming the obvious, that officials had such a duty, the question of foreseeability comes into play. To the extent that officials should have foreseen that such an incident could have occurred, they should have had it cleaned up reasonably quickly. Second, the issue of the school's duty and possible breach, in terms of supervising the area, must be answered. The third concern is the nature of the child's injuries. If the child's only injury was a wet pair of pants, then it is highly unlikely that his claim will proceed. However, if the child broke his leg on falling, then there is a greater likelihood that this may be deemed an injury for which compensation can be awarded.

89. *Cerny v. Cedar Bluffs Junior/Senior Pub. School*, 628 N.W.2d 697 [155 Educ. L. Rep. 827] (Neb. 2001).

90. *Cerny v. Cedar Bluffs Junior/Senior Pub. School*, 679 N.W.2d 198 [187 Educ. L. Rep. 783] (Neb.2004).

91. *Johnson v. School Dist. of Millard*, 573 N.W.2d 116 [123 Educ. L. Rep. 904] (Neb.1998).

Insofar as the existence of a physical harm is present in most of the cases discussed in this section, one additional, unusual case, from Louisiana exemplifies causation by illustrating the nature of an injury. An appellate court affirmed that a school board was liable for the emotional injuries that a kindergarten-aged child suffered when a physical education teacher told him that he hanged his friends with a jump rope.[92] The court thought that since the evidence revealed that the child was a well-adjusted five-year-old before the teacher pretended that he hanged his friends to death with a jump rope while he was not present, he and his parents were entitled to remuneration for the emotional harm that he experienced.

Causation

The final element in establishing liability for negligence is that school personnel must be the legal, or proximate cause, of injuries brought about by their breaches. Put another way, as situations evolve, the last person (or group of persons) in a temporal chain of events who could have taken steps to prevent an injury from occurring is typically considered as at least contributing to the legal cause.

Two cases from New York demonstrate judicial analysis with regard to causation. As two middle school students engaged in roughhousing during recess, shortly after they stopped fighting, one child threw a stick and injured the eye of the other. When parents filed a negligence claim, an appellate court was persuaded that since there was insufficient actual or constructive notice of dangerous conduct that such an injury would have occurred, educators did not breach their duty of adequate supervision.[93] The court thought that any negligence on the part of educators did not proximately cause the student's injury because the time span between the fight and the stick-throwing incident was so short that greater supervision could not have prevented the injury. The court also wrote that the student's supervisory negligence claim was without merit since he was a willing participant in the incident.[94]

A board challenged the denial of its motion for summary judgment in a case filed by a high school student who was assaulted in school after school hours by a former student. An appellate court in New York reversed in favor of the board on the ground that it was not liable absent a showing that the attack was foreseeable.[95] The court believed not only that although there were previous trespassing incidents by former students after school hours, none involved physical violence against stu-

92. *Spears on Behalf of Spears v. Jefferson Parish School Bd.*, 646 So.2d 1104 [96 Educ. L. Rep. 884] (La.Ct.App.1994). [Case No. 52]

93. *Janukajtis v. Fallon*, 726 N.Y.S.2d 451 [154 Educ. L. Rep. 912] (N.Y.App.Div. 2001). For a similar outcome, *see Convey v. City of Rye School Dist.*, 710 N.Y.S.2d 641 [146 Educ. L. Rep. 350] (N.Y.App.Div.2000).

94. *Lopez v. Freeport Union Free School Dist.*, 734 N.Y.S.2d 97 [159 Educ. L. Rep. 732] (N.Y.App.Div.2001) (finding no liability when a child fell from a jungle gym).

95. *Nossoughi v. Ramapo Cent. School Dist.*, 731 N.Y.S.2d 78 [157 Educ. L. Rep. 806] (N.Y.App.Div.2001).

dents but also that any negligence by the school officials was not the proximate cause of the plaintiff's injuries.

Insofar as two sets of circumstances, those involving athletics and off-campus activities, give rise to special concerns, these topics are addressed under their own headings.

Athletics

It almost goes without saying that the greater the risk of injuries to students in activities such as interscholastic sports involving physical contact, the more carefully that school officials must provide supervision. Moreover, proper instruction before students engage in risky activities is particularly important.[96] Even so, it is not essential for educators to instruct students about specific dangers of doing things that are clearly forbidden.[97]

An older leading case involved a physical education teacher's permitting two husky male students who were untrained in boxing to fight one round and part of another while he sat in the bleachers. When one of the students was fatally injured, an appellate court in New York affirmed that the teacher was liable both because he failed to teach them the proper principles of defense and since he was unable to supervise them properly from his seat in the bleachers.[98]

On the other hand, the Supreme Court of Missouri affirmed that when individuals are engaged in sports involving physical contact, such as wrestling, it is necessary to show in great detail what duty instructors failed to provide in actions to recover damages for injuries.[99] The court decreed that general charges of failure to teach or designate rules are insufficient since plaintiffs must show precisely how the omissions of educators led to the injuries that the children sustained or how the performance of omitted acts would have prevented the harm from occurring. In refusing to impose liability on the teacher, the court recognized that students who engage in activities such as wrestling are presumed to have assumed the risks inherent in the activity, a topic discussed below under the defenses to negligence.

In a tragic case from Texas, parents claimed that school officials acted with deliberate indifference where their daughter died following the completion of a run during training activities for her high school basketball team.[100] Along with deciding that the parents failed to prove that school officials acted with deliberate indifference to their daughter's well-being, a federal trial court granted a motion for qualified immunity for both the team's coach and trainer.

96. *Benitez v. New York City Bd. of Educ.*, 543 N.Y.S.2d 29 [54 Educ. L. Rep. 933] (N.Y. 1989) (also discussing assumption of risk). [Case No. 51]

97. *Payne v. North Carolina Dep't of Human Res.*, 382 S.E.2d 449 [55 Educ. L. Rep. 753] (N.C.Ct.App.1989).

98. *La Valley v. Stanford*, 70 N.Y.S.2d 460 (N.Y.App.Div.1947).

99. *Smith v. Consolidated School Dist. No. 2*, 408 S.W.2d 50 (Mo.1966).

100. *Livingston v. DeSoto Indep. School Dist.*, 391 F.Supp.2d 463 [203 Educ. L. Rep. 665] (N.D. Tex. 2005).

Immunity as a defense aside, it is understandable that school officials seek to limit liability for student participation in activities that can cause injuries. As long as officials carefully craft release forms, courts are unwilling to impose liability.[101] At the same time, courts are likely to invalidate releases that are too broad or vague. For instance, the Supreme Court of Washington vitiated release forms that officials in different districts required students to sign before engaging in school-related activities such as interscholastic athletics. According to the court, the releases, which sought to protect boards from all future negligence, violated public policy for a variety of reasons.[102] Similarly, an appellate court in New York invalidated a release form that was executed by parents of a child who participated in a youth wrestling activity which stipulated only that they absolved the president of the tournament and head coach of all risks beyond those inherent in wrestling.[103] The court affirmed that the release was void *ab initio* and did not bar their negligence action because it failed to limit liability plainly and precisely.

Educators must also provide adequate supervision at school-sponsored extracurricular activities. One of the most dramatic, albeit older, cases in this area arose when, as part of a club's initiation ceremony, a student who was subjected to an electric shock died. The Supreme Court of South Dakota contended that a teacher was personally liable since he actively participated in the initiation activities, even to the point of testing the electrical appliance.[104]

A dispute from New York illustrates how school officials have the duty to protect spectators who attend athletic events even if they occur off-campus; this case also serves as a segue to the next section. A high school student who was injured as a spectator at a school-sponsored ice hockey game when a puck struck her in the nose filed a personal injury action against the rink, its owner, and her school board, claiming that the defendants breached their duty of care to keep her safe. On further review of the denial of the owner's motion for summary judgment, an appellate court in New York affirmed that the student's suit should have been able to proceed.[105] The court noted that genuine issues of material fact remained over whether the protective screening around the rink satisfied the owner's duty to protect the student and other spectators from flying pucks.

Off-Premises Activities

The liability of school board personnel and/or boards for negligence depends on whether they have met their duty of care. The duty to

101. *Aaris v. Las Virgenes Unified School Dist.*, 75 Cal.Rptr.2d 801 [126 Educ. L. Rep. 350] (Cal.Ct.App.1998). *See also Sharon v. City of Newton*, 769 N.E.2d 738 [165 Educ. L. Rep. 742] (Mass.2002).

102. *Wagenblast v. Odessa School Dist. No. 105–157–166J*, 758 P.2d 968 [48 Educ. L. Rep. 676] (Wash.1988).

103. *Alexander v. Kendall Cent. School Dist.*, 634 N.Y.S.2d 318 [105 Educ. L. Rep. 262] (N.Y.App.Div.1995).

104. *De Gooyer v. Harkness*, 13 N.W.2d 815 (S.D.1944).

105. *Guenther v. West Seneca Cent. School Dist.*, 796 N.Y.S.2d 465 [199 Educ. L. Rep. 363] (N.Y. App. Div. 2005).

supervise students on school grounds is clear. Efforts to extend the scope of duty beyond the premises are increasing. In this regard, it is important to emphasize that common law sets the duty of school officials as being coextensive with, and concomitant to, their physical custody and control over children.

When boards provide transportation for children, their doing so in effect extends their boundaries via the bus to stops where students board and leave buses.[106] As can be expected, the use of school buses to transport students has generated a fair amount of litigation. As long as bus stops are not located in unreasonably dangerous places, boards are unlikely to be liable for injuries to children that occur there.[107] Boards also have no duty to ensure that students reach designated bus stops safely prior to the arrival of school buses[108] and, as long as the distance from home is reasonable, children can be required to walk to bus stops.[109]

On the homeward trip, bus drivers have the duty to see that children have crossed a road to the opposite side of the street if necessary.[110] In such a case, an appellate court in Georgia rejected a board's motion for summary judgment in the wrongful death action that a mother brought against it, the school bus driver, and another driver after the other driver struck and killed her daughter.[111] After the mother and other driver reached a settlement agreement, the court affirmed that material issues of fact existed as to whether the bus driver initiated the boarding procedure for children. In New York, parents of a student who was injured when he was struck by a car as he exited a bus sued the bus company, driver, and school board. An appellate court affirmed that the bus company's failure to equip the vehicle as a school bus did not violate a law regulating school buses since it was inapplicable to a bus that was not used solely to transport students.[112]

Where a second-grade student, who was dropped off early by his school bus driver, died as a result of injuries that he sustained while attempting to climb into his house through a window, his parents sued the board for negligence. The Supreme Court of Ohio ruled that since a genuine issue of material fact existed as to whether the driver violated a state statute that prohibited school bus drivers from starting their vehicles until after the children leaving them have reached places of safety, the suit should have been able to proceed.[113]

---

106. *Pratt v. Robinson*, 384 N.Y.S.2d 749 (N.Y.1976).

107. *See, e.g., Hackler By and Through Hackler v. Unified School Dist. No. 500, of Kansas City*, 777 P.2d 839 [55 Educ. L. Rep. 311] (Kan.1989); *Moshier v. Phoenix Cent. School Dist.*, 605 N.Y.S.2d 581 [88 Educ. L. Rep. 200] (N.Y.App.Div.1993).

108. *Cavalier v. Ward*, 723 So.2d 480 [131 Educ. L. Rep. 1166] (La.Ct.App.1998).

109. *Flowers v. Independent School Dist. of Tama*, 16 N.W.2d 570 (Iowa 1944).

110. *Johnson v. Svoboda*, 260 N.W.2d 530 (Iowa 1977).

111. *DeKalb County School Dist. v. Allen*, 561 S.E.2d 202 [163 Educ. L. Rep. 1002] (Ga.Ct. App.2002).

112. *Sigmond v. Liberty Lines Transit*, 689 N.Y.S.2d 239 [135 Educ. L. Rep. 218] (N.Y.App. Div.1999).

113. *Turner v. Central Local School Dist.*, 706 N.E.2d 1261 [132 Educ. L. Rep. 909] (Ohio 1999).

In a case that overlaps with field trips, the parents of first-graders and chaperones that were injured when the driver of a school bus lost control of his vehicle challenged a jury verdict in favor of the school and driver. Reversing in favor of the plaintiffs, an appellate panel in Indiana explained that the trial court committed a reversible error in not instructing the jury that it reasonably could have inferred that the driver should not have lost control of his bus as much as he did on a clear, dry spring day.[114]

School-sponsored field trips require special supervisory precautions because educators typically take children to unfamiliar places. While there are no specific guidelines for field trips, a rule of thumb is that the younger students are, the greater the amount, and degree, of supervision that educators must provide. When a sixth-grader was raped by acquaintances after she left the park where a class field trip occurred, the supervising teacher had left the park without her, stopped by her house, and returned to school. Although the teacher contacted the child's mother, she did not disclose the incident to officials at the school. The Court of Appeals of New York was convinced that the board was liable since evidence supported a jury's verdict that the rape was a foreseeable result of the danger created by the failure of educators to supervise the outing adequately.[115]

On a field trip to a zoo, a parent whose son was assaulted by children from another school sued the board for negligent supervision. The federal trial court in the District of Columbia rejected the board's motion to dismiss the claim on the basis that its staff owed a duty to supervise its students in order to prevent foreseeable harm such as the type that befell the child.[116]

Difficulties can arise when students are permitted, as part of open campus policies, to leave school. Connecticut's highest court held that immunity prevented a suit for negligence based on a board policy that permitted tenth, eleventh, and twelfth-grade students to leave campus during unscheduled times.[117] The court found no specific ministerial duty to supervise high school students at all times. An appellate court in Arizona reached a similar result when parents of two children who were killed in a car accident challenged the failure of school officials to enforce their board's closed campus policy. The court affirmed that the board could not be liable because the failure of educators to enforce the policy did not breach their general duty to avoid exposing students to foreseeable, unreasonable risks of harm.[118]

114. *Aldana v. School City of East Chicago*, 769 N.E.2d 1201 [165 Educ. L. Rep. 769] (Ind.Ct. App.2002), *transfer denied*, 783 N.E.2d 699 (Ind. 2002).

115. *Bell v. Board of Educ. of the City of N.Y.*, 665 N.Y.S.2d 42 [122 Educ. L. Rep. 1031] (N.Y.1997).

116. *Thomas v. City Lights School*, 124 F.Supp.2d 707 [150 Educ. L. Rep. 169] (D.D.C.2000).

117. *Heigl v. Board of Educ. of Town of New Canaan*, 587 A.2d 423 [66 Educ. L. Rep. 674] (Conn.1991).

118. *Tollenaar v. Chino Valley School Dist.*, 945 P.2d 1310 [121 Educ. L. Rep. 1154] (Ariz.Ct. App.1997).

Two appellate courts in Louisiana reached different outcomes when students were molested after leaving school. The first court reviewed whether a school board owed a duty to insure the safety of a child who ordinarily walked home alone from school after an extracurricular activity. The board stationed crossing guards at the highway where the student was injured at the end of the school day but not at the completion of after-school activities. The court affirmed that since the one-hour time period that the guard was on duty was appropriate, it would have been unreasonable to impose a duty on school officials to require them to have students walk home in groups.[119] In the second case, after a junior high school student checked herself out of school in violation of a board policy that authorized only the principal or vice-principal to allow a child to leave during regular class hours, she was sexually molested by a stranger while walking home through a bad neighborhood. An appellate court in Louisiana affirmed that the board and officials breached their duty since the scope of their supervisory responsibilities encompassed the foreseeable risk that a female student walking through a bad neighborhood might fall victim to a criminal who frequented the area.[120] Neither court reviewed the defense of assumption of risk that is examined in the next section.

Defenses

Even if an injured party has established that the elements of negligence are present, school boards and their employees have three primary defenses available to limit or eliminate liability. The defenses recognize that even though boards and officials have the duty to look after students, they cannot be accountable for all conceivable harms that befall the children in their care.

Immunity

As discussed above, immunity is the most frequent defense employed by school systems. Immunity is based on the common law principle, now supplemented widely by various statutes dealing with such aspects as recreational[121] and discretionary function[122] immunity, that the government, in and through its various branches and departments such as school boards, cannot be liable for the tortious acts of their officers or employees.

119. *Jackson v. Colvin*, 732 So.2d 530 [135 Educ. L. Rep. 296] (La.Ct.App.1998).

120. *D.C. v. St. Landry Parish School Bd.*, 802 So.2d 19 [160 Educ. L. Rep. 686] (La.Ct.App. 2001), *writ denied*, 793 So.2d 169 (La. 2001).

121. *See, e.g., Auman v. School Dist. of Stanley–Boyd*, 635 N.W.2d 762 [159 Educ. L. Rep. 321] (Wis.2001).

122. *See, e.g., Cooper v. Paulding County School Dist.*, 595 S.E.2d 671 [187 Educ. L. Rep. 1091] (Ga. Ct. App. 2004); *Arteman v. Clinton Community Unit School Dist.*, 763 N.E.2d 756 [163 Educ. L. Rep. 913] (Ill.2002).

Contributory/Comparative Negligence

Both contributory and comparative negligence are premised on the notion that parties played parts in causing their injuries. The difference between these similar sounding defenses, which now apply in an almost equal number of jurisdictions, can be profound. Contributory negligence, which traces it origins in the United States back almost two hundred years,[123] completely bars individuals from recovering for their injuries if they contributed in any way to the harm that they suffered.[124]

As courts and legislatures increasingly recognized that the defense of contributory negligence led to inequitable results, an increasing number of jurisdictions adopted the standard of comparative negligence. Comparative negligence permits juries to apportion liability based on a percentage of relative fault between the parties as most states that rely on this approach allow plaintiffs to recover for the harm that they suffered if they are not more than 50 percent liable.[125] Some states apply pure comparative negligence, which permits plaintiffs to recover even if they contributed more than 50 percent to their injuries.[126]

In a related concern involving liability, issues arise as to the appropriate standard to apply when children contribute to their injuries. Rather than expecting children to meet the same standard of care as adults, courts take their age and physical condition into account when the defense of comparative negligence is raised. As a general rule, courts agree that children between the ages of seven and fourteen[127] are incapable of negligence for their own behavior while those over the age of fourteen may be accountable on case-by-case bases. In such a case, an appellate court in Louisiana declared that a six-year-old child did not negligently cause his own injury even though he ran out into the street into the side of a car while returning to school to wait for his mother.[128] The court observed that the six-year-old did not share in the fault for his injury because he acted in the manner that could have been expected of a child of his age.[129] In addition, where a seventeen-year-old student was injured while performing in a school play, an appellate panel in Indiana decided that since a person of this age is expected to exercise the reasonable and ordinary care of an adult, rather than that of a person of like age, intelligence, and experience under like or similar circumstances,

---

123. *Smith v. Smith*, 19 Mass. 621 (Mass.1825).

124. *See, e.g., Daniel v. City of Morganton*, 479 S.E.2d 263 [114 Educ. L. Rep. 1251] (N.C.Ct. App.1997).

125. *See, e.g., Siders v. Reynoldsburg School Dist.*, 650 N.E.2d 150 [100 Educ. L. Rep. 708] (Ohio Ct.App.1994); *Millus v. Milford*, 735 N.Y.S.2d 202 [160 Educ. L. Rep. 855] (N.Y.App. Div. 2001); *Johnson ex rel. Johnson v. Dumas*, 811 So.2d 1085 [163 Educ. L. Rep. 1049] (La.Ct.App.2002); *Taney v. Indep. School Dist. No. 624*, 673 N.W.2d 497 [184 Educ. L. Rep. 568] (Minn. Ct. App. 2004).

126. *Church v. Massey*, 697 So.2d 407, 412 [120 Educ. L. Rep. 604] (Miss.1997) (criticizing an improper jury instruction on pure comparative negligence).

127. *Simmons ex rel. Simmons v. Columbus County Bd. of Educ.*, 615 S.E.2d 69, 76 [199 Educ. L. Rep. 955] (N.C. Ct. App. 2005) (noting that "In North Carolina, children between the ages of seven and fourteen are presumed to be incapable of contributory negligence.").

128. *Sutton v. Duplessis*, 584 So.2d 362 [69 Educ. L. Rep. 968] (La.Ct.App.1991).

129. For a similar outcome, *see Lewis v. Dependent School Dist. No. 10 of Pottawatomie County*, 808 P.2d 710 [66 Educ. L. Rep. 1283] (Okla.Ct.App.1990).

the school board could assert the affirmative defense of contributory negligence when the case returned to trial.[130]

Assumption of Risk

Assumption of risk, which is also based on comparative fault, can reduce an injured party's recovery in proportion to the degree to which his or her culpable conduct contributed to an accident if the individual voluntarily exposed himself or herself to a known and appreciated risk of harm. As noted elsewhere in this chapter, this defense frequently applies in cases where students are hurt while participating in sports.

Before turning to cases involving sports, it is worth examining a dispute wherein an appellate court in Maryland applied the defense of assumption of risk in favor of a school board where a high school student, who deceived school officials about her voluntarily leaving school without permission and was sexually assaulted by her uncle-in-law, sued it for negligent supervision.[131] The court affirmed that since the student willingly left the building with her uncle and knew of his intentions when she did so, her having assumed the risk of her injuries meant that she could not recover from the board.

To the extent that assumption of risk is a far-reaching defense in cases involving sports, it is worth considering its application in specific examples. In New York, an appellate court affirmed that a cheerleader who was injured during practice could not recover from her school board since she assumed the risks of her sport and was practicing voluntarily under the supervision of her coach.[132] Another appellate court in New York agreed that a board could not be liable for injuries that an experienced high school baseball player sustained when he was hit in the eye by a pitch from a batting machine after he asked the coach to increase the velocity of the pitches. The court was satisfied that since the player understood what he was doing when he voluntarily participated in the activity, he could not recover for his injuries.[133] Other courts reached similar results involving baseball,[134] basketball,[135] equestrienne activities,[136] field hockey,[137] football,[138] gymnastics,[139] ice hockey,[140] lacrosse,[141]

---

130. *Penn Harris Madison School Corp. v. Howard*, 832 N.E.2d 1013 [200 Educ. L. Rep. 869] (Ind. Ct. App. 2005).

131. *Tate v. Board of Educ. of Prince George's County*, 843 A.2d 890 [186 Educ. L. Rep. 437] (Md. Ct. App. 2004).

132. *Fisher v. Syosset Cent. School Dist.*, 694 N.Y.S.2d 691 [137 Educ. L. Rep. 761] (N.Y.App.Div.1999). For a similar result, *see Aaris v. Las Virgenes Unified School Dist.*, 75 Cal.Rptr.2d 801 [126 Educ. L. Rep. 350] (Cal.Ct.App.1998).

133. *Harris v. Cherry Valley–Springfield School Dist.*, 760 N.Y.S.2d 768 [178 Educ. L. Rep. 470] (N.Y. App.Div. 2003).

134. *Yanero v. Davis*, 65 S.W.3d 510 [161 Educ. L. Rep. 1058] (Ky.2001).

135. *Davis v. Savona Cent. School Dist.*, 675 N.Y.S.2d 269 [127 Educ. L. Rep. 995]

(N.Y.App. iv.1998), *leave to appeal denied*, 685 N.Y.S.2d 421 (N.Y.1999); *Milea v. Our Lady of Miracles*, 736 N.Y.S.2d 84 [160 Educ. L. Rep. 861] (N.Y.App.Div.2002).

136. *Papa ex rel. Papa v. Russo*, 719 N.Y.S.2d 723 [150 Educ. L. Rep. 911] (N.Y.App.Div. 2001), *leave to appeal denied*, 757 N.Y.S.2d 817 (N.Y.2003).

137. *Sandler ex rel. Sandler v. Half Hollow Hills West High School*, 672 N.Y.S.2d 120 [125 Educ. L. Rep. 1330] (N.Y.App.Div.1998).

138. *Hammond v. Board of Educ. of Carroll County*, 639 A.2d 223 [90 Educ. L. Rep. 256] (Md.Ct.Spec.App.1994); *Benitez v.*

139.–141. See notes 139–141 on page 400.

softball,[142] swimming,[143] and wrestling.[144]

Courts have been unwilling to apply assumption of risk as a defense in school settings where individual coaches did not warn a student sufficiently about the dangers of diving into a pool,[145] had students warm up in a hazardous location prior to the start of a volleyball game,[146] conducted a track practice in a high school hallway that unreasonably increased a student's risk of injury,[147] did not provide adequate safety equipment for physical education classes dealing with such activities as in-line skating[148] and softball[149] or interscholastic sports such as football.[150]

Educational Malpractice

Beginning in the 1970's, parents and others sought to render school boards liable for perceived failures in educational results allegedly due to pedagogical errors committed during a child's stay in school. Malpractice is a term of art for negligence of professional personnel, usually those who work in a one-to-one relationship with clients such as physicians or lawyers.

To date, all efforts to establish "educational malpractice" as a tort in regular education have failed[151] since it is "... a tort theory beloved of

New York City Bd. of Educ., 543 N.Y.S.2d 29 [54 Educ. L. Rep. 933] (N.Y. 1989). [Case No. 51]

139. *Weber v. William Floyd School Dist.*, 707 N.Y.S.2d 231 [144 Educ. L. Rep. 610] (N.Y. App.Div.2000).

140. *Greenberg by Greenberg v. North Shore Cent. School Dist. No. 1*, 619 N.Y.S.2d 151 [96 Educ. L. Rep. 206] (N.Y.App.Div.1994).

141. *Ciccone v. Bedford Cent. School Dist.*, 800 N.Y.S.2d 452 [201 Educ. L. Rep. 287] (N.Y. App. Div. 2005), *leave to appeal denied*, 810 N.Y.S.2d 416 (N.Y. 2005).

142. *Schoppman v. Plainedge Union Free School Dist.*, 746 N.Y.S.2d 325 [168 Educ. L. Rep. 445] (N.Y.App.Div.2002); Kelly v. McCarrick, 841 A.2d 869 [185 Educ. L. Rep. 662] (Md. Ct. Spec. App. 2004), *cert. denied sub nom. Kelly v. Archdioceses of Wash.*, 851 A.2d 594 (Md. 2004).

143. *Aronson v. Horace Mann–Barnard School*, 637 N.Y.S.2d 410 [106 Educ. L. Rep. 1281] (N.Y.App.Div.1996) *leave to appeal denied*, 651 N.Y.S.2d 15 (N.Y.1996).

144. *Lilley v. Elk Grove Unified School Dist.*, 80 Cal.Rptr.2d 638 [130 Educ. L. Rep. 1297] (Cal.Ct.App.1998).

145. *Kahn v. East Side Union High School Dist.*, 75 P.3d 30 [180 Educ. L. Rep. 312] (Cal. 2003).

146. *Gilbert ex rel. Gilbert v. Lyndonville Cent. School Dist.*, 730 N.Y.S.2d 638

[157 Educ. L. Rep. 283] (N.Y. App. Div. 2001).

147. *Kane ex rel. Kane v. North Colonie Cent. School Dist.*, 708 N.Y.S.2d 203 [145 Educ. L. Rep. 1096] (N.Y.App.Div.2000).

148. *Jackson v. Lawrence Pub. School Dist.*, 735 N.Y.S.2d 570 [160 Educ. L. Rep. 491] (N.Y.App.Div.2001). *But see Arteman v. Clinton Community Unit School Dist.*, 763 N.E.2d 756 [163 Educ. L. Rep. 913] (Ill.2002) (refusing to impose liability for a rollerblading accident in a physical education class based on discretionary function immunity).

149. *Muniz v. Warwick School Dist.*, 743 N.Y.S.2d 113 [165 Educ. L. Rep. 731] (N.Y.App.Div. 2002); *Zmitrowitz ex rel. Zmitrowitz v. Roman Catholic Diocese of Syracuse*, 710 N.Y.S.2d 453 [145 Educ. L. Rep. 760] (N.Y.App.Div.2000).

150. *Harvey v. Ouachita Parish School Bd.*, 674 So.2d 372 [110 Educ. L. Rep. 507] (La.Ct. App. 1996).

151. Insofar as children with disabilities have statutorily protected rights, some courts have allowed such suits to proceed. *See, e.g., Snow v. State*, 469 N.Y.S.2d 959 (N.Y.App.Div.1983); *M.C. on Behalf of J.C. v. Central Reg'l School Dist.*, 81 F.3d 389 [108 Educ. L. Rep. 522] (3d Cir.1996), *cert. denied*, 519 U.S. 866, 117 S.Ct. 176, 136 L.Ed.2d 116 (1996). Other courts have disagreed. *See, e.g., Suriano v. Hyde Park Cent.*

commentators, but not of courts."[152]

In a leading case, parents charged that school officials wrongly permitted their son, who could read only at the eighth-grade level, to graduate from high school. The student and his parents sought redress for having attended school for twelve years yet only being qualified for employment requiring little or no ability to read or write. An appellate court in California, in rejecting the suit, discussed at length the duty of care concept in the law of negligence.[153] The court reasoned that the claim was not actionable since there was no workable rule of care against which to measure the alleged conduct of school officials, no injury within the meaning of the law of negligence, and no perceptible connection between the educators' conduct and the student's alleged injury. In other words, the court posited that the student's claims were too amorphous to be justiciable under a theory of negligence. The court also dismissed a charge of intentional misrepresentation because even though the student and his parents had the opportunity to do so, they could not allege facts to show the requisite element of reliance on the asserted misrepresentation.

Along with the reasons cited above, other courts have recognized the difficulties of measuring damages and the public policy considerations that the acceptance of such cases would, in effect, have positioned them as overseers of day-to-day operation of schools.[154] To this end, courts have pointed out that since aggrieved parents can seek redress through the administrative channels of local boards and state-level educational agencies, they are not helpless bystanders as school officials make decisions affecting the education of their children. Of course, as evidenced in the voluminous litigation on the tort of negligence, if a specific act of a school employee directly, or intentionally, causes an injury to a student, liability may apply.[155]

Intentional Torts

Assault and Battery

These two intentional torts are placed under the same heading since they are often closely related. At common law, assault is placing another

---

School Dist., 611 N.Y.S.2d 20 [90 Educ. L. Rep. 1163] (N.Y.App.Div.1994).

152. *Ross v. Creighton Univ.*, 740 F.Supp. 1319, 1327 [62 Educ. L. Rep. 85] (N.D. Ill. 1990).

153. *Peter W. v. San Francisco Unified School Dist.*, 131 Cal.Rptr. 854 (Cal.Ct.App. 1976).

154. For other representative case, *see*, *e.g.*, *Simon v. Celebration Co.*, 883 So.2d 826 [192 Educ. L. Rep. 996] (Fla. Dist. Ct. App. 2004); *Key v. Coryell*, 86 Ark.App. 334 (Ark. Ct. App. 2004); *Christensen v. Southern Normal School*, 790 So.2d 252 (Ala. 2001); *Rich for Rich v. Kentucky Country Day*, 793 S.W.2d 832 [62 Educ. L. Rep. 772]

(Ky.Ct.App.1990); *Hunter v. Board of Educ. of Montgomery County*, 439 A.2d 582 (Md. 1982) [Case No. 53]; *Donohue v. Copiague Union Free School Dist.*, 418 N.Y.S.2d 375 (N.Y.1979).

155. For cases suggesting that educational malpractice might lie for intentional behavior, *see*, *e.g.*, *B.M. by Burger v. State*, 649 P.2d 425 [5 Educ. L. Rep. 1265] (Mont.1982), *appeal after remand*, 698 P.2d 399 [24 Educ. L. Rep. 541] (Mont.1985). Other courts disagreed with such an approach. *See*, *e.g.*, *Brantley v. District of Columbia*, 640 A.2d 181 [90 Educ. L. Rep. 658] (D.C. 1994); *Doe v. Town of Framingham*, 965 F.Supp. 226 [119 Educ. L. Rep. 109] (D.Mass.1997).

in the reasonable apprehension of an immediate, unwanted touching.[156] Thus, if a teacher threatens misbehaving children that he or she will walk to the back of classrooms and slap them the following day, the educator did not commit assault. No assaults would have occurred in such situations not only because the threats were of future, rather than immediate contact, but also since common law assault cannot be based on mere words. Moreover, parties must be aware that they are being assaulted.[157] For example, if a teacher throws objects at a group of students but misses them and hits children who did not see the items coming, then the teacher may well have battered the children who were struck and assaulted the ones at whom the items were hurled. Battery, on the other hand, is the unconsented to touching.[158]

School boards and teachers can face civil liability for assault and/or battery in situations involving corporal punishment and sexual misconduct with students. In cases where students who are subjected to corporal punishment sue for battery, courts ordinarily do not award damages unless educators acted with legal malice, defined by one court as "the intentional doing of a wrongful act without just cause or excuse, either with an intent to injure the other party or under such circumstances that the law will imply an evil intent."[159]

False Imprisonment

False imprisonment occurs when one intentionally and unlawfully confines another against his or her will, even if the other person does not suffer any physical harm.[160] Set out for perhaps the first time well over a century ago, the Supreme Court of Indiana recognized the authority of school personnel to detain students as a form of discipline as a defense to false imprisonment.[161] More than eighty years later, the Court of Appeals of New York relied on this case when a student was injured while attempting to climb out of a window as the bus driver proceeded to a police station because of damage that children did to the vehicle.[162] The court asserted that even if a jury agreed that the driver falsely imprisoned the student, the latter would have been unable to recover for his injuries if he acted unreasonably in attempting to climb out of the bus. Where a bus driver became lost and was four hours late arriving at school, an appellate court in Florida affirmed that neither the driver nor school board was liable for false imprisonment because there was no intent to restrain the student, a special needs child, against his will.[163]

The Supreme Court of Iowa affirmed that a student did not establish a claim of false imprisonment where school officials sent him home

---

156. RESTATEMENT (SECOND) OF TORTS § 21.

157. *Spacek v. Charles*, 928 S.W.2d 88 [112 Educ. L. Rep. 525] (Tex.Ct.App.1996).

158. RESTATEMENT (SECOND) OF TORTS § 13.

159. *Hinson v. Holt*, 776 So.2d 804, 812 [151 Educ. L. Rep. 343] (Ala.Civ.App.1998), *citing Empiregas v. Feely*, 524 So. 2d 626, 628 (Ala.1988).

160. RESTATEMENT (SECOND) OF TORTS § 35.

161. *Fertich v. Michener*, 11 N.E. 605 (Ind.1887).

162. *Sindle v. New York City Transit Auth.*, 352 N.Y.S.2d 183 (1973).

163. *School Bd. of Miami–Dade County, Florida v. Trujillo*, 906 So.2d 1109 [200 Educ. L. Rep. 910] (Fla. Dist. Ct. App. 2005), *reh'g denied* (2005).

on an unsupervised bus ride as discipline for violating rules while on a band trip in Texas.[164] The court maintained that this claim was without merit since the student willingly accompanied an educator to the bus station, boarded the vehicle without objection, and failed to produce evidence that he put up a fight to stay on the trip or to receive another punishment. Three years earlier, a federal trial court in Arkansas determined that a student who disrupted a choir class and had to sit in the choir library for three periods did not have a claim for false imprisonment.[165] In remarking that the student was neither physically threatened nor forced to enter this room, and was able to do her homework there, the court concluded that she was not subject to false imprisonment because if she refused the teacher's order to enter the room, she would have been subjected to a harsher form of discipline. In addition, where parents in Missouri gave their informed consent to have their child placed in a private residential facility with full knowledge of its restrictions after he was arrested and charged with terroristic threatening and criminal mischief, the Eighth Circuit affirmed that they could not sue the school and a variety of defendants for false imprisonment.[166]

Courts are willing to find that students were subjected to false imprisonment under egregious circumstances. In such cases, when a coach locked a football player in a locker room[167] and a teacher chained a student with poor attendance to a tree for an hour and one-half even though he claimed that it was a joke,[168] courts affirmed that the students presented actionable claims.

Defamation

Defamation involves the intentional, or at least negligent, unprivileged communication of a false statement to a third party that harms the reputation of the person being spoken about.[169] Spoken defamation is slander; written defamation is libel. Depending on the jurisdiction, some states may go so far as to require that an allegedly defamatory remark must contain an objectively verifiable assertion of fact rather than a mere opinion.[170]

School officials have three key protections at their disposal when dealing with defamation: truth, privilege, and opinion. If a statement is true, and does not invade a person's right to privacy, there can be no claim for defamation.[171] If there is a question of fact as to whether a

---

164. *Ette ex rel. Ette v. Linn–Mar Community School Dist.*, 656 N.W.2d 62 [173 Educ. L. Rep. 662] (Iowa 2002).

165. *Wallace v. Bryant School Dist.*, 46 F.Supp.2d 863 [135 Educ. L. Rep. 488] (E.D.Ark. 1999).

166. *Blair v. Wills*, 420 F.3d 823 [201 Educ. L. Rep. 97] (8th Cir. 2005), *reh'g and reh'g en banc denied* (2005).

167. *Newman v. Obersteller*, 915 S.W.2d 198 [107 Educ. L. Rep. 352] (Tex.Ct.App. 1996).

168. *Banks v. Fritsch*, 39 S.W.3d 474 [152 Educ. L. Rep. 379] (Ky.Ct.App.2001).

169. Restatement (Second) of Torts § 558.

170. *See, e.g., Lifton v. Board of Educ. of City of Chicago*, 416 F.3d 571 [200 Educ. L. Rep. 39] (7th Cir. 2005).

171. For statements reiterating this rule in dicta, *see, e.g., Gatto v. St. Richard School*, 774 N.E.2d 914, 924 [169 Educ. L. Rep. 371] (Ind.Ct.App.2002); *James v. De-*

statement is true, and in an area that overlaps with privilege, then such a matter is ordinarily reserved for a jury. In an illustrative case, where a former director of technology in Iowa sued an associate superintendent over the latter's allegation that he was dangerous, the Eighth Circuit affirmed that whether the allegation was true was a proper matter for a jury to consider.[172] In another case, where a principal made derogatory comments about a seventy-year-old teacher with thirty-four years of experience, who served as head foreign languages teacher on a one-year renewable contract, while in a meeting with parents about her role as chaperone in an overseas trip, an appellate court in Massachusetts denied the school committee's motion for summary judgment.[173] The court ascertained that insofar as genuine issue of material fact remained as to whether the principal's assessment of the teacher's performance was false, it refused to grant the motion for summary judgment.

School officials are afforded privilege with regard to defamation. Put another way, statements such as recommendations or evaluations that are supportable by evidence, but not necessarily true, made to appropriate persons in the line of duty are not actionable because they are privileged. In an early case, the Supreme Court of Nebraska ruled that a letter from the state superintendent of schools to another administrator that described a teacher as unfit since he was under the influence of liquor was not actionable because it was sent in connection with his official duties.[174] More recently, courts agreed that defamation suits were not actionable based on privilege where a superintendent investigated a board president and vice-president's use of a district credit card,[175] where a school director wrote a letter to a newspaper questioning whether a school business manager engaged in budgetary misconduct,[176] and where the director of an early childhood education program commented to television reporters about why some staff members had their employment terminated.[177]

If a statement is clearly an opinion, such as where parents and students criticize a teacher[178] or school officials[179] or where a letter writer commented on the close relationship between a member of a school committee and a construction manager who was involved in a school project,[180] courts refused to impose liability. An exception arises if

Grandis, 138 F.Supp.2d 402, 416 [153 Educ. L. Rep. 618] (W.D.N.Y.2001).

172. *Smith v. Des Moines Pub. Schools*, 259 F.3d 942 [156 Educ. L. Rep. 56] (8th Cir.2001).

173. *Dragonas v. School Comm. of Melrose*, 833 N.E.2d 679 [201 Educ. L. Rep. 296] (Mass. App. Ct. 2005), *review denied*, 836 N.E.2d 1096 (Mass. 2005).

174. *De Bolt v. McBrien*, 147 N.W. 462 (Neb.1914).

175. *Gallegos v. Escalon*, 993 S.W.2d 422 [135 Educ. L. Rep. 852] (Tex.Ct.App. 1999).

176. *Matta v. Burton*, 721 A.2d 1164 [131 Educ. L. Rep. 788] (Pa. Cmwlth. Ct.

1998), *appeal discontinued*, 736 A.2d 606 (Pa.1999).

177. *Enriquez v. Khouri*, 13 S.W.3d 458 [142 Educ. L. Rep. 1102] (Tex.Ct.App.2000).

178. *Ansorian v. Zimmerman*, 627 N.Y.S.2d 706 [101 Educ. L. Rep. 366] (N.Y.App.Div.1995).

179. *Nampa Charter School, Inc. v. De-LaPaz*, 89 P.3d 863 [187 Educ. L. Rep. 1056] (Idaho 2004).

180. *Alves v. Hometown Newspapers*, 857 A.2d 743 [192 Educ. L. Rep. 215] (R.I. 2004).

a statement can reasonably be understood to be based on undisclosed defamatory underlying facts.[181] Perhaps the most notable case in this regard was *Milkovich v. Lorain Journal Company*, wherein a high school wrestling coach sued a newspaper for defamation when an editorial suggested that he committed perjury. In acknowledging that since the statements about the coach were not opinions because they could have been proven to be true or false, the Supreme Court noted that "where a statement of 'opinion' on a matter of public concern reasonably implies false and defamatory facts regarding public figures or officials, those individuals [can recover damages if they] show that such statements were made with knowledge of their false implications or with reckless disregard of their truth."[182]

As suits against school personnel alleging defamation are increasing, a key element of successful claims is a showing that plaintiffs suffered significant harm to their professional reputations. Mere hurt feelings are not enough. By way of example, an appellate court in Louisiana affirmed that a principal was not liable for defamation when he wrote a letter to a superintendent recommending that a teacher not be re-employed and when he was overheard referring to her and another teacher as "nuts."[183] In failing to uncover anything defamatory in the letter, which, it suggested, would have been covered by privilege, the court posited that the principal's oral remarks were not slanderous because he made them in an informal conversation, and although unflattering, did not cause the teacher any harm. In another dispute, where a principal sued the man who had an affair with his wife for defamation, and the latter posted false rumors about him in an internet chat room, an appellate court in Missouri affirmed a default judgment in his favor.[184] The court agreed that the rumors were defamatory since they harmed the principal's professional reputation.

In a dispute from Maryland, a high school teacher-coach who was suspended with pay and transferred after two female members of his cross-country team falsely accused him of sexual misconduct based on their desire to have a different coach sued them and their parents for defamation. The state's highest court initially reinstated the claim, explaining that since the students' complaints were not absolutely privileged despite the strong public opinion that they and their parents should be protected from suit for reporting his alleged sexual misconduct, the defamation claim could have proceeded to trial in light of the harm that the teacher-coach suffered.[185] However, the same court later held that the educator's claim was barred by absolute privilege.[186] The court was convinced that the teacher-coach's claim could not proceed since adequate procedural safeguards were in place to minimize the

181. *Baker v. Lafayette College*, 532 A.2d 399 [42 Educ. L. Rep. 598] (Pa.1987).

182. 497 U.S. 1, 20, 110 S.Ct. 2695, 111 L.Ed.2d 1 [60 Educ. L. Rep. 1061] (1990).

183. *McGowen v. Prentice*, 341 So.2d 55, 56 (La.Ct.App.1976).

184. *Scott v. LeClercq*, 136 S.W.3d 183 [189 Educ. L. Rep. 436] (Mo. Ct. App. 2004).

185. *Flynn v. Reichardt*, 749 A.2d 197 [143 Educ. L. Rep. 585] (Md.Ct.App.2000).

186. *Reichardt v. Flynn*, 823 A.2d 566 [177 Educ. L. Rep. 357] (Md. Ct. App. 2003).

occurrence of defamatory statements in school administrative proceedings.

A case from the Supreme Court of New Jersey reveals how First Amendment concerns can be intertwined with defamation claims while serving as a segue to the next part of this section. The court affirmed that a teacher-chaperone could not sue another teacher with whom she shared duties while on a school trip after the latter sent their principal a letter discussing the plaintiff's alleged improprieties.[187] The court was of the opinion that the letter was not actionable because to the extent that it involved a matter of public concern, namely the safety of students, it was entitled to substantial First Amendment protection absent a showing of actual malice by the letter writer.

Insofar as defamation is speech, some First Amendment considerations apply. In the interest of free discussion of matters of public concern, the Supreme Court treats public officials differently from private persons. In order for public officials to succeed in defamation, plaintiffs must demonstrate that communicators acted with actual malice in making harmful and false statements that were known to be false or that defendants acted with reckless disregard of a statement's truth or falsity.[188] An interesting case arose in this regard in California where an appellate court affirmed that where the former superintendent of a system of charter schools sued some of its officers for libel over their posting statements on the organization's web-site urging that he be investigated over his alleged ties to a terrorist group.[189] The court agreed that since the alleged libel pertained to the former superintendent's role as a public official, he had to prove actual malice in order to prevail.[190]

The courts have generally accorded the status of public officials to board members[191] and superintendents[192] but are divided with regard to teachers[193] and principals.[194] In such a dispute, an appellate court in

187. *Rocci v. Ecole Secondaire Macdonald–Cartier*, 755 A.2d 583 [146 Educ. L. Rep. 283] (N.J.2000).

188. *New York Times Co. v. Sullivan*, 376 U.S. 254, 84 S.Ct. 710, 11 L.Ed.2d 686 (1964).

189. *Ghafur v. Bernstein*, 32 Cal. Rptr.3d 626 [200 Educ. L. Rep. 842] (Cal. Ct. App. 2005).

190. *See also Jee v. New York Post Co.*, 688 N.Y.S.2d 49 [134 Educ. L. Rep. 551] (N.Y.App. Div. 1999), *appeal denied*, 697 N.Y.S.2d 565 (N.Y.1999) (affirming that a principal who challenged a reporter's investigation and the credibility of individuals who provided him with information could not sue for defamation since there was no evidence that the allegedly defamatory statements were published with malice or that the reporter knew them to be false and published them with a reckless disregard for the truth).

191. *Peavy v. Harman*, 37 F.Supp.2d 495 (N.D.Tex.1999). *But see Roberts v.*

Board of Educ., 25 F.Supp.2d 866 [131 Educ. L. Rep. 128] (N.D.Ill.1998).

192. *Purvis v. Ballantine*, 487 S.E.2d 14 [119 Educ. L. Rep. 709] (Ga.Ct.App.1997).

193. For a case finding that a teacher was not a public official, *see Dec v. Auburn Enlarged School Dist.*, 672 N.Y.S.2d 591 [126 Educ. L. Rep. 365] (N.Y.App.Div.1998). For cases recognizing teachers as public officials, *see, e.g., Kelley v. Bonney*, 606 A.2d 693 [74 Educ. L. Rep. 896] (Conn.1992); *Elstrom v. Independent School Dist. No. 270*, 533 N.W.2d 51 [100 Educ. L. Rep. 733] (Minn.Ct.App.1995); *Tweedall v. Fritz*, 987 F.Supp. 1126 [124 Educ. L. Rep. 122] (S.D.Ind.1997); *Visentin v. Haldane Cent. School Dist.*, 782 N.Y.S.2d 517 [192 Educ. L. Rep. 561] (N.Y. Sup. Ct. 2004).

194. For cases affirming that principals were not public officials, *see Ellerbee v. Mills*, 422 S.E.2d 539 [78 Educ. L. Rep. 1104] (Ga.1992), *cert. denied*, 507 U.S. 1025, 113 S.Ct. 1833, 123 L.Ed.2d 460

South Carolina affirmed that since an assistant principal was not a public official who had to prove actual malice on the part of a minister who used a racial slur in connection with him while in the presence of others, he was entitled to monetary damages.[195] Where a father led a campaign that apparently resulted in a high school football coach being fired while their two sons competed for the same position, an appellate court in Illinois remanded the dispute for trial since it was unclear whether the parent acted with actual malice.[196] The court thought that the timing of the father's critical remarks about the coach to school board officials and a local newspaper raised triable issues of fact as to whether he acted with actual malice.

Intentional Infliction of Emotional Distress

Intentional infliction of emotional distress, although being raised with some regularity, is generally unsuccessful. In order to prevail in such a claim, an injured party must establish that a defendant acted intentionally or recklessly, that the conduct was extreme and outrageous, that the defendant's action(s) caused the plaintiff severe emotional distress, that the conduct exceeded all possible bounds of decency, and that it was utterly intolerable in a civilized community.[197]

Where a teacher was passed over for a coaching position in favor of a candidate who did not have a certificate, an appellate court in Ohio affirmed that the board's conduct did not constitute the extreme and outrageous conduct required to support action for intentional infliction of emotional distress.[198] The court observed that the record revealed that the board used adequate standards in determining that the teacher was not qualified for the coaching position. Further, an appellate court in Texas affirmed that female high school students could not sue a television station for broadcasting part of a videotape that their band director made in an attempt to discover who was going through their belongings, but which showed them changing their clothes for, among other causes of action, intentional infliction of emotional distress and defamation.[199] The court refused to permit the suit to proceed since the broadcasts, which were on a matter of legitimate public concern, neither subjected the students to intentional infliction of emotional distress nor defama-

(1993); *Beeching v. Levee*, 764 N.E.2d 669 [162 Educ. L. Rep. 938] (Ind.Ct.App.2002). For cases affirming that while principals were public officials, defendants were not liable for defamation since they did not act with reckless disregard for the truth in making statements, *see Jordan v. World Pub. Co.*, 872 P.2d 946 [90 Educ. L. Rep. 1227] (Okla.Ct.App.1994); *Palmer v. Bennington School Dist.*, 615 A.2d 498 [78 Educ. L. Rep. 881] (Vt.1992).

195. *Goodwin v. Kennedy*, 552 S.E.2d 319 [157 Educ. L. Rep. 387] (S.C.Ct.App. 2001).

196. *Myers v. Levy*, 808 N.E.2d 1139 [187 Educ. L. Rep. 952] (Ill. App. Ct. 2004), *appeal denied*, 823 N.E.2d 967 (Ill. 2004).

197. RESTATEMENT (SECOND) OF TORTS § 46 (1965).

198. *Katterhenrich v. Federal Hocking Local School Dist. Bd. of Educ.*, 700 N.E.2d 626 [129 Educ. L. Rep. 776] (Ohio Ct.App. 1997), *appeal not allowed*, 684 N.E.2d 707 (Ohio 1997).

199. *Doe v. Mobile Video Tapes*, 43 S.W.3d 40 [153 Educ. L. Rep. 805] (Tex.Ct. App.2001).

tion.[200]

In a tragic case from New York, an appellate court modified a jury verdict in favor of a mother who sued a school board for pain and suffering as well as for intentional infliction of emotional distress after her fourteen-year-old son drowned while on an eighth-grade field trip.[201] The court agreed that officials failed to supervise the student and did not realize that he was missing until after everyone had left the park, which closed at 5 P.M. School officials returned to the park at 9 P.M. to search for the child, but did not notify his mother until about 1 A.M. the next day, at which time maintenance workers discovered his body in a wave pool. In the intervening hours, even though the student's body was at the bottom of the pool, lifeguards used the pool for relay races and other activities. Even so, the court indicated that since the mother failed to establish that she suffered contemporaneous or consequential physical injury as required to support her claims of emotional distress over the death of her son, she could not recover on that claim.

On the other hand, an appellate court in Florida reinstated a high school teacher's claim for intentional infliction of emotional distress against students who allegedly participated in the production and distribution of a newsletter in which the author threatened to kill her and rape her and all of her children.[202] The court was satisfied that the teacher presented a cause of action against the students for intentional infliction of emotional distress since their alleged behavior was so outrageous in character and so extreme in degree as to go beyond all bounds of decency.

[Case No. 47]   Liability for Violation of Civil Rights of Students

WOOD v. STRICKLAND

Supreme Court of the United States, 1975.
420 U.S. 308, 95 S.Ct. 992, 43 L.Ed.2d 214.

[The school board suspended three 10th grade students for approximately three months, up to the end of their semester, for "spiking" the punch at a meeting of an extracurricular school organization attended by parents and students. Two students filed suit under Section 1983 seeking, among other things, damages against two administrators and board members for allegedly violated their constitutional rights to due process. This excerpt only includes that part of the case relating to liability of school officials.]

MR. JUSTICE WHITE delivered the opinion of the Court. . . .

The District Court instructed the jury that a decision for respondents had to be premised upon a finding that petitioners acted with

---

200. For similar results, *see, e.g., Dollard v. Board of Educ. of Town of Orange,* 777 A.2d 714 [156 Educ. L. Rep. 273] (Conn.Ct.App.2001); *Stamper v. Charlotte–Mecklenburg Bd. of Educ.,* 544 S.E.2d 818 [152 Educ. L. Rep. 832] (N.C.Ct.App.2001).

201. *Maracallo v. Board of Educ. of the City of N.Y.,* 800 N.Y.S.2d 23 [200 Educ. L. Rep. 861] (N.Y. App. Div. 2005).

202. *Nims v. Harrison,* 768 So.2d 1198 [148 Educ. L. Rep. 518] (Fla.Dist.Ct.App. 2000).

malice in expelling them and defined "malice" as meaning "ill will against a person—a wrongful act done intentionally without just cause or excuse." In ruling for petitioners after the jury had been unable to agree, the District Court found "as a matter of law" that there was no evidence from which malice could be inferred.

The Court of Appeals, however, viewed both the instruction and the decision of the District Court as being erroneous. Specific intent to harm wrongfully, it held, was not a requirement for the recovery of damages. Instead, "[i]t need only be established that the defendants did not, in the light of all the circumstances, act in good faith. The test is an objective, rather than a subjective one."

Petitioners as members of the school board assert here, as they did below, an absolute immunity from liability under § 1983 and at the very least seek to reinstate the judgment of the District Court. If they are correct and the District Court's dismissal should be sustained, we need go no further in this case. Moreover, the immunity question involves the construction of a federal statute, and our practice is to deal with possibly dispositive statutory issues before reaching questions turning on the construction of the Constitution. We essentially sustain the position of the Court of Appeals with respect to the immunity issue.

The nature of the immunity from awards of damages under § 1983 available to school administrators and school board members is not a question which the lower federal courts have answered with a single voice. There is general agreement on the existence of a "good faith" immunity, but the courts have either emphasized different factors as elements of good faith or have not given specific content to the good-faith standard.

This Court had decided three cases dealing with the scope of the immunity protecting various types of governmental officials from liability for damages under § 1983. In *Tenney v. Brandhove*, the question was found to be one essentially of statutory construction. Noting that the language of § 1983 is silent with respect to immunities, the Court concluded that there was no basis for believing that Congress intended to eliminate the traditional immunity of legislators from civil liability for acts done within their sphere of legislative action. That immunity, "so well grounded in history and reason . . .", was absolute and consequently did not depend upon the motivations of the legislators. In *Pierson v. Ray*, finding that "[t]he legislative record gives no clear indication that Congress meant to abolish wholesale all common-law immunities" in enacting § 1983, we concluded that the common-law doctrine of absolute judicial immunity survived. Similarly, § 1983 did not preclude application of the traditional rule that a policeman, making an arrest in good faith and with probable cause, is not liable for damages, although the person arrested proves innocent. Consequently the Court said: "Although the matter is not entirely free from doubt, the same consideration would seem to require excusing him from liability for acting under a statute that he reasonably believed to be valid but that was later held unconstitutional, on its face or as applied." Finally, last Term we held that the chief executive officer of a State, the senior and subordinate officers of the State's National Guard, and the president of a state-controlled university were not absolutely immune from liability under § 1983, but instead were entitled to immunity, under prior precedent and in light of the obvious need to avoid discouraging effective official action by public officers charged with a considerable range of responsibility and discretion, only if they acted in good faith as defined by the Court:

> [I]n varying scope, a qualified immunity is available to officers of the executive branch of Government, the variation being dependent upon the scope of discretion and responsibilities of the office and all the circumstances as they reasonably appeared at the time of the action on which liability is sought to be based. It is the existence of reasonable grounds for the belief formed at the time and in light of all the circumstances, coupled with good-faith belief, that affords a basis for qualified immunity of executive officers for acts performed in the course of official conduct.

Common-law tradition, recognized in our prior decisions, and strong public-policy reasons also lead to a construction of § 1983 extending a qualified good-faith immunity to school board members from liability for damages under that section. Although there have been differing emphases and formulations of the common-law immunity of public school officials in cases of student expulsion or suspension, state courts have generally recognized that such officers should be protected from tort liability under state law for all good-faith, non-malicious action taken to fulfill their official duties.

As the facts of this case reveal, school board members function at different times in the nature of legislators and adjudicators in the school disciplinary process. Each of these functions necessarily involves the exercise of discretion, the weighing of many factors, and the formulation of long-term policy. "Like legislators and judges, these officers are entitled to rely on traditional sources for the factual information on which they decide and act." As with executive officers faced with instances of civil disorder, school officials, confronted with student behavior causing or threatening disruption, also have an "obvious need for prompt action, and decisions must be made in reliance on factual information supplied by others."

Liability for damages for every action which is found subsequently to have been violative of a student's constitutional rights and to have caused compensable injury would unfairly impose upon the school decision maker the burden of mistakes made in good faith in the course of exercising his discretion within the scope of his official duties. School board members, among other duties, must judge whether there have been violations of school regulations and, if so, the appropriate sanctions for the violations. Denying any measure of immunity in these circumstances "would contribute not to principled and fearless decision-making but to intimidation." The imposition of monetary costs for mistakes which were not unreasonable in the light of all the circumstances would undoubtedly deter even the most conscientious school decisionmaker from exercising his judgment independently, forcefully, and in a manner best serving the long-term interest of the school and the students. The most capable candidates for school board positions might be deterred from seeking office if heavy burdens upon their private resources from monetary liability were a likely prospect during their tenure.

These considerations have undoubtedly played a prime role in the development by state courts of a qualified immunity protecting school officials from liability for damages in lawsuits claiming improper suspensions or expulsions. But at the same time, the judgment implicit in this common-law development is that absolute immunity would not be justified since it would not sufficiently increase the ability of school officials to exercise their discretion in a forthright manner to warrant the absence of a remedy for students subjected to intentional or otherwise inexcusable deprivations.

... Absent legislative guidance, we now rely on those same sources in determining whether and to what extent school officials are immune from damage suits under § 1983. We think there must be a degree of immunity if the work of the schools is to go forward; and, however worded, the immunity must be such that public school officials understand that action taken in the good-faith fulfillment of their responsibilities and within the bounds of reason under all the circumstances will not be punished and that they need not exercise their discretion with undue timidity....

The disagreement between the Court of Appeals and the District Court over the immunity standard in this case has been put in terms of an "objective" versus a "subjective" test of good faith. As we see it, the appropriate standard necessarily contains elements of both. The official must himself be acting sincerely and with a belief that he is doing right, but an act violating a student's constitutional rights can be no more justified by ignorance or disregard of settled, indisputable law on the part of one entrusted with supervision of students' daily lives than by the presence of actual malice. To be entitled to a special exemption from the categorical remedial language of § 1983 in a case in which his action violated a student's constitutional rights, a school board member, who has voluntarily undertaken the task of supervising the operation of the school and the activities of the students, must be held to a standard of conduct based not only on permissible intentions, but also on knowledge of the basic, unquestioned constitutional rights of his charges. Such a standard neither imposes an unfair burden upon a person assuming a responsible public office requiring a high degree of intelligence and judgment for the proper fulfillment of its duties, nor an unwarranted burden in light of the value which civil rights have in our legal system. Any lesser standard would deny much of the promise of § 1983. Therefore, in the specific context of school discipline, we hold that a school board member is not immune from liability for damages under § 1983 if he knew or reasonably should have known that the action he took within his sphere of official responsibility would violate the constitutional rights of the student affected, or if he took the action with the malicious intention to cause a deprivation of constitutional rights or other injury to the student. That is not to say that school board members are "charged with predicting the future course of constitutional law." A compensatory award will be appropriate only if the school board member has acted with such an impermissible motivation or with such disregard of the student's clearly established constitutional rights that his action cannot reasonably be characterized as being in good faith. . . .

Notes

1.   Section 1983 grants rights of redress to those who have had their civil rights violated by public officials. Do you agree that upholding the board's argument for absolute immunity would have denied much of section 1983's promise?

2.   On remand, the Eighth Circuit held that since officials violated the students' right to procedural due process, they were entitled to have their records cleared and to try to prove their claim of damages against individual board members. *Strickland v. Inlow*, 519 F.2d 744 (8th Cir. 1975).

[Case No. 48]   Damages When Student Is Denied Due Process before Suspension

CAREY v. PIPHUS

Supreme Court of the United States, 1978.
435 U.S. 247, 98 S.Ct. 1042, 55 L.Ed.2d 252.

Mr. Justice Powell delivered the opinion of the Court.

In this case, brought under 42 U.S.C.A. § 1983, we consider the elements and prerequisites for recovery of damages by students who were suspended from public elementary and secondary schools without procedural due process. . . . We . . . hold that in the absence of proof of actual injury, the students are entitled to recover only nominal damages.

I

Respondent Jarius Piphus was a freshman at Chicago Vocational High School during the 1973–1974 school year. On January 23, 1974, during school hours, the school principal saw Piphus and another student standing outdoors on school property passing back and forth what the principal described as an irregularly shaped cigarette. The principal approached the students unnoticed and smelled what he believed was the strong odor of burning marihuana. He also saw Piphus try to pass a packet of cigarette papers to the other student. When the students became aware of the principal's presence, they threw the cigarette into a nearby hedge.

The principal took the students to the school's disciplinary office and directed the assistant principal to impose the "usual" 20–day suspension for violation of the school rule against the use of drugs. The students protested that they had not been smoking marihuana, but to no avail. Piphus was allowed to remain at school, although not in class, for the remainder of the school day while the assistant principal tried, without success, to reach his mother.

A suspension notice was sent to Piphus' mother, and a few days later two meetings were arranged among Piphus, his mother, his sister, school officials, and representatives from a Legal Aid Clinic. The purpose of the meetings was not to determine whether Piphus had been smoking marihuana, but rather to explain the reasons for the suspension. Following an unfruitful exchange of views, Piphus and his mother, as guardian *ad litem,* filed suit against petitioners in Federal District Court ... charging that Piphus had been suspended without due process of law in violation of the Fourteenth Amendment. The complaint sought declaratory and injunctive relief, together with actual and punitive damages in the amount of $3,000. Piphus was readmitted to school under a temporary restraining order after eight days of his suspension.

Respondent Silas Brisco was in the sixth grade at Clara Barton Elementary School in Chicago during the 1973–1974 school year. On September 11, 1973, Brisco came to school wearing one small earring. The previous school year the school principal had issued a rule against the wearing of earrings by male students because he believed that this practice denoted membership in certain street gangs and increased the likelihood that gang members would terrorize other students. Brisco was reminded of this rule, but he refused to remove the earring, asserting that it was a symbol of black pride, not of gang membership.

The assistant principal talked to Brisco's mother, advising her that her son would be suspended for 20 days if he did not remove the earring. Brisco's mother supported her son's position, and a 20–day suspension was imposed. Brisco and his mother, as guardian *ad litem,* filed suit in Federal District Court ... charging that Brisco had been suspended without due process of law in violation of the Fourteenth Amendment. The complaint sought declaratory and injunctive relief, together with actual and punitive damages in the amount of $5,000. Brisco was readmitted to school during the pendency of proceedings for a preliminary injunction after 17 days of his suspension.

... We granted certiorari to consider whether, in an action under § 1983 for the deprivation of procedural due process, a plaintiff must prove that he actually was injured by the deprivation before he may recover substantial "nonpunitive" damages.

II

42 U.S.C.A. § 1983, enacted as § 1 of the Civil Rights Act of 1871, 17 Stat. 13, provides:

> Every person who, under color of any statute, ordinance, regulation, custom, or usage, of any State or Territory, subjects, or causes to be subjected, any citizen of the United States or other person within the jurisdiction thereof to the deprivation of any rights, privileges, or immunities secured by the Constitution and laws, shall be liable to the party injured in an action at law, suit in equity, or other proper proceeding for redress.

The legislative history of § 1983, demonstrates that it was intended to "create a species of tort liability" in favor of persons who are deprived of "rights, privileges, or immunities secured" to them by the Constitution....

A

Insofar as petitioners contend that the basic purpose of a § 1983 damages award should be to compensate persons for injuries caused by the deprivation of constitutional rights, they have the better of the argument. Rights, constitutional and otherwise, do not exist in a vacuum. Their purpose is to protect persons from injuries to particular interests, and their contours are shaped by the interests they protect.

Our legal system's concept of damages reflects this view of legal rights. "The cardinal principle of damages in Anglo–American law is that of *compensation* for the injury caused to plaintiff by defendant's breach of duty." The Court implicitly has recognized the applicability of this principle to actions under § 1983 by stating that damages are available under that section for actions "found ... to have been violative of ... constitutional rights *and to have caused compensable injury....*"

The Members of the Congress that enacted § 1983 did not address directly the question of damages, but the principle that damages are designed to compensate persons for injuries caused by the deprivation of rights hardly could have been foreign to the many lawyers in Congress in 1871. Two other sections of the Civil Rights Act of 1871 appear to incorporate this principle, and no reason suggests itself for reading § 1983 differently. To the extent that Congress intended that awards under § 1983 should deter the deprivation of constitutional rights, there is no evidence that it meant to establish a deterrent more formidable than that inherent in the award of compensatory damages.

B

It is less difficult to conclude that damages awards under § 1983 should be governed by the principle of compensation than it is to apply this principle to concrete cases. But over the centuries the common law of torts has developed a set of rules to implement the principle that a person should be compensated fairly for injuries caused by the violation of his legal rights. These rules, defining the elements of damages and the prerequisites for their recovery, provide the appropriate starting point for the inquiry under § 1983 as well.

It is not clear, however, that common-law tort rules of damages will provide a complete solution to the damages issue in every § 1983 case. In some cases, the interests protected by a particular branch of the common law of torts may parallel closely the interests protected by a particular constitutional right. In such cases, it may be appropriate to apply the tort rules of damages directly to the § 1983 action. In other cases, the interests protected by a particular constitutional right may not also be protected by an analogous branch of the common law torts. In those cases, the task will be the more difficult one of adapting common-law rules of damages to provide fair compensation for injuries caused by the deprivation of a constitutional right.

Although this task of adaptation will be one of some delicacy—as this case demonstrates—it must be undertaken. The purpose of § 1983 would be defeated if injuries caused by the deprivation of constitutional rights went uncompensated simply because the common law does not recognize an analogous cause of action. In order to further the purpose of § 1983, the rules governing compensation for injuries caused by the deprivation of constitutional rights should be tailored to the interests protected by the particular right in question—just as the common-law rules of damages themselves were defined by the interests protected in the various branches of tort law. We agree with Mr. Justice Harlan that "the experience of judges in dealing with private [tort] claims supports the conclusion that courts of law are capable of making the types of judgment concerning causation and magnitude of injury necessary to accord meaningful compensation for invasion of [constitutional] rights." With these principles in mind, we now turn to the problem of compensation in the case at hand.

C

The Due Process Clause of the Fourteenth Amendment provides:

"nor shall any State deprive any person of life, liberty, or property, without due process of law;...."

This Clause "raises no impenetrable barrier to the taking of a person's possessions," or liberty, or life. Procedural due process rules are meant to protect persons not from the deprivation, but from the mistaken or unjustified deprivation of life, liberty, or property. Thus, in deciding what process constitutionally is due in various contexts, the Court repeatedly has emphasized that "procedural due process rules are shaped by the risk of error inherent in the truth-finding process...." Such rules "minimize substantively unfair or mistaken deprivations of" life, liberty, or property by enabling persons to contest the basis upon which the State proposes to deprive them of protected interests....

The parties ... disagree as to the ... holding of the Court of Appeals that respondents are entitled to recover substantial—although unspecified—damages to compensate them for "the injury which is 'inherent in the nature of the wrong,'" even if their suspensions were justified and even if they fail to prove that the denial of procedural due process actually caused them some real, if intangible, injury. Respondents, elaborating on this theme, submit that the holding is correct because injury fairly may be "presumed" to flow from every denial of procedural due process. Their argument is that in addition to protecting against unjustified deprivations, the Due Process Clause also guarantees the "feeling of just treatment" by the government. They contend that the deprivation of protected interests without procedural due process, even where the premise for the deprivation is not erroneous, inevitably arouses strong feelings of mental and emotional distress in the individual who is denied this "feeling of just treatment." They analogize their case to that of defamation *per se,* in which "the plaintiff is relieved from the necessity of producing any proof whatsoever that he has been injured" in order to recover substantial compensatory damages.

Petitioners do not deny that a purpose of procedural due process is to convey to the individual a feeling that the government has dealt with him fairly, as well as to minimize the risk of mistaken deprivations of protected interests. They go so far as to concede that, in a proper case, persons in respondents' positions might well recover damages for mental and emotional distress caused by the denial of procedural due process. Petitioners' argument is the more limited one that such injury cannot be presumed to occur, and that plaintiffs at least should be put to their proof on the issue, as plaintiffs are in most tort actions.

We agree with petitioners in this respect. As we have observed in another context, the doctrine of presumed damages in the common law of defamation *per se* "is an oddity of tort law, for it allows recovery of purportedly compensatory damages without evidence of actual loss." . . . The doctrine has been defended on the grounds that those forms of defamation that are actionable *per se* are virtually certain to cause serious injury to reputation, and that this kind of injury is extremely difficult to prove. Moreover, statements that are defamatory *per se* by their very nature are likely to cause mental and emotional distress, as well as injury to reputation, so there arguably is little reason to require proof of this kind of injury either. But these considerations do not support respondents' contention that damages should be presumed to flow from every deprivation of procedural due process.

First, it is not reasonable to assume that every departure from procedural due process, no matter what the circumstances or how minor, inherently is as likely to cause distress as the publication of defamation *per se* is to cause injury to reputation and distress. Where the deprivation of a protected interest is substantively justified but procedures are deficient in some respect, there may well be those who suffer no distress over the procedural irregularities. Indeed, in contrast to the immediately distressing effect of defamation *per se,* a person may not even know that procedures *were* deficient until he enlists the aid of counsel to challenge a perceived substantive deprivation.

Moreover, where a deprivation is justified but procedures are deficient, whatever distress a person feels may be attributable to the justified deprivation rather than to deficiencies in procedure. But the injury caused by a justified deprivation, including distress, is not properly compensable under § 1983. This ambiguity in causation, which is absent in the case of defamation *per se,* provides additional need for requiring the plaintiff to convince the trier of fact that he actually suffered distress because of the denial of procedural due process itself.

Finally, we foresee no particular difficulty in producing evidence that mental and emotional distress actually was caused by the denial of procedural due process itself. Distress is a personal injury familiar to the law, customarily proved by showing the nature and circumstances of the wrong and its effect on the plaintiff. In sum, then, although mental and emotional distress caused by the denial of procedural due process itself is compensable under § 1983, we hold that neither the likelihood of such injury nor the difficulty of proving it is so great as to justify awarding compensatory damages without proof that such injury actually was caused. . . .

III

Even if respondents' suspensions were justified, and even if they did not suffer any other actual injury, the fact remains that they were deprived of their right to procedural due process. "It is enough to invoke the procedural safeguards of the Fourteenth Amendment that a significant property interest is at stake, whatever the ultimate outcome of a hearing. . . ."

Common-law courts traditionally have vindicated deprivations of certain "absolute" rights that are not shown to have caused actual injury through the award of a nominal sum of money. By making the deprivation of such rights actionable for nominal damages without proof of actual injury, the law recognizes the importance to organized society that those rights be scrupulously observed; but at the same time, it remains true to the principle that substantial damages should be awarded only to compensate actual injury or, in the case of exemplary or punitive damages, to deter or punish malicious deprivations of rights.

Because the right to procedural due process is "absolute" in the sense that it does not depend upon the merits of a claimant's substantive assertions, and because of the importance to organized society that procedural due process be observed, we believe that the denial of procedural due process should be actionable for nominal damages without proof of actual injury. We therefore hold that if, upon remand, the District Court determines that respondents' suspensions were justified, respondents nevertheless will be entitled to recover nominal damages not to exceed one dollar from petitioners. . . .

Notes

1. Note that procedural due process is considered an "absolute" right, the denial of which is actionable without proof of injury, with nominal damages to be awarded regardless of whether a suspension was justified.

2. Why might an individual who violated a school rule file suit on the basis of procedural due process?

3. An argument can be made that *Wood* might have had the effect of encouraging damages claims against school officials in cases involving discipline of students or school employees. Has this fear been borne out? Bear in mind that attorney fees can be awarded to a prevailing party in a civil rights action.

[Case No. 49]   Liability for Injury to Student before Start of School Day

TITUS v. LINDBERG

Supreme Court of New Jersey, 1967.
228 A.2d 65.

JACOBS, J. The Appellate Division affirmed a judgment for the plaintiffs against all three defendants, Lindberg, Smith and the Board of Education. We granted certification on the application of Smith and the Board of Education.

On October 25, 1963 the plaintiff Robert A. Titus, who was then nine years old and a student at the Fairview School in Middletown Township, rode off from home on his bicycle to school. He arrived at the school grounds at about 8:05 A.M., entered along the bus driveway, and headed for the bicycle rack on the west side of the school building. As he came around a corner of the building, he was struck by a paper clip which the defendant Richard Lindberg, then thirteen years old, had shot from an elastic band. Robert was seriously injured.

Lindberg was not then a student at Fairview but attended the Thompson School which was some distance away. Fairview had been designated by the school system's transportation coordinator as the pickup site for three schools including Thompson, and Lindberg was one of many students who customarily boarded school buses there. Up to two years earlier, Lindberg had attended Fairview and its records described him as "very rough" and a "bully." On the morning of the incident he arrived early at Fairview, fooled around with an elastic band for a while, and struck a student in the back with a paper clip about 5 minutes before he shot the one which injured Robert.

Though the school doors at Fairview did not officially open until 8:15 A.M., it was customary for quite a few Fairview students to start arriving on the school grounds at about 8 A.M. Some would arrive on their bicycles, as did Robert, and others would arrive on foot. Oftentimes the students played the game of "keep away" before the school bell rang. An early arrival would obtain a ball from a classroom and a team of students would try to keep it away from a second team. The first bell rang at 8:15 A.M., the students were supposed to be in their seats by 8:30 A.M. when the late bell rang, and classes began at 8:35 A.M.

The defendant Smith had been principal of Fairview since 1960. He testified that he "did the supervising of the arrival of the children" and that, although he had known of prior pranks and deportment problems connected with Lindberg, he was not aware of any earlier incidents involving conduct such as his shooting of paper clips. Smith's practice was to arrive at the school grounds at 8 A.M. and he had instructed his teachers to arrive at that time and prepare for and be in their classes at 8:15 A.M. so that they could maintain order as the students filed in. On his arrival at 8 A.M. he would supervise deliveries by the milk truck and would watch out for the safety of children in the immediate area. He would then walk from the east side of the school to the west side where the buses began to arrive at 8:15 A.M. Sometimes he would walk through a corridor within the building and at other times he would walk along the outside of the building. At the time of the incident, he was walking inside the building. As he passed one of the windows of the building, he looked out and saw a group gathered around the stricken Robert. He went to the scene to administer assistance.

There were 560 students at Fairview and approximately 70 or 80 additional students arrived at the school grounds to board the buses. There were, in addition to administrative and part-time personnel, 19 full-time classroom teachers on the Fairview staff but none of them had been assigned any responsibilities in connection with the supervision of students before their entry into the classrooms. Smith testified that he made the rules governing the conduct of students on the school grounds and that he was charged with that responsibility. Although he stated that he told the students that school arrival time was from 8:15 A.M. to 8:30 A.M., he acknowledged his awareness that students began arriving at 8 A.M. and stated flatly that he maintained "supervision outside the building on the grounds between eight and 8:30." . . .

There is no dispute that Lindberg was soundly held liable for the injury caused by his conduct. And while there is dispute as to the liability of Smith, we are satisfied that the evidence fairly presented a jury question as to whether he had negligently failed to discharge his responsibilities with consequential injury to Robert. The duty of school personnel to exercise reasonable supervisory care for the safety of students entrusted to them, and their accountability for injuries resulting from failure to discharge that duty, are well-recognized in our State and elsewhere. . . .

Apparently Smith does not dispute the foregoing principles although he does seem to question that his responsibilities began before 8:15 A.M. We have no doubt on that score. In the first place he assumed the responsibility for supervising the school grounds beginning at 8 A.M. and was from that point on obligated to exercise due care. In the second place, and wholly apart from the assumption, it cannot in any fair sense be said that his legal responsibility began only upon the opening of the classrooms at 8:15 A.M. Obviously the students would be expected to and could properly come to the school grounds during some short period before the classrooms actually opened. They customarily began coming at 8 A.M. and that was reasonable. Smith undoubtedly knew of their coming and of their "keep away" games. When all this is coupled with the fact that Fairview was also a pickup site for the older students, the dangers and the need for reasonable supervision from 8 A.M. on were entirely apparent. . . .

Smith contends that he was entitled to a direction on the ground that there was insufficient evidence to enable a jury to find negligence on his part. The record discloses the contrary. He had not announced any rules with respect to the congregation of his students and their conduct prior to entry into the classrooms. He had assigned none of the teachers or other personnel to assist him in supervising the students and he undertook the sole responsibility. He then failed to take any measures towards overseeing their presence and activities, except at the point of the milk delivery and by walking from east to west around or through the building. While he was walking through the building there was no semblance of supervision on the grounds outside and that was precisely when the injury to Robert occurred. Before then Lindberg had been fooling around and had struck another student while no supervisor was anywhere about. Bearing all of these circumstances in mind, it clearly cannot be said that the finding that Smith failed to take suitable supervisory precautions lacked reasonable support in the evidence.

Smith advances the further contention that, even if lack of due supervision be assumed, Lindberg's deliberate conduct rather than Smith's negligence was the "sole competent producing cause of the injury." The jury presumably found that conduct of the type engaged in by Lindberg was reasonably to be anticipated and guarded against and that Smith's failure to do so was a substantial factor in the occurrence. That being so, there was ample basis for finding proximate causation and holding Smith liable in addition to Lindberg. . . .

Notes

1. Principals are increasingly being named in tort actions for injuries suffered by pupils in school. Until the 1960's, principals usually were not included because of the common law requisite that to be liable for the tort of negligence, one's action must be the proximate, or immediate, cause of the injury.

2. Is a principal's failure to arrange for adequate recess or lunch-time supervision a proper basis for a charge of negligence?

[Case No. 50] Liability for Injury to Student Harmed by Snowball

LAWES v. BOARD OF EDUCATION OF THE CITY OF NEW YORK

Court of Appeals of New York, 1965.
266 N.Y.S.2d 364.

BERGAN, JUDGE. Plaintiff Nuvia Alicia Lawes, a pupil at Public School No. 144 in Brooklyn, was struck by a snowball thrown by a fellow pupil while she was on her way from her home to her classroom after lunch on February 17, 1960. Plaintiff, then 11 years old, suffered a serious eye injury. A judgment for $45,000 has been rendered against the Board of Education and affirmed by a divided Appellate Division.

The snowball was thrown on school property in a yard between the street and school entrance, but this was not during a recreation period. Children were then on the property on their way into the school after having been home to lunch. The school had made a rule against snowball throwing and plaintiff's teacher had warned her pupils not to throw snowballs.

If a school is to become liable to one pupil for a snowball thrown at him by a fellow pupil, the rule governing such responsibility should be laid down clearly and be precise enough to be generally understood in the schools.

No one grows up in this climate without throwing snowballs and being hit by them. If snow is on the ground as children come to school, it would require intensive policing, almost child by child, to take all snowball throwing out of play. It is unreasonable to demand or expect such perfection in supervision from ordinary teachers or ordinary school management; and a fair test of reasonable care does not demand it.

The classic New York statement of the measure of school care for children is laid out in Judge Loughran's noted opinion in *Hoose v. Drumm*: "Teachers have watched over the play of their pupils time out of mind. At recess periods, not less than in the class room, a teacher owes it to his charges to exercise such care of them as a parent of ordinary prudence would observe in comparable circumstances."

A parent of ordinary prudence would not invariably stop his children from making and throwing snowballs. Indeed, he might encourage it. He would stop dangerous throwing, if he learned hard frozen snow or ice had come into play, or the pelting of one child by several others, but ordinary snowball throwing would not necessarily be stopped.

A reasonable measure of a school's responsibility for snowball throwing is to control or prevent it during recreation periods according to its best judgment of conditions, and to take energetic steps to intervene at other times if dangerous play comes to its notice while children are within its area of responsibility.

The facts in the present case do not spell out any notice of special danger. There is no proof whatever in the record that teachers had notice of any other snowball throwing on the day plaintiff was hit. Proof that a snowball was thrown on the previous day is very thin and, even if fully credited, would not give fair notice of the kind of continued danger which should have been prevented by the active intervention of teachers.

A fellow pupil and friend of plaintiff testified that she was struck by a snowball on February 16 and that she reported this to a teacher. She did not testify that she reported that she was injured. She said: "I told her I got hit. Somebody hit me with a snowball."

The teacher denied having been told this and the Education Department records marked for identification, which the trial court refused to receive, show that this pupil reported in writing that she had been struck by a snowball, not before, but some five weeks after, plaintiff's injury.

No requirement on this kind of a record is imposed on teachers to enforce the rule against snowballs by standing outside in the cold to watch to see that children do not violate the rule as they come into the school. And it is an undue burden on the school to impose a liability because teachers did not stand outside for active intervention in the circumstances shown by this record.

A school is not liable for every thoughtless or careless act by which one pupil may injure another. Nor is liability invariably to fall on it because a school rule has been violated and an injury has been caused by another pupil. . . .

In its result the judgment in this case imposes a greatly enlarged risk of liability on a school without showing notice of a particular danger at a particular time. A long line of decisions should cause us to proceed warily toward such an enlarged area of liability. . . .

The order should be reversed and the complaint dismissed, without costs.

Notes

1.   New York has an indemnification statute that requires school boards to pay judgments obtained against teachers for their negligence in the course of their employment. N.Y. Educ. Law § 3811.

2.   What precautions should school officials take to prevent students from throwing snowballs? Should the precautions be different after the first snowfall as opposed to after the snow has been on the ground for a period of time?

Note the discussion in the text of this chapter of another snowball case from New York.

[Case No. 51]   Standard of Care, Assumption of Risk

BENITEZ v. NEW YORK CITY BOARD OF EDUCATION

Court of Appeals of New York.
543 N.Y.S.2d 29 [54 Educ. L. Rep. 933].

Bellacosa, Judge.

In this personal injury action seeking damages arising from a paralyzing high school football injury, the jury returned a verdict for plaintiff Benitez on four separate theories of negligence against the New York City Board of Education (Board) and its Public Schools Athletic League (PSAL). The Trial Justice granted a postverdict motion rejecting two of the four negligence theories. In a split decision, the Appellate Division affirmed the judgment for Benitez in the sum of $878,330 and subsequently granted the Board and PSAL leave to appeal.

We reverse and dismiss the complaint because plaintiff adduced insufficient evidence that defendants breached any duty of reasonable care which can be said to have proximately caused his injuries. A board of education, its subordinate employees and interscholastic athletic organizations must exercise only reasonable care to protect student athletes in sports competitions from injuries arising out of unassumed, concealed, or unreasonably increased risks. The trial court incorrectly resolved the duty/causation issue and did so under an erroneous higher duty of care instruction.

Benitez was a 19–year-old senior star athlete at George Washington High School (GW) when he suffered a broken neck in 1983 during a varsity football game against another Division A team, John F. Kennedy High School (JFK). GW had been placed in Division A prior to the 1982 season by the Football Committee of the PSAL. The PSAL determined, pursuant to established guidelines, that GW was better suited for Division A competition than the less competitive Division B league where GW had been dominant the three previous seasons. GW exhausted its administrative appeals, arguing throughout that Division A competition was "potentially dangerous to the safety and welfare of the team" and that the players might "suffer serious injuries". Before the start of the 1983 season, GW again sought to be assigned to Division B, citing among its grounds safety concerns and the injury toll suffered by the team during the 1982 season. Under PSAL administrative guidelines and because the injuries suffered by GW players were akin in number and degree with those of other Division A teams, this request for reassignment was also denied.

Following the 1983 denial, GW's coach advised the school's new principal to drop the football program but was told that such action would result in the barring of all GW athletic teams from interscholastic competition for the year. Prior to the 1983 GW–JFK game, the coach and the assistant principal in charge of physical education and health advised GW's principal that the game was a mismatch and should not be played because of the high risk of injury. The coach testified as a witness for plaintiff that, despite the principal's decision to play the season and the game, he viewed it as the coach's responsibility to pull a team off the field in the face of unsafe competition. He felt at the time it was unsafe for his team to be playing JFK; he knew his players were fatigued; he did not have the personnel to rest Benitez; and he was aware that injuries are most likely to occur when players are tired. He did not unilaterally cancel the game because he feared it might cost him his job.

Plaintiff Benitez had received numerous college football scholarship offers before his injury. He testified that he played football voluntarily and that he was fully trained by a qualified coach, particularly with respect to proper blocking techniques. His injury occurred with 1 minute and 17 seconds left in the first half of the game while correctly executing a block during a kick-off return by his team. Prior to his injury, he engaged, as was customary for him, in the great majority of plays for his team's offensive, defensive and special squads. Plaintiff conceded he was fatigued at the time of his injury but had not so informed his coach.

Benitez initiated this action against the Board, PSAL and City of New York alleging negligence in placing and retaining GW in Division A; allowing GW to play the JFK game in the face of an obvious mismatch; and allowing him to play virtually the entire first half of the game without adequate rest. Prior to submission of the case to the jury, the Trial Justice dismissed the case as against the City of New York. The court subsequently instructed the jury, over objection, that the defendants were obligated to exercise the same level of care "as a parent of ordinary prudence would exercise under the same circumstances".

The jury verdict in Benitez' favor apportioned 30% of the fault against him and 70% against the defendants. The Trial Justice granted, in part, a motion for a judgment notwithstanding the verdict and dismissed the causes relating to the placement and retention of GW in Division A, reasoning that these were discretionary determinations. Declining to direct a defendants' verdict on the remaining negligence theories, the Trial Justice stated: "[c]ertainly, the jury had a right to indicate that from the facts that were given, that they acted negligently in permitting him to play; particularly, if the coach indicated that he was fatigued. And, if he was playing him in a manner knowing that he was fatigued, certainly the jury could find that he was negligent in doing that."

In affirming, the Appellate Division majority reasoned that despite Benitez' voluntary participation and assumption of the risks inherent in football, the coach knew it was unsafe for Benitez to be playing full time, while tired, in a mismatched game and that the failure to rest him substantially increased the likelihood of injury and was its proximate cause. Additionally, the risk of injury was said to have been unreasonably enhanced by the "indirect compulsion" of the teacher-student relationship and the student's concern that he not jeopardize his college scholarship opportunities by removing himself from the game.

The dissenting Justice stated that the standard of care applicable to this situation was unsettled, but regardless of whether it was a "reasonable care" or a "prudent parent" standard, neither was breached in this case. Viewing fatigue and injury as risks inherent in football and assumed by plaintiff, the dissenter asserted that the assumption of risk defense was unrebutted. He rejected application of the "implied compulsion" theory as there was no evidence that the 19–year-old plaintiff was acting in other than a voluntary manner.

Leave was granted by the Appellate Division on a certified question which need not be answered, as the order appealed from finally determines the action. We reverse and dismiss the complaint.

The trial court erroneously instructed the jury that a school owes a student voluntarily competing in an interscholastic high school football game the more protective duty and standard of care of a prudent parent. In the context of wholly voluntary participation in intramural, interscholastic and other school-sponsored extracurricular athletic endeavors, we have required the exercise of the less demanding ordinary reasonable care standard.

To be sure, application of the personal injury principles of duty, breach and proximate cause in the context of sports injuries almost invariably includes a discussion also of assumption of risk. The common Latin aphorism cited in the cases translates as follows: one who consents to an act does not suffer a compensable injury. As Judge Cardozo put it in the "Flopper" amusement ride case, "[o]ne who takes part in such a sport accepts the dangers that inhere in it so far as they are obvious and necessary, just as a fencer accepts the risk of a thrust by his antagonist or a spectator at a ball game the chance of contact with the ball." As an integral part of athletic competitions, persons are generally held by their actual and implied consents to the risks of "injury-causing events which are known, apparent or reasonably foreseeable consequences of the participation." In this context, however, important legal distinctions are drawn between compulsory physical education courses and voluntary participation in interscholastic athletic activity as well as between professional and amateur status.

Assumption of risk in competitive athletics "is not an absolute defense but a measure of the defendant's duty of care." The policy underlying this tort rule is intended to facilitate free and vigorous participation in athletic activities. But even with professional athletes, it is "qualified to the extent that participants do not consent to acts which are reckless or intentional" Awareness of the risk assumed is to be assessed against the background of the skill and experience of the particular plaintiff, and in that assessment a higher degree of awareness will be imputed to a professional than to one with less than professional experience in the particular sport. Manifestly, a high school athlete, even an outstanding one, does not assume all the risks of a professional sportsperson, but neither does a 19–year-old senior star football player and college scholarship prospect fall within the extra protected class of those warranting strict parental duties of supervision.

... this court accepted a distinction between the circumstances of a physical education course, where participation is compulsory, and purely voluntary activity in interscholastic sports. We dismissed the complaint in that case in circumstances remarkably parallel to this case, albeit in a different sport—baseball. Players who voluntarily join in extracurricular interscholastic sports assume the risks to which their roles expose them but not risks which are "unreasonably increased or concealed." The distinction has continued validity and usefulness in correctly deciding this and like cases.

We hold that a board of education, its employees, agents and organized athletic councils must exercise ordinary reasonable care to protect student athletes voluntarily involved in extracurricular sports from unassumed, concealed or unreasonably increased risks.

On the record before us, we conclude as a matter of law that there was no showing of inherent compulsion and that Benitez' injury was not the consequence of a failed duty of care on the part of the defendants.

The theory of inherent compulsion provides that the defense of assumption of the risk is not a shield from liability, even where the injured party acted despite obvious and evident risks, when the element of voluntariness is overcome by the compulsion of a superior. Two factors are generally present to sustain a finding of liability on an inherent compulsion theory despite the injured party's knowledge of the risk, "a direction by a superior to do the act" and "an economic compulsion or other circumstance which equally impels" compliance with the direction. Though the risk is foreseen, an assurance of safety generally implicit in the supervisor's direction supplants the plaintiff's assumption of the risk by requiring action despite prudent cautionary concerns.

The coach undeniably supervised plaintiff, who may have feared that if he did not play or if he asked to be rested his athletic standing or scholarship opportunities might be jeopardized. However, there was no evidence at all that plaintiff was concerned about an unreasonably heightened risk of competition or that his coach directed him to disregard a risk he would not have otherwise assumed anyhow. While plaintiff testified he was tired, he acknowledged that he was participating voluntarily, that he did not inform his coach of his fatigue, and that he was playing without complaint under the same conditions as he had for the previous season and one half. In sum, plaintiff Benitez failed to present any evidence that he had no choice but to follow the coach's direction to play despite his concern over enhanced risk factors known by or communicated to the coach.

Moreover, while issues of proximate cause are generally fact matters to be resolved by a jury, "where only one conclusion may be drawn from the established facts ... the question of legal cause may be decided as a matter of law." Fatigue and, unfortunately, injury are inherent in team competitive sports, especially football. Benitez was concededly an excellent athlete, properly equipped and well-trained. He was playing voluntarily in the same manner as he had for the previous year and one half against Division A competition and had not requested rest or complained. Within the breadth and scope of his consent and participation, plaintiff put himself at risk in the circumstances of this case for the injuries he ultimately suffered. On his own proof, he thus failed to meet the burden of showing some negligent act or inaction, referenced to the applicable duty of care owed to him by these defendants, which may be said to constitute "a substantial cause of the events which produced the injury." The injury in this case, in sum, was a luckless accident arising from the vigorous voluntary participation in competitive interscholastic athletics.

Accordingly, the order of the Appellate Division should be reversed and the complaint dismissed, with costs. The certified question should not be answered as unnecessary.

Notes

1. Following *Benitez*, courts in New York continue to apply the reasonably prudent parent standard for young children. In a case with no record of an appeal, a trial court ruled that a jury was properly instructed that officials in a preschool owed children the duty of a prudent parent rather than that of ordinary reasonable care. *Enright by Enright v. Busy Bee Playschool*, 164 Misc.2d 415, 625 N.Y.S.2d 453 [99 Educ. L. Rep. 1073] (N.Y.Sup.Ct.1995). Another appellate court affirmed the denial of a motion for summary judgment in a suit against a church that housed a Head Start Program in a facility that where lead paint was peeling in classrooms based on the reasonable parent standard. *Espinal by Castillo v. 570 W. 156th Assocs.*, 667 N.Y.S.2d 223 [123 Educ. L. Rep. 847] (N.Y.Sup.Ct.1997), *aff'd*, 685 N.Y.S.2d 199 (N.Y.App.Div.1999). Where a

first-grade student was injured when he tripped on a crack in the sidewalk used as a play area for recess, a third court was satisfied that officials had exercised the same degree of care and supervision as a reasonably prudent parent. *Santana v. City of N.Y.*, 722 N.Y.S.2d 545 [152 Educ. L. Rep. 237] (N.Y.App.Div.2001). Is it wise applying a higher standard of care for young children?

2.   Where school officials sent a fifteen-year-old ninth-grade student home alone from a band trip via a 1,100–mile cross-country bus trip, the Supreme Court of Iowa held that since the law charged them with the care and control of children, they had to exercise the same standard of care as a parent of ordinary prudence under comparable circumstances. Do you agree? *Ette v. Linn–Mar Community School Dist.*, 656 N.W.2d 62 [173 Educ. L. Rep. 662] (Iowa 2002).

3.   In reaffirming the significance of the defense of assumption risk, an appellate court in England, in *Regina (Hampstead Heath Winter Swimming Club and Another) v. Corporation of London and Another*, Queens Bench Division, [2005] 1 W.L.R. 2930, 2943, available at 2005 WL 959620, criticized "[t]he pursuit of an unrestrained culture of blame and compensation has many evil consequences and one is certainly the interference with the liberty of the citizen." The court went on to describe assumption of risk as the legal vehicle that opposes society's "imposing a grey and dull safety regime on everyone," in the sense that it affords people the opportunities to choose whether they wish to engage in risky activities. Do you agree with this sentiment?

[Case No. 52] An Injury for Which Compensation Can Be Awarded

SPEARS v. JEFFERSON PARISH SCHOOL BOARD

Court of Appeal of Louisiana.
646 So.2d 1104 [96 Educ. L. Rep. 884].

GOTHARD, JUDGE.

This appeal arises out of an action filed by the plaintiffs, Joyce and Samuel Spears individually and on behalf of their minor son, Justin, for injuries sustained while Justin was a kindergarten student at Woodland West Elementary School, a part of the Jefferson Parish School System. Liability of the defendant was established by a joint stipulation of the parties and the matter went to trial on the issue of quantum. In due course the trial court rendered judgment, accompanied by written reasons, in favor of the plaintiffs as follows:

Past treatment expenses
$5,498.00

Future treatment
$2,160.00

General damages—Justin
$100,000.00

Loss of Consortium Mr. and Mrs. Spears $5,000.00 each
$10,000.00

Total award
$117,658.00

Defendant appeals that judgment.

FACTS

On February 28, 1989, Justin Spears was a kindergarten student at Woodland West Elementary School. Because it was a rainy day, the students were seated on the floor of the Cafeteria watching a movie during their regularly scheduled Physical Education class under the supervision of Coach John Brooks and Coach Johnny Peyton. Justin and two of his friends began to be slightly disruptive. At that time Coach Brooks called the boys over to sit near him. The boys began to play with his hair and his ears. Coach Brooks told the boys that if they did not stop annoying him he would "kill them." Because the coach was experiencing management problems with the three boys, he took two of them into an adjacent office with him while he did some paperwork, leaving the rest of the class to watch the movie. Justin stayed behind talking to Coach Peyton. The boys began asking Coach Brooks how he would kill them. Coach Brooks told them he would probably tie the jump rope around their neck and push them off a chair in the office. Because Justin was talking to Coach Peyton during this discussion, Coach Brooks ask the boys if they wanted to play a trick on Justin and they agreed.

The testimony differs as to the events that followed, but it is clear that Coach Brooks led Justin to believe that his friends were dead. He told Justin he had hanged them by their neck with the jump rope, and at least one of the boys was lying on the floor pretending to be dead. When Justin saw the boy lying there he became upset and began to cry. Coach Brooks told Justin it was just a joke and that the boys were not really dead.

Plaintiffs introduced live testimony from Justin and both of his parents. They also introduced depositions from two psychologists who treated Justin. According to the evidence, Justin was a normal, well-adjusted five-year-old before the incident. However, in the weeks following the incident he began to exhibit infantile behavior. He refused to go to the bathroom alone and refused to wipe himself. He was afraid that Coach Brooks would come out of the mirror in the bathroom and harm him. Justin would no longer sleep in his own room. He became overly dependent on his mother and was not comfortable when she was out of sight.

Justin was treated by Dr. Lynne Shwery, a psychologist at Children's Hospital. Dr. Shwery testified at her deposition that she treated Justin from the time of the incident until he moved with his family to Virginia in June, 1991. She opined that Justin had "experienced an event that was outside the range of usual human experience and that would be markedly distressing to almost anyone." She diagnosed Justin as having Post–Traumatic Stress Disorder and explained that Justin was fearful and anxious. He had come to the realization that the world was not a safe place and that all adults could not be trusted.

From the time of the family's relocation to Virginia in 1991, Justin was treated by Dr. Tonya Fridy; that treatment was still on going at the time of trial. Dr. Fridy's professional diagnosis concurred with that of Dr. Shwery's. Additionally, Dr. Fridy stated that Justin had separation anxiety and social phobia disorder and would probably need three to five more years of therapy.

The defendant offered testimony from their own expert, Dr. Vincent Carbone. He conducted an evaluation of Justin and concluded that Justin was "a very anxious child who was very fearful of things in his environment," but Dr. Carbone did not agree that Justin was suffering from Post–Traumatic Stress Disorder.

After considering all of the evidence, the trial court rendered judgment in favor of plaintiff, accompanied by written reasons which included the finding that "this child has been effectively robbed of a normal, carefree childhood due to the careless actions of the coach".

In brief to this court the defendant assigns nine errors which can be placed into three arguments. First, it is argued that the trial court erred in its findings of fact concerning the magnitude of Justin's injuries and thus the award of damages is excessive. Second, it is argued that the award of loss of consortium to the parents is incorrect. The final argument concerns an evidentiary ruling on the defendant's assertion that Justin's parents failed to mitigate the damages.

When reviewing the factual findings of the trial court we are restricted by the manifest error standard of *Rosell v. ESCO*. Where there is conflicting testimony, reasonable inferences of fact should not be disturbed, even when the appellate court may feel its own evaluations and inferences are as reasonable as those of the trial court. Where there are two permissible views of the evidence, the fact finder's choice between them cannot be manifestly erroneous or clearly wrong. Further, when factual findings are based on credibility of witnesses, the manifest error/clearly wrong standard demands great deference to the trier of fact. The rule that questions of credibility are for the trier of fact also applies to the evaluation of expert testimony, unless the stated reasons of the expert are patently unsound. Here the opinions of experts are supported by sound reasons and there is ample support for the trial court's findings of fact. Consequently, we find no manifest error in the trial court's reliance on the expert testimony in its formulation of factual findings in this matter.

Our review of the amount awarded as general damages is subject to *Youn v. Maritime Overseas Corp.*, in which the [United States] Supreme Court, stated:

> ... an appellate court should rarely disturb an award of general damages. Reasonable persons frequently disagree about the measure of general damages in a particular case. It is only when the award is, in either direction, beyond that which a reasonable trier of fact could assess for the effects of the particular injury to the particular plaintiff under the particular circumstances that the appellate court should increase or reduce the award.

Given the circumstances of this case and the standard of review mandated by the Supreme Court, we do not find the trial court's award of general damages in the amount of $100,000.00 to Justin was an abuse of discretion. For the same reasons we cannot find that the award of $2,160.00 for future therapy was an abuse of discretion. Therefore, we will not overturn those portions of the judgment.

The defendant also complains of the award of $5,000.00 each to Justin's parents for loss of consortium. ... At trial the plaintiffs introduced evidence concerning the loss of consortium claim.

In reasons for judgment the trial court stated:

> With respect to the claim for loss of consortium filed on behalf of Mr. and Mrs. Spears the Court believes that they personally have suffered heartache and anxiety as a result of the trauma to their child. The Spears have enjoyed little quality time alone because of Justin's need to be constantly in their physical presence. The Court believes that $5000.00 per parent is adequate to compensate them for their loss of consortium.

Defendant argues that the factual finding by the trial court does not warrant an award for loss of consortium, but rather, an award for mental anguish ... which is precluded by the stipulation.

Loss of consortium in the context of the parent/child relationship means loss of the aid, assistance and companionship of the child, or loss of affection, society and service. We agree with the defendant's assertion that mental anguish suffered by the parents because of the injury to their son is not compensable in a loss of consortium claim. Further, we agree that the trial court was incorrect in awarding damages based on the reasons stated.

However, we find that the record contains evidence to support a claim for loss of consortium. It is clear from the record that the incident adversely affected the relationship between Justin and his parents. The child, who was developing normally before the incident, became a behavior problem as a direct result of defendant's actions. Injuries incurred by the child rendered the family life difficult afterward since Justin no longer wished to go on family outings. Consequently, we do not find error in the award on loss of consortium damages to the parents.

The final assignment of error concerns certain evidentiary rulings made by the trial court during the testimony of defense expert witness, Dr. Vincent Carbone. During that testimony the defendant attempted to show that the Spears were overprotective parents who projected their parental fears to Justin, making the injury worse than it might have been and slowing the child's recovery. The plaintiffs' counsel objected to this line of questioning, arguing that the evidence would be only relevant to show a failure to mitigate the damages or to establish causation. Plaintiffs' counsel further argued that since failure to mitigate damages is an affirmative defense and had not been pled, and causation was not at issue, the evidence was inadmissible. The trial court sustained the objection, but allowed the defendant to proffer the evidence.

On appeal defendant argues that the trial court erred in ruling that mitigation of damages is an affirmative defense and that the Spears did not fail to mitigate their damages. Also, defendant argues that the proffer offered at the end of the testimony disrupted the flow of the evidence and prejudiced the defense in the presentation of its case.

. . .

Because the trial court considered the mitigation to be a viable issue before the court and made a judgment based on a factual finding supported by evidence contained in the record, we cannot find error in the evidentiary rulings at trial or the finding the Spears did not fail to mitigate the damages. Nor do we find any merit to defendant's argument that the offer of the proffer at the end of the expert's testimony upset the flow of evidence to such an extent that it prejudiced the presentation of defendant's case. The defendant was allowed to offer all of the evidence it wished to offer and it was all considered by the trial court.

For the foregoing reasons the judgment of the trial court is affirmed. Costs are assessed to the appellant.

AFFIRMED

Notes

1.   What do you think about the outcome in this case? Is it fair?

2.   What kind of professional development activities should school officials provide for teachers to avoid situations like this one?

[Case No. 53]   Educational Malpractice

HUNTER v. BOARD OF EDUCATION OF MONTGOMERY COUNTY

Court of Appeals of Maryland, 1982.
439 A.2d 582 [2 Educ. L. Rep. 114].

DIGGES, JUDGE. This case primarily presents the troubling but nevertheless important question, . . . of whether an action can be successfully asserted against a school board and various individual employees for improperly evaluating, placing or teaching a student. . . .

. . . The action was instituted . . . shortly after Ross' sixteenth birthday. As best we can gather from the declaration, the parents . . . complain that the school system negligently evaluated the child's learning abilities and caused him to repeat first grade materials while being physically placed in the second grade. It is alleged that this misplacement, which continued at least through grade school, generally caused the student to feel "embarrassment," to develop "learning deficiencies," and to experience "depletion of ego strength." . . .

It is clear . . . that the gravamen of petitioners' claim in this case sounds in negligence, asserting damages for the alleged failure of the school system to properly educate young Hunter, and we first focus our attention on this aspect of it. In so doing, we note that these so-called "educational malpractice" claims have been unanimously rejected by those few jurisdictions considering the topic. . . . These decisions generally hold that a cause of action seeking damages for acts of negligence in the educational process is precluded by considerations of public policy, among them being the absence of a workable rule of care against which the defendant's conduct may be measured, the inherent uncertainty in determining the cause and nature of any damages, and the extreme burden which would be imposed on the already strained resources of the public school system to say nothing of those of the judiciary. Thus ... where a high school graduate sought recovery in tort for a claimed inadequate education, the California court, viewing the problem as whether an actionable duty of care existed, noted that the "wrongful conduct and injuries allegedly involved in educational malfeasance" were neither comprehensible nor assessable within the judicial framework and explained as follows:

Unlike the activity of the highway or the marketplace, classroom methodology affords no readily acceptable standards of care, or cause, or injury. The science of pedagogy itself is fraught with different and conflicting theories of how or what a child should be taught, and any layman might—and commonly does—have his own emphatic views on the subject. The "injury" claimed here is plaintiff's inability to read and write. Substantial professional authority attests that the achievement of literacy in the schools, or its failure, is influenced by a host of factors which affect the pupil subjectively, from outside the formal teaching process, and beyond the control of its ministers. They may be physical, neurological, emotional, cultural, environmental; they may be present but not perceived, recognized but not identified.

We find in this situation no conceivable "workability of a rule of care" against which defendants' alleged conduct may be measured ... no reasonable "degree of certainty that ... plaintiff suffered injury" within the meaning of the law of negligence ..., and no such perceptible "connection between the defendant's conduct and the injury suffered," as alleged, which would establish a causal link between them within the same meaning.

Although the just-articulated policy considerations alone sufficed to negate a legal duty of care ... the court aptly identified additional, practical consequences of imposing such a duty upon the persons and agencies who administer our public educational system:.... [T]he New York Court of Appeals addressed the identical proposition ..., but viewed the issue as presenting solely a question of public policy.... The New York court concluded that the action should not be permitted because to do so would "constitute blatant interference with the responsibility for the administration of the public school system lodged by [State] Constitution and statute in school administrative agencies." ...

We find ourselves in substantial agreement with the reasoning employed by the [California and New York] courts, for an award of money damages, in our view, represents a singularly inappropriate remedy for asserted errors in the educational process. The misgivings expressed in these cases concerning the establishment of legal cause and the inherent immeasurability of damages that is involved in such educational negligence actions against the school systems are indeed well founded. Moreover, to allow petitioners' asserted negligence claims to proceed would in effect position the courts of this State as overseers of both the day-to-day operation of our educational process as well as the formulation of its governing policies. This responsibility we are loathe to impose on our courts. Such matters have been properly entrusted by the General Assembly to the State Department of Education and the local school boards who are invested with authority over them. . . .

Note

1. Widespread attempts to differentiate "educational malpractice" from negligence so as to avoid the centuries-old principles of negligence law have been uniformly unsuccessful.

2. Should claims for educational malpractice be actionable? How would, or should, liability be assessed?

Chapter 8

CONTRACTUAL LIABILITY OF SCHOOL BOARDS AND EMPLOYEES

Introduction

Clearly, the law of contracts applies to public school boards.[1] Even so, to the extent that a detailed treatment of the nature of contracts is beyond the scope of this book, this chapter provides a brief overview of the law of contracts, examining issues primarily other than those involving school employees.

Contracts Generally

The basic elements of contracts are mutual assent, reflected by offer and acceptance; consideration; legally competent parties; legal subject matter; and agreement in a form required by law. Mutual assent, which refers to a "meeting of the minds,"signifies that parties must agree on such essential elements as the subject or subjects covered, price, and time of performance. For example, where a teacher lied on her employment application, albeit to officials in a religiously affiliated non-public school, an appellate court in Louisiana held that since her answers improperly induced them to hire her by causing them to believe that she possessed principles that she lacked, her doing so vitiated their consent such that the parties had not entered into a valid contract insofar as there was no meeting of the minds.[2] Further, if a party modifies an offer, that party has, in effect, made a counteroffer that must be accepted by the first party in order to be binding. Put another way, it is important to recognize that a counteroffer, if made prior to acceptance, is a rejection of an original offer.[3] Thus, one who wishes to accept an offer should do so first unequivocally before making a counteroffer which seeks to modify the terms of the agreement.

Consideration, or that which each side pays for a promise or performance, is something of value, usually money or its equivalent in goods or services. Promises to make gifts or to perform gratuitous services are not contracts because they are not supported by consideration. In a broader sense, consideration is present if promisees, in return for promises, do anything legal which they are not required to do, or do not do something which they can legally do. In one of the classic cases in the

---

1. *Perritt Ltd. Partnership v. Kenosha Unified School Dist. No. 1*, 153 F.3d 489 [128 Educ. L. Rep. 1023] (7th Cir.1998).

2. *LaCross v. Cornerstone Christian Academy of Lafayette*, 896 So.2d 105 [197 Educ. L. Rep. 451] (La. Ct. App. 2004), *writ denied*, 896 So.2d 1037 (La. 2005).

3. *Foster v. Ohio State Univ.*, 534 N.E.2d 1220 [51 Educ. L. Rep. 1344] (Ohio Ct.App.1987).

law of contacts, admittedly not set in an educational context, the Court of Appeals of New York illustrated the parameters of consideration. The court affirmed that where a young man kept his promise to his uncle to refrain from drinking alcohol or using tobacco until he was twenty-one years of age, in exchange for $5,000, the two had entered into a contract since by refraining from doing something that he was legally free to do, he provided consideration in return for his promise.[4]

Legal competency, in the context of school settings, means that the parties must be authorized to enter into agreements. This stands for the proposition that contracts must be ones that boards have the legal ability to form and the other parties are empowered to enter. Contracts that exceed board powers, also known as *ultra vires*, literally, "beyond the powers," are not enforceable. Legality of subject matter also refers to the fact that parties cannot create binding contracts if the contracts require the parties to perform acts that are prohibited by law.

Contracts must be in the proper form in order to be enforceable. In other words, even though oral contracts may be as binding as written ones, in order to be enforceable, certain types of contracts, discussed below, must be in writing. At the same time, under the parole evidence rule, absent evidence to the contrary such as memos suggesting that a key term such as price may change, since written agreements are intended to be treated as the final agreements between parties, courts refuse to permit individuals to modify their agreements by introducing contemporaneous oral statements that change the content of contracts.[5] Even if agreements are not contained on single pieces of paper, courts will accept that parties formed contracts as long as all essential terms are in writing and there are express references to other writings or such connections between documents as to demonstrate that they relate to the same contracts.[6]

Under the common law principle known as the statute of frauds, that has been made statutory in most jurisdictions,[7] four types of contracts that are important for schools must be in writing in order to be enforceable. First, agreements that, by their terms, cannot be performed within one year must be in writing.[8] Second, agreements to purchase or sell interests in real property such as building sites for schools must be in writing.[9] Third, contracts for the purchase of goods worth more than

---

4. *Hamer v. Sidway*, 124 N.Y. 538 (N.Y. 1891).

5. *Russell v. Halteman's Adm'x*, 153 S.W.2d 899 (Ky. 1941).

6. *Mariani v. School Directors of Dist. 40, LaSalle County*, 506 N.E.2d 981 [39 Educ. L. Rep. 225] (Ill. App. Ct. 1987), *appeal denied*, 515 N.E.2d 111 [43 Educ. L. Rep. 251] (Ill. 1987).

7. *See, e.g., Mays-Maune & Assoc. v. Werner Bros.*, 139 S.W.3d 201 [190 Educ. L. Rep. 1058] (Mo. Ct. App. 2004) (affirming that since the statutory requirement that

contracts be in writing is mandatory, strict compliance is required in order to bind school boards).

8. *See, e.g., Kirschling v. Lake Forest School Dist.*, 687 F.Supp. 927 [47 Educ. L. Rep. 977] (D. Del. 1988); *Senghas v. L'Anse Creuse Pub. Schools*, 118 N.W.2d 975 (Mich. 1962).

9. *Board of Educ., Gadsden Indep. School Dist. No. 16 v. James Hamilton Const. Co.*, 891 P.2d 556 [98 Educ. L. Rep. 1037] (N.M. Ct. App. 1994), *cert. denied*, 890 P.2d 807 (N.M. 1995).

$500.00 must be in writing.[10] Fourth, promises to answer the debts of others, such as where school systems merge and newly created boards agree to pay the debts of their predecessor such as mortgages and salaries must be in writing.[11]

If parties make mutual mistakes in written contracts, courts may correct, or reform, their errors. In such a case, where a secretary used the wrong form, indicating that a superintendent was hired for one year, rather than two, the Supreme Court of Arkansas affirmed that a board could not subsequently claim that the agreement was for one year.[12] The court explained that since the parties wished to enter into a two-year contract, having their signatures affixed to the wrong form did not change their intended agreement. If an error is unilateral, as where a moving company's bid to transport the contents of school was one-third of the amount that it billed a board, an appellate court decided that it could not recover for its mistake.[13] An appellate court in Minnesota reasoned that recovery was inappropriate since there was no evidence that board officials acted in any way to mislead or take advantage of the moving company since they made further inquiries into the bid and confirmed the company's confidence in its offer.

Board Authority to Enter into Contracts

The contractual liability of school boards depends in part on whether they had the authority to enter into agreements. As reflected by a case from Texas, once a board enters into a contract, its status with regard to potential liability may change. An appellate court affirmed that when a board exercised its authority to enter into a contract with a company to install synthetic turf on its football field, it waived its immunity from liability with respect to the company's breach of contract claim.[14]

In addition to the contractual authority of boards to enter into various types of contracts, they must also comply with applicable statutory mandates.[15] In one case, a dispute arose over whether a county board of education violated state law by hiring private legal counsel rather than relying on the county's prosecuting attorney to handle its legal affairs. The Supreme Court of Appeals of West Virginia affirmed that the board could exercise discretion in choosing whether to use the services of the county prosecuting attorney or hire its own legal counsel.[16] In

---

10. *Double AA Builders, Ltd. v. Grand State Constr.*, 114 P.3d 835, 841 (Ariz. Ct. App. 2005).

11. *American Cas. Co. of Reading, Pa. v. Devine*, 157 So.2d 661 (Ala. 1963); *Parsons v. Kelso*, 125 S.W. 227 (Mo. Ct. App. 1910).

12. *Hampton School Dist. No. 1 of Calhoun County v. Phillips*, 470 S.W.2d 934 (Ark.1971).

13. *A.A. Metcalf Moving & Storage Co. v. North St. Paul–Maplewood Oakdale Schools*, 587 N.W.2d 311 [131 Educ. L. Rep. 504] (Minn.Ct.App.1998).

14. *Longview Indep. School Dist. v. Vibra–Whirl*, 169 S.W.3d 511 [201 Educ. L. Rep. 403] (Tex. App. 2005).

15. *Berkheimer Assoc. ex rel. North Coventry Township v. Norco Motors*, 842 A.2d 966 [185 Educ. L. Rep. 977] (Pa. Cmwlth. Ct. 2004), *appeal dismissed*, 860 A.2d 125 (Pa. 2004).

16. *Longwell v. Board of Educ. of the County of Marshall*, 583 S.E.2d 109 [179 Educ. L. Rep. 484] (W. Va. 2003).

another case, four days before a new consolidated school district came into being, its board and one of the component systems entered into a new employment contract with the superintendent. When the new board tried to set aside the reorganization, it refused to honor the superintendent's contract. The Supreme Court of Colorado affirmed that the superintendent could not recover on the contract since the old board exceeded its authority in entering into the agreement.[17]

As noted earlier, since boards are created to carry out state constitutional mandates to provide for public education, they have only those powers, including contractual ability, that legislatures expressly grant them along with those necessarily implied to enable them to carry out their express powers[18] such as entering into collective bargaining agreements.[19] As important as it may be, the express power of boards to enter into contracts does not necessarily imply the ability to include a clause for arbitration of disputes growing out of construction contracts.[20]

State statutes ordinarily delineate the contractual powers of school boards. It is a well established rule of statutory construction that when a law specifically sets out a body's powers, or the manner in which they are to be exercised, it precludes all other powers or manners of exercise by implication.

An area of growing controversy with regard to board power involves agreements where they "contract out" services such as food and maintenance to private companies in order to try to save money. In an illustrative case, the Supreme Court of Minnesota affirmed that a board could not unilaterally contract out food services work while a collective bargaining agreement remained in effect.[21] More recently, the Supreme Court of Vermont reached a similar result with regard to a board's attempt to contract out for custodial services.[22] Conversely, the Court of Appeals of New York ruled that a law permitting boards to subcontract services that its commissioner of education might have approved, such as printing, authorized it to subcontract out its printing services without subjecting itself to the operative collective bargaining agreement.[23]

Where statutes neither explicitly nor implicitly cover the manner in which boards are to execute their functions, they may be permitted to

---

17. *Achenbach v. School Dist. No. RE-2, Brush*, 491 P.2d 57 (Colo.1971).

18. *National Educ. Ass'n-Wichita v. Unified School Dist. No. 259, Sedgwick County*, 674 P.2d 478 [15 Educ. L. Rep. 948] (Kan.1983); *Swinney v. Deming Bd. of Educ.*, 873 P.2d 238 [91 Educ. L. Rep. 347] (N.M.1994).

19. *Savage Educ. Ass'n v. Trustees of Richland County Elementary Dist. No. 7*, 692 P.2d 1237 [22 Educ. L. Rep. 506] (Mont.1984).

20. *W.M. Schlosser Co. v. School Bd. of Fairfax County, Va.*, 980 F.2d 253 [79 Educ. L. Rep. 382] (4th Cir.1992).

21. *Independent School Dist. No. 88, New Ulm v. School Serv. Employees Union Local 284*, 503 N.W.2d 104 [84 Educ. L. Rep. 827] (Minn.1993).

22. *Milton Educ. and Support Ass'n v. Milton Bd. of School Trustees*, 824 A.2d 605 [177 Educ. L. Rep. 410] (Vt.2003).

23. *Vestal Employees Ass'n, NEA/NY, NEA v. Public Employment Relations Bd. of State of N.Y.*, 705 N.Y.S.2d 564 [143 Educ. L. Rep. 331] (N.Y.2000).

contract out certain services.[24] Yet, if the services have been performed by board personnel and a collective bargaining statute is in effect, a board must bargain on the matter. In a disagreement over a food service program, the Supreme Court of Wisconsin affirmed that since the same work would have had to have been completed either way, it had no choice but to reject a board's claim that the question was primarily related to the formulation or management of public policy that would have given a union undue control over its affairs.[25] In treating the dispute as one dealing with conditions of employment, the court observed that the board was not obligated to accept the union's proposal.

If a statute sets out the manner or form in which boards must enter into contracts, agreements that are created in any other way are invalid.[26] As such, where state laws require specified board contracts to be in writing, even though oral contracts for the same subject matter would have been valid if formed by individuals or private corporations, they are without legal effect.[27] Also, as discussed below, other contracts that boards enter may have to be awarded to the lowest bidders.

Inevitably boards attempt, in good faith, to form contracts that turn out to be invalid due to their failure to follow statutory guidelines. Yet, good faith does not validate illegal contracts.[28] In a closely related matter, most jurisdictions treat contracts as implying good faith covenants of good faith and fair dealing.[29]

Insofar as laws restricting board powers to enter into contracts are designed to protect the public, the degree of protection that they afford depends on the strictness with which courts construe applicable statutes. Where a statute in California required boards to take official actions by formal votes at legally called public meetings, an appellate court interpreted the law as meaning that a contract to purchase property for a school site could not be authorized in an executive session.[30] In a variation of this issue, an appellate court in Pennsylvania affirmed that while a formal recorded board vote is not required, there must be solid proof of compliance with state law before a contract becomes enforce-

---

24. *Nassau Educ. Chapter of Civil Service Employees Ass'n v. Great Neck Union Free School Dist.*, 439 N.E.2d 876 [6 Educ. L. Rep. 365] (N.Y.1982).

25. *Unified School Dist. No. 1 of Racine County v. Wisconsin Employment Relations Comm'n*, 259 N.W.2d 724 (Wis.1977).

26. *Minor v. Sully Buttes School Dist. No. 58–2*, 345 N.W.2d 48 [16 Educ. L. Rep. 624] (S.D.1984).

27. *Board of School Commr's of the City of Indianapolis v. State ex rel. Wolfolk*, 199 N.E. 569 (Ind.1936); *Richard D. Kimball Co. v. City of Medford*, 166 N.E.2d 708 (Mass.1960). *But see Burk v. Livingston Parish School Bd.*, 182 So. 656 (La.1938) (ordering a board to make full payment on an oral contract where the work was completed).

28. *Conners v. City of Lowell*, 140 N.E. 742 (Mass.1923).

29. *Christensen v. Kingston School Comm.*, 360 F.Supp.2d 212 [196 Educ. L. Rep. 854] (D. Mass. 2005); *Blanck v. Hager*, 360 F.Supp.2d 1137 [196 Educ. L. Rep. 872] (D. Nev. 2005); *Tollefson v. Roman Catholic Bishop*, 268 Cal.Rptr. 550 [59 Educ. L. Rep. 803] (Cal. Ct. App. 1990). *But see Hispanic College Fund v. National Collegiate Athletic Ass'n*, 826 N.E.2d 652, 658 [197 Educ. L. Rep. 770] (Ind. Ct. App. 2005), *transfer denied*, 841 N.E.2d 181 (Ind. 2005) ("Indiana law does not impose a generalized duty of good faith and fair dealing on every contract.").

30. *Santa Monica Unified School Dist. v. Persh*, 85 Cal.Rptr. 463 (Cal.Ct.App. 1970).

able.[31] Another court in Pennsylvania warned that individuals or companies that rely "on agreements with an agent of the school district without first obtaining approval by a vote of the majority of the members at a public meeting do so at their peril."[32]

As reflected by a case from Arizona, good intentions are irrelevant to a contract's validity. An appellate court affirmed that a board was not contractually obligated to accept high school students tuition-free from another district based on an agreement that the board entered into twenty-seven years earlier.[33] The court found that the contract was not only legislatively unauthorized, but impliedly prohibited by a statute that specified procedures for dealing with nonresident students.[34] On the other hand, where a state statute did not require a board to obtain prior approval from voters, the Supreme Court of New Hampshire affirmed that two boards could enter into a three-year tuition agreement under which one district sent its students to a high school in another district.[35] The court rejected a challenge from taxpayers who opposed the contract in determining that voters in the sending district ratified the agreement.

At issue in a dispute over the construction of a school administration center was whether a board authorized its president to sign the prime contract. An appellate court in Texas refused to void the contract in positing that a jury could properly have discovered the presence of authorization from such evidence as the minutes of the meeting at which the board accepted the prime contractor's low bid, testimony that the contractor did not perform any work until the board's architect approved it, and testimony from board members that officials made payments under the contract.[36]

Oral contracts can present special concerns. In one case, the Supreme Court of Ohio pointed out that a principal's oral promise to provide a teacher with a duty-free lunch period in exchange for her agreeing to teach journalism classes and serve as newspaper adviser was not binding on the board since he had no authority to enter into such an arrangement.[37] Previously, an appellate court in Ohio indicated that a superintendent's oral representations to parents that if their children were accepted as students on a tuition basis, they would have been able

31. *Parents Against Abuse In Schools v. Williamsport Area School Dist.*, 594 A.2d 796 [69 Educ. L. Rep. 466] (Pa.Cmwlth.Ct. 1991). *But see Hazleton Area School Dist. v. Krasnoff*, 672 A.2d 858 [107 Educ. L. Rep. 886] (Pa.Cmwlth.Ct.1996), *appeal denied*, 685 A.2d 548 (Pa.1996) (requiring an affirmative vote of a majority of a board on a contract increasing its indebtedness).

32. *Berkheimer Assoc. ex rel. N. Coventry Township v. Norco Motors*, 842 A.2d 966, 971 [185 Educ. L. Rep. 977] (Pa. Cmwlth. Ct. 2004), *appeal denied*, 860 A.2d 125 (Pa. 2004).

33. *Oracle School Dist. No. 2 v. Mammoth High School Dist. No. 88*, 633 P.2d 450 (Ariz.Ct.App. 1981).

34. For another case reflecting the rule that estoppel cannot be invoked against a public agency, *see Public Improvements v. Board of Educ. of City of N.Y.*, 453 N.Y.S.2d 170 [5 Educ. L. Rep. 1231] (N.Y.1982).

35. *Foote v. Manchester School Dist.*, 883 A.2d 283 [202 Educ. L. Rep. 206] (N.H. 2005).

36. *Calvin V. Koltermann, Inc. v. Underream Piling Co.*, 563 S.W.2d 950 (Tex. Civ.App.1977).

37. *Wolf v. Cuyahoga Falls City School Dist. Bd. of Educ.*, 556 N.E.2d 511 [61 Educ. L. Rep. 267] (Ohio 1990).

to attend classes until graduation was not binding even though it was based on conversations with individual board members.[38] The court was of the opinion that the parties did not enter into a contract since the board as a whole did not approve the agreement.

On the other hand, the Third Circuit affirmed that an oral contract between a school board and a construction firm was enforceable.[39] The court acknowledged that the board agreed to allow the company to bid on three building projects based on the drawings, specifications, and equipment lists that officials prepared. When the board withdrew the projects from bidding due to a lack of state subsidies, the company sought reimbursement for its services. A federal trial court rejected the board's claims that the agreement was not binding since it was made at a conference rather than formal meeting and that only written contracts could be enforced against boards for this type of work.[40]

Contracts Extending Beyond a Board's Term

The authority of school boards to enter into contracts that may extend beyond their terms is frequently called into question. Insofar as boards are ongoing legal entities, the fact that they undergo changes in membership does not alter their ability to act prospectively. Yet, if this concept were carried to its logical conclusion, boards could possibly deprive successor boards of a great deal of authority. Recognizing the dangers inherent in such situations, courts consistently agree that boards do not have unlimited powers to bind their successors even if they enter into agreements with other government agencies.[41] Put another way, if new board members could repudiate actions of their predecessors, the resulting uncertainty and instability could lead to chaos. The courts carefully examine fact situations where it appears that either of these extremes has occurred.

Two contract cases illustrate difficulties where boards exceeded their authority. Outgoing board members sought to grant a contract extension to a superintendent for an extra four-year term starting a year before the end of his current term. When new members of the board disagreed, Kentucky's highest court declared that the old board lacked the power to create a new term for the superintendent before his time in office expired.[42] The court wrote that any other result would have made it possible for a superintendent to secure the votes of the majority of board members, splice terms, and perpetuate himself in office indefinitely,

38. *Walker v. Lockland City School Dist. Bd. of Educ.,* 429 N.E.2d 1179 [2 Educ. L. Rep. 203] (Ohio Ct.App.1980).

39. *Titan Environmental Constr. Sys. v. School Dist. of Philadelphia,* 421 F.Supp. 1289 (E.D. Pa. 1976), *aff'd without reported opinion,* 564 F.2d 90 (3d Cir.1977).

40. *See also Robert W. Anderson Housewrecking and Excavating v. Board of Trustees, School Dist. No. 25, Fremont County,* 681 P.2d 1326 [17 Educ. L. Rep. 1232] (Wyo.1984).

41. *See Greene County School Dist. v. Greene County,* 607 S.E.2d 881 [195 Educ. L. Rep. 349] (Ga. 2005) (affirming that since a school board's agreement to convey property to a county in exchange for a reduction in the county's commission for collecting taxes for it was not a valid intergovernmental contract it did not bind the subsequent board of commissioners).

42. *Board of Educ. of Pendleton County v. Gulick,* 398 S.W.2d 483 (Ky.1966).

thereby defeating the right of the people to select, even if indirectly, a successor to this important office. In like fashion, an appellate court in New Jersey affirmed that a board, which hired a superintendent for a two-year probationary term, could not, after eight-and a half months, grant him a three-year contract including tenure.[43] The court examined the board's proceedings and maintained that it relied on an illegal modus operandi since the real reason for the change was that members of the majority block, mindful of a coming election, sought to give the superintendent tenure while they could even though it meant shortening his probationary period by almost two-thirds.

The general rule appears to be that absent express or implied statutory limits on their authority, or if there is no fraud or collusion, boards can enter into contracts that extend for reasonable periods beyond their terms. Such a result is especially likely if contracts begin during the terms of incumbent boards but is less certain if this is not the case. Courts have reached mixed results. For example, if a contract lies totally within the term of a succeeding board, it is invalid.[44] In other instances, courts have construed statutes to empower boards, as continuing bodies, to bind their successors even though the services would be performed wholly within the terms of the new boards.[45] At common law, board attempts to bind their successors in discretionary matters, even if arguably for the good of schools, are likely to fail if they are tainted by improper considerations. In such a case, a party wishing to obviate a board's attempt to bind its successor must show that an agreement extending beyond the term of a contracting board is not reasonably necessary or offered no definable advantage.[46]

Competitive Bidding

In General

Most states have laws, often with multiple versions addressing different bodies, requiring all or certain public contracts, including those for schools, to be subject to competitive bidding. The laws typically require that contracts be awarded to the "lowest responsible bidder"[47] or the "lowest and best bidder,"[48] with some states using both terms.[49]

---

43. *Thomas v. Board of Educ. of Morris Township*, 215 A.2d 35 (N.J.Super.Ct.App.Div.1965).

44. *Independent School Dist. v. Pennington*, 165 N.W. 209 (Iowa 1917).

45. *King City Union High School Dist. v. Waibel*, 37 P.2d 861 (Cal.Ct.App.1934).

46. *Michie v. Board of Trustees of Carbon County School Dist. No. 1*, 847 P.2d 1006 [81 Educ. L. Rep. 581] (Wyo.1993).

47. *See, e.g.*, ALA.CODE 1975 § 16–2–8; WEST'S ANN. CAL. EDUC. CODE § 17060, IDAHO CODE § 33–601; 105 ILL. COM. STAT. ANN. 5/10–9; INDIANA CODE ANN. § 20–9.1–2–9; IOWA CODE ANN. § 260C.38; KAN. STAT. ANN. § 72–6760; LA. REV. STAT. ANN. § 15:1035;

MINN STAT. ANN. § 123B.52; MISS. CODE ANN. § 37–41–31; MO. REV. STAT. ANN. 177.086; N.J. STAT. ANN. § 9:11–2; NEW MEXICO STAT. ANN. § 49–6–13; N.Y. MCKINNEY'S EDUC. L. § 305; OHIO REV. CODE ANN. § 3318.10; 24 PA. STAT. ANN. § 7–751; TEX. CODE ANN., EDUC. CODE § 44.033; W. VA. CODE § 10–2A–4.

48. IND. CODE. ANN. § 5–16–1–1.9; KY. REV. STAT. ANN. § 162.070; MISS. CODE ANN. § 37–39–7; OHIO REV. CODE § 3381.11; TENN. CODE. ANN. § 49–2–203; W. VA. CODE ANN. § 10–4–3.

49. *See* Indiana, Mississippi, Ohio, and West Virginia, *id.*

While most contracts for professional services[50] or repair services[51] are ordinarily not subject to competitive bidding, exceptions to this rule exist.[52]

The Supreme Court of Arizona reached a noteworthy outcome about the nature of bids in relation to final contracts where a contractor sued a school board for breach after the latter sought to cancel a bid before executing a final written agreement. According to the court, since the common law rule that a public agency that accepts a bid on a public contract is not bound until a formal contract exists applied, the board did not breach the agreement.[53]

Another interesting question about competitive bidding arose when a school board agreed to an exclusive ten-year contract with a national soft drink company to provide vending machines to sell its products at a school. A competing company unsuccessfully alleged that since it did not have the opportunity to bid for the contract, the board violated a state law that prohibits any "person" from regulating commerce to prevent competition in the sale of merchandise. The Supreme Court of Montana observed that the statute did not apply because the board was not a "person" engaged as a business.[54]

Competitive bidding statutes are designed to insure, as far as possible, both that boards do not become victims of wrongdoing and that they receive the most for their money. The Supreme Court of Mississippi stipulated that bidding laws, which were born of experience, are designed to protect boards and taxpayers from permitting officials to favor one contractor over another at their expense.[55]

Where statutes prevent school boards from seeking separate bids for certain types of contracts, courts are generally unwilling to waive such provisions.[56] To the extent that courts usually construe statutory provisions designed to safeguard public funds strictly, non-conforming contracts are rendered void.[57]

50. *Cress v. State*, 152 N.E. 822 (Ind. 1926); *Malloy v. Boyertown Area School Bd.*, 657 A.2d 915 [100 Educ. L. Rep. 198] (Pa.1995); *Shively v. Belleville Township High School Dist. No. 201*, 769 N.E.2d 1062 [167 Educ. L. Rep. 836] (Ill. App. Ct. 2002); *B & C Electric v. East Baton Rouge Parish School Bd.*, 849 So.2d 616 [179 Educ. L. Rep. 539] (La. Ct. App. 2003).

51. *Tiger Air & Heat v. Jefferson Parish School Bd.*, 832 So.2d 324 [172 Educ. L. Rep. 1056] (La. Ct. App. 2002), *writ denied*, 839 So.2d 35 (La.2003).

52. *See, e.g., Motta v. Philipsburg School Bd. Trustees, Dist. #1*, 110 P.3d 1055 (Mont. 2005) (mistating that since an agreement to provide workshops for administrators, teachers, and other selected community members was a professional services contract, the board was required to advertise for bids and award it to the lowest responsible bidder).

53. *Ry-Tan Const. v. Washington Elementary School Dist. No. 6*, 111 P.3d 1019 [198 Educ. L. Rep. 327] (Ariz. 2005).

54. *Montana Vending v. Coca–Cola Bottling Co. of Mont.*, 78 P.3d 499 [182 Educ. L. Rep. 345] (Mont. 2003).

55. *Beall v. Board of Supervisors*, 3 So.2d 839 (Miss.1941).

56. *See, e.g., Mechanical Contractors Ass'n of E. Pa. v. Commonwealth Dep't of Educ.*, 860 A.2d 1145 [193 Educ. L. Rep. 532] (Pa. Cmwlth. Ct. 2004), *reconsideration denied* (2004) (stating that the Department of Education could not issue a waiver to a school board exempting it from the requirement that it seek separate bids for plumbing, heating, ventilation, and electrical work on building projects).

57. *Buchanan Bridge Co. v. Campbell*, 54 N.E. 372 (Ohio 1899).

Insofar as state pre-qualifications for bidders, such as descriptions of qualifications and posting bonds, are generally treated as mandatory, contracts lacking them are void. In one case, where a bidder in Louisiana denied that it ever failed to complete a contract, the Fifth Circuit asserted that a board could disqualify it before awarding the project because the company did not pre-qualify.[58]

Lowest Responsible Bidder

Disputes have arisen over board difficulties evaluating what constitutes the "lowest responsible" or "lowest and best" bidders. Low bidders generally lack the right to sue[59] since the purpose of competitive bidding statutes is not to grant rights to bidders, but to benefit taxpayers who can file suit to ensure compliance with a law.[60] In an illustrative case, the Eighth Circuit affirmed that a school board in Missouri could reject the lowest bidder as long as it did not act arbitrarily, capriciously, or based on improper motives.[61] Moreover, it appears that boards may include statements in bid notices that they reserve the right to reject all bids.[62] Boards that reject all bids must typically issue another bid notice in order to procure contractors or suppliers.[63]

In evaluating whether bidders are responsive, meaning that their bids conform in all respects to an awarding authority's specifications,[64] boards are free to consider factors that go beyond financial ability and can consider characteristics such as financial standing, reputation, experience, general ability, promptness, and quality of previous work.[65] For instance, the Supreme Court of Rhode Island was of the view that a school committee did not act in bad faith, unreasonably, or arbitrarily in awarding a contract to a bidder who did not submit the lowest bid.[66] The

58. *Systems Contractors Corp. v. Orleans Parish School Bd.*, 148 F.3d 571 [127 Educ. L. Rep. 722] (5th Cir.1998). *See also Crest Const. Corp. v. Shelby County Bd. of Educ.*, 612 So.2d 425 [80 Educ. L. Rep. 1139] (Ala.1992).

59. *See Laidlaw Transit v. Anchorage School Dist.*, 118 P.3d 1018 [201 Educ. L. Rep. 714] (Alaska 2005) (affirming that where a matching bid was treated as responsive, an unsuccessful bidder had no right to sue). *But see Advance Elec. Co., Inc. v. Montgomery Township Bd. of Educ.*, 797 A.2d 216 [165 Educ. L. Rep. 243] (N.J.Super.Ct.App.Div.2002), *certification denied*, 807 A.2d 195 (N.J.2002) (affirming that in light of the importance of bidding statutes for public school projects, an unsuccessful bidder may challenge a bid award by seeking to enforce the policy behind the law).

60. *R. S. Noonan v. School Dist. of City of York*, 162 A.2d 623 (Pa.1960); *Black Ash Servs. v. DuBois Area School Dist.*, 764 A.2d 672 [150 Educ. L. Rep. 228] (Pa. Cmwlth. Ct.2000).

61. *Hanten v. School Dist. of Riverview Gardens*, 183 F.3d 799 [136 Educ. L. Rep.

761] (8th Cir. 1999). *See also Bud Mahas Const. v. Clark County School Dist.*, 767 F.Supp. 1045 [69 Educ. L. Rep. 286] (D.Nev.1991).

62. *Metropolitan School Dist. of Martinsville v. Mason*, 451 N.E.2d 349 [12 Educ. L. Rep.502] (Ind. Ct.App.1983).

63. *Painting & Decorating Contractors of Am. v. Ellensburg School Dist.*, 638 P.2d 1220 [2 Educ. L. Rep. 271] (Wash.1982).

64. *Bigley v. MSD of Wayne Township Schools*, 823 N.E.2d 278 [195 Educ. L. Rep. 935] (Ind. Ct. App. 2004), *transfer denied*, 831 N.E.2d 742 (Ind. 2005).

65. *Hibbs v. Arensberg*, 119 A. 727, 729 (Pa.1923). [Case No. 54] For a more recent case, *see Steingass Mechanical Contracting v. Warrensville Heights Bd. of Educ.*, 784 N.E.2d 118 [173 Educ. L. Rep. 981] (Ohio Ct. App. 2003).

66. *H.V. Collins Co. v. Tarro*, 696 A.2d 298 (R.I.1997).

court was satisfied that the committee carefully considered factors such as relative experience of bidders, expertise, qualifications, and quality of work in granting the contract to the bidder it considered to be superior where the criteria were sufficiently objective, measurable, and enunciated. At the same time, the Supreme Court of Pennsylvania posited that a board was not obligated to reject the low bidder that failed to meet the bid specification that its surety issue a bid bond with an "A-" rating or better.[67] The court added that since the board had discretion to waive the defects and, on request, the contractor furnished a bond of required quality, the submission of a bid with a lower-rated surety did not give the contractor an impermissible competitive advantage over other bidders.

On matters of propriety and reputation, where a board in New York feared that there was a link between a bidder and persons suspected of, and later indicted for, perjury in connection with bid rigging involving other public agencies, it was able to withhold a contract even though the party was the lowest bidder.[68] The court remarked that it was not necessary to conduct a hearing for the rejected bidder before the disqualification. Other courts in New York contended that although a board may disqualify a bidder for engaging in bidding improprieties,[69] one may not exclude an individual who asserted the privilege against self-incrimination before a grand jury.[70] Another appellate court in New York confirmed that an individual with a prior criminal conviction was not a responsible bidder[71] while the Second Circuit affirmed that the New York City School Construction authority did not violate the rights of a prospective low bidder whose company was subject to a criminal investigation.[72]

Conditions of Bidding

Consistent with their own policies, state, and federal law, school boards are free to set their own conditions such as requiring prime contractors to perform a minimum percentage of work with their own employees.[73] In another type of pre-condition implicating constitutional concerns, the Eighth Circuit affirmed that since a board in Missouri's preference for union labor, expressed in its construction bid specifications, did not violate the constitutional right of non-union employees to associate freely, it did not transgress the rights of a firm that was denied

67. *Gaeta v. Ridley School Dist.*, 788 A.2d 363 [160 Educ. L. Rep. 847] (Pa.2002).

68. *Arglo Painting Corp. v. Board of Educ. of City of N.Y.*, 263 N.Y.S.2d 124 (N.Y.Sup.Ct. 1965).

69. *Caristo Constr. Corp. v. Rubin*, 225 N.Y.S.2d 502 (N.Y.1962).

70. *Turley v. Lefkowitz*, 342 F.Supp. 544 (W.D.N.Y.1972), aff'd, 414 U.S. 70, 94 S.Ct. 316, 38 L.Ed.2d 274 (1973).

71. *Crescent Bus Corp. v. Board of Educ. of City of N.Y.*, 463 N.Y.S.2d 259 [11 Educ. L. Rep. 979] (N.Y.App.Div.1983).

72. *John Gil Const. v. Riverso*, 7 Fed. Appx. 134 [157 Educ. L. Rep. 581] (2d Cir. 2001).

73. *Valley Crest Landscape v. City Council*, 49 Cal.Rptr.2d 184 (Cal.Ct.App. 1996); *Benjamin R. Harvey Co. v. Board of Educ., Spring Lake Heights School Dist.*, 817 A.2d 1023 (N.J.Super.Ct.Law Div. 2002).

a contract even though it was the lowest bidder.[74] Previously, the Supreme Court of Alaska thought that a borough's requiring successful bidders on a high school renovation project to enter into a project labor agreement with local unions did not violate either the state constitution or its procurement code.[75] The court concluded that non-union contractors did not have a constitutionally protected right to equal protection to be free of bid specifications requiring participation in such an agreement.

As reflected by a dispute from New Jersey, a board may require bidders to submit a financial statement.[76] An appellate court ascertained that where the lowest bidder was one of two, out of a total of twenty-six, bidders who failed to submit financial statements, it, and a taxpayer, lacked standing to sue.

If an item is absent from the lowest bid, some courts agree that one may still be accepted if the missing information is furnished before a contract is signed. Where the lowest bidder did not submit a graphic representation of the schedule of work with a bid, but did so before the contract was awarded, the Supreme Judicial Court of Massachusetts was convinced that the contract was valid because when the bid was submitted, the missing information did not affect its total price.[77] In like fashion, appellate courts in New York agreed that a bidder's failure to include a certificate of non-collusive bidding did not render the lowest bid invalid,[78] and where a bid included a breakdown of unit prices rather than a total bid amount,[79] boards were free to grant them the contracts. More recently, the Supreme Court of South Carolina affirmed that a low bidder was entitled to correct a sealed bid on $16,000,000 school construction project in order to add $613,000 for a roof buildup where the board's procurement code only prohibited corrections if they caused a bidder to have the low bid.[80] In conceding that the bidder had the low bid both before and after the correction and used the same bid amount from a roofing contractor as three other bidders, the court held that the unsuccessful bidder's claim was without merit.

Prior to accepting bids, boards typically expect the parties to sign the necessary paperwork. Where a low bidder failed to comply with the specifications of signing a bid, an appellate court in Washington affirmed that the company was not entitled to a writ of mandamus to require the

74. *Hanten v. School Dist. of Riverview Gardens*, 183 F.3d 799 [136 Educ. L. Rep. 761] (8th Cir. 1999).

75. *Laborers Local No. 942 v. Lampkin*, 956 P.2d 422 [126 Educ. L. Rep. 437] (Alaska 1998).

76. *Albert F. Ruehl Co. v. Board of Trustees of Schools for Indus. Educ.*, 203 A.2d 410 (N.J.Super.Ct. Law Div.1964).

77. *Gil-Bern Constr. Corp. v. City of Brockton*, 233 N.E.2d 197 (Mass.1968).

78. *Consolidated Sheet Metal Works v. Board of Educ.*, 308 N.Y.S.2d 773 (N.Y.Sup. Ct.1970).

79. *Daniel Finley Allen & Co. v. East Williston Union Free School Dist.*, 533 N.Y.S.2d 19 [49 Educ. L. Rep. 724] (N.Y.App.Div.1988). *See also Sweet Assoc. v. Gallman*, 318 N.Y.S.2d 528 (N.Y.App.Div. 1971) (permitting a board to break a bid down into separate bids in order to save money).

80. *Martin Engineering v. Lexington County School Dist. One*, 615 S.E.2d 110 [199 Educ. L. Rep. 963] (S.C. 2005). [Case No. 55]

board to accept its bid.[81] The court explained that the board could not legally have accepted the bid since it was not binding without the signature. Later, an appellate court in Louisiana applied the same principle where a board improperly accepted a bid from a corporation that failed to submit the specified corporate resolution authorizing the signing of the bid.[82] The court was persuaded that the requirement of proof of the resolution was necessary for the bid to be valid. In addition, boards can demand strict adherence to deadlines for filing bids. To this end, appellate courts in New York[83] and Michigan[84] upheld board refusals to consider bids that were submitted two and five minutes late, respectively.

Bid laws commonly identify maximum expenditures that may be made without bids.[85] Difficulties can arise when projects involve separate contracts, each totaling less than the amount required for competitive bidding, but, when combined, exceed the limit. If the purpose of breaking bids into separate contracts is to save money, as illustrated by a case before the Supreme Court of Utah, the judiciary is likely to rule in favor of boards.[86] Where a board awarded a construction contract but failed to include a sprinkler system in the bid due to the lack of funds, it rebid the cost of the sprinkler system and materials only, intending to use its own personnel for installation. The court affirmed that the board did not violate the state bidding statute since it proceeded in the most efficient and economical manner.

The extent to which administrative bodies can place restrictions on bidders may depend on a state's public policy. In a dispute over whether a state building commission could include a provision requiring a contractor to pay a scale of minimum wages, the Supreme Court of Alabama decided that it lacked the authority to do so.[87] The court construed the law as delegating authority to the commission to do such things as designate the quality and nature of materials used and the quality of work. The court was of the opinion that the wage requirement would have violated the state's competitive bidding statute. Almost a quarter of a century later, the Supreme Court of Louisiana adopted a similar position where a board imposed such a requirement.[88] Conversely, where

---

81. *A. A. B. Electric v. Stevenson Pub. School Dist. No. 303*, 491 P.2d 684 (Wash. Ct.App.1971).

82. *Stafford Constr. Co. v. Terrebonne Parish School Bd.*, 560 So.2d 558 [60 Educ. L. Rep. 269] (La. Ct. App.1990).

83. *George A. Nole & Son v. Board of Educ. of City School Dist. of Norwich*, 514 N.Y.S.2d 274 [38 Educ. L. Rep. 1075] (N.Y.App.Div.1987).

84. *Great Lakes Heating, Cooling, Refrigeration and Sheet Metal Corp. v. Troy School Dist.*, 494 N.W.2d 863 [80 Educ. L. Rep. 238] (Mich.Ct.App.1992).

85. *See, e.g., Committee to Keep Our Public Schools Pub. v. Schweiker*, 803 A.2d 869 [168 Educ. L. Rep. 412] (Pa. Cmwlth.

Ct. 2002), *aff'd*, 838 A.2d 565 [183 Educ. L. Rep. 968] (Pa. 2003) (affirming that the School Reform Commission had the authority to suspend the statute requiring open bidding on all purchases of $10,000 or more for furniture, equipment, text books, and other school supplies).

86. *Utah Plumbing & Heating Contractors Ass'n v. Board of Educ.*, 429 P.2d 49 (Utah 1967). [Case No. 56]

87. *Wallace v. Board of Educ. of Montgomery County*, 197 So.2d 428 (Ala.1967).

88. *Louisiana Associated Gen. Contractors v. Calcasieu Parish School Bd.*, 586 So.2d 1354 [70 Educ. L. Rep. 715] (La. 1991).

the state legislature required employers to pay prevailing wages on public construction jobs, Maryland's highest court affirmed that "lowest responsible bidder" meant "lowest responsible bidder utilizing the prevailing wage rate" in a locality.[89]

As reflected by the remainder of the cases in this subsection, courts have considered constitutional issues when dealing with bidding laws for public projects that can implicate school boards. The Supreme Court of Ohio affirmed that bids for public construction contracts can be required to include written assurances of employment nondiscrimination.[90] The court decreed that a bidder's failure to offer such assurances was a valid ground for rejecting the low bid. On the other hand, a federal trial court in California distinguished between the power of a state and a local board to institute affirmative action policies.[91] Where a board policy required bidders for general contracting jobs to be minority-owned or to utilize minority-owned businesses for at least 25 percent of their base bid amounts, the court interpreted the condition as violating the state law calling for contracts to be awarded to the lowest responsible bidder.

A federal trial court in New York invalidated a state law that required giving preferences to state citizens who were residents for a year prior to seeking employment on public construction projects as violating equal protection.[92] The court specified that there was no compelling reason for treating resident aliens differently from citizens. In a brief memorandum opinion in *Lefkowitz v. C.D.R. Enterprises* (*Lefkowitz*),[93] the Supreme Court summarily affirmed.

A year after *Lefkowitz*, in another non-education case, the Court struck down a statute from Alaska that would have granted preference to state citizens over citizens of other states without reaching the merits of the equal protection claim.[94] The Court ruled that since the state's high rate of unemployment was not due to an influx of nonresidents, officials had little or no connection to much of the activity that the law covered. Conversely, in *Fullilove v. Klutznik*,[95] a plurality of the Court upheld a statute authorizing federal public works projects in a dispute from New York that granted preferences to businesses owned by racial minorities.

89. *Demory Brothers v. Board of Pub. Works*, 329 A.2d 674, 679 (Md.1974). *See also Mortenson v. Leatherwood Constr.*, 137 S.W.3d 529 [189 Educ. L. Rep. 938] (Mo. Ct. App. 2004).

90. *Weiner v. Cuyahoga Community College Dist.*, 249 N.E.2d 907 (Ohio 1969), *cert. denied*, 396 U.S. 1004, 90 S.Ct. 554, 24 L.Ed.2d 495 (1970).

91. *Associated Gen. Contractors of Cal. v. San Francisco Unified School Dist.*, 431 F.Supp. 854 (N.D.Cal.1977), *aff'd*, 616 F.2d 1381 (9th Cir.1980), *cert. denied*, 449 U.S. 1061, 101 S.Ct. 783, 66 L.Ed.2d 603 (1980).

92. *C.D.R. Enterprises v. Board of Educ. of City of N.Y.*, 412 F.Supp. 1164 (E.D.N.Y. 1976).

93. 429 U.S. 1031, 97 S.Ct. 721, 50 L.Ed.2d 742 (1977).

94. *Hicklin v. Orbeck*, 437 U.S. 518, 98 S.Ct. 2482, 57 L.Ed.2d 397 (1978). *See also White v. Massachusetts Council of Constr. Employers*, 460 U.S. 204, 103 S.Ct. 1042, 75 L.Ed.2d 1 (1983). *United Bldg. and Constr. Trades Council of Camden County and Vicinity v. Mayor and Council of City of Camden*, 465 U.S. 208, 104 S.Ct. 1020, 79 L.Ed.2d 249 (1984).

95. 448 U.S. 448, 100 S.Ct. 2758, 65 L.Ed.2d 902 (1980).

In *City of Richmond v. J.A. Croson Company*,[96] the Court vitiated a plan from Virginia that was designed to set aside at least 30 percent of the dollar amounts of city government contracts for minority businesses. Applying strict scrutiny, the Court reasoned that the plan's deficiencies included the lack of identified past discrimination in the construction industry to justify the "unyielding" racial quota and its being insufficiently narrowly tailored to remedy the effects of past discrimination. A year later, in a dispute from Washington, D.C., the Court upheld a preference policy for minority ownership of new radio or television stations in *Metro Broadcasting v. Federal Communications Commission*[97] as long as it could have been shown that it had a substantial relationship to an important Congressional interest. On the other hand, in *Adarand Contractors v. Pena*,[98] a subcontracting firm in Colorado that was denied the guardrail portion of a federal highway project successfully challenged the constitutionality of a program designed to offer contracts to disadvantaged business enterprises. The Court invalidated the program on the ground that its use of race was not sufficiently narrowly tailored to achieve a compelling governmental interest.

Along the same line of thought, an appellate court in Florida noted that an unsuccessful bidder for a school board's eye vision care contract waived its right to contest the use of raced-based criteria in the request for proposals.[99] The court declared that since the bidder failed to challenge the criteria within the set time of the publication of the specifications in a bid solicitation protest, its claim failed. Additionally, the Supreme Court of Indiana believed that a pool supplier could not challenge an award of public contract under the state's Public Purchasing Statute where it was neither a citizen nor taxpayer of the municipality.[100] The court indicated that under the statute at issue, only a citizen or a taxpayer of a municipality may challenge the award of a government contract.

Mistaken Bids

Disputes also arise when, after boards accept, or try to accept, mistaken bids, bidders refuse either to enter into contracts or to be bound by the terms of their agreements. Cases involving mistaken bids are governed by the general rule of contract law that individuals (or boards) cannot accept bids (or offers) if they knew, or reasonably should have known, that they were mistaken. Although it might be argued that bidders should be responsible for their errors, some mistakes do not necessarily indicate carelessness. Rather, it is the common practice of bidders to wait until the latest possible time before submitting bids in order to take full advantage of last-minute changes in the cost and

---

96. 488 U.S. 469, 109 S.Ct. 706, 102 L.Ed.2d 854 (1989).

97. 497 U.S. 547, 110 S.Ct. 2997, 111 L.Ed.2d 445 (1990).

98. 515 U.S. 200, 115 S.Ct. 2097, 132 L.Ed.2d 158 (1995).

99. *Optiplan v. School Bd. of Broward County*, 710 So.2d 569 [126 Educ. L. Rep. 550] (Fla.Dist.Ct. App.1998).

100. *Brownsburg Community School Corp. v. Natare Corp.*, 824 N.E.2d 336 (Ind. 2005).

availability of labor and materials. Insofar as subcontractors follow the same procedure, main contractors are often required to compute their bids hurriedly, with little opportunity to check all figures for accuracy, and under extreme pressure in order to submit them before bid deadlines expire.

Where a clerical error led a contracting firm to bid more than 10 percent less than it should have, four days after the board accepted the bid, the company sought to withdraw from the contract. The Supreme Court of Nebraska affirmed that under the circumstances, the firm could withdraw.[101] The court pointed out that the only loss that the board would have incurred was that which it sought to gain through taking undue advantage of the bidder. While the opinion is unclear as to whether the board actually knew of the mistake when it accepted the bid, the court commented that it was so low that board officials reasonably should have suspected that an error occurred and should have investigated that possibility before attempting to enter into the contract.

A case from Louisiana exemplifies a unilateral mistake that a court refused to correct. A bakery sought to escape the consequences of nonperformance of a contract with a school board primarily on the basis that its bid was mistaken because the manager of its local office overlooked the increase in the cost of flour. An appellate court rejected the company's claim that the board should have been aware of the error since its bid for supplying bread was nine cents a loaf lower than others. The court affirmed that insofar as the alleged error was in the judgment of company officials, not a mathematical calculation, the contract was binding.[102] Also, the court was unable to uncover any evidence that the board suspected an error in the bid.

In the first of two cases that segue into the next section, the Supreme Court of Ohio discussed the impact of submitting a bid bond with a bid.[103] The court found that when a bid bond was in force, a board could recover from the contractor that submitted the mistaken low bid. The court maintained that while the bid bond contract was separate from the offer, it became effective when the offer was accepted and remained in effect until the parties entered a performance contract. The court observed that excusing the bidder would have rendered the bid bond meaningless. In like fashion, an appellate court in Oklahoma affirmed that the judiciary lacked the equitable power to relieve a contractor of the forfeiture of its bid bond once company officials realized that it contained an error.[104] The court determined that the apparently successful bidder had to forfeit the bond pursuant to the state's competitive bidding statute if the contract was not executed even though

---

101. *School Dist. of Scottsbluff v. Olson Constr. Co.*, 45 N.W.2d 164 (Neb.1950). [Case No. 57]

102. *Caddo Parish School Bd. v. Cotton Baking Co.*, 342 So.2d 1196 (La.Ct.App. 1977).

103. *Board of Educ. v. Sever-Williams Co.*, 258 N.E.2d 605 (Ohio 1970), *cert. de-*

nied, 400 U.S. 916, 91 S.Ct. 175, 27 L.Ed.2d 155 (1970).

104. *J.D. Graham Const. v. Pryor Pub. Schools Indep. School Dist. No. 1, Mayes County*, 854 P.2d 917 [83 Educ. L. Rep. 1144] (Okla.Civ.App.1993).

company officials advised the board of the error in the bid and tried to withdraw it before the board awarded the contract.

Withdrawal of Bids

If bids are withdrawn properly, bid bonds should be cancelled and contractors should not be obligated to enter into performance contracts. Where a bidder notified city officials that there was a substantial clerical error in a bid on the day bids were submitted and opened, school officials asked for, and promptly received, the work sheets that clearly revealed the error. When, three weeks later, the board still awarded the contract to the bidder to build a junior high school based on the erroneous bid, appellate courts in New York affirmed that since the bid was rescinded, the bid bond had to be cancelled because the contractor had no legal obligation to fulfill its bond.[105] The courts were of the view that where the amount made enforcement of the contract unconscionable, the city should not have been permitted to enforce the bid.

On the other hand, a bidder in Florida unsuccessfully sought to withdraw a bid after all bids were opened and the results announced, but before the board accepted the bid. Even though no state law prevented the bidder from withdrawing, an appellate court affirmed that there was a fundamental reason, grounded in public policy, that forbade it from permitting the bidder to do so.[106] The court expressed its concern that if a bidder could withdraw without justification or cause after bids were opened and the results announced, this could have led to the perpetration of frauds which would have obviated the benefits of the state's bidding law.

Where a procedure is prescribed for withdrawing mistaken bids, bidders must comply with directions. If courts allowed mistaken bids to be withdrawn too easily, some bidders might try to manipulate the system and so thwart the purposes of competitive-bidding statutes. While bids are ordinarily treated merely as offers that may be withdrawn prior to acceptance, due to the public interest involved, states may impose restrictions on bidders' ability to withdraw bids.

In a case that highlights the need for bidders to comply with directions, a dispute arose where a public school building authority had a rule permitting bids to be withdrawn as long as a company representative personally appeared at its office with a written request to do so prior to the time set for their being opened. The Supreme Court of Pennsylvania refused to permit a bidder to withdraw even though its bid was a great deal lower than others.[107] The court posited that the bidder made no attempt to withdraw except via an unverified telegram that did not specify the reason for wishing to do so. In recognizing that the bidder's attitude was one of indifference and unconcern, the court found that due

---

105. *City of Syracuse v. Sarkisian Bros.,* 451 N.Y.S.2d 945 [5 Educ. L. Rep. 216] (N.Y. App.Div. 1982), *aff'd,* 454 N.Y.S.2d 71 (1982).

106. *Hotel China & Glassware Co. v. Board of Pub. Instruction,* 130 So.2d 78 (Fla.Dist.Ct.App. 1961).

107. *Modany v. State Pub. School Bldg. Auth.,* 208 A.2d 276 (Pa.1965).

to concerns for the general welfare it could not condone such looseness in public contractual relations. The court thought that permitting the bidder to withdraw would not only have placed a premium on negligence but would also have opened the door for fraudulent conduct between bidders or between bidders and public bodies inviting bids.

Changing Contracts Let on Bids

Under the general law of contracts, both parties are bound and neither may escape all or any part of an agreement without the consent of the other. While parties are free to modify or amend their contracts as they wish, this rule generally does not apply to contracts between boards and bidders pursuant to competitive-bidding laws. The reason for this variation is that if boards and bidders entering into competitive-bid contracts can change them at will, they can circumvent the very benefits that the laws are designed to afford. Even so, situations may arise wherein the public interest is best served by authorizing boards and bidders to agree to limited contractual modifications.

The courts permit parties some flexibility in modifying contracts. In other words, modifications are typically acceptable if the changes are neither so extensive nor so great as to amount essentially to abandoning original agreements and entering into new ones. In such a case, an appellate court in Illinois affirmed that when a board acted in good faith in agreeing to contractual changes based on new data, judicial intervention was unwarranted.[108]

Applying the general rule of non-modification can be difficult since it can be a challenge in evaluating the substantiality of contractual changes. In the first of two cases exemplifying issues that can arise in this regard, the Supreme Court of South Dakota considered a provision that permitted a school board to authorize changes in a building contract as work progressed. As the building was under construction, the board wished to build a stage opening but did not advertise for bids. After the contractor agreed to build the opening for about an extra 5 percent of the original contract price, it unsuccessfully sought payment from the board. The court asserted that since this change was not merely incidental, but constituted a supplemental agreement for independent work, and was made contrary to public policy requiring competitive bidding, the contractor could not claim that the board made an implied promise to pay for labor and materials.[109]

Where a board let a contract to erect five school buildings under competitive bids, the agreement provided an insufficient amount to pay for all of the construction. After the board and contractor agreed to eliminate one building and make other changes that reduced the contract's amount, a taxpayer enjoined the enforcement of the revised agreement. Maryland's highest court agreed that since the variation in

108. *Stahelin v. Board of Educ., School Dist. No. 4, DuPage County*, 230 N.E.2d 465 (Ill.Ct.App. 1967).

109. *Seim v. Independent Dist. of Monroe*, 17 N.W.2d 342 (S.D.1945).

the general plan was so substantial that it constituted, for all intents and purposes, a new contract that was not let on competitive bids, it was invalid.[110] More than forty years later, the Supreme Court of Arkansas reached a like result. Where a general contractor made a unilateral error in a bid amounting to less than 4 percent of a contract, the court was satisfied that since the magnitude of the error did not render the agreement unenforceable, the contractor was not entitled to rescission in light of its mistake.[111]

In Utah, the eventual low bidder on a school construction project submitted a contingency letter with its bid explaining that since it had difficulty calculating the price and availability of materials, it would have to modify its fee accordingly as the information became available. Inexplicably, the letter remained unread until six weeks after the parties signed a contract. When the contractor sought to recover additional funds, the state's highest court refused its request on the ground that the original contract was valid.[112] The court contended that since school officials read and accepted the bid, and the parties signed a contract that did not mention the contingency letter, the contractor was not entitled to recover additional funds for the increased cost of materials.

Recovery under Contracts

Express and Implied Contracts

Even in cases where contracts are void, since boards often have received goods or services, questions arise as to whether suppliers are entitled to remedies. In answering this question, it is necessary to distinguish among different kinds of contracts. Although the distinctions are sometimes less than clear, contracts fall into three classes. The first type of contract is one wherein parties expressly delineate their rights and duties, either orally or in writing. An implied-in-fact contract, the second type, "arises when the circumstances make it reasonably certain that an agreement was intended"[113] even though the parties did not reach an express agreement to enter into a contract. For example, when one accepts goods or services under conditions that show that they were not meant to be gratuitous, courts often imply that since the parties intended to enter into a contract, they were bound; such a contract is no less binding because it is implied.

The difference between contracts that are express and implied-in-fact is the manner in which they are formed. In the former, a contract is formed by words; in the latter, by conduct.[114] The third type of contract,

---

110. *Hanna v. Board of Educ.*, 87 A.2d 846 (Md.1952).

111. *Mountain Home School Dist. No. 9 v. T.M.J. Builders*, 858 S.W.2d 74 [84 Educ. L. Rep. 1174] (Ark.1993).

112. *Jaye Smith Constr. Co. v. Board of Educ., Granite School Dist.*, 560 P.2d 320 (Utah 1977).

113. *Manno v. St. Felicitas Elementary School*, 831 N.E.2d 1071, 1077 [200 Educ. L. Rep. 349] (Ohio Ct. App. 2005).

114. *Ryan v. Warren Township High School Dist. No. 121*, 510 N.E.2d 911 [40 Educ. L. Rep. 896] (Ill. Ct.App.1987).

implied-in-law, embraces so-called quasi-contracts.[115] A contract that is implied-in-law is not a contract in the true sense of the word. Rather, such a contract is created by law for reasons of justice and equity, obligating parties that receive benefits from others that would have resulted in unjust enrichment if they were not required to pay. Under some circumstances, the courts permit parties to recover as if they had entered into contracts.

Classifying contracts is important since the measure of recovery is different in each category. In cases involving express contracts, recovery is based on the terms of the agreements. In cases of implied-in-fact contracts, recovery depends on the reasonable value of goods or services rendered. By contrast, in express contracts, the stated amounts are generally recoverable regardless of whether they are reasonable, with courts holding parties to improvident agreements as long as they are not unconscionable or adhesion contracts, that they freely formed. In disputes dealing with implied-in-fact contracts, since there is no set price or agreement, the law does not imply a promise to pay more than the reasonable value. Consequently, in implied-in-law cases, the measure of recovery, if any is permitted,[116] is calculated based on the amount of benefit conferred on the party receiving the property or services, not by its price or reasonable value.

Implied-in-law contracts are imposed on parties that receive benefits since the law considers it inequitable to enrich one party at the expense of another. If a party has not received a benefit, there can be no recovery regardless of market price or reasonable value. Insofar as the courts often confuse implied-in-fact and implied-in-law cases, they sometimes fail to apply the appropriate measure of recovery. Indeed, in many cases, it is difficult to tell whether courts are referring to contracts that are implied-in-fact or in-law or whether they are permitting recovery on implied or quasi-contracts. Moreover, courts tend to apply the terms reasonable value and benefits received more or less indiscriminately, even though the terms or the amounts of recovery are not necessarily the same. Similarly, courts often apply *quantum meruit*, literally, "as much as it deserves," to disputes involving either type of implied contract, as it historically pertained to quasi-contracts.[117]

A case from Arkansas illuminates the interplay between an implied contract and *quantum meruit*. A superintendent signed a lease-purchase agreement for books and materials in excess of $113,000 with the understanding that federal funds could be used in payment. Even though another administrator and the book salesman encouraged the superintendent to sign the contract, they were both aware that federal funds

115. *Boyd v. Black School Township*, 23 N.E. 862 (Ind.1890).

116. For cases denying recover under quasi-contracts, *see Strain–Japan R–16 School Dist. v. Landmark Sys.*, 51 S.W.3d 916 [156 Educ. L. Rep. 719] (Mo. Ct. App. 2001); *Mays-Maune & Assoc. v. Werner Bros.*, 139 S.W.3d 201 [190 Educ. L. Rep. 1058] (Mo. Ct. App. 2004).

117. *See Alternatives Unlimited v. New Baltimore City Bd. of School Commr's*, 843 A.2d 252 [186 Educ. L. Rep. 341] (Md. Ct. Spec. App. 2004) (treating a *quantum meruit* claim as redundant to the extent that it was based on the theory of quasi-contract).

could not be used in this agreement. Insofar as the school board was apparently unaware of the situation at its inception, students used the materials for at least a year. When company officials asked the board to pay for the materials, it refused, claiming that the superintendent exceeded his authority in entering into the contract. Then, the board put the materials into storage and notified company officials to pick up their property. In concluding that neither party was without fault, the court decided that since they formed an implied contract, *quantum meruit* applied.[118] The court thus gave the company the option of taking back the used books or having the board keep them in return for $13,500 in payment.

Invalid Contracts in General

Statutory requirements controlling school contracts are designed to protect boards and taxpayers. To this end, requirements that certain contracts must be in writing are intended to avoid misunderstandings that can easily arise under oral contracts. In like manner, competitive-bidding laws are designed to insure that goods and services can be procured at the lowest price possible and to guard against collusion at a board's expense. When boards receive benefits under contracts that are invalid due to their failure to meet statutory requirements, the courts are faced with the options of relaxing statutory protections or permitting boards to retain benefits without compensating the other parties.

If school boards have the authority to enter into express contracts that are invalid due to irregularities in execution, they are liable under the theory of implied contracts for the reasonable value of the goods or services. The only limitations against recovery are that the form or manner of letting contracts cannot violate statutory restrictions, the ability of boards to enter contracts, and/or public policy. Insofar as the application of this rule has caused courts considerable difficulty, they have reached varying results. The outcomes of cases often seem to turn on what courts consider to be the better public policy, either strict enforcement of the statutory protections afforded boards or the equitable claims of aggrieved parties. Courts permitting recovery ordinarily agree that allowing boards to assert contractual invalidity while retaining benefits can be unconscionable.[119] On the other hand, courts that deny recoveries on implied contracts typically do so on the basis that reaching any other outcomes would open the door to raids on school funds[120] or that they expect strict compliance with state contract law[121] since making exceptions runs the risk of nullifying the very protections that the law seeks to provide.

---

118. *Responsive Environments Corp. v. Pulaski County Special School Dist.*, 366 F.Supp. 241 (E.D. Ark.1973). [Case No. 58]

119. *Burk v. Livingston Parish School Bd.*, 182 So. 656 (La.1938).

120. *Oberwarth v. McCreary County Bd. of Educ.*, 121 S.W.2d 716 (Ky.1938); *Good-*

year v. Junior College Dist. of St. Louis, 540 S.W.2d 621 (Mo.Ct.App.1976).

121. *Strain-Japan R-16 School Dist. v. Landmark Sys.*, 51 S.W.3d 916 [156 Educ. L. Rep. 719] (Mo.Ct.App.2001).

There can be no implied contracts if boards lack authority to enter into express contracts.[122] The concept of implied contracts is designed to permit boards to recover when they failed to follow statutory requirements rather than to exceed their powers. As courts have used the vehicle of implied contracts to remove a measure of the protection afforded by statutory requisites, it is a modification that justly alleviates the hardship on those who furnish goods or services to boards in good faith.

Ultra Vires Contracts

The weight of authority is that a party cannot recover based on *quantum meruit* if a school board's action is *ultra vires*. The fact that most courts refuse to imply the existence of contracts where express agreements are *ultra vires* reflects the limit beyond which the judiciary refuses to go in sacrificing statutory protection to avoid hardships on those who acted in good faith by conferring benefits on boards. In denying recoveries, the courts reason that individuals or companies dealing with boards are bound to know the limits of their contractual powers as statutory provisions define the limits of their authority.

Whether contracts are *ultra vires* is an issue that is not free from difficulty unless something is expressly prohibited by statute[123] or school boards set specific conditions precedent to their entering into valid contracts.[124] Courts ordinarily strike down contracts as *ultra vires* when boards make unauthorized expenditures,[125] violate specific statutory provisions,[126] exceed state constitutional debt limits,[127] or lack sufficient funds to pay for expenditures.[128] In considering whether contracts are *ultra vires*, courts sometimes merely declare categorically that agreements are impermissible since laws that address the scope of boards' contractual limits cannot be drawn so as to consider their specific authority in all conceivable transactions. Accordingly, in close cases, it is difficult to know whether boards have exceeded their contractual authority until disputes are litigated.

Where an architectural firm proceeded with work pursuant to a contract that exceeded the amount of money covered by the appropriation, the Supreme Judicial Court of Massachusetts affirmed that since the firm did so at its own risk, it could not recover even though it acted

122. *Reams v. Cooley*, 152 P. 293 (Cal. 1915).

123. *Board of Educ. v. Chicago Teachers Union, Local 1, Am. Fed'n of Teachers*, 326 N.E.2d 158 (Ill.Ct.App.1975).

124. *CADO Business Sys. of Ohio v. Board of Educ. of Cleveland City School Dist.*, 457 N.E.2d 939 [15 Educ. L. Rep. 358] (Ohio Ct.App.1983); *Ryan v. Warren Township High School Dist. No. 121*, 510 N.E.2d 911 [40 Educ. L. Rep. 896] (Ill.Ct. App.1987).

125. *Smith v. Dorsey*, 599 So.2d 529 [75 Educ. L. Rep. 692] (Miss.1992).

126. *Robert W. Anderson Housewrecking and Excavating v. Board of Trustees, School Dist. No. 25*, 681 P.2d 1326 [17 Educ. L. Rep. 1232] (Wyo.1984); *Swinney v. Deming Bd. of Educ.*, 873 P.2d 238, 240 [91 Educ. L. Rep. 347] (N.M.1994).

127. *Moe v. Millard County School Dist.*, 179 P. 980 (Utah 1919).

128. *School Dist. No. 9 Fractional of Waterford and Pontiac Townships v. McLintock*, 237 N.W. 539 (Mich.1931).

in good faith.[129] Conversely, where school board members unanimously approved entering a contract with an architectural firm, encouraged it to begin work, and executed a written contract, an appellate court in Pennsylvania affirmed that it was not unlawful for the board to pay for work that was actually done before the contract was executed since there was no fraud involved.[130]

School boards in Kansas sued to cancel lease-purchase agreements for photocopying equipment after they experienced difficulty in obtaining service. An appellate court affirmed a grant of summary judgment in favor of the boards on the ground that the agreements were void and unenforceable because they failed to contain mandatory disclosures of such matters as the amount of capital cost required to purchase the items if paid in cash, annual average effective interest costs, and amount included in payments for service, maintenance, and insurance for other charges exclusive of capital and interest costs.[131] The court specified that when a contract is declared void for failing to comply with an express statutory requirement, it could not intervene to render the agreement, or part thereof, valid.

Ratification of Invalid Contracts

School boards, like other corporate and quasi-corporate bodies, can act only through their agents. As such, some of the general rules governing agency relationships apply to acts of agents of school boards. One rule of agency is that even where agents act outside the scope of their duties, and their acts are not binding on the principals, the latter may then ratify acts, binding themselves as if the agents had the authority in the first place. This rule applies to acts purportedly carried out on behalf of school systems by others than their boards or to those of boards which, due to irregularities, were not binding. The rule is subject to the exception that boards must have had the ability to act as they did since *ultra vires* acts cannot be ratified.[132]

When school boards ratify unauthorized acts, most courts do not require them to take formal steps since they accept that boards did so when they acted in a manner consistent with the underlying agreements[133] or complied with statutory requirements. However, as revealed by a case from Pennsylvania, where only four, rather than the required five, board members approved a contract, an appellate court affirmed that it was not ratified even though district officials made some payments under the agreement.[134] Further, an appellate court in Kentucky

---

129. *Murphy v. City of Brockton*, 305 N.E.2d 103 (Mass.1973). *See also School Dist. No. One of Pima County v. Hastings*, 472 P.2d 44 (Ariz.1970).

130. *Kennedy v. Ringgold School Dist.*, 309 A.2d 269 (Pa.Cmwlth.Ct.1973).

131. *Unified School Dist. No. 207 v. Northland Nat'l Bank*, 887 P.2d 1138 [96 Educ. L. Rep. 1156] (Kan.Ct.App.1994).

132. *Arkansas Nat'l Bank v. School Dist. No. 99, Washington County*, 238 S.W. 630 (Ark.1922); *St. Paul Foundry Co. v. Burnstad School Dist. No. 31*, 269 N.W. 738 (N.D.1936).

133. *Frank v. Board of Educ.*, 100 A. 211 (N.J. Err. & App.1917). [Case No. 59]

134. *Grippo v. Dunmore School Bd.*, 365 A.2d 678 (Pa.Cmwlth.Ct.1976).

judged that since a board "must act through its records," an entry in board minutes could constitute ratification if a board would "bear a loss because [an agent] failed to perform his duty."[135]

The fact that school boards can retain benefits even when they are aware of the material facts in transactions does not necessarily constitute ratification if it is impossible for them to reject the benefits. If, for instance, improvements such as fixtures cannot be removed from school property, the fact that boards permit them to be used does not amount to ratification.[136] The basis for the rule is that if boards are obliged to refrain from using such improvements or are found to have ratified transactions, then school activities could be seriously disrupted. On the other hand, when dealing with non-permanent goods, such as school supplies and furniture, some courts, even in the same jurisdiction, disagree over whether board acceptance and use of these items means that they can be required to pay for such materials.[137]

Another issue arises as to whether those who acted on behalf of boards were truly their agents. In disputes of this sort, the parties claiming to be agents bear the burden of proof. In a case from North Carolina, a principal directed a salesperson to see a choral director who signed orders for decorative lamps to be used in fund-raising efforts. After the choral director ended his employment with the board, the principal sent payment to the novelty company and returned the unsold lamps. Faced with a discrepancy in the amount of money that the principal remitted, an appellate court rejected the company's claim to recover the money. The court affirmed that the board was not liable because insofar as it had not entered into the contract, and the principal lacked the authority to act on its behalf, it had not ratified the agreement.[138]

An appellate court in Louisiana took a different approach in a dispute where a teacher who served as a class sponsor conferred with the principal before signing a contract for entertainment at a prom. When the principal discovered that the contract was for a sound system, not a live band, and deemed the arrangement inappropriate, he and the teacher informed the contractor that its services would not be needed. In light of a term in the contract calling for payment if the contract was cancelled, an appellate court ruled that since the principal had the implied authority to bind the board and he properly delegated it to the teacher, the board was liable.[139]

135. *Ramsey v. Board of Educ. of Whitley County*, 789 S.W.2d 784, 786–787 [60 Educ. L. Rep. 1284] (Ky.Ct.App.1990).

136. *Young v. Board of Educ.*, 55 N.W. 1112 (Minn.1893); *Panther Oil and Grease Mfg. Co. v. Blount County Bd. of Educ.*, 134 So.2d 220 (Ala.Ct.App.1961).

137. *A.H. Andrews Co. v. Delight Special School Dist.*, 128 S.W. 361 (Ark.1910) (finding that a board's acceptance, and continued use, of school desks did not solve an irregularity in the execution of a contract).

See also Richards v. School Township of Jackson, 109 N.W. 1093 (Iowa 1906). *But see First Nat'l Bank v. Whisenhunt*, 127 S.W. 968 (Ark.1910) (affirming that a board's unauthorized purchase of maps was not ratified by their acceptance and use).

138. *Community Projects for Students v. Wilder*, 298 S.E.2d 434 [8 Educ. L. Rep. 521] (N.C.Ct.App. 1982).

139. *Herbert v. Livingston Parish School Bd.*, 438 So.2d 1141 [14 Educ. L. Rep. 237] (La.Ct.App. 1983).

Ratification renders contracts as valid as if they were made strictly in accordance with a school board's authority. Most courts agree that boards cannot partially ratify agreements as they must approve actions either in whole or not at all. An older case reflects this general rule. Where a certificated teacher began working under a contract that a board knew was invalid, and paid part of his salary, an appellate court in Kansas maintained that its doing so ratified the contract for the entire employment period.[140]

In building projects, boards often rely on architects to inform them when performance contracts are complete. Where a problem arose with a gymnasium floor before a new building was completed, the architect accepted the contractor's additional work as satisfactory. The board, relying on the architect's advice, made final payment unconditionally. When the contractor refused to honor a warranty that it would remedy defects that appeared within a year of final payment, the Supreme Court of Montana remarked that the board's issuing a final, unconditional payment constituted its ratification of the architect's acceptance of the floor.[141] The court decreed that if the floor was defective when accepted, the warranty did not apply since it only covered flaws that appeared within a year. The court added that the board lacked a remedy against the contractor because it waived its prior right not to accept the floor.

Board Contracts and Conflict of Interest

Individuals, including school board members and employees, must avoid conflicts of interest, a principle that has become statutory, constitutional, or both, in many jurisdictions.[142] Conflict of interest laws typically provide that it is unlawful for persons in public offices, including school board members, to have pecuniary interests, either directly or indirectly, in contracts on which they may be called on to act or vote.

Perhaps the most challenging issue in cases dealing with conflicts of interest is deciding what constitutes an interest in a school contract. If school board members entered into contracts with district officials to construct, furnish, or repair buildings or to provide supplies or services, there would be little doubt that these were conflicts of interest.

A more difficult situation develops when corporations or companies in which board members or school employees have substantial interests form contracts with their districts. To the extent that corporations are separate legal entities, distinct from their stockholders, the question becomes whether their interests in school contracts equate to an individual's interests. In an early case, the Supreme Court of Wisconsin agreed

---

140. *Jones v. School Dist. No. 144*, 51 P. 927 (Kan.Ct.App.1898).

141. *Grass Range High School Dist. v. Wallace Diteman*, 465 P.2d 814 (Mont. 1970).

142. *See, e.g.*, Ariz. Stat. Ann. § 38–503; Cal. Educ. Code Ann. § 35233; Kan. Stat. Ann. § 754304; Ky. Rev. Stat. Ann. § 160.180; Mich. Comp. Laws Ann. § 388.1769b; Miss. Code Ann. § 25–4–105; N.J. Stat. Ann. § 18A:12–22; N.Y. McKinney's Educ. L. § 2590–n; N.D. Cent. Code § 15.1–07–17; S.D. Codified Laws § 6–1–1; Wash. Rev. Code Ann. § 42.52.030; W. Va. Code § 6–6–7. *See also, e.g.*, Ga. Constit. Art. 1, § 2, Par. 1; Miss. Constit. Art. 4 § 109.

that a school treasurer violated the state's conflict of interest law when, after a contract had been let, he notified the contractor that a corporation in which he had a substantial interest could, and did, furnish a significant portion of the necessary building materials. When the corporation sued the contractor for the price of materials, the latter successfully defended itself on the ground that the treasurer's interest in the corporation rendered the contract void.[143] The court explained that this type of contract violated both the spirit and express provisions in the law.

The Supreme Court of South Dakota affirmed that a board's contract with a business that repaired a school bus was *ultra vires* as a conflict of interest where one of its members was a company shareholder, officer, and director.[144] In noting that the board could have used other firms to repair the bus, the court agreed that the board member, and two other persons associated with the company, had to reimburse the board.

Controversies often arise when boards deal with employment contracts for spouses, family members, or prospective members, with most courts agreeing that such agreements are conflicts of interest. The Supreme Court of Kentucky upheld the constitutionality of an anti-nepotism law which prevented boards from hiring relatives of their members.[145] The court reasoned that either a board member, or her daughter, both of whom were long serving with the district, had to relinquish her position. In a similar vein, the Supreme Court of Oklahoma originally ruled that a candidate whose wife was a teacher in a district was ineligible to run for the board under the state's anti-nepotism statute.[146] On rehearing, the court pointed out that the candidate, who was elected to the board pending the outcome of the case, could serve the remainder of his term in accordance with newly enacted provisions which suspended the operation of the anti-nepotism statute. In both instances, the courts agreed that the statutes did not violate the equal protection rights of the board members.

Within less than five weeks, the Supreme Court of Mississippi resolved two cases involving board members who were married to school employees. In the first, the court rejected a board member's claim that his voting against hiring his wife as teacher did not violate the state constitutional prohibition against having a direct or indirect interest in board contracts.[147] The court was of the view that since it was the board member's interest in his wife's contract, not his vote, that was forbidden, they had to return her salary and pay a fine. Unlike the second case, the court did not address the board member's ability to continue serving. Shortly thereafter, the court affirmed a grant of summary judgment on the issue of liability where a board member whose husband was a

---

143. *Bissell Lumber Co. v. Northwestern Cas. & Sur. Co.*, 207 N.W. 697 (Wis.1926).

144. *Ayres v. Junek*, 247 N.W.2d 488 (S.D.1976).

145. *Chapman v. Gorman*, 839 S.W.2d 232 [78 Educ. L. Rep. 1128] (Ky.1992).

146. *Sharp v. Tulsa County Election Bd.*, 890 P.2d 836 [98 Educ. L. Rep. 424] (Okla.1994).

147. *Waller v. Moore ex rel. Quitman County School Dist.*, 604 So.2d 265 [77 Educ. L. Rep. 1029] (Miss.1992).

teacher in the district during her tenure on the board violated the state's public servant conflicts of interest statute.[148] The court observed that the board member had to be removed from office and fined while her husband had to forfeit his job and salary because even though she did not vote for him, or influence others to do so, she still violated the law.

On the other hand, the Supreme Court of Georgia affirmed that the public trust provision of the state constitution did not preclude school board members who were married to employees of a county school system from voting on matters affecting compensation and benefits for staff.[149] The court acknowledged that the state constitution did not articulate a duty that required board members to refrain from participating in such a vote. In addition, the Supreme Court of Virginia affirmed that a conflict of interest did not prevent a board from hiring the sister-in-law of one of its members since she was not a regular employee when he was appointed.[150]

In a related concern, the Supreme Court of Kansas interpreted state law as meaning that an individual could not serve as both a teacher and school board member in the same district.[151] Overturning an adjudication of the state government's ethics commission that this did not violate the state's conflict of interest statute, the court pointed out that permitting one person to operate in both capacities was inconsistent with the meaning and intent of the common law rule of incompatibility of office. Interestingly, the court did not explicitly rely on the state's conflict of interest law in reaching its judgment. Previously, the Supreme Court of Colorado indicated that a board policy precluding its members from teaching in the district, but permitting their spouses to do so, did not violate members' rights to equal protection.[152] The court agreed with the board that it could have believed that its conflict of interest policy should have encompassed board members but not their spouses so as to avoid having to face complaints over incompatibility of interests. In another case involving an administrative directive rather than a state law, an appellate court in Ohio affirmed that a board did not abuse its discretion in refusing to recommend the low bidder on a painting contract because the company was owned by one of its teachers.[153]

As reflected by two cases from New Jersey, conflict of interest disputes over real estate are not uncommon. In the first, an appellate court affirmed that school board members could not be rendered personally liable for one member's allegedly improper opposition to a development plan.[154] The plaintiff unsuccessfully claimed that the board mem-

---

148. *Towner v. Moore ex rel. Quitman County School Dist.*, 604 So.2d 1093 [77 Educ. L. Rep. 1056] (Miss.1992).

149. *Ianicelli v. McNeely*, 527 S.E.2d 189 [143 Educ. L. Rep. 1073] (Ga.2000).

150. *Williams v. Augusta County School Bd.*, 445 S.E.2d 118 [92 Educ. L. Rep. 686] (Va.1994).

151. *Unified School Dist. No. 501, Shawnee County, Kan. v. Baker*, 6 P.3d 848 [146 Educ. L. Rep. 902] (Kan.2000).

152. *Montrose County School Dist. Re–1J v. Lambert*, 826 P.2d 349 [73 Educ. L. Rep. 271] (Colo. 1992).

153. *Darnell Painting Co. v. Toledo Bd. of Educ.*, 669 N.E.2d 311 [111 Educ. L. Rep. 1354] (Ohio Ct. App.1995).

154. *Lake Lenore Estates, Assoc. v. Township of Parsippany-Troy Hills Bd. of* ber opposed the development plan based on concerns that it would have had an adverse impact on his adjacent property. A second appellate court in New Jersey invalidated a vote on whether to build two adult-sized baseball fields with lighting towers on a school board's property.[155] In ascertaining that a member had both a direct and indirect personal interest in the outcome of the vote, the court concluded that he was ineligible to participate in the vote.

[Case No. 54] Lowest Responsible Bidder Changing Contracts after Letting

HIBBS v. ARENSBERG

Supreme Court of Pennsylvania, 1923.
119 A. 727.

[Suit was brought to restrain a board from proceeding under a contract which was let to a bidder other than the lowest bidder. The plaintiff also alleged that the contract was changed after it had been let. This is an appeal of a judgment in favor of the board]

KEPHART, J. . . .

It is averred, in the bill to restrain the school directors from awarding the contract to construct a badly needed school building in a school district in Fayette county, that the architect's plans and specifications do not fully state the kind, quality, and quantity of materials required. One special item reads:

> "The face brick . . . to be a thoroughly vitrified, wire-cut, face brick of such color as will be selected by the architect and school board; . . . to cost not more than $34.00 per thousand."

We see no reason why an intelligent bid could not be made on this item. Vitrified, wire-cut, face brick has a definite meaning; the contract preserved the right of inspection and rejection of materials; and there was little opportunity to slight the quality. If a certain make of brick had been selected, or several makes, we can readily see a charge of a different character might be presented.

That the directors later decided to use a little more expensive brick would not condemn the letting, or cause the directors to be liable for the increased price, or avoid the purchase. There was no such departure from the general purpose as would require reletting. Unforeseen contingencies or new ideas sometimes make it necessary to change the character or quality of material or a part of a structure from the original plans. A certain flexibility in the power of officials to take care of these matters is intended to be granted, that the law relating to public letting may not become an instrument of oppression through a too rigid construction. These officers must act honestly, reasonably, and intelligently, and a

---

Educ., 712 A.2d 200 [127 Educ. L Rep. 342] (N.J.Super.Ct.App.Div.1998).

155. *Friends Retirement Concepts v. Board of Educ. Borough of Somerville*, 811

A.2d 962 [172 Educ. L. Rep. 340] (N.J.Super.Ct.Law Div.2002).

new departure must not so vary from the original plan or be of such importance as to constitute a new undertaking, which the act controls, and where fairness could only be reached through competitive bidding. Courts, however, will be slow to interfere unless it appears the officers are not acting in good faith. . . .

. . . [But there were some] mistakes in the letting. The architect did not supply a sufficient number of copies of the plans and specifications for all those who expressed a wish to bid. Reputable contractors were deprived of the opportunity to submit prices. Competitive bidding could not be secured under these conditions. We cannot too strongly condemn the motives of some architects and public officials in following this practice; it opens the door to the grossest kind of fraud. A favored contractor, apprised in advance, may easily have the limited number of plans and specifications on file lifted by persons not bona fide bidders, or, through a combination none too infrequent, the favored contractor submits a price (the lowest) that is high enough to give an excessive profit and pays to other higher bidders a commission "or rake-off" as their part of the gain for participating in the combination. Of course, there are other methods. Officials must have on file enough sets of plans and specifications to supply those who demand them within a reasonable time prior to the day on which the bids are to be submitted. The time within which a request is made should be sufficient to enable the architect to furnish additional copies if those first furnished have been exhausted. The court was in error in passing over this fact as not being of sufficient consequence to restrain the work.

At the first meeting of the board, after the bids were submitted they were all deemed too high. A week later, at an adjourned meeting, the bid of the Republic Construction Company, fourth lowest bidder, was accepted by the vote of four of the directors. Two of the board were not present, and another, though present, did not vote. . . .

The contract was awarded to the fourth lowest bidder without investigating the responsibility of the three lower bidders. This is contrary to the Act of July 10, 1919, which directs the contract be let to the lowest responsible bidder. The term "lowest responsible bidder" does not mean the lowest bidder in dollars; nor does it mean the board may capriciously select a higher bidder regardless of responsibility or cost. What the law requires is the exercise of a sound discretion by the directors. They should call to their assistance the means of information at hand to form an intelligent judgment. They should investigate the bidders to learn their financial standing, reputation, experience, resources, facilities, judgment and efficiency as builders. This was not done. The court below censures the board for omitting this important step, but it holds, inasmuch as they had ample knowledge of the successful bidder and the merit of its work, the contract could be awarded. This might do in private affairs, but will not pass when public funds are at stake; it is not the exercise of discretion. Though the directors were not bound in law to give the contract to the lowest bidder, who might be irresponsible, they were bound to investigate, and if a bidder measured up to the law's requirement as a responsible party, the board could not capriciously award the contract to another. Giving a bond alone does not make up for responsibility; we have too many bonding companies willing to indemnify almost anything. But there should be a sufficient reason, where a bidder is lowest and responsible, why the job was not given to him. And where such reason appears, the action of the board is generally conclusive. . . .

We have indicated in this opinion where we think the court below was in error in permitting the work to go ahead. On the record presented the school board was without authority to award the contract and bind the school district.

Notes

1.   In *In re Scranton City School Dist. Audit*, 47 A.2d 288 (Pa.1946), school board officials sought to divide a project involving an expenditure of $12,673.63 into a number of contracts, each less than $300 in amount, in order to have it completed in a short time and to save money. Under Pennsylvania law, contracts for less than $300 were not required to be let to the lowest responsible bid. The court struck the board's action down as violating the competitive bidding statute. Would you have reached the same outcome?

2.   After a school board advertised for bids to supply milk and reserved the right to reject any of them, officials accepted a bid from a local firm even though it was $1,500 more than the lowest bid from a company located elsewhere. The court ruled that since the competitive bid statute covered only construction supplies, the board's action was legal. *Gosselin's Dairy v. School Comm. of Holyoke*, 205 N.E.2d 221 (Mass.1965).

[Case No. 55]   Permitting a Bid Modification

MARTIN ENGINEERING v. LEXINGTON COUNTY SCHOOL DISTRICT ONE

Supreme Court of South Carolina, 2005.
615 S.E.2d 110 [199 Educ. L. Rep. 963].

JUSTICE WALLER

We certified this case from the Court of Appeals pursuant to Rule 204(b), SCACR. At issue is whether Lexington County School District One (District) properly allowed Respondent Sharp Construction Company (Sharp), to amend its bid on the Lexington High School Additions and Renovations Project (Project). The circuit court granted District summary judgment, holding the correction was properly allowed. We affirm.

FACTS

In August 2003, District received bids for the Project. Sharp was the low bidder with a bid of $16,300,000.00. Appellant, Martin Engineering, was the second lowest bidder with a bid of $17,375,000.00. Immediately after the bids were opened, Sharp advised District it had inadvertently neglected to include a roofing subcontractor's bid in its overall bid. It requested to be allowed to correct its bid by adding the roofing cost, $613,500.00, to its bid. Alternatively, Sharp requested to withdraw its bid. District allowed Sharp to adjust its bid, resulting in an overall bid by Sharp of $16,913,500.00, some $461,500.00 less than Martin's bid. Martin filed a complaint in the circuit court seeking an injunction. The circuit court held the adjustment was properly allowed in compliance with District's Procurement Code and Regulations.

ISSUES

1.   Did the circuit court err in holding District properly allowed the upward adjustment?

2.   Did the court err in finding Sharp would suffer a substantial loss if it were not allowed to correct its bid?

1.   CORRECTION OF BID

District's Procurement Code, Article 2, Section 2–102 controls Competitive Sealed Bidding. In particular, section 2–102(10), "Correction or Withdrawal of Bids: Cancellation of Awards" states: Corrections or withdrawal of inadvertently erroneous bids before or after award, or cancellation of awards or contracts based on such bid mistakes may be permitted where appropriate. After bid openings, no change in bid prices or other provisions of bids prejudicial to the interest of the school district or fair competition will be permitted. A bidder must submit a written request to either correct or withdraw a bid to the school district. Each written request must document the fact that the bidder's mistake is clearly an error that will cause him substantial loss. In order to maintain the integrity of the competitive sealed bidding process, a bidder will not be permitted to correct a bid mistake after bid opening that would cause such bidder to have the low bid, unless the mistake, in the judgment of the school district, is clearly evident from examining the bid document: for example, extension of unit prices or errors in addition. All decisions to permit the correction of (sic) withdrawal of bids, or to cancel awards or contracts based on bids mistakes, will be supported by a written determination.

Martin contends that unless an error is clearly evident by examining the bid document itself, no correction is permissible. We disagree. It is patent from the language of § 2–102(10) that only a correction which *causes the bidder to have the low bid* [emphasis in original] requires the mistake be *clearly evident from examining the bid document*. On the other hand, where the bid correction does not *cause* the bidder to have the low bid, nothing in § 2–102 requires District to confine its review to the bid document itself.

Here, the item Sharp failed to include in its bid the bid of its roofing subcontractor, Watts. There was evidence that three different roofing contractors had utilized the identical roof bid from Watts in bidding on District's project. Moreover, Sharp had listed Watts as a sub-contractor in its bid. This evidence was in existence prior to the time the bids were opened. From this evidence, we find it was within District's discretion to determine that correction of Sharp's inadvertently erroneous bid was proper, and that the correction would not be prejudicial to the interests of the school district or fair competition.

Martin asserts the integrity of the bidding process and the need for fair competition require clear rules for post opening bid corrections. While we are not unmindful of the need to preserve the integrity of the bidding process, we find no violation of the rules in this case. Martin has not shown that the procedures followed by District render the upward correction unfair or unjust, nor has he demonstrated in what manner the correction was prejudicial to the District or to fair competition.

As noted by District's order in this case, "It is true that Sharp's omission of the price for the build-up roof was not apparent from the bid form itself. However, the mistake is clear, and the amount Sharp intended to bid for the roof is evident, by examining the roofing subcontractor's sub-bid, which was submitted to several of the bidders, including Sharp and Martin." We agree with the District that allowing the correction in this case neither jeopardized the integrity of the sealed bidding process, nor was it prejudicial to the interests of the District or fair competition. To the contrary, to accept Martin's argument that District must reject Sharp's bid and accept its bid, some $461,500.00 higher than Sharp's corrected bid, would clearly be prejudicial to the District requiring it to expend substantially more money.

Martin cites case law from other jurisdictions as supporting its claim that post-opening bid amendments are impermissible unless an error is readily apparent on the face of the bid. We find cases from other jurisdictions, addressing other state procurement codes, are simply inapplicable to District's procurement code.

2. SUBSTANTIAL LOSS

Martin next asserts Sharp failed to produce evidence that the bid mistake would cause him "substantial loss" as required by section 2–102(10) ("each written request must document that the bidder's mistake is clearly an error that will cause him substantial loss"). Accordingly, Martin contends the circuit court erred in finding "it patently reasonable to determine that omitting $613,000 in this Project would constitute a substantial loss." We disagree.

It is uncontroverted that Sharp neglected to include $613,000.00 for the roof build up in its bid on the project. Although it is unclear precisely the extent to which this affects Sharp's overall profit margin, we find that $613,000.00 constitutes a substantial loss.

The circuit court's order granting District summary judgment is

AFFIRMED.

Notes

1. Do you think that the outcome in this case was fair?

2. Should all contracts relating to public schools be let out for bids?

[Case No. 56]   Use of Regular Maintenance Personnel in School Construction

UTAH PLUMBING AND HEATING CONTRACTORS ASSOCIATION v. BOARD OF EDUCATION OF WEBER COUNTY SCHOOL DISTRICT

Supreme Court of Utah, 1967.
429 P.2d 49.

CROCKETT, CHIEF JUSTICE. Plaintiffs, an organization of plumbing contractors and three other trade associations ... sued to enjoin defendant Weber County Board of Education from installing a sprinkling system on the Roy High School football field. Plaintiffs contend that the defendant's use of its own maintenance employees to put in the sprinkling system was a violation of Section 53111, U.C.A.1953, which requires advertising for bids "[w]henever any schoolhouse is to be built" or any improvement constructed costing over $20,000....

After the contract for the school had been awarded and construction was well under way, additional funds from the State became available. It was then that the School Board decided they should install the sprinkling system on the football field at the least possible cost. By advertising for bids for the materials only, and using their regularly employed maintenance people during their free time from other duties, the job could be done for approximately $3200, about $2700 of it for materials, which they purchased from the lowest bidder.

The position essayed by plaintiffs is that the board was obliged to consider the sprinkling system as part of the "building of the schoolhouse" which cost $2,600,000, and that it should have been included in the advertisements for bids for its construction; or alternatively, even though constructed later, it still must be considered as part of the entire project and advertised for bids.

... The powers of the Board of Education are derived from statute and consist only of those expressly granted or those reasonably implied as necessary to carry out the duties imposed upon it. A number of sections of our code grant authority to school boards for the construction and maintenance of facilities for the operation of public school systems. Under the heading, "Further Powers of Boards of Education," Section 53620 U.C.A.1953, provides:

> Every board of education shall have power ... to construct and erect school buildings and to furnish the same, ... to purchase, exchange, repair and improve high school apparatus, books, furniture, fixtures and all other school supplies. It ... may do all things needful for the maintenance, prosperity and success of the schools, and the promotion of education; ....

The extensive discretion reposed in the school board by this section is apparent.

We are aware that in decisions construing the powers of school districts, the terms "school building" and "schoolhouse" are often given a broad meaning to encompass the entire functioning school plant, including athletic facilities. However, from this fact and the fact that under the grants of power to the board of education just referred to above, it has authority to construct and maintain athletic facilities, it does not necessarily follow that the sprinkling system in question must be regarded as coming within the language of Section 53111, first referred to above, requiring bids "[w]henever any schoolhouse is to be built." Whether it does or not may depend upon the circumstances. For example, it seems quite obvious that if the schoolhouse itself has already been built, the construction of some additional facility or improvement to the school plant, such as the installation of some additional blackboards, visual aid equipment, or of a sprinkling system in the athletic field, would not be within the meaning of the phrase "building a schoolhouse." If it were so, the school administration would often be hampered in adapting school buildings and facilities to changing needs such as supplying the deficiencies listed above in this very building with which we are concerned. This would be squarely contrary to the plain intent of Section 53620, above quoted which authorizes the Board to improve apparatus, books, furniture, fixtures and do all things needful for the maintenance, prosperity and success of the schools, and the promotion of education....

The principle that the School Board may not fragment a building contract into separate units to avoid the requirement of bids nor otherwise circumvent the requirements of the statutes is sound. From what we have said it should be apparent that as we view the evidence there is a reasonable basis therein to substantiate the trial court's refusal to find that the defendant Board did so. On the other hand, the evidence supports its findings to the contrary. Pertinent to this issue is the fact that the Board did request bids on the pipe and materials and bought them from the lowest bidder. This is evidence of its good faith and its desire to properly and lawfully perform its duty in administering the school system in "the most efficient and economical" manner possible. It is our opinion that its initiative and frugality in the premises should be approved and commended, rather than censured....

Notes

1. While the judges disagreed over whether the association had standing, they agreed on the merits of the case.

2. What do you think about using regular school employees on school repair and construction projects? If the amount of money involved exceeds that is required to be let on competitive bids, is your answer still the same? Put another way, should school boards consider the impact that such situations may have on local economies?

[Case No. 57]   Mistaken Bids

SCHOOL DISTRICT OF SCOTTSBLUFF v. OLSON CONSTRUCTION COMPANY

Supreme Court of Nebraska, 1950.
45 N.W.2d 164.

CARTER, JUSTICE. This is an action against the Olson Construction Company and its bondsman, Maryland Casualty Company, because of the failure of the former to comply with its bid and to contract for the construction of the buildings for the doing of which the bid was submitted. The trial court held against the plaintiff school district and for the defendants. The plaintiff appeals.

The school district advertised for bids for the construction of a new vocational agriculture and grandstand building and an addition to the Bryant Elementary School. The defendant Olson Construction Company was the successful bidder at $177,153.00. Pursuant to the instructions to bidders, contained in the advertisement for bids, the bid was accompanied by a bid bond in the amount of 5 percent of the bid, the defendant Maryland Casualty Company appearing as the surety thereon. The closing time for the acceptance of bids was fixed as of April 15, 1948, at 8 p.m. The bid of the Olson Construction Company was submitted on the evening of April 15, 1948, prior to 8 p.m. It was accepted and the contract awarded to the Olson Construction Company by the school board of the school district before the adjournment of the board thereafter on that day. The Olson Construction Company refused to comply with its bid and this action was brought to recover from the Olson Construction Company and its bondsman the sum of $8,857.65, the same being 5 percent of the bid, the amount the defendants obligated themselves to pay if the Olson Construction Company failed to enter into a contract to perform the work in accordance with its bid. The bid of the Olson Construction Company was $177,153.00 which showed an itemization of $68,410.00 for the construction of the vocational agriculture and grandstand building. The only other bid was in the amount of $203,758.00 and showed an itemization of $89,905.00 on the vocational agriculture and grandstand building. The architect's estimate on the latter building was $89,340.00. The defense of the Olson Construction Company is based on a typographical error in computing the total of its bid, which resulted in a reduction of the intended bid by an amount of $23,600.

The evidence shows that on April 15, 1948, John H. Miller, the vice president and secretary of the Olson Construction Company, was in Scottsbluff for the purpose of preparing the bid in final form for submission to the school district. In preparing the bid, form estimate sheets were used. Each of these form estimate sheets listed different items such as materials, labor, unit price, bids of subcontractors, and similar items. In order to arrive at the bid to be submitted it was necessary to tabulate the various sheets and add them up to secure the total amount of the bid. This latter work was assigned to one Erma Price, an experienced employee of the company. In tabulating the amounts shown on the estimate sheets relating to the bid on the vocational agriculture and grandstand building she inadvertently dropped a figure from the amount for which the structural steel was subcontracted, so that it was listed on the adding machine as $2,689 instead of $26,289. This resulted in a total being entered upon this particular estimate sheet in the amount of $6,624.50 instead of $30,224.50, even though one of the items alone amounted to $26,289. The erroneous total of $6,624.50 was carried into the total bid and resulted in the bid of $177,153.00 instead of $200,753.00 which the bid would have been except for the error. The evidence shows that Mrs. Price checked the items back after the addition was completed and again overlooked the error made in tabulating the amounts on the adding machine. The evidence shows also that Miller and those engaged with him in preparing the bid were in a hurry because of the approaching deadline for the filing of bids. The delay in preparation is shown to have been the result of slowness on the part of sub-contractors in submitting their bids, and delays in calculating certain items due to the rising costs of labor and materials.

The evidence is that the error was not observed by anyone connected with the preparation of the bid. The sealed bid was filed with the school district by a construction superintendent who was not familiar with its contents. Miller left Scottsbluff shortly before 8 p.m. on the last day for the filing of bids. It was not until he learned on the next day of the great variance of the two bids filed that he suspected a mistake in one of them. He immediately requested that the estimate sheets be sent to him at the home office at Lincoln. They were received the following Monday and the error was immediately discovered. The architect for the school district and the school district were immediately informed of the mistake. A number of conferences were had with reference to the matter. The school district decided to insist upon compliance with the bid and upon refusal of the Olson Construction Company to do so this suit was instituted.

The record establishes that the claimed error of $23,600 in the amount of the bid was a clerical mistake in tabulating and computing the bid. It was not an error of judgment in computing the quantity or cost of materials and labor. The mistake was unilateral, there being no allegations or evidence of mutual mistake. The school district contends that under such circumstances a bidder may not be relieved of his bid except where it is shown that the party receiving the bid knew or ought to have known, because of the amount of the bid or otherwise, that the bidder had made a mistake. While we think it could be said that the difference in the bids on the vocational agriculture and grandstand building was such as to indicate to the school district that a mistake had been made and thereby bring it within the rules applicable to mutual mistake, the bidder has the right under the facts shown by the record to withdraw its bid even though it was the result of unilateral error.

The rule under such circumstances is: When the mistake is so fundamental in character that the minds of the parties have not, in fact, met, or where an unconscionable advantage has been gained by mere mistake, equity will intervene to prevent intolerable injustice where there has been no failure to exercise reasonable care on the part of the bidder and where no intervening rights have accrued. In the case before us the mistake was discovered and notice thereof given to the school district within four days after the opening of the sealed bids. It was a fundamental mistake as distinguished from an incidental one. While the bid of the Olson Construction Company had been accepted and the contract awarded to it, no contract had been entered into; it was wholly executory. Failure to use reasonable care on the part of the Olson Construction Company is not shown and rights of third persons had not intervened. The parties could have been placed in statu quo at the time of the withdrawal of the bid. The reason for the latter statement is well stated in *Kutsche v. Ford*, wherein it is said: " 'In the instant case it may be thought that the school district cannot be said to be placed in statu quo when it is considered that the building cost nearly $6,000 more than plaintiff's bid. To place in statu quo does not mean that one shall profit out of the mistake of another. It does not appear that plaintiff's mistake has made the school building cost more than it otherwise would have cost. The school district, if placed back where it was before the bid, loses nothing except what it seeks to gain out of plaintiff's mistake. To compel plaintiff to forfeit his deposit, because of his mistake, would permit the school district to lessen the proper cost of the school building at the expense of plaintiff, and that, in equity, is no reason at all for refusing plaintiff relief. . . .' "

Numerous cases support the granting of relief to a bidder on the ground of unilateral mistake under the circumstances shown to exist in the present case. . . .

The essential conditions to relief from a unilateral mistake by rescission are: The mistake must be of so fundamental a nature that it can be said that the minds of the parties never met and that the enforcement of the contract as made would be unconscionable. The matter as to which the mistake was made must relate to the material feature of the contract. The mistake must have occurred notwithstanding the exercise of reasonable care by the party making it. Relief by way of rescission must be without undue prejudice to the other party, except for the loss of his bargain. . . .

The judgment of the trial court is supported by the law and the evidence. The judgment is affirmed.

Notes

1. Whether an error is material may depend on the margin of profit included in a bid as well as on the percent of the total bid encompassed by the error. *Boise Junior College Dist. v. Mattefs Constr. Co.*, 450 P.2d 604 (Idaho 1969).

2. Where specifications required bidders to submit certified checks, the Supreme Court of Iowa decided that a school board was justified in rejecting a

low bid where the accompanying check was not signed by a bank official but the word certified, along with the date and name of bank, was stamped on its face. *Menke v. Board of Educ., Indep. School Dist. of West Burlington*, 211 N.W.2d 601 (Iowa 1973).

[Case No. 58] Implied Contract*Quantum Meruit*

RESPONSIVE ENVIRONMENTS CORP. v. PULASKI COUNTY SPECIAL SCHOOL DISTRICT

United States District Court, Eastern District of Arkansas, 1973.
366 F.Supp. 241.

PAUL X. WILLIAMS, DISTRICT JUDGE. On February 22, 1968 Leroy Gattin, Superintendent of the Pulaski County, Arkansas, Special School District signed a "Lease Purchase Agreement" for a quantity of school library books as itemized in the agreement.

On March 14, 1968 the authorized agent of plaintiff, Responsive Environments Corporation, signed the same instrument. . . .

There is no question but that the district received the books covered by the lease-purchase agreement, distributed them to its various schools, used the books for a year or more and never paid anything for either the books or their use.

When called upon to pay for the books as provided by the contract, the Pulaski County Special School District responded that it considered the contract to be beyond the authority of the Superintendent and to be void and unenforceable. The District caused the books to be gathered up from the various schools and stored in a suitable place and notice to be given to Responsive Environments Corporation to come get them. . . .

. . . The Court finds that neither party to the contract is without fault. The conduct of both is subject to criticism.

The plaintiff's salesman, Mr. Marder, was so anxious to sell his company's books that he oversold his merchandise and carelessly misled the purchasers by his sales pitch. He represented that he had the approval of the State Department, when in truth he and Mr. Payne both had been informed that the lease-purchase form he proposed to use did not meet the requirements of the Arkansas Law and that Title II funds could not be used for payment at that time.

On the other hand, Superintendent Gattin relying upon the advice of Mr. Payne and Mr. Cox [subordinate administrators] was willing to make the deal if federal funds were used to pay for the books. His philosophy was clearly and aptly expressed when he testified that "Federal Funds are free."

In this case we have the plaintiff seeking the pot of gold at the end of the Federal rainbow and the defendant willing to go along if the acquisition was paid for by federal funds.

Both the present plaintiff and the R.E.C. are wholly owned by PrenticeHall. During the rainbow days, the plaintiff was acquiring and selling a large number of books_many of which were not the kind or quality desired nor needed by school libraries, but which in this case Mr. Gattin was willing to receive if payment came from the gold at the end of the rainbow.

It is elementary that the business affairs of a school district in Arkansas are by statute entrusted to its board of school directors.

In this case there is no evidence that the contract in question was ever approved or sanctioned by the school board except the action of the board authorizing the Superintendent to execute proper forms to secure federal funds. . . .

The Court finds that this action of the board did not authorize Mr. Gattin to enter into the contract here sued on. The Court finds that Mr. Gattin did not have authority to enter into the said contract and further finds that the school board did not ratify or adopt the action taken by Mr. Gattin. On the contrary, the board expressly refused to go along with the venture and changed some of its personnel and later even the Superintendent himself.

The Court finds that the subject matter was not *"ultra-vires"*; the board could have ratified the contract, but deliberately chose not to do so. . . .

. . . [T]he use of the books, in however slight degree, was beneficial to the defendant, for admittedly it needed a stronger library program and admittedly, at least a portion of the books were a desirable acquisition.

While the Court finds that both the plaintiff and the defendant are at fault and that no legal contract was made, ratified or consummated, at the same time the Court finds that the conduct of the parties was such that an implied contract arose that required the defendant school district to pay under the theory of *quantum meruit*. . . .

"*Quantum meruit* refers to that class of obligations imposed by law, without regard to the intention or assent of the parties bound, for reasons dictated by reason and justice. The form of the action is contract, but they are not contracts, because the parties do not fix the terms and their intentions are disregarded. One class of such cases is those where a party wrongfully compels another to render him valuable services, and a promise to pay is implied, because on equitable grounds one ought not to be permitted to keep that which is received without compensation." . . .

The Court finds that under the facts and circumstances in this case the plaintiff deserves the option to either have its books back or to receive in payment that sum of money which it deserves.

The next question which addresses itself to the Court is the fair amount which should be awarded to the plaintiff if it elects to take money. . . .

After considering all factors the Court finds that plaintiff is entitled to receive $13,500.00 in full settlement for the books which the School

District has received from the plaintiff. [The contract price was $113,260.] . . .

Notes

1.   What do you think about the superintendent's conduct in this case?

2.   "The doctrine of implied contract cannot be invoked to do rough justice and fasten liability where the legal requirements specifically prohibit." [sic] *Lutzken v. City of Rochester*, 184 N.Y.S.2d 483, 486 (N.Y.App.Div.1959).

[Case No. 59]   Invalid Contract–Ratified

FRANK v. BOARD OF EDUCATION OF JERSEY CITY

Court of Errors and Appeals of New Jersey, 1917.
100 A. 211.

BLACK, J. . . . There is but a single question presented by the record in this case to be answered; viz., whether a municipal corporation is liable to pay for work done and materials furnished it by an unauthorized agent, when the municipality had the power to make a contract for such purposes. If so, whether an agency to purchase such supplies in fact can be implied from the acts and conduct of the parties and a ratification of the contract for such supplies be also implied from like acts and conduct. The application of elemental and well-recognized principles in the law of agency to the facts, as disclosed by the record in this case, leads us to answer these questions in the affirmative. . . .

The facts on which the ruling of the trial court was based are these: The above work and materials were actually furnished by the respondent to the appellant, by order of John T. Rowland, Jr., supervising architect of the appellant, except two items. He had been permitted by the appellant "for a number of years" to order labor and materials of the nature sued for in this case. His orders had been recognized by the appellant, and the amounts therefor had been paid by it. "Many previous orders of the same kind were duly paid for by the defendant," furnished by the respondent. The item of $46.70 for repairing motor generator was for labor, which was furnished by the respondent to the appellant by order of Charles C. Wilson, vice principal of the Jersey City high school, which was under appellant's control. All the items except the item of $5.00 for one pole tester were "emergency" work; i.e., they were furnished at the time the emergency existed, requiring immediate performance, and before a meeting of the appellant could be held to pass upon the necessity of doing the same and ordering it to be done.

The respondent had done other work and furnished materials of a similar character for the appellant under and by similar orders. Such work had been regularly paid for, in due course, by the appellant, when the bills for the same were presented without question as to the regularity of the requests or the authority of the said Rowland and Wilson. The work done and materials furnished, sued for in this suit, were done and furnished, relying on the fact that previous orders by

Rowland and Wilson, under similar circumstances, had been paid for by the appellant. The respondent knew that this practice existed and was permitted to exist by the appellant. This practice had been so "for a number of years." The appellant knew that the work and materials had been furnished it by the respondent at or about the times they had been so furnished and it did not, until three years after the last work had been performed, deny the authority of the said Rowland and Wilson to order the work and materials. The appellant has had the use and benefit of the work so done and materials furnished. . . .

. . . [In a statute] there is express authority for the appointment of an agent, a business manager. The term is immaterial. A supervising architect or vice principal might just as well be called an agent or business manager. There is also the recognition by the legislature of the fact that the board of education probably could not act in many cases without appointing such agents, since the very necessity of some cases requires that such a board should act through agents. . . . It would be quite impracticable to require either a formal resolution for every possible small expenditure, or for the board to act by a majority in person. In the state of facts these orders under consideration are called "emergency" orders. . . .

The literature of the law of agency is rich in adjudged cases. The principles pertinent to the subject under discussion are these: An agency, as between individuals or business corporations, may be implied from prior habit, or from a course of dealings of a similar nature between the parties. The agency may be implied from the recognition or acquiescence of the alleged principal as to acts done in his behalf by the alleged agent, especially if the agent has repeatedly been permitted to perform acts like the one in question. But when it is implied, and in so far as it is implied, the power of the agent must be determined from no one fact alone but from all the facts and circumstances for which the principal is responsible. So ratification may be implied from any acts, words, or conduct on the part of the principal which reasonably tend to show an intention on the part of the principal to ratify the unauthorized acts or transactions of the alleged agent, provided the principal in doing the acts relied on as a ratification acted with knowledge of the material facts. The rule is particularly applicable where it appears that the principal has repeatedly recognized and affirmed similar acts by the agent. So a municipal corporation may ratify the unauthorized acts and contracts of its agents or officers which are within the scope of the corporate powers, but not otherwise. . . .

We think, as the board of education had the power, under the statute, to contract for the work done and material supplied in this case, there was created by conduct an implied agency, an agency in fact, on the part of Messrs. Rowland and Wilson, and further, that by implication the contracts of these unauthorized agents have been ratified by the acts and conduct of the school board. . . .

Notes

1. In *Everett v. Board of Pub. Instruction of Volusia County*, 186 So. 209 (Fla.1939), a janitor sued to recover on a contract he formed with the supervising principal of the school. Although the janitor was recommended for the position, the board appointed someone else even though its members knew that he rendered services under the contract and they did nothing to indicate that his services were unwanted. The court found that the janitor presented a cause of action in *quantum meruit*.

2. "School district officers cannot be permitted by the law to enter into a written contract with a teacher, none of them denying its validity for 10 weeks, or half the term, but recognizing it by making payments upon it, in which payments all join, and then, after the teacher, in the utmost good faith and reliance upon the contract, has taught that length of time, discharge him without cause, and plead in bar of payment under the contract that they never met and consulted, nor took corporate action in hiring him, or made any record in a book of the execution of the contract. It appears very clearly in this case that a majority of the school board assented to this contract in the first place, as evidenced by their executing it. It was afterward ratified by all three of them. It was not necessary that there should be a direct proceeding with the express intent to ratify. It may be done indirectly, and by acts of recognition or acquiescence, or acts inconsistent with repudiation or disapproval." *Crane v. Bennington School Dist.*, 28 N.W. 105, 107 (Mich.1886).

Chapter 9

TEACHER CERTIFICATION, EMPLOYMENT, AND CONTRACTS

Introduction

The primary source of law regulating the qualifications, employment, and contracts of teachers and other school employees is established at the state level. Even so, federal law, especially in the area of anti-discrimination, has a major impact on the employment rights of educators in public schools. As such, this chapter reviews issues associated with the employment of educators, most notably teachers, in public schools.

The Teacher's Certificate

Generally

All jurisdictions have laws[1] that require public school teachers to have certification or licenses[2] based on such qualifications as having completed professional preparation programs,[3] achieving appropriate scores on requisite examinations,[4] and/or passing criminal background checks.[5] Whether referred to as certification or licensure, insofar as state endorsements are not contracts, mere possession of credentials does not satisfy the statutory definition of a teacher since one must typically both possess a valid certificate and perform the statutory duties of educators.[6]

---

1. *See, e.g.,* ALA. CODE 1975 § 16–23–1 *et seq.*; ALASKA STAT. § 14.20.010 *et seq.*; CAL. EDUC. CODE ANN. § 44203; 105 ILL. STAT. 5/21–0.01 *et seq.*; KY. REV. STAT. ANN. § 161.010 *et seq.*; MONT. CODE ANN. § 20–4–101 *et seq.*; N.Y. MCKINNEY'S EDUC. LAW § 3001; OHIO REV. CODE ANN. § 3319.22 et seq.; 70 OKLA. STAT. ANN. § 6–106; PA. STAT. ANN. § 12–1201 *et seq.*; TEX. EDUC. ANN. § 21.041; WYO. STAT. ANN. § 21–7–501 *et seq.*

2. Amid debate over whether educators should receive permanent certification, or licenses, subject to regular renewal as in other professions such as law or medicine, unless otherwise noted, this book uses the term certification to apply to both.

3. *Irizarry v. Anker,* 558 F.2d 1122 (2d Cir.1977) (upholding a board's refusal to go beyond a catalogue description in denying course credit to an applicant); *State ex rel. Thompson v. Ekberg,* 613 P.2d 466 (Okla. 1980) (requiring a principal to have a masters degree). [Case No. 60]

4. *See* the discussion of teacher examinations beginning at note 31 *infra* and accompanying text.

5. *See, e.g.,* ARK. STAT. ANN. § 6–17–410; CAL. EDUC. CODE ANN. § 44339 *et seq.*; CONN. GEN. STAT. ANN. § 10–221d; KY. REV. STAT. ANN. § 160.380; MICH. COMP. LAWS ANN. § 380.1230a; MINN. STAT. ANN. § 122A.18; MISS. CODE ANN. § 37–13–89; OHIO REV. CODE ANN. § 3319.39; OR. REV. STAT. ANN. § 326.603; R.I. GEN. LAWS ANN. § 16–2–18.1; TENN. CODE ANN. § 49–5–413; TEX. EDUC. ANN. § 22.083. For a case rejecting a challenge to background checks, *see Hilliard v. Ferguson,* 30 F.3d 649 [93 Educ. L. Rep. 116] (5th Cir.1994).

6. *Sealey v. Board of Educ.,* 14 S.W.3d 597 [143 Educ. L. Rep. 1091] (Mo. Ct. App. 1999), *reh'g denied* (1999). *See also Houston v. Nelson,* 147 S.W.3d 589 [193 Educ. L. Rep. 332] (Tex. App. 2004).

Certification laws differ widely as to substantive requirements and procedures since legislatures vest varying amounts of discretion in state boards and departments of education, chief state school officers, and local school boards.

Certification requirements are subject to judicial scrutiny under federal and state anti-discrimination statutes and the Fourteenth Amendment. To this end, since the right to engage in a legitimate occupation is a liberty interest, state officials can only deny individuals jobs if there are reasonable standards in place to protect public health, safety, and welfare.[7] Employment is also sometimes denoted as a property right.[8] However, where an educational agency's action is rooted in the ministerial application of objective criteria, rather than an exercise of discretion, courts are reluctant to intervene on behalf of aggrieved teachers. In one such case, an appellate court in Pennsylvania dismissed the challenge of a teacher who failed the Praxis II test in Spanish Content Knowledge that was required for certification.[9] The court explained that since the teacher had no expectation that she would have received a certificate, educational officials did not deprive her of any right or privilege, including the opportunity to litigate her disagreement. A year earlier, another appellate court in Pennsylvania upheld the denial of an administrative certificate to a teacher who had only one year of experience where the applicable statute required a minimum of five years of professional experience and the completion of an approved program of graduate study.[10] As part of its analysis, the court refused to grant the teacher credit for any of her teaching experience at a charter school.

In a preliminary question, in *Ambach v. Norwick*, the Supreme Court upheld a statute from New York that required individuals who wished to become public school teachers to be United States citizens. Recognizing that "[t]he importance of public schools in the preparation of individuals for participation as citizens, and in the preservation of the values on which our society rests, long has been recognized by our decisions ...,"[11] the Court wrote that a state may regard teachers as having an obligation to promote civic virtues and understanding in their classes. On other basic matters, courts have refused to eliminate loyalty oaths,[12] residency requirements,[13] and mental and physical examinations

7. *Meyer v. Nebraska*, 262 U.S. 390, 43 S.Ct. 625, 67 L.Ed. 1042 (1923).

8. *See, e.g., Leetham v. McGinn*, 524 P.2d 323 (Utah 1974); *Connecticut Educ. Ass'n v. Tirozzi*, 554 A.2d 1065 [52 Educ. L. Rep. 604] (Conn.1989).

9. *Dauer v. Department of Educ.*, 874 A.2d 159 [198 Educ. L. Rep. 621] (Pa. Cmwlth. Ct. 2005).

10. *Davenport v. Department of Educ.*, 850 A.2d 802 [188 Educ. L. Rep. 917] (Pa. Cmwlth. Ct. 2004).

11. 441 U.S. 68, 76, 99 S.Ct. 1589, 60 L.Ed.2d 49 (1979).

12. *Gough v. State*, 667 A.2d 1057 [105 Educ. L. Rep. 584] (N.J.Super.Ct.App.Div.1995).

13. *Wardwell v. Board of Educ. of City School Dist. of City of Cincinnati*, 529 F.2d 625 (6th Cir.1976); *Mogle v. Sevier County School Dist.*, 540 F.2d 478 (10th Cir.1976), *cert. denied*, 429 U.S. 1121, 97 S.Ct. 1157, 51 L.Ed.2d 572 (1977). *But see Owen v. Board of Educ. of Kankakee School Dist. No. 111*, 632 N.E.2d 1073 [90 Educ. L. Rep. 732] (Ill.Ct.App.1994) (remanding a dispute over a residency requirement, as applied to an assistant principal, as to whether the board actually had a policy in place).

for job candidates.[14] In a case from California, an appellate court interpreted a statute that barred individuals who were convicted of felonies from receiving teaching credentials. Reversing in favor of an applicant for a teaching credential, the court held that since his conviction for discharging a firearm in a grossly negligent manner was reduced to a misdemeanor, and since he was placed on probation, the statute did not serve as a bar to his seeking certification.[15]

If candidates meet the legal standards for certification, state agencies may not arbitrarily reject their applications[16] or impose new conditions such as age requirements.[17] As reflected by an older case from Maryland, when the state legislature delegated its authority to an examining and certificating agency, the judiciary chose not to become involved. The state's highest court refused to issue a writ of mandamus to a candidate who challenged requirements that changed after he entered a preparation program.[18] The court noted that because the state board had the authority to enact bylaws to effectuate the state's educational policies, it would not interfere and grant certification to a candidate who failed to meet the requirement of graduating in the upper four-fifths of his class and earn a grade of "C" or better in "practical teaching."

In North Carolina, a dispute arose when the state board of education adopted a regulation indicating that all public school teaching certificates would expire after five years and that educators who wished to renew their credentials had to earn six units of credit during the five-year period immediately preceding renewal. The Supreme Court of North Carolina upheld this regulation on the ground that there was a reasonable basis for the belief of state officials that the quality of teachers' classroom performances would have improved if they broadened or kept their knowledge up-to-date.[19] Similarly, the Supreme Court of Connecticut affirmed that state officials could replace the statutory scheme, which permitted teachers to receive certification for life, revocable only for cause, with one that conferred five-year renewable certificates premised on successful completion of professional development activities.[20] While acknowledging that teachers had constitutionally protected property interests in their certificates, the court decided that the new system did not deprive them of due process. The court was satisfied that since the legislative goal of enhancing the quality of public edu-

14. *Sullivan v. River Valley School Dist.*, 197 F.3d 804 [140 Educ. L. Rep. 127] (6th Cir.1999), *cert. denied*, 530 U.S. 1262, 120 S.Ct. 2718, 147 L.Ed.2d 983 (2000) (also rejecting the applicant's claim that he was disabled under the Americans with Disabilities Act).

15. *Gebremicael v. California Comm'n on Teacher Credentialing*, 13 Cal.Rptr.3d 777 [187 Educ. L. Rep. 943] (Cal. Ct. App. 2004).

16. *Keller v. Hewitt*, 41 P. 871 (Cal. 1895); *State ex rel. Hopkins v. Wooster*, 208 P. 656 (Kan.1922).

17. *State ex rel. Johnson v. Matzen*, 210 N.W. 151 (Neb.1926).

18. *Metcalf v. Cook*, 178 A. 219 (Md. 1935).

19. *Guthrie v. Taylor*, 185 S.E.2d 193 (N.C.1971).

20. *Connecticut Educ. Ass'n v. Tirozzi*, 554 A.2d 1065 [52 Educ. L. Rep. 604] (Conn.1989).

cation was an important one, the plan was not unduly restrictive or onerous.

Where school officials knowingly employed a woman to teach subjects for which she was not certificated, and continually reassured her that this was not a problem, they were still able to discharge her due to her lack of qualifications. The Supreme Court of Wisconsin affirmed that since the teacher was responsible for being certificated, and local administrators could not waive the requirement, she was not entitled to equitable relief.[21] In like manner, an appellate court in New York confirmed that a school board could discharge a teacher even after officials obtained permission from the state department of education that would have permitted him to continue to remain on the job since he refused to complete course work toward certification nine years after he started working.[22] Another appellate court in New York agreed that a teacher could be denied certification in earth science since the biology course that he completed did not satisfy state requirements.[23] Conversely, the Court of Appeals of New York affirmed that a teacher who taught for seven years and was awarded tenure could not be denied a permanent certificate on the ground that she did not complete student teaching.[24] The court ruled that the state's commissioner of education did not abuse his discretion in waiving the student teaching requirement under the circumstances.

In the first of two cases that segue into the next section, the Supreme Court of South Carolina relied solely on the denial of procedural due process in preventing the cancellation of a teaching certificate when a private testing agency notified the state department of education that a score should have been canceled.[25] The court found that the regulation providing for automatic invalidation was unconstitutional where the only evidence against the teacher was an unexplained note from the testing company.

The Fourth Circuit outlined the necessary steps to comply with Section 504 of the Rehabilitation Act of 1973 (Section 504)[26] and, by extension, the Americans with Disabilities Act (ADA),[27] when an individual with disabilities cannot meet certification requirements. A candidate in Virginia who had been diagnosed as having learning disabilities failed the communications skills portion of the National Teacher Examination (NTE), which is designed to measure academic achievement of teachers,

---

21. *Grams v. Melrose–Mindoro Joint School Dist. No. 1,* 254 N.W.2d 730 (Wis. 1977).

22. *Chapman v. Board of Educ. of Yonkers City School Dist.,* 394 N.Y.S.2d 52 (N.Y.App.Div. 1977). *See also Smith v. Andrews,* 504 N.Y.S.2d 286 [37 Educ. L. Rep. 893] (N.Y.App.Div. 1986), *appeal denied,* 513 N.Y.S.2d 1025 [38 Educ. L. Rep. 1136] (N.Y.1987).

23. *Emminger v. Education Dep't of State of N.Y.,* 627 N.Y.S.2d 127 [100 Educ. L. Rep. 687] (N.Y.App.Div.1995).

24. *Bradford Cent. School Dist. v. Ambach,* 451 N.Y.S.2d 654 [5 Educ. L. Rep. 189] (N.Y. 1982). *See also Matteson v. State Bd. of Educ.,* 136 P.2d 120 (Cal.Ct.App. 1943).

25. *Brown v. South Carolina State Bd. of Educ.,* 391 S.E.2d 866 [60 Educ. L. Rep. 1004] (S.C. 1990). [Case No. 61]

26. 29 U.S.C.A. § 794(a). This statute is in the appendix.

27. 42 U.S.C.A. §§ 12101 *et seq.* Portions of this statute are in the appendix.

eight times, twice after she received special aids and a longer time period. Following lengthy litigation, the court determined that the teacher was entitled to a trial on the merits of whether she was otherwise qualified under Section 504.[28]

In an emerging issue, the No Child Left Behind Act (NCLB) requires school boards to hire teachers who are "highly qualified."[29] Matters are complicated by virtue of the fact under the NCLB, the standards vary depending on whether a teacher is in regular or special education,[30] the level at which an individual teaches, and whether one is an experienced or new teacher. While there has been no reported litigation on the issue of teachers who are "highly qualified," it is likely that cases will soon appear.

Examinations for Certificates

Where state legislatures require candidates to take competitive examinations for certification, questions arise as to the appropriate procedures. In an early case, an appellate court in New York directed a testing firm to provide an unsuccessful candidate for a license as high school department chair with model answers to essay questions and other parts of the examination.[31] The court thought that refusing to permit the candidate to review the standard against which his performance was measured was unreasonable.

A year later, the New York's highest court refused to annul failure ratings in an interview test that was part of a licensing examination for elementary school principals who claimed that it lacked sufficiently objective standards.[32] The court was of the opinion that since the skills necessary to become a principal cannot be adequately measured with precision, and the interview examination procedures were appropriate, they were sufficient. The same court also considered whether eligibility lists based on competitive examinations could be avoided in appointing elementary school principals who possessed characteristics that were deemed necessary in inner-city schools. In an experiment with decentralization and community involvement, the board of education created a post of "demonstration elementary school principal," following its normal procedure and temporarily appointing candidates. The court overturned judgments that this approach violated the state's constitutional mandate of a merit system since it did not test for special qualifications.[33] The court pointed out that the principals could remain on the job pending the rapid development of criteria and bases for their assessment.

28. *Pandazides v. Virginia Bd. of Educ.*, 13 F.3d 823 [88 Educ. L. Rep. 963] (4th Cir.1994).

29. 20 U.S.C.A. § 7801(23) (dealing with teachers in regular education). This section of the statute is in the appendix.

30. 20 U.S.C.A. § 1401(10) (dealing with teachers in special education). This section of the statute is in the appendix.

31. *Schwartz v. Bogen*, 281 N.Y.S.2d 279 (N.Y.App.Div.1967).

32. *Nelson v. Board of Examiners of Bd. of Educ.*, 288 N.Y.S.2d 454 (N.Y.1968).

33. *Council of Supervisory Ass'ns of Pub. Schools v. Board of Educ.*, 297 N.Y.S.2d 547 (N.Y. 1969).

In a case from South Carolina on teacher testing, the Supreme Court summarily upheld the use of the NTE.[34] The Court reasoned that state educational officials could rely on the NTE since it was validated to test the qualifications of prospective educators.

The first of four cases from Texas saw the Fifth Circuit uphold the legislature's general power to require candidates to pass a Pre–Professional Skills Test. The court dissolved a preliminary injunction against the test, ordering a trial on the merits of the claims which alleged that it was not only invalid but also had an unlawful disparate impact on minority students. As part of its analysis, the court reiterated the basic rule that a state is "not obligated to educate or certify teachers who cannot pass a fair and valid test of basic skills necessary for professional training"[35] and that disparate impact alone did not violate the Fourteenth Amendment's Equal Protection Clause. Shortly thereafter, the Supreme Court of Texas upheld a statute that required teachers to pass a basic skills test in order to keep their certificates in the face of allegations that it impaired contract rights.[36] The court rejected the argument that because the test did not include a specific provision for hearings or avenues of appeal, it was a retroactive law that violated due process. The court emphasized that both because no contract was involved in the case of a license and since decertification was not automatic, it could be governed by the law covering revocation for cause. In a later case, the Fifth Circuit affirmed both that statistical analysis provided by minority candidates who failed to pass Texas' compulsory certification test was inapplicable under Title VII of the Civil Rights Act of 1964,[37] discussed below, since they were not employees[38] and that neither the state nor the local school board acted with intent to discriminate when minority teachers were unable to pass the same test.[39]

In a long-running controversy from Alabama over testing, the Eleventh Circuit vacated a consent decree that stipulated that teacher certification examinations violated Title VII because they included impermissible racial bias against African Americans.[40] In like manner, in another lengthy dispute, the Ninth Circuit upheld the validity of the California Basic Educational Skills Test that all educators are required to pass before they can teach or fill other positions in public schools in the face of a claim that it violated the rights of minority candidates.[41]

34. *United States v. State of S.C.*, 445 F.Supp. 1094 (D.S.C.1977), *aff'd, sub nom. National Educ. Ass'n v. United States*, 434 U.S. 1026, 98 S.Ct. 756, 54 L.Ed.2d 775 (1978). [Case No. 62]

35. *United States v. LULAC*, 793 F.2d 636, 639 [37 Educ. L. Rep. 772] (5th Cir. 1986).

36. *State v. Project Principle*, 724 S.W.2d 387 [37 Educ. L. Rep. 961] (Tex. 1987).

37. 42 U.S.C.A. §§ 2000 *et seq.* Portions of this statute are in the appendix.

38. *Fields v. Hallsville Indep. School Dist.*, 906 F.2d 1017 [61 Educ. L. Rep. 442]

(5th Cir. 1990), *cert. denied*, 498 U.S. 1026, 111 S.Ct. 676, 112 L.Ed.2d 668 (1991).

39. *Frazier v. Garrison I.S.D.*, 980 F.2d 1514 [79 Educ. L. Rep. 420] (5th Cir.1993).

40. *Allen v. Alabama State Bd. of Educ.*, 164 F.3d 1347 [131 Educ. L. Rep. 920] (11th Cir. 1999), *vacated*, 216 F.3d 1263 [146 Educ. L. Rep. 628] (11th Cir. 2000).

41. *Association of Mexican–American Educators v. State of Cal.*, 231 F.3d 572 [148 Educ. L. Rep. 639] (9th Cir.2000).

The court maintained that the examination was constitutional because it used properly validated methods to demonstrate that it had a manifest relationship to teaching since it was job related to the extent that it actually measured skills, knowledge, or ability required for successful job performance.[42]

In a case on the issue of disability and eligibility to take a test, the Third Circuit affirmed that a school board in Pennsylvania could not refuse a blind person the opportunity to take a qualifying examination for teachers.[43] The court posited that since the right to take the examination arose under state law, the board violated the Fourteenth Amendment by arbitrarily creating the irrebuttable presumption that no blind person could qualify to teach. When the applicant was finally allowed to take, and pass, the examination, the court affirmed that she was entitled to seniority as of the time she would have been employed but for the illegal postponement of her taking the test.

A federal trial court in Minnesota, in another disagreement that also overlaps with the rights of the disabled, granted the state licensing board's motion for summary judgment in refusing to waive the mathematics section of an examination for a candidate with dyslexia.[44] The court asserted that since the mathematics portion of the test related to an essential job function, the candidate's inability to pass it meant that she was not an otherwise qualified individual who was entitled to protection under federal and state disability laws. In like fashion, a federal trial court in New York rejected the claim of a teacher that officials failed to accommodate her disability under the ADA.[45] In observing that the teacher refused to take a required certification examination, the court held that she was not otherwise qualified for a job.

Suspension-Revocation of Certificates

State agencies have the authority both to grant credentials and to take them away for a variety of reasons, such as where one teacher assaulted a child[46] and another directed inappropriate and verbally abusive language at students,[47] as long as they can demonstrate that their actions were not arbitrary and capricious.[48] Courts typically uphold the mandatory revocation of teaching credentials when educators are convicted of crimes,[49] including those for moral turpitude.[50]

42. *See also Feldman v. Board of Educ. of City School Dist. of City of N.Y.*, 686 N.Y.S.2d 842 [134 Educ. L. Rep. 262] (N.Y.App.Div.1999) (affirming the termination of the licenses of teachers who failed the NTE).

43. *Gurmankin v. Costanzo*, 556 F.2d 184 (3d Cir.1977).

44. *Jacobsen v. Tillmann*, 17 F.Supp.2d 1018 [129 Educ. L. Rep. 1094] (D.Minn. 1998).

45. *Falchenberg v. New York City Dep't of Educ.*, 375 F.Supp.2d 344 [199 Educ. L. Rep. 813] (S.D.N.Y. 2005).

46. *In re Appeal of Morrill*, 765 A.2d 699 [150 Educ. L. Rep. 758] (N.H.2001).

47. *Knight v. Winn*, 910 So.2d 310 [201 Educ. L. Rep. 989] (Fla. Dist. Ct. App. 2005), *reh'g denied* (2005).

48. *Von Gizycki v. Levy*, 771 N.Y.S.2d 174 [185 Educ. L. Rep. 325] (N.Y. App. Div. 2004).

49. *Vogulkin v. State Bd. of Educ.*, 15 Cal.Rptr. 335 (Cal.Ct.App.1961).

50. *Bowalick v. Commonwealth*, 840 A.2d 519 [184 Educ. L. Rep. 903] (Pa. Cmwlth. Ct. 2004).

In an older case, the Second Circuit upheld an order of the commissioner of education that a local board not re-employ a tenured teacher from New York pending the revocation of his certification after he was convicted of, and served a prison term for, conspiring to promote bribery of public officials.[51] Moreover, an appellate court in Pennsylvania affirmed the revocation of a teacher's certificate based on a guilty plea to a charge of mail fraud.[52] Insofar as the applicable statute required only that a teacher engage in a crime involving moral turpitude and did not mandate a pre-revocation hearing beyond establishing that such a crime was committed, the court was content that commonwealth officials acted within the bounds of their authority.[53] According to another appellate court in Pennsylvania, an educator did not have to be convicted of a criminal offense before officials could revoke her certification for submitting false, and forged, information with a job application.[54] The court's analysis was consistent with the general rule that public school employees can be expected to meet higher standards of conduct than their peers in the private sector since there is no right to public employment.

An appellate court in Georgia declared that the state Professional Standards Commission could revoke an educator's certification for improperly coaching his students on a standardized test.[55] The court referred to evidence that an instructional specialist identified portions of the test that he discovered in the teacher's classroom and that he admitted using materials, which he could not have possessed other than during the hours when the test occurred, as diagnostic measures for his students. Earlier, another appellate court in Georgia, in a long-running suit, affirmed the revocation of a coach-teacher's certification over his role in a grade-changing scandal that sought to render ineligible players able to play football.[56]

Cases involving violent behavior by teachers and/or other educators have led to mixed results. Where a teacher from Georgia engaged in violent behavior, an appellate court upheld the six-month suspension of his license for violating the state's Code of Ethics.[57] The court agreed that since the teacher was involved in two altercations on school property within four months, one with the cafeteria manager over food prices and the second after avoiding a car accident with a student, his uncontrolled anger and inappropriate behavior warranted a suspension because his actions seriously impaired his ability to function professionally as an educator. A second appellate court in Georgia upheld the one-year

51. *Pordum v. Board of Regents of State of N.Y.,* 491 F.2d 1281 (2d Cir.1974), *cert. denied,* 419 U.S. 843, 95 S.Ct. 74, 42 L.Ed.2d 71 (1974).

52. *Startzel v. Commonwealth, Dep't of Educ.,* 562 A.2d 1005 [55 Educ. L. Rep. 637] (Pa. Cmwlth.Ct.1989).

53. *See also Pardue v. Department of Educ.,* 815 A.2d 1162 [173 Educ. L. Rep. 898] (Pa. Cmwlth.Ct.2003) (affirming the suspension of a teacher's certification due to her being arrested for criminal stalking and harassment).

54. *Nanko v. Department of Educ.,* 663 A.2d 312 [102 Educ. L. Rep. 1149] (Pa. Cmwlth. Ct.1995).

55. *Professional Standards Comm'n v. Smith,* 571 S.E.2d 443 [171 Educ. L. Rep. 623] (Ga.Ct.App.2002).

56. *Brewer v. Schacht,* 509 S.E.2d 378 [131 Educ. L. Rep. 1138] (Ga.Ct.App.1998).

57. *Professional Standards Comm'n v. Valentine,* 603 S.E.2d 792 [192 Educ. L. Rep. 978] (Ga. Ct. App. 2004), *cert. denied* (2004).

suspension of a superintendent's certificate after he brandished a fire-arm during a confrontation with a flagman at a road construction site.[58] The court agreed with state officials that the superintendent's conduct constituted "good and sufficient cause" under the state's provisional standards and that the applicable statute was not unconstitutionally vague.

An appellate court in Arizona affirmed the revocation of a high school teacher's certificate following a series of incidents where he displayed aggressive, threatening, and intimidating behavior at or involving teenagers or young children.[59] The court commented that even though not all of the incidents resulted in criminal convictions, the teacher demonstrated that he was unfit to teach.

Another major ground for the revocation of certification involves sexual misconduct and impropriety, especially with students. In such a case, the Supreme Court of New Hampshire affirmed the revocation of a teacher's certificate for lack of good moral character after he pled no contest for simple assault following his being accused of inappropriate sexual contact with a thirteen-year-old female from his church that he was tutoring in his home.[60] The court ascertained there was sufficient evidence of a nexus between the former teacher's outside conduct and his fitness and ability to teach.[61] In a similar dispute, an appellate court in Ohio affirmed the revocation of a former art teacher's certificate by reason of unbecoming conduct.[62] Even though the teacher had an excellent professional reputation spanning thirty years, he engaged in sexual conduct in an adult bookstore and pled no contest to a charge of public indecency in an incident that received media attention and impacted his professional life. The court indicated that since the teacher's actions created a nexus between his conduct and ability to teach when he solicited students to write letters on his behalf, the revocation of his certificate for at least two years was not unwarranted. Further, an appellate court in Illinois affirmed the five-year suspension of an assistant principal's teaching and administrative certificates for immorality where he fathered a child with one of his fourteen-year-old students.[63]

A case from Florida illustrates how the internet may be an emerging source of sexual impropriety involving teachers. An appellate court affirmed that a teacher's sending profanity-laced, sexually explicit material over the internet directly to sixteen seventh-grade students warrant-

58. *Professional Standards Comm'n v. Alberson*, 614 S.E.2d 132 [199 Educ. L. Rep. 437] (Ga. Ct. App. 2005).

59. *Winters v. Arizona Bd. of Educ.*, 83 P.3d 1114 [185 Educ. L. Rep. 354] (Ariz. Ct. App. 2004).

60. *In re Appeal of Morrill*, 765 A.2d 699 [150 Educ. L. Rep. 758] (N.H.2001).

61. For other cases where teachers had their certificates revoked for engaging in sexual misconduct with students, *see, e.g.*, *Groht v. Sobol*, 604 N.Y.S.2d 279 [87 Educ. L. Rep. 555] (N.Y.App.Div.1993); *Howard v.*

Missouri State Bd. of Educ., 913 S.W.2d 887 [106 Educ. L. Rep. 942] (Mo.Ct.App. 995); *Welcher v. Sobol*, 642 N.Y.S.2d 370 [109 Educ. L. Rep. 896] (N.Y.App.Div.1996).

62. *Hoffman v. State Bd. of Educ.*, 763 N.E.2d 210 [161 Educ. L. Rep. 955] (Ohio Ct.App. 2001).

63. *Hayes v. State Teacher Certification Bd.*, 835 N.E.2d 146 [202 Educ. L. Rep. 259] (Ill. App. Ct. 2005), *appeal denied*, 217 Ill.2d 562 (Ill. 2005). The former assistant principal also faced dismissal and criminal proceedings.

ed the permanent revocation of her certification as a penalty clearly authorized by statute.[64] The court added that the revocation was appropriate since it was not inconsistent with the Education Practices Commission's (EPC) past practices. A year earlier, another appellate court in Florida affirmed the revocation of a teacher's certificate based on evidence that he inappropriately accessed pornographic internet sites on a school computer and that he battered his wife.[65] The court remarked that the EPC had the authority to revoke the certificate based on uncontroverted evidence in the complaint against the teacher.

In a case with an interesting twist, the Supreme Court of Minnesota refused to reinstate posthumously the certification of a teacher who died while litigation was pending over his inappropriate sexual contact with a student.[66] The court believed that the teacher's due process rights were not violated with respect to collateral estoppel in his license revocation hearing as to whether he engaged in non-consensual sexual conduct with a student since there was little risk of an erroneous deprivation of his right and the state had an interest in expeditiously barring contact between students and teachers who may be dangerous to the well-being of children.

When faced with the difficult matter of revoking teaching certificates, some courts refused to do so if such penalties would have been disproportionate to the offenses[67] or, as exemplified below, officials did not protect the due process rights of teachers. Even as they exercise their authority to revoke certifications, state officials must establish cause[68] and appropriate procedural due process since educators may have protected property interests in their certification.[69] Insofar as revocation of an educator's certification deprives one of employment, the courts carefully explore the procedures used in taking such steps. The considerations of required procedures before discharge from a position, discussed in Chapter 11, apply here, and must be augmented as warranted by the more serious penalty of the loss of certification.

As reflected in the next four cases, courts considered different procedural issues that arise in conducting certificate revocation hearings. In a dramatic fact pattern, an appellate court in Wisconsin reinstated the licenses of a teacher-social worker who was acquitted of all criminal

64. *Wax v. Horne*, 844 So.2d 797 [177 Educ. L. Rep. 699] (Fla. Dist. Ct. App.2003).

65. *Stueber v. Gallagher*, 812 So.2d 454 [164 Educ. L. Rep. 496] (Fla. Dist. Ct. App. 2002). *But see Bowalick v. Commonwealth*, 840 A.2d 519 [184 Educ. L. Rep. 903] (Pa. Cmwlth. Ct. 2004) (declaring that a teacher who was convicted of assault over a domestic dispute with his wife was entitled to a hearing as to whether his behavior met the statutory definition of moral turpitude necessary to revoke his certification).

66. *Falgren v. State Bd. of Teaching*, 545 N.W.2d 901 [108 Educ. L. Rep. 890] (Minn.1996).

67. *McKinney v. Castor*, 667 So.2d 387 [107 Educ. L. Rep. 402] (Fla.Dist.Ct.App. 1995) (rejecting a lifetime revocation of a principal's certificate as inappropriate in a disagreement over monitoring prescription drugs that were dispensed to students).

68. *Brown v. South Carolina State Bd. of Educ.*, 391 S.E.2d 866 [60 Educ. L. Rep. 1004] (S.C. 1990); *Joyell v. Commissioner of Educ.*, 696 A.2d 1039 [119 Educ. L. Rep. 1078] (Conn. Ct. App.1997).

69. *Scott v. Stewart*, 560 S.E.2d 260 (W.Va.2001); *Gee v. Professional Practices Comm'n*, 491 S.E.2d 375 [121 Educ. L. Rep. 849] (Ga.1997).

charges other than carrying a concealed weapon following an incident in which she fatally shot her former son-in-law.[70] The court was of the view that the teacher's shooting of her son-in-law, in order to protect her daughter and granddaughters from threats he made on their lives, and the carrying of a concealed weapon, were not "immoral conduct" justifying the revocation of her licenses. Moreover, the court contended that the unconscionable pattern of delay and deception by officials in the state's department of public instruction on remand of an earlier judgment violated the teacher's rights to due process.

An appellate court in Pennsylvania reinstated the certificate of a teacher who was accused of engaging in sexual intercourse with a child under the age of eighteen and furnishing alcoholic beverages to persons under the age of twenty-one in the presence of her nine-year-old son.[71] The court decreed that the Professional Standards and Practices Commission, in acting solely on the basis of an indictment, and the nature of the charges against her, violated the teacher's constitutional rights to due process by depriving her of a property interest without providing a meaningful pre-or post-deprivation hearing.

In California, an appellate court affirmed that a teacher who was being investigated for sexual misconduct with students had no statutory or due process right to obtain the addresses and other identifying information of the complainant and witnesses or to cross-examine these individuals.[72] The court rejected the teacher's request for the material in declaring that his doing so would have exceeded the scope of protections afforded in the state statute dealing with such allegations.

An appellate court in New York affirmed the revocation of a teacher's certification for engaging in inappropriate conduct with male students even though he admitted to having done so only after a private investigator who worked for the board falsely told him that there was incriminating evidence of his behavior and that if he failed to admit it or if he sought counsel, the board would pursue a criminal conviction rather than merely seek his resignation.[73] The court specified that since the revocation process was designed not to punish the teacher, but rather to protect the welfare of his students, his admission of improper sexual activity could have been used as evidence supporting the removal of his certification.

Certificates in Relation to Contracts

To the extent that educators lacking certification are not competent to enter contracts with school boards,[74] such agreements are of no legal

70. *Epstein v. Benson*, 618 N.W.2d 224 [147 Educ. L. Rep. 1059] (Wis.Ct.App.2000).

71. *Slater v. Pennsylvania Dep't of Educ.*, 725 A.2d 1248 [133 Educ. L. Rep. 521] (Pa. Cmwlth. Ct.1999).

72. *California Teachers Ass'n v. California Comm'n on Teacher Credentialing*, 4 Cal.Rptr.3d 369 [180 Educ. L. Rep. 239] (Cal. Ct. App.2003).

73. *Stedronsky v. Sobol*, 572 N.Y.S.2d 445 [68 Educ. L. Rep. 1089] (N.Y. App. Div.1991).

74. *Seamonds v. School Dist. No. 14, Fremont County*, 68 P.2d 149 (Wyo.1937).

effect.[75] In addition, as highlighted by a case from the Court of Appeals of New York, state law typically prevents boards from using school funds to pay individuals who lack valid certificates.[76] To this end, in an older case, Kentucky's highest court explained that a teacher who neither had certification nor was eligible for it since she had not reached her eighteenth birthday at the start of a school year, was ineligible to receive a salary before she turned eighteen.[77] The court conceded that the board would have to pay her for the teaching she did after her birthday and the receipt of her certification.[78] Later, an appellate court in New York was persuaded that a probationary teacher's full-time appointment could have been terminated since she lacked certification to serve as an elementary school counselor.[79] The court concluded that even though the teacher did not receive the requisite notice that her contract was being terminated, she was ineligible for back pay since she was unqualified for the job she performed.

On the other hand, an appellate court in Pennsylvania stated that a teacher whose certificate expired and was not renewed due to "bureaucratic delays" could not be dismissed on this basis.[80] However, where a teacher is responsible for the lack of certification, a board may terminate an individual's contract.[81] In such a case, where a teacher was permitted to work temporarily after having passed an examination under a special act, the Supreme Judicial Court of Massachusetts affirmed that his school committee had the right not to renew his contract because he neither sought, nor obtained, certification.[82]

Where a teacher who taught fourth grade for eighteen years was offered a contract to teach seventh and eighth grades, she claimed that her board violated the state's tenure law since she was not qualified for those grades. The Supreme Court of South Dakota discerned, as a matter of law, that since the teacher was qualified because her certificate encompassed the grades for which the board had the power to offer her an assignment, her refusal meant that her statutory rights expired.[83]

Employment

Generally

As noted earlier, teaching certificates attest that individuals have met the minimum state qualifications to apply for jobs in public schools;

75. *Goose River Bank v. Willow Lake School Township*, 44 N.W. 1002 (N.D.1890).

76. *Meliti v. Nyquist*, 391 N.Y.S.2d 398 (N.Y.1976).

77. *Floyd County Bd. of Educ. v. Slone*, 307 S.W.2d 912 (Ky.1957). *See also Flanary v. Barrett*, 143 S.W. 38 (Ky.1912).

78. *See also Sorenson v. School Dist. No. 28*, 418 P.2d 1004 (Wyo.1966) (denying a salary for a teacher who lacked certification).

79. *Sullivan v. Windham–Ashland–Jewett Cent. School Dist.*, 628 N.Y.S.2d 454 [101 Educ. L. Rep. 1007] (N.Y.App.Div. 1995).

80. *Pointek v. Elk Lake School Dist.*, 360 A.2d 804 (Pa.Cmwlth.Ct.1976).

81. *Brubaker v. Community Unit School Dist. No. 16, Sangamon and Morgan Counties*, 360 N.E.2d 1228 (Ill.Ct.App.1977).

82. *Luz v. School Comm. of Lowell*, 313 N.E.2d 925 (Mass.1974).

83. *Collins v. Wakonda Indep. School Dist. No. 1*, 252 N.W.2d 646 (S.D.1977). *See also Enstad v. North Cent. of Barnes Pub. School Dist. No. 65*, 268 N.W.2d 126 (N.D. 1978).

they do not attest to the skill levels of candidates. Where state law requires educators to be certified, local boards may neither employ staff who do not meet this standard nor use school funds to pay such individuals.

Local boards may require teachers to have additional qualifications such as extra course preparations[84] or certifications[85] beyond what is required by law as long as they are neither arbitrary nor capricious, are reasonably related to the jobs they seek, and are not barred by constitutional or statutory considerations. For example, in *Harrah Independent School District v. Martin*,[86] the Supreme Court affirmed that a school board in Oklahoma could choose not to renew the contract of a teacher who was aware of, but refused to, comply with a policy, enacted pursuant to state law, requiring her to participate in continuing education requirements. In a dispute with constitutional ramifications, *Shelton v. Tucker*,[87] the Court held that a school board in Arkansas could not require job applicants to list the names of all organizations that they were members of because doing so would have unduly restricted their freedom of association.

Where state laws require boards to act on employee nominations by superintendents, they still retain the power to set qualifications. In such a situation, under a Florida statute that stipulated that a superintendent's recommendations could only be rejected for good cause, an appellate court affirmed that a board could refuse to appoint an administrator who had a master's degree in business administration but no experience in either school finance or a school system.[88] Subsequently, when a superintendent refused to re-nominate a painter based on reasonable suspicion that he violated board policy by using drugs and rejected the superintendent's options of help, another appellate court in Florida affirmed that the board need not re-hire the employee.[89] The court reflected that since only the superintendent had the authority to nominate an individual, and had not done so, the board was not free to act.

Discriminatory Employment Practices

Title VII of the Civil Rights Act of 1964 (Title VII)[90] is the most significant federal anti-discrimination statute dealing with employment. In relevant part, Title VII reads that:

It shall be an unlawful employment practice for an employer—

84. *Montgomery County Bd. of Educ. v. Messer*, 79 S.W.2d 224 (Ky.1935).

85. *Cowen v. Harrison County Bd. of Educ.*, 465 S.E.2d 648 [106 Educ. L. Rep. 383] (W.Va. 1995).

86. 440 U.S. 194, 99 S.Ct. 1062, 59 L.Ed.2d 248 (1979). [Case No. 63]

87. 364 U.S. 479, 81 S.Ct. 247, 5 L.Ed.2d 231 (1960).

88. *Sinclair v. School Bd. of Baker County*, 354 So.2d 916 (Fla.Dist.Ct.App. 1978).

89. *Cox v. School Bd. of Osceola County*, 669 So.2d 353 [107 Educ. L. Rep. 1066] (Fla.Dist. Ct.App.1996).

90. 42 U.S.C.A. §§ 2000 *et seq.*

(1) to fail or refuse to hire or to discharge any individual, or otherwise to discriminate against any individual with respect to his compensation, terms, conditions, or privileges of employment, because of such individual's race, color, religion, sex, or national origin; or

(2) to limit, segregate, or classify his employees or applicants for employment in any way which would deprive or tend to deprive any individual of employment opportunities or otherwise adversely affect his status as an employee, because of such individual's race, color, religion, sex, or national origin.[91]

The Pregnancy Discrimination Act, enacted in response to two Supreme Court cases which upheld the denial of pregnancy-related benefits,[92] now incorporated into Title VII, prohibits discrimination "... on the basis of pregnancy, childbirth, or related medical conditions...."[93] Three other major federal laws also forbid workplace discrimination. The Age Discrimination in Employment Act[94] protects workers who are forty or over. The ADA, reflecting language of Section 504, requires employers to make reasonable accommodation for employees who are otherwise qualified to work. The Family and Medical Leave Act[95] provides a range of protections for employees who need to take time off to care for family members or themselves who are in need of medical attention.

A second category of statutes outlaw discrimination in programs receiving federal financial aid. The most notable of these is Title VI of the Civil Rights Act of 1964 (Title VI), according to which "[n]o person in the United States shall, on the ground of race, color, or national origin, be excluded from participation in, be denied the benefits of, or be subjected to discrimination under any program or activity receiving Federal financial assistance."[96] Litigation involving Titles VI and VII are often filed together. Another major federal law in this regard is Section 504, cited earlier, which forbids discrimination against individuals with disabilities. In addition, although Title IX of the Educational Amendments of 1972 (Title IX)[97] proscribes discrimination based on gender, it is beyond the scope of this chapter since it applies primarily to students, not employees. Insofar as most litigation involving employment focuses on Title VII, it receives the lion's share of attention in this chapter.

Title VII Generally

The Supreme Court crafted two different tests for alleged discrimination in the workplace involving Title VII: disparate impact and dispa-

---

91. 42 U.S.C.A. § 2000e–2(a).

92. *Geduldig v. Aiello*, 417 U.S. 484, 94 S.Ct. 2485, 41 L.Ed.2d 256 (1974) (under the Fourteenth Amendment); *General Elec. Co. v. Gilbert*, 429 U.S. 125, 97 S.Ct. 401, 50 L.Ed.2d 343 (1976) (under Title VII).

93. 42 U.S.C.A. § 2000e(k).

94. 29 U.S.C.A. §§ 621 *et seq.* Portions of this statute are in the appendix.

95. 29 U.S.C.A. §§ 2611 *et seq.*

96. 42 U.S.C.A. § 2000d. This statute is in the appendix.

97. 20 U.S.C.A. § 1681. Portions of this statute are in the appendix.

rate treatment, both of which can be present in the same claim. In *Griggs v. Duke Power Company (Griggs)*,[98] the Court interpreted Title VII as prohibiting not only overt discrimination, but also practices that appear to be fair in form but discriminatory in their impact. In other words, the Court proscribed what appear to be otherwise neutral criteria that are shown, often through reliance on quantitative data, to have a disparate impact on members of a particular group or class. At issue in *Griggs* was a power company in North Carolina's requirement that all of its employees have a high school education and perform satisfactorily on tests before being assigned to departments that had, in the past, practiced racial discrimination. In *Griggs,* the Court struck down both of the company's requirements since they were unrelated to successful job performance and had a disparate impact on African Americans.[99] The Court ruled that Congress did not command that persons be hired simply since they were formerly subject to discrimination or because they were members of a minority group. Rather, the Court decided that employers had to remove artificial, arbitrary, or unnecessary barriers which discriminate on the basis of race or other impermissible classifications.

In explicating its disparate impact standard, in *Washington v. Davis*,[100] the Court was of the opinion that while this theory serves as a sufficient basis on which to present a prima facie case of employment discrimination under Title VII, plaintiffs also had to offer proof of intent to discriminate in order to prevail in equal protection claims. In a controversy over the use of written examinations for police officer candidates, the Court found that while the test had a disparate impact on minority candidates, it was not unlawful. The Court upheld the use of examinations because there was no evidence that officials acted with a discriminatory purpose. The Court was also satisfied that the positive relationship between the test results and training school performances of candidates was sufficient to validate their use even aside from their possible relationship to actual job duties as police officers. Insofar as the dispute arose in Washington, D.C., the case was filed under the Fifth Amendment, which applies to the federal government, rather than the Fourteenth Amendment, which applies to states.

The Court clarified the steps and burdens of proof in Title VII cases involving disparate treatment, wherein individuals allege treatment different from other similarly situated individuals, in *McDonnell Douglas Corp. v. Green (McDonnell Douglas)*.[101] In Title VII cases, plaintiffs must prove that employers acted with intent; they are not required to do so in disputes relying on the disparate impact theory. *McDonnell Douglas* was filed by a civil rights activist who, after engaging in disruptive and illegal

---

98. 401 U.S. 424, 91 S.Ct. 849, 28 L.Ed.2d 158 (1971).

99. *But see United States v. State of S.C.,* 445 F.Supp. 1094 (D.S.C.1977), *aff'd, sub nom. National Educ. Ass'n v. United States,* 434 U.S. 1026, 98 S.Ct. 756, 54 L.Ed.2d 775 (1978) (upholding the use of the NTE as a valid measure for evaluating

the competence of teacher candidates). [Case No. 62]

100. 426 U.S. 229, 96 S.Ct. 2040, 48 L.Ed.2d 597 (1976).

101. 411 U.S. 792, 93 S.Ct. 1817, 36 L.Ed.2d 668 (1973). *See also Texas Dep't of Community Affairs v. Burdine,* 450 U.S. 248, 101 S.Ct. 1089, 67 L.Ed.2d 207 (1981).

activity as part of his protest against being dismissed by an airplane manufacturer, claimed that the firm's general hiring practices were racially motivated. Vacating and remanding in favor of the employee, the Court determined that Title VII did not restrict his right to sue to only those charges on which the Equal Employment Opportunity Commission (EEOC) had made findings of reasonable cause.

Based on the Court's Title VII jurisprudence in cases alleging disparate treatment, the initial burden is on plaintiffs to establish prima facie cases of discrimination by filing claims with the EEOC within 300 days of when the alleged unlawful employment practice occurred.[102] Such a complaint must allege the existence of five elements, depending on whether one merges the last two into one or leaves them as separate items. The elements are membership in a protected class; application for a position; qualification for the job; rejection; and an employer continues to seek applicants with the plaintiff's qualifications. These elements, with appropriate adaptations, constitute a prima facie case of discrimination for adverse personnel decisions.

If plaintiffs establish prima facie cases, defendants must articulate legitimate, nondiscriminatory reasons for acting such as bona fide occupational qualifications. If defendants can do so, they raise genuine issues of fact, which returns the burden to plaintiffs to prove that the explanations were pretexts.[103] As demonstrated by a case from the Eleventh Circuit, if a plaintiff files suit after having adjudicated a claim before the EEOC, one may bring only those claims that were included in her EEOC charge or that are likely, reasonably related, or growing out of such allegations.[104] In affirming that an applicant for a custodial position was properly dismissed, the court indicated that the rule was designed to afford both the EEOC and an employer the chance to settle a dispute and to give the latter fair notice of the conduct about which an individual is complaining.

As can be expected, plaintiffs often rely on statistics in attempting to prove that defendants engaged in patterns or practices of employment discrimination. In these instances, gross statistical disparities among groups may constitute prima facie proof of patterns or practices of discrimination. Even so, comparisons must be made by qualified professionals in the context of proper labor markets. Plaintiffs must also demonstrate that discrimination was the defendants' standard operating procedure, "the regular rather than the unusual practice."[105]

Employment actions need not be based solely on objective criteria. While the use of subjective criteria may afford evidence of discrimination, since it is not conclusive,[106] the same types of statistical analyses

---

102. 42 U.S.C.A.§ 2000e–5(e)(1). *See, e.g., Black v. Columbus Pub. Schools,* 211 F.Supp.2d 975 [168 Educ. L. Rep. 202] (S.D. Ohio 2002), *aff'd in relevant part,* 79 Fed. Appx. 735 [182 Educ. L. Rep. 785] (6th Cir. 2003).

103. *See St. Mary's Honor Ctr. v. Hicks,* 509 U.S. 502, 113 S.Ct. 2742, 125 L.Ed.2d 407 (1993) (reiterating that a plaintiff bears the ultimate burden of proof in a discrimination case).

104. *Geldon v. South Milwaukee School Dist.,* 414 F.3d 817 [199 Educ. L. Rep. 625] (7th Cir. 2005).

105. *International Brotherhood of Teamsters v. United States,* 431 U.S. 324, 336, 97 S.Ct. 1843, 52 L.Ed.2d 396 (1977).

106. *McCarthney v. Griffin–Spaulding County Bd. of Educ.,* 791 F.2d 1549 [32 Educ. L. Rep. 910] (11th Cir.1986).

apply to results of subjective and objective methods,[107] both of which must be defensible even if they are not the best options available. Yet, overall or bottom-line results do not suffice as a defense against the use of discriminatory preliminary elements since "[t]he principal focus of [Title VII] is the protection of the individual employee, rather than the protection of the minority group as a whole."[108]

In the words of the Fourth Circuit, "Title VII is not a 'bad acts' statute."[109] If an act or policy impacts disproportionately on members of a protected group, it may run afoul of Title VII.[110] For instance, the Fourth Circuit directed a school board in Virginia to discontinue its practice of word-of-mouth hiring and hiring of relatives because insofar as most of its employees were predominantly white, this approach had a disparate impact on minorities.[111]

Occasionally, adverse employment actions are based on several factors, only one of which is illegal. In these so-called mixed-motive cases, once Title VII plaintiffs prove that illegal elements played a part in employment actions, defendants can prevail only by showing that they would have acted in the same way even if the forbidden considerations were not part of the decision-making process.[112] In a case with mixed motives and mixed results, the Eleventh Circuit recognized that while a school board in Alabama offered an affirmative defense as to why it chose not to hire an African American, he might have been entitled to damages if he could have shown that the board's action was based on racial discrimination.[113]

Rather than engage in an exhaustive discussion of disputes arising under Title VII, insofar as the substantive analysis does not vary significantly from one case to another, the following headings review representative disputes from among the literally thousands of actions that have been litigated under this far-reaching statute. Many discrimination claims also can be filed under state statutes that are modeled after Title VII.

Race/National Origin

In *Hazelwood School District v. United States*,[114] the Supreme Court considered the relationship between Title VII and racial discrimination

107. *Watson v. Fort Worth Bank and Trust*, 487 U.S. 977, 108 S.Ct. 2777, 101 L.Ed.2d 827 (1988).

108. *Connecticut v. Teal*, 457 U.S. 440, 453, 102 S.Ct. 2525, 73 L.Ed.2d 130 (1982).

109. *Holder v. City of Raleigh*, 867 F.2d 823, 828 (4th Cir.1989).

110. *See, e.g., Knight v. Hayward Unified School Dist.*, 33 Cal.Rptr.3d 287 [201 Educ. L. Rep. 275] (Cal. Ct. App. 2005) (reiterating the general rule in rejecting the claim that a health insurance company's refusal to pay for in vitro fertilization constituted disability discrimination because it applied equally to all).

111. *Thomas v. Washington County School Bd.*, 915 F.2d 922 [63 Educ. L. Rep. 76] (4th Cir. 1990). [Case No. 64]

112. *See Price Waterhouse v. Hopkins*, 490 U.S. 228, 109 S.Ct. 1775, 104 L.Ed.2d 268 (1989), as modified by the Civil Rights Act of 1991. The Act provides that if an employer demonstrates that it would have taken the same action absent the discriminatory factor, a plaintiff remains eligible for attorney fees and costs.

113. *Harris v. Shelby County Bd. of Educ.*, 99 F.3d 1078 [113 Educ. L. Rep. 1124] (11th Cir. 1996).

114. 433 U.S. 299, 97 S.Ct. 2736, 53 L.Ed.2d 768 (1977).

in teacher employment. The Court thought that a federal trial court in Missouri misconceived the role of statistics in employment discrimination cases in its racial comparison of the district's teachers and students. The Court reasoned that the Eighth Circuit correctly concluded that the proper comparison should have been between the racial compositions of the teaching staff and the qualified public school teacher population in the labor market. Despite this, the Court vacated and remanded on the ground that the Eighth Circuit erred in substituting its judgment for that of the trial court in declaring that the board engaged in a pattern or practice of discrimination. The Court also directed the trial judge to determine the proper labor market area for comparison. Further, the Eighth Circuit remanded a dispute from Arkansas for a consideration of the relevant labor market in evaluating the propriety of the proportionality requirement that a federal trial court imposed on a school board in a class action discrimination suit by African American teachers.[115] The next year, the Fifth Circuit affirmed that African American teachers in Mississippi failed to prove that the board in a formerly segregated district had not discontinued its discriminatory employment practices where the percentages of black teachers increased over the time at issue and there was no evidence supporting their claim that they were subjected to discriminatory treatment.[116]

To the extent that Title VII cases involving race and national origin often deal with almost identical issues, they are addressed together under this heading. Courts reviewed a variety of procedural and substantive disputes, more often than not entering judgments in favor of school boards. Regarding procedural matters, courts required individuals to file complaints in a timely manner,[117] dismissed allegations for failure to state a claim in a complaint that was much longer than it needed to be,[118] and clarified the standards for the admissibility of evidence.[119]

Courts allowed suits to proceed where employees met the burden of presenting prima facie cases of racial discrimination such as where an African American was dismissed for taking part in a protest over the firing of another African American[120] and when a white teacher with seventeen years of experience was demoted from the position as chair of her department in favor of an African American with less experience and seniority.[121] In a case involving discrimination based on national origin, a federal trial court in Ohio asserted that a Mexican American custodian presented a prima facie case where a supervisor made a series of derogatory remarks, over a period of twenty-two years, despite her

115. *Scoggins v. Board of Educ. of Nashville, Arkansas Pub. Schools*, 853 F.2d 1472 [48 Educ. L. Rep. 772] (8th Cir.1988).

116. *Quarles v. Oxford Mun. Separate School Dist.*, 868 F.2d 750 [52 Educ. L. Rep. 38] (5th Cir.1989).

117. *Black v. Columbus Pub. Schools*, 211 F.Supp.2d 975 [168 Educ. L. Rep. 202] (S.D.Ohio 2002).

118. *Bennett v. Schmidt*, 153 F.3d 516 [129 Educ. L. Rep. 32] (7th Cir.1998).

119. *Freeman v. Madison Metropolitan School Dist.*, 231 F.3d 374 [148 Educ. L. Rep. 629] (7th Cir.2000).

120. *Copeland v. Rosen*, 38 F.Supp.2d 298 [133 Educ. L. Rep. 885] (S.D.N.Y.1999).

121. *Mohr v. Chicago School Reform Bd. of Trustees*, 99 F.Supp.2d 934 [145 Educ. L. Rep. 280] (N.D.Ill.2000).

having lodged unsuccessful complaints with her employer.[122] Conversely, a federal trial court in Kansas rejected a claim of discrimination based on national origin when school officials chose not to renew a teacher's contract.[123] The court acknowledged that since the teacher, who spoke with a Hispanic accent, failed to address concerns that she spoke too rapidly and that her accent made it difficult for students to follow her, her self-appraisal of her teaching skills was insufficient to create genuine issues of material fact which could have precluded the board's motion for summary judgment.

Examples of unsuccessful Title VII claims included cases where an African American employee was disciplined differently from a white worker who committed a similar offense but was unable to show that the board's action was a pretext for discrimination,[124] where a superintendent presented race neutral, non-pretextual reasons for terminating the contract of a principal who failed to carry out his duties and to maintain discipline in a school,[125] where employees could not prove that staff members who used racial epithets were treated differently,[126] when a superintendent's ill-advised remarks about Native Americans were insufficient to establish discriminatory intent in discharging a teacher who was late to work regularly,[127] and where a minority applicant was not hired by an all-white interview team since she failed to establish a prima facie claim of disparate impact and her attorney misrepresented statistical data.[128] Other cases addressed disputes such as where a white substitute teacher claimed that a board's refusal to hire her for a full-time job was motivated by race,[129] where an applicant failed to present evidence to support her claim that she was not hired for a teaching position because she was both a Muslim and Lebanese,[130] where an African American teacher failed to prove that she met a school board's legitimate performance expectations,[131] and where an African American

---

122. *Lagunovich v. Findlay City School Sys.*, 181 F.Supp.2d 753 [161 Educ. L. Rep. 458] (N.D.Ohio 2001). *See also Lewis v. State of Del. Dep't of Pub. Instruction*, 948 F.Supp. 352 [115 Educ. L. Rep. 683] (D.Del. 1996). *But see Salvadori v. Franklin School Dist.*, 293 F.3d 989 [166 Educ. L. Rep. 454] (7th Cir.2002) (affirming that a Fillipana teacher was unable to prove that the her dismissal was pretextual where school officials offered evidence that she had not performed satisfactorily).

123. *Forsythe v. Board of Educ. of Unified School Dist. No. 489*, 956 F.Supp. 927 [117 Educ. L. Rep. 161] (D.Kan.1997), *clarification denied*, 174 F.R.D. 694 (D.Kan. 1997).

124. *Silvera v. Orange County School Bd.*, 244 F.3d 1253 [152 Educ. L. Rep. 75] (11th Cir. 2001), *cert. denied*, 534 U.S. 976, 122 S.Ct. 402, 151 L.Ed.2d 305 (2001), *reh'g denied*, 535 U.S. 1013, 122 S.Ct. 1598, 152 L.Ed.2d 513 (2002). *See also Conward v. Cambridge School Comm.*, 171 F.3d 12 [133 Educ. L. Rep. 367] (1st Cir.1999).

125. *Joseph v. New York City Bd. of Educ.*, 171 F.3d 87 [133 Educ. L. Rep. 380] (2d Cir.1999), *cert. denied*, 528 U.S. 876, 120 S.Ct. 182, 145 L.Ed.2d 154 (1999).

126. *Sims-Eiland v. Detroit Bd. of Educ.*, 173 F.Supp.2d 682 [159 Educ. L. Rep. 620] (E.D. Mich. 2001); *Daso v. The Grafton School*, 181 F.Supp.2d 485, 493 [161 Educ. L. Rep. 388] (D.Md.2002).

127. *Clearwater v. Independent School Dist. No. 166*, 231 F.3d 1122 [148 Educ. L. Rep. 728] (8th Cir.2000).

128. *Bennett v. Roberts*, 295 F.3d 687 [167 Educ. L. Rep. 47] (7th Cir.2002).

129. *Koszola v. Board of Educ. of City of Chicago*, 385 F.3d 1104 [192 Educ. L. Rep. 372] (7th Cir. 2004).

130. *Raad v. Alaska State Comm'n for Human Rights*, 86 P.3d 899 [186 Educ. L. Rep. 551] (Alaska 2004).

131. *Shanklin v. Fitzgerald*, 397 F.3d 596 [195 Educ. L. Rep. 103] (8th Cir. 2005), *reh'g denied* (2005).

custodian whose board claimed that he falsified his time record alleged that he was dismissed for complaining that his children, who attended school in the district, were subject to racial bullying and harassment.[132]

Religion

In perhaps its most important case involving the religious rights of public school employees, *Ansonia Board of Education v. Philbrook (Ansonia)*[133] the Supreme Court interpreted Title VII as requiring school boards to make reasonable accommodations to meet the religious needs of staff, even if they are not the ones that the employees sought. Where a teacher in Connecticut needed, on average, six days per school year to fulfill religious duties to his church by visiting hospital patients, he challenged his board's refusal to modify provisions in its collective bargaining agreement which permitted him to use only three of his eighteen paid days of leave to do so. The teacher suggested that the board either permit him to use six days for his religious needs or allow him to pay for his own substitute when absent. As the dispute continued, the teacher stopped taking unauthorized leave, scheduled required hospital visits on church holy days, and worked on holy days. The Court wrote that Title VII did not require the board to prove that the teacher's alternatives would have caused it an undue hardship. Rather, the Court posited that once school officials offered the teacher a reasonable accommodation, even if it was unacceptable, then they were not required to do anything else. The Court added that even if the teacher had to take days off without pay, the option other than using the three days stipulated in his contract, this had no direct impact on his employment status. On remand, the Second Circuit contended that, as administered, the bargaining agreement did not discriminate against the teacher on the basis of religion.[134]

Another case involving the nexus between the religious rights of teachers under the First Amendment and collective bargaining agreements arose in New York. An appellate court ascertained that a provision in a bargaining contract that granted teachers a maximum of three days per year for religious observance was constitutional.[135] When board officials tried to have the teachers use personal time rather than the days allotted in the agreement, the court commented that the provision did not offend the Establishment Clause because it neither impermissibly advanced religion by coercing union members to profess a religious belief nor imposed any requirements regarding which religious holidays might be invoked.

In the first of two other cases that were not unlike *Ansonia*, a federal trial court in Texas granted a school board's motion for summary

---

132. *Dockery v. Unified School Dist. No. 231*, 382 F.Supp.2d 1234 [201 Educ. L. Rep. 582] (D. Kan. 2005).

133. 479 U.S. 60, 107 S.Ct. 367, 93 L.Ed.2d 305 [35 Educ. L. Rep. 365] (1986).

134. *Philbrook v. Ansonia Bd. of Educ.*, 925 F.2d 47 [65 Educ. L. Rep. 715] (2d Cir.1991), *cert. denied*, 501 U.S. 1218, 111 S.Ct. 2828, 115 L.Ed.2d 998 (1991).

135. *Maine-Endwell Teachers' Ass'n v. Board of Educ.*, 771 N.Y.S.2d 246 [185 Educ. L. Rep. 327] (N.Y. App. Div. 2004).

judgment in a dispute filed by a former instructor. When the instructor refused to meet his job obligation of working at least one full weekend each month since his religious beliefs prevented him from doing so between sunset on Friday and Saturday, the board terminated his employment.[136] The court remarked that insofar as the board proved that requiring other employees to work in place of the instructor would have imposed an undue hardship on them, his claim was without merit.[137] In like fashion, the Sixth Circuit affirmed that a school board in Ohio was not liable under Title VII for failing to accommodate a carpenter's religious observance of the Sabbath since such an accommodation, which would have permitted him to work on Sundays, rather than Saturdays, would have been an undue burden on the school system.[138] The court was of the view that the undue burden arose not only because the carpenter's collective bargaining agreement dictated that people working Sunday had to be paid double-time, while staff who worked on Saturday were only paid time-and-a-half, but also due to the fact that even if he was only paid time-and-a-half for Sunday work, the board would have had to pay at least one other employee double-time to open the building. The court concluded that since this would have amounted to more than de minimis costs, it was sufficient to defeat the carpenter's religious accommodation claim.

A case from California highlighted the issue of the extent to which public employees can express their religious preferences in the workplace. The Ninth Circuit invalidated a prohibition against permitting an employee of the state department of education to display religious materials on the interior walls of his cubbyhole at work.[139] The court observed that such a restriction was unnecessary to serve the department's interest in efficiency where there was no evidence of disruption in general or that any employee but the plaintiff engaged in the religious activity.

Claims of religious discrimination under Title VII often fail where school officials provide legitimate, non-discriminatory rationales for their actions. In such a case, a former high school paraprofessional sued his ex-principal, claiming that he was dismissed from his job in violation not only of his right to his freedom to practice his Islamic faith but also without due process.[140] In granting the principal's motion for summary judgment, a federal trial court in New York maintained that the paraprofessional was unable to prove one of the elements of a prima facie case, that he performed his duties satisfactorily. The court pointed out that during the two years prior to his dismissal, the paraprofessional's

136. *Bynum v. Fort Worth Indep. School Dist.*, 41 F.Supp.2d 641 [134 Educ. L. Rep. 860] (N.D. Tex.1999).

137. *See also Favero v. Huntsville Indep. School Dist.*, 939 F.Supp. 1281 [113 Educ. L. Rep. 747] (S.D.Tex.1996), *aff'd without reported opinion*, 110 F.3d 793 (5th Cir.1997) (affirming that a board did not have to give bus drivers extra leave to participate in religious observances since this would have imposed an undue hardship).

138. *Creusere v. Board of Educ. of City School Dist. of City of Cincinnati*, 88 Fed. Appx. 813 [185 Educ. L. Rep. 500] (6th Cir. 2003).

139. *Tucker v. California Dep't of Educ.*, 97 F.3d 1204 [113 Educ. L. Rep. 102] (9th Cir. 1996).

140. *Sharif v. Buck*, 338 F.Supp.2d 435 [192 Educ. L. Rep. 762] (W.D.N.Y. 2004).

evaluations revealed that he needed to improve and that he received verbal and written warnings along with two written reprimands for neglect of duty and insubordination. The court also commented that the principal was not liable for violating the paraprofessional's right to due process because there was no evidence that he was personally involved insofar as the operative collective bargaining required only that the administrator refer the matter to the board's department of human resources which had the duty to notify the employee about his dismissal.

Religious disputes have also arisen over instructional issues. For example, an appellate court in California rejected the claim of a teacher who alleged that officials violated his rights to free speech when they directed him not to talk about religion during the school day where he refused to teach about evolution[141] while a court in Minnesota upheld a board's reassigning a teacher to teach a different biology course after he refused to do so.[142] In addition, the Seventh Circuit affirmed that school officials in Indiana did not violate an individual's rights when they removed his name from an approved list of substitutes because he insisted on presenting his own religious views in class.[143] Along the same line, a federal trial court in California largely rejected the claims of an elementary school teacher who alleged that officials violated his rights by not permitting him to use supplemental classroom materials with religious content and talking about religion with his students.[144] However, the court stated that if the plaintiff could prove that officials permitted other similarly situated teachers to include religious expression in their lessons and supplemental handouts but prevented him from doing so, then he would have had evidence to present a case that they violated his right to equal protection.

On a different matter, in cases not involving Title VII, the Ninth Circuit noted that a school board in Idaho violated the religious rights of an acting assistant principal because he and his wife chose to home school their children.[145] The court was convinced that the board's employment action was nothing more than punishing the plaintiff for exercising his right to the free exercise of religion. Subsequently, the Sixth Circuit affirmed that a school superintendent could be personally liable for refusing to hire a substitute teacher to a promised full-time position unless the teacher removed his child from a Catholic school and enrolled him in a public school.[146] According to the court, the teacher not only had a protected constitutional right to liberty in directing the

141. *Peloza v. Capistrano Unified School Dist.*, 37 F.3d 517 [94 Educ. L. Rep. 1159] (9th Cir. 1994), *cert. denied*, 515 U.S. 1173, 115 S.Ct. 2640, 132 L.Ed.2d 878 (1995).

142. *LeVake v. Independent School Dist. No. 656*, 625 N.W.2d 502 [153 Educ. L. Rep. 356] (Minn. Ct. App. 2001), *review denied* (2001), *cert. denied*, 534 U.S. 1081, 122 S.Ct. 814, 151 L.Ed.2d 698 (2002).

143. *Helland v. South Bend Community School Corp.*, 93 F.3d 327 [111 Educ. L. Rep. 1108] (7th Cir. 1996).

144. *Williams v. Vidmar*, 367 F.Supp.2d 1265 [198 Educ. L. Rep. 292] (N.D. Cal. 2005).

145. *Peterson v. Minidoka County School Dist. No. 331*, 118 F.3d 1351 [120 Educ. L. Rep. 71] (9th Cir.1997), *opinion amended*, 132 F.3d 1258 (9th Cir.1997).

146. *Barrett v. Steubenville City Schools*, 388 F.3d 967 [193 Educ. L. Rep. 124] (6th Cir. 2004), *cert. denied*, ___ U.S. ___, 126 S.Ct. 334, 163 L.Ed.2d 47 [202 Educ. L. Rep. 27] (2005).

education of his son by sending him to the school of his choice, but also that the superintendent could be liable because this right was well-established when he acted as he did. A year earlier, the Fifth Circuit judged that the claims of a teacher whose superintendent refused to hire her as an assistant principal because her son attended a religious school could proceed to trial over whether he violated her right to educate her child as she saw fit.[147]

In Arkansas, a dispute involving religion took on a different twist in a case where a teacher challenged not only a superintendent's practice of reciting prayers at mandatory teacher meetings but also that he was required to attend in-service sessions at a religious college where prayers were part of the meeting.[148] The Eighth Circuit was persuaded that a trial court abused its discretion in prohibiting prayer at meetings only when the teacher attended and directing school officials to permit him to skip any in-service training sessions where prayers would be offered. The court ordered the board to end its endorsement of a particular religious message at such meetings.

The Eighth Circuit affirmed that school officials violated the free speech rights of an elementary teacher in South Dakota by refusing her permission to meet with a Good News Club that met on school premises after school. The court reversed an earlier order that would have permitted the teacher to meet with the club, but only at schools other than where she taught. Holding that the teacher's after-school participation amounted to private speech, the court explained that the after-school participation did not put the school board at risk of violating the Establishment Clause.[149]

Sex

The judicial trend appears to be that while Title IX, which is also discussed in Chapter 13, outlaws discrimination based on sex, it is ordinarily applied to cases involving students since employees must file suit pursuant to Title VII.[150] This may change, though, in light of the Supreme Court's ruling in *Jackson v. Birmingham Board of Education* (*Jackson*).[151] In *Jackson*, the Court permitted a male to proceed with his retaliation claim that he was removed from his position as head coach of a girls' basketball team after he complained about the facilities available

---

147. *Barrow v. Greenville Indep. School Dist.*, 332 F.3d 844 [177 Educ. L. Rep. 922] (5th Cir. 2003), *reh'g and reh'g en banc denied*, 75 Fed.Appx. 982 (5th Cir. 2003), *on remand*, 2003 WL 21653871 (N.D. Tex. 2003).

148. *Warnock v. Archer*, 380 F.3d 1076 [191 Educ. L. Rep. 620] (8th Cir. 2004).

149. *Wigg v. Sioux Falls School Dist. 49–5*, 382 F.3d 807 [192 Educ. L. Rep. 15] (8th Cir. 2004), *reh'g and reh'g en banc denied* (2004).

150. *Lakoski v. James*, 66 F.3d 751 [103 Educ. L. Rep. 652] (5th Cir.1995), *cert. de-*

nied, 519 U.S. 947, 117 S.Ct. 357, 136 L.Ed.2d 249 (1996), *reh'g denied*, 519 U.S. 1035, 117 S.Ct. 598, 136 L.Ed.2d 525 (1996); *Waid v. Merrill Area Pub. Schools*, 91 F.3d 857 [111 Educ. L. Rep. 644] (7th Cir.1996), *appeal after remand*, 130 F.3d 1268 [122 Educ. L. Rep. 625] (7th Cir. 1997); *Gibson v. Hickman*, 2 F.Supp.2d 1481 [127 Educ. L. Rep. 173] (M.D. Ga.1998).

151. 544 U.S. 167, 125 S.Ct. 1497, 161 L.Ed.2d 361 (2005), *on remand*, 416 F.3d 1280 (11th Cir. 2005).

to his team. The Court was of the opinion that Title IX created a private right of action for retaliation even in the absence of express Congressional intent to do so.

Federal courts were not initially receptive to claims of sexual discrimination under Title VII.[152] As courts became open to such charges,[153] two broad theories of discrimination emerged: hostile work environment and quid pro quo harassment. In claims filed under hostile work environment, which are more numerous than quid pro quo cases, plaintiffs must prove that employers' creation of hostile and offensive working environments result in intolerable conditions. In cases of quid pro quo harassment, plaintiffs must show that defendants engaged in unwelcomed conduct of a sexual nature that was directly connected to tangible aspects of the economic benefits of employment.

The Supreme Court addressed its first case on sexual discrimination in *Meritor Savings Bank FSB v. Vinson (Meritor).*[154] In *Meritor*, a female bank employee in Washington, D.C., who went on sick leave and was fired, filed suit against officials based on her supervisor's demands for sexual relations. The employee acquiesced to the supervisor's repeated demands and allowed herself to be subjected to other forms of inappropriate sexual conduct out of fear of losing her job. The Court, discerning that Title VII is not limited to economic or tangible discrimination, affirmed that "[w]ithout question, when a supervisor sexually harasses a subordinate because of the subordinate's sex, that supervisor 'discriminate(s)' on the basis of sex"[155] and that "a claim of 'hostile environment' sex discrimination is actionable under Title VII."[156] In *Meritor,* the Court enunciated the five elements in a claim of sexual discrimination based on the existence of a hostile work environment, an offense that is ordinarily established by a series of incidents. While the same criteria also can apply in cases of quid pro quo harassment, since its parameters are more readily established than hostile work environment, discussion here is limited to the latter.

The first element in a hostile work environment sexual discrimination claim is that plaintiffs must belong to a protected category. Insofar as most suits are filed by women, this element is satisfied on its face when a claim is filed by a woman. Second, plaintiffs must have been subjected to unwelcomed sexual harassment. In other words, "the conduct must be unwelcome in the sense that the employee did not solicit or incite it, and in the sense that the employee regarded the conduct as undesirable or offensive."[157] Third, the harassment must have been based on sex. This can be established in a variety of ways such as when

152. *Barnes v. Costle*, 561 F.2d 983 (D.C.Cir.1977); *Corne v. Bausch & Lomb*, 390 F.Supp. 161 (D.Ariz.1975); *Tomkins v. Public Serv. Electric & Gas Co.*, 568 F.2d 1044 (3d Cir.1977).

153. *Rogers v. EEOC*, 454 F.2d 234 (5th Cir.1971), *cert. denied*, 406 U.S. 957, 92 S.Ct. 2058, 32 L.Ed.2d 343 (1972); *Bundy v. Jackson*, 641 F.2d 934 (D.C.Cir.1981).

154. 477 U.S. 57, 106 S.Ct. 2399, 91 L.Ed.2d 49 (1986), *on remand, sub nom. Vinson v. Taylor*, 801 F.2d 1436 (D.C.Cir. 1986).

155. *Id.* at 64.

156. *Id.* at 73.

157. *Henson v. City of Dundee*, 682 F.2d 897, 903 (11th Cir.1982).

"harassing behavior lack[s] a sexually explicit content but [is] directed at women and motivated by animus against women"[158] or by "behavior that is not directed at a particular individual or group of individuals, but is disproportionately/more offensive or demeaning to one sex."[159] Fourth, the harassment must affect a term, condition, or privilege of employment to such a degree that it creates an abusive work environment. In other words, the harassment must be so pervasive as to alter working conditions to the point that, under the totality of the circumstances, it seriously affects one's psychological well-being. The fifth element is that employers knew or should have known of the harassment but failed to take prompt remedial action.

In *Harris v. Forklift Systems (Harris)*[160] the Supreme Court elaborated on the concept of harassment through an abusive work environment in response to questions that it left unanswered in *Meritor*. *Harris* was filed by a female executive in Tennessee who quit her job after the company president made inappropriate sexual comments to her about business dealings, suggesting that she must have engaged in sexual relations with a client in order to obtain a contract. In agreeing that the president's behavior was actionable, the Court decided that whether an environment is hostile or abusive is to be determined by examining such factors as frequency and severity of the conduct as well as whether it was physically threatening or humiliating, rather than merely offensive utterances, and whether it unreasonably interfered with one's work performance. The Court thought that in order for an employer to be liable under Title VII, an abusive work environment need not seriously affect an employee's psychological well-being or lead to a tangible job loss. On remand, the Sixth Circuit and a federal trial court in Tennessee affirmed a judgment in favor of the employee.[161]

In *Oncale v. Sundowner Offshore Services (Oncale)*,[162] the Court addressed same-sex sexual harassment for the first time. The Court found that same-sex sexual harassment, involving a male roustabout on an eight-man platform crew in Louisiana who alleged that he was forcibly subjected to humiliating sex-related actions by some of his male co-workers in the presence of the rest of the crew and was physically assaulted and threatened with rape by another worker, was actionable under Title VII.[163]

Burlington Industries v. Ellerth (Burlington)[164] and *Faragher v. City of Boca Raton (Faragher)*,[165] handed down on the same day as *Oncale*,

---

158. *Robinson v. Jacksonville Shipyards*, 760 F.Supp. 1486, 1522 (M.D.Fla. 1991).

159. *Id.* at 1522–1523.

160. 510 U.S. 17, 114 S.Ct. 367, 126 L.Ed.2d 295 (1993).

161. 14 F.3d 601 (6th Cir.1993), *on remand*, 1994 WL 792661 (M.D.Tenn.1994).

162. 523 U.S. 75, 118 S.Ct. 998, 140 L.Ed.2d 201 (1998).

163. For a case of same sex harassment in a school setting, *see Madon v. Laconia*

School Dist., 952 F.Supp. 44 [116 Educ. L. Rep. 253] (D.N.H.1996) (permitting a Title VII complaint to proceed against a principal but not the school board).

164. 524 U.S. 742, 118 S.Ct. 2257, 141 L.Ed.2d 633 (1998), *on remand*, 165 F.3d 31 (7th Cir. 1998).

165. 524 U.S. 775, 118 S.Ct. 2275, 141 L.Ed.2d 662 (1998), *on remand*, 166 F.3d 1152 (11th Cir.1999).

involved similar factual circumstances dealing with retaliation. In *Burlington,* a woman in Illinois quit her job as a salesperson after a supervisor subjected her to constant sexual harassment. The Court framed the issue as whether "an employee who refuses the unwelcome and threatening sexual advances of a supervisor, yet suffers no adverse, tangible job consequences, can recover against the employer without showing the employer is negligent or otherwise at fault for the supervisor's actions."[166] Answering in the affirmative, the Court indicated that an employee who refuses a supervisor's unwelcomed and threatening sexual advances, but suffers no adverse, tangible job consequences may recover from an employer without showing that it was negligent or otherwise at fault for the supervisor's actions. The Court asserted that employers may raise affirmative defenses to liability or damages claims which require them to show that they exercised reasonable care to prevent, and promptly correct, sexually harassing behavior and employees unreasonably failed to take advantage of preventive or corrective opportunities or to otherwise avoid harm. The Court rounded out its judgment by reflecting that "[g]iven [that] our explanation that the labels quid pro quo and hostile work environment are not controlling for purposes of establishing employer liability, [the plaintiff] should have an adequate opportunity to prove she has a claim for which Burlington is liable."[167]

In *Faragher,* a lifeguard at a city pool in Florida quit after supervisors created a sexually hostile work atmosphere by repeatedly subjecting her and other female lifeguards to uninvited and offensive touching, by making lewd remarks, and by speaking of women in offensive terms. The Court agreed that while an employer is subject to vicarious liability under Title VII for actionable discrimination by a supervisor, an employer may raise an affirmative defense that looks to the reasonableness of its action in seeking to prevent and correct harassing conduct along with the reasonableness of the employee's conduct in trying to avoid harm. As such, the Court declared that the city was vicariously liable to the lifeguard based on officials' failure to exercise reasonable care to prevent the supervisor's harassing behavior. On remand, the Eleventh Circuit reinstated a federal trial court ruling in favor of the lifeguard.[168]

Relying on *Faragher,* the Fourth Circuit believed that since a principal in Virginia's assigning extra work to a school psychologist was not a tangible employment action that created a hostile work environment sufficient to give rise to impute board liability, it had no choice but to vacate an earlier judgment in her favor and return the dispute to a lower court for further action.[169] In like manner, a teacher in Florida sued a board, claiming that it was liable where a principal created a hostile work environment by making comments of a sexual nature to her

---

166. *Burlington Indus. v. Ellerth* 524 U.S. 742, 747, 118 S.Ct. 2257, 141 L.Ed.2d 633 (1998), *on remand,* 165 F.3d 31 (7th Cir. 1998).

167. *Id.* at 765–766.

168. *Faragher v. City of Boca Raton,* 166 F.3d 1152 (11th Cir.1999).

169. *Reinhold v. Commonwealth of Va.,* 151 F.3d 172 [128 Educ. L. Rep. 588] (4th Cir.1998).

on numerous occasions.[170] A federal trial court granted the board's motion for summary judgment, recognizing that the board not only had a policy prohibiting sexual harassment but also that the teacher did not even file a complaint pursuant to its grievance procedures.

In *Clark County School District v. Breeden*, the Supreme Court addressed whether a single incident can give rise to liability in a case involving retaliation based on an allegedly sexually harassing remark. The dispute arose when a woman in Nevada who worked in a department that hired other staff filed suit for retaliation after she was transferred for complaining when she learned that a supervisor made a sexually explicit comment about her to another person. In rejecting the woman's claim in a brief per curiam order, the Court decreed that "[n]o reasonable person could have believed that the incident recounted above violated Title VII's standards."[171]

Title VII claims for sexual discrimination permit courts to award such relief as back pay but not reinstatement[172] or punitive damages.[173] Courts also rejected Title VII claims where a complaint was not filed in a timely manner,[174] where an assault complaint did not include sexual harassment,[175] and where boards offered legitimate, non-discriminatory reasons for adverse employment actions.[176]

A federal trial court in Louisiana addressed another uncommon situation involving a claim of gender discrimination under Title VII where a male was passed over in favor of a female for a job as a middle school assistant principal.[177] In rejecting the school board's motion for summary judgment, the court reasoned that genuine issues of material fact as to the qualifications of the male and the successful female candidate, and whether his sex was a motivating factor in the board's action precluded its motion for summary judgment. The court acknowledged that the male presented evidence that he was interviewed by females only, that discrepancies existed as to the statements of one of the interviewees and one of his former principals, and that there was a significant difference between his qualifications and those of the woman who was selected for the job.

170. *Masson v. School Bd. of Dade County, Fla.*, 36 F.Supp.2d 1354 [133 Educ. L. Rep. 489] (S.D.Fla.1999).

171. 532 U.S. 268, 271, 121 S.Ct. 1508, 149 L.Ed.2d 509 [152 Educ. L. Rep. 492] (2001), *reh'g denied*, 533 U.S. 912, 121 S.Ct. 2264, 150 L.Ed.2d 248 (2001), *on remand*, 258 F.3d 958 (9th Cir.2001).

172. *Prine v. Sioux City Community School Dist.*, 95 F.Supp.2d 1005 [144 Educ. L. Rep. 239] (N.D.Iowa 2000).

173. *Jonasson v. Lutheran Child and Family Servs.*, 115 F.3d 436 [118 Educ. L. Rep. 853] (7th Cir.1997) (also awarding compensatory damages); *Molnar v. Booth*, 229 F.3d 593 [148 Educ. L. Rep. 54] (7th Cir.2000).

174. *Cross v. Chicago School Reform Bd. of Trustees*, 80 F.Supp.2d 911 [141 Educ. L. Rep. 662] (N.D.Ill.2000).

175. *Howard-Ahmad v. Chicago School Reform Bd. of Trustees*, 161 F.Supp.2d 857 [157 Educ. L. Rep. 588] (N.D.Ill.2001).

176. *Jackson v. Delta Special School Dist. No. 2*, 86 F.3d 1489 [110 Educ. L. Rep. 574] (8th Cir.1996); *Robbins v. Jefferson County School Dist. R–1*, 186 F.3d 1253 [137 Educ. L. Rep. 489] (10th Cir.1999).

177. *Louis v. East Baton Rouge Parish School Bd.*, 303 F.Supp.2d 799 [185 Educ. L. Rep. 938] (M.D. La. 2003).

In a case involving a novel factual setting, the First Circuit reviewed a dispute where a female teacher in Puerto Rico was sexually harassed by one of her students. In ascertaining that while the teacher could have filed suit under Title IX, her claim was cognizable under Title VII.[178] The court rejected the defendants' motion for summary judgment over whether the commonwealth officials could have been liable due to the presence of remaining issues of material fact. At the same time, the court granted the defendants' motion for summary judgment since the teacher failed to establish a prima facie case of Title VII retaliation in light of her forced resignation prior to the termination of her contract. The court thought that the school's director was not entitled to qualified immunity under the teacher's suit.

On a different matter related to classifications based on sex, even though it is a topic that has received a great deal of attention in the popular press, federal statutory law does not afford protection to individuals based on their sexual orientation. However, courts have extended such protection to teachers in at least two instances. In the first, a federal trial court ruled that since school officials in Ohio discriminated against a gay teacher in not renewing his contract because of his sexual orientation, he was entitled to reinstatement on a two-year contract and an award of damages for back pay and emotional distress as well as attorney fees.[179] Moreover, a federal trial court in New York wrote that school officials violated the equal protection rights of a lesbian teacher by not protecting her from harassment by students.[180] Along with denying motions for qualified immunity for both the school board and principal, the court specified that the teacher was entitled to attorney fees.

In another kind of dispute involving sexual orientation, the Eighth Circuit affirmed that a school board in Minnesota did not create a hostile work environment in permitting a transgendered male teacher to use a woman's faculty restroom.[181] In rejecting a female faculty member's claim, the court noted that she neither suffered an adverse employment action nor did the arrangement affect a term, condition, or privilege of her employment since she had convenient access to numerous other restrooms. The court also affirmed that the teacher did not have a claim for religious discrimination since she failed to inform the board of her belief and she did not suffer an adverse employment action.

Privacy

As reflected in Chapter 13, the judiciary has focused considerably more attention on the privacy rights of students than teachers. This

---

178. *Plaza-Torres v. Rey*, 376 F.Supp.2d 171 [200 Educ. L. Rep. 166] (D. Puerto Rico 2005).

179. *Glover v. Williamsburg Local School Dist. Bd. of Educ.*, 20 F.Supp.2d 1160 [130 Educ. L. Rep. 661] (S.D. Ohio 1998).

180. *Lovell v. Comsewogue School Dist.*, 214 F.Supp.2d 319 [168 Educ. L. Rep. 749] (E.D. N.Y. 2002).

181. *Cruzan v. Special School Dist, #1*, 294 F.3d 981 [166 Educ. L. Rep. 492] (8th Cir.2002).

aside, disputes involving drug testing and other searches of teachers and other school employees have begun to emerge. The privacy rights of school employees are based on the Fourteenth Amendment's liberty clause which protects the bodily integrity of individuals and the Fourth Amendment's protection against unreasonable searches and seizures.

While the Supreme Court has not addressed a case dealing with drug testing or searches of public school employees, it has examined these questions in three non-school cases. *O'Connor v. Ortega*[182] involved the search of a doctor's locked office purportedly to conduct an inventory and to look for evidence that he allegedly sexually harassed two females. Hospital officials also alleged that the doctor inappropriately disciplined a medical resident. In upholding the search, the Court essentially adopted the reasonableness standard of *New Jersey v. T.L.O.*[183] The Court posited that hospital officials had the authority to enter a locked office at any time for business-related purposes such as conducting an inventory, looking for files or records, or investigating alleged acts of wrongdoing. At the same time, the Court suggested that extending searches of this nature to the personal property of employees, such as briefcases or purses, would have required reasonable suspicion.

Two years later, the Court reviewed companion cases involving public employees. In *Skinner v. Railway Labor Executives' Association*,[184] the Court permitted testing of railroad employees for drugs and alcohol after serious accidents even without showings of individualized suspicion. In *National Treasury Employees Union v. Von Raab*,[185] the Court upheld the United States Customs Service's practice of drug testing employees who applied for promotions or transfers to drug interdiction positions that would have required them to carry firearms. While the preceding three cases are not dispositive in school settings, they should be of interest to those who are concerned about the privacy rights of educators.

One of the more significant issues involving the privacy rights of teachers, and other school employees, involves their Fourth Amendment rights to be free from unreasonable searches and seizures. At the same time, it is worth recalling that since "[a] teacher's employment in the public schools is a privilege, not a right,"[186] absent language to the contrary in state statutes or collective bargaining agreements, boards probably have a great amount of authority in defining their employees' privacy expectations with regard to drug testing. Not surprisingly, courts have reached mixed results over drug testing of teachers and other school employees.

As to suspicionless testing, in the first case handed down by a court of last resort, the Court of Appeals of New York struck down a board

---

182. 480 U.S. 709, 107 S.Ct. 1492, 94 L.Ed.2d 714 (1987).

183. 469 U.S. 325, 105 S.Ct. 733, 83 L.Ed.2d 720 [21 Educ. L. Rep. 1122] (1985). [Case No. 108]

184. 489 U.S. 602, 109 S.Ct. 1402, 103 L.Ed.2d 639 (1989).

185. 489 U.S. 656, 109 S.Ct. 1384, 103 L.Ed.2d 685 (1989).

186. *Board of Educ. of City of Los Angeles v. Wilkinson*, 270 P.2d 82, 85 (Cal. Ct. App. 1954).

policy that sought to subject all probationary teachers in a school district to urinalysis to detect potential drug abuse as a pre-condition to receiving tenure. The court held that the policy violated the constitutional bar to unreasonable searches and seizures in the absence of individualized suspicion.[187]

Three years later, a federal trial court in Georgia reached the same result.[188] In enjoining a policy and invalidating an underlying statute as unconstitutional, the court explained that the state's sole rationale for requiring suspicionless drug testing for all applicants for state employment, namely its generalized interest in insuring integrity of work force, was not sufficiently compelling to outweigh the privacy rights of applicants for teaching and other positions even if they had diminished expectations of privacy under the Fourth Amendment. Later, the Fifth Circuit vitiated a policy that would have required random drug testing of school employees, including teachers.[189] The court observed that the policy, which required testing for school employees who were injured on the job, violated the Fourth Amendment's prohibition against unreasonable searches insofar as there was no special needs exception present to the requirement of individualized suspicion. The court was convinced that the policy was unacceptable because testing did not respond to any identified problem of drug use by employees and there was an insufficient nexus between worker injuries and drug use.

On the other hand, the Sixth Circuit became the first federal appellate court to uphold suspicionless drug testing of teachers, reinstating a board policy in Tennessee that required all individuals who wished to work in safety-sensitive positions to submit to such testing as a pre-condition of employment.[190] The court also upheld that part of the policy calling for drug testing based on reasonable suspicion while rejecting alcohol testing of employees because the standards were much more stringent than they were for even drunk drivers.

Five years later, a federal trial court in Kentucky relied on the Sixth Circuit's precedent in denying a teacher's request for a preliminary injunction in a suit challenging a school board's policy for random suspicionless drug testing of 25 percent of all employees.[191] The court pointed out that while the Sixth Circuit had not required evidence of a drug problem to justify such a policy, one had existed among staff and faculty. The court was also satisfied that the policy included sufficient procedural safeguards to protect teacher privacy. A variety of courts have upheld suspicionless drug testing of other school employees such as

187. *Patchogue–Medford Congress of Teachers v. Board of Educ. of Patchogue–Medford Union Free School Dist.*, 517 N.Y.S.2d 456 [40 Educ. L. Rep. 917] (N.Y. 1987).

188. *Georgia Ass'n of Educators v. Harris*, 749 F.Supp. 1110 [64 Educ. L. Rep. 122] (N.D. Ga. 1990).

189. *United Teachers of New Orleans v. Orleans Parish School Bd.*, 142 F.3d 853 [126 Educ. L. Rep. 104] (5th Cir. 1998).

190. *Knox County Educ. Ass'n v. Knox County Bd. of Educ.*, 158 F.3d 361 [130 Educ. L. Rep. 62] (6th Cir.1998), *cert. denied*, 528 U.S. 812, 120 S.Ct. 46, 145 L.Ed.2d 41 (1999).

191. *Crager v. Board of Educ. of Knott County*, 313 F.Supp.2d 690 [187 Educ. L. Rep. 892] (E.D. Ky. 2004).

school bus attendants,[192] a mechanic's helper,[193] public school bus drivers following accidents that resulted in bodily injury or $1,000 in property damage except where buses were struck while legally parked,[194] and custodians and other safety-sensitive school personnel in an elementary school.[195]

Turning to a more recent case involving suspicion-based testing, the Eleventh Circuit affirmed the dismissal of a teacher in Georgia who refused to be drug tested following the discovery of marijuana in her car.[196] The court concluded that the board acted pursuant to a county-wide safe school plan which called for a drug free workplace.

In a case from New York involving the search and seizure of a school employee, the Second Circuit maintained that a teacher who was suspended with pay and reassigned to an administrative position after having been charged with stalking a student with whom he was sexually involved nine years earlier had no expectation of privacy in his classroom or its contents.[197] In affirming a grant of summary judgment in favor of the school board, the court recognized that since the teacher had been suspended and asked to turn in his classroom keys, he had a diminished expectation of privacy. The court added that school officials had reasonable investigatory and non-investigatory grounds to search the teacher's classroom after he had been given two opportunities to remove personal items from the classroom.[198]

Statutory Protections Against Discrimination

In addition to Title VII, teachers and other school employees have a variety of statutory protections safeguarding their rights in the workplace. Key statutes in this regard protect educators against discrimination based on age, disability, and the need to care for one's self and family members who are ill.

192. *Jones v. McKenzie*, 878 F.2d 1476 [54 Educ. L. Rep. 1138] (D.C. Cir. 1989) (permitting testing without probable cause).

193. *English v. Talladega County Bd. of Educ.*, 938 F.Supp. 775 [113 Educ. L. Rep. 291] (N.D. Ala. 1996). *See also Cox v. McCraley*, 993 F.Supp. 1452 [125 Ed. Law Rep. 456] (M.D. Fla. 1998) (upholding a policy which required an employee who was on an annual contract to submit to a drug test, enter a drug assistance program, or resign after he was informed that officials had reasonable suspicion that he violated a board policy regarding drug and/or alcohol abuse).

194. *Cornette v. Commonwealth*, 899 S.W.2d 502 [101 Educ. L. Rep. 474] (Ky. Ct. App. 1995).

195. *Aubrey v. School Bd. of Lafayette Parish*, 148 F.3d 559 [127 Educ. L. Rep. 710] (5th Cir. 1998).

196. *Hearn v. Board of Pub. Educ.*, 191 F.3d 1329 [138 Educ. L. Rep. 662] (11th Cir.1999), *reh'g and suggestion for reh'g en banc denied*, 204 F.3d 1124 (11th Cir.1999), *cert. denied*, 529 U.S. 1109, 120 S.Ct. 1962, 146 L.Ed.2d 794 (2000).

197. *Shaul v. Cherry Valley–Springfield Cent. School*, 363 F.3d 177 [186 Educ. L. Rep. 604] (2d Cir. 2004).

198. For an interesting case, albeit from higher education, *see Biby v. Board of Regents, of Univ. of Neb. at Lincoln*, 419 F.3d 845 [201 Educ. L. Rep. 36] (8th Cir. 2005) (affirming that officials did not violate any clearly established constitutional rights by conducting a warrantless search of an employee's computer for work-related materials).

Age

According to the Age Discrimination in Employment Act (ADEA):

It shall be unlawful for an employer—

(1) to fail or refuse to hire or to discharge any individual or otherwise discriminate against any individual with respect to his compensation, terms, conditions, or privileges of employment, because of such individual's age;

(2) to limit, segregate, or classify his employees in any way which would deprive or tend to deprive any individual of employment opportunities or otherwise adversely affect his status as an employee, because of such individual's age; or

(3) to reduce the wage rate of any employee in order to comply with this chapter.[199]

Even in protecting workers over the age of forty, the ADEA permits employers to rely on seniority or bona fide occupational qualifications[200] in order to avoid liability. Insofar as the protections of Title VII and the ADEA are very much alike, judicial analyses often rely on analogous reasoning such that in order to be actionable, qualified employees must be over the age of forty, must have been treated less favorably than others not in the protected class, must have suffered an adverse employment action,[201] and must file suit within ninety-days of receiving a right-to-sue letter from the EEOC.[202] Once employees present prima facie cases, employers can seek to rebut them by providing legitimate non-discriminatory reasons for acting.[203] Accordingly, if two employees are over the age of forty, as where a fifty-three-year-old coach was passed over in favor of a forty-three-year-old, an individual cannot claim the protection of the ADEA.[204] In such a case, the Seventh Circuit upheld a school board in Illinois' refusal to hire a sixty-three-year-old applicant whose thirty years of experience would have exceeded the limit that it placed on the amount it would spend on a new teacher. The court rejected the EEOC's disparate impact theory that connecting years of experience to hiring decisions disparately affected age. The court was of the view that an economic basis for a hiring decision represented a nondiscriminatory reason.[205] Additionally, where school officials articu-

199. 29 U.S.C.A. § 623(a). Portions of this statute are in the appendix.

200. 29 U.S.C.A. § 623(f).

201. *Widoe v. District No. 111 Otoe County School*, 147 F.3d 726 [127 Educ. L. Rep. 576] (8th Cir.1998); *Gavigan v. Clarkstown Cent. School Dist.*, 84 F.Supp.2d 540 [142 Educ. L. Rep. 179] (S.D.N.Y. 2000) (both finding that employees presented prima facie cases).

202. 42 U.S.C.A. § 2000e–5. *See, e.g.*, *Bedden-Hurley v. New York City Bd. of Educ.*, 385 F.Supp.2d 274 [202 Educ. L. Rep. 656] (S.D.N.Y. 2005) (rejecting a claim

as time-barred since it was not filed within the ninety-day filing period).

203. *Sanchez v. Denver Pub. Schools*, 164 F.3d 527 [131 Educ. L. Rep. 679] (10th Cir.1998); *Horwitz v. Board of Educ. of Avoca School Dist. No. 37*, 260 F.3d 602 [156 Educ. L. Rep. 116] (7th Cir.2001).

204. *Ranieri v. Highland Falls–Ft. Montomery School Dist.*, 198 F.Supp.2d 542 [165 Educ. L. Rep. 98] (S.D.N.Y.2002).

205. *E.E.O.C. v. Francis W. Parker School*, 41 F.3d 1073 [96 Educ. L. Rep. 77] (7th Cir. 1994), *reh'g and suggestion for* lated the legitimate non-discriminatory reason that a younger female teacher performed better on her interviews than a fifty-year-old-male as both sought an administrative position in the district, a federal trial court in New York granted its motion for summary judgment in his case which claimed that they violated his rights under both the ADEA and Title VII.[206]

On the other hand, along with making derogatory statements about her role as a chaperone in an overseas trip, where a principal told a seventy-year-old, with thirty-four years of experience, who served as head foreign languages teacher on a one-year renewable contract, that her position was to be abolished so that the money spent on her salary could be used for other purposes, an appellate court in Massachusetts denied the school committee's motion for summary judgment.[207] The court thought that insofar as genuine issue of material fact remained as to whether the principal's assessment of the teacher's performance, which also caused her to file a defamation action, was false and not a good faith review, such that a discriminatory animus could have been inferred, it would not grant the committee's motion on the age discrimination case that she initiated after she was not reappointed as head foreign languages teacher.

In a noteworthy non-school case, the Supreme Court ruled that the ADEA authorizes aggrieved employees to sue under a "disparate-impact" theory of liability, which does not require them to prove that an employer engaged in intentional discrimination if they can show that they were adversely affected by an employer's action due to age. In *Smith v. City of Jackson, Mississippi*,[208] when city officials granted proportionately larger pay raises to younger police officers, older ones claimed that doing so violated the ADEA. On further review of dismissals in favor of the city, the Supreme Court was of the opinion that while the ADEA permits recoveries based on disparate impact, the officers could not have recovered since the city based its action on the statute's "reasonable factors other than age"[209] provision.

Another controversial area involving the ADEA concerns benefits and early retirement incentive plans where age is a factor. The Supreme Court, in another non-school case, *General Dynamics Land System v. Cline*,[210] upheld the benefits plan in a collective bargaining agreement that eliminated health care benefits for retired employees except for individuals who were fifty or older. In rejecting an ADEA claim by employees ages forty to fifty, the Court reasoned that the ADEA did not stop an employer from favoring older employees over younger employees. Other courts have invalidated plans that tied the amount of benefits to

reh'g en banc denied, cert. denied, 515 U.S. 1142, 115 S.Ct. 2577, 132 L.Ed.2d 828 (1995).

206. *Brierly v. Deer Park Union Free School Dist.*, 359 F.Supp.2d 275 [196 Educ. L. Rep. 534] (E.D.N.Y. 2005).

207. *Dragonas v. School Comm. of Melrose*, 833 N.E.2d 679 [201 Educ. L. Rep.

296] (Mass. App. Ct. 2005), *review denied*, 836 N.E.2d 1096 (Mass. 2005).

208. 544 U.S. 228, 125 S.Ct. 1536, 161 L.Ed.2d 410 (2005).

209. *Id.* at 1546.

210. 540 U.S. 581, 124 S.Ct. 1236, 157 L.Ed.2d 1094 (2004).

years of age.[211] Even so, the Eighth Circuit affirmed that a school system in Iowa violated the ADEA when it enacted a retirement-incentive plan which excluded employees who were over the age of sixty-five.[212] The court decided that a denial of benefits solely on age was inconsistent with the ADEA's purpose of prohibiting arbitrary age discrimination. In like fashion, the federal trial court in Minnesota invalidated a board's early retirement plan since it provided early retirees lump sum payments that varied according to their ages.[213]

Disability

As discussed in Chapter 14, federal law provides extensive protection for students with disabilities. Section 504, which covers both students and school employees, as well as others who may be in schools, applies to those who have, had, or are believed to have had impairments that substantially limit major life activities.[214] Individuals who are otherwise qualified, meaning that they are qualified despite their impairments, cannot be denied the benefits of, or participation in, programs that receive federal financial assistance as long as they can do so by means of reasonable accommodations.[215] Title I of the ADA prohibits discrimination by private sector employers with fifteen or more employees. Title II of the Act applies to public accommodations, in language similar to that of Section 504, requiring reasonable accommodations for otherwise qualified individuals with the result that it is being used extensively in cases alleging employment discrimination just as disputes involving students are now more commonly filed under the Rehabilitation Act.[216]

When otherwise qualified employees allege discrimination based on disabilities, employers must make reasonable accommodations unless doing so would cause undue hardships. Put another way, employers can claim one of three defenses to avoid compliance: if making accommodations would result either in "a fundamental alteration in the nature of [a] program;"[217] if they impose "undue financial burden[s];"[218] or if having individuals present creates a substantial risk of injury to themselves or others.[219]

---

211.   See Abrahamson v. Board of Educ. of Wappingers Falls Cent. School Dist., 374 F.3d 66 [189 Educ. L. Rep. 503] (2d Cir. 2004); Auerbach v. Board of Educ. of the Harborfields Cent. School Dist. of Greenlawn, 136 F.3d 104 [123 Educ. L. Rep. 1142] (2d Cir.1998).

212.   Jankovitz v. Des Moines Indep. Community School Dist., 421 F.3d 649 [201 Educ. L. Rep. 428] (8th Cir. 2005).

213.   Overlie v. Owatonna Indep. School Dist., 341 F.Supp.2d 1081 [193 Educ. L. Rep. 483] (D. Minn. 2004).

214.   34 C.F.R. § 104.3(j)(2)(i) ("Major life activities means functions such as caring for one's self, performing manual tasks, walking, seeing, hearing, speaking, breathing, learning, and working.").

215.   34 C.F.R. § 104.12.

216.   See, e.g., Temple v. Board of Educ. of City of N.Y., 322 F.Supp.2d 277 [189 Educ. L. Rep. 681] (E.D.N.Y. 2004) (rejecting a teacher's claim that under the ADA that systemic lupus erythematosus was a physical impairment that substantially limited a major life function).

217.   Southeastern Community College v. Davis, 442 U.S. 397, 410, 99 S.Ct. 2361, 60 L.Ed.2d 980 (1979); Alexander v. Choate, 469 U.S. 287, 105 S.Ct. 712, 83 L.Ed.2d 661 (1985).

218.   Davis, id. at 412.

219.   See School Bd. of Nassau County, Fla. v. Arline, 480 U.S. 273, 287–88, 107 S.Ct. 1123, 94 L.Ed.2d 307 [37 Educ. L. Rep. 448] (1987). [Case No. 65]

In *School Board of Nassau County, Florida v. Arline (Arline)*,[220] the Supreme Court first applied Section 504 in a K–12 setting when it affirmed that school officials violated a teacher's rights by discharging her due to recurrences of tuberculosis. In declaring that the teacher was otherwise qualified for the job, the Court enunciated a four-part test for use in cases involving contagious diseases; these elements consider the nature of the risk, its duration, its severity, and the probabilities that the disease will be transmitted and will cause varying degrees of harm. On remand, a federal trial court in Florida agreed that since the teacher was otherwise qualified, she was entitled to reinstatement and back pay,[221] typical remedies in such litigation.

In a case from Kansas, the federal trial court rejected the claim of a teacher who was seriously hearing-impaired after his school board refused to hire a full-time classroom aide to help him to preserve classroom discipline.[222] The court decreed that since being able to discipline students was an essential job function, providing the teacher with an aide was not a reasonable accommodation under the ADA. A federal trial court in New York reached a similar outcome in a case where a custodian who suffered from narcolepsy and sleep apnea claimed that his board violated the ADA in dismissing him from his job.[223] The court agreed that the board could terminate the custodian's employment because rather than refer to his illness, officials articulated a legitimate non-discriminatory reason in light of his poor performance and misconduct in fifteen of nineteen areas in which he was evaluated. In another case from New York, a federal trial court dismissed the claim of a guidance counselor who suffered from learning disabilities known as dyslexia and dysgraphia which affected her ability to write.[224] The court determined that since the counselor resigned rather than be denied tenure, her claim that school officials violated her rights under the ADA when they informed a possible employer about her writing ability did not qualify as retaliation under the statute.

Courts permitted suits to proceed or entered judgments in favor of employees in disputes where an otherwise qualified employee needed rest periods during the day and a transfer to a school closer to home,[225] another sought a room change due to rheumatoid arthritis,[226] and where an injured groundskeeper challenged a board's refusal for reinstatement.[227] Courts reached mixed results with regard to employees who suffered from cancer as the federal trial court in New Mexico permitted

---

220. *Id.*

221. *Arline v. School Bd. of Nassau County*, 692 F.Supp. 1286 [49 Educ. L. Rep. 195] (M.D. Fla.1988).

222. *Henry v. Unified Sch. Dist.*, 328 F.Supp.2d 1130 [191 Educ. L. Rep. 289] (D. Kan. 2004).

223. *Sanzo v. Uniondale Union Free School Dist.*, 381 F.Supp.2d 113 [201 Educ. L. Rep. 503] (E.D.N.Y. 2005).

224. *Hanig v. Yorktown Cent. School Dist.*, 384 F.Supp.2d 710 [202 Educ. L. Rep. 156] (S.D.N.Y. 2005).

225. *Young v. Central Square Cent. School Dist.*, 213 F.Supp.2d 202 [168 Educ. L. Rep. 264] (N.D.N.Y.2002).

226. *Ross v. Board of Educ. of Prince George's County*, 195 F.Supp.2d 730 [164 Educ. L. Rep. 240] (D.Md.2002).

227. *Johnson v. Paradise Valley Unified School Dist.*, 251 F.3d 1222 [154 Educ. L. Rep. 461] (9th Cir.2001).

the claim of a former school administrator with breast cancer to proceed,[228] while one in Missouri disagreed in refusing to treat it as a disabling impairment.[229] Moreover, an appellate court in New York, relying only partly on state law, affirmed that a teacher who had cancer surgery was not discriminated against on the basis of disability, or gender, since her condition had not limited a major life function.[230]

In an emerging medical issue, courts are also split on carpal tunnel syndrome. The Ninth Circuit reversed in favor of a janitor in Nevada who alleged that a board violated his rights by not offering him the reasonable accommodation of making him a school safety officer before terminating his employment.[231] Conversely, a federal trial court in Connecticut rejected the claim of a part-time employee that a board refused to hire to a full-time job in light of her charge that officials discriminated against her due to her disability since it did not think that carpal tunnel syndrome substantially limited her major life activity of working.[232]

Courts denied relief in a variety of cases including where a staff member had schizophrenia,[233] where an employee sought to perform only light duties,[234] where a disruptive teacher refused to undergo psychological testing,[235] and where an employee had a disabling kidney disorder,[236] typically agreeing that requested accommodations were not reasonable, that conditions did not limit major life activities, or that individuals were not otherwise qualified.[237]

In the first case directly implicating the rights of a school employee with AIDS/HIV, a teacher challenged his school board's refusal to reinstate him to his job due to his illness. On appeal of the denial of his request for an injunction, the Ninth Circuit reversed in favor of the teacher.[238] The court indicated that school officials violated the teacher's

---

228. *Keller v. Board of Educ. of City of Albuquerque*, 182 F.Supp.2d 1148 [161 Educ. L. Rep. 507] (D.N.M.2001) (also relying on the ADA).

229. *Treiber v. Lindbergh School Dist.*, 199 F.Supp.2d 949 [165 Educ. L. Rep. 136] (E.D. Mo.2002).

230. *Sirota v. New York City Bd. of Educ.*, 725 N.Y.S.2d 332 [154 Educ. L. Rep. 263] (N.Y. App.Div.2001).

231. *Wellington v. Lyon County School Dist.*, 187 F.3d 1150 [137 Educ. L. Rep. 890] (9th Cir.1999).

232. *Cutler v. Hamden Bd. of Educ.*, 150 F.Supp.2d 356 [155 Educ. L. Rep. 525] (D.Conn. 2001).

233. *Boyer v. KRS Computer and Business School*, 171 F.Supp.2d 950 [159 Educ. L. Rep. 117] (D.Minn.2001) (also rejecting a claim of alcoholism since the employee was sober for sixteen years).

234. *Hinson v. U.S.D. No. 500*, 187 F.Supp.2d 1297 [162 Educ. L. Rep. 801] (D.Kan.2002). *But see Butterfield v. Sidney*

Pub. Schools, 32 P.3d 1243 [157 Educ. L. Rep. 929] (Mont.2001) (relying on Section 504's regulations and state law in deciding that a board acted improperly in refusing to reinstate a custodian with a back injury).

235. *Sullivan v. River Valley School Dist.*, 197 F.3d 804 [140 Educ. L. Rep. 127] (6th Cir. 1999), *cert. denied*, 530 U.S. 1262, 120 S.Ct. 2718, 147 L.Ed.2d 983 (2000).

236. *Gammage v. West Jasper School Bd. of Educ.*, 179 F.3d 952 [136 Educ. L. Rep. 131] (5th Cir.1999).

237. *Falchenberg v. New York City Dep't of Educ.*, 375 F.Supp.2d 344 [199 Educ. L. Rep. 813] (S.D.N.Y. 2005) (rejecting the ADA claim of a teacher who refused to take a certification examination after officials failed to accommodate her dyslexia where her choosing not to do so meant that she was not otherwise qualified for a job).

238. *Chalk v. United States Dist. Ct., Cent. Dist. of Cal.*, 840 F.2d 701 [45 Educ. L. Rep. 58] (9th Cir. 1988).

rights under Section 504 since there was no adequate medical evidence that he would have passed the disease on to his students or coworkers and that the public fear of AIDS was not a sufficient ground to deny his request to order officials to permit him to return to his job. Subsequently, the federal trial court in Puerto Rico dismissed the case of a teacher with HIV who filed suit under the ADA claiming that his contract was not renewed because of his condition.[239] The court was satisfied that school officials relied on legitimate nondiscriminatory grounds that the teacher was frequently late for work and was unable to control students.

Family and Medical Leave Act

The Family and Medical Leave Act (FMLA) protects employees who may have to choose between job security and personal, and family, health concerns. Under the FMLA, school boards, as public agencies that employ fifty or more employees for each working day during each of twenty or more calendar workweeks in a current or preceding calendar year, must provide unpaid leave to eligible staff members for medical or child care purposes during a set twelve-month period.[240] In order to be covered by the FMLA, school employees, including part-time staff, must have worked for at least twelve months, providing at least 1,250 hours of service during the year immediately preceding the start of their leaves.[241]

Subject to any greater protections that they may have under other federal or state laws or collective bargaining agreements, school employees are entitled to twelve weeks of unpaid leave during any twelve-month period as provided for in the employer's FMLA policy.[242] If school board policies permit paid leave for fewer than twelve weeks, the remainder of leave may be without pay. School employees who have accrued paid vacation, personal, or family leave days may choose to or boards may require them to substitute these days for unpaid leave.[243] If leave plans do not allow for substitutions, then they are not permitted.[244] In creating one-year policies, boards may use the calendar year, any twelve-month leave period such as the fiscal year, a twelve-month span measured forward from the first FMLA leave date, or a rolling twelve-month period backward from the first FMLA leave date.[245]

School employees can request leave under two broad categories. The first, child care, covers the birth, adoption, or foster care assumption of a child within twelve months of the event.[246] The second, a "serious health condition," covers the illness of a spouse, child, or parent, or one rendering an employee unable to perform job functions.[247] Educators who request leave must provide school officials with thirty-days notice or as much as is practicable.[248] Staff members who seek leave for foresee-

239. *Velez Cajigas v. Order of St. Benedict*, 115 F.Supp.2d 246 [147 Educ. L. Rep. 928] (D. Puerto Rico 2000).

240. 29 U.S.C.A. §§ 2611(4)(A)(I), (B).

241. 29 U.S.C.A. § 2611 (2)(A).

242. 29 U.S.C.A. § 2612 (a)(c).

243. 29 U.S.C.A. § 2612(d)(1)(2).

244. 29 C.F.R. § 825.207(b)(c).

245. 29 C.F.R. § 825.200(b).

246. 29 U.S.C.A. § 2612(a)(1)(A)(B).

247. 29 U.S.C.A. § 2611(11).

248. 29 U.S.C.A. § 2612(e)(1).

able treatments due to serious medical conditions must make reasonable efforts to schedule them so as not to cause undue disruptions to the operations of their employers.[249] Even so, school boards can waive this requirement.

As part of the certification that school boards may request from health care providers before granting leaves, staff members should include the date when the condition began, its likely duration, and a statement of inability to perform job functions as designated in a description given to the health care provider.[250] If dealing with care for a family member, this certification should include an estimate of how long it will take to provide care.[251] If school board officials doubt the validity of certifications, they may require staff members, at their own expense, to obtain second opinions.[252] If the two opinions conflict, boards may, at their expense, have employees submit to the opinion of a third health care provider that is mutually acceptable to both parties; this third evaluation binds both parties.[253]

The FMLA includes special rules for school personnel who work primarily in instructional capacities. Under these provisions, if teachers request intermittent or reduced schedule leaves for foreseeable medical care and would be absent for more than 20 percent of the total of working days during leave periods, school systems have two options. Boards can either require teachers to take leaves for periods not to exceed the length of their planned treatments or may temporarily transfer them to other jobs with equivalent pay and benefits.[254]

Special rules also apply to leaves taken near the end of school terms. First, if teachers wish to begin leaves more than five weeks prior to the end of a term, boards may require them to wait until the end of the term if the leaves are at least three weeks long and they would return to work during the three weeks before the end of the term. Second, if teachers request leaves less than five weeks before the end of a term, boards may require them to wait until the end of the term if their requested leaves are more than two weeks long and their returns would be during the two weeks prior to the end of the term. Third, if requested leaves are less than three weeks before the end of a term and greater than five working days, boards may require teachers to take leaves that last until the end of the term.[255]

The key protection available under the FMLA is that school employees who are returning from leaves must be restored to their same or equivalent positions with equivalent pay and benefits.[256] Under this provision, school employees are not entitled to additional seniority, employment benefits, or any other rights, benefits, or positions that they would not have been entitled to but for taking leave.[257] If school board officials have good faith reasons to eliminate the jobs of individuals who

249. 29 U.S.C.A. § 2612(e)(2).

250. 29 U.S.C.A. §§ 2613(b)(1–3).

251. 29 U.S.C.A. § 2613(b)(4)(A).

252. 29 U.S.C.A. § 2613(c).

253. 29 U.S.C.A. § 2613(d).

254. 29 U.S.C.A. § 2618(c).

255. 29 U.S.C.A. § 2618(d).

256. 29 C.F.R. § 825.215.

257. 29 U.S.C.A. § 2614(a)(3).

are on leave, and do not act out of retaliation, then, subject to proving that they acted with proper motives, the positions can be terminated.[258]

Along with protecting school employees from being fired for asserting their rights,[259] the FMLA requires boards to make, keep, and preserve records demonstrating their compliance.[260] As part of this process, the Department of Labor has the right to conduct an annual review of the FMLA records of school boards and may examine them more frequently if necessary to investigate alleged violations.[261] School boards that violate the FMLA may not only have to reinstate or promote employees but may also be liable for up to twelve weeks of wages, benefits, and reasonable attorney fees.[262]

To date, there has been relatively little litigation under the FMLA. In cases dealing with substantive issues, one suit examined whether a former school employee had a health condition that was covered under the law[263] while another reviewed whether school officials improperly denied an employee's request for maternity leave.[264] As to procedural matters, one case considered whether the denial of a former administrator's claim under the ADA precluded a filing under the FMLA[265] and whether the Eleventh Amendment barred a public employee from suing her board.[266]

Veterans Preference

Courts generally uphold reasonable laws that benefit veterans in light of the overriding public interest in rewarding those who sacrificed to defend the nation. Title VII also exempts such laws from scrutiny under its mandates. The Supreme Court rejected a challenge to an extreme form of veterans preference in public employment in *Personnel Administrator of Massachusetts v. Feeney (Feeney)*.[267] The Court upheld a statute giving a lifetime preference in public employment to qualified veterans even though doing so resulted in preventing a grossly disproportionate number of qualified women from attaining civil service positions. In "noting that most states, as well as the federal government,

---

258. 29 U.S.C.A. § 2614(a)(3)(B).

259. 29 U.S.C.A. § 2615(b).

260. 29 U.S.C.A. § 2616.

261. 29 U.S.C.A. § 2616.

262. 29 U.S.C.A. § 2617.

263. *Jones v. Denver Pub. Schools*, 427 F.3d 1315 [203 Educ. L. Rep. 76] (10th Cir. 2005) (affirming that a former employee's condition was not covered).

264. *Walker v. Elmore County Bd. of Educ.*, 379 F.3d 1249 [191 Educ. L. Rep. 124] (11th Cir. 2004) (affirming a grant of summary judgment in favor of a school board where a teacher claimed that officials denied her maternity leave under the FMLA).

265. *Bourgo v. Canby School Dist.*, 167 F.Supp.2d 1173 [158 Educ. L. Rep. 314] (D.Or.2001) (judging that the denial of a former administrator's claim under the ADA did not preclude a filing under the FMLA).

266. *Touvell v. Ohio Dep't of Mental Retardation and Development Disabilities*, 422 F.3d 392 (6th Cir. 2005) (affirming that a former employee of a state agency could not sue under the FMLA alleging that officials interfered with her to entitlement to leave for self-care).

267. 442 U.S. 256, 99 S.Ct. 2282, 60 L.Ed.2d 870 (1979), *on remand*, 475 F.Supp. 109 (D. Mass.1979), *aff'd*, 445 U.S. 901, 100 S.Ct. 1075, 63 L.Ed.2d 317 (1980).

give some sort of hiring preference to veterans,"[268] since courts are reluctant to offer such an absolute hiring preference or to extend the case's reach in situations involving classifications based on gender,[269] *Feeney's* precedential value is limited.

In an example of limiting the reach of a veteran's preference law, an appellate court in Pennsylvania found that a statute did not cover an applicant who challenged an examination given by a school board.[270] According to the court, the law applied only to examinations that are administered by the Civil Service Commission. Earlier, another appellate court in Pennsylvania affirmed that the statute applied only to appointments, not promotions.[271] In a later case, an appellate court in Kansas affirmed that since the state's veterans hiring preference statute applied only to public agencies, it was inapplicable to not-for-profit corporations and employers.[272]

Teacher Contracts

In General

Employment agreements between boards and their teachers must conform to all general rules for contracts,[273] except as they may be modified by state laws.[274] As with certificated employees who must be classified in a manner consistent with state law, contracts cannot supersede statutory requirements.[275]

Insofar as state laws grant school boards the authority to employ staff, they alone must exercise that function and may not delegate hiring to anyone,[276] including superintendents.[277] Superintendents, or individual board members may, of course, interview and recommend teachers,

268. *Player v. Village of Bensenville*, 722 N.E.2d 792, 795 (Ill. App. Ct. 1999).

269. *White v. McGill*, 585 N.E.2d 945 [72 Educ. L. Rep. 346] (Ohio Ct.App.1990).

270. *Zablow v. Board of Educ. of School Dist. of Pittsburgh*, 729 A.2d 124 [134 Educ. L. Rep. 526] (Pa.Cmwlth.Ct.1999).

271. *Belle Vernon Area School Dist. v. Teamsters Local Union No. 782, Int'l. Brothers of Teamsters*, 670 A.2d 1201 [106 Educ. L. Rep. 1203] (Pa.Cmwlth.Ct.1996).

272. *Little v. State*, 121 P.3d 990 [202 Educ. L. Rep. 858] (Kan. Ct. App. 2005).

273. *Wright v. Mead School Dist. No. 354*, 944 P.2d 1 [121 Educ. L. Rep. 312] (Wash.Ct.App. 1997), *review denied*, 954 P.2d 277 (Wash.1998); *Wells v. Board of Trustees of Laramie County School Dist. No. 1*, 3 P.3d 861 [145 Educ. L. Rep. 785] (Wyo.2000).

274. *Drain v. Board of Educ. of Frontier County School Dist. No. 46*, 508 N.W.2d 255 [87 Educ. L. Rep. 612] (Neb.1993).

275. *Motevalli v. Los Angeles Unified School Dist.*, 18 Cal.Rptr.3d 562 [191 Educ. L. Rep. 838] (Cal. Ct. App. 2004), *review*

denied (2004) (affirming the non-renewal of the contract of a teacher with emergency certification who refused to cooperate with random weapons searches of students).

276. *McAndrew v. School Comm. of Cambridge*, 480 N.E.2d 327 [26 Educ. L. Rep. 404] (Mass.Ct.App.1985).

277. *Big Sandy School Dist. No. 100–J v. Carroll*, 433 P.2d 325 (Colo.1967). *See also Fremont Re–1 School Dist. v. Jacobs*, 737 P.2d 816, 818–819 [40 Educ. L. Rep. 465] (Colo. 1987) (mandating that a school board "may delegate to subordinate officers and boards powers and functions which are ministerial or administrative in nature, where there is a fixed and certain standard or rule which leaves little or nothing to the judgment or discretion of the subordinate. However, legislative or judicial powers, involving judgment and discretion on the part of the municipal body, which have been vested by statute in a municipal corporation may *not* be delegated unless such has been expressly authorized by the legislature.")

but boards retain the final hiring authority.[278] Additionally, where state law requires boards to obtain recommendations from superintendents before hiring teachers, they must do so.[279]

To the extent that employee contracts are governed by state laws,[280] staff members are bound to comply with statutory provisions since they are deemed incorporated in contracts.[281] Perhaps the most common requirement for school contracts is that they must be in writing.[282] The rule of incorporation applies to local board policies, covered in the next section, and collective bargaining agreements[283] which can modify board policies.[284] Yet, since most statutory contract rights cover typical duties, regular employment provisions do not apply to extracurricular activities.[285]

As with other contracts, if boards lack the authority to enter into agreements in the first instance, they may not ordinarily ratify them. Even if boards merely fail to comply with formalities in forming contracts, such as reducing them to writing, and state laws do not prohibit them from doing so, school officials cannot use their own failure to follow the law to the disadvantage of teachers.[286]

Questions frequently arise as to the interrelationships between the common law of contracts and statutes designed to protect employees against arbitrary and/or capricious board actions. Generally, statutes do not operate in situations where employees act voluntarily, by intent or gross neglect, to take themselves out of coverage. In one such case, where a teacher failed to return his contract in a timely manner, an appellate court in Washington affirmed that it would not remedy his failure to do so.[287]

278. *Fortney v. School Dist. of West Salem*, 321 N.W.2d 225 [4 Educ. L. Rep. 1281] (Wis.1982); *Crawford v. Board of Educ., Barberton City Schools*, 453 N.E.2d 627 [13 Educ. L. Rep. 475] (Ohio 1983).

279. *Tripp v. Martin*, 79 S.E.2d 521 (Ga.1954); *Katterhenrich v. Federal Hocking Local School Dist. Bd. of Educ.*, 700 N.E.2d 626 [129 Educ. L. Rep. 776], (Ohio Ct.App.1997) (affirming that a board's failure to comply with such a provision was harmless where it believed that the candidate was unqualified).

280. *Gere v. Council Bluffs Community School Dist.*, 334 N.W.2d 307 [11 Educ. L. Rep. 629] (Iowa 1983).

281. *School Comm. of Town of North Kingstown v. Crouch*, 808 A.2d 1074 [171 Educ. L. Rep. 258] (R.I.2002); *Zattiero v. Homedale School Dist. No. 370*, 51 P.3d 382 [167 Educ. L. Rep. 946] (Idaho 2002); *Hallissey v. School Admin. Dist. No. 77*, 755 A.2d 1068 [146 Educ. L. Rep. 293] (Me. 2000).

282. *See, e.g., Board of Educ. of Perry County v. Jones*, 823 S.W.2d 457 [72 Educ. L. Rep. 1190] (Ky.1992); *But see Kirschling v. Lake Forest School Dist.*, 687 F.Supp. 927 [47 Educ. L. Rep. 977] (D.Del.1988) (up-

holding an oral agreement based on state law).

283. *Oregon School Employees Ass'n, Chapter 89 v. Rainier School Dist. No. 13*, 808 P.2d 83 [66 Educ. L. Rep. 1270] (Or. 1991); *LaSorsa by LaSorsa v. UNUM Life Ins. Co. of Am.*, 955 F.2d 140 [72 Educ. L. Rep. 756] (1st Cir.1992); *Hunting v. Clark County School Dist. No. 161*, 931 P.2d 628 [116 Educ. L. Rep. 422] (Idaho 1997).

284. *Gilmore v. Bonner County School Dist. No. 82*, 971 P.2d 323 [132 Educ. L. Rep. 197] (Idaho 1999).

285. *State ex rel. Savarese v. Buckeye Local School Dist. Bd. of Educ.*, 660 N.E.2d 463 [106 Educ. L. Rep. 871] (Ohio 1996); *Cruse v. Clear Creek I.S.D.*, 976 F.Supp. 1068 [121 Educ. L. Rep. 972] (S.D.Tex. 1997).

286. *Flaherty v. Independent School Dist. No. 2144, Chisago Lakes Schools*, 577 N.W.2d 229 [125 Educ. L. Rep. 878] (Minn. Ct.App.1998).

287. *Corcoran v. Lyle School Dist. No. 406, Klickitat County*, 581 P.2d 185 (Wash. Ct.App. 1978).

In a related matter, courts generally agree that contracts that are terminated by mutual agreement, as in voluntary resignations, are generally not covered by statutory procedures.[288] In these cases, when employees resign, since they are technically offering to dissolve existing contracts,[289] boards must accept their offers. As in other contract situations, offers to resign can be withdrawn before being accepted[290] but ordinarily not after boards act.[291] If resignations are tendered orally when statutes require them to be in writing, they cannot be binding even if purportedly accepted by formal board resolutions.[292] In a case that also could fit in the section on the non-renewal of contracts, the Supreme Court of Arkansas held that remedies under the state's Teacher Fair Dismissal Act did not apply to an oral resignation.[293] The court was persuaded that since a board's acceptance of a resignation did not amount to a non-renewal, suspension, or other disciplinary action within the meaning of the statute, it was inapplicable.

Resignations may be invalid if submitted under coercion or duress such as where illegal pressures induced employees to act in ways that they were unable to apply their free will and judgment. If board officials merely suggest that employees should resign or threaten to pursue lawful courses of action, such as instituting dismissal proceedings, this does not constitute duress if employees are given the time and opportunities to deliberation before acting.[294]

Resignations may be transformed into constructive discharges if school officials deliberately make working conditions so intolerable that employees have no choice but to resign. Of course, employees bear the heavy burden of demonstrating that officials intentionally engaged in specific and substantial deviations from normal operations such that they amounted to harassment. For example, the Eighth Circuit remarked that a teacher in South Dakota with years of satisfactory evaluations who was at the top of the pay scale was subjected to "an intense pattern of classroom observation, criticism, and evaluation"[295] that led to his being constructively discharged due to his age. Conversely, where a teacher with a history of conflict with regard to the relationship that she and her son had with the board voluntarily resigned, a federal

---

288. *Brinson v. School Dist. No. 431*, 576 P.2d 602 (Kan.1978); *Brown v. Board of Educ. of Morgan County School Dist.*, 560 P.2d 1129 (Utah 1977); *Upshaw v. Alvin Indep. School Dist.*, 31 F.Supp.2d 553 [132 Educ. L. Rep. 96] (S.D. Tex. 1999).

289. *Shade v. Board of Trustees of Redondo Union High School Dist. in Los Angeles County*, 70 P.2d 490 (Cal.Ct.App. 1937).

290. *Totevski v. Board of Educ. of Hempstead Pub. School Dist.*, 680 N.Y.S.2d 824 [131 Educ. L. Rep. 253] (N.Y.Sup.Ct. 1998).

291. *Schmitt v. Hicksville UFSD No. 17*, 606 N.Y.S.2d 761 [88 Educ. L. Rep. 1139] (N.Y.App. Div.1994). *But see Pierce v. Douglas School Dist. No. 4*, 686 P.2d 332 [19 Educ. L. Rep. 716] (Or.1984) (recognizing that a board was not required to accept a teacher's resignation in order for it to become effective).

292. *Petrella v. Siegel*, 537 N.Y.S.2d 124 [51 Educ. L. Rep.1010] (N.Y.1988).

293. *Williams v. Little Rock School Dist.*, 66 S.W.3d 590 [162 Educ. L. Rep. 604] (Ark.2002).

294. *Dusanek v. Hannon*, 677 F.2d 538 [4 Educ. L. Rep. 409] (7th Cir.1982), *cert. denied*, 459 U.S. 1017, 103 S.Ct. 379, 74 L.Ed.2d 512 (1982).

295. *Lee v. Rapid City Area School Dist. No. 5–14*, 981 F.2d 316, 328 [79 Educ. L. Rep. 748] (8th Cir.1992).

trial court in Texas stated that in doing so she waived her rights to due process in her claim for constructive discharge.[296] Other courts agreed that educators who resigned waived rights such as those related to recall in situations involving layoffs[297] and to payments for unused sick leave.[298]

Where school board officials agree to conditions in resignations, they may not later disavow what were, in effect, contractual agreements. In such a case, where a chief school administrator offered to resign in return for six months of salary, the Supreme Court of South Carolina ruled that a board could not then refuse to pay the money.[299]

The extent to which school boards may contract for payments to employees who agree to resign is unclear. On the one hand, such payments might be subject to challenges as illegal gifts in return for payments for services not rendered. On the other hand, payments could be described as settlements to avoid costly litigation.[300] In an illustrative case, the Eighth Circuit affirmed that a mother in Texas could not sue a school board in Nebraska that entered into a confidential settlement agreement with the teacher who molested her son and provided him with a positive letter of recommendation rather than terminate his contract.[301] The court explained that the behavior of board officials in Nebraska did not rise to the level of deliberate indifference so as to warrant liability under section 1983 when the teacher sexually molested the child in Texas. Conversely, in an egregious case, the Supreme Court of California was of the opinion that a board can be liable for providing a good recommendation to an undeserving school employee.[302] When officials learned that an administrator allegedly sexually molested a student, they gave him a favorable letter of recommendation in exchange for his resignation. The administrator then relied on the letter to obtain a job in another school system where he allegedly engaged in sexual misconduct with the student whose claim was at issue. The court reinstated the student's claim against the board that gave the administrator the good letter of recommendation. Even so, as reflected by a case from Ohio, not all provisions in settlements are upheld when challenged due to public policy. An appellate court voided a settlement agreement executed in connection with a resignation where a school board agreed not to disclose information related to a teacher's pedophilia.[303]

296. *Upshaw v. Alvin Indep. School Dist.*, 31 F.Supp.2d 553 [132 Educ. L. Rep. 96] (S.D.Tex. 1999).

297. *Tomiak v. Hamtramck School Dist.*, 397 N.W.2d 770 [36 Educ. L. Rep. 897] (Mich.1986).

298. *Turnbough v. Mammoth Spring School Dist. No. 2*, 78 S.W.3d 89 [167 Educ. L. Rep. 492] (Ark.2002). *But see Schwartz v. Gary Community School Corp.*, 762 N.E.2d 192 [161 Educ. L. Rep. 631] (Ind.Ct.App. 2002) (declaring that a school board that incorrectly treated a school psychologist's letter as a resignation owed him pay for accumulated sick leave).

299. *Cain v. Noel*, 235 S.E.2d 292 (S.C. 1977).

300. *Ingram v. Boone*, 458 N.Y.S.2d 671 [8 Educ. L. Rep. 1076] (N.Y.App.Div.1983).

301. *Shrum ex rel. Kelly v. Kluck*, 249 F.3d 773 [153 Educ. L. Rep. 600] (8th Cir. 2001).

302. *But see Randi W. v. Muroc Joint Unified School Dist.*, 929 P.2d 582 [115 Educ. L. Rep. 502] (Cal.1997).

303. *Bowman v. Parma Bd. of Educ.*, 542 N.E.2d 663 [55 Educ. L. Rep. 707] (Ohio Ct. App. 1988).

Rules and Regulations Included

School boards have implied, if not express, authority to adopt reasonable rules and regulations pertaining to employees. As long as local policies neither contravene state directives, nor infringe on federal or state constitutional or statutory rights, such as those dealing with personnel evaluation,[304] they are incorporated, explicitly or by reference, into employment contracts and are upheld as long as they are reasonable. At the same time, where teachers are not made aware of rules or policies by reference in their contracts or other means, boards may not be able to discipline them for violations absent proof that individuals knew of or should have known of them through proper diligence.[305]

The Supreme Court has made it clear that although individuals have no right to work for the state on their own terms, they do have a right not to be excluded or treated differently pursuant to provisions that are arbitrary or discriminatory.[306] Put another way, as discussed in Chapters 10 and 11, while no one has an abstract right to public employment, individuals do have the right not to be excluded or treated differently for unconstitutional reasons. In such a case, the Supreme Court of Nebraska maintained that a teacher with twenty years of experience who took time off from work due to the illness, and eventual death of her mother, had not violated a board policy. The court concluded that since the board's action "... was arbitrary and capricious at best, and reprehensible at worst,"[307] the teacher was entitled to reinstatement with back pay.

Problems may develop when school boards seek to bind teachers under regulations that they adopted after individuals were hired. Two older cases addressed disputes of this kind. The Supreme Court of California rejected a teacher's claim that a regulation requiring staff to take graduate course work or have their pay reduced was inapplicable to her contract.[308] The court observed that board rules, which were in effect when the teacher's contract was renewed, were part of her agreement. Moreover, the Supreme Court of Indiana, rejecting a teacher's request for a leave of absence to campaign for public office, asserted that if staff could be bound only by rules and regulations that existed when their contracts were formed, conditions in districts would have to remain static for at least a year.[309] Other courts reached similar results.[310]

Along the same line, in *Harrah Independent School District v.*

---

304. *Baker v. Board of Educ., County of Hancock,* 534 S.E.2d 378 [147 Educ. L. Rep. 376] (W.Va. 2000).

305. *Miller v. South Bend Special School Dist. No. 1, McHenry County,* 124 N.W.2d 475 (N.D.1963).

306. *Wieman v. Updegraff,* 344 U.S. 183, 73 S.Ct. 215, 97 L.Ed. 216 (1952); *Perry v. Sindermann,* 408 U.S. 593, 92 S.Ct. 2694, 33 L.Ed.2d 570 (1972).

307. *Drain v. Board of Educ. of Frontier County School Dist. No. 46,* 508 N.W.2d 255, 261 [87 Educ. L. Rep. 612] (Neb.1993).

308. *Rible v. Hughes,* 150 P.2d 455 (Cal. 1944).

309. *School City of East Chicago v. Sigler,* 36 N.E.2d 760 (Ind.1941).

310. *Chatham v. Johnson,* 195 So.2d 62 (Miss.1967); *Wisconsin State Employees Ass'n v. Wisconsin Natural Resources Bd.,* 298 F.Supp. 339 (W.D.Wis.1969).

Martin,[311] the Supreme Court upheld the dismissal of a tenured teacher who refused to comply with a board's continuing education requirement which expected staff with only bachelors' degrees to earn five semester hours of credit every three years. When the state legislature removed the penalty that teachers who did not comply with such policies could have their pay reduced, a board in Oklahoma afforded recalcitrant staff the option of taking courses or facing dismissal. In upholding a teacher's dismissal, the Court commented that the policy was rationally related to the board's objective of enforcing the continuing education obligations of its staff.

As could have been expected, litigation occurs when educators seek to require boards to make certain that their policies comply with state laws. Under circumstances of this nature, courts have addressed many cases dealing with such issues as affording due process rights to all employees below the rank of superintendent[312] as well as entering judgments in favor of staff members where boards failed to comply with evaluation,[313] notice,[314] and due process[315] requirements. Courts also resolved a significant amount of litigation in favor of boards such as in cases where they agreed that a board did not have to provide a basketball coach with a formal evaluation of his performance before his coaching contract was not renewed,[316] a temporary teacher with statutory procedural rights,[317] or a superintendent with due process in terminating his contract.[318]

In a case with an interesting twist, an appellate court in Wisconsin posited that curriculum plans and safety rules were not board rules, regulations, or policies that were incorporated by reference into a teacher's employment contract.[319] The court thus decided that since a student who was injured in a technical education shop was not a third-party beneficiary of the provisions of faculty handbook governing safety procedures, he could not recover based on, among other things, breach of contract. The court added that the teacher's duty to instruct students as to safety procedures and to supervise them while enforcing these rules was not a term of his contract.

311. 440 U.S. 194, 99 S.Ct. 1062, 59 L.Ed.2d 248 (1979). [Case No. 63]

312. *Small v. Board of Trustees, Glacier County School Dist. No. 9,* 31 P.3d 358 [156 Educ. L. Rep. 1434] (Mont.2001); *Cimochowski v. Hartford Pub. Schools,* 802 A.2d 800 [167 Educ. L. Rep. 799] (Conn.2002).

313. *Bonilla v. Board of Educ. of City of N.Y.,* 728 N.Y.S.2d 69 [155 Educ. L. Rep. 1305] (N.Y. App.Div.2001).

314. *Bentley v. School Dist. No. 025 of Custer County,* 586 N.W.2d 306 [130 Educ. L. Rep. 900] (Neb.1998).

315. *Thomas v. Evangeline Parish School Bd.,* 733 So.2d 102 [135 Educ. L. Rep. 866] (La.Ct. App.1999), *writ denied,* 744 So.2d 626 (La.1999).

316. *Board of Educ. of Erlanger–Elsmere School Dist. v. Code,* 57 S.W.3d 820 [158 Educ. L. Rep. 878] (Ky.2001).

317. *Zalac v. Governing Bd. of Ferndale Unified School Dist.,* 120 Cal.Rptr.2d 615 [165 Educ. L. Rep. 277] (Cal.Ct.App.2002).

318. *Milstead v. Jackson Parish School Bd.,* 726 So.2d 979 [133 Educ. L. Rep. 280] (La.Ct. App. 1998), *writ denied,* 742 So.2d 557 (La.1999).

319. *Schilling by Foy v. Employers Mut. Cas. Co.,* 569 N.W.2d 776 [121 Educ. L. Rep. 1145] (Wis.Ct.App.1997), *review denied,* 576 N.W.2d 280 (Wis.1997).

Duties Covered by Implication

Contracts vary greatly over the extent to which they specify teacher duties. While collective bargaining agreements tend to include more provisions than individual contracts, they often do not answer the difficult question of the implied duties that teachers may have to perform. This chapter does not examine the myriad of cases surrounding the duty of teachers to provide adequate supervision of students during school hours and activities since these matters are covered in the discussion of negligence in Chapter 7.

In one of the first cases to consider this matter, an appellate panel in New York affirmed, without providing its own rationale, a trial court's detailed analysis of the implied duties of teachers in relying substantially on a directive of the state commissioner of education.[320] In upholding rules, which expected teachers to perform duties beyond classroom instruction, the court wrote that boards can assign teachers only to duties related to their respective subject matter fields or those in their contracts such as supervising a study hall or conducting student conferences. In clarifying that school officials could, for instance, assign English teachers to direct school plays, physical education teachers to coach intramural and interschool athletic teams, and band instructors to accompany students on band trips, they could not require mathematics teachers to coach athletic teams or compel any teacher to perform such duties as janitorial service or driving school buses.[321] Consistent with collective bargaining agreements, and presaging arrangements that largely obviated, but did not totally eliminate, litigation over disputes in this regard, the court ascertained that boards could arrange for teachers to perform extra duties in return for more pay. As evidence of the impact that bargaining has had in this area, the Supreme Court of New Hampshire pointed out that a school board committed an unfair labor practice in refusing to negotiate a salary scale for extracurricular positions since such compensation is a mandatory subject of bargaining.[322]

Disputes over co-curricular and extracurricular activities generated litigation, with mixed results, over the extent to which boards could require educators to perform extra duties. The Supreme Court of Pennsylvania was of the view that a teacher could not be required to supervise a voluntary high school bowling club.[323] The court acknowledged that the teacher could not have been required to perform this duty since it was not sufficiently related to the school program. On the other hand, in a pre-bargaining case, an appellate court in Illinois affirmed that teachers could be required to supervise extracurricular activities in

320. *Parrish v. Moss*, 106 N.Y.S.2d 577 (N.Y.Sup.Ct.1951), *aff'd*, 107 N.Y.S.2d 580 (N.Y. App. Div.1951).

321. *See also McGrath v. Burkhard*, 280 P.2d 864 (Cal.Ct.App.1955) (rejecting the argument that extending implied duties to include such activities as attending athletic events required teachers to perform essentially police work).

322. *Appeal of Berlin Educ. Ass'n, NHEA/NEA*, 485 A.2d 1038 [22 Educ. L. Rep. 192] (N.H. 1984).

323. *Pease v. Millcreek Township School Dist.*, 195 A.2d 104 (Pa.1963).

the evenings or on Saturdays at a rate of compensation lower than their regular salaries.[324] Another appellate court in Illinois has since affirmed that a teacher who was assigned an unreasonable number of extra duties could resign as volleyball coach while retaining her status as teacher along with other extracurricular activities.[325]

Having conceded that supervision of extracurricular activities was part of their duties, a trial court in New Jersey contended that the concerted resignations of teachers from these assignments constituted an illegal strike.[326] On further review, an appellate court noted that the question of whether the teachers had to perform the duties under their collective bargaining contract should have been referred to the state's Public Employment Relations Commission.[327] In the absence of bargaining, the Fifth Circuit affirmed that a school board in Texas was justified in terminating the contract of a teacher for insubordination when he refused to serve as a ticket-taker and to supervise students at high school football games.[328]

Another area that generated controversies was extra duty for special events such as open houses and parent-teacher conferences. An appellate court in Pennsylvania upheld the dismissal of a temporary teacher who refused to be present at an open house at her school even though she knew that she was expected to attend.[329] The court thought that the teacher's unexplained refusal to participate in an activity that was a significant part of the school program, since it brought parents to school to talk with teachers and to examine the work of their children, was a valid basis for her dismissal. West Virginia's highest court, in a case in which it did not consider whether a teacher's attendance at a parent-teacher conference was required or optional, indicated that even if it were optional, an educator had the duty to cooperate with school officials by informing them of reasons why she might not attend such an event.[330] The court was convinced that while a teacher could be disciplined for missing a parent-teacher conference, dismissal was too severe of a sanction. Yet, the Supreme Court of Colorado upheld a teacher's dismissal for a wide array of offenses, including missing parent-teacher conferences, on the ground of neglect of duty.[331]

Educators may also be expected to help when special circumstances develop. In an illustrative case, the Supreme Court of Iowa upheld the

324. *District 300 Educ. Ass'n v. Board of Educ. of Dundee Community Unit School Dist. No. 300*, 334 N.E.2d 165 (Ill.App.Ct. 1975).

325. *Lewis v. Board of Educ. of N. Clay Community Unit School Dist. No. 25*, 537 N.E.2d 435 [53 Educ. L. Rep. 596] (Ill.Ct. App.1989).

326. *Board of Educ. of City of Asbury Park v. Asbury Park Educ. Ass'n*, 368 A.2d 396 (N.J. Super. Ct. App. Div.1976).

327. *Board of Educ. of City of Asbury Park v. Asbury Park Educ. Ass'n*, 382 A.2d 392 (N.J. Super.Ct.App.Div.1977).

328. *Blair v. Robstown Indep. School Dist.*, 556 F.2d 1331 (5th Cir.1977).

329. *Johnson v. United School Dist. Joint School Bd.*, 191 A.2d 897 (Pa.Super.Ct.1963).

330. *Fox v. Board of Educ. of Doddridge County*, 236 S.E.2d 243 (W.Va.1977).

331. *Board of Educ. of Jefferson County School Dist. R–1 v. Wilder*, 960 P.2d 695 [128 Educ. L. Rep. 378] (Colo.1998).

termination of a principal's contract when he refused to perform the duties of an attendance officer.[332] The court found that in construing "other duties" in state law and in the principal's contract, it could not be said that board officials exceeded their discretion in assigning him tasks ordinarily performed by attendance officers since "other duties" is not restricted to instructional activities.

Nonrenewal of Teacher Contracts

When contracts expire, they dissolve unless there are some grounds on which renewals can be required such as if one party fails to perform a condition necessary for an agreement to be terminated properly. At the end of contract periods, since the parties are placed in essentially the same position that they were in before the agreements began, the non-renewals of limited contracts can be distinguished from tenured or continuing contracts. Of course, if teachers are working under at-will employment contracts, school officials may terminate them at any time.[333] When dealing with tenure or continuing contracts, since employees have acquired substantive due process rights, they are entitled to procedural safeguards before they can be dismissed. Chapter 11 reviews the hearing requirements that are necessary in order to dismiss employees with tenure or continuing contracts.

The Supreme Court first examined the extent to which the Fourteenth Amendment's due process clause applied to the non-renewal of the contracts of non-tenured educators in the context of companion cases from public institutions of higher education. Although these cases are set in higher education, they are important for educators in elementary and secondary schools because they help to set the parameters on the contractual rights of teachers and other staff members. *Board of Regents of State Colleges v. Roth (Roth)*[334] considered whether a non-tenured faculty member had a Fourteenth Amendment right to an explanation and a hearing when his contract was not renewed. In *Perry v. Sindermann (Perry)*,[335] the Court discussed the circumstances under which a public employee might gain the procedural rights of tenure absent an express statutory or contractual provision for such protection.

Roth was filed by a faculty member in Wisconsin who served under a one-year fixed contract. After the faculty member challenged the non-renewal of his contract, the Supreme Court rejected the notion that he was entitled to a statement of reasons and a hearing in order to protect against having such decisions made based on improper motives. The Court declared that the requirements of procedural due process apply only to deprivations of interests encompassed within the concepts of "liberty" and "property" in the Fourteenth Amendment since the "...

---

332. *Gere v. Council Bluffs Community School Dist.*, 334 N.W.2d 307 [11 Educ. L. Rep. 629] (Iowa 1983).

333. *Cape v. Greenville County School Dist.*, 618 S.E.2d 881 [202 Educ. L. Rep. 370] (S.C. 2005), *reh'g denied* (S.C. 2005).

334. 408 U.S. 564, 92 S.Ct. 2701, 33 L.Ed.2d 548 (1972). [Case No. 66]

335. 408 U.S. 593, 92 S.Ct. 2694, 33 L.Ed.2d 570 (1972). [Case No. 67]

range of interests protected by procedural due process is not infinite."[336] The Court was satisfied that the nature of the interest at stake was the crucial factor as to whether it was constitutionally protected because although the faculty member was not rehired and remained free to seek another job, he did not suffer a deprivation of his liberty interest.

In *Roth*, the Court maintained that the faculty member did not suffer a harm to his liberty interest, which is at issue when an individual's reputation is at stake since university officials neither seriously damaged his standing in his community by making a charge, such as dishonesty, nor did they impose a stigma on him that prevented him from obtaining other employment in his field, circumstances that would have established the right to a hearing. Regarding property interests, the Court concluded that since they do not derive from the Constitution but, rather, are created and defined by independent sources such as state law, the specific terms of the faculty member's contract did not secure any interest in his being employed beyond the one-year term of his contract.

Perry was filed by a faculty member who taught at three different colleges in the state system of Texas for ten consecutive years. Having served under a series of four one-year contracts at a junior college, he challenged the non-renewal of his contract, without a written explanation or a hearing, after he criticized policies of the state board of regents. At issue was whether the faculty member had a protected property interest in his job. The Court amplified the concept of property interest for due process purposes by clarifying that such an interest could derive not only from express legislative or contractual wording but also from existing rules or understandings, as a kind of unwritten common law in a given university that some faculty have the equivalent of tenure. However, the Court also recognized that a claim of de facto tenure, which could be examined only at a hearing, must be more than a mere subjective expectancy of re-employment. The Court determined that while the faculty member might not have had tenure, since any lack of a contractual right to re-employment was immaterial where his claim that his contract was not renewed was based on his exercising his constitutional right to freedom of speech, he was entitled to the protection of due process.

The Court went on to delineate the concept of liberty interests in *Bishop v. Wood*[337] wherein a probationary police officer in North Carolina who was dismissed without a hearing was informed of the reasons for the adverse employment action in a private meeting. In addition to the common stigma claim, the officer claimed that the reasons for his dismissal were false. The Court, in upholding the officer's dismissal, affirmed that he did not suffer from an actionable stigma since the reasons were not made public until he filed suit. In addition, the Court believed that the falsity allegation did not require a hearing because insofar as the officer received the reasons in private, his reputation was

---

336. *Board of Regents of State Colleges v. Roth*, 408 U.S. 564, 570, 92 S.Ct. 2701, 33 L.Ed.2d 548 (1972). [Case No. 66]

337. 426 U.S. 341, 96 S.Ct. 2074, 48 L.Ed.2d 684 (1976).

not affected by their truth or falsity. The Court reasoned that the Constitution could not be construed as requiring federal judicial review of the many personnel actions that officials at public agencies make on daily bases and that since state law had not conferred a property right on the officer, the rejection of his liberty interest claim meant that he was left without a federal remedy.

A year later, in *Codd v. Velger*,[338] a brief per curiam order directing the Second Circuit to reinstate the judgment of a federal trial court in New York, the Court held that officials did not stigmatize a former police officer by placing material in his personnel file that was related to an apparent suicide attempt and releasing the file, with his permission, to a prospective employer. The Court emphasized that since the purpose of hearings on stigmatization claims is to afford employees opportunities to refute the charges and clear their names, if the truth of a charge is not at issue, there is no constitutional need for hearings. The Court specified that employees are entitled to hearings only if employers create and disseminate false and defamatory impressions about individuals whose employment is terminated and that any harm that might have taken place was not occasioned by the lack of hearing.

As could have been anticipated, many disputes arose when non-tenured employees sought to establish that they had property or liberty interests in their jobs entitling them to due process hearings. While liberty and property interests can arise in the same case,[339] as reflected in the following review of representative litigation, these allegations usually appear separately.

The fact that states require school board officials to provide reasons for the non-renewal of contracts does not in itself create a federal right.[340] State procedural rights are enforceable in state courts which are empowered to interpret the existence and extent of rights allegedly created by state laws.[341] Property rights granted by states are shaped by the procedures provided in legislation or state-constitutional interpretations in evaluating such rights. For example, the Supreme Court of New Jersey granted teachers whose contracts were not renewed the right to be informed of reasons, suggesting that while these can be communicated at informal hearings, it would not place restrictions on the ability of boards to act as they saw fit.[342] In like fashion, the Supreme Court of Texas ruled that where a state statute stipulated that if the annual contracts of teachers were not renewed, boards had to notify them of the reasons for doing so along with opportunities for hearings since under these circumstance educators had protected property interests.[343] Earli-

---

338. 429 U.S. 624, 97 S.Ct. 882, 51 L.Ed.2d 92 (1977).

339. *Perez v. Denver Pub. Schools*, 919 P.2d 960 [111 Educ. L. Rep. 537] (Colo.Ct. App.1996); *Sickon v. School Bd. of Alachua County, Fla.*, 719 So.2d 360 [130 Educ. L. Rep. 944] (Fla. Dist. Ct.App.1998); *Townsend v. Vallas*, 256 F.3d 661 [155 Educ. L. Rep. 142] (7th Cir. 2001).

340. *Ryan v. Aurora Bd. of Educ.*, 540 F.2d 222 (6th Cir.1976), *cert. denied*, 429

U.S. 1041, 97 S.Ct. 741, 50 L.Ed.2d 753 (1977).

341. *Sigmon v. Poe*, 564 F.2d 1093 (4th Cir.1977).

342. *Donaldson v. Board of Educ. of N. Wildwood*, 320 A.2d 857 (N.J.1974).

343. *Grounds v. Tolar Indep. School Dist.*, 856 S.W.2d 417 [84 Educ. L. Rep. 559] (Tex.1993).

er, the same court overturned the non-renewal of a teacher's contract since the reason that board officials proffered was not on a list of eighteen specified in a board's rules.[344]

Where legislatures create statewide tenure systems, local boards cannot change their allocations of powers and rights, whether by collective bargaining or otherwise. Thus, de facto tenure is not possible.[345] Put another way, a property right such as tenure can be based only on an affirmative government action[346] and must be perfected by a body, such as a school board,[347] that is authorized to do so. Employees usually do not have property rights in jobs unless they have statutory entitlements to them[348] such as under tenure provisions or unless changes in duties amount to demotions giving rise to procedural due process rights to hearings.[349]

Courts rejected claims that employees had property rights in an array of cases. Among the controversies that courts examined were those where contracts expired,[350] where principals were paid under a salary schedule,[351] where a superintendent was paid his entire salary under a contract even though he was relieved of duty,[352] and where a coach's athletic contract was not renewed.[353]

As to liberty interests, it is difficult for employees to establish that they suffered from stigmas unless board members and/or school officials make public statements or release derogatory information about their employment status.[354] The constitutional requirement is that employees whose contracts are not renewed must demonstrate that they were seriously harmed, not merely that they were rejected and deemed to be of insufficient merit for re-employment in the district. Even where statements have gone beyond internal channels, if they describe perceived professional weakness or unsatisfactory performance in general, they usually do not rise to the constitutional level since, as reflected in

344. *Seifert v. Lingleville Indep. School Dist.*, 692 S.W.2d 461 [26 Educ. L. Rep. 512] (Tex. 1985).

345. *Ryan v. Aurora City Bd. of Educ.*, 540 F.2d 222 (6th Cir.1976); *Meyr v. Board of Educ. of Affton School Dist.*, 572 F.2d 1229 (8th Cir.1978). [Case No. 68]

346. *Confederation of Police v. City of Chicago*, 547 F.2d 375 (7th Cir.1977).

347. *Castro v. New York City Bd. of Educ.*, 777 F.Supp. 1113 [71 Educ. L. Rep. 465] (S.D.N.Y.1990), *aff'd without written opinion*, 923 F.2d 844 (2d Cir.1990), *cert. denied*, 498 U.S. 1099, 111 S.Ct. 992, 112 L.Ed.2d 1076 (1991).

348. *Ulichny v. Merton Community School Dist.*, 249 F.3d 686 [153 Educ. L. Rep. 573] (7th Cir.2001).

349. *Smith v. Ouachita Parish School Bd.*, 702 So.2d 727 [122 Educ. L. Rep. 1069]

(La.Ct. App.1997), *writ denied*, 706 So.2d 978 (La.1998).

350. *Corns v. Russell County Va. School Bd.*, 52 F.3d 56 [99 Educ. L. Rep. 761] (4th Cir.1995); *State ex rel. McGinty v. Cleveland City School Dist. Bd. of Educ.*, 690 N.E.2d 1273 [123 Educ. L. Rep. 1270] (Ohio 1998).

351. *Gardner v. Coffeeville School Dist.*, 982 F.Supp. 1221 [123 Educ. L. Rep. 72] (N.D. Miss. 1997).

352. *Harrington v. Lauer*, 888 F.Supp. 616 [101 Educ. L. Rep. 775] (D.N.J.1995), *on reconsideration in part*, 893 F.Supp. 352 [102 Educ. L. Rep. 974] (D.N.J.1995) (addressing section 1983 liability).

353. *Puchalski v. School Dist. of Springfield*, 161 F.Supp.2d 395 [156 Educ. L. Rep. 1092] (E.D.Pa.2001).

354. *Hayes v. Phoenix–Talent School Dist. No. 4*, 893 F.2d 235 [58 Educ. L. Rep. 45] (9th Cir.1990).

the following review, most courts agreed that a liberty interest is not at issue absent specific and substantial charges.

Courts refused to find that school officials acted in ways that stigmatized employees or that they were entitled to name-clearing hearings in cases where teachers were denied tenure[355] or when a teacher was not provided with reasons for being denied tenure.[356] Other cases involved charges of using ineffective teaching methods,[357] being reassigned to another school in a district in connection with testing irregularities,[358] being temporarily suspended pending the completion of a criminal investigation,[359] and having contracts not renewed for refusing to take a drug test,[360] being absent frequently,[361] and hitting a student.[362]

On the other hand, courts agreed that the existence of stigmas entitled employees to name-clearing hearings in disagreements over charges of a serious mental disorder,[363] moral unfitness,[364] wilful neglect of duty,[365] and responsibility for rapid deterioration of a school.[366] Additional cases considered such controversies as where officials accused a teacher of fabricating or causing sex crimes involving students,[367] where there were unjustified allegations of child abuse,[368] where comments on an evaluation were so harsh that they would likely have convinced other boards not to hire an individual,[369] and where a teacher was named on a registry of child abusers.[370]

A related concern is the effect of including a constitutionally protected right as a factor in not renewing the contract of a non-tenured

---

355. *Calvin v. Rupp,* 471 F.2d 1346 (8th Cir.1973); *Meyr v. Board of Educ. of Affton School Dist.,* 572 F.2d 1229 (8th Cir.1978).

356. *Cato v. Collins,* 539 F.2d 656 (8th Cir.1976).

357. *LaBorde v. Franklin Parish School Bd.,* 510 F.2d 590 (5th Cir.1975); *Shirck v. Thomas,* 486 F.2d 691 (7th Cir.1973).

358. *Thomas v. Smith,* 897 F.2d 154 [58 Educ. L. Rep. 1114] (5th Cir.1989).

359. *Strasburger v. Board of Educ., Hardin County Community Unit School Dist. No. 1,* 143 F.3d 351 [126 Educ. L. Rep. 577] (7th Cir.1998), *cert. denied,* 525 U.S. 1069, 119 S.Ct. 800, 142 L.Ed.2d 661 [132 Educ. L. Rep. 283] (1999).

360. *Cox v. McCraley,* 993 F.Supp. 1452 [125 Educ. L. Rep. 456] (M.D.Fla.1998).

361. *Cohen v. Litt,* 906 F.Supp. 957 [105 Educ. L. Rep. 515] (S.D.N.Y.1995) (also unsuccessfully alleging violations of a property interest).

362. *Burton v. Town of Littleton,* 426 F.3d 9 [202 Educ. L. Rep. 86] (1st Cir. 2005) (also rejecting the teacher's ADEA claim).

363. *Lombard v. Board of Educ. of City of N.Y.,* 502 F.2d 631 (2d Cir.1974), *cert. denied,* 420 U.S. 976, 95 S.Ct. 1400, 43 L.Ed.2d 656 (1975).

364. *McGhee v. Draper,* 564 F.2d 902 (10th Cir.1977).

365. *Huntley v. Community School Bd. of Brooklyn, N.Y. School Dist. No. 14,* 543 F.2d 979 (2d Cir.1976), *cert. denied,* 430 U.S. 929, 97 S.Ct. 1547, 51 L.Ed.2d 773 (1977).

366. *Staton v. Mayes,* 552 F.2d 908 (10th Cir.1977), *cert. denied,* 434 U.S. 907, 98 S.Ct. 309, 54 L.Ed.2d 195 (1977).

367. *Burke v. Chicago School Reform Bd. of Trustees,* 169 F.Supp.2d 843 [158 Educ. L. Rep. 631] (N.D.Ill.2001).

368. *Winegar v. Des Moines Indep. Community School Dist.,* 20 F.3d 895 [90 Educ. L. Rep. 580] (8th Cir.1994), *cert. denied,* 513 U.S. 964, 115 S.Ct. 426, 130 L.Ed.2d 340 (1994).

369. *Donato v. Plainview–Old Bethpage Cent. School Dist.,* 96 F.3d 623 [112 Educ. L. Rep. 624] (2d Cir.1996), *cert. denied,* 519 U.S. 1150, 117 S.Ct. 1083, 137 L.Ed.2d 218 (1997), *on remand,* 985 F.Supp. 316 [123 Educ. L. Rep. 617] (E.D.N.Y.1997).

370. *Matter of Allegations of Sexual Abuse at East Park High School,* 714 A.2d 339 [128 Educ. L. Rep. 302] (N.J.Super.Ct.App.Div.1998).

teacher. The Supreme Court addressed such a so-called mixed-motives case in *Mt. Healthy City Board of Education v. Doyle* (*Mt. Healthy*).[371] A teacher in Ohio with a record of being difficult in school claimed that a board violated his rights by not renewing his contract because he called a radio talk show and criticized a memo from his principal dealing with a faculty dress code. The Court rejected the Sixth Circuit's position that inclusion of a protected activity as a substantial part of the basis for the non-renewal of the teacher's contract entitled him to reinstatement with back pay. The Court pointed out that the Sixth Circuit would have placed the teacher in a better position as a result of the exercise of his purportedly constitutionally protected conduct than he would have occupied had he done nothing. According to the Court, this meant that if a teacher shows that protected conduct about a school matter was a substantial or motivating factor in a board's choosing not to renew a contract, a board must be given the opportunity to demonstrate that it would have reached the same decision not to re-employ the individual in the absence of the protected conduct. On remand, the Sixth Circuit ascertained that the board would not have renewed the teacher's contract regardless of whether he placed the call to the radio station.[372]

Some courts, in non-education cases, have suggested that parts of *Mt. Healthy*[373] were superseded legislatively[373] while others, in educational disputes, chose not to extend it[374] or distinguished it away.[375] The Supreme Court applied *Mt. Healthy* in non-education cases[376] and one dispute involving education, *Givhan v. Western Line Consolidated School District* (*Givhan*).[377] On remand in *Givhan*, the Fifth Circuit affirmed that since one motivating factor behind a board in Mississippi's choosing not to rehire a teacher was her exercise of protected speech in criticizing school officials, it violated her rights since it would not have terminated her contract but for her having spoken out.[378] Subsequently, the First Circuit affirmed that although one motivating factor behind a school board in Maine's non-renewal of a teacher's contract was her exercise of protected free speech, it did not violate her rights[379] while the Third Circuit decided that a board in Pennsylvania might have been able to defeat a teacher's claim of malicious prosecution if officials could have proven that they would have dismissed her even in the absence of her

---

371. 429 U.S. 274, 97 S.Ct. 568, 50 L.Ed.2d 471 (1977). [Case No. 69]

372. *Doyle v. Mt. Healthy City School Dist. Bd. of Educ.*, 670 F.2d 59 [2 Educ. L. Rep. 973] (6th Cir.1982).

373. *See N.L.R.B. v. Fluor Daniel, Inc.*, 161 F.3d 953 (6th Cir.1998) (suggesting that the Civil Rights Act of 1991, 42 U.S.C.A. § 2000e–2(m), superseded aspects of *Mt. Healthy* in Title VII cases). *See also Rivera v. United States*, 924 F.2d 948 (9th Cir. 1991).

374. *Zugarek v. Southern Tioga School Dist.*, 214 F.Supp.2d 468 [168 Educ. L. Rep. 756] (M.D. Pa.2002).

375. *Belanger v. Madera Unified School Dist.*, 963 F.2d 248 [75 Educ. L. Rep. 118] (9th Cir. 1992), *cert. denied*, 507 U.S. 919, 113 S.Ct. 1280, 122 L.Ed.2d 674 (1993).

376. *Waters v. Churchill*, 511 U.S. 661, 114 S.Ct. 1878, 128 L.Ed.2d 686 (1994).

377. 439 U.S. 410, 99 S.Ct. 693, 58 L.Ed.2d 619 (1979).

378. *On remand*, 592 F.2d 280 (5th Cir. 1979), *appeal after remand*, 691 F.2d 766 [7 Educ. L. Rep. 242] (5th Cir.1982).

379. *Wytrwal v. Saco School Bd.*, 70 F.3d 165 [104 Educ. L. Rep. 1023] (1st Cir.1995).

exercising protected speech.[380]

[Case No. 60]   Contract with Uncertificated Principal

STATE EX REL. THOMPSON v. EKBERG

Supreme Court of Oklahoma, 1980.
613 P.2d 466.

SIMMS, JUSTICE: Plaintiff appeals from a defendants' judgment in a taxpayer's suit brought ... by electors in the Vian School District of Vian, Oklahoma, to recover damages against the Vian School Board (Board) members ... for the wrongful hiring of Moxom as principal of the Vian High School.

Moxom was hired to serve as principal for the 1974–75 school year at a salary of $11,200 per year. Moxom did not have a standard master's degree as required for his certification by 70 O.S.Supp.1972, § subsection 9. The Board hired Moxom only after a representative of the State Department of Education, Ben Chapman, advised the Board that the degree requirement would be waived. Moxom was then working toward his master's degree, and the Board had little time in which to hire a principal before the school year began. Moxom then served as principal for the school year, acquiring his master's degree sometime thereafter.

Appellant (plaintiff below) claims that the purported waiver of the certification requirement was ineffective, and therefore the appellees are liable for double the amount of the salary for the wrongful act of hiring an uncertified principal. 70 O.S.1971, § 5–125.

The trial court found the purported "waiver" or "permission" effective and gave judgment for the defendants.

70 O. S. Supp.1972, § 3–104, in its applicable provision, reads:

The control of the State Department of Education and the supervision of the public school system of Oklahoma shall be vested in the State Board of Education and, subject to limitations otherwise provided by law, the State Board of Education shall: ...

9. Have full and exclusive authority in all matters pertaining to standards of qualifications and the certification of persons for instructional, supervisory, and administrative positions and services in the public schools of the state, and shall formulate rules and regulations governing the issuance and revocation of certificates. ...

... Provided, further, that the requirements for a certificate for county superintendent of schools, district superintendent of schools and principal, shall include not less than a standard master's degree. ...

---

380. *Merkle v. Upper Dublin School*   (3d Cir.2000).
Dist., 211 F.3d 782 [144 Educ. L. Rep. 83]

Defendants claim that the State Board of Education's grant of full and exclusive authority in matters pertaining to qualifications allows it to waive the specific requirement of a master's degree for a principal, and that, in fact, this waiver is given routinely by [it].

A plain reading of the statute shows a legislative intent that no person is to be certified to be a principal unless he or she holds a standard master's degree. This is a specific exception to the general words of grant of authority, and as a rule, general words in a statute are limited by subsequent more specific terms. To hold otherwise and allow the State Board of Education discretion to ignore the requirement, would make the requirement meaningless. This Court will not presume the legislature has done a vain and useless act. Further, statutes must be interpreted to render every word and sentence operative, rather than in a manner which would render a specific statutory provision nugatory.

Finally, the grant of authority to the State Board of Education is specifically subject to limitations otherwise provided by law. The requirement that a principal hold a standard master's degree is one such limitation.

We hold, therefore, that the State Board of Education has no authority to waive the requirement of a master's degree for a certificate for a principal, and such purported waiver is of no effect.

Plaintiffs base the liability of the defendants on 70 O.S.1971, § 5–15, providing a recovery of double the amount of money wrongfully paid, specifically including money paid on an unlawful school employment contract. This statute is penal in nature and must be strictly construed.

The policy of this statute was discussed in [a 1953 case]:

The statutes above quoted determine the public policy of this state, which is that boards of education may not knowingly hire and pay uncertified teachers or superintendents or other employees, and if such is done, the members of such board shall be jointly liable for the return of the amount of public money thus expended.

Liability under the statute is only imposed where the Board "knowingly" hires a principal without certification. Under the facts presented, the Board could not reasonably have known that the waiver given was ineffective to satisfy the certificate requirement. We hold today that the requirement of a master's degree for a principal cannot be waived. This holding stands as notice to all school boards that any such purported waiver is of no effect, and that any money expended under such purported waiver is an unlawful expenditure that will subject the parties involved to liability under 70 O.S.1971, § 5–125.

Judgment of the trial court affirmed.

Notes

1. The court did not discuss whether Mr. Chapman was an agent of the state department who was authorized to make statements on its behalf. Was it reasonable for the board to believe that Mr. Chapman was its agent?

2.   Can an agent bind his principal to violate the law? Was it clear that the waiver violated the law?

[Case No. 61]   Procedural Due Process in Teacher Certification Determination

BROWN v. SOUTH CAROLINA STATE BOARD OF EDUCATION

Supreme Court of South Carolina, 1990.
391 S.E.2d 866 [60 Educ. L. Rep. 1004].

GREGORY, CHIEF JUSTICE. This appeal is from a circuit court order affirming respondent's (Board's) invalidation of appellant's teaching certificate. We reverse and remand.

Appellant took the National Teacher's Examination (NTE) for elementary school teachers which is administered by Educational Testing Service (ETS). On March 28, 1987, ETS reported to the State Department of Education (Department) that appellant had achieved a passing score. The Department then issued appellant a teaching certificate valid through June 1990.

With certificate in hand, appellant applied for a teaching position with the Dorchester County School District No. 4. The superintendent of schools who interviewed appellant noted that her NTE scores were at the 78th percentile nationally, well above the required score of 50 percent. Because of this and other qualifications, appellant was offered a position as a second grade teacher. She performed satisfactorily on the job.

On January 25, 1988, the Department received a report from ETS stating simply that appellant's March 28, 1987, NTE scores had been "canceled" and directing the Department to "delete them from your records." The Department then advised appellant that because her NTE scores had been canceled, her teaching certificate was no longer valid and she could qualify for certification only upon presentation of a valid passing NTE score. At appellant's request, a hearing was scheduled and the invalidation was suspended until that time.

A hearing was held before the Teacher Recruitment, Training, and Certification Committee of the Board. The only evidence produced at the hearing to support invalidation of appellant's teaching certificate was the notification from ETS that her NTE scores had been canceled. The Committee recommended appellant's teaching certificate be invalidated and the Board affirmed that decision. On appeal to the circuit court, the Board's decision was affirmed and this appeal followed.

Appellant contends the regulation under which her teaching certificate was invalidated is unconstitutional because it violates her right to procedural due process. Reg. 43–50 provides:

If any testing company invalidates a test score, the State Board of Education shall accept that determination and, if a teaching certificate has been issued based upon the invalid score, shall automatically invalidate that certificate effective the date of receipt of notification of the score invalidity by the Office of Teacher Education and Certification.

The fourteenth amendment Due Process Clause requires procedural due process be afforded an individual deprived of a property or liberty interest by the State. The right to hold specific employment and the right to follow a chosen profession free from unreasonable governmental interference come within the liberty and property interests protected by the Due Process Clause. The liberty interest at stake is the individual's freedom to practice his or her chosen profession; the property interest is the specific employment. When the State seeks to revoke or deny a professional license, these interests are implicated and procedural due process requirements must be met. The State must afford notice and the opportunity for a hearing appropriate to the nature of the case.

Where important decisions turn on questions of fact, due process requires an opportunity to confront and cross-examine adverse witnesses. Procedural due process often requires confrontation and cross-examination of one whose word deprives a person of his or her livelihood. Moreover, the evidence used to prove the State's case must be disclosed to the individual so that he or she has an opportunity to show it is untrue.

We hold Reg. 43–59 unconstitutional because it does not provide for notice and an opportunity to be heard when the State deprives a teacher of his or her teaching certificate. The fact that appellant was granted a hearing as a matter of favor in this case does not save the regulation from constitutional attack under the Due Process Clause. Further, the hearing appellant was granted did not comport with procedural due process since the Board did not disclose any evidence substantiating cancellation of the NTE scores in order to allow appellant the opportunity to contest the allegations against her.

The Board contends appellant cannot complain she was deprived of due process because she failed to avail herself of ETS procedure to contest the cancellation of her scores. On the record before us, however, ETS procedure does not provide for any hearing whereby appellant could confront her accusers. The Board further contends it could not obtain information from ETS regarding cancellation of appellant's scores absent her consent which she refused to give. The record, however, reveals no attempt by the Board to obtain information regarding cancellation of appellant's test scores from ETS. . . .

REVERSED and REMANDED.

Notes

1.   Was Regulation 43–59 struck down because it contained an intrinsic flaw or due to the way in which it was implemented?

2.   What is your opinion about the educational and legal ramifications of a state's accepting a testing company's unexplained notification as a condition for disqualifying a teacher?

3.   Why do you think that ETS was unwilling to supply the state board with the information it needed?

[Case No. 62]   National Teacher Examination as Certification Requirement

UNITED STATES v. STATE OF SOUTH CAROLINA

United States District Court, District of South Carolina, 1977.
445 F.Supp. 1094.

The United States brought this action on September 15, 1975, against the State of South Carolina, the South Carolina State Board of Education, the South Carolina State Retirement System, the South Carolina Budget and Control Board, and three local school boards in their individual capacities and as representatives of a defendant class of all local school boards in the State. The defendants are charged with violations of the Fourteenth Amendment to the Constitution of the United States and Title VII of the Civil Rights Act of 1964 through the use of minimum score requirements on the National Teacher Examinations (hereinafter "NTE") to certify and determine the pay levels of teachers within the State. . . .

For over thirty years the State of South Carolina and its agencies have used scores on the NTE to make decisions with respect to the certification of teachers and the amount of state aid payable to local school districts. Local school boards within the State use scores on the NTE for selection and compensation of teachers. From 1969 to 1976, a minimum score of 975 was required by the State for its certification and state aid decisions. In June, 1976, after an exhaustive validation study by Educational Testing Service (ETS), and, after a critical review and evaluation of this study by the Board of Education's Committee on Teacher Recruitment, Training and Compensation and the Department Staff, the State established new certification requirements involving different minimum scores in various areas of teaching specialization that range from 940 to 1198. . . .

. . . [B]ut there are no uniform standards with respect to test scores used by the local school boards in selecting from among the pool of certified applicants.

Plaintiffs challenge each of the uses of the NTE. They contend that more blacks than whites historically have failed to achieve the required minimum score, and that this result creates a racial classification in violation of the constitutional and statutory provisions cited in their complaints. . . .

I.   Constitutional Issues

We first consider whether the use by the State and its Board of Education of a minimum score requirement on the NTE violates the equal protection clause of the Fourteenth Amendment.

. . . Plaintiffs allege that the disparate racial impact of defendants' certification and compensation systems creates a racial classification in violation of the Fourteenth Amendment. In order to sustain that allegation, the Supreme Court's decision in *Washington v. Davis* requires plaintiffs to prove that the State intended to create and use a racial classification. If plaintiffs fail to prove intent (or defendants adequately rebut that proof), then we must evaluate this classification under the rational relationship standard required by the Fourteenth Amendment as to all such classifications.

A. Discriminatory Intent

Because of its paramount importance under *Washington v. Davis*, we look first at whether the plaintiffs have proved that any of the challenged decisions of defendants were motivated by an intent to discriminate. The purpose or intent that we must assess is the purpose or intent that underlies the particular act or acts under review. In its decision in *Village of Arlington Heights v. Metropolitan Housing Development Corp.*, the Supreme Court suggested that evidence as to several factors might have probative value in proving intent: historical background, the sequence of events leading up to the challenged decision (including substantive and procedural departures from the norm), legislative history, and testimony from officials. . . .

1. Certification

South Carolina requires persons who teach in the public schools to hold a certificate issued by the State Board of Education. From 1945 to the present the State has had four certification systems, each requiring prospective teachers to take the NTE. Candidates are able to take the NTE an unlimited number of times. (The tests are given by the State three or four times each year).

The record before us indicates that during this period, the racial composition of the South Carolina teacher force has closely paralleled the racial composition of the State's population. . . .

From 1945 through 1968, the State issued four grades of certificates: A, B, C and D. From 1945 through 1956, candidates were awarded certificates based on their relative standing with respect to test scores of all candidates in the State for the year: A certificates went to the top 25%; B certificates to the middle 50%; C certificates to the next 15%; and D certificates to the bottom 10%. Under this system, every candidate who met the other requirements was licensed.

In 1957, a new system of absolute, rather than relative, requirements was instituted. Under this system, a score of 500 or more on the Common Examinations portion of the NTE was required for an A certificate; a score of 425 to 499 for a B certificate; a score of 375 to 424 for a C certificate; and a score of 332 to 374 for a D certificate. Those with scores below 332 were not licensed. During the academic year 1967–68, that restriction eliminated less than 1% of the candidates from predominantly white colleges and approximately 3% of the candidates from predominantly black colleges. The reason for these low percentages is that the 332 minimum score, when placed on the NTE score scale of 300 to 900 points, is very near the lowest attainable score.

In 1969, the certification system was further revised by replacing the four-tiered system with two types of certificates: the professional certificate and the warrant. The minimum score requirement was set at 975 for the professional certificate, including a score of at least 450 on the Common Examinations and at least 450 on the applicable Area Examination; and 850 for the warrant, including a score of at least 400 on the Common Examinations and 400 on the applicable Area Examination. Those who attained scores below 400 were not licensed. In the academic year 1969–70, the minimum score requirement of 400 on the Common Examinations eliminated approximately 41% of the graduates of predominantly black colleges and less than 1% of the graduates of predominantly white colleges. Similar results were obtained in succeeding years, despite the fact that a score of 400 is usually below the 11th percentile nationally, and almost 90% of the candidates who take these tests get a higher score.

In 1976, the certification system was again revised, the two-tiered system being replaced with a single certificate with separate minimum score requirements in each of the 18 fields of teaching specialty replacing the single minimum score requirement. These combined scores on both Common Examinations and Area Examinations ranged from 940 in Agriculture to 1178 in Library and Media Specialties; and are set forth in detail hereinafter. There are no statistics in the record indicating the impact of the new score requirements because they will be applied first to the class of 1977; however, plaintiffs predict that, under these requirements, the disparate impact may be even greater....

The 1945 decision: In 1941, a committee was appointed by the General Assembly to review the certification and compensation of teachers. The committee recommended that a thorough study of the certification system be made and suggested that the use of an NTE score requirement be explored because of the great variation in teacher training institutions. The State Board undertook a two-year study that resulted in a four-volume report, made available in 1944. That report recommended four different teacher credentials based on relative NTE scores. On the basis of the report, the State Board adopted the four-tiered system described above under which no candidate was denied licensing. At that time, South Carolina maintained a dual public school system with segregated student bodies and faculties. After the decision to institute the new certification system, but before its effective date, the State Board tested 50% of the teachers in the State, which revealed that 90% of the white teachers, and only 27% of the black teachers, would qualify for A or B certificates (the two top grades). The remaining candidates 10% of the whites and 73% of the blacks would receive C and D certificates. After receiving these data, the State Board did not rescind its decision to institute the new certification system.

We are unable to find any discriminatory intent from these facts. Although the historical background of segregated schools might provide some basis for the inference urged by plaintiffs, any such inference has been rebutted. The committee based its recommendation concerning the NTE in part on its conclusion that the tests "can be scored objectively and impartially and their use would not be subject to the accusation that they are used for purposes of discrimination." The Board's extensive study is viewed as an earnest effort in its time, and provided reasonable support for its decision to institute an NTE requirement. The Board's knowledge of differential impact, without more, does not support a finding of discriminatory intent.

The 1956 decision: From 1945 through 1956, the State Board received from ETS statistical summaries of the test scores of South Carolina candidates showing that blacks as a group had lower average scores than whites as a group. In 1954 and 1955, the Supreme Court handed down its historic decisions in *Brown v. Board of Education*, which announced the end of the "separate but equal" rationale for segregated school systems. South Carolina did not thereafter integrate its schools, but instead adopted policies which maintained its dual school system until well into the 1960's. In 1956, the School Board adopted the absolute score system without a professional study relating the scores to effective teaching or academic achievement in the teacher preparation program.

Again, we find nothing in the record to support a finding of discriminatory intent. Plaintiffs have not persuaded the court that the State's reluctance to integrate its schools infected its decisions on teacher certification. The minimum score requirement of 332 was so low as to preclude us from presuming or even inferring that this was the case. Only 3% of the candidates from black colleges (and 1% of the candidates from white colleges) were denied certificates under this system during the last year it was in effect; and its effect in earlier years was not substantially different. The State Board did not move to change the system when it discovered that very few blacks were excluded, and significantly, this system was maintained for over 11 years.

The 1969 decision: From 1957 through 1969, the State Board continued to receive from ETS statistical data indicating disparate impact by race. During this period, the State continued to maintain its essentially dual school system through a variety of administrative measures. In 1968, the State Board received a report from a committee formed in 1967 to study the certification system. The committee included black and white members who were educators, teachers, state administrators and others. The committee had before it, inter alia, two documents, one which was critical of the NTE as a predictor of performance in student teaching, and the other which set out the ETS position that the test scores should not be used as a sole criterion for certification if other measures were available. The committee reviewed the academic programs and admission requirements at the State's 25 teacher training institutions and determined that not all had the same resources and strengths. The committee recommended that the minimum score levels be raised to 975 for professional certificates and 850 for warrants. From the data supplied by ETS, the committee would have been able to predict the impact of its recommendations on black teacher candidates as a group and on white candidates as a group (although it is unclear that such a prediction was ever made). The State Board adopted the committee's recommendations.

We are unable to find any intent to discriminate with respect to this decision. Plaintiffs offer no direct evidence of such an intent, even though one obvious source, the black members of the committee, was apparently available to them. The State's authority to re-define minimal competence from time to time cannot reasonably be questioned.

The 1976 decision: ETS urged that the State validate its cutoff score adopted in 1969. In 1971, ETS issued Guidelines that made its position clear. In the absence of any affirmative response by the State, in 1974 ETS announced its intention to cease the reporting of scores to South Carolina. In 1975, a three-judge court issued an interim decision in the case styled *United States v. North Carolina*, which required objective proof by the State of a rational relationship between the minimum score requirement on the NTE and the State's objective of certifying only minimally competent teachers. Shortly thereafter, the State Board authorized an extensive validity study which was conducted by ETS over a period of three months. The results of the study are set out in a two-volume, 300–page report, which was delivered to the State Board in January, 1976. The Board adopted the study report's recommendation that there be separate minimum score requirements by teaching field, and set new higher score levels based on the data produced by the study.

The 1976 decision carries a separate importance inasmuch as a finding with respect to it is the only basis for injunctive relief. Intent with respect to prior decisions is relevant only to damages. Plaintiffs offer no additional proof with respect to the defendants' alleged intent to discriminate in establishing the new certification requirements in 1976. They apparently rely on the cumulative historical background and the imminence of litigation with regard to the prior system. Even if we had found intent to discriminate with respect to one of the State's earlier decisions, this cumulative history would be without probative value as to the 1976 decision.

While historical circumstances may illuminate the purpose of a particular State action, recent events are far more probative than distant events. With the exception of the 1969 adoption of minimum cutoff scores, the "history" relied on by plaintiffs occurred over 20 years ago. Plaintiffs' elaborate web of historical circumstances, from which the court is being asked to infer discriminatory purpose, is noticeably silent about recent events. Significantly, the cases relied on by the Supreme Court in *Village of Arlington Heights v. Metropolitan Housing Development Corp.* and by plaintiffs in this case (for the proposition that historical circumstances do bear upon invidious purpose) involved events occurring within four years of the state act or decision under review.

With respect to the constitutional challenge to South Carolina's use of the NTE for certification purposes, we conclude that the plaintiffs have not demonstrated the required discriminatory intent with respect to any of the specific decisions setting certification standards based on NTE scores. This is especially true in connection with the State's 1976 change in requirements where there is no indication whatsoever that the State and its officers were motivated by anything more than a desire to use an accepted and racially neutral standardized test to evaluate the teacher applicants competing for relatively few jobs in South Carolina.

The NTE are developed and administered by ETS, an independent non-profit organization of recognized professional reputation. ETS recommends that minimum score requirements not be used as a sole determinant of certification decisions where other appropriate information or criteria are available.

In this case, the plaintiffs have come forth with no other reasonably appropriate criteria upon which certification may be properly based.

Neither have plaintiffs been able to establish any defect in the NTE indicating that the examinations themselves discriminate on the basis of race. The choices as to subject matter and question format are reasonable and well-documented on the record, and although other subject matters or other examination forms might be possible or even preferable, there is no proof of any inherent discrimination. The inference that plaintiffs would have us draw from the statistics which indicate that blacks as a group have lower average scores than whites is rebutted by the evidence with respect to the construction of the tests and their content validity. Since we find that the NTE create classifications only on permissible bases (presence or absence of knowledge or skill and ability in applying knowledge), and that they are not used pursuant to any intent to discriminate, their use in making certification decisions by the State is proper and legal.

2. Pay Scales

[Similar analysis led to a like conclusion on pay scales based on level of certificate.] . . .

B. Application of Rational Relationship Standard

In the absence of discriminatory intent, the classifications of teachers for both certification and pay purposes may be assessed under the "rational relationship" standard required by the Fourteenth Amendment of all classifications.

The Supreme Court has defined this standard in the following terms:

> Although no precise formula has been developed, the Court has held that the Fourteenth Amendment permits the States a wide scope of discretion in enacting laws which affect some groups of citizens differently than others. The constitutional safeguard is offended only if the classification rests on grounds wholly irrelevant to the achievement of the State's objective. State legislatures are presumed to have acted within their constitutional power despite the fact that, in practice, their laws result in some inequality. A statutory discrimination will not be set aside if any state of facts reasonably may be conceived to justify it.

We conclude that the State's use of the NTE for both certification and pay purposes meets the "rational relationship" standard of *McGowan v. Maryland*, and consequently does not violate the equal protection clause of the Fourteenth Amendment. No more rigorous constitutional standard need be applied to a case which does not involve express differentiation by race of other "suspect" classification, and does not involve discriminatory intent. We find however, that were an intermediate standard applied, the defendants' use of the NTE bears a "fair and substantial relationship to the achievement of an important and constitutionally permissible governmental objective."

Nevertheless, we find that the defendants have offered a legitimate and important governmental objective for their use of the NTE. The State has the right to adopt academic requirements and to use written achievement tests designed and validated to disclose the minimum amount of knowledge necessary to effective teaching. The evidence in the record supports a finding that South Carolina officials were concerned with improving the quality of public school teaching, certifying only those applicants possessed of the minimum knowledge necessary to teach effectively, utilizing an objective measure of applicants coming from widely disparate teacher training programs, and providing appropriate financial incentives for teachers to improve their academic qualifications and thereby their ability to teach. We conclude that these are entirely legitimate and clearly important governmental objectives.

In considering whether defendants' use of the NTE bears a fair and substantial relationship to these governmental objectives, we conclude that it does.

The record supports the conclusion that the NTE are professionally and carefully prepared to measure the critical mass of knowledge in academic subject matter. The NTE do not measure teaching skills, but do measure the content of the academic preparation of prospective teachers. Like the test at issue in *Washington v. Davis*, the NTE program "is neutral on its face and rationally may be said to serve a purpose the Government is constitutionally empowered to pursue." Plaintiffs have not contended nor proved that the NTE are racially biased or otherwise deficient when measured against the applicable professional and legal standards.

Furthermore, there is ample evidence in the record of the content validity of the NTE. The NTE have been demonstrated to provide a useful measure of the extent to which prospective teachers have mastered the content of their teacher training programs. The Supreme Court has held that a substantial relationship between a test and a training program—such as is found here—is sufficient to withstand challenge on constitutional grounds. State officials surely have the right to require graduation from approved teacher training programs as a prerequisite to being certified to teach in South Carolina. Plaintiffs have acknowledged the substantial relationship between the academic training program and the job of teaching by advocating that a requirement of graduation from an approved program alone is sufficient to protect the public interest.

Also, the minimum score of 975 selected by South Carolina in 1969, and the range of scores selected in 1976 were permissible exercises of judgment by the responsible officials. In fact the minimum scores adopted by the State in 1976 are for the most part substantially lower than those recommended for adoption by ETS. As in *Washington v. Davis*, "there is no evidence that the required passing grade was set at an arbitrarily high level." The evidence supports the conclusion that the 975 score was selected in large part because it enabled the State to deny certification to only those who scored in the lowest 10% of all candidates taking the NTE throughout the United States; and that score reflected the judgment as to minimal competence of a committee of independent responsible professionals. Such exercise of judgment, although subjective and imperfect, may nonetheless serve to support a minimum test score requirement challenged on equal protection grounds. Although we agree that a professionally designed and executed validity study is not necessarily required to demonstrate the relationship between a challenged use of a test and the governmental objective for which it is being used, we find support for our conclusions with respect to the NTE in the validity study conducted in this case and discussed below in connection with our analysis of plaintiffs' contentions under Title VII....

II.   Title VII Issues

. . .

A.   Certification

Plaintiffs have proved that the use of NTE scores by the State in its certification decisions disqualifies substantially disproportionate numbers of blacks. The burden of proof was thereby shifted to the defendants, and in an effort to meet this burden the State commissioned an extensive validity study by ETS. The design of this study is novel, but consistent with the basic requirements enunciated by the Supreme Court, and we accordingly hold such study sufficient to meet the burden placed on defendants under Title VII.

The study seeks to demonstrate content validity by measuring the degree to which the content of the tests matches the content of the teacher training programs in South Carolina. It also seeks to establish a minimum score requirement by estimating the amount of knowledge (measured by the ability to answer correctly test questions that have been content validated) that a minimally qualified teacher candidate in South Carolina would have....

The design of the validity study is adequate for Title VII purposes. The Supreme Court made clear once again in *Washington v. Davis* that a content validity study that satisfies professional standards also satisfies Title VII. The defendants called as an expert witness Dr. Robert M. Guion, the principal author of Standards for Educational and Psychological Tests published by the American Psychological Association and a nationally recognized authority in the field of testing and measurement who testified in an unqualified fashion that in his expert opinion the ETS study design met all of the requirements of the APA Standards, the

Division 14 Principles, and the EEOC Guidelines. Two other experts testified similarly, and ETS sought and obtained favorable opinions on the study design, before its implementation, from another two independent experts. The ETS decision to validate against the academic training program rather than job performance is specifically endorsed in principle in *Davis* . . . .

The principal issue raised by plaintiffs in attacking the validity study is whether the execution of the design was such that the results can be trusted. Plaintiffs deposed 81 of the 456 panel members selected at random and, on the basis of those depositions, claim that the panel members did not prepare for the tasks they were asked to undertake, and did not understand or follow the instructions.

Admittedly, there is a showing from these depositions which indicates some misunderstanding did exist; however, our review of these depositions shows that the misunderstandings were much less extensive than claimed by plaintiffs. When so many people are involved some misunderstanding and failure adequately to follow instructions are inevitable.

The new cutoff scores adopted by the State which are substantially below the scores recommended by ETS after completion of its validation study provide a substantial margin of error. . . .

We find that the results of the validity study are sufficiently trustworthy to sustain defendants' burden under Title VII. First, the possible error rate was not high. Second, the key question is not whether some of the panel members failed to understand the instructions or for other reasons failed to follow the instructions, but whether they would have reached any different result if they had understood and followed the instructions. Plaintiffs misconceive their burden once defendants have made a reasonable showing that the study was executed in a responsible, professional manner designed to produce trustworthy results. In order to rebut the presumption that trustworthy results were indeed produced, plaintiffs must not only show that the study was not executed as intended, but also that the results were adversely affected. . . .

There remains, however, the question whether the State has satisfied the "business necessity" requirement set out in *Griggs v. Duke Power Co.* This "business necessity" doctrine appears neither in the explicit language nor the legislative history of Title VII. . . .

We think that *Griggs* did not import into Title VII law the concept of "compelling interest" developed as a part of the "strict scrutiny" standard for assessing certain classifications under the Fourteenth Amendment. Under this concept, the Court would balance the disparate impact on blacks against the business purpose of the employer and uphold the business practice only if it were sufficiently "compelling" to overcome the disparate impact. It is our view that the Supreme Court intended an examination of the alternatives available with respect to the legitimate employment objective identified by the employer to determine whether there is available to the employer an alternative practice that would achieve his business purpose equally well but with a lesser disparate impact by race. In examining alternatives, the risk and cost to the employer are relevant.

Here, plaintiffs have suggested only one alternative to the use of the NTE for certification purposes. Plaintiffs contend that mere graduation from an approved program should be sufficient and would have a lesser disparate impact on blacks. We cannot find that this alternative will achieve the State's purpose in certifying minimally competent persons equally well as the use of a content-validated standardized test. The record amply demonstrates that there are variations in admissions requirements, academic standards and grading practices at the various teacher training institutions within the State. The approval that the State gives to the teacher training program is to general subject matter areas covered by the program, not to the actual course content of the program, and not to the means used within the program to measure whether individual students have actually mastered the course content to which they have been exposed. The standardized test scores do reflect individual achievement with respect to specific subject matter content, which is directly relevant to (although not sufficient in itself to assure) competence to teach, and thus the use of these scores for certification purposes survives the business necessity test under Title VII.

B. Pay Scales

There remains, finally, the question whether the uses of the NTE for salary purposes are a violation of Title VII. Where the salary system was linked to the certification system, some salary benefits were available only by improving the grade of the certificate; and that, in turn, could be done only by achieving certain minimum NTE scores. That system continued in effect after March 24, 1972, when Title VII was made applicable to states, and in 1976, the distribution of teachers within the four grades of the pay scale system showed a substantial disparate impact by race. A higher proportion of whites (98%) were classified in the two higher grades (A and B) and a higher proportion of blacks (51%) were classified in the lower grades (C and D). By such showing plaintiffs have satisfied their burden of proof under Title VII to shift the burden of proof to the defendants to show a rational relationship to a legitimate employment objective and to show business necessity. The State identifies its legitimate employment objective as providing an incentive for improvement, so that teachers without adequate knowledge to teach effectively will upgrade their capability; and the State offers the same evidence of a rational relationship between its pay scales and this objective as it did with respect to the constitutional challenges. We think that evidence is sufficient to establish the relationship.

We believe that a distinction for pay purposes between those who are qualified as well as between those who are not qualified survives the business necessity test. There appears to be no alternative available to the State, within reasonable limits of risk and cost, for providing the incentive necessary to motivate thousands of persons to acquire, generally on their own time and at their own expense, the necessary additional academic training so that they will be minimally competent teachers.

Having made the investment of four years in an undergraduate education, it seems reasonable to try to upgrade the talent of unqualified teachers where possible, rather than rejecting them altogether. . . .

Ordered that judgment be entered in favor of the defendants.

Notes

1. The Supreme Court summarily affirmed this judgment.

2. If a state other than South Carolina instituted a similar certification plan, would there have been any basis for a challenge?

[Case No. 63] Constitutionality of Professional Growth Requirement for Teachers

HARRAH INDEPENDENT SCHOOL DISTRICT v. MARTIN

Supreme Court of the United States, 1979.
440 U.S. 194, 99 S.Ct. 1062, 59 L.Ed.2d 248.

PER CURIAM. Respondent Martin was employed as a teacher by petitioner School District under a contract that incorporated by reference the School Board's rules and regulations. Because respondent was tenured, Oklahoma law required the School Board to renew her contract annually unless she was guilty of, among other things, "wilful neglect of duty." The same Oklahoma statute provided for hearing and appeal procedures in the event of nonrenewal. One of the regulations incorporated into respondent's contract required teachers holding only a bachelor's degree to earn five semester hours of college credit every three years. Under the terms of the regulation, noncompliance with the continuing-education requirement was sanctioned by withholding salary increases.

Respondent, hired in 1969, persistently refused to comply with the continuing-education requirement and consequently forfeited the increases in salary to which she would have otherwise been entitled during the 1972–1974 school years. After her contract had been renewed for the 1973–1974 school term, however, the Oklahoma Legislature enacted a law mandating certain salary raises for teachers regardless of the compliance with the continuing-education policy. The School Board, thus deprived of the sanction which it had previously employed to enforce the provision, notified respondent that her contract would not be renewed for the 1974–1975 school year unless she completed five semester hours by April 10, 1974. Respondent nonetheless declined even to enroll in the necessary courses and, appearing before the Board in January 1974, indicated that she had no intention of complying with the requirement in her contract. Finding her persistent noncompliance with the continuing-education requirement "wilful neglect of duty," the Board voted at its April 1974 meeting not to renew her contract for the following school year. . . .

. . .

The School District has conceded at all times that respondent was a "tenured" teacher under Oklahoma law, and therefore could be dismissed only for specified reasons. She was accorded the usual elements of procedural due process. . . .

. . . [R]espondent's claim is simply that she, as a tenured teacher, cannot be discharged under the School Board's purely prospective rule establishing contract nonrenewal as the sanction for violations of the continuing-education requirement incorporated into her contract.

The School Board's rule is endowed with a presumption of legislative validity, and the burden is on respondent to show that there is no rational connection between the Board's action and its conceded interest in providing its students with competent, well-trained teachers. Respondent's claim that the Board acted arbitrarily in imposing a new penalty for noncompliance with the continuing-education requirement simply does not square with the facts. By making pay raises mandatory, the state legislature deprived the Board of the sanction that it had earlier used to enforce its teachers' contractual obligation to earn continuing-education credits. The Board thus turned to contract nonrenewal, but applied this sanction purely prospectively so that those who might have relied on its past practice would nonetheless have an opportunity to bring themselves into compliance with the terms of the contracts. . . .

The School District's concern with the educational qualifications of its teachers cannot under any reasoned analysis be described as impermissible, and respondent does not contend that the Board's continuing-education requirement bears no rational relationship to that legitimate governmental concern. Rather, respondent contests "the permissibility of the classification by which [she] and three other teachers were required to achieve [by April 1974] the number of continuing education credits that all other teachers were given three years to achieve."

The Board's objective in sanctioning violations of the continuing-education requirement was, obviously, to encourage future compliance with the requirement. Admittedly, imposition of a penalty for noncompliance placed respondent and three other teachers in a "class" different from those teachers who had complied with their contractual obligations in the past. But any sanction designed to enforce compliance with a valid rule, whatever its source, falls only on those who break the rule. Respondent and those in her "class" were the only teachers immediately affected by the Board's action because they were the only teachers who had previously broken their contractual obligation. . . .

That the Board was forced by the state legislature in 1974 to penalize noncompliance differently than it had in the past in no way alters the equal protection analysis of respondent's claim. Like all teachers employed in the School District, respondent was given three years to earn five continuing-education credits. Unlike most of her colleagues, however, respondent refused to comply with the requirement, thus forfeiting her right to routine pay raises. Had the legislature not mandated salary increases in 1974, the Board presumably would have penalized respondent's continued refusal to comply with the terms of her contract by denying her an increase in salary for yet another year. The Board, having been deprived by the legislature of the sanction previously employed to enforce the continuing-education requirement, merely substituted in its place another, albeit more onerous, sanction. The classification created by both sanctions, however, was between those who had acquired five continuing-education credits within the allotted time and those who had not.

At bottom, respondent's position is that she is willing to forgo routine pay raises, but she is not willing to comply with the continuing-education requirement or to give up her job. The constitutional permissibility of a sanction imposed to enforce a valid governmental rule, however, is not tested by the willingness of those governed by the rule to accept the consequences of noncompliance. The sanction of contract nonrenewal is quite rationally related to the Board's objective of enforcing the continuing education obligation of its teachers. Respondent was not, therefore, deprived of equal protection of the laws.

The petition for certiorari is granted, and the judgment of the Court of Appeals is

Reversed.

Notes

1.   Should Ms. Martin have been given more time to meet the requirement that she flaunted? The Court noted that she declined even to enroll in courses and in January said she did not intend to comply.

2.   As reflected by a case from Illinois, school boards can make reasonable in-service requirements conditions of employment. *Last v. Board of Educ. of Community Unit School Dist. No. 321*, 185 N.E.2d 282 (Ill.Ct.App.1962). Professional associations also advocate increased preparation for teachers. What impact did the National Education Association's support for Ms. Martin have on the cause of education?

[Case No. 64]   Discriminatory Initial Employment Practices

THOMAS v. WASHINGTON COUNTY SCHOOL BOARD

United States Court of Appeals, Fourth Circuit, 1990.
915 F.2d 922 [63 Educ. L. Rep. 76].

BUTZNER, SENIOR CIRCUIT JUDGE: Patricia A. Thomas appeals a judgment of the district court that dismissed her action against the Washington County School Board, alleging racial discrimination in violation of Title VII of the Civil Rights Act of 1964. In her complaint Thomas sought remedies for two alleged violations of the Act: first, a teaching position and monetary relief for the Board's denial of employment and, second, injunctive relief to restrain the Board from continuing its hiring practices. We affirm the district court's dismissal of the hiring claim, vacate the judgment with respect to the omission of injunctive relief, and remand for further proceedings.

I

Thomas is a black woman who was raised and educated in Washington County, Virginia. She graduated *cum laude* from Emory & Henry College and shortly thereafter was certified by the Commonwealth of Virginia to teach social studies in secondary schools. In 1982, while in her final year of college, she applied for a teaching position in Washington County. Although she kept her application current, the Board failed to notify her of job openings on three separate occasions over a two year period. Those jobs were filled by white teachers.

One position was filled by someone more qualified than Thomas and another position was filled by someone transferring from another school within the county. It does not appear that there was any discrimination against Thomas in those instances. A third position, however, was filled by Mary Sue Smith, one of two white applicants interviewed for the position. Smith also graduated from Emory & Henry College with excellent grades, although not *cum laude*. She was the wife of a Washington County school teacher. She heard of the opening through word-of-mouth and was hired after having only one interview—the norm was three. Thomas heard of the vacancies after the Board filled them. She filed a complaint with the EEOC alleging racial discrimination. The EEOC issued a right to sue letter and this action followed.

The Board's evidence disclosed that Thomas's application was overlooked because the cover sheet indicated she had not yet been certified to teach. There was information within Thomas's file to indicate that she was certified, but apparently the file was not opened.

The district court found that the Board's failure to consider Thomas for the vacancies was a mistake rather than an act of intentional discrimination. This was a factual finding and is subject to review under a clearly erroneous standard. The court's finding of mistake was based largely on credibility determinations and is supported by the evidence. Consequently, it is binding upon us.

II

The district court did not grant Thomas's request for an injunction to require the Board to change its discriminatory hiring procedure. Instead the court admonished the Board:

> As a practical matter, however, the defendant should seriously consider plaintiff's application the next time a position in her field becomes vacant. The defendant was successful in this case primarily because it showed that it was ignorant of plaintiff's credentials and qualifications. Defendant now knows that plaintiff is a qualified teacher and cannot plead ignorance again. The defendant should remember that it is still subject to Title VII and act accordingly.

Although Thomas is presently teaching in nearby Tennessee, she is, as the district court recognized, a prospective applicant for a teaching position in Washington County. Consequently, she is entitled to hiring practices that conform to the requirements of Title VII.

The legal premise for Thomas's claim is sound. Congress enacted Title VII "to achieve equality of employment opportunities" through the removal of "artificial, arbitrary, and unnecessary barriers to employment when the barriers operate invidiously to discriminate on the basis of racial or other impermissible classification." *Griggs v. Duke Power Co.* held that a plaintiff need not prove intentional discrimination, for Title VII also proscribes "practices that are fair in form, but discriminatory in operation." "The necessary premise of the disparate impact approach is that some employment practices, adopted without a deliberately discriminatory motive, may in operation be functionally equivalent to intentional discrimination."

The factual basis of Thomas's claim is disclosed by evidence that establishes that the Board has erected barriers that invidiously discriminate on the basis of race. The Washington County school system was desegregated in 1963. At that time there were six black elementary teachers. There remained six black elementary teachers and no black high school teachers until 1981 when Dennis Hill, following an EEOC complaint, was hired as a physical education teacher and coach for one of the high schools. He remained the only black high school teacher in the county schools. Apart from Hill, no black teacher was hired from 1975 until 1988, after this action was filed. In 1988, the superintendent, having learned that an elderly black teacher was retiring, requested Hill to recruit another black teacher. Wittingly or unwittingly, the Board has limited black teachers over the years to a rather rigid quota.

Between 1981 and 1988, at least 46 relatives of school employees were hired, including Smith. Notices of teaching vacancies are generally not advertised; they are posted in each school in the Washington County school system. Several black applicants testified that they learned of vacancies only after they had been filled. These policies and practices amount to nepotism and word-of-mouth hiring, which, in the context of a predominantly white work force, serve to freeze the effects of past discrimination.

Courts generally agree that, whatever the benefits of nepotism and word-of-mouth hiring, those benefits are outweighed by the goal of providing everyone with equal opportunities for employment.... Nepotism and word-of-mouth hiring constitute badges of discrimination in the context of a predominantly white work force.

Nepotism is not per se violative of Title VII. Given an already integrated work force, nepotism might have no impact on the racial composition of that work force. In such cases, nepotism, word-of-mouth hiring, and similar practices might simply amount to "bad acts" which discriminate against all outsiders without having any disparate impact on racial or religious minorities. "Title VII is not a 'bad acts' statute" and does not proscribe that type of discrimination. However, when the work force is predominantly white, nepotism and similar practices which operate to exclude outsiders may discriminate against minorities as effectively as any intentionally discriminatory policy.

Thomas proved the existence of "artificial, arbitrary, and unnecessary barriers to employment [that] operate invidiously to discriminate on the basis of racial ... classifications." *Griggs*. Two of the Board's practices bear a causal relationship to her unsuccessful efforts to secure employment. They are the Board's practice of nepotism and the general practice of posting notice of vacancies only in the schools. Thomas did not learn of the vacancies until after they were filled. She is therefore entitled to injunctive relief to remedy these unlawful practices.

The district court's admonition, while well intentioned, fell short of affording the relief Title VII contemplates.... "The trial judge in a Title VII case bears a special responsibility in the public interest to resolve the employment dispute, for once the judicial machinery has been set in train, the proceeding takes on a public character in which remedies are devised to vindicate the policies of the Act, not merely to afford private relief to the employee." ...

The district court quite properly found that Thomas did not offer sufficient statistical evidence to prove discrimination under the disparate impact theory by the means of statistics. The county's population is 98.2% white and 1.8% black. Black teachers constitute only .5% of the secondary schools' faculties. The Board's policy of generally limiting its pool of applicants to county residents, coupled with the lack of proof of the number of qualified applicants living in the county, other than Thomas, made the data base inadequate for statistical purposes. However, although disparate impact cases usually focus on statistics, they are neither the exclusive nor a necessary means of proof. The paucity of statistics is no bar to the prospective injunctive relief Thomas seeks, for Thomas has proved by other means that the Board's hiring practices have a disparate impact on minorities and violate Title VII. She produced evidence of at least 46 cases of nepotism, a stipulation from the Board which revealed a practice of posting vacancies in schools and offices with public notice only in exceptional circumstances, and testimony from other black applicants which indicated they were not being given an opportunity to compete for teaching jobs, largely because the Board's practices of nepotism and word-of-mouth hiring kept them unaware of job openings.

III

We affirm the district court's judgment insofar as it denies Thomas's claim that the Board intentionally discriminated against her when it failed to hire her.

Thomas has shown that as a prospective applicant she is entitled to injunctive relief to conform the Board's hiring policies to Title VII. We vacate the district court's judgment insofar as it dismisses her complaint and remand the case for further proceedings.

The district court is directed to fashion an injunction requiring the Board to publicly advertise vacancies and fill them by a selection process that is not influenced by race. The district court should also prohibit the Board from giving preference to relatives of employees. The court should prescribe any other conditions that it deems proper to achieve equality of employment opportunities without regard to race for all qualified applicants certified by the state. The court may limit the injunction to a reasonable number of years. . . .

Notes

1.   Note that while the plaintiff was the catalyst for a substantial legal change in board practices, she did not receive a tangible benefit.

2.   Is there professional support for the hiring policies that were practiced in this case? Keep in mind that the courts cannot intervene unless the result of "bad acts" conflicts with constitutional or statutory mandates.

3.   The Civil Rights Act of 1991 authorized courts to award damages, both compensatory and punitive, to persons who are discriminated against in violation of Title VII. Previously, Title VII only provided remedies of injunctions and lost pay. Could Ms. Thomas have demonstrated that she was entitled to damages due to, say, emotional distress as a result of the board's actions or should it have been subject to punitive damages?

[Case No. 65]   Employment Rights of Teachers with Disabilities

SCHOOL BOARD OF NASSAU COUNTY, FLORIDA v. ARLINE

Supreme Court of the United States, 1987.
480 U.S. 273, 107 S.Ct. 1123, 94 L.Ed.2d 307 [37 Educ. L. Rep. 448].

JUSTICE BRENNAN delivered the opinion of the Court.

Section 504 of the Rehabilitation Act of 1973 prohibits a federally funded state program from discriminating against a handicapped individual solely by reason of his or her handicap. This case presents the questions whether a person afflicted with tuberculosis, a contagious disease, may be considered a "handicapped individual" within the meaning of § 504 of the Act, and, if so, whether such an individual is "otherwise qualified" to teach elementary school.

I

From 1966 until 1979, respondent Gene Arline taught elementary school in Nassau County, Florida. She was discharged in 1979 after suffering a third relapse of tuberculosis within two years. After she was denied relief in state administrative proceedings, she brought suit in federal court, alleging that the school board's decision to dismiss her because of her tuberculosis violated § 504 of the Act.

A trial was held in the District Court . . . According to the medical records . . . Arline was hospitalized for tuberculosis in 1957. For the next 20 years, Arline's disease was in remission. Then, in 1977, a culture revealed that tuberculosis was again active in her system; cultures taken in March 1978 and in November 1978 were also positive.

The superintendent of schools for Nassau County, Craig Marsh, then testified as to the school board's response to Arline's medical reports. After both her second relapse, in the spring of 1978, and her third relapse in November 1978, the school board suspended Arline with pay for the remainder of the school year. At the end of the 1978–1979 school year, the school board held a hearing, after which it discharged Arline, "not because she had done anything wrong," but because of the "continued reoccurence [sic] of tuberculosis." In her trial memorandum, Arline argued that it was "not disputed that the [school board dismissed her] solely on the basis of her illness. Since the illness in this case qualifies the Plaintiff as a 'handicapped person' it is clear that she was dismissed solely as a result of her handicap in violation of Section 504." The District Court held, however, that although there was "[n]o question that she suffers a handicap," Arline was nevertheless not "a handicapped person under the terms of that statute." The court found it "difficult ... to conceive that Congress intended contagious diseases to be included within the definition of a handicapped person." The court then went on to state that, "even assuming" that a person with a contagious disease could be deemed a handicapped person, Arline was not "qualified" to teach elementary school.

The Court of Appeals reversed, holding that "persons with contagious diseases are within the coverage of section 504," and that Arline's condition "falls ... neatly within the statutory and regulatory framework" of the Act. The court remanded the case "for further findings as to whether the risks of infection precluded Mrs. Arline from being 'otherwise qualified' for her job and, if so, whether it was possible to make some reasonable accommodation for her in that teaching position" or in some other position. We granted certiorari and now affirm.

II

In enacting and amending the Act, Congress enlisted all programs receiving federal funds in an effort "to share with handicapped Americans the opportunities for an education, transportation, housing, health care, and jobs that other Americans take for granted." To that end, Congress not only increased federal support for vocational rehabilitation, but also addressed the broader problem of discrimination against the handicapped by including § 504, an antidiscrimination provision patterned after Title VI of the Civil Rights Act of 1964. Section 504 of the Rehabilitation Act reads in pertinent part:

> "No otherwise qualified handicapped individual in the United States, as defined in section 706(7) of this title, shall, solely by reason of his handicap, be excluded from participation in, be denied the benefits of, or be subjected to discrimination under any program or activity receiving Federal financial assistance...." 29 U.S.C. § 794.

In 1974 Congress expanded the definition of "handicapped individual" for use in § 504 to read as follows:

> "[A]ny person who (i) has a physical or mental impairment which substantially limits one or more of such person's major life activities, (ii) has a record of such an impairment, or (iii) is regarded as having such an impairment." 29 U.S.C. § 706(7)(B).

The amended definition reflected Congress' concern with protecting the handicapped against discrimination stemming not only from simple prejudice, but also from "archaic attitudes and laws" and from "the fact that the American people are simply unfamiliar with and insensitive to the difficulties confront[ing] individuals with handicaps." To combat the effects of erroneous but nevertheless prevalent perceptions about the handicapped, Congress expanded the definition of "handicapped individual" so as to preclude discrimination against "[a] person who has a record of, or is regarded as having, an impairment [but who] may at present have no actual incapacity at all."

In determining whether a particular individual is handicapped as defined by the Act, the regulations promulgated by the Department of Health and Human Services are of significant assistance. As we have previously recognized, these regulations were drafted with the oversight and approval of Congress; they provide "an important source of guidance on the meaning of § 504." The regulations are particularly significant here because they define two critical terms used in the statutory definition of handicapped individual. "Physical impairment" is defined as follows:

> "[A]ny physiological disorder or condition, cosmetic disfigurement, or anatomical loss affecting one or more of the following body systems: neurological; musculoskeletal; special sense organs; respiratory, including speech organs; cardiovascular; reproductive, digestive, genito-urinary; hemic and lymphatic; skin; and endocrine."

In addition, the regulations define "major life activities" as "functions such as caring for one's self, performing manual tasks, walking, seeing, hearing, speaking, breathing, learning, and working."

III

Within this statutory and regulatory framework, then, we must consider whether Arline can be considered a handicapped individual. According to ... testimony ... Arline suffered tuberculosis "in an acute form in such a degree that it affected her respiratory system," and was hospitalized for this condition. Arline thus had a physical impairment as that term is defined by the regulations, since she had a "physiological disorder or condition ... affecting [her] ... respiratory [system]." This impairment was serious enough to require hospitalization, a fact more than sufficient to establish that one or more of her major life activities were substantially limited by her impairment. Thus, Arline's hospitalization for tuberculosis in 1957 suffices to establish that she has a "record of ... impairment" within the meaning of 29 U.S.C. § 706(7)(B)(ii), and is therefore a handicapped individual.

Petitioners concede that a contagious disease may constitute a handicapping condition to the extent that it leaves a person with "diminished physical or mental capabilities," Brief for Petitioners 15, and concede that Arline's hospitalization for tuberculosis in 1957 demonstrates that she has a record of a physical impairment. Petitioners maintain, however, that Arline's record of impairment is irrelevant in this case, since the school board dismissed Arline not because of her diminished physical capabilities, but because of the threat that her relapses of tuberculosis posed to the health of others.

We do not agree with petitioners that, in defining a handicapped individual under § 504, the contagious effects of a disease can be meaningfully distinguished from the disease's physical effects on a claimant in a case such as this. Arline's contagiousness and her physical impairment each resulted from the same underlying condition, tuberculosis. It would be unfair to allow an employer to seize upon the distinction between the effects of a disease on others and the effects of a disease on a patient and use that distinction to justify discriminatory treatment.

Nothing in the legislative history of § 504 suggests that Congress intended such a result. That history demonstrates that Congress was as concerned about the effect of an impairment on others as it was about its effect on the individual. Congress extended coverage, in 29 U.S.C. § 706(7)(B)(iii), to those individuals who are simply "regarded as having" a physical or mental impairment. The Senate Report provides as an example of a person who would be covered under this subsection "a person with some kind of visible physical impairment which in fact does not substantially limit that person's functioning." Such an impairment might not diminish a person's physical or mental capabilities, but could nevertheless substantially limit that person's ability to work as a result of the negative reactions of others to the impairment.

Allowing discrimination based on the contagious effects of a physical impairment would be inconsistent with the basic purpose of § 504, which is to ensure that handicapped individuals are not denied jobs or other benefits because of the prejudiced attitudes or the ignorance of others. By amending the definition of "handicapped individual" to include not only those who are actually physically impaired, but also those who are regarded as impaired and who, as a result, are substantially limited in a major life activity, Congress acknowledged that society's accumulated myths and fears about disability and disease are as handicapping as are the physical limitations that flow from actual impairment. Few aspects of a handicap give rise to the same level of public fear and misapprehension as contagiousness. Even those who suffer or have recovered from such noninfectious diseases as epilepsy or cancer have faced discrimination based on the irrational fear that they might be contagious. The Act is carefully structured to replace such reflexive reactions to actual or perceived handicaps with actions based on reasoned and medically sound judgments: the definition of "handicapped individual" is broad, but only those individuals who are both handicapped and otherwise qualified are eligible for relief. The fact that some persons who have contagious diseases may pose a serious health threat to others under certain circumstances does not justify excluding from the coverage of the Act all persons with actual or perceived contagious diseases. Such exclusion would mean that those accused of being contagious would never have the opportunity to have their condition evaluated in light of medical evidence and a determination made as to whether they were "otherwise qualified." Rather, they would be vulnerable to discrimination on the basis of mythology—precisely the type of injury Congress sought to prevent. We conclude that the fact that a person with a record of a physical impairment is also contagious does not suffice to remove that person from coverage under § 504.

IV

The remaining question is whether Arline is otherwise qualified for the job of elementary schoolteacher. To answer this question in most cases, the district court will need to conduct an individualized inquiry and make appropriate findings of fact. Such an inquiry is essential if § 504 is to achieve its goal of protecting handicapped individuals from deprivations based on prejudice, stereotypes, or unfounded fear, while giving appropriate weight to such legitimate concerns of grantees as avoiding exposing others to significant health and safety risks. The basic factors to be considered in conducting this inquiry are well established. In the context of the employment of a person handicapped with a contagious disease, we agree with amicus American Medical Association that this inquiry should include ... "[findings of] facts, based on reasonable medical judgments given the state of medical knowledge, about (a) the nature of the risk (how the disease is transmitted), (b) the duration of the risk (how long is the carrier infectious), (c) the severity of the risk (what is the potential harm to third parties) and (d) the probabilities the disease will be transmitted and will cause varying degrees of harm."

In making these findings, courts normally should defer to the reasonable medical judgments of public health officials. The next step in the "otherwise-qualified" inquiry is for the court to evaluate, in light of these medical findings, whether the employer could reasonably accommodate the employee under the established standards for that inquiry. See n. 17, supra.

Because of the paucity of factual findings by the District Court, we, like the Court of Appeals, are unable at this stage of the proceedings to resolve whether Arline is "otherwise qualified" for her job. The District Court made no findings as to the duration and severity of Arline's condition, nor as to the probability that she would transmit the disease. Nor did the court determine whether Arline was contagious at the time she was discharged, or whether the School Board could have reasonably accommodated her. Accordingly, the resolution of whether Arline was otherwise qualified requires further findings of fact.

We hold that a person suffering from the contagious disease of tuberculosis can be a handicapped person within the meaning of § 504 of the Rehabilitation Act of 1973, and that respondent Arline is such a person. We remand the case to the District Court to determine whether Arline is otherwise qualified for her position. The judgment of the Court of Appeals is Affirmed.

Notes

1.   The Court first applied Section 504 in an educational dispute in *South-eastern Community College v. Davis*, 442 U.S. 397, 99 S.Ct. 2361, 60 L.Ed.2d 980 (1979). [Case No. 117].

2.   Was this decision wise? Was it safe for the school community?

[Case No. 66]   Procedural Due Process for Non-tenured Faculty Members Who Are Not Reappointed, I

BOARD OF REGENTS OF STATE COLLEGES v. ROTH

Supreme Court of the United States, 1972.
408 U.S. 564, 92 S.Ct. 2701, 33 L.Ed.2d 548.

MR. JUSTICE STEWART delivered the opinion of the Court.

In 1968 the respondent, David Roth, was hired for his first teaching job as assistant professor of political science at Wisconsin State University–Oshkosh. He was hired for a fixed term of one academic year. The notice of his faculty appointment specified that his employment would begin on September 1, 1968, and would end on June 30, 1969. The respondent completed that term. But he was informed that he would not be rehired for the next academic year.

The respondent had no tenure rights to continued employment. . . . There are no statutory or administrative standards defining eligibility for re-employment. State law thus clearly leaves the decision whether to rehire a non-tenured teacher for another year to the unfettered discretion of University officials.

. . .

The respondent . . . brought this action in a federal district court alleging that the decision not to rehire him for the next year infringed his Fourteenth Amendment rights. He attacked the decision both in substance and procedure. First, he alleged that the true reason for the decision was to punish him for certain statements critical of the University administration, and that it therefore violated his right to freedom of speech. Second, he alleged that the failure of University officials to give him notice of any reason for nonretention and an opportunity for a hearing violated his right to procedural due process of law.

. . . The only question presented to us at this stage in the case is whether the respondent had a constitutional right to a statement of reasons and a hearing on the University's decision not to rehire him for another year. We hold that he did not.

I

The requirements of procedural due process apply only to the deprivation of interests encompassed within the Fourteenth Amendment's protection of liberty and property. When protected interests are implicated the right to some kind of prior hearing is paramount. But the range of interests protected by procedural due process is not infinite.

... [T]o determine whether due process requirements apply in the first place, we must look not to the "weight" but to the nature of the interest at stake. We must look to see if the interest is within the Fourteenth Amendment's protection of liberty and property....

Yet, while the Court has eschewed rigid or formalistic limitations on the protection of procedural due process, it has at the same time observed certain boundaries. For the words "liberty" and "property" in the Due Process Clause of the Fourteenth Amendment must be given some meaning.

II

"While this Court has not attempted to define with exactness the liberty ... guaranteed [by the Fourteenth Amendment] the term has received much consideration, and some of the included things have been definitely stated. Without doubt, it denotes not merely freedom from bodily restraint but also the right of the individual to contract, to engage in any of the common occupations of life, to acquire useful knowledge, to marry, establish a home and bring up children, to worship God according to the dictates of his own conscience, and generally to enjoy those privileges long recognized ... as essential to the orderly pursuit of happiness by free men." In a Constitution for a free people, there can be no doubt that the meaning of "liberty" must be broad indeed.

There might be cases in which a State refused to re-employ a person under such circumstances that interests in liberty would be implicated. But this is not such a case.

The State, in declining to rehire the respondent, did not make any charge against him that might seriously damage his standing and associations in his community. It did not base the nonrenewal of his contract on a charge, for example, that he had been guilty of dishonesty, or immorality. Had it done so, this would be a different case. For "[w]here a person's good name, reputation, honor or integrity is at stake because of what the government is doing to him, notice and an opportunity to be heard are essential." In such a case, due process would accord an opportunity to refute the charge before University officials. (The purpose of such notice and hearing is to provide the person an opportunity to clear his name. Once a person has cleared his name at a hearing, his employer, of course, may remain free to deny him future employment for other reasons.) In the present case, however there is no suggestion whatever that the respondent's interest in his "good name, reputation, honor or integrity" is at stake.

Similarly, there is no suggestion that the State, in declining to re-employ the respondent, imposed on him a stigma or other disability that foreclosed his freedom to take advantage of other employment opportunities. The State, for example, did not invoke any regulations to bar the respondent from all other public employment in State universities. Had it done so, this, again, would be a different case. For "[t]o be deprived not only of present government employment but of future opportunity for it is no small injury ..." The Court has held, for example, that a State, in regulating eligibility for a type of professional employment, cannot foreclose a range of opportunities "in a manner ... that contravene[s] ... due process," and, specifically, in a manner that denies the right to a full prior hearing. In the present case, however, this principle does not come into play.

To be sure, the respondent has alleged that the nonrenewal of his contract was based on his exercise of his right to freedom of speech. But this allegation is not now before us. The District Court stayed proceedings on this issue, and the respondent has yet to prove that the decision not to rehire him was, in fact, based on his free speech activities.

Hence, on the record before us, all that clearly appears is that the respondent was not rehired for one year at one University. It stretches the concept too far to suggest that a person is deprived of "liberty" when he simply is not rehired in one job but remains as free as before to seek another.

III

The Fourteenth Amendment's procedural protection of property is a safeguard of the security of interests that a person has already acquired in specific benefits. These interests—property interests—may take many forms.

Thus the Court has held that a person receiving welfare benefits under statutory and administrative standards defining eligibility for them has an interest in continued receipt of those benefits that is safeguarded by procedural due process.... Similarly, in the area of public employment, the Court has held that a public college professor dismissed from an office held under tenure provisions, *Slochower v. Board of Education*, and college professors and staff members dismissed during the terms of their contracts, *Wieman v. Updegraff*, have interests in continued employment that are safeguarded by due process. Only last year, the Court held that this principle "proscribing summary dismissal from public employment without a hearing or inquiry required by due process" also applied to a teacher recently hired without tenure or a formal contract but nonetheless with a clearly implied promise of continued employment.

Certain attributes of "property" interests protected by procedural due process emerge from these decisions. To have a property interest in a benefit, a person clearly must have more than an abstract need or desire for it. He must have more than a unilateral expectation of it. He must, instead, have a legitimate claim of entitlement to it. It is a purpose of the ancient institution of property to protect those claims upon which people rely in their daily lives, reliance that must not be arbitrarily undermined. It is a purpose of the constitutional right to a hearing to provide an opportunity for a person to vindicate those claims.

Property interests, of course, are not created by the Constitution. Rather, they are created and their dimensions are defined by existing rules or understandings that stem from an independent source such as state law-rules or understandings that secure certain benefits and that support claims of entitlement to those benefits. Thus the welfare recipients ... had a claim of entitlement to welfare payments that was grounded in the statute defining eligibility for them. The recipients had not yet shown that they were, in fact, within the statutory terms of eligibility. But we held that they had a right to a hearing at which they might attempt to do so.

Just as the welfare recipients' "property" interest in welfare payments was created and defined by statutory terms, so the respondent's "property" interest in employment at the Wisconsin State University–Oshkosh was created and defined by the terms of his appointment. Those terms secured his interest in employment up to June 30, 1969. But the important fact in this case is that they specifically provided that the respondent's employment was to terminate on June 30. They did not provide for contract renewal absent "sufficient cause." Indeed, they made no provision for renewal whatsoever.

Thus the terms of the respondent's appointment secured absolutely no interest in re-employment for the next year. They supported absolutely no possible claim to entitlement to re-employment. Nor, significantly, was there any state statute or University rule or policy that secured his interest in re-employment or that created any legitimate claim to it. In these circumstances, the respondent surely had an abstract concern in being rehired, but he did not have a property interest sufficient to require the University authorities to give him a hearing when they declined to renew his contract of employment.

IV

Our analysis of the respondent's constitutional rights in this case in no way indicates a view that an opportunity for a hearing or a statement of reasons for nonretention would, or would not, be appropriate or wise in public colleges and universities. For it is a written Constitution that we apply. Our role is confined to interpretation of that Constitution.

Notes

1.   Specific charges and a hearing before removal constitute the heart of tenure protection. Had the Supreme Court upheld the lower courts in *Roth*, would any practical differences have remained between teachers who are tenured and those who have not yet achieved this status?

2.   *Roth* is important because of its scope. Based on *Roth*, a public employee whose employment is not continued beyond the term of a contract may seek to come under its umbrella by alleging an impairment of a liberty or a property interest.

[Case No. 67]   Procedural Due Process for Non-tenured Faculty Members Who Are Not Reappointed, II

PERRY v. SINDERMANN

Supreme Court of the United States, 1972.
408 U.S. 593, 92 S.Ct. 2694, 33 L.Ed.2d 570.

MR. JUSTICE STEWART delivered the opinion of the Court.

From 1959 to 1969 the respondent, Robert Sindermann, was a teacher in the state college system of the State of Texas. After teaching for two years at the University of Texas and for four years at San Antonio Junior College, he became a professor of Government and Social Science at Odessa Junior College in 1965. He was employed at the college for four successive years, under a series of one-year contracts. He was successful enough to be appointed, for a time, the cochairman of his department.

During the 1968–1969 academic year, however, controversy arose between the respondent and the college administration. The respondent was elected president of the Texas Junior College Teachers Association. In this capacity, he left his teaching duties on several occasions to testify before committees of the Texas Legislature, and he became involved in public disagreements with the policies of the college's Board of Regents. In particular, he aligned himself with a group advocating the elevation of the college to four-year status—a change opposed by the Regents. And, on one occasion, a newspaper advertisement appeared over his name that was highly critical of the Regents.

Finally, in May 1969, the respondent's one-year employment contract terminated and the Board of Regents voted not to offer him a new contract for the next academic year. The Regents issued a press release setting forth allegations of the respondent's insubordination. But they provided him no official statement of the reasons for the nonrenewal of his contract. And they allowed him no opportunity for a hearing to challenge the basis of the nonrenewal.

. . .

I

The first question presented is whether the respondent's lack of a contractual or tenure right to re-employment, taken alone, defeats his claim that the nonrenewal of his contract violated the First and Fourteenth Amendments. We hold that it does not.

For at least a quarter century, this Court has made clear that even though a person has no "right" to a valuable governmental benefit and even though the government may deny him the benefit for any number of reasons, there are some reasons upon which the government may not act. It may not deny a benefit to a person on a basis that infringes his constitutionally protected interests—especially his interest in freedom of speech. For if the government could deny a benefit to a person because of his constitutionally protected speech or associations, his exercise of those freedoms would in effect be penalized and inhibited. This would allow the government to "produce a result which [it] could not command directly." Such interference with constitutional rights is impermissible. . . .

In this case, of course, the respondent has yet to show that the decision not to renew his contract was, in fact, made in retaliation for his exercise of the constitutional right of free speech. . . .

. . . The respondent has alleged that his nonretention was based on his testimony before legislative committees and his other public statements critical of the Regents' policies. And he has alleged that this public criticism was within the First and Fourteenth Amendment's protection of freedom of speech. Plainly, these allegations present a bona fide constitutional claim. For this Court has held that a teacher's public criticism of his superiors on matters of public concern may be constitutionally protected and may, therefore, be an impermissible basis for termination of his employment. . . .

II

The respondent's lack of formal contractual or tenure security in continued employment at Odessa Junior College, though irrelevant to his free speech claim, is highly relevant to his procedural due process claim. But it may not be entirely dispositive.

We have held today in *Board of Regents v. Roth* that the Constitution does not require opportunity for a hearing before the nonrenewal of a non-tenured teacher's contract, unless he can show that the decision not to rehire him somehow deprived him of an interest in "liberty" or that he had a "property" interest in continued employment, despite the lack of tenure or a formal contract. In *Roth* the teacher had not made a showing on either point to justify summary judgment in his favor.

Similarly, the respondent here has yet to show that he has been deprived of an interest that could invoke procedural due process protection. As in *Roth,* the mere showing that he was not rehired in one particular job, without more, did not amount to a showing of a loss of liberty. Nor did it amount to a showing of a loss of property.

But the respondent's allegations—which we must construe most favorably to the respondent at this stage of the litigation—do raise a genuine issue as to his interest in continued employment at Odessa Junior College. He alleged that this interest, though not secured by a formal contractual tenure provision, was secured by a no less binding understanding fostered by the college administration. In particular, the respondent alleged that the college had a de facto tenure program, and that he had tenure under that program. He claimed that he and others legitimately relied upon an unusual provision that had been in the college's official Faculty Guide for many years:

"Teacher Tenure: Odessa College has no tenure system. The Administration of the College wishes the faculty member to feel that he has permanent tenure as long as his teaching services are satisfactory and as long as he displays a cooperative attitude toward his co-workers and his superiors, and as long as he is happy in his work."

Moreover, the respondent claimed legitimate reliance upon guidelines promulgated by the Coordinating Board of the Texas College and University System that provided that a person, like himself, who had been employed as a teacher in the state college and university system for seven years or more has some form of job tenure. Thus the respondent offered to prove that a teacher, with his long period of service, at this particular State College had no less a "property" interest in continued employment than a formally tenured teacher at other colleges, and had no less a procedural due process right to a statement of reasons and a hearing before college officials upon their decision not to retain him.

We have made clear in *Roth* that "property" interests subject to procedural due process protection are not limited by a few rigid, technical forms. Rather, "property" denotes a broad range of interests that are secured by "existing rules or understandings." A person's interest in a benefit is a "property" interest for due process purposes if there are such rules or mutually explicit understandings that support his claim of entitlement to the benefit and that he may invoke at a hearing.

A written contract with an explicit tenure provision clearly is evidence of a formal understanding that supports a teacher's claim of entitlement to continued employment unless sufficient "cause" is shown. Yet absence of such an explicit contractual provision may not always foreclose the possibility that a teacher has a "property" interest in re-employment. For example, the law of contracts in most, if not all, jurisdictions long has employed a process by which agreements, though not formalized in writing, may be "implied." Explicit contractual provisions may be supplemented by other agreements implied from "the promisor's words and conduct in the light of the surrounding circumstances." And, "[t]he meaning of [the promisor's] words and acts is found by relating them to the usage of the past."

A teacher, like the respondent, who has held his position for a number of years, might be able to show from the circumstances of this service—and from other relevant facts—that he has a legitimate claim of entitlement to job tenure. Just as this Court has found there to be a "common law of a particular industry or of a particular plant" that may supplement a collective-bargaining agreement, so there may be an unwritten "common law" in a particular university that certain employees shall have the equivalent of tenure. This is particularly likely in a college or university, like Odessa Junior College, that has no explicit tenure system even for senior members of its faculty, but that nonetheless may have created such a system in practice.

In this case, the respondent has alleged the existence of rules and understandings, promulgated and fostered by state officials, that may justify his legitimate claim of entitlement to continued employment absent "sufficient cause." We disagree with the Court of Appeals insofar as it held that a mere subjective "expectancy" is protected by procedural due process, but we agree that the respondent must be given an opportunity to prove the legitimacy of his claim of such entitlement in light of "the policies and practices of the institution." Proof of such a property interest would not, of course, entitle him to reinstatement. But such proof would obligate college officials to grant a hearing at his request, where he could be informed of the grounds for his nonretention and challenge their sufficiency. . . .

Notes

1.   How may *Perry* benefit teachers in states lacking tenure statutes?

2.   In many states, school boards are not required to provide teachers whose contracts are not renewed with explanations of their actions. Still other states require boards to offer such teachers explanations only if they ask for them. What do you think of these two different approaches? Which do you prefer?

[Case No. 68]   Non-reappointment of Teacher–Various Claims

MEYR v. BOARD OF EDUCATION OF AFFTON SCHOOL DISTRICT

United States Court of Appeals, Eighth Circuit, 1978.
572 F.2d 1229.

VAN OOSTERHOUT, SENIOR CIRCUIT JUDGE. This is a timely appeal from the final judgment of the district court dismissing plaintiff's complaint. . . .

For a reversal the plaintiff [whose probationary contract was not renewed] urges that the trial court erred in the following respects:

I.   Holding plaintiff had no property interest in continued employment.

II.   Holding that plaintiff's liberty interests had not been infringed by the defendants.

III.   Holding that termination was not based, even partially, upon plaintiff's exercise of her first amendment free speech rights.

We affirm for the reasons hereinafter set out. . . .

I

The court committed no error in determining plaintiff had no property right in continued employment. . . .

. . . [T]he record reflects that the plaintiff had not acquired tenure at the time notice of non-renewal was served.

Plaintiff urges that the Board is required to provide the benefits conferred by Board Policy No. 4118 III D, which reads:

If the Board determines that a teacher is not doing satisfactory work, the Board through its administrative representative shall give the teacher a written statement definitely setting forth his alleged incompetency and specifying the nature thereof. . . .

and by Board Policy No. 4119 which reads:

Teachers not considered satisfactory shall be notified by their supervisor and be given such reasonable time to improve as the Board of Education may determine.

Board Policy No. 4118 III D is substantially identical to Mo. Ann. Stat. § 168.126 (Vernon Supp.1977), which the Missouri Court of Appeals in *White v. Scott County School District* holds to be applicable only to termination within the contract period and not to a failure to renew an existing contract of a probationary teacher.

We find nothing in Policy No. 4119 which indicates that it is applicable to probationary teachers whose contracts are not renewed. As a probationary teacher under Missouri law plaintiff has no property interest in continued employment....

The record clearly reflects that the school had suffered a substantial decrease in enrollment, that it was economically necessary to substantially reduce the teaching staff and that the policy of the Board was to limit acquisition of tenure to exceptionally qualified teachers. Such policy was reasonable under the circumstances to protect the rights of teachers who had attained tenure. Many probationary contracts were not renewed in pursuance of this policy.

The Board's minutes reflect a clear intention not to renew plaintiff's contract for the school year commencing in the fall of 1976. The Board had a right to do so without a finding of incompetency and without assigning any other reason for its action. Plaintiff continued to serve under her existing contract until its expiration.

II

Plaintiff has not in her affidavit or otherwise set out any material facts as distinguished from legal conclusions to support her contention that her liberty interests have been violated by the Board's failure to renew her teaching contract.

The failure to receive tenure does not constitute the deprivation of a liberty interest protected by the fourteenth amendment.

Plaintiff has failed to show that she has any evidence to support her claim that she was stigmatized by any action of the defendants in refusing to renew her probationary contract.

The record reflects that when the President and President-elect of the Affton school teachers acting as a grievance committee, at the request of the plaintiff, went to the superintendent to investigate the non-renewal of plaintiff's contract, they were told that many probationary teachers were not re-employed by reason of the economic necessity of reducing the teaching staff, and that Mrs. Meyr was not re-employed for the additional reason that she was not considered a satisfactory teacher because of excessive absences and tardiness and poor staff relations. Nevertheless, economic necessity for reduction of the teaching staff remained the prime reason for not renewing plaintiff's contract. The Board's minutes above quoted do not set forth the additional factors as a basis for not rehiring, and as heretofore emphasized the Board's action was not to renew and was not termination of the plaintiff's existing contract prior to expiration. Such does not constitute the publication by defendants of stigmatizing information. The posting of the vacancy in the position held by Mrs. Meyr does not, standing alone, support stigmatization. Mrs. Meyr herself told many people she had not been re-employed.

In any event, the burden is on Mrs. Meyr to prove the charges made by the superintendent were false. Plaintiff admits that she had a substantial number of absences and tardiness and has set out no facts in her affidavits to disprove such charges. Plaintiff has not shown that she has any evidence to establish the falsity of any charges made against her. Plaintiff has not indicated that she has any evidence that stigmatizing information was given to school districts in which she applied for employment. She admits in her deposition the fact that she had too many years of experience, which resulted in entitlement to a higher salary and was a substantial factor in her failure to obtain a teaching contract. She admits that she was employed as a substitute teacher by several school districts. . . .

III

The trial court committed no error in determining that plaintiff's exercise of her right of free speech was not a substantial factor in the non-renewal of her contract.

Initially, in this case, the burden was properly placed upon respondent to show that his conduct was constitutionally protected, and that this conduct was a "substantial factor"—or, to put it in other words, that it was a "motivating factor" in the Board's decision not to rehire him.

Judged by such standard, we are satisfied that the plaintiff by affidavit or otherwise has failed to establish that her exercise of free speech was a substantial or motivating factor in the Board's decision not to renew.

Plaintiff in a speech to the mothers' club in January 1976 criticized the Board for not supplying equipment the plaintiff deemed essential for her physical education classes. Board member Lemp was present at this meeting and was upset by such remarks and reported the incident to Superintendent Onkle. Plaintiff under the first amendment had a right to make such remark. School boards and other public boards are as a matter of public knowledge frequently subjected to public criticism for making or failing to make appropriations for various projects or for failure to grant salary increases. The statement made by the plaintiff is not the kind of statement that could be reasonably supposed to upset the school board officials.

The power to determine whether a contract should be renewed is in the school board. The superintendent can make recommendations which the board can accept or reject.

Each of the board members serving at the time here material, except Mrs. Lemp, filed affidavits stating that they had no knowledge of plaintiff's statement at the time they voted not to renew plaintiff's contract and that no consideration was given to such statement. Mrs. Lemp in her affidavit states plaintiff's speech was not a factor in her vote not to renew, and Superintendent Onkle filed a similar affidavit.

Plaintiff in her affidavit has merely claimed by way of conclusion that the speech was a substantial factor in inducing the Board's action. She points to no evidence available to her to disprove the sworn statements made by the Board members, and we consequently see no reasonable possibility that plaintiff could meet the burden of refuting these statements. . . .

The judgment is affirmed.

Notes

1.   The board had a policy of limiting new tenured appointments to exceptionally qualified teachers. Was this policy important to the resolution of the case?

2.   Note the emphasis that the court placed on the lack of evidence supporting Mrs. Myer's claims as to stigmatization and the infringement of her free speech rights. What kinds of evidence might have supported Mrs. Myer's claims?

3.   Was it sound administrative practice for the superintendent to discuss the plaintiff's non-reappointment with officials of the teachers' association? Should this discussion have been of any legal consequence?

[Case No. 69]   Non-reappointment of a Teacher–Partially Based on an Unconstitutional Reason

MT. HEALTHY CITY SCHOOL DISTRICT BOARD OF EDUCATION v. DOYLE

Supreme Court of the United States, 1977.
429 U.S. 274, 97 S.Ct. 568, 50 L.Ed.2d 471.

MR. JUSTICE REHNQUIST delivered the opinion of the Court.

Respondent Doyle sued petitioner Mt. Healthy Board of Education in the United States District Court for the Southern District of Ohio. Doyle claimed that the Board's refusal to renew his contract in 1971 violated his rights under the First and Fourteenth Amendments to the United States Constitution. After a bench trial the District Court held that Doyle was entitled to reinstatement with back pay. The Court of Appeals for the Sixth Circuit affirmed . . .

Doyle was first employed by the Board in 1966. He worked under one-year contracts for the first three years, and under a two-year contract from 1969 to 1971. In 1969 he was elected president of the Teachers' Association, in which position he worked to expand the subjects of direct negotiation between the Association and the Board of Education. During Doyle's one-year term as president of the Association, and during the succeeding year when he served on its executive committee, there was apparently some tension in relations between the Board and the Association.

Beginning early in 1970, Doyle was involved in several incidents not directly connected with his role in the Teachers' Association. In one instance, he engaged in an argument with another teacher which culminated in the other teacher's slapping him. Doyle subsequently refused to accept an apology and insisted upon some punishment for the other teacher. His persistence in the matter resulted in the suspension of both teachers for one day, which was followed by a walkout by a number of other teachers, which in turn resulted in the lifting of the suspensions.

On other occasions, Doyle got into an argument with employees of the school cafeteria over the amount of spaghetti which had been served him; referred to students, in connection with a disciplinary complaint, as "sons of bitches"; and made an obscene gesture to two girls in connection with their failure to obey commands made in his capacity as cafeteria supervisor. Chronologically the last in the series of incidents which respondent was involved in during his employment by the Board was a telephone call by him to a local radio station. It was the Board's consideration of this incident which the court below found to be a violation of the First and Fourteenth Amendments.

In February of 1971, the principal circulated to various teachers a memorandum relating to teacher dress and appearance, which was apparently prompted by the view of some in the administration that there was a relationship between teacher appearance and public support for bond issues. Doyle's response to the receipt of the memorandum—on a subject which he apparently understood was to be settled by joint teacher-administration action—was to convey the substance of the memorandum to a disc jockey at WSAI, a Cincinnati radio station, who promptly announced the adoption of the dress code as a news item. Doyle subsequently apologized to the principal, conceding that he should have made some prior communication of his criticism to the school administration.

Approximately one month later the superintendent made his customary annual recommendations to the Board as to the rehiring of non-tenured teachers. He recommended that Doyle not be rehired. The same recommendation was made with respect to nine other teachers in the district, and in all instances, including Doyle's, the recommendation was adopted by the Board. Shortly after being notified of this decision, respondent requested a statement of reasons for the Board's actions. He received a statement citing "a notable lack of tact in handling professional matters which leaves much doubt as to your sincerity in establishing good school relationships." That general statement was followed by references to the radio station incident and to the obscene gesture incident.

The District Court found that all of these incidents had in fact occurred. It concluded that respondent Doyle's telephone call to the radio station was "clearly protected by the First Amendment," and that because it had played a "substantial part" in the decision of the Board not to renew Doyle's employment, he was entitled to reinstatement with back pay. The District Court did not expressly state what test it was applying in determining that the incident in question involved conduct protected by the First Amendment, but simply held that the communication to the radio station was such conduct. The Court of Appeals affirmed in a brief *per curiam* opinion.

Doyle's claims under the First and Fourteenth Amendments are not defeated by the fact that he did not have tenure. Even though he could have been discharged for no reason whatever, and had no constitutional right to a hearing prior to the decision not to rehire him, he may nonetheless establish a claim to reinstatement if the decision not to rehire him was made by reason of his exercise of constitutionally protected First Amendment freedoms.

That question of whether speech of a government employee is constitutionally protected expression necessarily entails striking "a balance between the interests of the teacher, as a citizen, in commenting upon matters of public concern and the interest of the State as an employer, in promoting the efficiency of the public services it performs through its employees." *Pickering v. Board of Education*. There is no suggestion by the Board that Doyle violated any established policy, or that its reaction to his communication to the radio station was anything more than an *ad hoc* response to Doyle's action in making the memorandum public. We therefore accept the District Court's finding that the communication was protected by the First and Fourteenth Amendments. We are not, however, entirely in agreement with that court's manner of reasoning from this finding to the conclusion that Doyle is entitled to reinstatement with back pay.

The District Court made the following "conclusions" on this aspect of the case:

> "(1) If a non-permissible reason, e.g., exercise of First Amendment rights, played a substantial part in the decision not to renew— even in the face of other permissible grounds—the decision may not stand (citations omitted).

> "(2) A non-permissible reason did play a substantial part. That is clear from the letter of the Superintendent immediately following the Board's decision, which stated two reasons—the one, the conversation with the radio station clearly protected by the First Amendment. A court may not engage in any limitation of First Amendment rights based on 'tact'—that is not to say that 'tactfulness' is irrelevant to other issues in this case."

At the same time, though, it stated that "in fact, as this Court sees it and finds, both the Board and the Superintendent were faced with a situation in which there did exist in fact reason ... independent of any First Amendment rights or exercise thereof, to not extend tenure."

Since respondent Doyle had no tenure, and there was therefore not even a state law requirement of "cause" or "reason" before a decision could be made not to renew his employment, it is not clear what the District Court meant by this latter statement. Clearly the Board legally could have dismissed respondent had the radio station incident never come to its attention. One plausible meaning of the court's statement is that the Board and the Superintendent not only could, but in fact would have reached that decision had not the constitutionally protected incident of the telephone call to the radio station occurred. We are thus brought to the issue whether, even if that were the case, the fact that the protected conduct played a "substantial part" in the actual decision not to renew would necessarily amount to a constitutional violation justifying remedial action. We think that it would not.

A rule of causation which focuses solely on whether protected conduct played a part, "substantial" or otherwise, in a decision not to rehire, could place an employee in a better position as a result of the exercise of constitutionally protected conduct than he would have occupied had he done nothing. The difficulty with the rule enunciated by the District Court is that it would require reinstatement in cases where a dramatic and perhaps abrasive incident is inevitably on the minds of those responsible for the decision to rehire, and does indeed play a part in that decision—even if the same decision would have been reached had the incident not occurred. The constitutional principle at stake is sufficiently vindicated if such an employee is placed in no worse a position than if he had not engaged in the conduct. A borderline or marginal candidate should not have the employment question resolved against him because of constitutionally protected conduct. But that same candidate ought not to be able, by engaging in such conduct, to prevent his employer from assessing his performance record and reaching a decision not to rehire on the basis of that record, simply because the protected conduct makes the employer more certain of the correctness of its decision.

This is especially true where, as the District Court observed was the case here, the current decision to rehire will accord "tenure." The long term consequences of an award of tenure are of great moment both to the employee and to the employer. They are too significant for us to hold that the Board in this case would be precluded, because it considered constitutionally protected conduct in deciding not to rehire Doyle, from attempting to prove to a trier of fact that quite apart from such conduct Doyle's record was such that he would not have been rehired in any event.

. . .

Initially, in this case, the burden was properly placed upon respondent to show that his conduct was constitutionally protected, and that this conduct was a "substantial factor"—or to put it in other words, that it was a "motivating factor" in the Board's decision not to rehire him. Respondent having carried that burden, however, the District Court should have gone on to determine whether the Board had shown by a preponderance of the evidence that it would have reached the same decision as to respondent's reemployment even in the absence of the protected conduct.

We cannot tell from the District Court opinion and conclusions, nor from the opinion of the Court of Appeals affirming the judgment of the

District Court, what conclusion those courts would have reached had they applied this test. The judgment of the Court of Appeals is therefore vacated, and the case remanded for further proceedings consistent with this opinion.

Notes

1.   Consider the consequences of having to retain teachers whose job performances were unsatisfactory simply because they injected First Amendment claims into their defenses. Note that the Court was aware of this problem.

2.   On remand, the Sixth Circuit determined that the board would not have renewed Mr. Doyle's contract regardless of whether he placed the call to the radio station. Do you think that the board acted fairly?

3.   Should the First Amendment protect teachers from disciplinary action for any and all calls to radio stations?

4.   In the next to last paragraph, the auxiliary verb is "would." How, if at all, would the result have been different if the auxiliary were "could?"

Chapter 10

TERMS AND CONDITIONS
OF EMPLOYMENT OF
TEACHERS

Introduction

In addition to the federal laws that were reviewed in the previous chapter, state statutes and regulations dealing with the terms and conditions of teacher employment have proliferated in such areas as salaries, personnel records, leaves, assignments and transfers, loyalty requirements, and collective bargaining. Where state laws permit negotiations, collective bargaining laws have had perhaps the broadest impact on teacher employment since they typically result in the development of policies that influence a range of items involving the daily terms and conditions of the professional lives of educators. In light of these issues, this chapter examines a range of legal matters dealing with the terms and conditions of teacher employment.

Salaries

In General

Absent statutory constraints or constitutional prohibitions on their implied power to set salaries for staff, school boards can act as they see fit.[1] Although some state legislatures have enacted laws directly or indirectly related to the salaries of teachers that narrow the power of local boards, because boards must adopt salary schedules and pay teachers commensurate with their education and experience, they have broad discretion in setting wages.[2] Courts have upheld the all but universal use of salary schedules as long as classifications are reasonable and teachers with like training and experience who perform similar services are treated uniformly.[3]

Placement on Salary Schedules

When school board officials place new teachers on salary schedules, they are ordinarily not obligated to grant them credit for the experiences

---

1. *Hansen v. Board of Educ. of School Dist. No. 65*, 502 N.E.2d 467 [36 Educ. L. Rep. 827] (Ill.App.Ct.1986).

2. *Osborn v. Harrison School Dist. No. 2*, 844 P.2d 1283 [80 Educ. L. Rep. 732] (Colo.Ct.App. 1992).

3. *United Teachers of Ukiah v. Board of Educ.*, 251 Cal.Rptr. 499 [49 Educ. L. Rep. 299] (Cal. Ct.App.1988) (affirming that a board violated state law by giving some, but not all, teachers credit for more than five years of prior teaching experience when they were hired).

that they had outside of the public school systems of their states.[4] If officials do grant teachers credit for past work, board policies usually do not require them to pay educators for experience that is not directly related to their jobs. For example, the Supreme Court of Arkansas rejected a teacher's claim that her board failed to pay her in accord with its salary schedule.[5] The court affirmed that the board, which hired the teacher as an elementary school counselor, could pay her based on her five years of teaching even though she worked in schools for seventeen years because she willingly signed a contract indicating that she was paid at this rate.

Once salary policies are in place, officials may not administer them in arbitrary or discriminatory manners such as by making new rules retroactive.[6] Boards may also grant credit for experiences other than teaching such as military service.[7] Further, as reflected by a case from the Supreme Court of South Dakota, a board had the authority to impose a term in a collective bargaining agreement that unilaterally allowed it to go over and above its salary schedule when it deemed it necessary to do so.[8]

Where qualifications and performance are equal, teachers must be treated the same,[9] even granting them credit for past years of service following a break in employment with regard to being placed on salary schedules.[10] In a case with a twist as to equality of performance, an appellate court in South Carolina affirmed that when teachers who worked in the statewide prison school system were not compensated any differently than their counterparts in the regular public schools, they were entitled to salary supplements.[11]

Insofar as titles alone are not controlling, the Supreme Court of Minnesota agreed that regular teachers and those in a special vocational-technical school could be paid differently.[12] The Supreme Judicial Court of Massachusetts reached a similar outcome in noting that not all supervisors had to be paid in like fashion.[13] Later, the Supreme Court of Idaho affirmed that a board did not violate the rights of teachers who served as department chairpersons in refusing to pay them extra com-

---

4. *Howard Union of Teachers v. State,* 478 A.2d 563 [18 Educ. L. Rep. 929] (R.I. 1984); *Fry v. Board of Educ.,* 112 P.2d 229 (Cal.1941).

5. *Stone v. Mayflower School Dist.,* 894 S.W.2d 881 [98 Educ. L. Rep. 1108] (Ark. 1995).

6. *Aebli v. Board of Educ.,* 145 P.2d 601 (Cal.Ct.App.1944); *Board of Educ. of Katonah–Lewisboro Union Free School Dist. v. Ambach,* 432 N.Y.S.2d 661 (N.Y.App.Div. 1980).

7. *See North Plainfield Educ. Ass'n on Behalf of Koumjian v. Board of Educ. of Borough of N. Plainfield, Somerset County,* 476 A.2d 1245 [18 Educ. L. Rep. 334] (N.J. 1984).

8. *Sisseton Educ. Ass'n v. Sisseton School Dist. No. 54–8,* 516 N.W.2d 301 [91 Educ. L. Rep. 328] (S.D.1994).

9. *Vittal v. Long Beach Unified School Dist.,* 87 Cal.Rptr. 319 (Cal.Ct.App.1970).

10. *Mifflinburg Area Educ. Ass'n ex rel. Ulrich v. Mifflinburg Area School Dist.,* 724 A.2d 339 [132 Educ. L. Rep. 507] (Pa.1999).

11. *Abraham v. Palmetto Unified School Dist. No. 1,* 538 S.E.2d 656 [149 Educ. L. Rep. 909] (S.C.Ct.App.2000).

12. *Frisk v. Board of Educ. of Duluth,* 75 N.W.2d 504 (Minn.1956).

13. *Murphy v. School Comm. of Lawrence,* 73 N.E.2d 835 (Mass.1947).

pensation.[14] The court acknowledged that since the operative bargaining pact did not create employment contracts with individuals, they were not entitled to additional compensation solely by reason of the extra duty pay schedules in the master agreement.

Disputes also arise over substitute teachers. In such a case, the Supreme Court of Ohio affirmed that a board was statutorily required to pay long-term substitute teachers only the minimum salary on its adopted salary schedule.[15] An appellate court in Pennsylvania struck down a provision in a bargaining agreement which required substitute teachers who were hired to full-time positions to give up all claims to salary schedule placements for any or all time spent as substitutes.[16] The court held that the provision violated a statute that required boards to give substitutes salary credits for long-term service if they are hired to work in the same districts where they served as substitutes. This is consistent with the general rule that collective bargaining agreements may not conflict with statutes.

Bases of Salary Classifications

School boards may not differentiate salaries based on race, sex, or marital status. Yet, boards may classify teachers for salary purposes as long as they do so on grounds that are reasonable, natural, and based on substantial differences that are germane to their duties. As such, an appellate court in California affirmed that a board's professional growth policy, which covered activities that were separate and distinct from bona fide elements of teaching experience, violated the state law governing uniform salaries for teachers since it did not treat years of training and years of experience uniformly.[17]

Perhaps the most significant salary issues arise in connection with discussions of pay increases. Courts generally uphold salary differences based on subjective judgments as long as the criteria that school officials apply are reasonably specific and relevant. For instance, a federal trial court in Illinois refused to exercise its jurisdiction where a teacher claimed that her superintendent failed to follow committee recommendations that she be granted a merit increase because others who were no more qualified than she received the increase and she did not receive any written reasons why she was not awarded a raise.[18] The court found that since the teacher did not have a legitimate expectation of a merit salary increase, she had neither a constitutionally protected property interest nor a right to procedural due process to standards defining merit or written reasons for her being denied a merit raise.

14. *Gilmore v. Bonner County School Dist. No. 82*, 971 P.2d 323 [132 Educ. L. Rep. 197] (Idaho 1999).

15. *State ex rel. Antonucci v. Youngstown City School Dist. Bd. of Educ.*, 722 N.E.2d 69 [140 Educ. L. Rep. 740] (Ohio 2000).

16. *Greater Johnstown School Dist. v. Greater Johnstown Educ. Ass'n*, 804 A.2d 680 [168 Educ. L. Rep. 843] (Pa.Cmwlth.Ct. 2002), *appeal denied*, 812 A.2d 1231 (Pa. 2002).

17. *Wygant v. Victor Valley Joint High School Dist.*, 214 Cal.Rptr. 205 [25 Educ. L. Rep. 396] (Cal.Ct.App.1985).

18. *Kanter v. Community Consol. School Dist. 65*, 558 F.Supp. 890 [10 Educ. L. Rep. 137] (N.D.Ill.1982).

The Supreme Court of New Jersey handed down three cases dealing with salaries. In the first, the court reiterated the general rule that an annual pay raise based on meritorious service is not a matter of statutory right but is subject to denial for inefficiency or other good cause.[19] The court next decided that when a board withheld salary increments from a teacher for unsatisfactory performance, she was not entitled to have them restored and returned to the board's salary schedule when she performed satisfactorily.[20] In the third case, the court ruled that while teacher evaluations are a managerial prerogative essential to the way that school boards discharge their duties, officials could not withhold a teacher's annual raise due to her excessive absences where an arbitrator determined that they acted for disciplinary, rather than educational, reasons.[21]

Recognizing that school boards have the authority to create extra incentives for teachers to receive salary supplements,[22] courts have upheld policies that awarded raises on items other than typical teaching duties. The Fourth Circuit affirmed that a school board in South Carolina could tie pay raises to scores that exceed the minimum on the National Teacher Examination.[23] Previously, an appellate court in California affirmed a board policy that teachers had to be present for 75 percent of a school year in order to receive their annual increments.[24] The court rejected a claim that the policy's making exceptions for those on military or sabbatical leave violated a teacher's right to equal protection since he was on sick leave. The court explained that the exceptions passed constitutional muster in light of the strong public policy in favor of granting credit to those on military leave and that teachers' sabbatical leave activities are intended to benefit school boards and, ultimately, students. On the other hand, an appellate court in New Jersey affirmed that military service credits for the purposes of protecting tenure are on a different footing than when they are applied to calculate compensation.[25] The court thus reasoned that since tenure protection applied to all teachers but the compensation protection covered only those who were employed by local or regional boards or county vocational schools, teachers who worked for state departments and agencies were not entitled to military service credits for compensation purposes.

19. *North Plainfield Educ. Ass'n on Behalf of Koumjian v. Board of Educ. of Borough of N. Plainfield, Somerset County,* 476 A.2d 1245 [18 Educ. L. Rep. 334] (N.J. 1984).

20. *Probst v. Board of Educ. of Borough of Haddonfield, Camden County,* 606 A.2d 345 [74 Educ. L. Rep. 137] (N.J.1992).

21. *Scotch Plains–Fanwood Bd. of Educ. v. Scotch Plains–Fanwood Educ. Ass'n,* 651 A.2d 1018 [96 Educ. L. Rep. 984] (N.J.1995). *See also Board of Educ. Township of Neptune in County of Monmouth v. Neptune Township Educ. Ass'n,* 675 A.2d 611 [115 Educ. L. Rep. 372] (N.J.1996) (de-claring that payments of fourth year salary increments following the expiration of a three-year contract violated state education law).

22. *Weatherford v. Martin,* 418 So.2d 777 [6 Educ. L. Rep. 275] (Miss.1982).

23. *Newman v. Crews,* 651 F.2d 222 (4th Cir.1981).

24. *Hunt v. Alum Rock Union Elementary School Dist.,* 86 Cal.Rptr. 663 (Cal.Ct. App.1970).

25. *In re Military Service Credit For State Teachers,* 875 A.2d 978 [199 Educ. L. Rep. 320] (N.J. Super. Ct. App. Div. 2005).

On the general question of extra pay for certain types of teachers, an appellate court in Louisiana affirmed that a school board was required to pay special education teachers only a 10 percent salary supplement for sixteen-days since a pre-existing clause in an amendment to their contract was inapplicable to their case.[26] The court noted that the amendment applied only to teachers who were actually employed when the contract went into effect.[27]

In addition to salary, school board officials may offer teachers other benefits based on various characteristics. In apparently the only reported case on point, when faced with a shortage of qualified personnel, the Supreme Judicial Court of Massachusetts upheld a dependency-allowance plan for teachers who were the sole support of spouses or children.[28] Where a school board permitted children of its non-resident faculty to attend school without paying tuition, New York's highest court affirmed that it could not unilaterally stop doing so.[29] The court indicated that the dispute was subject to arbitration under the operative collective bargaining agreement between the board and its teachers. Subsequently, the Eighth Circuit observed that a board's policy of allowing children of certified and administrative employees to attend school in the district even if they lived outside of it, while not allowing children of other nonresident employees to attend school there, was rationally related to its desire to recruit or retain quality teachers and administrators.[30] The court was thus satisfied that the policy did not violate the equal protection rights of nonresident employees whose children were not permitted to attend schools in the district.

Changes in Salary Classifications

School boards and their unions can modify salary classifications, and scales, from one collective bargaining agreement to the next. While bargaining has certainly not eliminated salary disputes, they were arguably more common before the advent of negotiations. In *Phelps v. Board of Education*,[31] the Supreme Court resolved a controversy from New Jersey over whether a board could reduce teacher salaries pursuant to a permissive statute that conflicted with the statewide tenure law's prohibition against reductions of salary without following tenure procedures. The Court pointed out that since the tenure law was a statement of legislative policy rather than a contract, the salary reductions for teachers was permissible because it was carried out in a nondiscriminatory manner.

26. *Phillips v. Orleans Parish School Bd.*, 755 So.2d 353 [144 Educ. L. Rep. 446] (La.Ct.App. 2000), *writ denied*, 761 So.2d 547 (La.2000).

27. *See also Weslaco Fed'n of Teachers v. Texas Educ. Agency*, 27 S.W.3d 258 [147 Educ. L. Rep. 730] (Tex. App.2000) (affirming that teachers were not entitled to a local supplement they received the previous year when their board failed to adopt a salary schedule in a timely manner).

28. *Cotter v. City of Chelsea*, 108 N.E.2d 47 (Mass.1952).

29. *Board of Educ. of New Paltz Cent. School Dist. v. New Paltz United Teachers*, 407 N.Y.S.2d 632 (N.Y.1978).

30. *Clayton v. White Hall School Dist.*, 875 F.2d 676 [53 Educ. L. Rep. 1107] (8th Cir.1989).

31. 300 U.S. 319, 57 S.Ct. 483, 81 L.Ed. 674 (1937). [Case No. 70]

In order to protect teachers, some states have enacted statutes that require them to be paid the same amount as the previous year unless school systems make across-the-board pay cuts or individuals reduce their responsibilities.[32] Even where there is apparent mutual consent on salary reductions, school officials must follow state law. To this end, the highest courts in Arkansas,[33] Tennessee,[34] and Washington[35] agreed that teachers could sue to recover the full salary to which they were entitled even though they signed contracts agreeing to work for lower wages.

Boards cannot reduce salary schedules during a school year[36] or for extra duty assignments. In an illustrative case, an appellate court in California affirmed that a board could not unilaterally eliminate the stipend that it paid teachers who were required to make calls on absent students since, in light of the fact that there was no material change in their duties, it sought, in effect, to reduce their pay impermissibly.[37]

Disagreements arise over changes in classifications of teachers on salary schedules. In such a case, an appellate court in California maintained that teachers who resigned or left their jobs at the end of a school year were not entitled to payment under the terms of a collective bargaining agreement which granted a one-time retroactive payment to individuals who retired or returned to work the following school year.[38] The court asserted that since the agreement between the board and union specifically excluded teachers who resigned or left voluntarily, and the payment was not salary for the purposes of the state's uniform salary law, they did not have their status changed impermissibly.

Individuals who receive benefits erroneously are generally not entitled to continue to receive them once the mistakes are discovered.[39] If the benefit is overpayment of salary, school boards can later deduct these sums from teachers' pay as long as the amounts are not substantial, no great hardship results, and doing so does not violate express contractual terms.[40]

Personnel Files

School boards must preserve personnel files for their teachers and staff. Consequently, since states have enacted Open Records Laws to

32. *See, e.g.,* 105 ILL. COMP. STAT. ANN. 5/24–11; KY. REV. STAT. ANN. § 161.760, OHIO REV. CODE ANN. § 3319.12. *See also Pigue v. Christian County Bd. of Educ.,* 65 S.W.3d 540 [161 Educ. L. Rep. 1080] (Ky.Ct.App. 2001) (upholding the statute).

33. *Marvel v. Coal Hill Pub. School Dist.,* 635 S.W.2d 245 [5 Educ. L. Rep. 667] (Ark.1982). [Case No. 71]

34. *McMinn County Bd. of Educ. v. Anderson,* 292 S.W.2d 198 (Tenn.1956).

35. *Malcolm v. Yakima County Consol. School Dist. 90,* 159 P.2d 394 (Wash.1945).

36. *Abraham v. Sims,* 42 P.2d 1029 (Cal.1935).

37. *A.B.C. Fed'n of Teachers v. A.B.C. Unified School Dist.,* 142 Cal.Rptr. 111 (Cal.Ct.App. 1977).

38. *California Teachers' Ass'n v. Governing Bd. of the Hilmar Unified School Dist.,* 115 Cal.Rptr.2d 323 [160 Educ. L. Rep. 449] (Cal.Ct.App.2002).

39. *Shoban v. Board of Trustees of Desert Ctr. Unified School Dist.,* 81 Cal.Rptr. 112 (Cal.Ct. App.1969).

40. *Green Local Teachers Ass'n v. Blevins,* 539 N.E.2d 653 [54 Educ. L. Rep. 296] (Ohio Ct. App.1987).

make personnel files and other public materials available,[41] disputes have arisen over who has access to this information.

A major concern with regard to the content of files is whether teachers have the right to challenge the inclusion of uncomplimentary materials. The Court of Appeals of New York, echoing the widely held view, was of the opinion that school officials can place letters that are critical of performance or conduct in teachers' files without affording them hearings since supervisors have legitimate rights and duties to do so.[42] Similarly, the Tenth Circuit affirmed that officials in Colorado could place a letter of reprimand in a teacher's file over inappropriate comments that he made in class about the behavior of students because the admonition was neither impermissibly vague nor broad and since his speech was not about a matter of public concern, it was not subject to constitutional protection.[43] Conversely, the Sixth Circuit directed officials in Ohio to remove a letter from a teacher's personnel file since it believed that they placed it there simply in retaliation for his protected union activities.[44]

In an extension of teachers' rights to challenge the correctness of items in their files that may be stigmatizing or that present barriers to future employment if they dealt with dismissals and are likely to be disclosed to future employers, the Second Circuit reiterated the general rule that educators have the right to name-clearing hearings.[45] However, the court thought that since the teacher in New York failed to prove that officials violated his protected liberty interest insofar as stigmatizing allegations were removed from his personnel file, their not being disclosed meant that there was no likelihood of any future disclosure of the stigmatizing allegations. In a non-education case, the Supreme Court affirmed that while an individual may be able to file a defamation claim under state law if false information is released, a federal cause of action does not arise based solely on injury to reputation that occurs due to the release of derogatory information that is not in the context of a discharge or the non-renewal of a contract.[46]

Whether, and to whom, confidential information must be divulged is ordinarily resolved on a case-by-case basis in light of competing considerations.[47] The Supreme Court of North Dakota, rejecting arguments to the contrary, affirmed that under the state's Open Records Law, person-

---

41. *See, e.g.,* ALA. CODE 1975 § 16–22–14; ARK. CODE ANN. § 6–17–1505; CAL. EDUC. CODE ANN. § 44031; FLA. STAT. ANN. § 1012.31; IDAHO CODE ANN. § 33–518; 20 ME. REV. STAT. ANN. § 13004; N.C. GEN. STAT. ANN. § 115C–319; N.D. CENT. CODE §§ 15.1–17–01 *et seq.*; OR. REV. STAT. § 342.850; VA. CODE ANN. § 22.1–295.1.

42. *Holt v. Board of Educ. of Webutuck Cent. School Dist.,* 439 N.Y.S.2d 839 (N.Y. 1981).

43. *Miles v. Denver Pub. Schools,* 944 F.2d 773 [69 Educ. L. Rep. 1060] (10th Cir.1991).

44. *Columbus Educ. Ass'n v. Columbus City School Dist.,* 623 F.2d 1155 (6th Cir. 1980).

45. *Brandt v. Board of Co-op. Educ. Servs.,* 845 F.2d 416 [46 Educ. L. Rep. 548] (2d Cir.1988).

46. *Siegert v. Gilley,* 500 U.S. 226, 111 S.Ct. 1789, 114 L.Ed.2d 277 (1991), *reh'g denied,* 501 U.S. 1265, 111 S.Ct. 2920, 115 L.Ed.2d 1084 (1991).

47. *Berst v. Chipman,* 653 P.2d 107 [7 Educ. L. Rep. 437] (Kan.1982).

nel files are public records available for inspection.[48] Moreover, the Supreme Court, in a case from higher education, *University of Pennsylvania v. Equal Employment Opportunity Commission* (EEOC),[49] affirmed that a faculty member's confidential tenure files were subject to subpoena by the EEOC when it is investigating discrimination claims.

In a case with a different focus, the Fifth Circuit rejected the claim of a teacher and her school board that the Family Educational Rights and Privacy Act (FERPA)[50] prevented officials from disclosing the contents of her college transcript.[51] The court affirmed that FERPA was inapplicable because it covered the records of only students, not employees. Even assuming that the teacher had a recognizable privacy interest in her transcript, the court commented that it was outweighed by the public's interest in evaluating the competence of teachers.[52] An appellate court in Minnesota reached a similar outcome in positing that while a union had standing to challenge the release of disciplinary information about teachers, its interest in non-disclosure was ultimately outweighed by the public's right to such information.[53]

As issues have arisen over the privacy rights of job applicants, courts have reached mixed results. On the one hand, appellate courts in Pennsylvania[54] and Indiana[55] agreed that boards did not have to release information about applicants. The court in Pennsylvania conceded that while applications might have been covered by a relevant statute, since the files included confidential information such as home addresses, social security numbers, and college transcripts, they were protected from disclosure. The court from Indiana interpreted its statute as applying only to present or former employees, not applicants. On the other hand, an appellate court in Ohio contended that the media could seek access to the names, applications, and resumes of applicants for a superintendency on the ground that a board failed to present a good reason why the information should not have been released.[56]

Leaves

The Family and Medical Leave Act,[57] discussed in Chapter 9, ensures that school employees have a federally protected right to take time

---

48. *Hovet v. Hebron Pub. School Dist.*, 419 N.W.2d 189 [44 Educ. L. Rep. 1325] (N.D.1988).

49. 493 U.S. 182, 110 S.Ct. 577, 107 L.Ed.2d 571 [57 Educ. L. Rep. 666] (1990).

50. 20 U.S.C. § 1232g.

51. *Klein Indep. School Dist. v. Mattox*, 830 F.2d 576 [42 Educ. L. Rep. 70] (5th Cir.1987), *cert. denied*, 485 U.S. 1008, 108 S.Ct. 1473, 99 L.Ed.2d 702 [46 Educ. L. Rep. 27] (1988). [Case No. 72]

52. *See also Brouillet v. Cowles Publishing Co.*, 791 P.2d 526 [60 Educ. L. Rep. 638] (Wash.1990) (affirming that FERPA did not prevent the disclosure of a teacher's records).

53. *Minneapolis Fed'n of Teachers, AFL–CIO, Local 59 v. Minneapolis Pub. Schools, Special School Dist. No. 1*, 512 N.W.2d 107 [89 Educ. L. Rep. 261] (Minn. Ct.App.1994).

54. *Cypress Media, Inc. v. Hazleton Area School Dist.*, 708 A.2d 866 [125 Educ. L. Rep. 527] (Pa.Cmwlth.Ct.1998).

55. *South Bend Tribune v. South Bend Community School Corp.*, 740 N.E.2d 937 [150 Educ. L. Rep. 253] (Ind.Ct.App.2000).

56. *State ex rel. Dayton Newspapers v. Dayton Bd. of Educ.*, 747 N.E.2d 255 [153 Educ. L. Rep. 756] (Ohio Ct.App.2000).

57. 29 U.S.C.A. §§ 2611 *et seq.*

off from work to look after their own medical needs and those of their family members. Even though state laws and collective bargaining agreements vary as to the extent to which teachers may take time off due to illness, it is well-established that they have rights to sick leave.[58]

Abuse of sick leave constitutes cause for disciplinary action against employees.[59] An appellate court in Pennsylvania ascertained that when two teachers used sick leave to go on a ski trip after school officials denied their requests for personal leave, their board had just cause to terminate their contracts.[60] Conversely, an appellate court in Illinois affirmed that while a teacher abused her sick leave by using it to attend a professional conference, her action was remediable under the law, which provided that before faculty members could be dismissed for such conduct, they had to have received written warnings to cease the objectionable behavior.[61]

Before granting requests for medical leaves, boards may ask teachers for evidence that they were ill, either as a matter of general policy[62] or where there is a question,[63] and may require them to undergo physical examinations to evaluate their health before returning to work.[64] In one case, the Eighth Circuit affirmed that a board in Iowa could require a driving instructor to obtain two medical opinions evaluating his mental competence before permitting him to return to work.[65]

Details of sick leave policies are ordinarily negotiable, typically as a mandatory topic of bargaining,[66] as long as agreements do not violate state law.[67] Where boards provide for various leaves, the legal issues that arise primarily deal with contractual interpretation. If educators do not take all of their sick leave, absent state statutes or bargaining provisions to the contrary, courts have reached mixed results over whether they can obtain payment for unused time. In cases that focused on disputes of this type, the Supreme Court of Arkansas affirmed that a teacher could not obtain payment for unused sick leave[68] while an appellate court in

---

58. *Averell v. Newburyport*, 135 N.E. 463 (Mass.1922).

59. *Reddick v. Leon County School Bd.*, 405 So.2d 757 [1 Educ. L. Rep. 464] (Fla. Dist.Ct.App. 1981); *Board of Educ. of Laurel County v. McCollum*, 721 S.W.2d 703 [36 Educ. L. Rep. 1026] (Ky.1986).

60. *Riverview School Dist. v. Riverview Educ. Ass'n, PSEA–NEA*, 639 A.2d 974 [90 Educ. L. Rep. 280] (Pa.Cmwlth.Ct.1994).

61. *Board of Educ. of Joliet Township High School Dist. No. 204 v. Illinois State Bd. of Educ.*, 770 N.E.2d 711 [167 Educ. L. Rep. 845] (Ill.App.Ct.2002), *appeal denied*, 786 N.E.2d 180 (Ill.2002).

62. *Crowston v. Jamestown Pub. School Dist. No. 1*, 335 N.W.2d 775 [12 Educ. L. Rep. 525] (N.D.1983).

63. *Brown v. Houston Indep. School Dist.*, 763 F.Supp. 905 [67 Educ. L. Rep. 1175] (S.D.Tex. 1991), *aff'd without published opinion*, 957 F.2d 866 [73 Educ. L. Rep. 375] (5th Cir.1992), *cert. denied*, 506

U.S. 868, 113 S.Ct. 198, 121 L.Ed.2d 140 (1992).

64. *Strong v. Board of Educ. of Uniondale Union Free School Dist.*, 902 F.2d 208 [60 Educ. L. Rep. 379] (2d Cir.1990), *cert. denied*, 498 U.S. 897, 111 S.Ct. 250, 112 L.Ed.2d 208 (1990).

65. *Scheideman v. West Des Moines Community School Dist.*, 989 F.2d 286 [82 Educ. L. Rep. 39] (8th Cir.1993).

66. *See, e.g., Waterloo Community School Dist. v. Public Employment Relations Bd.*, 650 N.W.2d 627 [169 Educ. L. Rep. 402] (Iowa 2002).

67. *Jefferson Classroom Teachers Ass'n v. Jefferson Elementary School Dist.*, 187 Cal.Rptr. 542 [7 Educ. L. Rep. 946] (Cal.Ct. App.1982).

68. *Turnbough v. Mammoth Spring School Dist. No. 2*, 78 S.W.3d 89 [167 Educ. L. Rep. 492] (Ark.2002).

Indiana reached the opposite result in a dispute involving a school psychologist.[69]

Turning to pregnancy, an appellate court in Indiana affirmed that since state law granted teachers a right to request a one-year leave of absence following childbirth, a board had to grant her request as long as she met statutory requirements.[70] The court added that the teacher was entitled to leave even though she initially did not ask for a full year since she gave the board ample notice that she was requesting the entire amount available under the statute. On a procedural matter, an appellate court in Texas reached a different outcome when a probationary teacher sued her board after she was not allowed to return to work following pregnancy leave. The court was of the view that since material issues of fact were present as to whether the teacher was dismissed or voluntarily abandoned her position and whether she was ever physically able to return to employment, she had to exhaust administrative remedies before filing suit.[71]

Teachers may also seek leave for personal, including religious,[72] and professional reasons such as sabbaticals. Boards retain discretion to grant or deny requests for leaves of absence.[73] Teachers must continue to meet professional requirements while on leave. In such a case, the Supreme Court of Colorado affirmed that a school board could terminate the contract of a staff member who was on leave for sex-reassignment surgery since she allowed her teaching license to lapse.[74]

As to sabbatical leaves, boards face potentially troublesome issues in evaluating eligibility and what positions teachers return to when they come back from leaves. Clearly, boards retain discretion in granting sabbaticals.[75] When teachers are scheduled to return to work, disputes arise over whether they are entitled to return to their exact same positions. Courts generally do not interpret the term "same position" as meaning the same exact academic position.[76] If one party breaches a sabbatical contract, either teachers[77] or boards[78] can sue. Once teachers return from sabbatical leaves, they retain the rights that they would

69. *Schwartz v. Gary Community School Corp.*, 762 N.E.2d 192 [161 Educ. L. Rep. 631] (Ind. Ct.App.2002), *transfer denied*, 774 N.E.2d 518 (Ind.2002).

70. *Board of School Trustees of Salem Community Schools v. Robertson*, 637 N.E.2d 181 [92 Educ. L. Rep. 962] (Ind.Ct. App.1994).

71. *Mercedes Indep. School Dist. v. Munoz*, 941 S.W.2d 215 [117 Educ. L. Rep. 373] (Tex. App.1996).

72. For a review of the use of leave time for religious purposes, *see* the discussion of *Ansonia Bd. of Educ. v. Philbrook*, 479 U.S. 60, 107 S.Ct. 367, 93 L.Ed.2d 305 [35 Educ. L. Rep. 365] (1986) at note 133 and accompanying text in Chapter 9.

73. *Giordano v. Ambach*, 509 N.Y.S.2d 203 [36 Educ. L. Rep. 416] (N.Y.App.Div. 1986).

74. *Snyder v. Jefferson County School Dist. R–1*, 842 P.2d 624 [79 Educ. L. Rep. 632] (Colo. 1992).

75. *Board of Educ. of Three Village Cent. Schools of Towns of Brookhaven and Smithtown v. Three Village Teachers' Ass'n*, 419 N.Y.S.2d 665 (N.Y.App.Div.1979).

76. *Taube v. St. Charles Parish School Bd.*, 787 So.2d 377 [155 Educ. L. Rep. 976] (La.Ct. App. 2001).

77. *Cahill v. Board of Educ. of City of Stamford*, 444 A.2d 907 [4 Educ. L. Rep. 163] (Conn. 1982).

78. *Trumansburg Cent. School Dist. v. Chalone*, 449 N.Y.S.2d 92 [3 Educ. L. Rep. 720] (N.Y. App.Div.1982).

have enjoyed had they remained in active service but do not gain enhanced rights.[79]

Assignments and Transfers

School boards have the discretion to assign teachers to individual schools since educators do not have rights to teach in specific buildings.[80] To the extent that some states have established statutory or regulatory guidelines for employee transfers, school officials must comply with the law.[81] Absent state-level constraints, local boards, often subject to terms in collective bargaining agreements, have the discretion[82] to establish their own rules with regard to assigning, and transferring, teachers to similar positions[83] within their areas of certification[84] even if, for example, an individual is relieved of coaching responsibilities in the process.[85]

As long as school boards comply with their own rules, courts ordinarily do not intervene. In a dispute from New Jersey, an appellate court wrote that a board could involuntarily transfer a tenured teacher when it abolished his position and required him to teach different subjects within his area of certification.[86] The court specified that the board did not violate the teacher's rights since he did not suffer a loss in pay or other job benefits and was not singled out for the transfer on a prohibited basis.

In Indiana, a federal trial court granted a school board's motion for summary judgment after it transferred a teacher during an investigation over whether he behaved inappropriately with two female students.[87] The court remarked that since officials provided the teacher with suitable employment, it did not force him to resign. Similarly, the Seventh Circuit affirmed that a board in Illinois did not violate the rights of a tenured physical education teacher when it temporarily transferred him to an administrative position, with full pay, pending an investigation after one of his students drowned due to an apparent lack of supervision in the pool area.[88]

---

79. *Gardner v. State ex rel. Dep't of Educ.*, 844 So.2d 311 [176 Educ. L. Rep. 955] (La.Ct.App. 2003).

80. *Gordon v. Nicoletti*, 84 F.Supp.2d 304 [142 Educ. L. Rep. 169] (D.Conn.2000); *Maupin v. Independent School Dist. No. 26*, 632 P.2d 396 (Okla.1981).

81. *Ex parte Ezell*, 545 So.2d 52 [54 Educ. L. Rep. 1023] (Ala.1989), *on remand*, 545 So.2d 55 [55 Educ. L. Rep. 334] (Ala. Civ.App.1989).

82. *Stevenson v. Lower Marion County School Dist. No. Three*, 327 S.E.2d 656 [23 Educ. L. Rep. 1101] (S.C.1985).

83. *Thomas v. Smith*, 897 F.2d 154 [58 Educ. L. Rep. 1114] (5th Cir.1989).

84. *Quarles v. McKenzie Pub. School Dist. No. 34*, 325 N.W.2d 662 [7 Educ. L.

Rep. 401] (N.D.1982); *Adlerstein v. Board of Educ. of City of N.Y.*, 466 N.Y.S.2d 973 [13 Educ. L. Rep. 836] (N.Y.App.Div.1983), *aff'd*, 485 N.Y.S.2d 1 [22 Educ. L. Rep. 1220] (N.Y.1984).

85. *Jett v. Dallas Indep. School Dist.*, 798 F.2d 748 [34 Educ. L. Rep. 384] (5th Cir.1986), *aff'd in part, remanded in part*, 491 U.S. 701, 109 S.Ct. 2702, 105 L.Ed.2d 598 [54 Educ. L. Rep. 30] (1989).

86. *Carpenito v. Board of Educ. of the Borough of Rumson*, 731 A.2d 538 [135 Educ. L. Rep. 567] (N.J.Super.Ct.App.Div.1999).

87. *Tweedall v. Fritz*, 987 F.Supp. 1126 [124 Educ. L. Rep. 122] (S.D.Ind.1997).

88. *Townsend v. Vallas*, 256 F.3d 661 [155 Educ. L. Rep. 142] (7th Cir.2001).

An older case reflects the general rule that teachers can be discharged for refusing to accept assignments in their areas of competence. When a physical education teacher who was relieved of his duties as football coach refused to continue to coach basketball, the Supreme Court of Pennsylvania upheld his dismissal.[89] More than sixty years later, an appellate court in Texas affirmed that when a tenured teacher refused to go to work for three months as a protest against being transferred, the board had sufficient cause to terminate her employment.[90]

Involuntary transfers are subject to heightened judicial examination if they involve educators' exercises of their First Amendment rights. The Ninth Circuit addressed a controversy involving the transfer of a counselor of Mexican American ancestry who criticized board policies relating to the classification of Mexican American children on the basis of tests that were given in English. A federal trial court in Arizona maintained that while the transfer was impermissible since it was partially in retaliation for the counselor's exercise of her First Amendment rights, she was not entitled to relief because it did not involve a loss of pay or status. In remanding, the panel concluded that the counselor was entitled to a remedy, emphasizing that she had neither harassed school officials nor was insubordinate.[91] Previously, the Supreme Court of California invalidated the transfer of a teacher who was critical of, but complied with, board policies.[92]

Individuals in administrative positions may be reassigned to other jobs,[93] including those lower in the hierarchy,[94] or teaching,[95] ordinarily without hearings,[96] absent statutory or contractual provisions to the contrary. If, as with other school staff, state laws provide detailed directives dealing with the demotion of administrators, officials must strictly apply the law.[97]

As with teachers, disputes arise over the free speech rights of principals, especially if their actions subject them to demotions. The Sixth Circuit affirmed that the free speech rights of a principal from Tennessee who was demoted to teaching for having criticized his superintendent's position on a dress code were outweighed by the latter's need

89. *Appeal of Ganaposki*, 2 A.2d 742 (Pa.1938).

90. *Miller v. Houston Indep. School Dist.*, 51 S.W.3d 676 [156 Educ. L. Rep. 708] (Tex. App. 2001), *reh'g overruled, review denied, reh'g of petition for review denied, cert. denied*, 535 U.S. 905, 122 S.Ct. 1203, 152 L.Ed.2d 142 (2002).

91. *Bernasconi v. Tempe Elementary School Dist. No. 3*, 548 F.2d 857 (9th Cir. 1977), *cert. denied*, 434 U.S. 825, 98 S.Ct. 72, 54 L.Ed.2d 82 (1977).

92. *Adcock v. Board of Educ. of San Diego Unified School Dist.*, 513 P.2d 900 (Cal.1973).

93. *McCoy v. McConnell*, 461 S.W.2d 948 (Tenn.1970).

94. *Scottsdale School Dist. v. Clark*, 512 P.2d 853 (Ariz.Ct.App.1973).

95. *Love-Lane v. Martin*, 201 F.Supp.2d 566 [165 Educ. L. Rep. 526] (M.D.N.C. 2002).

96. *Sharp v. Lindsey*, 285 F.3d 479 [163 Educ. L. Rep. 88] (6th Cir.2002); *McCoy v. Lincoln Intermediate Unit No. 12*, 391 A.2d 1119 (Pa.Cmwlth.Ct.1978), *cert. denied*, 441 U.S. 923, 99 S.Ct. 2033, 60 L.Ed.2d 397 (1979).

97. *Edgar v. School Bd. of Calhoun County*, 549 So.2d 726 [56 Educ. L. Rep. 680] (Fla.Dist.Ct. App.1989).

for a good working relationship with staff.[98] In like manner, the Seventh Circuit affirmed that a board in Wisconsin could demote a principal to assistant principal since, as a policy-making employee, her criticism of its attempts to gain additional state aid for disadvantaged students was not protected free speech.[99]

A final factor that is sometimes involved in teacher assignments is race. Insofar as this topic is discussed in detail in Chapter 15, it suffices to say that the courts have reached mixed results in examining the role of race as a factor in transfers and reassignments in eliminating racial segregation.[100]

Loyalty

Loyalty Oaths

In the years after World War II, loyalty oaths for teachers and other public employees proliferated. As provisions became increasingly extensive, they focused more on what teachers should have avoided doing rather than on what they should have done. Some oaths barred teachers from participating in outside associations while others contained stipulations requiring them to attest that they did not engage in specified activities before being hired. Oaths often included criminal penalties for making false statements along with being rendered ineligible for teaching.

In its first case on point, *Wieman v. Updegraff*,[101] the Supreme Court unanimously struck down a loyalty oath statute from Oklahoma primarily since it disqualified individuals from public employment if, during the preceding five years, they belonged to organizations deemed subversive, regardless of whether they knew of their character. In conceding that membership could have been innocent, the Court did not believe that public employees should have been punished for joining groups if they were unaware of their activities and purposes.

Almost a decade later, in *Cramp v. Board of Public Instruction of Orange County, Florida*, the Court, again unanimously, struck down an oath as unconstitutionally vague since it barred individuals from giving "... aid, support, advice, counsel or influence to the Communist Party."[102] Although not questioning the state's power to safeguard the public service from disloyalty, the Court decreed that state officials had to describe proscribed conduct in language that was subject to objective measurement.

---

98. *Sharp v. Lindsey*, 285 F.3d 479 [163 Educ. L. Rep. 88] (6th Cir.2002).

99. *Vargas-Harrison v. Racine Unified School Dist.*, 272 F.3d 964 [159 Educ. L. Rep. 459] (7th Cir.2001).

100. *See, e.g., Wygant v. Jackson Bd. of Educ.*, 476 U.S. 267, 106 S.Ct. 1842, 90 L.Ed.2d 260 [32 Educ. L. Rep. 20] (1986), *reh'g denied*, 478 U.S. 1014, 106 S.Ct. 3320, 92 L.Ed.2d 728 [35 Educ. L. Rep. 20]

(1986); *Jacobson v. Cincinnati Bd. of Educ.*, 961 F.2d 100 [74 Educ. L. Rep. 51] (6th Cir.1992), *cert. denied*, 506 U.S. 830, 113 S.Ct. 94, 121 L.Ed.2d 55 (1992). [Case No. 73]

101. 344 U.S. 183, 73 S.Ct. 215, 97 L.Ed. 216 (1952).

102. 368 U.S. 278, 281, 82 S.Ct. 275, 7 L.Ed.2d 285 (1961).

Five years later, in *Elfbrandt v. Russell*,[103] the Court introduced a new criterion for loyalty legislation: officials could not impose penalties unless they could demonstrate that individual members of organizations joined them with the specific intent to further or participate in the groups' unlawful ends. Fearing that teachers might have been inhibited from participating in a variety of activities if the new criterion were not added, the Court held that to presume that members share in the unlawful aims of organizations to which they belong is an unconstitutional inference.

A year later, in *Knight v. Board of Regents of University of State of New York*, (*Knight*) the Supreme Court summarily upheld the constitutionality of an oath that required individuals to support the federal and state constitutions while faithfully discharging their job duties.[104] The trial court determined that since the oath did not impose restrictions on political or philosophical expressions and was not unconstitutionally vague, the state had the authority to require educators to subscribe to such an oath.

Citing *Knight* as the leading case, the Supreme Court, in a per curiam opinion, upheld a similar requirement from Florida in *Connell v. Higginbotham* since it demanded no more of public employees than was required of all state and federal officers. The Justices also agreed that the state could not summarily dismiss those who refused to pledge that they did "... not believe in the overthrow of the government ... by force or violence."[105]

A year later, in *Biklen v. Board of Education*,[106] the Court upheld the oath from *Knight* in a religious challenge from a teacher in New York. After a federal trial court was convinced that the state had a compelling interest in teachers' agreeing to support the federal and state constitutions, the Court affirmed, in a memorandum opinion, that since a teacher had the adequate opportunity to make the oath or affirmation and thus retain her position, she was not entitled to a hearing before her contract was terminated.

In a plurality judgment involving only seven members, *Cole v. Richardson*, the Court upheld an oath from Massachusetts which required individuals to "... oppose the overthrow of the government of the United States of America or of this Commonwealth by force, violence or by any illegal or unconstitutional method."[107] The Court also unanimously sustained language that required individuals to uphold and defend the federal and commonwealth constitutions since this only applied, rather than expanded, the obligation of the oath's first provision.

---

103. 384 U.S. 11, 86 S.Ct. 1238, 16 L.Ed.2d 321 (1966).

104. 269 F.Supp. 339 (S.D.N.Y.1967), *aff'd*, 390 U.S. 36, 88 S.Ct. 816, 19 L.Ed.2d 812 (1968). [Case No. 74]

105. 403 U.S. 207, 209, 91 S.Ct. 1772, 29 L.Ed.2d 418 (1971).

106. 333 F.Supp. 902 (N.D.N.Y.1971), *aff'd*, 406 U.S. 951, 92 S.Ct. 2060, 32 L.Ed.2d 340 (1972).

107. 405 U.S. 676, 677–78, 92 S.Ct. 1332, 31 L.Ed.2d 593 (1972).

New York's Feinberg Law

New York State enacted the Feinberg Law, which, although not prescribing an oath, was designed to implement and enforce older statutes. The new law made membership in subversive organizations prima facie evidence of disqualification for employment in public schools, further requiring the Board of Regents, along with local boards, to take measures to file reports on the loyalty of all teachers. In *Adler v. Board of Education (Adler)*,[108] the Supreme Court upheld the facial constitutionality of the statute. According to the Court, if an organization was declared subversive, and if employees were notified, they would have been free to choose between membership in the group and public employment.

After the Feinberg Law was extended to personnel of public institutions of higher learning, complex administrative procedures emerged. However, in *Keyishian v. Board of Regents of University of State of New York*, the Supreme Court invalidated this system, including the Feinberg Law, its administrative regulations, and the two older statutes that it was enacted to implement, since "[t]he regulatory maze created by New York [wa]s wholly lacking in 'terms susceptible of objective measurement.' "[109] The Court ruled that unlike *Adler*, which involved a review of a declaratory judgment suit, it had yet to consider a charge of unconstitutional vagueness that had not been raised in the earlier case.

The Fifth Amendment

During the 1950's, Congressional and state legislative investigative committees were common. When a congressional committee investigating communist activities tried to question a faculty member at a public college in New York City, he refused to answer, pleading the Fifth Amendment's provision against self-incrimination. Even so, a section in the city charter provided that whenever employees utilized this privilege to avoid answering questions about their official conduct, their employment was automatically terminated. In *Slochower v. Board of Higher Education of New York City*,[110] the Supreme Court noted that the provision violated due process. Hastening to add that it did not think that the faculty member had a right to teach in higher education, or that a proper inquiry might not have shown that dismissal was warranted, the Court found that a summary dismissal without a hearing violated due process.

Two years later, in *Beilan v. Board of Public Education, School District of Philadelphia*,[111] the Court upheld a teacher's dismissal when he refused to answer whether, in the previous eight years, he had been an officer of the Communist Political Association. Agreeing that he was

108. 342 U.S. 485, 72 S.Ct. 380, 96 L.Ed. 517 (1952).

109. 385 U.S. 589, 604, 87 S.Ct. 675, 17 L.Ed.2d 629 (1967). [Case No. 75]

110. 350 U.S. 551, 76 S.Ct. 637, 100 L.Ed. 692 (1956).

111. 357 U.S. 399, 78 S.Ct. 1317, 2 L.Ed.2d 1414 (1958).

insubordinate and lacked both frankness and candor, the Court contended that since fitness to teach depends on a broad range of factors, of which classroom conduct is but one, the board had the authority to dismiss the teacher.

Collective Bargaining

In General

Modeled largely after the process in private sector industrial labor relations, collective bargaining is the vehicle whereby school boards and their employees negotiate over terms and conditions of employment. Public sector bargaining received a big boost in 1958 when New York City permitted municipal employees to bargain collectively for the first time. A year later, Wisconsin became the first state to mandate bargaining by public employees.[112] Three years later, a brief strike by teachers in New York City led to a wave of teacher activism[113] that culminated in more than thirty states enacting statutes granting teachers the right to organize and bargain collectively with their school boards over terms and conditions of employment.[114] The extent to which boards may engage in bargaining varies from one jurisdiction to the next.

School boards cannot divest themselves of their discretionary authority by agreeing to contracts that are formed through other than legally sanctioned processes of bargaining or by addressing items for which they lack legislative approval. States have the power to permit teachers to engage in, or to refrain from, actions designed to bring about changes in employment conditions. The Constitution of the United States not only guarantees freedom of speech and of association but also restricts the conditions that can be placed on public employees. While the First Amendment does not require school boards to recognize or bargain with unions, it does protect teachers who join labor organizations[115] and cannot discipline them for doing so or for engaging in protected union activities.

Bargaining Units

In order to negotiate with their school boards, employee unions must organize bargaining units. Once local unions are organized, state

---

112. Gus Tyler, Why They Organize, in Education and Collective Bargaining: Readings in Policy and Research 19–20 (Anthony M. Cresswell & Michael J. Murphy eds. 1976).

113. Charles Taylor Kirchner & Douglas E. Mitchell, The Changing Idea of a Teacher's Union 1 (1988).

114. *See, e.g.,* Cal. Gov't Code § 3540; Colo. Rev. Stat. Ann. § 8–2–101; Conn. Gen. Stat. Ann. § 10–153a; Del. Code Ann. tit. 14, § 4001; Idaho Code Ann. § 33–1271; 115 Ill. Comp. Stat. Ann. 5/1; Ind. Code Ann. § 20–7.5–1–1; Iowa Code Ann. § 20.1; Kan. Stat. Ann. § 75–4321; Me. Rev. Stat. Ann. tit. 26, § 966; Md. Code Ann., Educ. §§ 4–312 *et seq.*;

Mich. Stat. Ann. § 423.209; Minn. Stat. Ann. § 179.10; Neb. Rev. Stat. Ann. § 81–1370; N.H. Rev. Stat. Ann. §§ 273–A:1 *et seq.*; N.J. Stat. Ann. § 34:13A–5.3; McKinney's Civil Serv. Law Ann. §§ 204 *et seq.*; N.D. Cent. Code Ann. § 34–08–02; Ohio Rev. Code Ann. § 4117.01 *et seq.*; Or. Rev. Stat. §§ 243.650 *et seq.*; Pa. Stat. Ann. tit. 24, § 11–1133; R.I. Gen. Laws Ann. §§ 28–9.3–1 *et seq.*; S.D. Cod. Laws Ann. §§ 3–18–1 *et seq.*; Vt. Stat. Ann. tit. 16 §§ 1981 *et seq.*; Wash. Rev. Code Ann. §§ 41.56.010 *et seq.*

115. *Stellmaker v. DePetrillo,* 710 F.Supp. 891 [53 Educ. L. Rep. 512] (D.Conn.1989).

public employment relations boards typically certify that, as a result of votes of eligible employees, they are recognized as the exclusive bargaining agents of their members.[116] Once boards recognize unions, bargaining is limited to sessions with the exclusive bargaining representatives of their employees.[117] At the same time, unions have the duty to represent all employees in good faith[118] during bargaining, even individuals who are not members, and who must pay so-called agency or representation fees,[119] discussed below. In a case dealing with the duty of fair representation, an appellate court in Massachusetts affirmed that a union's refusal to pursue a former substitute teacher's grievances against her school was not a breach of its duty of fair representation.[120] The court held that since there was no evidence to support the teacher's claim of bad faith against the union, her grievances were unfounded.

As a means of avoiding conflicts of interest, different bargaining units form around communities of interest such that teachers, typically referred to as professional staff, are in one unit, while other employees, usually referred to as classified staff, including office workers, maintenance staff, and the like, are in another. For instance, an appellate court in New York affirmed that a teachers' union did not have the duty to represent retired teachers since it reasoned that retired employees do not belong to the same community of interest as active employees.[121]

Managerial or administrative and confidential employees who work in personnel offices with information and/or others involved in bargaining are usually not permitted to form unions.[122] In fact, the Supreme Court of Nebraska decided that a union violated state law when it tried to include principals and supervisors in the same unit.[123]

Scope of Bargaining

Collective bargaining is subject to legislative control and judicial interpretation. Insofar as state statutes vary in scope and specificity,

116. *Appeal of Londonderry School Dist.*, 707 A.2d 137 [124 Educ. L. Rep. 948] (N.H.1998).

117. *Independence-Nat'l Educ. Ass'n v. Independence School Dist.*, 162 S.W.3d 18 [198 Educ. L. Rep. 357] (Mo. Ct. App. 2005), *transfer denied* (2005).

118. *See, e.g., Sutton v. Cleveland Bd. of Educ.*, 958 F.2d 1339 [73 Educ. L. Rep. 624] (6th Cir.1992); *Leer v. Washington Educ. Ass'n*, 172 F.R.D. 439 [118 Educ. L. Rep. 1046] (W.D. Wash.1997); *Jones v. Illinois Educ. Labor Relations Bd.*, 650 N.E.2d 1092 [100 Educ. L. Rep. 660] (Ill.App.Ct.1995); *Fratus v. Marion Community Schools Bd. of Trustees*, 749 N.E.2d 40 [154 Educ. L. Rep. 642] (Ind.2001).

119. *O'Brien v. City of Springfield*, 319 F.Supp.2d 90 [189 Educ. L. Rep. 142] (D. Mass. 2003).

120. *Saxonis v. City of Lynn*, 817 N.E.2d 793 [193 Educ. L. Rep. 309] (Mass. App. Ct. 2004), *review denied*, 822 N.E.2d 304 (Mass. 2005), *cert. denied*, ___ U.S. ___, 126 S.Ct. 350, 163 L.Ed.2d 59 (2005).

121. *Baker v. Board of Educ., Hoosick Falls Cent. Sch. Dist.*, 770 N.Y.S.2d 782 [184 Educ. L. Rep. 940] (N.Y. App. Div. 2004).

122. *Barrington School Comm. v. Rhode Island State Labor Relations Bd.*, 608 A.2d 1126 [75 Educ. L. Rep. 1130] (R.I.1992); *Chicago Teachers Union, IFT–AFT, AFL–CIO v. Illinois Educ. Labor Relations Bd.*, 695 N.E.2d 1332 [127 Educ. L. Rep. 369] (Ill.App.Ct.1998). *But see, e.g., Pennsylvania School Bds. Ass'n v. Commonwealth Ass'n of School Adm'rs*, 805 A.2d 476, 491 [169 Educ. L. Rep. 289, 304] (Pa.2002).

123. *Papillion/La Vista Schools Principals and Supervisors Org. v. Papillion/LaVista Dist. No. 27*, 562 N.W.2d 335 [117 Educ. L. Rep. 736] (Neb.1997).

some refer only expansively to terms and conditions of employment while others leave gray areas requiring judicial interpretation.

Topics for bargaining can be classified under three broad headings.[124] Consistent with practices in private sector labor law, mandatory topics include such matters as salaries and other terms and conditions of employment. On the other hand, boards and unions are prohibited from engaging in managerial prerogatives such as setting staffing needs and curriculum. A third category of topics, those that are permissive, is most readily subject to judicial interpretation.

In a case that reflects the difficulty in evaluating which of the three areas within which an item for bargaining fits, the Supreme Court of Alaska explained that "logically and semantically it is nearly impossible to assign specific items"[125] beyond salaries, fringe benefits, number of hours worked, and amount of leave time to the categories of negotiable or non-negotiable. The court, in strongly suggesting that more specific guidance from the legislature would have been helpful, categorized fifty items which had been raised in the three cases it consolidated for judgment. The non-negotiable topics included relief from nonprofessional chores, class size and teacher load, personnel evaluation, and calendar. Acknowledging the difficulty in seeking to place all topics neatly into these three sometimes overlapping categories, the following sections review major topics under each, highlighting judicial exceptions in various jurisdictions.

Mandatory Topics of Bargaining

In considering whether proposals are subject to mandatory bargaining, the Supreme Court of Iowa offered a two-part test.[126] First, the court pointed out that proposals had to fall within the meaning of subjects listed in the state's collective bargaining statute. Second, the court indicated that proposals could not be outside of the scope of bargaining. In light of its analysis, the court asserted that issues concerning staff who taught more than 300 minutes per day and pooling sick leave were mandatory topics while those dealing with evaluations and the time and place of wage payments were not subject to mandatory bargaining.[127]

Beyond terms and conditions of employment, such as salaries[128] and

124.   *See Colonial School Bd. v. Colonial Affiliate, NCCEA/DSEA/NEA,* 449 A.2d 243 [6 Educ. L. Rep. 87] (Del.Super.Ct.1982).

125.   *Kenai Peninsula Borough School Dist. v. Kenai Peninsula Educ. Ass'n,* 572 P.2d 416, 422 (Alaska 1977).

126.   For similar tests, *see In re Hillsboro–Deering School Dist.,* 737 A.2d 1098 [138 Educ. L. Rep. 447] (N.H.1999); *Webster Educ. Ass'n v. Webster School Dist.,* 631 N.W.2d 202 [155 Educ. L. Rep. 1381] (S.D. 2001).

127.   *Waterloo Community School Dist. v. Public Employment Relations Bd.,* 650 N.W.2d 627 [169 Educ. L. Rep. 402] (Iowa

2002); *Kenai Peninsula Borough School Dist. v. Kenai Peninsula Educ. Ass'n,* 572 P.2d 416, 422 (Alaska 1977).

128.   *See, e.g., Fort Stewart Schools v. Federal Labor Relations Auth.,* 495 U.S. 641, 110 S.Ct. 2043, 109 L.Ed.2d 659 [60 Educ. L. Rep. 9] (1990) (affirming that proposals for salary, leave, and mileage reimbursement for teachers at schools owned and operated by the Army were mandatory subjects of bargaining); *Education Minnesota-Greenway, Local 1330 v. Independent School Dist. No. 316,* 673 N.W.2d 843 [184 Educ. L. Rep. 578] (Minn.App. 2004).

fringe benefits,[129] over which boards are statutorily bound to bargain, courts agree that an array of topics are mandatory topics of negotiations. Among the items that courts have made subjects of mandatory bargaining due to their impact on financial aspects of employment are reimbursing teachers for graduate studies,[130] the impact of a smoke-free work environment,[131] holiday pay,[132] subcontracting of services,[133] early retirement incentives,[134] a reduction-in-force plan,[135] stipends that teachers received for mileage and released time while serving on professional development committees,[136] a proposed dress code policy,[137] and a merit system for hiring set forth in a bargaining agreement.[138]

Prohibited Topics of Bargaining

Among the topics that courts interpreted as beyond the power of boards to bargain over are whether to consolidate two department chairmanships[139] or to abolish positions[140] as well as policies governing assignments and transfers,[141] granting tenure,[142] withholding salary increments,[143] creating school calendars,[144] appointing principals[145] and

129. *International Brotherhood of Firemen and Oilers, Local 1201, AFL–CIO v. Board of Educ. of School Dist. of Philadelphia,* 457 A.2d 1269 [10 Educ. L. Rep. 203] (Pa.1983).

130. *Barnett v. Durant Community School Dist.,* 249 N.W.2d 626 (Iowa 1977).

131. *Local 1186 of Council No. 4, AFSCME, AFL–CIO v. State Bd. of Labor Relations,* 620 A.2d 766 [81 Educ. L. Rep. 206] (Conn.1993).

132. *Cadott Educ. Ass'n v. Wisconsin Employment Relations Comm'n,* 540 N.W.2d 21 [104 Educ. L. Rep. 1345] (Wis. Ct.App.1995).

133. *Matter of Watkins Glen Cent. School Dist. (Watkins Glen Faculty Ass'n),* 628 N.Y.S.2d 824 [101 Educ. L. Rep. 1022] (N.Y.App.Div.1995); *Morrisville School Dist. v. Pennsylvania Labor Relations Bd.,* 687 A.2d 5 [115 Educ. L. Rep. 29] (Pa. Cmwlth.Ct.1996), *appeal denied,* 700 A.2d 445 (Pa.1997).

134. *Ringgold School Dist. v. Ringgold Educ. Ass'n,* 694 A.2d 1163 [119 Educ. L. Rep. 190] (Pa.Cmwlth.Ct.1997).

135. *Webster Educ. Ass'n v. Webster School Dist.,* 631 N.W.2d 202 [155 Educ. L. Rep. 1381] (S.D.2001).

136. *Governing Bd. of Special Educ. Dist. of Lake County v. Sedol Teachers' Union, Lake County Fed'n of Teachers, Local 504, IFT–AFT, AFL–CIO,* 772 N.E.2d 847 [167 Educ. L. Rep. 886] (Ill.App.Ct.2002), *appeal denied,* 786 N.E.2d 183 (Ill.2002).

137. *Polk County Bd. of Educ. v. Polk County Educ.,* 139 S.W.3d 304 [190 Educ. L.

Rep. 1072] (Tenn. Ct. App. 2004), *appeal denied* (2004).

138. *Walter v. Scherzinger,* 121 P.3d 644 [202 Educ. L. Rep. 844] (Or. 2005).

139. *Dunellen Bd. of Educ. v. Dunellen Educ. Ass'n,* 311 A.2d 737 (N.J.1973).

140. *School Comm. of Boston v. Boston Teachers Union, Local 66, Am. Fed'n of Teachers,* 389 N.E.2d 970 (Mass. 1979).

141. *Blount County Educ. Ass'n v. Blount County Bd. of Educ.,* 78 S.W.3d 307 [167 Educ. L. Rep. 504] (Tenn.Ct.App. 2002). *See also School Dist. of Seward Educ. Ass'n v. School Dist.,* 199 N.W.2d 752 (Neb.1972).

142. *Cohoes City School Dist. v. Cohoes Teachers Ass'n,* 390 N.Y.S.2d 53 (N.Y.1976); *School Comm. of Danvers v. Tyman,* 360 N.E.2d 877 (Mass.1977); *Mindemann v. Independent School Dist. No. 6 of Caddo County,* 771 P.2d 996 [53 Educ. L. Rep. 270] (Okla.1989).

143. *Board of Educ. of Township of Bernards v. Bernards Township Educ. Ass'n,* 399 A.2d 620 (N.J.1979).

144. *Kenai Peninsula Borough School Dist. v. Kenai Peninsula Educ. Ass'n,* 572 P.2d 416 (Alaska 1977); *Montgomery County Educ. Ass'n v. Board of Educ. of Montgomery County,* 534 A.2d 980 [43 Educ. L. Rep. 720] (Md.1987); *Public Employee Relations Bd. v. Washington Teachers' Union Local 6, AFT,* 556 A.2d 206 [52 Educ. L. Rep. 1075] (D.C.1989).

145. *Berkshire Hills Reg'l School Dist. Comm. v. Berkshire Hills Educ. Ass'n,* 377 N.E.2d 940 (Mass.1978).

department heads,[146] and reworking a board's organizational structure.[147]

The amount of time that teachers must work in inclement weather has led to some interesting disputes, thereby serving as a segue into the next section on permissive topics of bargaining. In a case that can only be described as having mixed results, an appellate court in Indiana observed that although a board did not have the duty to bargain over make-up days and adopting a policy on school closings, its practice of issuing supplemental contracts to teachers for make-up days did not elevate the subject of make-up days to the status of a mandatory topic of bargaining.[148] Yet, the court also posited that the board's refusal to initiate discussions with the teachers' union about make-up days and a school closing plan was an unfair labor practice. Similarly, an appellate court in New Jersey maintained that while a board did not have to negotiate over whether to have class on days that had been scheduled as recess days in order to make up for time missed due to snow, it did not follow that the impact of the changes was not subject to bargaining.[149]

Permissive Topics of Bargaining

Where subjects are not excluded from bargaining, questions arise as to whether they must be subject to negotiations. Although many disputes begin in administrative proceedings, they are typically resolved by the courts. In considering whether topics are subject to mandatory or permissive bargaining, some courts, rather than simply proclaiming matters subject to mandatory bargaining, have suggested guidelines beyond such basic restatements as conditions of employment, managerial prerogatives, and basic policy issues. The courts caution that such judgments must be made on case-by-case bases. In such a case, the Supreme Court of Kansas thought that the key was to consider "how direct the impact of an issue is on the well-being of the individual teacher, as opposed to its effect on the operation of the school system as a whole."[150] The Supreme Court of Pennsylvania set the test as "whether the impact of the issue on the interest of the employee in wages, hours and terms and conditions of employment outweighs its probable effect on the basic policy of the system as a whole."[151] Moreover, an appellate court in California offered a useful distinction in noting that non-mandatory, or permissive topics, are those neither covered by state statute nor identified by the judiciary.[152]

146. *Maine School Admin. Dist. No. 61 Bd. of Dirs. v. Lake Region Teachers Ass'n,* 567 A.2d 77 [57 Educ. L. Rep. 940] (Me. 1989).

147. *State ex rel. Quiring v. Board of Educ. of Indep. School Dist. No. 173, Mountain Lake,* 623 N.W.2d 634 [152 Educ. L. Rep. 271] (Minn.Ct.App.2001).

148. *Union County School Corp. Bd. of School Trustees v. Indiana Educ. Employment Relations Bd.,* 471 N.E.2d 1191 [21 Educ. L. Rep. 989] (Ind.Ct.App.1984).

149. *Piscataway Township Educ. Ass'n v. Piscataway Township Bd. of Educ.,* 704 A.2d 981 [123 Educ. L. Rep. 764] (N.J.Super.Ct.App.Div.1998), *certification denied,* 718 A.2d 1214 (N.J. 1998).

150. *National Educ. Ass'n of Shawnee Mission v. Board of Educ. of Shawnee Mission Unified School Dist. No. 512,* 512 P.2d 426, 435 (Kan.1973).

151. *Pennsylvania Labor Relations Bd. v. State College Area School Dist.,* 337 A.2d 262, 268 (Pa.1975).

Among the permissive topics that courts have recognized are broad zipper clauses, which allow parties to renegotiate items in mid-contract,[153] drug testing,[154] the timing and effective dates of lay-offs,[155] adoption of year-around schooling,[156] lump-sum payments for unused sick days,[157] and teacher requirements to take assessment tests before having their licenses renewed.[158] One of the more controversial topics of bargaining is class size since some courts treat it as excluded from bargaining[159] while others treat it as a mandatory[160] or permissive[161] topic of negotiations.

Teacher evaluations highlight differences between substance and procedure. Whether, and by whom, evaluations are to occur is usually considered to be a policy matter excluded from bargaining.[162] However, some courts are of the opinion that procedures used in the evaluation processes are subject to mandatory[163] bargaining while others treat it as a permissive[164] topic.

Restraints on Boards

In perhaps the most significant restraint on school boards and teachers with regard to labor relations, two state legislatures expressly forbid collective bargaining between governmental units and employees.[165] Even so, boards may not dismiss or fail to rehire teachers solely

152. *South Bay Union School Dist. v. Public Employment Relations Bd.*, 279 Cal. Rptr. 135 [66 Educ. L. Rep. 357] (Cal.Ct. App.1991).

153. *Mt. Vernon Educ. Ass'n, IEA–NEA v. Illinois Educ. Labor Relations Bd.*, 663 N.E.2d 1067 [109 Educ. L. Rep. 305] (Ill. App.Ct.1996).

154. *Drivers, Chauffeurs and Helpers Local Union No. 639 v. District of Columbia*, 631 A.2d 1205 [86 Educ. L. Rep. 283] (D.C.1993).

155. *West Bend Educ. Ass'n v. Wisconsin Employment Relations Comm'n*, 357 N.W.2d 534, 122 L.R.R.M. (BNA) 2705 [21 Educ. L. Rep. 305] (Wis.1984).

156. *Racine Educ. Ass'n v. Wisconsin Employment Relations Comm'n*, 571 N.W.2d 887 [122 Educ. L. Rep. 1281] (Wis. Ct.App.1997).

157. *Perrenod v. Liberty Bd. of Educ. for Liberty Cent. School Dist.*, 636 N.Y.S.2d 210 [106 Educ. L. Rep. 302] (N.Y.App.Div.1996).

158. *Massachusetts Fed'n of Teachers, AFT, AFL–CIO v. Board of Educ.*, 767 N.E.2d 549 [164 Educ. L. Rep. 393] (Mass. 2002).

159. *West Irondequoit Teachers Ass'n v. Helsby*, 358 N.Y.S.2d 720 (N.Y.1974); *Kenai Peninsula Borough School Dist. v. Kenai*

Peninsula Educ. Ass'n, 572 P.2d 416 (Alaska 1977).

160. *Decatur Bd. of Educ., Dist. No. 61 v. Illinois Educ. Labor Relations Bd.*, 536 N.E.2d 743 [52 Educ. L. Rep. 1153] (Ill.App. Ct.1989), *appeal denied*, 545 N.E.2d 107 (Ill.1989).

161. *Fargo Educ. Ass'n v. Fargo Pub. School Dist. No. 1*, 291 N.W.2d 267 (N.D. 1980).

162. *Bethlehem Township Bd. of Educ. v. Bethlehem Township Educ. Ass'n*, 449 A.2d 1254 [6 Educ. L. Rep. 748] (N.J.1982).

163. *Arlington Community School Dist. v. Iowa Pub. Employment Relations Bd.*, 392 N.W.2d 495 [34 Educ. L. Rep. 607] (Iowa 1986); *City of Beloit by Beloit City School Bd. v. Wisconsin Employment Relations Comm'n*, 242 N.W.2d 231 (Wis.1976); *Milberry v. Board of Educ. of School Dist. of Philadelphia*, 354 A.2d 559 (Pa.1976).

164. *Alton Community Unit School Dist. No. 11, Counties of Madison and Jersey v. Illinois Educ. Labor Relations Bd.*, 567 N.E.2d 671 [66 Educ. L. Rep. 397] (Ill.App.Ct.1991); *In re Pittsfield School Dist.*, 744 A.2d 594 [141 Educ. L. Rep. 847] (N.H.1999).

165. N.C. Gen. Stat. Ann. § 95–98, ("Any agreement, or contract, between the governing authority of any city, town, counbecause of constitutionally protected union activities.[166] Likewise, consistent with provisions in state constitutions to this effect, boards cannot require teachers to join unions as a condition of employment[167] or as a basis for benefits such as salary increases.[168]

So-called union shops, which are prevalent in the private sector and which typically require all employees to join unions within a set time after being hired, are either not permitted or expressly forbidden in public employment. As such, two issues arise as to how unions interact with their members. The first of these two concerns relates to the collection of dues via employee "check-offs," on appropriate forms, of their willingness to permit their boards to collect their dues via payroll deductions and pass them on to their unions. Most states with collective bargaining statutes permit "dues check-offs" to assist unions in their activities.[169]

An important issue involving union activities deals with the question of "free riders" and financial support for union costs associated with bargaining. In order to balance equities, agency or representation fee arrangements require individuals who are not union members to pay a fair share for the services that unions render on their behalf in negotiating employment contracts.

Abood v. Detroit Board of Education (Abood)[170] is the first of four Supreme Court cases on agency fees. In *Abood*, the Court specified that the Constitution does not prohibit agency fee provisions in bargaining agreements as long as unions do not use these funds to support ideologi-

---

ty, or other municipality, or between any agency, unit, or instrumentality thereof, or between any agency, instrumentality, or institution of the State of North Carolina, and any labor union, trade union, or labor organization, as bargaining agent for any public employees of such city, town, county or other municipality, or agency or instrumentality of government, is hereby declared to be against the public policy of the State, illegal, unlawful, void and of no effect"); *Winston–Salem/Forsyth County Unit of North Carolina Ass'n of Educators v. Phillips*, 381 F.Supp. 644 (M.D.N.C.1974); Tex. Gov't Code Ann. § 617.002. ("'(a) An official of the state or of a political subdivision of the state may not enter into a collective bargaining contract with a labor organization regarding wages, hours, or conditions of employment of public employees. (b) A contract entered into in violation of Subsection (a) is void. (c) An official of the state or of a political subdivision of the state may not recognize a labor organization as the bargaining agent for a group of public employees'').

166. *Fort Frye Teachers Ass'n v. SERB*, 809 N.E.2d 1130 [188 Educ. L. Rep. 433] (Ohio 2004) (remarking that the non-renewal of a teacher's contract based on his union activities was an unfair labor prac-

tice); *Classroom Teachers of Dallas/Texas State Teachers Ass'n/National Educ. Ass'n v. Dallas Indep. School Dist.*, 164 F.Supp.2d 839 [157 Educ. L. Rep. 677] (N.D.Tex.2001) (finding that anti-union threats, harassment, and illegal threats of dismissal did not amount to an adverse employment action); *Morfin v. Albuquerque Pub. Schools*, 906 F.2d 1434 [61 Educ. L. Rep. 470] (10th Cir.1990); *Hale v. Walsh*, 747 P.2d 1288 [44 Educ. L. Rep. 719] (Idaho Ct.App. 1987) (involving higher education); *Hickman v. Valley Local School Dist. Bd. of Educ.*, 619 F.2d 606 (6th Cir.1980); *Durango School Dist. No. 9–R v. Thorpe*, 614 P.2d 880 (Colo. 1980).

167. *Shelton v. Tucker*, 364 U.S. 479, 81 S.Ct. 247, 5 L.Ed.2d 231 (1960).

168. *Benson v. School Dist. No. 1 of Silver Bow County*, 344 P.2d 117 (Mont. 1959).

169. *But see City of Charlotte v. Local 660, Intern. Ass'n of Firefighters*, 426 U.S. 283, 96 S.Ct. 2036, 48 L.Ed.2d 636 (1976) (declaring that public employee unions do not have a constitutional right to "check-offs").

170. 431 U.S. 209, 97 S.Ct. 1782, 52 L.Ed.2d 261 (1977). [Case No. 76]

cal activities that members and non-members oppose and that are unrelated to the process of negotiations. The Court explained that since individuals who object to how their funds are being spent must notify unions of their concerns, they should do so in general terms so that they do not have to reveal their positions on particular matters.

Six years later, in a non-education case, the Court decreed that agency fees could be used for conventions, business meetings and occasional social activities, and publications that communicate about nonpolitical activities.[171] The Court also approved of advanced reductions of fees for non-members. At the same time, the Court forbade unions from using agency fees for organizing activities and litigation not connected to bargaining while disapproving the use of rebates in dealing with fees even if unions paid interest on these funds.

The Court next examined procedures established to effectuate the preceding cases in *Chicago Teachers Union, Local No. 1, AFT, AFL–CIO v. Hudson*.[172] The Court disapproved of a rebate system because it did not avoid the risk that funds of non-union members might have temporarily been used for improper purposes. Under this system the unions offered inadequate information to justify the amount of agency fees and did not afford a reasonably prompt answer about expenditures and fees by an impartial third-party decision-maker.

In a case from Michigan involving a faculty union in a public institution of higher learning, *Lehnert v. Ferris Faculty Association*,[173] the Court considered which activities unions may charge to non-members. According to the Court, chargeable items must be germane to bargaining, must be justified by the government's vital policy interest in labor peace and avoiding "free riders," and must not significantly add to the burdening of free speech inherent in allowing an agency or union shop. The Court permitted a local union to bill non-members for costs associated with otherwise chargeable activities of its state and national affiliates even when those activities, such as for publications dealing not only with bargaining but with teaching and education generally, professional development, employment opportunities, and miscellaneous matters were neither political nor public in nature. The Court refused to permit the union to charge non-members for the costs associated with lobbying and general public relations activities.

The Ninth Circuit, in a case from California, subsequently reiterated that since non-union members have an absolute right to be free from supporting speech with which they do not agree, unions must develop fair, prompt, and effective procedures to identify what sums these individuals must pay and how their money is to be used.[174] State courts

---

171. *Ellis v. Brotherhood of Railway, Airline and Steamship Clerks, Freight Handlers, Express and Station Employees*, 466 U.S. 435, 104 S.Ct. 1883, 80 L.Ed.2d 428 (1984).

172. 475 U.S. 292, 106 S.Ct. 1066, 89 L.Ed.2d 232 [30 Educ. L. Rep. 649] (1986), *on remand*, 922 F.2d 1306 [65 Educ. L. Rep.

81] (7th Cir.1991), *cert. denied*, 501 U.S. 1230, 111 S.Ct. 2852, 115 L.Ed.2d 1020 (1991).

173. 500 U.S. 507, 111 S.Ct. 1950, 114 L.Ed.2d 572 [67 Educ. L. Rep. 421] (1991).

174. *Grunwald v. San Bernardino City Unified School Dist.*, 994 F.2d 1370 [83 Educ. L. Rep. 963] (9th Cir.1993), *cert. de-*

continue to apply similar analyses in upholding dues "check-off" provisions as long as adequate safeguards are in place.[175]

The second important concern of unions is being able to communicate with members at their places of work, especially if rival groups seek access to the same individuals. In *Perry Education Association v. Perry Local Educators' Association*, a case from Indiana, the Court considered "whether the First Amendment ... is violated when a union that has been elected by public school teachers as their exclusive bargaining representative is granted access to certain means of communication while such access is denied to a rival union."[176] Responding that this was not a constitutional violation, the Court found that the privilege of exclusive access to intra-school system mail facilities was properly characterized as an appropriate restriction on the use of public property that was not, by designation or in fact, a general public forum or a limited public forum. Even if the mailing system were to be considered a limited public forum by virtue of its occasional use by groups, such as the Cub Scouts and YMCAs, the Court wrote that the Constitution would require only that similar organizations be granted access. The Court did not agree that the rival union fell into the category of groups entitled to access because insofar as the union had a unique function, the board acted rationally in the interest of labor peace by agreeing to limit access solely to the exclusive bargaining representative of its staff. The Court ascertained that the rival union was excluded not because of its views, but due to its status in relation to the board and its teachers. In asserting that the rival union had alternative channels of communication available, such as bulletin boards, meeting rooms, and the United States mail, and that they had equal access to mailboxes during election periods, the Court was satisfied that the board did not violate its rights.

Three years later, in *Texas State Teachers Association v. Garland Independent School District*,[177] the Supreme Court summarily affirmed a judgment from the Fifth Circuit, which reasoned that since a school board had not created either a public or limited public forum in its schools or mail facilities, denying a teacher organization access to them during school hours did not violate teachers' First Amendment rights since they had alternative means of communication available. The court thought that board policies purporting to deny faculty members the right to discuss teacher organizations during non-class time and preventing

---

nied, 510 U.S. 964, 114 S.Ct. 439, 126 L.Ed.2d 373 (1993). *See also Mitchell v. Los Angeles Unified School Dist.*, 963 F.2d 258 [75 Educ. L. Rep. 126] (9th Cir.1992), *cert. denied*, 506 U.S. 940, 113 S.Ct. 375, 121 L.Ed.2d 287 (1992) (stating that a union's opt out procedures to give dissenting non-union employees the opportunity to object to full agency fees protected their First Amendment rights).

175. *Laborers Local No. 942 v. Lampkin*, 956 P.2d 422 [126 Educ. L. Rep. 437] (Alaska 1998); *Hayden v. Linton–Stockton Classroom Teachers Ass'n*, 686 N.E.2d 143

[122 Educ. L. Rep. 527] (Ind.Ct.App.1997); *Browne v. Wisconsin Employment Relations Comm'n*, 485 N.W.2d 376 [75 Educ. L. Rep. 502] (Wis.1992), *reconsideration denied*, 491 N.W.2d 770 (Wis.1992).

176. 460 U.S. 37 44, 103 S.Ct. 948, 74 L.Ed.2d 794 [9 Educ. L. Rep. 23] (1983), *on remand*, 705 F.2d 462 (7th Cir.1983).

177. *Texas State Teachers Ass'n v. Garland Indep. School Dist.*, 784 F.2d 1113 [30 Educ. L. Rep. 1108] (5th Cir.1986), *aff'd*, 479 U.S. 801, 107 S.Ct. 41, 93 L.Ed.2d 4 [34 Educ. L. Rep. 1004] (1986).

them from using school mail facilities to mention employee organizations were unconstitutional. In a case from higher education, the Court clarified that federal postal law did not permit a union to use a university's internal mail system since its attempt to organize was not a current university activity that would entitle it to such access.[178] The Seventh Circuit reached the same result in a case involving public education in Indiana.[179]

Dispute Resolution

The ordinary means of redressing disputes relating to the administration of collective bargaining contracts is through grievances that, depending on state laws and local contracts, may pass through several stages before being subject to arbitration. Arbitration is properly used to denote the process whereby parties agree to be bound by the decision of a third party that they select. Insofar as arbitration is an alternative to judicial review, to the extent that courts are satisfied that arbitrators draw their judgments from the essence of the underlying bargaining agreements, more often than not they are content to leave the adjudications in place.

Arbitration should not be confused with mediation, conciliation, fact-finding, or other forms of conflict resolution that do not culminate in legally binding outcomes. Further, there is an important distinction between interest arbitration, which focuses on an agreement's terms, and rights or grievance arbitration that is concerned with a provision's application to an existing agreement. Grievance arbitration is prevalent in both the public and private sectors. On the other hand, while interest arbitration is virtually unused in the private sector, it constitutes one way to resolve impasses in the public sector when work stoppages, regardless of whether they are legally sanctioned, pose a serious danger to the public welfare.

As reflected by an opinion of the Supreme Court of New Jersey, the judiciary initially had concerns about the role of the public in the formulation and application of policy if arbitrators resolve too many matters related to bargaining. In a case restricting the scope of educational matters that were negotiable and/or arbitrable, the court mused that "[t]here would be little room for community involvement if agreements concerning educational policy matters could be negotiated behind closed doors and disputes concerning that agreement settled by an arbitrator who lacks public accountability."[180] The Supreme Court of Pennsylvania later illustrated how this concern lessened when it commented that a law, which gave selected school administrators the right

---

178. *Regents of Univ. of Cal. v. Public Employment Relations Bd.*, 485 U.S. 589, 108 S.Ct. 1404, 99 L.Ed.2d 664 [45 Educ. L. Rep. 972] (1988), *on remand*, 248 Cal.Rptr. 815 (Cal.Ct. App.1988).

179. *Fort Wayne Community Schools v. Fort Wayne Educ. Ass'n*, 977 F.2d 358 [78

Educ. L. Rep. 29] (7th Cir.1992), *cert. denied*, 510 U.S. 826, 114 S.Ct. 90, 126 L.Ed.2d 57 (1993).

180. *Ridgefield Park Educ. Ass'n v. Ridgefield Park Bd. of Educ.*, 393 A.2d 278, 286–87 (N.J. 1978).

to bargain collectively and engage in binding arbitration, was not an unlawful delegation of legislative powers.[181]

A case from the Court of Appeals of New York exemplifies how the issue of non-delegability of board power cannot be raised to stay the process where broad arbitration clauses are in collective bargaining contracts and arbitrators fashion sufficiently narrow remedies. Even though the ultimate decision on class composition is ordinarily up to a board's discretion, when a board summarily altered the make-up of a class, the court held that the dispute could proceed to arbitration since the bargaining agreement provided for it in any dispute concerning proper contractual interpretation.[182]

Questions of lawful delegation of governmental power arise in connection with arbitration, especially interest arbitration. Courts do not agree whether the ultimate authority to prescribe the provisions of a contract with a school board can be placed in the hands of a separate body created to resolve impasses. Where parties rely on interest arbitration, courts typically emphasize the need for enabling statutes to include standards and parameters circumscribing the focus and scope of the process.[183]

As to grievance arbitration, most courts have followed the lead of the highest court of Connecticut,[184] which was the first to uphold the power of a local board to enter into a contract with a teachers' association to arbitrate grievances. Boards, of course, can agree to arbitrate grievances only if there is a statute to that effect. If boards voluntarily agree to grievance arbitration in states that do not forbid the practice, the results are usually binding as long as matters are not beyond their ability to delegate. Courts are increasingly reluctant to allow boards to escape the consequences of what they may have agreed to in bargaining.

In light of disagreements over the scope of arbitration, the Court of Appeals of New York set forth a two-part test for evaluating whether a dispute is arbitrable.[185] The first considers the "may they do so" test, addressing the subject matter of a dispute and whether the parties expressed a lawful intent to bargain. The second examines the "did they do so" test in reviewing whether the parties agreed to arbitrate a grievance, acknowledging that this does not employ a presumption for or against arbitration. In the underlying dispute, the court ruled that disagreements over health insurance benefits were subject to arbitration.

Including grievance arbitration clauses in collective bargaining contracts has spawned a great deal of litigation. To the extent that arbitration developed in the private sector as a substitute for judicial review,

---

181. *Pennsylvania School Bds. Ass'n v. Commonwealth Ass'n of School Adm'rs*, 805 A.2d 476, 491 [169 Educ. L. Rep. 289, 304] (Pa.2002).

182. *Babylon Union Free School Dist. v. Babylon Teachers Ass'n*, 579 N.Y.S.2d 629 [72 Educ. L. Rep. 988] (N.Y.1991).

183. *City of Amsterdam v. Helsby*, 371 N.Y.S.2d 404 (N.Y.1975).

184. *Norwalk Teachers' Ass'n v. Board of Educ.*, 83 A.2d 482 (Conn.1951).

185. *In re Board of Educ. of Watertown City School Dist. (Watertown Educ. Ass'n)*, 688 N.Y.S.2d [134 Educ. L. Rep. 984] (N.Y. 1999). [Case No. 77]

and the parties voluntarily agree to it, courts are reluctant to intervene in labor disputes. Consequently, absent contractual language to the contrary, in interpreting labor agreements in the private sector, the presumption has been that the parties agreed to arbitrate a dispute, with doubts being resolved in favor of coverage.[186] The courts have largely transferred this perspective to educational disputes.[187] The judiciary has broadly construed general arbitration clauses in bargaining contracts, granting stays under unrestricted arbitration clauses only where statutes have vested a power solely in boards or where permitting the process to proceed would violate public policy.[188]

When arbitration is used, the role of the courts is severely curtailed. Insofar as the parties have bargained for an arbitrator's interpretation, the courts ordinarily do not deal with the merits of disputes. If the subject matter of a grievance is arguably covered by a contract, whether the petitioner is right or wrong is a question for an arbitrator to evaluate.[189] Neither ambiguities as to coverage nor arbitrators' alleged errors of interpretation of law or fact, absent irrationality[190] or other impermissible grounds such as fraud, or bad faith, generally are subject to litigation. The courts review arbitration awards only to assure that they rationally draw their essence from bargaining agreements[191] and that remedies are not contrary to law or boards' managerial prerogative such as dismissing an employee for immorality where a teacher-coach sent love letters to students.[192] Arbitrators need to have flexibility in considering remedies. This fact is integral to the theory underlying the use of arbitration as a means of resolving disputes in the array of situations that develop in ongoing relationships between organized employees and management.[193] The parties, of course, may place restrictions as to remedies in their contracts.

Among the issues that courts have agreed were subject to arbitra-

---

186. *United Steelworkers of Am. v. Warrior & Gulf Navigation Co.*, 363 U.S. 574, 80 S.Ct. 1347, 4 L.Ed.2d 1409 (1960). Consistent with this case, in the private sector the parties can agree to have as arbitrator resolve the question of arbitrability.

187. *See, e.g., Davis v. Chester Upland School Dist.*, 786 A.2d 186 [160 Educ. L. Rep. 170] (Pa.2001).

188. *Board of Educ., West Babylon Union Free School Dist. v. West Babylon Teachers Ass'n*, 438 N.Y.S.2d 291 (N.Y. 1981).

189. *United Steelworkers of America v. American Mfg. Co.*, 363 U.S. 564, 80 S.Ct. 1343, 4 L.Ed.2d 1403 (1960).

190. "An arbitrator's interpretation [must] be upheld if it can, in any rational way, be derived from the language and context of the agreement.... [R]eversal is not warranted even if a court believes that the decision, though rational, is incorrect." *Greater Johnstown Area Vocational–Techni-*

cal School v. Greater Johnstown Area Vocational–Technical Educ. Ass'n, 553 A.2d 913, 915 [51 Educ. L. Rep. 983] (Pa.1989).

191. *School Dist. of City of Erie v. Erie Educ. Ass'n*, 873 A.2d 73 [197 Educ. L. Rep. 658] (Pa. Cmwlth.Ct. 2005); *Norristown v. Norristown Educ. Support Personnel Ass'n*, 847 A.2d 795 [187 Educ. L. Rep. 704] (Pa. Cmwlth. Ct. 2004). *But see Flandreau Pub. School Dist. #50–3 v. G.A. Johnson Const.*, 701 N.W.2d 430 [200 Educ. L. Rep. 396] (S.D. 2005) (affirming that a trial court, not an arbitrator, had the authority to consider whether a dispute was subject to arbitration).

192. *Manheim Cent. Educ. Ass'n v. Manheim Cent. School Dist.*, 572 A.2d 31 [59 Educ. L. Rep. 445] (Pa.Cmwlth.Ct. 1990), *appeal denied*, 582 A.2d 326 (Pa. 1990).

193. *See United Steelworkers of Am. v. Warrior & Gulf Navigation Co.*, 363 U.S. 574, 80 S.Ct. 1347, 4 L.Ed.2d 1409 (1960).

tion were a teacher's placement on a salary scale,[194] a teacher's voluntary transfer,[195] whether a union complied with time requirements for filing a grievance,[196] withholding a salary increment from a principal who was absent excessively,[197] permitting employees to receive both early-retirement bonuses and payments for unused sick leave[198] and extra-duty assignments,[199] a board's terminating a teacher's contract for failing to renew his certificate,[200] a proposed bumping system that was to be used as part of a reduction-in-force,[201] and teachers' entitlements to the value of selected shares of stock that a board received due to the demutualization of its health insurer.[202]

On the other hand, courts agreed that the non-renewal of a teacher's contract,[203] a teacher's being dismissed for not renewing his teaching certificate,[204] using a sick-leave bank for extended post maternity leave,[205] a school nurse's duty to dispense medication for students with special needs,[206] and selecting teachers to work during summer school[207] were not properly subject to arbitration. Another group of courts believed that arbitrators exceeded the scope of their authority in directing a board to negotiate the rate of compensation for teachers who had to work beyond the end of the school day,[208] ordering the reinstatement of a non-permanent teacher,[209] and concerning a plan with regard to controversial reading materials.[210]

194. *Souderton Area School Dist. v. Souderton Area Educ. Ass'n*, 639 A.2d 904 [90 Educ. L. Rep. 275] (Pa.Cmwlth.Ct. 1994), *appeal denied*, 655 A.2d 519 (Pa. 1994).

195. *Orleans Parish School Bd. v. United Teachers of New Orleans*, 689 So.2d 645 [116 Educ. L. Rep. 1320] (La.Ct.App.1997), *writ denied*, 692 So.2d 1091 (La.1997).

196. *Dalton v. Schneider*, 667 N.Y.S.2d 523 [123 Educ. L. Rep. 860] (N.Y.App.Div. 1997).

197. *Edison Township Bd. of Educ., Middlesex County v. Edison Township Principals and Supervisors Ass'n*, 701 A.2d 459 [121 Educ. L. Rep. 1075] (N.J.Super.Ct.App.Div.1997).

198. *United School Dist. v. United Educ. Ass'n*, 782 A.2d 40 [157 Educ. L. Rep. 782] (Pa. Cmwlth.Ct.2001).

199. *Apollo–Ridge School Dist. v. Apollo–Ridge Educ. Ass'n*, 799 A.2d 911 [166 Educ. L. Rep. 275] (Pa.Cmwlth.Ct.2002).

200. *Mount Adams School Dist. v. Cook*, 81 P.3d 111 [183 Educ. L. Rep. 1017] (Wash. 2003).

201. *School Comm. of Westport v. American Fed'n of State, County and Mun. Employees, Council 93, Local 2667*, 810 N.E.2d 848 [188 Educ. L. Rep. 962] (Mass. App. Ct. 2004).

202. *Region 14 Bd. of Educ. v. Nonnewaug Teachers' Ass'n*, 866 A.2d 1252 [195 Educ. L. Rep. 909] (Conn. 2005).

203. *Warwick School Comm. v. Warwick Teachers' Union, AFL–CIO*, 705 A.2d 984 [123 Educ. L. Rep. 1228] (R.I.1998).

204. *Mount Adams School Dist. v. Cook*, 81 P.3d 111 [183 Educ. L. Rep. 1017] (Wash. 2003).

205. *Pocantico Hills Cent. School Dist. v. Pocantico Hills Teachers Ass'n*, 694 N.Y.S.2d 417 [137 Educ. L. Rep. 759] (N.Y.App.Div.1999), *leave to appeal denied*, 705 N.Y.S.2d 6 (N.Y. 2000).

206. *Woonsocket Teachers' Guild, Local 951, AFT v. Woonsocket School Comm.*, 770 A.2d 834 [153 Educ. L. Rep. 319] (R.I.2001).

207. *Chicago Teachers Union, Local No. 1 Am. Fed'n of Teachers, AFL–CIO v. Illinois Educ. Labor Relations Bd.*, 778 N.E.2d 1232 [171 Educ. L. Rep. 539] (Ill.App.Ct. 2002), *appeal denied*, 787 N.E.2d 171 (Ill. 2003).

208. *Central Dauphin School Dist. v. Central Dauphin Educ. Ass'n*, 767 A.2d 16 [151 Educ. L. Rep. 532] (Pa.Cmwlth.Ct. 2001).

209. *North Miami Educ. Ass'n v. North Miami Community Schools*, 736 N.E.2d 749 [148 Educ. L. Rep. 445] (Ind.Ct.App.2000), *decision clarified on reh'g*, 746 N.E.2d 380 [153 Educ. L. Rep. 352] (Ind.Ct.App.2001), *transfer denied*, 761 N.E.2d 417 (Ind.2001).

210. *School Admin. Dist. No. 58 v. Mount Abram Teachers Ass'n*, 704 A.2d 349 [123 Educ. L. Rep. 255] (Me.1997).

A final form of dispute resolution occurs when contract negotiations break down and neither party is willing to compromise. At this point, the parties can declare an impasse[211] and, depending on the jurisdiction, proceed to mediation and/or fact-finding.[212] When a breakdown occurs following the expiration of a contract, some courts ruled that original agreements may be deemed to continue by the implied mutual assent of the parties[213] while others declared that boards must continue to pay step increases to employees;[214] still other courts refused to order boards to pay step increases.[215] The next section examines whether cessations in bargaining can lead to work stoppages or strikes.

Strikes and Other Concerted Activities

Strikes have been fairly common in the private sector. Even so, courts and legislatures ordinarily frown on strikes by teachers and other public employees. In the earliest case on point, the Supreme Court of Errors of Connecticut, although recognizing that educators had the right to bargain collectively, concluded that teacher strikes were illegal.[216] In addition to common law barriers against teacher strikes, courts have overwhelmingly sustained statutory prohibitions against strikes[217] absent express legislative permission authorizing work stoppages.[218] Accordingly, some courts conceded that teachers have a qualified right to strike.[219]

In a case with a twist, an appellate court in Ohio considered the meaning of a strike. The court affirmed that where school bus drivers refused to be available to drive students to extracurricular activities

211. For cases discussing impasse, *see, e.g., Mountain Valley Educ. Ass'n v. Maine School Admin. Dist. No. 43*, 655 A.2d 348 [98 Educ. L. Rep. 256] (Me.1995); *State ex rel. Boggs v. Springfield Local School Dist. Bd. of Educ.*, 694 N.E.2d 1346 [125 Educ. L. Rep. 1337] (Ohio 1998).

212. *See, e.g.,* OHIO REV. CODE ANN. § 4117.14 (C) for an example of a statute dealing with break downs in bargaining.

213. *State ex rel. Boggs v. Springfield Local School Dist. Bd. of Educ.*, 757 N.E.2d 339 [158 Educ. L. Rep. 435] (Ohio 2001), *reconsideration denied*, 761 N.E.2d 49 (Ohio 2002).

214. *Board of Trustees of Univ. of Me. Sys. v. Associated Colt Staff of Univ. of Me. Sys.*, 659 A.2d 842 [101 Educ. L. Rep. 279] (Me.1995); *See also Cobleskill Cent. School Dist. v. Newman*, 481 N.Y.S.2d 795 [21 Educ. L. Rep. 645] (N.Y.App.Div.1984).

215. *Board of Educ. of Township of Neptune in County of Monmouth v. Neptune Township Educ. Ass'n*, 675 A.2d 611 [115 Educ. L. Rep. 372] (N.J.1996). *See also Providence Teachers Union v. Providence School Bd.*, 689 A.2d 388 [116 Educ. L. Rep. 703] (R.I.1997).

216. *Norwalk Teachers' Ass'n v. Board of Educ.*, 83 A.2d 482 (Conn.1951). *See also Pinellas County Classroom Teachers Ass'n v. Board of Pub. Instruction of Pinellas County*, 214 So.2d 34 (Fla.1968).

217. *Anchorage Educ. Ass'n v. Anchorage School Dist.*, 648 P.2d 993 [5 Educ. L. Rep. 1010] (Alaska 1982); *Mountain Valley Educ. Ass'n v. Maine School Admin. Dist. No. 43*, 655 A.2d 348 [98 Educ. L. Rep. 256] (Me.1995); *Franklin v. St. Louis Bd. of Educ.*, 904 S.W.2d 433 [103 Educ. L. Rep. 509] (Mo.Ct.App.1995); *Curley v. Board of School Directors of Greater Johnstown School Dist.*, 641 A.2d 719 [91 Educ. L. Rep. 238] (Pa.Cmwlth.Ct.1994); *Warwick School Comm. v. Warwick Teachers' Union, Local 915*, 613 A.2d 1273 [77 Educ. L. Rep. 861] (R.I.1992).

218. *Jefferson County Bd. of Educ. v. Jefferson County Educ. Ass'n*, 393 S.E.2d 653 [61 Educ. L. Rep. 765] (W.Va.1990).

219. *Reichley v. North Penn School Dist.*, 626 A.2d 123 [83 Educ. L. Rep. 1030] (Pa.1993); *Martin v. Montezuma–Cortez School Dist. RE–1*, 841 P.2d 237 [79 Educ. L. Rep. 256] (Colo. 1992).

since they did not have a duty to do so, their refusal to render this voluntary service could not be viewed as a strike.[220]

When teachers threaten to strike, courts typically use their discretion in evaluating requests for injunctions. The Supreme Court of Michigan was the first court to apply restraint in granting injunctions when it required a board to show that a strike would have resulted in "violence, irreparable injury, or breach of the peace" since injunctions on other grounds are "basically contrary to [state] public policy."[221] The Supreme Court of New Hampshire, while agreeing strikes of public employees were illegal, followed the lead of Michigan and pointed out that an injunction should not have automatically been issued since it had to consider operational factors such as whether negotiations were conducted in good faith and whether recognized methods of settlement failed.[222] An appellate court in Minnesota, in revoking a temporary injunction in favor of a union on the ground that it failed to show irreparable harm, explained that any right the teachers had to strike matured when they filed the notice of intent to strike rather than when it was actually exercised.[223] In another case, the Supreme Court of Arkansas affirmed that taxpayers did not have a right to enjoin a strike by teachers absent a showing of irreparable harm.[224]

The courts can punish violations of judicial orders to end strikes by placing unions and their leaders in contempt even without jury trials.[225] In addition, when union officials violate court orders, they and their unions can be fined[226] and suffer the loss of dues "check-off" privileges.[227] Leaders can also be imprisoned for contempt.[228] Yet, statements that one intends to violate an injunction against a strike are not an acceptable basis for contempt decrees.[229]

Teachers who participate in illegal strikes may face penalties including loss of pay,[230] having to reimburse boards for expenses caused incident to strikes,[231] and, as reflected by the Supreme Court's judgment

---

220. *Shelby Ass'n of School Support, OEA/NEA v. Shelby City Bd. of Educ.*, 662 N.E.2d 37 [107 Educ. L. Rep. 980] (Ohio Ct.App.1995).

221. *School Dist. for City of Holland v. Holland Educ. Ass'n*, 157 N.W.2d 206, 210 (Mich. 1968).

222. *Timberlane Reg'l School Dist. v. Timberlane Reg'l Educ. Ass'n*, 317 A.2d 555 (N.H.1974). [Case No. 78]

223. *Central Lakes Educ. Ass'n v. Independent School Dist. No. 743, Sauk Centre*, 411 N.W.2d 875 [41 Educ. L. Rep. 1072] (Minn.Ct.App.1987).

224. *Wilson v. Pulaski Ass'n of Classroom Teachers*, 954 S.W.2d 221 [122 Educ. L. Rep. 334] (Ark.1997).

225. *Rankin v. Shanker*, 295 N.Y.S.2d 625 (N.Y.1968).

226. *Wilmington Fed'n of Teachers v. Howell*, 374 A.2d 832 (Del.1977); *Labor Re-*

lations Comm'n v. Fall River Educ. Ass'n, 416 N.E.2d 1340 (Mass.1981).

227. *Buffalo Teachers Fed'n v. Helsby*, 676 F.2d 28 [4 Educ. L. Rep. 14] (2d Cir. 1982).

228. *In re Block*, 236 A.2d 589 (N.J. 1967). *See also Board of Educ. v. Newark Teachers Union, Local No. 481*, 276 A.2d 175 (N.J.Super.Ct.App.Div.1971), *cert. denied*, 404 U.S. 950, 92 S.Ct. 275, 30 L.Ed.2d 267 (1971).

229. *Board of Educ. of Brunswick City School Dist. v. Brunswick Educ. Ass'n*, 401 N.E.2d 440 (Ohio 1980).

230. *Head v. Special School Dist. No. 1*, 182 N.W.2d 887 (Minn.1970), *cert. denied*, 404 U.S. 886, 92 S.Ct. 196, 30 L.Ed.2d 168 (1971); *Board of Educ. of Marshallton–McKean School Dist. v. Sinclair*, 373 A.2d 572 (Del.1977).

231. *Passaic Township Bd. of Educ. v. Passaic Township Educ. Ass'n*, 536 A.2d in a case from Wisconsin, *Hortonville Joint School District No. 1 v. Hortonville Education Association*,[232] the loss of their jobs. However, the Supreme Court of Colorado affirmed that since a strike by public school teachers was legal, their board could not recover from them for tortious interference with their contracts between it and other teachers.[233]

On the other hand, a court in New Jersey refused to expunge the records of teachers who were incarcerated for between one and five days because they refused to comply with an injunction that prohibited them from striking.[234] In a matter of first impression, the court determined that while its ability to expunge records was limited to criminal cases, even if it could have exercised such authority in this dispute, it would have not done so because the history of strikes in the district suggested the likelihood that another would occur in the near future.

Along with actual work stoppages, courts have granted orders forbidding teachers from engaging in such activities as mass resignations[235] and absences to protest labor issues,[236] treating these as the equivalents of strikes. In a related concern, since unions have engaged in picketing as a form of protest when dealing with labor issues, the practice has generated litigation. If employees picket solely to induce breaches of contracts[237] or to obstruct government functions,[238] they can be restrained. Courts do not enjoin informational picketing unless it can be shown that it is likely to cause a disruption.[239]

The fact that picketing may be peaceful neither validates its use nor renders it legal when employees offer to perform essential services. In such a case, the Supreme Court of Illinois agreed that custodians could be enjoined from picketing since it agreed that their doing so disrupted normal school operations.[240] The same court later affirmed that a judge could issue a temporary restraining order without notice or a hearing when striking teachers engaged in picketing.[241] The court indicated that the United States Constitution does not afford the same kind of freedom to those who communicate ideas by picketing as it does to those who communicate ideas by pure speech. Conversely, an appellate court in Oregon refused to enjoin picketing where a board terminated the contract of its athletic director and refused to submit the matter to arbitra-

---

1276 [44 Educ. L. Rep. 1185] (N.J. Super. Ct. App. Div.1987).

232. 426 U.S. 482, 96 S.Ct. 2308, 49 L.Ed.2d 1 (1976).

233. *Martin v. Montezuma–Cortez School Dist. RE–1*, 841 P.2d 237 [79 Educ. L. Rep. 256] (Colo.1992).

234. *Board of Educ., Township of Middleton v. Middletown Teachers Educ. Ass'n*, 839 A.2d 159 [184 Educ. L. Rep. 433] (N.J. Super. Ct. Ch. Div. 2003).

235. *Board of Educ. of the City of N.Y. v. Shanker*, 286 N.Y.S.2d 453 (N.Y.App.Div. 1967).

236. *Pruzan v. Board of Educ. of City of N.Y.*, 217 N.Y.S.2d 86 (N.Y.1961).

237. *Board of Educ. of Martins Ferry City School Dist. v. Ohio Educ. Ass'n*, 235 N.E.2d 538 (Ohio Common Pleas 1967).

238. *State v. Heath*, 177 N.W.2d 751 (N.D.1970).

239. *Board of Educ. of Danville Community Consol. School Dist. No. 118 v. Danville Educ. Ass'n*, 376 N.E.2d 430 (Ill.App. Ct.1978).

240. *Board of Educ. v. Redding*, 207 N.E.2d 427 (Ill.1965). *See also City of Pana v. Crowe*, 316 N.E.2d 513 (Ill.1974).

241. *Board of Educ. v. Kankakee Fed'n of Teachers Local No. 886*, 264 N.E.2d 18 (Ill.1970), *cert. denied*, 403 U.S. 904, 91 S.Ct. 2203, 29 L.Ed.2d 679 (1971).

tion.[242] The court rejected the board's claim that it would have been irreparably harmed if the arbitrator denied the union's grievance on the merits since it did not agree with the conjecture that it might have obtained a victory was a showing of injury.

[Case No. 70] Salary Reduction—Legislation Impairing Obligation of Contract

PHELPS v. BOARD OF EDUCATION

Supreme Court of the United States, 1937.
300 U.S. 319, 57 S.Ct. 483, 81 L.Ed. 674.

MR. JUSTICE ROBERTS delivered the opinion of the Court.

The people of New Jersey have ordained by their Constitution that the Legislature "shall provide for the maintenance and support of a thorough and efficient system of free public schools." In fulfillment of this command a comprehensive school law was adopted in 1903 by which boards of education were set up for cities, towns, and school districts throughout the state.... This general school law was amended by the Act of April 21, 1909, section 1 of which provided: "The service of all teachers, principals, supervising principals of the public schools in any school district of this state shall be during good behavior and efficiency, after the expiration of a period of employment of three consecutive years in that district, unless a shorter period is fixed by the employing board.... No principal or teacher shall be dismissed or subjected to reduction of salary in said school district except for inefficiency, incapacity, conduct unbecoming a teacher or other just cause, and after a written charge of the cause or causes shall have been preferred against him or her, ... and after the charge shall have been examined into and found true in fact by said board of education, upon reasonable notice to the person charged, who may be represented by counsel at the hearing."

An Act of February 4, 1933, premising that existing economic conditions require that boards of education be enabled to fix and determine the amount of salary to be paid to persons holding positions in the respective school districts, authorizes each board to fix and determine salaries to be paid officers and employees for the period July 1, 1933, to July 1, 1934, "notwithstanding any such person be under tenure"; prohibits increase of salaries within the period named; forbids discrimination between individuals in the same class of service in the fixing of salaries or compensation; and sets a minimum beyond which boards may not go in the reduction of salaries. On June 23, 1933, the board adopted a resolution reducing salaries for the school year July 1, 1933, to July 1, 1934, by a percentage of the existing salaries graded upward in steps as the salaries increased in amount, except with respect to clerks, the compensation of each of whom was reduced to a named amount....

242. *Arlington School Dist. No. 3 v. Arlington Educ. Ass'n*, 55 P.3d 546 [170 Educ. L. Rep. 394] (Or.Ct.App.2002).

The position of the appellants is that by virtue of the Act of 1909 three years of service under contract confer upon an employee of a school district a contractual status indefinite in duration which the legislature is powerless to alter or to authorize the board of education to alter. The Supreme Court holds that the Act of 1909 "established a legislative status for teachers, but we fail to see that it established a contractual one that the Legislature may not modify.... The status of tenure teachers, while in one sense perhaps contractual, is in essence dependent on a statute, like that of the incumbent of a statutory office, which the Legislature at will may abolish, or whose emoluments it may change."

This court is not bound by the decision of a state court as to the existence and terms of a contract, the obligation of which is asserted to be impaired, but where a statute is claimed to create a contractual right we give weight to the construction of the statute by the courts of the state. Here those courts have concurred in holding that the act of 1909 did not amount to a legislative contract with the teachers of the state and did not become a term of the contracts entered into with employees by boards of education. Unless these views are palpably erroneous we should accept them.

It appears from a stipulation of facts submitted in view of evidence that after a teacher has served in a school district under yearly contracts for three years it has not been customary to enter into additional further formal contracts with such teacher. From time to time, however, promotions were granted and salary raised for the ensuing year by action of the board. In the case of many of the appellants there have been several such increases in salary.

Although after the expiration of the first three years of service the employee continued in his then position and at his then compensation unless and until promoted or given an increase in salary for a succeeding year, we find nothing in the record to indicate that the board was bound by contract with the teacher for more than the current year. The employee assumed no binding obligation to remain in service beyond that term. Although the act of 1909 prohibited the board, a creature of the state, from reducing the teacher's salary or discharging him without cause, we agree with the courts below that this was but a regulation of the conduct of the board and not a term of a continuing contract of indefinite duration with the individual teacher.

The resolution of June 23, 1933, grouped the existing salaries paid by the board into six classes the lowest of which comprised salaries between $1200 and $1999; and the highest included salaries ranging between $4000 and $5600. The reduction in the lowest class for the coming year was 10 per cent; that in highest class 15 per cent. Salaries in the intermediate classes were reduced 11, 12, 13, and 14 per cent. It resulted that in some instances a teacher receiving the lowest salary in a given bracket would have his compensation reduced to a figure lower than the reduced compensation of one receiving the highest salary in the next lower bracket. From this circumstance it is argued that the board's action arbitrarily discriminated between the employees and so denied them the equal protection of the laws guaranteed by the Fourteenth Amendment.

We think it was reasonable and proper that the teachers employed by the board should be divided into classes for the application of the percentage reduction. All in a given class were treated alike. Incidental individual inequality resulting in some instances from the operation of the plan does not condemn it as an unreasonable or arbitrary method of dealing with the problem of general salary reductions or deny the equality guaranteed by the Fourteenth Amendment. . . .

Notes

1. Note the Court's statement that although it was not bound by the judgment of a state court as to the existence and terms of a contract, it gave weight to its interpretation of the statute that was alleged to have created a contractual right.

2. If a legislature can change the tenure status and retirement allowances of teachers at will, their rights appear to be flimsy. Are individual teachers or groups of teachers seriously threatened by precipitous legislative action in these areas?

[Case No. 71]   Right of Teacher to Minimum Salary

MARVEL v. COAL HILL PUBLIC SCHOOL DISTRICT

Supreme Court of Arkansas, 1982.
635 S.W.2d 245 [5 Educ. L. Rep. 667].

HICKMAN, JUSTICE. The question in this case is whether a full-time school teacher can be denied the minimum salary due to teachers because of a written contract for a lesser amount. The trial court found such a contract enforceable. We disagree and reverse.

Deborah Marvel had been a part-time librarian and teacher for the Coal Hill Public School District when her contract was negotiated for the 1979–1980 school year. She said that Mr. Nolan Williams, the superintendent of schools, told her she would serve as part-time librarian and part-time teacher but would receive the same salary that full-time teachers did. (She had been paid in the past as an aide, but was now to be paid as a teacher.) Williams refuted that. But the contract only provided for a salary of $9,800.00 and the minimum a full-time teacher with her experience would receive is $11,450.00. She accepted the position and signed the contract but chose to sue for the difference, which was $1,650.00, plus interest.

The parties disagreed as to whether Miss Marvel signed the contract under protest but that is irrelevant. It is not disputed that she was a "teacher" within the meaning of Ark. Stats. Ann. § 80–1326 (Repl. 1980), and performed all the duties of a full-time teacher. She performed the ancillary duties of all teachers such as hall monitor, attending ball games and faculty meetings. She kept grade, class planning and attendance records. In order to qualify as full-time, she was required to work six periods a day. She acted as a teacher five periods a day and as a librarian two periods. It is also undisputed that the school district filed with the State Department of Education a salary schedule, as required by Ark. Stats. Ann. 80–1324 and 80–850.7 (Repl.1980), and that her salary as a full-time teacher would have been $11,450.00.

The superintendent said the reason Miss Marvel was not paid the minimum salary is because the part of her salary for teaching remedial reading was Title I money (federal money) and the grant did not allow her to be paid more.

The trial court held that the contract did not violate Arkansas law which requires that school districts promulgate minimum salary schedules.... The court found that since she was paid fairly for librarian duties from general funds that the district complied with the law, and found further that Miss Marvel knowingly and freely entered into a binding agreement.

The trial court was wrong in its interpretation of the law. Miss Marvel was a full-time teacher and the district could not receive her services and refuse to pay her the minimum salary it paid other full-time teachers. Title I provisions cannot be used to avoid Ark. Stats. Ann. 80–1327 and 80–850.7, which require each school district to set a schedule of minimum salaries and abide by it.

If the district's position were to prevail, then no teacher could be sure of equal treatment when he or she was hired or retained at least to the extent that a minimum salary would apply to all hired for full-time duties. The school district received the benefit of the services of a full-time teacher and it should not be allowed to manipulate the law to avoid its legal responsibility.

The judgment is reversed....

Notes

1. Accepting as true the superintendent's statements about the use of Title I money, there still was no prohibition against supplementing those salary funds with state (or local) money.

2. Why did the court not need to resolve the disagreement as to whether Ms. Marvel signed the contract under protest?

[Case No. 72] Right of Public to See Teacher's College Transcript

KLEIN INDEPENDENT SCHOOL DISTRICT v. MATTOX

United States Court of Appeals, Fifth Circuit, 1987.
830 F.2d 576 [42 Educ. L. Rep. 70].

GARZA, CIRCUIT JUDGE:

I.   Facts and Proceedings

During the months of October and November of 1985, Dr. Donald Collins, the Superintendent of the Klein Independent School District, received two letters requesting copies of the "personnel file and other related public records" of Rebecca J. Holt. Ms. Holt is a public school-teacher employed by the school district. The requests were made pursuant to the Texas Open Records Act. Dr. Collins asked the Attorney General's Office for the State of Texas whether the contents of Ms. Holt's personnel file, particularly her college transcript, were public records subject to disclosure under state law. An Assistant Attorney General sent an opinion to Dr. Collins informing him that, in addition to the other documents, Ms. Holt's college transcript must be released according to the Texas Open Records Act. Moreover, such disclosure was not proscribed by the Family Educational Rights and Privacy Act of 1974 (FERPA)....

On July 14, 1986, Ms. Holt and the school district brought suit against Jim Mattox, the Attorney General for the State of Texas, alleging that he issued an opinion which, if followed, would cause the school district to act in violation of Ms. Holt's rights secured under FERPA and the First Amendment to the United States Constitution....

On November 21, 1986, the district court granted the defendant's motion for summary judgment, and entered a final order dismissing the case....

II. Discussion

... The appellants present two issues to this Court. The first issue is whether the lower court erred in ruling that they are not entitled to maintain this action pursuant to FERPA.... The second issue is whether the court erred in finding that Ms. Holt's interest in maintaining the confidentiality of her academic record did not outweigh the public's interest in learning whether she is qualified to teach.

A. FERPA

. . .

FERPA was designed to regulate the release of student records. A student's or parent's consent is required where personally identifiable information from the education records of a student is to be disclosed. The Secretary of Education is empowered to enforce the various provisions of FERPA. An educational agency or institution that unlawfully releases a student's record may lose federal funding. This is the only express remedy provided in the statute. FERPA neither explicitly provides for a private cause of action, nor does its legislative history indicate that its drafters intended one.

Naturally, we are alerted to the problem that Ms. Holt is employed by the school district, and is not a student and never has been a student of the subject school district. It is fundamental from a reading of FERPA that a "student" is a "person with respect to whom an educational agency or institution maintains education records or personally identifiable information, but does not include a person who has not been in attendance at such agency or institution." ...

It cannot be disputed that the statute was enacted to prevent an educational agency or institution from releasing the record of one of its own students. Excluded from FERPA's protections are records relating to an individual who is employed by an educational agency or institution. Because Ms. Holt has not attended any school within the Klein Independent School District, the agency which has been directed to release her transcript, she cannot be considered a "student" under the FERPA definition. Rather, Ms. Holt's capacity with the school district is that of an employee. Because she is an employee and not a student of the institution requested to disclose her transcript, she does not fall within that class of people for whose benefit FERPA was created. Ms. Holt is not a "student" and her college transcript is not an "education record" protected from disclosure pursuant to FERPA's provisions....

B.   Balancing the Interests

The district court found that Ms. Holt had a privacy interest in her college transcript. The Supreme Court has written that there are two different kinds of privacy interests. "One is the individual interest in avoiding disclosure of personal matters, and another is the interest in independence in making certain kinds of important decisions."

Under the autonomy branch of privacy, constitutional protection has been limited to intimate personal relationships or activities, and freedoms to make fundamental choices involving oneself, one's family, and one's relationships with others. The appellants seek constitutional protection from an action quite dissimilar from that which has been held to be protected. Their claim is based not upon a challenge to the state's ability to restrict her freedom of action in a private matter, but rather on a claim that the state directed a college record to be released. Obviously, this is not a question concerning the autonomy branch of the right to privacy.

Regarding the interest in confidentiality, the Supreme Court has defined this branch as "the individual interest in avoiding disclosure of personal matters." ... Without engaging in an inquiry into whether Ms. Holt has a recognizable privacy interest in her college transcript, we believe that, under the balancing test, even if she did have an interest it is significantly outweighed by the public's interest in evaluating the competence of its schoolteachers.

The district court ... [stated] that Ms. Holt has a constitutional right to avoid disclosure of personal matters. The court then balanced Ms. Holt's privacy interest against the public's interest in knowing about her educational background. Although her file may contain "embarrassing or confidential information," the court noted, the public interest in learning whether those who teach young children are qualified clearly outweighs her limited right to disclosural privacy.

The appellants contend that the public's interest can be vindicated through less intrusive means than presented in this case. The appellants propose that since her teaching certificate represents the informed judgment of the Texas Board of Education that she is qualified to teach, disclosure of the certificate itself fully serves the public's interest in being assured that those who teach are qualified. Therefore, the certificate and not a college transcript suffices, and to require disclosure of the transcript operates to invade Ms. Holt's interest in maintaining the confidentiality of her academic career.

The public's interest in disclosure of a schoolteacher's transcript is set forth in section 1 of the Texas Open Records Act.

Pursuant to the fundamental philosophy of the American constitutional form of representative government which holds to the principle that government is the servant of the people, and not the master of them, it is hereby declared to be the public policy of the State of Texas that all persons are, unless otherwise expressly provided by law, at all times entitled to full and complete information regarding the affairs of government and the official acts of those who represent them as public officials and employees. The people, in delegating authority, do not give their public servants the right to decide what is good for the people to know and what is not good for them to know. The people insist on remaining informed so that they may retain control over the instruments they have created. To that end, the provisions of this Act shall be liberally construed with the view of carrying out the above declaration of public policy.

The Open Records Act, however, does make provision for safeguarding the personal privacy of the individual. Section 3(a)(2) of the statute exempts from public disclosure "information in personnel files, the disclosure of which would constitute a clearly unwarranted invasion of personal privacy[.]" We do not find that the disclosure of a schoolteacher's college transcript rises to the level of that information which constitutes an unwarranted invasion of personal privacy, as provided in section 3(a)(2). . . .

We agree with the district court in tipping the balance in favor of the right of the public to know the academic records of the schoolteachers of their children. The appellants' reasoning concerning the regulations imposed by the Texas Legislature and the screening procedures of the Texas Board of Education is unavailing. Recently, there has been grave concern in Texas about the quality of public education, notwithstanding the state's regulations. Many teachers who had been certified and were teaching in Texas classrooms could not pass a basic test of minimal competency. In light of this apparent lack of competency prevalent in the state, the public must have full and complete information concerning the teachers who serve the public in educating their children.

III.   Conclusion

Finding no merit in the appellants' claims and agreeing with the district court that the defendant was entitled to judgment as a matter of law, we AFFIRM the court's decision to grant summary judgment in this case.

Notes

1. The Supreme Court denied *certiorari*, 485 U.S. 1008, 108 S.Ct. 1473, 99 L.Ed.2d 701 (1988).

2. Even if Ms. Holt once had been a student in the district, only records related to those days would come under FERPA protection.

3. Why do you think that the board joined Ms. Holt's appeal?

[Case No. 73]   Constitutionality of Race–Based Teacher Transfer Plan

JACOBSEN v. CINCINNATI BOARD OF EDUCATION

United States Court of Appeals, Sixth Circuit, 1992.
961 F.2d 100 [74 Educ. L. Rep. 51], *cert. denied,*
506 U.S. 830, 113 S.Ct. 94, 121 L.Ed.2d 55.

ALAN E. NORRIS, CIRCUIT JUDGE. Eight Cincinnati public school teachers and the Cincinnati Federation of Teachers ("CFT"), the union that represents them, brought suit in the district court challenging the teacher transfer policy adopted by the Cincinnati Board of Education ("Board") to ensure that the faculty of its schools reflects system-wide racial balance. After an evidentiary hearing, the district court concluded that the policy did not violate either plaintiffs' Fourteenth Amendment right to equal protection or the terms of the collective bargaining agreement ("CBA") negotiated by the CFT and the Board. Accordingly, the district court denied plaintiffs' request to enjoin the transfer policy. For the reasons outlined below, we affirm the judgment of the district court.

This dispute has its genesis in the 1970s, when concerted efforts to eradicate indicia of racial segregation within the Cincinnati public school system began. On January 14, 1974, the Board adopted a policy designed to ensure that the teaching staff of a given school approximated the racial balance of the teaching staff of the system as a whole. Shortly thereafter, the Board issued a statement indicating how this general policy would be implemented. Among other things, the statement provided that the percentage of black teachers in any school should not be five percent greater or less than the percentage of black teachers throughout the system. In order to implement this racial balance, the policy restricts the ability of some teachers to voluntarily transfer to other school buildings, and requires the reassignment of others. It is this portion of the policy which plaintiffs challenge.

In the same year that these efforts to balance the racial composition of the faculty were initiated, a group of school children and their parents filed a lawsuit against the Board, contending that the school system was unlawfully segregated. That suit was ultimately settled by the parties, and the district court adopted the settlement agreement as a consent decree. Paragraph 5 of the settlement agreement reads as follows:

The Cincinnati Board of Education currently has in force a policy which requires that the staff in each of its schools has a racial composition which is within 5% of the racial composition of the staff in the district as a whole. The Board shall maintain that policy in effect and take steps necessary to assure that it is enforced.

The CFT actively participated in the resolution of [the settled suit] and did not object to the maintenance of the staff racial balance policy. The position of the CFT is reflected in the CBA negotiated with the Board. Section 250, paragraph 1, of the CBA contains the following provision regarding teacher transfers: "Teacher requests for transfer will be honored if positions are available and the teacher is qualified for a particular vacancy, provided that the transfer is consistent with the racial balance of the staff."

We begin by noting that school authorities have broad discretion to implement educational policy. This authority includes the power to prescribe a ratio of white to minority students that reflects the composition of the overall school district, particularly when such a policy is implemented in order to prepare students for life in a pluralistic society. And we believe that this discretionary authority includes the power to assign faculty to achieve a racial ratio reflecting the racial composition of the system's teachers. The Supreme Court has recognized that the attainment of an integrated teaching staff is a legitimate concern in achieving a school system free of racial discrimination.

Here, the district court found that the policy adopted by the Board is race conscious in the sense that it allows the Board to determine the schools at which a teacher may teach solely on the basis of his or her race. However, the court went on to find that the policy is "specific race neutral in that there is no disparate impact as to race in its application. It is applied equally to both black and white teachers. In some instances, it will benefit or harm white teachers; in others, it will benefit or harm black teachers." We agree with that characterization. We are therefore unable to agree with plaintiffs' contention that the policy establishes preferences based on race that require us to examine the policy with strict scrutiny to determine whether it conflicts with guarantees afforded them under the Constitution.

Under analogous circumstances, the Court of Appeals for the Third Circuit offered these observations concerning the appropriate level of scrutiny to which such a policy should be subjected:

No case has suggested that the mere utilization of race as a factor, together with seniority, school need, and subject qualification, is prohibited. Since the classification is not preferential, it might most appropriately be reviewed for its rational relationship to a legitimate government objective, under which standard it would be patently valid. At most, since there is some element of racial classification, albeit not of preference, the appropriate level of scrutiny would be the intermediate level suggested by four members of the Court in *Bakke*, in which the classification was indeed preferential.

The appropriate question under that standard is whether the classification "serve[s] important governmental objectives" and is "substantially related to achievement of those objectives."

In our view, this intermediate level of scrutiny is the proper one, since the Cincinnati teacher transfer policy, like the policy challenged in Kromnick, does not prefer one race over another. Accordingly, we must determine whether the policy is substantially related to an important governmental objective. We believe the policy at issue meets that test. It was implemented to achieve a racially integrated faculty throughout the Cincinnati public school system. Not only is this a legitimate objective, it has been endorsed in the past by the CFT. In fact, section 250 of the CBA, which appellants mistakenly contend has been violated by the Board, expressly allows for the accommodation of such a transfer policy.

We therefore hold that plaintiffs have failed to demonstrate how their interest in selecting the schools to which they are assigned outweighs the Board's interest in fostering an integrated, pluralistic school system.

The judgment of the district court is affirmed.

Notes

1. In an equal protection case such as this, a court first must consider which level of scrutiny to apply.

2. What is your impression of the role of the union in pursuit of the claim of unconstitutionality in this case?

3. Would this case serve as a precedent for resolving a dispute where a factor in an involuntary transfer was a teacher's sex, years of experience (age), or religion?

[Case No. 74]   Constitutionality of Teachers' Oath

KNIGHT v. BOARD OF REGENTS OF THE UNIVERSITY OF THE STATE OF NEW YORK

United States District Court, Southern District of New York, 1967.
269 F.Supp. 339.

TYLER, DISTRICT JUDGE. Plaintiffs are twenty-seven faculty members at Adelphi University, a private, non-profit institution of higher learning located in Garden City, New York and tax exempt under Section 420 of the New York Real Property Tax Law, McKinney's Consol.Laws, c. 50–A.

Section 3002 of the New York Education Law, McKinney's Consol.Laws, c. 16, requires every citizen teacher, instructor or professor in any public school or in any private school the real property of which is in whole or in part exempt from taxation to execute an oath. In pertinent part, Section 3002 reads as follows:

Oath to support federal and state constitutions. It shall be unlawful for any citizen of the United States to serve as teacher, instructor or professor in any school or institution in the public school system of the state or in any school, college, university or other educational institution in this state, whose real property, in whole or in part, is exempt from taxation under section four of the tax law unless and until he or she shall have taken and subscribed the following oath or affirmation: "I do solemnly swear (or affirm) that I will support the constitution of the United States of America and the constitution of the State of New York, and that I will faithfully discharge, according to the best of my ability, the duties of the position of ... (title of position and name or designation of school, college, university or institution to be here inserted), to which I am now assigned."

Although this statutory requirement dates back to 1934, through inadvertence Adelphi had not previously requested that its faculty members execute the oath. In October, 1966, however, upon being made aware of the statute, the administrative offices of Adelphi asked all the members of its teaching staff to sign and return the oath. Plaintiffs have refused to do so, instead bringing this action to enjoin the enforcement of the oath provision....

So far as we can determine, the precise question of whether an oath such as that provided for by Section 3002 may constitutionally be required of teachers has not been ruled upon by the Supreme Court. That Court, however, has recently stated that Georgia's requirement that her legislators take a similar oath in no way impinges upon the First Amendment's protection of free speech. Moreover, the Court, in striking down so called "negative loyalty oath" requirements of the states, has never suggested that the First Amendment proscribes any form of oath or affirmation required of teachers.

Plaintiffs rely heavily upon *West Virginia State Board of Education v. Barnette*, in which the Supreme Court held unconstitutional a state statute requiring school children to salute and pledge allegiance to the American flag. The pledge of allegiance there involved, however, was far more elaborate than the affirmation required by New York of teachers in public and tax supported educational institutions. Furthermore, the decision in *Barnette* was based on the First Amendment's guarantee of religious freedom. The plaintiffs there were members of a religious group who claimed that the requirement of the oath and accompanying salute violated their religious beliefs. No such claim or allegation is made here....

Plaintiffs also urge that section 3002 suffers the vice of vagueness. In support of this theory, they rely upon the line of Supreme Court cases striking down "negative loyalty oaths" or "non-Communist oaths". As plaintiffs' counsel candidly conceded at oral argument, however, such oaths, which typically require an affiant to state that he is not now and has never been a member of certain organizations, present a very different problem.

The language of Section 3002 is simple and clear in its import. It requires no more than that the subscriber affirm that he will support the constitutions of the United States and the State of New York and that he will be a dedicated teacher. The statutory language of support of the constitutional governments can be substantially equated to that allegiance which, by the common law, every citizen was understood to owe his sovereign.... In our view, a state can reasonably ask teachers in public or tax exempted institutions to subscribe to professional competence and dedication.

Plaintiffs, conceding that it is constitutionally permissible to demand from public officials, federal and state, an oath or affirmation substantially the same as that set forth in Section 3002, suggest that different considerations apply to teachers. In sum, it is said that teachers' speech must be totally "free of interference". But, as may be implied from what has already been said, we interpret the statute to impose no restrictions upon political or philosophical expressions by teachers in the State of New York. A state does not interfere with its teachers by requiring them to support the governmental systems which shelter and nourish the institutions in which they teach, nor does it restrict its teachers by encouraging them to uphold the highest standards of their chosen profession. Indeed, it is plain that a state has a clear interest in assuring "... careful and discriminating selection of teachers" by its publicly supported educational institutions. . . .

Notes

1. What was the legal basis for making the oath applicable to the faculty of private schools?

2. Was this oath a threat to academic freedom?

3. The faculty members argued that they should have been classified differently from other public employees with regard to such oaths. Do you agree?

[Case No. 75] Constitutionality of State Program Designed to Remove Subversive Faculty Members

KEYISHIAN v. BOARD OF REGENTS OF THE UNIVERSITY OF THE STATE OF NEW YORK

Supreme Court of the United States, 1967.
385 U.S. 589, 87 S.Ct. 675, 17 L.Ed.2d 629.

MR. JUSTICE BRENNAN delivered the opinion of the Court.

Appellants were members of the faculty of the privately owned and operated University of Buffalo, and became state employees when the University was merged in 1962 into the State University of New York, an institution of higher education owned and operated by the State of New York. As faculty members of the State University their continued employment was conditioned upon their compliance with a New York plan, formulated partly in statutes and partly in administrative regulations, which the State utilizes to prevent the appointment or retention of "subversive" persons in state employment.

Appellants Hochfield and Maud were Assistant Professors of English, appellant Keyishian, an instructor in English, and appellant Garver, a lecturer in philosophy. Each of them refused to sign, as regulations then in effect required, a certificate that he was not a Communist, and that if he had ever been a Communist, he had communicated that fact to the President of the State University of New York. Each was notified that his failure to sign the certificate would require his dismissal. Keyishian's one-year-term contract was not renewed because of his failure to sign the certificate. . . .

I

We considered some aspects of the constitutionality of the New York plan 15 years ago in *Adler v. Board of Education*. That litigation arose after New York passed the Feinberg Law which added § 3022 to the Education Law, McKinney's Consol.Laws, c. 16. The Feinberg Law was enacted to implement and enforce two earlier statutes. The first was a 1917 law, now § 3021 of the Education Law, under which "the utterance of any treasonable or seditious word or words or the doing of any treasonable or seditious act" is a ground for dismissal from the public school system. The second was a 1939 law which was § 12–a of the Civil Service Law when *Adler* was decided and, as amended, is now § 105 of that law. This law disqualifies from the civil service and from employment in the educational system any person who advocates the overthrow of government by force, violence, or any unlawful means, or publishes material advocating such overthrow or organizes or joins any society or group of persons advocating such doctrine.

The Feinberg Law charged the State Board of Regents with the duty of promulgating rules and regulations providing procedures for the disqualification or removal of persons in the public school system who violate the 1917 law or who are ineligible for appointment to or retention in the public school system under the 1939 law. The Board of Regents was further directed to make a list, after notice and hearing, of "subversive" organizations, defined as organizations which advocate the doctrine of overthrow of government by force, violence, or any unlawful means. Finally, the Board was directed to provide in its rules and regulations that membership in any listed organization should constitute prima facie evidence of disqualification for appointment to or retention in any office or position in the public schools of the State.

The Board of Regents thereupon promulgated rules and regulations containing procedures to be followed by appointing authorities to discover persons ineligible for appointment or retention under the 1939 law, or because of violation of the 1917 law. The Board also announced its intention to list "subversive" organizations after requisite notice and hearing, and provided that membership in a listed organization after the date of its listing should be regarded as constituting prima facie evidence of disqualification, and that membership prior to listing should be presumptive evidence that membership has continued, in the absence of a showing that such membership was terminated in good faith. Under the regulations, an appointing official is forbidden to make an appointment until after he has first inquired of an applicant's former employers and other persons to ascertain whether the applicant is disqualified or ineligible for appointment. In addition, an annual inquiry must be made to determine whether an appointed employee has ceased to be qualified for retention, and a report of findings must be filed.

Adler was a declaratory judgment suit in which the Court held, in effect, that there was no constitutional infirmity in former § 12–a or in the Feinberg Law on their faces and that they were capable of constitutional application. But the contention urged in this case that both § 3021 and § 105 are unconstitutionally vague was not heard or decided. Section 3021 of the Education Law was challenged in *Adler* as unconstitutionally vague, but because the challenge had not been made in the pleadings or in the proceedings in the lower courts, this Court refused to consider it. . . . Appellants in this case timely asserted below the unconstitutionality of all these sections on grounds of vagueness and that question is now properly before us for decision. Moreover, to the extent that *Adler* sustained the provision of the Feinberg Law constituting membership in an organization advocating forceful overthrow of government a ground for disqualification, pertinent constitutional doctrines have since rejected the premises upon which that conclusion rested. *Adler* is therefore not dispositive of the constitutional issues we must decide in this case.

II

A 1953 amendment extended the application of the Feinberg Law to personnel of any college or other institution of higher education owned and operated by the State or its subdivisions. In the same year, the Board of Regents, after notice and hearing, listed the Communist Party of the United States and of the State of New York as "subversive organizations." In 1956 each applicant for an appointment or the renewal of an appointment was required to sign the so-called "Feinberg Certificate" declaring that he had read the Regents Rules and understood that the Rules and the statutes constituted terms of employment, and declaring further that he was not a member of the Communist Party, and that if he had ever been a member he had communicated that fact to the President of the State University. This was the certificate that appellants Hochfield, Maud, Keyishian, and Garver refused to sign.

In June 1965, shortly before the trial of this case, the Feinberg Certificate was rescinded and it was announced that no person then employed would be deemed ineligible for continued employment "solely" because he refused to sign the certificate. In lieu of the certificate, it was provided that each applicant be informed before assuming his duties that the statutes, §§ 3021 and 3022 of the Education Law and § 105 of the Civil Service Law, constituted part of his contract. He was particularly to be informed of the disqualification which flowed from membership in a listed "subversive" organization. The 1965 announcement further provides: "Should any question arise in the course of such inquiry such candidate may request . . . a personal interview. Refusal of a candidate to answer any question relevant to such inquiry by such officer shall be sufficient ground to refuse to make or recommend appointment." A brochure is also given new applicants. It outlines and explains briefly the legal effect of the statutes and invites any applicant who may have any question about possible disqualification to request an interview. The covering announcement concludes that "a prospective appointee who does not believe himself disqualified need take no affirmative action. No disclaimer oath is required."

The change in procedure in no wise moots appellants' constitutional questions raised in the context of their refusal to sign the now abandoned Feinberg Certificate. The substance of the statutory and regulatory complex remains and from the outset appellants' basic claim has been that they are aggrieved by its application.

III

Section 3021 requires removal for "treasonable or seditious" utterances or acts. . . .

. . . We cannot gainsay the potential effect of this obscure wording on "those with a conscientious and scrupulous regard for such undertakings." . . . The teacher cannot know the extent, if any, to which a "seditious" utterance must transcend mere statement about abstract doctrine, the extent to which it must be intended to and tend to indoctrinate or incite to action in furtherance of the defined doctrine. The crucial consideration is that no teacher can know just where the line is drawn between "seditious" and nonseditious utterances and acts.

Other provisions of § 105 also have the same defect of vagueness. Subdivision 1(a) of § 105 bars employment of any person who "by word of mouth or writing wilfully and deliberately advocates, advises or teaches the doctrine" of forceful overthrow of government. This provision is plainly susceptible of sweeping and improper application. It may well prohibit the employment of one who merely advocates the doctrine in the abstract without any attempt to indoctrinate others, or incite others to action in furtherance of unlawful aims. And in prohibiting "advising" the "doctrine" of unlawful overthrow does the statute prohibit mere "advising" of the existence of the doctrine, or advising another to support the doctrine? Since "advocacy" of the doctrine of forceful overthrow is separately prohibited, need the person "teaching" or "advising" this doctrine himself "advocate" it? Does the teacher who informs his class about the precepts of Marxism or the Declaration of Independence violate the prohibition?

Similar uncertainty arises as to the application of subdivision 1(b) of § 105. That subsection requires the disqualification of an employee involved with the distribution of written material "containing or advocating, advising or teaching the doctrine" of forceful overthrow, and who himself "advocates, advises, teaches, or embraces the duty, necessity or propriety of adopting the doctrine contained therein." Here again, mere advocacy of abstract doctrine is apparently included. And does the prohibition of distribution of matter "containing" the doctrine bar histories of the evolution of Marxist doctrine or tracing the background of the French, American, or Russian revolutions? The additional requirement, that the person participating in distribution of the material be one who "advocates, advises, teaches, or embraces the duty, necessity or propriety of adopting the doctrine" of forceful overthrow, does not alleviate the uncertainty in the scope of the section, but exacerbates it.

Like the language of § 105, subd. 1(a), this language may reasonably be construed to cover mere expression of belief. For example, does the university librarian who recommends the reading of such materials thereby "advocate ... the propriety of adopting the doctrine contained therein"?

We do not have the benefit of a judicial gloss by the New York courts enlightening us as to the scope of this complicated plan. In light of the intricate administrative machinery for its enforcement, this is not surprising. The very intricacy of the plan and the uncertainty as to the scope of its proscriptions make it a highly efficient in terrorem mechanism. It would be a bold teacher who would not stay as far as possible from utterances or acts which might jeopardize his living by enmeshing him in this intricate machinery. The uncertainty as to the utterances and acts proscribed increases that caution in "those who believe the written law means what it says." The result must be to stifle "that free play of the spirit which all teachers ought especially to cultivate and practice...." That probability is enhanced by the provisions requiring an annual review of every teacher to determine whether any utterance or act of his, inside the classroom or out, came within the sanctions of the laws....

There can be no doubt of the legitimacy of New York's interest in protecting its education system from subversion. But "even though the governmental purpose be legitimate and substantial, that purpose cannot be pursued by means that broadly stifle fundamental personal liberties when the end can be more narrowly achieved." The principle is not inapplicable because the legislation is aimed at keeping subversives out of the teaching ranks....

Our Nation is deeply committed to safeguarding academic freedom, which is of transcendent value to all of us and not merely to the teachers concerned. That freedom is therefore a special concern of the First Amendment, which does not tolerate laws that cast a pall of orthodoxy over the classroom. "The vigilant protection of constitutional freedoms is nowhere more vital than in the community of American schools." The classroom is peculiarly the "marketplace of ideas." The Nation's future depends upon leaders trained through wide exposure to that robust exchange of ideas which discovers truth "out of a multitude of tongues, [rather] than through any kind of authoritative selection." ...

The regulatory maze created by New York is wholly lacking in "terms acceptable of objective measurement." ... Vagueness of wording is aggravated by prolixity and profusion of statutes, regulations, and administrative machinery, and by manifold cross-references to interrelated enactments and rules.

We therefore hold that § 3021 of the Education Law and subdivisions 1(a), 1(b) and 3 of § 105 of the Civil Service Law as implemented by the machinery created pursuant to § 3022 of the Education Law are unconstitutional.

IV

Appellants have also challenged the constitutionality of the discrete provisions of subdivision 1(c) of § 105 and subdivision 2 of the Feinberg Law, which make Communist Party membership, as such, prima facie evidence of disqualification. The provision was added to subdivision 1(c) of § 105 in 1958 after the Board of Regents, following notice and hearing, listed the Communist Party of the United States and the Communist Party of the State of New York as "subversive" organizations. Subdivision 2 of the Feinberg Law was, however, before the Court in *Adler* and its constitutionality was sustained. But constitutional doctrine which has emerged since that decision has rejected its major premise. That premise was that public employment, including academic employment, may be conditioned upon the surrender of constitutional rights which could not be abridged by direct government action. . . .

We proceed then to the question of the validity of the provisions of subdivision 1 of § 105 and subdivision 2 of § 3022, barring employment to members of listed organizations. Here again constitutional doctrine has developed since *Adler*. Mere knowing membership without a specific intent to further the unlawful aims of an organization is not a constitutionally adequate basis for exclusion from such positions as those held by appellants.

In *Elfbrandt v. Russell*, we said, "Those who join an organization but do not share its unlawful purposes and who do not participate in its unlawful activities surely pose no threat, either as citizens or as public employees." We there struck down a statutorily required oath binding the state employee not to become a member of the Communist Party with knowledge of its unlawful purpose, on threat of discharge and perjury prosecution if the oath were violated. We found that "[a]ny lingering doubt that proscription of mere knowing membership, without any showing of 'specific intent,' would run afoul of the Constitution was set at rest by our decision in *Aptheker v. Secretary of State*."

These limitations clearly apply to a provision, like § 105, subd. 1(c), which blankets all state employees, regardless of the "sensitivity" of their positions. But even the Feinberg Law provision, applicable primarily to activities of teachers, who have captive audiences of young minds, are subject to these limitations in favor of freedom of expression and association; the stifling effect on the academic mind from curtailing freedom of association in such manner is manifest, and has been documented in recent studies. *Elfbrandt* and *Aptheker* state the governing standard: legislation which sanctions membership unaccompanied by specific intent to further the unlawful goals of the organization or which is not active membership violates constitutional limitations. . . .

We therefore hold that Civil Service Law § 105, subd. 1(c), and Education Law § 3022, subd. 2, are invalid insofar as they proscribe mere knowing membership without any showing of specific intent to further the unlawful aims of the Communist Party of the United States or of the State of New York. . . .

Notes

1. This case marked the demise of most efforts by states to check on teacher loyalty.

2. At what point does the legitimacy of New York, or any other state's interest in protecting its education system, end and the personal liberties of teachers begin?

[Case No. 76] Union Rights to Collect Dues from Non–Members

ABOOD v. DETROIT BOARD OF EDUCATION

Supreme Court of the United States, 1977.
431 U.S. 209, 97 S.Ct. 1782, 52 L.Ed.2d 261.

MR. JUSTICE STEWART delivered the opinion of the Court.

The State of Michigan has enacted legislation authorizing a system for union representation of local governmental employees. A union and a local government employer are specifically permitted to agree to an "agency shop" arrangement, whereby every employee represented by a union even though not a union member must pay to the union, as a condition of employment, a service fee equal in amount to union dues. The issue before us is whether this arrangement violates the constitutional rights of government employees who object to public-sector unions as such or to various union activities financed by the compulsory service fees.

I

After a secret ballot election, the Detroit Federation of Teachers (Union) was certified in 1967 pursuant to Michigan law as the exclusive representative of teachers employed by the Detroit Board of Education (Board). The Union and the Board thereafter concluded a collective-bargaining agreement effective from July 1, 1969, to July 1, 1971. Among the agreement's provisions was an "agency shop" clause, requiring every teacher who had not become a Union member within 60 days of hire (or within 60 days of January 26, 1970, the effective date of the clause) to pay the Union a service charge equal to the regular dues required of Union members. A teacher who failed to meet this obligation was subject to discharge. Nothing in the agreement, however, required any teacher to join the Union, espouse the cause of unionism, or participate in any other way in Union affairs.

On November 7, 1969 more than two months before the agency-shop clause was to become effective Christine Warczak and a number of other named teachers filed a class action in a state court, naming as defendants the Board, the Union, and several Union officials. Their complaint, as amended, alleged that they were unwilling or had refused to pay dues and that they opposed collective bargaining in the public sector. The amended complaint further alleged that the Union "carries on various social activities for the benefit of its members which are not available to non-members as a matter of right," and that the Union is engaged "in a number and variety of activities and programs which are economic, political, professional, scientific and religious in nature of which Plaintiffs do not approve, and in which they will have no voice, and which are not and will not be collective bargaining activities, i. e., the negotiation and administration of contracts with Defendant Board, and that a substantial part of the sums required to be paid under said Agency Shop Clause are used and will continue to be used for the support of such activities and programs, and not solely for the purpose of defraying the cost of Defendant Federation of its activities as bargaining agent for teachers employed by Defendant Board."

The complaint prayed that the agency-shop clause be declared invalid under state law and also under the United States Constitution as a deprivation of, inter alia, the plaintiffs' freedom of association protected by the First and Fourteenth Amendments, and for such further relief as might be deemed appropriate.

Upon the defendants' motion for summary judgment, the trial court dismissed the action for failure to state a claim upon which relief could be granted. The plaintiffs appealed, and while their appeal was pending the Michigan Supreme Court ruled in *Smigel v. Southgate Community School Dist.*, that state law prohibited an agency shop in the public sector. Accordingly, the judgment in the Warczak case was vacated and remanded to the trial court for further proceedings consistent with the *Smigel* decision.

Meanwhile, D. Louis Abood and other named teachers had filed a separate action in the same state trial court. The allegations in the complaint were virtually identical to those in Warczak and similar relief was requested. This second action was held in abeyance pending disposition of the Warczak appeal, and when that case was remanded the two cases were consolidated in the trial court for consideration of the defendants' renewed motion for summary judgment.

On November 5, 1973, that motion was granted. The trial court noted that following the Smigel decision, the Michigan Legislature had in 1973 amended its Public Employment Relations Act so as expressly to authorize an agency shop. This amendment was applied retroactively by the trial court to validate the agency-shop clause predating 1973 as a matter of state law, and the court ruled further that such a clause does not violate the Federal Constitution.

The plaintiffs' appeals were consolidated by the Michigan Court of Appeals, which ruled that the trial court had erred in giving retroactive application to the 1973 legislative amendment. The appellate court proceeded, however, to consider the constitutionality of the agency-shop clause, and upheld its facial validity on the authority of this Court's decision in *Railway Employes' Dept. v. Hanson* which upheld the constitutionality under the First Amendment of a union-shop clause, authorized by the Railway Labor Act, requiring financial support of the exclusive bargaining representative by every member of the bargaining unit. Noting, however, that Michigan law also permits union expenditures for legislative lobbying and in support of political candidates, the state appellate court identified an issue explicitly not considered in *Hanson* the constitutionality of using compulsory service charges to further "political purposes" unrelated to collective bargaining. Although recognizing that such expenditures "could violate plaintiffs' First and Fourteenth Amendment rights," the court read this Court's more recent decisions to require that an employee who seeks to vindicate such rights must "make known to the union those causes and candidates to which he objects." Since the complaints had failed to allege that any such notification had been given, the court held that the plaintiffs were not entitled to restitution of any portion of the service charges. The trial court's error on the retroactivity question, however, led the appellate court to reverse and remand the case. After the Supreme Court of Michigan denied review, the plaintiffs appealed to this Court, and we noted probable jurisdiction.

But both sides acknowledged in their briefs submitted to the Michigan Court of Appeals that a successor collective-bargaining agreement effective in 1973 contained substantially the identical agency-shop provision. The Court of Appeals appears to have taken judicial notice of this agreement in rendering its decision, for otherwise its ruling that the 1973 amendment was not retroactive would have disposed of the case without the need to consider any constitutional questions. Since the state appellate court considered the 1973 agreement to be part of the record in making its ruling, we proceed upon the same premise.

The fact that the 1973 agreement may have expired since the state appellate court rendered its decision does not affect the continuing vitality of this controversy for Art. III purposes. Some of the plaintiffs in both Warczak and Abood either refused to pay the service charge or paid it under protest. Their contention that they cannot constitutionally be compelled to contribute the service charge, or at least some portion of it, thus survives the expiration of the collective-bargaining agreement itself.

II

A

Consideration of the question whether an agency-shop provision in a collective-bargaining agreement covering governmental employees is, as such, constitutionally valid must begin with two cases in this Court that on their face go far toward resolving the issue. The cases are *Railway Employes' Dept. v. Hanson* ... and *Machinists v. Street*.

In the *Hanson* case a group of railroad employees brought an action in a Nebraska court to enjoin enforcement of a union-shop agreement. The challenged clause was authorized, and indeed shielded from any attempt by a State to prohibit it, by the Railway Labor Act. The trial court granted the relief requested. The Nebraska Supreme Court upheld the injunction on the ground that employees who disagreed with the objectives promoted by union expenditures were deprived of the freedom of association protected by the First Amendment. This Court agreed that "justiciable questions under the First and Fifth Amendments were presented," but reversed the judgment of the Nebraska Supreme Court on the merits....

The record in *Hanson* contained no evidence that union dues were used to force ideological conformity or otherwise to impair the free expression of employees, and the Court noted that "(i)f 'assessments' are in fact imposed for purposes not germane to collective bargaining, a different problem would be presented." But the Court squarely held that "the requirement for financial support of the collective-bargaining agency by all who receive the benefits of its work ... does not violate ... the First ... Amendmen(t)."

The Court faced a similar question several years later in the Street case, which also involved a challenge to the constitutionality of a union shop authorized by the Railway Labor Act. In Street, however, the record contained findings that the union treasury to which all employees were required to contribute had been used "to finance the campaigns of candidates for federal and state offices whom (the plaintiffs) opposed, and to promote the propagation of political and economic doctrines, concepts and ideologies with which (they) disagreed."

The Court recognized that these findings presented constitutional "questions of the utmost gravity" not decided in *Hanson*, and therefore considered whether the Act could fairly be construed to avoid these constitutional issues. The Court concluded that the Act could be so construed, since only expenditures related to the union's functions in negotiating and administering the collective-bargaining agreement and adjusting grievances and disputes fell within "the reasons ... accepted by Congress why authority to make union-shop agreements was justified." The Court ruled, therefore, that the use of compulsory union dues for political purposes violated the Act itself. Nonetheless, it found that an injunction against enforcement of the union-shop agreement as such was impermissible under *Hanson*, and remanded the case to the Supreme Court of Georgia so that a more limited remedy could be devised.

The holding in *Hanson*, as elaborated in *Street*, reflects familiar doctrines in the federal labor laws. The principle of exclusive union representation, which underlies the National Labor Relations Act as well as the Railway Labor Act, is a central element in the congressional structuring of industrial relations. The designation of a single representative avoids the confusion that would result from attempting to enforce two or more agreements specifying different terms and conditions of employment. It prevents inter-union rivalries from creating dissension within the work force and eliminating the advantages to the employee of collectivization. It also frees the employer from the possibility of facing conflicting demands from different unions, and permits the employer and a single union to reach agreements and settlements that are not subject to attack from rival labor organizations.

The designation of a union as exclusive representative carries with it great responsibilities. The tasks of negotiating and administering a collective-bargaining agreement and representing the interests of employees in settling disputes and processing grievances are continuing and difficult ones. They often entail expenditure of much time and money. The services of lawyers, expert negotiators, economists, and a research staff, as well as general administrative personnel, may be required. Moreover, in carrying out these duties, the union is obliged "fairly and equitably to represent all employees ..., union and non-union," within the relevant unit. A union-shop arrangement has been thought to distribute fairly the cost of these activities among those who benefit, and it counteracts the incentive that employees might otherwise have to become "free riders" to refuse to contribute to the union while obtaining benefits of union representation that necessarily accrue to all employees.

To compel employees financially to support their collective-bargaining representative has an impact upon their First Amendment interests. An employee may very well have ideological objections to a wide variety of activities undertaken by the union in its role as exclusive representative. His moral or religious views about the desirability of abortion may not square with the union's policy in negotiating a medical benefits plan. One individual might disagree with a union policy of negotiating limits on the right to strike, believing that to be the road to serfdom for the working class, while another might have economic or political objections to unionism itself. An employee might object to the union's wage policy because it violates guidelines designed to limit inflation, or might object to the union's seeking a clause in the collective-bargaining agreement proscribing racial discrimination. The examples could be multiplied. To be required to help finance the union as a collective-bargaining agent might well be thought, therefore, to interfere in some way with an employee's freedom to associate for the advancement of ideas, or to refrain from doing so, as he sees fit. But the judgment clearly made in *Hanson* and *Street* is that such interference as exists is constitutionally justified by the legislative assessment of the important contribution of the union shop to the system of labor relations established by Congress. "The furtherance of the common cause leaves some leeway for the leadership of the group. As long as they act to promote the cause which justified bringing the group together, the individual cannot withdraw his financial support merely because he disagrees with the group's strategy. If that were allowed, we would be reversing the Hanson case, sub silentio."

B

The National Labor Relations Act leaves regulation of the labor relations of state and local governments to the States. Michigan has chosen to establish for local government units a regulatory scheme which, although not identical in every respect to the NLRA or the Railway Labor Act, is broadly modeled after federal law. Under Michigan law employees of local government units enjoy rights parallel to those protected under federal legislation: the rights to self-organization and to bargain collectively,; and the right to secret-ballot representation elections,

Several aspects of Michigan law that mirror provisions of the Railway Labor Act are of particular importance here. A union that obtains the support of a majority of employees in the appropriate bargaining unit is designated the exclusive representative of those employees. A union so designated is under a duty of fair representation to all employees in the unit, whether or not union members. And in carrying out all of its various responsibilities, a recognized union may seek to have an agency-shop clause included in a collective-bargaining agreement. Indeed, the 1973 amendment to the Michigan Law was specifically designed to authorize agency shops in order that "employees in the bargaining unit ... share fairly in the financial support of their exclusive bargaining representative...."

The governmental interests advanced by the agency-shop provision in the Michigan statute are much the same as those promoted by similar provisions in federal labor law. The confusion and conflict that could arise if rival teachers' unions, holding quite different views as to the proper class hours, class sizes, holidays, tenure provisions, and grievance procedures, each sought to obtain the employer's agreement, are no different in kind from the evils that the exclusivity rule in the Railway Labor Act was designed to avoid. The desirability of labor peace is no less important in the public sector, nor is the risk of "free riders" any smaller.

Our province is not to judge the wisdom of Michigan's decision to authorize the agency shop in public employment. Rather, it is to adjudicate the constitutionality of that decision. The same important government interests recognized in the *Hanson* and *Street* cases presumptively support the impingement upon associational freedom created by the agency shop here at issue. Thus, insofar as the service charge is used to finance expenditures by the Union for the purposes of collective bargaining, contract administration, and grievance adjustment, those two decisions of this Court appear to require validation of the agency-shop agreement before us.

While recognizing the apparent precedential weight of the *Hanson* and *Street* cases, the appellants advance two reasons why those decisions should not control decision of the present case. First, the appellants note that it is government employment that is involved here, thus directly implicating constitutional guarantees, in contrast to the private employment that was the subject of the *Hanson* and *Street* decisions. Second, the appellants say that in the public sector collective bargaining itself is inherently "political," and that to require them to give financial support to it is to require the "ideological conformity" that the Court expressly found absent in the *Hanson* case.

Because it is employment by the State that is here involved, the appellants suggest that this case is governed by a long line of decisions holding that public employment cannot be conditioned upon the surrender of First Amendment rights. But, while the actions of public employers surely constitute "state action," the union shop, as authorized by the Railway Labor Act, also was found to result from governmental action in *Hanson*. The plaintiffs' claims in *Hanson* failed, not because there was no governmental action, but because there was no First Amendment violation. The appellants' reliance on the "unconstitutional conditions" doctrine is therefore misplaced.

The appellants' second argument is that in any event collective bargaining in the public sector is inherently "political" and thus requires a different result under the First and Fourteenth Amendments. This contention rests upon the important and often-noted differences in the nature of collective bargaining in the public and private sectors. A public employer, unlike his private counterpart, is not guided by the profit motive and constrained by the normal operation of the market. Municipal services are typically not priced, and where they are they tend to be regarded as in some sense "essential" and therefore are often price-inelastic. Although a public employer, like a private one, will wish to keep costs down, he lacks an important discipline against agreeing to increases in labor costs that in a market system would require price increases. A public-sector union is correspondingly less concerned that high prices due to costly wage demands will decrease output and hence employment.

The government officials making decisions as the public "employer" are less likely to act as a cohesive unit than are managers in private industry, in part because different levels of public authority department managers, budgetary officials, and legislative bodies are involved, and in part because each official may respond to a distinctive political constituency. And the ease of negotiating a final agreement with the union may be severely limited by statutory restrictions, by the need for the approval of a higher executive authority or a legislative body, or by the commitment of budgetary decisions of critical importance to others.

Finally, decision-making by a public employer is above all a political process. The officials who represent the public employer are ultimately responsible to the electorate, which for this purpose can be viewed as comprising three overlapping classes of voters taxpayers, users of particular government services, and government employees. Through exercise of their political influence as part of the electorate, the employees have the opportunity to affect the decisions of government representatives who sit on the other side of the bargaining table. Whether these representatives accede to a union's demands will depend upon a blend of political ingredients, including community sentiment about unionism generally and the involved union in particular, the degree of taxpayer resistance, and the views of voters as to the importance of the service involved and the relation between the demands and the quality of service. It is surely arguable, however, that permitting public employees to unionize and a union to bargain as their exclusive representative gives the employees more influence in the decision-making process than is possessed by employees similarly organized in the private sector.

The distinctive nature of public-sector bargaining has led to widespread discussion about the extent to which the law governing labor relations in the private sector provides an appropriate model. To take but one example, there has been considerable debate about the desirability of prohibiting public employee unions from striking, a step that the

State of Michigan itself has taken, But although Michigan has not adopted the federal model of labor relations in every respect, it has determined that labor stability will be served by a system of exclusive representation and the permissive use of an agency shop in public employment. As already stated, there can be no principled basis for according that decision less weight in the constitutional balance than was given in *Hanson* to the congressional judgment reflected in the Railway Labor Act. The only remaining constitutional inquiry evoked by the appellants' argument, therefore, is whether a public employee has a weightier First Amendment interest than a private employee in not being compelled to contribute to the costs of exclusive union representation. We think he does not.

Public employees are not basically different from private employees; on the whole, they have the same sort of skills, the same needs, and seek the same advantages. "The uniqueness of public employment is not in the employees nor in the work performed; the uniqueness is in the special character of the employer." The very real differences between exclusive-agent collective bargaining in the public and private sectors are not such as to work any greater infringement upon the First Amendment interests of public employees. A public employee who believes that a union representing him is urging a course that is unwise as a matter of public policy is not barred from expressing his viewpoint. Besides voting in accordance with his convictions, every public employee is largely free to express his views, in public or private orally or in writing. With some exceptions not pertinent here, public employees are free to participate in the full range of political activities open to other citizens. Indeed, just this Term we have held that the First and Fourteenth Amendments protect the right of a public school teacher to oppose, at a public school board meeting, a position advanced by the teachers' union. In so ruling we recognized that the principle of exclusivity cannot constitutionally be used to muzzle a public employee who, like any other citizen, might wish to express his view about governmental decisions concerning labor relations.

There can be no quarrel with the truism that because public employee unions attempt to influence governmental policymaking, their activities and the views of members who disagree with them may be properly termed political. But that characterization does not raise the ideas and beliefs of public employees onto a higher plane than the ideas and beliefs of private employees. It is no doubt true that a central purpose of the First Amendment " 'was to protect the free discussion of governmental affairs.' " But our cases have never suggested that expression about philosophical social, artistic, economic, literary, or ethical matters to take a nonexhaustive list of labels is not entitled to full First Amendment protection. Union members in both the public and private sectors may find that a variety of union activities conflict with their beliefs. Nothing in the First Amendment or our cases discussing its meaning makes the question whether the adjective "political" can properly be attached to those beliefs the critical constitutional inquiry.

The differences between public-and private-sector collective bargaining simply do not translate into differences in First Amendment rights. Even those commentators most acutely aware of the distinctive nature of public-sector bargaining and most seriously concerned with its policy implications agree that "(t)he union security issue in the public sector ... is fundamentally the same issue ... as in the private sector.... No special dimension results from the fact that a union represents public rather than private employees." We conclude that the Michigan Court of Appeals was correct in viewing this Court's decisions in Hanson and Street as controlling in the present case insofar as the service charges are applied to collective-bargaining, contract administration, and grievance-adjustment purposes.

C

Because the Michigan Court of Appeals ruled that state law "sanctions the use of non-union members' fees for purposes other than collective bargaining," and because the complaints allege that such expenditures were made, this case presents constitutional issues not decided in *Hanson* or *Street*. Indeed, Street embraced an interpretation of the Railway Labor Act not without its difficulties, precisely to avoid facing the constitutional issues presented by the use of union-shop dues for political and ideological purposes unrelated to collective bargaining. Since the state court's construction of the Michigan statute is authoritative, however, we must confront those issues in this case.

Our decisions establish with unmistakable clarity that the freedom of an individual to associate for the purpose of advancing beliefs and ideas is protected by the First and Fourteenth Amendments. Equally clear is the proposition that a government may not require an individual to relinquish rights guaranteed him by the First Amendment as a condition of public employment. The appellants argue that they fall within the protection of these cases because they have been prohibited, not from actively associating, but rather from refusing to associate. They specifically argue that they may constitutionally prevent the Union's spending a part of their required service fees to contribute to political candidates and to express political views unrelated to its duties as exclusive bargaining representative. We have concluded that this argument is a meritorious one.

One of the principles underlying the Court's decision in *Buckley v. Valeo* was that contributing to an organization for the purpose of spreading a political message is protected by the First Amendment. Because "(m)aking a contribution ... enables like-minded persons to pool their resources in furtherance of common political goals," the Court reasoned that limitations upon the freedom to contribute "implicate fundamental First Amendment interests."

The fact that the appellants are compelled to make, rather than prohibited from making, contributions for political purposes works no less an infringement of their constitutional rights. For at the heart of the First Amendment is the notion that an individual should be free to believe as he will, and that in a free society one's beliefs should be shaped by his mind and his conscience rather than coerced by the State. And the freedom of belief is no incidental or secondary aspect of the First Amendment's protections ...

These principles prohibit a State from compelling any individual to affirm his belief in God, or to associate with a political party, as a condition of retaining public employment. They are no less applicable to the case at bar, and they thus prohibit the appellees from requiring any of the appellants to contribute to the support of an ideological cause he may oppose as a condition of holding a job as a public school teacher.

We do not hold that a union cannot constitutionally spend funds for the expression of political views, on behalf of political candidates, or toward the advancement of other ideological causes not germane to its duties as collective-bargaining representative. Rather, the Constitution requires only that such expenditures be financed from charges, dues, or assessments paid by employees who do not object to advancing those ideas and who are not coerced into doing so against their will by the threat of loss of governmental employment.

There will, of course, be difficult problems in drawing lines between collective-bargaining activities, for which contributions may be compelled, and ideological activities unrelated to collective bargaining, for which such compulsion is prohibited.... We have no occasion in this case, however, to try to define such a dividing line. The case comes to us after a judgment on the pleadings, and there is no evidentiary record of any kind. The allegations in the complaints are general ones, and the parties have neither briefed nor argued the question of what specific Union activities in the present context properly fall under the definition of collective bargaining. The lack of factual concreteness and adversary presentation to aid us in approaching the difficult line-drawing questions highlights the importance of avoiding unnecessary decision of constitutional questions. All that we decide is that the general allegations in the complaints, if proved, establish a cause of action under the First and Fourteenth Amendments.

III

In determining what remedy will be appropriate if the appellants prove their allegations, the objective must be to devise a way of preventing compulsory subsidization of ideological activity by employees who object thereto without restricting the Union's ability to require every employee to contribute to the cost of collective-bargaining activities. This task is simplified by the guidance to be had from prior decisions. In *Street*, the plaintiffs had proved at trial that expenditures were being made for political purposes of various kinds, and the Court found those expenditures illegal under the Railway Labor Act. Moreover, in that case each plaintiff had "made known to the union representing his craft or class his dissent from the use of his money for political causes which he opposes." The Court found that "(i)n that circumstance, the respective unions were without power to use payments thereafter tendered by them for such political causes." Since, however, *Hanson* had established that the union-shop agreement was not unlawful as such, the Court held that to enjoin its enforcement would "(sweep) too broadly." The Court also found that an injunction prohibiting the union from expending dues for political purposes would be inappropriate, not only because of the basic policy reflected in the Norris–La Guardia Act against enjoining labor unions, but also because those union members who do wish part of their dues to be used for political purposes have a right to associate to that end "without being silenced by the dissenters."

After noting that "dissent is not to be presumed" and that only employees who have affirmatively made known to the union their opposition to political uses of their funds are entitled to relief, the Court sketched two possible remedies: First, "an injunction against expenditure for political causes opposed by each complaining employee of a sum, from those moneys to be spent by the union for political purposes, which is so much of the moneys exacted from him as is the proportion of the union's total expenditures made for such political activities to the union's total budget"; and second, restitution of a fraction of union dues paid equal to the fraction of total union expenditures that were made for political purposes opposed by the employee.

The Court again considered the remedial question in *Railway Clerks v. Allen*. In that case employees who had refused to pay union-shop dues obtained injunctive relief in state court against enforcement of the union-shop agreement. The employees had not notified the union prior to bringing the lawsuit of their opposition to political expenditures, and at trial, their testimony was principally that they opposed such expenditures, as a general matter. The Court held that the employees had adequately established their cause of action by manifesting "opposition to any political expenditures by the union" and that the requirement in Street that dissent be affirmatively indicated was satisfied by the allegations in the complaint that was filed. The Court indicated again the appropriateness of the two remedies sketched in Street; reversed the judgment affirming issuance of the injunction; and remanded for determination of which expenditures were properly to be characterized as political and what percentage of total union expenditures they constituted.

The Court in *Allen* described a "practical decree" that could properly be entered, providing for (1) the refund of a portion of the exacted funds in the proportion that union political expenditures bear to total union expenditures, and (2) the reduction of future exactions by the same proportion. Recognizing the difficulties posed by judicial administration of such a remedy, the Court also suggested that it would be highly desirable for unions to adopt a "voluntary plan by which dissenters would be afforded an internal union remedy." This last suggestion is particularly relevant to the case at bar, for the Union has adopted such a plan since the commencement of this litigation.

Although *Street* and *Allen* were concerned with statutory rather than constitutional violations, that difference surely could not justify any lesser relief in this case. Judged by the standards of those cases, the Michigan Court of Appeals' ruling that the appellants were entitled to no relief at this juncture was unduly restrictive. For all the reasons outlined in Street, the court was correct in denying the broad injunctive relief requested. But in holding that as a prerequisite to any relief each appellant must indicate to the Union the specific expenditures to which he objects, the Court of Appeals ignored the clear holding of *Allen*. As in *Allen*, the employees here indicated in their pleadings that they opposed ideological expenditures of any sort that are unrelated to collective bargaining. To require greater specificity would confront an individual employee with the dilemma of relinquishing either his right to withhold his support of ideological causes to which he objects or his freedom to maintain his own beliefs without public disclosure. It would also place on each employee the considerable burden of monitoring all of the numerous and shifting expenditures made by the Union that are unrelated to its duties as exclusive bargaining representative.

The Court of Appeals thus erred in holding that the plaintiffs are entitled to no relief if they can prove the allegations contained in their complaints, and in depriving them of an opportunity to establish their right to appropriate relief, such, for example, as the kind of remedies described in *Street* and *Allen*. In view of the newly adopted Union internal remedy, it may be appropriate under Michigan law, even if not strictly required by any doctrine of exhaustion of remedies, to defer further judicial proceedings pending the voluntary utilization by the parties of that internal remedy as a possible means of settling the dispute.

The judgment is vacated, and the case is remanded for further proceedings not inconsistent with this opinion.

It is so ordered.

Note

Are fair share fees fundamentally fair? Put another way, should teachers be required to pay such fees when they choose not to be union members?

[Case No. 77]   Arbitration in Public Sector Labor Contracts

IN RE BOARD OF EDUCATION OF WATERTOWN CITY SCHOOL

District v. Watertown Education Association.
Court of Appeals of New York, 1999.

688 N.Y.S.2d 463 [134 Educ. L. Rep. 984].

ROSENBLATT, J.:

The questions of law common to the two appeals before us involve public sector arbitration under the Taylor Law. In each appeal the ultimate question is whether the claimed grievance is arbitrable, but the cases raise broader concerns that involve presumptions relating to arbitrability in the public sector, the respective roles of courts and arbitrators, and an examination of this Court's decision in *Matter of Acting Supt. of Schools of Liverpool Cent. School District.*

The Watertown Dispute

In this litigation the Watertown City School District and the Watertown Education Association are opponents. The Association is the collective bargaining representative of teachers and other employees in the District. The parties entered into a collective bargaining agreement (CBA) that defined various terms and conditions of employment. It contained provisions relating to health insurance benefits that included the District's choice of insurance carriers and the percentage breakdown of premium costs allocable to the parties.

Shortly before the CBA went into effect, the District, along with other school districts (including Indian River, the district involved in the companion appeal), entered into a Municipal Cooperation Agreement to provide health insurance benefits for employees of participating districts. The insurance was provided through the Jefferson–Lewis Health Plan, an entity managed by a Board of Trustees comprised of the chief executive officers of the Plan participants, including the Watertown City School District and the Indian River Central School District. Subsequently, owing to financial considerations, the Plan raised the employees' co-payment cap. The Association filed a grievance alleging, in essence, that this change constituted an impermissible, unilateral reduction in employee benefits and a violation of the District's obligations under the CBA. After the District denied the grievance, the Association made a demand for arbitration, which the District then sought to stay, claiming that the dispute was not covered by the CBA. The Association cross-moved to compel arbitration.

The CBA contained a broad arbitration clause which provided that "any alleged violation of this Agreement, or any dispute with respect to its meaning or application" was arbitrable. Notwithstanding this language, Supreme Court ruled in favor of the District, granted its application for a stay, and denied the Association's cross-application to compel arbitration, holding that the parties had not agreed to arbitrate the dispute at issue. The Appellate Division affirmed, for reasons stated in the decision at Supreme Court.

The Indian River Dispute

This dispute is identical to Watertown. The parties are the School District and the Indian River Education Association (by its President). They entered into a CBA which contained a broad arbitration clause identical to the one in Watertown. The Indian River School District acquired health insurance coverage for its members under the same Municipal Cooperation Agreement as in Watertown. The Indian River CBA also contained a clause setting the percentage breakdown for health insurance premiums allocable to the parties. The case followed a procedural history similar to Watertown. Following the District's denial of the Association's grievance when the Plan raised the employees' co-payment, the Association sought arbitration, the District resisted it, and Supreme Court, in an order issued the same day as in Watertown, ruled with the District. It granted the District's application for a stay, and in language similar to its holding in Watertown, denied the Association's cross-application to compel arbitration. Supreme Court noted that in light of its decision it need not consider whether the Association failed to comply with a condition precedent to arbitration. The Appellate Division affirmed, without opinion, citing Watertown.

We reverse both Appellate Division orders and direct that both cases proceed to arbitration.

The Taylor Law

Based on their status as employee organizations and public employers, both parties couch their arguments in the context of the Taylor Law.

In 1967 the State Legislature enacted the Taylor Law, which governs labor relations in the public sector. It deals with rights and relationships involved in public employment, such as organizing, collective bargaining, the prohibition of strikes by public employees, and the creation of the Public Employment Relations Board. The Taylor Law contemplates two types of arbitration: compulsory and permissive. The former is found in Civil Service Law § 209 and involves what has been termed "interest arbitration." This deals, in essence, with terms and conditions of employment not previously agreed upon. Normally those disputed issues are settled by negotiation, but the Legislature provided that if an impasse occurs in collective negotiations involving public employees, the compulsory arbitration provisions of Civil Service Law § 209 come into play.

In addition to imposing these obligations, the Taylor Law permits public sector parties to submit CBA grievances to arbitration (Civil Service Law § 204). This species of arbitration-grievance arbitration-is at issue in this case. The question whether a particular grievance is arbitrable under the Taylor Law has occupied the courts of this State in scores of cases over the last three decades.

The Liverpool Two–Step Format

In 1977 this Court decided *Matter of Acting Sup. of Schools of Liverpool Cent. School Dist. [United Liverpool Faculty Assn.]*, which established criteria for determining whether and when a particular public sector grievance is subject to arbitration.

The Liverpool protocol entails a two-step inquiry. Initially the Court must determine whether arbitration claims with respect to the particular subject matter are authorized by the terms of the Taylor Law. The second step involves "a determination of whether such authority was in fact exercised and whether the parties did agree by the terms of their particular arbitration clause to refer their differences in this specific area to arbitration" Succinctly, the test centers on two distinct inquiries as to the public parties' purported entry into the arbitral forum: may they do so and, if yes, did they do so.

Liverpool's First Step

The first ("may-they-do-so") step calls for an examination, by the court, of the subject matter of the dispute. Drawing on earlier decisions that discussed the lawfully permissible scope of arbitrability, the Court in *Liverpool* pointed out that owing to public policy or to statutory or constitutional restrictions there are certain matters that are off-limits for arbitration. Although this inquiry deals with whether the parties may arbitrate, it typically involves an assertion by the public employer that it may not or should not lawfully submit itself to a particular grievance arbitration. The inquiry is less concerned with the wording of the parties' intent to arbitrate than with the lawfulness of that intent.

Commentators have described this concern as having been born of a number of factors, including a reluctance to deprive the government of what has been its ultimate decision-making prerogatives.

In the 22 years following *Liverpool*, however, this Court has over-whelmingly rejected contentions by public employers that particular issues fall outside the scope of permissible grievance arbitration . . . [examples omitted]

This is not to say that the concept of public policy (or statutory or constitutional) restrictions on public sector arbitration are extinct. To be sure, there are instances in which arbitration has been prohibited. . . . [examples omitted] Moreover, our courts have vacated arbitral awards or portions thereof as having been against public policy. . . . In all, however, the decisional law reflects the reality of greatly increased public sector arbitration, and its acceptance, compatible with the government's public policy concerns.

Liverpool's Second Step

If the first step is scaled, and the subject matter declared lawfully fit for arbitration, the Liverpool protocol next calls for a determination as to whether the parties agreed to arbitrate the grievance. The second ("did-they-do-so") step invokes the sort of conventional judicial analysis that is influenced by the wording of the CBA. Descending from the higher reaches of public policy, this step typically turns on drafting skills and language entirely within the control of the parties.

Here, too, in the vast majority of post-Liverpool cases, this Court has determined that the public sector parties had, by the broad arbitration clause language of the collective bargaining contracts, agreed to arbitrate the particular grievances involved . . . [examples omitted]

This case catalog is revealing. It not only speaks to the litigational aftermath of the two Liverpool steps, but also sheds light on an additional theme in Liverpool, notably, the approach in evaluating the intention of the parties with regard to public sector arbitration.

Liverpool and Presumptions Regarding Arbitrability

In 1960, 17 years before Liverpool, the United States Supreme Court decided United *Steelworkers of Am. v. Warrior & Gulf Nav. Co.*-a case that involved private sector parties and a Federal statute—in which it adopted a "presumption of arbitrability." The Supreme Court observed that the Federal Labor Management Relations Act was imbued with a congressional policy in favor of arbitration to resolve labor disputes and that courts should interpret arbitration clauses accordingly, "unless it may be said with positive assurance that the arbitration clause is not susceptible of an interpretation that covers the asserted dispute. Doubts should be resolved in favor of coverage." This has been a consistent theme in Federal labor law cases.

In pre-Liverpool cases that involved the application of Federal law, this Court applied the *Steelworkers* "presumption of arbitrability". Emphasizing, however, the relatively brief acquaintance that the State had with Taylor Law grievance arbitration, and lacking an adequate, reassuring experience, the Court, in Liverpool, expressed hesitancy over the prospect of prematurely expanding the arbitral portals in public sector cases.

In *Liverpool* the Court emphasized that arbitration did "not yet carry the same historical or general appearance" or "demonstration of efficacy" in the public sector as it did in the private sector. In the absence of unequivocal agreement to the contrary, it was to be taken that a public employer, being charged with nondelegable responsibilities, did not intend to arbitrate grievances.

That was 1977, and it epitomized a wait-and-see attitude. We have waited, and we have seen. Arbitration in the public arena is no longer unfamiliar or unaccepted. It is a reality, and it is widespread.

The enormous growth in the use of collective bargaining agreements has generated vast experience in drafting arbitration clauses. Public sector parties may now use phrases that have been litigated into familiarity. They are free to negotiate language that will define disputes in areas of the broadest permissible scope. Parties are likewise free to negotiate exclusions, and to word arbitration clauses with sufficient clarity for a court to be able to tell, on a threshold determination, whether they intended a permissible subject or type of dispute to be arbitrable or not.

Liverpool did not expressly create a "presumption" against public sector arbitrability. To the extent, however, that one may be implied or fairly so characterized, an anti-arbitrational presumption is no longer justified either in law, or in the public sector labor environment. The lengthy chronicle of this Court's cases after Liverpool proclaims as much, as does the huge increase of public sector arbitration over the last quarter century.

Liverpool's approach calls for a two-step analysis necessary in public sector arbitrations which, by its nature involves concerns of public policy not at issue in Steelworkers. We will stay with the Liverpool format because it has been workable for over two decades, with results that have largely comported with the Steelworkers presumption with respect to CBA interpretation. We will preserve the two-step *Liverpool* analysis for judicial threshold consideration, free of any presumptions.

Merits Considerations by The Courts

It is also clear that the merits of the grievance are not the courts' concern. Even an apparent weakness of the claimed grievance is not a factor in the court's threshold determination. It is the arbitrator who weighs the merits of the claim. CPLR 7501 explicitly provides: "In determining any matter arising under this article, the court shall not consider whether the claim with respect to which arbitration is sought is tenable, or otherwise pass upon the merits of the dispute." This was added by section 47 of chapter 532 of the Laws of 1963 for the purpose of abrogating what was left of the so-called *"Cutler–Hammer"* rule, in which our courts had taken a more expansive view of the merits, in determining arbitrability.

While some case records contain enough information for a court to make a penetrating analysis of the scope of the substantive provisions of the CBA, an undertaking of that kind is not the function of the court. A judicial inquiry of that sort would involve an inapt flirtation with the merits, or an inappropriate use of the judicial scalpel to split the hairs that mark the perimeters of the contractual provisions. History, legislation, and experience dictate that courts not revert to the business of merits inquiries of the kind that existed under the *Cutler–Hammer* doctrine before the enactment of CPLR 7501.

The "Reasonable Relationship" Test

In the two cases before us, there is no dispute as to the first step. Both sides have recognized the subject matter as arbitrable. As for the second step, the courts below assessed the Associations' claims and ruled that they were not arbitrable. In both cases, and in the face of broad arbitration clauses, they addressed the nature of the dispute, and, acting as would an arbitrator, interpreted the scope of the substantive provision of the contract. They then found the grievances to be outside of the parties' agreement to arbitrate. This was error. A court confronted with a contest of this kind should merely determine whether there is a reasonable relationship between the subject matter of the dispute and the general subject matter of the CBA. If there is none, the issue, as a matter of law, is not arbitrable. If there is, the court should rule the matter arbitrable, and the arbitrator will then make a more exacting interpretation of the precise scope of the substantive provisions of the CBA, and whether the subject matter of the dispute fits within them.

The parties in the cases before us chose to arbitrate any alleged violation of the CBA or any dispute with respect to its meaning or application. Given a clause of this breadth, and the presence of language dealing specifically with health insurance benefits, we determine that the reduction of benefits by increasing the employees' co-payments was an arbitrable issue. We reach this conclusion even though, as the District stresses, it was the Plan, a non-party, that reduced the benefits. The Districts assert that even though the Plan is governed by a Board of Trustees comprised of District CEOs, the Districts do not control the amount or type of health insurance benefits that the Plan provides. Whether this is so, and whether the District violated the CBA with regard to maintaining a certain level of benefits, is for the arbitrator.

We have considered Indian River Central School District's remaining argument in support of a stay of arbitration, and find it to be without merit.

Accordingly, in each proceeding, the order of the Appellate Division should be reversed, with costs, the petition to stay arbitration denied and the cross-application to compel arbitration granted.

Order reversed, with costs, petition to stay arbitration denied and cross application to compel arbitration granted.

Notes

1. New York's Taylor Law is one of the most comprehensive statutes dealing with public sector employment.

2. Is arbitration an appropriate vehicle for resolving labor disputes in education?

[Case No. 78]   Injunction against Teachers' Strike

TIMBERLANE REGIONAL SCHOOL DISTRICT v. TIMBERLANE REGIONAL EDUCATION ASSOCIATION

Supreme Court of New Hampshire, 1974.
317 A.2d 555.

KENISON, CHIEF JUSTICE. The major issue in this case is whether the presiding justice properly denied the plaintiff's petition to enjoin the defendants from engaging in or aiding and abetting a strike. . . .

The Timberlane Regional Education Association (hereinafter TREA) is the collective bargaining agent for some, if not all, of the teachers in the Timberlane Regional School District and is affiliated with the New Hampshire Education Association, whose membership consists of school teachers employed throughout the State. The TREA and the Timberlane Regional School Board (hereinafter board) agreed to meet during the spring and summer of 1973 for the purpose of negotiating a contract for the 1974–75 school year.

The board proceeded to hire a professional negotiator and delayed meeting with the TREA until July 31, 1973. The parties met throughout the fall and early winter and, by January 14, 1974, had reached a tentative agreement on approximately one-quarter of the items submitted for negotiation by the TREA. The majority of the remaining items, which included salary schedules, sick and emergency leave, teacher rights and responsibilities, teacher evaluation, academic freedom and grievance procedures, had been declared non-negotiable by the board. It became apparent that an impasse was developing in regard to these items, and the members of the TREA voted to submit their differences with the board to a mediator for resolution. The TREA contacted the Federal Mediation Service which agreed to undertake mediation if both parties so requested. The board, however, declined to accept this offer,

and several other attempts to find a mutually agreeable mediator came
to naught.

The parties resumed negotiations on February 15, 1974, and met
again on February 18, 20 and 23. These meetings resulted in a tentative
agreement on several of the remaining items, but their differences with
respect to great majority of these items were unresolved. During the
course of negotiations on February 23, 1974, the TREA discovered for
the first time that on February 16, 1974, the board had submitted salary
proposals to the budget committee, despite the fact that an agreement
had not been worked out between the parties on this matter. The board
then stated at the end of this session that it would go no further and
declined to negotiate on the evening of February 23, or at any time on
February 24, and 25, 1974.

The members of the TREA met on February 25, 1974, and voted to
call for mediation because of an impasse in negotiations and to refuse to
teach until mediation began. Last minute efforts to achieve compromise
between the positions of the parties came to no avail, and the strike
commenced on February 26, 1974. Approximately two-thirds of the
teaching staff in the district did not report to work, and pickets were set
up in the vicinity of the schools. The board was initially able to keep all
of the schools in the district open by hiring substitute teachers, and
student attendance did not drop appreciably. The board, however, was
ultimately forced to shut down the Timberlane Regional High and Junior
High Schools.

"[P]ublic employer collective bargaining is now an established fact
at the federal level and in the majority of state and local governments.
The transition from uniform disapproval to majority acceptance of public
employer collective bargaining began in 1955, when New Hampshire
adopted legislation authorizing town governments to engage in collective
bargaining with public employee unions." Nevertheless, in most jurisdictions, a strike by public employees is prohibited either by statute or by
judicial decision. New Hampshire is no exception to this rule, for this
court held in *Manchester v. Manchester Teachers Guild*, that such strikes
are illegal under the common law of this State and characterized this
prohibition as a matter of public policy solely within the province of the
legislature.

We are aware of the general dissatisfaction with the effect of this
prohibition on labor negotiations between government and public employees. In the private sector, the right to strike is viewed as an integral
part of the collective bargaining process. . . . In the public sector, however, the denial of the right to strike has the effect of heavily weighing the
collective bargaining process in favor of the government. Without legislation providing alternative methods for resolving impasses in negotiation,
there is no ultimate sanction available to the public employees for
compelling the good faith of the government, and as a consequence, the
only recourse available to them, if they are being treated unfairly, is to
terminate their employment or to engage in an illegal strike.

It is not a proper judicial function to make policy judgments as to the merits of providing public employees with the right to strike or of developing alternative processes such as compulsory mediation or arbitration to resolve government labor disputes. This decision must be made by the legislature.

However, in the absence of legislation, the courts are necessarily compelled to consider the problems inherent in labor relations between the government and public employees when called upon to issue an injunction to prevent an illegal strike. The injunction is an extraordinary remedy which is only granted under circumstances where a plaintiff has no adequate remedy at law and is likely to suffer irreparable harm unless the conduct of the defendant is enjoined. The availability of injunctive relief is a matter within the sound discretion of the court exercised on a consideration of all the circumstances of each case and controlled by established principles of equity.

In view of the nature of this remedy, a growing number of jurisdictions have applied equitable principles to deny the government the use of an injunction against illegal strikes by teachers unless there is a showing of irreparable harm to the public. One of the first cases in formulating this new approach was *School Dist. for Holland v. Holland Educ. Ass'n,* in which the Michigan Supreme Court indicated that the refusal of the government to bargain in good faith would be a factor of importance in the determination of whether or not to issue an injunction. This position was embraced by the Rhode Island Supreme Court in *School Committee of Westerly v. Westerly Teachers Ass'n, R.I.,* which held that an injunction would not issue "unless it clearly appears from specific facts ... that irreparable harm will result...."

We are persuaded by these recent developments that it would be detrimental to the smooth operation of the collective bargaining process to declare that an injunction should automatically issue where public teachers have gone on strike. The essence of the collective bargaining process is that the employer and the employees should work together in resolving problems relating to the employment. The courts should intervene in this process only where it is evident the parties are incapable of settling their disputes by negotiation or by alternative methods such as arbitration and mediation. Judicial interference at any earlier stage could make the courts "an unwitting third party at the bargaining table and a potential coercive force in the collective bargaining processes." Accordingly, it is our view that in deciding to withhold an injunction the trial court may properly consider among other factors whether recognized methods of settlement have failed, whether negotiations have been conducted in good faith, and whether the public health, safety and welfare will be substantially harmed if the strike is allowed to continue.

We have reviewed the ... record and are satisfied that the trial court took these matters into account in denying the injunction for the present. We agree ... that the parties had not yet exhausted the possibilities of finding compromise in the collective bargaining process at the time the injunction was refused....

Notes

1.   What are the pros and cons of granting public school teachers the right to strike? Are the arguments equally valid for public transportation workers, police, and/or firefighters?

2.   Can teachers bargain effectively if they have no right to call for a strike? Can school boards bargain effectively if they cannot respond with lockouts or close-downs?

3.   Do you agree with this court's position as to the proper role of the judiciary in connection with collective bargaining disputes involving public employees?

Chapter 11

TENURE, DISMISSAL, AND TEACHER RETIREMENT

Introduction

At common law, the authority of school boards to hire teachers and other employees includes the right to discharge staff subject to constitutional, statutory, or contractual constraints. Even absent express contractual provisions identifying grounds for which educators may be discharged, common law permits dismissals for sufficient cause. What constitutes sufficient cause is, of course, a question of fact on a case-by-case basis.

The fact that state statutes grant school boards the right to employ teachers does not confer on them the ability to act arbitrarily or capriciously. Teachers who comply with express and/or implied contractual conditions have the right to retain their jobs until their contracts expire or they retire. As such, it is important to keep in mind the critical distinction between school board decisions not to renew the expired contracts of untenured teachers and discharging tenured faculty members.

Insofar as this chapter focuses primarily on dismissals involving tenured teachers, it is important to recognize that boards can dismiss tenured staff under two broad categories, for cause and not for cause, the latter typically referred to as a reduction-in-force. After reviewing the significance and status of tenure statutes, this chapter examines legal issues surrounding the dismissal of teachers before considering their rights at retirement.

Tenure Statutes

Most states have enacted legislation granting school boards the non-delegable authority[1] to grant tenure,[2] sometimes referred to as continuing contract status,[3] to teachers. Further, some jurisdictions extend tenure rights to administrators[4] who meet statutory requirements by

1. *Remus v. Board of Educ. for Tonawanda City School Dist.*, 727 N.Y.S.2d 43 [155 Educ. L. Rep. 759] (N.Y.2001).

2. *See, e.g.*, ALASKA STAT. § 14.20.150; Cal. Educ. Code Ann. § 33123; Ga. Code Ann. § 20–2–242; 105 Ill. Comp. Stat. Ann. 5/2–3.47; Md. Code Ann. Educ. § 6–202; Mich. Comp. Laws Ann. § 38.91; Mont. Code Ann. § 20–6–711; N.J. Stat. Ann. § 18A:13–42; N.Y. Educ. Law § 3012–A; Tenn. Code Ann. § 49–2–203. *BUT SEE, E.G.*,

Ark. Code Ann. § 6–17–1503(B) ("THIS SUB-CHAPTER IS NOT A TEACHER TENURE LAW IN THAT IT DOES NOT CONFER LIFETIME APPOINTMENT OF TEACHERS").

3. *See, e.g.*, 105 ILL. COMP. STAT. ANN. 5/11D–10; IOWA CODE ANN. § 279.15; OHIO REV. CODE ANN. § 4419.09 (C); OKLA. STAT. ANN. TITLE 70 § 6–101.

4. *Nelson v. Board of Educ. of Township of Old Bridge*, 689 A.2d 1342 [116 Educ. L.

satisfactorily serving probationary periods.[5] Courts have long upheld the constitutionality of tenure laws,[6] acknowledging that they must be liberally construed in favor of educators since their purpose is to afford "protection [for] competent and qualified teachers in the security of their positions"[7] as well as to ensure them measures of protection from unjust dismissals.[8] To this end, courts tend to agree that educators do not waive their rights to tenure as teachers when they accept positions as administrators in the same district.[9]

In a case that it described as "highly unusual,"[10] an appellate court in New York affirmed that where a board granted a teacher tenure in an improper area, the remedy was to remit the case back to the board so that officials could examine her lesson plans, evaluations, and in-class work in order to reclassify her into an accepted tenure area rather than terminate her employment. However, the state's highest court affirmed that where a probationary teacher who admitted consuming alcoholic beverages with students while serving as a chaperone during an overseas exchange program rejected her superintendent's offer to extend her probationary period for an extra year because the effective date of tenure had not yet occurred, the board could rescind its conditional tenure appointment and terminate her contract without having to meet the statutory guidelines otherwise applicable to a formal dismissal.[11]

Insofar as boards can confer tenure only by taking affirmative actions,[12] courts are unwilling to grant tenure by default or estoppel.[13] In an illustrative case, an appellate court in California affirmed the denial of permanent status to a teacher who spent two years teaching under an emergency license.[14] The court agreed that state law was clear that time spent teaching under an emergency permit did not count toward perma-

---

Rep. 1062] (N.J.1997); *Bell v. Board of Educ. of Vestal Cent. School Dist.*, 472 N.Y.S.2d 899 [16 Educ. L. Rep. 894] (N.Y. 1984).

5. *Picogna v. Board of Educ. of Township of Cherry Hill*, 671 A.2d 1035 [107 Educ. L. Rep. 859] (N.J.1996).

6. *Teachers' Tenure Act Cases*, 197 A. 344 (Pa.1938); *State ex rel. Bishop v. Board of Educ.*, 40 N.E.2d 913 (Ohio 1942).

7. *Sherwood Nat'l Educ. Ass'n v. Sherwood–Cass R–VIII School Dist.*, 168 S.W.3d 456, 459–460 [201 Educ. L. Rep. 394] (Mo. Ct. App. 2005), *reh'g and/or transfer denied* (2005), *transfer denied* (2005).

8. *Palmer v. Louisiana State Bd. of Elementary and Secondary Educ.*, 842 So.2d 363 [175 Educ. L. Rep. 845] (La.2003); *State ex rel. Donah v. Windham Exempted Village School Dist. Bd. of Educ.*, 630 N.E.2d 687 [90 Educ. L. Rep. 367] (Ohio 1994).

9. *East Canton Educ. Ass'n. v. McIntosh*, 709 N.E.2d 468 [134 Educ. L. Rep. 284] (Ohio 1999). *But see Pittman v. Chicago Bd. of Educ.*, 64 F.3d 1098 [103 Educ. L.

Rep. 68] (7th Cir.1995), *cert. denied*, 517 U.S. 1243, 116 S.Ct. 2497, 135 L.Ed.2d 189 (1996).

10. *Abrantes v. Board of Educ. of Norwood–Norfolk Cent. School Dist.*, 649 N.Y.S.2d 957, 959 [114 Educ. L. Rep. 608] (N.Y.App.Div.1996), *leave to appeal denied*, 657 N.Y.S.2d 405 (N.Y. 1997).

11. *Remus v. Board of Educ. for Tonawanda City School Dist.*, 727 N.Y.S.2d 43 [155 Educ. L. Rep. 759] (N.Y.2001).

12. *Ray v. Board of Educ. of Oak Ridge Schools*, 72 S.W.3d 657 [164 Educ. L. Rep. 954] (Tenn. Ct.App.2001).

13. *Scheer v. Independent School Dist. No. I–26 of Ottawa County*, 948 P.2d 275 [122 Educ. L. Rep. 833] (Okla.1997); *Roese v. Board of Educ. of the S. Country Cent. School Dist.*, 724 N.Y.S.2d 501 [153 Educ. L. Rep. 950] (N.Y.App.Div. 2001); *Ray v. Board of Educ. of Oak Ridge Schools*, 72 S.W.3d 657 [164 Educ. L. Rep. 954] (Tenn. Ct.App.2001).

14. *Smith v. Governing Bd. of Elk Grove Unified School Dist.*, 16 Cal.Rptr.3d nent status, except for teachers who were credentialed in other states. The court refused to intercede on behalf of the teacher and grant her tenure by estoppel since board officials had not misled her about the effect of teaching under an emergency permit. Yet, where state law imposes statutory requirements such as notice, they are construed strictly against boards and have resulted in teachers being awarded tenure because school officials failed to follow the law.[15]

The general rule is that tenure statutes cover only those positions that are explicitly identified.[16] Strict construction of tenure statutes is evident in judicial refusal to extend their protection to supplementary positions such as coaching.[17] Accordingly, when coaches are relieved of their duties but do not suffer the loss of tenure, courts are unwilling to intervene on their behalf.[18]

In *State ex rel. Anderson v. Brand (Brand)*, the Supreme Court held that a state may make tenure contractual rather than place it on legislative status.[19] The Court refused to allow a board in Indiana to repudiate a teacher's tenure where an unusually worded statute was repealed after she acquired tenure. In upholding the teacher's right to tenure, the Court suggested that the legislature could have changed the statute for prospective employees but not for those who were already covered by its original provisions.

Courts generally uphold legislative authority to change tenure laws based on the rationale that states cannot permanently bind themselves to specific employment practices.[20] In such a case, the Supreme Court of Illinois upheld the legislature's elimination of tenure for principals in Chicago.[21] In a related dispute, the Seventh Circuit, echoing the Supreme Court's analysis in *Brand*, agreed that a legislature could rescind tenure even if it meant that principals who were returned to the least senior positions on the list of tenured teachers might lose their jobs.[22]

To the extent that statutes typically require teachers to work full-time for set periods of time, typically three or four years, before becoming eligible for tenure, questions arise about substitutes. As with many areas, the courts reached mixed results. On the one hand, courts are

---

1 [189 Educ. L. Rep. 814] (Cal. Ct. App. 2004), *review denied* (2004).

15. *Farrington v. School Comm. of Cambridge*, 415 N.E.2d 211 (Mass.1981).

16. *Frye v. Independent School Dist. No. 625*, 494 N.W.2d 466 [80 Educ. L. Rep. 210] (Minn.1992); *Franson v. Bald Eagle Area School Dist.*, 668 A.2d 633 [105 Educ. L. Rep. 1125] (Pa.Cmwlth. Ct.1995), *appeal denied*, 677 A.2d 840 (Pa.1996).

17. *Davis v. Russell*, 852 So.2d 774 [180 Educ. L. Rep. 963] (Ala. Civ. App. 2002).

18. *Kingsford v. Salt Lake City School Dist.*, 247 F.3d 1123 [153 Educ. L. Rep. 68] (10th Cir. 2001); *Campbell v. Talladega City Bd. of Educ.*, 628 So.2d 842 [88 Educ. L. Rep. 516] (Ala. Civ.App.1993); *Lagos v.*

Modesto City Schools Dist., 843 F.2d 347 [46 Educ. L. Rep. 60] (9th Cir.1988), *cert. denied*, 488 U.S. 926, 109 S.Ct. 309, 102 L.Ed.2d 328 (1988). [Case No. 79]

19. 303 U.S. 95, 58 S.Ct. 443, 82 L.Ed. 685 (1938).

20. *Morgan v. Potter*, 298 N.W. 763 (Wis.1941). *See also Phelps v. Board of Educ.*, 300 U.S. 319, 57 S.Ct. 483, 81 L.Ed. 674 (1937).

21. *Fumarolo v. Chicago Bd. of Educ.*, 566 N.E.2d 1283 [65 Educ. L. Rep. 1181] (Ill.1990).

22. *Pittman v. Chicago Bd. of Educ.*, 64 F.3d 1098 [103 Educ. L. Rep. 68] (7th Cir.

reluctant to permit short-term service as substitutes[23] or time spent working under emergency status[24] to be credited toward meeting probationary periods prior to acquiring tenure. Other courts made exceptions and took time spent as substitutes into consideration if educators rendered substantial service.[25] In one case, the Supreme Court of Missouri affirmed that since an amendment to the state tenure law permitted a part-time teacher to accrue credit toward permanent status on a prorated basis, she was entitled to a permanent contract.[26]

Teacher Discharge

Discharge for Cause Generally

Insofar as tenure statutes provide that teacher contracts continue without the need for express renewals, boards must follow specified procedures when they wish to terminate the employment of tenured teachers. While procedures vary widely from one jurisdiction to another, they involve three basic elements: timely notice that dismissal is being contemplated, specification of charges, and a hearing at which the allegations are examined and a judgment rendered on the record regarding a teacher's future employment. Most statutes also include provisions for appeals that often culminate in judicial review.

Tenure statutes typically provide that tenured teachers may be dismissed on specified grounds. Conversely, teachers who have not earned tenure can have their employment terminated for any lawful reason[27] without hearings.[28] Recognizing that states employ a variety of terms for the same topics, the three sometimes overlapping grounds for which teachers can be dismissed for cause are insubordination, conduct unbecoming a professional, and incompetence. The overlapping nature of these bases for dismissal aside, when boards review specific charges, they cannot act on any others unless there is a phrase such as "other good and just cause" in the applicable statute. Although some states also include the catch-all phrase "other good and just cause," described by an appellate court in Colorado as any action that "... includes any cause

1995), *cert. denied*, 517 U.S. 1243, 116 S.Ct. 2497, 135 L.Ed.2d 189 (1996).

23. *Reis v. Biggs Unified School Dist.*, 24 Cal.Rptr.3d 393 [195 Educ. L. Rep. 261] (Cal. Ct. App. 2005); *Zalac v. Governing Bd. of Ferndale Unified School Dist.*, 120 Cal. Rptr.2d 615 [165 Educ. L. Rep. 277] (Cal. Ct.App.2002); *Emanuel v. Independent School Dist. No. 273, Edina School Dist.*, 615 N.W.2d 415 [146 Educ. L. Rep. 860] (Minn.Ct.App.2000); *Bochner v. Providence School Comm.*, 490 A.2d 37 [24 Educ. L. Rep. 294] (R.I.1985). For older cases, *see Tyler v. School Dist. No. 1, City and County of Denver*, 493 P.2d 22 (Colo.1972); *Hudson v. Independent School Dist. No. 77*, 258 N.W.2d 594 (Minn.1977).

24. *Smith v. Governing Bd. of Elk Grove Unified Sch. Dist.*, 16 Cal.Rptr.3d 1

[189 Educ. L. Rep. 814] (Cal. Ct. App. 2004), *reh'g and review denied* (2004).

25. *Harkins v. Ohio County Bd. of Educ.*, 369 S.E.2d 224 [47 Educ. L. Rep. 347] (W.Va.1988).

26. *Dial v. Lathrop R–II School Dist.*, 871 S.W.2d 444 [89 Educ. L. Rep. 1033] (Mo.1994).

27. *Shiers v. Richland Parish School Bd.*, 902 So.2d 1173 [198 Educ. L. Rep. 1009] (La. Ct. App. 2005), *writ denied*, 916 So.2d 1066 (La. 2005); *Haviland v. Yonkers Pub. Schools*, 800 N.Y.S.2d 578 [201 Educ. L. Rep. 667] (N.Y. App. Div. 2005).

28. *Von Gizycki v. Levy*, 771 N.Y.S.2d 174 [185 Educ. L. Rep. 325] (N.Y. App. Div. 2004).

bearing a reasonable relationship to a teacher's fitness to discharge her duties,"[29] this review focuses on the three major categories that are present in most laws.

State legislatures retain the authority to enumerate the grounds for which tenured teachers may be discharged. To this end, local boards may not add reasons of their own choosing. Even so, from a practical point of view, most courts give broad interpretations to such words as incompetence, immorality, and conduct unbecoming a teacher. Moreover, since teachers cannot be disciplined for exercising their constitutional rights such as First Amendment guarantees, this heading includes a section on their rights to free speech.

Tenure statutes, local board policies, and collective bargaining agreements often provide for warnings before serious disciplinary actions can be imposed on teachers who engaged in remediable offenses. Absent specific remediation provisions, boards are under no obligation to warn teachers and to offer them opportunities to correct their behavior.[30] In considering whether misconduct is remediable, an appellate court in Illinois applied a two-part test in explaining that the issue is whether a teacher's conduct "(1) has caused significant damage to students, the faculty, or the school and (2) could not have been corrected even if superiors had given the teacher the statutorily prescribed warning."[31] The court decided that since a tenured teacher's refusal to accept a classroom assignment was irremediable, the board could terminate his contract. Where courts are convinced that misconduct can be corrected or punishments are disproportionate to offenses, they typically provide teachers with opportunities to improve.[32]

As reflected by a case from New York, criminal conduct is treated as irremediable per se.[33] An appellate court thus vacated that part of an arbitration award that would have reinstated a dean of students who was guilty of drug possession if he successfully completed a treatment program.[34] The court maintained that the order was irrational and defied common sense since it would have returned the dean to a position administering a program that was designed to discourage students from using drugs.

Insubordination

In order to be subject to charges of insubordination, teachers must intentionally fail to comply with legitimate orders of supervisors or with

29. *Fredrickson v. Denver Pub. School Dist.*, 819 P.2d 1068, 1073 [71 Educ. L. Rep. 274] (Colo.Ct.App.1991). *See also Spurlock v. Board of Trustees, Carbon County School Dist. No. 1*, 699 P.2d 270 [25 Educ. L. Rep. 577] (Wyo.1985).

30. *Roberts v. Lincoln County School Dist. No. One*, 676 P.2d 577 [16 Educ. L. Rep. 331] (Wyo.1984).

31. *Board of Educ. of City of Chicago v. Harris*, 578 N.E.2d 1244, 1248 [70 Educ. L. Rep. 156] (Ill.App.Ct.1991), *appeal denied*, 584 N.E.2d 126 (Ill.1991).

32. *See, e.g., Hall v. Board of Trustees of Sumter County School Dist. No. 2*, 499 S.E.2d 216 [125 Educ. L. Rep. 1362] (S.C.Ct.App.1998); *Smith v. Board of Educ., Onteora Cent. School Dist.*, 633 N.Y.S.2d 625 [104 Educ. L. Rep. 1279] (N.Y.App.Div. 1995), *leave to appeal denied*, 642 N.Y.S.2d 858 (N.Y.1996).

33. *McBroom v. Board of Educ., Dist. No. 205*, 494 N.E.2d 1191 [33 Educ. L. Rep. 404] (Ill. App.Ct.1986).

34. *City School Dist. of City of N.Y. v. Campbell*, 798 N.Y.S.2d 54 [199 Educ. L. Rep. 908] (N.Y. App. Div. 2005).

valid rules and regulations of which they were, or reasonably should have been, aware.[35] The Supreme Court of Tennessee, for example, reasoned that a teacher could not be discharged for failing to return to duty when her superintendent ordered her to do so where she was medically unable to work due to stress, fear, and intimidation after a star basketball player failed her class.[36]

When teachers are unaware of rules, or rules are unreasonable, courts agree that educators cannot be dismissed for insubordination. In such a case, an appellate court in Illinois affirmed that a board could not dismiss a tenured teacher for scheduling a vacation during a winter break that the board cancelled due to a strike since she and others were unaware of this ad hoc rule.[37] While some courts think that a single incident can justify a dismissal for insubordination,[38] others disagree, declaring that a teacher must engage in persistent or continuing behavior.[39]

While teachers have been dismissed for insubordination for an array of reasons, four areas stand out: discipline, corporal punishment, sexual misconduct with students, and refusal to comply with legitimate instructional methodologies and policies, including evaluations. Each of these topics is now explored in some detail.

Discipline: Courts addressed a variety of claims wherein teachers faced sanctions for alleged violations of state law and/or board policy when disciplining students. Where state law forbade cruelty to students, an appellate court in Illinois upheld a teacher's dismissal for using a cattle prod on a student since it was satisfied that this behavior met the statutory definition.[40] Further, an appellate court in Louisiana upheld a teacher's dismissal for brandishing a starter pistol to gain control over several hostile students in positing that this was unacceptable conduct.[41] Similarly, an appellate court in Alabama upheld the dismissal of a teacher-principal who fired a shot into a floor as a scare tactic to break up a fight where board policy prohibited staff members from bringing firearms on to school property.[42] On the other hand, where a teacher in

35. *Sims v. Board of Trustees, Holly Springs, Mun. Separate School Dist.*, 414 So.2d 431 [4 Educ. L. Rep. 933] (Miss.1982).

36. *McGhee v. Miller*, 753 S.W.2d 354 [47 Educ. L. Rep. 1228] (Tenn.1988), *appeal after remand*, 785 S.W.2d 817 [59 Educ. L. Rep. 567] (Tenn.1990), *appeal after remand*, 837 S.W.2d 596 [78 Educ. L. Rep. 156] (Tenn.1992).

37. *Board of Educ. of Round Lake Area Schools v. Community Unit School Dist. No. 116*, 685 N.E.2d 412 [121 Educ. L. Rep. 821] (Ill.App.Ct.1997).

38. *Ware v. Morgan County School Dist. No. RE–3*, 748 P.2d 1295 [44 Educ. L. Rep. 778] (Colo.1988); *Hall v. Board of Trustees of Sumter County School Dist. No. 2*, 499

S.E.2d 216 [125 Educ. L. Rep. 1362] (S.C.Ct.App.1998).

39. *Sims v. Board of Trustees, Holly Springs, Mun. Separate School Dist.*, 414 So.2d 431 [4 Educ. L. Rep. 933] (Miss.1982).

40. *Rolando v. School Directors of Dist. No. 125, LaSalle County*, 358 N.E.2d 945 (Ill.App.Ct. 1976).

41. *Myres v. Orleans Parish School Bd.*, 423 So.2d 1303 [8 Educ. L. Rep. 545] (La. Ct.App. 1982), *writ denied*, 430 So.2d 657 (La.1983), *reconsideration denied*, 433 So.2d 155 (La.1983).

42. *Burton v. Alabama State Tenure Comm'n*, 601 So.2d 113 [76 Educ. L. Rep. 293] (Ala.Civ. App.1992).

Louisiana was seriously threatened by a student who was armed with a large board, an appellate court believed that since he acted reasonably in getting a gun from his car in order to protect himself when pursued, he should not have lost his job.[43]

Corporal punishment: Not surprisingly, the use of corporal punishment or physical force has generated controversy. Where a primary school music teacher disregarded express directives from supervisors about the use of force in class and intentionally hit or tapped a student on the hand with a three-foot pointer, the Supreme Court of Colorado agreed that her school board could dismiss her for insubordination.[44] In like fashion, an appellate court in Tennessee affirmed the dismissal of a third-grade teacher who slapped students, placed her hands on their faces to get them to pay attention, and hit them on their heads with a soft-cover textbook.[45] The court agreed that the teacher was insubordinate because she failed to follow instructions from her principal and assistant principal to refrain from placing her hands on any of her students.

On the other hand, an appellate court in Colorado rejected a board's attempt to dismiss a tenured teacher who refused to comply with a principal's directive not to ever touch a student physically for disciplinary reasons.[46] The court pointed out that the teacher was not insubordinate when she intervened to stop two children who struck her while disrupting class because the principal's order would have unequivocally divested her of authority that she had pursuant to board policy. Moreover, the Supreme Court of Alabama ordered the reinstatement of a teacher who was about to be dismissed for using corporal punishment.[47] The court disagreed with the board's assessment that the teacher should have been dismissed when, in response to a disrespectful gesture from a student whom others described as difficult, she tapped him on the face. Subsequently, an appellate court in New York affirmed that in the face of insufficient evidence to support a finding that a teacher improperly used physical force against a student in violation of state regulations, the penalty of dismissal was excessive and shocking to one's conscience.[48]

Sexual misconduct with students: It almost goes without saying that any time teachers engage in sexual conduct with students, they also violate board policies against sexual harassment, a topic explored later in this section and in more detail in Chapter 13. Even so, it is worth noting that courts have upheld the dismissals of teachers for insubordination in

---

43. *Landry v. Ascension Parish School Bd.*, 415 So.2d 473 [4 Educ. L. Rep. 1361] (La.Ct.App. 1982), *writ denied*, 420 So.2d 448 (La.1982).

44. *Board of Educ. of West Yuma School Dist. RJ–1 v. Flaming*, 938 P.2d 151 [118 Educ. L. Rep. 1202] (Colo.1997).

45. *Ketchersid v. Rhea County Bd. of Educ.*, 174 S.W.3d 163 [203 Educ. L. Rep. 423] (Tenn. Ct. App. 2005), *appeal denied* (Tenn. 2005) (also affirming that the teacher was incompetent and inefficient).

46. *Fredrickson v. Denver Pub. School Dist.*, 819 P.2d 1068 [71 Educ. L. Rep. 274] (Colo.Ct.App.1991).

47. *Ex parte Alabama State Tenure Comm'n*, 555 So.2d 1071 [58 Educ. L. Rep. 841] (Ala.1989), *on remand*, 555 So.2d 1075 [58 Educ. L. Rep. 845] (Ala. Civ. App. 1989).

48. *Weinstein v. Department of Educ. of City of N.Y.*, 798 N.Y.S.2d 383 [199 Educ. L. Rep. 916] (N.Y. App. Div. 2005).

a variety of settings involving sexual overtones such as where they spanked female teenagers and discussed matters of an explicitly sexual nature with them,[49] made sexually suggestive statements in class,[50] used sexually explicit materials,[51] and touched female students when explicitly warned not to do so.[52] In addition, an appellate court in Arizona upheld a male teacher's dismissal for insubordination for lying and for refusing to cooperate with his school board's investigation of the relationship he had with a seventeen-year-old student.[53] In like manner, the Sixth Circuit affirmed that a school board in Michigan could deny tenure to a female high school physical education teacher who had a sexual relationship with a student within nine months after the latter graduated.[54] The court observed that the teacher repeatedly denied that she engaged in improper conduct with the student despite evidence to the contrary.

Instructional issues: An older case from the First Circuit illustrates difficulties that can arise when teachers seek to use ideas or language that may be offensive to others. After a teacher in Massachusetts assigned an article for classroom discussion that a psychiatrist wrote for a reputable publication that included a term, offensive to many, for an incestuous son, the court decreed that he could not lose his job for insubordination.[55] Although conceding that some regulation of classroom speech is proper, the court found that it was inappropriate to discipline the teacher not only because he had insufficient notice that he could not use such material but also since the word appeared in at least five books in the library.[56] The Supreme Court of California was also of the opinion that a teacher could not be dismissed for reading a story in class that he wrote and that contained language objectionable to school officials.[57] The court determined that the reading was only a single incident and that it was done in good faith as a teaching technique that was not barred by any school rule. Conversely, the Seventh Circuit upheld the dismissal of a teacher for distributing brochures to eighth-grade students referring to the pleasures of marijuana use and encouraging them to free themselves of the moral environment of their home lives and experience a new sense of love and community.[58]

Courts support the notion that certain classroom behavior is so clearly improper that boards need no specific rules before disciplining

---

49. *Penn-Delco School Dist. v. Urso*, 382 A.2d 162 (Pa.Cmwlth.Ct.1978).

50. *Simon v. Jefferson Davis Parish School Bd.*, 289 So.2d 511 (La.Ct.App.1974); *Pryse v. Yakima School Dist. No. 7*, 632 P.2d 60 (Wash.Ct.App.1981).

51. *Bernstein v. Norwich City School Dist. Bd of Educ.*, 726 N.Y.S.2d 474 [154 Educ. L. Rep. 916] (N.Y.App.Div.2001).

52. *Forte v. Mills*, 672 N.Y.S.2d 497 [126 Educ. L. Rep. 362] (N.Y.App.Div.1998).

53. *Welch v. Board of Educ. of Chandler Unified School Dist. No. 80 of Maricopa County*, 667 P.2d 746 [12 Educ. L. Rep. 1290] (Ariz.Ct.App.1983).

54. *Flaskamp v. Dearborn Pub. Schools*, 385 F.3d 935 [192 Educ. L. Rep. 359] (6th Cir. 2004).

55. *Keefe v. Geanakos*, 418 F.2d 359 (1st Cir.1969).

56. *See also Mailloux v. Kiley*, 448 F.2d 1242 (1st Cir.1971).

57. *Lindros v. Governing Bd. of Torrance Unified School Dist.*, 510 P.2d 361 (Cal.1973), *cert. denied*, 414 U.S. 1112, 94 S.Ct. 842, 38 L.Ed.2d 739 (1973).

58. *Brubaker v. Board of Educ., School Dist. 149, Cook County, Ill.*, 502 F.2d 973 (7th Cir.1974), *cert. denied*, 421 U.S. 965, 95 S.Ct. 1953, 44 L.Ed.2d 451 (1975).

teachers. The Sixth Circuit agreed that a school board in Kentucky could dismiss a tenured teacher for insubordination after she showed a violent and sexually suggestive movie, the content of which she never previewed or discussed, since it did not contain a proper educational purpose.[59] The court rejected the teacher's claim that she engaged in protected First Amendment speech which others sometimes rely on in alleging that they have rights to academic freedom.[60] In another academic matter, an appellate court in Arkansas affirmed that even absent a specific prohibition, a teacher could be dismissed for unprofessional conduct when she offered to, but did not, sell raffle tickets to students in return for higher grades.[61] Further, an appellate court in New York upheld a teacher's dismissal for unprofessional conduct when she improperly disclosed words on a standard achievement test to her students.[62]

Courts tend to be unresponsive to claims of academic freedom when teachers are charged with insubordination and/or inefficiency. Courts rendered judgments against teachers who refused to follow directions with regard to curricular activities,[63] course content,[64] supplemental reading materials,[65] and the teaching of any subject having to do with love of country, the flag, or other patriotic matters.[66] Courts also limited the ability of teachers to vent, or expound on their personal views, whether speaking against the police following an automobile accident[67] or where proselytizing[68] or praying out loud in class.[69]

Policies on student assessments and grading are integral to school operations. Although teachers assign grades, their power may be subject to some restrictions. The courts seem to agree that teachers can be required to conform to reasonable rules and be evaluated on this aspect of their jobs.[70] In one case, West Virginia's highest court ascertained that

59. *Fowler v. Board of Educ. of Lincoln County, Ky.*, 819 F.2d 657 [39 Educ. L. Rep. 1011] (6th Cir.1987), *cert. denied*, 484 U.S. 986, 108 S.Ct. 502, 98 L.Ed.2d 501 [43 Educ. L. Rep. 21] (1987).

60. *See also Krizek v. Board of Educ. of Cicero–Stickney Township High School Dist. No. 201, Cook County*, 713 F.Supp. 1131 [54 Educ. L. Rep. 491] (N.D.Ill.1989) (involving a non-tenured teacher).

61. *Gatewood v. Little Rock Pub. Schools*, 616 S.W.2d 784 (Ark.Ct.App.1981).

62. *Altsheler v. Board of Educ. of Great Neck Union Free School Dist.*, 476 N.Y.S.2d 281 [17 Educ. L. Rep. 1199] (N.Y.1984), *reargument dismissed*, 483 N.Y.S.2d 1026 [22 Educ. L. Rep. 1237] (N.Y.1984).

63. *In re Proposed Termination of James E. Johnson's Teaching Contract with Indep. School Dist. No. 709*, 451 N.W.2d 343 [58 Educ. L. Rep. 1031] (Minn.Ct.App. 1990).

64. *Bradley v. Pittsburgh Bd. of Educ.*, 910 F.2d 1172 [62 Educ. L. Rep. 426] (3d Cir.1990).

65. *Kirkland v. Northside Indep. School Dist.*, 890 F.2d 794 [57 Educ. L. Rep. 396] (5th Cir.1989), *cert. denied*, 496 U.S. 926, 110 S.Ct. 2620, 110 L.Ed.2d 641 (1990).

66. *Palmer v. Board of Educ. of City of Chicago*, 603 F.2d 1271 (7th Cir.1979), *cert. denied*, 444 U.S. 1026, 100 S.Ct. 689, 62 L.Ed.2d 659 (1980).

67. *Petrie v. Forest Hills School Dist. Bd. of Educ.*, 449 N.E.2d 786 [11 Educ. L. Rep. 618] (Ohio Ct.App.1982).

68. *La Rocca v. Board of Educ. of Rye City School Dist.*, 406 N.Y.S.2d 348 (N.Y.App.Div. 1978), *appeal denied*, 413 N.Y.S.2d 1025 (N.Y.1978), *appeal dismissed*, 413 N.Y.S.2d 1030 (N.Y.1978).

69. *Fink v. Board of Educ. of Warren County School Dist.*, 442 A.2d 837 [3 Educ. L. Rep. 105] (Pa.Cmwlth.Ct.1982), *appeal dismissed*, 460 U.S. 1048, 103 S.Ct. 1493, 75 L.Ed.2d 927 [19 Educ. L. Rep. 21] (1983).

70. *Brown v. Wood County Bd. of Educ.*, 400 S.E.2d 213 [65 Educ. L. Rep. 608] (W.Va.1990).

an administrator's merely asking a teacher to re-evaluate a grade did not raise constitutional issues.[71]

Courts upheld the dismissals of tenured teachers for insubordination where individuals refused to follow directives not to leave classes unattended,[72] teach in a separate school for part of a day,[73] sign a supplement to a contract containing excerpts of board policies,[74] comply with guidelines to make timely reports on lost books and to retain final examinations,[75] obey rules such as getting approval for specified articles to appear in a school newspaper,[76] refuse to accept a student into a class,[77] perform hall duty,[78] accept an assignment in one's tenured area but in a different school,[79] implement a professional growth plan,[80] and turn in lesson plans.[81]

On the other hand, courts refuted board attempts to dismiss teachers for insubordination where individuals refused to submit to a psychological examination not required by law for reinstatement;[82] took time off from work due to the illness, and eventual death, of her mother;[83] refused to request unpaid medical leave of absence for evaluating her psychological fitness since her wait for a dismissal hearing at which to defend herself was proper exercise of her procedural rights;[84] and where a board, rather than a hearing officer, terminated a teacher's contract.[85]

Incompetence/Neglect of Duty

Incompetence, also sometimes referred to as neglect of duty, is a ground for dismissal in common law[86] as well as under most statutes. Abstractly, incompetence is a term of art lacking a precise definition that has been given a variety of meanings extending far beyond those related

71. *Meckley v. Kanawha County Bd. of Educ.*, 383 S.E.2d 839 [56 Educ. L. Rep. 328] (W.Va. 1989).

72. *Robbins v. Board of Educ. of Argo Community High School Dist.*, 313 F.Supp. 642 (N.D. Ill.1970).

73. *Board of Trustees of School Dist. No. 4, Big Horn County v. Colwell*, 611 P.2d 427 (Wyo.1980).

74. *Sims v. Board of Trustees, Holly Springs, Municipal Separate School Dist.*, 414 So.2d 431 [4 Educ. L. Rep. 933] (Miss. 1982).

75. *Moffitt v. Batesville School Dist.*, 643 S.W.2d 557 [8 Educ. L. Rep. 877] (Ark. 1982).

76. *Nicholson v. Board of Educ. Torrance Unified School Dist.*, 682 F.2d 858 [5 Educ. L. Rep. 733] (9th Cir.1982).

77. *Hatton v. Wicks*, 744 F.2d 501 [20 Educ. L. Rep. 400] (5th Cir.1984). [Case No. 80]

78. *Lockhart v. Board of Educ. of Arapahoe County School Dist. No. 6*, 735 P.2d 913 [39 Educ. L. Rep. 349] (Colo.Ct.App. 1986).

79. *Adlerstein v. Board of Educ. of City of N.Y.*, 485 N.Y.S.2d 1 [22 Educ. L. Rep. 1220] (N.Y. 1984).

80. *Hope v. Charlotte–Mecklenburg Bd. of Educ.*, 430 S.E.2d 472 [83 Educ. L. Rep. 481] (N.C.Ct.App.1993).

81. *School Dist. No. 1, City and County of Denver v. Cornish*, 58 P.3d 1091 [171 Educ. L. Rep. 1028] (Colo.Ct.App.2002).

82. *In re Mary Silvestri's Teaching Contract with Indep. School Dist. No. 695*, 480 N.W.2d 117 [72 Educ. L. Rep. 1050] (Minn. Ct.App.1992).

83. *Drain v. Board of Educ. of Frontier County School Dist. No. 46*, 508 N.W.2d 255 [87 Educ. L. Rep. 612] (Neb.1993).

84. *Board of Educ. of City of Chicago v. Weed*, 667 N.E.2d 627 [111 Educ. L. Rep. 1306] (Ill. App. Ct.1996).

85. *Board of Educ. of Community Consol. School Dist. No. 54 v. Spangler*, 767 N.E.2d 452 [166 Educ. L. Rep. 294] (Ill.App. Ct.2002).

86. *City of Crawfordsville v. Hays*, 42 Ind. 200 (Ind.1873).

to subject matter, teaching methods, or preserving discipline, ordinarily over time rather than as a single event, that has not been rendered inappropriate for vagueness when boards seek to terminate the contracts of tenured teachers.[87] Insofar as there is a legal presumption that certificated teachers are competent, the longer they serve without documented difficulties, the stronger the presumption becomes. To this end, the burden of proof of incompetence or neglect of duty is on boards when officials claim that teachers have failed to perform satisfactorily.

The Supreme Court of Nebraska ruled that the standard to be used in evaluating incompetence was not that of perfection, but, not unlike the reasonable educator in negligence cases, of performance required of others executing the same or like duties.[88] This court later indicated that incompetence can be defined as demonstrated deficiencies or shortcomings in educators' knowledge in subject matter or administrative skills.[89] In this case, the court affirmed that a school board improperly dismissed a superintendent over claims that he erred in preparing drafts of budget documents and did not provide him with evaluations and notice of his alleged deficiencies.[90] Other courts agreed that tenured teachers must be given notice of their deficiencies and opportunities to improve.[91]

Failure to preserve student discipline is frequently offered as a cause for teacher dismissal due to incompetence.[92] For instance, an appellate court in Tennessee affirmed that a board could dismiss a tenured teacher for incompetence, inefficiency, insubordination, and neglect of duty where there was sufficient evidence that she was unable to control her class, used questionable grading methods, and required extraordinary assistance from administrators and parents to enforce discipline.[93] Other dismissals for incompetence for inappropriate discipline included cases where a principal tied a child with a behavioral disorder to a desk, bound his ankles and wrists with duct tape, and left him in an open doorway in public view for about two hours[94] and where a teacher bound one

87. *California Teachers Ass'n v. Governing Bd.*, 192 Cal.Rptr. 358 [11 Educ. L. Rep. 574] (Cal.Ct.App.1983), *cert. denied sub nom. Takahashi v. Governing Board of the Livingston Union School Dist.*, 465 U.S. 1008, 104 S.Ct. 1003, 79 L.Ed.2d 235 (1984); *Board of Educ. of W. Yuma School Dist. RJ–1 v. Flaming*, 938 P.2d 151 [118 Educ. L. Rep. 1202] (Colo.1997).

88. *Sanders v. Board of Educ. of S. Sioux City Community School Dist. No. 11*, 263 N.W.2d 461 (Neb.1978).

89. *Boss v. Fillmore County School Dist. No. 19*, 559 N.W.2d 448 [116 Educ. L. Rep. 380] (Neb.1997).

90. For a similar statements of the standards in evaluating whether tenure can be revoked for incompetence, *see Sekor v. Board of Educ. of the Town of Ridgefield*, 689 A.2d 1112 [116 Educ. L. Rep. 1049] (Conn.1997); *Ruchert v. Freeman School Dist.*, 22 P.3d 841 [153 Educ. L. Rep. 424]

(Wash.Ct.App.2001), *review denied*, 35 P.3d 381 (Wash.2001).

91. *Jones v. New York City Bd. of Educ.*, 592 N.Y.S.2d 441 [80 Educ. L. Rep. 700] (N.Y.App. Div.1993); *Board of Educ. of Benton Harbor Area Schools v. Wolff*, 361 N.W.2d 750 [22 Educ. L. Rep. 1257] (Mich. Ct.App.1984).

92. *Linstad v. Sitka School Dist.*, 963 P.2d 246 [129 Educ. L. Rep. 504] (Alaska 1998); *Johnson v. Francis Howell R–3 Bd. of Educ.*, 868 S.W.2d 191 [88 Educ. L. Rep. 1253] (Mo.Ct.App. 1994).

93. *Childs v. Roane County Bd. of Educ.*, 929 S.W.2d 364 [113 Educ. L. Rep. 505] (Tenn.Ct. App.1996).

94. *Sylvester v. Cancienne*, 664 So.2d 1259 [105 Educ. L. Rep. 1350] (La.App.Ct. 1995), *writ not considered*, 666 So.2d 663 (La.1996). *But see James v. Trumbull County Bd. of Educ.*, 663 N.E.2d 1361 [109 Educ. L. Rep. 349] (Ohio Ct.App.1995) (affirming student with electrical cord and placed soap on the tongue of another.[95]

In preserving classroom decorum, teachers also must apply board policies that limit student expression and/or their own instructional techniques. In a controversial case on this topic, the Eighth Circuit upheld the dismissal of a teacher in Missouri who permitted students to make videotapes that included in excess of one hundred and fifty uses of profanity and racial slurs on the basis that she persistently violated board policy prohibiting such behavior.[96] Earlier, when a tenured teacher in Pennsylvania disregarded directives that he stop using a classroom management technique that he developed, the Third Circuit affirmed that the board could terminate his contract.[97]

As discussed in the previous chapter, evaluations of classroom performance have led to a fair amount of litigation. The general rule with regard to the substance of evaluations is that as long as they are based on professional criteria and are applied by competent evaluators, results are not subject to judicial review absent claims that low ratings are influenced by, or in retaliation for, teachers exercising their constitutional rights.

In expansive interpretations of evaluations, courts upheld the dismissals of tenured teachers due to the lack of student progress,[98] a teacher's inability to impart curricular knowledge as reflected in a high rate of failures,[99] and the combination of a teacher's weak rapport with students and her poor communication skills with parents.[100] In what was then a novel case involving evidence of incompetence or inefficiency, an appellate court in Texas affirmed that the use of videotapes in the evaluation process did not violate a teacher's right to privacy.[101] The court specified that affording the teacher access to the tapes, though not in edited form, sufficed as notice of evidence to be considered when the board initiated dismissal proceedings. Fifteen years later, an appellate court in Kentucky rejected a teacher's request that she be able to take part in an in camera review of videotapes of her performance that were made to monitor her behavior with her students after children complained that she treated them inappropriately.[102] The court remanded for

---

that a tenured teacher could not be dismissed for wilful and persistent violations of board policy for placing hot sauce in the mouth of a student with multiple disabilities since the board failed to identify a rule or regulation that she violated).

95. *Johanson v. Board of Educ. of Lincoln County School Dist. No. 1*, 589 N.W.2d 815 [132 Educ. L. Rep. 916] (Neb.1999).

96. *Lacks v. Ferguson Reorganized School Dist. R–2*, 147 F.3d 718 [127 Educ. L. Rep. 568] (8th Cir.1998), *suggestion for reh'g en banc denied*, 154 F.3d 904 (8th Cir.1998), *cert. denied*, 526 U.S. 1012, 119 S.Ct. 1158, 143 L.Ed.2d 223 (1999). [Case No. 81]

97. *Bradley v. Pittsburgh Bd. of Educ.*, 913 F.2d 1064 [62 Educ. L. Rep. 894] (3d Cir.1990).

98. *Whaley v. Anoka–Hennepin Indep. School Dist. No. 11*, 325 N.W.2d 128 [7 Educ. L. Rep. 206] (Minn.1982).

99. *In re Proposed Termination of James E. Johnson's Teaching Contract with Indep. School Dist. No. 709*, 451 N.W.2d 343 [58 Educ. L. Rep. 1031] (Minn.Ct.App. 1990).

100. *Raitzik v. Board of Educ. of City of Chicago*, 826 N.E.2d 568 [197 Educ. L. Rep. 685] (Ill. App. Ct. 2005).

101. *Roberts v. Houston Indep. School Dist.*, 788 S.W.2d 107 [60 Educ. L. Rep. 251] (Tex.Ct. App.1990). [Case No. 82]

102. *Medley v. Board of Educ., Shelby County*, 168 S.W.3d 398 [201 Educ. L. Rep. 380] (Ky. Ct. App. 2004), *review denied* (2005).

further consideration as to whether the teacher could examine the tapes in her official capacity as an educator who had a legitimate educational interest in viewing their content under the Family Educational Rights and Privacy Act.

Courts also have upheld the dismissals of teachers and other school employees for a variety of other matters. Courts agreed that educators could be dismissed for inability to define standards for student assessment and not keeping records of the same,[103] for failing to comply with a board's special education paperwork requirements,[104] for supervising a strip search of students,[105] for excessive absences,[106] for telling dirty jokes to students and referring to another teacher in front of other pupils by a derogatory name,[107] and for failing to prevent the loss or theft of more than $25,000 of gate receipts at a high school's athletic events.[108]

Conduct Unbecoming a Teacher

"[T]eacher[s] serve[] as [] role model[s] for [their] students, exerting a subtle but important influence over their perceptions and values."[109] Most, if not all, courts agree with this statement of the Supreme Court, expecting educators' character and conduct to be above that of persons not working in sensitive relationships with children. Accordingly, with judicial approval, boards have dismissed teachers for offenses variously referred to as conduct unbecoming an educator, immorality, and/or moral turpitude. While there has been a discernible trend toward affording teachers more freedom in their personal lives than in the more distant past, it is difficult to draw a line between their rights as private citizens and the obligations they accept as educators. The bottom line is that, generally speaking, the private lives of educators are their own business unless or until their actions impact their professional lives. In one noteworthy area in this regard, the courts have long agreed that being an unwed mother does not per se constitute grounds for dismissal.[110] Further, although not condoning such behavior, courts have generally refused to sanction educators for engaging in adultery with other

103. *Davis v. Board of Educ. of City of Chicago,* 659 N.E.2d 86 [105 Educ. L. Rep. 1175] (Ill.App.Ct.1995).

104. *Hellmann v. Union School Dist.,* 170 S.W.3d 52 [201 Educ. L. Rep. 955] (Mo. Ct. App. 2005).

105. *Rogers v. Board of Educ. of City of New Haven,* 749 A.2d 1173 [143 Educ. L. Rep. 968] (Conn.2000).

106. *McKinnon v. Board of Educ. of N. Bellmore Union Free School Dist.,* 709 N.Y.S.2d 104 [145 Educ. L. Rep. 1100] (N.Y.App.Div.2000) (also including a charge of misconduct).

107. *Oleske v. Hilliard City School Dist. Bd. of Educ.,* 764 N.E.2d 1110 [162 Educ. L.

Rep. 958] (Ohio App.2001, *appeal not allowed,* 761 N.E.2d 48 (Ohio 2002).

108. *Smith v. Bullock County Bd. of Educ.,* 906 So.2d 938 [200 Educ. L. Rep. 905] (Ala. Civ. App. 2004), *cert. denied* (Ala. 2005).

109. *Ambach v. Norwick,* 441 U.S. 68, 78–79, 99 S.Ct. 1589, 60 L.Ed.2d 49 (1979).

110. *Andrews v. Drew Municipal Separate School Dist.,* 507 F.2d 611 (5th Cir. 1975); *New Mexico State Bd. of Educ. v. Stoudt,* 571 P.2d 1186 (N.M.1977); *Avery v. Homewood City Bd. of Educ.,* 674 F.2d 337 [3 Educ. L. Rep. 506] (5th Cir.1982), *cert. denied,* 461 U.S. 943, 103 S.Ct. 2119, 77 L.Ed.2d 1300 [21 Educ. L. Rep. 17] (1983).

school employees.[111]

Conduct unbecoming an educator, as with incompetence, is basically a term of art, its meaning shaped by contemporary concepts of improper personal conduct. Courts have thus refused to vitiate the term immorality as unconstitutionally vague as a ground for dismissal.[112] The Supreme Court of Pennsylvania, in often quoted language,[113] pointed out as much when it described immorality as "a course of conduct as offends the morals of the community and is a bad example to the youth whose ideals a teacher is supposed to foster and to elevate."[114] In the underlying dispute, the court reinstated the teacher's dismissal in connection with her public behavior, including playing dice with customers for drinks, in a bar that her husband owned.

If teachers are subject to discipline, school officials must demonstrate that their behavior reduced their occupational effectiveness. Put another way, officials must prove that there is a rational nexus between teachers' inappropriate conduct and their professional duties to such an extent that it impairs or destroys their professional effectiveness.[115]

The Supreme Court of California identified relevant factors in considering whether a teacher's behavior renders one unfit if activities occurred outside of school settings. The court addressed "the likelihood that the conduct may have adversely affected students or fellow teachers, the degree of such adversity anticipated, the proximity or remoteness in time of the conduct, the type of teaching certificate held by the party involved, the extenuating or aggravating circumstances, if any, surrounding the conduct, the praiseworthiness or blameworthiness of the motives resulting in the conduct, the likelihood of the recurrence of the questioned conduct, and the extent to which disciplinary action may inflict an adverse impact or chilling effect upon the constitutional rights of the teacher involved or other teachers."[116] Twenty-five years later, an appellate court in California explicitly applied these criteria in affirming the dismissal of a male teacher for sexually harassing female students.[117]

In specific cases, the Supreme Court of Colorado affirmed the dismissal of a tenured teacher for immorality because she violated board policy by drinking beer with students while acting in her official capacity

111. *Bertolini v. Whitehall City School Dist. Bd. of Educ.*, 744 N.E.2d 1245 [152 Educ. L. Rep. 259] (Ohio Ct.App.2000), *stay denied*, 739 N.E.2d 817 (Ohio 2000), *appeal not allowed*, 742 N.E.2d 146 (Ohio 2001); *Erb v. Iowa State Bd. of Pub. Instruction*, 216 N.W.2d 339 (Iowa 1974).

112. *Sullivan v. Meade Indep. School Dist. No. 101*, 530 F.2d 799 (8th Cir.1976); *Weissman v. Board of Educ. of Jefferson County School Dist. No. R–1*, 547 P.2d 1267 (Colo.1976); *Ross v. Robb*, 662 S.W.2d 257 [15 Educ. L. Rep. 606] (Mo.1983).

113. *See, e.g., Kinniry v. Abington School Dist.*, 673 A.2d 429, 432 [108 Educ. L. Rep. 312] (Pa.Cmwlth.Ct.1996).

114. *Horosko v. Mount Pleasant Township School Dist.*, 6 A.2d 866, 868 (Pa. 1939), *cert. denied*, 308 U.S. 553, 60 S.Ct. 101, 84 L.Ed. 465 (1939).

115. *Woo v. Putman County Bd. of Educ.*, 504 S.E.2d 644 [129 Educ. L. Rep. 853] (W.Va. 1998).

116. *Morrison v. State Bd. of Educ.*, 461 P.2d 375, 386–87 (Cal.1969).

117. *Governing Bd. of ABC Unified School Dist. v. Haar*, 33 Cal.Rptr.2d 744 [94 Educ. L. Rep. 384] (Cal.Ct.App.1994).

as cheerleader sponsor.[118] The court agreed that insofar as the teacher knowingly violated the policy, it had the authority to terminate her employment since her conduct had a direct bearing on her relationship to students and the school community. In another dispute involving alcohol, the Supreme Court of Iowa upheld a teacher's dismissal for allowing her son to have a party at her house at which he and others drank alcohol. After the students left the teacher's house, four of them were killed when the driver lost control of his car and hit a tree. Among its reasons for affirming the teacher's dismissal, the court referred to her "unprofessional conduct in allowing students to use [her] property for a party where alcohol was illegally used by students ... failure to protect the safety and well-being of students, inability to be effective as a teacher, [being] a poor role model, and poor and ineffective leadership."[119]

Courts usually agree that educator misbehavior in class or on school premises has enough of a connection to their duties as to meet the nexus criterion as a matter of law, that is, without need for proof of connection. In such situations, courts have upheld the dismissals of teachers for making racially derogatory remarks to, or about, students in class[120] and for being rude to children.[121] However, isolated remarks that are considered to be disrespectful of students, such as calling one a "slob" for not paying attention and for being slumped down in her chair,[122] are usually insufficient to justify dismissals.

The judiciary has little difficulty disciplining educators for inappropriate sexual contact with students, even for incidents that did not surface for years.[123] Among the actions involving sexuality that led to dismissals for conduct unbecoming are exposing oneself on many occasions over four years to female students,[124] surreptitiously taking photographs of young girls and using them in a sexually gratifying manner,[125] engaging in sexual[126] and romantic[127] relations with students, hugging

---

118. *Blaine v. Moffat County School Dist. re No. 1*, 748 P.2d 1280 [44 Educ. L. Rep. 763] (Colo.1988).

119. *Walthart v. Board of Directors of Edgewood–Colesburg Community School Dist.*, 694 N.W.2d 740, 741–42 [197 Educ. L. Rep. 388] (Iowa 2005).

120. *Loeffelman v. Board of Educ. of Crystal City School Dist.*, 134 S.W.3d 637 [188 Educ. L. Rep. 510] (Mo. Ct. App. 2004); *Emri v. Evesham Township Bd. of Educ.*, 327 F.Supp.2d 463 [191 Educ. L. Rep. 142] (D. N.J. 2004); *Resetar v. State Bd. of Educ.*, 399 A.2d 225 (Md.1979), *cert. denied*, 444 U.S. 838, 100 S.Ct. 74, 62 L.Ed.2d 49 (1979).

121. *Emri v. Evesham Township Bd. of Educ.*, 327 F.Supp.2d 463 [191 Educ. L. Rep. 142] (D. N.J. 2004) (the teacher here also made racist remarks to students).

122. *Trustees of Lincoln County School Dist. No. 13, Eureka v. Holden*, 754 P.2d 506 [46 Educ. L. Rep. 1036] (Mont.1988).

123. *Toney v. Fairbanks North Star Borough School Dist., Bd. of Educ.*, 881 P.2d 1112 [95 Educ. L. Rep. 380] (Alaska 1994); *Parker v. Board of Educ. of Byron Center Pub. Schools*, 582 N.W.2d 859 [128 Educ. L. Rep. 878] (Mich.Ct.App.1998).

124. *Miller v. Grand Haven Bd. of Educ.*, 390 N.W.2d 255 [33 Educ. L. Rep. 1247] (Mich.Ct. App.1986).

125. *Montefusco v. Nassau County*, 39 F.Supp.2d 231 [134 Educ. L. Rep. 127] (E.D.N.Y.1999).

126. *Johnson v. Board of Trustees, Beaverhead County High School Dist.*, 771 P.2d 137 [52 Educ. L. Rep. 1264] (Mont.1989); *Parker v. Board of Educ. of Byron Center Pub. Schools*, 582 N.W.2d 859 [128 Educ. L. Rep. 878] (Mich.Ct.App.1998); *Toney v. Fairbanks North Star Borough School Dist., Bd. of Educ.*, 881 P.2d 1112 [95 Educ. L. Rep. 380] (Alaska 1994).

127. *Board of Educ. of City School Dist. of City of N.Y. v. Mills*, 680 N.Y.S.2d 683

and allegedly trying to kiss a female student,[128] writing overtly sexual letters to female students,[129] and placing a hand on a female student's knee.[130]

Even if there are circumstances that may reduce the personally controllable reasons for inappropriate conduct, teachers can be dismissed for conduct unbecoming an educator. Courts have upheld dismissals for drug dependency derived from an effort to combat obesity[131] and for shoplifting possibly as a result of temporary mental instability.[132]

Turning to criminal behavior as a basis for dismissal, the Supreme Court of Alaska reiterated the general rule that there need not always be a separate nexus between educators' moral turpitude and their fitness to perform their duties because they can be held to a higher standard than non-educators. The court thus affirmed that a board had the authority to dismiss a teacher for engaging in a sexual relationship with a fifteen-year-old minor, years earlier in another state, even though his behavior did not lead to a conviction.[133] In like fashion, an appellate court in Pennsylvania affirmed the revocation of a teacher's certificate in the face of a not-guilty verdict on criminal charges where he was accused of having improperly touched two male students.[134] The court was of the view that the criminal acquittal was not *res judicata* in the teacher's being disciplined where the revocation was supported by substantial evidence.

Other courts have upheld suspensions of teachers who were indicted for possession of cocaine with intent to distribute[135] and welfare fraud.[136] An appellate court in Louisiana went so far as to affirm that even though a tenured teacher completed probation for his guilty plea for possession of marijuana and cocaine, and the criminal proceedings were dismissed, his school board had the authority to terminate his contract for moral turpitude.[137] The court asserted that even though the charges were dropped because the teacher completed probation, nothing changed

[131 Educ. L. Rep. 248] (N.Y.App.Div.1998), *leave to appeal denied*, 689 N.Y.S.2d 16 (N.Y.1999); *Andrews v. Independent School Dist. No. 57*, 12 P.3d 491 [148 Educ. L. Rep. 1061] (Okla.Civ. App.2000).

128. *Baltrip v. Norris*, 23 S.W.3d 336 [146 Educ. L. Rep. 573] (Tenn.Ct.App. 2000).

129. *Board of Educ. of Sparta Community Unit School Dist. No. 140 v. Illinois State Bd. of Educ.*, 577 N.E.2d 900 [69 Educ. L. Rep. 846] (Ill.App.Ct.1991).

130. *Rivers v. Board of Trustees, Forrest County Agricultural High School*, 876 So.2d 1043 [190 Educ. L. Rep. 731] (Miss. Ct. App. 2004).

131. *Martin v. Guillot*, 875 F.2d 839 [53 Educ. L. Rep. 1113] (11th Cir.1989).

132. *Board of Directors of Lawton–Bronson Community School Dist. v. Davies*,

489 N.W.2d 19 [77 Educ. L. Rep. 482] (Iowa 1992).

133. *Toney v. Fairbanks North Star Borough School Dist., Bd. of Educ.*, 881 P.2d 1112 [95 Educ. L. Rep. 380] (Alaska 1994).

134. *Boguslawski v. Department of Educ.*, 837 A.2d 614 [183 Educ. L. Rep. 928] (Pa. Cmwlth. Ct. 2003).

135. *Dupree v. School Comm. of Boston*, 446 N.E.2d 1099 [10 Educ. L. Rep. 336] (Mass.Ct. App.1983), *review denied*, 451 N.E.2d 1166 (Mass.1983).

136. *Perryman v. School Comm. of Boston*, 458 N.E.2d 748 [15 Educ. L. Rep. 533] (Mass.Ct. App.1983).

137. *Dubuclet v. Home Ins. Co.*, 660 So.2d 67 [103 Educ. L. Rep. 547] (La.Ct. App.1995), *writ denied*, 664 So.2d 446 (La. 1995).

the fact that he engaged in inappropriate behavior.[138] In like manner, appellate courts in Pennsylvania[139] and Michigan[140] affirmed that tenured teachers could be dismissed following convictions for trafficking in counterfeit goods and embezzlement at a part-time job, respectively, since their actions negatively impacted their reputations in their school communities. Further, an appellate court in New York affirmed the dismissal of a tenured teacher who had prior convictions for fraud based on similar misconduct after she was convicted of grand larceny.[141] The court stated that since the penalty was not so disproportionate to the offense so as to shock the conscience, there was no reason why she should have been reinstated.

Free Speech Rights of Teachers

Concerns arise about the employment status of teachers who exercise their First Amendment rights to freedom of speech as private citizens. Beginning with *Pickering v. Board of Education of Township High School District (Pickering)*,[142] the Supreme Court has handed down a series of judgments that helped to clarify the parameters of this important topic.

At issue in *Pickering* was a school board in Illinois' attempt to dismiss a teacher for writing a letter to a local newspaper which criticized its handling of a bond issue and its allocation of financial resources between the school's educational and athletic programs. The Supreme Court identified the need to find the appropriate "[b]alance between the interests of the teacher, as a citizen, in commenting upon matters of public concern and the interest of the State, as an employer, in promoting the efficiency of the public services it performs through its employees."[143] In rejecting the board's claim that the letter was detrimental to the best interests of the schools, the Court wrote that the teacher's right to free speech was primary since this was a matter of public concern.

In *Pickering*, the Supreme Court examined a variety of factors which led it to rule in favor of the teacher. Along with recognizing that the teacher had the right to speak out on a legitimate matter of public concern as a private citizen, the Court commented that he did not have a close working relationship with those he criticized, that his letter did not have a detrimental impact on the administration of the district, and that it did not negatively affect his regular duties. Deciding that the interests of the board and schools were not synonymous, the Court acknowledged

---

138. *See Board of Educ. of Hopkins County v. Wood*, 717 S.W.2d 837 [35 Educ. L. Rep. 824] (Ky.1986) (dismissing a tenured teacher for smoking marijuana in his apartment with others, including two fifteen-year-old students, during the summer months when school was not in session).

139. *Kinniry v. Abington School Dist.*, 673 A.2d 429 [108 Educ. L. Rep. 312] (Pa. Cmwlth.Ct. 1996).

140. *Satterfield v. Board of Educ. of the Grand Rapids Pub. Schools*, 556 N.W.2d 888 [114 Educ. L. Rep. 1192] (Mich.Ct.App. 1996).

141. *Green v. New York City Dep't of Educ.*, 793 N.Y.S.2d 405 [197 Educ. L. Rep. 714] (N.Y. App. Div. 2005).

142. 391 U.S. 563, 88 S.Ct. 1731, 20 L.Ed.2d 811 (1968). [Case No. 83]

143. *Id.* at 569.

not only that the public interest in having free and unhindered debate on matters of public importance was crucial but also that since "teachers are, as a class, the members of a community most likely to have informed and definite opinions as to how funds allotted to the operation of the schools should be spent,"[144] it was essential that they be able to speak freely on such questions.

The Supreme Court revisited the free speech rights of teachers eleven years later in *Mt. Healthy City Board of Education v. Doyle* (*Mt. Healthy*),[145] wherein it considered the effect of including a constitutionally protected right as a factor in not renewing the contract of a non-tenured teacher. The board chose not to renew the contract of a teacher who had a record of being difficult in school despite his claim that it violated his rights because he called into a radio talk show and criticized a memo from his principal dealing with a faculty dress code. The Court rejected the Sixth Circuit's finding that including a protected activity as a substantial part of the justification for the non-renewal of a probationary teacher's contract entitled him to reinstatement with back pay. The Court remarked that the Sixth Circuit would have placed the teacher in a better position as a result of exercising his protected speech than had he done nothing. The Court conceded that where a teacher shows that protected conduct about a school matter was a substantial or motivating factor where a board chooses not to renew a contract, it must be given the opportunity to show that it would have chosen not to re-employ in the absence of the protected conduct. On remand, the board reported that it would not have renewed the teacher's contract regardless of whether he placed the call to the radio talk show.[146]

Two years later, in *Givhan v. Western Line Consolidated School District* (*Givhan*),[147] the Court determined that the *Pickering* balancing test also applies to teachers who express themselves during private conversations with their supervisors. When school officials chose not to renew the contract of a non-tenured teacher in Mississippi, she was informed that it was in response for, among other reasons, her allegedly making petty and unreasonable demands on the principal and addressing him in a manner variously described as insulting, hostile, loud, and arrogant. The teacher also complained that the board, which operated under a court-ordered desegregation plan, was racially discriminatory in its employment policies and practices. In refusing to reinstate the teacher, the Court reasoned that the Fifth Circuit erred in declaring that school officials were justified in not renewing her contract, suggesting that under *Mt. Healthy*, they may have had sufficient cause on other grounds that would have required further proceedings. The Court thought that under *Pickering*, the judiciary must consider working relationships of personnel as well as the contents of communications in

---

144. *Id.* at 572.

145. 429 U.S. 274, 97 S.Ct. 568, 50 L.Ed.2d 471 (1977). [Case No. 69]

146. *Doyle v. Mt. Healthy City School Dist. Bd. of Educ.*, 670 F.2d 59 [2 Educ. L. Rep. 973] (6th Cir.1982).

147. 439 U.S. 410, 99 S.Ct. 693, 58 L.Ed.2d 619 (1979).

evaluating whether private communications exceeded the scope of First Amendment protection.

At issue in *Connick v. Myers (Connick),*[148] the Court's next case on employee speech, was whether *Pickering* protects public employees who communicate their views about workplace matters to peers. Here a former assistant district attorney challenged her being dismissed on the same day that she was scheduled for a transfer to another division because she circulated a questionnaire about office operations among staff. The Court distinguished *Givhan* in conceding that while the teacher's statements involved issues of public concern, the attorney's were primarily based on an internal disagreement with her supervisors and the questionnaire interfered with the close working relationships in the office. In noting that the attorney's dismissal did not violate her rights, the Court established a two-step test to evaluate whether speech is entitled to First Amendment protections. First, the Court explained that the judiciary must consider whether the speech involved an issue of public concern by examining its content and form along with the context within which it was expressed. Second, the Court posited that if speech does deal with a matter of public concern, the judiciary must balance employees' interests as citizens in speaking out on matters of public concern against those of employers in promoting effective and efficient public services. Almost a decade later, in *Waters v. Churchill,*[149] a case from Illinois involving a nurse who criticized internal policies at a public hospital, the Supreme Court, in a plurality opinion, reiterated that public employees who publicly dispute internal policies that are not of public concern may not be entitled to constitutional protection.

Examples of subjects that have met the criterion of public concern include criticisms of or questions about a delay by school officials in implementing federally mandated programs for students with disabilities,[150] a medication policy,[151] a policy that prevented teachers from making critical statements about school officials unless spoken directly to the person(s) being criticized,[152] a principal's failure to implement a school improvement plan,[153] and a board's child abuse reporting policy.[154] Other matters that were deemed to be of public concern included a teacher's use of a racially derogatory word in class during a discussion on interracial marriage,[155] a secretary's questions about whether a

148. 461 U.S. 138, 103 S.Ct. 1684, 75 L.Ed.2d 708 (1983).

149. 511 U.S. 661, 114 S.Ct. 1878, 128 L.Ed.2d 686 (1994).

150. *Southside Pub. Schools v. Hill,* 827 F.2d 270 [41 Educ. L. Rep. 439] (8th Cir. 1987).

151. *Johnsen v. Independent School Dist. No. 3 of Tulsa County,* 891 F.2d 1485 [57 Educ. L. Rep. 1154] (10th Cir.1989).

152. *Westbrook v. Teton County School Dist. No. 1,* 918 F.Supp. 1475 [108 Educ. L. Rep. 215] (D.Wyo.1996).

153. *Harris v. Victoria Indep. School Dist.,* 168 F.3d 216 [132 Educ. L. Rep. 662] (5th Cir. 1999), *reh'g and reh'g en banc denied,* 336 F.3d 343 [179 Educ. L. Rep. 81] (5th Cir. 1999), *cert. denied,* 528 U.S. 1022, 120 S.Ct. 533, 145 L.Ed.2d 413 (1999).

154. *Calvit v. Minneapolis Pub. Schools,* 122 F.3d 1112 [120 Educ. L. Rep. 952] (8th Cir.1997).

155. *Labalokie v. Capital Area Intermediate Unit,* 926 F.Supp. 503 [110 Educ. L. Rep. 146] (M.D.Pa.1996).

board's awarding of a contract presented a conflict of interest,[156] a teacher's inviting a speaker to class to talk about industrial hemp,[157] the head of a bus drivers' union-like organization expressing her concerns about student safety due to overcrowding on buses and the lack of pretrip inspections,[158] a school nurse's challenging a grossly unsatisfactory employment rating in retaliation for her advocating on behalf of students with disabilities in her district,[159] and a secretary's responding to a question from a reporter over whether the school's principal had resigned.[160]

A recent case from Ohio highlights how the elements of a free speech claim come together. The Sixth Circuit affirmed that school officials retaliated against a teacher by not renewing her contract after she exercised her First Amendment right to free speech. At issue were parental complaints about the teacher's use of such novels as *Fahrenheit 451*, *To Kill a Mockingbird*, and *Siddhartha* even though the school board paid for the books and approved their use. The court identified the three elements of a First Amendment retaliation claim as whether an employee was engaged in a constitutionally protected activity, whether the employer's action caused an injury that would have been likely to chill a person of ordinary firmness from continuing it, and whether the employer's action was, at least in part, a response to the protected activity.[161] The court also applied *the Pickering–Connick* test, which requires public employees to prove that if their activity was speech, whether they were disciplined for addressing issues of public concern, and whether their interests outweighed those of their employers in ruling that the board acted inappropriately by not renewing the teacher's contract.

In a significant number of cases, courts refused to treat the speech of school employees as protected since it failed to involve matters of public concern. Among these cases were instances criticizing a superintendent[162] or a board's hiring of a superintendent;[163] questioning a school's policies with regard to class size;[164] challenging the non renewals of teaching[165] and coaching contracts;[166] complaining about unfavorable

156. *Kirchmann v. Lake Elsinore Unified School Dist.*, 67 Cal.Rptr.2d 268 [120 Educ. L. Rep. 523] (Cal.Ct.App.1997).

157. *Cockrel v. Shelby County School Dist.*, 270 F.3d 1036 [158 Educ. L. Rep. 551] (6th Cir. 2001).

158. *Cook v. Gwinnett County School Dist.*, 414 F.3d 1313 [199 Educ. L. Rep. 637] (11th Cir. 2005).

159. *McGreevy v. Stroup*, 413 F.3d 359 [199 Educ. L. Rep. 593] (3d Cir. 2005).

160. *Salge v. Edna Indep. School Dist.*, 411 F.3d 178 [198 Educ. L. Rep. 807] (5th Cir. 2005).

161. *Evans-Marshall v. Board of Educ. of the Tipp City Exempted Village School Dist.*, 428 F.3d 223 [203 Educ. L. Rep. 88] (6th Cir. 2005).

162. *Burkybile v. Board of Educ. of Hastings–On–Hudson Union Free School Dist.*, 411 F.3d 306 [199 Educ. L. Rep. 26] (2d Cir. 2005), *cert. denied*, ___ U.S. ___, 126 S.Ct. 801, 163 L.Ed.2d 628 (2005).

163. *Vukadinovich v. Board of School Trustees of Michigan City Area Schools*, 978 F.2d 403 [78 Educ. L. Rep. 269] (7th Cir. 1992), *cert. denied*, 510 U.S. 844, 114 S.Ct. 133, 126 L.Ed.2d 97 (1993).

164. *Cliff v. Board of School Commr's of City of Indianapolis*, 42 F.3d 403 [96 Educ. L. Rep. 365] (7th Cir.1994).

165. *Padilla v. South Harrison R–II School Dist.*, 181 F.3d 992 [136 Educ. L. Rep. 728] (8th Cir.1999), *reh'g and reh'g en banc denied*, 192 F.3d 805 (8th Cir.1999); *Alba v. Ansonia Bd. of Educ.*, 999 F.Supp. 687 [126 Educ. L. Rep. 807] (D. Conn.1998).

166. *Lancaster v. Independent School Dist. No. 5*, 149 F.3d 1228 [128 Educ. L. Rep. 67] (10th Cir.1998).

evaluation ratings;[167] challenging a board's passing an applicant over for a newly-created staff position in retaliation for speaking out about alcohol and drug use by school bus drivers;[168] referring to others by using such epithets as "sick and demented," "ignorant and abusive," "mentally ill," "mindless criminals," and "alcoholic;"[169] challenging the accuracy of school attendance records;[170] questioning a board's tobacco policy;[171] claiming that school officials created a racially hostile work environment;[172] and criticizing the quality of leadership and the education children receive in a district.[173] Other cases where courts rejected the claims of school employees concerned such matters as writing a letter to a local newspaper criticizing a hiring process;[174] failing to comply with procedures when administering state-wide standardized tests;[175] making an allegedly racist remark about immigration during a class;[176] opposing a board policy designed to seek aid for disadvantaged students;[177] engaging in disruptive speech such as where a principal wrote a letter to and spoke critically about a superintendent's dress code policy;[178] circulating a survey among faculty members evaluating a school's administration and speaking critically of its quality at a school board meeting;[179] sending inflammatory and disparaging letters to members of a school board for years;[180] and expressing one's political views in a middle school class.[181] Further, where an award-winning kindergarten teacher was dismissed for sending unauthorized and inappropriate correspondence to parents and students, failing to grade report cards, and not completing other end-of-year tasks, the Seventh Circuit affirmed that school officials did not retaliate against her for speech in which she criticized them for the early renewal of her principal's contract or over her proposal to restructure the kindergarten program.[182] The court

167. *Fales v. Garst*, 235 F.3d 1122, 1124 [150 Educ. L. Rep. 41] (8th Cir.2001).

168. *Wheeler v. Natale*, 178 F.Supp.2d 407 [160 Educ. L. Rep. 797] (S.D.N.Y.2001).

169. *Farhat v. Jopke*, 370 F.3d 580 [188 Educ. L. Rep. 108] (6th Cir. 2004).

170. *Brewster v. Board of Educ. of Lynwood Unified School Dist.*, 149 F.3d 971 [128 Educ. L. Rep. 50] (9th Cir.1998), *cert. denied*, 526 U.S. 1018, 119 S.Ct. 1252, 143 L.Ed.2d 349 (1999).

171. *Hill v. Silsbee Indep. School Dist.*, 933 F.Supp. 616 [112 Educ. L. Rep. 150] (E.D. Tex. 1996).

172. *Wallace v. School Bd. of Orange County*, 41 F.Supp.2d 1321 [134 Educ. L. Rep. 879] (M.D. Fla.1998).

173. *McCullough v. Wyandanch Union Free School Dist.*, 187 F.3d 272 [137 Educ. L. Rep. 505] (2d Cir.1999), *on remand*, 132 F.Supp.2d 87 [151 Educ. L. Rep. 874] (E.D.N.Y.2001).

174. *Quick v. Bozeman School Dist. No. 7*, 983 P.2d 402 [137 Educ. L. Rep. 819] (Mont.1999).

175. *Rodriguez v. Laredo Indep. School Dist.*, 82 F.Supp.2d 679 [141 Educ. L. Rep. 1080] (S.D.Tex.2000), *reconsideration denied*, 143 F.Supp.2d 727 [155 Educ. L. Rep. 177] (S.D.Tex. 2001).

176. *Sivek v. Baljevic*, 758 A.2d 473 [147 Educ. L. Rep. 203] (Conn. Super. Ct. 1999), *aff'd* 758 A.2d 441 (Conn. App. Ct. 2000).

177. *Vargas–Harrison v. Racine Unified School Dist.*, 272 F.3d 964 [159 Educ. L. Rep. 459] (7th Cir.2001).

178. *Sharp v. Lindsey*, 285 F.3d 479 [163 Educ. L. Rep. 88] (6th Cir.2002).

179. *Levich v. Liberty Cent. School Dist.*, 361 F.Supp.2d 151 [197 Educ. L. Rep. 70] (S.D.N.Y. 2004).

180. *Jackson v. State of Alabama State Tenure Comm'n*, 405 F.3d 1276 [197 Educ. L. Rep. 499] (11th Cir. 2005).

181. *Calef v. Budden*, 361 F.Supp.2d 493 [197 Educ. L. Rep. 93] (D.S.C. 2005).

182. *Lifton v. Board of Educ. of City of Chicago*, 416 F.3d 571 [200 Educ. L. Rep. 39] (7th Cir. 2005).

concluded that when the teacher resigned following a demand that she produce a doctor's note after taking five consecutive sick days, the board did not constructively discharge her from her job.

Two specific areas that engender controversy are the lifestyles and political activities of teachers. In a case involving lifestyle and sexual preferences, the Second Circuit affirmed that under the *Pickering* balancing test, the New York City Board of Education's interest in the orderly operation of a high school outweighed a tenured teacher's interest in commenting on matters of public concern through his membership in the North American Man/Boy Love Association. The court reported that the association identified its primary goal as seeking to bring about a change in the attitudes and laws governing sexual activity between men and boys while advocating the abolition of laws governing the age of consent for such activities and that limit freedom of expression, including child pornography laws. The court was also of the opinion that the teacher's dismissal, even absent evidence that he engaged in any illegal or inappropriate conduct with students, based on disruption caused by public furor over his activities in the group, did not amount to impermissible "heckler's veto."[183] The court was satisfied that the board's action was not motivated by the desire to retaliate against him for his membership in the association.

On the other hand, the federal trial court in Utah was convinced that school officials violated the equal protection and free speech rights of a teacher who was a lesbian by prohibiting her from discussing her sexual orientation outside of class since officials did not forbid other teachers from talking about their heterosexual orientations in this manner.[184] The court observed that since the principal's not assigning the teacher to coach volleyball constituted retaliation for exercising her First Amendment rights, officials had to offer her a contract for the job. In a related dispute, the Supreme Court of Utah affirmed the dismissal of a case against the teacher which claimed that she violated the state constitution and statutes governing the conduct of teachers and psychologists by leading discussions of alternate lifestyles in a psychology course that she taught.[185] The court agreed that since the statute did not create a private right of action, the taxpayers lacked standing to sue.

In another case about lifestyles, the Ninth Circuit affirmed that when a school board in California erected a bulletin board on which it provided information about Gay and Lesbian Awareness Month, a teacher did not have a First Amendment right to post material with a different point of view.[186] The court ascertained that since the informa-

---

183. *Melzer v. Board of Educ. of City School Dist. of City of N.Y.*, 336 F.3d 185, 198 [179 Educ. L. Rep. 32] (2d Cir.2003), *cert. denied*, 540 U.S. 1183, 124 S.Ct. 1424, 158 L.Ed.2d 87 [185 Educ. L. Rep. 415] (2004).

184. *Weaver v. Nebo School Dist.*, 29 F.Supp.2d 1279 (D. Utah 1998).

185. *Miller v. Weaver*, 66 P.3d 592 [175 Educ. L. Rep. 334] (Utah 2003).

186. *Downs v. Los Angeles Unified School Dist.*, 228 F.3d 1003 [147 Educ. L. Rep. 855] (9th Cir.2000), *cert. denied*, 532 U.S. 994, 121 S.Ct. 1653, 149 L.Ed.2d 636 (2001).

tion was attributable to the board as an expression of its policy, it could properly exclude materials reflecting a different perspective.

When teachers become involved in situations with political connotations, boards cannot enforce rules prohibiting all types of political activities on school premises. In one such case, a board unsuccessfully tried to stop a teachers' organization from circulating a petition addressed to state and local authorities protesting threatened cutbacks in expenditures for education. In language that relied on the then recently resolved *Tinker v. Des Moines Independent Community School District*,[187] wherein the Court upheld the rights of students to wear black armbands in protest of American activity in Vietnam, the Supreme Court of California pointed out that the board could have prevented the teachers from acting only on a showing of a "clear and substantial threat to order and efficiency"[188] in schools. Similarly, the Second Circuit upheld the right of a teacher in New York to wear a black armband in class as a protest against American involvement in Vietnam.[189] The same court later agreed that a school board in New York could not dismiss a teacher for refusing to participate in the flag-salute ceremony where she simply stood silently at attention during its recitation.[190] Further, Massachusetts' highest court maintained that requiring teachers to lead their classes in the Pledge of Allegiance would have violated their First Amendment rights.[191]

In another aspect of political activities, the Supreme Court of Kentucky invalidated a provision in a comprehensive school reform act which prohibited school employees from participating in campaigns for the elections of local school board members. The court vitiated portions of the law in contending that they were unconstitutionally vague and overbroad insofar as it was unclear which activities were forbidden.[192] Four years later, a federal trial court in Pennsylvania struck down a board policy that would have prevented teachers from engaging in political activities on district property at any time.[193] The court decreed that insofar as the policy would have violated the teachers' First Amendment rights by preventing off-duty educators from soliciting votes at official polling places located on school property, it was unconstitutional.

The Supreme Court addressed a matter of speech that is related to employee rights of association and collective bargaining that was discussed in the previous chapter. In *Texas State Teachers Association v.*

187. 393 U.S. 503, 89 S.Ct. 733, 21 L.Ed.2d 731 (1969).

188. *Los Angeles Teachers Union v. Los Angeles City Bd. of Educ.*, 455 P.2d 827, 836 (Cal. 1969).

189. *James v. Board of Educ. of Cent. School Dist. No. 1, Addison*, 461 F.2d 566 (2d Cir.1972), *cert. denied*, 409 U.S. 1042, 93 S.Ct. 529, 34 L.Ed.2d 491 (1972). [Case No. 84]

190. *Russo v. Central School Dist. No. 1, Towns of Rush*, 469 F.2d 623 (2d Cir.

1972), *cert. denied*, 411 U.S. 932, 93 S.Ct. 1899, 36 L.Ed.2d 391 (1973).

191. *Opinions of the Justices to the Governor*, 363 N.E.2d 251 (Mass.1977).

192. *State Bd. for Elementary and Secondary Educ. v. Howard*, 834 S.W.2d 657 [76 Educ. L. Rep. 1211] (Ky.1992).

193. *Castle v. Colonial School Dist.*, 933 F.Supp. 458 [112 Educ. L. Rep. 120] (E.D.Pa.1996).

Garland Independent School District,[194] the Court summarily affirmed that board policies purporting to deny faculty members the right to discuss teacher organizations during non-class time and preventing them from using school mail facilities to mention employee organizations were unconstitutional.

Procedural Due Process

As interpreted by the Supreme Court in *Cleveland Board of Education v. Loudermill (Loudermill)*,[195] absent exigent circumstances, wherein they can be suspended with pay,[196] the Fourteenth Amendment requires school boards to provide educators who have property interests in their jobs, whether through tenure or unexpired contracts, to procedural due process, beginning with notice.[197] More specifically, the Court specified that "tenured public employee[s] [are] entitled to oral or written notice of the charges against [them], an explanation of the employer's evidence, and an opportunity to present [their] side of the story."[198] Depending on state law, though, tenured teachers are not necessarily entitled to full pre-termination hearings as long as they are afforded opportunities to have hearings after they are dismissed from their jobs.[199]

To the extent that non-tenured teachers do not have the same property interests in their jobs and are not entitled to the same procedural protections as their tenured colleagues,[200] it should not be surprising that jurisdictions have adopted statutes of varying degrees of particularity in establishing due procedures dealing with the dismissals of teachers.[201] Insofar as the courts strictly enforce statutory due process rights, the failure of school boards to comply ordinarily renders adverse

---

194. *Texas State Teachers Ass'n v. Garland Indep. School Dist.*, 784 F.2d 1113 [30 Educ. L. Rep. 1108] (5th Cir.1986), *aff'd*, 479 U.S. 801, 107 S.Ct. 41, 93 L.Ed.2d 4 [34 Educ. L. Rep. 1004] (1986).

195. 470 U.S. 532, 105 S.Ct. 1487, 84 L.Ed.2d 494 [23 Educ. L. Rep. 473] (1985), *on remand*, 763 F.2d 202 [25 Educ. L. Rep. 158] (6th Cir.1985), *on remand*, 651 F.Supp. 92 [37 Educ. L. Rep. 502] (N.D.Ohio 1986), *aff'd*, 844 F.2d 304 [46 Educ. L. Rep. 523] (6th Cir.1988), *cert. denied*, 488 U.S. 941, 109 S.Ct. 363, 102 L.Ed.2d 353 (1988), *cert. denied*, 488 U.S. 946, 109 S.Ct. 377, 102 L.Ed.2d 365 [50 Educ. L. Rep. 15] (1988). [Case No. 85]

196. *See Bauman v. Board of Educ. of Watkins Glen Cent. School Dist.*, 800 N.Y.S.2d 461 [201 Educ. L. Rep. 290] (N.Y. App. Div. 2005) (affirming that while a tenured principal was entitled to pay while suspended, the board had no duty to provider her with expired stipends for extra duty assignments because it was free to terminate those at any time).

197. *See, e.g., Tweedall v. Fritz*, 987 F.Supp. 1126 [124 Educ. L. Rep. 122] (S.D.Ind.1997) (judging that one day notice was sufficient where a teacher was accused of touching students inappropriately).

198. *Cleveland Board of Educ. v. Loudermill*, 470 U.S. 532, 546, 105 S.Ct. 1487, 84 L.Ed.2d 494 [23 Educ. L. Rep. 473] (1985). [Case No. 85]

199. *See, e.g., Baird v. Board of Educ. for Warren Community Unit Sch. Dist.*, 389 F.3d 685 [193 Educ. L. Rep. 402] (7th Cir. 2004).

200. *Pennycuff v. Fentress County Bd. of Educ.*, 404 F.3d 447 [197 Educ. L. Rep. 29] (6th Cir. 2005), *reh'g and reh'g en banc denied*.

201. *See, e.g.,* ALA. CODE 1975 § 16-24-9; ARIZ. REV. STAT. ANN. § 15-539; ARK. CODE ANN. § 6-17-1503; COLO. REV. STAT. ANN. § 22-63-202; 105 ILL. COMP. STAT. ANN. 5/24-12; KAN. STAT. ANN. § 72-5438; N.Y. EDUC. LAW § 3020-a; OHIO REV. CODE ANN. § 3319.16; 24 PA. STAT. ANN. § 11-1127; W. VA. CODE ANN. § 18A-2-8.

employment actions invalid.[202] In emphasizing its importance, the Supreme Court, in a non-school case, held that constitutional due process, which may not be as precise in its requirements as state law, and focuses on the issue of fairness, must be interpreted in light of factual contexts and different types of proceedings.[203]

In another non-education case, the Supreme Court was of the view that "identification of the specific dictates of due process generally requires consideration of three distinct factors: First, the private interest that will be affected by the official action; second, the risk of an erroneous deprivation of such interest through the procedures used, the probable value, if any, of additional or substitute procedural safeguards; and finally, the Government's interest, including the function involved and the fiscal and administrative burdens that the additional or substitute procedural requirement would entail."[204]

The Supreme Court's having stopped short of setting a precise formula for due process aside, at the core of procedural due process is notice and a hearing at which teachers must have the chance to address the charges that they face.[205] In most jurisdictions, initial hearings are conducted by local school boards, hearing officers, or state administrative agencies. While hearings need not conform to strict judicial processes,[206] evidence that might not be admitted in court may be admissible as long as it does not violate the fundamentals of fair hearings.[207] Whether hearings are adequate is ultimately a matter of judicial interpretation.

Notice

Teachers often challenge the adequacy of the notice that contains the charges they face. Clearly, teachers must be notified of all charges against them[208] with sufficient specificity,[209] including names, dates, facts, and/or other information that officials relied on in seeking to take adverse employment actions,[210] so that they can prepare responses.[211]

202. *Jackson v. El Dorado School Dist.*, 48 S.W.3d 558 [155 Educ. L. Rep. 936] (Ark.Ct.App. 2001); *Neshaminy Fed'n of Teachers v. Neshaminy School Dist.*, 462 A.2d 629 [12 Educ. L. Rep. 807] (Pa.1983).

203. *Morrissey v. Brewer*, 408 U.S. 471, 92 S.Ct. 2593, 33 L.Ed.2d 484 (1972).

204. *Mathews v. Eldridge*, 424 U.S. 319, 96 S.Ct. 893, 47 L.Ed.2d 18 (1976).

205. *Bertolini v. Whitehall City School Dist. Bd. of Educ.*, 744 N.E.2d 1245 [152 Educ. L. Rep. 259] (Ohio Ct.App.2000), *stay denied*, 739 N.E.2d 817 (Ohio 2000), *appeal not allowed*, 742 N.E.2d 146 (Ohio 2001); *Post v. Salem–Keizer School Dist.*, 45 P.3d 116 [164 Educ. L. Rep. 471] (Or.2002); *Sanders v. Board of Educ. of City School Dist. of City of N.Y.*, 794 N.Y.S.2d 95 [197 Educ. L. Rep. 724] (N.Y. App. Div. 2005).

206. *Knox County Bd. of Educ. v. Willis*, 405 S.W.2d 952 (Ky.1966). [Case No. 86]; *Cope v. Board of Educ. of Town of W.*

Hartford, 495 A.2d 718 [26 Educ. L. Rep. 699] (Conn.Ct.App. 1985).

207. *Carangelo v. Ambach*, 515 N.Y.S.2d 665 [39 Educ. L. Rep. 752] (N.Y.App.Div.1987), *appeal denied*, 522 N.Y.S.2d 109 [43 Educ. L. Rep. 756] (N.Y. 1987).

208. *Clark County School Dist. v. Riley*, 14 P.3d 22 [149 Educ. L. Rep. 615] (Nev. 2000); *McDaniel v. Princeton City School Dist. Bd. of Educ.*, 45 Fed.Appx. 354 [169 Educ. L. Rep. 129] (6th Cir.2002).

209. *Washington v. Independent School Dist. No. 625*, 590 N.W.2d 655 [133 Educ. L. Rep. 589] (Minn.Ct.App.1999).

210. *Blackburn v. Board of Educ. of Breckinridge County*, 564 S.W.2d 35 (Ky.Ct. App.1978).

211. *Cliff v. Board of School Commr's of City of Indianapolis*, 42 F.3d 403 [96

Accordingly, the Supreme Court of Wyoming struck down a charge of inability to establish rapport with students as too vague.[212]

If charges against teachers involve a pattern of conduct, notice must include the time period covered and the specifics.[213] Further, officials must provide teachers with notice far enough in advance of any disciplinary proceedings so that they will have adequate time to prepare defenses.[214] Thus, where state law required boards to give teachers written notice by a specified date, the federal trial court in Vermont denied a board's motion for summary judgment in a suit by a non-tenured teacher who claimed that the oral notice that she received, almost two months late, was insufficient to terminate her employment.[215]

To the extent that state statutes provide specifics with regard to notice, courts generally expect school officials to comply strictly with these requirements. When officials failed to comply with notice requirements, school employees have been reinstated as a matter of law[216] and may have been entitled to new contracts[217] and/or damages.[218] Where rights are limited by statute such as when employees are placed on administrative leave,[219] where they engage in behavior that exceeds the limits of their employment,[220] or where they have other remedies available under collective bargaining agreements,[221] notice may not be required.

Hearings

Loudermill clarified the minimum requirements of constitutional due process that boards must provide for teachers with property interests in their jobs before they can terminate their employment, specifying that they are entitled to "[s]ome kind of hearing"[222] prior to discharge. The Court indicated that informal pre-termination hearings need not be elaborate since post-termination hearings should follow at which educators could present their cases. The Seventh Circuit illustrated this

Educ. L. Rep. 365] (7th Cir.1994), *reh'g and suggestion for reh'g en banc denied*, 42 F.3d 403 [96 Educ. L. Rep. 365] (7th Cir.1994); *Rubin v. Lafayette Parish School Bd.*, 649 So.2d 1003 [97 Educ. L. Rep. 965] (La.Ct. App.1994), *writ denied*, 654 So.2d 351 (La. 1995).

212. *Powell v. Board of Trustees of Crook County School Dist. No. 1*, 550 P.2d 1112 (Wyo. 1976).

213. *Allen v. Texarkana Pub. Schools*, 794 S.W.2d 138 [62 Educ. L. Rep. 779] (Ark.1990).

214. *Clark County School Dist. v. Riley*, 14 P.3d 22 [149 Educ. L. Rep. 615] (Nev. 2000) (affirming that four days notice was insufficient).

215. *Latouche v. North Country Union High School Dist.*, 131 F.Supp.2d 568 [151 Educ. L. Rep. 817] (D.Vt.2001).

216. *Morrison v. Board of Educ. of Weatherford Pub. Schools*, 47 P.3d 888 [165 Educ. L. Rep. 810] (Okla.Ct.Civ.App.2002).

217. *State ex rel. Chapnick v. East Cleveland City School Dist. Bd. of Educ.*, 755 N.E.2d 883 [157 Educ. L. Rep. 302] (Ohio 2001).

218. *McDaniel v. Princeton City School Dist. Bd. of Educ.*, 45 Fed.Appx. 354 [169 Educ. L. Rep. 129] (6th Cir.2002).

219. *Pavlik v. Chinle Unified School Dist. No. 24*, 985 P.2d 633 [138 Educ. L. Rep. 547] (Ariz. Ct.App.Div.1999).

220. *McGehee v. DePoyster*, 708 So.2d 77 [125 Educ. L. Rep. 246] (Miss.1998).

221. *Rich v. Montpelier Supervisory Dist. (Rich)*, 709 A.2d 501 [125 Educ. L. Rep. 736] (Vt.1998); *Barrera v. Frontier Cent. School Dist.*, 672 N.Y.S.2d 218 [125 Educ. L. Rep. 1332] (N.Y. App. Div.1998).

222. *Rich, Id.* at 542.

principle in a case from Illinois when it affirmed that a board's failure to provide a principal with elaborate, trial-type rights, including the ability to cross-examine witnesses, at his pre-termination hearing, did not deprive him of due process because he lacked a protectable property interest in employment beyond the term of his contract.[223]

Turning to the nature of hearings, where statutes, contracts, or board policies call for pre-termination hearings, they must ordinarily precede individuals' removals from the payroll.[224] Even so, the absence of full adversarial pre-termination hearings does not per se invalidate board actions. Along with providing employees with appropriate notice of the charges that they face, board officials must present all of the evidence they relied on so that teachers can respond.[225] Although events are not automatically excluded from evidence if they occurred during previous school years, in order to be inadmissible, teachers must prove that the passage of time prejudiced their defenses such as when witnesses were unavailable or their memories were unclear.[226] If boards rely on past events, their notice must inform teachers of their intent to do so.[227]

Hearings may be open to the public[228] or closed.[229] At hearings, educators can question witnesses[230] and be assisted by counsel[231] but are not entitled to unlimited time to make their cases.[232] On their part, boards must make particularized findings of fact based on a record[233] containing competent, probative, credible evidence.[234] While courts generally uphold administrative adjudications unless they are contrary to

223. *Head v. Chicago School Reform Bd. of Trustees*, 225 F.3d 794 (7th Cir. 2000).

224. *Vanelli v. Reynolds School Dist. No. 7*, 667 F.2d 773 [2 Educ. L. Rep. 366] (9th Cir.1982). [Case No. 87]

225. *Haddock v. Board of Educ., Unified School Dist. No. 462, Cowley County*, 661 P.2d 368 [10 Educ. L. Rep. 405] (Kan. 1983).

226. *Tomczik v. State Tenure Comm'n*, 438 N.W.2d 642 [53 Educ. L. Rep. 248] (Mich.Ct.App. 1989).

227. *Allen v. Texarkana Pub. Schools*, 794 S.W.2d 138 [62 Educ. L. Rep. 779] (Ark.1990).

228. *Gibson v. Caruthersville School Dist. No. 8*, 336 F.3d 768 [179 Educ. L. Rep. 84] (8th Cir.2003) (referring to an open hearing).

229. *Unke v. Independent School Dist. No. 147, Dilworth*, 510 N.W.2d 271 [88 Educ. L. Rep. 784] (Minn.Ct.App.1994) (declaring that a board violated the state's open meeting law by failing to close a meeting during a discussion of private data involving a school counselor).

230. *Gibson v. Caruthersville School Dist. No. 8*, 336 F.3d 768 [179 Educ. L. Rep. 84] (8th Cir.2003); *Lafferty v. Board of Educ. of Floyd County*, 133 F.Supp.2d 941 [152 Educ. L. Rep. 562] (E.D.Ky.2001).

231. *Gibson v. Caruthersville School Dist. No. 8*, 336 F.3d 768 [179 Educ. L. Rep. 84] (8th Cir.2003); *Coleman v. Reed*, 147 F.3d 751 [127 Educ. L. Rep. 583] (8th Cir. 1998).

232. *Halpern v. Board of Educ. of City of Bristol*, 703 A.2d 1144 [124 Educ. L. Rep. 338] (Conn.1997), *cert. denied*, 523 U.S. 1138, 118 S.Ct. 1842, 140 L.Ed.2d 1092 (1998). *See also Clark v. Board of Directors of School Dist. of Kansas City*, 915 S.W.2d 766 [107 Educ. L. Rep. 368] (Mo.Ct.App. 1996) (positing that although a board's imposing time limits during a hearing may have been unreasonable, its doing so did not prevent a tenured teacher from having a full and fair opportunity to rebut charges that he inappropriately disciplined students).

233. *Harmon v. Mifflin County School Dist.*, 713 A.2d 620 [127 Educ. L. Rep. 916] (Pa.1998); *Barnett v. Board of Educ. of Town of Fairfield*, 654 A.2d 720 [97 Educ. L. Rep. 1086] (Conn. 1995).

234. *Jones v. Sully Buttes Schools*, 340 N.W.2d 697 [14 Educ. L. Rep. 809] (S.D. 1983); *Ross v. Springfield School Dist. No. 19*, 657 P.2d 188 (Or.1982).

the manifest weight of evidence, there is an increasing judicial tendency to examine the evidence in cases involving adverse employment actions.

Insofar as some state statutes permit trials de novo to review dismissals and grant courts original, rather than appellate, jurisdiction, the adequacy of administrative hearings is not directly involved. Other statutes provide that although judicial review is of the record of hearings, courts are empowered to make additional inquiries or take additional testimony in their discretion. In such a case, the Supreme Court of Kansas reasoned that the legislature may provide that an external hearing committee, rather than a local board, had the authority to render a final judgment as to whether a tenured teacher is to be dismissed.[235] The court acknowledged that as long as a board can appeal a committee's action to a judge, its general power is not unconstitutionally impaired.

As with notice requirements, if statutes or board policies prescribe details for conducting hearings, they must be strictly followed or they are likely to be rendered null and void. Pursuant to state statutory provisions or judicial orders,[236] when hearings are conducted before hearing officers rather than boards, teachers may be entitled to see, and respond to, reports before the meetings at which boards are to act.[237]

Issues often arise over the impartiality of board members or hearing officers. In *Hortonville Joint School District No. 1 v. Hortonville Education Association*,[238] a dispute from Wisconsin wherein the Supreme Court upheld board authority to dismiss striking teachers, it discussed the question of impartiality. The Court emphasized that mere familiarity with the facts of a case in light of performing one's statutory duties did not disqualify the board members from acting as decision-makers, especially since they did not have a personal or official stake in dismissing the teachers that would have disqualified them on due process grounds.

In order to disqualify decision-makers, educators must meet the heavy burden of proving that board members or hearing officers are incapable of fairly judging controversies. Yet, even where board members or hearing officers had some involvement in or knowledge of controversies, such as where boards are named in suits,[239] courts typically reject claims that they are unable to act impartially at full and fair hearings.[240] If employees can prove that board members are biased, then courts can find that they were deprived of their rights to due process.[241]

235. *Unified School Dist. No. 380, Marshall County v. McMillen*, 845 P.2d 676 [80 Educ. L. Rep. 1034] (Kan.1993).

236. *Winston v. Board of Educ. of Borough of S. Plainfield*, 309 A.2d 89 (N.J.Super.Ct. App.Div.1973), *aff'd*, 319 A.2d 226 (N.J.1974); *Powell v. Brown*, 238 S.E.2d 220 (W.Va.1977).

237. *Buck v. Board of Educ. of City of N.Y.*, 553 F.2d 315 (2d Cir.1977), *cert. denied*, 438 U.S. 904, 98 S.Ct. 3122, 57 L.Ed.2d 1147 (1978).

238. 426 U.S. 482, 96 S.Ct. 2308, 49 L.Ed.2d 1 (1976).

239. *Green v. Clarendon County*, 923 F.Supp. 829 [109 Educ. L. Rep. 681] (D.S.C. 1996).

240. *Felder v. Charleston County School Dist.*, 489 S.E.2d 191 [120 Educ. L. Rep. 616] (S.C. 1997); *Riter v. Woonsocket School Dist. No. 55–4*, 504 N.W.2d 572 [85 Educ. L. Rep. 249] (S.D. 1993).

241. *Crump v. Board of Educ. of Hickory Admin. School Unit*, 392 S.E.2d 579 [60

Remedies for Wrongful Discharge

Section 1983, discussed in greater detail in Chapter 7, permits individuals to seek redress for violations of their federally protected civil rights. Not surprisingly, school employees rely on section 1983 when filing suits against their boards for claims of unlawful dismissal. Insofar as prevailing parties in civil rights cases can recover attorney fees,[242] section 1983 is an attractive vehicle for redress of adverse employment actions that can be linked to deprivations of the Constitution and/or federal statutory rights.

School employees with property interests in their jobs who suffer adverse employment actions are entitled to recover for damages that they sustained just as if they were in breach of contract suits.[243] The theory of contractual recovery is that it places injured parties in the positions that they would have occupied but for the breaches. At the same time, contract law requires injured parties to mitigate damages. As happened in a case from Arkansas, where a school board breached the contract of a principal but he obtained a new job at a higher salary in another school district, an appellate court affirmed that he was not entitled to recover damages because, by mitigating his damages, he did not suffer any loss.[244]

If teachers are unable to procure other jobs, they are entitled to recover the full back pay that they would have earned but for being discharged,[245] subject to mitigating their losses.[246] Even with the obligation to mitigate, teachers are not required to accept just any positions which may be offered. Rather, educators are obliged to accept only jobs of the same general character as they filled.[247] Moreover, teachers are not bound to accept work in other geographic locations even if the jobs are as good or better than the ones from which they were discharged since individuals are not required to make sacrifices in mitigating their damages.[248] In taking reasonable steps to avoid or minimize their losses,

Educ. L. Rep. 1259] (N.C.1990), *appeal after remand*, 420 S.E.2d 462 [77 Educ. L. Rep. 555] (N.C.Ct. App.1992) (denying supplemental relief in the form of back pay, front pay, reinstatement, and attorney fees), *dismissal allowed, review denied*, 424 S.E.2d 400 (N.C.1992).

242. 42 U.S.C.A. § 1988. *See McDaniel v. Princeton City School Dist. Bd. of Educ.*, 45 Fed.Appx. 354 [169 Educ. L. Rep. 129] (6th Cir.2002).

243. *Okebiyi v. Crew*, 757 N.Y.S.2d 299 [175 Educ. L. Rep. 648] (N.Y. App. Div. 2003).

244. *Larry v. Grady School Dist.*, 119 S.W.3d 528 [183 Educ. L. Rep. 270] (Ark. Ct. App. 2003).

245. *Grant v. Board of Educ. of City of Chicago*, 668 N.E.2d 1188 [112 Educ. L. Rep. 390] (Ill. App.Ct.1996), *appeal denied*, 675 N.E.2d 632 (Ill.1996); *Farmer v. Kelleys Island Bd. of Educ.*, 630 N.E.2d 721 [90 Educ. L. Rep. 387] (Ohio 1994), *opinion clarified*, 638 N.E.2d 79 [93 Educ. L. Rep. 281] (Ohio 1994).

246. *Hosford v. School Comm. of Sandwich*, 659 N.E.2d 1178 [106 Educ. L. Rep. 313] (Mass. 1996).

247. *Zeller v. Prior Lake Pub. Schools*, 108 N.W.2d 602 (Minn.1961); *Selland v. Fargo Pub. School Dist. No. 1*, 302 N.W.2d 391 (N.D.1981).

248. *Kenaston v. School Admin. Dist. No. 40*, 317 A.2d 7 (Me.1974); *Board of School Trustees of Baugo Community Schools v. Indiana Educ. Employment Relations Bd.*, 412 N.E.2d 807 (Ind.Ct.App. 1980).

educators who are improperly discharged may have to accept offers from their boards for part-time teaching duties.[249] The burden of proof is on boards to show that teachers have not made enough effort to mitigate damages.[250]

Insofar as educators must make reasonable efforts to secure other employment in order to help boards reduce the flow of public funds incident to litigation, courts have upheld awards that mitigated recoveries when they returned to work.[251] For example, an appellate court in California affirmed that a school board was entitled to deduct the amount of money a teacher might have earned from an award of back pay after she returned to work from a compulsory leave following her arrest on drug charges and successful completion of a diversion program that led to the dismissal of the charges that she faced.[252] In noting that she made no effort to seek a teaching job during her suspension, even though she had valid credentials and an otherwise unblemished record in an area of high demand, the court rejected the teacher's claim that her perception that she was not hireable was a sufficient basis to demonstrate futility in her attempt to mitigate damages.[253]

Along with back pay, educators who have been improperly subjected to adverse employment actions have been reinstated to their previous positions with front pay[254] and their seniority rights protected.[255] Even so, not all courts agree that employees are automatically entitled to reinstatement,[256] especially where it would be not only disruptive but also destructive of a learning environment.[257]

When teachers breach their employment contracts, school boards may be entitled to damages. In such a case, the Supreme Court of Montana affirmed that a board could recover liquidated damages from a teacher who breached his contract by informing officials that he would not return to work only two weeks before the start of the term.[258] The

---

249. *Gross v. Board of Educ. of Elmsford Union Free School Dist.*, 571 N.Y.S.2d 200 [68 Educ. L. Rep. 473] (N.Y.1991).

250. *Assad v. Berlin–Boylston Reg'l School Comm.*, 550 N.E.2d 357 [58 Educ. L. Rep. 1008] (Mass.1990).

251. *Unzueta v. Ocean View School Dist.*, 8 Cal.Rptr.2d 614 [74 Educ. L. Rep. 1202] (Cal. Ct. App.1992); *Marshall School Dist. v. Hill*, 939 S.W.2d 319 [116 Educ. L. Rep. 1253] (Ark. Ct. App.1997).

252. *Martin v. Santa Clara Unified School Dist.*, 125 Cal.Rptr.2d 337 [169 Educ. L. Rep. 609] (Cal. Ct. App.2002).

253. *See also California Teachers Ass'n v. Governing Bd. of the Golden Valley Unified School Dist.*, 119 Cal.Rptr.2d 642 [164 Educ. L. Rep. 818] (Cal.Ct.App.2002) (directing the trial court, on remand, to consider whether the teacher failed to mitigate her damages by seeking other employment through the exercise of reasonable diligence).

254. *DePace v. Flaherty*, 183 F.Supp.2d 633 [161 Educ. L. Rep. 845] (S.D.N.Y.2002); *Clark County School Dist. v. Riley*, 14 P.3d 22 [149 Educ. L. Rep. 615] (Nev.2000); *Werthman v. School Bd. of Seminole County, Fla.*, 599 So.2d 220 [75 Educ. L. Rep. 683] (Fla.Dist.Ct.App. 1992).

255. *Harms v. Independent School Dist. No. 300, LaCrescent*, 450 N.W.2d 571 [58 Educ. L. Rep. 734] (Minn.1990).

256. *Hicks v. Gayville-Volin School Dist.*, 668 N.W.2d 69 [179 Educ. L. Rep. 889] (S.D.2003). *Mustafa v. Clark County School Dist.*, 157 F.3d 1169 [129 Educ. L. Rep. 990] (9th Cir.1998); *Bowman v. Ferrell*, 627 So.2d 335 [87 Educ. L. Rep. 1107] (Miss.1993).

257. *Jackson v. Delta Special School Dist. No. 2*, 86 F.3d 1489 [110 Educ. L. Rep. 574] (8th Cir.1996).

258. *Arrowhead School Dist. No. 75 v. Klyap*, 79 P.3d 250 [182 Educ. L. Rep. 915] (Mont. 2003).

court indicated that the board was entitled to damages since the teacher failed to prove that the inclusion of such a clause in his contract was unconscionable.[259]

Dismissal Not For Cause: Reduction-in-Force

Almost all jurisdictions have statutes directly dealing with the abolition of teaching or other educational positions without fault on the part of individual employees, more commonly referred to as reduction-in-force (RIF).[260] The grounds for RIF, the order in which employees are released, can "bump" others, and call-back rights are matters of state law subject to modifications by board policies and collective bargaining agreements.

Unless school boards modify their RIF policies incident to collective bargaining agreements, this is an area controlled by statute. RIFs are most commonly statutorily authorized for declines in student enrollments,[261] financial exigencies,[262] elimination of positions or programs,[263] and board discretion.[264] Although courts generally defer to board discretion[265] on the good faith need for RIFs, if challenged, educational officials must prove that they carried out justifiable RIFs,[266] in accord with applicable state law,[267] their own policies[268] and/or bargaining con-

259. For an earlier case with the same result, *see Bowbells Pub. School Dist. No. 14 v. Walker*, 231 N.W.2d 173 (N.D. 1975).

260. *See, e.g.,* Alaska Stat. Ann. § 14.20.177; Cal. Educ. Code Ann. §§ 44955 *et seq.*; Conn. Gen. Stat. §§ 10–151 *et seq.*; Ga. Code Ann. § 20–4–35; Haw. Rev. Stat. § 302A–609; 105 Ill. Comp. Stat. 5/24–12; Ky. Rev. Stat. Ann. § 161.800; La. Rev. Stat. Ann. § 17:81.4; Mich. Comp. Laws § 38.105; N.J. Stat. Ann. § 18A:28–9; N.Y. Educ. Law §§ 3013 *et seq.*; Ohio Rev. Code Ann. § 3319.17; Pa. Stat. Ann. Tit. 24 § 11–1124; R.I. Gen. Laws § 16–13–6; Utah Code Ann. § 53A–8–107; Wash. Rev. Code § 28A.405.210; Wis. Stat. Ann. § 118.23.

261. *Willie v. Board of Trustees*, 59 P.3d 302 (Idaho 2002); *Nickel v. Saline County School Dist. No. 163*, 559 N.W.2d 480 [116 Educ. L. Rep. 393] (Neb.1997).

262. *State ex rel. Quiring v. Board of Educ. of Indep. School Dist. No. 173, Mountain Lake, Minn.*, 623 N.W.2d 634 [152 Educ. L. Rep. 271] (Minn.Ct.App.2001); *Boner v. Eminence R–1 School Dist.*, 55 F.3d 1339 [100 Educ. L. Rep. 886] (8th Cir.1995); *Impey v. Board of Educ. of Borough of Shrewsbury*, 662 A.2d 960 [102 Educ. L. Rep. 639] (N.J.1995).

263. *State ex rel. Quiring v. Board of Educ. of Indep. School Dist. No. 173, Mountain Lake, Minn.*, 623 N.W.2d 634 [152 Educ. L. Rep. 271] (Minn.Ct.App.2001). In a case with a twist, the Supreme Court of

Louisiana affirmed that even though a school board could dismiss a shop teacher who brought a gun to school, he was entitled to back pay since the superintendent failed to notify him that the board eliminated the only class that he was certified to teach as part of a RIF. *Howard v. West Baton Rouge Parish School. Bd.*, 865 So.2d 708 [185 Educ. L. Rep. 778] (La. 2004).

264. *Ballato v. Board of Educ. of Town of Stonington*, 633 A.2d 323 [87 Educ. L. Rep. 171] (Conn.Ct.App.1993), *certification denied*, 638 A.2d 37 (Conn.1994).

265. *State ex rel. Quiring v. Board of Educ. of Indep. School Dist. No. 173, Mountain Lake, Minn.*, 623 N.W.2d 634 [152 Educ. L. Rep. 271] (Minn.Ct.App.2001).

266. *Borr v. McKenzie County Pub. School Dist. No. 1*, 560 N.W.2d 213 [116 Educ. L. Rep. 787] (N.D.1997); *Stone County School Bd. v. McMaster*, 573 So.2d 753 [65 Educ. L. Rep. 666] (Miss.1990).

267. *Wood County Bd. of Educ. v. Smith*, 502 S.E.2d 214 [127 Educ. L. Rep. 1112] (W.Va. 1998); *Barnett v. Board of Educ. of Town of Fairfield*, 654 A.2d 720 [97 Educ. L. Rep. 1086] (Conn.1995); *Junction City School Dist. v. Alphin*, 938 S.W.2d 239 [116 Educ. L. Rep. 499] (Ark.Ct.App. 1997).

268. *Chilson v. Kimball School Dist. No. 7–2*, 663 N.W.2d 667 [177 Educ. L. Rep. 1204] (S.D. 2003); *Gettysburg School Dist.*

tracts.[269] In addition, courts expect policies to include descriptions of the criteria that boards rely on[270] and how they are weighed[271] in implementing RIFs. In an illustrative case, the Supreme Court of Appeals of West Virginia ordered a board to re-employ teachers of hospital or home-bound students with disabilities when it realized that officials violated state law by eliminating their full-time jobs without showing any need to do so and replacing them with part-time hourly employees.[272]

Once a school board determines that a RIF is necessary, the next step is to set the order of release. While RIFs are ordinarily based on seniority, since seniority rights are not derived from common law, they must be based on statutes or collective bargaining agreements. Courts typically treat seniority as a rational, but not exclusive, criterion in selecting teachers for RIFs.[273] To this end, the Supreme Court of Nebraska upheld a board's retention of a tenured business education teacher with three years experience rather than one who worked for six years due to the greater contribution that the former made to the school's extracurricular activities program.[274]

As evidenced by a case from the Court of Appeals of New York, the judiciary can construe tenure statutes broadly to include seniority rights within the category of probationary teachers.[275] The court also observed that since merely abolishing positions is not equivalent to dismissals, boards must consider whether qualified employees are eligible for other available positions.

Boards bear the burden of proving that positions are unnecessary when they are eliminated during RIFs.[276] However, boards are not usually required to interchange a large number of courses or modify established positions to create jobs for teachers who were subjected to RIFs.[277] In evaluating seniority, absent modifications based on board policy or bargaining agreements, the first criterion is actual full-time

53–1 v. Larson, 631 N.W.2d 196 [155 Educ. L. Rep. 1375] (S.D. 2001).

269. *State ex rel. Ohio Ass'n of Pub. School Emp./AFSCME, Local 4, AFL–CIO v. Batavia Local School Dist. Bd. of Educ.*, 729 N.E.2d 743 [144 Educ. L. Rep. 689] (Ohio 2000).

270. *Wilder v. Grant County School Dist. No. 0001*, 658 N.W.2d 923 [175 Educ. L. Rep. 328] (Neb.2003); *Zalac v. Governing Bd. of Ferndale Unified School Dist.*, 120 Cal.Rptr.2d 615 [165 Educ. L. Rep. 277] (Cal.Ct.App.2002).

271. *Nickel v. Saline County School Dist. No. 163*, 559 N.W.2d 480 [116 Educ. L. Rep. 393] (Neb.1997).

272. *State ex rel. Boner v. Kanawha County Bd. of Educ.*, 475 S.E.2d 176 [112 Educ. L. Rep. 504] (W.Va.1996). *See also Wood County Bd. of Educ. v. Smith*, 502 S.E.2d 214 [127 Educ. L. Rep. 1112] (W.Va. 1998).

273. *Board of Educ. of County of Wood v. Enoch*, 414 S.E.2d 630 [73 Educ. L. Rep. 299] (W.Va.1992).

274. *Dykeman v. Board of Educ. of School Dist. of Coleridge, Cedar County*, 316 N.W.2d 69 [2 Educ. L. Rep. 862] (Neb. 1982). [Case No. 88]

275. *Lezette v. Board of Educ., Hudson City School Dist.*, 360 N.Y.S.2d 869 (N.Y. 1974).

276. *Penasco Indep. School Dist. No. 4 v. Lucero*, 526 P.2d 825 (N.M.App.1974); *Bauer v. Board of Educ., Unified School Dist. No. 452, Johnson*, 765 P.2d 1129 [50 Educ. L. Rep. 1255] (Kan. 1988).

277. *Peters v. Board of Educ. of Rantoul Township High School Dist. No. 193 of Champaign County*, 454 N.E.2d 310 [13 Educ. L. Rep. 1039] (Ill.1983); *Butler v. Board of Educ., Unified School Dist. No. 440, Harvey County*, 769 P.2d 651 [52 Educ. L. Rep. 332] (Kan.1989).

service.[278] Beyond that, board methods must be reasonable and not prohibited by statute. For instance, where state law specified that teachers with less seniority within the tenure areas to be abolished were to be part of a RIF, an appellate court in New York invalidated a provision in a bargaining contract that would have allowed individuals to change their tenure areas voluntarily so that they could accrue seniority.[279] A later case in New York extended the statutory protections that applied to teachers based on seniority to tenured teaching assistants.[280]

When tenured teachers lose their jobs as part of RIFs, non-tenured teachers typically cannot be retained in similar positions nor may board policies grant them the status of tenured faculty.[281] In such a case, the Supreme Court of Pennsylvania wrote that the statutory prescription of seniority in RIF situations applies to positions as they exist.[282] In other words, the court decreed that incumbents of eliminated positions were entitled to retain jobs for which they were certificated even if those positions had been occupied by staff members with less seniority.

A controversial case involving the intersection of RIF, seniority, and affirmative action was days away from oral argument at the Supreme Court when the parties reached a settlement agreement. At issue was a dispute from New Jersey wherein a school board, mistakenly acting on its belief that its affirmative action program required it to terminate the contract of a white, rather than an African American, teacher, based solely on race, dismissed the white woman even though the two had virtually identical credentials. The Third Circuit affirmed that since the board's RIF plan, which was adopted to promote racial diversity rather than remedying discrimination or the effects of past discrimination, violated the rights of non-minorities, it was unconstitutional.[283]

Individuals who lose their jobs in RIFs are responsible to assure board officials that their certifications for other positions are valid when it is time for bumping, a term of art that makes it possible for employees with more seniority, and the same credentials, to perhaps be able to save their jobs at the expense of less senior colleagues.[284] While it involved administrators, rather than teachers, a case from Minnesota illustrates

278. *Schoenfeld v. Board of Co-op. Educ. Servs. of Nassau County,* 469 N.Y.S.2d 133 [14 Educ. L. Rep. 1062] (N.Y.App.Div.1983).

279. *Szumigala v. Hicksville Union Free School Dist. Bd. of Educ.,* 539 N.Y.S.2d 83 [52 Educ. L. Rep. 698] (N.Y.App.Div. 1989).

280. *Madison-Oneida Bd. of Co-op. Educ. Servs. v. Mills,* 770 N.Y.S.2d 443 [184 Educ. L. Rep. 532] (N.Y.App.Div. 2003).

281. *Babb v. Independent School Dist. No. I–5 of Rogers County, Okla.,* 829 P.2d 973 [74 Educ. L. Rep. 977] (Okla.1992).

282. *Duncan v. Rochester Area School Bd.,* 571 A.2d 365 [59 Educ. L. Rep. 121] (Pa.1990). *See also Dallap v. Sharon City*

School Dist., 571 A.2d 368 [59 Educ. L. Rep. 124] (Pa.1990).

283. *Taxman v. Board of Educ. of the Township of Piscataway,* 91 F.3d 1547 [111 Educ. L. Rep. 696] (3d Cir.1996), *cert. granted,* 521 U.S. 1117, 117 S.Ct. 2506, 138 L.Ed.2d 1010 [122 Educ. L. Rep. 389] (1997), *cert. dismissed,* 522 U.S. 1010, 118 S.Ct. 595, 139 L.Ed.2d 431 [122 Educ. L. Rep. 570] (1997).

284. *Moe v. Independent School Dist. No. 696, Ely, Minn.,* 623 N.W.2d 899 [152 Educ. L. Rep. 288] (Minn.Ct.App.2001); *School Comm. of Westport v. American Fed'n of State, County and Mun. Employees,* 810 N.E.2d 848 [188 Educ. L. Rep. 962] (Mass.Ct.App. 2004) (involving paraprofessionals).

this principle. An appellate court permitted a middle school principal with less seniority to preserve her job while a more senior elementary school principal was released as part of a RIF due to a job consolidation.[285] The court remarked that since the more senior principal lacked the appropriate qualifications for the job under state law and was ineligible for the position that she was in, she was properly released as part of the RIF. According to the court, the board was not required to change job duties of remaining supervisory positions to accommodate the more senior principal's licensure. In another case, a tenured drafting teacher unsuccessfully alleged that his school board's failure to transfer him to a different job after his position was eliminated as part of a RIF constituted age discrimination. An appellate court in New York affirmed that officials acted properly in not offering the teacher a job in social studies or industrial arts since he was not tenured in those areas.[286] Additionally, the court was satisfied that the board eliminated the program for economic reasons, not age discrimination.

As highlighted by a case from Illinois, being eligible for certification is not the same as having certification. An appellate court affirmed that a teacher who eventually received certification was ineligible to bump a less senior teacher who was qualified.[287] Subsequently, the Supreme Court of Indiana affirmed that a board could retain a less than fully qualified staff member without tenure over a similarly situated tenured colleague where the former was closer to qualifying for the needed second certificate for a new position.[288]

An appellate court in New York affirmed that tenure bumping rights applied only to those who were qualified for jobs, not for new positions. In so ruling, the court agreed that a teacher who lost her job as chair of a social studies department was not entitled to reinstatement to a district level position as chair of social studies.[289] In like fashion, the Court of Appeals of New York affirmed that a psychologist was not entitled to re-employment as an elementary school counselor because he did not have certification for the newly created position.[290]

Subject to board policy[291] and collective bargaining agreements, RIF statutes typically provide that the positions of certificated employees[292] who have been released cannot be filled until they have first been offered

285. *Hinckley v. School Bd. of Indep. School Dist. No. 2167*, 678 N.W.2d 485 [187 Educ. L. Rep. 262] (Minn. Ct. App. 2004).

286. *Davis v. School Dist. of City of Niagara Falls*, 772 N.Y.S.2d 180 [185 Educ. L. Rep. 723] (N.Y. App. Div. 2004).

287. *Hancon v. Board of Educ. of Barrington Community Unit School Dist. No. 220*, 474 N.E.2d 407 [23 Educ. L. Rep. 192] (Ill.App.Ct.1985).

288. *Stewart v. Fort Wayne Community Schools*, 564 N.E.2d 274 [64 Educ. L. Rep. 893] (Ind.1990), *cert. denied*, 502 U.S. 856, 112 S.Ct. 169, 116 L.Ed.2d 133 (1991).

289. *Donato v. Board of Educ. of the Plainview–Old Bethpage Cent. School Dist.*, 729 N.Y.S.2d 187 [156 Educ. L. Rep. 291] (N.Y.App.Div.2001).

290. *Davis v. Mills*, 748 N.Y.S.2d 890 [171 Educ. L. Rep. 323] (N.Y.2002).

291. *Brum v. Board of Educ. of Wood County*, 599 S.E.2d 795 [190 Educ. L. Rep. 1034] (W.Va. 2004).

292. *Greater Johnstown School Dist. v. Greater Johnstown Educ. Ass'n*, 647 A.2d 611 [94 Educ. L. Rep. 352] (Pa.Cmwlth.Ct. 1994).

their jobs back.[293] State law may even specify how many months or years of seniority that individuals retain while on preferred eligibility, or call-back, lists.[294] Under preferred eligibility provisions, employees are usually called back to work in the order of seniority such that the first to be released from their jobs are the first to be called back.[295]

Two cases exemplify the significance of complying with statutory guidelines with regard to teacher eligibility under call-back provisions. If, as in California, state law requires teachers to have two years of experience in school systems before acquiring call-back rights, then those with less seniority have no rights to preferred eligibility for reinstatement.[296] Further, an appellate court in New York ordered a board to place a teacher on a preferred eligibility list even though after he was laid off as part of a RIF, his program was terminated and the board that took over dismissed him for unsatisfactory performance.[297] The court determined that the board could not consider the teacher's work after he was laid off in evaluating whether he met his statutory duty of providing faithful and competent service.

Retirement

In General

All jurisdictions have statutes addressing teacher retirement.[298] Fortunately, legal issues that were crucial in the early stages of the development of teacher retirement systems have been long settled as courts upheld their constitutionality[299] and the authority of retirement boards to act as they see fit in managing retirement funds.[300] Yet, litigation continues over eligibility for participation in state retirement systems and proposed changes in benefits.

293. *See Cook v. Board of Educ. of Eldorado Community Unit School Dist. No. 4*, 820 N.E.2d 481 [194 Educ. L. Rep. 922] (Ill. App. Ct. 2004) (deciding that a genuine issue of material fact regarding how broadly the school board defined the category of positions in which teacher's aide/library aide worked precluded her involuntary dismissal).

294. *Avila v. Board of Educ. of N. Babylon Union Free School Dist.*, 658 N.Y.S.2d 703 [119 Educ. L. Rep. 205] (N.Y.App.Div. 1997), *leave to appeal denied*, 666 N.Y.S.2d 563 (N.Y.1997).

295. *Board of Educ. of County of Mercer v. Owensby*, 526 S.E.2d 831 [143 Educ. L. Rep. 1065] (W.Va.1999); *Fontaine v. Wissahickon School Dist.*, 658 A.2d 851 [100 Educ. L. Rep. 625] (Pa. Cmwlth.Ct.1995).

296. *California Teachers Ass'n v. Mendocino Unified School Dist.*, 111 Cal. Rptr.2d 879 [156 Educ. L. Rep. 1183] (Cal. Ct.App.2001).

297. *Bojarczuk v. Mills*, 774 N.Y.S.2d 593 [186 Educ. L. Rep. 955] (N.Y.App.Div. 2004).

298. *See, e.g.*, ALA. CODE § 16–25–110; CAL. EDUC. CODE §§ 22100 *et seq.*; FLA. STAT. ANN. § 238.01; GA. CODE ANN. § 47–3–44; ILL.COMP. STAT. ANN. 5/16–106; KY. REV. STAT. ANN. §§ 161.220 *et seq.*; N.Y. EDUC. LAW § 501 § 501; OHIO REV. CODE ANN. §§ 3307.01 *et seq.*; OKLA. STAT. ANN. tit. 70 §§ 17–101 *et seq.*; PA. STAT. ANN. Tit. 24 §§ 8102 *et seq.*; W. VA. CODE ANN. § 18–7A–1.

299. *Trumper v. School Dist. No. 55 of Musselshell County*, 173 P. 946 (Mont. 1918); *Shinnick v. State*, 128 N.E. 91 (Ohio 1920); *School Dist. No. 1, Multnomah County v. Teachers' Retirement Fund Ass'n of School Dist. No. 1, Multnomah County*, 96 P.2d 419 (Or.1939).

300. *Kraus v. Riley*, 80 P.2d 864 (Mont. 1938); *Crawford v. Teachers' Retirement Fund Ass'n of School Dist. No. 1, Multnomah County*, 99 P.2d 729 (Or.1940).

Teacher retirement systems include two financial elements: one is the amount derived from employee contributions, the other from employer contributions. The former is known technically as an annuity, the latter as a pension. Typical retirement systems mandate deductions from employee salaries with states contributing the remainder necessary to provide for retirement allowances. In addition to provisions for retirement benefits, state plans also ordinarily cover other key areas such as death benefits for survivors.[301]

Except for changes in existing retirement provisions, or where constitutional provisions may intrude, legislatures have plenary power to establish plans as they see fit. Local retirement systems typically preceded state-level programs in many jurisdictions.[302] Insofar as local plans were often unsound actuarially and because states have more economic ability to finance retirement plans, with the exception of a few large municipalities,[303] they were blended into state systems.

Membership Eligibility and Benefits

Local boards cannot adopt rules that contravene state retirement laws. If states set eligibility requirements for retirement programs, local boards can neither deviate from these provisions[304] nor institute incentive plans for early retirement that might threaten the actuarial soundness of state systems.[305]

Litigation has occurred, with mixed results, over whether employees have had sufficient notice when they seek to join retirement systems retroactively. Whether employees can join retirement systems retroactively depends on the nature of the notice that they received. If board officials can demonstrate that employees received appropriate notice, individuals cannot join retroactively.[306] Conversely, if employees can prove that they did not receive appropriate notice, they can join state retirement systems at a later point.[307]

Turning to issues involving service credit in retirement systems, the Supreme Court of Wisconsin affirmed that two teachers who left the

301. *Venet v. Teachers' Retirement Sys. of City of N.Y.*, 552 N.Y.S.2d 275 [59 Educ. L. Rep. 161] (N.Y.App.Div.1990), *appeal denied*, 559 N.Y.S.2d 982 (N.Y.1990); *Pepper v. Peacher*, 742 P.2d 21 [41 Educ. L. Rep. 1107] (Okla.1987) (holding that death benefits were not revoked by divorce where the name of the beneficiary was not changed).

302. *See, e.g., Board of Educ. of Louisville v. City of Louisville*, 157 S.W.2d 337 (Ky.1941).

303. *See, e.g., Venet v. Teachers' Retirement Sys. of City of N.Y.*, 552 N.Y.S.2d 275 [59 Educ. Law Rep. 161] (N.Y.App.Div. 1990), *appeal denied*, 559 N.Y.S.2d 982 (N.Y.1990).

304. *Herzig v. Board of Educ. of the Town of W. Hartford*, 204 A.2d 827 (Conn. 1964).

305. *Fair Lawn Educ. Ass'n v. Fair Lawn Bd. of Educ.*, 401 A.2d 681 (N.J. 1979).

306. *Liebert v. Board of Educ. for Scotia–Glenville Cent. School Dist.*, 704 N.Y.S.2d 352 [142 Educ. L. Rep. 477] (N.Y.App.Div.2000), *leave to appeal denied*, 712 N.Y.S.2d 447 (N.Y.2000); *Capone v. Board of Educ. of Lafayette Cent. School Dist.*, 697 N.Y.S.2d 895 [139 Educ. L. Rep. 1006] (N.Y.App.Div.1999).

307. *Higgins v. Public School Employees' Retirement Sys.*, 736 A.2d 745 [137 Educ. L. Rep. 1041] (Pa.Cmwlth.Ct.1999); *Serio v. Board of Educ. of Valley Stream Union Free School Dist. No. 13*, 703 N.Y.S.2d 232 [142 Educ. L. Rep. 465] (N.Y.App.Div.2000); *Bettis v. Potosi R–III School Dist.*, 51 S.W.3d 183 [156 Educ. L. Rep. 329] (Mo.Ct.App. 2001).

profession and took separation benefits retained their membership rights in the state's system when they returned to work.[308] The court found that the teachers' service credit was sufficient to sustain their memberships as a matter of right.

In a related concern, courts in Massachusetts,[309] Ohio,[310] and Pennsylvania[311] denied individuals who taught in non-public schools opportunities to join their state retirement systems while an appellate court in Pennsylvania affirmed that officials of the state retirement system properly denied retirement credit to a member who worked with students from non-public schools in her capacity with a not-for-profit corporation.[312] An appellate court in Ohio affirmed that a teacher who was employed as a part-time teaching assistant at a public university for two years was ineligible to purchase service credit.[313] Further, the Supreme Court of Alaska was of the opinion that the board of the state's teacher retirement service erred in granting service credit to two teachers who worked both outside of the state and with the Bureau of Indian Affairs.[314]

Courts have reached mixed results with regard to military service, as some have permitted veterans to purchase credit[315] while others disagreed.[316] Other courts reached opposite outcomes with regard to credit for out-of-state service as some grant it[317] but others refuse to do so.[318] Still other courts granted substitute[319] and part-time[320] teachers

308. *Solie v. Employee Trust Funds Bd.*, 695 N.W.2d 463 [197 Educ. L. Rep. 798] (Wis. 2005).

309. *Dube v. Contributory Retirement Appeal Bd.*, 733 N.E.2d 1089 [146 Educ. L. Rep. 414] (Mass.Ct.App.2000).

310. *State ex rel. State Teachers Retirement Bd. v. West Geauga Local School Dist. Bd. of Educ.*, 722 N.E.2d 93 [140 Educ. L. Rep. 743] (Ohio Ct.App.1998), *appeal allowed*, 705 N.E.2d 367 (Ohio 1999), *appeal dismissed as improvidently allowed*, 718 N.E.2d 928 (Ohio 1999).

311. *Cain v. Public School Employees' Retirement Sys.*, 651 A.2d 660 [96 Educ. L. Rep. 632] (Pa.Cmwlth.Ct.1994), *appeal denied*, 659 A.2d 560 (Pa.1995).

312. *Thorpe v. Public School Employees' Retirement Bd.*, 879 A.2d 341 [200 Educ. L. Rep. 814] (Pa. Cmwlth. Ct. 2005).

313. *State ex rel. Palmer v. State Teachers Retirement Bd.*, 629 N.E.2d 1377 [89 Educ. L. Rep. 946] (Ohio Ct.App.1993).

314. *Bartley v. State, Dep't of Admin., Teacher's Retirement Bd.*, 110 P.3d 1254 [197 Educ. L. Rep. 849] (Alaska 2005).

315. *Dailey v. Public School Retirement Sys. of Mo.*, 707 F.Supp. 1087 [52 Educ. L. Rep. 582] (E.D.Mo.1989); *Morris v. Commonwealth, Public School Employees' Retirement Sys.*, 538 A.2d 1385 [45 Educ. L. Rep. 1131] (Pa.Cmwlth.Ct.1988), *appeal denied*, 557 A.2d 345 (Pa.1989); *Watkins v.*

Oldham, 731 S.W.2d 829 [40 Educ. L. Rep. 551] (Ky.Ct.App.1987).

316. *Fishman v. Teachers' Retirement Sys.*, 408 N.E.2d 113 (Ill.App.Ct.1980), *cert. denied*, 452 U.S. 915, 101 S.Ct. 3048, 69 L.Ed.2d 418 (1981); *Newcomb v. New York State Teachers' Retirement Sys.*, 373 N.Y.S.2d 554 (N.Y.1975).

317. *Hopkins v. Public School Employees' Retirement Bd.*, 674 A.2d 1197 [109 Educ. L. Rep. 271] (Pa.Cmwlth.Ct.1996) (commenting that a youth correctional facility qualified as public educational institution for the purpose of whether a teacher could purchase retirement credits). *See also Teacher Retirement Sys. of Texas v. Cottrell*, 583 S.W.2d 928 (Tex.Civ.App. 1979) (affirming that a teacher was entitled to purchase service credits for his three years of out-of-state teaching in the public school system at West Point).

318. *Day v. Public School Employees' Retirement Sys.*, 682 A.2d 398 [112 Educ. L. Rep. 1012] (Pa.Cmwlth.Ct.1996) (denying retirement credit for an out-of-state maternity leave of absence which was neither certified by an out-of-state employer nor credited by its retirement system).

319. *Board of State Teachers Retirement Sys. of Ohio v. Cuyahoga Falls City School Dist. Bd. of Educ.*, 498 N.E.2d 167 [35 Educ. L. Rep. 266] (Ohio Ct.App.1985).

320. *Madden v. Contributory Retirement Appeal Bd.*, 729 N.E.2d 1095 [144 Educ. L.

eligibility to join retirement systems. Courts have also rejected claims that independent contractors could join retirement systems[321] and that lump-sum buy-outs of employee contracts should have counted toward retirement benefits.[322]

On a specific matter, in a non-education case, the Supreme Court struck down the practice of treating women differently from men regarding financial aspects of retirement.[323] In the context of public employment, the Court interpreted Title VII as barring the use of retirement plans that required women to contribute more than men for equal benefits. The Court added that neither Title VII nor its judgment was intended to revolutionize the insurance and pension industries. Rather, the Court thought that it did not imply either that it would have been unlawful for employers to set aside equal retirement contributions for each of their employees and have retirees purchase benefits in the open market or that insurance companies would have been prevented from considering the composition of employers' work forces in calculating the costs of retirement and/or death benefit plans. Five years later, the Court concluded that Title VII prohibited employers from offering their employees the option of receiving retirement benefits from one of several companies that they selected, all of which paid women lower monthly benefits than men who made the same contributions.[324]

Changes in Provisions—Calculations of Benefits

The legality of changes in retirement plans depends on whether arrangements are considered contractual between states and teachers. The general rule is that legislation does not create contractual rights unless legislative intent to this effect is clear. In this way, retirement statutes have been regarded as expressions of legislative policy, subject to future change if circumstances warrant. In such a case, the First Circuit contended that legislative changes to Maine's retirement system did not violate the contractual rights of teachers since they had not started receiving their pension benefits under state law.[325] Additionally, the Supreme Court of Ohio upheld changes in the state's statutory classification that placed members into groups as non-retired and retired, asserting that teachers do not possess their contract rights until their pensions vest by operation of law.[326]

Rep. 721] (Mass.2000); *Hawes v. Public School Employees' Retirement Bd.*, 778 A.2d 1277 [156 Educ. L. Rep. 1147] (Pa.Cmwlth. Ct.2001) (permitting service as a part-time teacher to count toward total service).

321. *Roesch v. Board of Educ. for Wayne–Finger Lakes Bd. of Co-op. Educ. Servs.*, 687 N.Y.S.2d 448 [134 Educ. L. Rep. 542] (N.Y.App.Div.1999).

322. *Horowitz v. New York State Teachers' Retirement Sys.*, 740 N.Y.S.2d 158 [163 Educ. L. Rep. 939] (N.Y.App.Div.2002); *Wallon v. New York State Teachers' Retire-*

ment Sys., 741 N.Y.S.2d 597 [164 Educ. L. Rep. 854] (N.Y.App.Div.2002).

323. *City of Los Angeles, Dep't of Water and Power v. Manhart*, 435 U.S. 702, 98 S.Ct. 1370, 55 L.Ed.2d 657 (1978).

324. *Arizona Governing Comm. for Tax Deferred Annuity and Deferred Comp. Plans v. Norris*, 463 U.S. 1073, 103 S.Ct. 3492, 77 L.Ed.2d 1236 (1983).

325. *Parker v. Wakelin*, 123 F.3d 1 [120 Educ. L. Rep. 966] (1st Cir.1997), *cert. denied*, 523 U.S. 1106, 118 S.Ct. 1675, 140 L.Ed.2d 813 (1998).

In its only case on point, *Dodge v. Board of Education*,[327] the Supreme Court examined legislation from Illinois providing for pensions for retired teachers that were paid entirely from tax funds. When the legislature reduced the allowance for all teachers, including those who had already retired, the Supreme Court of Illinois rejected their claim that this violated their contractual rights since no contract existed. The Court affirmed that since the gratuitous payments were non-contractual, the teachers did not have any vested rights to the funds. The substantial weight of authority is now against permitting the allowances of those already retired to be changed to their disadvantage.[328]

Most courts have adopted an attitude toward retirement benefits that is different from that of their predecessors. Insofar as modern courts view retirement benefits as inducements to enter and remain in public service,[329] they treat them as property rights governed by statute for employees whose rights have vested.[330] In such a case, the Supreme Court of Appeals of West Virginia agreed with two members who alleged that the board of the state's retirement system erred in refusing to include lump-sum payments for accumulated vacation pay in the final calculation of their final average salaries for the purposes of computing their benefits.[331] The court reasoned that since the rule that the board applied went into effect after the petitioners made their requests for benefits, it was inapplicable. Conversely, where a school system in New York granted a disproportionate salary increase to an administrator who was about to retire, an appellate court held that officials at the state's retirement system had a rational basis for excluding this financial incentive in calculating his retirement benefits.[332] Also, the Supreme Court of Michigan rejected the claim of retired public school employees who challenged an increase in their prescription drug co-payments and the deductibles under the master health care plan as diminishing or impairing their accrued financial benefits.[333] The court responded that since the statute establishing health care benefits for public school

326. *State ex rel. Horvath v. State Teachers Retirement Bd.*, 697 N.E.2d 644 [127 Educ. L. Rep. 1017] (Ohio 1998), *reconsideration denied*, 700 N.E.2d 334 (Ohio 1998), *cert. denied*, 525 U.S. 1179, 119 S.Ct. 1115, 143 L.Ed.2d 111 (1999).

327. 302 U.S. 74, 58 S.Ct. 98, 82 L.Ed. 57 (1937).

328. *Newcomb v. Ogden City Pub. School Teachers' Retirement Comm'n*, 243 P.2d 941 (Utah 1952).

329. *Rosinski v. Teachers Retirement Ass'n Bd. of Trustees*, 495 N.W.2d 14 [80 Educ. L. Rep. 979] (Minn.Ct.App.1993).

330. *See, e.g., Tubbs v. State ex rel., Teachers' Retirement Sys. of Okla.*, 57 P.3d 571 [171 Educ. L. Rep. 360] (Okla.2002) (permitting a pension to be divided after a divorce); *Pierce v. State*, 910 P.2d 288 (N.M. 1995) (ascertaining that state retirement

laws create vested property rights, but not contract rights); *National Educ. Ass'n-R.I. by Scigulinsky v. Retirement Bd. of R.I. Employees' Retirement Sys.*, 972 F.Supp. 100 [120 Educ. L. Rep. 1006] (D.R.I.1997) (distinguishing the rights of vested and non-vested employees).

331. *Summers v. West Virginia Consol. Pub. Retirement Bd.*, 618 S.E.2d 408 [201 Educ. L. Rep. 774] (W. Va. 2005).

332. *Cooper v. New York State Teachers' Retirement Sys.*, 795 N.Y.S.2d 802 [198 Educ. L. Rep. 680] (N.Y. App. Div. 2005). For an earlier case with the same result, *see Wallon v. New York State Teachers' Retirement Sys.*, 741 N.Y.S.2d 597 [164 Educ. L. Rep. 854] (N.Y. App. Div. 2002).

333. *Studier v. Michigan Pub. School Employees' Retirement Bd.*, 698 N.W.2d 350 [199 Educ. L. Rep. 398] (Mich. 2005).

retirees did not create a contract between them and the state for the purposes of federal and state constitutional provisions that prohibit the impairment of contracts, such that these were not accrued financial benefits, their claim was without merit.

At issue in one case was a state constitutional provision which made retirement benefits contractual so that they could not be reduced by legislative action.[334] When the state retirement board sought to adopt new mortality tables that would have reduced the benefits of members, the Court of Appeals of New York declared that this would have violated the state constitution.[335] In rejecting the claim that not permitting the changes would have bankrupted the system, the court pointed out that if that were to have been the case, then legislators would have had to provide the funds needed to pay the allowances of those who were already members. The same court later invalidated a statute that would have required the retirement system to invest funds in municipal bonds that were floated as part of a plan to alleviate a severe fiscal emergency in New York City.[336] The court noted that such an approach was unacceptable since it could have interfered with the integrity and security of the sources that paid for the protected benefits.

The fact that periods of rapid inflation can place retired personnel in poor economic conditions beyond their control has caused a relaxation of the prohibition against expenditures to raise retirement allowances. To this end, the Supreme Court of Wisconsin distinguished a moral obligation from gratuity, defining the former as "an obligation which, though lacking in any foundation cognizable in law, springs from a sense of justice and equity ... but not from a mere sense of doing benevolence or charity."[337] Insofar as the state statute authorized local boards to provide additional payments, the court indicated that they did not fall within the constitutional inhibition that applied only to the state treasury.

[Case No. 79]   No Right to Tenure in Coaching Position

LAGOS v. MODESTO CITY SCHOOLS DISTRICT

United States Court of Appeals, Ninth Circuit, 1988.
843 F.2d 347 [46 Educ. L. Rep. 60].

NOONAN, CIRCUIT JUDGE:

John Lagos sues under 42 U.S.C. § 1983 asserting that he has been injured by the defendants conspiring to deny him renewal of his year-to-year position as head baseball coach at Thomas Downey High School, a public school in Modesto, California. Lagos' complaint alleges that he

---

334. *Ballentine v. Koch,* 651 N.Y.S.2d 362 (N.Y.1996); *Winston v. City of N.Y.,* 759 F.2d 242 [24 Educ. L. Rep. 27] (2d Cir. 1985); *Sheffield v. Alaska Public Employees' Ass'n,* 732 P.2d 1083 (Alaska 1987).

335. *Birnbaum v. New York State Teachers' Retirement Sys.,* 176 N.Y.S.2d 984 (N.Y.1958). [Case No. 89]

336. *Sgaglione v. Levitt,* 375 N.Y.S.2d 79 (N.Y.1975).

337. *State ex rel. Holmes v. Krueger,* 72 N.W.2d 734, 738 (Wis.1955).

was hired in 1974 by the Modesto City Schools District to teach physical education and mathematics and to be the head wrestling coach at Thomas Downey High School. In 1975 he became assistant varsity baseball coach and from 1978 until June 1985 he was head varsity baseball coach. The defendants, charged with depriving Lagos of his civil rights, are the school district, four named members of the school district board, the principal, vice principal and the athletic director of the high school, and another teacher at the school who in 1985 was made head varsity baseball coach in Lagos' stead. Lagos alleges that he has been deprived of property and liberty without due process and denied the equal protection of the laws. In the complaint filed on his behalf and verified by his brother, Panos Lagos, he states that he is entitled to damages of not less than $1,500,000, attorneys fees, exemplary damages and punitive damages.

Lagos' employment as baseball coach was by virtue of a contract good for one year that was not renewed in June of 1985. Lagos seeks to get around the contract by stating that when in 1974 he left Marysville he was orally assured by the then principal of Downey High School that he would "be ultimately placed in his 'strength' position" coaching baseball; that he was never told that his baseball position would be a one year position; that in 1983 the present principal told him that he would "pull for him"; that he was replaced because of the defendants' "personal likes and preferences"; and that it was "the custom, practice and procedure" of the school district that it would keep coaches in their coaching positions as long as they "performed their tasks satisfactorily."

Lagos' amended complaint was dismissed by the district court for failure to state a cause of action. We review anew. Lagos' efforts to surmount the obvious barrier of the time limitation built into his one-year contract merit no discussion except for his claim that there was a practice which converted the one-year contract into something more. This contention runs squarely into California Education Code Section 44923, which provides:

> In the event a permanent employee of the school district has tenure as a full-time employee of the district, any assignment or employment of such employee in addition to his full-time assignment may be terminated by the governing board of the district at any time.

Lagos was a permanent employee of the school district having tenure as a full-time teacher of mathematics. His assignment as baseball coach falls within the language of the statute. The statute gave notice to Lagos that there was no custom in California of creating tenure for coaches who were already employed as full-time teachers in a school.

Lagos argues that he had a constitutionally protected property interest in his coaching job. We have held that California does not recognize a property interest in a community college district superintendent in his job as superintendent. We noted that provisions of the California Education Code defined and confined the superintendent's rights.

In *San Bernardino Physicians Services Medical Group*, we held that a medical services group's contract with a county did not constitute constitutionally protected property. In broad dictum we suggested that employment contracts were more easily protectible than other contracts and that crucial factors in treating them as property were the security with which they were held under state law and the importance they had to the employee as an individual. The Supreme Court has affirmed a case holding on its particular facts that a school athletic director and football coach had property in his employment contract. in *Vail* [*v. Board of Education*], the athletic director was persuaded to give up the job in Joliet he had held for thirteen years, take a salary cut, and move to Paris, Illinois to rejuvenate its athletic program, a feat he did not believe could be accomplished in one year. His new contract was formally for one year but the board of education promised him that it would renew him for a second year. The board, instead, terminated him in the first year, invoking Illinois law which required only 60 days' notice to terminate a new teacher. Upholding the director's section 1983 claim, the district court found that he had in fact a two-year employment contract, which constituted property, arbitrarily and therefore unconstitutionally taken by the board. The court of appeals did not find the district court's finding of fact clearly erroneous. As a matter of law the court of appeals held that a two-year contract was not unlawful in Illinois, that the board had exercised its legal discretion to give such a contract, and that *Vail* was not claiming any right of tenure, "which would have been extinguished by the actions of the Board." Judge Posner dissented on the ground that this "squabble" between a school and its football coach should not have been in the federal courts. He protested that if the majority was right, every breach of a public employment contract by a public body could be turned into a constitutional tort a result "contrary to every principle of federalism and good sense."

As the Supreme Court divided evenly, "no principle" was "settled" by *Vail*. In *Smith v. Board of Education* another panel of the Seventh Circuit considered whether a high school head football coach for 26 years had tenure in his coaching job, protectible as property under the Constitution, and held that he did not. The facts alleged in Smith are close to those alleged by the plaintiff in this case. In Smith, as in this case, they do not state a cause of action.

Lagos' contract was good for one year. He alleges nothing from which it could be inferred that he was promised the head coaching position for life. An individual's interest in his employment is a reasonable factor to be considered in determining whether he has property in his job, and there is no doubt that Lagos had a high emotional investment in his coaching position. But an individual's interest cannot unilaterally create property. The security with which the job is held is also relevant. Lagos had no security. The board hired him from year to year. The allegation of a custom to the contrary is refuted as a matter of law by the California Education Code Section 44923. Lagos continues to enjoy tenure as a mathematics teacher. California expressly does not grant tenure in assignments additional to regular full-time assignments.

California created no property for Lagos of which he has been arbitrarily deprived.

Lagos also has no constitutionally recognized liberty interest infringed by the defendants. He has not been stigmatized by his non-renewal; he has not been so burdened that he cannot take advantage of other employment opportunities. Who is a good coach is apt to be the subject of debate. It is no shame to lose one's job in such an argument. We were assured in oral argument that John Lagos' coaching record was "excellent." We can understand his pain at not being renewed, at not having the continued opportunity to do what he loves to do. But his disappointment is not a loss of that liberty which the Constitution guarantees.

Lagos' equal protection claim has not been pressed on appeal. His pendent state claim for defamation has been rightly dismissed. The district court was correct in granting the defendants' motion to dismiss the entire case.

As a result of his disappointment Lagos has made the school district and the individual defendants defend a federal law suit both in the district court and on appeal. He has subjected them to the payment of their attorneys fees. He has asked for very large actual damages. When queried in oral argument how he had arrived at these damages, counsel replied that they were based on the loss of Lagos' coaching stipend (not more than $1500 per year) and the fact that "in an Alameda County case" he knew of someone getting a $300,000 verdict in what seemed to him analogous circumstances. It is extraordinarily difficult to see what justification existed for the verified complaint's assertion that Lagos' damages were not less than $1.5 million. We do not sympathize with any effort to make uncomfortable or intimidate the individual defendants or the board by claiming an astronomical amount not based on any identifiable facts.

AFFIRMED.

Notes

1. Should supplemental positions such as coaches be eligible for tenure?

2. Suppose that there was no extra pay for the coaching position, but that it was part of the teacher's regular load. Would this have been a legally significant difference?

[Case No. 80]   Right of Teacher to Refuse to Accept Student

HATTON v. WICKS

United States Court of Appeals, Fifth Circuit, 1984.
744 F.2d 501 [20 Educ. L. Rep. 400].

JERRE S. WILLIAMS, CIRCUIT JUDGE. This is an unusual case in which an established sixth grade teacher, under contract and who had taught sixth grade at the same school for ten years, was discharged for refusing to accept into her class a thirteen year old "disciplinary problem student" who chose her as his teacher in what the discharged teacher calls a "lineup" of the available teachers. The use of the word "lineup" to describe what actually occurred is, to some extent at least, a stigmatizing overstatement. Appellant Ethel Hatton was an established and qualified school teacher under contract to teach in the Columbus Municipal Separate School District, Columbus, Mississippi. She was called into the office of the principal of her school, appellee Marshall Wicks, together with two other available sixth grade teachers. Also present in the office was the thirteen year old male student and that student's mother. The principal asked the student which of the three teachers he would like to have as his sixth grade teacher, and he chose the appellant. The principal then stated that it was settled and the student would be in appellant's class. When the mother presented the thirteen year old boy for enrollment in appellant's class the next Monday, appellant refused to enroll him.

In the afternoon of the same day, appellant was summoned to appellee's office for a conference. When appellee told her at the conference that she was under an obligation to accept the student in her class, she indicated she would not do so and walked out of the meeting without further discussion.

Appellee later wrote her a letter granting her a conference with him, setting a date ten days later. She failed to appear at this conference. In the meantime the child had been assigned to another teacher.

Appellant was discharged for these two instances of what the principal and other school authorities call "insubordination." She was afforded hearings before the Superintendent of Schools, and the entire School Board, and then a review by the Department of Education of the State of Mississippi. All three of these tribunals upheld her discharge.

Five years later appellant brought this suit in the United States District Court under 42 U.S.C. § 1983 claiming substantive due process of law violations on the ground that the public school authorities did not have the constitutional right under the Fourteenth Amendment to discharge her under the facts outlined above. After a full trial, the district court held that there had been no constitutional violation in her discharge. We affirm.

There is no procedural due process of law challenge in this case. Appellant does not challenge the adequacy of the administrative hearings which she was given in accordance with Mississippi law. She challenges only the result of those hearings which upheld her discharge.

Appellant raises the question of whether there was "substantial evidence" in the administrative proceedings and in the district court to establish the existence of a constitutional due process violation. The issue is not one of "substantial evidence", however. The critical and controlling facts in this case are not in dispute at all. They are as reported above. The sole question which is before us, then, is whether the existence of these facts and these events constitutes a violation of appellant Hatton's civil rights under the due process of law clause of the Fourteenth Amendment. That question obviously is a question of law, a question of the interpretation and application of the Constitution. As such we are not bound to a clearly erroneous standard of review of the findings and conclusions of the district court.

No issue was raised concerning the motive for appellant's discharge. The finding, not disputed, is that appellant was discharged for insubordination for twice failing to accept the pupil in her class when ordered to do so by the principal. Thus we do not have the typical mixed motive case so we need not inquire whether or not she would have been discharged absent these circumstances. Neither party challenges the finding of the district court that the discharge was for the overt circumstances shown in this case.

Appellant takes the position that she could not be fired for "insubordination" because under Mississippi law insubordination requires "a constant or continuing intentional refusal to obey a direct or implied order, reasonable in nature and given by or with proper authority." Whether or not her actions constituted insubordination under the Mississippi law does not control this case. Mississippi cannot by defining "insubordination" or other grounds for discharge of teachers create or eliminate federal constitutional rights. The federal rights are independent of the state law. It is not amiss, however, to point out that her two refusals to accept this pupil into her class may constitute insubordination under the Mississippi definition.

Whether or not appellant was insubordinate under Mississippi law, the issue before this Court is whether she has established that her discharge under the admitted facts and circumstances of this case constituted a violation of her substantive due process right under the Fourteenth Amendment. The district court concluded that she had not established a violation of such a constitutional right, and we agree.

The action of the principal may have been somewhat unusual in giving this particular pupil the opportunity to choose which teacher he wished to have in the sixth grade. It should be pointed out, however, that such choice was under the supervision of the principal, who had ruled out two other teachers who otherwise would have been available because their classes were housed in temporary buildings outside the main school building, and the principal felt that this particular pupil might create less problems if he remained in the main school building. Further, while no one disputes appellant's claim that this particular pupil was a "disciplinary problem", he did not constitute such a serious problem that he could not attend regular school classes with other students. After appellant's refusal to accept this student, the student was assigned to another sixth grade class as a regular pupil in that class. Finally, the record reveals that the pupil had rational and sensible reasons for choosing the class of this particular teacher rather than the other two sixth grade teachers who accompanied appellant to the principal's office.

The record reveals that this particular student was being given an opportunity that students generally did not have. But we cannot quarrel with a conclusion of a school administrator that treating a particular student with such care might be to the advantage not only of the pupil but also of the other students in the school as well.

This discussion of the circumstances yields the constitutional answer. This Court would be intruding in the details of the administration of the school if it found a constitutional violation in this case. Appellant was not placed in a lineup. She and two other teachers were simply brought into the principal's room to enable this pupil to decide which class he wanted to go into for the sixth grade. The principal then directed that his choice be implemented, and appellant refused. Later when he attempted to talk to her about it again, she again refused and walked out on him. She makes no showing that she is entitled to any privilege over any other teacher who might have this pupil assigned to her or his classroom. There was not the slightest hint of racial, religious, or gender discrimination, or interference with her free speech or other personal rights. She was simply assigned a pupil for her class who had the right to be assigned to such a class. She refused the assignment twice and was discharged. It must be recognized that under these circumstances a teacher who refuses to carry out her or his obligations in this manner is "interfering with the regular operation of the schools," and is engaged in conduct which "materially and substantially impedes the operation or effectiveness of the educational program." Appellant's asserted section 1983 claim must fail.

AFFIRMED.

Notes

1.   Why do you think Hatton filed suit in federal court under Section 1983 rather than state courts after losing before the state department of education?

2.   The definition of insubordination enunciated by the Supreme Court of Mississippi in *Sims v. Board of Trustees, Holly Springs Municipal Separate School Dist.*, cited in the case, was taken directly from the Supreme Court of *Minnesota in Ray v. Minneapolis Bd. of Educ.*, 202 N.W.2d 375 (Minn.1972).

3.   Should there be any conditions under which a teacher can refuse to instruct a student? Consider the last paragraph of the opinion.

[Case No. 81]   Discipline of Teacher—Incompetence—Neglect of Duty, Use of Controversial Instructional Approach

LACKS v. FERGUSON REORGANIZED SCHOOL DISTRICT R–2

United States Court of Appeals, Eighth Circuit, 1998.
147 F.3d 718 [127 Educ. L. Rep. 568].

RICHARD S. ARNOLD, CHIEF JUDGE.

In this case Ferguson–Florissant Reorganized School District ("the school board") appeals the District Court's grant of summary judgment in favor of the plaintiff, Cecilia Lacks, on Lacks's claim under Missouri law that her termination by the board was not supported by substantial evidence. The school board also appeals a jury verdict in favor of Lacks on First Amendment and race discrimination claims. We reverse and remand for the entry of judgment in favor of the defendant school district. We hold, among other things, that a school district does not violate the First Amendment when it disciplines a teacher for allowing students to use profanity repetitiously and egregiously in their written work.

I

Cecilia Lacks began teaching at Berkeley Senior High School in the fall of 1992 after teaching at other schools in the same school district since 1972. Lacks taught English and journalism classes, and she sponsored the school newspaper. In October 1994, Lacks divided her junior English class into small groups and directed them to write short plays, which were to be performed for the other students in the class and videotaped. The plays written by the students contained profanity, including the repeated uses of ... [vulgar language and racial slurs]. When the plays were videotaped, these words were used more than 150 times in approximately forty minutes. Lacks later admitted that the plays contained an unusual amount of profanity, and one of her witnesses later described the use of profanity in the plays as "extreme," "disgusting," "upsetting," and "embarrassing." Lacks was aware of the content of the plays before they were performed, because she had previously reviewed at least one of the scripts and had attended rehearsals of the plays the day before. On October 10, the students performed their plays and were videotaped at the direction of Lacks. Two other school district employees were also present during the videotaping of the plays: Donna Clark, a part-time teacher, and Mike Minks, an audiovisual technician. Clark and Minks eventually received letters of reprimand from the school administration for allowing the students to use profanity.

The following January, as a result of complaints by one of Lacks's students, the existence of the videotapes came to the attention of Vernon Mitchell, the principal of Berkeley High School. Mitchell initiated an inquiry into the matter, and he and two school district administrators met with Lacks and her union representative twice over the next two weeks. During the investigation, the administrators learned that as part of a poetry-writing exercise, Lacks had permitted a student to read aloud in a classroom two of his poems which contained profanity and graphic descriptions of oral sex.

Following the investigation, Dr. Robert Fritz, the district superintendent, formally charged Lacks with "willful or persistent violation of and failure to obey [the school district's] policies" under Mo. Ann. Stat. § 168.114. Fritz alleged that Lacks violated several school board policies and recommended her termination by the school board. Lacks requested a hearing, and the school board heard testimony from Lacks and fifteen other witnesses over five evenings in early March 1995. The school board also examined numerous exhibits and viewed the videotaped performances of the students' plays. At the hearing, the school board narrowed its earlier allegations to one charge: violation of board policy 3043, which requires teachers to enforce the section of the Student Discipline Code which prohibits profanity. On March 23, the board issued a decision which found that Lacks was aware of the school board's policy preventing profanity, that she could have chosen teaching methods which prohibited profanity, and that her failure to do so constituted a "willful and persistent practice violative of Board policy to a degree that cannot be ... tolerated." Based on its findings, the school board terminated Lacks's teaching contract.

In May 1995, Lacks brought suit in a Missouri state court, seeking judicial review of the school board's decision under Mo. Ann. Stat. § 168.120. She also alleged that the school board violated her due process rights under the United States and Missouri Constitutions, violated her rights under the First Amendment and 42 U.S.C. § 1983, and discriminated against her on the basis of race in violation of Missouri law and Title VII of the federal Civil Rights Act. The school board removed the entire case to the District Court pursuant to 28 U.S.C. § 1441. The District Court granted the school board's motion to dismiss Lacks's due process claims for failure to state a claim upon which relief could be granted, but it denied the school board's motion to dismiss Lacks's First Amendment claim. The District Court also entered partial summary judgment in favor of Lacks on her claim for review of the school board's termination of her teaching contract. In its order, the District Court held that Lacks did not willfully violate board policy 3043, because she believed that profanity was permitted in the context of creative expression in the classroom. Accordingly, the District Court awarded Lacks reinstatement with back pay, attorneys' fees, and costs.

The parties proceeded to trial in November 1996 on Lacks's First Amendment and race discrimination claims. The school board moved for judgment as a matter of law at the close of Lacks's case and its own case, and the District Court denied the motion both times. The District Court submitted the case to the jury, which returned a verdict in favor of Lacks for $500,000 on the First Amendment claim and $250,000 on the race discrimination claim. The school board now appeals.

II

We can easily dispose of the school board's argument that the District Court improperly allowed the board to remove the case because it lacked jurisdiction to review the school board's decision ... we hold that the District Court properly allowed the school board to remove this case.

III

A

Under Missouri law, when a school board terminates a contract with a teacher under Mo. Ann. Stat. § 168.114, including termination for the willful or persistent violation of a school board regulation, the teacher may appeal the school board's decision to a state circuit court and seek judicial review of the school board's decision. The court must affirm the decision of the school board unless the decision (1) violates a constitutional provision; (2) is made in excess of statutory authority or jurisdiction; (3) is unsupported by "competent and substantial evidence upon the whole record"; (4) is made for any other reason unauthorized by law; (5) is made upon unlawful procedure or without a fair trial; (6) is arbitrary, capricious or unreasonable; or (7) involves an abuse of discretion. This scope of review is limited. The reviewing court must affirm the school board if the board "reasonably could have reached the decision it did." The court may not substitute its judgment of the evidence for that of the school board, and it must consider all evidence in the light most favorable to the decision of the board. The determination of the credibility of the witnesses is a function of the school board, not the reviewing court.

The District Court granted summary judgment in favor of Lacks because it found insufficient evidence in the record that Lacks "willfully or persistently" violated board policy 3043. The parties agree with the District Court that proof of "willful or persistent" violation is twofold: The school board must prove both an intent to act and an intent to violate or disobey a particular regulation. In other words, in order to prevail the school board must prove that Lacks violated the board policy prohibiting profanity, and that she knew that the board policy applied to the profanity used by her students. After a careful review of the evidence, we hold that the record contains sufficient evidence for the school board to have concluded that Lacks willfully violated board policy.

Lacks admitted that she allowed students to use profanity in the classroom in the context of performing the plays they had written and reading aloud the poems they had composed. At the hearing, and in her brief, Lacks defended this practice by arguing that she thought that the board's policy on profanity applied only to "student behavior" and not to students' creative assignments. She also argued that her teaching method, which she describes as the "student-centered method" and which she explained at length at the hearing, required her to allow her students creative freedom, which included the use of profanity. Lacks could not say with certainty that she would be able to teach at Berkeley High School if her students were not given the freedom to use profanity in their creative activities. As evidence that Lacks believed that the anti-profanity policy did not apply to students' creative assignments, the District Court noted that testimony at the hearing indicated some confusion within the school district as to whether reading aloud literature which contained profanity might violate the school board's prohibition on profanity. For example, Larilyn Lawrence, a curriculum coordinator for language arts at the school district, believed that a videotaped production of a play with students using profanity could fall within acceptable course parameters. On the other hand, Barbara Davis, the assistant superintendent for curriculum instruction, testified that teachers in the school district should not allow students to read aloud profanity contained in literary works.

The school board also heard testimony from Lacks's principal, Vernon Mitchell, that he told Lacks that profanity was not permitted in the school newspaper. Mitchell testified that he specifically spoke to

Lacks in 1993 about profanity in the school newspaper, and told her that use of profanity in the newspaper was not allowed. Mitchell said that he had reviewed a draft of the newspaper and was concerned that the students were including profanity in the paper by writing "S blank blank T" and "F blank blank K" rather than writing every letter of the profane words. Mitchell testified that he discussed the use of profanity in the newspaper with Lacks "[t]wo or three times." Mitchell also noted that signs posted in Lacks's classroom read "No Profanity." When the board issued its opinion terminating Lacks's contract, it based its decision in part on its finding that Lacks had been warned about the use of profanity by Mitchell.

Lacks claimed that Mitchell never warned her about the use of profanity in the newspaper. However, under Missouri law, assessing the credibility of witnesses is the function of the school board, not the reviewing court. Because the school board heard testimony that Lacks was directly warned by the principal in her school that including "S blank blank T" and "F blank blank K" in the student newspaper violated the school board's profanity policy, the board could have reasonably found that Lacks knew that profanity was not allowed in students' creative activities. While Lacks did produce some evidence that confusion existed in the school district as to the profanity policy, and while she denied that she had been warned about it, we must read the record in the light most favorable to the school board's decision, together with all reasonable inferences.

The policy prohibiting profanity was explicit and contained no exceptions. It was not ambiguous. The board was free to find that Mitchell gave Lacks an express and particularized direction about the student newspaper. We think it was not unreasonable for the board to treat student writing for the newspaper and student writing for the class as alike. Isolated instances of profanity had been overlooked or tolerated in the past, but what went on in Lacks's classroom went far beyond the reading aloud of a novel containing the occasional "damn." The board might have chosen a lesser form of discipline, especially in view of Lacks's long and devoted service. It was not required to do so by law. We hold that the board's decision was reasonable and supported by substantial evidence on the record as a whole. The judgment in the plaintiff's favor on this claim must be reversed.

B

When the jury returned a verdict in favor of Lacks on her First Amendment claim, it provided answers to two interrogatories posed by the District Court's instructions. Under the District Court's instructions, answering "no" to either of the interrogatories allowed Lacks to prevail on the First Amendment claim. With respect to the first interrogatory— "Did [Lacks] have reasonable notice that allowing students to use profanity in their creative writing was prohibited?"—the jury answered "no." With respect to the second interrogatory—"Did defendant school district have a legitimate academic interest in prohibiting profanity by students in their creative writing, regardless of any other competing interests?"—the jury also answered "no." District Court subsequently entered judgment in favor of Lacks with respect to her First Amendment claim. We reverse and hold, as a matter of law, that the answer to both of those questions was "yes."

Lacks argued at trial and on appeal that she was acting as a facilitator for her students' speech, and that, under First Amendment law, she cannot be punished for not prohibiting her students' use of profanity unless she was provided with reasonable notice that profanity was prohibited in students' creative exercises, and unless the prohibition on profanity in creative activity served a legitimate academic interest. At least one court has held that, under the First Amendment, a school district must provide a teacher with notice as to what types of expression are prohibited in a classroom before it holds the teacher responsible for failing to limit that type of expression. We are satisfied that Lacks was provided with enough notice by the school board that profanity was not to be allowed in her classroom, whether in the context of a creative exercise or not. Lacks testified at trial that she understood that, under her contract with the school district, she was required to enforce the Student Discipline Code, and she testified that she was familiar with the rules and policies of the school board. The Student Discipline Code clearly prohibits profanity and obscene gestures, and it contains no exception for creative activities. Moreover, Lacks's principal, Vernon Mitchell, testified at trial, as he did at the school board hearing, that he informed Lacks that the use of profanity by the students was not permitted in the student newspaper, one form of creative activity. Mitchell told Lacks: "There is no way I would allow profanity in the newspaper."

In fact, Lacks received more notice than has been required in other cases. In *Bethel School District No. 403 v. Fraser*, a student was disciplined for using sexually suggestive language in a speech before a high school assembly. Before the student gave the speech, he told some of his teachers what he was going to say, and he was told that the speech was "inappropriate and that he probably should not deliver it" and that giving the speech could have "severe consequences." The Court rejected the student's argument that his due process rights had been violated because he had not received sufficient notice that delivery of the speech would result in discipline: "Given the school's need to be able to impose disciplinary sanctions for a wide range of unanticipated conduct disruptive of the educational process, the school disciplinary rules need not be as detailed as a criminal code which imposes criminal sanctions." In the present case, not only did Lacks admit that she was familiar with the school district's disciplinary rules and understood her obligation to enforce them, her principal also testified that he told her that the rules applied to one form of student creative activity. Therefore, as a matter of law, Lacks had sufficient notice that under the board's rules, she was not to permit profanity in her classroom. Perhaps the jury did not believe the principal's testimony about the warning he gave Lacks. Even so, the policy against profanity was explicit. Lacks well knew what the plays were like before she allowed the students to perform them. In acting as she did, she took the risk that the board would enforce the policy as written. Under the circumstances, the notice given was fair and constitutionally sufficient.

We also hold, as a matter of law, that the school board had a legitimate academic interest in prohibiting profanity by students in their creative writing. The Supreme Court has written that public education " 'must inculcate the habits and manner of civility as values in themselves conducive to happiness and as indispensable to the practice of self-government in the community and the nation.' " While students in public schools do not "shed their constitutional rights to freedom of speech or expression at the schoolhouse gate," students' First Amendment rights "in schools and classrooms must be balanced against the society's countervailing interest in teaching students the boundaries of socially appropriate behavior." Accordingly, the Supreme Court has held that "educators do not offend the First Amendment by exercising editorial control over the style and content of student speech in school-sponsored expressive activities so long as their actions are reasonably related to legitimate pedagogical concerns."

A flat prohibition on profanity in the classroom is reasonably related to the legitimate pedagogical concern of promoting generally acceptable social standards. The Supreme Court has told us that "schools must teach by example the shared values of a civilized social order." The school board itself, in its opinion terminating Lacks's employment with the school district, wrote that the purpose of the board's disciplinary policies is "to establish, to foster, and to reflect the norms and standards of the community it serves." Allowing one student to call another a [profanity] and a [prostitute] in front of the rest of the class, and allowing a student to read aloud a poem that describes sexual encounters in the most graphic detail, as the students did in Lacks's classroom, hardly promotes these shared social standards. We consider the matter too plain for argument.

As a matter of law, the school board had the right to establish and require the enforcement of a rule which prohibits classroom profanity in any context, and it provided Lacks with enough notice of its disciplinary policies. Therefore, the judgment in the plaintiff's favor on her First Amendment claim is reversed.

C

At trial, Lacks set out to prove her race discrimination case by "direct" evidence of discrimination under *Price Waterhouse v. Hopkins* rather than the indirect, burden-shifting method of *McDonnell Douglas Corp. v. Green*. The jury found that Lacks had proved by a preponderance of the evidence that race was a motivating factor in the school board's decision to terminate her, and that the school board did not prove by a preponderance of the evidence that it would have discharged Lacks regardless of her race. We reverse, and hold as a matter of law that race was not a motivating factor in the school board's decision to terminate Lacks. In reaching that conclusion, we are mindful that the evidence must be viewed in the light most favorable to the jury's verdict, and that all reasonable inferences in support of the verdict must be allowed.

. . .

. . . Because Lacks has produced insufficient evidence that the school board's decision to terminate her was motivated by race, the judgment in Lacks's favor on her race discrimination claims cannot stand. On this record, the inference that the school board acted because of Lacks's race is wholly unreasonable. In our view, the extreme nature of the language used and the exhaustive hearing given Lacks by the board leave no room for anyone reasonably to conclude that Lacks was disciplined because of her race.

The judgment of the District Court is reversed, and the cause remanded with directions to dismiss the complaint with prejudice.

It is so ordered.

Notes

1. Should teachers in elementary and secondary education have greater rights to academic freedom?

2. Given the teacher's years of experience, was the penalty of dismissal too harsh?

3. For a similar result, *see Boring v. Buncombe County Bd. of Educ.*, 136 F.3d 364 [124 Educ. L. Rep. 56] (4th Cir.1998), *cert. denied*, 525 U.S. 813, 119 S.Ct. 47, 142 L.Ed.2d 36 (1998), wherein the Fourth Circuit upheld the transfer of an award-winning drama coach and teacher in North Carolina for directing a controversial play that some members of the community found objectionable.

4. The Eighth Circuit resolved another interesting employment case arguably involving academic freedom in *Cowan v. Strafford R–VI School Dist.*, 140 F.3d 1153 [125 Educ. L. Rep. 613] (8th Cir.1998). The court affirmed an award of damages, but not reinstatement, in favor of a second grade teacher whose contract was not renewed where a board acted on its fear of the encroachment of New Ageism, when she presented each member of her second grade class with a "magic rock" and a letter telling them that it would help them in whatever they did.

[Case No. 82]   Discharge of Teacher Evaluation Procedure

ROBERTS v. HOUSTON INDEPENDENT SCHOOL DISTRICT

Court of Appeals of Texas, 1990.
788 S.W.2d 107 [60 Educ. L. Rep. 251].

EVANS, CHIEF JUSTICE. This is an appeal from a judgment upholding a school district's administrative decision to terminate appellant's employment for inefficiency or incompetency in the performance of duties. The cause was submitted to the trial court on an agreed stipulation of facts and exhibits, and on appeal, only a question of law is presented for review.

The stipulation of facts shows that appellant, Verna Roberts, had a continuing teacher's contract with the Houston Independent School

District (school district). On numerous occasions during school years 1982–1983 and 1983–1984, the school district's assessment team, composed of an associate superintendent and an instructional supervisor, evaluated appellant's teaching performance. These evaluations included both written assessments and videotaping of appellant's classroom performance. The evaluation team used videotapes so that the teacher could more easily follow and understand the evaluation team's observations and criticisms. Appellant objected to the use of videotaping in her classroom.

Both the written evaluations and videotapes revealed problems with appellant's teaching performance. Appellant was told of these problems, but according to the assessment team, she did not correct or improve her performance. Based on appellant's classroom performance, the assessment team recommended that the school district terminate her employment at the end of the 1983–84 school year. (Appellant's contract allowed for termination for inefficiency or incompetence in the performance of duties.) The deputy superintendent accepted this recommendation and, in turn, recommended termination to the general superintendent. The deputy superintendent and three members of the assessment team met with appellant and notified her of the recommendation and the reason for their recommendation. On March 9, 1984, the board of education authorized the general superintendent to notify appellant that it had proposed her employment be terminated at the end of the 1983–84 school year . . .

Appellant then notified the school district of her desire to contest the proposed termination and asked for a public hearing, which was scheduled for June 2, 1984. About 45 days before the hearing, appellant and her attorney were notified of the date, time, place, and procedures to be used at the termination proceedings. Appellant and her attorney were later given a witness list, a description of the testimony to be provided at the hearing, and a copy of the exhibits to be used. Appellant was not, however, given a copy of the videotape exhibits. Appellant asked for copies of all videotapes made of her classroom performance, but the school district refused. The school district did make the tapes available for appellant's review and inspection at its administrative offices.

On June 2, 1984, the school board heard testimony from appellant's supervisors, and it reviewed approximately 100 documents offered as evidence of appellant's classroom performance. The school board also viewed a 30–minute videotape, which included excerpts from the five separate videotapes made of appellant's classroom performance. The five tapes were all used by the assessment team in its evaluation of appellant's classroom performance.

Appellant chose not to testify at the hearing, and she did not present any witnesses or evidence on her own behalf. She limited her presentation to the cross-examination of appellee's witnesses. The hearing lasted approximately six hours, and at the end of the hearing, the school board voted unanimously to terminate appellant's employment at the end of the 1983–84 school year.

In her first point of error, appellant claims the trial court's judgment is flawed, as a matter of law, because she was denied both procedural and substantive due process in the termination proceedings.

I. Procedural Due Process

Appellant, as the holder of a continuing contract with the school district, possessed a property interest in her continued employment. The state may not deprive a person of a property interest without due process of law. At the very least, the law requires that a public employee with a protected right in continued employment be given notice and an opportunity to reply prior to termination.

The record reflects that appellant did receive notice and had an opportunity to respond before the termination of her employment.

On February 29, 1984, the deputy superintendent and members of the assessment team met with appellant, and explained their recommendation that the school district terminate her employment at the end of the 1983–84 school year. On March 12, 1984, the general superintendent wrote to appellant, notifying her of the proposed termination of her employment. In that letter, the general superintendent discussed the sections of appellant's contract upon which the school district was basing the proposed termination, and he enumerated specific complaints about her teaching performance. The superintendent stated that appellant had 10 days after receipt of the letter to notify him of her desire to contest the proposed termination, and that she could obtain copies of the evaluation reports and memoranda "touching or concerning" her "fitness or conduct as a teacher."

Appellant also received notice of the time, date, and place of the termination hearing. The school district notified appellant of the witnesses and testimony it would be offering, and gave appellant an opportunity to cross-examine each school district witness and produce evidence on her own behalf.

Appellant's principal contention is that she did not have notice of the contents of the edited videotape. We reject this contention. Appellant was told she could view the unedited videotapes at the school district's offices during regular business hours at any time between May 17, 1984, and June 2, 1984. This was about 10 days before the hearing. Appellant had also previously reviewed the tapes with the members of her assessment team after each evaluation. Although appellant was not given an opportunity, before the hearing, to view the composite tape that had been edited from the five evaluation tapes, she was given ample opportunity to view the five videotapes from which the composite was made. She simply chose not to do so.

II. Substantive Due Process

Appellant argues that the administrative hearing, which resulted in her termination, violated her right of due process because "of the nature of the evidence presented and the resulting inability of (appellant) to defend against the evidence as presented."

In evaluating a substantive due process claim, based on allegedly arbitrary state action in academic matters, a reviewing court must ascertain whether the state's action was "such a substantial departure from accepted academic norms as to demonstrate that the person or committee responsible did not actually exercise professional judgment." In a suit challenging an academic dismissal, the reviewing court must determine from the record whether there was "some rational academic basis for the decision." If there was a rational academic basis for the decision, the court may not override the state's action, even though the evidence may indicate such action was arbitrarily made.

Here, the school board listened to six hours of testimony and other evidence before deciding to terminate appellant's employment. The board reviewed appellant's teaching evaluations, listened to testimony of appellant's supervisors, and viewed a 30–minute composite videotape of appellant's teaching. Appellant was represented by her attorney during the hearing, she was given an opportunity to testify and to present witnesses on her own behalf, and she was allowed to cross-examine the witnesses called by the school district. Appellant could have even shown portions of the unedited videotapes, had she chosen to do so.

We conclude that the school board did not act arbitrarily or deviate from accepted academic norms in reaching its judgment to terminate appellant's employment.

Appellant further complains that the board saw the composite videotape without any showing that the tape was authentic, and that the tape was not made available to her for copying before the hearing.

Although an administrative proceeding must meet minimum requirements of due process, strict rules applicable to courts of law do not apply to such proceedings. In the absence of some showing that the school district acted arbitrarily in considering the composite videotape, or that the videotape falsely or inaccurately presented appellant's teaching performance, we can only conclude that the administrative proceedings complied with applicable substantive due process requirements.

We overrule appellant's first point of error.

In her second point of error, appellant contends that the trial court erred in granting a judgment for the school district because the termination proceedings violated her right of privacy. Under this point, appellant argues that she had an expectation of privacy in her classroom to be free from intrusion by videotaping, and that by videotaping her performance, over her objection, the school district violated her right of privacy as well as its own policy. . . .

Appellant has not cited any authority, and we have found none, relating to her claim of "involuntary videotaping" of her performance as a teacher. Based on the record before us, we conclude that appellant has not demonstrated that she had a "reasonable expectation of privacy" in her public classroom. The record shows that appellant was videotaped in a public classroom, in full view of her students, faculty members, and administrators. At no point, did the school district attempt to record appellant's private affairs.

The activity of teaching in a public classroom does not fall within the expected zone of privacy. To fall within the "zone of privacy," the activity must be one about which the individual possesses a reasonable expectation of privacy in the activity.

The right of privacy has been defined as the right of an individual to be left alone, to live a life of seclusion, to be free from unwarranted publicity. There is no invasion of the right of privacy when one's movements are exposed to public views generally.

The second point of error is overruled.

Appellant contends, in her third point of error, that the school district violated its own policy against involuntary videotaping. Under this point, she refers to the school district's Administrative Procedure Guide, section 572.720, which provides:

> No mechanical or electronic device shall be utilized to listen to or record the procedures unless requested or permitted by the teacher.

The school district responds to this argument by suggesting that a newer administrative procedure manual has repealed section 572.720, and that the new manual provides:

> The Teacher Quality Assurance Program was adopted by the Board of Education on October 7, 1982, and amended on August 4, 1983. The adoption and amendment supercede all prior policies and procedures on teacher evaluation in effect and will repeal and replace any policies or procedures in conflict. . . .

If videotaping is used . . ., the principal is to make arrangements for the videotaping. The taping session period should be a minimum of one hour/class session with the teacher. Videotaping can provide the teacher with an opportunity to see herself as the assessment team does.

Appellant contends these two sections are not in conflict, and that the section first quoted effectively prohibits videotaping "unless requested or permitted by the teacher."

We agree with the school district's interpretation of its own administrative procedures. The language in the new section expressly authorizes the principal to make arrangements for videotaping, and the quoted section does not require that the teacher must request or give consent to the videotaping. We accordingly conclude that the videotaping of appellant did not violate any of the school district's policies or procedures.

The third point of error is overruled.

The judgment of the trial court is affirmed.

Notes

1. Note that Roberts did not take advantage of the opportunity to again view the videotapes before the hearing. Further, she did not testify at the hearing or present witnesses or evidence on her behalf.

2. Is the use of videotaping classes a sound tool for evaluating teacher performance?

[Case No. 83]   Right of Teacher to Write Public Letter Critical of Board

PICKERING v. BOARD OF EDUCATION OF TOWNSHIP HIGH SCHOOL DISTRICT 205

Supreme Court of the United States, 1968.
391 U.S. 563, 88 S.Ct. 1731, 20 L.Ed.2d 811.

MR. JUSTICE MARSHALL delivered the opinion of the Court.

Appellant Marvin L. Pickering, a teacher in Township High School District 205, Will County, Illinois, was dismissed from his position by the appellee Board of Education for sending a letter to a local newspaper in connection with a recently proposed tax increase that was critical of the way in which the Board and the district superintendent of schools had handled past proposals to raise new revenue for the schools. Appellant's dismissal resulted from a determination by the Board, after a full hearing, that the publication of the letter was "detrimental to the efficient operation and administration of the schools of the district" and hence, under the relevant Illinois statute, that "interests of the schools require[d] [his dismissal]." . . .

The letter constituted, basically, an attack on the school board's handling of the 1961 bond issue proposals and its subsequent allocation of financial resources between the schools' educational and athletic programs. It also charged the superintendent of schools with attempting to prevent teachers in the district from opposing or criticizing the proposed bond issue.

The Board dismissed Pickering for writing and publishing the letter. Pursuant to Illinois law, the Board was then required to hold a hearing on the dismissal. At the hearing the Board charged that numerous statements in the letter were false and that the publication of the statements unjustifiably impugned the "motives, honesty, integrity, truthfulness, responsibility and competence" of both the Board and the school administration. The Board also charged that the false statements damaged the professional reputations of its members and of the school administrators, would be disruptive of faculty discipline, and would tend to foment "controversy, conflict and dissension" among teachers, administrators, the Board of Education, and the residents of the district. . . .

To the extent that the Illinois Supreme Court's opinion may be read to suggest that teachers may constitutionally be compelled to relinquish the First Amendment rights they would otherwise enjoy as citizens to comment on matters of public interest in connection with the operation of the public schools in which they work, it proceeds on a premise that has been unequivocally rejected in numerous prior decisions of this Court. . . . At the same time it cannot be gainsaid that the State has interests as an employer in regulating the speech of its employees that differ significantly from those it possesses in connection with regulation of the speech of the citizenry in general. The problem in any case is to arrive at a balance between the interests of the teacher, as a citizen, in commenting upon matters of public concern and the interest of the State, as an employer, in promoting the efficiency of the public services it performs through its employees.

... Because of the enormous variety of fact situations in which critical statements by teachers and other public employees may be thought by their superiors, against whom the statements are directed, to furnish grounds for dismissal, we do not deem it either appropriate or feasible to attempt to lay down a general standard against which all such statements may be judged. However, in the course of evaluating the conflicting claims of First Amendment protection and the need for orderly school administration in the context of this case, we shall indicate some of the general lines along which an analysis of the controlling interests should run.

An examination of the statements in appellant's letter objected to by the Board reveals that they, like the letter as a whole, consist essentially of criticism of the Board's allocation of school funds between educational and athletic programs, and of both the Board's and the superintendent's methods of informing, or preventing the informing of, the district's taxpayers of the real reasons why additional tax revenues were being sought for the schools. The statements are in no way directed towards any person with whom appellant would normally be in contact in the course of his daily work as a teacher. Thus no question of maintaining either discipline by immediate superiors or harmony among coworkers is presented here. Appellant's employment relationships with the Board and, to a somewhat lesser extent, with the superintendent are not the kind of close working relationships for which it can persuasively be claimed that personal loyalty and confidence are necessary to their proper functioning....

We next consider the statements in appellant's letter which we agree to be false. The Board's original charges included allegations that the publication of the letter damaged the professional reputations of the Board and the superintendent and would foment controversy and conflict among the Board, teachers, administrators, and the residents of the district. However, no evidence to support these allegations was introduced at the hearing. So far as the record reveals, Pickering's letter was greeted by everyone but its main target, the Board, with massive apathy and total disbelief. The Board must, therefore, have decided, perhaps by analogy with the law of libel, that the statements were *per se* harmful to the operation of the schools.

However, the only way in which the Board could conclude, absent any evidence of the actual effect of the letter, that the statements contained therein were *per se* detrimental to the interest of the schools was to equate the Board members' own interests with that of the schools. Certainly an accusation that too much money is being spent on athletics by the administrators of the school system (which is precisely the import of that portion of appellant's letter containing the statements that we have found to be false) cannot reasonably be regarded as *per se* detrimental to the district's schools. Such an accusation reflects rather a difference of opinion between Pickering and the Board as to the preferable manner of operating the school system, a difference of opinion that clearly concerns an issue of general public interest.

In addition, the fact that particular illustrations of the Board's claimed undesirable emphasis on athletic programs are false would not normally have any necessary impact on the actual operation of the schools, beyond its tendency to anger the Board. For example, Pickering's letter was written after the defeat at the polls of the second proposed tax increase. It could, therefore, have had no effect on the ability of the school district to raise necessary revenue, since there was no showing that there was any proposal to increase taxes pending when the letter was written.

More importantly, the question whether a school system requires additional funds is a matter of legitimate public concern on which the judgment of the school administration, including the School Board, cannot, in a society that leaves such questions to popular vote, be taken as conclusive. On such a question free and open debate is vital to informed decision-making by the electorate. Teachers are, as a class, the members of a community most likely to have informed and definite opinions as to how funds allotted to the operation of the schools should be spent. Accordingly, it is essential that they be able to speak out freely on such questions without fear of retaliatory dismissal.

In addition, the amounts expended on athletics which Pickering reported erroneously were matters of public record on which his position as a teacher in the district did not qualify him to speak with any greater authority than any other taxpayer. The Board could easily have rebutted appellant's errors by publishing the accurate figures itself, either via a letter to the same newspaper or otherwise. We are thus not presented with a situation in which a teacher has carelessly made false statements about matters so closely related to the day-to-day operations of the schools that any harmful impact on the public would be difficult to counter because of the teacher's presumed greater access to the real facts. Accordingly, we have no occasion to consider at this time whether under such circumstances a school board could reasonably require that a teacher make substantial efforts to verify the accuracy of his charges before publishing them.

What we do have before us is a case in which a teacher has made erroneous public statements upon issues then currently the subject of public attention, which are critical of his ultimate employer but which are neither shown nor can be presumed to have in any way either impeded the teacher's proper performance of his daily duties in the classroom or to have interfered with the regular operation of the schools generally. In these circumstances we conclude that the interest of the school administration in limiting teachers' opportunities to contribute to public debate is not significantly greater than its interest in limiting a similar contribution by any member of the general public. . . .

In sum, we hold that, in a case such as this, absent proof of false statements knowingly or recklessly made by him, a teacher's exercise of his right to speak on issues of public importance may not furnish the basis for his dismissal from public employment. . . .

Notes

1.   At what point are teachers ethically free to criticize local school officials in the public press? How, if at all, do the responsibilities of teachers differ from those of other citizens in this regard?

2.   In light of *Pickering*, the Court vacated, and remanded, judgments upholding the dismissals of teachers for criticisms of school authorities. On remand, the Court of Appeals of New York ruled in favor of a teacher, *Puentes v. Board of Educ. of Union Free School Dist. No. 21 of Town of Bethpage*, 302 N.Y.S.2d 824 (N.Y.1969), while the Supreme Court of Alaska reinstated its original judgment, *Watts v. Seward School Bd.*, 454 P.2d 732 (Alaska 1969), *cert. denied*, 397 U.S. 921, 90 S.Ct. 899, 25 L.Ed.2d 101 (1970).

[Case No. 84]   Right of Teacher to Wear Black Armband in Class

JAMES v. BOARD OF EDUCATION OF CENTRAL DISTRICT NO. 1, ADDISON

United States Court of Appeals, Second Circuit, 1972.
461 F.2d 566.

IRVING R. KAUFMAN, CIRCUIT JUDGE. . . .

. . . We are asked to decide whether a Board of Education, without transgressing the first amendment, may discharge an 11th grade English teacher who did no more than wear a black armband in class in symbolic protest against the Vietnam War, although it is agreed that the armband did not disrupt classroom activities, and as far as we know did not have any influence on any students and did not engender protest from any student, teacher or parent. We hold that the Board may not take such action.

The facts essential to a resolution of the conflicting interests are undisputed. On June 7, 1969, Charles James was employed as an 11th grade English teacher at Addison High School, located near Elmira, New York. He previously had taught in the New York City public schools. After moving to the Elmira area, James, a practicing Quaker, joined the Elmira Meeting of the Religious Society of Friends.

When November 14 and December 12, 1969, were designated as "moratorium" days by the opponents of the Vietnam War, the Elmira Meeting determined to observe the two days by wearing black armbands. On November 14 James affixed one of the armbands, which had been prepared by the Meeting, to the sleeve of his jacket. He since has stated that he "resolved to wear one of the black armbands as an expression of [his] religious aversion to war in any form and as a sign of [his] regret over the loss of life in Vietnam."

Shortly after school began that day, Carl Pillard, the Principal, entered James's homeroom, noticed the armband, but made no comment. Pillard waited until midway through the second period when James was teaching poetry, apparently without any incident or discussion whatsoever relating to Vietnam or the armband, to summon James to his office and to request him to remove the armband. When James refused to remove it, Pillard sent him to the District Principal, Edward J. Brown. Brown ordered James to remove the armband or risk suspension or dismissal because the armband would tend to be disruptive and would possibly encourage pupils to engage in disruptive demonstrations. When James again refused to remove the armband, Brown summarily suspended him and ordered James to leave the school at once.

The following day James received a letter from the Board of Education of Central District No. 1, reinstating him on "the understanding that [he] engage in no political activities while in the school." James resumed his teaching duties, but, steadfastly abiding by his principles, whether religious (Quakers are doctrinally opposed to war) or political in nature, he came to school wearing an armband on December 12, the second moratorium day. He was summarily suspended as soon as Brown learned that James again had worn an armband. Here, too, the record is barren of a scintilla of evidence indicating that there were any incidents or threats to school discipline, that any students or teachers had complained of or were offended by James's first or second symbolic protest, or that the armband constituted more than a silent expression of James's own feelings. On January 13, however, without affording James a hearing, the Board of Education of Central District No. 1 discharged him from his teaching position in accordance with [a statute covering probationary teachers]. . . .

We come now to the crucial issue we must decide—did the Board of Education infringe James's first amendment right to freedom of speech?

Any meaningful discussion of a teacher's first amendment right to wear a black armband in a classroom as a symbolic protest against this nation's involvement in the Vietnam War must begin with a close examination of the case which dealt with this question as it applied to a student.

With respect to both teacher and student, the responsibility of school authorities to maintain order and discipline in the schools remains the same. The ultimate goal of school officials is to insure that the discipline necessary to the proper functioning of the school is maintained among both teachers and students. Any limitation on the exercise of constitutional rights can be justified only by a conclusion, based upon reasonable inferences flowing from concrete facts and not abstractions, that the interests of discipline or sound education are materially and substantially jeopardized, whether the danger stems initially from the conduct of students or teachers. Although it is not unreasonable to assume that the views of a teacher occupying a position of authority may carry more influence with a student than would those of students inter sese, that assumption merely weighs upon the inferences which may be drawn. It does not relieve the school of the necessity to show a reasonable basis for its regulatory policies. As the Court has instructed in discussing the state's power to dismiss a teacher for engaging in conduct ordinarily protected by the first amendment: "The problem in any case is to arrive at a balance between the interest of the teacher, as a citizen, in commenting upon matters of public concern and the interest of the State, as an employer, in promoting the efficiency of the public services it performs through its employees."

It is to be noted that in this case, the Board of Education has made no showing whatsoever at any stage of the proceedings that Charles James, by wearing a black armband, threatened to disrupt classroom activities or created any disruption in the school. Nor does the record demonstrate any facts "which might reasonably have led school authorities to forecast substantial disruption of or material interference with school activities ..." All we can learn from the record is that in the opinion of Edward Brown, the District Principal, "wearing the armband would tend to be disruptive and would possibly encourage pupils to engage in disruptive demonstrations." "But," the Supreme Court warned in *Tinker,* "in our system, undifferentiated fear or apprehension of disturbance is not enough to overcome the right to freedom of expression." ...

That does not end our inquiry, however. The interest of the state in promoting the efficient operation of its schools extends beyond merely securing an orderly classroom. Although the pros and cons of progressive education are debated heatedly, a principal function of all elementary and secondary education is indoctrinative—whether it be to teach the ABC's or multiplication tables or to transmit the basic values of the community. "[S]ome measure of public regulation is inherent in the very provision of public education." Accordingly, courts consistently have affirmed that curriculum controls belong to the political process and local school authorities....

Appellees argue that this broad power extends to controlling a teacher's speech in public schools, that "assumptions of the 'free marketplace of ideas' on which freedom of speech rests do not apply to school-aged children, especially in the classroom where the word of the teacher may carry great authority." Certainly there must be some restraints because the students are a "captive" group. But to state the proposition without qualification is to uncover its fallacy. More than a decade of Supreme Court precedent leaves no doubt that we cannot countenance school authorities arbitrarily censoring a teacher's speech merely because they do not agree with the teacher's political philosophies or leanings. This is particularly so when that speech does not interfere in any way with the teacher's obligations to teach, is not coercive and does not arbitrarily inculcate doctrinaire views in the minds of the students.

As we have indicated, there is merit to appellees' argument that *Tinker* does not control this case, because a teacher may have a far more pervasive influence over a student than would one student over another.

Although sound discussions of ideas are the beams and buttresses of the first amendment, teachers cannot be allowed to patrol the precincts of radical thought with the unrelenting goal of indoctrination, a goal compatible with totalitarianism and not democracy. When a teacher is only content if he persuades his students that his values and only his values ought to be their values, then it is not unreasonable to expect the state to protect impressionable children from such dogmatism. But, just as clearly, those charged with overseeing the day-to-day interchange between teacher and student must exercise that degree of restraint necessary to protect first amendment rights. The question we must ask in every first amendment case is whether the regulatory policy is drawn as narrowly as possible to achieve the social interests that justify it, or whether it exceeds permissible bounds by unduly restricting protected speech to an extent "greater than is essential to the furtherance of" those interests. Thus, when a teacher presents a colorable claim that school authorities have infringed on his first amendment rights and arbitrarily transgressed on these transcendent values, school authorities must demonstrate a reasonable basis for concluding that the teacher's conduct threatens to impair their legitimate interests in regulating the school curriculum. What we require, then, is only that rules formulated by school officials be reasonably related to the needs of the educational process and that any disciplinary action taken pursuant to those rules have a basis in fact.

Several factors present here compel the conclusion that the Board of Education arbitrarily and unjustifiably discharged James for wearing the black armband. Clearly, there was no attempt by James to proselytize his students. It does not appear from the record that any student believed the armband to be anything more than a benign symbolic expression of the teacher's personal views. Moreover, we cannot ignore the fact that James was teaching 11th grade (high school) English. His students were approximately 16 or 17 years of age, thus more mature than those junior high school students in *Tinker.* . . .

Finally, James was first removed from class while he was teaching poetry. There is no suggestion whatsoever that his armband interfered with his teaching functions, or, for that matter, that his teaching ever had been deficient in any respect.

We emphasize that we do not question the broad discretion of local school authorities in setting classroom standards, nor do we question their expertise in evaluating the effects of classroom conduct in light of the special characteristics of the school environment. The federal courts, however, cannot allow unfettered discretion to violate fundamental constitutional rights. . . .

The dangers of unrestrained discretion are readily apparent. Under the guise of beneficent concern for the welfare of school children, school authorities, albeit unwittingly, might permit prejudices of the community to prevail. It is in such a situation that the will of the transient majority can prove devastating to freedom of expression. Indeed, James has alleged in his complaint that another teacher, "without incurring any disciplinary sanction, prominently displayed the slogan 'Peace with Honor' on a bulletin board in his classroom." This slogan has been associated with our foreign policy. If the allegation is true, and we must assume that it is in light of the summary dismissal of the complaint, it exemplifies the concern we have expressed. The Board's actions under such circumstances would indicate that its regulation against political activity in the classroom may be no more than the fulcrum to censor only that expression with which it disagrees. By requiring the Board of Education to justify its actions when there is a colorable claim of deprivation of first amendment rights, we establish a prophylactic procedure that automatically tempers abuse of properly vested discretion. . . .

It is appropriate, however, lest our decision today (which is based on the total absence of any facts justifying the Board of Education's actions) be misunderstood, that we disclaim any intent to condone partisan political activities in the public schools which reasonably may be expected to interfere with the educational process. . . .

Notes

1. The present case relied heavily on *Tinker*. Are there situations where teachers should not possess as much freedom of speech as students?

2. *Pickering* involved an exercise of freedom of expression by a teacher outside of school. Are there actions which teachers should be permitted outside of school but not in classes?

3. Following the Supreme Court's denial of *certiorari*, 409 U.S. 1042, 93 S.Ct. 529, 34 L.Ed.2d 491 (1972), the school board asserted that since wearing the armband was disruptive, James could be discharged. A federal trial court disagreed. *James v. Board of Educ. of Cent. Dist. No. 1*, 385 F.Supp. 209 (W.D.N.Y.1974).

[Case No. 85] Procedural Due Process before Removal from Payroll of Employee Dischargeable Only for Cause

CLEVELAND BOARD OF EDUCATION v. LOUDERMILL
PARMA BOARD OF EDUCATION v. DONNELLY

Supreme Court of the United States, 1985.
470 U.S. 532, 105 S.Ct. 1487, 84 L.Ed.2d 494 [23 Educ. L. Rep. 473].

JUSTICE WHITE delivered the opinion of the Court.

In these cases we consider what pretermination process must be accorded a public employee who can be discharged only for cause.

I

In 1979 the Cleveland Board of Education . . . hired respondent James Loudermill as a security guard. On his job application, Loudermill stated that he had never been convicted of a felony. Eleven months later, as part of a routine examination of his employment records, the Board discovered that in fact Loudermill had been convicted of grand larceny in 1968. By letter dated November 3, 1980, the Board's Business Manager informed Loudermill that he had been dismissed because of his dishonesty in filling out the employment application. Loudermill was not afforded an opportunity to respond to the charge of dishonesty or to challenge his dismissal. On November 13, the Board adopted a resolution officially approving the discharge.

Under Ohio law, Loudermill was a "classified civil servant." Such employees can be terminated only for cause, and may obtain administrative review if discharged. pursuant to this provision, Loudermill filed an appeal with the Cleveland Civil Service Commission on November 12. The Commission appointed a referee, who held a hearing on January 29, 1981. Loudermill argued that he had thought that his 1968 larceny conviction was for a misdemeanor rather than a felony. The referee recommended reinstatement. On July 20, 1981, the full Commission heard argument and orally announced that it would uphold the dismissal. . . .

Although the Commission's decision was subject to judicial review in the state courts, Loudermill instead brought the present suit in the Federal District Court for the Northern District of Ohio. The complaint alleged that § 124.34 was unconstitutional on its face because it did not provide the employee an opportunity to respond to the charges against him prior to removal. As a result, discharged employees were deprived of liberty and property without due process. . . .

The other case before us arises on similar facts and followed a similar course. Respondent Richard Donnelly was a bus mechanic for the Parma Board of Education. In August 1977, Donnelly was fired because he had failed an eye examination. He was offered a chance to retake the examination but did not do so. Like Loudermill, Donnelly appealed to the Civil Service Commission. After a year of wrangling about the timeliness of his appeal, the Commission heard the case. It ordered Donnelly reinstated, though without backpay. In a complaint essentially identical to Loudermill's, Donnelly challenged the constitutionality of the dismissal procedures. . . .

II

Respondents' federal constitutional claim depends on their having had a property right in continued employment. *Board of Regents v. Roth.* If they did, the State could not deprive them of this property without due process.

Property interests are not created by the Constitution, "they are created and their dimensions are defined by existing rules or understandings that stem from an independent source such as state law. . . ." The Ohio statute plainly creates such an interest. Respondents were "classified civil service employees," entitled to retain their positions "during good behavior and efficient service," who could not be dismissed "except . . . for . . . misfeasance, malfeasance, or nonfeasance in office." The statute plainly supports the conclusion . . . that respondents possessed property rights in continued employment. . . .

The Parma Board argues, however, that the property right is defined by, and conditioned on, the legislature's choice of procedures for its deprivation. The Board stresses that in addition to specifying the grounds for termination, the statute sets out procedures by which termination may take place. The procedures were adhered to in these cases. According to petitioner, "[t]o require additional procedures would in effect expand the scope of the property interest itself." ...

... More recently, however, the Court has clearly rejected [this argument]. In *Vitek v. Jones* we pointed out that "minimum [procedural] requirements [are] a matter of federal law, they are not diminished by the fact that the State may have specified its own procedures that it may deem adequate for determining the preconditions to adverse official action." This conclusion was reiterated in *Logan v. Zimmerman Brush Co.* where we reversed the lower court's holding that because the entitlement arose from a state statute, the legislature had the prerogative to define the procedures to be followed to protect that entitlement.

In light of these holdings, it is settled that the "bitter with the sweet" approach misconceives the constitutional guarantee. If a clearer holding is needed, we provide it today. The point is straightforward: the Due Process Clause provides that certain substantive rights—life, liberty, and property—cannot be deprived except pursuant to constitutionally adequate procedures. The categories of substance and procedure are distinct. Were the rule otherwise, the Clause would be reduced to a mere tautology. "Property" cannot be defined by the procedures provided for its deprivation any more than can life or liberty. The right to due process "is conferred, not by legislative grace, but by constitutional guarantee. While the legislature may elect not to confer a property interest in [public] employment, it may not constitutionally authorize the deprivation of such an interest, once conferred, without appropriate procedural safeguards."

In short, once it is determined that the Due Process Clause applies, "the question remains what process is due." The answer to that question is not to be found in the Ohio statute.

III

An essential principle of due process is that a deprivation of life, liberty, or property "be preceded by notice and opportunity for hearing appropriate to the nature of the case." ... We have described "the root requirement" of the Due Process Clause as being "that an individual be given an opportunity for a hearing *before* he is deprived of any significant property interest." This principle requires "some kind of a hearing" prior to the discharge of an employee who has a constitutionally protected property interest in his employment. *Board of Regents v. Roth, Perry v. Sindermann.* ... [T]his rule has been settled for some time now. Even decisions finding no constitutional violation in termination procedures have relied on the existence of some pretermination opportunity to respond....

The need for some form of pretermination hearing, recognized in these cases, is evident from a balancing of the competing interests at stake. These are the private interests in retaining employment, the governmental interest in the expeditious removal of unsatisfactory employees and the avoidance of administrative burdens, and the risk of an erroneous termination.

First, the significance of the private interest in retaining employment cannot be gainsaid. We have frequently recognized the severity of depriving a person of the means of livelihood. While a fired worker may find employment elsewhere, doing so will take some time and is likely to be burdened by the questionable circumstances under which he left his previous job.

Second, some opportunity for the employee to present his side of the case is recurringly of obvious value in reaching an accurate decision. Dismissals for cause will often involve factual disputes. Even where the facts are clear, the appropriateness or necessity of the discharge may not be; in such cases, the only meaningful opportunity to invoke the discretion of the decisionmaker is likely to be before the termination takes effect. (This is not to say that where state conduct is entirely discretionary the Due Process Clause is brought into play. Nor is it to say that a person can insist on a hearing in order to argue that the decisionmaker should be lenient and depart from legal requirements. The point is that where there is an entitlement, a prior hearing facilitates the consideration of whether a permissible course of action is also an appropriate one.)

The cases before us illustrate these considerations. Both respondents had plausible arguments to make that might have prevented their discharge. The fact that the Commission saw fit to reinstate Donnelly suggests that an error might have been avoided had he been provided an opportunity to make his case to the Board. As for Loudermill, given the Commission's ruling we cannot say that the discharge was mistaken. Nonetheless, in light of the referee's recommendation, neither can we say that a fully informed decisionmaker might not have exercised its discretion and decided not to dismiss him, notwithstanding its authority to do so. In any event, the termination involved arguable issues (Loudermill's dismissal turned not on the objective fact that he was an ex-felon or the inaccuracy of his statement to the contrary, but on the subjective question whether he had lied on his application form. His explanation for the false statement is plausible in light of the fact that he received only a suspended 6–month sentence and a fine on the grand larceny conviction.), and the right to a hearing does not depend on a demonstration of certain success.

The governmental interest in immediate termination does not outweigh these interests. As we shall explain, affording the employee an opportunity to respond prior to termination would impose neither a significant administrative burden nor intolerable delays. Furthermore, the employer shares the employee's interest in avoiding disruption and erroneous decisions; and until the matter is settled, the employer would continue to receive the benefit of the employee's labors. It is preferable to keep a qualified employee on than to train a new one. A governmental employer also has an interest in keeping citizens usefully employed rather than taking the possibly erroneous and counterproductive step of forcing its employees onto the welfare rolls. Finally, in those situations where the employer perceives a significant hazard in keeping the employee on the job, it can avoid the problem by suspending with pay.

IV

The foregoing considerations indicate that the pretermination "hearing," though necessary, need not be elaborate. We have pointed out that "[t]he formality and procedural requisites for the hearing can vary, depending upon the importance of the interests involved and the nature of the subsequent proceedings." In general, "something less" than a full evidentiary hearing is sufficient prior to adverse administrative action. Under state law, respondents were later entitled to a full administrative hearing and judicial review. The only question is what steps were required before the termination took effect.

... Here, the pretermination hearing need not definitively resolve the propriety of the discharge. It should be an initial check against mistaken decisions—essentially, a determination of whether there are reasonable grounds to believe that the charges against the employee are true and support the proposed action.

The essential requirements of due process ... are notice and an opportunity to respond. The opportunity to present reasons, either in person or in writing, why proposed action should not be taken is a fundamental due process requirement. The tenured public employee is entitled to oral or written notice of the charges against him, an explanation of the employer's evidence, and an opportunity to present his side of the story. To require more than this prior to termination would intrude to an unwarranted extent on the government's interest in quickly removing an unsatisfactory employee.

V

Our holding rests in part on the provisions in Ohio law for a full post-termination hearing. In his cross-petition Loudermill asserts, as a separate constitutional violation, that his administrative proceedings took too long. The Court of Appeals held otherwise, and we agree. The Due Process Clause requires provision of a hearing "at a meaningful time." At some point, a delay in the post-termination hearing would become a constitutional violation. In the present case, however, the complaint merely recites the course of proceedings and concludes that the denial of a "speedy resolution" violated due process. This reveals nothing about the delay except that it stemmed in part from the thoroughness of the procedures. A 9–month adjudication is not, of course, unconstitutionally lengthy per se. Yet Loudermill offers no indication that his wait was unreasonably prolonged other than the fact that it took nine months. The chronology of the proceedings set out in the complaint, coupled with the assertion that nine months is too long to wait, does not state a claim of a constitutional deprivation.

VI

We conclude that all the process that is due is provided by a pretermination opportunity to respond, coupled with post-termination administrative procedures as provided by the Ohio statute. Because respondents allege in their complaints that they had no chance to respond, the District Court erred in dismissing for failure to state a claim. The judgment of the Court of Appeals is affirmed, and the case is remanded for further proceedings consistent with this opinion. So ordered.

Notes

1. Compare the minimum requirements of constitutional procedural due process that must precede the termination of a public employee's contract where a property interest exists with those that must precede the short-term suspension of a student where a property interest (found in state compulsory education statutes) exists.

2. Bear in mind that since a property right is an individualized benefit that can be withdrawn only for cause, school boards must provide due process when they attempt to do so.

3. Would extensive post-termination procedures, and remedies including reinstatement, back pay, and attorney fees, remedy pre-termination constitutional due process deficiencies? Here the Court did not give attention to post-termination procedures beyond noting their existence as an integral part of Loudermill's property right.

[Case No. 86]   Discharge of Teacher—Classroom Performance; Board Procedures

KNOX COUNTY BOARD OF EDUCATION v. WILLIS

Court of Appeals of Kentucky, 1966.
405 S.W.2d 952.

Clay, Commissioner. Appellant, Knox County Board of Education, terminated appellee's teaching contract after a hearing upon charges brought under KRS 161.790. On appeal to the circuit court the action of the Board was reversed, from which judgment the Board appeals to this court.

The charges against appellee were for "inefficiency, incompetency and neglect of duty". The notice of charges with which appellee was served made specific reference to and included a copy of a "supervisor's report". This report criticized appellee's conduct of classes, her lack of control and discipline over her students, and the destruction of classroom furniture. At the hearing substantial evidence was introduced concerning the inadequacy of records kept by appellee, although this deficiency did not appear in the charges. The Board found that appellee (1) failed and refused to keep proper order in her classes; (2) allowed the children to damage and destroy furniture and to use improper language, and failed to take appropriate corrective and disciplinary measures; and (3) failed to keep proper records. On the basis of these findings, the Board terminated her contract.

The circuit court on appeal found these proceedings arbitrary in almost every respect.

The first ground of alleged arbitrariness was the failure of the Board to furnish appellee with rules and regulations governing procedure in the conduct of the hearing. Apparently the Board did not have such rules and regulations, as the trial court found. Our first question is whether, as appellee insists, the Board is without power to conduct, or acts arbitrarily in conducting, a hearing such as this without written rules of procedure.

We find nothing in the statutes which *requires* a board of education to adopt formal procedural rules for the conduct of a hearing. While KRS 160.290(2) provides that each board "shall make and adopt ... rules, regulations and by-laws" for the regulation and management of schools and the transaction of its business, we must construe this language sensibly to require such rules and regulations as are necessary and proper. Otherwise a school board could not legally perform *any* act without a pre-established written rule specifically pertaining to it. If we adopt appellee's theory, it would require each board to draft a comprehensive code of procedure for hearings on the termination of teachers' contracts, and if such code failed to cover a single phase of procedure sought to be invoked, the board could not proceed. We simply cannot construe this statute so unrealistically. The average school board would certainly lack the competency to draft such a code.

We believe that KRS 161.790(2), (3) adequately outlines the procedure required for such a hearing, although a board could adopt consistent supplementary rules. As pointed out in *Board of Education v. Chattin, Ky.* a proper hearing of this nature simply requires "orderly procedure" and "fundamental fairness" and not "the esoteric formalities of a medieval jousting match". Within the scope of "fundamental fairness" we must recognize the necessity for procedural flexibility, particularly since these proceedings ordinarily must be conducted by laymen. As suggested in that case, under proper circumstances resort may be had to our Rules of Civil Procedure.

Appellee's plea for the requirement of technical rules of procedure is really an academic one. She makes no claim that the hearing was not a fair one, that she was denied any right to be fully heard, or that she was prejudiced by the manner in which the hearing was conducted. We find nothing illegal or arbitrary in the conduct of this hearing without written rules of procedure.

The trial court correctly found that the Board acted arbitrarily in sustaining the charges against appellee for failure to keep proper records. She was given no fair notice of this charge, as required by KRS 161.790(2). However, the Board sustained two other charges against her. If she was given adequate notice of these other charges and there was substantial evidence to support them, the Board's action may be upheld even though the charge of failing to keep records was not properly prosecuted.

The trial court found the Board acted arbitrarily in sustaining the charges against appellee which involved the failure to keep proper order in her classroom and the failure to take appropriate corrective and disciplinary measures against students who were guilty of flagrant misconduct. The basis of this determination was that the charges against appellee were not sufficiently specific, and the evidence did not support the findings.

The charges against appellee were for "inefficiency, incompetency and neglect of duty". We agree that these charges, appearing in the "Notice of Termination of Contract", were not sufficiently specific under KRS 161.790(2). However, the notice incorporates a "supervisor's report" wherein certain details are set forth. It is apparently appellee's contention that the details must appear in the formal charges and that an interoffice communication does not have sufficient formal dignity to constitute adequate charges. It is also contended by appellee, and the trial court found, that the "supervisor's report" was not sufficiently detailed.

It is our opinion that the formal charges against appellee, coupled with the facts stated in the "supervisor's report", gave appellee fair notice that the charges of inefficiency, incompetency and neglect were based upon the manner in which she conducted her classes, with particular emphasis upon her failure to maintain any sort of discipline. We cannot go along with appellee's argument that the "supervisor's report" cannot be considered as part and parcel of the charges. This report was incorporated in the formal notice just as an exhibit to a pleading. The informality of the report has no bearing on the adequacy of the charges since we are seeking fair notice to the teacher.

We are also disinclined to agree with the trial court that the "supervisor's report" did not contain sufficient detail. We are convinced that it did give appellee fair notice that the charges were based upon the method of conducting her classes, which resulted in the specified abnormal conditions.

There was ample evidence of intolerable conduct on the part of students in her classroom, and there was ample evidence of a neglect upon her part in controlling her classes and students. Such being the case, we cannot find that the Board acted arbitrarily in upholding these grounds as justification for terminating appellee's contract. It may be noted in passing that there is no claim that this proceeding was politically or otherwise motivated except in the interest of efficient school administration. . . .

The judgment is reversed, with directions to enter a judgment sustaining the action of the Knox County Board of Education.

Notes

1. In *Tichenor v. Orleans Parish School Bd.*, 144 So.2d 603 (La.Ct.App. 1962), an appellate court in Louisiana held that a teacher who refused supervision may be discharged on the ground of incompetency and wilful neglect of duty. The court described incompetence a relative term meaning disqualification, inability, or incapacity.

2. The Supreme Court of Nebraska annulled a teacher's discharge because of inadequate notice of the charges where he had received a vague and conclusory letter, even though he had access to his personnel file. *Irwin v. Board of Educ. of School Dist. No. 25 of Holt County*, 340 N.W.2d 877 [14 Educ. L. Rep. 1102] (Neb.1983).

[Case No. 87]　Discharge of Teacher—Immoral Conduct; Board Procedures

VANELLI v. REYNOLDS SCHOOL DISTRICT NO. 7

United States Court of Appeals, Ninth Circuit, 1982.
667 F.2d 773 [2 Educ. L. Rep. 366].

KENNEDY, CIRCUIT JUDGE: In this case we examine again the procedural protections afforded by the due process clause when a public employee is dismissed. . . .

Appellant, George Vanelli, was hired by the school district to teach sophomore English at Reynolds High School during the 1975–76 school year under a probationary contract which ran for one academic year, and which reserved the school board's right to discharge the teacher "for any cause deemed in good faith sufficient by the Board." Midway through the year, some female students complained of offensive conduct by Vanelli. An assistant principal called him to discuss the matter and when Vanelli arrived he was given a letter notifying him of suspension. The meeting lasted a few minutes and Vanelli did not attempt to present his side of the case, though he did request to appear at the school board meeting on March 11, 1976, to respond to the charges leveled against him. He was told not to attend and that he would be given an opportunity to respond at a later date. Vanelli made no attempt to present a written rebuttal to the board, apparently because he was under the reasonable impression the board would not consider it.

The school board met for approximately 45 minutes on Sunday, March 11, and, after the school administrators had presented the case against Vanelli, the board voted to terminate his contract without giving him an opportunity to respond to the charges either in person or in writing. Another school board meeting was scheduled for April 7, 1976, to review the termination decision. At that hearing, Vanelli was represented by an attorney and was permitted to cross-examine the witnesses, all of whom testified under oath. Four of the five girls who filed the complaints were present (the fifth was ill), and the hearing was tape recorded.

Despite certain objections to the procedures at the hearing, the board upheld the earlier dismissal. Soon thereafter, Vanelli sought employment at other high schools, but found difficulty in securing a permanent position due to the circumstances surrounding his dismissal from Reynolds.

The fourteenth amendment's guarantee of procedural due process applies when a constitutionally protected liberty or property interest is at stake.... It is well established that an employee dismissed during the term of a one-year contract and in breach of its provisions has a legitimate claim of entitlement and a property interest in continued employment.... Accordingly, we hold appellant's midyear dismissal implicated a property interest protectible under the due process clause.

Appellant's interest in liberty is similarly implicated if a charge impairs his reputation for honesty or morality. The procedural protections of due process apply if the accuracy of the charge is contested, there is some public disclosure of the charge, and it is made in connection with the termination of employment or the alteration of some right or status recognized by state law. Under these principles, appellant's midyear dismissal implicated a protectible liberty interest.

We must decide next whether the timing and procedures of the hearing provided by the school district adequately protected appellant's property and liberty interests. We are met at the outset with the school district's contention that a post-termination hearing is sufficient compliance with the due process clause. Under the circumstances of this case, however, we cannot agree.

There is a strong presumption that a public employee is entitled to some form of notice and opportunity to be heard before being deprived of a property or liberty interest. Apart from this general presumption, a court should analyze whether the timing of a hearing comports with due process, given the exigencies and circumstances of any particular case, according to the three part balancing test outlined in *Mathews v. Eldridge*. The factors to consider include the private interest that will be affected, the risk of an erroneous deprivation of that interest through the procedures used, and the fiscal and administrative burdens that any additional procedural requirements would entail.

Application of this balancing test necessarily compels our determination that under these circumstances a pre-termination hearing is constitutionally required. The weight of the private interest affected is apparent. Teaching had been Vanelli's livelihood for over sixteen years, and the stigma arising from a midyear dismissal on the grounds here asserted would seriously impair opportunities for future employment. The interest of the school district in dismissing, rather than merely suspending, Vanelli without affording him a hearing is less clear. The lower court found no emergency situation requiring immediate dismissal, and on this record we cannot say the finding was clearly erroneous. The risk of an erroneous deprivation was substantial, since appellant was dismissed without an opportunity to confront the evidence and was denied the opportunity to respond to the charges at the school board meeting. The administrative burdens of permitting appellant to appear at the March 11 school board meeting and rebut the charges made against him or present a written rebuttal were minimal. In denying appellant's request to attend the March 11 meeting and thereby proceeding to dismiss him without any opportunity to be heard in person or in writing, the board deprived him of property and liberty interests without due process.

Appellant characterizes the April 7 hearing as a mere review of the March 11 termination decision and, accordingly, claims his right to a de novo trial was violated. Under the circumstances of this case, however, we cannot agree that the April 7 hearing was unconstitutionally infirm because of the board's participation in the prior termination decision. Irrespective of whether the April 7 hearing is labeled a review of a prior hearing or a de novo hearing, the critical inquiry is whether it comported with due process. The key component of due process, when a decisionmaker is acquainted with the facts, is the assurance of a central fairness at the hearing. Essential fairness is a flexible notion, but at a minimum one must be given notice and an opportunity to be heard "at a meaningful time and in a meaningful manner." An individual must have an opportunity to confront all the evidence adduced against him, in particular that evidence with which the decisionmaker is familiar.

The April 7 post-termination hearing met the standards of fairness required by the due process clause. Appellant's counsel was present, he was permitted to cross-examine all the witnesses (except for one who was ill), and was given ample opportunity to rebut all evidence which the school board had heard on March 11. No issues were raised at the prior meeting which were not thoroughly examined at the subsequent hearing. The board members did not have any personal or financial stake in the action, nor was any personal animosity alleged. For these reasons, we uphold the validity of the subsequent dismissal action. . . .

Judgment vacated and case remanded for redetermination of damages and attorneys' fees . . .

Notes

1. Four female students complained that Vanelli, in the summary words of the court, stared at their physical attributes and made statements with sexual overtones. Other specific incidents seemed innocuous or susceptible to differing interpretations.

2. This case represents a fairly common occurrence. The court upheld the school board's decision, but its overreaction was costly.

[Case No. 88]   Reduction in Force—Selection of Teacher

DYKEMAN v. BOARD OF EDUCATION OF SCHOOL DISTRICT OF COLERIDGE, CEDAR COUNTY

Supreme Court of Nebraska, 1982.
316 N.W.2d 69 [2 Educ. L. Rep. 862].

BOSLAUGH, JUSTICE. This is an appeal . . . to review an order of the Board of Education of the School District of Coleridge, Cedar County,

Nebraska, terminating the contract of the plaintiff pursuant to a reduction in force. The District Court found that the action of the Board was not arbitrary or capricious . . .

The plaintiff had been employed by the district for 6 years as a business education teacher. In 1980 the Board determined that it was necessary to reduce its staff for the next school year and that a teacher in the business education department of the high school should be dropped from the staff. There were two teachers employed to teach business education, both of whom were tenured, and whose teaching certificates contained identical endorsements.

In deciding which teacher should be dropped from the staff, the Board considered the contribution that each made to the activities program. The plaintiff was co-sponsor of the annual staff [sic] and sponsor of the sophomore class. For her duties in connection with the activities program, the plaintiff was paid an additional $228, amounting to 2.5 percent of her annual base salary. The other teacher, who had been employed for 3 years and was retained, was the assistant volleyball coach, head girls' basketball coach, and co-sponsor of the "C" Club. For these duties he was paid an additional $1,592.50, which amounted to 17.5 percent of his annual base salary.

The reduction in force policy which the Board had adopted pursuant to Neb.Rev.Stat. § 79–1254.05 provided in part: "Within the separate category of tenured teachers, the process of selecting personnel for termination will involve consideration of (listed in order of priority):

"1. Certification and area(s) of endorsement.

"2. Program to be offered.

"3. Contribution to the activity program.

"4. Length of uninterrupted service.

"5. Special qualifications that may require specific training and/or experience. Part-time employees shall have lowest priority for retention."

The plaintiff contends that a school board may not consider the contribution teachers make to an activities program in making a reduction in force. . . .

Although § 79–1254.05 does not specifically authorize consideration of a teacher's contribution to an activities program as a criterion to be used in making a reduction in force, neither does it prohibit its use as a criterion. Certainly, extracurricular activities such as athletics are generally considered to be important parts of any educational program. It has been held that a school board may impose extracurricular activity duties upon a teacher as a condition to continued employment in the system.

It is generally held that the selection of a teacher to be eliminated from the staff through a reduction in force is an executive or administrative function as distinguished from quasi-judicial action.

In the absence of statutory or contractual restrictions, the decision of a school board in such a matter is generally subject to but a limited review. School boards should have broad discretionary powers in such matters free from judicial interference in the absence of a finding that their actions were arbitrary and capricious.

In making a selection of the teacher to be dismissed pursuant to a reduction in force, the school board may exercise its discretion and consider noneducational factors as well as educational ones.

The board of education is given the general authority to manage and direct the schools within the district. This includes the power to conduct nonteaching and extracurricular duties as a part of the educational program. It follows that the board may consider a teacher's contribution to the activities program when deciding upon a reduction in force.

The judgment of the District Court is affirmed.

Notes

1. Nebraska, like other states, required school boards to articulate the criteria to be used in reduction-in-force situations. Do you approve of the ones used in this case?

2. Why did the court include data as to amounts of extra pay for extra duties earned by the two business education teachers?

[Case No. 89]   Membership in Retirement System as Contractual

BIRNBAUM v. NEW YORK STATE TEACHERS' RETIREMENT SYSTEM

Court of Appeals of New York, 1958.
176 N.Y.S.2d 984.

CONWAY, CHIEF JUDGE. . . .

This is an action for a declaratory judgment brought by plaintiffs on behalf of themselves and all other school teachers in the State of New York similarly situated. They challenge the validity of the action of the defendant, the New York State Teachers Retirement System, in adopting on or about January 9, 1946, an actuarial table for computing the annuity benefits of the members of the defendant pursuant to subdivisions 4 and 5 of section 508 of the Education Law of the State of New York. Their contention is that the action of the defendant constitutes a breach of the contractual relationship established by section 7 of article V of the Constitution of the State of New York, as to members of the retirement system prior to the effective date (July 1, 1940) of the constitutional provision.

The complaint alleges, and the answer admits, that since 1920 the Education Law has established a retirement system for public school-teachers within the State whereby the teachers make regular contributions to a retirement fund and receive in return upon their retirement an annuity; that the plaintiffs have made the required contributions, the plaintiff Birnbaum since 1935 and the plaintiff Cate since 1922; that they are eligible to retire after having completed 25 years of service and having attained the age of 60 years or over; and that the mortality table adopted on January 9, 1946, reduces by approximately 5% the amount to be paid to the plaintiffs pursuant to the table in use on July 1, 1940, when section 7 of article V of the Constitution went into effect.

The answer pleads two affirmative defenses. The first is that the plaintiffs have no present interest in the subject matter of the action and will have none until and when, if ever, they seek retirement and apply for their retirement benefits. The second is that subdivision 4 of section 508 of the Education Law mandates the periodical adjustment of annuity benefits payable upon retirement according to mortality and actuarial tables adopted pursuant to subdivisions 4 and 5 of section 508 of the Education Law, and that such section constitutes and forms part of the contract between each member of the retirement system and the New York State Teachers Retirement System....

... The Education Law provides that the "annuity ... shall be the actuarial equivalent of his accumulated contributions at the time of his [the member's] retirement".

The term "actuarial equivalent" has reference to the mathematical formula for computing annuity payments according to the mortality table calculated and adopted pursuant to the provisions of subdivisions 4 and 5 of section 508 of the Education Law.

The issue in this case relates solely to the use of new mortality tables to compute the "annuity" which is payable upon retirement from funds contributed by the member. When the Teachers Retirement System adopted new mortality tables in 1946, the new tables were made applicable to the computation of all annuities of all members who had not previously retired. The new tables, as mentioned earlier, have the effect of reducing the annuities of all members of the system by approximately 5%.

As a practical matter, the controversy here comes to this: Plaintiffs argue that the contractual arrangement which the Constitution envisaged was the usual annuity policy whereby an insurance company, on the day the policy is issued, agrees that it will pay periodically a fixed and stated amount commencing on a certain date and that, viewed in that light, it was intended that a teacher who was a member of the Retirement System on July 1, 1940, after making the required contributions to the Retirement System over the required period of time, should receive an annuity computed from mortality tables in use on July 1, 1940 (the date the constitutional amendment became effective). The defendant Retirement System, on the other hand, maintains that it was intended that the Retirement System should determine, at the time of retirement, the amount of annuity which the member's contributions will purchase at the time of retirement, employing the mortality table in effect at the time of making such calculation....

... [T]his court [has] held that where the statutory conditions for retirement from the civil service have been met "and the award of the pension or benefit has been made, or as of right should have been made

... the interest becomes vested and takes on the attributes of a contract, which, in the absence of statutory reservations, may not legally be diminished or otherwise adversely affected by subsequent legislation". We pointed out, however, that "[w]here the statutory scheme creates a fund wholly or largely out of public moneys, the interest of the member down to the point where there has been compliance with all precedent conditions and the award has been or as of right should have been made can hardly be deemed contractual" and that "whatever its legal nature may be, there seems to be no doubt that it is subject to change or even to revocation at the will of the Legislature." Thereafter, in 1938, section 7 of article V of the New York State Constitution was adopted by the Constitutional Convention and approved by the people. It reads: "After July first, nineteen hundred forty, membership in any pension or retirement system of the state or of a civil division thereof shall be a contractual relationship, the benefits of which shall not be diminished or impaired."

It seems clear that the foregoing constitutional provision was designed to overcome the dictum in the *Roddy* case, to the effect that prior to retirement, pension and retirement systems of the State or of a civil division thereof, created wholly or largely out of public moneys, were subject to the will of the Legislature. By the constitutional amendment the people determined to confer contractual protection upon the benefits of pension and retirement system of the State and of the civil divisions thereof, and to prohibit their diminution or impairment prior to retirement. . . .

While it is clear that section 508 contemplates a periodic review of the mortality tables to be used in determining the amounts of annuities to be allowed on the basis of the contributions of members, the section nowhere declares that mortality tables adopted after a person has become a member of the system are to be employed in determining the annuity benefits to which such person is entitled upon retirement. Nor do we see that we should read such an intention into the statute. The constitutional amendment, as demonstrated above, prohibits official action during a public employment membership in a retirement system which adversely affects the amount of the retirement benefits payable to the members on retirement under laws and conditions existing at the time of his entrance into retirement system membership. If we are to construe section 508 of the Education Law as authorizing that which the Constitution prohibits, then, the statute must be held to have been superseded by the constitutional amendment. It seems to us that there is no necessity for so holding since it is reasonable to construe the Education Law as authorizing (1) a periodic review by the State Teachers Retirement System of the mortality tables being used to compute annuities, (2) the adoption of new mortality tables, and (3) the use of the new mortality tables in the computation of the annuities of only such persons as enter the system thereafter.

Defendant argues that if this court holds that new mortality tables adopted by the Retirement System are applicable only to those persons who joined the system subsequent to the date of such adoption, the system will be plunged into bankruptcy. The answer to that argument must be that if the people intended to decree, by the constitutional amendment, that mortality tables adopted by the system after one has become a member are not to be applied in the computation of the annuity of such person, we are not at liberty to hold otherwise simply because the system may become bankrupt as a result.... If bankruptcy now threatens to overtake the Teachers Retirement System, the system must turn to the Legislature for financial assistance. It may not ask us to ignore the will of the people as expressed in their Constitution....

Notes

1. What are the pros and cons of designating retirement rights as contractual in nature?

2. Should school employees have the option of choosing between the state retirement system and private investment companies?

Chapter 12

COMPULSORY ATTENDANCE, CURRICULUM, AND OTHER INSTRUCTIONAL ISSUES

Introduction

The face of American public education has changed dramatically since the emergence of compulsory attendance laws in the mid-Nineteenth Century. As school systems continue to evolve to meet the needs of the communities that they serve, a variety of legal matters surfaced dealing with what can be broadly classified as the instructional program or curriculum, however broadly these terms are defined. In light of the array of questions that surface with regard to providing educational programming for students, this chapter examines legal issues under the broad umbrella of curricular and instructional issues.

Compulsory Education

In General

In 1852, Massachusetts became the first jurisdiction in the United States to enact a compulsory attendance law.[1] Courts have generally upheld compulsory education statutes[2] against charges that they unreasonably infringed on individual constitutional liberties.[3] In permitting compulsory attendance laws to remain in effect along with a variety of exceptions, for example, for parents who wish to send their children to non-public schools or educate them via home schooling, the courts recognize that these statutes represent a valid exercise of state police power[4] that is served by the creation of an enlightened citizenry.

Based on the concept of *in loco parentis*, literally "in the place of the parent," compulsory attendance laws rely on the common law presump-

---

1. *See* MASS. GEN. LAWS ANN. 76 § 1 (historical notes St.1852, c. 240, §§ 1, 2, 4).

2. *See, e.g.,* ALA. CODE ANN. § 16–28–3; ALASKA STAT. ANN. § 14.30.010; CAL. EDUC. CODE § 48200; DEL. CODE ANN. tit. 14 § 2702; GA. CODE ANN. § 20–2–690.1; HAW. REV. STAT. ANN. § 302A–1132; 105 ILL. COMP. STAT. ANN. 5/26–1; KY. REV. STAT. ANN. § 159.010; LA. REV. STAT. ANN. § 17:221; MD. CODE ANN., EDUC. § 7–301; MASS. GEN. LAWS ch. 76, § 1; N.J. STAT. ANN. § 18A:38–25; N.Y. EDUC. LAW § 3205; OHIO REV. CODE ANN. § 3321.01; OKLA. STAT. ANN. tit. 70, § 10–105; 24 PA. CONSOL. STAT. ANN. § 13–1327; TEX. EDUC. CODE ANN. § 25.085; VT. STAT. ANN. tit. 16, § 1121; WIS. STAT. ANN. § 118.15.

3. *Parr v. State*, 157 N.E. 555 (Ohio 1927); *Concerned Citizens for Neighborhood Schools v. Board of Educ. of Chattanooga*, 379 F.Supp. 1233 (E.D.Tenn.1974); *Mazanec v. North Judson-San Pierre School Corp.*, 614 F.Supp. 1152 [27 Educ. L. Rep. 140] (N.D.Ind.1985); *Brown v. District of Columbia*, 727 A.2d 865 [134 Educ. L. Rep. 206] (D.C.1999). *But see Wisconsin v. Yoder*, 406 U.S. 205, 92 S.Ct. 1526, 32 L.Ed.2d 15 (1972). [Case No. 90]

4. *Matter of Shannon B.*, 522 N.Y.S.2d 488 [43 Educ. L. Rep. 1068] (N.Y.1987).

tion that parents voluntarily submit their children to the authority of school officials.[5] Yet, a question can be raised about the continuing viability of the presumed voluntary nature of *in loco parentis* in light of compulsory attendance laws, not to mention other school rules,[6] which require parents to send their children to school at the risk of punishment for noncompliance.[7]

An alternative justification for compulsory attendance rests on another common law principle, *parens patriae*, literally "father of the country," under which state legislatures have the authority to enact reasonable laws for the welfare of their residents.[8] Placing the dispute over the tension between the authority of state officials and parents vis-a-vis the education of children aside in the interest of addressing the practical issues associated with compulsory attendance laws, suffice it to say that the courts agree that parents[9] must ensure that their children are educated.

Whether parents satisfy their responsibility to send their children to school, or whether students who are classified as truants are absent from school without justification[10] is a duty shared by school officials and the courts.[11] In one dispute, where school officials failed to prove that a mother committed an essential element of the crime of failing to send her daughter to school regularly because they did not demonstrate that she did so knowingly or purposefully, the Supreme Court of Missouri reversed her conviction for having allegedly violated the state's compulsory attendance statute.[12] Further, an appellate court in Wisconsin held that a mother could raise the affirmative defense that her son disobeyed her when she ordered him to attend school.[13] In reversing the mother's conviction, the panel explained that the trial court erred in not permitting the mother to raise the disobedience defense.

As state and local officials enforce compulsory education laws, their goal is to strike a balance between the rights of individuals and the state. In seeking to preserve this balance, there is a point beyond which state

---

5. *State ex rel. Burpee v. Burton*, 45 Wis. 150 (Wis.1878).

6. *See, e.g., Baker v. Owen*, 395 F.Supp. 294 (M.D.N.C.1975), *aff'd*, 423 U.S. 907, 96 S.Ct. 210, 46 L.Ed.2d 137 (1975) (affirming that parental disapproval of corporal punishment did not preclude its being used on a child).

7. *Eukers v. State*, 728 N.E.2d 219 [143 Educ. L. Rep. 1029] (Ind.Ct.App.2000).

8. In *Wisconsin v. Yoder*, 406 U.S. 205, 92 S.Ct. 1526, 32 L.Ed.2d 15 (1972), the Court rejected the applicability of *parens patriae* to compulsory attendance but upheld the general principle that the state has the authority to regulate education. [Case No. 90]

9. While recognizing that many laws speak of guardians along with parents, this chapter uses the term parents to include both parents and guardians.

10. *See, e.g., G.N. v. State*, 833 N.E.2d 1071 [201 Educ. L. Rep. 681] (Ind. Ct. App. 2005) (upholding a student's conviction as truant where evidence proved that he violated the state's compulsory attendance law).

11. *See, e.g., In re C.M.T.*, 861 A.2d 348 [193 Educ. L. Rep. 805] (Pa. Super. Ct. 2004); *In re Commissioner of Social Servs. On Behalf of Leslie C.*, 614 N.Y.S.2d 855 (N.Y. Fam. Ct. 1994); Matter of T.K., 462 N.W.2d 893 (S.D. 1990).

12. *State v. Self*, 155 S.W.3d 756 [195 Educ. L. Rep. 1019] (Mo. 2005).

13. *State v. McGee*, 698 N.W.2d 850 [199 Educ. L. Rep. 429] (Wis. Ct. App. 2005), *review denied*, 705 N.W.2d 660 (Wis. 2005).

officials may not go without violating the constitutional rights of parents and students. Insofar as exactly where this point is cannot be established in the abstract, the judiciary has intervened in cases where parents, and students, claim that public officials intruded into their personal rights.

The most basic constitutional limitation on compulsory education laws is that parents can satisfy them by means other than having their children attend public schools since the primary goal of these statutes is to ensure that students obtain a minimum level of education rather than focus on where they are educated. The Supreme Court first enunciated this principle in *Pierce v. Society of the Sisters of the Holy Names of Jesus and Mary (Pierce)*.[14] In *Pierce*, the Court struck down a law from Oregon which would have required children, other than those needing what today would be described as special education, between the ages of eight and sixteen to attend public schools.

Pierce was filed by officials in two non-public schools, one religiously affiliated and the other a military academy, who sought to avoid having their schools forced out of business, relying on their property rights under the Fourteenth Amendment. In addition to agreeing with the due process claim that the school officials advanced, the Court, finding that since parents had the right to direct the upbringing of their children, decided that they could satisfy the compulsory attendance law by sending their children to non-public schools. At the same time, the Court acknowledged that state officials could "reasonably [ ] regulate all schools, to inspect, supervise, and examine them, their teachers and pupils."[15] In practice, other than health and safety code issues, state officials typically impose fewer restrictions on non-public schools than on public schools.

Wisconsin v. Yoder (Yoder)[16] represents perhaps the most noteworthy exception to judicial support for compulsory attendance laws. In *Yoder,* the Supreme Court ruled in favor of Amish parents who challenged state officials who refused to exempt their children from formal education beyond eighth grade. The parents argued that since their children would have received all of the preparation that they needed in their home communities, it was unnecessary for them to attend public high schools. Relying on the First Amendment's Free Exercise Clause, the Court agreed that the community's almost three-hundred-year way of life would have been gravely endangered, if not destroyed, by requiring them to comply with the compulsory education law.

In *Yoder*, the Court reiterated that while there is no doubt as to the state's power to impose reasonable regulations over basic education, in balancing the competing interests, greater weight had to be placed on the First Amendment and the traditional interests of parents with respect to the religious upbringing of their children. The Court concluded that since the Amish way of life and religion were inseparable, requiring the children to attend public high school may have destroyed

14. 268 U.S. 510, 45 S.Ct. 571, 69 L.Ed. 1070 (1925). [Case No. 91]

15. *Id.* at 268 534.

16. 406 U.S. 205, 92 S.Ct. 1526, 32 L.Ed.2d 15 (1972). [Case No. 90]

their religious beliefs. In a partial dissent, Justice Douglas questioned whether children had rights apart from their parents, in light of his fear that students could have been "harnessed" to the lifestyles of their parents without opportunities to express their own desires.

Following *Yoder*, it is clear that few, if any, members of other religions can meet its test for avoiding compulsory education requirements. Other than the Amish, courts consistently deny religion-based applications for exceptions to substantial or material parts of compulsory education requirements such as home schooling[17] and sex-AIDS education.[18] In one case, the federal trial court in Connecticut asserted that school officials did not violate the Free Exercise Clause by rejecting a father's request that his son be excused from a mandatory health education course and by assigning him a failing grade when he refused to do so.[19]

Equivalent Instruction—Home Schooling

Parents who choose not to send their children to public schools must provide them with equivalent instruction elsewhere either by having them educated in non-public schools or via home schooling. As with other areas involving compulsory attendance, the courts have generally upheld statutes and regulations dealing with equivalent instruction.[20] The Supreme Court of Ohio made an exception to this rule in noting that the state's minimum standards were so pervasive and all-encompassing "that total compliance by a non-public school would have effectively eradicated the distinction between public and non-public education."[21] Subsequently, the Supreme Courts of Georgia[22] and Wisconsin[23] agreed that where laws and regulations lacked sufficient clarity with regard to standards for non-public schools, they were unenforceable.

In an area that has become contentious in view of the growth of home schooling, courts have examined whether children who are so educated are receiving equivalent instruction due to their lack of interac-

---

17. *Johnson v. Charles City Community Schools Bd. of Educ.*, 368 N.W.2d 74 [25 Educ. L. Rep. 524] (Iowa 1985), *cert. denied sub nom. Pruessner v. Benton*, 474 U.S. 1033, 106 S.Ct. 594, 88 L.Ed.2d 574 [29 Educ. L. Rep. 493] (1985).

18. *See, e.g., Ware v. Valley Stream High School Dist.*, 551 N.Y.S.2d 167 [58 Educ. L. Rep. 1242] (N.Y.1989) (affirming the denial of a board's motion for summary judgment where genuine issues of material fact existed over the burden that exposure to an AIDS curriculum would have had on the religious beliefs of students and their parents).

19. *Leebaert ex rel. Leebaert v. Harrington*, 193 F.Supp.2d 491 [163 Educ. L. Rep. 755] (D.Conn.2002).

20. *State v. Shaver*, 294 N.W.2d 883 (N.D.1980); *State ex rel. Douglas v. Faith Baptist Church of Louisville*, 301 N.W.2d 571 (Neb.1981), *appeal dismissed*, 454 U.S. 803, 102 S.Ct. 75, 70 L.Ed.2d 72 (1981); *New Life Baptist Church Academy v. Town of East Longmeadow*, 885 F.2d 940 [56 Educ. L. Rep. 82] (1st Cir.1989), *cert. denied*, 494 U.S. 1066, 110 S.Ct. 1782, 108 L.Ed.2d 784 (1990).

21. *State v. Whisner*, 351 N.E.2d 750, 768 (Ohio 1976). *See also State ex rel. Nagle v. Olin*, 415 N.E.2d 279 (Ohio 1980).

22. *Roemhild v. State*, 308 S.E.2d 154 [14 Educ. L. Rep. 383] (Ga.1983).

23. *State v. Popanz*, 332 N.W.2d 750 [10 Educ. L. Rep. 789] (Wis.1983). [Case No. 92] tion with other students. While an older case from New Jersey suggested that children who were home schooled did not receive an equivalent education,[24] a later one expressly rejected the need to consider social development in evaluating whether instruction is equivalent.[25] The court posited that while children need group activity to develop socially, it did not necessarily have to take place in school.

After a flurry of activity in the 1980's, home schooling is legal throughout the nation as more than thirty states have enacted explicit statutes.[26] The remaining jurisdictions make home schooling legal under laws dealing with alternative,[27] comparable,[28] equivalent,[29] or other[30] instruction (including tutors)[31] and/or private,[32] church,[33] or parochial[34] school exceptions. At the outset, it is important to note that home schooling, wherein parents educate their own children, is not the same as home-bound instruction that students with disabilities are eligible to receive if they are unable to attend schools.[35]

Following legislative and regulatory approval of home schooling, courts have still had to address an array of issues such as teacher qualifications, curricular content, and state oversight. Although most states do not have explicit educational requirements for parents who home school their children, the Supreme Court of North Dakota reasoned that state officials could have expected them to meet reasonable certification requirements.[36] On the other hand, the Supreme Court of Michigan indicated that teacher certification requirements violated the free exercise rights of parents because state officials failed to show that they were the least restrictive means of achieving the state's claimed interest.[37] According to the court, this approach violated the rights of parents who home schooled their children since the state legislature did

---

24. *Stephens v. Bongart,* 189 A. 131 (N.J.Juv. & Dom.Rel.Ct.1937); *Knox v. O'Brien,* 72 A.2d 389 (N.J. County Ct.1950).

25. *State v. Massa,* 231 A.2d 252 (N.J. County Ct.1967).

26. *See, e.g.,* Ark. Code Ann. § 6–15–501; Col. Rev. Stat. Ann. § 22–33–104.5; Del. Code Ann. tit. 14 § 2703; Ga. Code Ann. § 20–2–690 (c); La. Rev. Stat. Ann. tit. 17 § 236.1; Me. Rev. Stat. Ann. 20-A, § 5001–A(3)(A)(3); Mich. Comp. Laws Ann. § 380.1561(3)(f); N.J. Stat. Ann. § 18A: 38–25; Ohio Rev. Code Ann. § 3321.04(A)(2); Pa. Stat. Ann. tit. 24 § 13–1327.1; Utah Code Ann. § 53A–11–102(1)(b)(ii); Va. Code Ann. § 22.1–254.1.

27. S.D. Codified Laws Ann. § 13–27–3.

28. Idaho Code Ann. § 33–202.

29. Conn. Gen. Stat. Ann. § 10–184; Nev. Rev. Stat. Ann. § 392.070; N.Y. Educ. Law § 3204(2).

30. Ind. Code Ann. §§ 20–8.1–3–17 ("... some other school which is taught in the English language.").

31. Ala. Code § 16–28–1(2) (addressing church schools and tutors).

32. For statutes covering home schooling as private schools, *see* Cal. Educ. Code § 48222; Ill. Comp. Stat. Ann. 105 5/26–1; Iowa Code Ann. §§ 299A.1 *et seq.* (competent private instruction); Mass Gen. Laws Ann. Ch. 76 § 1; Okla. Stat. Ann. tit. 70 § 10–105(A) (private or other schools); Tex. Educ. Code Ann. § 25.086 (private or parochial schools).

33. Ky. Rev. Stat. Ann. § 159.030(b) (private, parochial, or church day schools); Neb. Rev. Stat. Ann. § 79–1701(2) (private, parochial, or denominational schools).

34. Kan. Stat. Ann. § 72–1111(a)(2) (private, denominational, or parochial schools providing instruction that is substantially equivalent to that in the public schools).

35. *See* 20 U.S.C.A. § 1401(26)(A).

36. *State v. Anderson,* 427 N.W.2d 316 [48 Educ. L. Rep. 649] (N.D.1988), *cert. denied,* 488 U.S. 965, 109 S.Ct. 491, 102 L.Ed.2d 528 (1988).

37. *People v. DeJonge,* 501 N.W.2d 127 [83 Educ. L. Rep. 773] (Mich.1993).

not require teachers in non-public schools to be certificated and permitted individuals who lacked state certification to serve as substitute teachers in public schools.

Most states do not require parents who home school their children to cover specified subject areas. Even so, litigation has arisen over the content of the curriculum. For instance, the Sixth Circuit, in a case from Kentucky, affirmed that a statute requiring children who were home schooled to pass an equivalency examination in order to receive credit for a home study program did not violate the due process, equal protection, or free exercise rights of a student and/or his parents based on the commonwealth's desire to ensure that it had an educated citizenry.[38] Applying the same kind of analysis, a federal trial court in Texas rejected a claim from a home schooling family that requiring students from non-accredited or home schools to pass proficiency examinations at their own expense in order to receive credit toward graduation violated a child's rights to equal protection and free exercise of religion.[39]

In the related matter of oversight, courts have recognized the right of state officials to ensure that students are progressing in school whether by means of standardized tests[40] or other measures such as portfolios[41] and annual reports.[42] On the other hand, both the Supreme Judicial Court of Massachusetts[43] and the Ninth Circuit[44] invalidated requirements that would have subjected home schooling families to state visitations in essentially agreeing that this kind of oversight was overly intrusive since the same information could have been obtained in other ways such as having parents submit written reports. At the same time, an appellate court in Massachusetts affirmed that when home schooling parents refused to provide school officials with the bare essentials of the educational plan they created for their children or to permit any evaluations of their educational attainment, officials had the right to proceed with having the children declared as being in need of protection and committed to the care of the Department of Social Services.[45] In like fashion, an appellate panel in Missouri affirmed that while a trial court erred in its discussion of the length of a school term, state officials had the authority to take jurisdiction over an autistic or nearly autistic child.[46] The court agreed that the parents could have been charged with

---

38. *Vandiver v. Hardin County Bd. of Educ.*, 925 F.2d 927 [65 Educ. L. Rep. 1045] (6th Cir. 1991).

39. *Hubbard By and Through Hubbard v. Buffalo Indep. School Dist.*, 20 F.Supp.2d 1012 [130 Educ. L. Rep. 647] (W.D.Tex. 1998).

40. *Murphy v. State of Ark.*, 852 F.2d 1039 [48 Educ. L. Rep. 159] (8th Cir.1988).

41. *Stobaugh v. Wallace*, 757 F.Supp. 653 [66 Educ. L. Rep. 245] (W.D.Pa.1990); *Battles v. Anne Arundel County Bd. of Educ.*, 904 F.Supp. 471 [105 Educ. L. Rep. 93] (D.Md.1995) *aff'd without reported opinion*, 95 F.3d 41 (4th Cir.1996).

42. *State v. Rivera*, 497 N.W.2d 878 [81 Educ. L. Rep. 1064] (Iowa 1993).

43. *Brunelle v. Lynn Pub. Schools*, 702 N.E.2d 1182 [130 Educ. L. Rep. 1322] (Mass.1998).

44. *Calabretta v. Floyd*, 189 F.3d 808 (9th Cir.1999).

45. *In re Ivan*, 717 N.E.2d 1020 [138 Educ. L. Rep. 511] (Mass.App.Ct.1999), *review denied*, 723 N.E.2d 33 (Mass.2000).

46. *In re J. B.*, 58 S.W.3d 575 [159 Educ. L. Rep. 356] (Mo.Ct.App.2001).

educational neglect since they failed to administer the required hours of instruction or to keep proper records of the child's work and progress.

Parents who practice home schooling have had limited success over whether their children have the right to participate in extracurricular activities. West Virginia's highest court was of the opinion that rules of the state athletic association that prohibited students who were home schooled from taking part in interscholastic athletics did not violate their rights under the Equal Protection Clause of the state constitution.[47] The court pointed out that since participation in extracurricular activities, including interscholastic athletics, did not rise to the level of a fundamental or constitutional right under the state constitution, the rule was rationally related to a legitimate state purpose. The court identified two key reasons in justifying its position. First, the court maintained that the rule prevented parents from withdrawing their children who may have been struggling academically simply to maintain athletic eligibility. Second, the court thought that since local boards received funding only for students who actually enrolled, and having to offer services to students who are home schooled would have strained their budgets, the rule protected the financial well-being of school systems.

In like manner, home schooled students and their parents in Michigan unsuccessfully challenged a rule of the state athletic association that would have required them to attend school before becoming eligible to participate in extracurricular interscholastic athletic programs. In affirming the denial of the plaintiffs' request to enjoin the rule, the court remarked that the home schooled students did not have a statutory right to participate in extracurricular interscholastic athletic programs because they are not required elements of the school program.[48] The court added that the enrollment requirement did not violate the students' rights to either the free exercise of religion or equal protection. Earlier, an appellate court in New York affirmed that a home schooled student was ineligible to participate in a local school's interscholastic sports program in light of a state regulation which conditioned eligibility on being regularly enrolled in school.[49] The court found that the regulation did not infringe on the student's rights to due process or equal protection.

Parents who engage in home schooling have also not had much success in claiming that their children could attend public schools on part-time bases. In such a case, the Tenth Circuit affirmed that a school board in Oklahoma's policy that prohibited part-time attendance did not violate a home schooled student's right to free exercise of religion.[50] The

47. *Jones v. West Va. State Bd. of Educ.*, 622 S.E.2d 289 [203 Educ. L. Rep. 862] (W.Va. 2005).

48. *Reid v. Kenowa Hills Pub. Schools*, 680 N.W.2d 62 [188 Educ. L. Rep. 438] (Mich. Ct. App. 2004).

49. *Bradstreet v. Sobol*, 650 N.Y.S.2d 402 [114 Educ. L. Rep. 927] (N.Y. App. Div. 1996). *See also Angstadt v. Midd–West School Dist.*, 377 F.3d 338 [190 Educ. L.

Rep. 48] (3d Cir. 2004) (affirming that a student who was educated in a cyber school had no right to participate in interscholastic basketball on the ground that she failed to establish the likelihood of success on the merits of the claim that she had a property interest in doing so).

50. *Swanson By and Through Swanson v. Guthrie Indep. School Dist. No. I–L*, 135 court agreed that the board did not violate the student's right because its action was rooted in a neutral policy of general application that neither prohibited her parents from home schooling her in accordance with their religious beliefs nor forced them to do anything contrary to those beliefs.[51]

Marriage and/or Parenthood

Students who are eligible to attend public schools cannot be excluded if they are married. In an older case that reflects this rule, where a young woman conceived a child out of wedlock but was married by the time that she gave birth, she sought to return to school after her husband deserted her and the child. The Supreme Court of Kansas, although conceding that school officials could bar individuals who were "... of a licentious or immoral character,"[52] observed that having a child out of wedlock did not prove that the woman was of such character. In the same year, the Supreme Court of Mississippi invalidated a board resolution that attempted to prohibit married persons from attending public schools. In ordering the student's admission, the court commented that since marriage is a domestic relation "... highly favored by law.... [as] refining and elevating, rather than demoralizing,"[53] there was no reason why she should have been excluded.

Courts have also struck down prohibitions aimed at limiting the participation of married students in extracurricular activities. The first three federal trial courts to address the issue agreed, in rapid succession, and without citing each other, that eligibility for school-sponsored activities could not be made dependent on marital status.[54] Other federal and state courts followed their lead.[55]

Litigation continued over the right of pregnant students to become members of the National Honor Society (NHS). In one case, the Third Circuit affirmed that school officials did not violate the rights of a pregnant student in Pennsylvania who was dismissed from the NHS since their action was based on premarital sexual activity.[56] Conversely, the Ninth Circuit affirmed an award of attorney fees in favor of a

---

F.3d 694 [123 Educ. L. Rep. 1087] (10th Cir. 1998).

51. *See also Thomas v. Allegany County Bd. of Educ.*, 443 A.2d 622 [3 Educ. L. Rep. 670] (Md. Ct. Spec. App. 1982) (rejecting parental claims that officials violated the rights of their children who attended non-public schools by not permitting them to participate in a music program offered only to full-time public school students; the court wrote that state law did not entitle students in non-public schools to be admitted to any part or portion of the public school system which they choose).

52. *Nutt v. Board of Educ. of City of Goodland*, 278 P. 1065, 1066 (Kan.1929).

53. *McLeod v. State ex rel. Colmer*, 122 So. 737, 738 (Miss.1929).

54. *Holt v. Shelton*, 341 F.Supp. 821 (M.D.Tenn.1972); *Davis v. Meek*, 344 F.Supp. 298 (N.D.Ohio 1972); *Moran v. School Dist. No. 7, Yellowstone County*, 350 F.Supp. 1180 (D.Mont.1972).

55. *Hollon v. Mathis Indep. School Dist.*, 358 F.Supp. 1269 (S.D.Tex.1973); *Bell v. Lone Oak Indep. School Dist.*, 507 S.W.2d 636 (Tex. Civ. App.1974); *Indiana High School Athletic Ass'n v. Raike*, 329 N.E.2d 66 (Ind. Ct. App.1975); *Beeson v. Kiowa County School Dist. RE–1*, 567 P.2d 801 (Colo. Ct. App.1977).

56. *Pfeiffer v. Marion Ctr. Area School Dist.*, 917 F.2d 779 [63 Educ. L. Rep. 727] (3d Cir. 1990).

pregnant, unmarried student in Arizona who was not living with the child's father and was excluded from the NHS.[57] The court upheld the award of attorney fees even though the amount exceeded the statutory cap since it was convinced that educators acted in bad faith in excluding the student. Similarly, a federal trial court in Kentucky granted a preliminary injunction to high school students who were excluded from the NHS after becoming pregnant and having children outside of wedlock.[58] The court was satisfied that the students showed the strong likelihood of success on the merits of their claims and that they would have suffered irreparable injury if it did not grant the requested relief.

Residence for School Purposes

State laws grant school-aged children who are district residents the right to attend school on tuition-free bases. The great weight of authority is that residence for school purposes does not necessarily mean that children must have legal domiciles in districts since domicile is a place where individuals intend to remain indefinitely.[59] The common law rule is that the legal domicile of minors is that of their parent(s) and that children are legally incapable of establishing their own domiciles absent special circumstances such as the death or legal separation of their parents.[60] While residence refers to the place where children actually live, neither physical presence alone[61] nor residing in a district solely in order to attend public school[62] is a sufficient basis to establish residence for purposes of attending school on a tuition-free basis. Accordingly, it is possible to have several residences, but it is only possible to have one domicile. In such a case, when a child moved from Illinois to attend school in North Carolina while living with an uncle, her attorney was unable to rebut the presumption that her domicile was the same as her mother's. An appellate court thus affirmed that since the residency requirements were uniformly applied, school officials did not violate the child's rights to due process or equal protection in forbidding her from attending school without having to pay tuition.[63]

In *Plyler v. Doe (Plyler)*,[64] the Supreme Court declared that under the Equal Protection Clause, Texas could not deny a free public school education to undocumented school-aged children. In so doing, the Court

57. *Cazares v. Barber*, 959 F.2d 753 [73 Educ. L. Rep. 931] (9th Cir.1992).

58. *Chipman v. Grant County School Dist.*, 30 F.Supp.2d 975 [131 Educ. L. Rep. 994] (E.D. Ky.1998).

59. *State ex rel. Doe v. Kingery*, 203 S.E.2d 358 (W. Va.1974).

60. *Wise v. Ohio Dep't of Educ.*, 80 F.3d 177 [108 Educ. L. Rep. 82] (6th Cir.1996); *In re Residence Hearing Before Bd. of School Directors, Cumberland Valley School Dist.*, 744 A.2d 1272 [141 Educ. L. Rep. 872] (Pa.2000).

61. *Catlin v. Sobol*, 93 F.3d 1112 [111 Educ. L. Rep. 1114] (2d Cir.1996), *on re-* mand, 988 F.Supp. 85 [124 Educ. L. Rep. 166] (N.D.N.Y.1997).

62. *Mina ex rel. Anghel v. Board of Educ. for Homewood–Flossmoor*, 809 N.E.2d 168 [188 Educ. L. Rep. 405] (Ill. App. Ct. 2004).

63. Graham v. Mock, 545 S.E.2d 263 [153 Educ. L. Rep. 796] (N.C.Ct.App.2001), *appeal dismissed, review denied*, 550 S.E.2d 776 (N.C.2001).

64. 457 U.S. 202, 102 S.Ct. 2382, 72 L.Ed.2d 786 [4 Educ. L. Rep. 953] (1982), *reh'g denied*, 458 U.S. 1131, 103 S.Ct. 14, 73 L.Ed.2d 1401 (1982). [Case No. 93]

invalidated a statute that would have deprived local boards of state funds for the education of children who were not legally admitted to the United States and that authorized officials to refuse to enroll these students. In applying the right to equal protection to the children, the Court determined that the constitutionality of a classification depended on whether it could be viewed as fairly furthering a substantial state interest. The Court was of the view that the uniqueness of education distinguishes it from general forms of social welfare, thereby triggering the necessity for a state to support withholding it by more substantial justification than required by the usual rational relationship test. The Court also ascertained both that the state's reasons for the statute failed to meet this test and that although the children were innocent of the conduct of their parents, the law's impact severely punished them as long as they were in the United States.

More than a decade after *Plyler*, a federal trial court in California enjoined the implementation of Proposition 187, a voter initiative that would have required state personnel, including educators, to verify the immigration status of persons with whom they came into contact.[65] While not addressing the education provisions directly, the Ninth Circuit upheld the injunction.[66] On partial reconsideration, the trial court, citing *Plyler*, specified that the portion of the initiative that would have denied access to schools to children was invalid since states cannot deny basic public education to children due to their immigration status or that of their parents.[67]

In a second case from Texas, *Martinez v. Bynum*, the Court rejected a challenge to the constitutionality of a statutory-residency requirement that denied tuition-free admission to public schools to minors who lived apart from their parents if they were in districts primarily to obtain a free education. In affirming that the statute violated neither the Fourteenth Amendment nor interfered with the constitutional right of interstate travel, the Court held that "[a] bona fide residence requirement, appropriately defined and uniformly applied, furthers the substantial state interest in assuring that services provided for its residents are enjoyed only by residents."[68]

The conditions under which students living in one district can attend classes in another under open-enrollment statutes vary from one jurisdiction to another. School officials may accept students from other districts on tuition bases as long as state laws permit them to do so.[69] Non-resident parents can be required to pay tuition under these circumstances[70] since children do not have a right to attend public schools for

---

65. *League of United Latin American Citizens v. Wilson*, 908 F.Supp. 755 (C.D.Cal.1995).

66. *Gregorio T. By and Through Jose T. v. Wilson*, 59 F.3d 1002 (9th Cir.1995).

67. *League of United Latin American Citizens v. Wilson*, 997 F.Supp. 1244 (C.D.Cal.1997).

68. 461 U.S. 321, 328, 103 S.Ct. 1838, 75 L.Ed.2d 879 [10 Educ. L. Rep. 11] (1983). [Case No. 94]

69. *Union Free High School Dist. No. 1, Town of Iron River v. Joint School Dist. No. 1 of Town of Maple*, 117 N.W.2d 273 (Wis. 1962).

70. *In re White*, 715 N.E.2d 203 [137 Educ. L. Rep. 361] (Ohio Ct.App.1998).

free once their families have moved.[71] In one such dispute, an appellate court in Ohio permitted a board's fraud claim against parents to proceed where officials sought to recover tuition from them due to the fact that they used false documentation to enroll their children in a district within which they did not live.[72]

As reflected in a case from the Supreme Court of Vermont, educational officials must be careful when considering whether parents are district residents who are eligible for free tuition for their children. In affirming that officials in the State Department of Education mistakenly identified parents as eligible for tuition payments in a district that did not operate its own schools, the panel agreed that a trial court did not abuse its discretion in denying a school board's motion for relief from the judgment without a hearing because local officials failed to file any response to the initial finding that the parents were eligible for free tuition.[73]

Absent state laws to the contrary, children living in orphanages, charitable homes, and/or who are adjudicated wards of the state are generally considered residents of the districts within which they reside.[74] Courts also agree that school boards cannot refuse to enroll homeless children whose shelters are located within their boundaries.[75] In a case on point from Texas, a federal trial court was persuaded that a rational relationship existed between a statute and the state's legitimate objectives of preserving the financial integrity of school districts while not expecting taxpayers to pay for educating children who were wards of other states.[76] Further, if courts appoint guardians with whom children live, educators must accept them on a tuition-free basis.[77]

A case from Pennsylvania illustrates that public officials can enforce a statute providing that a child who lives in an institution and whose expenses are paid for in whole or part by another jurisdiction are not entitled to tuition-free attendance in local public schools.[78] Along these same lines, an appellate court in Illinois contended that when a board placed a student that it expelled in a residential facility, it still had to pay for his tuition even though officials argued that he could not have

71. *Dunbar v. Hamden Bd. of Educ.,* 267 F.Supp.2d 178 [179 Educ. L. Rep. 258] (D. Conn. 2003).

72. *Shaker Heights City School Dist. Bd. of Educ. v. Cloud,* 738 N.E.2d 473 [148 Educ. L. Rep. 1031] (Ohio Ct.App.2000).

73. *Sandgate School Dist. v. Cate,* 883 A.2d 774 [202 Educ. L. Rep. 215] (Vt. 2005).

74. *Catlin v. Sobol,* 93 F.3d 1112 [111 Educ. L. Rep. 1114] (2d Cir.1996), *on remand,* 988 F.Supp. 85 [124 Educ. L. Rep. 166] (N.D.N.Y.1997); *State ex rel. Bd. of Christian Serv. of Lutheran Minn. Conference v. School Bd. of Consol. School Dist. No. 3,* 287 N.W. 625 (Minn. 1939).

75. *See, e.g., Harrison v. Sobol,* 705 F.Supp. 870 [52 Educ. L. Rep. 91] (S.D.N.Y.

1988); *Orozco ex rel. Arroyo v. Sobol,* 703 F.Supp. 1113 [51 Educ. L. Rep. 865] (S.D.N.Y.1989); *Lampkin v. District of Columbia,* 27 F.3d 605 [92 Educ. L. Rep. 811] (D.C.Cir.1994), *cert. denied,* 513 U.S. 1016, 115 S.Ct. 578, 130 L.Ed.2d 493 (1994), *on remand,* 879 F.Supp. 116 [99 Educ. L. Rep. 137] (D.D.C.1995), *injunction terminated,* 886 F.Supp. 56 [100 Educ. L. Rep. 1031] (D.D.C.1995).

76. *East Texas Guidance & Achievement Ctr. v. Brockette,* 431 F.Supp. 231 (E.D.Tex. 1977).

77. *University Ctr. v. Ann Arbor Pub. Schools,* 191 N.W.2d 302 (Mich.1971).

78. *Steven M. v. Gilhool,* 700 F.Supp. 261 [50 Educ. L. Rep. 785] (E.D.Pa.1988).

attended classes if he had not been excluded from school.[79] More recently, New York's highest court addressed the status of students who lived with their mother before they were evicted from their home.[80] The court decreed that the district where the children previously lived with their mother, rather than the one in which they resided in a homeless shelter when they were placed in foster care, was their district of residence within the meaning of state law. The court asserted that the district where they lived with their mother was responsible for the cost of educating the children after they were placed in a family home.

Vaccinations

Requirements related to vaccinations as a condition of attending school have been subject to a fair amount of litigation. In the first of two older, but still relevant, cases, the Supreme Court decided that a statute empowering local authorities to require everyone to be vaccinated was constitutional.[81] Later, in refusing to hear an appeal of a case from Texas, the Court let stand a judgment that parents did not have a constitutional right to have their child attend school without being vaccinated.[82]

Courts uniformly uphold statutes requiring or authorizing school officials to adopt vaccination policies, typically for smallpox and diphtheria.[83] Where children who are not vaccinated are barred from schools, the remedies against parents are normally fines and threats of imprisonment. In one instance, the Supreme Court of Arkansas upheld an order removing a child from parental custody on the ground that their refusal to cooperate deprived a child of his right to an education.[84]

Where statutes provide for exceptions from compulsory vaccination requirements, parents have had more success. For example, the federal trial court in New Hampshire vitiated a provision that school officials may excuse a child for religious reasons at their discretion as unconstitutionally vague due to the lack of criteria guiding their actions.[85] More recently, the Eighth Circuit reviewed a consolidated appeal which relied on the Establishment Clause in striking down a statute from Arkansas that invalidated a religious-beliefs exemption requiring immunization of school children against Hepatitis B but which otherwise upheld, after

---

79. *Carbondale Community High School Dist. No. 165 v. Herrin Community Unit School Dist. No. 4*, 708 N.E.2d 844 [134 Educ. L. Rep. 538] (Ill.App.Ct.1999).

80. *Longwood Cent. School Dist. v. Springs Union Free School Dist.*, 774 N.Y.S.2d 857 [187 Educ. L. Rep. 205] (N.Y. 2004).

81. *Jacobson v. Commonwealth of Mass.*, 197 U.S. 11, 25 S.Ct. 358, 49 L.Ed. 643 (1905).

82. *Zucht v. King*, 260 U.S. 174, 43 S.Ct. 24, 67 L.Ed. 194 (1922).

83. *Board of Educ. of Mt. Lakes v. Maas*, 152 A.2d 394 (N.J.Su-

per.Ct.App.Div.1959); *McCartney v. Austin*, 298 N.Y.S.2d 26 (N.Y.App.Div.1969); *Itz v. Penick*, 493 S.W.2d 506 (Tex.1973), *appeal dismissed*, 412 U.S. 925, 93 S.Ct. 2754, 37 L.Ed.2d 152 (1973); *Syska v. Montgomery County Bd. of Educ.*, 415 A.2d 301 (Md. Ct. Spec. App. 1980), *appeal dismissed*, 450 U.S. 961, 101 S.Ct. 1475, 67 L.Ed.2d 610 (1981).

84. *Cude v. State of Ark.*, 377 S.W.2d 816 (Ark.1964).

85. *Avard v. Dupuis*, 376 F.Supp. 479 (D.N.H.1974).

severance, the underlying immunization requirement.[86] The court dismissed the appeal as moot since the legislature broadened the exemption to encompass philosophical and religious objections.[87]

In a case with a twist, a federal trial court in New York explained that parents were not entitled to an exemption under a state law that excuses persons whose opposition to immunization stems from genuine and sincere religious beliefs because their objections were medical, not religious.[88] Conversely, in another case from New York, a mother who was a member of a religious congregation that opposed the introduction of any foreign material into the human body sought a religious exemption from the state's immunization requirement. Even though educators were convinced that the mother's sincerely held religious beliefs were based on a personal philosophy rather than a legitimate religion, a federal trial court denied a board's motion to dismiss her claim since she established the likelihood of success on the merits insofar as her views appeared to be religious in nature as opposed to merely philosophical or scientific.[89] When parents seeking religious exemptions comply with statutory requirements, courts do not hesitate to enter judgments in their favor,[90] even if they are not required to substantiate the religious bases for their requests.[91]

Student Records

The Family Educational Rights and Privacy Act (FERPA),[92] also known as the Buckley Amendment, after its primary sponsor, New York Senator James Buckley, covers all educational institutions receiving federal financial assistance, most notably public schools. FERPA created two major obligations for educational institutions that receive funds administered by the United States Department of Education (DOE). First, FERPA assures eligible students, typically those over the age of eighteen, and parents of dependent children access to their educational records. Second, FERPA protects the confidentiality of these records by prohibiting their disclosure without prior consent of parents or eligible students, subject to two major exceptions. The first permits school officials to reveal "directory information"[93] about students, unless they,

86. The earlier cases were *McCarthy v. Boozman*, 212 F.Supp.2d 945 [168 Educ. L. Rep. 258] (W.D. Ark.2002) and *Boone v. Boozman*, 217 F.Supp.2d 938 [169 Educ. L. Rep. 247] (E.D. Ark.2002).

87. *McCarthy v. Ozark School Dist.*, 359 F.3d 1029 [185 Educ. L. Rep. 453] (8th Cir. 2004).

88. *Farina v. Board of Educ. of City of N.Y.*, 116 F.Supp.2d 503 [148 Educ. L. Rep. 168] (S.D.N.Y.2000).

89. *Turner v. Liverpool Cent. School*, 186 F.Supp.2d 187, 188–189 [162 Educ. L. Rep. 256] (N.D.N.Y.2002).

90. *In re LePage*, 18 P.3d 1177 [151 Educ. L. Rep. 605] (Wyo.2001); *Jones v.*

State, Dep't of Health, 18 P.3d 1189 [151 Educ. L. Rep. 610] (Wyo.2001).

91. *Department of Health v. Curry*, 722 So.2d 874 [131 Educ. L. Rep. 870] (Fla.Dist. Ct. App.1998).

92. 20 U.S.C. § 1232g. This statute is in the appendix.

93. Directory information includes "the student's name, address, telephone listing, date and place of birth, major field of study, participation in officially recognized activities and sports, weight and height of members of athletic teams, dates of attendance, degrees and awards received, and the most recent previous educational agency or institution attended by the student." 20 U.S.C. § 1232g(a)(5)(A).

or their parents, object to the release of some or all of the information.[94] The second allows limited disclosure to entities[95] such as the juvenile justice system[96] and accrediting agencies[97] or, under certain circumstances, in response to subpoenas[98] or in emergencies "to protect the health or safety of the student or other persons."[99]

FERPA defines "education records" as "records, files, documents and other materials which ... contain information directly related to a student and [which] are maintained by an educational ... agency or institution or by a person acting for such ... agency or institution."[100] FERPA excludes "records of instructional ... personnel ... which are in the sole possession of the maker ... and which are not accessible or revealed to any other person except a substitute."[101] Insofar as the DOE is responsible for enforcing FERPA, complaints must be filed with its Family Policy Compliance Office.[102] Parents and eligible students also have enforcement rights and are entitled to "an opportunity for a hearing ... to challenge the content of ... education records."[103]

As important as FERPA is with regard to student records, the Supreme Court did not address its first two cases involving the statute until more than twenty-five years after it went into effect. In *Owasso Independent School District v. Falvo (Falvo)*,[104] a mother in Oklahoma challenged a school board's permitting the use of peer grading, whereby children grade each others' papers and call the scores out to teachers. The Court noted that since peer-grading does not turn the student papers into educational records covered by FERPA, the board did not violate the law by permitting teachers to use the practice over the mother's objection. Interestingly, in *Falvo*, in ruling that school officials could continue to allow teachers to use peer grading, the Court proceeded on the assumption that FERPA permitted injured parties to file private causes of action, a position that it explicitly rejected in the next case.

At issue in *Gonzaga University v. Doe (Gonzaga)*,[105] handed down four months after *Falvo*, was the claim of an undergraduate male student who alleged that university administrators violated his rights when, in the face of apparently unsubstantiated accusations of sexual misconduct involving a female friend, they released his records to state

---

94. 20 U.S.C. § 1232g(a)(5)(A)(B) identifies the content of "directory information" and the notice which must be given to students, and parents of students under 18 and who have not yet graduated from high school, about the directory information to be revealed and the right to object to release.

95. For a complete list of exceptions, *see* 20 U.S.C. 1232g(b)(1)(A)–(J).

96. 20 U.S.C. § 1232g(b)(1)(E)(ii).

97. 20 U.S.C. § 1232g(b)(1)(G).

98. 20 U.S.C. § 1232g(a)(2)(B). *See Baker v. Mitchell–Waters*, 826 N.E.2d 894 [197 Educ. L. Rep. 777] (Ohio Ct. App. 2005) (affirming that FERPA and the equivalent state statute did not exempt documents

from discovery where parents claimed that school officials were verbally and physically abusive to their son).

99. 20 U.S.C. § 1232g(b)(1)(I).

100. 20 U.S.C. § 1232g(a)(4)(A).

101. 20 U.S.C. § 1232g(a)(4)(B)(1).

102. 20 U.S.C. § 1232g(f)(g).

103. 20 U.S.C. § 1232g(a)(2).

104. 534 U.S. 426, 122 S.Ct. 934, 151 L.Ed.2d 896 [161 Educ. L. Rep. 33] (2002). [Case No. 95]

105. 536 U.S. 273, 122 S.Ct. 2268, 153 L.Ed.2d 309 [165 Educ. L. Rep. 458] (2002).

officials without his knowledge or consent. The male was later denied certification as a public school teacher. The Supreme Court posited that although the student's records were disclosed impermissibly, he did not have a private cause of action under section 1983 since his sole avenue of redress was to file a complaint with the DOE. As a result of these two cases, especially *Gonzaga*, it is unlikely that school systems will face much litigation under FERPA since the Court essentially repudiated its position from *Falvo* by interpreting the law as not intending to create individually enforceable rights.

Curriculum

Establishment of the Elements

All states have statutory and regulatory guidelines related to what must be taught as part of public school curricula and, in some instances, how subjects should be taught along with prohibitions against covering specified topics such as those advancing religious perspectives.[106] Except for constitutional restraints, since legislatures have plenary power over public school curricula, they can require schools to teach that which is "plainly essential to good citizenship" while prohibiting that which is "manifestly inimical to the public welfare."[107]

State officials may, and to differing degrees do, delegate curricular powers to local school boards. Local boards must thus deal with the innumerable aspects of school programs that are not specifically covered by state law.

In *Meyer v. Nebraska*, the Supreme Court invalidated a prohibition against teaching a foreign language in grades lower than the ninth under which a teacher in a non-public school was convicted of teaching German. The Court rejected the statute's purported goal of promoting civic development by "inhibiting training and education of the immature in foreign tongues and ideals before they could learn English and acquire American ideals, and 'that the English language should be and become the mother tongue of all children reared in this state.' "[108] In pointing out that the statute limited the rights of modern language teachers to teach, of students to gain knowledge, and of parents to control the education of their children, the Court emphasized that there was no showing of harm that the state had the right to prevent. The Court added that no emergency had arisen that rendered the knowledge of a language other than English to be so clearly harmful as to warrant its prohibition. While conceding that it did not question the state's power over the curriculum in public schools, the thrust of the Court's analysis

---

106. *See, e.g., School Dist. of Abington Township v. Schempp*, 374 U.S. 203, 83 S.Ct. 1560, 10 L.Ed.2d 844 (1963) (striking down prayer and Bible reading in public school) [Case No. 4]; *Epperson v. Arkansas*, 393 U.S. 97, 89 S.Ct. 266, 21 L.Ed.2d 228 (1968) (striking down statutes that prohibited the teaching of evolution). [Case No. 6]

107. *Pierce v. Society of the Sisters of the Holy Names of Jesus and Mary*, 268 U.S. 510, 534, 45 S.Ct. 571, 69 L.Ed. 1070 (1925). [Case No. 91]

108. 262 U.S. 390, 401, 43 S.Ct. 625, 67 L.Ed. 1042 (1923).

involved the constitutional right to pursue an occupation not contrary to the public interest.

The power of local school boards to offer courses beyond those mandated by the state rests on their implied, rather than plenary or inherent, powers. That boards have such implied power is well established beginning with the so-called "Kalamazoo case," wherein the Supreme Court of Michigan, absent express legislative authority, declared that a local board had the power to operate a high school.[109] A review of relevant appellate cases, a sample of which are reflected herein, warrants the generalization that local boards have vast discretion to supplement courses required by state-level authorities.[110] Perhaps in no other sphere of school operations have the courts more liberally interpreted implied powers of local boards than in curricular matters, not only with regard to individual elements but also as to methods of carrying out both specific and general mandates.

Community residents cannot compel school boards to offer courses of instruction[111] or use specific books in particular ways since such choices lay within their discretion absent state directives to the contrary and as long as they are not depriving students of their constitutional rights.[112] Likewise, absent proof that materials or books are sectarian or subversive, citizens cannot require boards to remove them from the curriculum.[113]

Where states specify courses of study, local boards must provide sufficient financial resources to support them properly.[114] At the same time, electives must be curtailed if necessary to operate required programs. While boards cannot eliminate state-mandated courses,[115] they have implied power to drop electives, even if they have been offered over long periods of time since the courts recognize that local officials have the authority to meet changing educational conditions by creating new courses and rearranging curricula.[116] Insofar as boards cannot be re-

109. *Stuart v. School Dist. No. 1 of Village of Kalamazoo*, 30 Mich. 69 (1874).

110. *See, e.g., State ex rel. Andrews v. Webber*, 8 N.E. 708 (Ind.1886); *State Tax Comm'n v. Board of Educ. of Holton*, 73 P.2d 49 (Kan.1937).

111. *Wright v. Houston Indep. School Dist.*, 486 F.2d 137 (5th Cir.1973); *Mercer v. Michigan State Bd. of Educ.*, 379 F.Supp. 580 (E.D. Mich.1974), *aff'd*, 419 U.S. 1081, 95 S.Ct. 673, 42 L.Ed.2d 678 (1974).

112. *See, e.g., Presidents Council, Dist. 25 v. Community School Bd. No. 25*, 457 F.2d 289 (2d Cir.1972), *cert. denied*, 409 U.S. 998, 93 S.Ct. 308, 34 L.Ed.2d 260 (1972); *Board of Educ., Island Trees Union Free School Dist. No. 26 v. Pico*, 457 U.S. 853, 857, 102 S.Ct. 2799, 73 L.Ed.2d 435 [4 Educ. L. Rep. 1013] (1982).

113. *See, e.g., Rosenberg v. Board of Educ. of City of N.Y.*, 92 N.Y.S.2d 344

(N.Y.Sup.Ct. 1949); *Todd v. Rochester Community Schools*, 200 N.W.2d 90 (Mich.Ct. App.1972); *Williams v. Board of Educ. of County of Kanawha*, 388 F.Supp. 93 (S.D.W.Va.1975), *aff'd*, 530 F.2d 972 (4th Cir.1975); *Grove v. Mead School Dist. No. 354*, 753 F.2d 1528 [22 Educ. L. Rep. 1141] (9th Cir.1985), *cert. denied*, 474 U.S. 826, 106 S.Ct. 85, 88 L.Ed.2d 70 (1985).

114. *See, e.g., Talbot v. Board of Educ. of N.Y.*, 14 N.Y.S.2d 340 (N.Y.Sup.Ct.1939); *Durant v. State of Mich.*, 650 N.W.2d 380 [169 Educ. L. Rep. 389] (Mich.Ct.App.2002).

115. *Jones v. Board of Trustees of Culver City School Dist.*, 47 P.2d 804 (Cal.App. 1935).

116. *Jones v. Holes*, 6 A.2d 102 (Pa. 1939).

quired to offer courses simply because they may be available elsewhere, officials do not violate student rights by refusing to offer electives.[117]

Methods and Materials

Almost all states have statutes impinging on teaching methodology. Even so, most prescriptions are general and suggestive rather than specific and exclusive. In general, curricular content and teaching methodology are essentially local, rather than state, responsibilities. When disputes arise over teaching methodology, the courts generally accept the authority of local boards and the expertise of school personnel as to pedagogical techniques.[118]

In the face of a challenge to the establishment and operation of a non-graded program in an elementary school, an appellate court in Michigan maintained that a local board's discretionary power was sufficiently broad to justify its action.[119] The court emphasized that since the state board, in exercising its general supervision over public education, had not prohibited local boards from creating non-graded schools, school officials had the authority to act as they did. In support of its position, the court cited a case from the Supreme Court of Michigan which upheld the discretionary authority of local boards to establish half-day sessions and to offer subjects on a compressed schedule due to the lack of funds.[120]

When the New York City Board of Education, as part of a collective bargaining contract, promulgated a directive which shortened the class day by two forty-five-minute periods per week, the state's highest court affirmed its authority to do so. The court was of the opinion that absent state regulations specifying a minimum length of the school day or week, the board was within its authority.[121] In a related claim, a federal trial court in New York rejected an allegation that the board's shortening of the school day violated the United States Constitution based on the principle of *res judicata*.[122] In dismissing the claim, the court thought that since the directive was a rational solution to a grave financial and labor problem, the board acted within the bounds of its discretion.

At common law, there was no question as to the legal rights of states to prescribe textbooks.[123] Yet, the statutory trend has been to delegate

117. *Board of Educ. of Okay Indep. School Dist. v. Carroll*, 513 P.2d 872 (Okla. 1973); *Zykan v. Warsaw Community School Corp.*, 631 F.2d 1300 (7th Cir.1980).

118. *See, e.g., Boring v. Buncombe County Bd. of Educ.*, 136 F.3d 364 [124 Educ. L. Rep. 56] (4th Cir.1998), *cert. denied*, 525 U.S. 813, 119 S.Ct. 47, 142 L.Ed.2d 36 (1998); *Lacks v. Ferguson Reorganized School Dist. R–2*, 147 F.3d 718 [127 Educ. L. Rep. 568] (8th Cir.1998), *suggestion for reh'g en banc denied*, 154 F.3d 904 (8th Cir.1998), *cert. denied*, 526 U.S. 1012, 119 S.Ct. 1158, 143 L.Ed.2d 223 (1999).

119. *Schwan v. Board of Educ. of Lansing School Dist.*, 183 N.W.2d 594 (Mich.Ct. App.1970).

120. *Welling v. Board of Educ. for Livonia School Dist.*, 171 N.W.2d 545 (Mich. 1969).

121. *New York City School Bds. Ass'n v. Board of Educ. of City School Dist. of City of N.Y.*, 383 N.Y.S.2d 208 (N.Y.1976).

122. *Zoll v. Anker*, 414 F.Supp. 1024 (S.D.N.Y.1976).

123. *Leeper v. State of Tenn.*, 53 S.W. 962 (Tenn.1899).

more and more power over textbook selection to local officials.[124] Selection of supplementary books and instructional materials is generally subject to the same rules. Insofar as school officials can select textbooks independent of the wishes of teachers, they need not accept recommendations of faculty committees.[125] While courts do not often review textbook selection, when they do, they typically defer to the choices of educators.[126]

If anything, the courts are more likely to review disputes over the removal of material than the failure of educators to add items,[127] especially since the constitutional rights at issue more closely involve students (and their parents) than teachers.[128] In *Board of Education, Island Trees Union Free School District No. 26 v. Pico*, the Supreme Court addressed the rights of students and their parents to challenge a school board's removal of books from a school library that they described as "anti-American, anti-Christian, anti-Semitic, and just plain filthy."[129] In a plurality, the Court remanded the dispute for a more specific finding as to why the board had the books removed since the trial court failed to address the issue adequately in granting the board's motion for summary judgment. Four of the five Justices voting for the remand believed that the removal of the books would have been unconstitutional if the decisive factor was that the board sought to ban ideas with which it disagreed. These Justices also agreed that the board could remove books if they were convinced that they were "pervasively vulgar" or did not meet standards of "educational suitability." In a similar kind of dispute, the Fourth Circuit affirmed that school officials in Delaware did not violate the First Amendment rights of students by rejecting their selection for a school play.[130]

One of the more extensive attacks on books used in public schools arose in Alabama. In stating that the books passed Establishment Clause analysis, the Eleventh Circuit rejected a parental claim that the use of forty-four state-approved books in history, social studies, and home economics amounted to the teaching of secular humanism.[131] The Sixth,[132] Seventh,[133] and Ninth[134] Circuits also rejected parental chal-

---

124. *See, e.g.,* Ky. Rev. Stat. Ann. § 160.345(g) (granting authority for textbook selection to school based decision making councils). ("The school council shall determine which textbooks, instructional materials, and student support services shall be provided in the school.")

125. *Minarcini v. Strongsville City School Dist.*, 541 F.2d 577 (6th Cir.1976).

126. *Monteiro v. Tempe Union High School Dist.*, 158 F.3d 1022 (9th Cir.1998).

127. *Pratt v. Independent School Dist. No. 831, Forest Lake, Minn.*, 670 F.2d 771 [2 Educ. L. Rep. 990] (8th Cir.1982).

128. *Johnson v. Stuart*, 702 F.2d 193 [9 Educ. L. Rep. 1148] (9th Cir.1983).

129. 457 U.S. 853, 857, 102 S.Ct. 2799, 73 L.Ed.2d 435 [4 Educ. L. Rep. 1013] (1982).

130. *Seyfried v. Walton*, 668 F.2d 214 [2 Educ. L. Rep. 379] (3d Cir.1981). [Case No. 96] For a case filed by a teacher, *see Boring v. Buncombe County Bd. of Educ.*, 136 F.3d 364 [124 Educ. L. Rep. 56] (4th Cir.1998), *cert. denied*, 525 U.S. 813, 119 S.Ct. 47, 142 L.Ed.2d 36 (1998) (upholding the transfer of an award-winning drama coach and teacher for directing a controversial play that some members of the community found objectionable).

131. *Smith v. Board of School Commr's of Mobile County*, 827 F.2d 684 [41 Educ. L. Rep. 452] (11th Cir.1987).

132. For another lengthy battle of this type, *see Mozert v. Hawkins County Pub. Schools*, 579 F.Supp. 1051 [16 Educ. L. Rep. 473] (E.D.Tenn.1984), *rev'd*, 765 F.2d 75 [25 Educ. L. Rep. 1063] (6th Cir.1985), *on remand*, 647 F.Supp. 1194 [36 Educ. L. Rep.

lenges that reading materials impermissibly burdened students' rights to free exercise of religion. The courts essentially concurred that since none of the books or materials were antagonistic toward religion or its place in culture and values, local officials had the authority to formulate the content of the curricula in their schools.

In a parental challenge from Florida, even though state educational officials approved a book for use in a humanities course, a local school board voted to discontinue its use after parents complained about vulgarity and sexual subject matter in two of the selections. Other parents then sought to prevent the removal, claiming that doing so would have violated their First Amendment rights, emphasizing that the course was an elective rather than required and that the disputed selections were not required readings. The Eleventh Circuit affirmed that since the book was part of the curriculum, the board could control its content and that of the library where it was kept.[135] Subsequently, parents in Arkansas charged that school officials violated the First and Fourteenth Amendments when they required students to obtain parental permission before they could access books from the popular *Harry Potter* series in a school library. In granting the parents' motion for summary judgment on the ground that the educators violated the students' First Amendment right to receive information, the court awarded them court costs.[136]

On the flip side, when dealing with teacher rights, the Tenth Circuit affirmed that school officials in Colorado did not violate a teacher's rights in restricting his indirect use of the Bible in a fifth-grade class. The teacher frequently read his Bible silently as students sat at their desks reading books of their choice. The Bible was always on the teacher's desk and he displayed a poster with the message "You have only to open your eyes to see the hand of God." The court also upheld the removal of two books about the Bible and life of Jesus from the teacher's classroom library of "about 239 books of varying content that [he] had compiled over his nineteen-years of teaching,"[137] while permitting others on Buddhism, Greek gods and goddesses, and Indian religions to remain in the collection. The court indicated that while the teacher's practices violated the Establishment Clause, the principal should not have removed the Bible from the school library. On the other hand, when a teacher sued his school board claiming that officials directed him not to teach about non-Christian religions in response to parental complaints about his doing so, the federal trial court in Maine

90] (E.D.Tenn.1986), *rev'd*, 827 F.2d 1058 [41 Educ. L. Rep. 473] (6th Cir.1987), *cert. denied*, 484 U.S. 1066, 108 S.Ct. 1029, 98 L.Ed.2d 993 [44 Educ. L. Rep. 1000] (1988).

133. *Fleischfresser v. Directors of School Dist. 200*, 15 F.3d 680 [89 Educ. L. Rep. 429] (7th Cir.1994).

134. *Brown v. Woodland Joint Unified School Dist.*, 27 F.3d 1373 [92 Educ. L. Rep. 828] (9th Cir.1994).

135. *Virgil v. School Bd. of Columbia County, Fla.*, 862 F.2d 1517 [50 Educ. L. Rep. 718] (11th Cir.1989).

136. *Counts v. Cedarville School Dist.*, 295 F.Supp.2d 996 [184 Educ. L. Rep. 305] (W.D. Ark. 2003).

137. *Roberts v. Madigan*, 921 F.2d 1047, 1049 [64 Educ. L. Rep. 1038] (10th Cir. 1990), *cert. denied*, 505 U.S. 1218, 112 S.Ct. 3025, 120 L.Ed.2d 896 (1992).

denied its motion for summary judgment.[138] The court reasoned that since issues of fact remained as to whether restrictions on the curriculum were motivated by officials' desire to eliminate references to non-Christian religions at the request of parents who objected to its being taught, the dispute had to proceed to a trial on the merits over whether they violated the teacher's First Amendment rights.

As to testing, where parents and teachers enjoined a planned city-wide examination that they claimed was compromised due to cheating, the Court of Appeals of New York reversed in favor of the board. The court discerned that since such educational matters as test selection and use are in the province of the discretion of school authorities, they are inappropriate for judicial resolution.[139] The court wrote that its interference would have placed the judiciary in the role of displacing, or at least overseeing, officials charged with the school system's management. An appellate court in Washington applied the same analysis in affirming that school personnel could not be charged for allegedly failing to meet the instructional criteria established by a state basic education statute.[140]

Bilingual-Bicultural Studies

In *Lau v. Nichols (Lau)*,[141] its only case involving bilingual education, the Supreme Court acknowledged that a class of non-English speaking students of Chinese origin in San Francisco were entitled to relief from the school board's policy of providing special English instruction for only about 1,000 of the over 2,800 eligible children. In rejecting the board's claim that it lacked the funds to implement a program, the Court responded that students who did not understand English and who did not receive specialized instruction were effectively precluded from obtaining a meaningful education. The Court did not resolve the dispute on equal protection grounds, instead relying on Title VI of the Civil Rights Act of 1964 (Title VI), which bars discrimination under federally assisted programs on a ground of "race, color, or national origin."[142] According to the Court, federal guidelines required instruction for correction of language deficiencies and that the board contractually agreed to abide by them in order to receive federal funds. The Court expressly refused to take a stance on what educational techniques educators should have used.

Two years after *Lau*, the Tenth Circuit reached a virtually identical result in a case involving students with Spanish-surnames who lived in New Mexico.[143] In recognizing that many students spoke Spanish at home and were growing up in a culture that was alien to the environ-

138. *Cole v. Maine School Admin. Dist. No. 1*, 350 F.Supp.2d 143 [195 Educ. L. Rep. 130] (D. Me. 2004).

139. *James v. Board of Educ. of City of N.Y.*, 397 N.Y.S.2d 934 (N.Y.1977).

140. *Camer v. Seattle School Dist. No. 1*, 762 P.2d 356 [49 Educ. L. Rep. 819] (Wash.Ct.App. 1988), *review denied*, 1989 WL 661505 (Wash.1989), *cert. denied*, 493 U.S. 873, 110 S.Ct. 204, 107 L.Ed.2d 157 (1989).

141. 414 U.S. 563, 94 S.Ct. 786, 39 L.Ed.2d 1 (1974).

142. 42 U.S.C. §§ 2000d *et seq.*

143. *Serna v. Portales Mun. Schools*, 499 F.2d 1147 (10th Cir.1974).

ment they faced in school, the court ordered officials to implement a bilingual education program. A year later, the same court rejected the notion that students had a constitutional right to bilingual-bicultural education.[144] On remand, the federal trial court in Colorado ordered the board to initiate a bilingual-bicultural program for students who spoke predominately Spanish. The Tenth Circuit reversed, observing that bilingual education is not a substitute for desegregation since Spanish-speaking students were constitutionally entitled to a non-segregated education that afforded them the opportunity to acquire English proficiency.

The Ninth Circuit[145] later affirmed that neither Title VI nor the Equal Educational Opportunities Act of 1974[146] conferred a right to bilingual-bicultural education. The court remarked that a program designed to cure language deficiencies of non-English-speaking students in Arizona met legal requirements even though there was no bar to a school board's instituting the bilingual-bicultural program advocated by the plaintiffs. However, in the same year, a federal trial court in New York, in contending that an English as a Second Language Program was deficient, directed school officials to provide instruction that complied with *Lau* for children who were of Puerto Rican ancestry[147]

Two state cases dealt with a different aspect of bilingual and bicultural studies. In the first, an appellate court in North Carolina affirmed that parents could not prevent their children from attending school because their board did not provide instruction in their heritage and culture.[148] The court rejected the argument that a deep-rooted conviction for Indian heritage was on a constitutional plane equal to religious beliefs. In another dispute involving heritage, a mother with Indian ancestry in New York withdrew her child from school because she objected to some comments that her daughter's teacher made about Indians. An appellate court affirmed that the mother lacked a sufficient reason for not complying with the state's compulsory education law when officials refused to meet her demands that curricular programs be instituted on the problems of Indians and that a steering committee be set up to implement a policy against racism in any form.[149]

The Fifth Circuit considered whether a program in Texas constituted appropriate action to overcome language barriers among Spanish-speaking students when officials allegedly impeded their equal participation in a school district's instructional programs. In remanding for further consideration, the court declared that the program had to be evaluated on such criteria as whether it was based on an arguably sound educational theory, was reasonably calculated to implement the theory,

---

144. *Keyes v. School Dist. No. 1, Denver, Colo.*, 521 F.2d 465 (10th Cir.1975).

145. *Guadalupe Org. v. Tempe Elementary School Dist.*, 587 F.2d 1022 (9th Cir. 1978).

146. 20 U.S.C.A. § 1703(f).

147. *Rios v. Read*, 480 F.Supp. 14 (E.D.N.Y.1978).

148. *Matter of McMillan*, 226 S.E.2d 693 (N.C.Ct.App.1976).

149. *Matter of Baum*, 401 N.Y.S.2d 514 (N.Y.App.Div.1978), *appeal denied*, 407 N.Y.S.2d 1026 (N.Y.1978).

and was a good faith effort consistent with local circumstances and resources.[150]

In the first of two cases from Illinois, the Seventh Circuit was satisfied that Spanish-speaking students who were identified as being of limited English proficiency could enforce the Equal Educational Opportunities Act in a class action suit against the state board of education.[151] On remand, a federal trial court contended that the class was entitled to certification. In a later dispute from Illinois involving minority and other students with limited English proficiency, a federal trial court rejected a school board's motion to dismiss a class action suit claiming that it failed to address the needs of these children by eliminating existing language barriers.[152] The court permitted the case to proceed since it agreed that the plaintiffs demonstrated the existence of language barriers, the board's failure to take appropriate action to overcome these barriers, and the resulting impediment to the ability of the students to participate equally in instructional programs.

In a case that may presage future litigation under the broader provisions of the expansive No Child Left Behind Act (NCLB),[153] an appellate court in Pennsylvania affirmed it was not practicable for the Commonwealth's Department of Education to provide native language testing.[154] The court specified that since native language testing is not mandatory under the NCLB and should be provided only to the extent that it is practicable, the Department did not violate the law especially since it was trying to determine which of the 125 native languages that are spoken in Pennsylvania it would be feasible to use in testing.

Required Elements

Controversies over whether subjects or activities can be required also involve issues concerned with what officials can do if parents direct their children not to comply. In these cases, it is important to examine the nature of both the activities and the punishments, if any, and how to balance them with the parental right to guide the upbringing of their children, especially if they conflict with a state's right to require the study of subjects essential to citizenship. Under older common law, the courts tended to give the parents the benefit of the doubt in matters not likely to have an adverse affect on a curriculum or their children.

Early on, the courts established the rule that school officials could not use corporal punishment to compel children to adopt courses of

150. *United States v. State of Tex.*, 680 F.2d 356 [5 Educ. L. Rep. 141] (5th Cir. 1982).

151. *Gomez v. Illinois State Bd. of Educ.*, 811 F.2d 1030 [37 Educ. L. Rep. 1073] (7th Cir. 1987), *on remand*, 117 F.R.D. 394 [42 Educ. L. Rep. 1211] (N.D.Ill. 1987).

152. *Leslie v. Board of Educ. for Ill. School Dist. U–46*, 379 F.Supp.2d 952 [201 Educ. L. Rep. 151] (N.D. Ill. 2005).

153. 20 U.S.C.A. § 6301. Portions of the NCLB are in the appendix.

154. *Reading School Dist. v. Department of Educ.*, 855 A.2d 166 [191 Educ. L. Rep. 341] (Pa. Cmwlth. Ct. 2004), *appeal denied*, 877 A.2d 463 (Pa. 2005).

action that were contrary to the wishes of their parents. Where a child was whipped because she obeyed her father and refused to study algebra, the record revealed that he asked that his daughter be excused since her health was delicate and the class met in the afternoon. The Supreme Court of Iowa, although affirming the reasonableness of the father's action, cautioned that normally it must be presumed that a child will submit to school regulations.[155] The court reiterated that a teacher can punish a student for following parental directions.

The general rule has been that parents have the right to make reasonable course selections for their children. When parents choose, educators must excuse children from taking such courses unless they are essential to citizenship. In a leading older case, where a father's objection to his daughter's studying rhetoric led to her being able to take a grammar class, he challenged officials for expelling her when he ordered her to discontinue studying the subject. The Supreme Court of Nebraska entered a judgment in favor of the father, directing officials to re-admit the child without her having to study grammar.[156] In another case, parents instructed their daughter not to attend a class in domestic science which was required of all females because they thought that she could have used the time spent traveling to the class more profitably in private music lessons. When officials expelled the child for not taking the course, the Supreme Court of Nebraska ordered her reinstatement, explaining that the parental request was reasonable.[157] The court pointed out that since the parents wished to have their daughter study music, they had the unquestionable right to have her do so.

If curricular requirements violate the constitutional rights of students and/or parents, school board officials lack the authority to require children to take specific courses. Of course, it follows that children cannot be expelled or suspended due to such refusals. In an older case from California, where a board included dancing as part of its physical education curriculum, the father of two students challenged the denial of their request that his children be excused from participating and their resulting expulsion from school. Entering a judgment in favor of the father, an appellate court was of the view that if a regulation was unduly burdensome or violated the fundamental right of a person or set of persons, it must be set aside as unconstitutional.[158]

More recent cases typically deal with religious objections to such matters as sex-AIDS education[159] in school curricula. For instance, the federal trial court in Connecticut held that school officials did not violate the free exercise rights of a father or his son by refusing the parental

---

155. *State v. Mizner*, 50 Iowa 145 (1878).

156. *State ex rel. Sheibley v. School–Dist. No. 1*, 48 N.W. 393 (Neb.1891).

157. *State ex rel. Kelley v. Ferguson*, 144 N.W. 1039 (Neb.1914).

158. *Hardwick v. Board of School Trustees of Fruitridge*, 205 P. 49 (Cal.Ct.App. 1921).

159. *See, e.g., Ware v. Valley Stream High School Dist.*, 551 N.Y.S.2d 167 [58 Educ. L. Rep. 1242] (N.Y.1989) (affirming the denial of a board's motion for summary judgment where genuine issues of material fact existed over the burden that exposure to an AIDS curriculum would have had on the religious beliefs of students and their parents).

request that his child be excused from a mandatory health education course and by assigning the student a failing grade when he did not attend class.[160] Conversely, the federal trial court in Maryland enjoined a proposed sex-education curriculum that opponents claimed endorsed a homosexual lifestyle in part on the basis that it violated the Establishment Clause.[161] In deciding that the proposed curriculum presented only one view on the subject, to the exclusion of other perspectives, and criticized specific Christian religions in the process, the court ruled that such one-sided information threatened the First Amendment rights of the students and their parents.

The courts are willing to impose limits on the power of parents who idiosyncratically select what their children are permitted to study in school.[162] This is especially true where religious claims are tenuous, where secular reasons are weak, or where parents or children pressure others to follow their lead in seeking to be excused.[163] Moreover, even as educators try to accommodate minor parental requests, they are not required to make major curricular adjustments. The Sixth Circuit treated this issue extensively where parents sought to have their children placed in a core reading program other than the one used by the school system.[164] The program, which was coordinated with other subjects, contained books with ideas that the parents objected to largely on religious grounds. The court decreed that students and their parents did not have the right not to be exposed to ideas in public schools as long as the positions they objected to were not promoted and children were not obligated to affirm or disaffirm their agreement with the ideas.

In the first of three other cases that reveal how issues involving sexuality in the curriculum can cause controversy, parents in Massachusetts challenged a highly explicit sex-education program that officials offered to high school students. In upholding the authority of local school officials over curricular content, the First Circuit noted that the parental right to direct the upbringing and education of their children does not encompass a broad-based right to restrict flow of information in public schools.[165]

The Ninth Circuit affirmed a school board in California's motion for summary judgment in a suit filed by parents of first, third, and fifth grade students against educators who distributed a sexually explicit survey to their children. The court posited both that parents had neither a fundamental due process right to be exclusive providers of information on sexual matters for their children nor due process or privacy rights to

160. *Leebaert ex rel. Leebaert v. Harrington,* 193 F.Supp.2d 491 [163 Educ. L. Rep. 755] (D.Conn.2002).

161. *Citizens for a Responsible Curriculum v. Montgomery County Pub. Schools,* 2005 WL 1075634 (D. Md. 2005).

162. *Kidder v. Chellis,* 59 N.H. 473 (1879); *Muka v. Cornell,* 368 N.Y.S.2d 874 (N.Y.App.Div. 1975).

163. *Davis v. Page,* 385 F.Supp. 395 (D.N.H.1974).

164. *Mozert v. Hawkins County Bd. of Educ.,* 827 F.2d 1058 [41 Educ. L. Rep. 473] (6th Cir.1987), *cert. denied,* 484 U.S. 1066, 108 S.Ct. 1029, 98 L.Ed.2d 993 (1988).

165. *Brown v. Hot, Sexy and Safer Productions,* 68 F.3d 525 [104 Educ. L. Rep. 106] (1st Cir.1995), *cert. denied,* 516 U.S. 1159, 116 S.Ct. 1044, 134 L.Ed.2d 191 (1996).

override public school officials as to the information to which students can be exposed.[166] The court argued that including the questions about sexual topics in the survey was rationally related to the board's legitimate interest in effective education and mental welfare of children.

Three weeks later, the Third Circuit reached a similar result in affirming a grant of summary judgment in favor of a school board in New Jersey where parents objected to the official use of a voluntary, anonymous survey that sought information about drug and alcohol use, sexual activity, experiences of physical violence, attempts at suicide, personal associations and relationships (including parental relationships), and views on matters of public interest from students in grades seven to twelve.[167] The court essentially agreed that officials neither violated the privacy rights of students nor the rights of parents to make important decisions about the care and control of their children.

Graduation Requirements

Setting graduation requirements for public school students rests within the powers of state education officials and, to the extent that it is expressly or impliedly delegated, to local school boards. As long as requirements are reasonable, students can be denied diplomas if they are unable to or refuse to meet curricular standards.

School officials have the authority to evaluate whether students completed the requisite courses and possess the necessary qualifications to earn diplomas. As illustrated in the following cases, once students have met the prescribed standards, issuance of diplomas is a mandatory or ministerial act. The Supreme Court of Iowa affirmed that while a student could not be denied a diploma for refusing to wear a cap and gown at a graduation ceremony, he could be denied the privilege of participating in the exercises.[168] The Supreme Court of Kansas asserted that a student who was accused of cheating on a final examination could not be denied a diploma since officials failed to prove that he had done so.[169] An appellate court in Missouri explained that a student could not be refused a certificate of attainment based on his failure to pay a fee for the support of the high school since it was convinced that the board exceeded its authority in setting this requirement.[170] Fifty years later, where a local board required students to attend class for eight semesters in order to qualify for high school diplomas, a student who left school after a disciplinary incident eight weeks before the end of his third year re-entered at the beginning of the next year with the credits he earned toward graduation. When officials denied the student a diploma due to the eight-semester rule, the same court agreed that it was unreasonable, especially since the superintendent's testimony showed clearly that it

166. *Fields v. Palmdale School Dist.*, 427 F.3d 1197 [203 Educ. L. Rep. 44] (9th Cir. 2005).

167. *C.N. v. Ridgewood Bd. of Educ.*, 430 F.3d 159 [203 Educ. L. Rep. 468] (3d Cir. 2005).

168. *Valentine v. Independent School Dist.*, 183 N.W. 434 (Iowa 1921).

169. *Ryan v. Board of Educ.*, 257 P. 945 (Kan.1927).

170. *State ex rel. Roberts v. Wilson*, 297 S.W. 419 (Mo.Ct.App.1927).

would not have been necessary for the student to earn any additional credits, pass any courses, or even attend any number of classes.[171] The court rejected the eight-semester enrollment rule as no more than an exercise in futility that would not have benefitted either the board or the student.

In a case of first impression from Tennessee, where male students were required to take a Reserve Officers Training Corps (ROTC) course in order to graduate, a conscientious objector, through his father, asked to be allowed to participate in a physical education course in its place. After officials denied the student's request, they allowed him to continue his other courses but refused to grant him a diploma solely because he did not complete the ROTC class. The Sixth Circuit affirmed that officials wrongfully withheld the diploma since their action was the direct result of the student's practice of his religious beliefs.[172] On the other hand, where students did not complete all of the course work necessary to graduate, the Supreme Court of Georgia found that they had no right to participate in a graduation ceremony.[173] The court added that the case was moot since the students had already taken part in the graduation ceremony.

In the face of school reform issues dealing with accountability for student performance, especially as are likely to emerge under the No Child Left Behind Act,[174] it is worth recalling that state and local school officials have the authority to require children to pass competency, sometimes called proficiency, tests before receiving their diplomas as long as they have had fair opportunities to learn the material on the tests. Although this question first emerged in higher education, the Supreme Court reiterated this principle in *Board of Curators of University of Missouri v. Horowitz,*[175] a dispute over whether a medical student could be dismissed during her final year of course work for failing to meet academic standards. All nine Justices agreed, albeit on different grounds, that under the circumstances, the student received procedural due process through warnings and chances to demonstrate improvement. Five of the Justices, citing a case from the Supreme Judicial Court of Massachusetts,[176] agreed that there were distinct differences between excluding students for disciplinary and academic reasons.

The leading case on competency testing in elementary and secondary schools arose in Florida, where the then Fifth, now Eleventh, Circuit initially refused to allow the use of such an examination on the basis that it was fundamentally unfair since the students had not been exposed to the material on which they were being tested.[177] The court

171. *State ex rel. Sageser v. Ledbetter,* 559 S.W.2d 230 (Mo.Ct.App.1977). [Case No. 97]

172. *Spence v. Bailey,* 465 F.2d 797 (6th Cir.1972).

173. *Dolinger v. Driver,* 498 S.E.2d 252 [125 Educ. L. Rep. 986] (Ga.1998).

174. *See* 20 U.S.C.A. § 6301 (Statement of Purpose, discussing the need for testing).

This section of the statute is in the appendix.

175. 435 U.S. 78, 98 S.Ct. 948, 55 L.Ed.2d 124 (1978).

176. *Barnard v. Inhabitants of Shelburne,* 102 N.E. 1095 (Mass.1913).

177. *Debra P. v. Turlington,* 644 F.2d 397 (5th Cir.1981).

also rejected the thirteen-month notice period that officials provided as insufficient to permit the students to prepare for the examination. Once it agreed that the test was valid for instructional purposes, students received sufficient notice, and there was no link between the disproportionate number of African American students who failed it and the effects of past discrimination in the schools, the court permitted officials to use the examination.[178]

Three cases from Texas illustrate the extent to which the judiciary is split over the use of competency tests as preconditions for high school graduation. An appellate court vacated an injunction that would have permitted students who met all of the requirements except passing the state competency examination from participating in a graduation ceremony.[179] The court maintained that this was a matter for educational officials, not the judiciary. A year later, a federal trial court agreed that graduation was reserved for students who met all of the requirements.[180] Conversely, in the same year, a second federal trial court in Texas disagreed.[181] The court permitted students who passed all of their required courses but failed the state's competency test to participate in graduation ceremonies in commenting that officials were prohibited from imposing new criteria on students without providing adequate notice and a sufficient nexus between the test and the curriculum. While the court granted the students' request for a preliminary injunction permitting them to participate in the ceremony, it did direct school officials to grant them their diplomas.[182]

More recently, the Supreme Judicial Court of Massachusetts refused to enjoin a regulation that required students to pass the tenth-grade English language arts and mathematics sections of the Massachusetts Comprehensive Assessment System (MCAS) examination as a prerequisite to graduation before the other sections of the MCAS were phased in.[183] The court affirmed that officials at the commonwealth's board of education could exercise their discretion by requiring students to demonstrate competence in English and arithmetic before being tested on competence in science, history, and other areas. A little bit more than a year later, the court again upheld the use of the MCAS in the face of a challenge from a different group of students.[184]

Turning to disciplinary matters in relation to academic performance, appellate courts in Pennsylvania agreed that where one student sold a

---

178. *Debra P. v. Turlington,* 730 F.2d 1405 [16 Educ. L. Rep. 1120] (11th Cir. 1984).

179. *Edgewood Indep. School Dist. v. Paiz,* 856 S.W.2d 269 [84 Educ. L. Rep. 556] (Tex.Ct. App. 1993).

180. *Williams v. Austin Indep. School Dist.,* 796 F.Supp. 251 [77 Educ. L. Rep. 111] (W.D. Tex.1992).

181. *Crump v. Gilmer Indep. School Dist.,* 797 F.Supp. 552 [77 Educ. L. Rep. 205] (E.D.Tex. 1992).

182. The chapter on special education reviews the related issue of competency testing of students with disabilities.

183. *Student No. 9 v. Board of Educ.,* 802 N.E.2d 105 [184 Educ. L. Rep. 553] (Mass. 2004).

184. *Hancock v. Commissioner of Educ.,* 822 N.E.2d 1134 [195 Educ. L. Rep. 591] (Mass. 2005).

controlled substance on the morning of graduation[185] and another was suspended for a variety of offenses but completed course work as part of a home tutoring program,[186] they could not be denied diplomas. In both instances, the courts were convinced that since the students met all of their graduation requirements, school officials could not deny them their diplomas.

On another matter, increasing numbers of school systems have required students to engage in some forms of community service before graduation. In the face of challenges to these types of programs, the Second,[187] Third,[188] and Fourth[189] Circuits have rejected suits that claimed that school officials forced students to engage in involuntary servitude outlawed by the Thirteenth Amendment.

A final case with regard to graduation ceremonies involved when they can be scheduled. The Second Circuit rejected the claim of an orthodox Jewish student in New York that having a high school graduation ceremony take place on a Saturday violated his right to the free exercise of religion. The court reiterated that as long as attendance at the ceremony was not a prerequisite for the student's receiving his diploma, school officials were free to schedule graduation ceremonies when they saw fit.[190]

Classification and Assignment of Students

School boards clearly have the power to classify students. Even so, insofar as procedures are sometimes challenged as arbitrary, the courts must resolve the legality of methods of classification. As illustrated by a case from the Supreme Court of Ohio, such disputes often involve the recurring question of whether a matter is educational or legal. At issue was a parental request that a student skip from fifth to seventh grade. The parent argued that since the child was tutored during the summer, he made such progress that he was qualified for the higher grade.[191] Although a trial court supported the parent, the state's highest court indicated that the judge erred since such questions are within the authority of educational officials, not the judiciary.

Not unexpectedly, disputes have arisen over the assignments of students to kindergarten classes. A parent in New York unsuccessfully

185. *Shuman v. Cumberland Valley School Dist. Bd. of Directors*, 536 A.2d 490 [44 Educ. L. Rep. 399] (Pa.Cmwlth.Ct. 1988), *appeal denied*, 593 A.2d 428 (Pa. 1991).

186. *Ream v. Centennial School Dist.*, 765 A.2d 1195 [150 Educ. L. Rep. 773] (Pa. Cmwlth. Ct.2001).

187. *Immediato v. Rye Neck School Dist.*, 73 F.3d 454 [106 Educ. L. Rep. 85] (2d Cir.1996), *cert. denied*, 519 U.S. 813, 117 S.Ct. 60, 136 L.Ed.2d 22 (1996).

188. *Steirer v. Bethlehem Area School Dist.*, 987 F.2d 989 [81 Educ. L. Rep. 734]

(3d Cir.1993), *cert. denied*, 510 U.S. 824, 114 S.Ct. 85, 126 L.Ed.2d 53 (1993).

189. *Herndon by Herndon v. Chapel Hill–Carrboro City Bd. of Educ.*, 89 F.3d 174 [110 Educ. L. Rep. 1037] (4th Cir.1996), *cert. denied*, 519 U.S. 1111, 117 S.Ct. 949, 136 L.Ed.2d 837 (1997).

190. *Smith by Smith v. Board of Educ., N. Babylon Union Free School Dist.*, 844 F.2d 90 [46 Educ. L. Rep. 518] (2d Cir. 1988).

191. *Board of Educ. of Sycamore v. State ex rel. Wickham*, 88 N.E. 412 (Ohio 1909).

argued that since public kindergarten was optional and his five-year-old had a state right to attend public school, the child should have been placed in first grade. An appellate court agreed with the father that his son had a right to attend school but affirmed that once kindergarten was established, whether he was assigned to it or to first grade was subject to criteria established by the local school board.[192] At the same time, an appellate court in Pennsylvania affirmed that where kindergarten was optional, a child who was below the requisite age for admission had neither a constitutionally protected right to attend kindergarten nor to a formal hearing before school officials acted.[193] In other cases, statutes basing admission to public schools solely on age have been consistently upheld.[194]

As far-ranging as the authority of school boards may be, their rules must not have discriminatory effects. For example, where seven-year-olds who did not attend kindergarten in their district were automatically registered in first grade, an appellate court invalidated the requirement that they had to pass a readiness test imposed on children who attended kindergarten.[195] In a different situation, the Supreme Court of Kansas was of the opinion that a board had the implied authority to require graduates of non-public schools to take an entrance examination before attending public high schools.[196] Three quarters of a century later, the Sixth Circuit upheld an almost identical provision for those transferring from home study situations in Kentucky.[197] Previously, a court in New York approved the use of a placement test for a child who attended a private kindergarten.[198] However, where a statute permitted, but did not require, local boards to assess the readiness of children to attend school prior to the statutory starting date, an appellate court in Illinois reasoned that a board was not required to continue doing so.[199]

Requirements for progress from grade to grade are generally not subject to judicial review. In one case, the Fourth Circuit affirmed that the courts should not intervene where school officials refused to promote students who failed a reading-level test.[200] The court accepted the evaluations of educators that even though the second-grade students in Virginia were capable of reading at the third-grade level, they should not have been promoted until they mastered the requisite reading skills. In like manner, the Eleventh Circuit affirmed that school officials in

192. *Isquith v. Levitt*, 137 N.Y.S.2d 497 (N.Y.App.Div.1955).

193. *Goldsmith v. Lower Moreland School Dist.*, 461 A.2d 1341 [12 Educ. L. Rep. 431] (Pa. Cmwlth.Ct.1983).

194. *See, e.g., Hammond v. Marx*, 406 F.Supp. 853 (D.Me.1975); *Wright v. Ector County Indep. School Dist.*, 867 S.W.2d 863 [88 Educ. L. Rep. 859] (Tex.Ct.App.1993).

195. *Morgan v. Board of Educ., Trico Community Unit School Dist. No. 176*, 317 N.E.2d 393 (Ill.App.Ct.1974).

196. *Creyhon v. Board of Educ.*, 163 P. 145 (Kan.1917).

197. *Vandiver v. Hardin County Bd. of Educ.*, 925 F.2d 927 [65 Educ. L. Rep. 1045] (6th Cir.1991).

198. *Silverberg v. Board of Educ. of Union Free School Dist. No. 18*, 303 N.Y.S.2d 816 (N.Y. Sup.Ct.1969).

199. *Morrison v. Chicago Bd. of Educ.*, 544 N.E.2d 1099 [56 Educ. L. Rep. 524] (Ill.Ct.App. 1989).

200. *Sandlin v. Johnson*, 643 F.2d 1027 (4th Cir.1981).

Alabama had the authority to initiate a new policy discontinuing the promotion of students who performed unsatisfactorily.[201]

Courts also reviewed controversies involving specialized offerings. The Fifth Circuit affirmed that a student in Georgia lacked a federal claim that he was not allowed to enroll in a particular course of study because school officials did not violate a specific state mandate to this effect.[202] Almost ten years later, a student challenged his being denied readmission to a special program in automobile mechanics that was conducted at an area vocational-technical school after being involved in a theft of automobile parts from a different location. The Eighth Circuit affirmed that school officials in Missouri could deny the student's request both because participation was conditioned on good citizenship and due to their interest in protecting the integrity of off-campus programs.[203]

Evaluation of the academic progress of students has led to increasing amounts of litigation. The courts generally agree that attendance can be a factor affecting final course grades.[204] In a leading case, the Supreme Court of Connecticut issued an extensive order which responded to an array of arguments in permitting a student to be denied academic credit due to excessive absences.[205] The Supreme Court of Missouri reached the same result even though it determined that a student had the right to a hearing before officials could impose a penalty.[206] The essential educational consideration that courts accept is that presence in class adds a dimension to subject matter learning and affords many less-tangible benefits such as interactions with teachers and fellow students. An appellate court in Michigan, although not believing that the matter was of constitutional significance, stated that even if it were, the case from Connecticut provided persuasive precedent.[207]

In recognizing that board officials have wide discretion to assign students to specific schools, the courts generally do not substitute their judgment for that of educators.[208] In fact, even if a school is more conveniently located for a child, courts do not necessarily agree that this is determinative of a child's right to attend a particular school.[209] In a

201. *Bester v. Tuscaloosa City Bd. of Educ.*, 722 F.2d 1514 [15 Educ. L. Rep. 118] (11th Cir. 1984).

202. *Arundar v. DeKalb County School Dist.*, 620 F.2d 493 (5th Cir.1980).

203. *Felton v. Fayette School Dist.*, 875 F.2d 191 [53 Educ. L. Rep. 850] (8th Cir. 1989).

204. *See, e.g., Knight v. Board of Educ. of Tri–Point Community Unit School Dist. No. 6J*, 348 N.E.2d 299 (Ill.Ct.App.1976).

205. *Campbell v. Board of Educ. of Town of New Milford*, 475 A.2d 289 [17 Educ. L. Rep. 840] (Conn.1984). [Case No. 98]

206. *State ex rel. Yarber v. McHenry*, 915 S.W.2d 325 [107 Educ. L. Rep. 361] (Mo.1995).

207. *Slocum v. Holton Bd. of Educ.*, 429 N.W.2d 607 [49 Educ. L. Rep. 740] (Mich. Ct.App. 1988).

208. *State ex rel. Lewis v. Board of Educ. of Wilmington School Dist.*, 28 N.E.2d 496 (Ohio 1940). *But see Bartlett v. Board of Trustees of White Pine County School Dist.*, 550 P.2d 416 (Nev.1976) (rejecting a board plan to close a school).

209. *Bernstein v. Board of Educ. of Prince George's County*, 226 A.2d 243 (Md. 1967); *Lillbask ex rel. Mauclaire v. Sergi*, 193 F.Supp.2d 503 [163 Educ. L. Rep. 767] (D.Conn.2002).

typical case, parents wished to have their children continue to attend the school nearest their homes when the local board rearranged assignments based on the need to reduce overcrowded conditions at a high school and the need for additional classroom space in the school from which the students were to be moved to remedy the overflow. The Supreme Court of Michigan agreed that it could not substitute its judgment for that of a school board.[210] The Supreme Court of Mississippi extended this rationale in affirming that a child does not have a right to attend the same school as a sibling as long as school officials did not act arbitrarily and capriciously in denying such a request.[211]

At issue in one case was a school board's revision of school attendance zones and reassigning students where race was not involved. The parents' main objection focused on a safety consideration, particularly that even though the village had yet to erect a proposed school building, the board did not change reassignment plans for students. In upholding the board's plan, the Court of Appeals of New York agreed that it had a rational basis for its plan because it relied on the report of a citizens advisory committee, board members personally visited classrooms, conducted safety discussions with village officials, and walked the proposed routes.[212] According to the court, requiring a quasi-judicial hearing every time a board revised school attendance lines would have posed serious problems for school officials. The Supreme Court of Washington applied a like rationale when the school board in Seattle created a plan for busing to correct de facto segregation.[213] A decade later, in a similar fact pattern, the Supreme Court struck down a statute adopted by statewide referendum that was designed to prevent student assignments to correct de facto segregation in *Washington v. Seattle School District No. 1*.[214] Key to the Court's analysis was that since state law permitted local boards to make all assignments except those for race-connected purposes, it violated the Equal Protection Clause.

A board's authority to make student assignments, combined with a child's lacking a vested right to attend a particular school aside, does not mean that courts never review these kinds of controversies. Parents of a high school student who studied Latin during her first year, was a member of the band, generally received high grades, and expected to go to a college that had an entrance requirement of a minimum of two units in two foreign languages or three units in Latin challenged her proposed reassignment to a school that had neither Latin nor a band. State law provided that after assignments were completed, board officials could make changes if doing so were in the best interests of students and did not interfere with the proper administration of the schools. Insofar as

210. *Hiers v. Brownell*, 136 N.W.2d 10 (Mich.1965). For a more recent case with the same outcome, *see Clay v. Harrison Hills City School Dist. Bd. of Educ.*, 723 N.E.2d 1149 [141 Educ. L. Rep. 1164] (Ohio Com.Pl.1999).

211. *Pascagoula Mun. Separate School Dist. v. Barton*, 776 So.2d 683 [151 Educ. L. Rep. 334] (Miss.2001).

212. *Older v. Board of Educ. of Union Free School Dist. No. 1 Town of Mamaroneck*, 318 N.Y.S.2d 129 (N.Y.1971).

213. *Citizens Against Mandatory Bussing v. Palmason*, 495 P.2d 657 (Wash.1972).

214. 458 U.S. 457, 102 S.Ct. 3187, 73 L.Ed.2d 896 [5 Educ. L. Rep. 58] (1982).

the board refused to reassign the student to her original school, the Supreme Court of North Carolina, observing that the law placed all of its emphasis on the welfare of students and the effect upon the school to which reassignment was requested, directed the board to reassign the student to her original school.[215]

Parents and interest groups challenged board policies for ability grouping, or tracking, of students in public schools, alleging that this practice violated federally protected rights. This issue first arose in the context of a broad assault on policies and practices in the Washington, D.C., public school system. Parents succeeded in demonstrating that tracking unconstitutionally deprived African American and poor children of their rights to equal educational opportunities with white and more affluent peers. It appears that based on examinations that the students took relatively early in their school careers, officials assigned them to curricular tracks designed to prepare them for different types of jobs. In remarking that the absence of compensatory education made it almost impossible for a child who was originally on one track to move to a higher one, the federal trial court struck down the practice as discriminatory. Raising general questions about the tests as a measure of ability, the court barred any system of ability grouping, which, through its failure to include and implement the concept of compensatory education, did not bring the great majority of children into the mainstream of public education.[216] Conversely, even in invalidating tracking in a dual-school system in Mississippi, the then Fifth Circuit acknowledged that ability grouping can be permitted as long as it is motivated by legitimate, non-discriminatory educational concerns.[217]

When dealing with disputes over the elimination of dual-school systems, courts were reluctant to permit groupings based on achievement test scores primarily because insofar as white students performed better on such tests than African Americans, desegregation would have been impeded if assignments were made on the basis of such tests.[218] While neither achievement nor ability grouping is per se unconstitutional,[219] they may be used even if doing so causes some segregation in an otherwise unitary system when overall segregation is remedied by providing better educational opportunities.[220] As courts remain alert to possible resegregation in desegregated systems,[221] they have permitted

215. *In re Hayes*, 135 S.E.2d 645 (N.C. 1964).

216. *Hobson v. Hansen*, 269 F.Supp. 401 (D.D.C.1967), *aff'd sub nom. Smuck v. Hobson*, 408 F.2d 175 (D.C.Cir.1969).

217. *Singleton v. Jackson Mun. Separate School Dist.*, 419 F.2d 1211 (5th Cir. 1969).

218. *United States v. Tunica County School Dist.*, 421 F.2d 1236 (5th Cir.1970); *United States v. Gadsden County School Dist.*, 572 F.2d 1049 (5th Cir.1978).

219. *McNeal v. Tate County School Dist.*, 508 F.2d 1017 (5th Cir.1975); *Castaneda v. Pickard*, 648 F.2d 989 (5th Cir.

1981), 781 F.2d 456 [29 Educ. L. Rep. 942] (5th Cir.1986); *Georgia State Conference of Branches of NAACP v. State of Ga.*, 775 F.2d 1403 [28 Educ. L. Rep. 339] (11th Cir.1985).

220. *United States v. Gadsden County School Dist.*, 572 F.2d 1049 (5th Cir.1978); *Montgomery v. Starkville Mun. Separate School Dist.*, 854 F.2d 127 [48 Educ. L. Rep. 413] (5th Cir.1988).

221. *Bester v. Tuscaloosa City Bd. of Educ.*, 722 F.2d 1514 [15 Educ. L. Rep. 118] (11th Cir.1984).

school officials to offer elective courses that are especially attractive to college-bound students.[222]

One objection that opponents to achievement tests typically raise is that they have a disparate impact on minority students. In order to prevail on disparate impact claims when challenging achievement tests, plaintiffs must demonstrate by a preponderance of the evidence that facially neutral practices have disproportionate effects. If plaintiffs succeed, the burden shifts to school boards to provide substantial legitimate justifications for their practices. Next, plaintiffs have the opportunity to show either that the practices are pretexts for discrimination or to proffer equally effective practices that would result in less racial disproportionality in achieving the legitimate goals of school systems.[223]

The use of I.Q. tests as a primary determinant for placing students who are mentally retarded has been challenged with differing results. To this end, federal trial courts, in disputes arising in San Francisco[224] and Chicago,[225] reached opposite conclusions as to whether certain tests were culturally biased.

Gifted Education

The only applicable federal statute, the Jacob K. Javits Gifted and Talented Act, does not afford federal statutory rights to specialized programs because even though it encourages local school boards to create programs, it does not provide funds to do so.[226] States, of course, are free to offer programs for children who are gifted and talented.

Insofar as state and local officials have the authority to classify students as gifted, they may rely on I.Q. tests as a criterion for use in their identification.[227] If programs for the gifted can accommodate only a limited number of students, officials can use a lottery to select who is to be admitted from among qualified applicants.[228] Amid disputes over the rights of gifted children, the courts have reached mixed results with regard to programs for these students.

On the one hand, the Supreme Court of Pennsylvania unanimously affirmed that pursuant to a commonwealth statute and regulations requiring an Individualized Education Program (IEP) for each gifted

---

222. *Andrews v. City of Monroe,* 730 F.2d 1050 [16 Educ. L. Rep. 1102] (5th Cir.1984).

223. *Quarles v. Oxford Mun. Separate School Dist.,* 868 F.2d 750 [52 Educ. L. Rep. 38] (5th Cir.1989).

224. *Larry P. v. Riles,* 495 F.Supp. 926 (N.D.Cal.1979), *aff'd in part,* 793 F.2d 969 (9th Cir.1984) (striking tests down).

225. *Parents in Action on Special Educ. v. Hannon,* 506 F.Supp. 831 (N.D.Ill.1980) (upholding the validity of texts).

226. 20 U.S.C.A. § 7253. States often follow an approach such as the one used in

Ohio which requires school board officials to identify, but not serve, students who are gifted. OHIO REV. CODE ANN. § 3324.04.

227. *Student Roe v. Commonwealth of Pa.,* 638 F.Supp. 929 [33 Educ. L. Rep. 1132] (E.D.Pa. 1986), *aff'd,* 813 F.2d 398 [38 Educ. L. Rep. 111] (3d Cir.1987), *cert. denied,* 483 U.S. 1021, 107 S.Ct. 3265, 97 L.Ed.2d 764 [39 Educ. L. Rep. 998] (1987).

228. *Bennett v. City School Dist. of New Rochelle,* 497 N.Y.S.2d 72 [29 Educ. L. Rep. 728] (N.Y.App.Div.1985).

student, a child had a right to gifted education.[229] Later, an appellate court in Pennsylvania affirmed that a school board was required to provide an education sufficient to confer a benefit on a gifted student that was tailored to his unique needs pursuant to an IEP.[230]

Conversely, a case from the Supreme Court of Connecticut is more typical of the states' treatment of gifted children.[231] The court unanimously affirmed that a gifted child's state constitutional right to a free public education did not include the right to special education. The court also ruled that the legislature's failure to mandate a program for a gifted child did not violate his (agreement) rights under the equal rights and equal protection provisions of the state constitution.

Sex

A contentious issue involves assignments of students based on sex. In an early case, the federal trial court in Massachusetts directed officials at the Boston Latin School to use the same admissions standards when evaluating the applications of both males and females.[232] The court reasoned that officials violated the equal protection rights of female students not only because they attended classes in a smaller building but also since some of the young women who were excluded had higher scores on the admissions examination than males who were admitted.

Where the board in San Francisco operated a prestigious academic high school, in order to attract equal numbers of males and females, admissions criteria required females to have higher grades than males. In the face of a challenge, the Ninth Circuit directed officials to discontinue the practice of differential admissions requirements.[233] The court ascertained that board officials did not present any evidence that a balance of the sexes furthered the goal of better academic education.

A female in Philadelphia filed suit seeking admission to the city's only all-male high school rather than its only all-female high school. Enrollment at the schools was voluntary, the standards at both were high, and the schools were of like size and prestige. After a federal trial court ordered the board to admit the female, the Third Circuit reversed in its favor.[234] The court relied on the fact that attendance at either single sex-school was voluntary and the facilities were equal. An equally divided Supreme Court affirmed in *Vorchheimer v. School District of Philadelphia.*[235]

In a case involving court-ordered desegregation, a board in Mississippi sought to open schools that were segregated by gender as the only

229. *Centennial School Dist. v. Commonwealth, Dep't of Educ.*, 539 A.2d 785 [46 Educ. L. Rep. 278] (Pa.1988).

230. *York Suburban School Dist. v. S.P.*, 872 A.2d 1285 [197 Educ. L. Rep. 653] (Pa. Cmwlth. Ct. 2005).

231. *Broadley v. Board of Educ. of City of Meriden*, 639 A.2d 502 [90 Educ. L. Rep. 265] (Conn.1994).

232. *Bray v. Lee*, 337 F.Supp. 934 (D.Mass.1972).

233. *Berkelman v. San Francisco Unified School Dist.*, 501 F.2d 1264 (9th Cir. 1974). [Case No. 99]

234. *Vorchheimer v. School Dist. of Philadelphia*, 532 F.2d 880 (3d Cir.1976).

235. 430 U.S. 703, 97 S.Ct. 1671, 51 L.Ed.2d 750 (1977).

way to keep white parents from taking their children out of the schools. On further review of an order upholding the practice, the Fifth Circuit reversed in writing that the involuntary assignment plan violated equal protection and the then recently enacted Equal Educational Opportunity Act.[236]

Parents in New York City unsuccessfully challenged their school board's transforming its only all-girl public high school into a co-educational facility. A federal trial court declared that insofar as Title IX did not require officials to create all-female schools, the change did not deprive their daughters of the right to equal educational opportunities.[237]

When demographics revealed that its student population was predominately African American, the board in Detroit sought to open all-black male academies in an attempt to remedy educational and social difficulties that young black males experienced. After the mother of a female tried to enroll her daughter in one of the schools, a federal trial court in Michigan refused to let the schools open as planned.[238] Relying on *Mississippi University for Women v. Hogan*,[239] wherein the Supreme Court affirmed that excluding an individual from a public institution solely due to sex violated equal protection, the court was of the view that the rationale for founding the all-male academies was insufficient to override the female's rights.

In *United States v. Commonwealth of Virginia*,[240] a dispute from higher education, the Supreme Court concluded that the Virginia Military Institute's failure to justify its policy of excluding women violated their rights to equal protection. While rejecting the idea that programs can be designed for only one gender, the Court left the door open to the possibility that single-sex schools can be constitutional as long as they provide equal educational opportunities for females and males.[241]

As cases involving student honor societies have reached the courts, the judiciary is content that faculty recommendations, however subjective, are acceptable criteria for membership. Students do not have a right to be selected even if they meet the academic requirements[242] unless they can claim to have been excluded based on unconstitutional criteria. In such a controversy, the Third Circuit examined the case of a female in Pennsylvania who was dismissed from an honor society for

236. *United States v. Hinds County School Bd.*, 560 F.2d 619 (5th Cir.1977).

237. *Jones on Behalf of Michele v. Board of Educ. of City School Dist. of City of N.Y.*, 632 F.Supp. 1319 [32 Educ. L. Rep. 141] (E.D.N.Y.1986).

238. *Garrett v. Board of Educ. of School Dist. of City of Detroit*, 775 F.Supp. 1004 [70 Educ. L. Rep. 1101] (E.D.Mich.1991).

239. 458 U.S. 718, 102 S.Ct. 3331, 73 L.Ed.2d 1090 [5 Educ. L. Rep. 103] (1982).

240. 518 U.S. 515, 116 S.Ct. 2264, 135 L.Ed.2d 735 (1996), *on remand*, 96 F.3d 114 (4th Cir. 1996).

241. For a like case involving the Citadel, *see Faulkner v. Jones*, 51 F.3d 440 [99 Educ. L. Rep. 99] (4th Cir.1995), *stay denied*, 66 F.3d 661 (4th Cir. Aug.1995), *cert. dismissed*, 516 U.S. 910, 116 S.Ct. 331, 133 L.Ed.2d 202 [105 Educ. L. Rep. 395] (1995), *cert. denied*, 516 U.S. 938, 116 S.Ct. 352, 133 L.Ed.2d 248 [105 Educ. L. Rep. 396] (1995).

242. *Karnstein v. Pewaukee School Bd.*, 557 F.Supp. 565 (E.D.Wis.1983).

becoming pregnant out-of-wedlock.[243] While conceding that an honor society that emphasized leadership and character could consider conduct of unmarried high school students, the court remanded for a consideration of whether school officials dismissed a male member who fathered a child out-of-wedlock. Federal trial court in Kentucky[244] and the Ninth Circuit[245] reached similar results.

Use of Race in Admissions Decisions

The use of race as an admissions criterion first surfaced in *Regents of University of California v. Bakke (Bakke).*[246] Even though it was set in higher education, *Bakke* became the bellwether in suits involving what is commonly referred to as affirmative action. In *Bakke*, the Supreme Court held that while the admissions program at issue, which set aside seats for minority applicants, was unacceptable, the use of race as a factor in admissions decisions was not per se constitutionally impermissible. *Bakke* opened the door to a steady stream of litigation on the use of race in admissions to educational institutions.

In addition to terminating judicial oversight of school desegregation efforts in Denver, the federal trial court in Colorado reviewed a state constitutional provision which prohibited the use of race in school assignments. In rejecting the school board's claim that it had the right to place children as officials saw fit, the court pointed out that educators could not engage in this sort of racial balancing.[247] Rather than review the question, the Tenth Circuit dismissed the case as moot.[248]

Parents challenged the Boston Latin School's use of an admissions policy that took race and ethnicity into consideration. The First Circuit vitiated the policy in rejecting the notion that it was meant to remedy the vestiges of past discrimination. The court also posited that since diversity was not a compelling interest, educational officials had to admit a white student because the policy violated her right to equal protection.[249] Along the same line, in a case from Maryland, the Fourth Circuit found in favor of the parents of a first-grade student who questioned the constitutionality of a policy at a magnet school that used race and ethnicity as factors in considering whether students could transfer into the program.[250] The court directed the school board to admit the child to the magnet school in noting that the use of race as a factor in the

243. *Pfeiffer v. Marion Ctr. Area School Dist.,* 917 F.2d 779 [63 Educ. L. Rep. 727] (3d Cir. 1990).

244. *Chipman v. Grant County School Dist.,* 30 F.Supp.2d 975 [131 Educ. L. Rep. 994] (E.D.Ky.1998).

245. *Cazares v. Barber,* 959 F.2d 753 [73 Educ. L. Rep. 931] (9th Cir.1992).

246. 438 U.S. 265, 98 S.Ct. 2733, 57 L.Ed.2d 750 (1978).

247. *Keyes v. Congress of Hispanic Educators,* 902 F.Supp. 1274 [104 Educ. L. Rep. 1067] (D. Colo.1995).

248. *Keyes v. School Dist. No. 1, Denver, Colo.,* 119 F.3d 1437 [120 Educ. L. Rep. 158] (10th Cir.1997).

249. *Wessman v. Gittens,* 160 F.3d 790 [130 Educ. L. Rep. 1009] (1st Cir. 1998).

250. *Eisenberg v. Montgomery County Pub. Schools,* 197 F.3d 123 [140 Educ. L. Rep. 88] (4th Cir. 1999), *cert. denied,* 529 U.S. 1019, 120 S.Ct. 1420, 146 L.Ed.2d 312 (2000).

transfer policy violated equal protection because its was insufficiently narrowly tailored to achieve the goal of a diversified student body.

On the other hand, the Ninth Circuit upheld a policy from California that included race and ethnicity as criteria in admitting students to a university's laboratory school.[251] The court affirmed that since the state had a compelling interest in providing effective education in urban schools, the use of race was narrowly tailored to achieve this goal.[252]

The Supreme Court's most recent pronouncements on race-conscious affirmative action plans in education were companion cases from the University of Michigan. In *Grutter v. Bollinger (Gruttzer)*,[253] the Court upheld the university's affirmative action admissions policy in its law school, determining that because diversity is a compelling governmental interest, officials could use race as a factor in admissions decisions because the criteria were sufficiently narrowly tailored to achieve the compelling state interest of having a racially diverse student body. Yet, in *Gratz v. Bollinger (Gratz)*,[254] the Court struck down the university's reliance on a point system in admissions to undergraduate programs because its use of race was not sufficiently narrowly tailored to achieve its goal of a diverse student body. Not surprisingly, in the aftermath of these cases courts continue to reach mixed results on the use of race in admissions in K–12 schools. Three of the four circuit courts that considered race as a criterion were satisfied that educators acted with compelling state interests.

In a case from Louisiana initially involving a consent decree, a magnet school, and a court-ordered desegregation plan, the Fifth Circuit discerned that a school board's race-based admissions policy was not narrowly tailored enough to remedy the present effects of past segregation.[255] While not citing either *Grutter* or *Gratz*, the court asserted that the plan was unacceptable because there was no evidence that officials considered any race-neutral means of selecting students that might arguably have increased participation by African Americans. The court was not convinced that the board's quota system complied with the dictates of the earlier consent decree.

The first of three cases that upheld the use of race involved a challenge by parents in Kentucky who questioned the use of a district-wide, race-conscious school choice plan. The Sixth Circuit affirmed that since the plan was narrowly tailored to achieve the compelling goal of preserving the presence of minority students in each school as a means

251. *Hunter ex rel. Brandt v. Regents of the Univ. of Cal.*, 190 F.3d 1061 [138 Educ. L. Rep. 127] (9th Cir. 1999), *cert. denied*, 531 U.S. 877, 121 S.Ct. 186, 148 L.Ed.2d 128 (2000).

252. *See also Brewer v. West Irondequoit Cent. School Dist.*, 212 F.3d 738 [144 Educ. L. Rep. 845] (2d Cir. 2000) (commenting, in upholding a urban-suburban interdistrict transfer program, that "indeed, such [voluntary racial] integration serves important societal functions.").

253. 539 U.S. 306, 123 S.Ct. 2325, 156 L.Ed.2d 304 [177 Educ. L. Rep. 801] (2003).

254. 529 U.S. 244, 123 S.Ct. 2411, 156 L.Ed.2d 257 [177 Educ. L. Rep. 851] (2003).

255. *Cavalier ex rel. Cavalier v. Caddo Parish School Bd.*, 403 F.3d 246 [196 Educ. L. Rep. 765] (5th Cir. 2005).

of successfully implementing racial integration, it was acceptable.[256] Parents in Massachusetts whose children were denied transfers on race-conscious grounds filed a discrimination claim against school officials. Sitting en banc, the First Circuit affirmed that since the plan was sufficiently narrowly tailored to meet the school committee's compelling interest in achieving the benefits of educational diversity, it was constitutional.[257]

A procedurally complex case from Washington state, which began prior to *Grutter* and *Gratz,* involved a parental challenge to their school board's "open choice" assignment plan. The parents claimed that the plan, which used race as a tiebreaker in assigning students to oversubscribed high schools, violated the Equal Protection Clause and state laws. After a federal trial court granted the school board's motion for summary judgment,[258] the Ninth Circuit reversed in favor of the parents[259] but withdrew its opinion when it agreed to conduct a rehearing[260] while certifying the question to the Supreme Court of Washington.[261] The Supreme Court of Washington maintained that while racial diversity in education is a compelling interest, the board's use of race as a tiebreaker was not narrowly tailored to further such an interest. In essentially conforming with the judgment of the Supreme Court of Washington, the Ninth Circuit reversed and remanded in favor of the parents with instructions to enjoin the plan.[262] The court was persuaded that the racial integration tiebreaker violated a state law which prohibited the preferential use of race in public education. An en banc panel of the Ninth Circuit, relying on *Gratz* and *Grutter,* then explained that the plan did not violate equal protection since its use of race was sufficiently narrowly tailored to achieve the compelling state interest of avoiding racial isolation while increasing diversity.[263] In deciding that the plan met the requirements of *Grutter and Gratz* insofar as it did not employ quotas and engaged in the good faith consideration of race-neutral alternatives, the court upheld it as constitutional.

In a case involving race and ethnicity that had an interesting twist, a non-native Hawaiian student challenged a private school, its charitable trust, and trustees claiming that its race-conscious admissions policy of accepting only students of native Hawaiian ancestry was unconstitution-

256. *McFarland ex rel. McFarland v. Jefferson County Pub. Schools,* 416 F.3d 513 (6th Cir. 2005), *reh'g and reh'g en banc denied* (2005).

257. *Comfort v. Lynn School Comm.,* 418 F.3d 1 [200 Educ. L. Rep. 541] (1st Cir. 2005), *cert. denied,* ___ U.S. ___, 126 S.Ct. 798, 163 L.Ed.2d 627 (2005).

258. *Parents Involved in Community Schools v. Seattle School Dist. No. 1,* 137 F.Supp.2d 1224 [153 Educ. L. Rep. 267] (W.D. Wash. 2001).

259. *Parents Involved in Community Schools v. Seattle School Dist., No. 1,* 285 F.3d 1236 [163 Educ. L. Rep. 572] (9th Cir. 2002).

260. *Parents Involved In Community Schools v. Seattle School Dist., No. 1,* 294 F.3d 1084 [167 Educ. L. Rep. 38] (9th Cir. 2002).

261. *Parents Involved in Community Schools v. Seattle School Dist. No. 1,* 294 F.3d 1085 [166 Educ. L. Rep. 511] (9th Cir. 2002).

262. *Parents Involved in Community Schools v. Seattle School Dist. No. 1,* 377 F.3d 949 [190 Educ.L. Rep. 79] (9th Cir. 2004).

263. *Parents Involved in Community Schools v. Seattle School Dist. No. 1,* 426 F.3d 1162 [202 Educ. L. Rep. 549] (9th Cir. 2005). [Case No. 100] al. The Ninth Circuit agreed with the plaintiff that since the school's race-based admissions policy did not constitute a valid affirmative action plan that might have supplied legitimate nondiscriminatory reason for its actions, it violated section 1981.[264]

Fees

Insofar as state constitutions typically provide that their legislatures must establish systems of free public schools, disputes arise over whether local boards can charge fees. A case from the Supreme Court of Arkansas illustrates the general rule that students and/or their parents cannot be charged registration fees in order to keep public schools open for a full term.[265] Another court specified that boards may not indirectly violate the spirit of the constitutional provision that a state must operate a system of free public schools by charging athletic, library, and other such fees as a condition to being admitted to schools.[266] Insofar as the courts have reached mixed results with regard to such items as transportation, textbooks, course materials, and summer programs, each of these topics is addressed separately.

Transportation

Absent express statutory directives to do so, and as reflected in a case from Louisiana,[267] most states do not charge fees for transporting students to and from school. If boards discontinue providing transportation for students in public schools, parents whose children attend non-public schools cannot claim such a right for their children.[268] Even if statutes permit school boards to provide free transportation or pay the allowance for students, they have no duty to reimburse parents for the cost of transportation expenses if their children make their own way to school.[269]

As reflected in its only case on transportation fees, *Kadrmas v. Dickinson Public Schools (Kadrmas)*,[270] the Supreme Court affirmed that a state has the authority to permit such charges. In *Kardrmas*, the Court upheld a statute from North Dakota that allowed school boards to charge students fees for transportation that did not exceed their actual estimated costs. According to the Court, the law did not violate equal protection because it not only encouraged local boards to provide bus service as a

264. *Doe v. Kamehameha Schools/Bernice Pauahi Bishop Estate*, 416 F.3d 1025 [200 Educ. L. Rep. 53] (9th Cir. 2005). This statute is in the appendix.

265. *Dowell v. School Dist. No. 1, Boone County*, 250 S.W.2d 127 (Ark.1952). See also Morris v. Vandiver, 145 So. 228 (Miss. 1933).

266. *Morris v. Vandiver*, 145 So. 228 (Miss. 1933).

267. *Moreau v. Avoyelles Parish School Bd.*, 897 So.2d 875, 883 [197 Educ. L. Rep. 463] (La. Ct. App. 2005), *writs denied*, 904

So.2d 704, 705 (La. 2005) ("the concept of free education in Louisiana includes as a *primary* element the transportation to and from school.)" (emphasis in original).

268. *Crowe ex rel. Crowe v. School Dist. of Pittsburgh*, 805 A.2d 691 [169 Educ. L. Rep. 314] (Pa.Cmwlth.2002).

269. *State ex rel. Fick v. Miller*, 584 N.W.2d 809 [129 Educ. L. Rep. 800] (Neb. 1998).

270. 487 U.S. 450, 108 S.Ct. 2481, 101 L.Ed.2d 399 [47 Educ. L. Rep. 383] (1988).

legitimate state purpose but was a rational way to avoid undermining its objective by means of a rule requiring the use of general revenues to subsidize an optional service that would have benefitted a minority of families. In conceding that transportation is different from fees for tuition and other items, some courts permitted these fees in agreeing that transportation is not at the heart of the obligation of states to provide students with a free public education.[271]

Textbooks

As important as textbooks are, courts disagree on whether all students in public schools are entitled to use them for free. On the one hand, the highest courts in Georgia,[272] Idaho,[273] Michigan,[274] West Virginia,[275] and Ohio[276] agreed that students cannot be charged fees for textbooks. The Supreme Court of Michigan, citing the case from Idaho, thought that since textbooks were necessary elements of school activities, officials should have provided them for students at no cost. The court in West Virginia, indicating that since books and school supplies are an essential part of free public schools, was of the opinion that denying them to students who cannot pay for them would have been akin to prohibiting them from attending school. The court added that a school board cannot purchase school books and sell them to students, even at wholesale prices, unless it is specially authorized to do so by statute.

On the other hand, the Supreme Courts in Illinois,[277] Indiana,[278] Wisconsin,[279] Arizona,[280] Colorado,[281] and North Dakota,[282] along with an appellate court in Indiana,[283] upheld book fees. Even where state law permitted a textbook fee to be charged, a federal trial court in Indiana

---

271. *See, e.g., Salazar v. Eastin*, 890 P.2d 43 [97 Educ. L. Rep. 1139] (Cal.1995); *Arcadia Unified School Dist. v. State Dep't of Educ.*, 825 P.2d 438 [72 Educ. L. Rep. 1137] (Cal.1992); *Sutton v. Cadillac Area Pub. Schools*, 323 N.W.2d 582 [6 Educ. L. Rep. 187] (Mich.Ct.App. 1982).

272. *Mathis v. Gordy*, 47 S.E. 171 (Ga. 1904).

273. *Paulson v. Minidoka County School Dist. No. 331*, 463 P.2d 935 (Idaho 1970). [Case No. 101]

274. *Bond v. Public Schools of Ann Arbor School Dist.*, 178 N.W.2d 484 (Mich. 1970).

275. *Randolph County Bd. of Educ. v. Adams*, 467 S.E.2d 150 [107 Educ. L. Rep. 324] (W.Va. 1995).

276. *State ex rel. Massie v. Gahanna–Jefferson Pub. Schools Bd. of Educ.*, 669 N.E.2d 839 [112 Educ. L. Rep. 421] (Ohio 1996) (permitting the board to charge a fee for any materials used in course of instruc-

tion with the exception of necessary textbooks).

277. *Hamer v. Board of Educ. of School Dist. No. 109*, 265 N.E.2d 616 (Ill.1970), *appeal after remand*, 299 N.E.2d 595 (Ill. App. Ct. 1973).

278. *Chandler v. South Bend Community School Corp.*, 312 N.E.2d 915 (Ind. Ct. App. 1974).

279. *Board of Educ. v. Sinclair*, 222 N.W.2d 143 (Wis.1974).

280. *Carpio v. Tucson High School Dist. No. 1 of Pima County*, 524 P.2d 948 (Ariz. 1974), *cert. denied*, 420 U.S. 982, 95 S.Ct. 1412, 43 L.Ed.2d 664 (1975).

281. *Marshall v. School Dist. RE No. 3 Morgan County*, 553 P.2d 784 (Colo.1976).

282. *Cardiff v. Bismarck Pub. School Dist.*, 263 N.W.2d 105 (N.D.1978).

283. *Chandler v. South Bend Community School Corp.*, 312 N.E.2d 915 (Ind.Ct. App.1974).

remarked that suspending a student from school for failing to pay such a fee violated his right to equal protection.[284]

Course Materials and Other Fees

In a trilogy of cases, the Supreme Court of Illinois upheld charges for clean towels where the use of the service was optional,[285] a mandatory fee for a wide variety of supplies and materials that would have been consumed by or retained by students,[286] and a lunchroom supervision fee for students who lived near school but chose to eat their lunches in the lunchroom.[287] Further, the Supreme Court of North Carolina upheld charging modest fees for purchasing supplementary supplies and materials for use by or on behalf of students whose parents were able to pay for them as long as local board officials provided them with notice of procedures.[288] Conversely, the Supreme Court of Montana prohibited school officials from charging fees in connection with activities that were reasonably related to recognized academic and educational goals of the school system.[289]

The Supreme Court of Ohio reasoned that statutes authorizing fees are to be strictly construed. The court thus invalidated a fee for "paper products, copier materials, and other necessary consumable educational supply items" as not covered by the phrase "any materials used in a course of instruction."[290] The court subsequently clarified its rationale in acknowledging that school boards could charge instructional fees for classroom materials such as consumable non-food instructional supplies including paper, paste, pencils, paint, and other expenditures for items that teachers used to aid in their instruction of students.[291]

Elective Courses and Summer School

The Supreme Courts of Montana[292] and New Mexico[293] agreed that students can be charged fees for taking electives classes. Conversely, the Supreme Court of California disagreed in contending that doing so violated the state constitutional guarantee to a free public school education.[294] In specifically addressing extracurricular sports[295] and music,

284. *Carder v. Michigan City School Corp.*, 552 F.Supp. 869 [8 Educ. L. Rep. 318] (N.D.Ind. 1982).

285. *Hamer v. Board of Educ. of School Dist. No. 109, Lake County*, 292 N.E.2d 569 (Ill.Ct. App.1973).

286. *Beck v. Board of Educ. of Harlem Consol. School Dist. No. 122*, 344 N.E.2d 440 (Ill.1976).

287. *Ambroiggio v. Board of Educ. of School Dist. No. 44*, 427 N.E.2d 1027 [1 Educ. L. Rep. 337] (Ill.Ct.App.1981).

288. *Sneed v. Greensboro City Bd. of Educ.*, 264 S.E.2d 106 (N.C.1980).

289. *Granger v. Cascade County School Dist. No. 1*, 499 P.2d 780 (Mont.1972).

290. *Association for the Defense of Washington Local School Dist. v. Kiger*, 537 N.E.2d 1292, 1292 [53 Educ. L. Rep. 676] (Ohio 1989). See also *Sneed v. Greensboro City Bd. of Educ.*, 264 S.E.2d 106 (N.C. 1980).

291. *State ex rel. Massie v. Gahanna–Jefferson Pub. Schools Bd. of Educ.*, 669 N.E.2d 839 [112 Educ. L. Rep. 421] (Ohio 1996).

292. *Granger v. Cascade County School Dist. No. 1*, 499 P.2d 780 (Mont.1972).

293. *Norton v. Board of Educ. of School Dist. No. 16, Hobbs Mun. Schools*, 553 P.2d 1277 (N.M. 1976).

294. *Hartzell v. Connell*, 679 P.2d 35 [17 Educ. L. Rep. 241] (Cal.1984).

the court observed that any educational activity must be offered free to all, regardless of its characterization as non-credit or extracurricular.[296] In a related concern, to the extent that extracurricular activities may tax the budgets of school systems, an appellate court in New York affirmed that where a board operated under a contingency budget, it was not required to fund interschool athletics, field trips, and other extracurricular activities.[297]

Disputes over specific programs have led to mixed results. The Supreme Judicial Court of Massachusetts[298] and an appellate court in California[299] agreed that where driver's education was offered, it had to be free of charge. On the other hand, appellate courts in New Jersey[300] and New York[301] disagreed, recognizing that absent statutory directives to the contrary, fees could have been charged for such elective courses.

Courts in California and South Carolina reached different results on fees for summer school programs. The former ascertained that a board had no power to charge fees unless the legislature authorized it to do so.[302] The latter disagreed in postulating that since a summer program was not included in the state constitutional provision for free public schools even though the classes could have been credited toward graduation, a board could assess fees.[303]

Interscholastic Activities

School boards can join and agree to be bound by the rules of state or regional associations for interscholastic activities. Even though associations are voluntary, privately governed bodies, because most are intertwined with the state, courts treat them as state actors.[304] Accordingly, courts typically inquire into matters such as equal protection and due process which would not otherwise apply to private groups.

There seems to be general agreement that interscholastic associations can enforce rules against individual schools or boards. For example, the Supreme Court of Ohio refused to intervene in a dispute over the

---

295. For an early case striking down a fee for athletic privileges, *see Morris v. Vandiver*, 145 So. 228 (Miss.1933).

296. *Attorney General v. East Jackson Pub. Schools*, 372 N.W.2d 638 [27 Educ. L. Rep. 304] (Mich.Ct.App.1985) (upholding a fee for participation in interscholastic athletics).

297. *Polmanteer v. Bobo*, 794 N.Y.S.2d 171 [197 Educ. L. Rep. 726] (N.Y. App. Div. 2005).

298. *Johnson v. School Comm. of Brockton*, 358 N.E.2d 820 (Mass.1977).

299. *California Ass'n for Safety Education v. Brown*, 36 Cal.Rptr.2d 404 [95 Educ. L. Rep. 1026] (Cal.Ct.App.1994), *review denied* (1995).

300. *Parsippany–Troy Hills Educ. Ass'n v. Board of Educ. of Parsippany–Troy Hills Township*, 457 A.2d 15 [9 Educ. L. Rep. 941] (N.J.Super.App.Div.1983), *certification denied*, 468 A.2d 182 (N.J.1983).

301. *Messina v. Sobol*, 553 N.Y.S.2d 529 [59 Educ. L. Rep. 868] (N.Y.App.Div.1990), *appeal dismissed*, 560 N.Y.S.2d 129 (N.Y. 1990).

302. *California Teachers Ass'n v. Board of Educ. of Glendale*, 167 Cal.Rptr. 429 (Cal.Ct.App. 1980).

303. *Washington v. Salisbury*, 306 S.E.2d 600 [13 Educ. L. Rep. 545] (S.C. 1983).

304. *See Brentwood Academy v. Tennessee Secondary School Athletic Ass'n*, 531

suspension of a team from competition since school officials violated a provision governing the recruitment of football players.[305] The Supreme Court of Pennsylvania, citing this case, refused to grant relief where the commonwealth's athletic association placed a high school on probation due to fighting among spectators after a football game.[306] Similarly, the Third Circuit rejected the claim of a student from Pennsylvania that it was unconstitutional to deprive him of the opportunity to play in post-season games because his team was suspended for rules violations.[307]

Association rules must meet constitutional standards. In light of this principle, the federal trial court in South Dakota invalidated a rule that disadvantaged small-school debating teams by classifying schools by enrollment as a violation of equal protection.[308] More recently, though, an appellate court in New York upheld a rule of the state athletic association that divided schools that have football teams into classes based on size because its action was not arbitrary and capricious.[309]

Participation in interscholastic sports and other extracurricular activities is not a constitutionally protected civil right.[310] This means that school officials can institute rules that place greater responsibilities on participants than on their peers who do not take part in these activities.

There is a strong presumption in favor of rules designed to protect the educational value and integrity of interscholastic sports as well as the health and welfare of student-athletes. To this end, a large number of cases uphold such rules as long as they are supported by rational bases. In such a dispute, where the father of a student-athlete in Alabama allegedly struck a referee in the face, an appellate court upheld the team's being placed on probation and forbidding it from playing whenever the father was present at a game.[311] At the same time, the Supreme Court of Oklahoma upheld the two-game suspension that prohibited a student-athlete from competing in football playoff games after he participated in an on-field fight in which he kicked at an opposing player's helmet.[312] The court agreed that there was no evidence suggesting that officials acted in anything other than good faith in conjunction with the rule of law by a referee who was positioned to see the play and who reacted immediately to the athlete's action.

U.S. 288, 121 S.Ct. 924, 148 L.Ed.2d 807 [151 Educ. L. Rep. 18] (2001). [Case No. 22]

305. *State ex rel. Ohio High School Athletic Ass'n v. Judges of Court of Common Pleas of Stark County*, 181 N.E.2d 261 (1962).

306. *School Dist. of Harrisburg v. Pennsylvania Interscholastic Athletic Ass'n*, 309 A.2d 353 (Pa.1973).

307. *Moreland v. Western Pa. Interscholastic Athletic League*, 572 F.2d 121 (3d Cir.1978).

308. *Baltic Indep. School Dist. v. South Dakota High School Activities Ass'n*, 362 F.Supp. 780 (D.S.D.1973).

309. *Suburban Scholastic Council v. Section 2 of N.Y. State Pub. High School*

Athletic Ass'n, 803 N.Y.S.2d 270 [203 Educ. L. Rep. 334] (N.Y. App. Div. 2005).

310. *See, e.g., Albach v. Odle*, 531 F.2d 983 (10th Cir.1976) [Case No. 102]; *Palmer v. Merluzzi*, 868 F.2d 90 [51 Educ. L. Rep. 1196] (3d Cir.1989) [Case No. 105]; *Pirschel v. Sorrell*, 2 F.Supp.2d 930 [127 Educ. L. Rep. 124] (E.D. Ky.1998); *Florida High School Athletic Ass'n v. Melbourne Cent. Catholic High School*, 867 So.2d 1281 [186 Educ. L. Rep. 1025] (Fla. Dist. Ct. App. 2004).

311. *Marshall v. Alabama High School Athletic Ass'n*, 717 So.2d 404 [129 Educ. L. Rep. 881] (Ala.Civ.App.1998).

312. *Brown ex rel. Brown v. Oklahoma Secondary School Activities Ass'n*, 125 P.3d 1219 [205 Educ. L. Rep. 898] (Okla. 2005).

The constitution does not require school officials to grant exceptions for students who wish to participate in extracurricular activities. As long as rules are reasonable, it is not the function of the courts to rewrite or administer them so as to provide for exceptions. The Supreme Court of North Dakota echoed this sentiment in refusing to grant an exception to transfer rules for students who changed schools primarily for academic reasons.[313] Further, although offering its opinion that it appeared to be harsh, the Supreme Court of Georgia upheld a rule stipulating that eligibility would have been for only eight consecutive semesters or four consecutive years from date of first entrance into ninth grade.[314] In this case, the student dropped out of school for a little over a year because he had been forced to work due to his mother's illness.

As important as rules are, courts do not uphold them if they are enforced arbitrarily. In an illustrative case, where a student-athlete in Indiana moved from the custody of one parent to another due to their divorce, the Seventh Circuit overturned the league's rendering him ineligible to participate since the league official responsible for eligibility changed his mind on three separate occasions with regard to the student.[315] In another case from Indiana, an appellate court agreed with a student-athlete that the denial of his request for a hardship exception to the transfer rule was arbitrary and capricious.[316] The court pointed out that in view of evidence that a family's changed financial circumstances following the divorce of the student's parents, through no fault of his own and without athletic motivation, he should have been permitted to retain his eligibility.

The major issues in the realm of athletics include transfers, residency and age requirements, longevity rules, academic qualifications, and gender equity. Student-athletes who transfer from one school system to another must generally have letters explaining that they are not doing so exclusively for athletic purposes.[317] Students who transfer for athletic reasons[318] ordinarily have to sit out a season of competition while those who transfer due to legitimate changes of residence, such as where families relocate[319] or where one switched to a Catholic school after converting to that faith,[320] are generally eligible immediately. Of course, where a rule rendered black students in formerly segregated school districts reluctant to transfer, it was struck down as applied.[321] Yet, in a formerly segregated district, a federal trial court in Alabama rejected the

313. *Crandall v. North Dakota High School Activities Ass'n,* 261 N.W.2d 921 (N.D.1978).

314. *Smith v. Crim,* 240 S.E.2d 884 (Ga. 1977).

315. *Crane by Crane v. Indiana High School Athletic Ass'n,* 975 F.2d 1315 [77 Educ. L. Rep. 722] (7th Cir.1992).

316. *Indiana High School Athletic Ass'n v. Durham,* 748 N.E.2d 404 [154 Educ. L. Rep. 279] (Ind.Ct.App.2001).

317. *See, e.g., Sutterby v. Zimar,* 594 N.Y.S.2d 607 [81 Educ. L. Rep. 508] (N.Y.Sup.Ct.1993).

318. *Revesz ex rel. Revesz v. Pennsylvania Interscholastic Athletic Ass'n,* 798 A.2d 830 [165 Educ. L. Rep. 694] (Pa.Cmwlth. 2002).

319. *Indiana High School Athletic Ass'n v. Wideman,* 688 N.E.2d 413 [122 Educ. L. Rep. 1268] (Ind.Ct.App.1997).

320. *Robbins by Robbins v. Indiana High School Athletic Ass'n,* 941 F.Supp. 786 [113 Educ. L. Rep. 1240] (S.D.Ind.1996).

321. *Rogers v. Board of Educ.,* 281 F.Supp. 39 (E.D.Ark.1968).

claims of black high school student-athletes who challenged a board policy that required all students who transferred under a majority to minority program to sit out a year of interscholastic athletics.[322] The court wrote that the policy's goal was to address the compelling problem of illegal recruiting and to revive schools in largely black areas. The court decided that any purported knowledge on the part of board members that the policy would have had a disparate impact on the students was not enough to prove intent to discriminate based on race, especially given the board's clear intent to benefit the predominately black schools.

As to residency, the Fifth Circuit rejected claims that a rule which required a student in Texas to reside in a district for a year before participating in interscholastic events burdened his right to travel and freedom of family association.[323] The same court previously rejected a claim that a student's losing a year of interscholastic eligibility due to his having participated in an athletic camp infringed on parental rights.[324] The Supreme Court of Florida upheld a rule for post-season play that reduced each team's player limit below that allowed for regular season play.[325] The Supreme Court of New Hampshire refused to overrule an adjudication of the state athletic association that a student not be permitted to run in a special event because he did not qualify in the preliminary despite his claim that he did not qualify because he had been fouled.[326]

To the extent that the two criteria often overlap, courts reach comparable results in upholding eligibility requirements based on age[327] and longevity in the sense that students are typically limited to eight semesters of eligibility in interscholastic sports.[328] Most courts are also unwilling to make exceptions for eligibility based on age with regard to students with disabilities.[329]

---

322. *Young By and Through Young v. Montgomery County (Alabama) Bd. of Educ.*, 922 F.Supp. 544 [109 Educ. L. Rep. 202] (M.D.Ala.1996).

323. *Niles v. University Interscholastic League*, 715 F.2d 1027 [13 Educ. L. Rep. 257] (5th Cir.1983), *cert. denied*, 465 U.S. 1028, 104 S.Ct. 1289, 79 L.Ed.2d 691 (1984).

324. *Kite v. Marshall*, 661 F.2d 1027 [1 Educ. L. Rep. 44] (5th Cir.1981), *cert. denied*, 457 U.S. 1120, 102 S.Ct. 2934, 73 L.Ed.2d 1333 (1982). [Case No. 103]

325. *The Florida High School Activities Ass'n v. Thomas*, 434 So.2d 306 [12 Educ. L. Rep. 1022] (Fla.1983).

326. *Snow v. New Hampshire Interscholastic Athletic Ass'n*, 449 A.2d 1223 [6 Educ. L. Rep. 736] (N.H.1982).

327. *Sandison v. Michigan High School Athletic Ass'n*, 64 F.3d 1026 [103 Educ. L. Rep. 56] (6th Cir.1995). *But see Baisden v.*

West Virginia Secondary Schools Activities Com'n, 568 S.E.2d 32 [168 Educ. L. Rep. 950] (W.Va.2002) (prohibiting a nineteen year-old with a learning disability from playing football).

328. *See, e.g., McPherson v. Michigan High School Athletic Ass'n*, 119 F.3d 453 [120 Educ. L. Rep. 96] (6th Cir.1997); *Indiana High School Athletic Ass'n. v. Reyes*, 694 N.E.2d 249 [125 Educ. L. Rep. 848] (Ind.1997).

329. *Thomas v. Greencastle Community School Corp.*, 603 N.E.2d 190 [78 Educ. L. Rep. 984](Ind. Ct. App. 1992); *Pottgen v. Missouri State High School Activities Ass'n*, 40 F.3d 926 [95 Educ. L. Rep. 867] (8th Cir.1994); *Dennin v. Connecticut Interscholastic Athletic Conference*, 913 F.Supp. 663 [106 Educ. L. Rep. 1130] (D.Conn.1996); *Washington v. Indiana High School Athletic Ass'n*, 181 F.3d 840 [136 Educ. L. Rep. 713] (7th Cir.1999); *Cruz ex rel. Cruz v. Pennsylvania Interscholastic Athletic Ass'n*, 157 F.Supp.2d 485 [156 Educ. L. Rep. 633]

The courts uniformly uphold academic eligibility requirements in any and all extracurricular activities.[330] The courts reach these results regardless of whether rules come from legislatures,[331] state boards of education,[332] or local school boards.[333] Disputes over the controversial practice of "no pass, no play," even though upheld, have dissipated.

An interesting case that overlaps with academic eligibility and residency may portend issues to come. The Third Circuit affirmed the dismissal of a federal trial court's refusal to grant an injunction to a student at a cyber school who sought to participate in a junior varsity basketball program at a school in the district within which she and her parents lived.[334] The court agreed that the board did not act unreasonably since its rules were consistent with Pennsylvania statutes and officials did not violate the student's due process rights because she did not have a property interest in participating in extracurricular activities.

There has been a significant amount of litigation on gender equity in sports. In a leading older case from Minnesota, the Eighth Circuit noted that eligibility to participate in a non-contact sport cannot be based on sex.[335] The court found that where there were no teams for females in tennis, skiing, and running, and females were qualified to compete with males in those non-contact sports, a rule of the state interscholastic athletic league barring mixed athletics was unenforceable.

The first court to lift restrictions against females who wished to participate in contact sports was in Pennsylvania. An appellate court, referring to the equal rights amendment in the commonwealth's constitution, struck down a bylaw of the state interscholastic athletic association which barred females from competing or practicing with boys in any athletic activity as unconstitutional on its face.[336] Later in the same year, the Supreme Court of Washington, relying in part on the case from Pennsylvania, and an almost identical provision in its state constitution, also invalidated sex barriers in contact sports.[337] Moreover, the Sixth Circuit, although stopping short of ordering co-educational teams in contact sports in Ohio, declared that a rule against such participation

(E.D.Pa.2001). *But see University Interscholastic League v. Buchanan,* 848 S.W.2d 298 [81 Educ. L. Rep. 1145] (Tex. App. 1993), *reh'g overruled* (1993) (affirming an injunction that permitted nineteen year-olds with learning disabilities to participate in interscholastic sports).

330. *State ex rel. Bartmess v. Board of Trustees of School Dist. No. 1,* 726 P.2d 801 [35 Educ. L. Rep. 564] (Mont.1986).

331. *Spring Branch Indep. School Dist. v. Stamos,* 695 S.W.2d 556 [27 Educ. L. Rep. 605] (Tex.1985), *appeal dismissed,* 475 U.S. 1001, 106 S.Ct. 1170, 89 L.Ed.2d 290 [30 Educ. L. Rep. 662] (1986) [Case No. 104]. *See also Texas Educ. Agency v. Dallas Indep. School Dist.,* 797 S.W.2d 367 [63 Educ. L. Rep. 670] (Tex.Ct.App.1990) (dismissing a claim over an ineligible player as moot since the season was over).

332. *Bailey v. Truby,* 321 S.E.2d 302 [20 Educ. L. Rep. 980] (W.Va.1984).

333. *Thompson v. Fayette County Pub. Schools,* 786 S.W.2d 879 [59 Educ. L. Rep. 1197] (Ky.Ct.App.1990).

334. *Angstadt v. Midd–West School Dist.,* 377 F.3d 338 [190 Educ. L. Rep. 48] (3d. Cir. 2004).

335. *Brenden v. Independent School Dist. 742,* 477 F.2d 1292 (8th Cir.1973).

336. *Commonwealth by Packel v. Pennsylvania Interscholastic Athletic Ass'n,* 334 A.2d 839 (Pa.Cmwlth.Ct.1975).

337. *Darrin v. Gould,* 540 P.2d 882 (Wash.1975).

was unacceptable because it was more restrictive than Title IX required.[338]

Massachusetts' highest court, in applying strict scrutiny, was of the opinion that officials acted inappropriately in barring boys from girls' teams.[339] Conversely, where there was no equal rights amendment in the state constitution, the Supreme Court of Rhode Island asserted that a lower standard of scrutiny should have been applied to evaluate whether a similar state association rule violated the state constitution.[340] In remanding, the court observed that promoting safety and the preservation of interscholastic competition for males and females were important governmental interests.

Where there are no teams for females in sports that are offered for males only, school officials have three choices: discontinue teams;[341] field separate teams by sex with substantial equality in funding, coaching, officiating and opportunities to play; or permit both sexes to compete for positions on the same teams. Where there is only one team, females have been able to participate in baseball,[342] football,[343] soccer,[344] swimming,[345] tennis,[346] and wrestling.[347]

If schools have two basketball teams, it does not appear to be necessary to allow females to try out for the boys' team.[348] At the same

338. *Yellow Springs Exempted Village School Dist. Bd. of Ed. v. Ohio High School Athletic Ass'n*, 647 F.2d 651 (6th Cir.1981).

339. *Attorney General v. Massachusetts Interscholastic Athletic Ass'n*, 393 N.E.2d 284 (Mass. 1979).

340. *Kleczek v. Rhode Island Interscholastic League*, 612 A.2d 734 [77 Educ. L. Rep. 349] (R.I.1992).

341. Male student athletes have unsuccessfully sought to prevent their teams from being disbanded as institutions seek to comply with Title IX. *See Horner v. Kentucky High School Athletic Ass'n*, 206 F.3d 685 [142 Educ. L. Rep. 728] (6th Cir.2000), *cert. denied*, 531 U.S. 824, 121 S.Ct. 69, 148 L.Ed.2d 34 (2000) (upholding the discontinuation of men's swimming while keep the women's team). *See also, e.g., Harper v. Board of Regents, Ill. State Univ.*, 35 F.Supp.2d 1118 [133 Educ. L. Rep. 89] (C.D.Ill.1999) (involving soccer and wrestling); *Chalenor v. University of N.D.*, 142 F.Supp.2d 1154 [154 Educ. L. Rep. 813] (D.N.D.2000) (involving wrestling); *Miami Univ. Wrestling Club v. Miami Univ.*, 195 F.Supp.2d 1010 [164 Educ. L. Rep. 279] (S.D.Ohio 2001) (involving soccer, tennis, and wrestling); *National Wrestling Coaches Ass'n v. Department of Educ.*, 366 F.3d 930 [187 Educ. L. Rep. 405] (D.C. Cir. 2004), *reh'g and reh'g en banc denied*, 383 F.3d 1047 (D.C. Cir. 2004), *cert. denied*, ___ U.S. ___, 125 S.Ct. 2537, 162 L.Ed.2d 274 (2005) (involving wrestling).

342. *Israel by Israel v. West Virginia Secondary Schools Activities Comm'n*, 388 S.E.2d 480 [58 Educ. L. Rep. 795] (W.Va. 1989) (positing that since baseball and softball are sufficiently different, it was a denial of equal protection to prohibit a female from playing baseball).

343. *Force v. Pierce City R–VI School Dist.*, 570 F.Supp. 1020 [13 Educ. L. Rep. 959] (W.D.Mo.1983); *Lantz by Lantz v. Ambach*, 620 F.Supp. 663 [28 Educ. L. Rep. 783] (S.D.N.Y.1985); *Balsley by Balsley v. North Hunterdon Reg'l School Dist. Bd. of Educ.*, 568 A.2d 895 [58 Educ. L. Rep. 675] (N.J.1990).

344. *Hoover v. Meiklejohn*, 430 F.Supp. 164 (D.Colo.1977); *Libby by Libby v. Illinois High School Ass'n*, 921 F.2d 96 [64 Educ. L. Rep. 708] (7th Cir.1990).

345. *Leffel v. Wisconsin Interscholastic Athletic Ass'n*, 444 F.Supp. 1117 (E.D.Wis. 1978).

346. *Leffel v. Wisconsin Interscholastic Athletic Ass'n*, 444 F.Supp. 1117 (E.D.Wis. 1978).

347. *Saint v. Nebraska School Activities Ass'n*, 684 F.Supp. 626 [46 Educ. L. Rep. 960] (D.Neb.1988).

348. *O'Connor v. Board of Educ. of School Dist. No. 23*, 645 F.2d 578 (7th Cir. 1981), *cert. denied*, 454 U.S. 1084, 102 S.Ct. 641, 70 L.Ed.2d 619 (1981), *on remand*, 545 F.Supp. 376 [6 Educ. L. Rep. 65] (N.D. Ill.1982).

time, courts disagree over whether school officials can permit a female volleyball team and exclude males from participating.[349]

Title IX and its regulations occupy a central role with regard to nondiscrimination in athletic activities. Consistent with their usual approach, and as illustrated by a dispute from Pennsylvania, courts avoid addressing constitutional questions if they can resolve disputes statutorily such as under Title IX.[350] Title IX's goal of gender equity also applies to reductions in options due to financial considerations as well as to additional opportunities for the underrepresented sex.[351]

As might have been expected, courts have reached mixed results over the constitutionality of having different seasons for females and males. The Supreme Court of Minnesota ruled that where limited athletic facilities made it necessary to schedule male and female high school teams in tennis and swimming during separate seasons and neither schedule was substantially better than the other, officials did not violate the females' rights to equal protection.[352] Six years later, the Ninth Circuit affirmed that since it was unnecessary to align the basketball and volleyball seasons with the national norm, school officials in Montana did not violate the equal protection rights of females.[353]

On the other hand, West Virginia's highest court, relying on the Equal Protection Clause of the state constitution, held that having the girls' basketball season scheduled outside of the traditional season was impermissible.[354] Similarly, the Second Circuit affirmed that when two school boards in New York scheduled girls' soccer in the spring, they violated the rights of female student-athletes by preventing them from participating in the state soccer playoffs.[355] The court was of the opinion that the boards were unable to demonstrate either that the disadvantages that the girls' soccer teams faced were offset by comparable advantages to scheduling or that their actions were justified by nondiscriminatory factors. However, in a suit from Michigan, the Sixth Circuit affirmed that the state athletic association's use of differential scheduling of girls' high school sports disadvantaged female student-athletes in

---

349. *Compare Gomes v. Rhode Island Interscholastic League*, 469 F.Supp. 659 (D.R.I.1979), *vacated as moot* [due to the end of the season and the student's graduation], 604 F.2d 733 (1st Cir.1979) (permitting participation in volleyball) with *Clark v. Arizona Interscholastic Ass'n*, 695 F.2d 1126 [8 Educ. L. Rep. 246] (9th Cir.1982), *cert. denied*, 464 U.S. 818, 104 S.Ct. 79, 78 L.Ed.2d 90 (1983) (denying participation in volleyball) and *Kleczek on Behalf of Kleczek v. Rhode Island Interscholastic League*, 768 F.Supp. 951 [69 Educ. L. Rep. 366] (D.R.I. 1991) (denying participation in field hockey).

350. *Williams v. School Dist. of Bethlehem, Pa.*, 998 F.2d 168 [84 Educ. L. Rep. 629] (3d Cir.1993), *cert. denied*, 510 U.S. 1043, 114 S.Ct. 689, 126 L.Ed.2d 656 (1994).

351. *Cohen v. Brown Univ.*, 879 F.Supp. 185 [99 Educ. L. Rep. 149] (D.R.I.1995), *aff'd in part, rev'd in part*, 101 F.3d 155 [114 Educ. L. Rep. 394] (1st Cir.1996), *cert. denied*, 520 U.S. 1186, 117 S.Ct. 1469, 137 L.Ed.2d 682 (1997).

352. *Striebel v. Minnesota State High School League*, 321 N.W.2d 400 [5 Educ. L. Rep. 245] (Minn. 1982).

353. *Ridgeway v. Montana High School Ass'n*, 858 F.2d 579 [49 Educ. L. Rep. 495] (9th Cir. 1988).

354. *State ex rel. Lambert by Lambert v. West Virginia State Bd. of Educ.*, 447 S.E.2d 901 [93 Educ. L. Rep. 1031] (W.Va. 1994).

355. *McCormick v. School Dist. of Mamaroneck*, 370 F.3d 275 [188 Educ. L. Rep. 62] (2d Cir. 2004).

comparison to their male counterparts, in violation of the Equal Protection Clause. On further review, though, the Supreme Court vacated[356] in light of its judgment in *Rancho Palos Verdes v. Abrams*,[357] in which it held that an individual was unable to file suit under section 1983 since the statute at issue provided a remedy.

In a related issue, a federal trial court in Florida ordered a school board to correct discrepancies with regard to equipment and supplies, game and practice time, schedules and locker room facilities in its boys' baseball and girls' softball programs.[358] The court added that Title IX requires school officials to administer athletic programs equitably.

[Case No. 90]   The Amish Exception and Compulsory Education

WISCONSIN v. YODER

Supreme Court of the United States, 1972.
406 U.S. 205, 92 S.Ct. 1526, 32 L.Ed.2d 15.

Mr. Chief Justice Burger delivered the opinion of the Court.

. . .

Respondents Jonas Yoder and Adin Yutzy are members of the Old Order Amish Religion, and respondent Wallace Miller is a member of the Conservative Amish Mennonite Church. They and their families are residents of Green County, Wisconsin. Wisconsin's compulsory school attendance law required them to cause their children to attend public or private school until reaching age 16 but the respondents declined to send their children, ages 14 and 15, to public school after completing the eighth grade. The children were not enrolled in any private school, or within any recognized exception to the compulsory attendance law, and they are conceded to be subject to the Wisconsin statute.

On complaint of the school district administrator for the public schools, respondents were charged, tried, and convicted of violating the compulsory attendance law in Green County Court and were fined the sum of $5 each. . . .

In support of their position, respondents presented as expert witnesses scholars on religion and education whose testimony is uncontradicted. They expressed their opinions on the relationship of the Amish belief concerning school attendance to the more general tenets of their religion, and described the impact that compulsory high school attendance could have on the continued survival of Amish communities as they exist in the United States today. . . .

A related feature of Old Order Amish communities is their devotion to a life in harmony with nature and the soil, as exemplified by the simple life of the early Christian era which continued in America during

---

356. *Michigan High School Athletic Ass'n v. Communities for Equity,* ___ U.S. ___, 125 S.Ct. 1973, 161 L.Ed.2d 845 (2005).

357. 544 U.S. 113, 125 S.Ct. 1453, 161 L.Ed.2d 316 (2005).

358. *Landow v. School Bd. of Brevard County,* 132 F.Supp.2d 958 [151 Educ. L. Rep. 909] (M.D.Fla.2000).

much of our early national life. Amish beliefs require members of the community to make their living by farming or closely related activities. Broadly speaking, the Old Order Amish religion pervades and determines the entire mode of life of its adherents. . . .

Amish objection to formal education beyond the eighth grade is firmly grounded in these central religious concepts. They object to the high school and higher education generally because the values it teaches are in marked variance with Amish values and the Amish way of life; they view secondary school education as an impermissible exposure of their children to a "worldly" influence in conflict with their beliefs. The high school tends to emphasize intellectual and scientific accomplishments, self-distinction, competitiveness, worldly success, and social life with other students. Amish society emphasizes informal learning-through-doing, a life of "goodness," rather than a life of intellect, wisdom, rather than technical knowledge, community welfare rather than competition, and separation, rather than integration with contemporary worldly society. . . .

I

There is no doubt as to the power of a State, having a high responsibility for education of its citizens, to impose reasonable regulations for the control and duration of basic education. Providing public schools ranks at the very apex of the function of a State. Yet even this paramount responsibility was, in *Pierce,* made to yield to the right of parents to provide an equivalent education in a privately operated system. There the Court held that Oregon's statute compelling attendance in a public school from age eight to age 16 unreasonably interfered with the interest of parents in directing the rearing of their offspring including their education in church-operated schools. As that case suggests, the values of parental direction of the religious upbringing and education of their children in their early and formative years have a high place in our society. Thus, a State's interest in universal education, however highly we rank it, is not totally free from a balancing process when it impinges on other fundamental rights and interests, such as those specifically protected by the Free Exercise Clause of the First Amendment and the traditional interest of parents with respect to the religious upbringing of their children so long as they, in the words of *Pierce,* "prepare [them] for additional obligations."

It follows that in order for Wisconsin to compel school attendance beyond the eighth grade against a claim that such attendance interferes with the practice of a legitimate religious belief, it must appear either that the State does not deny the free exercise of religious belief by its requirement, or that there is a state interest of sufficient magnitude to override the interest claiming protection under the Free Exercise Clause. Long before there was general acknowledgment of the need for universal formal education, the Religion Clauses had specifically and firmly fixed the right to free exercise of religious beliefs, and buttressing this fundamental right was an equally firm, even if less explicit, prohibition against the establishment of any religion by government. The values underlying these two provisions relating to religion have been zealously protected, sometimes even at the expense of other interests of admittedly high social importance. The invalidation of financial aid to parochial schools by government grants for a salary subsidy for teachers is but one example of the extent to which courts have gone in this regard, notwithstanding that such aid programs were legislatively determined to be in the public interest and the service of sound educational policy by States and by Congress. . . .

The essence of all that has been said and written on the subject is that only those interests of the highest order and those not otherwise served can overbalance legitimate claims to the free exercise of religion. We can accept it as settled, therefore, that however strong the State's interest in universal compulsory education, it is by no means absolute to the exclusion or subordination of all other interests.

II

We come then to the quality of the claims of the respondents concerning the alleged encroachment of Wisconsin's compulsory school attendance statute on their rights and the rights of their children to the free exercise of the religious beliefs they and their forbears have adhered to for almost three centuries. In evaluating those claims we must be careful to determine whether the Amish religious faith and their mode of life are, as they claim, inseparable and interdependent. A way of life, however virtuous and admirable, may not be interposed as a barrier to reasonable state regulation of education if it is based on purely secular considerations; to have the protection of the Religion Clauses, the claims must be rooted in religious belief. Although a determination of what is a "religious" belief or practice entitled to constitutional protection may present a most delicate question, the very concept of ordered liberty precludes allowing every person to make his own standards on matters of conduct in which society as a whole has important interests. Thus, if the Amish asserted their claims because of their subjective evaluation and rejection of the contemporary secular values accepted by the majority, much as Thoreau rejected the social values of his time and isolated himself at Walden Pond, their claim would not rest on a religious basis. Thoreau's choice was philosophical and personal rather than religious, and such belief does not rise to the demands of the Religion Clause.

Giving no weight to such secular considerations, however, we see that the record in this case abundantly supports the claim that the traditional way of life of the Amish is not merely a matter of personal preference, but one of deep religious conviction, shared by an organized group, and intimately related to daily living. . . .

In sum, the unchallenged testimony of acknowledged experts in education and religious history, almost 300 years of consistent practice, and strong evidence of a sustained faith pervading and regulating respondents' entire mode of life support the claim that enforcement of the State's requirement of compulsory formal education after the eighth grade would gravely endanger if not destroy the free exercise of respondents' religious beliefs.

III

. . .

The State advances two primary arguments in support of its system of compulsory education. It notes, as Thomas Jefferson pointed out early in our history, that some degree of education is necessary to prepare citizens to participate effectively and intelligently in our open political system if we are to preserve freedom and independence. Further, education prepares individuals to be self-reliant and self-sufficient participants in society. We accept these propositions.

However, the evidence adduced by the Amish in this case is persuasively to the effect that an additional one or two years of formal high school for Amish children in place of their long established program of informal vocational education would do little to serve those interests. Respondents' experts testified at trial, without challenge, that the value of all education must be assessed in terms of its capacity to prepare the child for life. It is one thing to say that compulsory education for a year or two beyond the eighth grade may be necessary when its goal is the preparation of the child for life in modern society as the majority live, but it is quite another if the goal of education be viewed as the preparation of the child for life in the separated agrarian community that is the keystone of the Amish faith.

The State attacks respondents' position as one fostering "ignorance" from which the child must be protected by the State. No one can question the State's duty to protect children from ignorance but this argument does not square with the facts disclosed in the record. Whatever their idiosyncrasies as seen by the majority, this record strongly shows that the Amish community has been a highly successful social unit within our society even if apart from the conventional "mainstream." Its members are productive and very law-abiding members of society; they reject public welfare in any of its usual modern forms. The Congress itself recognized their self-sufficiency by authorizing exemption of such groups as the Amish from the obligation to pay social security taxes. . . .

The State, however, supports its interest in providing an additional one or two years of compulsory high school education to Amish children because of the possibility that some such children will choose to leave the Amish community, and that if this occurs they will be ill-equipped for life. The State argues that if Amish children leave their church they should not be in the position of making their way in the world without the education available in the one or two additional years the State requires. However, on this record, that argument is highly speculative. There is no specific evidence of the loss of Amish adherents by attrition, nor is there any showing that upon leaving the Amish community Amish children, with their practical agricultural training and habits of industry and self-reliance, would become burdens on society because of educational shortcomings. Indeed, this argument of the State appears to rest primarily on the State's mistaken assumption, already noted, that the Amish do not provide any education for their children beyond the eighth grade, but allow them to grow in "ignorance." To the contrary, not only do the Amish accept the necessity for formal schooling through the eighth grade level, but continue to provide what has been characterized by the undisputed testimony of expert educators as an "ideal" vocational education for their children in the adolescent years. . . .

The requirement for compulsory education beyond the eighth grade is a relatively recent development in our history. Less than 60 years ago, the educational requirements of almost all of the States were satisfied by completion of the elementary grades, at least where the child was regularly and lawfully employed. The independence and successful social functioning of the Amish community for a period approaching almost three centuries and more than 200 years in this country is strong evidence that there is at best a speculative gain, in terms of meeting the duties of citizenship, from an additional one or two years of compulsory formal education. Against this background it would require a more particularized showing from the State on this point to justify the severe interference with religious freedom such additional compulsory attendance would entail.

We should also note that compulsory education and child labor laws find their historical origin in common humanitarian instincts, and that the age limits of both laws have been coordinated to achieve their related objectives. . . .

IV

. . .

Contrary to the suggestion of the dissenting opinion of Mr. Justice Douglas, our holding today in no degree depends on the assertion of the religious interest of the child as contrasted with that of the parents. It is the parents who are subject to prosecution here for failing to cause their children to attend school, and it is their right of free exercise, not that of their children, that must determine Wisconsin's power to impose criminal penalties on the parent. The dissent argues that a child who expresses a desire to attend public high school in conflict with the wishes of his parent should not be prevented from doing so. There is no reason for the Court to consider that point since it is not an issue in the case. The children are not parties to this litigation. The State has at no point tried this case on the theory that respondents were preventing their children from attending school against their expressed desires, and indeed the record is to the contrary. The State's position from the outset has been that it is empowered to apply its compulsory attendance law to Amish parents in the same manner as to other parents—that is, without regard to the wishes of the child. That is the claim we reject today. . . .

V

For the reasons stated we hold, with the Supreme Court of Wisconsin, that the First and Fourteenth Amendments prevent the State from compelling respondents to cause their children to attend formal high school to age 16. Our disposition of this case, however, in no way alters our recognition of the obvious fact that courts are not school boards or legislatures, and are ill-equipped to determine the "necessity" of discrete aspects of a State's program of compulsory education. This should suggest that courts must move with great circumspection in performing the sensitive and delicate task of weighing a State's legitimate social concern when faced with religious claims for exemption from generally applicable educational requirements. It cannot be over-emphasized that we are not dealing with a way of life and mode of education by a group claiming to have recently discovered some "progressive" or more enlightened process for rearing children for modern life.

Aided by a history of three centuries as an identifiable religious sect and a long history as a successful and self-sufficient segment of American society, the Amish in this case have convincingly demonstrated the sincerity of their religious beliefs, the interrelationship of belief with their mode of life, the vital role which belief and daily conduct play in the continued survival of Old Order Amish communities and their religious organization, and the hazards presented by the State's enforcement of a statute generally valid as to others. Beyond this, they have carried the even more difficult burden of demonstrating the adequacy of their alternative mode of continuing informal vocational education in terms of precisely those overall interests that the State advances in support of its program of compulsory high school education. In light of this convincing showing, one which probably few other religious groups or sects could make, and weighing the minimal difference between what the State would require and what the Amish already accept, it was incumbent on the State to show with more particularity how its admittedly strong interest in compulsory education would be adversely affected by granting an exemption to the Amish.

Nothing we hold is intended to undermine the general applicability of the State's compulsory school attendance statutes or to limit the power of the State to promulgate reasonable standards that, while not impairing the free exercise of religion, provide for continuing agricultural vocational education under parental and church guidance by the Old Order Amish or others similarly situated. The States have had a long history of amicable and effective relationships with church-sponsored schools, and there is no basis for assuming that, in this related context, reasonable standards cannot be established concerning the content of the continuing vocational education of Amish children under parental guidance, provided always that state regulations are not inconsistent with what we have said in this opinion.

Affirmed.

Notes

1. The Court noted that the Amish faith pervaded and directed the entire lives of its believers, whom it also described as productive and law-abiding citizens. Might the Court have reached the same result if the religion was less pervasive and/or if its members created social problems?

2. Would the Court have reached the same result in *Yoder* today? Consider your answer in light of *Employment Div., Dep't of Human Res. of Or. v. Smith*, 494 U.S. 872, 886, n. 3, 110 S.Ct. 1595, 108 L.Ed.2d 876 (1990) where, in

upholding the dismissal of two Native American drug counselors for ingesting peyote as part of a religious ritual on the basis the Court ruled that "generally applicable, religion-neutral laws that have the effect of burdening a particular religious practice need not be justified by a compelling government interest."

3. Justice Douglas expressed concern that no one asked the children whether they wished to maintain the Amish lifestyle of their parents. In light of this, what can, or should, be done to accommodate the wishes of students under these circumstances? Should children who do not wish to follow the lifestyles of their parents be emancipated? If so, who should pay for the living costs of such emancipated minors?

4. Although home schooling proponents often cite *Yoder* for support, the courts are unreceptive. For example, in *Johnson v. Charles City Community Schools Bd. of Educ.*, 368 N.W.2d 74 [25 Educ. L. Rep. 524] (Iowa 1985), *cert. denied sub nom. Pruessner v. Benton*, 474 U.S. 1033, 106 S.Ct. 594, 88 L.Ed.2d 574 [29 Educ. L. Rep. 493] (1985), the Supreme Court of Iowa rejected a home schooling advocate's reliance on *Yoder*. The court noted that unlike the Amish, who have preserved their way of life for hundreds of years, the plaintiffs operated a home school for only five years by the time it heard the case.

[Case No. 91] Compulsory Education, Parental Rights, and Non–Public Schools

PIERCE v. SOCIETY OF THE SISTERS OF THE HOLY NAMES OF JESUS AND MARY

Supreme Court of the United States, 1925.
268 U.S. 510, 45 S.Ct. 571, 69 L.Ed. 1070.

MR. JUSTICE MCREYNOLDS delivered the opinion of the Court.

These appeals are from decrees, based upon undenied allegations, which granted preliminary orders restraining appellants from threatening or attempting to enforce the Compulsory Education Act ... under the initiative provision of her Constitution by the voters of Oregon. They present the same points of law; there are no controverted questions of fact. Rights said to be guaranteed by the federal Constitution were specially set up, and appropriate prayers asked for their protection.

The challenged act ... requires every parent, guardian, or other person having control or charge or custody of a child between 8 and 16 years to send him "to a public school for the period of time a public school shall be held during the current year" in the district where the child resides; and failure so to do is declared a misdemeanor. There are exemptions—not specially important here—for children who are not normal, or who have completed the eighth grade, or whose parents or private teachers reside at considerable distances from any public school, or who hold special permits from the county superintendent. The manifest purpose is to compel general attendance at public schools by normal children ... who have not completed the eight grade. And without doubt enforcement of the statute would seriously impair, perhaps destroy, the profitable features of appellees' business and greatly diminish the value of their property.

Appellee the Society of Sisters is an Oregon corporation, organized in 1880, with power to care for orphans, educate and instruct the youth, establish and maintain academies or schools, and acquire necessary real and personal property. It has long devoted its property and effort to the secular and religious education and care of children, and has acquired the valuable good will of many parents and guardians. It conducts interdependent primary and high schools and junior colleges, and maintains orphanages for the custody and control of children between 8 and 16. In its primary schools many children between those ages are taught the subjects usually pursued in Oregon public schools during the first eight years. Systematic religious instruction and moral training according to the tenets of the Roman Catholic Church are also regularly provided. All courses of study, both temporal and religious, contemplate continuity of training under appellee's charge; the primary schools are essential to the system and the most profitable. It owns valuable buildings, especially constructed and equipped for school purposes. The business is remunerative—the annual income from primary schools exceeds $30,000—and the successful conduct of this requires long time contracts with teachers and parents. The Compulsory Education Act of 1922 has already caused the withdrawal from its schools of children who would otherwise continue, and their income has steadily declined. The appellants, public officers, have proclaimed their purpose strictly to enforce the statute.

After setting out the above facts, the Society's bill alleges that the enactment conflicts with the right of parents to choose schools where their children will receive appropriate mental and religious training, the right of the child to influence the parents' choice of a school, the right of schools and teachers therein to engage in a useful business or profession, and is accordingly repugnant to the Constitution and void. And, further, that unless enforcement of the measure is enjoined the corporation's business and property will suffer irreparable injury.

Appellee Hill Military Academy is a private corporation organized in 1908 under the laws of Oregon, engaged in owning, operating, and conducting for profit an elementary, college preparatory, and military training school for boys between the ages of 5 and 21 years. The average attendance is 100, and the annual fees received for each student amount to some $800. The elementary department is divided into eight grades, as in the public schools; the college preparatory department has four grades, similar to those of the public high schools; the courses of study conform to the requirements of the state board of education.... The business and incident good will are very valuable. In order to conduct its affairs, long time contracts must be made for supplies, equipment, teachers, and pupils. Appellants, law officers of the state and county, have publicly announced that the Act ... is valid and have declared their intention to enforce it. By reason of the statute and threat of enforcement appellee's business is being destroyed and its property depreciated; parents and guardians are refusing to make contracts for the future instruction of their sons, and some are being withdrawn.

The Academy's bill states the foregoing facts and then alleges that the challenged act contravenes the corporation's rights guaranteed by the Fourteenth Amendment and that unless appellants are restrained from proclaiming its validity and threatening to enforce it irreparable injury will result. The prayer is for an appropriate injunction.

No answer was interposed in either cause, and after proper notices they were heard by three judges on motions for preliminary injunctions upon the specifically alleged facts. The court ruled that the Fourteenth Amendment guaranteed appellees against the deprivation of their property without due process of law consequent upon the unlawful interference by appellants with the free choice of patrons, present and prospective. It declared the right to conduct schools was property and that parents and guardians, as a part of their liberty, might direct the education of children by selecting reputable teachers and places. Also, that appellees' schools were not unfit or harmful to the public, and that enforcement of the challenged statute would unlawfully deprive them of patronage and thereby destroy appellees' business and property. Finally, that the threats to enforce the act would continue to cause irreparable injury; and the suits were not premature.

No question is raised concerning the power of the state reasonably to regulate all schools, to inspect, supervise and examine them, their teachers and pupils; to require that all children of proper age attend some school, that teachers shall be of good moral character and patriotic disposition, that certain studies plainly essential to good citizenship must be taught, and that nothing be taught which is manifestly inimical to the public welfare.

The inevitable practical result of enforcing the act under consideration would be destruction of appellees' primary schools, and perhaps all other private primary schools for normal children within the state of Oregon. Appellees are engaged in a kind of undertaking not inherently harmful, but long regarded as useful and meritorious. Certainly there is nothing in the present records to indicate that they have failed to discharge their obligations to patrons, students, or the state. And there are no peculiar circumstances or present emergencies which demand extraordinary measures relative to primary education.

Under the doctrine of *Meyer v. Nebraska*, we think it entirely plain that the Act of 1922 unreasonably interferes with the liberty of parents and guardians to direct the upbringing and education of children under their control. As often heretofore pointed out, rights guaranteed by the Constitution may not be abridged by legislation which has no reasonable relation to some purpose within the competency of the state. The fundamental theory of liberty upon which all governments in this Union repose excludes any general power of the state to standardize its children by forcing them to accept instruction from public teachers only. The child is not the mere creature of the state; those who nurture him and direct his destiny have the right, coupled with the high duty, to recognize and prepare him for additional obligations.

Appellees are corporations, and therefore, it is said, they cannot claim for themselves the liberty which the Fourteenth Amendment guarantees. Accepted in the proper sense, this is true. But they have business and property for which they claim protection. These are threatened with destruction through the unwarranted compulsion which appellants are exercising over present and prospective patrons of their schools. And this court has gone very far to protect against loss threatened by such action....

Generally, it is entirely true, as urged by counsel, that no person in any business has such an interest in possible customers as to enable him to restrain exercise of proper power of the state upon the ground that he will be deprived of patronage. But the injunctions here sought are not against the exercise of any proper power. Appellees asked protection against arbitrary, unreasonable, and unlawful interference with their patrons and the consequent destruction of their business and property....

The suits were not premature. The injury to appellees was present and very real, not a mere possibility in the remote future. If no relief had been possible prior to the effective date of the act, the injury would have become irreparable. Prevention of impending injury by unlawful action is a well-recognized function of courts of equity.

The decrees below are affirmed.

Notes

1. *Pierce* has been described as a kind of Magna Carta for non-public schools. Is this an accurate description?

2. Following *Pierce*, state level public school officials have granted great deference to educational leaders in religiously-affiliated non-public schools when it comes to curricular decision-making. Should state officials exercise greater control over curriculum-related matters in non-public schools?

[Case No. 92] Constitutionality of Compulsory Education Statute

STATE v. POPANZ

Supreme Court of Wisconsin, 1983.
332 N.W.2d 750 [10 Educ. L. Rep. 789].

ABRAHAMSON, JUSTICE. This is an appeal from a judgment of conviction of ... Lawrence C. Popanz on two counts of violating Wisconsin's compulsory school attendance law, [which] requires a person having control of a child who is between the ages of 6 and 18 years to cause the child to attend public or private school regularly....

The issue presented on certification is whether the phrase "private school" as used in sec. 118.15(1)(a) is impermissibly vague and sec. 118.15(1)(a) as applied to prosecutions involving "private schools" violates the fourteenth amendment to the United States Constitution and art. I, sec. 8, of the Wisconsin constitution....

There is no simple litmus-paper test to determine whether a criminal statute is void for vagueness. The principles underlying the void for vagueness doctrine ... stem from concepts of procedural due process. Due process requires that the law set forth fair notice of the conduct prohibited or required and proper standards for enforcement of the law and adjudication. . . .

A criminal statute must be sufficiently definite to give a person of ordinary intelligence who seeks to avoid its penalties fair notice of conduct required or prohibited. "Vague laws may trap the innocent by not providing fair warning."

A criminal statute must also provide standards for those who enforce the laws and those who adjudicate guilt. A statute should be sufficiently definite to allow law enforcement officers, judges, and juries to apply the terms of the law objectively to a defendant's conduct in order to determine guilt without having to create or apply their own standards. The danger posed by a vague law is that officials charged with enforcing the law may apply it arbitrarily or the law may be so unclear that a trial court cannot properly instruct the jury as to the applicable law. . . .

Like this defendant, we have searched the statutes, administrative rules and regulations and official Department of Public Instruction writings for a definition of "private school" or criteria which an entity must meet to be classified as a "private school" for purposes of sec. 118.15(1)(a). We have found neither a definition nor prescribed criteria. Nor does the phrase "private school" have a well-settled meaning in common parlance or in decisions of this court which could be used for purposes of applying sec. 118.15(1)(a). We therefore decline to adopt the definition of "private school" proposed by the court of appeals or by the State Superintendent of Public Instruction in an amicus brief. . . .

We are not convinced that these definitions are the only ones a citizen, an administrator, or a court using dictionary definitions, court decisions and the statutes could deduce. In any event the legislature or its delegated agent should define the phrase "private school"; citizens or the courts should not have to guess at its meaning.

Since there is no definition of "private school," as that term is used in sec. 118.15(1)(a), the determination of what constitutes a "private school" apparently rests solely in the discretion of the school attendance officer of the district. . . . The record shows that in this school district a person seeking to comply with sec. 118.15(1)(a) apparently must consult the district school administrator to find out what that administrator considers a "private school" and must comply with the procedure set forth by that particular administrator to have a school classified as a private school. . . .

The lack of definition of "private school" delegates the basic policy matter, the determination of whether or not children are attending a private school, to local school officials whose decisions may rest on *ad hoc* and subjective standards. Sec. 118.15(1)(a) thus poses the danger of arbitrary and discriminatory enforcement, contrary to the basic values underlying the principles of due process.

The persons who must obey the law should not have to guess at what the phrase "private school" means. They should have some objective standards to guide them in their attempts to "steer between lawful and unlawful conduct." Furthermore, standards cannot lie only in the minds of persons whose duty it is to enforce the laws. We must conclude that the statute fails to provide fair notice to those who would seek to obey it and also lacks sufficient standards for proper enforcement.

The Department of Public Instruction, recognizing that there are no standards for determining what constitutes a "private school" under sec. 118.15(1)(a), suggests that the school attendance officer file a charge under that section if he or she "felt the attendance was not at a 'private school,'" leaving the final determination of what constitutes a "private school" to the courts.... We do not think that sec. 118.15(1)(a) or any other statutes or any rules equip the courts to define "private school" or to instruct a jury on what constitutes a private school. Defining the contours of laws subjecting a violator to criminal penalty is a legislative, not a judicial, function. The legislature, not the courts, should clarify sec. 118.15(1)(a).

We hold that sec. 118.15(1)(a) is void for vagueness insofar as it fails to define "private school." The court of appeals' decision in *State v. White* ... is hereby overruled....

Judgment of the circuit court reversed; cause remanded with directions to dismiss the complaint.

Notes

1. The court refused to approve a definition of "private school" despite requests from the state department of education in an amicus brief and the intermediate appellate court.

2. Did the court exercise appropriate judicial restraint or fail to apply judicial leadership?

[Case No. 93] Educational Rights on Non–Documented Children

PLYLER v. DOE ET AL.

Supreme Court of the United States, 1982.
457 U.S. 202, 102 S.Ct. 2382, 72 L.Ed.2d 786 [4 Educ. L. Rep. 953].

JUSTICE BRENNAN delivered the opinion of the Court.

The question presented by these cases is whether, consistent with the Equal Protection Clause of the Fourteenth Amendment, Texas may deny to undocumented school-age children the free public education that it provides to children who are citizens of the United States or legally admitted aliens.

I

. . .

In May 1975, the Texas Legislature revised its education laws to withhold from local school districts any state funds for the education of children who were not "legally admitted" into the United States. The 1975 revision also authorized local school districts to deny enrollment in their public schools to children not "legally admitted" to the country. These cases involve constitutional challenges to those provisions.

No. 80–1538

Plyler v. Doe

This is a class action, filed in the United States District Court for the Eastern District of Texas in September 1977, on behalf of certain school-age children of Mexican origin residing in Smith County, Tex., who could not establish that they had been legally admitted into the United States. The action complained of the exclusion of plaintiff children from the public schools of the Tyler Independent School District. The Superintendent and members of the Board of Trustees of the School District were named as defendants; the State of Texas intervened as a party-defendant. After certifying a class consisting of all undocumented school-age children of Mexican origin residing within the School District, the District Court preliminarily enjoined defendants from denying a free education to members of the plaintiff class. In December 1977, the court conducted an extensive hearing on plaintiffs' motion for permanent injunctive relief.

In considering this motion, the District Court made extensive findings of fact. The court found that neither § 21.031 nor the School District policy implementing it had "either the purpose or effect of keeping illegal aliens out of the State of Texas." Respecting defendants' further claim that § 21.031 was simply a financial measure designed to avoid a drain on the State's fisc, the court recognized that the increases in population resulting from the immigration of Mexican nationals into the United States had created problems for the public schools of the State, and that these problems were exacerbated by the special educational needs of immigrant Mexican children. The court noted, however, that the increase in school enrollment was primarily attributable to the admission of children who were legal residents. It also found that while the "exclusion of all undocumented children from the public schools in Texas would eventually result in economies at some level," funding from both the State and Federal Governments was based primarily on the number of children enrolled. In net effect then, barring undocumented children from the schools would save money, but it would "not necessarily" improve "the quality of education." The court further observed that the impact of § 21.031 was borne primarily by a very small subclass of illegal aliens, "entire families who have migrated illegally and—for all practical purposes—permanently to the United States." Finally, the court noted that under current laws and practices "the illegal alien of today may well be the legal alien of tomorrow," and that without an education, these undocumented children, "[a]lready disadvantaged as a result of poverty, lack of English-speaking ability, and undeniable racial prejudices, ... will become permanently locked into the lowest socio-economic class."

The District Court held that illegal aliens were entitled to the protection of the Equal Protection Clause of the Fourteenth Amendment, and that § 21.031 violated that Clause. Suggesting that "the state's exclusion of undocumented children from its public schools ... may well be the type of invidiously motivated state action for which the suspect classification doctrine was designed," the court held that it was unnecessary to decide whether the statute would survive a "strict scrutiny" analysis because, in any event, the discrimination embodied in the statute was not supported by a rational basis. The District Court also concluded that the Texas statute violated the Supremacy Clause.

The Court of Appeals for the Fifth Circuit upheld the District Court's injunction. The Court of Appeals held that the District Court had erred in finding the Texas statute pre-empted by federal law. With respect to equal protection, however, the Court of Appeals affirmed in all essential respects the analysis of the District Court, concluding that 21.031 was "constitutionally infirm regardless of whether it was tested using the mere rational basis standard or some more stringent test." We noted probable jurisdiction.

No. 80–1934

In re Alien Children Education Litigation

During 1978 and 1979, suits challenging the constitutionality of § 21.031 and various local practices undertaken on the authority of that provision were filed in the United States District Courts for the Southern, Western, and Northern Districts of Texas. Each suit named the State of Texas and the Texas Education Agency as defendants, along with local officials. In November 1979, the Judicial Panel on Multidistrict Litigation, on motion of the State, consolidated the claims against the state officials into a single action to be heard in the District Court for the Southern District of Texas. A hearing was conducted in February and March 1980. In July 1980, the court entered an opinion and order holding that § 21.031 violated the Equal Protection Clause of the Fourteenth Amendment. The court held that "the absolute deprivation of education should trigger strict judicial scrutiny, particularly when the absolute deprivation is the result of complete inability to pay for the desired benefit." The court determined that the State's concern for fiscal integrity was not a compelling state interest, that exclusion of these children had not been shown to be necessary to improve education within the State, and that the educational needs of the children statutorily excluded were not different from the needs of children not excluded. The court therefore concluded that § 21.031 was not carefully tailored to advance the asserted state interest in an acceptable manner. While appeal of the District Court's decision was pending, the Court of Appeals rendered its decision in No. 80–1538. Apparently on the strength of that opinion, the Court of Appeals ... summarily affirmed the decision of the Southern District. We noted probable jurisdiction and consolidated this case with No. 80–1538 for briefing and argument.

II

The Fourteenth Amendment provides that "[n]o State shall ... deprive any person of life, liberty, or property, without due process of law; nor deny to *any person within its jurisdiction* the equal protection of the laws." (Emphasis added.) Appellants argue at the outset that undocumented aliens, because of their immigration status, are not "persons within the jurisdiction" of the State of Texas, and that they therefore have no right to the equal protection of Texas law. We reject this argument. Whatever his status under the immigration laws, an alien is surely a "person" in any ordinary sense of that term. Aliens, even aliens whose presence in this country is unlawful, have long been recognized as "persons" guaranteed due process of law by the Fifth and Fourteenth Amendments. Indeed, we have clearly held that the Fifth Amendment protects aliens whose presence in this country is unlawful from invidious discrimination by the Federal Government.

Appellants seek to distinguish our prior cases, emphasizing that the Equal Protection Clause directs a State to afford its protection to persons *within its jurisdiction* while the Due Process Clauses of the Fifth and Fourteenth Amendments contain no such assertedly limiting phrase. In appellants' view, persons who have entered the United States illegally are not "within the jurisdiction" of a State even if they are present within a State's boundaries and subject to its laws. Neither our cases nor the logic of the Fourteenth Amendment supports that constricting construction of the phrase "within its jurisdiction." We have never suggested that the class of persons who might avail themselves of the equal protection guarantee is less than coextensive with that entitled to due process. To the contrary, we have recognized that both provisions were fashioned to protect an identical class of persons, and to reach every exercise of state authority.

In concluding that "all persons within the territory of the United States," including aliens unlawfully present, may invoke the Fifth and Sixth Amendments to challenge actions of the Federal Government, we reasoned from the understanding that the Fourteenth Amendment was designed to afford its protection to all within the boundaries of a State. Our cases applying the Equal Protection Clause reflect the same territorial theme ...

There is simply no support for appellants' suggestion that "due process" is somehow of greater stature than "equal protection" and therefore available to a larger class of persons. To the contrary, each aspect of the Fourteenth Amendment reflects an elementary limitation on state power. To permit a State to employ the phrase "within its jurisdiction" in order to identify subclasses of persons whom it would define as beyond its jurisdiction, thereby relieving itself of the obligation to assure that its laws are designed and applied equally to those persons, would undermine the principal purpose for which the Equal Protection Clause was incorporated in the Fourteenth Amendment. The Equal Protection Clause was intended to work nothing less than the abolition of all caste-based and invidious class-based legislation. That objective is fundamentally at odds with the power the State asserts here to classify persons subject to its laws as nonetheless excepted from its protection.

Although the congressional debate concerning § 1 of the Fourteenth Amendment was limited, that debate clearly confirms the understanding that the phrase "within its jurisdiction" was intended in a broad sense to offer the guarantee of equal protection to all within a State's boundaries, and to all upon whom the State would impose the obligations of its laws. Indeed, it appears from those debates that Congress, by using the phrase "person within its jurisdiction," sought expressly to ensure that the equal protection of the laws was provided to the alien population. . . .

Use of the phrase "within its jurisdiction" thus does not detract from, but rather confirms, the understanding that the protection of the Fourteenth Amendment extends to anyone, citizen or stranger, who *is* subject to the laws of a State, and reaches into every corner of a State's territory. That a person's initial entry into a State, or into the United States, was unlawful, and that he may for that reason be expelled, cannot negate the simple fact of his presence within the State's territorial perimeter. Given such presence, he is subject to the full range of obligations imposed by the State's civil and criminal laws. And until he leaves the jurisdiction—either voluntarily, or involuntarily in accordance with the Constitution and laws of the United States—he is entitled to the equal protection of the laws that a State may choose to establish.

Our conclusion that the illegal aliens who are plaintiffs in these cases may claim the benefit of the Fourteenth Amendment's guarantee of equal protection only begins the inquiry. The more difficult question is whether the Equal Protection Clause has been violated by the refusal of the State of Texas to reimburse local school boards for the education of children who cannot demonstrate that their presence within the United States is lawful, or by the imposition by those school boards of the burden of tuition on those children. It is to this question that we now turn.

III

The Equal Protection Clause directs that "all persons similarly circumstanced shall be treated alike." But so too, "[t]he Constitution does not require things which are different in fact or opinion to be treated in law as though they were the same." The initial discretion to determine what is "different" and what is "the same" resides in the legislatures of the States. A legislature must have substantial latitude to establish classifications that roughly approximate the nature of the problem perceived, that accommodate competing concerns both public and private, and that account for limitations on the practical ability of the State to remedy every ill. In applying the Equal Protection Clause to most forms of state action, we thus seek only the assurance that the classification at issue bears some fair relationship to a legitimate public purpose.

But we would not be faithful to our obligations under the Fourteenth Amendment if we applied so deferential a standard to every classification. The Equal Protection Clause was intended as a restriction on state legislative action inconsistent with elemental constitutional premises. Thus we have treated as presumptively invidious those classifications that disadvantage a "suspect class," or that impinge upon the exercise of a "fundamental right." With respect to such classifications, it is appropriate to enforce the mandate of equal protection by requiring the State to demonstrate that its classification has been precisely tailored to serve a compelling governmental interest. In addition, we have recognized that certain forms of legislative classification, while not facially invidious, nonetheless give rise to recurring constitutional difficulties; in these limited circumstances we have sought the assurance that the classification reflects a reasoned judgment consistent with the ideal of equal protection by inquiring whether it may fairly be viewed as furthering a substantial interest of the State. We turn to a consideration of the standard appropriate for the evaluation of § 21.031.

A

Sheer incapability or lax enforcement of the laws barring entry into this country, coupled with the failure to establish an effective bar to the employment of undocumented aliens, has resulted in the creation of a substantial "shadow population" of illegal migrants—numbering in the millions—within our borders. This situation raises the specter of a permanent caste of undocumented resident aliens, encouraged by some to remain here as a source of cheap labor, but nevertheless denied the benefits that our society makes available to citizens and lawful residents. The existence of such an underclass presents most difficult problems for a Nation that prides itself on adherence to principles of equality under law.

The children who are plaintiffs in these cases are special members of this underclass. Persuasive arguments support the view that a State may withhold its beneficence from those whose very presence within the United States is the product of their own unlawful conduct. These arguments do not apply with the same force to classifications imposing disabilities on the minor children of such illegal entrants. At the least, those who elect to enter our territory by stealth and in violation of our law should be prepared to bear the consequences, including, but not limited to, deportation. But the children of those illegal entrants are not comparably situated. Their "parents have the ability to conform their conduct to societal norms," and presumably the ability to remove themselves from the State's jurisdiction; but the children who are plaintiffs in these cases "can affect neither their parents' conduct nor their own status." Even if the State found it expedient to control the conduct of adults by acting against their children, legislation directing the onus of a parent's misconduct against his children does not comport with fundamental conceptions of justice. . . .

Of course, undocumented status is not irrelevant to any proper legislative goal. Nor is undocumented status an absolutely immutable characteristic since it is the product of conscious, indeed unlawful, action. But § 21.031 is directed against children, and imposes its discriminatory burden on the basis of a legal characteristic over which children can have little control. It is thus difficult to conceive of a rational justification for penalizing these children for their presence within the United States. Yet that appears to be precisely the effect of § 21.031.

Public education is not a "right" granted to individuals by the Constitution. But neither is it merely some governmental "benefit" indistinguishable from other forms of social welfare legislation. Both the importance of education in maintaining our basic institutions, and the lasting impact of its deprivation on the life of the child, mark the distinction. The "American people have always regarded education and [the] acquisition of knowledge as matters of supreme importance." We have recognized "the public schools as a most vital civic institution for the preservation of a democratic system of government" and as the primary vehicle for transmitting "the values on which our society rests." "[A]s . . . pointed out early in our history, . . . some degree of education is necessary to prepare citizens to participate effectively and intelligently in our open political system if we are to preserve freedom and independence." And these historic "perceptions of the public schools as inculcating fundamental values necessary to the maintenance of a democratic political system have been confirmed by the observations of social scientists." In addition, education provides the basic tools by which individuals might lead economically productive lives to the benefit of us all. In sum, education has a fundamental role in maintaining the fabric of our society. We cannot ignore the significant social costs borne by our Nation when select groups are denied the means to absorb the values and skills upon which our social order rests.

In addition to the pivotal role of education in sustaining our political and cultural heritage, denial of education to some isolated group of children poses an affront to one of the goals of the Equal Protection Clause: the abolition of governmental barriers presenting unreasonable obstacles to advancement on the basis of individual merit. Paradoxically, by depriving the children of any disfavored group of an education, we foreclose the means by which that group might raise the level of esteem in which it is held by the majority. But more directly, "education prepares individuals to be self-reliant and self-sufficient participants in society." Illiteracy is an enduring disability. The inability to read and write will handicap the individual deprived of a basic education each and every day of his life. The inestimable toll of that deprivation on the social economic, intellectual, and psychological well-being of the individual, and the obstacle it poses to individual achievement, make it most difficult to reconcile the cost or the principle of a status-based denial of basic education with the framework of equality embodied in the Equal Protection Clause. . . .

B

These well-settled principles allow us to determine the proper level of deference to be afforded § 21.031. Undocumented aliens cannot be treated as a suspect class because their presence in this country in violation of federal law is not a "constitutional irrelevancy." Nor is education a fundamental right; a State need not justify by compelling necessity every variation in the manner in which education is provided to its population. But more is involved in these cases than the abstract question whether § 21.031 discriminates against a suspect class, or whether education is a fundamental right. Section 21.031 imposes a lifetime hardship on a discrete class of children not accountable for their disabling status. The stigma of illiteracy will mark them for the rest of their lives. By denying these children a basic education, we deny them the ability to live within the structure of our civic institutions, and foreclose any realistic possibility that they will contribute in even the smallest way to the progress of our Nation. In determining the rationality of § 21.031, we may appropriately take into account its costs to the Nation and to the innocent children who are its victims. In light of these countervailing costs, the discrimination contained in § 21.031 can hardly be considered rational unless it furthers some substantial goal of the State.

IV

It is the State's principal argument, and apparently the view of the dissenting Justices, that the undocumented status of these children *vel non* establishes a sufficient rational basis for denying them benefits that a State might choose to afford other residents. The State notes that while other aliens are admitted "on an equality of legal privileges with all citizens under non-discriminatory laws," the asserted right of these children to an education can claim no implicit congressional imprimatur. Indeed, in the State's view, Congress' apparent disapproval of the presence of these children within the United States, and the evasion of the federal regulatory program that is the mark of undocumented status, provides authority for its decision to impose upon them special disabilities. Faced with an equal protection challenge respecting the treatment of aliens, we agree that the courts must be attentive to congressional policy; the exercise of congressional power might well affect the State's prerogatives to afford differential treatment to a particular class of aliens. But we are unable to find in the congressional immigration scheme any statement of policy that might weigh significantly in arriving at an equal protection balance concerning the State's authority to deprive these children of an education.

The Constitution grants Congress the power to "establish an uniform Rule of Naturalization." Drawing upon this power, upon its plenary authority with respect to foreign relations and international commerce, and upon the inherent power of a sovereign to close its borders, Congress has developed a complex scheme governing admission to our Nation and status within our borders. The obvious need for delicate policy judgments has counseled the Judicial Branch to avoid intrusion into this field. But this traditional caution does not persuade us that unusual deference must be shown the classification embodied in § 21.031. The States enjoy no power with respect to the classification of aliens. This power is "committed to the political branches of the Federal Government." Although it is "a routine and normally legitimate part" of the business of the Federal Government to classify on the basis of alien status and to "take into account the character of the relationship between the alien and this country," only rarely are such matters relevant to legislation by a State....

To be sure, like all persons who have entered the United States unlawfully, these children are subject to deportation. But there is no assurance that a child subject to deportation will ever be deported. An illegal entrant might be granted federal permission to continue to reside in this country, or even to become a citizen. In light of the discretionary federal power to grant relief from deportation, a State cannot realistically determine that any particular undocumented child will in fact be deported until after deportation proceedings have been completed. It would of course be most difficult for the State to justify a denial of education to a child enjoying an inchoate federal permission to remain.

We are reluctant to impute to Congress the intention to withhold from these children, for so long as they are present in this country through no fault of their own, access to a basic education. In other contexts, undocumented status, coupled with some articulable federal policy, might enhance state authority with respect to the treatment of undocumented aliens. But in the area of special constitutional sensitivity presented by these cases, and in the absence of any contrary indication fairly discernible in the present legislative record, we perceive no national policy that supports the State in denying these children an elementary education. The State may borrow the federal classification. But to justify its use as a criterion for its own discriminatory policy, the State must demonstrate that the classification is reasonably adapted to "the purposes for which the state desires to use it." We therefore turn to the state objectives that are said to support § 21.031.

V

Appellants argue that the classification at issue furthers an interest in the "preservation of the state's limited resources for the education of its lawful residents." Brief for Appellants 26. Of course, a concern for the preservation of resources standing alone can hardly justify the classification used in allocating those resources. The State must do more than justify its classification with a concise expression of an intention to discriminate. Apart from the asserted state prerogative to act against undocumented children solely on the basis of their undocumented status—an asserted prerogative that carries only minimal force in the circumstances of these cases—we discern three colorable state interests that might support § 21.031.

First, appellants appear to suggest that the State may seek to protect itself from an influx of illegal immigrants. While a State might have an interest in mitigating the potentially harsh economic effects of sudden shifts in population, § 21.031 hardly offers an effective method of dealing with an urgent demographic or economic problem. There is no evidence in the record suggesting that illegal entrants impose any significant burden on the State's economy. To the contrary, the available evidence suggests that illegal aliens underutilize public services, while contributing their labor to the local economy and tax money to the state fisc. The dominant incentive for illegal entry into the State of Texas is the availability of employment; few if any illegal immigrants come to this country, or presumably to the State of Texas, in order to avail themselves of a free education. Thus, even making the doubtful assumption that the net impact of illegal aliens on the economy of the State is negative, we think it clear that "[c]harging tuition to undocumented children constitutes a ludicrously ineffectual attempt to stem the tide of illegal immigration," at least when compared with the alternative of prohibiting the employment of illegal aliens.

Second, while it is apparent that a State may "not ... reduce expenditures for education by barring [some arbitrarily chosen class of] children from its schools," appellants suggest that undocumented children are appropriately singled out for exclusion because of the special burdens they impose on the State's ability to provide high-quality public education. But the record in no way supports the claim that exclusion of undocumented children is likely to improve the overall quality of education in the State. As the District Court in No. 80–1934 noted, the State failed to offer any "credible supporting evidence that a proportionately small diminution of the funds spent on each child [which might result from devoting some state funds to the education of the excluded group] will have a grave impact on the quality of education." And, after reviewing the State's school financing mechanism, the District Court in No. 80–1538 concluded that barring undocumented children from local schools would not necessarily improve the quality of education provided in those schools. Of course, even if improvement in the quality of education were a likely result of barring some *number* of children from the schools of the State, the State must support its selection of *this* group as the appropriate target for exclusion. In terms of educational cost and need, however, undocumented children are "basically indistinguishable" from legally resident alien children.

Finally, appellants suggest that undocumented children are appropriately singled out because their unlawful presence within the United States renders them less likely than other children to remain within the boundaries of the State, and to put their education to productive social or political use within the State. Even assuming that such an interest is legitimate, it is an interest that is most difficult to quantify. The State has no assurance that any child, citizen or not, will employ the education provided by the State within the confines of the State's borders. In any event, the record is clear that many of the undocumented children disabled by this classification will remain in this country indefinitely, and that some will become lawful residents or citizens of the United States. It is difficult to understand precisely what the State hopes to achieve by promoting the creation and perpetuation of a subclass of illiterates within our boundaries, surely adding to the problems and costs of unemployment, welfare, and crime. It is thus clear that whatever savings might be achieved by denying these children an education, they are wholly insubstantial in light of the costs involved to these children, the State, and the Nation.

VI

If the State is to deny a discrete group of innocent children the free public education that it offers to other children residing within its borders, that denial must be justified by a showing that it furthers some substantial state interest. No such showing was made here. Accordingly, the judgment of the Court of Appeals in each of these cases is

Affirmed.

Notes

1. What do you think about the Court's position that the parents of the students at issue already paid taxes in a variety of forms? Is this sound judicial reasoning?

2. In light of issues surrounding immigration, do you think that the Court would reach the same result today?

[Case No. 94] Constitutionality of Residence Requirement for Tuition–Free Admission to Public Schools

MARTINEZ v. BYNUM

Supreme Court of the United States, 1983.
461 U.S. 321, 103 S.Ct. 1838, 75 L.Ed.2d 879 [10 Educ. L. Rep. 11].

JUSTICE POWELL delivered the opinion of the Court.

This case involves a facial challenge to the constitutionality of the Texas residency requirement governing minors who wish to attend public free schools while living apart from their parents or guardians.

I

Roberto Morales was born in 1969 in McAllen, Texas, and is thus a United States citizen by birth. His parents are Mexican citizens who reside in Reynosa, Mexico. He left Reynosa in 1977 and returned to McAllen to live with his sister, petitioner Oralia Martinez, for the primary purpose of attending school in the McAllen Independent School District. Although Martinez is now Morales's custodian, she is not—and does not desire to become—his guardian. As a result, Morales is not entitled to tuition-free admission to the McAllen schools. . . .

II

This Court frequently has considered constitutional challenges to residence requirements. On several occasions the Court has invalidated requirements that condition receipt of a benefit on a minimum period of residence within a jurisdiction, but it always has been careful to distinguish such durational residence requirements from bona fide residence requirements. In *Shapiro v. Thompson*, for example, the Court invalidated one-year durational residence requirements that applicants for public assistance benefits were required to satisfy despite the fact that they otherwise had "met the test for residence in their jurisdictions." . . .

We specifically have approved bona fide residence requirements in the field of public education. The Connecticut statute before us in *Vlandis v. Kline*, for example, was unconstitutional because it created an irrebuttable presumption of nonresidency for state university students whose legal addresses were outside of the State before they applied for admission. The statute violated the Due Process Clause because it in effect classified some bona fide state residents as nonresidents for tuition purposes. . . .

A bona fide residence requirement, appropriately defined and uniformly applied, furthers the substantial state interest in assuring that services provided for its residents are enjoyed only by residents. Such a requirement with respect to attendance in public free schools does not violate the Equal Protection Clause of the Fourteenth Amendment. It does not burden or penalize the constitutional right of interstate travel, for any person is free to move to a State and to establish residence there. A bona fide residence requirement simply requires that the person does establish residence before demanding the services that are restricted to residents.

There is a further, independent justification for local residence requirements in the public-school context. . . . The provision of primary and secondary education, of course, is one of the most important functions of local government. Absent residence requirements, there can be little doubt that the proper planning and operation of the schools would suffer significantly. The State thus has a substantial interest in imposing bona fide residence requirements to maintain the quality of local public schools.

III

The central question we must decide here is whether § 21.031(d) is a bona fide residence requirement. Although the meaning may vary according to context, "residence" generally requires both physical presence and an intention to remain. . . . This classic two-part definition of residence has been recognized as a minimum standard in a wide range of contexts time and time again. . . .

Section 21.031 is far more generous than this traditional standard. It compels a school district to permit a child such as Morales to attend school without paying tuition if he has a bona fide intention to remain in the school district indefinitely, for he then would have a reason for being there other than his desire to attend school: his intention to make his home in the district. Thus § 21.031 grants the benefits of residency to all who satisfy the traditional requirements. The statute goes further and extends these benefits to many children even if they (or their families) do not intend to remain in the district indefinitely. As long as the child is not living in the district for the sole purpose of attending school, he satisfies the statutory test. For example, if a person comes to Texas to work for a year, his children will be eligible for tuition-free admission to the public schools.... In short, § 21.031 grants the benefits of residency to everyone who satisfies the traditional residence definition and to some who legitimately could be classified as nonresidents. Since there is no indication that this extension of the traditional definition has any impermissible basis, we certainly cannot say that § 21.031(d) violates the Constitution.

IV

The Constitution permits a State to restrict eligibility for tuition-free education to its bona fide residents. We hold that § 21.031 is a bona fide residence requirement that satisfies constitutional standards. The judgment of the Court of Appeals accordingly is affirmed.

Notes

1. Can you reconcile the holdings in *Plyler* and *Martinez*?

2. The Texas statute in *Martinez* parallels the general common-law view.

3. Insofar as education is a state function, why should a child who resides in the state not be able to attend any public school in the state tuition-free? Should school boards in "better" districts advertise for out-of-district students as long as their parents are willing to pay tuition?

[Case No. 95]   Student Records

OWASSO INDEPENDENT SCHOOL DISTRICT NO. I–011 v. FALVO

Supreme Court of the United States.
534 U.S. 426, 122 S.Ct. 934, 151 L.Ed.2d 896 [161 Educ. L. Rep. 33].

JUSTICE KENNEDY delivered the opinion of the Court.

Teachers sometimes ask students to score each other's tests, papers, and assignments as the teacher explains the correct answers to the entire class. Respondent contends this practice, which the parties refer to as peer grading, violates the Family Educational Rights and Privacy Act of 1974 (FERPA or Act). We took this case to resolve the issue.

I

Under FERPA, schools and educational agencies receiving federal financial assistance must comply with certain conditions. § 1232g(a)(3). One condition specified in the Act is that sensitive information about students may not be released without parental consent. The Act states that federal funds are to be withheld from school districts that have "a policy or practice of permitting the release of education records (or personally identifiable information contained therein ...) of students without the written consent of their parents." § 1232g(b)(1). The phrase "education records" is defined, under the Act, as "records, files, documents, and other materials" containing information directly related to a student, which "are maintained by an educational agency or institution or by a person acting for such agency or institution." § 1232g(a)(4)(A).

The definition of education records contains an exception for "records of instructional, supervisory, and administrative personnel ... which are in the sole possession of the maker thereof and which are not accessible or revealed to any other person except a substitute." § 1232g(a)(4)(B)(i). The precise question for us is whether peer-graded classroom work and assignments are education records.

Three of respondent Kristja J. Falvo's children are enrolled in Owasso Independent School District No. I–011, in a suburb of Tulsa, Oklahoma. The children's teachers, like many teachers in this country, use peer grading. In a typical case the students exchange papers with each other and score them according to the teacher's instructions, then return the work to the student who prepared it. The teacher may ask the students to report their own scores. In this case it appears the student could either call out the score or walk to the teacher's desk and reveal it in confidence, though by that stage, of course, the score was known at least to the one other student who did the grading. Both the grading and the system of calling out the scores are in contention here.

Respondent claimed the peer grading embarrassed her children. She asked the school district to adopt a uniform policy banning peer grading and requiring teachers either to grade assignments themselves or at least to forbid students from grading papers other than their own. The school district declined to do so, and respondent brought a class action.... against the school district, Superintendent Dale Johnson, Assistant Superintendent Lynn Johnson, and Principal Rick Thomas (petitioners). Respondent alleged the school district's grading policy violated FERPA and other laws not relevant here. The United States District Court for the Northern District of Oklahoma granted summary judgment in favor of the school district's position. The court held that grades put on papers by another student are not, at that stage, records "maintained by an educational agency or institution or by a person acting for such agency or institution," 20 U.S.C. § 1232g(a)(4)(A), and thus do not constitute "education records" under the Act. On this reasoning it ruled that peer grading does not violate FERPA.

The Court of Appeals for the Tenth Circuit reversed.... the Court of Appeals held that peer grading violates the Act. The grades marked by students on each other's work, it held, are education records protected by the statute, so the very act of grading was an impermissible release of the information to the student grader.

We granted certiorari to decide whether peer grading violates FERPA. Finding no violation of the Act, we reverse.

II

At the outset, we note it is an open question whether FERPA provides private parties, like respondent, with a cause of action enforceable under § 1983. We have granted certiorari on this issue in another case. The parties, furthermore, did not contest the § 1983 issue before the Court of Appeals. That court raised the issue *sua sponte,* and petitioners did not seek certiorari on the question. We need not resolve the question here as it is our practice "to decide cases on the grounds raised and considered in the Court of Appeals and included in the question on which we granted certiorari." In these circumstances we assume, but without so deciding or expressing an opinion on the question, that private parties may sue an educational agency under § 1983 to enforce the provisions of FERPA here at issue. Though we leave open the § 1983 question, the Court has subject-matter jurisdiction because respondent's federal claim is not so "completely devoid of merit as not to involve a federal controversy."With these preliminary observations concluded, we turn to the merits.

The parties appear to agree that if an assignment becomes an education record the moment a peer grades it, then the grading, or at least the practice of asking students to call out their grades in class, would be an impermissible release of the records under § 1232g(b)(1). without deciding the point, we assume for the purposes of our analysis that they are correct. The parties disagree, however, whether peer-graded assignments constitute education records at all. The papers do contain information directly related to a student, but they are records under the Act only when and if they "are maintained by an educational agency or institution or by a person acting for such agency or institution." § 1232g(a)(4)(A).

Petitioners, supported by the United States as amicus curiae, contend the definition covers only institutional records—namely, those materials retained in a permanent file as a matter of course. They argue that records "maintained by an educational agency or institution" generally would include final course grades, student grade point averages, standardized test scores, attendance records, counseling records, and records of disciplinary actions—but not student homework or classroom work. Respondent, adopting the reasoning of the Court of Appeals, contends student-graded assignments fall within the definition of education records. That definition contains an exception for "records of instructional, supervisory, and administrative personnel ... which are in the sole possession of the maker thereof and which are not accessible or revealed to any other person except a substitute." § 1232g(a)(4)(B)(i). The Court of Appeals reasoned that if grade books are not education records, then it would have been unnecessary for Congress to enact the exception. Grade books and the grades within, the court concluded, are "maintained" by a teacher and so are covered by FERPA. The court recognized that teachers do not maintain the grades on individual student assignments until they have recorded the result in the grade books. It reasoned, however, that if Congress forbids teachers to disclose students' grades once written in a grade book, it makes no sense to permit the disclosure immediately beforehand. The court thus held that student graders maintain the grades until they are reported to the teacher.

The Court of Appeals' logic does not withstand scrutiny. Its interpretation, furthermore, would effect a drastic alteration of the existing allocation of responsibilities between States and the National Government in the operation of the Nation's schools. We would hesitate before interpreting the statute to effect such a substantial change in the balance of federalism unless that is the manifest purpose of the legislation. This principle guides our decision.

Two statutory indicators tell us that the Court of Appeals erred in concluding that an assignment satisfies the definition of education records as soon as it is graded by another student. First, the student papers are not, at that stage, "maintained" within the meaning of § 1232g(a)(4)(A). The ordinary meaning of the word "maintain" is "to keep in existence or continuance; preserve; retain." . . . Even assuming the teacher's grade book is an education record—a point the parties contest and one we do not decide here—the score on a student-graded assignment is not "contained therein," § 1232g(b)(1), until the teacher records it. The teacher does not maintain the grade while students correct their peers' assignments or call out their own marks. Nor do the student graders maintain the grades within the meaning of § 1232g(a)(4)(A). The word "maintain" suggests FERPA records will be kept in a filing cabinet in a records room at the school or on a permanent secure database, perhaps even after the student is no longer enrolled. The student graders only handle assignments for a few moments as the teacher calls out the answers. It is fanciful to say they maintain the papers in the same way the registrar maintains a student's folder in a permanent file.

The Court of Appeals was further mistaken in concluding that each student grader is "a person acting for" an educational institution for purposes of § 1232g(a)(4)(A). The phrase "acting for" connotes agents of the school, such as teachers, administrators, and other school employees. Just as it does not accord with our usual understanding to say students are "acting for" an educational institution when they follow their teacher's direction to take a quiz, it is equally awkward to say students are "acting for" an educational institution when they follow their teacher's direction to score it. Correcting a classmate's work can be as much a part of the assignment as taking the test itself. It is a way to teach material again in a new context, and it helps show students how to assist and respect fellow pupils. By explaining the answers to the class as the students correct the papers, the teacher not only reinforces the lesson but also discovers whether the students have understood the material and are ready to move on. We do not think FERPA prohibits these educational techniques. We also must not lose sight of the fact that the phrase "by a person acting for [an educational] institution" modifies "maintain." Even if one were to agree students are acting for the teacher when they correct the assignment, that is different from saying they are acting for the educational institution in maintaining it.

Other sections of the statute support our interpretation. FERPA, for example, requires educational institutions to "maintain a record, kept with the education records of each student." § 1232g(b)(4)(A). This record must list those who have requested access to a student's education records and their reasons for doing so. The record of access "shall be available only to parents, [and] to the school official and his assistants who are responsible for the custody of such records."

Under the Court of Appeals' broad interpretation of education records, every teacher would have an obligation to keep a separate record of access for each student's assignments. Indeed, by that court's logic, even students who grade their own papers would bear the burden of maintaining records of access until they turned in the assignments. We doubt Congress would have imposed such a weighty administrative burden on every teacher, and certainly it would not have extended the mandate to students.

Also, FERPA requires "a record" of access for each pupil. This single record must be kept "with the education records." This suggests Congress contemplated that education records would be kept in one place with a single record of access. By describing a "school official" and "his assistants" as the personnel responsible for the custody of the records, FERPA implies that education records are institutional records kept by a single central custodian, such as a registrar, not individual assignments handled by many student graders in their separate classrooms.

FERPA also requires recipients of federal funds to provide parents with a hearing at which they may contest the accuracy of their child's education records. The hearings must be conducted "in accordance with regulations of the Secretary," which in turn require adjudication by a disinterested official and the opportunity for parents to be represented by an attorney. It is doubtful Congress would have provided parents with this elaborate procedural machinery to challenge the accuracy of the grade on every spelling test and art project the child completes.

Respondent's construction of the term "education records" to cover student homework or classroom work would impose substantial burdens on teachers across the country. It would force all instructors to take time, which otherwise could be spent teaching and in preparation, to correct an assortment of daily student assignments. Respondent's view would make it much more difficult for teachers to give students immediate guidance. The interpretation respondent urges would force teachers to abandon other customary practices, such as group grading of team assignments. Indeed, the logical consequences of respondent's view are all but unbounded. At argument, counsel for respondent seemed to agree that if a teacher in any of the thousands of covered classrooms in the Nation puts a happy face, a gold star, or a disapproving remark on a classroom assignment, federal law does not allow other students to see it.

We doubt Congress meant to intervene in this drastic fashion with traditional state functions. Under the Court of Appeals' interpretation of FERPA, the federal power would exercise minute control over specific teaching methods and instructional dynamics in classrooms throughout the country. The Congress is not likely to have mandated this result, and we do not interpret the statute to require it.

For these reasons, even assuming a teacher's grade book is an education record, the Court of Appeals erred, for in all events the grades on students' papers would not be covered under FERPA at least until the teacher has collected them and recorded them in his or her grade book. We limit our holding to this narrow point, and do not decide the broader question whether the grades on individual student assignments, once they are turned in to teachers, are protected by the Act.

The judgment of the Court of Appeals is reversed, and the case is remanded for further proceedings consistent with this opinion.

It is so ordered.

Notes

1.   Justice Scalia concurred with the Court's judgment that peer-graded papers were not educational records within the meaning of FERPA. However, he wrote separately because he was concerned that the Court's suggestion that the term educational record only included those documents maintained in a central repository at a school was unnecessary to resolve the dispute. Do you agree with Justice Scalia?

2.   What do you think of the practice of peer-grading? Is it useful?

3.   In a case involving student records, an appellate court in Washington affirmed that educators did not have to provide parents whose son was disciplined for his part in a fight on a school bus with a redacted copy of the surveillance video containing the altercation. The court held that the tape was exempt from disclosure under a provision of state law that addressed personal information in school files and that even if the identifying features of students on the bus were obliterated, meaningful information would have remained on the tape. Was the tape an educational record that should have been released to the parents? *Lindeman v. Kelso School Dist. No. 458*, 111 P.3d 1235 [198 Educ. L. Rep. 347] (Wash. Ct. App. 2005).

[Case No. 96]   Power of School Authorities to Choose Spring Play

SEYFRIED v. WALTON

United States Court of Appeals, Third Circuit, 1981.
668 F.2d 214 [2 Educ. L. Rep. 379].

ALDISERT, CIRCUIT JUDGE. The question presented is whether a public school superintendent's decision to cancel a high school dramatic production because of its sexual theme violated the students' first amendment right of expression. Plaintiffs, parents of three students in the play, sued the school district, the school board, and the district superintendent, seeking compensatory and equitable relief under 42 U.S.C. § 1983. The district court, sitting without a jury, held that the school superintendent's decision to cancel the production as inappropriate for school sponsorship was no different from other administrative decisions involving allocation of educational resources and that the cancellation did not offend the students' first amendment rights. We accept the reasoning given by the district court and we will affirm. . . .

I.

. . . Caesar Rodney High School, located in Dover, Delaware, sponsors autumn and spring theatrical productions each year. In December

1980, the director of the spring production, an English teacher at the school, selected the musical "Pippin" for presentation the following spring. Because the play contained certain sexually explicit scenes, the director consulted the assistant principal before reaching a final decision. After the director edited the script, she and the assistant principal agreed that the revised scenes, although still sexually suggestive, were appropriate for a high school production.

In March 1981, shortly after rehearsals for the spring production had begun, the father of a "Pippin" cast member complained to his brother, the president of the school board, that the play mocked religion. The board president directed the district superintendent to look into the matter. After reviewing the edited script, the superintendent determined that the play did not mock religion, but that it was inappropriate for a public high school because of its sexual content. He directed the principal to stop production of the play. After hearing the views of interested parents, the school board refused to overturn the superintendent's decision. As a result, the school did not present a spring play in 1981.

Parents of three members of the "Pippin" cast and crew then filed a civil rights action under 42 U.S.C. § 1983, claiming that the students' first amendment rights of expression had been unconstitutionally abridged. After a two-day trial, the district court entered judgment in favor of the defendants. Plaintiffs appeal.

II.

Appellants' principal contention is that the students of the "Pippin" cast and crew had a first amendment right to produce the play. Although we agree that, in general, dramatic expression is "speech" for purposes of the first amendment, we also agree with the district court that the decision to cancel the production of "Pippin" in these circumstances did not infringe on the students' constitutional rights.

In his well reasoned opinion, Judge Stapleton noted that a school community "exists for a specialized purpose—the education of young people," including the communication of both knowledge and social values. The first amendment, he concluded, must therefore be "applied in light of the special characteristics of the school environment...."

We believe that the district court properly distinguished student newspapers and other "non-program related expressions of student opinion" from school-sponsored theatrical productions. The critical factor in this case is the relationship of the play to the school curriculum. As found by the district court, both the staff and the administration view the spring production at Caesar Rodney as "an integral part of the school's educational program." Participation in the play, though voluntary, was considered a part of the curriculum in the theater arts.... Viewed in this light, the selection of the artistic work to be given as the spring production does not differ in principle from the selection of course curriculum, a process which courts have traditionally left to the expertise of educators. Just as a student has no First Amendment right to study a particular aspect or period of history in his or her senior history course, he or she has no First Amendment right to participate in the production of a particular dramatic work or version thereof.

The district court also noted the likelihood that the school's sponsorship of a play would be viewed as an endorsement of the ideas it contained. A school has an important interest in avoiding the impression that it has endorsed a viewpoint at variance with its educational program. The district court cautioned that administrators may not so chill the school's atmosphere for student and teacher expression that they cast "a pall of orthodoxy" over the school community, but it found no such danger here. The court found that no student was prohibited from expressing his views on any subject; no student was prohibited from reading the script, an unedited version of which remains in the school library; and no one was punished or reprimanded for any expression of ideas. In light of these facts, the court could find no reasonable threat of a chilling effect on the free exchange of ideas within the school community. These findings are amply supported by the record.

We agree with the district court that those responsible for directing a school's educational program must be allowed to decide how its limited resources can be best used to achieve the goals of educating and socializing its students. "Limitations of time and resources ... dictate that choices be made.... [S]ince the objective of the process is the 'inculcation of both knowledge and social values' in young people, these decisions as to what will be taught will necessarily involve an acceptance or preference of some values over others."

Because of the burden of responsibility given to school administrators, courts are reluctant to interfere with the operation of our school systems.... We agree with the district court that the conflict here does not "directly and sharply implicate" the first amendment rights of the students. We hold, therefore, that the court properly entered judgment for the defendants....

Notes

1. The superintendent overruled the dramatic arts teacher's decision to produce "Pippin." The teacher did not legally challenge the action. Could she have? If so, on what grounds?

2. Note how the superintendent became involved. Could this be fairly characterized as censorship? Would your answer be different if the superintendent, rather than the teacher, was the one who was supposed to select the spring play?

3. As a result of this controversy, the school did not produce a spring play. Who gained and who lost in this situation?

[Case No. 97]   Power of Board to Establish Graduation Requirements

STATE EX REL. SAGESER v. LEDBETTER

Missouri Court of Appeals, 1977.
559 S.W.2d 230.

STONE, PRESIDING JUDGE. In this proceeding ... relator Ronnie Sageser (hereinafter Ronnie) sought a writ of mandamus to compel ... the members of the board of education of the Sarcoxie R–2 School District (hereinafter collectively referred to as the board), W.D. Ledbetter, the superintendent of schools for that district, and Jess Bair, the principal of Sarcoxie High School at the time of suit, to execute and deliver to relator Ronnie a diploma evidencing his graduation from that school....

[For "showing disrespect" to a teacher, Ronnie had been suspended by the former principal Smith during his junior year.]

Either the next day by relator Ronnie's account, or "about five days later" according to principal Smith, the latter called Ronnie's home and requested that he report to the principal's office. Upon trial, principal Smith recalled that, when Ronnie did report, "his attitude [was] that of indifference toward returning to school and behaving"—in short, that "his attitude hadn't improved," so Smith told Ronnie "to go home until his attitude improved." Ronnie's recollection was that, in the course of this meeting, principal Smith had exclaimed, "You don't even know what you are doing here, do you" and, when Ronnie agreed and answered "No," the principal "just said, '[w]hy don't you just check out your books and go home.'" Although the principal declared that Ronnie's check-out and withdrawal were voluntary and without compulsion by any school official, certain portions of the principal's testimony cast doubt upon that characterization of Ronnie's withdrawal. (E.g., when asked on cross-examination "[d]id you instruct Ronald Sageser to check out of school," principal Smith responded "I don't remember whether I did or didn't"; and, in one entry book, Ronnie's name was listed with the comment "dropped 4/1/74.") But, regardless of whether the principal's above-quoted utterances to Ronnie constituted a mere suggestion, an admonition or a command, Ronnie did "go home" after having completed a "checkout form" obtainable only from the principal or upon his authorization. This "checkout form" was dated April 1, 1974, which was approximately eight weeks prior to the last day of the 1973–74 school year.

Ronnie reentered Sarcoxie High School in September 1974, was listed as a senior, continued in school through the 1974–75 academic year, and (with his academic credits from the three previous years) earned the twenty units of credit required for graduation. However, he was denied a diploma (so superintendent Ledbetter declared) because he had not completed "eight semesters of attending" as prescribed "in the policy that is made by the Board of Education" (hereinafter the eight-semester requirement).

When Ronnie's parents learned that he would not graduate with his class, one of the parents attended a meeting of the board of education and requested that the board waive the eight-semester requirement and give Ronnie's diploma to him, but the board refused to do so. However, acknowledging that Ronnie had satisfied all other requirements for graduation, superintendent Ledbetter declared that, if Ronnie would *enroll* for "[e]xactly the amount of time that was lacking from the time he dropped out [April 1, 1974] until the end of school which, I believe, [was] eight weeks, give or take a day or two," he would receive his diploma.

Since the Sarcoxie eight-semester requirement hatched this controversy, it becomes both appropriate and necessary to note the evidence concerning its origin, meaning and prior enforcement. We observe initially that the eight-semester requirement was *not* imposed or ordained by statute, but was a requirement for graduation formulated and prescribed by the Sarcoxie Board of Education (so superintendent Ledbetter declared) pursuant to a *recommendation* nestling in a footnote to the last sentence of paragraph 17, "High School Graduation Requirements," in the *Handbook for Classification and Accreditation of Public School Districts in Missouri* (1973) published by the Missouri State Board of Education, that sentence and footnote reading as follows:

> "The local board of education may require more than 20 units, adopt specific course requirements, and/or specify the number of semesters of attendance** required for graduation from their local school district."

> "**Eight semesters of attendance after grade eight are *recommended.*" (All emphasis herein is ours.)

Inasmuch as the proper disposition of this appeal does not involve or depend upon the wisdom vel non of this recommendation, the acceptance of which mandatorily herded all high school students, without regard to ability, aptitude, ambition, intellect, motivation, performance or prior scholastic record, onto the same conveyor belt geared to the pace of the mediocre or average student, we eschew comment concerning its adoption by the Sarcoxie board. . . .

Respondents' position in this proceeding (as *initially* stated by superintendent Ledbetter) was that, by reason of Ronnie's absence during approximately the last eight weeks of his Junior school year, he did not satisfy the four-year requirement and will not be entitled to receive a diploma until he does. Thus, Ledbetter initially declared that relator Ronnie would be required to attend Sarcoxie High School for "exactly" the additional number of school days that he missed in his Junior year from his suspension or "checkout" on April 1, 1974, to the end of that school year. However, Ledbetter subsequently conceded not only that the eight-semester requirement did *not* demand or necessitate any *attendance* but also that relator Ronnie already had earned the twenty units of credit which constituted and satisfied the "measure of academic achievement" required for graduation, from which it followed that it would not be necessary for Ronnie to earn any additional units of credit, pass any courses in which he might be enrolled, or for that matter even attend any classes. Thus, it becomes plain that the additional requirement of *enrollment* for eight weeks imposed by the school authorities would do no more than work an exercise in futility which would benefit neither the school district nor relator Ronnie and thus would fly in the teeth of the commonsense maxim that the law does not require the doing of a useless thing.

Although the foregoing is dispositive of this appeal, the earnest presentations of counsel move us to note other record evidence pointing to and supporting the same conclusion.... Supt. Ledbetter conceded that, during the three years prior to trial of this proceeding, four girls, identified by name in the transcript, had been graduated with a diploma although they had not *attended* eight semesters. One of those four girls who had become pregnant, had missed the last few weeks of the 1973–74 school year, but had graduated with her class in 1975. Relator Ronnie likewise had missed the last few weeks of the 1973–74 school year, but contrawise had been denied graduation with the 1975 class.

Although respondents assert that mandamus is inappropriate, the transcript establishes that relator had satisfied all academic requirements for graduation and that respondents rely solely, albeit mistakenly, on the eight-semester requirement to justify and support their denial of a diploma to relator Ronnie. Within reasonable limits a school board may determine graduation requirements but where, as here, a rule is applied or enforced unreasonably, capriciously, arbitrarily or inequitably to deny a diploma to a qualified candidate, mandamus is an appropriate remedy....

Notes

1. Is this decision based on a finding of an unauthorized rule, an unreasonable rule, an unreasonable application of an authorized and reasonable rule, or an unreasonable application of a rule the reasonableness of which was not here determined?

2. What do you think of the behavior of the superintendent and former principal?

3. Should there be a required minimum period of attendance for high school graduation? Should graduation be based on the completion of a fixed number of courses? Should graduation be based on passing tests regardless of either or both of the preceding? What should be the roles of the state and the local board in setting graduation requirements?

[Case No. 98]   Power of Board to Include Attendance in Determining Course Grades

CAMPBELL v. BOARD OF EDUCATION
OF TOWN OF NEW MILFORD

Supreme Court of Connecticut, 1984.
475 A.2d 289 [17 Educ. L. Rep. 840].

PETERS, ASSOCIATE JUSTICE. This case concerns the validity of the policy of a local school board that imposes academic sanctions for nonattendance upon high school students. In a class action brought by the named plaintiff, John A. Campbell, for himself and others similarly situated, the plaintiff class sought injunctive and declaratory relief, mandamus, and compensatory damages from the named defendant, the New Milford board of education, and others. The plaintiff claimed that the defendants' policy was ultra vires in light of governing state statutes, and unconstitutional in light of operative provisions of the Connecticut constitution and the United States constitution. The trial court rendered judgment for the defendants and the plaintiff has appealed.

The underlying facts are undisputed. The New Milford attendance policy, set out in an annually distributed student handbook, provides two sets of academic sanctions for students who are absent from school. Course credit is withheld from any student who, without receiving an administrative waiver, is absent from any year-long course for more than twenty-four class periods. In the calculation of the twenty-four maximum absences, all class absences are included except absences on school-sponsored activities or essential administrative business. In addition to the twenty-four absence limit, the course grade of any student whose absence from school is unapproved is subject to a five-point reduction for each unapproved absence after the first. In any one marking period, the grade may not, however, be reduced to a grade lower than 50, which is a failing grade. The grade reduction for unexcused absences is, like the twenty-four maximum absence policy, subject to administrative waiver. The policy of the school board entails extensive opportunities for counseling after a student's first confirmed unapproved absence from a class and thereafter.

The stated purpose of the attendance policy is educational rather than disciplinary. A student's disciplinary suspension from school, for reasons unrelated to attendance, is considered an approved rather than an unapproved absence. Such an absence cannot result in the diminution of a class grade although it may be counted, unless waived, as part of the twenty-four maximum absences for class credit. A student's absence from school, whether approved or unapproved, is not a ground for suspension or expulsion.

A student's report card lists, for each course, grades for each marking period, a final examination grade, a final grade, the amount of credit awarded, and the number of approved and unapproved absences. The report card conspicuously bears the following legend: "A circled grade indicates that the grade was reduced due to unapproved absences." In the case of the named plaintiff, his report card indicated grade reductions by the circling of grades in each of his academic courses, with the result that in three of the courses his final grade was lowered from passing to failing. In a fourth course, Architectural Drafting II, where the plaintiff's final grade was passing despite an indicated reduction for unapproved absences, the report card assigned him no credit because of a total of thirty-eight absences, thirty-one of which were approved and seven of which were unapproved. Any report card thus discloses, on its face, those grades which are affected by the enforcement of the attendance policy. . . .

I

The plaintiff's first argument on appeal is that the defendant school board's policy is invalid because it conflicts with a number of state statutes. This argument is twofold, that the attendance policy is ultra vires because it exceeds the authority conferred upon local school boards by state law and that the policy is preempted by state statutes with which it is inconsistent. We find neither argument persuasive.

The authority of local boards of education derives from their role as agents of the state. "[T]he furnishing of education for the general public, required by article eighth, § 1, of the Connecticut constitution, is by its very nature a state function and duty." This responsibility has been delegated to local boards which, as "agencies of the state in charge of education in the town . . . possess only such powers as are granted to them by the General Statutes expressly or by necessary implication." . . .

. . . The authority to adopt uniform rules concerning irregularity of attendance is necessarily implied in the conjunction of statutory provisions authorizing local implementation of the educational mission of the state. Significantly, § 10–220 expressly charges local boards with responsibility for the oversight of the school attendance of children from the ages of seven to sixteen made mandatory by § 10–184. Furthermore, the plaintiff's concession that school teachers, upon the instruction of local school boards, may properly consider class participation in the assignment of grades, logically implies the existence of an educational nexus between classroom presence and grading. If local school boards can delegate to others the authority to impose academic sanctions for nonattendance, the decision to adopt uniform school-wide rules for such sanctions can hardly be deemed ultra vires.

None of the out-of-state cases upon which the plaintiff relies compels the conclusion that school-wide academic sanctions for nonattendance should generally be adjudged to be ultra vires. It may well be improper to reduce a student's grade for nonattendance as an additional punishment for unrelated conduct leading to a suspension from class; but this school board's program does not permit such double punishment. It would indubitably be unlawful to apply a nonattendance program in an unreasonable, capricious, arbitrary or inequitable manner; but no such allegation has been factually demonstrated. It would finally be troublesome to bar a truant student from further class attendance and from taking a final examination; but the defendant board's program neither removes such a student from class nor excuses further compliance with the state's compulsory education law. In short, the plaintiff has cited no authority for his claim that attendance rules promulgated by local school boards, if carefully drafted and fairly applied, are to be deemed per se ultra vires. Our own research has likewise revealed no such caselaw. We agree that such regulations fall within the authority granted to local school boards by the statutes of this state.

In the alternative, the plaintiff maintains that the defendant school board's attendance policy is preempted by state statutes governing school attendance. . . .

The defendant school board's reply . . . calls upon us to recognize a distinction between sanctions which are disciplinary in nature and sanctions which relate to academic requirements. The question is not whether we concur in the judgment of the defendant board of education that "[l]earning experiences that occur in the classroom are . . . essential components of the learning process" or that "[t]ime lost from class tends to be irretrievable in terms of opportunity for instructional interaction." The policy decision that academic credentials should reflect more than the product of quizzes, examinations, papers and classroom participation nonetheless constitutes an academic judgment about academic requirements. We agree with the defendants' characterization of their policy. . . .

II

Even if the defendant school board's attendance policy is authorized by the relevant state statutes, the plaintiff class asserts that the policy cannot pass constitutional muster. The plaintiff relies on provisions of our state and federal constitutions to raise three different constitutional claims: a right to substantive due process, a right to procedural due process, and a right to equal protection of the laws. The trial court, upon consideration of these claims, found no infringement of the plaintiff's constitutional rights. We agree.

A

The plaintiff's challenge to the New Milford attendance policy as violative of the requirements of substantive due process claims infringement of students' fundamental rights to public education, of students' liberty interests in their academic reputation and of students' property interests in grades reflecting academic achievement. . . .

Of these substantive due process claims, the most serious is the charge of impairment of a fundamental right, because, if such an impairment were properly before us, the validity of the questioned governmental regulation would require strict scrutiny to determine whether the regulation was compellingly justified and narrowly drafted. We must therefore decide the applicability of the fundamental rights guaranteed by article eighth, § 1, to a school board's policy of imposing uniform school-wide academic sanctions for nonattendance. In *Horton v. Meskill* we held, in the context of state-wide disparities in the financing of public school education, that "elementary and secondary education is a fundamental right, [and] that pupils in the public schools are entitled to the equal enjoyment of that right." The plaintiff argues that *Horton v. Meskill* implies that strict scrutiny must be the test for any and all governmental regulations affecting public school education. We disagree. The underlying issue in *Horton v. Meskill* was the provision of "a substantially equal educational opportunity" for Connecticut students in the state's "free public elementary and secondary schools." This school board policy, which is neither disciplinary nor an infringement of equal educational opportunity, does not jeopardize any fundamental rights under our state constitution.

The standard by which the plaintiff's remaining substantive due process claims must be measured is therefore the more usual rational basis test. In order to succeed on these claims, the plaintiff bears the heavy burden of proving that the challenged policy has no reasonable relationship to any legitimate state purpose and that the plaintiff class has suffered a specific injury as a result of the policy's enforcement. The plaintiff has established neither the legal nor the factual predicate for meeting this burden of proof.

The plaintiff argues that it is unconstitutionally arbitrary and capricious for the defendant school board to require student grades to reflect more than academic achievement. With respect to the plaintiff's liberty interest, we can find no factual impairment of whatever rights the plaintiff might possibly assert. Inspection of the report card of the named plaintiff discloses the relationship between his academic performance and the reduction in his grades and class credit that resulted from application of the attendance policy. The plaintiff has failed to show how a student's reputation could be injured by a report card in this form. With respect to the plaintiff's property interest, we find it difficult to understand how a uniform school-wide policy that links class grades with attendance can be on its face more arbitrary, as a constitutional matter, than are similar judgments by individual teachers who may justifiably, according to the plaintiff, adjust classroom grades to reflect classroom participation. Furthermore, the trial court made no findings of fact that application of the attendance policy was arbitrary or capricious in the only two specific cases about which evidence was adduced at trial. On this record, the plaintiff class has not proven infringement of its liberty or property interest in a fair grading system.

The plaintiff argues finally that impermissible vagueness in the waiver provisions that ameliorate the potential rigor of the defendant board's attendance policy requires the conclusion that the policy is substantively unconstitutional. The policy of grade reduction is subject to waiver for "outstanding performance," and denial of class credit may be waived in extenuating circumstances calling for "special consideration." These provisions for waiver are unconstitutional, according to the plaintiff, because they permit school administrators to exercise unbridled discretion and hence invite arbitrary action. It is, however, by no means clear that provisions for waiver, which necessarily depend upon the equities of particular circumstances, require the same degree of precision as must accompany the imposition of sanctions in the first instance. Significantly, the plaintiff's challenge for vagueness does not contest any part of the attendance policy other than its provisions of waiver. In any case, the plaintiff class has again failed to make the factual showing necessary to prove that it has suffered a constitutional injury. The record contains no findings that any member of the class in fact misunderstood the waiver policy or was deprived of a waiver because of ambiguity in its statement. The plaintiff's claim of unconstitutional vagueness therefore cannot succeed.

B

The plaintiff also claims a deprivation of procedural due process. The plaintiff maintains that the New Milford attendance policy fails to provide constitutionally mandated basic procedural safeguards because students are not given notice of the dates of their alleged absences and are not afforded the opportunity to contest the imposition of an academic penalty, either at an internal hearing or before the board of education. These omissions, according to the plaintiff, jeopardize accurate and fair application of the defendants' policy.

Before we can consider this claim on its merits, we must clarify the standards that govern procedural fairness in a school setting. We have already held that the defendants' policy is academic rather than disciplinary in intent and effect, and that the policy impairs no fundamental rights. The Supreme Court of the United States has recently determined that flexible standards of procedural due process call for "far less stringent procedural requirements in the case of an academic dismissal" than for a dismissal based on disciplinary reasons. *Board of Curators of the University of Missouri v. Horowitz.* That court found it compelling that academic evaluations of a student necessarily depend upon professional judgments that are "more subjective and evaluative than the typical factual questions presented in the average disciplinary decision." For similar reasons, it is appropriate for this court to defer to the policy judgments of the academic administrators who formulated the defendant school board's attendance program. Such deferral does not of course obviate the fundamental requirements of procedural due process that a student must be given adequate notice of the program, and a meaningful timely opportunity to be heard. It does, however, mean that notice and hearings need not take any one particular form in order to pass constitutional muster.

In this case, the plaintiff does not argue that students at New Milford High School were not provided with sufficient notice of the existent attendance policy or of the academic sanctions that would ensue from recurrent class absences. The plaintiff asserts only that students had inadequate opportunities to contest whether absences had occurred, whether they were excused or unexcused, or whether they should be waived. The defendants introduced evidence to the contrary. In the absence of express findings by the trial court, we must conclude that the plaintiff class has not met the requirement that the challenged attendance program must be shown to have adversely affected a constitutionally protected right under the facts of this particular case rather than of some possible or hypothetical facts not proven to exist.

C

The plaintiff's final constitutional claim invokes the equal protection provisions of article first, § 20, of the Connecticut constitution and the fourteenth amendment to the United States constitution. The plaintiff urges us to hold that because the defendant board's attendance policy permits waiver of grade reductions for unexcused absences, the policy creates two unequal classes of students: students who are denied a waiver and students who are granted a waiver. In part the plaintiff's argument depends upon the assertion that the defendants' classification, because it allegedly affects a fundamental right to education, must meet the test of strict scrutiny. That assertion we have rejected, supra. Even if the applicable test is whether the waiver provision bears a reasonable relationship to legitimate governmental ends, the plaintiff argues that the waiver provision is constitutionally flawed because it ties eligibility for waiver to a student's "outstanding performance for the latter portion of the marking period." It is irrational, and a violation of equal protection, according to the plaintiff, to waive grade reduction for students who do "outstanding" work and to impose such sanctions on students whose work is, because of academic difficulties unrelated to class absence, only average.

The defendants offer several answers to this argument. Factually, they deny the premise that the waiver provision favors students on account of their ability rather than on account of their effort, since work may be considered "outstanding" in light of a particular student's past performance. Legally, they note that the waiver provision imports a reasonable element of flexibility into the assessment of a student's total classroom performance. Finally, they remind us that a district-wide policy is more likely to assure equality of treatment for all students than is a policy administered on an ad-hoc basis by individual classroom teachers. We find the defendants' arguments persuasive and therefore reject the plaintiff's equal protection claim.

There is no error.

Notes

1. What do you think about the quality of the plaintiff's arguments and the evidence used to support his position?

2. How, if at all, should "approved" and "unapproved" absences be handled differently as regards academics? Where should absences caused by suspension fit?

3. An appellate court in New York rejected the argument that the denial of credit after a number of cuts is equivalent to dropping a student from enrollment contrary to the compulsory education law. *Bitting v. Lee*, 564 N.Y.S.2d 791 [65 Educ. L. Rep. 480] (N.Y.App.Div.1990). What do you think?

[Case No. 99]   Power of Board to Use Academic and Sex Admission Standards

BERKELMAN v. SAN FRANCISCO
UNIFIED SCHOOL DISTRICT

United States Court of Appeals, Ninth Circuit, 1974.
501 F.2d 1264.

ALFRED T. GOODWIN, CIRCUIT JUDGE: . . .

Lowell High School is an academic, or college-preparatory, public high school which accepts each year those applicants for admission whose prior academic achievement places them within approximately the top 15 per cent of the junior-high-school graduates in the district.

The issues on appeal, phrased broadly, are: (1) whether a school district may admit students to a preferred high school on the basis of past academic achievement if the percentage of black, Spanish–American, and low-income students who qualify for admission is substantially disproportionate to the percentage of black, Spanish–American, and low-income students in the school district at large; (2) whether a school district, in order to maintain equal numbers of boys and girls in the school, may apply higher admission requirements to girls than to boys.

I

The district operates eleven high schools. Seven are "comprehensive" high schools, to which students are assigned substantially on the basis of residence. The other four high schools have special educational objectives and accept qualified students from anywhere in the district. Lowell, one of these special schools, offers advanced, college-preparatory courses. Others serve students who need special help because of language or other problems, who work part-time, or who desire vocational training.

Except for students admitted under a pilot minority-admissions program, or under the balancing-of-the-sexes policy at issue in this case, admission to Lowell is based solely upon a student's junior-high-school grade-point average in four college-preparatory subjects. All applicants in the district are ranked numerically by their junior-high-school grade-point averages, and students are admitted in their numerical order until their class is filled. Grade averages are not weighted according to schools in which they were earned. All junior-high grades are accepted at face value, regardless of neighborhood or demographic factors that might produce nonuniformity of grading among junior-high schools.

The statistical data stipulated into this record indicate a lower proportion of low-income students at Lowell than in the high school population city-wide. The data also show that 7.5% of Lowell's students are black, while 25.9% of the district's high school students are black; 5.2% of Lowell's students are Spanish–American, and 13% of the district's high-school students are Spanish–American. The minority percentages in Lowell's student body would be even lower than they are but for the minority-admissions program instituted in 1970.

However, the district-court record reveals that Lowell has not become an exclusive province of the affluent and white. Chinese students contribute 29.8% of Lowell's student body, while they make up only 17.9% of the district's high-school population. Further, 3.2% of Lowell's students are Japanese, and 3.8% are Filipino, while the respective city-wide percentages are 1.9% and 4.5%.

There was no evidence that the Board's actions in connection with its administration of Lowell were racially motivated. The admission standard is neither an intentionally discriminatory standard, nor a neutral standard applied in an intentionally discriminatory manner. . . .

However, if an admission standard operates in fact to exclude a disproportionate number of black and Spanish–American students from Lowell, the court has a duty to test the constitutionality of that standard. Where a nonsuspect classification (past academic achievement) is alleged to operate to the detriment of a disadvantaged class or classes (black and Spanish–American students), neither "strict" nor "minimal" scrutiny provides useful guidance as a standard of review. The task is to examine the school district's assertion that the standard of past academic achievement substantially furthers the purpose of providing the best education possible for the public-school students in the district. If the past-achievement standard does substantially further that purpose, then the district has not unconstitutionally discriminated in its Lowell admission policy.

The advantages of an "academic" high school offering advanced courses to students who have excelled in a traditional curriculum are obvious. Lowell provides in one school a program which cannot be duplicated in ten other schools any more than special courses for students with specific educational needs can be economically taken from the other special high schools in the city and spread among all eleven schools. The student whose past performance has demonstrated ability to move at an advanced rate in an advanced program will receive a "better" education than he or she would receive if required to work in subject matter and at a pace which does not provide as great an educational challenge. Likewise, a student with an interest in vocational training receives a "better" education if permitted to take vocational courses than if required to continue against his wishes with the "traditional" high-school program. The school district has determined that it is educationally "better" to consolidate special offerings for the benefit of those who can meet the performance standards than to dispense with the effort entirely because budget considerations make is impossible to offer every program at every school.

Conditioning admission to Lowell upon the level of past academic achievement substantially furthers the district's purpose of operating an academic high school. Those students who have best mastered their junior-high-school courses are well prepared for more advanced courses at the high-school level. Of course, it does not necessarily follow that all applicants who fall below the cutoff line are educationally disqualified for Lowell's program. The cutoff is the result of space and budget limitations, not the result of a perfect determination of who can and who cannot benefit from the program.

Those students not admitted to Lowell are neither denied a quality education nor relegated to an inadequate school. Rather, they attend one of San Francisco's seven "comprehensive" high schools. Unlike a "tracking" system in which the challenged classifications are "predictive" and isolate students of "less promising" ability, the classification here is based upon past achievement impartially measured. There is slight potential for psychic injury to a student from attending a comprehensive high school with the majority of the city's high-school students. We conclude that the district's legitimate interest in establishing an academic high school, admission to which is based upon past achievement, outweighs any harm imagined or suffered by students whose achievement had not qualified them for admission to that school.

Our decision does not mean that we are not troubled by the underrepresentation of some racial and ethnic groups at Lowell. Uncertainty on this score, however, does not mean that the maintenance of Lowell High is itself unconstitutional or that conditioning admission on the basis of past academic achievement is unconstitutional.

Nor does the alleged underrepresentation at Lowell of students of low-income families render the admission policy unconstitutional. Low-income persons have no greater status under the equal-protection clause of the Fourteenth Amendment than members of racial minorities. It follows that since the admission policy is not made unconstitutional by its impact upon black students, it is likewise not made unconstitutional by a similar impact upon low-income students.

II

Appellants also attack as discrimination on the basis of sex the school district's policy of requiring higher admission standards for girls than for boys. The school district asserts that the standards were designed to produce an equal number of boys and girls at Lowell....

... No actual proof that a balance of the sexes furthers the goal of better academic education was offered by the school district.

We note that had the advanced courses been offered in each high school, rather than in a separate high school, and had the school authorities applied the same or similar admission standards to such courses, the admission standards would have been an illegal discrimination on the basis of sex under Title IX of the Education Amendments of 1972. Although Congress condemned discrimination on the basis of sex in any education program, the prohibition with regard to sex discrimination in admissions to educational institutions was not extended to public secondary schools. This omission, however, indicates nothing more than that Congress did not know the manner, extent, or rationale of separate education below the college level, and could not anticipate the effect of a prohibition upon such single-sex schools. On the other hand, its reasons for prohibiting sex discrimination in educational programs in general bears directly upon this case. Congress recognized that, because education provides access to jobs, sex discrimination in education is potentially destructive to the disfavored sex. Lowell High, as a conduit to better university education and hence to better jobs, is exactly that type of educational program with regard to which Congress intended to eliminate sex discrimination when it passed Title IX.

On the basis of the foregoing, we hold that the use of higher admission standards for female than for male applicants to Lowell High School violates the Equal Protection Clause of the Fourteenth Amendment. . . .

Notes

1. Why do you think that school officials did not offer any proof that a balance of the sexes was educationally desirable? What educational rationale is offered by those who favor single sex private schools?

2. Observe the court's statements about Title IX. If it does not apply to secondary schools, why did the court place such emphasis on this stance?

3. Would admissions standards other than grade averages be more valid? If so, what do you suggest?

[Case No. 100]   Use of Race in Admissions Decisions

PARENTS INVOLVED IN COMMUNITY SCHOOLS v. SEATTLE SCHOOL DISTRICT NO. 1

426 F.3d 1162 [202 Educ. L. Rep. 549] (9th Cir. 2005).

Opinion by JUDGE FISHER:

This appeal requires us to consider whether the use of an integration tiebreaker in the open choice, noncompetitive, public high school assignment plan crafted by Seattle School District Number 1 (the "District") violates the federal Constitution's Equal Protection Clause. Our review is guided by the principles articulated in the Supreme Court's recent decisions regarding affirmative action in higher education, *Grutter v. Bollinger* and *Gratz v. Bollinger* and the Court's directive that "[c]ontext matters when reviewing race-based governmental action under the Equal Protection Clause." We conclude that the District has a compelling interest in securing the educational and social benefits of racial (and ethnic) diversity, and in ameliorating racial isolation or concentration in its high schools by ensuring that its assignments do not simply replicate Seattle's segregated housing patterns. We also conclude that the District's Plan is narrowly tailored to meet the District's compelling interests.

I. Background

A. Seattle Public Schools: A Historical Perspective

Seattle's historical struggle with the problem of racial isolation in its public school system provides the context for the District's implementation of the current challenged assignment plan. Seattle is a diverse community. Approximately 70 percent of its residents are white, and 30 percent are nonwhite. Seattle public school enrollment breaks down nearly inversely, with approximately 40 percent white and 60 percent nonwhite students. A majority of the District's white students live in neighborhoods north of downtown, the historically more affluent part of the city. A majority of the city's nonwhite students, including approximately 84 percent of all African–American students, 74 percent of all Asian–American students, 65 percent of all Latino students and 51 percent of all Native–American students, live south of downtown.

The District operates 10 four-year public high schools.... Since the 1960s, while courts around the country ordered intransigent school districts to desegregate, Seattle's School Board voluntarily explored measures designed to end de facto segregation in the schools and provide all of the District's students with access to diverse and equal educational opportunities.

In the late 1950s and early 1960s, school assignments were made strictly on the basis of neighborhood. In 1962, Garfield High School reported 64 percent minority enrollment and it accommodated 75 percent of all African–American students. Meanwhile, the eight high schools serving other major areas of the city remained more than 95 percent white.

The District responded to this imbalance, and racial tensions in the de facto segregated schools, in various ways. In the early 1960s, the District first experimented with small-scale exchange programs in which handfuls of students switched high schools for five-week periods. In 1963, expanding on this concept, the District implemented a "Voluntary Racial Transfer" program through which a student could transfer to any school with available space if the transfer would improve the racial balance at the receiving school. In the 1970s, the District increased its efforts again, this time adopting a desegregation plan in the middle schools that requested volunteers to transfer between minority-and majority-dominated neighborhood schools and called for mandatory transfers when the number of volunteers was insufficient, though this portion of the plan was never implemented. The District also took steps to desegregate Garfield High School.... for the 1977–78 school year, the District instituted a magnet-school program....

During the summer of 1977, the District and community representatives reviewed five model plans. Ultimately, the District incorporated elements of each model into its final desegregation plan, adopted in December 1977 and known as the "Seattle Plan." The Seattle Plan divided the district into zones, within which majority-dominated elementary schools were paired with minority-dominated elementary schools to achieve desegregation....

Seattle became the first major city to adopt a comprehensive desegregation program voluntarily without a court order....

The Seattle Plan furthered the District's school desegregation goals, but its operation was unsatisfactory in other ways. In 1988, a decade after its implementation, the District abandoned the Seattle Plan and adopted a new plan that it referred to as "controlled choice." Under the controlled choice plan, schools were grouped into clusters that met state and district desegregation guidelines, and families were permitted to rank schools within the relevant cluster, increasing the predictability of assignments. Because of Seattle's housing patterns, the District's planners explained that "it was impossible to fashion clusters in a geographically contiguous manner"; some cluster schools were near students' homes, but others were in "racially and culturally different neighborhoods." Although roughly 70 percent of students received their first choices, the controlled choice plan still resulted in mandatory busing for 16 percent of the District's students.

In 1994, the Board directed District staff to devise a new plan for all grade levels to simplify assignments, reduce costs and increase community satisfaction, among other things. The guiding factors were to be choice, diversity and predictability. Staff developed four basic options, including the then-existing controlled choice plan, a regional choice plan, a neighborhood assignment plan with a provision for voluntary, integration-positive transfers and an open choice plan.

Board members testified that they considered all the options as they related to the District's educational goals—with special emphasis, at the secondary school level, on the goals of choice and racial diversity. Neighborhood and regional plans were viewed as unduly limiting student choice, on which the District placed high value because student choice was seen to increase parental involvement in the schools and promote improvements in quality through a marketplace model. The District sought to maintain its commitment to racially integrated education by establishing diversity goals while moving away from the rigid desegregation guidelines and mandatory assignments prevalent in the 1970s and 1980s.

The Board adopted the current open choice plan (the "Plan") for the 1998–99 school year. Under the Plan, students entering the ninth grade may select any high school in the District. They are assigned, where possible, to the school they list as their first choice. If too many students choose the same school as their first choice, resulting in "oversubscription," the District assigns students to each oversubscribed school based on a series of tiebreakers. If a student is not admitted to his or her first choice school as a result of the tiebreakers, the District tries to assign the student to his or her second choice school, and so on. Students not assigned to one of their chosen schools are assigned to the closest school with space available; students who list more choices are less likely to receive one of these "mandatory" assignments. The most recent version of the Plan, which the School Board reviews annually, is for the 2001–02 school year and is the subject of this litigation.

B.   The Plan

The District has sought to make each of its 10 high schools unique, with programs that respond to the continually changing needs of students and their parents. Indeed, the District implemented the Plan as part of a comprehensive effort to improve and equalize the attractiveness of all the high schools, including adoption of a weighted funding formula, a facilities plan and a new teacher contract that would make teacher transfers easier. Nevertheless, the high schools vary widely in desirability. Three of the northern schools ... are highly desirable and oversubscribed, meaning that more students wish to attend those schools than capacity allows. The magnitude of the oversubscription is noteworthy: For the academic year 2000–01, approximately 82 percent of students selected one of the oversubscribed schools as their first choice, while only about 18 percent picked one of the undersubscribed high schools as their first choice. Only when oversubscription occurs does the District become involved in the assignment process.

If a high school is oversubscribed, all students applying for ninth grade are admitted according to a series of four tiebreakers, applied in the following order: First, students who have a sibling attending that school are admitted. In any given oversubscribed school, the sibling tiebreaker accounts for somewhere between 15 to 20 percent of the admissions to the ninth grade class. Second, if an oversubscribed high school is racially imbalanced—meaning that the racial make up of its student body differs by more than 15 percent from the racial make up of the students of the Seattle public schools as a whole—and if the sibling preference does not bring the oversubscribed high school within plus or minus 15 percent of the District's demographics, the race-based tiebreaker is "triggered" and the race of the applying student is considered. (For the purposes of the race-based tiebreaker, a student is deemed to be of the race specified in his or her registration materials.) Thus, if a school has more than 75 percent nonwhite students (i.e., more than 15 percent above the overall 60 percent nonwhite student population) and less than 25 percent white students, or when it has less than 45 percent nonwhite students (i.e., more than 15 percent below the overall 60 percent nonwhite student population) and more than 55 percent white students, the school is considered racially imbalanced.

Originally, schools that deviated by more than 10 percent were deemed racially imbalanced. For the 2001–02 school year, however, the triggering number was increased to 15 percent, softening the effect of the tiebreaker. For that year, the race-based tiebreaker was used in assigning entering ninth grade students only to three oversubscribed schools.... Accordingly, in seven of the 10 public high schools in 2001–02, race was not relevant in making admissions decisions.

The race-based tiebreaker is applied to both white and nonwhite students....

In addition to changing the trigger point for the 2001–02 school year to plus or minus 15 percent, the District also developed a "thermostat," whereby the tiebreaker is applied to the entering ninth grade student population only until it comes within the 15 percent plus or minus variance. Once that point is reached, the District "turns-off" the race-based tiebreaker, and there is no further consideration of a student's race in the assignment process. The tiebreaker does not apply, and race is not considered, for students entering a high school after the ninth grade (e.g., by transfer). . . .

In the third tiebreaker, students are admitted according to distance from the student's home to the high school. Distance between home and school is calculated within 1/100 of a mile, with the closest students being admitted first. In any given oversubscribed school, the distance-based tiebreaker accounts for between 70 to 75 percent of admissions to the ninth grade.

In the fourth tiebreaker, a lottery is used to allocate the remaining seats. Because the distance tiebreaker serves to assign nearly all the students in the District, a lottery is virtually never used.

C.   Procedural History

Parents Involved in Community Schools ("Parents"), a group of parents whose children were not, or might not be, assigned to the high schools of their choice under the Plan, claimed that the District's use of the race-based tiebreaker for high school admissions is illegal under the Washington Civil Rights Act ("Initiative 200"), the Equal Protection Clause of the Fourteenth Amendment and Title VI of the Civil Rights Act of 1964.

Both Parents and the District moved for summary judgment on all claims. In a published opinion dated April 6, 2001, the district court upheld the use of the racial tiebreaker under both state and federal law, granting the District's motion. Parents timely appealed, and on April 16, 2002, a three-judge panel of this court issued an opinion reversing the district court's decision, holding that the Plan violated Washington state law and discussing federal law only as an aid to construing state law. The panel subsequently withdrew its opinion and certified the state law question to the Washington Supreme Court. The Washington Supreme Court disagreed with the panel's decision, holding that the open choice plan did not violate Washington law. Thereafter, a majority of the three-judge panel of this court held that although the District demonstrated a compelling interest in achieving the benefits of racial diversity, the Plan violated the Equal Protection Clause because it was not narrowly tailored. We granted en banc rehearing and now affirm the district court.

II.   Discussion

A.   Strict Scrutiny

We review racial classifications under the strict scrutiny standard, which requires that the policy in question be narrowly tailored to achieve a compelling state interest. The strict scrutiny standard is not "strict in theory, but fatal in fact." "Although all governmental uses of race are subject to strict scrutiny, not all are invalidated by it." We employ strict scrutiny to "smoke out" impermissible uses of race by ensuring that the government is pursuing a goal important enough to warrant use of a highly suspect tool. This heightened standard of review provides a framework for carefully examining the importance and the sincerity of the reasons advanced by the governmental decisionmaker for the use of race in that particular context. In evaluating the District's Plan under strict scrutiny, we also bear in mind the Court's directive that "[c]ontext matters when reviewing race-based governmental action under the Equal Protection Clause."

B. Compelling State Interest

Under strict scrutiny, a government action will not survive unless motivated by a "compelling state interest." Because strict scrutiny requires us to evaluate the "fit" between the government's means and its ends, it is critical to identify precisely the governmental interests—the ends—to which the government's use of race must fit.

Although the Supreme Court has never decided a case involving the consideration of race in a voluntarily imposed school assignment plan intended to promote racially and ethnically diverse secondary schools, its decisions regarding selective admissions to institutions of higher learning demonstrate that one compelling reason for considering race is to achieve the educational benefits of diversity. The compelling interest that the Court recognized in *Grutter* was the promotion of the specific educational and societal benefits that flow from diversity.... In evaluating the relevance of diversity to higher education, the Court focused principally on two benefits that a diverse student body provides: (1) the learning advantages of having diverse viewpoints represented in the "robust exchange of ideas" that is critical to the mission of higher education; and (2) the greater societal legitimacy that institutions of higher learning enjoy by cultivating a group of national leaders who are representative of our country's diversity. The Court also mentioned the role of diversity in challenging stereotypes. The Court largely deferred to the law school's educational judgment not only in determining that diversity would produce these benefits, but also in determining that these benefits were critical to the school's educational mission.

Against this background, we consider the specific interests that the District's Plan seeks to advance. These interests are articulated in the "Board Statement Reaffirming Diversity Rationale" as:

> Diversity in the classroom increases the likelihood that students will discuss racial or ethnic issues and be more likely to socialize with people of different races. Diversity is thus a valuable resource for teaching students to become citizens in a multi-racial/multi-ethnic world. Providing students the opportunity to attend schools with diverse student enrollment also has inherent educational value from the standpoint of education's role in a democratic society.... Diversity brings different viewpoints and experiences to classroom discussions and thereby enhances the educational process. It also fosters racial and cultural understanding, which is particularly important in a racially and culturally diverse society such as ours.

The District's commitment to the diversity of its schools and to the ability to voluntarily avoid racially concentrating enrollment patterns also helps ensure that all students have access to those schools, faculties, course offerings, and resources that will enable them to reach their full potential.

Based on the foregoing rationale, the Seattle School District's commitment is that no student should be required to attend a racially concentrated school. The District is also committed to providing students with the opportunity to voluntarily choose to attend a school to promote integration. The District provides these opportunities for students to attend a racially and ethnically diverse school, and to assist in the voluntary integration of a school, because it believes that providing a diverse learning environment is educationally beneficial for all students.

The District's interests fit into two broad categories: (1) the District seeks the affirmative educational and social benefits that flow from racial diversity; and (2) the District seeks to avoid the harms resulting from racially concentrated or isolated schools.

1. Educational and Social Benefits that Flow from Diversity

The District has established that racial diversity produces a number of compelling educational and social benefits in secondary education. First, the District presented expert testimony that in racially diverse schools, "both white and minority students experienced improved critical thinking skills—the ability to both understand and challenge views which are different from their own."

Second, the District demonstrated the socialization and citizenship advantages of racially diverse schools. School officials, relying on their experience as teachers and administrators, and the District's expert all explained these benefits on the record.... The research further supports the proposition that these benefits are "long lasting." Even Parents' expert conceded that "[t]here is general agreement by both experts and the general public that integration is a desirable policy goal mainly for the social benefit of increased information and understanding about the cultural and social differences among various racial and ethnic groups." That is, diversity encourages students not only to think critically but also democratically.

Third, the District's expert noted that "research shows that a[ ] desegregated educational experience opens opportunity networks in areas of higher education and employment ... [and] strongly shows that graduates of desegregated high schools are more likely to live in integrated communities than those who do not, and are more likely to have cross-race friendships later in life."

The District's interests in the educational and social benefits of diversity are similar to those of a law school as articulated in *Grutter*. The contextual differences between public high schools and universities, however, make the District's interests compelling in a similar but also significantly different manner.

The Supreme Court in *Grutter* noted the importance of higher education in "preparing students for work and citizenship." For a number of reasons, public secondary schools have an equal if not more important role in this preparation. First, underlying the history of desegregation in this country is a legal regime that recognizes the principle that public secondary education serves a unique and vital socialization function in our democratic society. As the Court explained in *Plyler v. Doe*, "[w]e have recognized the public schools as a most vital civic institution for the preservation of a democratic system of government, and as the primary vehicle for transmitting the values on which our society rests." ... Under Washington law, such civic training is mandated by the state constitution. . . .

Second, although one hopes that all students who graduate from Seattle's public schools would have the opportunity to attend institutions of higher learning if they so desire, a substantial number of Seattle's public high school graduates do not attend college. For these students, their public high school educational experience will be their sole opportunity to reap the benefits of a diverse learning environment. We reject the notion that only those students who leave high school and enter the elite world of higher education should garner the benefits that flow from learning in a diverse classroom. Indeed, it would be a perverse reading of the Equal Protection Clause that would allow a university, educating a relatively small percentage of the population, to use race when choosing its student body but not allow a public school district, educating all children attending its schools, to consider a student's race in order to ensure that the high schools within the district attain and maintain diverse student bodies.

Third, the public school context involves students who, because they are younger and more impressionable, are more amenable to the benefits of diversity. . . .

The dissent insists that racial diversity in a public high school is not a compelling interest, arguing that *Grutter* endorsed a law school's compelling interest in diversity only in some broader or more holistic sense. . . . To attain this broader interest, the dissent contends, the District may only consider race along with other attributes such as socioeconomic status, ability to speak multiple languages or extracurricular talents. We read *Grutter*, however, to recognize that racial diversity, not some proxy for it, is valuable in and of itself. . . .

In short, the District has demonstrated that it has a compelling interest in the educational and social benefits of racial diversity similar to those articulated by the Supreme Court in *Grutter* as well as the additional compelling educational and social benefits of such diversity unique to the public secondary school context.

2. Avoiding the Harms Resulting from Racially Concentrated or Isolated Schools

The District's interest in achieving the affirmative benefits of a racially diverse educational environment has a flip side: avoiding racially concentrated or isolated schools. In particular, the District is concerned with making the educational benefits of a diverse learning environment available to all its students and ensuring that "no student should be required to attend a racially concentrated school.".... Research regarding desegregation has found that racially concentrated or isolated schools are characterized by much higher levels of poverty, lower average test scores, lower levels of student achievement, with less-qualified teachers and fewer advanced courses—"[w]ith few exceptions, separate schools are still unequal schools."

In Seattle, the threat of having to attend a racially concentrated or isolated school is not a theoretical or imagined problem. As the district court found, the District "established that housing patterns in Seattle continue to be racially concentrated," and would result in racially concentrated or isolated schools if school assignments were based solely on a student's neighborhood or proximity to a particular high school. Accordingly, the District's Plan strives to ensure that patterns of residential segregation are not replicated in the District's school assignments.... Although Parents make much of the fact that "Seattle has never operated a segregated school system," and allege that "this is not a school desegregation case," each court to review the matter has concluded that because of Seattle's housing patterns, high schools in Seattle would be highly segregated absent race conscious measures.

The district court found that, "[t]he circumstances that gave rise to the court-approved school assignment policies of the 1970s [e.g., ... segregated housing patterns] continue to be as compelling today as they were in the days of the district's mandatory busing programs.... [I]t would defy logic for this court to find that the less intrusive programs of today violate the Equal Protection Clause while the more coercive programs of the 1970s did not." Thus, it concluded that "[p]reventing the re-segregation of Seattle's schools is ... a compelling interest." Several other courts have also conceived of a school district's voluntary reduction or prevention of de facto segregation as a compelling interest.... We join these courts in recognizing that school districts have a compelling interest in ameliorating real, identifiable de facto racial segregation.

The dissent, however, contends first that the District is not "desegregating" but rather is engaged in racial balancing.... Further, for the dissent, segregation requires a state actor intentionally to separate the races; and in the absence of such offensive state conduct, the Supreme Court cases detailing the remedies for Fourteenth Amendment violations are of no relevance.... Thus, without a court finding of de jure segregation the elected school board members of the District may not take voluntary, affirmative steps towards creating a racially diverse student body. We disagree. The fact that de jure segregation is particularly offensive to our Constitution does not diminish the real harms of separation of the races by other means. "Segregation of white and colored children in public schools has a detrimental effect upon the colored children. The impact is greater when it has the sanction of law...." The benefits that flow from integration (or desegregation) exist whether or not a state actor was responsible for the earlier racial isolation. Brown's statement that "in the field of public education ...

[s]eparate educational facilities are inherently unequal" retains its validity today. The District is entitled to seek the benefits of racial integration and avoid the harms of segregation even in the absence of a court order deeming it a violator of the U.S. Constitution.

Support for this conclusion comes from statements in the Supreme Court's school desegregation cases, which repeatedly refer to the voluntary integration of schools as sound educational policy within the discretion of local school officials. . . .

In sum, we hold that the District's interests in obtaining the educational and social benefits of racial diversity in secondary education and in avoiding racially concentrated or isolated schools resulting from Seattle's segregated housing pattern are clearly compelling.

C.   Narrow Tailoring

We must next determine whether the District's use of the race-based tiebreaker is narrowly tailored to achieve its compelling interests. The narrow tailoring inquiry is intended to " 'smoke out' illegitimate uses of race" by ensuring that the government's classification is closely fitted to the compelling goals that it seeks to achieve. Here, our analysis is framed by the Court's narrow tailoring analysis in *Grutter* and *Gratz*, which, though informed by considerations specific to the higher education context, substantially guides our inquiry. . . .

In *Gratz*, the Court held unconstitutional the University of Michigan's undergraduate admissions program, which automatically assigned 20 points on the admissions scale to an applicant from an underrepresented racial or ethnic minority group. In *Grutter*, by contrast, the Court upheld the University of Michigan Law School's admissions policy, which took race into account as one of several variables in an individual's application. The law school's policy also attempted to ensure that a "critical mass" of underrepresented minority students would be admitted in order to realize the benefits of a diverse student body.

In its analysis, the Court identified five hallmarks of a narrowly tailored affirmative action plan: (1) individualized consideration of applicants; (2) the absence of quotas; (3) serious, good-faith consideration of race-neutral alternatives to the affirmative action program; (4) that no member of any racial group was unduly harmed; and (5) that the program had a sunset provision or some other end point. . . .

Hallmarks two through five are applicable here despite significant differences between the competitive admissions plans at issue in *Gratz* and *Grutter* and the District's high school assignment Plan. The first hallmark, however, is less relevant to our analysis because of the contextual differences between institutions of higher learning and public high schools.

1.   Individualized, Holistic Consideration of Applicants

a.   An applicant's qualifications

In the context of university admissions, where applicants compete for a limited number of spaces in a class, the Court in *Grutter* and *Gratz* focused its inquiry on the role race may play in judging an applicant's qualifications. The Court's underlying concern was that the "admissions policy is flexible enough to consider all pertinent elements of diversity in light of the particular qualifications of each applicant, and to place them on the same footing for consideration, although not necessarily according them the same weight." . . .

In *Grutter* and *Gratz*, in order to prevent race from being used as a mechanical proxy for an applicant's qualifications, the Court required individualized, holistic consideration of each applicant across a broad range of factors (of which race may be but one). . . . This focus on an applicant's qualifications—whether these qualifications are such things as an applicant's test scores, grades, artistic or athletic ability, musical talent or life experience—is not applicable when there is no competition or consideration of qualifications at issue.

All of Seattle's high school students must and will be placed in a Seattle public school. Students' relative qualifications are irrelevant because regardless of their academic achievement, sports or artistic ability, musical talent or life experience, any student who wants to attend Seattle's public high schools is entitled to an assignment; no assignment to any of the District's high schools is tethered to a student's qualifications. Thus, no stigma results from any particular school assignment. Accordingly, the dangers that are present in the university context—of substituting racial preference for qualification-based competition—are absent here . . . .

b.   Differences in compelling interests

The Court's requirement of individualized, holistic review in *Grutter* is also more relevant to the compelling interest advanced by the law school ("the robust exchange of ideas" fostered by viewpoint diversity) than it is to the District's (racial diversity and avoiding racially concentrated or isolated schools). The Court noted that the law school did not "limit in any way . . . the broad range of qualities and experiences that may be considered valuable contributions to student body diversity." To this end, the law school's policy made clear that "[t]here are many possible bases for diversity admissions, and provide[d] examples of admittees who have lived or traveled widely abroad, are fluent in several languages, have overcome personal adversity and family hardship, have exceptional records of extensive community service, and had successful careers in other fields." These multiple bases for diversity ensure the "classroom discussion is livelier, more spirited, and simply more enlightening and interesting when the students have the greatest possible variety of backgrounds."

Although the District's Plan, like the plan in *Grutter*, is designed to achieve the educational and social benefits of diversity, including bringing "different viewpoints and experiences to classroom discussions," . . . viewpoint diversity in the law school and high school contexts serves different albeit overlapping ends. In the law school setting, viewpoint diversity fosters the "robust exchange of ideas." In the high school context, viewpoint diversity fosters racial and civic understanding. . . .

In addition, the law school takes other diversity factors, besides race and ethnicity, into consideration in order to achieve its other compelling interest—cultivating a group of national leaders. For example, extensive travel, fluency in foreign languages, extensive community service and successful careers in other fields demonstrate that a candidate is somehow exceptional or out of the ordinary. . . . In contrast, the District is required to educate all high school age children, both the average and the extraordinary, regardless of individual leadership potential.

The District also has a second compelling interest that is absent from the university context—ensuring that its school assignments do not replicate Seattle's segregated housing patterns. The holistic review necessary to achieve viewpoint diversity in the university context, across a broad range of factors (of which race may be but one), is not germane to the District's compelling interest in preventing racial concentration or racial isolation. Because race itself is the relevant consideration when attempting to ameliorate de facto segregation, the District's tiebreaker must necessarily focus on the race of its students. . . . We therefore conclude that if a noncompetitive, voluntary student assignment plan is otherwise narrowly tailored, a district need not consider each student in a individualized, holistic manner.

The dissent insists that absent such individualized consideration, the District's plan cannot serve a compelling interest and is not narrowly tailored to protect individuals from group classifications by race. . . . This is a flawed reading of the Fourteenth Amendment. The District's compelling interest is to avoid the harms of racial isolation for all students in the Seattle school district. As we have explained, to accomplish that objective the District may look to the racial consequences of honoring the preferred choices of individual students (and their parents). It is true that for some students their first choice of school, based on geographical proximity, will be denied because other students' choices are granted in order to advance the overall interest in maintaining racially diverse school enrollments. The Fourteenth Amendment in this context does not preclude the District from honoring racial diversity at the expense of geographical proximity. We must not forget that "race unfortunately still matters," and it is race that is the relevant consideration here.

In sum, the contextual differences between public high schools and selective institutions of higher learning make the first of the *Grutter* hallmarks ill-suited for our narrow tailoring inquiry. The remaining hallmarks, however, are relevant and control our analysis.

2.   Absence of Quotas

In *Grutter*, the Court approved the law school's plan, in part, because it did not institute a quota, whereby a fixed number of slots are reserved exclusively for minority groups, thereby insulating members of those groups from competition with other candidates. Although the law school's plan did not seek to admit a set number or percentage of minority students, during the height of the admission's season, the law school would consult "daily reports" that kept track of the racial composition of the incoming class. The Court held that this attention to numbers did not transform the law school plan into a quota, but instead demonstrated that the law school sought to enroll a critical mass of minority students in order "to realize the educational benefits of a diverse student body." Id. Similarly, we conclude that the District's 15 percent plus or minus variance is not a quota because it does not reserve a fixed number of slots for students based on their race, but instead it seeks to enroll a critical mass of white and nonwhite students in its oversubscribed schools in order to realize its compelling interests.

a.   No fixed number of slots

The District's race-based tiebreaker does not set aside a fixed number of slots for nonwhite or white students in any of the District's schools. The tiebreaker is used only so long as there are members of the underrepresented race in the applicant pool for a particular oversubscribed school. If the number of students of that race who have applied to that school is exhausted, no further action is taken, even if the 15 percent variance has not been satisfied. That is, if the applicant pool has been exhausted, no students are required or recruited to attend a particular high school in order to bring it within the 15 percent plus or minus range for that year.

Moreover, the number of white and nonwhite students in the high schools is flexible and varies from school to school and from year to year. This variance in the number of nonwhite and white students throughout the District's high schools is because, under the Plan, assignments are based on students' and parents' preferences. The tiebreakers come into play in the assignment process only when a school is oversubscribed. . . .

b.   Critical mass

Within this flexible system, where parental and student choices drive the assignments to particular schools, the District seeks to enroll and maintain a relatively stable critical mass of white and nonwhite students in each of its oversubscribed high schools in order to achieve its compelling interest in racial diversity and to prevent the assignments from replicating Seattle's segregated housing patterns. Faced with the question of what constituted a critical mass of students in this particular context, the District determined that a critical mass was best achieved by adopting the 15 percent plus or minus variance tied to demographics of students in the Seattle public schools. Thus, when an oversubscribed high school has more than 75 percent nonwhite students (i.e., more than 15 percent above the overall 60 percent nonwhite student population) and less than 25 percent white students, or when it has less than 45 percent nonwhite students (i.e., more than 15 percent below the overall 60 percent nonwhite student population) and more than 55 percent white students, the school is considered racially concentrated or isolated, meaning that it lacks a critical mass of students needed "to realize the educational benefits of a diverse student body."

Parents attack the District's use of the 15 percent plus or minus variance tied to the District's school population demographics because they believe that the District cannot use race at all in its assignment process. We have rejected this argument, however, applying *Grutter* and *Gratz*. Alternatively, Parents contend that the District's goal of enrolling between 75 and 45 percent nonwhite students and between 25 and 55 percent white students in its oversubscribed schools establishes a quota, not a critical mass. They note that the critical mass sought by the law school in *Grutter* was smaller, consisting of between 12 and 20 percent of underrepresented minority students in each law school class.

Parents' argument, however, ignores *Grutter's* admonition that the narrow tailoring inquiry be context-specific. First, like the District's enrollment goals, which are tied to the demographics of the Seattle schools' total student population, the law school's goal of enrolling between 12 to 20 percent of underrepresented minorities in a given year was tied to the demographics of its applicant pool. Second, in tying the use of the tiebreaker to the District's demographics with a 15 percent plus or minus trigger point, the District adopted a common benchmark in the context of voluntary and court-ordered school desegregation plans. . . .

Even Parents' expert testified that school districts throughout the country determine whether a district is sufficiently desegregated by looking to the "population of the district" in question. . . . Given this empirically and time-tested notion of critical mass in the public high school desegregation context, it would make little sense to force the District to utilize the same percentages that constituted a critical mass in the elite law school context to determine what constitutes a critical mass for Seattle public high schools. . . .

Accordingly, we conclude that the District's 15 percent plus or minus trigger point tied to the demographics of the Seattle school population is not a quota. It is a context-specific, flexible measurement of racial diversity designed to attain and maintain a critical mass of white and nonwhite students in Seattle's public high schools.

3.   Necessity of the Plan and Race–Neutral Alternatives

Narrow tailoring also requires us to consider the necessity of the race-based plan or policy in question and whether there are equally effective, race-neutral alternatives.

a.   Necessity of the Plan

The District argues that the compelling interests that it seeks are directly served by the race-based tiebreaker. The tiebreaker allows the District to balance students' and parents' choices among high schools with its broader compelling interests—achieving the educational and social benefits of diversity and the benefits specific to the secondary school context, and discouraging a return to enrollment patterns based on Seattle's racially segregated housing pattern.

i.   Need for race-based tiebreaker

When the District moved from its controlled choice plan to the current Plan, it predicted that families would tend to choose schools close to their homes. Indeed, this feature was seen as a positive way to increase parental involvement. However, unfettered choice—especially with tiebreakers based on neighborhood or distance from a school— created the risk that Seattle's high school enrollment would again do no more than reflect its segregated housing patterns.

It is this de facto residential segregation across a white/nonwhite axis that the District has battled historically and that it seeks to ameliorate by making the integration tiebreaker a part of its open choice Plan. The District, mindful of both Seattle's history and future, appro- priately places its focus here. In the 2001–02 school year, the integration tiebreaker operated in three high schools (that is, three high schools were oversubscribed and deviated by more than 15 percent from the ratio of white to nonwhite students district-wide). The integration tie- breaker served to alter the imbalance in the schools in which it operated in a minimally intrusive manner. The tiebreaker, therefore, successfully achieved the District's compelling interests.

ii.   White/Nonwhite distinction

Parents argue that the District paints with too broad a brush by distinguishing only between white and nonwhite students, without tak- ing into account the diversity within the "nonwhite" group. However, the District's choice to increase diversity along the white/nonwhite axis is rooted in Seattle's history and current reality of de facto segregation resulting from Seattle's segregated housing patterns. The white/non- white distinction is narrowly tailored to prioritize movement of students from the north of the city to the south of city and vice versa. This white/nonwhite focus is also consistent with the history of public school desegregation measures throughout the country, as reflected in a current federal regulation defining "[m]inority group isolation" as "a condition in which minority group children constitute more than 50 percent of the enrollment of the school," without distinguishing among the various categories included within the definition of "minority group." . . .

b.   Race-neutral alternatives

In *Grutter*, the Court explained that narrow tailoring "require[s] serious, good faith consideration of workable race-neutral alternatives that will achieve the diversity the university seeks." On the other hand, "[n]arrow tailoring does not require exhaustion of every conceivable race-neutral alternative." Id. Furthermore, the Court made clear that the university was not required to adopt race-neutral measures that would have forced it to sacrifice other educational values central to its mission. Implicit in the Court's analysis was a measure of deference toward the university's identification of those values. Here, the record reflects that the District reasonably concluded that a race-neutral alter- native would not meet its goals.

i. Using poverty as an alternative measure of diversity

The record demonstrates that the School Board considered using a poverty tiebreaker in place of the race-based tiebreaker. It concluded, however, that this proxy device would not achieve its compelling interest in achieving racial diversity, and had other adverse effects. Although there was no formal study of the proposal by District staff, Board members' testimony revealed two legitimate reasons why the Board rejected the use of poverty to reach its goal of racial diversity. First, the Board concluded that it is insulting to minorities and often inaccurate to assume that poverty correlates with minority status. Second, for the group of students for whom poverty would correlate with minority status, the implementation would have been thwarted by high school students' understandable reluctance to reveal their socioeconomic status to their peers.

Because racial diversity is a compelling interest, the District may permissibly seek it if it does so in a narrowly tailored manner. We do not require the District to conceal its compelling interest of achieving racial diversity and avoiding racial concentration or isolation through the use of "some clumsier proxy device" such as poverty.

ii. The Urban League plan

Parents also assert that the District should have more formally considered an Urban League proposal, which did not eliminate the integration tiebreaker but merely considered it after other factors. The Urban League plan was a comprehensive plan seeking to enhance the quality of education in Seattle's schools by focusing on educational organization, teacher quality, parent-teacher interaction, raising curricular standards, substantially broadening the availability of specialized and magnet programs (which could attract a broader cross-section of students to undersubscribed schools) and supporting extra-curricular development. The plan proposed decreasing the School District's reliance on race in the assignment process by pairing neighborhoods with particular schools and creating a type of neighborhood/regional school model. Under the Urban League plan, preference initially would be given to students choosing a school in their paired region, and the existing racial tiebreaker would be demoted from second to third in the process of resolving any remaining oversubscription. The plan also suggested adding an eleventh high school.

Board members testified that they rejected the plan because of the high value the District places on parental and student choice. Moreover, given Seattle's segregated housing patterns, by prioritizing a neighborhood/regional school model where students are assigned to schools close to their homes, the Urban League plan did not sufficiently ensure the achievement of the District's compelling interests in racial diversity and avoidance of racial concentration or isolation. As one member of the School Board testified, "[it] would become Controlled Choice all over again. That's basically what Controlled Choice was, [ ] a regional plan; it controlled your options by using regions or geography." It was therefore permissible for the District to reject a plan that neither comported with its priorities nor achieved its compelling interests.

iii. Lottery

Parents additionally contend in this court that the District should have considered using a lottery to assign students to the oversubscribed high schools. As an initial matter, we note that Parents did not argue before the district court that a lottery was a workable race-neutral alternative that would achieve the Districts' compelling interests. Parents now argue on appeal, however, that a lottery would achieve the District's compelling interests without having to resort to the race-based tiebreaker. They ask us to assume that because approximately 82 percent of all students want to attend one of Seattle's oversubscribed schools, the makeup of this 82 percent, as well as that of the applicant pool for each school, mirrors the demographics of the District (60 percent white and 40 percent nonwhite). Employing this assumption, Parents also ask us to assume that a random lottery drawing from this pool would produce a student body in each of the oversubscribed schools that falls within the District's 15 percent plus or minus variance. These assumptions, however, are not supported—indeed, are undercut—by the factual record. For example, Superintendent Olchefske explained that District patterns indicate that more people choose schools close to home. That would mean that the pool of applicants would be skewed in favor of the demographic of the surrounding residential area. That is, the applicant pool for the north area oversubscribed high schools would have a higher concentration of white students and the applicant pool for the south area oversubscribed high school would have a higher concentration of nonwhite students. Thus, random sampling from such a racially skewed pool would produce a racially skewed student body. . . .

Although the District has the burden of demonstrating that its Plan is narrowly tailored, it need not "exhaust[ ] every conceivable race-neutral alternative." Parents' belated and bald assertion that a lottery could achieve the District's compelling interests, without any evidence to support their claim, fails to demonstrate that a lottery is a viable race-neutral alternative. . . .

c. The District's use of race

. . .

In sum, the District made a good faith effort to consider feasible race-neutral alternatives and permissibly rejected them in favor of a system involving a sibling preference, a race-based tiebreaker and a proximity preference. Over the long history of the District's efforts to achieve desegregated schools, it has experimented with many alternatives, including magnet and other special-interest programs, which it continues to employ, and race-conscious districting. But when a racially diverse school system is the goal (or racial concentration or isolation is the problem), there is no more effective means than a consideration of race to achieve the solution. . . .

4. Undue Harm

A narrowly tailored plan ensures that no member of any racial group is unduly harmed. Parents argue that every student who is denied his or her choice of schools because of the integration tiebreaker suffers a constitutionally significant burden. We agree with the Supreme Court of Washington, however, in its assessment that the District's Plan imposes a minimal burden that is shared equally by all of the District's students. As that court noted, it is well established that "there [is] no right under Washington law to attend a local school or the school of the student's choice." Indeed, public schools, unlike universities, have a tradition of compulsory assignment. . . .

Moreover, it is undisputed that the race-based tiebreaker does not uniformly benefit one race or group to the detriment of another. At some schools, white students are given preference over nonwhite students, and, at other schools, nonwhite students are given preference over white students . . .

In sum, because (1) the District is entitled to assign all students to any of its schools, (2) no student is entitled to attend any specific school and (3) the tiebreaker does not uniformly benefit any race or group of individuals to the detriment of another, the tiebreaker does not unduly harm any students in the District.

5. Sunset Provision

A narrowly tailored plan must be limited not only in scope, but also in time. The Court held in *Grutter* that this durational requirement can be met by "periodic reviews to determine whether racial preferences are still necessary to achieve student body diversity." The District's Plan includes such reviews. It revisits the Plan annually and has demonstrated its ability to be responsive to parents' and students' choice patterns and to the concerns of its constituents. For example, in 2000, when a higher than normal number of students selected the same schools, the Board responded by increasing the race-based trigger from 10 percent to a 15 percent deviation from the school population, adopting the thermostat that turns off the tiebreaker as soon as the school has come within the 15 percent plus or minus trigger point and by using the tiebreaker solely for the incoming ninth grade class.

With respect to the dissent's concern for a "logical end point," like Justice O'Connor this court shares in the hope that "25 years from now, the use of racial preferences will no longer be necessary to further the interest approved today." We expect that the District will continue to review its Plan, and we presume, as did the Court in *Grutter*, that school officials will demonstrate a good faith commitment to monitoring the continued need for the race-based tiebreaker and terminating its use when that need ends.

III. Conclusion

For the foregoing reasons, we hold that the Plan adopted by the Seattle School District for high school assignments is constitutional and the use of the race-based tiebreaker is narrowly tailored to achieve the District's compelling interests. Accordingly, we AFFIRM the district court's judgment.

AFFIRMED

Notes

1. This is the most comprehensive judicial analysis of *Gratz* and *Grutter* since the cases were handed down.

2. In *Grutter v. Bollinger,* 539 U.S. 306, 343, 123 S.Ct. 2325, 156 L.Ed.2d 304 [177 Educ. L. Rep. 801] (2003), in upholding the University of Michigan's affirmative action admissions policy in its law school, the Court suggested that "[w]e expect that 25 years from now, the use of racial preferences will no longer be necessary to further the interest approved today." What do you think about this statement?

3. What should the role of race be in admissions decisions?

[Case No. 101]   Power of Board to Charge Fees to Students

PAULSON v. MINIDOKA COUNTY SCHOOL DISTTRICT NO. 331

Supreme Court of Idaho, 1970.
93 Idaho 469, 463 P.2d 935.

McQUADE, JUSTICE. This action was instituted by Jack Paulson, and his sons Dan and Kirk Paulson, ... They sought to compel the defendants Minidoka County School District, its trustees and superintendent, hereinafter referred to collectively as the "school," to furnish a transcript of grades to Dan Paulson who graduated from Minidoka County High School in June, 1968. Dan and Kirk both attended the high school during the school year 1967–1968. Dan graduated that school year, and Kirk attended school during the 1968–1969 term. The issues in the present case arose from the adoption in 1967 by the Board of Trustees of the Minidoka County School District of ... [a] schedule of fees to be charged each student attending the high school.... In July, 1968, the fee schedule was amended so that although the same total of $25.00 per student was charged, the fees were itemized only as "Text Book Fees"— $12.50 and "School Activity Fees"—$12.50, total $25.00.

Dan and Kirk Paulson have each year refused to pay these fees. The school would not accept partial payment allocated to any one particular item, but insisted that the fees be paid in their entirety. Failure to pay the fees, however, did not in any way affect the student's right to attend classes. Not only were non-paying students allowed to attend classes, but they were also furnished textbooks free of charge. Until 1968–1969 all students were regularly given a student activity card and thereby allowed to attend social and athletic events even though the fees were not paid. Yearbooks were not furnished, nor were non-paying students allowed to purchase a yearbook since the school's policy was that the entire $25.00 fee be paid. Upon graduation Dan Paulson was furnished a cap and gown and presented a diploma.

Although a student could thus accumulate an "education" without payment of the fees, the impediment is that the school refuses to furnish a transcript of courses studied and grades achieved. When Dan applied to Idaho State University for admission, the school would not furnish a University required transcript. Dan was, however, provisionally admitted and this action was instituted to compel the high school to furnish a transcript. . . .

Our task in this case is to determine the application of art. 9, sec. 1 of the Constitution of the State of Idaho to this particular factual situation. That section is:

> "The stability of a republican form of government depending mainly upon the intelligence of the people, it shall be the duty of the legislature of Idaho, to establish and maintain a general, uniform and thorough system of public, free common schools."

Because of the delicacy and difficulty in resolving constitutional problems we settle such questions on a case-by-case basis. We, today, affirm the judgment of the lower court; and we hold that public high schools in Idaho are "common schools" within the meaning of art. 9, sec. 1; that the $25.00 fee *as it was charged in this case* offended the requirement that the "common schools" be "free;" and that the appellants were under a clear legal duty to furnish transcripts to eligible graduates of Minidoka County High School. . . .

The appellants, however, argue at some length that the high school in this case was "free" despite the mandatory $25.00 fee. One half of the $25.00 fee is assigned as payment for what appellants themselves call extra-curricular activities. If a student of Minidoka County High School wishes a transcript of his scholastic achievement he must pay the entire $25.00, one-half of which is expressly consigned to fund extra-curricular activities. Items which are "extra-curricular" are, by definition, outside of or in addition to the regular academic courses or curriculum of a school. A levy for such purposes, imposed generally on all students whether they participate in extra-curricular activities or not, becomes a charge on attendance at the school. Such a charge contravenes the constitutional mandate that the school be free. But it should be noted that, because social and extra-curricular activities are not necessary elements of a high school career, the constitution does not prohibit appellants from setting fees to cover costs of such activities to be paid by students who wish to exercise an option to participate in them.

The other half of the $25.00 fee, the $12.50 "textbook fee," stands on different ground. Textbooks are necessary elements of any school's activity. They represent a fixed expense peculiar to education, the benefits from which inure to every student in equal proportion (ignoring differences in ability and motivation) solely as a function of his being a student. Unlike pencils and paper, the student has no choice in the quality or quantity of textbooks he will use if he is to earn his education. He will use exactly the books, prescribed by the school authorities, that his classmates use; and no voluntary act of his can obviate the need for books nor lessen their expense. School books are, thus, indistinguishable from other fixed educational expense items such as school building maintenance or teachers' salaries. The appellants may not charge students for such items because the common schools are to be "free" as our constitution requires. (Appellants argue that if books must be provided free of charge then it becomes impossible to draw a line and even school clothing must be given away. This contention is answered by pointing out that clothing is not an item peculiarly necessary for the use of free schools-everyone must be clothed if he walks the streets-and it is an item of expense which is especially subject to personal taste in terms of the cost, quality and quantity of it used by any individual student.)

Appellants contend, however, that they are giving and have given the respondents "free high school educations," which is all that is required by the constitution. The appellants would separate the transcript from the educational experience it evidences and they argue that they are merely making availability of a transcript contingent upon payment of the fees. They also reason that they are under no clear legal duty to furnish a transcript and are not subject to mandamus. This argument evidences a serious misapprehension of the constitutional requirement of free schools. If the constitution said that all that was necessary was a "free common school education" the case might be different, but the constitution instead demands "free common schools." The *school* and the entire product to be received from it by the student must be "free."

The appellants failed to provide "free common schools" when they made access to the official reports of the students' records contingent on the $25.00 fee charged in this case. This fee bears no apparent relationship to the actual costs of printing and distributing the transcripts. It instead serves an enforcement purpose only. The appellants have withheld Dan's transcript to coerce payment of the lump-sum $25.00 fee. Because they may not charge the fee it follows that they may not penalize nonpayment of the fee by withholding an incidental but necessary transcript.

The legal duty to make available a transcript arises from the practicality that, in our society, the ability to obtain a transcript without cost is a necessary incident of a high school education. A reasonable fee, after the first free transcript, representing actual average costs, would be proper and may be charged for the duplication and issuance of subsequent transcripts. . . .

Notes

1. Was it necessary for the court to cover so many specifics to resolve the basic question that this case presented?

2. Should all public school activities, including interscholastic sports be free for students? Is it fair to charge fees for these activities?

[Case No. 102]   Constitutionality of Eligibility Requirement for Interscholastic Athletics—General Considerations

ALBACH v. ODLE

United States Court of Appeals, Tenth Circuit, 1976.
531 F.2d 983.

PER CURIAM. This appeal seeks to test the application of transfer rules adopted by the New Mexico Activities Association. The rules automatically bar from interscholastic high school athletic competition for one year any student who transfers from his home district to a boarding school or from a boarding school to his home district.…

The trial court dismissed the complaint on various grounds, one of which was that it failed to raise a substantial federal question. We affirm.

Controlling precedent is found in *Oklahoma High School Athletic Ass'n v. Bray*, where this court stated:

> "… In the case at bar, once the pleadings were pierced at pretrial, it became apparent that Bray's grievance with the Athletic Association lay only with the application of its residence rule, the Board's refusal to grant an exception for hardship, and a general attack upon the amount of power delegated by the high schools to the Association. Such complaints are not within federal cognizance,.…"

The court held that if Bray had not voluntarily dismissed the action, the trial court would have been compelled to dismiss for lack of a substantial federal question. Appellant's allegations are virtually identical with those noted above.

Appellant cites numerous cases in support of the contention that high school athletic regulations must survive constitutional scrutiny. The cases are distinguished by the fact that, in the context of athletic regulations, clearly defined constitutional principles are at issue. The supervision and regulation of high school athletic programs remain within the discretion of appropriate state boards, and are not within federal cognizance under 42 U.S.C.A. § 1983 unless the regulations deny an athlete a constitutionally protected right or classify him or her on a suspect basis.

Appellant also argues that *Goss v. Lopez* somehow negates our decision in *Bray*. We disagree. *Goss* recognizes a student's entitlement to a public education as a property interest which is constitutionally protected. A ten-day suspension from school without a hearing was found to violate a student's right to due process under the Fourteenth Amendment. But it is necessary to note that in framing the property interest the Court in *Goss* speaks in terms of the "educational process." The educational process is a broad and comprehensive concept with a variable and indefinite meaning. It is not limited to classroom attendance but includes innumerable separate components, such as participation in athletic activity and membership in school clubs and social groups, which combine to provide an atmosphere of intellectual and moral advancement. We do not read *Goss* to establish a property interest subject to constitutional protection in each of these separate components.

Affirmed.

Notes

1.   How can one account for the rash of cases attacking rules covering eligibility for participation in interscholastic athletics? This opinion succinctly covers many established constitutional principles relevant to the area.

2.   Are eligibility rules for interscholastic athletics too restrictive?

[Case No. 103]   Constitutionality of Eligibility Requirement for Interscholastic Athletics—Parent Rights

KITE v. MARSHALL

United States Court of Appeals, Fifth Circuit, 1981.
661 F.2d 1027 [1 Educ. L. Rep. 44].

POLITZ, CIRCUIT JUDGE: These consolidated actions challenge the validity of Section 21 of Article VIII of the Constitution and Contest Rules of the University Interscholastic League (UIL) of Texas. The challenged section suspends for one year the varsity athletics eligibility of any high school student who attends certain training camps. The district court enjoined the enforcement of section 21 and subsequently declared the rule unconstitutional as applied. We reverse.

UIL is a voluntary, non-profit association of public schools below collegiate rank in the State of Texas. . . . Its stated objective is "to foster among the public schools of Texas interschool competitions as an aid in the preparation for citizenship." In pursuit of this goal, UIL promulgates rules and regulations governing various aspects of competition in speech, journalism, literary and academic contests, drama, music and athletics. Although a private organization, UIL's functioning constitutes state action subject to the limitations of the fourteenth amendment to the Constitution. We must determine whether section 21 violates either the due process or equal protection clause of that amendment.

The district court found section 21 to be constitutionally infirm because it infringed protected parental authority in the child-rearing arena. Appellees exhort us to affirm the trial court's conclusions, principally relying on the "family choice doctrine" which has its genesis in *Prince v. Massachusetts*, *Pierce v. Society of Sisters*, and *Meyer v. Nebraska*. We cannot accept the invitation.

The *Meyer* and *Pierce* decisions are based on the premise that the state has no power to "standardize its children," or to "foster a homogeneous people," by foreclosing the opportunity of individuals "to heed the music of different drummers." . . .

Appellees cite as controlling precedent a line of Supreme Court decisions which purportedly recognize the existence of a "private realm of family life which the state cannot enter," absent compelling reasons. Uncertainty abounds, not only as to the constitutional spring from which this family privacy right flows, but also as to its definition and character.

Recent decisions by the Supreme Court declaring that parents have no constitutional right to educate their children in private segregated academies, *Runyon v. McCrary*, or to demand approval before the administration of corporal punishment in school, *Ingraham v. Wright*, ... clearly signal that parental authority falls short of being constitutionally absolute. Confronted with these situations which, at first blush, appear to rest at the heart of parental decision making, the Supreme Court refrained from clothing parental judgment with a constitutional mantle.

The instant case presents a similar inquiry. Reduced to essentials, the legal questions posed are: (1) whether parents possess a fundamental right to send their children to summer athletic camps; and (2) whether the children have a constitutional right to attend such activities. As is frequently the case, in the very postulation of the questions the answer lies. A negative response to both questions is mandated. This case implicates no fundamental constitutional right.

The determination that no fundamental right to participate in summer athletic camp exists establishes the level of scrutiny to which we must subject section 21. The regulation will pass constitutional muster if it is found to have a rational basis.

Due Process

The UIL contends that its rules are designed to make competition among its 1,142 member schools as fair and equitable as possible. The UIL program, including the athletics component, is only a part of the overall educational process. Several reasons are advanced in support of section 21, including the need to control over-zealous coaches, parents and communities, the achieving of a competitive balance between those who can afford to attend summer camp and those who cannot, the avoidance of various excessive pressures on students, and the abrogation of the use of camps as recruiting mechanisms.

It cannot be argued seriously that section 21 is wholly arbitrary and totally without value in the promotion of a legitimate state objective. We do not evaluate the ultimate wisdom, *vel non*, of section 21, or the sagacity of its methodology. The school authorities have concluded that section 21 serves the purpose of making interscholastic athletics fairer and more competitive. We are not prepared to say that section 21 bears no meaningful relationship to the achievement of that ideal. The due process clause of the fourteenth amendment has not been offended.

Equal Protection

Traditionally, the equal protection analysis has been performed against the backdrop of the standards of strict scrutiny and minimum rationality. To withstand strict scrutiny, a statute must necessarily relate to a compelling state interest. The rational basis test requires only that the legislation or regulation under challenge rationally promote a legitimate governmental objective.

A state action viewed under the rational basis banner is presumed to be valid. In such a situation, "the burden is not upon the state to establish the rationality of its restriction, but is upon the challenger to show that the restriction is wholly arbitrary." Accordingly, only when a demonstration is made that the classification contained in the regulation is wholly arbitrary or does not teleologically relate to a permissible governmental objective is the equal protection clause violated. When "the classification created by the regulatory scheme neither trammels fundamental rights or interests nor burdens an inherently suspect class, equal protection analysis requires that the classification be rationally related to a legitimate state interest."

In view of the Supreme Court's prevailing opinions ... we believe that the minimum rationality test provides the guide for our equal protection evaluation.

Admittedly section 21 operates to treat student-athletes who attend summer athletic camps differently from those students who do not. The former lose eligibility in all varsity sports for the next year. But the categorization is not premised on impermissible, suspect grounds. Nor does the classification impinge upon the exercise of fundamental rights. The rule seeks to achieve a balance in interscholastic athletics. It is not unconstitutional.

The judgment of the district court, in these consolidated cases, is reversed.

Note

Suppose the parents sent their son to a summer drama school. Could school officials have enforced a ban on his trying out for the school play?

[Case No. 104] Power of State to Set Academic Requirements for Participants in Extracurricular Activities

SPRING BRANCH I.S.D. v. STAMOS

Supreme Court of Texas, 1985.
695 S.W.2d 556 [27 Educ. L. Rep. 605].

RAY, JUSTICE. This is a direct appeal brought by the Attorney General, representing the Texas Education Agency, and others, seeking immediate appellate review of an order of the trial court which held unconstitutional, and enjoined enforcement of, a provision of the Texas Education Code.... We hold that the statutory provision is not unconstitutional and reverse the judgment of the trial court.

Chris Stamos and others brought this suit on behalf of Nicky Stamos and others, seeking a permanent injunction against enforcement of the Texas "no pass, no play" rule by the Spring Branch and Alief

Independent School Districts. The Texas Education Agency and the University Interscholastic League intervened. The district court issued a temporary restraining order and later, after a hearing, a temporary injunction enjoining all parties from enforcing the rule. This court issued an order staying the district court's order and setting the cause for expedited review.

THE "NO PASS, NO PLAY" RULE

The Second Called Session of the 68th Legislature adopted a package of educational reforms known as "H.B. 72." A major provision of these educational reforms was the so-called "no pass, no play" rule, which generally requires that students maintain a "70" average in all classes to be eligible for participation in extracurricular activities. The rule is incorporated in section 21.920 of the Texas Education Code and provides as follows:

§ 21.920.   Extracurricular Activities

(a) The State Board of Education by rule shall limit participation in and practice for extracurricular activities during the school day and the school week. The rules shall, to the extent possible, preserve the school day for academic activities without interruption for extracurricular activities. In scheduling those activities and practices, a district must comply with the rules of the board.

(b) A student, other than a mentally retarded student, enrolled in a school district in this state shall be suspended from participation in any extracurricular activity sponsored or sanctioned by the school district during the grade reporting period after a grade reporting period in which the student received a grade lower than the equivalent of 70 on a scale of 100 in any academic class. The campus principal may remove this suspension if the class is an identified honors or advanced class. A student may not be suspended under this subsection during the period in which school is recessed for the summer or during the initial grade reporting period of a regular school term on the basis of grades received in the final grade reporting period of the preceding regular school term.

. . .

ISSUES RAISED

The sole issue before this court is the constitutionality of the no pass, no play rule. The district court held the rule unconstitutional on the grounds that it violated equal protection and due process guarantees. The burden is on the party attacking the constitutionality of an act of the legislature. There is a presumption in favor of the constitutionality of an act of the legislature.

This court has long recognized the important role education plays in the maintenance of our democratic society. Article VII of the Texas Constitution "discloses a well-considered purpose on the part of those who framed it to bring about the establishment and maintenance of a comprehensive system of public education, consisting of a general public free school system and a system of higher education." Section 1 of article VII of the Constitution establishes a mandatory duty upon the legislature to make suitable provision for the support and maintenance of public free schools. The Constitution leaves to the legislature alone the determination of which methods, restrictions, and regulations are necessary and appropriate to carry out this duty, so long as that determination is not so arbitrary as to violate the constitutional rights of Texas' citizens.

Equal Protection

Stamos challenges the constitutionality of the "no pass, no play" rule on the ground that it violates the equal protection clause of the Texas Constitution. The first determination this court must make in the context of equal protection analysis is the appropriate standard of review. When the classification created by a state regulatory scheme neither infringes upon fundamental rights or interests nor burdens an inherently suspect class, equal protection analysis requires that the classification be rationally related to a legitimate state interest. Therefore, we must first determine whether the rule burdens an inherently suspect class or infringes upon fundamental rights or interests.

The no pass, no play rule classifies students based upon their achievement levels in their academic courses. We hold that those students who fail to maintain a minimum level of proficiency in all of their courses do not constitute the type of discrete, insular minority necessary to constitute a "suspect" class. Thus, the rule does not burden an inherently "suspect" class. . . .

Stamos also argues that the rule is subject to strict scrutiny under equal protection analysis because it impinges upon a fundamental right, i.e., the right to participate in extracurricular activities. We note that the overwhelming majority of jurisdictions have held that a student's right to participation in extracurricular activities does *not* constitute a fundamental right.

Stamos cites the case of *Bell v. Lone Oak Independent School District* for the proposition that students have a fundamental right to participate in extracurricular activities. In *Bell,* a school regulation prohibited married students from participating in extracurricular activities. Because the regulation impinged upon the fundamental right of marriage, the court of appeals held the regulation subject to strict scrutiny and struck it down because the school district had shown no compelling interest to support its enforcement. The presence of a fundamental right (marriage) distinguishes *Bell* from the present cause.

Fundamental rights have their genesis in the express and implied protections of personal liberty recognized in federal and state constitutions. A student's "right" to participate in extracurricular activities does not rise to the same level as the right to free speech or free exercise of religion, both of which have long been recognized as fundamental rights under our state and federal constitutions. We adopt the majority rule and hold that a student's right to participate in extracurricular activities *per se* does *not* rise to the level of a fundamental right under our constitution.

Because the no pass, no play rule neither infringes upon fundamental rights nor burdens an inherently suspect class, we hold that it is *not* subject to "strict" or heightened equal protection scrutiny. . . .

The no pass, no play rule distinguishes students based upon whether they maintain a satisfactory minimum level of performance in each of their classes. Students who fail to maintain a minimum proficiency in all of their classes are ineligible for participation in school-sponsored extra-curricular activities for the following six-week period, with no carry over from one school year to the next. The rule provides a strong incentive for students wishing to participate in extracurricular activities to maintain minimum levels of performance in all of their classes. In view of the rule's objective to promote improved classroom performance by students, we find the rule rationally related to the legitimate state interest in providing a quality education to Texas' public school students. . . .

The distinctions recognized in the rule for mentally retarded students and students enrolled in honors or advanced courses likewise do not render the rule violative of the equal protection guarantees of the Texas Constitution. While the statute itself does not deprive students of their right to equal protection of the law, we recognize that the discretion given to school principals in the rule's provision dealing with honors or advanced courses may well give rise to arbitrary or discriminatory application violative of equal protection principles. We are faced with no allegations of discriminatory application of the rule's honors exception in the present case.

Procedural Due Process

We begin our analysis of the due process arguments in this cause by recognizing that the strictures of due process apply only to the threatened deprivation of liberty and property interests deserving the protection of the federal and state constitutions. The federal courts have made it clear that the federal constitution's due process guarantees do not protect a student's interest in participating in extracurricular activities. We must, then, examine our state constitution to determine whether its due process guarantees extend to a student's desire to participate in school-sponsored extracurricular activities.

A property or liberty interest must find its origin in some aspect of state law. Nothing in either our state constitution or statutes entitles students to an absolute right to participation in extracurricular activities. We are in agreement, therefore, with the overwhelming majority of jurisdictions that students do not possess a constitutionally protected interest in their participation in extracurricular activities. Therefore, the strictures of procedural due process do *not* apply to the determination by a campus principal, pursuant to section 21.920(b) of the Texas Education Code, as to whether a student who fails an identified honors or advanced course shall be permitted to participate in extracurricular activities.

Substantive Due Process

Stamos cites *Spann v. City of Dallas* to support his argument that the rule violates principles of fundamental fairness and notions of substantive due process by giving school principals discretion to determine whether students who fail honors or advanced courses may participate in extracurricular activities. In *Spann,* this court declared void a city ordinance that required persons seeking to construct commercial buildings within residential areas to first obtain the consent of both neighboring residents and the city building inspector. There, we found that the ordinance provided no standards for builders or building inspectors with regard to the proper design for such buildings. By leaving the approval for such buildings "subject to the arbitrary discretion of the inspector," the ordinance violated the would-be builders' property right to use their property as they saw fit. This court emphasized that the ordinance in *Spann* infringed upon well-recognized property rights by permitting wholly arbitrary limitations upon the uses which owners could make of their property.

In the present case, appellees liken the school principals' unfettered discretion in determining both which classes shall constitute "advanced" or "honors" courses and whether students failing such classes may participate in extracurricular activities to the building inspectors' unfettered discretion over approving commercial building plans. *Spann* is distinguishable for the obvious reason that a recognized property interest was affected by the Dallas ordinance. As stated previously, students have no constitutionally protected interest in participation in extracurricular activities. Because no constitutionally protected interest is implicated by this delegation of authority to school principals, no violation of due process, substantive or procedural, results therefrom.

We do not agree with Stamos' argument that a school principal's exercise of discretion pursuant to the "honors" exception to the rule is shielded from all review. Arbitrary, capricious, or discriminatory exercise of a school principal's discretion pursuant to subsection 21.920(b) of the Texas Education Code may well give rise to claims based upon equal protection grounds. Accreditation audits of schools and school districts may also afford relief against improper utilization of the "honors" exception. We also note there are no findings of fact before us that any of the student-plaintiffs received failing grades in honors or advanced courses. . . .

Accordingly, we reverse the district court's judgment with regard to the constitutionality of section 21.920 of the Texas Education Code and dissolve the temporary injunction ordered by the district court.

Notes

1. West Virginia's highest court upheld a similar rule that was promulgated under the general supervisory powers of the state board of education. *Bailey v. Truby,* 321 S.E.2d 302 [20 Educ. L. Rep. 980] (W. Va.1984). The court rejected an argument that the rule infringed on the powers of county boards since they could not diminish the state board's constitutional power to pursue academic excel-

lence. The court responded that county boards could set higher standards than its state counterpart.

2.   Parents and others challenged a local board policy that required a 2.0 grade point average in five of six classes in order for student-athletes to remain eligible to participate in extracurricular activities. An appellate court affirmed that the policy was reasonably designed to minimize outside activities which distract from academic matters while offering incentive so that student-athletes could earn grades that would help them to retain eligibility. *Thompson v. Fayette County Pub. Schools*, 786 S.W.2d 879 [59 Educ. L. Rep. 1197] (Ky. Ct. App.1990).

Chapter 13

STUDENT RIGHTS

Introduction

As expansive as the topic of student rights has become, it is worth acknowledging that 1969 is a watershed year in this important area. In that year, for the first time, in *Tinker v. Des Moines Independent Community School District*,[1] the Supreme Court recognized the First Amendment free speech rights of public school students. In ensuing years, courts have addressed a wide array of disputes involving student rights such as challenges to school rules and discipline, whether on campus or off, to disputes over the Fourth and First Amendment rights of students, to litigation dealing with sexual harassment. In light of the important questions that these topics present, this chapter focuses on the rights of students.

Student Rights and School Rules

Generally

Courts grant school officials broad discretion to act to ensure safe and orderly learning environments. To this end, school boards have the authority to adopt reasonable policies and procedures regulating student conduct. Insofar as the Federal Constitution directs courts to respond only to real cases or controversies, rather than act in advisory capacities, a vast amount of litigation illustrates the general proposition that even though the judiciary generally defers to school officials, whether rules are enforceable depends on the fact-specific analysis of case law.

To the extent that school board policies with regard to student discipline and/or codes of conduct are presumptively valid, the burden of showing that they are unreasonable rests on students and their parents. The closer that rules encroach on the constitutional rights of students, the greater the need for justification by school officials since, even in light of the broad discretion that educators enjoy, students do not shed their constitutional rights at the schoolhouse gate.

If school rules infringe on fundamental constitutional rights such as freedom from unreasonable searches and seizures or freedom of speech or expression, the burden of proof shifts back to school officials to demonstrate that such rules are justified by a compelling need. Under these circumstances, courts have invalidated rules that are not rationally related to their expressed objectives, are too vague as to what conduct they forbid, or are over-broad in that they encompass constitutionally

---

1. 393 U.S. 503, 89 S.Ct. 733, 21 L.Ed.2d 731 (1969). [Case No. 110]

protected activities along with those that may be restricted.[2] Further, as the severity of punishments increases, courts take closer looks at rules and their accompanying procedures.

Whether all rules are written is immaterial if offenses, such as cheating, are punishable under general norms of school behavior. Inasmuch as courts concede that educators cannot develop written rules for all possible student infractions, they typically defer to the authority of school officials as long as they impose discipline that meets the requirements of due process. Put another way, when students know,[3] or reasonably should have known, school rules and punishments are appropriate to the offenses,[4] whether misbehavior occurs in school or away from school, then the courts are unlikely to intervene on their behalf as long as school officials provide them with the requisite level of due process.[5] Accordingly, while students have a right to know what conduct is prohibited, school disciplinary rules need not meet the stringent criteria that courts apply in criminal statutes.[6] Additionally, when school officials question students about their misbehavior in school,[7] courts agree that they are not entitled to receive *Miranda* warnings from educators[8] or school resource officers[9] about their Fifth Amendment right against self-incrimination.[10] However, in distinguishing between educators and police officials, the Supreme Court of Pennsylvania observed that since school police officers who interrogated a juvenile regarding the break-in and vandalism of a classroom were law enforcement officers, they violated his rights by not providing him with a *Miranda* warning.[11]

Out-of-School Conduct

The authority of school officials to discipline students for their off-campus misconduct has led to a substantial amount of litigation with the

2. *See, e.g., Saxe v. State College Area School Dist.*, 240 F.3d 200 [151 Educ. L. Rep. 86] (3d Cir.2001) (invalidating an anti-harassment policy as over-broad); *Killion v. Franklin Reg'l School Dist.*, 136 F.Supp.2d 446 [153 Educ. L. Rep. 90] (W.D.Pa.2001) (striking down a policy that allowed officials to discipline students for abuse directed towards teachers or administrators as vague).

3. *Martinez v. School Dist. No. 60*, 852 P.2d 1275 [83 Educ. L. Rep. 454] (Colo.Ct. App. 1992).

4. *Kolesnick By and Through Shaw v. Omaha Pub. School Dist.*, 558 N.W.2d 807 [115 Educ. L. Rep. 1054] (Neb.1997).

5. *Goss v. Lopez*, 419 U.S. 565, 95 S.Ct. 729, 42 L.Ed.2d 725 (1975). [Case No. 107]

6. *Wiemerslage Through Wiemerslage v. Maine Township High School Dist. 207*, 29 F.3d 1149 [93 Educ. L. Rep. 64] (7th Cir. 1994).

7. *Shuman ex rel. Shertzer v. Penn Manor School Dist.*, 422 F.3d 141 [201 Educ. L. Rep. 459] (3d Cir. 2005) (affirming that while questioning a student's involvement in an inappropriate sexual incident at school was a seizure within the meaning of the Fourth Amendment, it was reasonable under the circumstances).

8. *Miranda v. Arizona*, 384 U.S. 436, 86 S.Ct. 1602, 16 L.Ed.2d 694 (1966).

9. *State v. J.H.*, 898 So.2d 240 [197 Educ. L. Rep. 941] (Fla. Dist. Ct. App. 2005); *In re L.A.*, 21 P.3d 952 [152 Educ. L. Rep. 804] (Kan.2001) (involving both an educator and security officer).

10. *See, e.g., J.D. v. Commonwealth*, 591 S.E.2d 721 [184 Educ. L. Rep. 1049] (Va. Ct. App. 2004); *Commonwealth v. Ira I.*, 791 N.E.2d 894 [178 Educ. L. Rep. 491] (Mass. 2003); *Bills by Bills v. Homer Consol. School Dist. No. 33–C*, 959 F.Supp. 507 [117 Educ. L. Rep. 1064] (N.D.Ill.1997); *In re S.K.*, 647 A.2d 952 [94 Educ. L. Rep. 365] (Pa. Super. Ct. 1994); *In Interest of J.C.*, 591 So.2d 315 [71 Educ. L. Rep. 1276] (Fla. Dist.Ct.App.1991); *Pollnow v. Glennon*, 757 F.2d 496 [23 Educ. L. Rep. 1219] (2d Cir. 1985).

11. *In re R.H.*, 791 A.2d 331 [162 Educ. L. Rep. 453] (Pa.2002).

vast majority of courts deferring to educators as long as rules satisfy due process.[12] Clearly, educators can govern student conduct that is detrimental to school operations even if it occurs at extracurricular activities such as football games.[13] It is, of course, more difficult to enforce conduct rules outside of school due to potential conflicts with the rights of parents and attenuated connections between student behavior and the educational process.

Perhaps the oldest case involving student discipline for off-premises behavior was resolved in 1859. After school, a high school student, in the presence of friends, insulted his teacher as he walked by, calling him by the name, "old Jack Seaver." When the teacher whipped the student in school the following day, he unsuccessfully challenged the educator's ability to do so. The Supreme Court of Vermont upheld the teacher's imposition of discipline since the student's behavior had "... a direct and immediate tendency to injure the school and bring the master's authority into contempt."[14]

Another older case, from Connecticut's highest court, explained that the true test of educators' ability to punish students for offenses that occur away from campus is "... not the time or place of the offense, but its effect upon the morale and efficiency of the school."[15] The court upheld a male student's being subjected to corporal punishment for annoying young female students who were on their way home from school. Over a half century later, the Supreme Court of Wyoming upheld the punishment of a student driver for harassing a school bus driver who was en route to school with his passengers.[16] In another case, where out-of-school conduct was a continuation of misbehavior that started in school, the highest court in Massachusetts agreed that school officials were justified in expelling a student who assaulted a peer.[17]

Regulations preventing drug use and/or alcohol consumption, whether on or off campus, especially by student-athletes, are typically upheld on two grounds. First, since participation in extracurricular activities is a privilege rather than a right, educators can impose higher standards of discipline on these students than on their peers who do not take part in these programs. Second, school officials can base rules in health and safety concerns. Under either case, school officials can suspend or

---

12. *But see Packer v. Board of Educ. of Thomaston*, 717 A.2d 117 [129 Educ. L. Rep. 400] (Conn. 1998) (affirming the reinstatement of a student who was expelled from both school and extracurricular activities for possessing marijuana off of school grounds after hours where the rule was unconstitutionally vague because it did not provide adequate notice).

13. *Fuller ex rel. Fuller v. Decatur Pub. School Bd. of Educ. School Dist. 61*, 251 F.3d 662 [154 Educ. L. Rep. 127] (7th Cir. 2001).

14. *Lander v. Seaver*, 32 Vt. 114, *5 [online Westlaw designation at 1859 WL 5454] (1859).

15. *O'Rourke v. Walker*, 128 A. 25, 26 (Conn.1925).

16. *Clements v. Board of Trustees of Sheridan County School Dist. No. 2, in Sheridan County*, 585 P.2d 197 (Wyo.1978).

17. *Nicholas B. v. School Comm. of Worcester*, 587 N.E.2d 211 [72 Educ. L.Rep. 1006] (Mass.1992).

dismiss students who violate team or activity rules regardless of whether parents approve of the behavior of their children.[18] For example, the Eighth Circuit affirmed that school officials did not violate the rights of two cheerleaders from Missouri who received ten-day out-of-school suspensions for consuming alcohol at the house of a third student before they performed at a school football jamboree.[19] The court held that even though the cheerleading advisor failed to follow board policy in investigating the allegation of the students' misconduct, neither she nor the board violated their rights since they received due process before being suspended.

It almost goes without saying that rules cannot be too broad such as where one forbade a student-athlete from being in a car where beer was being transported.[20] Yet, presence at an event where alcohol is being consumed can provide the justification for an athlete's disqualification[21] as can drinking alcohol at a school-sponsored event.[22] Moreover, rules must be applied equally to males and females[23] and when school officials dismiss players from teams, they must rely on sufficient evidence[24] and fair processes.[25]

The off-campus activities of students that clearly threaten the health or safety of those in school can lead to their being subjected to punishments. As such, courts have upheld sanctions for such off-campus misbehavior as drug sales,[26] possession of tobacco[27] or drugs[28] on a school sponsored trip, and aggravated assaults.[29] In such a case, an appellate court in Illinois upheld a high school football player's being barred from playing after he violated his school's zero tolerance policy by being picked up by the police, in front of a convenience store, at 3:00 A.M. because he displayed obvious signs of intoxication.[30] Similarly, the Sev-

18. *Braesch v. DePasquale*, 265 N.W.2d 842 (Neb.1978), *cert. denied*, 439 U.S. 1068, 99 S.Ct. 836, 59 L.Ed.2d 34 (1979); *Palmer v. Merluzzi*, 868 F.2d 90 [51 Educ. L. Rep. 1196] (3d Cir.1989) [Case No. 105]; *Pirschel v. Sorrell*, 2 F.Supp.2d 930 [127 Educ. L. Rep. 124] (E.D. Ky. 1998); *L.P.M. v. School Bd. of Seminole County*, 753 So.2d 130 [143 Educ. L. Rep. 411] (Fla.Dist.Ct.App.2000).

19. *Jennings v. Wentzville R–IV School Dist.*, 397 F.3d 1118 [195 Educ. L. Rep. 461] (8th Cir. 2005).

20. *Bunger v. Iowa High School Athletic Ass'n*, 197 N.W.2d 555 (Iowa 1972).

21. *Clements v. Board of Educ. of Decatur Pub. School Dist. No. 61*, 478 N.E.2d 1209 [25 Educ. L. Rep. 866] (Ill.App.Ct. 1985); *Bush v. Dassel–Cokato Bd. of Educ.*, 745 F.Supp. 562 [63 Educ. L. Rep. 145] (D.Minn.1990).

22. *Katchak v. Glasgow Indep. School Sys.*, 690 F.Supp. 580 [48 Educ. L. Rep. 533] (W.D. Ky.1988).

23. *Schultzen v. Woodbury Cent. Community School Dist.*, 187 F.Supp.2d 1099 [162 Educ. L. Rep. 766] (N.D.Iowa 2002).

24. *Butler v. Oak Creek–Franklin School Dist.*, 172 F.Supp.2d 1102 [159 Educ. L. Rep. 166] (E.D.Wis.2001).

25. *Butler v. Oak Creek–Franklin School Dist.*, 172 F.Supp.2d 1102 [159 Educ. L. Rep. 166] (E.D.Wis.2001).

26. *Howard v. Colonial School Dist.*, 621 A.2d 362 [81 Educ. L. Rep. 878] (Del.Super.Ct. 1992), *aff'd without published opinion*, 615 A.2d 531 (Del.1992).

27. *Ette ex rel. Ette v. Linn–Mar Community School Dist.*, 656 N.W.2d 62 [173 Educ. L. Rep. 662] (Iowa 2002) (sending an eighth-grade student home from a band trip for possessing cigarettes).

28. *Rhodes v. Guarricino*, 54 F.Supp.2d 186 [137 Educ. L. Rep. 258] (S.D.N.Y.1999).

29. *Pollnow v. Glennon*, 594 F.Supp. 220 [20 Educ. L. Rep. 880] (S.D.N.Y.1984), *aff'd*, 757 F.2d 496 [23 Educ. L. Rep. 1219] (2d Cir.1985).

30. *Jordan ex rel. Edwards v. O'Fallon Township High School Dist. No. 203 Bd. of Educ.*, 706 N.E.2d 137 [133 Educ. L. Rep. 214] (Ill.App.Ct.1999).

enth Circuit upheld the expulsions of student spectators in Illinois who participated in a fight at a high school football game.[31]

Zero Tolerance Policies

Faced with ongoing difficulties associated with student substance abuse and violence in schools, boards have adopted zero tolerance policies in attempts to remediate, if not eliminate, these kinds of problems. When reviewing zero tolerance policies, courts look to ensure that school officials acted with discretion in disciplining students.

Courts reach mixed results with regard to students who have knives at school. On the one hand, where school officials in Tennessee discovered a hunting knife in the glove compartment of a student's car, but it did not belong to him, the Sixth Circuit ruled that his proposed suspension or expulsion for weapons possession, pursuant to a zero tolerance policy under which students could be disciplined for not knowingly possessing weapons, was invalid because it was not rationally related to a legitimate state interest.[32] Similarly, an appellate court in Pennsylvania affirmed that educators exceeded their authority when they sought to expel a seventh-grade student for a year because he found a Swiss army knife in a school hallway and did not turn it in immediately.[33] The court pointed out that the policy ignored the clear legislative intent that zero tolerance policies not be applied blindly. On the other hand, the Fourth Circuit affirmed that educators could suspend a student who had a knife in his locker even though he took it from a suicidal schoolmate.[34] The court was satisfied that school officials provided the student with due process before he was suspended.

The Eleventh Circuit affirmed that a school board in Florida's zero tolerance policy with regard to school-related violent crime could not render it liable for constitutional violations where police arrested and strip searched a student after she distributed anonymous pamphlets in which the author wondered about what might have happened if he shot the principal, teachers, or other students.[35] The court refused to impose liability on school officials for the actions of the police. Previously, the feral trial court in South Dakota upheld a student's being disciplined for violating her school's zero tolerance policy with regard to the use of profanity.[36]

31. *Fuller ex rel. Fuller v. Decatur Pub. School Bd. of Educ. School Dist. 61*, 251 F.3d 662 [154 Educ. L. Rep. 127] (7th Cir. 2001).

32. *Seal v. Morgan*, 229 F.3d 567 [148 Educ. L. Rep. 34] (6th Cir.2000).

33. *Lyons v. Penn Hills School Dist.*, 723 A.2d 1073 [132 Educ. L. Rep. 490] (Pa.Cmwlth.Ct.1999). *See also Colvin ex rel. Colvin v. Lowndes County, Miss. School Dist.*, 114 F.Supp.2d 504 [147 Educ. L. Rep. 601] (N.D. Miss.1999) (overturning the expulsion of a student with a disability for bringing a Swiss Army knife to school but otherwise agreeing that a school board had the authority to enact such a rule).

34. *Ratner v. Loudoun County Pub. Schools*, 16 Fed.Appx. 140 (4th Cir.2001), *cert. denied*, 534 U.S. 1114, 122 S.Ct. 922, 151 L.Ed.2d 886 (2002).

35. *Cuesta v. School Bd. of Miami–Dade County*, 285 F.3d 962 [163 Educ. L. Rep. 101] (11th Cir.2002).

36. *Anderson v. Milbank School Dist. 25–4*, 197 F.R.D. 682 (D.S.D.2000).

Punishments

Generally

Courts realize that educators need to use their discretion when disciplining students who break school rules.[37] As noted earlier, as long as discipline policies and procedures satisfy due process, courts usually uphold the actions of educators as long as they are not arbitrary, capricious, or unreasonable. It is long established that courts take the sex, age, and size as well as the mental, emotional, and physical conditions of students and the nature of their offenses into consideration when imposing penalties.[38] In an illustrative case, where a student received a ten-day suspension for using inappropriate and disrespectful language to school officials, a federal trial court in Michigan rejected his claim that the educators violated his rights to due process even though he missed his graduation ceremony and other senior events.[39] The court reasoned that since the student received all of the process to which he was due and the punishment was rationally related to his offense, his claim was without merit.

In reviewing disciplinary actions, courts consider whether punishments involve the withholding of the right to attend school or a privilege such as participation in an extracurricular activity. While courts expect educators to provide students with greater due process protections when they seek to deny them the right to attend school, they cannot arbitrarily or capriciously exclude students from extracurricular activities. Even so, school officials can impose higher standards, such as drug testing,[40] as a condition for participation in extracurricular activities.

Courts ordinarily do not review student conduct rules with the same scrutiny that they apply to criminal laws. For instance, in *Wood v. Strickland*, which involved the attempted expulsion of students in Arkansas for consuming alcoholic beverages at school or school-sponsored activities, the Supreme Court asserted that the federal judiciary is not supposed to "... supplant the interpretation of [a] regulation of those officers who adopted it and are entrusted with its enforcement."[41] In *Board of Education of Rogers, Arkansas v. McCluskey*, a brief per curiam judgment that upheld the suspensions of students who were intoxicated

37. *Spacek v. Charles*, 928 S.W.2d 88 [112 Educ. L. Rep. 525] (Tex.Ct.App.1996).

38. *Berry v. Arnold School Dist.*, 137 S.W.2d 256 (Ark.1940); *Holman By and Through Holman v. Wheeler*, 677 P.2d 645 [16 Educ. L. Rep. 658] (Okla.1983), *superseded by statute on other grounds as stated in Leding v. Pittsburg County Dist. Ct.*, 928 P.2d 957 (Okla.Civ.App. 1996).

39. *Posthumus v. Board of Educ. of Mona Shores Pub. Schools*, 380 F.Supp.2d 891 [201 Educ. L. Rep. 184] (W.D. Mich. 2005) (also rejecting the student's claim that his speech was entitled to First Amendment protection).

40. *See, e.g., Vernonia School Dist. 47J v. Acton*, 515 U.S. 646, 115 S.Ct. 2386, 132 L.Ed.2d 564 [101 Educ. L. Rep. 37] (1995); *Board of Education of Independent School District No. 92 of Pottawatomie v. Earls*, 536 U.S. 822, 122 S.Ct. 2559, 153 L.Ed.2d 735 [166 Educ. L. Rep. 79] (2002), *on remand*, 300 F.3d 1222 [168 Educ. L. Rep. 581] (10th Cir.2002). [Case No. 109]

41. 420 U.S. 308, 325, 95 S.Ct. 992, 43 L.Ed.2d 214 (1975), *reh'g denied*, 421 U.S. 921, 95 S.Ct. 1589, 43 L.Ed.2d 790 (1975), *on remand sub nom. Strickland v. Inlow*, 519 F.2d 744 (8th Cir.1975) [Case No. 47]

at school, the Court was of the view that "... a school board's interpretation of its rules [may be] so extreme as to be a violation of due process,"[42] a situation that was not present in the case at bar. In a dispute from Illinois, the Seventh Circuit decided that school officials who expelled a student for six weeks due to public indecency and possession of pornography after he was photographed in a shower following wrestling practice did not violate his right to substantive due process.[43] The court thought that even though officials exercised what it described as questionable judgment in excluding the student from school, they did not violate his rights since he received a hearing and the punishment did not rise to the level of conscience shocking.

As to the common practice of verbal warnings, in an older case, an appellate court in Illinois reiterated the rule that teachers can verbally chastise students as long as they do not make disparaging remarks that are malicious or wanton.[44] The Third[45] and Eighth[46] Circuits echoed similar sentiments in affirming that teachers did not violate the rights of students where their actions did not rise to the level required to support claims that they violated the substantive due process rights of the children by engaging in behavior that was shocking to the conscience.

Among the many cases dealing with punishments, courts refused to overturn such penalties as having a child clean a toilet with his bare hands;[47] being adjudicated delinquent for threatening a teacher[48] or being disruptive at school;[49] being charged with making a false fire alarm report at school;[50] violating a statute against the possession of a weapon at school for bringing a paintball gun and markers to school;[51] being expelled for bringing a weapon to school;[52] being named a ward of the court for bringing a knife to school;[53] making obscene remarks to a teacher;[54] receiving a grade of zero for the first offense of plagiarism on an assignment;[55] being dismissed from a marching band for missing a performance;[56] and being seated at an isolated desk due to disruptive behavior.[57]

42.　458 U.S. 966, 970, 102 S.Ct. 3469, 73 L.Ed.2d 1273 [5 Educ. L. Rep. 136] (1982), *reh'g denied*, 458 U.S. 1132, 103 S.Ct. 16, 73 L.Ed.2d 1402 (1982), *on remand*, 688 F.2d 596 (8th Cir.1982).

43.　*Tun v. Whitticker*, 398 F.3d 899 [195 Educ. L. Rep. 479] (7th Cir. 2005).

44.　*Wexell v. Scott*, 276 N.E.2d 735 (Ill. App. Ct. 1971).

45.　*S.M. ex rel. L.G. v. Lakeland School Dist.*, 33 Fed.Appx. 635 [164 Educ. L. Rep. 83] (3d Cir.2002).

46.　*Costello v. Mitchell Pub. School Dist. 79*, 266 F.3d 916 [157 Educ. L. Rep. 520] (8th Cir.2001).

47.　*Harris v. Robinson*, 273 F.3d 927 [159 Educ. L. Rep. 533] (10th Cir.2001).

48.　*In re J.H.*, 797 A.2d 260 [165 Educ. L. Rep. 254] (Pa.Super.Ct.2002).

49.　*M.C. v. State*, 695 So.2d 477 [119 Educ. L. Rep. 296] (Fla.Dist.Ct.App.1997), *review denied*, 700 So.2d 686 (Fla.1997).

50.　*In re C.R.K.*, 56 S.W.3d 288 [158 Educ. L. Rep. 475] (Tex.Ct.App.2001).

51.　*In re M.H.M.*, 864 A.2d 1251 [195 Educ. L. Rep. 238] (Pa. Super. Ct. 2004), *appeal denied*, 880 A.2d 1239 (Pa. 2005).

52.　*J.M. v. Webster County Bd. of Educ.*, 534 S.E.2d 50 [147 Educ. L. Rep. 351] (W.Va. 2000).

53.　*In re Randy G.*, 28 P.3d 239 [155 Educ. L. Rep. 1292] (Cal.2001).

54.　*In Interest of D.A.D.*, 481 S.E.2d 262 [116 Educ. L. Rep. 449] (Ga.Ct.App.1997).

55.　*Zellman ex rel. M.Z. v. Independent School Dist. No. 2758*, 594 N.W.2d 216 [134 Educ. L. Rep. 1017] (Minn.Ct.App.1999).

56.　*Mazevski v. Horseheads Cent. School Dist.*, 950 F.Supp. 69 [115 Educ. L. Rep. 885] (W.D. N.Y.1997).

57.　*Cole by Cole v. Greenfield–Cent. Community Schools*, 657 F.Supp. 56 [39 Educ. L. Rep. 76] (S.D.Ind.1986).

In a case with an interesting twist, the Supreme Court of Appeals of West Virginia reversed an order of the state's Human Rights Commission which posited that a teacher committed racial discrimination when she punished a student who committed a variety of in-class related offenses including tardiness and rudeness.[58] The court declared both that the Human Rights Commission's order was clearly erroneous in light of the numerous misrepresentations in its findings of fact, which served as the basis of its adjudication, and that the student failed to produce sufficient evidence to prove that the teacher's attempts to discipline her were more than likely due to her race. The court added that discipline imposed on minority students in public schools does not alone equate to racial discrimination.

On the other hand, courts invalidated a variety of penalties as too harsh under the circumstances. For example, courts refused to uphold such penalties as a conviction for disorderly conduct where a student threatened to shoot up a school since no one took him seriously and there were no weapons in his home,[59] assault for throwing a partially eaten apple at a teacher,[60] or an adjudication as a juvenile delinquent for having a butter knife in a locker since it was incapable of being used as a deadly weapon.[61]

Corporal Punishment

At common law, teachers have the right to administer reasonable corporal punishment. In fact, absent growing statutory prohibitions against corporal punishment,[62] educators may employ the practice even against parental wishes[63] as long as local board policies authorize its use.[64] If not contrary to state-level provisions, board policies generally control.[65] Yet, the use of unreasonable corporal punishment or behavior that violates board policy or state law can serve as cause for dismissing teachers.[66]

58. *Cobb v. West Va. Human Rights Comm'n*, 619 S.E.2d 274 [202 Educ. L. Rep. 373] (W. Va. 2005).

59. *State v. McCooey*, 802 A.2d 1216 [167 Educ. L. Rep. 814] (N.H.2002).

60. *In re Gavin T.*, 77 Cal.Rptr.2d 701 [128 Educ. L. Rep. 313] (Cal.Ct.App.1998).

61. *In re Melanie H.*, 706 A.2d 621 [124 Educ. L. Rep. 608] (Md.Ct.App.1998).

62. *See, e.g.*, CAL. EDUC. CODE § 49000; IOWA CODE ANN. § 280.21; MICH. COMP. LAWS ANN. § 37G; NEB. REV. STAT. ANN. § 79–295, N.D. CENT. CODE 15.1–19–02 UTAH CODE ANN. § 53A–11–802; VA. CODE ANN. § 22.1–279.1; WASH. REV. CODE ANN. § 28A.150.300; W. VA. CODE ANN. § 18A–5–1; WIS. STAT. ANN. § 118.31. Other states explicitly give local boards the option of prohibiting corporal punishment. *See, e.g.*, FLA. STAT. ANN. § 1006.07, N.M. STAT. ANN. § 22–5–4.3, OHIO REV. CODE ANN. § 3319.41.

63. *Baker v. Owen*, 395 F.Supp. 294 (M.D.N.C.1975), *aff'd*, 423 U.S. 907, 96 S.Ct. 210, 46 L.Ed.2d 137 (1975) (affirming that parental disapproval of corporal punishment did not preclude its use on a child).

64. *Ware v. Estes*, 328 F.Supp. 657 (N.D.Tex.1971), *aff'd*, 458 F.2d 1360 (5th Cir.1972), *cert. denied*, 409 U.S. 1027, 93 S.Ct. 463, 34 L.Ed.2d 321 (1972).

65. *McKinney v. Greene*, 379 So.2d 69 (La.Ct.App.1979).

66. *See, e.g.*, *Bott v. Board of Educ., Deposit Cent. School Dist.*, 392 N.Y.S.2d.2d 274 (N.Y. 1977); *Friedland v. Ambach*, 522 N.Y.S.2d 696 [43 Educ. L. Rep. 1089] (N.Y.

In its only case on the merits of the issue, *Ingraham v. Wright*,[67] the Supreme Court determined that corporal punishment was not per se unconstitutional. Ruling that the Eighth Amendment's prohibition against cruel and unusual punishments was designed to protect those guilty of crimes and did not apply to paddling students in order to preserve discipline, the Court rejected an analogy between children and inmates. In concluding that most states that addressed corporal punishment at that time permitted its use, and that professional and public opinion have long been divided on the practice, the Court refused to strike it down as unconstitutional.

Turning to fact-specific cases, the Fourth,[68] Tenth,[69] and Eleventh[70] Circuits, as well as federal trial courts,[71] agreed that students can proceed with substantive due process claims where punishments are "... so brutal, demeaning, and harmful as literally to shock the conscience of a court,"[72] even if they are against peers rather than educators. In such a case, the Fourth Circuit affirmed the denial of a wrestling coach's claim for qualified immunity where a student sued him and other school officials after the coach encouraged members of his team to beat the plaintiff repeatedly.[73] On two occasions, though, the Fifth Circuit disagreed, maintaining that state statutory and common law provisions offered better redress in the way of damages and possible criminal liability rather than vitiate the use of corporal punishment.[74] As reflected in the cases identified above, most litigation involving corporal punishment has been resolved in favor of teachers based on the presumption of correctness which complaining students and parents were unable to overcome.[75]

As illustrated by cases from the Second,[76] Third,[77] and Seventh[78] Circuits, there are times when teachers may have to use force to remove

App. Div. 1987); *Tucker v. Board of Educ., Community School Dist. No. 10*, 604 N.Y.S.2d 506 [87 Educ. L. Rep. 565] (N.Y. 1993); *Galbreath v. Board of Educ.*, 111 F.3d 123 (2d Cir.1997), *cert. denied*, 522 U.S. 1001, 118 S.Ct. 571, 139 L.Ed.2d 410 (1997); *Madison v. Houston Indep. School Dist.*, 47 F.Supp.2d 825 [135 Educ. L. Rep. 535] (S.D.Tex.1999), *aff'd without published opinion*, 207 F.3d 658 [143 Educ. L. Rep. 726] (5th Cir.2000).

67. 430 U.S. 651, 97 S.Ct. 1401, 51 L.Ed.2d 711 (1977). [Case No. 106]

68. *Hall v. Tawney*, 621 F.2d 607 (4th Cir.1980).

69. *Garcia v. Miera*, 817 F.2d 650 [39 Educ. L. Rep. 33] (10th Cir.1987), *cert. denied*, 485 U.S. 959, 108 S.Ct. 1220, 99 L.Ed.2d 421 [45 Educ. L. Rep. 486] (1988).

70. *Neal v. Fulton County Bd. of Educ.*, 229 F.3d 1069 [148 Educ. L. Rep. 86] (11th Cir.2000), *reh'g en banc denied*, 244 F.3d 143 (11th Cir.2000).

71. *See, e.g., Nicol v. Auburn–Washburn USD 437*, 231 F.Supp.2d 1107 (D.Kan. 2002).

72. *Hall v. Tawney*, 621 F.2d 607, 613 (4th Cir.1980).

73. *Meeker v. Edmundson*, 415 F.3d 317 [200 Educ. L. Rep. 16] (4th Cir. 2005).

74. *Cunningham v. Beavers*, 858 F.2d 269 [49 Educ. L. Rep. 490] (5th Cir.1988), *cert. denied*, 489 U.S. 1067, 109 S.Ct. 1343, 103 L.Ed.2d 812 (1989); *Moore v. Willis Indep. School Dist.*, 233 F.3d 871 [149 Educ. L. Rep. 337] (5th Cir.2000), *reh'g en banc denied*, 248 F.3d 1145 (5th Cir.2001).

75. *See also Fox v. Cleveland*, 169 F.Supp.2d 977 [158 Educ. L. Rep. 638] (W.D.Ark.2001); *Campbell v. Gahanna–Jefferson Bd. of Educ.*, 717 N.E.2d 347 [137 Educ. L. Rep. 1104] (Ohio Ct. App.1998); *Burnham v. Stevens*, 734 So.2d 256 [135 Educ. L. Rep. 1129] (Miss.Ct.App. 1999); *Rinehart v. W. Local School Dist. Bd. of Educ.*, 621 N.E.2d 1365 [86 Educ. L. Rep. 393] (Ohio Ct. App.1993).

76. *Smith ex rel. Smith v. Half Hollow Hills Cent. School Dist.*, 298 F.3d 168 [167 Educ. L. Rep. 619] (2d Cir.2002).

disruptive students. In fact, in the case from the Seventh Circuit, the court specified that when a teacher in Illinois grabbed a student by her wrist and elbow to escort her from a classroom, he did not violate her rights to substantive due process amounting to corporal punishment. Similarly, federal trial and state appellate courts agree that teachers did not commit corporal punishment where they paddled a child on the buttocks,[79] restrained a child with Asperger's Syndrome,[80] grabbed the arm of a student who was attempting to retrieve a shirt and pulled him toward a door,[81] grabbed and twisted a child's wrist in an effort to compel her to turn over a twenty-dollar bill she found on the floor,[82] and grasped a student in an attempt to preserve discipline.[83]

Suspension and Expulsion

Suspension and expulsion are clearly the most serious penalties that school officials can impose on students. Allowing for variations in terminology from one jurisdiction to another, suspensions generally refer to temporary exclusions for specified periods or until students and their parents satisfy specific conditions while expulsions indicate permanent removals from school. As discussed in greater detail below, the elements of due process depend to a significant extent on the length of the exclusion being considered.

Due Process and Punishments

Courts generally defer to educators who use reasonable forms of discipline in schools. In these situations, cases often hinge on whether officials provided students with adequate procedural due process protections. While due process does not require educators to afford students all of the safeguards that are present in criminal,[84] or, for that matter, civil,[85] proceedings, essential elements depend on the circumstances and gravity of potential punishments. At the very least, students who are subject to significant disciplinary penalties are entitled to notice and opportunities to respond in the presence of fair and impartial third-party decision-makers.[86]

77. *Gottlieb ex rel. Calabria v. Laurel Highlands School Dist.*, 272 F.3d 168 [159 Educ. L. Rep. 16] (3d Cir.2001).

78. *Wallace by Wallace v. Batavia School Dist. 101*, 68 F.3d 1010 [104 Educ. L. Rep. 132] (7th Cir.1995).

79. *Fox v. Cleveland*, 169 F.Supp.2d 977 [158 Educ. L. Rep. 638] (W.D.Ark.2001).

80. *Brown ex rel. Brown v. Ramsey*, 121 F.Supp.2d 911 [149 Educ. L. Rep. 392] (E.D. Va. 2000).

81. *Widdoes v. Detroit Pub. Schools*, 619 N.W.2d 12 [148 Educ. L. Rep. 1039] (Mich. Ct.App. 2000), *appeal denied*, 625 N.W.2d 785 (Mich.2001).

82. *Bisignano v. Harrison Cent. School Dist.*, 113 F.Supp.2d 591 [147 Educ. L. Rep. 529] (S.D.N.Y.2000).

83. *Young v. St. Landry Parish School Bd.*, 759 So.2d 800 (La.Ct.App.1999).

84. In addition to the earlier discussion on this topic, *see Brewer by Dreyfus v. Austin Indep. School Dist.*, 779 F.2d 260 [29 Educ. L. Rep. 56] (5th Cir.1985).

85. *Colquitt v. Rich Township High School Dist. No. 227*, 699 N.E.2d 1109 [129 Educ. L. Rep. 733] (Ill.App.Ct.1998).

86. *See, e.g., In re Z.K.*, 695 N.W.2d 656 [197 Educ. L. Rep. 820] (Minn. Ct. App. 2005) (overturning the expulsion of middle school students for shooting another juve-

The Fifth Circuit provided perhaps the earliest set of guidelines, albeit from higher education, as to the nature of the notice and hearing that were required prior to long-term exclusions in a case where a student faced expulsion from a public college for non-academic reasons.[87] The court was of the opinion that notice should contain a statement of the specific charges and grounds which, if proven, would justify an expulsion. The court also ascertained that since assessing misconduct depends on collecting facts that can be easily colored by witnesses, a fair and impartial third-party decision-maker must hear both sides in considerable detail. Expressly rejecting any requirement of "... a full-dress judicial hearing, with the right to cross-examine witnesses,"[88] the court commented that "... the rudiments of an adversary proceeding ... [require that] ... student[s] should be given the names of the witnesses against him and an oral or written report on the facts to which each witness testifies. [They] should also be given the opportunity to present ... [their] own defense against the charges and to produce either oral testimony or written affidavits of witnesses in [their] behalf."[89] The Fifth Circuit subsequently applied these criteria in striking down a student's thirty-day suspension because he had not received any sort of hearing.[90] In a related development, the Seventh Circuit did not agree that students were entitled to the names of witnesses and information about their testimony[91] while the Second Circuit indicated that witnesses were not essential where the credibility of evidence was not at issue.[92] However, the Ninth Circuit affirmed that school officials had to produce witnesses and permit them to be cross-examined before students who committed a variety of disciplinary infractions could be expelled.[93]

Shortly thereafter, in *Goss v. Lopez* (*Goss*),[94] the Supreme Court set out the minimum constitutional requirements in situations involving suspensions of ten-days or less. In a dispute from Ohio, students who did not receive a hearing challenged their ten-day suspensions for allegedly disruptive conduct. Ruling in favor of the students, the Court mandated that due process requires that they be given "... oral or written notice of the charges against [them] and, if [they] denies them, an explanation of the evidence the authorities have and an opportunity to present [their] side of the story."[95] The Court remarked that there is no need for a delay between school officials' giving students notice and the time of their hearings. The Court acknowledged that in most instances, discipli-

---

nile with a BB gun because insofar as they were not specifically advised that state law afforded them the right to free or low-cost legal assistance, their waivers of their right to a hearing before the school board were not knowing and intelligent).

87. *Dixon v. Alabama State Bd. of Educ.*, 294 F.2d 150 (5th Cir.1961), *cert. denied*, 368 U.S. 930, 82 S.Ct. 368, 7 L.Ed.2d 193 (1961).

88. *Id.* at 159.

89. *Id.*

90. *Williams v. Dade County School Bd.*, 441 F.2d 299 (5th Cir.1971).

91. *Linwood v. Board of Educ. of City of Peoria, School Dist. No. 150, Ill.*, 463 F.2d 763 (7th Cir.1972), *cert. denied*, 409 U.S. 1027, 93 S.Ct. 475, 34 L.Ed.2d 320 (1972).

92. *Winnick v. Manning*, 460 F.2d 545 (2d Cir.1972).

93. *Black Coalition v. Portland School Dist. No. 1*, 484 F.2d 1040 (9th Cir.1973).

94. 419 U.S. 565, 95 S.Ct. 729, 42 L.Ed.2d 725 (1975). [Case No. 107]

95. *Id.* at 581.

narians may well have informally discussed students' alleged acts of misconduct with them shortly after they occurred.[96]

The *Goss* Court also explained that if the presence of students constitutes threats of disruption, they may be removed immediately with the due process requirements to be fulfilled as soon as practicable. The Court expressly rejected the notion that students should be represented by counsel, be able to present witnesses, and be able to confront and cross-examine adverse witnesses in short-term exclusions from school.[97] The Court emphasized that "[l]onger suspensions or expulsions for the remainder of the school term, or permanently, may require more formal procedures ... [and that] in unusual situations, although involving only a short suspension, something more than the rudimentary procedures will be required."[98] States picked up on the Court's suggestion and have developed statutory guidelines when students are subject to long-term suspensions and/or expulsions.

Two years later, in upholding the constitutionality of corporal punishment in *Ingraham v. Wright*,[99] the Supreme Court addressed procedural due process. In observing that although corporal punishment implicates a constitutionally protected liberty interest, traditional common law remedies afforded adequate due process. Refusing to impose a constitutional requirement of advanced procedural safeguards, citing impracticability and cost as factors outweighing any incremental benefit, the Court was not convinced that corporal punishment deprived the students of property rights because their schooling was not interrupted and state courts could have set procedural, and substantive, restrictions on its use.[100]

Shortly after *Goss*, federal trial courts began to apply its procedural requirements to student disciplinary transfers[101] and three-day suspensions.[102] These courts agreed that where the property interests of students were involved, they were of sufficient magnitude to qualify for the minimal constitutional due process protections. Later, a federal trial court in Texas reached the same outcome where a student received a three-day suspension for taking allegedly compromising photographs of the principal's car while it was parked in front of a female teacher's house.[103]

96. *Smith on Behalf of Smith v. Severn*, 129 F.3d 419 [122 Educ. L. Rep. 106] (7th Cir.1997).

97. Previously, in *In re Gault*, 387 U.S. 1, 87 S.Ct. 1428, 18 L.Ed.2d 527 (1967), the Court stated that a fifteen-year-old who was committed to a facility for juvenile delinquents had the right to notice of charges, to counsel, to confront and cross-examine witnesses as well as the privilege against self-incrimination.

98. *Goss v. Lopez*, 419 U.S. 565, 584, 95 S.Ct. 729, 42 L.Ed.2d 725 (1975). [Case No. 107]

99. 430 U.S. 651, 97 S.Ct. 1401, 51 L.Ed.2d 711 (1977). [Case No. 106]

100. *Smith v. West Va. State Bd. of Educ.*, 295 S.E.2d 680 [6 Educ. L. Rep. 1138] (W.Va.1982).

101. *Everett v. Marcase*, 426 F.Supp. 397 (E.D.Pa.1977).

102. *Hillman v. Elliott*, 436 F.Supp. 812 (W.D.Va.1977).

103. *Riggan v. Midland Indep. School Dist.*, 86 F.Supp.2d 647 [142 Educ. L. Rep. 836] (W.D. Tex. 2000).

In cases where students were involved in criminal misconduct, the Fifth[104] and Eleventh[105] Circuits disagreed in determining that since they were transferred to alternative schools within their districts and did not suffer the losses of property interests, they were not entitled to hearings. On the other hand, the Sixth Circuit remanded a like dispute where a student was transferred due to criminal misbehavior for consideration of whether the failure of school officials to afford him a hearing violated his rights.[106]

The argument that more extensive processes are necessary if disciplinary penalties indirectly lead to academic sanctions is not necessarily persuasive. In such a case, an appellate court in Illinois refused to intervene where a student's missing examinations due to a three-day suspension led to a grade reduction since its timing was not intended to make it a more onerous penalty.[107] The Seventh Circuit reached a similar result where the effect of a three-day suspension delayed a student's graduation.[108] In the first of three cases from Pennsylvania, an appellate court found that a student whose suspension overlapped with graduation by one day did not have a constitutionally protected property right to attend the ceremony since it was only symbolic and not an essential component of his education.[109] Later, where school officials who caught a student selling drugs expelled him from school on the morning that he was due to graduate, an appellate court directed them to issue him a diploma because he completed all of the academic requirements for graduation.[110] Further, where a student was suspended for a variety of offenses but completed her course work, examinations, and all of the requirements necessary for graduation, an appellate court affirmed that she could not be denied her high school diploma.[111]

Courts do not agree as to the precise demands of constitutional procedural due process in connection with possible penalties that are more severe than the ten-day suspension involved in *Goss*. The lodestar is the elusive criterion of fairness under the circumstances. As such, most jurisdictions rely on the Supreme Court's perspective as set forth in *Mathews v. Eldridge*, that "[d]ue process is flexible and calls for such procedural protections as the particular situation demands."[112] For instance, where a student in Georgia received a nine-day suspension for fighting, screaming obscenities, and refusing to cooperate with and

---

104. *Nevares v. San Marcos Consol. Indep. School Dist.*, 111 F.3d 25 [117 Educ. L. Rep. 470] (5th Cir.1997).

105. *C.B. By and Through Breeding v. Driscoll*, 82 F.3d 383 [108 Educ. L. Rep. 1126] (11th Cir.1996), *reh'g and suggestion for reh'g en banc denied*, 99 F.3d 1157 (11th Cir.1996).

106. *Buchanan v. City of Bolivar, Tenn.*, 99 F.3d 1352 [114 Educ. L. Rep. 25] (6th Cir.1996).

107. *Donaldson v. Board of Educ., Danville School Dist. No. 118*, 424 N.E.2d 737 (Ill.App.Ct. 1981).

108. *Lamb v. Panhandle Community Unit School Dist. No. 2*, 826 F.2d 526 (7th Cir.1987).

109. *Mifflin County School Dist. v. Stewart*, 503 A.2d 1012 [30 Educ. L. Rep. 403] (Pa. Cmwlth. Ct.1986).

110. *Shuman v. Cumberland Valley School Dist. Bd. of Directors*, 536 A.2d 490 [44 Educ. L. Rep. 399] (Pa. Cmwlth. Ct.1988).

111. *Ream v. Centennial School Dist.*, 765 A.2d 1195 [150 Educ. L. Rep. 773] (Pa. Cmwlth. Ct.2001).

112. 424 U.S. 319, 334, 96 S.Ct. 893, 47 L.Ed.2d 18 (1976).

assaulting faculty members in connection with her possession of look-alike drugs at school, the Eleventh Circuit affirmed that educators met the requirements of due process when her mother participated in a telephone call with them on the day that the incident occurred.[113]

Due Process Hearings

The courts do not expect students to receive full judicial proceedings.[114] Even so, students facing expulsions are entitled to notice informing them of the time and place of some form of hearings.[115] School officials should also inform students of the charges and the nature of the evidence that they face[116] but not necessarily to pre-hearing notice of particular code or rule infractions. In specific cases, courts upheld expulsions where one student and his parents received repeated warnings that he faced expulsion for possession of marijuana[117] and another was arrested and charged with two counts of illegal sales of controlled substances.[118] Both courts agreed that the students were expelled only after hearings that were presided over by fair and impartial third-party decision-makers who based their actions on the contents of the records.[119]

Other courts decided that students are not entitled to have attorneys present as trial counsel,[120] to know the identity of[121] and/or to confront witnesses,[122] especially where there may be clear and serious

113. *C.B. By and Through Breeding v. Driscoll*, 82 F.3d 383 [108 Educ. L. Rep. 1126] (11th Cir.1996).

114. *See, e.g., Boykins v. Fairfield Bd. of Educ.*, 492 F.2d 697 (5th Cir.1974); *Newsome v. Batavia Local School Dist.*, 842 F.2d 920 (6th Cir.1988); *Baxter v. Round Lake Area Schools*, 856 F.Supp. 438 [93 Educ. L. Rep. 599] (N.D.Ill.1994); *James v. Unified School Dist. No. 512*, 899 F.Supp. 530 [104 Educ. L. Rep. 188] (D.Kan.1995).

115. *Hill v. Rankin County, Miss. School Dist.*, 843 F.Supp. 1112 [89 Educ. L. Rep. 815] (S.D. Miss.1993); *Bivins v. Albuquerque Pub. Schools*, 899 F.Supp. 556 [104 Educ. L. Rep. 195] (D.N.M.1995); *Donovan v. Ritchie*, 68 F.3d 14 [104 Educ. L. Rep. 80] (1st Cir.1995); *Hammock ex rel. Hammock v. Keys*, 93 F.Supp.2d 1222 [143 Educ. L. Rep. 915] (S.D.Ala.2000).

116. *C.B. By and Through Breeding v. Driscoll*, 82 F.3d 383 [108 Educ. L. Rep. 1126] (11th Cir.1996).

117. *L.Q.A. By and Through Arrington v. Eberhart*, 920 F.Supp. 1208 [108 Educ. L. Rep. 680] (M.D.Ala.1996), *aff'd without reported opinion*, 111 F.3d 897 (11th Cir. 1997). *See also South Gibson School Bd. v. Sollman*, 768 N.E.2d 437 [165 Educ. L. Rep. 316] (Ind.2002); *E.M. Through S.M. v. Briggs*, 922 P.2d 754 [112 Educ. L. Rep. 472] (Utah 1996).

118. *Rossi v. West Haven Bd. of Educ.*, 359 F.Supp.2d 178 [196 Educ. L. Rep. 522] (D. Conn. 2005).

119. *Newsome v. Batavia Local School Dist.*, 842 F.2d 920 [45 Educ. L. Rep. 1037] (6th Cir.1988); *Ruef v. Jordan*, 605 N.Y.S.2d 530 [88 Educ. L. Rep. 198] (N.Y.App.Div.1993).

120. *See, e.g., Osteen v. Henley*, 13 F.3d 221 [88 Educ. L. Rep. 939] (7th Cir.1993); *Newsome v. Batavia Local School Dist.*, 842 F.2d 920 [45 Educ. L. Rep. 1037] (6th Cir. 1988); *Lake Central School Corp. v. Scartozzi*, 759 N.E.2d 1185 [160 Educ. L. Rep. 231] (Ind.Ct.App.2001).

121. *Brewer v. Austin Indep. School Dist.*, 779 F.2d 260 [29 Educ. L. Rep. 56] (5th Cir.1985); *Paredes by Koppenhoefer v. Curtus*, 864 F.2d 426 [51 Educ. L. Rep. 20] (6th Cir.1988); *Snyder on Behalf of Snyder v. Farnsworth*, 896 F.Supp. 96 [103 Educ. L. Rep. 230] (N.D.N.Y.1995); *Coplin v. Conejo Valley Unified School Dist.*, 903 F.Supp. 1377 [104 Educ. L. Rep. 1204] (C.D. Cal.1995), *aff'd in an unpublished opinion*, 116 F.3d 483 (9th Cir.1997).

122. *Newsome v. Batavia Local School Dist.*, 842 F.2d 920 [45 Educ. L. Rep. 1037] (6th Cir. 1988); *Paredes by Koppenhoefer v. Curtus*, 864 F.2d 426 [51 Educ. L. Rep. 20] (6th Cir.1988).

danger to student witnesses.[123] As reflected by a case from the Sixth Circuit, there is a delicate balance between the rights of the accused to confront witnesses and the danger to accusers. The court noted that the necessity of protecting student witnesses from reprisal and ostracism generally outweighs the value to the truth-seeking process of allowing them to cross-examine their accusers.[124]

Still other courts agreed that students do not have rights to hearing officers who are not school employees[125] or, as noted earlier, to *Miranda* warnings when questioned by school officials. In a case that addressed various elements of due process, the Eighth Circuit affirmed that a middle school student in Arkansas failed to prove that school officials violated his procedural due process rights in connection with his expulsion following an altercation with a teacher and principal. The court wrote that school officials did not violate the student's rights because they fully informed his mother of the grounds for his expulsion and he received a hearing at which he was represented by counsel who had a full opportunity to examine and cross-examine witnesses.[126] The court pointed out that even though educators violated board rules by not supplying the student's attorney with statements of two witnesses in advance of the hearing, this did not amount to a constitutional violation.[127]

On the other hand, some courts agreed that students do have a right to have an attorney present;[128] to cross-examine witnesses;[129] to the presence of an impartial, non-school, third-party decision-maker;[130] and to have a redacted version of disciplinary records.[131]

In a related concern, a federal trial court in Illinois pointed out that students facing long-term suspensions or expulsions did not have a right to stenographic or mechanical recordings of proceedings.[132] Almost thirty years later, an appellate court in the same state denied a student's request for a verbatim transcript of his expulsion hearing.[133] Similarly, the federal trial court in Massachusetts agreed that a student who was excluded from school for disruptive behavior was not entitled to make a

---

123. *Dillon v. Pulaski County Special School Dist.*, 468 F.Supp. 54 (E.D.Ark. 1978); *John A. v. San Bernardino City Unified School Dist.*, 654 P.2d 242 [7 Educ. L. Rep. 1059] (Cal.1982).

124. *Newsome v. Batavia Local School Dist.*, 842 F.2d 920 [45 Educ. L. Rep. 1037] (6th Cir.1988).

125. *John A. v. San Bernardino City Unified School Dist.*, 654 P.2d 242 [7 Educ. L. Rep. 1059] (Cal.1982).

126. *London v. Directors of DeWitt Pub. School*, 194 F.3d 873 [139 Ed. L. Rep. 145] (8th Cir.1999).

127. For a similar result in a case involving a student's three-day suspension for drawing a Confederate flag, *see West v. Derby Unified School Dist. No. 260*, 206 F.3d 1358 [143 Educ. L. Rep. 43] (10th Cir.2000),

cert. denied, 531 U.S. 825, 121 S.Ct. 71, 148 L.Ed.2d 35 (2000).

128. *Givens v. Poe*, 346 F.Supp. 202 (W.D.N.C.1972); *Gonzales v. McEuen*, 435 F.Supp. 460 (C.D.Cal.1977).

129. *Colquitt v. Rich Township High School Dist. No. 227*, 699 N.E.2d 1109 [129 Educ. L. Rep. 733] (Ill.App.Ct.1998).

130. *Gonzales v. McEuen*, 435 F.Supp. 460 (C.D.Cal.1977).

131. *Graham v. West Babylon Union Free School Dist.*, 692 N.Y.S.2d 460 [136 Educ. L. Rep. 1012] (N.Y.App.Div.1999).

132. *Whitfield v. Simpson*, 312 F.Supp. 889 (E.D.Ill.1970).

133. *Colquitt v. Rich Township High School Dist. No. 227*, 699 N.E.2d 1109 [129 Educ. L. Rep. 733] (Ill.App.Ct.1998).

stenographic or mechanical recording of the hearing that resulted in his expulsion.[134] Yet, the highest court of Massachusetts was of the view that where students request that testimony given at closed hearings be recorded electronically, it must be honored.[135]

Many challenges to disciplinary actions question whether school officials fully complied with statutory provisions or board policies. If infractions are minor and have not prejudiced student rights, courts tend not to overturn the punishments. In an illustrative case, where a student did not receive the necessary written notice, but knew of the rules and charges, the Supreme Court of Vermont refused to invalidate his expulsion.[136] Earlier, where a student in Mississippi admitted that he brought a switchblade to school in violation of board policy, the Fifth Circuit affirmed that it was not necessary for all witnesses and their testimony to have been identified before the hearing.[137] Additionally, where officials in Minnesota may not have provided a precise rationale for a contemplated three-day suspension of students who distributed an unofficial newspaper that contained vulgarity at school, but the evidence against them was so overwhelming that a second hearing would not have altered the outcome, the Eighth Circuit reasoned that officials did not violate their rights to due process.[138] On the other hand, where a state regulation stipulated that school officials could not impose long-term suspensions without first trying other forms of punishment, the Supreme Court of Washington set aside a student's lengthy exclusion for one incident of drinking champagne.[139]

The Fourth Amendment

Searches of Students and their Property

The spread of violence, coupled with the presence of contraband such as weapons and drugs in schools, has led to legal conflicts over the extent to which educators could search students and their property in attempts to keep schools safe. According to the Fourth Amendment, "[t]he right of the people to be secure in their persons, houses, papers, and effects, against unreasonable searches and seizures, shall not be violated. . . ." This clause and the one following it, which pertains to search warrants, have been invoked in almost innumerable criminal cases but did not play much of a role in schools until the 1970's.

In an early case, an appellate court in California upheld a search based on an odor that emanated from a student's locker.[140] Two other

---

134. *Pierce v. School Comm. of New Bedford*, 322 F.Supp. 957 (D.Mass.1971).

135. *Nicholas B. v. School Comm. of Worcester*, 587 N.E.2d 211 [72 Educ. L. Rep. 1006] (Mass.1992).

136. *Rutz v. Essex Junction Prudential Comm.*, 457 A.2d 1368 [10 Educ. L. Rep. 207] (Vt. 1983).

137. *McClain v. Lafayette County Bd. of Educ.*, 673 F.2d 106 [3 Educ. L. Rep. 298]

(5th Cir.1982), *reh'g denied*, 687 F.2d 121 [6 Educ. L. Rep. 346] (5th Cir.1982).

138. *Bystrom By and Through Bystrom v. Fridley High School*, 686 F.Supp. 1387 [47 Educ. L. Rep. 905] (D.Minn.1987), *aff'd without reported opinion*, 855 F.2d 855 [48 Educ. L. Rep. 1144] (8th Cir.1988).

139. *Quinlan v. University Place School Dist. 83*, 660 P.2d 329 [9 Educ. L. Rep. 1090] (Wash.Ct.App.1983).

early cases, from federal trial courts in Pennsylvania[141] and New York,[142] questioned the propriety of strip searches of students in schools for missing property. Other early cases involved the use of sniff dogs in school as Tenth Circuit, in a case from New Mexico,[143] and a federal trial court in Indiana[144] upheld their use while a federal trial court in Texas declared that they could not be used to search students.[145] Moreover, the Fifth Circuit reached mixed results in a case from Texas, permitting the use of dogs in searches of cars owned by students and their lockers but not the students themselves.[146]

The Supreme Court first addressed the Fourth Amendment in a school setting in *New Jersey v. T.L.O. (T.L.O.).*[147] When a fourteen-year-old first-year high school student, identified as T.L.O., and a friend were accused of violating school rules by smoking cigarettes in a school lavatory, the latter, who admitted to smoking, was not brought to the office for a search. Insofar as T.L.O. denied smoking and claimed that she did not smoke at all, the teacher who confronted her brought her to the assistant principal's office. On opening T.L.O.'s purse, since the assistant principal saw her cigarettes "in plain view," a term of art borrowed from criminal law, he removed them and accused her of lying. Continuing with the search, the assistant principal discovered cigarette rolling papers, a small amount of marijuana, a pipe, a number of plastic bags, a substantial quantity of one-dollar bills, an index card that appeared to be a list of students who owed T.L.O. money, and two letters that implicated her in dealing marijuana.

Once T.L.O. confessed to selling marijuana at her high school, a trial court refused to suppress the evidence, adjudicated her delinquent, and sentenced her to a year on probation.[148] An appellate court affirmed the denial of the motion to suppress the search of T.L.O.'s purse but vacated and remanded since neither the record nor the findings and conclusions below were sufficient to evaluate whether she knowingly and voluntarily waived her Fifth Amendment rights before confessing.[149] The Supreme Court of New Jersey decreed that the search of T.L.O.'s purse violated the Fourth Amendment.[150]

140. *People v. Lanthier*, 488 P.2d 625 (Cal.1971).

141. *Potts v. Wright*, 357 F.Supp. 215 (E.D.Pa.1973).

142. *Bellnier v. Lund*, 438 F.Supp. 47 (N.D.N.Y.1977).

143. *Zamora v. Pomeroy*, 639 F.2d 662 (10th Cir.1981).

144. *Doe v. Renfrow*, 475 F.Supp. 1012 (N.D.Ind.1979), *rev'd in part on other grounds*, 631 F.2d 91 (7th Cir.1980) (*per curiam*), *cert. denied*, 451 U.S. 1022, 101 S.Ct. 3015, 69 L.Ed.2d 395 (1981).

145. *Jones v. Latexo Indep. School Dist.*, 499 F.Supp. 223 (E.D.Tex.1980).

146. *Horton v. Goose Creek Indep. School Dist.*, 690 F.2d 470 [6 Educ. L. Rep. 950] (5th Cir. 1982), *cert. denied*, 463 U.S. 1207, 103 S.Ct. 3536, 77 L.Ed.2d 1387 (1983).

147. 469 U.S. 325, 105 S.Ct. 733, 83 L.Ed.2d 720 [21 Educ. L. Rep. 1122] (1985). [Case No. 108]

148. *In re T.L.O.*, 428 A.2d 1327 (N.J.Juv. & Dom.Rel.Ct.1980).

149. *In re T.L.O.*, 448 A.2d 493 (N.J.Super.Ct.App.Div.1982).

150. *In re T.L.O.*, 463 A.2d 934 [12 Educ. L. Rep. 1184] (N.J.1983).

On appeal, in *New Jersey v. T.L.O.*, the Supreme Court reversed in favor of the State of New Jersey. Positing that the Fourth Amendment's prohibition against unreasonable searches and seizures applies in public schools, the Court devised a two-part test to evaluate the legality of a search: "[f]irst, one must consider 'whether the ... action was justified at its inception;' second, one must determine whether the search as actually conducted 'was reasonably related in scope to the circumstances which justified the interference in the first place.' "[151] The Court added that "a search will be permissible in its scope when the measures adopted are reasonably related to the objectives of the search and not excessively intrusive in light of the age and sex of the student and the nature of the infraction."[152]

The Court further clarified that a search is justified at its inception "... when there are reasonable grounds for suspecting that the search will turn up evidence that the student has violated or is violating either the law or the rules of the school."[153] A subjective measure based on specific facts that must be more than a mere hunch,[154] reasonable suspicion is significantly less than the probable cause standard that applies to the police. Inasmuch as school, also known as administrative, searches are designed to ensure school safety where there are generally large numbers of young people and relatively few adults present, educators need only articulable justification in order to proceed.

A related concern in addressing the totality of circumstances is that school officials may have to depend on the reliability of witnesses in considering whether to search. In assessing the sufficiency of cause to conduct a search, courts consider such factors as the source(s) of information, a student's record, the seriousness and prevalence of a problem, and the urgency of making a search without delay.

Courts have upheld searches based on information supplied by students,[155] parents,[156] school employees,[157] and the police.[158] In one illustrative case, an appellate court in New York was satisfied that a search was reasonable when a student's book bag made a metallic thud as it was placed on a cabinet.[159] Twelve years later, a federal trial court in New York rejected the claim of a sixth-grade student who alleged that officials violated his Fourth Amendment rights not to be subjected to

151. *New Jersey v. T.L.O.*, 469 U.S. 325, 341, 105 S.Ct. 733, 83 L.Ed.2d 720 [21 Educ. L. Rep. 1122] (1985). [Case No. 108]

152. *Id.* at 342.

153. *Id.* at 342.

154. *R.S.M. v. State*, 911 So.2d 283 [202 Educ. L. Rep. 440] (Fla. Dist. Ct. App. 2005) (declaring that a school official's hunch that something was wrong did not constitute reasonable suspicion to justify a search).

155. *See, e.g., Wofford v. Evans*, 390 F.3d 318 [193 Educ. L. Rep. 701] (4th Cir. 2004); *State v. J.H.*, 898 So.2d 240 [197 Educ. L. Rep. 941] (Fla. Dist. Ct. App. 2005); *In re L.A.*, 21 P.3d 952 [152 Educ. L.

Rep. 804] (Kan.2001); *Commonwealth v. Snyder*, 597 N.E.2d 1363 [76 Educ. L. Rep. 843] (Mass.1992).

156. *United States v. Aguilera*, 287 F.Supp.2d. 1204 [183 Educ. L. Rep. 137] (E.D. Cal. 2003); *In re Joseph G.*, 38 Cal. Rptr.2d 902 [97 Educ. L. Rep. 1109] (Cal. Ct.App.1995).

157. *Cornfield v. Consolidated High School Dist. No. 230*, 991 F.2d 1316 [82 Educ. L. Rep. 379] (7th Cir.1993).

158. *In re D.E.M.*, 727 A.2d 570 [133 Educ. L. Rep. 990] (Pa.Super.Ct.1999).

159. *Matter of Gregory M.*, 606 N.Y.S.2d 579 [88 Educ. L. Rep. 1127] (N.Y.1993).

unreasonable searches or seizures when he was forced to undergo psychological testing after he wrote and read to classmates a story in which named fellow students were murdered or sexually assaulted.[160] In granting the school board's motion for dismissal, the court thought that officials voiced a legitimate concern that the student might have committed violent acts.

When searches are based on anonymous tips, courts have not all agreed. On the one hand, the Supreme Court of Hawaii held that an anonymous Crime Stoppers' tip that was relayed to a high school vice principal who passed it on to the principal that a minor had marijuana and was selling it on campus did not provide a sufficient justification for school security personnel to search the student.[161] The court explained that although the tip identified the student, the principal was not aware of any of the circumstances under which it came in other than that it was from Crime Stoppers.'[162] Conversely, an appellate court in California affirmed that the search of a student's backpack was permissible after a school's campus security officer received an anonymous telephone call reporting that it contained a knife.[163] The court upheld the search because the student admitted to having the knife without reference to the reliability of the anonymous telephone call. Also, an appellate court in Florida upheld a search by a school security specialist, based on an uncorroborated, anonymous tip, that led to the discovery of marijuana and money since it was based on reasonable suspicion.[164]

Recognizing that different types of searches involve varying levels of intrusiveness, courts have generally sustained searches of students' cars,[165] lockers,[166] and backpacks[167] for routine administrative purposes connected with the general welfare of the schools. However, the Eighth Circuit determined that a school board policy in Arkansas, which permitted random, suspicionless searches of students and their belongings, violated their Fourth Amendment. Acting pursuant to the policy, school officials ordered members of a seventh-grade class to empty everything from their pockets and place all of their belongings, including backpacks

160. *D.F. ex rel. Finkle v. Board of Educ. of Syosset Cent. School Dist.*, 386 F.Supp.2d 119 [203 Educ. L. Rep. 160] (E.D.N.Y. 2005).

161. *In re Doe*, 91 P.3d 485 [188 Educ. L. Rep. 979] (Hawai'i 2004).

162. For other cases rejecting anonymous tips, *see, e.g., See also In re K.C.B.*, 141 S.W.3d 303 [191 Educ. L. Rep. 892] (Tex. App. 2004); *People v. Kline*, 824 N.E.2d 295 (Ill. App. Ct. 2005), *appeal denied*, 833 N.E.2d 6 (Ill. 2005).

163. *In re Cody S.*, 16 Cal.Rptr.3d 653 [190 Educ. L. Rep. 436] (Cal. Ct. App. 2004).

164. *State v. Bullard*, 891 So.2d 1158 [195 Educ. L. Rep. 678] (Fla. Dist. Ct. App. 2005).

165. *See, e.g., Anders ex rel. Anders v. Fort Wayne Community Schools*, 124 F.Supp.2d 618 [150 Educ. L. Rep. 155]

(N.D.Ind.2000); *Covington County v. G.W.*, 767 So.2d 187 [147 Educ. L. Rep. 752] (Miss.2000); *F.S.E. v. State*, 993 P.2d 771 [141 Educ. L. Rep. 1176] (Okla. Ct. Crim. App. 1999).

166. *Zamora v. Pomeroy*, 639 F.2d 662 (10th Cir.1981); *Commonwealth v. Carey*, 554 N.E.2d 1199 [60 Educ. L. Rep. 920] (Mass.1990); *In Interest of Isiah B.*, 500 N.W.2d 637 [83 Educ. L. Rep. 419] (Wis. 1993), *cert. denied*, 510 U.S. 884, 114 S.Ct. 231, 126 L.Ed.2d 186 (1993); *Commonwealth v. Cass*, 709 A.2d 350 [125 Educ. L. Rep. 705] (Pa.1998); *In re F.B.*, 726 A.2d 361 [133 Educ. L. Rep. 528] (Pa.1999).

167. *In re F.B.*, 726 A.2d 361 [133 Educ. L. Rep. 528] (Pa.1999); *In re Murray*, 525 S.E.2d 496 [142 Educ. L. Rep. 546] (N.C.Ct. App.2000).

and purses, on their desks. When the search uncovered marijuana in a student's purse, she was subject to criminal prosecution. Relying on the three part *Acton-Earls* test, discussed below, rather than *T.L.O.*, the court contended that since the policy failed to demonstrate the required "special needs" that would have been required before the search could have proceeded, school officials violated the student's rights because their actions were not justified by individualized suspicion.[168]

Police Searches

In the first case involving police in a school search, after a vice principal's check of a locker uncovered a large amount of marijuana, the student unsuccessfully sought to suppress the evidence. The Supreme Judicial Court of Massachusetts affirmed that since a memorandum between the police and school officials containing guidelines for reporting criminal behavior did not make educators police agents, the vice principal was not acting as an agent of law enforcement.[169] In addition, the court contended that the vice principal satisfied the more stringent standard of probable cause to search the juvenile for drugs largely based on the strong smell of marijuana emanating from the student. Similarly, an appellate court in North Carolina affirmed that a deputy sheriff who acted in conjunction with school officials did not violate the Fourth Amendment.[170] The court maintained that the search, which took place in a school's weight room, was appropriate since the deputy had reasonable suspicion inasmuch as he smelled the strong odor of marijuana when the student walked past him in the hall. The court concluded that the search, which was limited to a pat down that included having the student empty his pockets, was reasonably related to the objective of preserving a drug-free educational environment and was not excessively intrusive in light of his age, gender, and the nature of the suspicion.

Juveniles who were charged with assault and battery as well as assault and battery with a dangerous weapon succeeded in having the statements to an assistant principal suppressed and the case dismissed without prejudice because officials failed to comply with discovery orders. On appeal, the Supreme Judicial Court of Massachusetts reversed in remarking that the prosecutor's failure to provide the juveniles with statements taken by the assistant principal did not warrant dismissal of the charges.[171] The court was of the opinion that since the assistant principal was not acting as an agent of the state when he questioned the students, and they were not in his custody, their comments were admissible because they were voluntary.

Off-Campus Searches

Rules applying to school searches can be extended to off-campus activities. For example, the Eighth Circuit affirmed that when a student

---

168. *Doe v. Little Rock School Dist.*, 380 F.3d 349 [191 Educ. L. Rep. 608] (8th Cir. 2004).

169. *Commonwealth v. Lawrence L.*, 792 N.E.2d 109 [178 Educ. L. Rep. 919] (Mass. 2003).

170. *In re S.W.*, 614 S.E.2d 424 [199 Educ. L. Rep. 451] (N.C. Ct. App. 2005), *review denied*, 623 S.E.2d 42 (N.C. 2005).

171. *Commonwealth v. Ira I.*, 791 N.E.2d 894 [178 Educ. L. Rep. 491] (Mass. 2003).

from Minnesota who was on a field trip was seen opening a bottle of juice with a knife, he could be expelled for possession of an illegal weapon after a search revealed that he was carrying a baton similar to those used by police officers.[172] The court ascertained that even though the student was searched by both police officers and school officials, reasonable suspicion, rather than probable cause, was the appropriate standard.[173] Other courts upheld off-campus searches where officials had reasonable suspicion that students violated either school rules[174] or the law.[175]

Metal Detectors

In order to avoid having school personnel search students, or as an aid in searches, many boards have adopted the use of metal detectors since they are highly reliable and minimally intrusive. Acknowledging that individualized reasonable suspicion is not required, courts have generally upheld the use of metal detectors,[176] including those that are hand-held and used in random searches.[177]

A dispute arose in Illinois when a student who just entered a school was about to leave once he saw that a metal detector was present. Before the student could leave, he responded to a police officer's command that he pass through the metal detector by revealing that he was carrying a gun. An appellate court affirmed that since the seizure of the gun that the student was carrying was not based on reasonable suspicion, it was inadmissible in his being charged with the unlawful use of a weapon.[178]

Sniff Dogs

Many school boards have also relied on trained dogs to sniff, or detect, the presence of contraband in educational settings. As reflected in

---

172. *Shade v. City of Farmington*, 309 F.3d 1054 [170 Educ. L. Rep. 529] (8th Cir.2002).

173. For a similar case, *see People v. Dilworth*, 661 N.E.2d 310 [107 Educ. L. Rep. 226] (Ill. 1996), *cert. denied*, 517 U.S. 1197, 116 S.Ct. 1692, 134 L.Ed.2d 793 (1996). *See also In re Patrick Y.*, 746 A.2d 405 [142 Educ. L. Rep. 401] (Md.2000); *In re D.E.M.*, 727 A.2d 570 [133 Educ. L. Rep. 990] (Pa.Super.Ct.1999).

174. *See, e.g., Rhodes v. Guarricino*, 54 F.Supp.2d 186 [137 Educ. L. Rep. 258] (S.D.N.Y. 1999); *Juran v. Independent Or. Cent. School Dist.*, 898 F.Supp. 728 [103 Educ. L. Rep. 1068] (D.Or.1995).

175. *See, e.g., Commonwealth v. Williams*, 749 A.2d 957 [143 Educ. L. Rep. 951] (Pa.Cmwlth. Ct. 2000); *People v. McKinney*, 655 N.E.2d 40 [103 Educ. L. Rep. 798] (Ill.Ct.App.1995).

176. *Thompson v. Carthage School Dist.*, 87 F.3d 979 [110 Educ. L. Rep. 602] (8th Cir.1996); *In re F.B.*, 726 A.2d 361 [133 Educ. L. Rep. 528] (Pa.1999); *cert. denied sub nom. F.B. v. Pennsylvania*, 528 U.S. 1060, 120 S.Ct. 613, 145 L.Ed.2d 508 (1999); *Latasha W. v. People*, 70 Cal.Rptr.2d 886 [123 Educ. L. Rep. 277] (Cal.Ct.App. 1998); *People v. Pruitt*, 662 N.E.2d 540 [108 Educ. L. Rep. 329] (Ill.App.Ct.1996), *appeal denied*, 667 N.E.2d 1061 (Ill.1996); *People v. Dukes*, 580 N.Y.S.2d 850 (N.Y.Crim.Ct. 1992).

177. *State v. J.A.*, 679 So.2d 316 [112 Educ. L. Rep. 1107] (Fla. Dist. Ct. App. 1996), *reh'g denied* (1996), *review denied*, 689 So.2d 1069 (Fla. 1997), *cert. denied*, 522 U.S. 831, 118 S.Ct. 98, 139 L.Ed.2d 53 (1997).

178. *People v. Parker*, 672 N.E.2d 813 [114 Educ. L. Rep. 920] (Ill.App.Ct.1996).

the following review of the litigation, most courts have upheld the use of sniff dogs.

A federal trial court in Indiana, in a classroom search,[179] and the Fifth Circuit, in a search of a car in a school parking lot in Texas,[180] rejected challenges to the use of sniff dogs. The courts agreed that having dogs sniff students were not searches within the meaning of the Fourth Amendment. Previously, the Tenth Circuit, in a case from New Mexico, upheld the use of sniff dogs in exploratory searches of student lockers.[181]

More recently, the Supreme Court of Pennsylvania and two federal trial courts, in Texas and Alabama, upheld the use of sniff dogs. In the case from Pennsylvania, the court ascertained that the use of a sniff dog in a general search that led to the discovery of drugs and drug paraphernalia in a student's locker was permissible.[182] The court specified that the search was constitutional because it was a minimally intrusive invasion of students' limited privacy interests in their lockers since they had been forewarned of the possibility that their lockers would be searched, the search followed stringent guidelines in which date and time of search were set several weeks in advance, the scope of search was predetermined, and the drug dog was used to limit the intrusiveness of the search.

In the case from Texas, a sniff dog alerted school officials to a possible rule violation involving illegal narcotics or alcohol in a student's truck that was parked at school. Even though the search failed to discover drugs, the court remarked that the student could be suspended since educators uncovered a machete in the toolbox of his truck in violation of a school rule that prohibited students from possessing illegal weapons.[183] Similarly, a federal trial court in Alabama was convinced that where a dog detected the odor of narcotics in a car in a school's parking lot, but none were discovered, a student could be placed in an alternative school since educators discovered an exacto knife and large pocket knife in violation of rules against weapons.[184] At the same time, in an interesting twist in cases involving sniffing, a federal trial court in Virginia decided,[185] and another in Texas added in dicta,[186] that when educators sniffed the hands of children, they did perform searches.

---

179. *Doe v. Renfrow*, 475 F.Supp. 1012 (N.D.Ind.1979), *rev'd in part on other grounds*, 631 F.2d 91 (7th Cir.1980), *cert. denied*, 451 U.S. 1022, 101 S.Ct. 3015, 69 L.Ed.2d 395 (1981).

180. *Jennings v. Joshua Indep. School Dist.*, 869 F.2d 870 [52 Educ. L. Rep. 488] (5th Cir. 1989), *opinion amended and superseded*, 877 F.2d 313 [54 Educ. L. Rep. 1107] (5th Cir.1989), *cert. denied*, 496 U.S. 935, 110 S.Ct. 3212, 110 L.Ed.2d 660 (1990), *appeal after remand*, 948 F.2d 194 [71 Educ. L. Rep. 36] (5th Cir.1991), *reh'g denied*, 952 F.2d 402 (5th Cir.1992), *cert. denied*, 504 U.S. 956, 112 S.Ct. 2303, 119 L.Ed.2d 226 (1992).

181. *Zamora v. Pomeroy*, 639 F.2d 662 (10th Cir.1981).

182. *Commonwealth v. Cass*, 709 A.2d 350 [125 Educ. L. Rep. 705] (Pa. 1998), *cert. denied*, 525 U.S. 833, 119 S.Ct. 89, 142 L.Ed.2d 70 (1998).

183. *Bundick v. Bay City Indep. School Dist.*, 140 F.Supp.2d 735 [154 Educ. L. Rep. 183] (S.D. Tex.2001).

184. *Marner v. Eufaula City School Bd.*, 204 F.Supp.2d 1318 [166 Educ. L. Rep. 224] (M.D. Ala. 2002).

185. *Burnham v. West*, 681 F.Supp. 1160 [46 Educ. L. Rep. 168] (E.D.Va.1987), *order supplemented*, 681 F.Supp. 1169 (E.D.Va.1988).

On the other hand, the Fifth Circuit invalidated the use of a sniff dog to search students in Texas in observing both that school officials lacked individualized reasonable suspicion and that having the dogs place their noses directly on students was particularly intimidating and invasive of their privacy.[187] In the same opinion, the court wrote that a sniff-search of student lockers and cars was permissible because insofar as they were only sniffing inanimate objects, the only legal inquiry was about their record of reliability.[188] Subsequently, the Ninth Circuit expanded the Fifth Circuit's rationale in affirming that stationing a sniff dog at classroom doors in California, in close proximity to students, was unreasonable because doing so violated their rights to privacy.[189] The court also upheld the dismissal of a student's damages claim for lack of standing since he no longer attended the school where the search occurred or any other school in the district.

Strip Searches

An even more intrusive form of searches involves strip searches. In perhaps the earliest case, a federal trial court in Pennsylvania indicated that school officials and a city police chief were not entitled to the dismissal of Fourth Amendment claims filed by eight junior high school students who were strip searched in an unsuccessful attempt to locate a classmate's missing ring.[190] In another early case, a federal trial court in New York believed that individualized suspicion was necessary where school officials wished to strip search fifth-grade students in an attempt to locate three dollars that were reported missing.[191]

Following *T.L.O.*, the majority,[192] but not all,[193] cases have struck down strip searches for personal items rather than drugs or other forms of contraband. In one case, the Seventh Circuit upheld a strip search of a student in Illinois when looking for drugs even though his mother refused to consent to a pat down and he became visibly agitated when

---

186. *Jones v. Latexo Indep. School Dist.*, 499 F.Supp. 223, 232–233 (E.D.Tex.1980).

187. *See also Jones v. Latexo Indep. School Dist.*, 499 F.Supp. 223 (E.D.Tex. 1980).

188. *Horton v. Goose Creek Indep. School Dist.*, 690 F.2d 470 [6 Educ. L. Rep. 950] (5th Cir.1982), *cert. denied*, 463 U.S. 1207, 103 S.Ct. 3536, 77 L.Ed.2d 1387 (1983). *See also Commonwealth v. Cass*, 709 A.2d 350 [125 Educ. L. Rep. 705] (Pa.1998).

189. *B.C. v. Plumas Unified School Dist.*, 192 F.3d 1260 [138 Educ. L. Rep. 1003] (9th Cir. 1999).

190. *Potts v. Wright*, 357 F.Supp. 215 (E.D.Pa.1973).

191. *Bellnier v. Lund*, 438 F.Supp. 47 (N.D.N.Y.1977).

192. *See, e.g., State ex rel. Galford v. Mark Anthony B.*, 433 S.E.2d 41 [84 Educ. L. Rep. 1138] (W.Va.1993); *Kennedy v. Dexter Consol. Schools*, 10 P.3d 115 [148 Educ. L. Rep. 1047] (N.M. 2000); *Thomas ex rel. Thomas v. Roberts*, 261 F.3d 1160 [156 Educ. L. Rep. 508] (11th Cir. 2001); *Bell v. Marseilles Elementary School*, 160 F.Supp.2d 883 [156 Educ. L. Rep. 1066] (N.D. Ill.2001); *Oliver by Hines v. McClung*, 919 F.Supp. 1206 [108 Educ. L. Rep. 619] (N.D. Ill. 1995).

193. *Williams ex rel. Williams v. Ellington*, 936 F.2d 881 [68 Educ. L. Rep. 302] (6th Cir.1991); *Cornfield by Lewis v. Consolidated High School Dist. No. 230*, 991 F.2d 1316 [82 Educ. L. Rep. 379] (7th Cir. 1993); *Jenkins v. Tallaedga City Bd. of Educ.*, 115 F.3d 821 [118 Educ. L. Rep. 867] (11th Cir.1997), *cert. denied sub nom. Jenkins by Hall v. Herring*, 522 U.S. 966, 118 S.Ct. 412, 139 L.Ed.2d 315 (1997); *Cuesta v. School Bd. of Miami–Dade County*, 285 F.3d 962 [163 Educ. L. Rep. 101] (11th Cir.2002).

searched.[194] The court decreed that since there was reasonable suspicion, school officials met both prongs of the *T.L.O.* test. In a case from Connecticut with a different slant, after educators searched a student's bag and discovered that she had cigarettes, in violation of school rules, but not the marijuana that they sought, they asked her mother to come to school to strip search her for marijuana. Even though the search did not lead to the discovery of marijuana or other illegal substances, the federal trial court granted the board's motion to dismiss the student's claim that they violated her Fourth Amendment rights since it judged that educators met both parts of the *T.L.O.* test.[195]

In a related concern, most,[196] but not all, courts[197] have refused to impose personal liability on educators for unreasonable strip searches since case law did not clearly establish that their actions were unconstitutional under the circumstances. In such a case, the Eleventh Circuit affirmed that while a strip search of elementary school students in Georgia, in an attempt to locate twenty-six dollars that were missing, was unreasonable, officials were not liable for the unconstitutional searches under the theory of inadequate training or supervision, and the board was not faced with situations that were so similar that there was a need for such training.[198] In a later exemplary case, a federal trial court in Texas refused to impose liability on school officials who subjected a student with Down's Syndrome to a strip search after she was sexually assaulted by another student in a boy's bathroom between classes.[199] The court discerned that the school board could not be liable because the search was not the result of an official custom or policy.

The Supreme Court of Kentucky refused to impose liability on educators who had middle school students in a physical education class drop their shorts below their knees and raise their shirts above their breasts, exposing their underwear in a fruitless search for a student's missing pair of shorts.[200] Similarly, the Sixth Circuit refused to impose liability on educators in Michigan who conducted an unsuccessful search for missing money.[201] The facts revealed that officials directed a physical

---

194. *Cornfield by Lewis v. Consolidated High School Dist. No. 230*, 991 F.2d 1316 [82 Educ. L. Rep. 379] (7th Cir.1993).

195. *Phaneuf v. Cipriano*, 330 F.Supp.2d 74 [191 Educ. L. Rep. 752] (D. Conn.2004).

196. *See, e.g., Williams ex rel. Williams v. Ellington*, 936 F.2d 881 [68 Educ. L. Rep. 302] (6th Cir.1991); *Jenkins v. Tallaedga City Bd. of Educ.*, 115 F.3d 821 [118 Educ. L. Rep. 867] (11th Cir.1997), *cert. denied sub nom. Jenkins by Hall v. Herring*, 522 U.S. 966, 118 S.Ct. 412, 139 L.Ed.2d 315 (1997); *Higginbottom ex rel. Davis v. Keithley*, 103 F.Supp.2d 1075 [146 Educ. L. Rep. 145] (S.D.Ind.1999).

197. *See, e.g., Kennedy v. Dexter Consol. Schools*, 10 P.3d 115 [148 Educ. L. Rep. 1047] (N.M. 2000); *Oliver by Hines v. McClung*, 919 F.Supp. 1206 [108 Educ. L.

Rep. 619] (N.D.Ill. 1995); *Konop v. Northwestern School Dist.*, 26 F.Supp.2d 1189 [131 Educ. L. Rep. 201] (D.S.D. 1998); *Bell v. Marseilles Elementary School*, 160 F.Supp.2d 883 [156 Educ. L. Rep. 1066] (N.D. Ill. 2001); *Fewless v. Board of Educ.*, 208 F.Supp.2d 806 [167 Educ. L. Rep. 153] (W.D. Mich. 2002).

198. *Thomas ex rel. Thomas v. Roberts*, 261 F.3d 1160 [156 Educ. L. Rep. 508] (11th Cir. 2001).

199. *Teague ex rel. C.R.T. v. Texas City Indep. School Dist.*, 386 F.Supp.2d 893 [203 Educ. L. Rep. 205] (S.D. Tex. 2005).

200. *Lamb v. Holmes*, 162 S.W.3d 902 [198 Educ. L. Rep. 755] (Ky. 2005).

201. *Beard v. Whitmore*, 402 F.3d 598 [196 Educ. L. Rep. 438] (6th Cir. 2005), *reh'g and reh'g en banc denied* (2005).

education teacher and another male teacher to strip search about twenty males by having them individually lower their pants and underwear while removing their shirts and having two female teachers strip search at least five girls by having them pull up their shirts and pull down their pants while standing in a circle.

Drug Testing

Three years after *T.L.O.*, a dispute from Indiana became the first case directly addressing drug testing of student-athletes. After five baseball players tested positive for marijuana, their school board implemented a random drug testing policy for student-athletes and cheerleaders. The Seventh Circuit affirmed the validity of testing on the grounds that it was reasonable under the Fourth Amendment and that school officials instituted sufficient safeguards to protect student privacy.[202] In upholding the policy, the court was of the view that since student-athletes and cheerleaders gained enhanced prestige in the community, it was not unreasonable to require them to submit to drug testing.

Ten years after *T.L.O.*, the Supreme Court revisited the Fourth Amendment in considering mass suspicionless drug testing of student-athletes in *Vernonia School District 47J v. Acton (Acton)*.[203] The Court also addressed the question of individualized suspicion that it left unanswered in *T.L.O.* Acting in response to fears of increased drug use among students, a school board in Oregon, following up on parental concerns, instituted a drug testing policy for student-athletes. The board focused on student-athletes both because they were leaders of the drug culture and there were at least two incidents wherein student-athletes were injured due to the effects of drugs. The policy, which contained elaborate safeguards to protect the privacy rights of the student-athletes, required any student who wished to try out for interscholastic athletic teams to submit to a urinalysis drug testing.

When a seventh-grade student was suspended from interscholastic athletics because he and his parents refused to sign a consent form for drug testing, they challenged his exclusion, claiming that educators violated his rights under the Fourth Amendment, and the state constitution since there was no basis on which to believe that he ever used drugs. After a federal trial court upheld the policy, the Ninth Circuit struck it down as unconstitutional.[204] When the school board appealed, the Supreme Court vacated and remanded in its favor.

In *Acton*, the Supreme Court applied a three-part balancing test in affirming the policy's constitutionality. First, the Court held that students have a lesser expectation of privacy than ordinary citizens. The Court explained that student-athletes in particular experience diminished privacy rights not only because they are subject to physical examina-

202. *Schaill v. Tippecanoe County School Corp.*, 864 F.2d 1309 [51 Educ. L. Rep. 92] (7th Cir.1988).

203. 515 U.S. 646, 115 S.Ct. 2386, 132 L.Ed.2d 564 [101 Educ. L. Rep. 37] (1995).

204. *Acton v. Vernonia School Dist. 47J*, 23 F.3d 1514 [91 Educ. L. Rep. 495] (9th Cir.1994).

tions before becoming eligible to play but also because they dress in open areas of locker rooms. Second, the Court posited that the urinalysis testing was minimally intrusive since it was coupled with safeguards that allowed little encroachment on the students' privacy. Third, given the perception of increased drug use, the Court agreed with school officials and parents that there was a significant need for the policy. On remand, the Ninth Circuit affirmed "... that the Oregon Supreme Court would not offer greater protection under the provisions of the Oregon Constitution in this case...."[205]

Even after *Acton*, the circuits remained divided over suspicionless testing of students involved in extracurricular activities including sports.[206] For instance, the Seventh Circuit twice upheld suspicionless drug testing even though it had second thoughts about doing so, suggesting that but for its being bound by the precedent from the first case, it would have reached a different result in the latter.[207] Yet, the same court invalidated drug and alcohol testing of students who received suspensions for three-days or more for fighting absent a nexus between use of the banned substances and violent behavior.[208] A year later, the Eighth Circuit originally upheld random testing but later vacated its judgment as moot when the student moved out of the district.[209]

The Tenth Circuit, in a case from Oklahoma that eventually made its way to the Supreme Court, struck down random drug testing as unconstitutional, thereby revealing how the disagreement between the circuits left educators without clear guidelines.[210] In a case not involving a student-athlete, the Third Circuit affirmed that educators did not violate the rights of a high school student who was suspected of being on drugs when, pursuant to board policy, she was subjected to urinalysis testing.[211] Even though the student tested negative for drugs, the court affirmed that officials did not violate her Fourth Amendment rights since testing was reasonably related to their objective of evaluating whether she used drugs. The court noted that even though officials might have relied on less invasive means, such as testing the student's breath or saliva, rather than her urine, the test was not excessively intrusive.

205. *Acton v. Vernonia School Dist. 47J*, 66 F.3d 217, 218 [103 Educ. L. Rep. 608] (9th Cir. 1995).

206. The Supreme Court of Colorado prohibited random testing of members of a school band, including those who participated for credit, on the basis that these students had greater expectations of privacy under the state constitution. *Trinidad School Dist. No. 1 v. Lopez*, 963 P.2d 1095 [129 Educ. L. Rep. 812] (Colo.1998).

207. *Todd v. Rush County Schools*, 133 F.3d 984 [125 Educ. L. Rep. 18] (7th Cir. 1998), *cert. denied*, 525 U.S. 824, 119 S.Ct. 68, 142 L.Ed.2d 53 (1998); *Joy v. Penn-Harris–Madison School Corp.*, 212 F.3d 1052 [144 Educ. L. Rep. 866] (7th Cir.2000).

208. *Willis v. Anderson Community School Corp.*, 158 F.3d 415 [130 Educ. L. Rep. 89] (7th Cir. 1998).

209. *Miller ex rel. Miller v. Wilkes*, 172 F.3d 574 [133 Educ. L. Rep. 765] (8th Cir. 1999).

210. *Earls ex rel. Earls v. Board of Educ. of Tecumseh Pub. School Dist.*, 242 F.3d 1264 [151 Educ. L. Rep. 752] (10th Cir.2001), *cert. granted*, 534 U.S. 1015, 122 S.Ct. 509, 151 L.Ed.2d 418 [158 Educ. L. Rep. 544] (2001).

211. *Hedges v. Musco*, 204 F.3d 109 [141 Educ. L. Rep. 1020] (3d Cir.2000).

A school board in Oklahoma adopted a student activities drug testing policy which required all middle and high school students to consent to urinalysis testing for drugs in order to participate in extracurricular activities. In practice, the policy applied only to students who took part in competitive extracurricular activities sanctioned by the state's secondary schools activities association. Students and their parents filed suit alleging that the policy violated the Fourth Amendment because, in adopting it, the board neither identified a special need to test individuals who participated in extracurricular activities nor addressed a proven problem or offered any benefits to students or their school.

Relying on *Acton*, a federal trial court granted the board's motion for summary judgment, but the Tenth Circuit entered a judgment in favor of the students. On further review in *Board of Education of Independent School District No. 92 of Pottawatomie v. Earls (Earls)*,[212] the Supreme Court reversed in favor of the board. As an initial matter, the Court pointed out that the students who were tested in *Earls* were not in regular classrooms and that results were not turned over to the police. This suggests that *Acton* and *Earls* are limited to the narrow range of disputes involving students in extracurricular activities.

Before applying *Acton*, the Court asserted that it relied on a fact-specific balancing of the intrusion on the Fourth Amendment rights of students against the promotion of legitimate governmental *qua* school interests. The Court first considered the nature of the students' alleged privacy interest, reasoning that they are not only limited due to the need of officials to preserve discipline and safety but also that individuals who participate in extracurricular activities voluntarily subject themselves to greater intrusions on their privacy than their non-participating peers. The Court was satisfied that given the limited privacy expectations of the students who were affected by the policy, it was constitutional.

Turning to the character of the intrusion, the Court reviewed key elements of the policy, recognizing that it included procedures that were virtually identical to those in *Acton*. If anything, the Court stated that this policy afforded even more protection since faculty members stood outside of closed restroom stalls, unlike *Acton* where males stood at a urinal, and produced urine samples which were then poured into different vials before being sent for testing. The Court also determined that the results were kept in separate confidential student files that were released on a need-to-know basis and were not turned over to law enforcement officials. The Court added that test results did not lead to the imposition of disciplinary or academic sanctions but only resulted in varying degrees of the loss of the privilege of participating in extracurricular activities. The Court was thus persuaded that since the urine samples were collected in a minimally intrusive manner, and the test results had limited uses, the invasion into the students' privacy was not constitutionally significant.

212. 536 U.S. 822, 122 S.Ct. 2559, 153 L.Ed.2d 735 [166 Educ. L. Rep. 79] (2002), *on remand*, 300 F.3d 1222 [168 Educ. L. Rep. 581] (10th Cir.2002). [Case No. 109]

As to the third part of the test, the nature and immediacy of the board's concern and the policy's efficacy in meeting them, the Court recounted how it acknowledged the importance of governmental concern to prevent drug use, a problem that had not abated since *Acton*. In so doing, the Court rejected the students' claims that drug use was not a problem at the school by relying on evidence to the contrary from board officials. The Court also wrote that it did not require a school to have a particularized or pervasive drug problem before permitting educators to conduct suspicionless testing. Aware of the nationwide epidemic of drug use and the effectiveness of testing, the Court rejected the students' argument that testing had to be based on individualized suspicion since this would have been less intrusive. Even in concluding that drug testing was a reasonably effective means of addressing the board's legitimate concerns in preventing, deterring, and detecting drug use, the Court "... express[ed] no opinion as to its wisdom."[213]

Following *Earls*, courts continue to uphold drug testing of student-athletes. In one such case, a federal trial court in Pennsylvania rejected claims by a member of a swim team that his being subjected to testing violated his Fourth Amendment rights.[214] The court thought that the coach's suspicions that the student was using drugs, coupled with evidence of his drug use and the potential harm that he would have faced if the coach had failed to intervene, rendered the compulsory drug testing reasonable.

As controversies continue with regard to testing, a case from the Supreme Court of Indiana reflects the trend that the judiciary generally upholds testing for alcohol and drugs but not for other substances. The court largely upheld a policy that permitted random testing of students who participated in athletics, extracurricular, and co-curricular activities as well as those who wished to drive to and from school for alcohol and other non-tobacco-related drugs because it merely barred individuals from participating in privileged activities in which they were portrayed as role models. In discerning that the policy was based on officials' valid interest in deterring student drug abuse, the court decided that it did not violate the unreasonable searches and seizures clause in the state constitution.[215] The court also declared that educators could not subject students to nicotine testing due to their negligible interest in this regard.[216] A year earlier, a federal trial court in Texas invalidated a drug testing policy which officials sought to apply to all students in junior and senior high school for the duration of the academic year as unreasonable.[217] The court decreed that the policy was unacceptable because even though the method of testing imposed a low level of intrusion on students' rights to privacy, there was no compelling interest to outweigh

---

213. *Id.* at 838.

214. *Dominic J. v. Wyoming Valley West High School*, 362 F.Supp.2d 560 [197 Educ. L. Rep. 154] (M.D. Pa. 2005).

215. *Linke v. Northwestern School Corp.*, 763 N.E.2d 972 [162 Educ. L. Rep. 525] (Ind.2002).

216. For a similar result, *see Penn–Harris–Madison School Corp. v. Joy*, 768 N.E.2d 940 [165 Educ. L. Rep. 323] (Ind.Ct. App.2002).

217. *Tannahill ex rel. Tannahill v. Lockney Indep. School Dist.*, 133 F.Supp.2d 919 [152 Educ. L. Rep. 549] (N.D.Tex. 2001).

their privacy interests. The court also reflected that drug use in the school was actually lower than in other schools in the state.

Controls over Student Free Speech–Expressive Activities

Over time, the Supreme Court created essentially two standards addressing state-imposed limits on free speech. In *Schenck v. United States*, a dispute involving national security in the wake of World War I, the Court maintained, in often quoted, or paraphrased, language that "[t]he most stringent protection of free speech would not protect a man in falsely shouting fire in a theatre and causing a panic."[218] The Court enunciated the so-called clear and present danger test, contending that "[t]he question . . . is whether the words used are used in such circumstances and are of such a nature as to create a clear and present danger. . . ."[219] Under this test, the mere possibility of disruption is not enough to limit free speech. Rather, speech cannot be limited unless there is an explicit concern that serious harm may follow to the public welfare.

In conceding that the clear and present danger test was not entirely appropriate for use in educational settings, the Court created a different measure for schools. More specifically, in *Tinker v. Des Moines Independent Community School District*[220] that Court declared that school officials had the authority to act only if student behavior causes material and substantial disruptions in school settings.

Even prior to *Tinker*, the courts deferred to the ability of school officials to control disruptive student expressive activity. In an early case, an appellate court in California upheld a student's expulsion from school since he refused to apologize for critical statements that he made about a school facility during a speech at a school gathering.[221]

As reflected in the ensuing discussion, courts have examined a wide range of challenging issues involving student speech whether dealing with symbolic speech, such as dress, which is entitled to greater protection as a form of pure speech, or the spoken and/or written word, both of which are entitled to less protection. As to the former, in a non-school case that sets forth useful guidelines, the Supreme Court identified two factors to be considered in evaluating whether speech connected with conduct qualifies as symbolic expression that is afforded constitutional protection: whether the expression is intended to convey a particularized message and whether the message will be understood by recipients.[222] Even with such guidelines, the Seventh Circuit aptly noted that "[m]any aspects of the law with respect to students' speech . . . are difficult to understand and apply."[223] While it can be difficult to make clear distinc-

---

218. 249 U.S. 47, 52, 39 S.Ct. 247, 63 L.Ed. 470 (1919).

219. *Id.*

220. 393 U.S. 503, 89 S.Ct. 733, 21 L.Ed.2d 731 (1969). [Case No. 110]

221. *Wooster v. Sunderland*, 148 P. 959 (Cal.Ct.App.1915).

222. *Spence v. Washington*, 418 U.S. 405, 94 S.Ct. 2727, 41 L.Ed.2d 842 (1974).

223. *Hosty v. Carter*, 412 F.3d 731 [199 Educ. L. Rep. 91] (7th Cir. 2005), cert. denied, ___ U.S. ___, 126 S.Ct. 1330, ___ L.Ed.2d ___ (2006). (finding that a dean was entitled to qualified immunity in a case tions in all cases and there can be a fair amount of overlapping between and among these issues, this section examines cases involving student expressive activities.

Political Expression

Amid the social upheaval of the 1960's, the Supreme Court's first case on a matter directly related to student speech was *Tinker v. Des Moines Independent Community School District (Tinker)*.[224] In *Tinker* the Court invalidated a two-day old board policy from Iowa which sought to prohibit students from wearing black armbands to school in protest of American activity in Vietnam.

In acknowledging that "[i]t can hardly be argued that either students or teachers shed their constitutional rights to freedom of speech or expression at the schoolhouse gate,"[225] the Court sought an acceptable middle ground to balance the rights of students against the needs of school officials to maintain order and discipline. As such, the Court ruled that the case involved "direct, primary First Amendment rights akin to 'pure speech' [that did not concern] ... speech or action that intrudes upon the work of the school or the rights of other students."[226] According to the Court, in order to prohibit students from expressing particular points of view, school officials had to be able to show that their actions were motivated by "... more than a desire to avoid the discomfort and unpleasantness that always accompany an unpopular viewpoint. Certainly where there is no finding and no showing that engaging in the forbidden conduct would 'materially and substantially interfere with the requirements of appropriate discipline in the operation of the school,' the prohibition cannot be sustained."[227]

In the first of many post-*Tinker* cases to consider prohibitions against students who wear clothing with symbolic messages at school, the Sixth Circuit upheld a ban in a school in Ohio where there were serious racial tensions.[228] In refusing to disturb the forty-year-old rule that applied to emblems and other insignia that were not related to school activities, one that was originally intended to reduce undesirable divisions created within the student body by fraternities and sororities, the court relied on evidence that students increasingly attempted to wear buttons and badges that expressed racially inflammatory messages that led to disruptions. Referring to the relatively non-oppressive rule, which was enforced uniformly, the court agreed that it was acceptable since it served the goal of meaningful integration. Less than six months later, the Fifth Circuit vitiated a directive that sought to prevent students from wearing black armbands to school in connection with a

from higher education over the contents of a student newspaper).

224. 393 U.S. 503, 89 S.Ct. 733, 21 L.Ed.2d 731 (1969). [Case No. 110]

225. *Id.* at 506.

226. *Id.* at 508–509.

227. *Id.* at 509 citing *Burnside v. Byars*, 363 F.2d 744, 749 (5th Cir.1966).

228. *Guzick v. Drebus*, 431 F.2d 594 (6th Cir.1970), *cert. denied*, 401 U.S. 948, 91 S.Ct. 941, 28 L.Ed.2d 231 (1971). [Case No. 111] protest over events in Vietnam.[229] The court rejected the board's improvised ad hoc policy against black armbands as constitutionally impermissible since officials neither expected, nor was there, any disruption in the district's schools.

Over the years, courts considered a wide array of cases involving student speech in schools. In Oregon, for example, litigation arose when students challenged their suspension and a directive to discontinue carrying signs and wearing buttons to school that referred to replacement teachers, who were hired as substitutes for striking faculty members, as "scabs." The Ninth Circuit was convinced that school officials violated the students' rights to wear the buttons since along with not being vulgar, there were no disruptions and none were reasonably forecast.[230]

On the other hand, where officials could reasonably forecast that serious disturbances might arise, courts entered judgments in their favor. In perhaps the earliest case on point, the Sixth Circuit upheld the suspension of a student who refused to stop wearing symbolic expression in the form of a Confederate Flag as a sleeve patch in a racially tense school that had recently been integrated.[231] Courts continue to uphold prohibitions against such symbols. In another dispute, the Fourth Circuit affirmed the suspensions of students in Virginia who violated school rules by wearing depictions of "Johnny Reb," a caricature of an emblematic Confederate soldier and former cartoon symbol of their high school after its use was discontinued due to complaints from black students and their parents.[232]

Disputes also emerged over students who wore expressive clothing as a subset of political speech apart from dress code issues.[233] In the first of two cases that are conceptually related to the previous discussions involving the Confederate Flag, the Sixth Circuit found that school officials in Kentucky violated the rights of students who were suspended for violating their school's dress code after they wore t-shirts to a concert on which Confederate Flags were depicted.[234] The court believed that the t-shirts, which also had the picture of a country music singer pictured on front and the phrase "Southern Thunder" on the back, through which students sought to commemorate the birthday of the singer's father, who was also a famous country singer, and to express their southern heritage, constituted protected First Amendment speech. Similarly, the Third

229. *Butts v. Dallas Indep. School Dist.*, 436 F.2d 728 (5th Cir.1971).

230. *Chandler v. McMinnville School Dist.*, 978 F.2d 524 [78 Educ. L. Rep. 282] (9th Cir. 1992). *But see Smith ex rel. Lanham v. Greene County School Dist.*, 100 F.Supp.2d 1354 [145 Educ. L. Rep. 368] (M.D.Ga.2000) (rebuffing this rationale in rejecting a claim that school officials violated the rights of a student for violating a school's dress code policy).

231. *Melton v. Young*, 465 F.2d 1332 (6th Cir.1972), *cert. denied*, 411 U.S. 951, 93 S.Ct. 1926, 36 L.Ed.2d 414 (1973).

232. *Crosby v. Holsinger*, 852 F.2d 801 [48 Educ. L. Rep. 156] (4th Cir.1988).

233. *See also Phillips v. Anderson County School Dist. Five*, 987 F.Supp. 488 [124 Educ. L. Rep. 85] (D.S.C.1997) (permitting school officials to prevent a student from wearing a jacket to school that looked like a Confederate flag because it might have caused a substantial disruption).

234. *Castorina ex rel. Rewt v. Madison County School Bd.*, 246 F.3d 536 [152 Educ. L. Rep. 524] (6th Cir.2001).

Circuit observed that students in New Jersey could enjoin their school board's racial harassment policy on the basis that its preventing them from wearing t-shirts displaying depictions of a comedian known for "redneck," a derogatory term for Southerners, violated their First Amendment rights to freedom of expression.[235] The court judged that since educators could not show that the shirts would have caused disruptions, they lacked the authority to prevent the students from wearing them to school. More recently, a federal trial court in West Virginia granted a high school student's request for a preliminary injunction after he was disciplined for wearing a t-shirt and belt buckle that displayed the Confederate Flag, purportedly in commemoration of his Southern heritage.[236] The court indicated that since the part of the school's policy that prohibited "items displaying the Rebel flag" under the "racist language and/or symbols or graphics" was unconstitutional over-broad under the First Amendment, it was unenforceable.

Two cases involving pictures of President George W. Bush and student t-shirts reached different results. The first case arose in Michigan where a high school student wore a t-shirt that displayed a photograph of the President with the caption "International Terrorist" without any problems until lunch time, at which time school officials directed him to turn it inside-out for the rest of the day or leave school. After the student contacted his father and left school, the principal called him and told him he was not allowed to wear the shirt to school.[237] A federal trial court enjoined the principal from prohibiting the student from wearing the t-shirt on the grounds that it constituted symbolic speech that was protected by the First Amendment and that he intended to convey a particularized message that was understood by its viewers. In rejecting the claim of school officials that this censorship was required because the shirt might have offended Iraqi students at the school, the court posited that since educators failed to demonstrate the likelihood that wearing it would have caused a substantial disruption, their actions were improper. Shortly thereafter, in Vermont, another federal trial court distinguished the two cases. Educators informed a middle school student who wore a t-shirt that was critical of President Bush and his alleged illegal drug use that he could wear the shirt only if he taped over portions that offended the school dress code insofar as it contained images depicting drugs and alcohol. After the student was sent home for the day for refusing to tape over the offending portions, he and his parents challenged his being disciplined. Although explaining that the student was not entitled to an injunction to prohibit officials from disciplining him for wearing the shirt, the court directed educators to expunge his record of any disciplinary actions because their initial act of censorship violated the First Amendment.[238] In addressing the differences between the cases, the

235. *Sypniewski v. Warren Hills Reg'l Bd. of Educ.*, 307 F.3d 243 [170 Educ. L. Rep. 83] (3d Cir.2002), *cert. denied*, 538 U.S. 1033, 123 S.Ct. 2077, 155 L.Ed.2d 1062 [176 Educ. L. Rep. 542] (2003).

236. *Bragg v. Swanson*, 371 F.Supp.2d 814 [199 Educ. L. Rep. 162] (S.D. W. Va. 2005).

237. *Barber ex rel. Barber v. Dearborn Pub. Schools*, 286 F.Supp.2d 847 [183 Educ. L. Rep. 79] (E.D. Mich. 2003).

238. *Guiles ex rel. Lucas v. Marineau*, 349 F.Supp.2d 871 [194 Educ. L. Rep. 880] (D. Vt. 2004).

court reflected that educators could require the student to cover specific images on the t-shirt not because they were critical of the President but since they acted pursuant to a neutral policy against wearing clothing that bore images of drugs and alcohol.

In the first of three cases involving student attitudes with regard to homosexuality, the federal trial court in Minnesota enjoined a principal from preventing a student from wearing a sweatshirt emblazoned with the message "Straight Pride" to school.[239] The court was of the opinion that since the student and his parents demonstrated the strong likelihood of success on the merits of their claim that the principal acted unreasonably, they were entitled to the injunction. In the second case, a high school student wore a t-shirt displaying the message that "Homosexuality is shameful." A federal trial court in California noted that officials violated the student's rights to freedom of speech and religion, but not equal protection, after he was suspended for wearing the t-shirt that expressed his religious condemnation of homosexuality.[240] The court was persuaded that the student's claim was valid based on his allegation that school officials tried to coerce him to change his views about homosexuality. In like fashion, a federal trial court in Ohio granted a middle school student's request for an injunction, holding that educators violated his free speech rights when they tried to prohibit him from wearing a t-shirt that expressed his religious convictions in messages reading "Homosexuality is a sin!"[241] The shirt also proclaimed that "Islam is a lie!" and "Abortion is murder!" The court rejected the notion that school officials had the authority to restrict the student's message as plainly offensive speech. Instead, the court pointed out that the student could wear the t-shirt because officials failed to prove that it caused a material disruption of school activities, there was a reasonable likelihood that it might have caused such a disruption, or that it invaded the rights of others.

Students seeking to form clubs for peers who are gay and those who are not, in a different form of expression, have experienced mixed success under an unlikely source, the Equal Access Act (EAA). In relevant part, the EAA stipulates that "[i]t shall be unlawful for any public secondary school which ... has a limited open forum to deny equal access or a fair opportunity to, or discriminate against, any students who wish to conduct a meeting ... on the basis of the religious, political, philosophical, or other content of the speech at such meetings."[242] When students who wished to form a Gay-Straight Alliance Club in California sued their school board, a federal trial court entered a judgment in their behalf.[243] The court was of the view that if officials in

---

239. *Chambers v. Babbitt,* 145 F.Supp.2d 1068 [155 Educ. L. Rep. 252] (D.Minn.2001).

240. *Harper ex rel. Harper v. Poway Unified School Dist.,* 345 F.Supp.2d 1096 [194 Educ. L. Rep. 208] (S.D. Cal. 2004).

241. *Nixon v. Northern Local School Dist. Bd. of Educ.,* 383 F.Supp.2d 965 [201 Educ. L. Rep. 904] (S.D. Ohio 2005).

242. 20 U.S.C.A. § 4071(a). This statute is in the appendix.

243. *Colin ex rel. Colin v. Orange Unified School Dist.,* 83 F.Supp.2d 1135 [142 Educ. L. Rep. 138] (C.D.Cal.2000).

public high schools allow even one non-curriculum-related student group to meet, they opened the door for others to do the same.

In the first of three related cases from Utah, high school students with a gay-positive point of view challenged a board policy that denied them an opportunity to meet at school during non-instructional time and to have access to school facilities. The federal trial court thought that the policy violated the group's EAA rights since it denied the students the opportunity to meet inasmuch as another non-curriculum-related student group was permitted to convene.[244] The same court later remarked that since the plaintiffs did not demonstrate how the policy had a disparate impact on their viewpoint, it did not have to examine the actual motives of board members regarding their allegations.[245] In the third case, the court reviewed the standards governing access to the limited forum that the board created for curriculum-related student clubs at the high school where a club sought to examine the impact, experience, and contributions of gays and lesbians in history and current events.[246] The court granted the club's request for a preliminary injunction since there was substantial likelihood that it would succeed on the merits of its First Amendment claim that the school official who was responsible for evaluating their application misapplied the appropriate standards or added a new one. Subsequently, federal trial courts in Indiana[247] and Kentucky[248] granted permanent and preliminary injunctions, respectively, to Gay/Straight Alliance clubs, permitting them to meet in public schools.

On the other hand, a federal trial court in Texas upheld a school board's rejection of a gay-straight student association's requests that members be permitted to post and distribute fliers about it at a high school, to use the school's public address system for announcements, and to be recognized as a student group that had the right to meet on campus.[249] The court maintained that school officials' investigation of the association's web site, which led to the discovery that it posted sexually explicit material, was reasonable and nondiscriminatory for the purposes of the First Amendment. The court stated that since the EAA includes exceptions for avoiding disruption and preserving order in schools in order to protect student well-being, educators acted lawfully in denying the association's requests. In addition, a Gay/Straight Alliance Club in Colorado unsuccessfully sought a motion for a preliminary injunction that would have ordered school officials to recognize the

---

244. *East High Gay/Straight Alliance v. Board of Educ.*, 81 F.Supp.2d 1166 [141 Educ. L. Rep. 776] (D.Utah 1999).

245. *East High Gay/Straight Alliance v. Board of Educ.*, 81 F.Supp.2d 1199 [141 Educ. L. Rep. 809] (D.Utah 1999).

246. *East High School Prism Club v. Seidel*, 95 F.Supp.2d 1239 [144 Educ. L. Rep. 260] (D. Utah 2000).

247. *Franklin Central Gay/Straight Alliance v. Franklin Township Community School Corp.*, 2002 WL 32097530 (S.D. Ind. 2002), *reconsideration denied*, 2002 WL 31921332 (S.D. Ind. 2002).

248. *Boyd County High School Gay Straight Alliance v. Board of Educ. of Boyd County, Ky.*, 258 F.Supp.2d 667 [177 Educ. L. Rep. 211] (E.D. Ky. 2003).

249. *Caudillo v. Lubbock Indep. School Dist.*, 311 F.Supp.2d 550 [187 Educ. L. Rep. 564] (N.D. Tex. 2004).

group. The federal trial court concluded that the school's policy of officially recognizing only "curricular" clubs did not violate the EAA.[250]

Inappropriate Student Expression

Seventeen years after *Tinker,* the Supreme Court revisited the acceptable limits of student expression in a dispute from Washington where a student delivered a lewd speech at a school assembly. The speech included elaborate, graphic, and explicit sexual metaphors that caused a substantial disruption. Ignoring warnings from two teachers that he not deliver the speech, the student received a three-day suspension and had his name removed from the list of possible speakers at his graduation. Even so, the student was elected by a write-in vote to serve as a speaker.

On further review of a judgment in favor of the student, in *Bethel School District No. 403 v. Fraser (Fraser),*[251] the Supreme Court reversed in favor of the school board. The Court reasoned that school officials had the authority to discipline the student for violating school rules because he delivered the speech after being advised not to do so. In its analysis, the Court distinguished the speech from *Tinker* where the armbands were a passive, nondisruptive expression of a political position, rather than a lewd and obscene speech totally lacking in any political viewpoint, incident to a student election that was delivered to an unsuspecting captive audience. In ascertaining that educators have the duty to inculcate habits and manners of civility and teach students the boundaries of socially appropriate behavior, the Court asserted that "[t]he determination of what manner of speech in the classroom or in school assembly is inappropriate properly rests with the school board."[252]

Four years later, the Sixth Circuit affirmed that officials in Tennessee could discipline a student for speech that was disrespectful of school authorities or disruptive of instructional activities. The court wrote that where the candidate for the presidency of a student council made discourteous and rude remarks at an election assembly, his speech was not entitled to First Amendment protection.[253] More recently, where a secretary overheard a student utter an expletive in school, the federal trial court in South Dakota upheld her suspension even though it did not create a disturbance because she violated a rule of which she was aware.[254] Previously, a federal trial court in South Dakota, in upholding a student's suspension for uttering an obscenity, regardless of whether she was merely repeating and returning words that were directed at her since her speech was clearly disruptive and heard by ninety students in a

---

250. *Palmer High School Gay/Straight Alliance v. Colorado Springs School Dist. No. 11*, 2005 WL 3244049 (D. Colo. 2005).

251. 478 U.S. 675, 106 S.Ct. 3159, 92 L.Ed.2d 549 [32 Educ. L. Rep. 1243] (1986). [Case No. 112]

252. *Id.* at 683.

253. *Poling v. Murphy*, 872 F.2d 757 [53 Educ. L. Rep. 37] (6th Cir.1989), *cert. denied*, 493 U.S. 1021, 110 S.Ct. 723, 107 L.Ed.2d 742 (1990).

254. *Anderson v. Milbank School Dist. 25–4*, 197 F.R.D. 682 (D.S.D.2000).

cafeteria, rejected her claim that school officials violated her right to freedom of speech.[255]

Along with the spoken word, as reflected by a case from the Eleventh Circuit, students can be disciplined for inappropriate non-political speech that might incite violence. The court affirmed that educators in Florida could discipline a student under a zero-tolerance policy for distributing anonymous pamphlets that contained an essay wondering what might have happened if the author had shot the school's principal and others.[256] The court also agreed that school officials could not be accountable for the student's having been strip searched and arrested since the board did not have a custom that could be the basis for such liability. Two years later, in Louisiana, a high school student was suspended for bringing his brother's drawing to school which depicted a public school soaked in gasoline targeted by a missile, students pointing guns at the principal, and racial and obscene expletives. Officials searched the student's brother and his book bag and, after discovering references to drugs, sex, death, and gangs and a razor blade, expelled him from school. Both students sued the school board on a variety of charges, most notably for violations of their rights under the First Amendment. In affirming a grant of summary judgment in favor of the defendants, the Fifth Circuit agreed that the drawing was not entitled to protection because in light of the unsettled nature of relevant First Amendment law, the contours of the student's rights were not so clearly established that the principal's actions could have been categorized as objectively unreasonable.[257]

Along with difficulties that can arise when students seek to wear representations of the Confederate Flag, school officials must also deal with its presence in other forms. Acting in response to racial tension, coupled with recommendations from a task force of parents, teachers, and community members, a school board in Kansas adopted a Racial Harassment and Intimidation policy. When a middle school student, who was informed of the policy on several occasions, drew and displayed a Confederate Flag, he and his father challenged his three-day suspension. The Tenth Circuit affirmed that the policy neither violated the student's right to free speech nor was it over-broad or unconstitutionally vague.[258] The Eleventh Circuit reached the same outcome in two different cases from Florida, agreeing that bans against displaying the Confederate Flag in schools were not unconstitutional since they were designed to promote racial harmony.[259]

255. *Heller v. Hodgin*, 928 F.Supp. 789 [110 Educ. L. Rep. 694] (S.D.Ind.1996).

256. *Cuesta v. School Bd. of Miami–Dade County*, 285 F.3d 962 [163 Educ. L. Rep. 101] (11th Cir.2002).

257. *Porter v. Ascension Parish School Bd.*, 393 F.3d 608 [194 Educ. L. Rep. 497] (5th Cir. 2004), *cert. denied*, ___ U.S. ___, 125 S.Ct. 2530, 161 L.Ed.2d 1112 (2005).

258. *West v. Derby Unified School Dist. No. 260*, 206 F.3d 1358 [143 Educ. L. Rep. 43] (10th Cir.2000), *cert. denied*, 531 U.S. 825, 121 S.Ct. 71, 148 L.Ed.2d 35 (2000).

259. *Denno v. School Bd. of Volusia County, Fla.*, 218 F.3d 1267 [145 Educ. L. Rep. 942] (11th Cir.2000), *reh'g and suggestion for reh'g en banc denied*, 235 F.3d 1347 (11th Cir.2000), *cert. denied*, 531 U.S. 958, 121 S.Ct. 382, 148 L.Ed.2d 295 (2000); *Scott v. School Bd. of Alachua County*, 324 F.3d 1246 [175 Educ. L. Rep. 88] (11th Cir.2003), *cert. denied*, 540 U.S. 824, 124 S.Ct. 156,

On the other hand, a student successfully challenged his being adjudicated delinquent for making a criminal threat after he handed a classmate three sheets of "dark poetry," which included one that read, "I am Dark, Destructive, and Dangerous. I slap on my face of happiness but inside I am evil. For I can be the next kid to bring guns to kill students at school."[260] The Supreme Court of California ascertained that insofar as the student had both a plausible First Amendment defense, and since the poem was ambiguous, the circumstances of its dissemination were such that school officials failed to establish that it presented a criminal threat. Earlier, the Ninth Circuit affirmed that educators in Washington did not violate a high school student's First Amendment rights in expelling him on an emergency basis after he showed his teacher a poem that he wrote, which was filled with imagery of violent death, suicide, and the shooting of fellow students, even if it was protected speech.[261] However, since the court added that officials violated the student's rights by placing, and keeping, documentation about the incident in his file after the perceived threat subsided, it directed them to remove those materials from his record.

In a case from Missouri, a high school student and his parents unsuccessfully sued their school board, alleging that his being disqualified as a candidate for student body president for the unauthorized distribution of condoms attached to stickers bearing his campaign slogan violated his First Amendment right to free speech. The Eighth Circuit affirmed that the election was a school-sponsored event over which officials had the authority to restrict even protected student expression that materially and substantially interfered with school discipline.[262] In a different kind of situation, a federal trial court in Ohio rejected a male student's free speech claim when school officials disciplined him for writing a sexually related message in the yearbook of a female friend.[263] Relying in part on *Fraser*, the court reiterated that school officials have the right to prevent students from engaging in vulgar or offensive speech, including sexual innuendo.

Publications

Courts have applied *Tinker* in cases involving student publications in school-sponsored, curricular-related activities. Consistent with *Tinker's* rationale, courts agree that while student expressive activities are entitled to First Amendment protection and that their content is not subject to the unrestricted will of school officials, educators need not permit all forms of student expression. Controversies in this area fall

157 L.Ed.2d 46 [182 Educ. L. Rep. 32] (2003).

260. *In re George T.*, 16 Cal.Rptr.3d 61, 64 [190 Educ. L. Rep. 550] (Cal. 2004).

261. For such a case, *see LaVine v. Blaine School Dist.*, 257 F.3d 981 [155 Educ. L. Rep. 1019] (9th Cir.2001), *reconsideration en banc denied*, 279 F.3d 719 (9th Cir.2002), *cert. denied*, 536 U.S. 959, 122 S.Ct. 2663, 153 L.Ed.2d 837 (2002).

262. *Henerey ex rel. Henerey v. City of St. Charles*, 200 F.3d 1128 [141 Educ. L. Rep. 95] (8th Cir.1999).

263. *Doe v. DePalma*, 163 F.Supp.2d 870 [157 Educ. L. Rep. 628] (S.D.Ohio 2000).

under two overlapping headings: school-sponsored curriculum-related publications and student-sponsored underground publications.

School-Sponsored/Curriculum Related

The first post-*Tinker* federal case that addressed attempted expulsions over student expression occurred in Illinois where high school students produced a newspaper off-campus but distributed it in school. The content of the newspaper was critical of school policies and officials. Reinstating the students, even in conceding that it contained stories that were disrespectful toward authority, the Seventh Circuit ruled that the expulsions were unjustified since the newspaper neither forecast, nor led to, disruptions in school.[264]

In another early case, the Second Circuit upheld a ban that prevented staff members of a high school newspaper in New York from distributing a questionnaire on sexual attitudes and habits where educators feared that doing so might have inflicted emotional harm on some students. Emphasizing that the issue was neither a ban against the distribution of sex-related information nor an attempt to restrict the expression of student views, the court decreed that the First Amendment did not include the "... right to importune others to respond to questions when there is reason to believe that such importuning may result in harmful consequences."[265]

Hazelwood School District v. Kuhlmeier (Hazelwood)[266] is the Court's only case involving school-sponsored publications. *Hazelwood* arose when a principal in Missouri deleted two articles, one on teenage pregnancy, the other about the divorce of a student's father, from a newspaper that was written and edited by members of a journalism class that was part of the school's curriculum. In recognizing that the newspaper was neither an open forum nor had become one by past practice, the Court found that the principal acted reasonably in light of factors such as possible identification of unnamed pregnant students, references to sexual activity and birth control in the first article that were inappropriate for some of the younger students, and a student's unilateral criticism of her father in the second article.

The Court distinguished *Hazelwood* from *Tinker* insofar as the issue was not so much the right of students to speak on specific topics as it was the duty of educators not to promote particular student speech. The latter area concerns the authority of school officials over school-sponsored publications, theatrical productions, and other expressive activities that could reasonably be perceived to bear a school's imprimatur. In key language that reflects the rational relations test, the Court explained

---

264. *Scoville v. Board of Educ. of Joliet Township High School Dist. 204*, 425 F.2d 10 (7th Cir.1970), *cert. denied*, 400 U.S. 826, 91 S.Ct. 51, 27 L.Ed.2d 55 (1970).

265. *Trachtman v. Anker*, 563 F.2d 512, 520 (2d Cir.1977), *cert. denied*, 435 U.S. 925, 98 S.Ct. 1491, 55 L.Ed.2d 519 (1978).

266. 484 U.S. 260, 108 S.Ct. 562, 98 L.Ed.2d 592 [43 Educ. L. Rep. 515] (1988). [Case No. 113]

that "... educators do not offend the First Amendment by exercising editorial control over the style and content of student speech in school-sponsored expressive activities so long as their actions are reasonably related to legitimate pedagogical concerns."[267]

A related issue is advertisements in student newspapers. In the first reported case on this topic, a federal trial court in New York decreed that since a school newspaper published articles questioning American policy in Vietnam, there was no logical reason to forbid it from printing a paid advertisement on the same topic.[268] After *Hazelwood*, questions of advertising raise issues over whether school-sponsored publications constitute an open forum for expression by students and/or the public or whether they bear the imprimatur of schools so that access may be more limited.

The Ninth Circuit, relying on *Hazelwood*, affirmed that since the student publications at issue were not an open forum, and officials in Nevada did not create a limited-purpose forum by opening them up for advertisers of lawful goods and services, educators could apply reasonable editorial control over the content of a student newspaper and exclude advertisements from a wide range of organizations, including, as here, a group that focused on family planning.[269] A similar action arose in Massachusetts when student editors refused to deviate from their school newspaper and yearbook policy under which they agreed not to publish any political or advocacy advertising, including those for candidates for student government.[270] The First Circuit affirmed that school officials were not liable for refusing to run advertisements promoting sexual abstinence since the student policy did not involve state action.

Underground Activities and School Distribution Policies

Along with school-sponsored publications, whether curricular or extracurricular, students have developed their own, so-called, underground publications that have led to litigation. Absent reasonable forecasts of material and/or substantial disruption, courts have permitted educators to impose reasonable time, manner, and place restrictions on the distribution of materials while also preventing them from disciplining students who operated within these guidelines. In a case that is instructive on the importance of such limits, the Supreme Court upheld an anti-noise ordinance that prohibited persons who were on grounds adjacent to buildings in which schools were in session from wilfully making noises that disturb the peace. According to the Court, "[t]he crucial question [in evaluating such restrictions] is whether the manner of expression is basically incompatible with the normal activity of a particular place at a particular time."[271]

---

267. *Id.* at 273.

268. *Zucker v. Panitz,* 299 F.Supp. 102 (S.D.N.Y.1969).

269. *Planned Parenthood of S. Nev. v. Clark County School Dist.,* 941 F.2d 817 [69 Educ. L. Rep. 252] (9th Cir.1991).

270. *Yeo v. Town of Lexington,* 131 F.3d 241 [122 Educ. L. Rep. 924] (1st Cir.1997), *cert. denied,* 524 U.S. 904, 118 S.Ct. 2060, 141 L.Ed.2d 138 (1998).

271. *Grayned v. City of Rockford,* 408 U.S. 104, 92 S.Ct. 2294, 33 L.Ed.2d 222 (1972).

When students in New York produced and distributed an essentially off-campus paper that contained a vulgar satire about the school community, the Second Circuit was persuaded that they could not be punished.[272] In dicta, the court suggested that while there are circumstances under which school officials can deem specific publications unacceptable, this was not the case in the dispute at bar. In a later case, the Eighth Circuit upheld the approval of discipline of students in Minnesota who circulated an unofficial newspaper that contained vulgar and indecent language while indirectly encouraging violence against teachers.[273]

The Second Circuit, in a dispute from Connecticut, discussed the extent to which educators can exercise prior restraint on publications that are to be distributed at schools.[274] The court approved, but modified, an earlier judgment that invalidated a board rule that required all materials to have prior approval from school officials. The court held that in order for a rule requiring prior submission of material for distribution to be valid, it must prescribe a definite, brief period within which the review is to be completed along with identifying to whom and how it is to be submitted for clearance. In like fashion, the Ninth Circuit, in a case from Washington, expressing doubts that a constitutionally sound pre-distribution policy could be effectively established, struck down a policy that would have required approval for all non-school-sponsored materials.[275] The court decided that the policy violated the First Amendment because of its content over-breadth.

Student Free Speech and the Internet

An emerging question with regard to student expressive activity is their use of the internet. As school officials develop technology and internet use policies, they would be wise to craft their words carefully. In such a case, a federal trial court in Pennsylvania granted parents' motion for summary judgment in their challenge to their son's being disciplined for postings on a website message board.[276] The court agreed that provisions in a school handbook relating to discipline, student responsibility, and technology were unconstitutionally vague and overbroad especially since they did not geographically limit the authority of educators to discipline expression that occurred on school premises or at school-related activities.

The relatively few cases that addressed threatening student expression on the internet have reached mixed results. A student unsuccessful-

---

272. *Thomas v. Board of Educ., Granville Cent. School Dist.*, 607 F.2d 1043 (2d Cir.1979), *cert. denied*, 444 U.S. 1081, 100 S.Ct. 1034, 62 L.Ed.2d 765 (1980).

273. *Bystrom By and Through Bystrom v. Fridley High School*, 686 F.Supp. 1387 [47 Educ. L. Rep. 905] (D.Minn.1987), *aff'd without reported opinion*, 855 F.2d 855 [48 Educ. L. Rep. 1144] (8th Cir.1988).

274. *Eisner v. Stamford Bd. of Educ.*, 440 F.2d 803 (2d Cir.1971).

275. *Burch v. Barker*, 861 F.2d 1149 [50 Educ. L. Rep. 339] (9th Cir.1988).

276. *Flaherty v. Keystone Oaks School Dist.*, 247 F.Supp.2d 698 [175 Educ. L. Rep. 188] (W.D. Pa.2003).

ly challenged his expulsion for creating a website, on his own computer while at home, that contained derogatory remarks about his algebra teacher, asking for collections to pay a hit man to kill her. The board expelled the student for violating his school's code of conduct by threatening, harassing, and showing disrespect to the teacher. The Supreme Court of Pennsylvania affirmed that since the student's offensive messages substantially disrupted school activities, educators did not violate his First Amendment rights.[277]

On the other hand, since material issues of fact remained as to why officials acted as they did, a federal trial court in Ohio denied a school board's motion for summary judgment in a dispute over the expulsion of a middle school student for using school computers, during class hours, to access a website that he created on his own computer, on his own time, at home, that contained insulting sentences and graphics directed towards three classmates.[278] The court commented that while the conduct code's catch-all phrase was invalid on its face, the remaining sections were not unconstitutionally vague and that officials did not chill the student's First Amendment rights to expression. Moreover, federal trial courts in Missouri[279] and Michigan[280] reached similar outcomes as both rejected the arguments of school officials that material on websites did not disrupt school activities in a way that would have permitted them to discipline students. A federal trial court in Pennsylvania went even further in observing that educators exceeded their authority in attempting to suspend a student for writing a letter that ridiculed a school's athletic director and e-mailing it to friends from his home computer.[281] The court contended that even though the message was lewd and vulgar, since the student created it out-of-school and did not bring it there, officials could not discipline him due to the lack of evidence that it would have caused a substantial likelihood of disruption.

Dress Codes and Student Grooming

Dress Codes

Amid evolving judicial and social perspectives on student dress and grooming, two early disputes reflect the attitudes of the times. In a case that was cited in *Tinker*, the Supreme Court of Arkansas upheld a school board rule that prohibited "[t]he wearing of transparent hosiery, low-necked dresses, or any style of clothing tending toward immodesty in dress, or the use of face paint or cosmetics."[282] Eight years later, the Supreme Court of North Dakota applied similar analysis in refusing to

---

277. *J.S. v. Bethlehem Area School Dist.*, 807 A.2d 847 [170 Educ. L. Rep. 302] (Pa.2002).

278. *Coy v. Board of Educ.*, 205 F.Supp.2d 791 [166 Educ. L. Rep. 535] (N.D.Ohio 2002).

279. *Beussink ex rel. Beussink v. Woodland R–IV School Dist.*, 30 F.Supp.2d 1175 [131 Educ. L. Rep. 1000] (E.D. Mo.1998).

280. *Mahaffey ex rel. Mahaffey v. Aldrich*, 236 F.Supp.2d 779 (E.D.Mich.2002).

281. *Killion v. Franklin Reg'l School Dist.*, 136 F.Supp.2d 446 [153 Educ. L. Rep. 90] (W.D.Pa. 2001).

282. *Pugsley v. Sellmeyer*, 250 S.W. 538, 538 (Ark.1923).

disturb a rule against wearing metal heel plates since doing so damaged school floors and was noisy.[283]

Where rules on dress and grooming are narrowly drawn to cover specific activities, much of the judicial disagreement dissolves. Courts continue to uphold dress code policies as long as they are rationally related to legitimate pedagogical concerns in support of a school's educational mission[284] and are neither vague nor over-broad.[285]

Disputes involving political expression and clothing discussed earlier aside, courts reach mixed results on the appropriateness of placing limits on student dress, most notably t-shirts that display questionable messages that do not cause disruptions. For example, the Supreme Judicial Court of Massachusetts thought that students could wear t-shirts with arguably vulgar, lewd, and/or offensive messages, such as "Coed Naked Band: Do It To the Rhythm" as long as their doing so did not cause disruptions at school.[286] On the other hand, the Sixth Circuit affirmed that educational officials did not act in a manifestly unreasonable manner that violated a student's First Amendment right to free speech by prohibiting him from wearing t-shirts containing symbols and words that promoted values patently contrary to the school's educational mission.[287] The court was of the opinion that one t-shirt was offensive because it mocked Jesus while the others featured a singer who encouraged destructive conduct and demoralizing values along with promoting drug use.

As illustrated by a case from a federal trial court in Georgia, the judiciary defers to educators in evaluating the appropriateness of student dress that is not offensive or vulgar.[288] The court upheld a student's being given a three-day suspension in determining that even though his having worn a t-shirt to school that contained the message "Even adults lie" on front may have been a factor in his being excluded from class, educators did not violate his free speech rights and the school's dress code was not over-broad. Earlier, a federal trial court in Oklahoma enjoined school officials from preventing students from wearing t-shirts with the message "[t]he best of the night's adventures are reserved for people with nothing planned."[289] In acknowledging limits between school officials and student expression, the court rejected the board's claim that since this was a phrase taken from an advertisement for a company that

283. *Stromberg v. French*, 236 N.W. 477 (N.D.1931).

284. *Blau v. Fort Thomas Pub. School Dist.*, 401 F.3d 381 [196 Educ. L. Rep. 118] (6th Cir. 2005).

285. *See, e.g., Littlefield v. Forney Ind. School Dist.*, 268 F.3d 275 [158 Educ. L. Rep. 36] (5th Cir.2001); *Long v. Board of Educ. of Jefferson County, Ky.*, 121 F.Supp.2d 621 [149 Educ. L. Rep. 157] (W.D.Ky.2000), *aff'd*, 21 Fed.Appx. 252 [160 Educ. L. Rep. 392] (6th Cir.2001).

286. *Pyle By and Through Pyle v. South Hadley School Comm.*, 861 F.Supp. 157, 158 [94 Educ. L. Rep. 729] (D.Mass.1994),

question certified by, 55 F.3d 20 [100 Educ. L. Rep. 579] (1st Cir. 1995), *question certified to state court*, 667 N.E.2d 869 [111 Educ. L. Rep. 481] (Mass.1996).

287. *Boroff v. Van Wert City Bd. of Educ.*, 220 F.3d 465 [146 Educ. L. Rep. 629] (6th Cir. 2000), *cert. denied*, 532 U.S. 920, 121 S.Ct. 1355, 149 L.Ed.2d 286 (2001).

288. *Smith ex rel. Lanham v. Greene County School Dist.*, 100 F.Supp.2d 1354 [145 Educ. L. Rep. 368] (M.D.Ga.2000).

289. *McIntire v. Bethel School, Indep. School Dist. No. 3*, 804 F.Supp. 1415, 1418 [78 Educ. L. Rep. 828] (W.D.Okla.1992).

sells rum, it violated its policy against wearing t-shirts that advertise alcoholic beverages, insofar as the message was open to many possible interpretations, was not disruptive, and did not otherwise violate the dress code.

When public school students in an eighth-grade gifted program submitted a design for their official class shirt that depicted a physically disabled boy with the word "Gifties" on the back, administrators disapproved of its design and forbade them from wearing them or the unofficial versions that they created. After several students who wore the shirts were punished, officials lifted the ban. Even so, students filed suit claiming that they were subjected to continued reprimands, detentions, and suspensions for frivolous reasons that, in effect, amounted to retaliation. A federal trial court in Illinois rejected the students' claims that the t-shirt design was an expression of the individuality of the gifted section of the eighth-grade class.[290] Although the students claimed that they were poking fun at themselves with the t-shirt's design, the court agreed with officials that since its depiction of a physically disabled person created a threat to the school's ability to preserve discipline, they were not entitled to free speech protections under the First Amendment.

Where clothing or items of dress signify affiliations that can be detrimental to school discipline, disputes arise over whether they can be banned. When students wore rosaries to school as necklaces, a federal trial court in Texas was convinced that educators violated their First Amendment right to pure speech because rosaries are a form of religious expression.[291] The court concluded that the dress code's prohibition of gang-related apparel was unconstitutionally vague because officials could not show that wearing rosaries would have caused actual or anticipated disruptions. Similarly, after a high school student in Iowa had a small tattoo of a cross on her hand removed via laser surgery rather than be disciplined for violating a board policy against gang symbols, the Eighth Circuit voided the policy for vagueness since it did not adequately define the term "gang symbols."[292]

Other litigation has occurred over so-called gang clothing and dress codes. In one case, an appellate court in New Mexico affirmed that a dress code did not violate the First Amendment because it was reasonably related to school officials' interest in reducing distractions caused by clothing and increased campus security, among other goals.[293] On the other hand, the Eighth Circuit struck down a school board regulation from Iowa against wearing gang symbols for vagueness and overbreadth.[294] Earlier, a federal trial court in Illinois upheld a board's

290. *Brandt v. City of Chicago*, 326 F.Supp.2d 916 [190 Educ. L. Rep. 817] (N.D. Ill. 2004).

291. *Chalifoux v. New Caney Indep. School Dist.*, 976 F.Supp. 659 [121 Educ. L. Rep. 751] (S.D. Tex.1997).

292. *Stephenson v. Davenport Community School Dist.*, 110 F.3d 1303 [117 Educ. L. Rep. 443] (8th Cir.1997).

293. *Phoenix Elem. School Dist. No. 1 v. Green*, 943 P.2d 836 [120 Educ. L. Rep. 1170] (Ariz. Ct.App.1997).

294. *Stephenson v. Davenport Community School Dist.*, 110 F.3d 1303 [117 Educ. L. Rep. 443] (8th Cir.1997).

authority to forbid male students from wearing earrings connected with gang membership even though females were permitted to wear such ornamentations.[295]

Turning to earrings specifically, an appellate court in Louisiana affirmed that educators could prohibit a male elementary school student, but not females, from wearing them since a school rule advanced the legitimate educational objective of inspiring discipline and a positive learning environment.[296] To date, the only two reported cases addressing body piercings, both of which arose in Kentucky and were resolved by the Sixth Circuit, upheld dress code policies that included prohibitions against body piercings other than earrings.[297] However, in neither case was the rule against body piercing the primary issue.

In other cases, the federal trial court in New Mexico rejected a student's claim that his high school dress code's prohibition against wearing "sagging" pants violated his First Amendment expressive rights.[298] The court noted that wearing "sagging" pants was not a form of speech. In like manner, the federal trial court in Maryland indicated that a policy prohibiting students from wearing hats to school did not violate the First Amendment speech rights of a young woman who wanted to wear a head wrap to school to celebrate her cultural heritage.[299] The court thought that the rule was permissible since it was content-neutral and furthered the important governmental interest of providing a safe, respectful school environment that was conducive to learning. Similarly, a state court from Connecticut rejected a challenge filed by students who were expelled for violating a school's dress code policy.[300] The court was of the view that since the policy of prohibiting students from wearing blue jeans was rationally related to the school board's goal of reducing disruption, taunting, theft, and loss of attention to course work, it did not violate their First Amendment rights to free expression.[301]

The father of a middle school student in Virginia sought to enjoin part of a dress code that prohibited messages on clothing, jewelry, and personal belongings related to weapons. The Fourth Circuit maintained that the trial court abused its discretion in concluding that the father

---

295. *Olesen v. Board of Educ. of School Dist. No. 228*, 676 F.Supp. 820 [44 Educ. L. Rep. 205] (N.D.Ill.1987).

296. *Jones v. W.T. Henning Elementary School*, 721 So.2d 530 [131 Educ. L. Rep. 330] (La.Ct. App.1998).

297. *See Blau v. Fort Thomas Pub. School Dist.*, 401 F.3d 381 [196 Educ. L. Rep. 118] (6th Cir. 2005); *Long v. Board of Educ. of Jefferson County, Ky.*, 121 F.Supp.2d 621 [149 Educ. L. Rep. 157] (W.D. Ky. 2000), *aff'd*, 21 Fed.Appx. 252 [160 Ed. Law Rep. 392] (6th Cir. 2001).

298. *Bivens v. Albuquerque Pub. Schools*, 899 F.Supp. 556 [104 Educ. L. Rep. 195] (D.N.M. 1995).

299. *Isaacs v. Board of Educ. of Howard County*, 40 F.Supp.2d 335 [134 Educ. L. Rep. 166] (D.Md.1999).

300. *Byars v. City of Waterbury*, 795 A.2d 630 [164 Educ. L. Rep. 311] (Conn.Super.Ct.2001).

301. *See also Bannister v. Paradis*, 316 F.Supp. 185 (D.N.H.1970) (upholding a ban against blue jeans); *Fowler v. Williamson*, 251 S.E.2d 889 (N.C.Ct.App.1979) (upholding a ban against wearing jeans to a graduation ceremony).

had not met the test for obtaining a preliminary injunction.[302] The court pointed out that the father demonstrated a strong likelihood of success on his claim that the policy was over-broad since there was no evidence that clothing worn by students with messages related to weapons ever substantially disrupted the school or interfered with the rights of others.

In the first of two dress code cases involving religious issues, an atheist mother in New Jersey unsuccessfully filed an equal protection challenge to her school board's mandatory dress code policy which would have permitted an exemption for students based on their sincerely held religious beliefs.[303] The Third Circuit affirmed that the exemption was acceptable because it was rationally drawn to advance the school board's legitimate interest in accommodating the right of students to the free exercise of religion without undermining the pedagogical goals of the school uniform policy. Yet, the federal trial court in Nevada reached a different outcome with regard to a similar exemption to a mandatory dress code that was authorized by state statute. The court struck down exceptions that would have excused students from wearing uniforms if doing so violated their religious beliefs on the ground that it granted school officials unfettered discretion in evaluating which religious exceptions were permissible.[304] The court also upheld that part of the code that required students to wear clothing that was devoid of all messages because it was content neutral, but permitted exceptions for displays of the school logo, and could have been justified due to health and safety concerns.

Student Grooming

As to grooming and hair-length for males, courts reached mixed results as some permitted restrictions[305] while others refused to allow limitations to stand.[306] In a case involving student-athletes, the Eleventh Circuit upheld a policy from Alabama that required basketball and football players to be clean-shaven.[307] The court was satisfied that the policy was acceptable since it was rationally aimed at presenting the school in a favorable light, not at improving performance. Subsequently, in two separate cases, the Supreme Court of Texas agreed that school officials could set hair-length restriction for males.[308]

---

302. *Newsom ex rel. Newsom v. Albemarle County*, 354 F.3d 249 [184 Educ. L. Rep. 24] (4th Cir. 2003).

303. *Wilkins v. Penns Grove-Carnyes*, 123 Fed.Appx. 493 [196 Educ. L. Rep. 449] (3d Cir. 2005).

304. *Jacobs v. Clark County School Dist.*, 373 F.Supp.2d 1162 [199 Educ. L. Rep. 701] (D. Nev. 2005).

305. *Freeman v. Flake*, 448 F.2d 258 (10th Cir.1971), *cert. denied*, 405 U.S. 1032, 92 S.Ct. 1292, 31 L.Ed.2d 489 (1972); *Sherling v. Townley*, 464 F.2d 587 (5th Cir. 1972); *Zeller v. Donegal School Dist. Bd. of Educ.*, 517 F.2d 600 (3d Cir.1975).

306. *Richards v. Thurston*, 424 F.2d 1281 (1st Cir.1970); *Bishop v. Colaw*, 450 F.2d 1069 (8th Cir.1971); *Massie v. Henry*, 455 F.2d 779 (4th Cir.1972); *Arnold v. Carpenter*, 459 F.2d 939 (7th Cir.1972).

307. *Davenport by Davenport v. Randolph County Bd. of Educ.*, 730 F.2d 1395 [16 Educ. L. Rep. 1116] (11th Cir.1984).

308. *Barber v. Colorado Indep. School Dist.*, 901 S.W.2d 447 [101 Educ. L. Rep. 1241] (Tex. 1995); *Board of Trustees of Bastrop Indep. School Dist. v. Toungate*, 958 S.W.2d 365 [123 Educ. L. Rep. 392] (Tex. 1997), *reh'g of cause overruled* (Tex.1998).

The most recent case involving grooming arose in a non-public school but reflects the general rule. The Supreme Court of Rhode Island, reversing an earlier order to the contrary, reasoned that school officials had the authority to enforce a policy limiting the hair length of male students.[309] The court posited that inasmuch as the policy did not violate public policy, it was an enforceable provision of the school's educational contract with students.

Sexual Harassment

A long-term problem that has increasingly been recognized in American schools deals with sexual harassment of students by teachers and peers. To this end, the Supreme Court has resolved three cases dealing with sexual harassment in school settings while lower federal and state courts continue to resolve a large number of disputes. The first two Supreme Court cases involved situations where teachers engaged in inappropriate sexual misconduct with students while the third dealt with peer-to-peer sexual harassment.

Sexual Harassment Involving Teachers and Students

The facts in *Franklin v. Gwinnett County Public Schools (Franklin)*[310] revealed egregious disregard for a student's well-being. A female high school sophomore in Georgia alleged that she and one of her male teachers developed a "special" friendship. The teacher conducted private meetings with the student, authorized her late entry to classes, and engaged her in sexually oriented conversations. On one occasion, after the two argued in the school parking lot, the teacher forcibly kissed the student on the mouth. During this time, the student's boyfriend personally notified the school's band director about the teacher's conduct, and at least one other student who told an assistant principal about it was admonished for doing so. Other female students informed a teacher and a guidance counselor that the teacher made sexual remarks to them. Even as officials were apparently unwilling to investigate the teacher's behavior, his conduct worsened to the point that he engaged the student in three acts of coercive sexual intercourse at school. When the principal was informed of the sexual activity, administrators discouraged the student from pursuing her complaint due to the negative publicity that it might have generated. In addition, the band director spoke with the student's boyfriend, in an attempt to dissuade her from acting on her complaint. Shortly after officials began an inquiry into the student's complaints, they closed their investigation when the teacher agreed to resign at the end of the academic year; the band director voluntarily retired.

After unsuccessfully filing a complaint with the Federal Office of Civil Rights (OCR), an unreported federal trial court opinion rejected the

---

309. *Gorman v. St. Raphael Academy,* 853 A.2d 28 [189 Educ. L. Rep. 784] (R.I. 2004).

310. 503 U.S. 60, 112 S.Ct. 1028, 117 L.Ed.2d 208 [72 Educ. L. Rep. 32] (1992), *on remand,* 969 F.2d 1022 [76 Educ. L. Rep. 396] (11th Cir.1992). [Case No. 114]

student's damages claim under Title IX of the Educational Amendments of 1972.[311] The Eleventh Circuit affirmed the dismissal of the student's complaint.[312]

In *Franklin*, a unanimous Supreme Court expanded the scope of Title IX, which was enacted to provide the federal government with a tool to fight gender-based discrimination, by applying it, for the first time, to sexual harassment in a school setting. In reversing in favor of the student, the Court interpreted Title IX as implying a private right of action. According to the Court, since nothing in congressional intent in enacting Title IX prevented individuals, students or otherwise, from bringing suits for monetary damages for sexual harassment, the student was free to pursue this remedy since precluding her from doing so would have left her without any other legal recourse.

The second case involving teacher-student sexual harassment arose in Texas after an eighth-grade student joined a book-discussion club at the high school she ultimately attended. The controversy arose when the teacher in charge made sexually suggestive comments, eventually directing his more inappropriate remarks at the student. The teacher later initiated sexual contact with the student when he visited her home on the pretext of giving her a book, culminating in their regularly engaging in sexual relations. None of the sexual encounters between the teacher and student took place on school property. The student did not complain at that time both because she was uncertain about how she should have behaved and since she wished to continue having the same teacher.

More than a year later, when parents of other students complained about the teacher's behavior, the principal warned him to be careful about what he said and informed the school guidance counselor about the incident but failed to notify the superintendent who also served as the district's Title IX coordinator. When a police officer happened to discover the teacher and student having sex, he was arrested. Unlike in *Franklin*, the school board promptly terminated the teacher's employment and the Texas Education Agency revoked his teaching license. The student and her mother filed suit in a federal trial court, seeking monetary damages under Title IX for the teacher's sexual harassment. After the trial court granted the board's motion for summary judgment, the Fifth Circuit affirmed that the board was not vicariously liable under Title IX for the teacher's sexual misconduct under common law agency theory.[313]

In *Gebser v. Lago Vista Independent School District* (*Gebser*),[314] the Supreme Court affirmed that a board could not be liable under Title IX for a teacher's misconduct unless an official who, at a minimum, has the authority to institute corrective measures, has actual notice of, and is deliberately indifferent to, a teacher's sexual misconduct. The Court

311. 20 U.S.C.A. § 1681. Portions of this statute are in the appendix.

312. *Franklin v. Gwinnett County Pub. Schools*, 911 F.2d 617 [62 Educ. L. Rep. 453] (11th Cir. 1990).

313. *Doe v. Lago Vista Indep. School Dist.*, 106 F.3d 1223, 125 Ed. Law Rep. 1074 (5th Cir. 1997).

314. 524 U.S. 274, 118 S.Ct. 1989, 141 L.Ed.2d 277 [125 Educ. L. Rep. 1055] (1998). [Case No. 115]

found that since the board behaved appropriately under the circumstances insofar as school officials acted promptly and decisively in punishing the teacher, the student and her mother could not proceed with their claim.

The Eighth Circuit, in one of many later cases, rejected the claim of a student in Nebraska that her school board was liable under Title IX when she had a homosexual relationship with a teacher.[315] The court contended that the board was not at fault since the student failed to make the necessary showing that school officials acted with deliberate indifference after being informed about the teacher's behavior.

In a case with an interesting twist, the Eleventh Circuit affirmed that a school board in Georgia was not liable under Title IX where a male student failed to prove that school officials acted with deliberate indifference to reports that he engaged in a sexual relationship with a female teacher.[316] The panel ascertained that the trial court incorrectly applied the stricter Title IX standard that governs cases of student-on-student harassment. Focusing instead on the teacher-on-student standard enunciated in *Gebser*, the court added that since board officials unsuccessfully warned the teacher to end the relationship, they had not acted with deliberate indifference because they responded appropriately to allegations about the relationship even though they were unable to prevent additional abuse.

Peer-to-Peer Sexual Harassment

Davis v. Monroe County Board of Education (Davis)[317] began when a female fifth-grade student in Georgia was subjected to a prolonged pattern of sexual harassment by a male classmate. Over five months, the male engaged in inappropriate behavior, including trying to touch the female's breasts and genital area along with verbal requests for sexual relations. Even though the student and her parents reported the male's behavior and repeatedly requested intervention, officials failed to intervene. Due to the male's behavior, the female's grades suffered since she was unable to concentrate on school work; her father also discovered that she had written a suicide note. Moreover, there was evidence that the female was not the only target of the male's behavior. The harassment did not stop until the male pled guilty to charges of sexual battery.

The student and her parents filed suit against the board of education under Title IX, seeking monetary damages and injunctive relief for peer-to-peer sexual harassment. A federal trial court granted the board's motion to dismiss for failure to state a claim upon which relief can be granted and the Eleventh Circuit affirmed.[318]

315. *Kinman v. Omaha Pub. School Dist.*, 171 F.3d 607 [133 Educ. L. Rep. 418] (8th Cir.1999).

316. *Sauls v. Pierce County School Dist.*, 399 F.3d 1279 [195 Educ. L. Rep. 767] (11th Cir. 2005).

317. 526 U.S. 629, 119 S.Ct. 1661, 143 L.Ed.2d 839 [134 Educ. L. Rep. 477] (1999), *on remand*, 206 F.3d 1377 [143 Educ. L. Rep. 724] (11th Cir.2000). [Case No. 116]

318. *Davis v. Monroe County Bd. of Educ.*, 74 F.3d 1186 [106 Educ. L. Rep. 486] (11th Cir. 1996), *reh'g en banc granted*,

In *Davis,* the Supreme Court reversed in favor of the female and her parents.[319] The Court decided that school boards, as recipients of federal financial assistance, "... are properly held liable in damages only when they are deliberately indifferent to sexual harassment, of which they have actual knowledge, that is so severe, pervasive, and objectively offensive that it can be said to deprive the victims of access to the educational opportunities or benefits provided by the school."[320] The Court also observed that damages are limited "... to circumstances wherein the recipient exercises substantial control over both the harasser and the context in which the known harassment occurs."[321] The Court stressed that while boards may be accountable if officials are deliberately indifferent, this does not mean that they can avoid liability only by eliminating actionable peer-harassment claims or by taking specified disciplinary steps.

In rejecting the dissent's argument that the Court placed too much of a burden on school officials, the majority responded that the standard is flexible enough to account for the level of authority that they must apply while also protecting them from potential liability in disciplining students who sexually harass peers. The Court conceded that while it remains to be seen whether the female could have proved that board officials acted with deliberate indifference, she may have been able to demonstrate that administrators subjected her to discrimination by failing to respond to her complaints for five months.

Later Developments

Litigation involving sexual harassment in the schools continues at a brisk pace. Courts continue to award damages to students for sexual harassment and/or misconduct under Title IX for harassment by peers[322] and school employees,[323] or where school officials failed to supervise students to prevent such behavior in school settings when they agree that educators could have prevented the misconduct.[324] For instance, a federal trial court in Michigan denied administrators' request for qualified immunity where they continually removed reprimands from the file of a male teacher who was accused of sexually molesting three female

opinion vacated, 91 F.3d 1418 [111 Educ. L. Rep. 1107] (11th Cir. 1996), *on reh'g,* 120 F.3d 1390 [120 Educ. L. Rep. 390] (11th Cir. 1997).

319. For an earlier case holding a board liable for peer-to-peer harassment, *see Oona R.-S.- by Kate S. v. McCaffrey,* 143 F.3d 473 [126 Educ. L. Rep. 589] (9th Cir.1998). *But see Rowinsky v. Bryan Indep. School Dist.,* 80 F.3d 1006 [108 Educ. L. Rep. 502] (5th Cir.1996), *cert. denied,* 519 U.S. 861, 117 S.Ct. 165, 136 L.Ed.2d 108 (1996) (denying relief in a case of peer-to-peer sexual harassment).

320. *Davis v. Monroe County Bd. of Educ.,* 526 U.S. 629, 650, 119 S.Ct. 1661, 143 L.Ed.2d 839 [134 Educ. L. Rep. 477]

(1999), *on remand,* 206 F.3d 1377 [143 Educ. L. Rep. 724] (11th Cir.2000). [Case No. 116]

321. *Id.* at 646.

322. *See, e.g., Vance v. Spencer County Pub. School Dist.,* 231 F.3d 253 [148 Educ. L. Rep. 616] (6th Cir.2000); *Ray v. Antioch Unified School Dist.,* 107 F.Supp.2d 1165 [146 Educ. L. Rep. 1036] (N.D.Cal.2000).

323. *See, e.g., Baynard v. Malone,* 268 F.3d 228 [158 Educ. L. Rep. 19] (4th Cir. 2001).

324. *Vaughn v. Orleans Parish School Bd.,* 802 So.2d 967 [160 Educ. L. Rep. 973] (La.Ct.App. 2001), *writ of error denied,* 818 So.2d 773 (La.2002).

students.[325] The court determined that this part of the suit could proceed because a genuine issue of material fact remained as to whether the school board had a custom of failing to prevent sexual abuse from occurring even after officials received repeated notices about the teacher's improper conduct. Conversely, where they believed that educators behaved responsibly, courts refused to impose liability on boards for harassment and/or sexual misconduct by peers[326] and school employees,[327] especially where there was no evidence that officials acted with deliberate indifference to staff misconduct.[328]

In a key concern with regard to the element of notice in sexual harassment cases, the Third Circuit considered who is an appropriate person to have actual notice of harassment for the purpose of alleging that educators acted with deliberate indifference.[329] In a dispute where a fifteen-year-old student had a sexual relationship with one of her male teachers, the court affirmed that the school's principal and assistant principal could not be deemed "appropriate persons" solely by virtue of their positions because they lacked actual knowledge of the relationship. The court refused to impose liability on the two administrators because in addition to having to have had actual notice of a teacher's misconduct, they would have had to have acted with deliberate indifference, meaning that they would have had to have made an official decision not to remedy the violation.

Where a student in Kansas claimed that school officials were deliberately indifferent to his being sexually harassed by peers, the federal trial court rejected the school board's motion to dismiss in acknowledging that same-sex, student-on-student sexual harassment was actionable

---

325. *Doe ex rel. Doe v. Warren Consol. Schools,* 307 F.Supp.2d 860 [186 Educ. L. Rep. 775] (E.D. Mich. 2003), *aff'd in relevant part, sub nom. Doe v. Warren Consol. Schools,* 93 Fed.Appx. 812 (6th Cir. 2004).

326. *See, e.g., Hawkins v. Sarasota County School Bd.,* 322 F.3d 1279 [174 Educ. L. Rep. 678] (11th Cir.2003); *Bruneau ex rel. Schofield v. South Kortright Cent. School Dist.,* 163 F.3d 749 [131 Educ. L. Rep. 593] (2d Cir.1998); *Nordo v. School Dist. of Philadelphia,* 172 F.Supp.2d 600 [159 Educ. L. Rep. 138] (E.D.Pa.2001); *Clark v. Bibb County Bd. of Educ.,* 174 F.Supp.2d 1369 [159 Educ. L. Rep. 675] (M.D.Ga.2001); *C.R.K. v. U.S.D. 260,* 176 F.Supp.2d 1145 [160 Educ. L. Rep. 105] (D.Kan.2001); *Burwell v. Pekin Community High School Dist. 303,* 213 F.Supp.2d 917 [168 Educ. L. Rep. 328] (C.D.Ill.2002); *Doe v. Lennox School Dist. No. 41–4,* 329 F.Supp.2d 1063 [191 Educ. L. Rep. 743] (D.S.D. 2003).

327. *See, e.g., Hartley v. Parnell,* 193 F.3d 1263 [139 Educ. L. Rep. 95] (11th Cir.1999); *Doe v. Gooden,* 214 F.3d 952 [145 Educ. L. Rep. 167] (8th Cir.2000); *P.H. v.*

School Dist. of Kansas City, Mo., 265 F.3d 653 [157 Educ. L. Rep. 42] (8th Cir.2001); *Johnson v. Elk Lake School Dist.,* 283 F.3d 138 [162 Educ. L. Rep. 679] (3d Cir.2002); *Craig v. Lima City Schools Bd. of Educ.,* 384 F.Supp.2d 1136 [202 Educ. L. Rep. 172] (N.D. Ohio 2005).

328. *See, e.g., Doe ex rel. Doe v. Dallas Indep. School Dist.,* 220 F.3d 380 [146 Educ. L. Rep. 80] (5th Cir.2000); *Davis ex rel. Doe v. DeKalb County School Dist.,* 233 F.3d 1367 [149 Educ. L. Rep. 376] (11th Cir.2000), *cert. denied,* 532 U.S. 1066, 121 S.Ct. 2217, 150 L.Ed.2d 210 (2001); *Doe v. City of Roseville,* 296 F.3d 431 [167 Educ. L. Rep. 115] (6th Cir. 2002), *cert. denied,* 537 U.S. 1232, 123 S.Ct. 1357, 155 L.Ed.2d 196 (2003); *Sauls v. Pierce County School Dist.,* 399 F.3d 1279 [195 Educ. L. Rep. 767] (11th Cir. 2005); *Williams ex rel. Hart v. Paint Valley Local School Dist.,* 400 F.3d 360 [196 Educ. L. Rep. 27] (6th Cir. 2005); *Doe v. D'Agostino,* 367 F.Supp.2d 157 [198 Educ. L. Rep. 250] (D. Mass. 2005).

329. *Bostic v. Smyrna School Dist.,* 418 F.3d 355 [200 Educ. L. Rep. 573] (3d Cir. 2005).

under Title IX.[330] After a jury entered a verdict in favor of the student, the board unsuccessfully filed a motion for a judgment as a matter of law. The court wrote that when viewing the evidence in a light most favorable to the plaintiff, it was sufficient for the jury to have returned a verdict in his favor where school officials acted with deliberate indifference to his plight.[331]

Sexual Orientation

Another area of growing concern deals with harassment based on sexual orientation. Former students in California, who were, or were perceived by others as being, lesbian, gay, and/or bisexual, sued school officials alleging that their failure to respond to complaints of student-on-student anti-homosexual harassment denied them their rights to equal protection under the Fourteenth Amendment rather than under Title IX. In affirming the denial of the officials' motion for summary judgment, the Ninth Circuit explained that at the time of the alleged incidents, the students' right to be free from intentional discrimination on the basis of sexual orientation was clearly established.[332]

The first of two cases that arose in New Jersey saw parents file suit on behalf of their son under the Individuals with Disabilities Education Act, claiming that he was bullied by other students, in part because of his lack of athleticism, physique, and perceived femininity. The Third Circuit indicated that school officials failed to provide the student with a free appropriate public education.[333] The court believed that insofar as school officials failed to offer substantial reasons for not crediting witnesses who testified on behalf of the student at a due process hearing, they had to reimburse his parents for the cost associated with their unilaterally placing him in a public school in a neighboring district.

Where a mother filed a complaint with New Jersey's Division of Civil Rights (DCR), alleging that school officials violated the Law Against Discrimination due to her son's having been repeatedly subject to harassment by peers at school on account of his perceived sexual orientation, the DCR agreed that since the response of school officials was inadequate, he was entitled to damages for emotional distress. On further review, an appellate court affirmed that in light of evidence establishing that school officials did not effectively respond to two assaults on the student based on his perceived sexual orientation, the award of $50,000 in damages was not excessive.[334]

330. *Theno v. Tonganoxie Unified School Dist. No. 464*, 377 F.Supp.2d 952 [200 Educ. L. Rep. 658] (D. Kan. 2005).

331. *Theno v. Tonganoxie Unified School Dist. No. 464*, 394 F.Supp.2d 1299 [204 Educ. L. Rep. 230] (D. Kan. 2005).

332. *Flores v. Morgan Hill Unified School Dist.*, 324 F.3d 1130 [175 Educ. L. Rep. 79] (9th Cir. 2003).

333. *Shore Reg'l High School Bd. of Educ. v. P.S. ex rel. P.S.*, 381 F.3d 194 [191 Educ. L. Rep. 641] (3d Cir. 2004).

334. *L.W. v. Toms River Reg'l Schools Bd. of Educ.*, 886 A.2d 1090 [204 Educ. L. Rep. 300] (N.J. Super. Ct. App. Div. 2005).

[Case No. 105]   The Authority of a School Board to Set Disciplinary Rules for Interscholastic Athletics

PALMER v. MERLUZZI

United States Court of Appeals, Third Circuit, 1989.
868 F.2d 90 [51 Educ. L. Rep. 1196].

STAPLETON, CIRCUIT JUDGE.

This is an appeal from a summary judgment in favor of the defendants, Peter Merluzzi, Superintendent of Schools for the Hunterdon Central High School District, and the Hunterdon Central Board of Education. Plaintiff Dan Palmer, a student and football player at Hunterdon, claims that his Constitutional rights to due process and equal protection were violated when Superintendent Merluzzi suspended him from playing interscholastic football for sixty days. We will affirm.

I

In September of 1986, Dan Palmer was a senior at Hunterdon Central High School and a starting wide receiver on the high school's football team. He was also enrolled in a high school course called "Careers in Broadcasting Technology." On the evening of September 28, 1986, in order to fill a course requirement, Palmer and three other students were assigned, without faculty supervision, to the school radio station, which is located on the school premises. The next morning, beer stains and a marijuana pipe were discovered at the radio station. Later that day, Palmer, school disciplinarian Dr. Grimm, and Mr. Buckley, Palmer's former football coach, met in Mr. Buckley's office and Palmer was questioned about this discovery. During that meeting, Palmer admitted that the evening before he had smoked marijuana and consumed beer at the radio station.

On September 30, 1986, Dr. Grimm sent Mr. and Mrs. Palmer a letter advising them that their son had been assigned a ten-day out-of-school suspension effective from September 30, 1986 to October 13, 1986. The letter asked the Palmers to call Dr. Grimm if they had additional questions and suggested that they and their son consider counseling. The Palmers took no action to contest the ten-day suspension.

After Dr. Grimm's meeting with Palmer, Superintendent Merluzzi conferred about the appropriateness of additional discipline with Dr. Grimm, Mr. Buckley, assistant principal Dr. Myers, Mr. Kleber, the faculty director of the radio station, and Palmer's current football Coach, Mr. Meert. Suspension from extra-curricular activities was discussed and all except Dr. Grimm agreed that such a step was appropriate. No specific number of days for such a suspension was discussed, however.

Thereafter, Merluzzi made telephone calls to two drug-counseling agencies. These agencies suggested sixty days as an average time for the rehabilitation of someone with a minor drug problem, and Merluzzi ultimately decided that sixty days would be an appropriate period for the students concerned to ponder their actions. All students who were involved in the incident at the radio station received the same punishment.

On October 13, the eve of the expiration of the ten-day suspension, the Board of Education met. Palmer's father, James Palmer, hearing "rumors" concerning the possible imposition of additional sanctions on his son, attended the meeting and spoke with Merluzzi shortly before it started. Merluzzi confirmed that he was inclined to impose a sixty-day extra-curricular suspension, but told James Palmer that he could raise the issue with the Board. James Palmer was accorded half an hour in closed session to present his views; he argued that the additional suspension would adversely affect his son's chances of playing football in college and would also reduce his chances of being awarded college scholarships. The Board declined to intervene and, after the meeting, Merluzzi informed all concerned parents that he was definitely going to impose the sixty-day extra-curricular suspension.

Subsequent to the imposition of the sixty day extra-curricular suspension, Palmer appealed to the New Jersey State Commissioner of Education for a review of the actions of the defendants. On October 20, 1986, an evidentiary hearing was conducted before Administrative Law Judge Bruce R. Campbell. Judge Campbell found that the "ten-day out-of-school suspension was procedurally faultless and consistent with announced policy." With respect to the sixty-day football suspension, however, he concluded that Palmer had been denied procedural due process ... because Palmer was not given notice of the proposed sixty-day suspension and afforded a hearing thereon. . . .

On appeal, the Commissioner of Education affirmed the ALJ's finding that "the actions of the Board's agents in suspending [Palmer] from school for 10 days in all respects comports with the due process requirements set forth in *Goss v. Lopez*." The commissioner did not, however, accept the ALJ's conclusion that "the decision to increase the penalty imposed on [Palmer] ... rises to the level of *requiring* that the Board provide to him an additional due process proceeding ..." (emphasis in original). In the course of reaching this conclusion, the commissioner noted that Palmer "could not or should not have been unaware of the fact that his role as a member of the football team, as well as his status as a student in the school, was in jeopardy when he decided to take the actions he did."

The district court granted summary judgment to the defendants, holding that for purposes of due process analysis, Palmer had no property or liberty interest in participating in the school's football program.

II

Resolution of this appeal does not require that we address the issue found dispositive by the ALJ and the district court—whether procedural due process is required whenever a public school student in New Jersey faces or receives for a breach of discipline solely a suspension from participation in his or her school's athletic program. Palmer did not commit an offense for which athletic suspension was the only potential sanction or the only sanction in fact imposed. Here there was a single proceeding on a single charge that resulted in two sanctions being imposed, a ten-day suspension from school and a sixty-day suspension from athletics. The ultimate issue before us is whether the process received by Palmer in that single proceeding was appropriate given the fact that he faced, and ultimately received, both of those sanctions. We conclude that it was.

The threshold issue is whether the interests that could be adversely affected in the proceeding against Palmer were such that the due process clause was implicated. The answer seems clear. In *Goss v. Lopez* the Supreme Court concluded that due process was required when a student faced a ten-day scholastic suspension. *A fortiori,* due process is required when a student faces a ten-day academic suspension *and* a sixty-day athletic suspension.

Having concluded that "some process" was due, we turn to the issue of how much was due. We know from *Goss* what process would have been due if only a ten-day academic suspension had been at stake. After balancing the competing interests involved, the Court decided that the student must be given "oral or written notice of the charges against him and, if he denies them, an explanation of the evidence the authorities have and an opportunity to present his side of the story." The Court continued, stating that "[t]here need be no delay between the time 'notice' is given and the time of the hearing. . . . We hold only that . . . the student first be told what he is accused of doing and what the basis of the accusation is." The Court also stopped short of requiring that the student be given "the opportunity to secure counsel, to confront and cross-examine witnesses supporting the charge, or to call his own witnesses to verify his version of the incident." As long as the student "at least ha[s] the opportunity to characterize his conduct and put it in what he deems the proper context" due process has been satisfied.

Palmer received the process required by *Goss.* The day after the incident at the radio station, in an informal hearing with Dr. Grimm and Mr. Buckley, he was advised of what had been found in the radio station and thus of the character of the offense being investigated. He then admitted his participation in the smoking of marijuana and the drinking of beer at the station. Palmer's involvement in the activities of that evening has never been disputed. During the conference, Palmer had the opportunity to put the events of the prior evening into what he perceived to be their proper context and could have argued for leniency had he so chosen.

Palmer does not argue before us that the hearing afforded him did not comport with the kind of informal hearing contemplated by *Goss.* Moreover, Palmer acknowledges that due process would not have been violated if only the ten-day suspension from school had been imposed. Rather, Palmer's argument is that a second notice and a second hearing were required because at the time of his conference with Dr. Grimm, he did not have adequate notice that a sixty-day athletic suspension might be imposed upon him.

We find this argument unpersuasive. The notice required by *Goss* is notice of "what [the student] is accused of doing and what the basis of the accusation is." We have been cited to no authority, and we know of none, suggesting that the *notice of the charge and supporting evidence* in a *Goss* situation must include a statement of the *penalties* that could be imposed in the course of the proceeding. We decline to adopt such a requirement in a situation like the one before us, in which the possible sanctions are knowable from previously published materials or are obvious from the circumstances.

In this case, Palmer was advised at the outset that he was suspected of consuming alcohol and a drug on school property. The Student Handbook, which was applicable to all students, specified that "alcohol and/or drug use" would, if a first offense, result in "10 days suspension" from school. The Interscholastic Athletic Program policy statement, which was applicable to Palmer and other students participating in that program, warned that "no student may participate who has not demonstrated good citizenship and responsibility." Based on these provisions, the nature of the offense, and common sense, we, like the New Jersey Commissioner of Education, are confident that Palmer must have realized from the outset that his football eligibility, as well as his status as a student, was at stake. Accordingly, we hold that Palmer's interview with Dr. Grimm and Mr. Buckley provided just as meaningful an opportunity to argue against the athletic suspension as against the scholastic suspension.

Having concluded that Palmer received the process contemplated by *Goss,* we turn to the issue of whether more than that process was required in this case because Palmer faced not only a ten-day suspension from school but a football suspension as well. As Palmer stresses, the Court in *Goss* expressly noted that it was addressing itself solely to the procedure that must be provided in connection with a "short suspension, not exceeding 10 days," and that "longer suspensions or expulsions for the remainder of the school term, or permanently, may require more formal procedures." Palmer urges, as we understand it, that his interest in avoiding an erroneous deprivation of his participation in the football program for sixty days was sufficiently great that before any decision was made concerning the sanction for his misconduct, he should have been given express notice of the fact that his football eligibility was in jeopardy and that he should have been given the opportunity to secure the advice of an attorney before presenting his defense. Although we acknowledge that the sixty-day football suspension had a substantial impact on Palmer, determination of the amount of process due in a given situation involves a balancing of interests and we conclude that, when the balance is struck, the procedure prescribed in *Goss* was sufficient under the circumstances of this case.

Due process is a flexible concept and the process due in any situation is to be determined by weighing (1) the private interests at stake, (2) the governmental interests at stake, and (3) the fairness and reliability of the existing procedures and the probable value, if any, of additional procedural safeguards. In *Goss*, the Court described the student's interest as one in avoiding "unfair or mistaken exclusion from the educational process with all its unfortunate consequences." Those consequences include not only the loss of the benefit of the educational process but also potential damage to "the students' standing with their fellow students and their teachers" and potential "interfer[ence] with later opportunities for higher education and employment."

From the school's and the public's point of view, *Goss* recognized the need for maintaining order and discipline in our schools without prohibitive costs and in a manner that will contribute to, rather than disrupt, the educational process. As we have noted, the Court concluded that an informal hearing process would reconcile the private and governmental interests and that requiring representation by counsel, cross-examination, and other, more formal procedural safeguards would not sufficiently increase the reliability and fairness of the process to warrant the additional expense and disruption of the educational process.

We accept for present purposes Palmer's contention that, while called an extra-curricular activity, the school's football program is an integral part of its educational program. Nevertheless, it is but one part of that program and in terms of lost educational benefit, the loss occasioned by a football suspension is far less than that occasioned by a suspension from school for a comparable period of time. In terms of the student's standing with teachers and peers, we believe the potential loss is likely to be a function of the nature of the offense rather than the penalty; it is therefore unlikely to be affected by the fact that the sanction includes an athletic as well as a school suspension. As a general proposition, we believe the same can be said for the potential for interference with later opportunities for higher education and employment. Indeed, Palmer does not argue otherwise. The loss that he emphasizes is the possible loss of the opportunity to play college football. Although we acknowledge that the loss of the opportunity to impress college scouts with one's senior year play can have a significant adverse effect on one's chances for a college football career, we believe it would be unduly disruptive of a school's educational process to require one disciplinary process for football players and similarly situated athletes and another disciplinary process for other students.

Since the governmental interest at stake here is the same as that in *Goss*, since the incremental efficacy of the process proposed over the process afforded is not materially different than the one in that case, and since we find the student's interest to be only slightly greater, we conclude that the process required by *Goss* was sufficient in the circumstances presented by this case.

III

Palmer also contends that his suspension violated his right to equal protection under the Fourteenth Amendment. Since participation in extra-curricular activities is not a fundamental right under the Constitution and since Palmer's suspension was not based on a suspect classification, we must examine Palmer's argument under the "rational relationship test." We conclude that the disciplinary actions taken by the school were rationally related to a valid state interest. The State has very strong interests in preserving a drug-free environment in its schools and in discouraging drug use by its students. We are unwilling to say that the sanctions imposed on Palmer were not reasonably designed to serve those legitimate interests.

IV

Since Palmer's suspensions from school and participation in inter-scholastic football did not violate any right secured by the Constitution, we will affirm the judgment of the district court.

Notes

1. Note that the student and his parents did not contest his ten-day exclusion from school. What do you think about this?

2. Is it fair to hold student-athletes to higher standards of conduct?

3. Was the punishment in this case fair?

[Case No. 106] Constitutional Rights of Students regarding Corporal Punishment

INGRAHAM v. WRIGHT

Supreme Court of the United States, 1977.
430 U.S. 651, 97 S.Ct. 1401, 51 L.Ed.2d 711.

Mr. Justice Powell delivered the opinion of the Court.

This case presents questions concerning the use of corporal punishment in public schools: first, whether the paddling of students as a means of maintaining school discipline constitutes cruel and unusual punishment in violation of the Eighth Amendment; and second, to the extent that paddling is constitutionally permissible, whether the Due Process Clause of the Fourteenth Amendment requires prior notice and an opportunity to be heard.

I

. . .

Petitioners' evidence may be summarized briefly. In the 1970–1971 school year many of the 237 schools in Dade County used corporal punishment as a means of maintaining discipline pursuant to Florida legislation and a local school board regulation. The statute then in effect authorized limited corporal punishment by negative inference, proscribing punishment which was "degrading or unduly severe" or which was inflicted without prior consultation with the principal or the teacher in charge of the school. The regulation . . . contained explicit directions and limitations. . . .

... Petitioners focused on Drew Junior High School, the school in which both Ingraham and Andrews were enrolled in the fall of 1970. In an apparent reference to Drew, the District Court found that "[t]he instances of punishment which could be characterized as severe, accepting the students' testimony as credible, took place in one junior high school." The evidence, consisting mainly of the testimony of 16 students, suggests that the regime at Drew was exceptionally harsh. The testimony of Ingraham and Andrews, in support of their individual claims for damages, is illustrative. Because he was slow to respond to his teacher's instructions, Ingraham was subjected to more than 20 licks with a paddle while being held over a table in the principal's office. The paddling was so severe that he suffered a hematoma requiring medical attention and keeping him out of school for several days. Andrews was paddled several times for minor infractions. On two occasions he was struck on his arms, once depriving him of the full use of his arm for a week.

The District Court made no findings on the credibility of the students' testimony. Rather, assuming their testimony to be credible, the court found no constitutional basis for relief. . . .

A panel of the Court of Appeals voted to reverse. . . . Upon rehearing, the en banc court rejected these conclusions and affirmed the judgment of the District Court. . . .

II

In addressing the scope of the Eighth Amendment's prohibition on cruel and unusual punishment this Court has found it useful to refer to "[t]raditional common law concepts," and to the "attitude[s] which our society has traditionally taken." So too, in defining the requirements of procedural due process under the Fifth and Fourteenth Amendments, the Court has been attuned to what "has always been the law of the land," and to "traditional ideas of fair procedure." We therefore begin by examining the way in which our traditions and our laws have responded to the use of corporal punishment in public schools.

The use of corporal punishment in this country as a means of disciplining school children dates back to the colonial period. It has survived the transformation of primary and secondary education from the colonials' reliance on optional private arrangements to our present system of compulsory education and dependence on public schools. Despite the general abandonment of corporal punishment as a means of punishing criminal offenders, the practice continues to play a role in the public education of school children in most parts of the country. Professional and public opinion is sharply divided on the practice, and has been for more than a century. Yet we can discern no trend toward its elimination.

At common law a single principle has governed the use of corporal punishment since before the American Revolution: teachers may impose reasonable but not excessive force to discipline a child. . . . The basic doctrine has not changed. The prevalent rule in this country today privileges such force as a teacher or administrator "reasonably believes to be necessary for [the child's] proper control, training, or education." ... To the extent that the force is excessive or unreasonable, the educator in virtually all States is subject to possible civil and criminal liability.

Although the early cases viewed the authority of the teacher as deriving from the parents, the concept of parental delegation has been replaced by the view—more consonant with compulsory education laws—that the State itself may impose such corporal punishment as is reasonably necessary "for the proper education of the child and for the maintenance of group discipline." ... All of the circumstances are to be taken into account in determining whether the punishment is reasonable in a particular case. Among the most important considerations are the seriousness of the offense, the attitude and past behavior of the child, the nature and severity of the punishment, the age and strength of the child, and the availability of less severe but equally effective means of discipline....

Of the 23 States that have addressed the problem through legislation, 21 have authorized the moderate use of corporal punishment in public schools. Of these States only a few have elaborated on the common law test of reasonableness, typically providing for approval or notification of the child's parent, or for infliction of punishment only by the principal or in the presence of an adult witness. Only two States, Massachusetts and New Jersey, have prohibited all corporal punishment in their public schools. Where the legislatures have not acted, the state courts have uniformly preserved the common law rule permitting teachers to use reasonable force in disciplining children in their charge.

Against this background of historical and contemporary approval of reasonable corporal punishment, we turn to the constitutional questions before us.

III

The Eighth Amendment provides, "Excessive bail shall not be required, nor excessive fines imposed, nor cruel and unusual punishments inflicted." Bail, fines and punishment traditionally have been associated with the criminal process, and by subjecting the three to parallel limitations the text of the Amendment suggests an intention to limit the power of those entrusted with the criminal law function of government. An examination of the history of the Amendment and the decisions of this Court construing the proscription against cruel and unusual punishment confirms that it was designed to protect those convicted of crimes. We adhere to this longstanding limitation and hold that the Eighth Amendment does not apply to the paddling of children as a means of maintaining discipline in public schools.

A

The history of the Eighth Amendment is well known. The text was taken, almost verbatim, from a provision of the Virginia Declaration of Rights of 1776, which in turn derived from the English Bill of Rights of

1689. The English version, adopted after the accession of William and Mary, was intended to curb the excesses of English judges under the reign of James II....

At the time of its ratification, the original Constitution was criticized in the Massachusetts and Virginia Conventions for its failure to provide any protection for persons convicted of crimes.... This criticism provided the impetus for inclusion of the Eighth Amendment in the Bill of Rights....

B

In light of this history, it is not surprising to find that every decision of this Court considering whether a punishment is "cruel and unusual" within the meaning of the Eighth and Fourteenth Amendments has dealt with a criminal punishment....

In the few cases where the Court has had occasion to confront claims that impositions outside the criminal process constituted cruel and unusual punishment, it has had no difficulty finding the Eighth Amendment inapplicable....

C

Petitioners acknowledge that the original design of the Cruel and Unusual Punishments Clause was to limit criminal punishments, but urge nonetheless that the prohibition should be extended to ban the paddling of school children. Observing that the Framers of the Eighth Amendment could not have envisioned our present system of public and compulsory education, with its opportunities for noncriminal punishments, petitioners contend that extension of the prohibition against cruel punishments is necessary lest we afford greater protection to criminals than to schoolchildren. It would be anomalous, they say, if schoolchildren could be beaten without constitutional redress, while hardened criminals suffering the same beatings at the hands of their jailors might have a valid claim under the Eighth Amendment. Whatever force this logic may have in other settings, we find it an inadequate basis for wrenching the Eighth Amendment from its historical context and extending it to traditional disciplinary practices in the public schools.

The prisoner and the schoolchild stand in wholly different circumstances, separated by the harsh facts of criminal conviction and incarceration....

The schoolchild has little need for the protection of the Eighth Amendment. Though attendance may not always be voluntary, the public school remains an open institution. Except perhaps when very young, the child is not physically restrained from leaving school during school hours; and at the end of the school day, the child is invariably free to return home. Even while at school, the child brings with him the support of family and friends and is rarely apart from teachers and other pupils who may witness and protest any instances of mistreatment.

The openness of the public school and its supervision by the community afford significant safeguards against the kinds of abuses from which the Eighth Amendment protects the prisoner. In virtually every community where corporal punishment is permitted in the schools, these safeguards are reinforced by the legal constraints of the common law. Public school teachers and administrators are privileged at common law to inflict only such corporal punishment as is reasonably necessary for the proper education and discipline of the child; any punishment going beyond the privilege may result in both civil and criminal liability.... As long as the schools are open to public scrutiny, there is no reason to believe that the common law constraints will not effectively remedy and deter excesses such as those alleged in this case.

We conclude that when public school teachers or administrators impose disciplinary corporal punishment, the Eighth Amendment is inapplicable. The pertinent constitutional question is whether the imposition is consonant with the requirements of due process.

IV

The Fourteenth Amendment prohibits any State deprivation of life, liberty or property without due process of law. Application of this prohibition requires the familiar two-stage analysis: we must first ask whether the asserted individual interests are encompassed within the Fourteenth Amendment's protection of "life, liberty or property"; if protected interests are implicated, we then must decide what procedures constitute "due process of law." Following that analysis here, we find that corporal punishment in public school implicates a constitutionally protected liberty interest, but we hold that the traditional common law remedies are fully adequate to afford due process.

A

"[T]he range of interests protected by procedural due process is not infinite." ...

... Among the historic liberties ... protected was a right to be free from, and to obtain judicial relief for, unjustified intrusions on personal security.

While the contours of this historic liberty interest in the context of our federal system of government have not been defined precisely, they always have been thought to encompass freedom from bodily restraint and punishment. It is fundamental that the state cannot hold and physically punish an individual except in accordance with due process of law.

This constitutionally protected liberty interest is at stake in this case. There is, of course a *de minimis* level of imposition with which the Constitution is not concerned. But at least where school authorities, acting under color of state law, deliberately decide to punish a child for misconduct by restraining the child and inflicting appreciable physical pain, we hold that Fourteenth Amendment liberty interests are implicated.

B

"[T]he question remains what process is due." Were it not for the common law privilege permitting teachers, to inflict reasonable corporal punishment on children in their care, and the availability of the traditional remedies for abuse, the case for requiring advance procedural safeguards would be strong indeed. But here we deal with a punishment—paddling—within that tradition, and the question is whether the common law remedies are adequate to afford due process.

. . . Whether in this case the common law remedies for excessive corporal punishment constitute due process of law must turn on an analysis of the competing interests at stake, viewed against the background of "history, reason, [and] the past course of decisions." The analysis requires consideration of three distinct factors: "first, the private interest that will be affected . . ., second, the risk of an erroneous deprivation of such interest . . . and the probable value, if any, of additional or substitute procedural safeguards; and, finally, the [state] interest, including the function involved and the fiscal and administrative burdens that the additional or substitute procedural requirement would entail."

1

Because it is rooted in history, the child's liberty interest in avoiding corporal punishment while in the care of public school authorities is subject to historical limitations. . . .

The concept that reasonable corporal punishment in school is justifiable continues to be recognized in the laws of most States. . . . It represents "the balance struck by this country," between the child's interest in personal security and the traditional view that some limited corporal punishment may be necessary in the course of a child's education. Under that longstanding accommodation of interests, there can be no deprivation of substantive rights as long as disciplinary corporal punishment is within the limits of the common law privilege.

This is not to say that the child's interest in procedural safeguards is insubstantial. The school disciplinary process is not "a totally accurate, unerring process, never mistaken and never unfair. . . ." In any deliberate infliction of corporal punishment on a child who is restrained for that purpose, there is some risk that the intrusion on the child's liberty will be unjustified and therefore unlawful. In these circumstances the child has a strong interest in procedural safeguards that minimize the risk of wrongful punishment and provide for the resolution of disputed questions of justification.

We turn now to a consideration of the safeguards that are available under applicable Florida law.

2

Florida has continued to recognize, and indeed has strengthened by statute, the common law right of a child not to be subjected to excessive corporal punishment in school. Under Florida law the teacher and principal of the school decide in the first instance whether corporal punishment is reasonably necessary under the circumstances in order to discipline a child who has misbehaved. But they must exercise prudence and restraint. For Florida has preserved the traditional judicial proceedings for determining whether the punishment was justified. If the punishment inflicted is later found to have been excessive—not reasonably believed at the time to be necessary for the child's discipline or training—the school authorities inflicting it may be held liable in damages to the child and, if malice is shown, they may be subject to criminal penalties.

Although students have testified in this case to specific instances of abuse, there is every reason to believe that such mistreatment is an aberration. The uncontradicted evidence suggests that corporal punishment in the Dade County schools was, "[w]ith the exception of a few cases, . . . unremarkable in physical severity." Moreover, because paddlings are usually inflicted in response to conduct directly observed by teachers in their presence, the risk that a child will be paddled without cause is typically insignificant. In the ordinary case, a disciplinary paddling neither threatens seriously to violate any substantive rights nor condemns the child "to suffer grievous loss of any kind."

In those cases where severe punishment is contemplated, the available civil and criminal sanctions for abuse—considered in light of the openness of the school environment—afford significant protection against unjustified corporal punishment. Teachers and school authorities are unlikely to inflict corporal punishment unnecessarily or excessively when a possible consequence of doing so is the institution of civil or criminal proceedings against them. . . .

3

But even if the need for advance procedural safeguards were clear, the question would remain whether the incremental benefit could justify the cost. Acceptance of petitioners' claims would work a transformation in the law governing corporal punishment in Florida and most other States. Given the impracticability of formulating a rule of procedural due process that varies with the severity of the particular imposition, the prior hearing petitioners seek would have to precede *any* paddling, however moderate or trivial.

Such a universal constitutional requirement would significantly burden the use of corporal punishment as a disciplinary measure. Hearings—even informal hearings—require time, personnel, and a diversion of attention from normal school pursuits. . . .

Elimination or curtailment of corporal punishment would be welcomed by many as a societal advance. But when such a policy choice may result from this Court's determination of an asserted right to due process, rather than from the normal processes of community debate and legislative action, the societal costs cannot be dismissed as insubstantial. . . .

... In view of the low incidence of abuse, the openness of our schools, and the common law safeguards that already exist, the risk of error that may result in violation of a schoolchild's substantive rights can only be regarded as minimal. Imposing additional administrative safeguards as a constitutional requirement might reduce that risk marginally, but would also entail a significant intrusion into an area of primary educational responsibility. We conclude that the Due Process Clause does not require notice and a hearing prior to the imposition of corporal punishment in the public schools, as that practice is authorized and limited by the common law.

Notes

1. The vote in *Ingraham* was five-to-four The dissent argued that the Eighth Amendment applied to some corporal punishment cases and that the rudimentary due process requirements of *Goss* should have applied. Do you agree?

2. In *Baker v. Owens*, 395 F.Supp. 294 (M.D.N.C.1975), *aff'd*, 423 U.S. 907, 96 S.Ct. 210, 46 L.Ed.2d 137 (1975), the Supreme Court summarily affirmed that school officials have the right to administer corporal punishment as they see fit, regardless of whether parents agree. What does this do to the presumed voluntary nature of state officials acting *in loco parentis*?

3. The efficacy of corporal punishment has been contested since long before there were public schools. To what extent is this issue properly a legislative, rather than judicial, concern? To what extent is it an educational, rather than legal, concern?

[Case No. 107]   Procedural Due Process for Short–Term Suspensions

GOSS v. LOPEZ

Supreme Court of the United States, 1975.
419 U.S. 565, 95 S.Ct. 729, 42 L.Ed.2d 725.

MR. JUSTICE WHITE delivered the opinion of the Court.

This appeal by various administrators of the Columbus, Ohio, Public School System (CPSS) challenges the judgment of a three-judge federal court, declaring that appellees—various high school students in the CPSS—were denied due process of law contrary to the command of the Fourteenth Amendment in that they were temporarily suspended from their high schools without a hearing either prior to suspension or within a reasonable time thereafter, and enjoining the administrators to remove all references to such suspensions from the students' records.

I

Ohio law, Rev. Code Ann. § 3313.64, provides for free education to all children between the ages of six and 21. Section 3313.66 of the Code empowers the principal of an Ohio public school to suspend a pupil for misconduct for up to 10 days or to expel him. In either case, he must notify the student's parents within 24 hours and state the reasons for his action. A pupil who is expelled, or his parents, may appeal the decision to the Board of Education and in connection therewith shall be permitted to be heard at the board meeting. The Board may reinstate in pupil following the hearing. No similar procedure is provided in section 3313.66 or any other provision of state law for a suspended student. Aside from a regulation tracking the statute, at the time of the imposition of the suspensions in this case the CPSS itself had not issued any written procedure applicable to suspensions. Nor, so far as the record reflects, had any of the individual high schools involved in this case. Each, however, had formally or informally described the conduct for which suspension could be imposed.

The nine named appellees, each of whom alleged that he or she had been suspended from public high school in Columbus for up to 10 days without a hearing pursuant to section 3313.66, filed an action under 42 U.S.C. § 1983 against the Columbus Board of Education and various administrators of the CPSS. The complaint sought a declaration that section 3313.66 was unconstitutional in that it permitted public school administrators to deprive plaintiffs of their rights to an education without a hearing of any kind, in violation of the procedural due process component of the Fourteenth Amendment. It also sought to enjoin the public school officials from issuing future suspensions pursuant to section 3313.66 and to require them to remove references to the past suspensions from the records of the students in question.

The proof below established that the suspensions arose out of a period of widespread student unrest in the CPSS during February and March 1971. Six of the named plaintiffs, Rudolph Sutton, Tyrone Washington, Susan Cooper, Deborah Fox, Clarence Byars, and Bruce Harris, were students at the Marion–Franklin High School and were each suspended for 10 days on account of disruptive or disobedient conduct committed in the presence of the school administrator who ordered the suspension. One of these, Tyrone Washington, was among a group of students demonstrating in the school auditorium while a class was being conducted there. He was ordered by the school principal to leave, refused to do so, and was suspended. Rudolph Sutton, in the presence of the principal, physically attacked a police officer who was attempting to remove Tyrone Washington from the auditorium. He was immediately suspended. The other four Marion–Franklin students were suspended for similar conduct. None was given a hearing to determine the operative facts underlying the suspension, but each, together with his or her parents, was offered the opportunity to attend a conference, subsequent to the effective date of the suspension, to discuss the student's future.

Two named plaintiffs, Dwight Lopez and Betty Crome, were students at the Central High School and McGuffey Junior High School, respectively. The former was suspended in connection with a disturbance in the lunchroom which involved some physical damage to school property. Lopez testified that at least 75 other students were suspended from his school on the same day. He also testified below that he was not a party to the destructive conduct but was instead an innocent bystander. Because no one from the school testified with regard to this incident, there is no evidence in the record indicating the official basis for concluding otherwise. Lopez never had a hearing.

Betty Crome was present at a demonstration at a high school other than the one she was attending. There she was arrested together with others, taken to the police station, and released without being formally charged. Before she went to school on the following day, she was notified that she had been suspended for a 10–day period. Because no one from the school testified with respect to this incident, the record does not disclose how the McGuffey Junior High School principal went about making the decision to suspend Crome, nor does it disclose on what information the decision was based. It is clear from the record that no hearing was ever held. There was no testimony with respect to the suspension of the ninth named plaintiff, Carl Smith. The school files were also silent as to his suspension, although as to some, but not all, of the other named plaintiffs the files contained either direct references to their suspensions or copies of letters sent to their parents advising them of the suspension.

On the basis of this evidence, the three-judge court declared that plaintiffs were denied due process of law because they were "suspended without hearing prior to suspension or within a reasonable time thereafter," and that Ohio Rev.Code Ann. section 3313.66 and regulations issued pursuant thereto were unconstitutional in permitting such suspensions. It was ordered that all references to plaintiffs' suspensions be removed from school files.

Although not imposing upon the Ohio school administrators any particular disciplinary procedures and leaving ... the District Court declared that there were "minimum requirements of notice and a hearing prior to suspension, except in emergency situations." In explication, the court stated that relevant case authority would: (1) permit "(i)mmediate removal of a student whose conduct disrupts the academic atmosphere of the school, endangers fellow students, teachers or school officials, or damages property"; (2) require notice of suspension proceedings to be sent to the students' parents within 24 hours of the decision to conduct them; and (3) require a hearing to be held, with the student present, within 72 hours of his removal. Finally, the court stated that, with respect to the nature of the hearing, the relevant cases required that statements in support of the charge be produced, that the student and others be permitted to make statements in defense or mitigation, and that the school need not permit attendance by counsel.

The defendant school administrators have appealed the three-judge court's decision.... We affirm.

II

At the outset, appellants contend that because there is no constitutional right to an education at public expense, the Due Process Clause does not protect against expulsions from the public school system. This position misconceives the nature of the issue and is refuted by prior decisions. The Fourteenth Amendment forbids the State to deprive any person of life, liberty or property without due process of law. Protected interests in property are normally "not created by the Constitution. Rather, they are created and their dimensions are defined" by an independent source such as state statutes or rules entitling the citizen to certain benefits.

Accordingly, a state employee who under state law, or rules promulgated by state officials, has a legitimate claim of entitlement to continued employment absent sufficient cause for discharge may demand the procedural protections of due process. So may welfare recipients who have statutory rights to welfare as long as they maintain the specified qualifications. . . .

Here, on the basis of state law, appellees plainly had legitimate claims of entitlement to a public education. Ohio Rev.Code §§ 3313.48 and 3313.64 direct local authorities to provide a free education to all residents between six and 21 years of age, and a compulsory attendance law requires attendance for a school year of not less than 32 weeks. It is true that § 3313.66 of the code permits school principals to suspend students for up to two weeks; but suspensions may not be imposed without any grounds whatsoever. All of the schools had their own rules specifying the grounds for expulsion or suspension. Having chosen to extend the right to an education to people of appellees' class generally, Ohio may not withdraw that right on grounds of misconduct absent fundamentally fair procedures to determine whether the misconduct has occurred.

Although Ohio may not be constitutionally obligated to establish and maintain a public school system, it has nevertheless done so and has required its children to attend. Those young people do not "shed their constitutional rights" at the schoolhouse door. "The Fourteenth Amendment, as now applied to the States, protects the citizen against the State itself and all of its creatures—Boards of Education not excepted." The authority possessed by the State to prescribe and enforce standards of conduct in its schools, although concededly very broad, must be exercised consistently with constitutional safeguards. Among other things, the State is constrained to recognize a student's legitimate entitlement to a public education as a property interest which is protected by the Due Process Clause and which may not be taken away for misconduct without adherence to the minimum procedures required by that clause.

The Due Process Clause also forbids arbitrary deprivations of liberty. "Where a person's good name, reputation, honor, or integrity is at stake because of what the government is doing to him," the minimal requirements of the clause must be satisfied. School authorities here suspended appellees from school for periods of up to 10 days based on charges of misconduct. If sustained and recorded, those charges could seriously damage the students' standing with their fellow pupils and their teachers as well as interfere with later opportunities for higher education and employment. It is apparent that the claimed right of the State to determine unilaterally and without process whether that misconduct has occurred immediately collides with the requirements of the Constitution.

Appellants proceed to argue that even if there is a right to a public education protected by the Due Process Clause generally, the clause comes into play only when the State subjects a student to a "severe detriment or grievous loss." The loss of 10 days, it is said, is neither severe nor grievous and the Due Process Clause is therefore of no relevance. Appellee's argument is again refuted by our prior decisions; for in determining "whether due process requirements apply in the first place, we must look not to the 'weight' but to the *nature* of the interest at stake." *Board of Regents v. Roth.* The Court's view has been that as long as a property deprivation is not *de minimis,* its gravity is irrelevant to the question whether account must be taken of the Due Process Clause. A 10–day suspension from school is not *de minimis* in our view and may not be imposed in complete disregard of the Due Process Clause.

. . . Neither the property interest in educational benefits temporarily denied nor the liberty interest in reputation, which is also implicated, is so insubstantial that suspensions may constitutionally be imposed by any procedure the school chooses, no matter how arbitrary.

III

"Once it is determined that due process applies, the question remains what process is due." . . .

There are certain bench marks to guide us. . . . *Mullane v. Central Hanover Trust Co.,* a case often invoked by later opinions, said that "[m]any controversies have raged about the cryptic and abstract words of the Due Process Clause but there can be no doubt that at a minimum they require that deprivation of life, liberty or property by adjudication be preceded by notice and opportunity for hearing appropriate to the nature of the case." . . . "The fundamental requisite of due process of law is the opportunity to be heard," a right that "has little reality or worth unless one is informed that the matter is pending and can choose for himself whether to . . . contest." At the very minimum, therefore, students facing suspension and the consequent interference with a protected property interest must be given *some* kind of notice and afforded *some* kind of hearing. . . .

It also appears from our cases that the timing and content of the notice and the nature of the hearing will depend on appropriate accommodation of the competing interests involved. The student's interest is to avoid unfair or mistaken exclusion from the educational process, with all of its unfortunate consequences. The Due Process Clause will not shield him from suspensions properly imposed, but it disserves both his interest and the interest of the State if his suspension is in fact unwarranted. The concern would be mostly academic if the disciplinary process were a totally accurate, unerring process, never mistaken and never unfair. Unfortunately, that is not the case, and no one suggests that it is. Disciplinarians, although proceeding in utmost good faith, frequently act on the reports and advice of others; and the controlling facts and the nature of the conduct under challenge are often disputed. The risk of error is not at all trivial, and it should be guarded against if that may be done without prohibitive cost or interference with the educational process.

The difficulty is that our schools are vast and complex. Some modicum of discipline and order is essential if the educational function is to be performed. Events calling for discipline are frequent occurrences and sometimes require immediate, effective action. Suspension is considered not only to be a necessary tool to maintain order but a valuable educational device. The prospect of imposing elaborate hearing requirements in every suspension case is viewed with great concern, and many school authorities may well prefer the untrammeled power to act unilaterally, unhampered by rules about notice and hearing. But it would be a strange disciplinary system in an educational institution if no communication was sought by the disciplinarian with the student in an effort to inform him of his defalcation and to let him tell his side of the story in order to make sure that an injustice is not done. . . .

We do not believe that school authorities must be totally free from notice and hearing requirements if their schools are to operate with acceptable efficiency. Students facing temporary suspension have interests qualifying for protection of the Due Process Clause, and due process requires, in connection with a suspension of 10 days or less, that the student be given oral or written notice of the charges against him and, if he denies them, an explanation of the evidence the authorities have and an opportunity to present his side of the story. The clause requires at least these rudimentary precautions against unfair or mistaken findings of misconduct and arbitrary exclusion from school.

There need be no delay between the time "notice" is given and the time of the hearing. In the great majority of cases the disciplinarian may informally discuss the alleged misconduct with the student minutes after it has occurred. We hold only that, in being given an opportunity to explain his version of the facts at this discussion, the student first be told what he is accused of doing and what the basis of the accusation is. Lower courts which have addressed the question of the *nature* of the procedures required in short suspension cases have reached the same conclusion. Since the hearing may occur almost immediately following the misconduct, it follows that as a general rule notice and hearing should precede removal of the student from school. We agree with the District Court, however, that there are recurring situations in which prior notice and hearing cannot be insisted upon. Students whose presence poses a continuing danger to persons or property or an ongoing threat of disrupting the academic process may be immediately removed from school. In such cases, the necessary notice and rudimentary hearing should follow as soon as practicable, as the District Court indicated. . . .

We stop short of construing the Due Process Clause to require, countrywide, that hearings in connection with short suspensions must afford the student the opportunity to secure counsel, to confront and cross-examine witnesses supporting the charge or to call his own witnesses to verify his version of the incident. Brief disciplinary suspensions are almost countless. To impose in each such case even truncated trial type procedures might well overwhelm administrative facilities in many places and, by diverting resources, cost more than it would save in educational effectiveness. Moreover, further formalizing the suspension process and escalating its formality and adversary nature may not only make it too costly as a regular disciplinary tool but also destroy its effectiveness as part of the teaching process.

On the other hand, requiring effective notice and informal hearing permitting the student to give his version of the events will provide a meaningful hedge against erroneous action. At least the disciplinarian will be alerted to the existence of disputes about facts and arguments about cause and effect. He may then determine himself to summon the accuser, permit cross-examination and allow the student to present his own witnesses. In more difficult cases, he may permit counsel. In any event, his discretion will be more informed and we think the risk of error substantially reduced.

Requiring that there be at least an informal give-and-take between student and disciplinarian, preferably prior to the suspension, will add little to the factfinding function where the disciplinarian has himself witnessed the conduct forming the basis for the charge. But things are not always as they seem to be, and the student will at least have the opportunity to characterize his conduct and put it in what he deems the proper context.

We should also make it clear that we have addressed ourselves solely to the short suspension, not exceeding 10 days. Longer suspensions or expulsions for the remainder of the school term, or permanently, may require more formal procedures. Nor do we put aside the possibility that in unusual situations, although involving only a short suspension, something more than the rudimentary procedures will be required.

IV

The District Court found each of the suspensions involved here to have occurred without a hearing, either before or after the suspension, and that each suspension was therefore invalid and the statute unconstitutional insofar as it permits such suspensions without notice or hearing. Accordingly, the judgment is affirmed....

Notes

1.   *Goss* applies only to suspensions of up to ten-days. What are the possible consequences of having a ten-day suspension noted on the permanent record cards of students?

2.   Section III of the opinion sets out in detail guidelines of the nature and extent of required hearings.

3.   Has *Goss* opened avenues for judicial intervention that have had a negative impact on the daily operations of schools?

[Case No. 108]   Constitutionality of Student Searches

NEW JERSEY v. T.L.O.

Supreme Court of the United States, 1985.
469 U.S. 325, 105 S.Ct. 733, 83 L.Ed.2d 720 [21 Educ. L. Rep. 1122].

JUSTICE WHITE delivered the opinion of the Court.

We granted certiorari in this case to examine the appropriateness of the exclusionary rule as a remedy for searches carried out in violation of the Fourth Amendment by public school authorities. Our consideration of the proper application of the Fourth Amendment to the public schools, however, has led us to conclude that the search that gave rise to the case now before us did not violate the Fourth Amendment. Accordingly, we here address only the questions of the proper standard for assessing the legality of searches conducted by public school officials and the application of that standard to the facts of this case.

I

On March 7, 1980, a teacher at Piscataway High School in Middlesex County, N.J., discovered two girls smoking in a lavatory. One of the two girls was the respondent T.L.O., who at that time was a 14–year-old high school freshman. Because smoking in the lavatory was a violation of a school rule, the teacher took the two girls to the Principal's office, where they met with Assistant Vice Principal Theodore Choplick. In response to questioning by Mr. Choplick, T.L.O.'s companion admitted that she had violated the rule. T.L.O., however, denied that she had been smoking in the lavatory and claimed that she did not smoke at all.

Mr. Choplick asked T.L.O. to come into his private office and demanded to see her purse. Opening the purse, he found a pack of cigarettes, which he removed from the purse and held before T.L.O. as he accused her of having lied to him. As he reached into the purse for the cigarettes, Mr. Choplick also noticed a package of cigarette rolling papers. In his experience, possession of rolling papers by high school students was closely associated with the use of marihuana. Suspecting that a closer examination of the purse might yield further evidence of drug use, Mr. Choplick proceeded to search the purse thoroughly. The search revealed a small amount of marihuana, a pipe, a number of empty plastic bags, a substantial quantity of money in one-dollar bills, an index card that appeared to be a list of students who owed T.L.O. money, and two letters that implicated T.L.O. in marihuana dealing.

Mr. Choplick notified T.L.O.'s mother and the police, and turned the evidence of drug dealing over to the police. At the request of the police, T.L.O.'s mother took her daughter to police headquarters, where T.L.O. confessed that she had been selling marihuana at the high school. On the basis of the confession and the evidence seized by Mr. Choplick, the State brought delinquency charges against T.L.O. . . . Contending that Mr. Choplick's search of her purse violated the Fourth Amendment, T.L.O. moved to suppress the evidence found in her purse as well her confession, which, she argued, was tainted by the allegedly unlawful search. . . .

II

In determining whether the search at issue in this case violated the Fourth Amendment, we are faced initially with the question whether that Amendment's prohibition on unreasonable searches and seizures applies to searches conducted by public school officials. We hold that it does.

It is now beyond dispute that "the Federal Constitution, by virtue of the Fourteenth Amendment, prohibits unreasonable searches and seizures by state officers." Equally indisputable is the proposition that the Fourteenth Amendment protects the rights of students against encroachment by public school officials. . . .

. . . We have held school officials subject to the commands of the First Amendment, see *Tinker v. Des Moines Independent Community School District,* and the Due Process Clause of the Fourteenth Amendment. More generally, the Court has recognized that "the concept of parental delegation" as a source of school authority is not entirely "consonant with compulsory education laws." *Ingraham v. Wright.* Today's public school officials do not merely exercise authority voluntarily conferred on them by individual parents; rather, they act in furtherance of publicly mandated educational and disciplinary policies. In carrying out searches and other disciplinary functions pursuant to such policies, school officials act as representatives of the State, not merely as surrogates for the parents, and they cannot claim the parents' immunity from the strictures of the Fourth Amendment.

III

To hold that the Fourth Amendment applies to searches conducted by school authorities is only to begin the inquiry into the standards governing such searches. Although the underlying command of the Fourth Amendment is always that searches and seizures be reasonable, what is reasonable depends on the context within which a search takes place. The determination of the standard of reasonableness governing any specific class of searches requires "balancing the need to search against the invasion which the search entails." On one side of the balance are arrayed the individual's legitimate expectations of privacy and personal security; on the other, the government's need for effective methods to deal with breaches of public order.

We have recognized that even a limited search of the person is a substantial invasion of privacy. We have also recognized that searches of closed items of personal luggage are intrusions on protected privacy interests, for "the Fourth Amendment provides protection to the owner of every container that conceals its contents from plain view." A search of a child's person or of a closed purse or other bag carried on her person, no less than a similar search carried out on an adult, is undoubtedly a severe violation of subjective expectations of privacy.

Of course, the Fourth Amendment does not protect subjective expectations of privacy that are unreasonable or otherwise "illegitimate." To receive the protection of the Fourth Amendment, an expectation of privacy must be one that society is "prepared to recognize as legitimate." . . .

. . . In short, schoolchildren may find it necessary to carry with them a variety of legitimate, noncontraband items, and there is no reason to conclude that they have necessarily waived all rights to privacy in such items merely by bringing them onto school grounds.

Against the child's interest in privacy must be set the substantial interest of teachers and administrators in maintaining discipline in the classroom and on school grounds. . . .

How, then, should we strike the balance between the schoolchild's legitimate expectations of privacy and the school's equally legitimate need to maintain an environment in which learning can take place? It is evident that the school setting requires some easing of the restrictions to which searches by public authorities are ordinarily subject. The warrant requirement, in particular, is unsuited to the school environment: requiring a teacher to obtain a warrant before searching a child suspected of an infraction of school rules (or of the criminal law) would unduly interfere with the maintenance of the swift and informal disciplinary procedures needed in the schools. . . . [W]e hold today that school officials need not obtain a warrant before searching a student who is under their authority.

The school setting also requires some modification of the level of suspicion of illicit activity needed to justify a search. Ordinarily, a search—even one that may permissibly be carried out without a warrant—must be based upon "probable cause" to believe that a violation of the law has occurred. However, "probable cause" is not an irreducible requirement of a valid search. The fundamental command of the Fourth Amendment is that searches and seizures be reasonable. . . .

We join the majority of courts that have examined this issue in concluding that the accommodation of the privacy interests of schoolchildren with the substantial need of teachers and administrators for freedom to maintain order in the schools does not require strict adherence to the requirement that searches be based on probable cause to believe that the subject of the search has violated or is violating the law. Rather, the legality of a search of a student should depend simply on the reasonableness, under all the circumstances, of the search. Determining the reasonableness of any search involves a twofold inquiry: first, one must consider "whether the . . . action was justified at its inception"; second, one must determine whether the search as actually conducted "was reasonably related in scope to the circumstances which justified the interference in the first place." Under ordinary circumstances, a search of a student by a teacher or other school official will be "justified at its inception" when there are reasonable grounds for suspecting that the search will turn up evidence that the student has violated or is violating either the law or the rules of the school. Such a search will be permissible in its scope when the measures adopted are reasonably related to the objectives of the search and not excessively intrusive in light of the age and sex of the student and the nature of the infraction.

This standard will, we trust, neither unduly burden the efforts of school authorities to maintain order in their schools nor authorize unrestrained intrusions upon the privacy of schoolchildren. By focusing attention on the question of reasonableness, the standard will spare teachers and school administrators the necessity of schooling themselves in the niceties of probable cause and permit them to regulate their conduct according to the dictates of reason and common sense. At the same time, the reasonableness standard should ensure that the interests of students will be invaded no more than is necessary to achieve the legitimate end of preserving order in the schools.

IV

There remains the question of the legality of the search in this case.... Our review of the facts surrounding the search leads us to conclude that the search was in no sense unreasonable for Fourth Amendment purposes.

The incident that gave rise to this case actually involved two separate searches, with the first—the search for cigarettes—providing the suspicion that gave rise to the second—the search for marihuana. Although it is the fruits of the second search that are at issue here, the validity of the search for marihuana must depend on the reasonableness of the initial search for cigarettes, as there would have been no reason to suspect that T.L.O. possessed marihuana had the first search not taken place. Accordingly, it is to the search for cigarettes that we first turn our attention....

... T.L.O. had been accused of smoking, and had denied the accusation in the strongest possible terms when she stated that she did not smoke at all. Surely it cannot be said that under these circumstances, T.L.O.'s possession of cigarettes would be irrelevant to the charges against her or to her response to those charges. T.L.O.'s possession of cigarettes, once it was discovered, would both corroborate the report that she had been smoking and undermine the credibility of her defense to the charge of smoking. To be sure, the discovery of the cigarettes would not prove that T.L.O. had been smoking in the lavatory; nor would it, strictly speaking, necessarily be inconsistent with her claim that she did not smoke at all. But it is universally recognized that evidence, to be relevant to an inquiry, need not conclusively prove the ultimate fact in issue, but only have "any tendency to make the existence of any fact that is of consequence to the determination of the action more probable or less probable than it would be without the evidence." The relevance of T.L.O.'s possession of cigarettes to the question whether she had been smoking and to the credibility of her denial that she smoked supplied the necessary "nexus" between the item searched for and the infraction under investigation....

Our conclusion that Mr. Choplick's decision to open T.L.O.'s purse was reasonable brings us to the question of the further search for marihuana once the pack of cigarettes was located. The suspicion upon which the search for marihuana was founded was provided when Mr. Choplick observed a package of rolling papers in the purse as he removed the pack of cigarettes.... The discovery of the rolling papers concededly gave rise to a reasonable suspicion that T.L.O. was carrying marihuana as well as cigarettes in her purse. This suspicion justified further exploration of T.L.O.'s purse, which turned up more evidence of drug-related activities: a pipe, a number of plastic bags of the type commonly used to store marihuana, a small quantity of marihuana, and a fairly substantial amount of money. Under these circumstances, it was not unreasonable to extend the search to a separate zippered compartment of the purse; and when a search of that compartment revealed an index card containing a list of "people who owe me money" as well as two letters, the inference that T.L.O. was involved in marihuana trafficking was substantial enough to justify Mr. Choplick in examining the letters to determine whether they contained any further evidence. In short, we cannot conclude that the search for marihuana was unreasonable in any respect. Accordingly, the judgment of the Supreme Court of New Jersey is

Reversed.

Notes

1. In footnote 5, 469 U.S. 325 at 338, the Court stated that it was addressing "... whether a school child has a legitimate expectation of privacy in lockers, desks, or other school property provided for the storage of school supplies." How far should the privacy rights of students extend?

2. In footnote 8, 469 U.S. 325 at 342, the Court wrote that it did "... not decide whether individualized suspicion is an essential element of the reasonableness standard we adopt for searches by school authorities." Should the Court have considered this issue? Would its doing so have altered the result?

3. T.L.O. has been applied in more than 200 cases, with the vast majority of courts ruling in favor of school officials.

[Case No. 109]   Drug Testing of Student–Athletes

BOARD OF EDUCATION OF INDEPENDENT SCHOOL DISTRICT NO. 92 OF POTTAWATOMIE COUNTY v. EARLS

Supreme Court of the United States, 2002.
536 U.S. 822, 122 S.Ct. 2559, 153 L.Ed.2d 735 [166 Educ. L. Rep. 79].

JUSTICE THOMAS delivered the opinion of the Court.

The Student Activities Drug Testing Policy implemented by the Board of Education of Independent School District No. 92 of Pottawatomie County (School District) requires all students who participate in competitive extra-curricular activities to submit to drug testing. Because this Policy reasonably serves the School District's important interest in detecting and preventing drug use among its students, we hold that it is constitutional.

I

The city of Tecumseh, Oklahoma, is a rural community located approximately 40 miles southeast of Oklahoma City. The School District administers all Tecumseh public schools. In the fall of 1998, the School District adopted the Student Activities Drug Testing Policy (Policy), which requires all middle and high school students to consent to drug testing in order to participate in any extra-curricular activity. In practice, the Policy has been applied only to competitive extra-curricular activities sanctioned by the Oklahoma Secondary Schools Activities Association, such as the Academic Team, Future Farmers of America, Future Homemakers of America, band, choir, pom-pom, cheerleading, and athletics. Under the Policy, students are required to take a drug test before participating in an extra-curricular activity, must submit to random drug testing while participating in that activity, and must agree to be tested at any time upon reasonable suspicion. The urinalysis tests are designed to detect only the use of illegal drugs, including amphetamines, marijuana, cocaine, opiates, and barbituates, not medical conditions or the presence of authorized prescription medications.

At the time of their suit, both respondents attended Tecumseh High School. Respondent Lindsay Earls was a member of the show choir, the marching band, the Academic Team, and the National Honor Society. Respondent Daniel James sought to participate in the Academic Team. Together with their parents, Earls and James brought a 42 U.S.C. § 1983 action against the School District, challenging the Policy both on its face and as applied to their participation in extra-curricular activities. They alleged that the Policy violates the Fourth Amendment as incorporated by the Fourteenth Amendment and requested injunctive and declarative relief. They also argued that the School District failed to identify a special need for testing students who participate in extra-curricular activities, and that the "Drug Testing Policy neither addresses a proven problem nor promises to bring any benefit to students or the school."

Applying the principles articulated in *Vernonia School Dist. 47J v. Acton*, in which we upheld the suspicionless drug testing of school athletes, the United States District Court for the Western District of Oklahoma rejected respondents' claim that the Policy was unconstitutional and granted summary judgment to the School District. The court noted that "special needs" exist in the public school context and that, although the School District did "not show a drug problem of epidemic proportions," there was a history of drug abuse starting in 1970 that presented "legitimate cause for concern." The District Court also held that the Policy was effective because "[i]t can scarcely be disputed that the drug problem among the student body is effectively addressed by making sure that the large number of students participating in competitive, extra-curricular activities do not use drugs."

The United States Court of Appeals for the Tenth Circuit reversed, holding that the Policy violated the Fourth Amendment. The Court of Appeals agreed with the District Court that the Policy must be evaluated in the "unique environment of the school setting," but reached a different conclusion as to the Policy's constitutionality. Before imposing a suspicionless drug testing program, the Court of Appeals concluded that a school "must demonstrate that there is some identifiable drug abuse problem among a sufficient number of those subject to the testing, such that testing that group of students will actually redress its drug problem." The Court of Appeals then held that because the School District failed to demonstrate such a problem existed among Tecumseh students participating in competitive extra-curricular activities, the Policy was unconstitutional. We granted *certiorari* and now reverse.

II

The Fourth Amendment to the United States Constitution protects "[t]he right of the people to be secure in their persons, houses, papers, and effects, against unreasonable searches and seizures." Searches by public school officials, such as the collection of urine samples, implicate Fourth Amendment interests. We must therefore review the School District's Policy for "reasonableness," which is the touchstone of the constitutionality of a governmental search.

In the criminal context, reasonableness usually requires a showing of probable cause. The probable-cause standard, however, "is peculiarly related to criminal investigations" and may be unsuited to determining the reasonableness of administrative searches where the "Government seeks to *prevent* the development of hazardous conditions." The Court has also held that a warrant and finding of probable cause are unnecessary in the public school context because such requirements " 'would unduly interfere with the maintenance of the swift and informal disciplinary procedures [that are] needed.' "

Given that the School District's Policy is not in any way related to the conduct of criminal investigations, respondents do not contend that the School District requires probable cause before testing students for drug use. Respondents instead argue that drug testing must be based at least on some level of individualized suspicion. It is true that we generally determine the reasonableness of a search by balancing the nature of the intrusion on the individual's privacy against the promotion of legitimate governmental interests. But we have long held that "the Fourth Amendment imposes no irreducible requirement of [individualized] suspicion." "[I]n certain limited circumstances, the Government's need to discover such latent or hidden conditions, or to prevent their development, is sufficiently compelling to justify the intrusion on privacy entailed by conducting such searches without any measure of individualized suspicion." Therefore, in the context of safety and administrative regulations, a search unsupported by probable cause may be reasonable "when 'special needs, beyond the normal need for law enforcement, make the warrant and probable-cause requirement impracticable.' "

Significantly, this Court has previously held that "special needs" inhere in the public school context. While schoolchildren do not shed their constitutional rights when they enter the schoolhouse, "Fourth Amendment rights ... are different in public schools than elsewhere; the 'reasonableness' inquiry cannot disregard the schools' custodial and tutelary responsibility for children." In particular, a finding of individualized suspicion may not be necessary when a school conducts drug testing.

In *Vernonia*, this Court held that the suspicionless drug testing of athletes was constitutional. The Court, however, did not simply authorize all school drug testing, but rather conducted a fact-specific balancing of the intrusion on the children's Fourth Amendment rights against the promotion of legitimate governmental interests. Applying the principles of *Vernonia* to the somewhat different facts of this case, we conclude that Tecumseh's Policy is also constitutional.

A

We first consider the nature of the privacy interest allegedly compromised by the drug testing. As in *Vernonia*, the context of the public school environment serves as the backdrop for the analysis of the privacy interest at stake and the reasonableness of the drug testing policy in general. . . .

A student's privacy interest is limited in a public school environment where the State is responsible for maintaining discipline, health, and safety. Schoolchildren are routinely required to submit to physical examinations and vaccinations against disease. Securing order in the school environment sometimes requires that students be subjected to greater controls than those appropriate for adults . . .

Respondents argue that because children participating in nonathletic extra-curricular activities are not subject to regular physicals and communal undress, they have a stronger expectation of privacy than the athletes tested in *Vernonia*. This distinction, however, was not essential to our decision in *Vernonia*, which depended primarily upon the school's custodial responsibility and authority.

In any event, students who participate in competitive extra-curricular activities voluntarily subject themselves to many of the same intrusions on their privacy as do athletes. Some of these clubs and activities require occasional off-campus travel and communal undress. All of them have their own rules and requirements for participating students that do not apply to the student body as a whole. For example, each of the competitive extra-curricular activities governed by the Policy must abide by the rules of the Oklahoma Secondary Schools Activities Association, and a faculty sponsor monitors the students for compliance with the various rules dictated by the clubs and activities. This regulation of extra-curricular activities further diminishes the expectation of privacy among schoolchildren. We therefore conclude that the students affected by this Policy have a limited expectation of privacy.

B

Next, we consider the character of the intrusion imposed by the Policy. Urination is "an excretory function traditionally shielded by great privacy." But the "degree of intrusion" on one's privacy caused by collecting a urine sample "depends upon the manner in which production of the urine sample is monitored."

Under the Policy, a faculty monitor waits outside the closed restroom stall for the student to produce a sample and must "listen for the normal sounds of urination in order to guard against tampered specimens and to insure an accurate chain of custody." The monitor then pours the sample into two bottles that are sealed and placed into a mailing pouch along with a consent form signed by the student. This procedure is virtually identical to that reviewed in *Vernonia*, except that it additionally protects privacy by allowing male students to produce their samples behind a closed stall. Given that we considered the method of collection in *Vernonia* a "negligible" intrusion, the method here is even less problematic.

In addition, the Policy clearly requires that the test results be kept in confidential files separate from a student's other educational records and released to school personnel only on a "need to know" basis. Respondents nonetheless contend that the intrusion on students' privacy is significant because the Policy fails to protect effectively against the disclosure of confidential information and, specifically, that the school "has been careless in protecting that information: for example, the Choir teacher looked at students' prescription drug lists and left them where other students could see them." But the choir teacher is someone with a "need to know," because during off-campus trips she needs to know what medications are taken by her students. Even before the Policy was enacted the choir teacher had access to this information. In any event, there is no allegation that any other student did see such information. This one example of alleged carelessness hardly increases the character of the intrusion.

Moreover, the test results are not turned over to any law enforcement authority. Nor do the test results here lead to the imposition of discipline or have any academic consequences. Rather, the only consequence of a failed drug test is to limit the student's privilege of participating in extra-curricular activities. Indeed, a student may test positive for drugs twice and still be allowed to participate in extra-curricular activities. After the first positive test, the school contacts the student's parent or guardian for a meeting. The student may continue to participate in the activity if within five days of the meeting the student shows proof of receiving drug counseling and submits to a second drug test in two weeks. For the second positive test, the student is suspended from participation in all extra-curricular activities for 14 days, must complete four hours of substance abuse counseling, and must submit to monthly drug tests. Only after a third positive test will the student be suspended from participating in any extra-curricular activity for the remainder of the school year, or 88 school days, whichever is longer.

Given the minimally intrusive nature of the sample collection and the limited uses to which the test results are put, we conclude that the invasion of students' privacy is not significant.

C

Finally, this Court must consider the nature and immediacy of the government's concerns and the efficacy of the Policy in meeting them. This Court has already articulated in detail the importance of the governmental concern in preventing drug use by schoolchildren. The drug abuse problem among our Nation's youth has hardly abated since *Vernonia* was decided in 1995. In fact, evidence suggests that it has only grown worse. As in *Vernonia,* "the necessity for the State to act is magnified by the fact that this evil is being visited not just upon individuals at large, but upon children for whom it has undertaken a special responsibility of care and direction." The health and safety risks identified in *Vernonia* apply with equal force to Tecumseh's children. Indeed, the nationwide drug epidemic makes the war against drugs a pressing concern in every school.

Additionally, the School District in this case has presented specific evidence of drug use at Tecumseh schools. Teachers testified that they had seen students who appeared to be under the influence of drugs and that they had heard students speaking openly about using drugs. A drug dog found marijuana cigarettes near the school parking lot. Police officers once found drugs or drug paraphernalia in a car driven by a Future Farmers of America member. And the school board president reported that people in the community were calling the board to discuss the "drug situation." We decline to second-guess the finding of the District Court that "[v]iewing the evidence as a whole, it cannot be reasonably disputed that the [board] was faced with a 'drug problem' when it adopted the Policy."

Respondents consider the proffered evidence insufficient and argue that there is no "real and immediate interest" to justify a policy of drug testing nonathletes. We have recognized, however, that "[a] demonstrated problem of drug abuse ... [is] not in all cases necessary to the validity of a testing regime," but that some showing does "shore up an assertion of special need for a suspicionless general search program." The School District has provided sufficient evidence to shore up the need for its drug testing program.

Furthermore, this Court has not required a particularized or pervasive drug problem before allowing the government to conduct suspicionless drug testing. For instance, in *Von Raab* the Court upheld the drug testing of customs officials on a purely preventive basis, without any documented history of drug use by such officials. In response to the lack of evidence relating to drug use, the Court noted generally that "drug abuse is one of the most serious problems confronting our society today," and that programs to prevent and detect drug use among customs officials could not be deemed unreasonable. Likewise, the need to prevent and deter the substantial harm of childhood drug use provides the necessary immediacy for a school testing policy. Indeed, it would make little sense to require a school district to wait for a substantial portion of its students to begin using drugs before it was allowed to institute a drug testing program designed to deter drug use.

Given the nationwide epidemic of drug use, and the evidence of increased drug use in Tecumseh schools, it was entirely reasonable for the School District to enact this particular drug testing policy. We reject the Court of Appeals' novel test that "any district seeking to impose a random suspicionless drug testing policy as a condition to participation in a school activity must demonstrate that there is some identifiable drug abuse problem among a sufficient number of those subject to the testing, such that testing that group of students will actually redress its drug problem." Among other problems, it would be difficult to administer such a test. As we cannot articulate a threshold level of drug use that would suffice to justify a drug testing program for schoolchildren, we refuse to fashion what would in effect be a constitutional quantum of drug use necessary to show a "drug problem."

Respondents also argue that the testing of nonathletes does not implicate any safety concerns, and that safety is a "crucial factor" in applying the special needs framework. They contend that there must be "surpassing safety interests," or "extraordinary safety and national security hazards," in order to override the usual protections of the Fourth Amendment. Respondents are correct that safety factors into the special needs analysis, but the safety interest furthered by drug testing is undoubtedly substantial for all children, athletes and nonathletes alike. We know all too well that drug use carries a variety of health risks for children, including death from overdose.

We also reject respondents' argument that drug testing must presumptively be based upon an individualized reasonable suspicion of wrongdoing because such a testing regime would be less intrusive. In this context, the Fourth Amendment does not require a finding of individualized suspicion and we decline to impose such a requirement on schools attempting to prevent and detect drug use by students. Moreover, we question whether testing based on individualized suspicion in fact would be less intrusive. Such a regime would place an additional burden on public school teachers who are already tasked with the difficult job of maintaining order and discipline. A program of individualized suspicion might unfairly target members of unpopular groups. The fear of lawsuits resulting from such targeted searches may chill enforcement of the program, rendering it ineffective in combating drug use. In any case, this Court has repeatedly stated that reasonableness under the Fourth Amendment does not require employing the least intrusive means, because "[t]he logic of such elaborate less-restrictive-alternative arguments could raise insuperable barriers to the exercise of virtually all search-and-seizure powers."

Finally, we find that testing students who participate in extracurricular activities is a reasonably effective means of addressing the School District's legitimate concerns in preventing, deterring, and detecting drug use. While in *Vernonia* there might have been a closer fit between the testing of athletes and the trial court's finding that the drug problem was "fueled by the 'role model' effect of athletes' drug use," such a finding was not essential to the holding. *Vernonia* did not require the school to test the group of students most likely to use drugs, but rather considered the constitutionality of the program in the context of the public school's custodial responsibilities. Evaluating the Policy in this context, we conclude that the drug testing of Tecumseh students who participate in extra-curricular activities effectively serves the School District's interest in protecting the safety and health of its students.

III

Within the limits of the Fourth Amendment, local school boards must assess the desirability of drug testing schoolchildren. In upholding the constitutionality of the Policy, we express no opinion as to its wisdom. Rather, we hold only that Tecumseh's Policy is a reasonable means of furthering the School District's important interest in preventing and deterring drug use among its schoolchildren. Accordingly, we reverse the judgment of the Court of Appeals.

It is so ordered.

Notes

1. As in *Acton*, the focus of the policy here was rehabilitative or therapeutic rather than punitive. If the policy focused on punishment would, or should, the Court have reached a different result?

2. In *Earls*, the Court lowered the bar with regard to the nature and immediacy of the governmental concern, making it easier for school officials to submit student-athletes to drug testing. Should educators be able to test students in other activities such as newspapers and school clubs?

3. Should students or school systems be required to pay for the not inconsiderable cost of mandatory drug testing? What if students cannot afford to pay?

[Case No. 110] Student Rights to Political Free Speech in Schools, I

TINKER v. DES MOINES INDEPENDENT COMMUNITY SCHOOL DISTRICT

Supreme Court of the United States, 1969.
393 U.S. 503, 89 S.Ct. 733, 21 L.Ed.2d 731.

MR. JUSTICE FORTAS delivered the opinion of the Court.

Petitioner John F. Tinker, 15 years old, and petitioner Christopher Eckhardt, 16 years old, attended high schools in Des Moines. Petitioner Mary Beth Tinker, John's sister, was a 13–year-old student in junior high school.

In December 1965, a group of adults and students in Des Moines, Iowa, held a meeting at the Eckhardt home. The group determined to publicize their objections to the hostilities in Vietnam and their support for a truce by wearing black armbands during the holiday season and by fasting on December 16 and New Year's Eve. Petitioners and their parents had previously engaged in similar activities, and they decided to participate in the program.

The principals of the Des Moines schools became aware of the plan to wear armbands. On December 14, 1965, they met and adopted a policy that any student wearing an armband to school would be asked to remove it, and if he refused he would be suspended until he returned without the armband. Petitioners were aware of the regulation that the school authorities adopted.

On December 16, Mary Beth and Christopher wore black armbands to their schools. John Tinker wore his armband the next day. They were all sent home and suspended from school until they would come back without their armbands. They did not return to school until after the planned period for wearing armbands had expired—that is, until after New Year's Day. . . .

First Amendment rights, applied in light of the special characteristics of the school environment, are available to teachers and students. It can hardly be argued that either students or teachers shed their constitutional rights to freedom of speech or expression at the schoolhouse gate. This has been the unmistakable holding of this Court for almost 50 years. . . .

. . . On the other hand, the Court has repeatedly emphasized the need for affirming the comprehensive authority of the States and of school officials, consistent with fundamental constitutional safeguards, to prescribe and control conduct in the schools. . . .

The problem presented by the present case does not relate to regulation of the length of skirts or the type of clothing, to hair style or deportment. It does not concern aggressive, disruptive action or even group demonstrations. Our problem involves direct, primary First Amendment rights akin to "pure speech."

The school officials banned and sought to punish petitioners for a silent, passive, expression of opinion, unaccompanied by any disorder or disturbance on the part of petitioners. There is here no evidence whatever of petitioners' interference, actual or nascent, with the school's work or of collision with the rights of other students to be secure and to be let alone. Accordingly, this case does not concern speech or action that intrudes upon the work of the school or the rights of other students.

Only a few of the 18,000 students in the school system wore the black armbands. Only five students were suspended for wearing them. There is no indication that the work of the school or any class was disrupted. Outside the classrooms, a few students made hostile remarks to the children wearing armbands, but there were no threats or acts of violence on school premises.

The District Court concluded that the action of the school authorities was reasonable because it was based upon their fear of a disturbance from the wearing of the armbands. But, in our system, undifferentiated fear or apprehension of disturbance is not enough to overcome the right to freedom of expression. Any departure from absolute regimentation may cause trouble. Any variation from the majority's opinion may inspire fear. Any word spoken, in class, in the lunchroom or on the campus, that deviates from the views of another person, may start an argument or cause a disturbance. But our Constitution says we must take this risk; and our history says that it is this sort of hazardous freedom-this kind of openness-that is the basis of our national strength and of the independence and vigor of Americans who grow up and live in this relatively permissive, often disputatious society.

In order for the State in the person of school officials to justify prohibition of a particular expression of opinion, it must be able to show that its action was caused by something more than a mere desire to avoid the discomfort and unpleasantness that always accompany an unpopular viewpoint. Certainly where there is no finding and no showing that the exercise of the forbidden right would "materially and substantially interfere with the requirements of appropriate discipline in the operation of the school," the prohibition cannot be sustained.

In the present case, the District Court made no such finding, and our independent examination of the record fails to yield evidence that the school authorities had reason to anticipate that the wearing of the armbands would substantially interfere with the work of the school or impinge upon the rights of other students. Even an official memorandum prepared after the suspension that listed the reasons for the ban on wearing the armbands made no reference to the anticipation of such disruption.

On the contrary, the action of the school authorities appears to have been based upon an urgent wish to avoid the controversy which might result from the expression, even by the silent symbol of armbands, of opposition to this Nation's part in the conflagration in Vietnam. It is revealing, in this respect, that the meeting at which the school principals decided to issue the contested regulation was called in response to a student's statement to the journalism teacher in one of the schools that he wanted to write an article on Vietnam and have it published in the school paper.

It is also relevant that the school authorities did not purport to prohibit the wearing of all symbols of political or controversial significance. The record shows that students in some of the schools wore buttons relating to national political campaigns, and some even wore the Iron Cross, traditionally a symbol of nazism. The order prohibiting the wearing of armbands did not extend to these. Instead, a particular symbol—black armbands worn to exhibit opposition to this Nation's involvement in Vietnam—was singled out for prohibition. Clearly, the prohibition of expression of one particular opinion, at least without evidence that it is necessary to avoid material and substantial interference with school work or discipline, is not constitutionally permissible. . . .

... The principal use to which the schools are dedicated is to accommodate students during prescribed hours for the purpose of certain types of activities. Among those activities is personal intercommunication among the students. This is not only an inevitable part of the process of attending school. It is also an important part of the educational process. A student's rights therefore, do not embrace merely the classroom hours. When he is in the cafeteria, or on the playing field, or on the campus during the authorized hours, he may express his opinions, even on controversial subjects like the conflict in Vietnam, if he does so "[without] materially and substantially interfering with ... appropriate discipline in the operation of the school" and without colliding with the rights of others. But conduct by the student, in class or out of it, which for any reason—whether it stems from time, place, or type of behavior—materially disrupts classwork or involves substantial disorder or invasion of the rights of others is, of course, not immunized by the constitutional guaranty of freedom of speech.

Under our Constitution, free speech is not a right that is given only to be so circumscribed that it exists in principle but not in fact. Freedom of expression would not truly exist if the right could be exercised only in an area that a benevolent government has provided as a safe haven for crackpots. The Constitution says that Congress (and the States) may not abridge the right to free speech. This provision means what it says. We properly read it to permit reasonable regulation of speech-connected activities in carefully restricted circumstances. But we do not confine the permissible exercise of First Amendment rights to a telephone booth or the four corners of a pamphlet, or to supervised and ordained discussion in a school classroom.

If a regulation were adopted by school officials forbidding discussion of the Vietnam conflict, or the expression by any student of opposition to it anywhere on school property except as part of a prescribed classroom exercise, it would be obvious that the regulation would violate the constitutional rights of students, at least if it could not be justified by a showing that the students' activities would materially and substantially disrupt the work and discipline of the school.... In the circumstances of the present case, the prohibition of the silent passive "witness of the armbands," as one of the children called it, is no less offensive to the constitution's guaranties.

As we have discussed the record does not demonstrate any facts which might reasonably have led school authorities to forecast substantial disruption of or material interference with school activities, and no disturbances or disorders on the school premises in fact occurred....

Reversed and remanded.

Notes

1. Both school officials and students cite *Tinker* almost ritualistically in student discipline cases since it establishes general guidelines applicable to many different situations.

2. The Court placed the burden of showing that student behavior might lead to a forecast of material and/or substantial disruption on school officials. To what extent should school officials be permitted to adopt preventive rules and when should they be required to wait for disruptions to occur before being able to act?

[Case No. 111] Student Rights to Political Free Speech in Schools, II

GUZICK v. DREBUS

United States Court of Appeals, Sixth Circuit, 1970.
431 F.2d 594.

O'SULLIVAN, SENIOR CIRCUIT JUDGE.

Plaintiff–Appellant, Thomas Guzick, Jr.—prosecuting this action by his father and next friend, Thomas Guzick—appeals from dismissal of his complaint in the United States District Court for the Northern District of Ohio, Eastern Division. Plaintiff's complaint sought an injunction and other relief against defendant Drebus, the principal of Shaw High School in East Cleveland, Ohio, as well as against the Superintendent and Board of Education for the schools of said city. Plaintiff also asked for declaratory relief and damages.

The complaint charged that Thomas Guzick, Jr., a seventeen year old, eleventh grade student at Shaw High School, had been denied the right of free speech guaranteed to him by the United States Constitution's First Amendment. He asserted that this right had been denied him when he was suspended for refusing to remove, while in the classrooms and the school premises, a button which solicited participation in an anti-war demonstration that was to take place in Chicago on April 5. The legend of the button was:

> "April 5 Chicago
> GI—Civilian
> Anti–War
> Demonstration
> Student Mobilization Committee"

. . .

On March 11, 1969, young Guzick and another student Havens, appeared at the office of defendant Drebus, principal of the high school, bringing with them a supply of pamphlets which advocated attendance at the same planned Chicago anti-war demonstration as was identified by the button. The boys were denied permission to distribute the pamphlets, and were also told to remove the buttons which both were then wearing. Guzick said that his lawyer, counsel for him in this litigation, told him that a United States Supreme Court decision entitled him to wear the button in school. Principal Drebus directed that he remove it and desist from wearing it in the school. Being told by Guzick that he would not obey, the principal suspended him and advised that such suspension would continue until Guzick obeyed. The other young man complied, and returned to school. Guzick did not, and has made no effort to return to school. This lawsuit promptly followed on March 17. . . .

The District Judge denied plaintiff's application for a preliminary injunction, and after a plenary evidentiary hearing, which was concluded on March 26, 1969, the complaint was dismissed. . . .

We affirm.

Plaintiff insists that the facts of this case bring it within the rule of *Tinker v. Des Moines Independent Community School District*. We are at once aware that unless *Tinker* can be distinguished, reversal is required. We consider that the facts of this case clearly provide such distinction.

The rule applied to appellant Guzick was of long standing—forbidding all wearing of buttons, badges, scarves and other means whereby the wearers identify themselves as supporters of a cause or bearing messages unrelated to their education. Such things as support the high school athletic teams or advertise a school play are not forbidden, The rule had its genesis in the days when fraternities were competing for the favor of the students and it has been uniformly enforced. The rule has continued as one of universal application and usefulness. While controversial buttons appeared from time to time, they were required to be removed as soon as the school authorities could get to them.

. . .

From the total evidence, including that of educators, school administrators and others having special relevant qualifications, the District Judge concluded that abrogation of the rule would inevitably result in collisions and disruptions which would seriously subvert Shaw High School as a place of education for its students, black and white.

1. The Rule of *Tinker*.

Contrasting with the admitted long standing and uniform enforcement of Shaw's no symbol rule, the majority opinion in *Tinker* was careful to point out,

> "It is also relevant that the school authorities [in *Tinker*] did not purport to prohibit the wearing of all symbols of political or controversial significance. . . ."

The armband demonstration in *Tinker* was a one time affair, with a date for its ending fixed in its original plan. Plaintiff here argues that Shaw's no symbol rule should be abrogated to accommodate his wish to be relieved from obeying it. . . .

Further distinguishing *Tinker* from our case are their respective settings. No potential racial collisions were background to *Tinker*, whereas here the changing racial composition of Shaw High from all white to 70% black, made the no symbol rule of even greater good than had characterized its original adoption. In our view, school authorities should not be faulted for adhering to a relatively non-oppressive rule that will indeed serve our ultimate goal of meaningful integration of our public schools. . . .

2. Shaw High School's need for its Rule.

In *Tinker* the Court concluded that a regulation forbidding expressions opposing the Vietnam conflict anywhere on school property would violate the students' constitutional rights,

> "at least *if it could not be justified* by a showing that the students' activities would materially and substantially disrupt the work and discipline of the school." (Emphasis supplied.) . . .

The District Judge was of the view that the situation at Shaw was "incendiary." The evidence justified such a view.

> "The Court has concluded that if all buttons were permitted at Shaw High, many students would seek to wear buttons conveying an inflammatory or provocative message or which would be considered as an insult or affront to certain of the other students. Such buttons have been worn at Shaw High School in the past. One button of this nature, for example, contained the message 'Happy Easter, Dr. King.' This button caused a fight last year in the school cafeteria at Shaw. Other buttons, such as 'Black Power,' 'Say it loud, Black and Proud,' and buttons depicting a black mailed fist have been worn at Shaw and would likely be worn again, if permitted. These buttons would add to the already incendiary situation and would undoubtedly provoke further fighting among the students and lead to a material and substantial disruption of the educational process at Shaw High."

Further distinction from *Tinker* is provided by the long standing and *universal application* of Shaw's rule. . . .

The District Judge here points out that for school authorities to allow some buttons and not others would create an unbearable burden of selection and enforcement. . . .

In our view, the potentiality and the imminence of the admitted rebelliousness in the Shaw students support the wisdom of the no-symbol rule. Surely those charged with providing a place and atmosphere for educating young Americans should not have to fashion their disciplinary rules only after good order has been at least once demolished.

3. Conclusion.

We will not attempt extensive review of the many great decisions which have forbidden abridgment of free speech. We have been thrilled by their beautiful and impassioned language. They are part of our American heritage. None of these masterpieces, however, were composed or uttered to support the wearing of buttons in high school classrooms. We are not persuaded that enforcement of such a rule as Shaw High School's no-symbol proscription would have excited like judicial classics. Denying Shaw High School the right to enforce this small disciplinary rule could, and most likely would, impair the rights of its students to an education and the rights of its teachers to fulfill their responsibilities. . . .

Notes

1. Can you distinguish *Guzick* from *Tinker*?

2. Could *Tinker* have been resolved differently if the board prohibited all controversial symbols rather than only black armbands? How does the concept of invalidity for being overly-broad square with *Guzick*?

[Case No. 112] Board Power to Discipline a Student for Vulgar Speech

BETHEL SCHOOL DISTRICT NO. 403 v. FRASER

Supreme Court of the United States, 1986.
478 U.S. 675, 106 S.Ct. 3159, 92 L.Ed.2d 549 [32 Educ. L Rep. 1243].

CHIEF JUSTICE BURGER delivered the opinion of the Court.

We granted certiorari to decide whether the First Amendment prevents a school district from disciplining a high school student for giving a lewd speech at a school assembly.

I

A

On April 26, 1983, respondent Matthew N. Fraser, a student at Bethel High School in Bethel, Washington, delivered a speech nominating a fellow student for student elective office. Approximately 600 high school students, many of whom were 14–year-olds, attended the assembly. Students were required to attend the assembly or to report to the study hall. The assembly was part of a school-sponsored educational program in self-government. Students who elected not to attend the assembly were required to report to study hall. During the entire speech, Fraser referred to his candidate in terms of an elaborate, graphic, and explicit sexual metaphor.

Two of Fraser's teachers, with whom he discussed the contents of his speech in advance, informed him that the speech was "inappropriate and that he probably should not deliver it" and that his delivery of the speech might have "severe consequences."

During Fraser's delivery of the speech, a school counselor observed the reaction of students to the speech. Some students hooted and yelled; some by gestures graphically simulated the sexual activities pointedly alluded to in respondent's speech. Other students appeared to be bewildered and embarrassed by the speech. One teacher reported that on the day following the speech, she found it necessary to forgo a portion of the scheduled class lesson in order to discuss the speech with the class.

A Bethel High School disciplinary rule prohibiting the use of obscene language in the school provides:

"Conduct which materially and substantially interferes with the educational process is prohibited, including the use of obscene, profane language or gestures."

The morning after the assembly, the Assistant Principal called Fraser into her office and notified him that the school considered his speech to have been a violation of this rule. Fraser was presented with copies of five letters submitted by teachers, describing his conduct at the assembly; he was given a chance to explain his conduct, and he admitted to having given the speech described and that he deliberately used sexual innuendo in the speech. Fraser was then informed that he would be suspended for three days, and that his name would be removed from the list of candidates for graduation speaker at the school's commencement exercises.

Fraser sought review of this disciplinary action through the School District's grievance procedures. The hearing officer determined that the speech given by respondent was "indecent, lewd, and offensive to the modesty and decency of many of the students and faculty in attendance at the assembly." The examiner determined that the speech fell within the ordinary meaning of "obscene," as used in the disruptive-conduct rule, and affirmed the discipline in its entirety. Fraser served two days of his suspension, and was allowed to return to school on the third day.

B

. . . Respondent alleged a violation of his First Amendment right to freedom of speech and sought both injunctive relief and monetary damages under 42 U.S.C. § 1983. . . . The District Court awarded respondent $278 in damages, $12,750 in litigation costs and attorney's fees, and enjoined the School District from preventing respondent from speaking at the commencement ceremonies. Respondent, who had been elected graduation speaker by a write-in vote of his classmates, delivered a speech at the commencement ceremonies on June 8, 1983.

The Court of Appeals for the Ninth Circuit affirmed the judgment of the District Court. . . .

. . . We reverse.

II

This Court acknowledged in *Tinker v. Des Moines Independent Community School Dist.*, that students do not "shed their constitutional rights to freedom of speech or expression at the schoolhouse gate." The Court of Appeals read that case as precluding any discipline of Fraser for indecent speech and lewd conduct in the school assembly. That court appears to have proceeded on the theory that the use of lewd and obscene speech in order to make what the speaker considered to be a point in a nominating speech for a fellow student was essentially the same as the wearing of an armband in *Tinker* as a form of protest or the expression of a political position.

The marked distinction between the political "message" of the armbands in *Tinker* and the sexual content of respondent's speech in this case seems to have been given little weight by the Court of Appeals. In upholding the students' right to engage in a nondisruptive, passive expression of a political viewpoint in *Tinker*, this Court was careful to note that the case did "not concern speech or action that intrudes upon the work of the schools or the rights of other students."

It is against this background that we turn to consider the level of First Amendment protection accorded to Fraser's utterances and actions before an official high school assembly attended by 600 students.

III

The role and purpose of the American public school system was well described by two historians, saying "public education must prepare pupils for citizenship in the Republic.... It must inculcate the habits and manners of civility as values in themselves conducive to happiness and as indispensable to the practice of self-government in the community and the nation." In *Ambach v. Norwick* we echoed the essence of this statement of the objectives of public education as the "inculcat[ion of] fundamental values necessary to the maintenance of a democratic political system."

These fundamental values of "habits and manners of civility" essential to a democratic society must, of course, include tolerance of divergent political and religious views, even when the views expressed may be unpopular. But these "fundamental values" must also take into account consideration of the sensibilities of others, and, in the case of a school, the sensibilities of fellow students. The undoubted freedom to advocate unpopular and controversial views in schools and classrooms must be balanced against the society's countervailing interest in teaching students the boundaries of socially appropriate behaviour. Even the most heated political discourse in a democratic society requires consideration for the personal sensibilities of the other participants and audiences.

In our Nation's legislative halls, where some of the most vigorous political debates in our society are carried on, there are rules prohibiting the use of expressions offensive to other participants in the debate.... Can it be that what is proscribed in the halls of Congress is beyond the reach of school officials to regulate?

The First Amendment guarantees wide freedom in matters of adult public discourse. A sharply divided Court upheld the right to express an antidraft viewpoint in a public place, albeit in terms highly offensive to most citizens. It does not follow, however, that simply because the use of an offensive form of expression may not be prohibited to adults making what the speaker considers a political point, that the same latitude must be permitted to children in a public school. In *New Jersey v. T.L.O.* we reaffirmed that the constitutional rights of students in public school are not automatically coextensive with the rights of adults in other settings....

Surely it is a highly appropriate function of public school education to prohibit the use of vulgar and offensive terms in public discourse. Indeed, the "fundamental values necessary to the maintenance of a democratic political system" disfavor the use of terms of debate highly offensive or highly threatening to others. Nothing in the Constitution prohibits the states from insisting that certain modes of expression are inappropriate and subject to sanctions. The inculcation of these values is truly the "work of the schools." The determination of what manner of speech in the classroom or in school assembly is inappropriate properly rests with the school board.

The process of educating our youth for citizenship in public schools is not confined to books, the curriculum, and the civics class; schools must teach by example the shared values of a civilized social order. Consciously or otherwise, teachers—and indeed the older students— demonstrate the appropriate form of civil discourse and political expression by their conduct and deportment in and out of class. Inescapably, like parents, they are role models. The schools, as instruments of the state, may determine that the essential lessons of civil, mature conduct cannot be conveyed in a school that tolerates lewd, indecent, or offensive speech and conduct such as that indulged in by this confused boy.

The pervasive sexual innuendo in Fraser's speech was plainly offensive to both teachers and students—indeed to any mature person. By glorifying male sexuality, and in its verbal content, the speech was acutely insulting to teenage girl students. The speech could well be seriously damaging to its less mature audience, many of whom were only 14 years old and on the threshold of awareness of human sexuality. Some students were reported as bewildered by the speech and the reaction of mimicry it provoked.

This Court's First Amendment jurisprudence has acknowledged limitations on the otherwise absolute interest of the speaker in reaching an unlimited audience where the speech is sexually explicit and the audience may include children. In *Ginsberg v. New York*, this Court upheld a New York statute banning the sale of sexually oriented material to minors, even though the material in question was entitled to First Amendment protection with respect to adults. And in addressing the question whether the First Amendment places any limit on the authority of public schools to remove books from a public school library, all Members of the Court, otherwise sharply divided, acknowledged that the school board has the authority to remove books that are vulgar. These cases recognize the obvious concern on the part of parents, and school authorities acting in loco parentis to protect children-especially in a captive audience-from exposure to sexually explicit, indecent, or lewd speech.

We have also recognized an interest in protecting minors from exposure to vulgar and offensive spoken language. . . .

We hold that petitioner School District acted entirely within its permissible authority in imposing sanctions upon Fraser in response to his offensively lewd and indecent speech. Unlike the sanctions imposed on the students wearing armbands in *Tinker,* the penalties imposed in this case were unrelated to any political viewpoint. The First Amendment does not prevent the school officials from determining that to permit a vulgar and lewd speech such as respondent's would undermine the school's basic educational mission. A high school assembly or classroom is no place for a sexually explicit monologue directed towards an unsuspecting audience of teenage students. Accordingly, it was perfectly appropriate for the school to disassociate itself to make the point to the pupils that vulgar speech and lewd conduct is wholly inconsistent with the "fundamental values" of public school education. . . .

IV

Respondent contends that the circumstances of his suspension violated due process because he had no way of knowing that the delivery of the speech in question would subject him to disciplinary sanctions. This argument is wholly without merit. We have recognized that "maintaining security and order in the schools requires a certain degree of flexibility in school disciplinary procedures, and we have respected the value of preserving the informality of the student-teacher relationship." Given the school's need to be able to impose disciplinary sanctions for a wide range of unanticipated conduct disruptive of the educational process, the school disciplinary rules need not be as detailed as a criminal code which imposes criminal sanctions. Two days' suspension from school does not rise to the level of a penal sanction calling for the full panoply of procedural due process protections applicable to a criminal prosecution. The school disciplinary rule proscribing "obscene" language and the prespeech admonitions of teachers gave adequate warning to Fraser that his lewd speech could subject him to sanctions.

The judgment of the Court of Appeals for the Ninth Circuit is

Reversed.

Notes

1. Justice Brennan concurred in the judgment, but wrote ". . . separately to express my understanding of the breadth of the Court's holding," *Bethel School Dist. No. 403 v. Fraser*, 478 U.S. 675, 688, 106 S.Ct. 3159, 92 L.Ed.2d 549, 32 Educ. L Rep. 1243 (1986), which he placed in the framework of some prior Supreme Court opinions. His concurrence repeated parts of the speech:

> Respondent gave the following speech at a high school assembly in support of a candidate for student government office:
>
>> I know a man who is firm-he's firm in his pants, he's firm in his shirt, his character is firm-but most . . . of all, his belief in you, the students of Bethel, is firm. Jeff Kuhlman is a man who takes his point and pounds it in. If necessary, he'll take an issue and nail it to the wall. He doesn't attack things in spurts-he drives hard, pushing and pushing until finally-he succeeds. Jeff is a man who will go to the very end—even the climax, for each and every one of you. So vote for Jeff for A.S.B. vice-president—he'll never come between you and the best our high school can be. *Id.* at 687.

In light of the contents of the speech, do you think that the punishment was appropriate?

2. The Court never defined vulgar or lewd, relying on a kind of "I know it when I see it approach," consistent with Justice Stewart's concurrence in *Jacobellis v. State of Ohio*, 378 U.S. 184, 197, 84 S.Ct. 1676, 12 L.Ed.2d 793 (1964) in a case dealing with ". . . hard-core-pornography. I shall not today attempt further to define the kinds of material I understand to be embraced

within that shorthand description; and perhaps I could never succeed in intelligibly doing so. But I know it when I see it, and the motion picture involved in this case is not that."

3. Should the student have been subjected to the same punishment if he had not mentioned the contents of his speech to teachers? Should a student be punished for delivering such a speech at a school-sponsored "Comedy Club" on a Saturday night that members of the audience had to purchase tickets to attend?

[Case No. 113] Power of School Officials to Regulate the Content of a Newspaper Produced by Journalism Class

HAZELWOOD SCHOOL DISTRICT v. KUHLMEIER

Supreme Court of the United States, 1988.
484 U.S. 260, 108 S.Ct. 562, 98 L.Ed.2d 592 [43 Educ. L. Rep. 515].

JUSTICE WHITE delivered the opinion of the Court.

This case concerns the extent to which educators may exercise editorial control over the contents of a high school newspaper produced as part of the school's journalism curriculum.

I

Petitioners are the Hazelwood School District in St. Louis County, Missouri; various school officials; Robert Eugene Reynolds, the principal of Hazelwood East High School, and Howard Emerson, a teacher in the school district. Respondents are three former Hazelwood East students who were staff members of Spectrum, the school newspaper. They contend that school officials violated their First Amendment rights by deleting two pages of articles from the May 13, 1983, issue of Spectrum.

Spectrum was written and edited by the Journalism II class at Hazelwood East. The newspaper was published every three weeks or so during the 1982–1983 school year. More than 4,500 copies of the newspaper were distributed during that year to students, school personnel, and members of the community.

The Board of Education allocated funds from its annual budget for the printing of Spectrum. These funds were supplemented by proceeds from sales of the newspaper. The printing expenses during the 1982–1983 school year totaled $4,668.50; revenue from sales was $1,166.84. The other costs associated with the newspaper—such as supplies, textbooks, and a portion of the journalism teacher's salary—were borne entirely by the Board.

The Journalism II course was taught by Robert Stergos for most of the 1982–1983 academic year. Stergos left Hazelwood East to take a job in private industry on April 29, 1983, when the May 13 edition of Spectrum was nearing completion, and petitioner Emerson took his place as newspaper adviser for the remaining weeks of the term.

The practice at Hazelwood East during the spring 1983 semester was for the journalism teacher to submit page proofs of each Spectrum issue to Principal Reynolds for his review prior to publication. On May 10, Emerson delivered the proofs of the May 13 edition to Reynolds, who objected to two of the articles scheduled to appear in that edition. One of the stories described three Hazelwood East students' experiences with pregnancy; the other discussed the impact of divorce on students at the school.

Reynolds was concerned that, although the pregnancy story used false names "to keep the identity of these girls a secret," the pregnant students still might be identifiable from the text. He also believed that the article's references to sexual activity and birth control were inappropriate for some of the younger students at the school. In addition, Reynolds was concerned that a student identified by name in the divorce story had complained that her father "wasn't spending enough time with my mom, my sister and I" prior to the divorce, "was always out of town on business or out late playing cards with the guys," and "always argued about everything" with her mother. Reynolds believed that the student's parents should have been given an opportunity to respond to these remarks or to consent to their publication. He was unaware that Emerson had deleted the student's name from the final version of the article.

Reynolds believed that there was no time to make the necessary changes in the stories before the scheduled press run and that the newspaper would not appear before the end of the school year if printing were delayed to any significant extent. He concluded that his only options under the circumstances were to publish a four-page newspaper instead of the planned six-page newspaper, eliminating the two pages on which the offending stories appeared, or to publish no newspaper at all. Accordingly, he directed Emerson to withhold from publication the two pages containing the stories on pregnancy and divorce. He informed his superiors of the decision, and they concurred.

Respondents subsequently commenced this action....

II

Students in the public schools do not "shed their constitutional rights to freedom of speech or expression at the schoolhouse gate." They cannot be punished merely for expressing their personal views on the school premises—whether "in the cafeteria, or on the playing field, or on the campus during the authorized hours"—unless school authorities have reason to believe that such expression will "substantially interfere with the work of the school or impinge upon the rights of other students."

We have nonetheless recognized that the First Amendment rights of students in the public schools "are not automatically coextensive with the rights of adults in other settings," and must be "applied in light of the special characteristics of the school environment." A school need not tolerate student speech that is inconsistent with its "basic educational mission," even though the government could not censor similar speech outside the school. Accordingly, we held in *Bethel School District No. 403 v. Fraser* that a student could be disciplined for having delivered a speech that was "sexually explicit" but not legally obscene at an official school assembly, because the school was entitled to "disassociate itself" from the speech in a manner that would demonstrate to others that such vulgarity is "wholly inconsistent with the 'fundamental values' of public school education." We thus recognized that "[t]he determination of what manner of speech in the classroom or in school assembly is inappropriate properly rests with the school board," rather than with the federal courts. It is in this context that respondents' First Amendment claims must be considered.

A

We deal first with the question whether Spectrum may appropriately be characterized as a forum for public expression. The public schools do not possess all of the attributes of streets, parks, and other traditional public forums that "time out of mind, have been used for purposes of assembly, communicating thoughts between citizens, and discussing public questions." Hence, school facilities may be deemed to be public forums only if school authorities have "by policy or by practice" opened those facilities "for indiscriminate use by the general public," or by some segment of the public, such as student organizations. If the facilities have instead been reserved for other intended purposes, "communicative or otherwise," then no public forum has been created, and school officials may impose reasonable restrictions on the speech of students, teachers, and other members of the school community. "The government does not create a public forum by inaction or by permitting limited discourse, but only by intentionally opening a nontraditional forum for public discourse."

The policy of school officials toward Spectrum was reflected in Hazelwood School Board Policy 348.51 and the Hazelwood East Curriculum Guide. Board Policy 348.51 provided that "[s]chool sponsored publications are developed within the adopted curriculum and its educational implications in regular classroom activities." The Hazelwood East Curriculum Guide described the Journalism II course as a "laboratory situation in which the students publish the school newspaper applying skills they have learned in Journalism I." The lessons that were to be learned from the Journalism II course, according to the Curriculum Guide, included development of journalistic skills under deadline pressure, "the legal, moral, and ethical restrictions imposed upon journalists within the school community," and "responsibility and acceptance of criticism for articles of opinion." Journalism II was taught by a faculty member during regular class hours. Students received grades and academic credit for their performance in the course.

School officials did not deviate in practice from their policy that production of Spectrum was to be part of the educational curriculum and a "regular classroom activit[y]." The District Court found that Robert Stergos, the journalism teacher during most of the 1982–1983 school year, "both had the authority to exercise and in fact exercised a great deal of control over Spectrum." For example, Stergos selected the editors of the newspaper, scheduled publication dates, decided the number of pages for each issue, assigned story ideas to class members, advised students on the development of their stories, reviewed the use of quotations, edited stories, selected and edited the letters to the editor, and dealt with the printing company. Many of these decisions were made without consultation with the Journalism II students. The District Court thus found it "clear that Mr. Stergos was the final authority with respect to almost every aspect of the production and publication of Spectrum, including its content." Moreover, after each Spectrum issue had been finally approved by Stergos or his successor, the issue still had to be reviewed by Principal Reynolds prior to publication. Respondents' assertion that they had believed that they could publish "practically anything" in Spectrum was therefore dismissed by the District Court as simply "not credible." These factual findings are amply supported by the record, and were not rejected as clearly erroneous by the Court of Appeals.

. . . School officials did not evince either "by policy or by practice" any intent to open the pages of Spectrum to "indiscriminate use" by its student reporters and editors, or by the student body generally. Instead, they "reserve[d] the forum for its intended purpos[e]" as a supervised learning experience for journalism students. Accordingly, school officials were entitled to regulate the contents of Spectrum in any reasonable manner. It is this standard, rather than our decision in *Tinker v. Des Moines Independent Community School Dist.,* that governs this case.

B

The question whether the First Amendment requires a school to tolerate particular student speech—the question that we addressed in *Tinker*—is different from the question whether the First Amendment requires a school affirmatively to promote particular student speech. The former question addresses educators' ability to silence a student's personal expression that happens to occur on the school premises. The latter question concerns educators' authority over school-sponsored publications, theatrical productions, and other expressive activities that students, parents, and members of the public might reasonably perceive to bear the imprimatur of the school. These activities may fairly be characterized as part of the school curriculum, whether or not they occur in a traditional classroom setting, so long as they are supervised by faculty members and designed to impart particular knowledge or skills to student participants and audiences.

Educators are entitled to exercise greater control over this second form of student expression to assure that participants learn whatever lessons the activity is designed to teach, that readers or listeners are not exposed to material that may be inappropriate for their level of maturity, and that the views of the individual speaker are not erroneously attributed to the school. Hence, a school may in its capacity as publisher of a school newspaper or producer of a school play "disassociate itself" not only from speech that would "substantially interfere with [its] work . . . or impinge upon the rights of other students," but also from speech that is, for example, ungrammatical, poorly written, inadequately researched, biased or prejudiced, vulgar or profane, or unsuitable for immature audiences. A school must be able to set high standards for the student speech that is disseminated under its auspices—standards that may be higher than those demanded by some newspaper publishers or theatrical producers in the "real" world—and may refuse to disseminate student speech that does not meet those standards. In addition, a school must be able to take into account the emotional maturity of the intended audience in determining whether to disseminate student speech on potentially sensitive topics, which might range from the existence of Santa Clause in an elementary school setting to the particulars of teenage sexual activity in a high school setting. A school must also retain the authority to refuse to sponsor student speech that might reasonably be perceived to advocate drug or alcohol use, irresponsible sex, or conduct otherwise inconsistent with "the shared values of a civilized social order," or to associate the school with any position other than neutrality on matters of political controversy. Otherwise, the schools would be unduly constrained from fulfilling their role as "a principal instrument in awakening the child to cultural values, in preparing him for later professional training, and in helping him to adjust normally to his environment."

Accordingly, we conclude that the standard articulated in *Tinker* for determining when a school may punish student expression need not also be the standard for determining when a school may refuse to lend its name and resources to the dissemination of student expression. Instead, we hold that educators do not offend the First Amendment by exercising editorial control over the style and content of student speech in school-sponsored expressive activities so long as their actions are reasonably related to legitimate pedagogical concerns.

This standard is consistent with our oft-expressed view that the education of the Nation's youth is primarily the responsibility of parents, teachers, and state and local school officials, and not of federal judges. It is only when the decision to censor a school-sponsored publication, theatrical production, or other vehicle of student expression has no valid educational purpose that the First Amendment is so "directly and sharply implicate[d]" as to require judicial intervention to protect students' constitutional rights.

III

We also conclude that Principal Reynolds acted reasonably in requiring the deletion from the May 13 issue of Spectrum of the pregnancy article, the divorce article, and the remaining articles that were to appear on the same pages of the newspaper.

The initial paragraph of the pregnancy article declared that "[a]ll names have been changed to keep the identity of these girls a secret." The principal concluded that the students' anonymity was not adequately protected, however, given the other identifying information in the article and the small number of pregnant students at the school. Indeed, a teacher at the school credibly testified that she could positively identify at least one of the girls and possibly all three. It is likely that many students at Hazelwood East would have been at least as successful in identifying the girls. Reynolds therefore could reasonably have feared that the article violated whatever pledge of anonymity had been given to the pregnant students. In addition, he could reasonably have been concerned that the article was not sufficiently sensitive to the privacy interests of the students' boyfriends and parents, who were discussed in the article but who were given no opportunity to consent to its publication or to offer a response. The article did not contain graphic accounts of sexual activity. The girls did comment in the article, however, concerning their sexual histories and their use or nonuse of birth control. It was not unreasonable for the principal to have concluded that such frank talk was inappropriate in a school-sponsored publication distributed to 14–year-old freshmen and presumably taken home to be read by students' even younger brothers and sisters.

The student who was quoted by name in the version of the divorce article seen by Principal Reynolds made comments sharply critical of her father. The principal could reasonably have concluded that an individual publicly identified as an inattentive parent—indeed, as one who chose "playing cards with the guys" over home and family—was entitled to an opportunity to defend himself as a matter of journalistic fairness. These concerns were shared by both of Spectrum's faculty advisers for the 1982–1983 school year, who testified that they would not have allowed the article to be printed without deletion of the student's name.

Principal Reynolds testified credibly at trial that, at the time that he reviewed the proofs of the May 13 issue during an extended telephone conversation with Emerson, he believed that there was no time to make any changes in the articles, and that the newspaper had to be printed immediately or not at all. It is true that Reynolds did not verify whether the necessary modifications could still have been made in the articles, and that Emerson did not volunteer the information that printing could be delayed until the changes were made. We nonetheless agree with the District Court that the decision to excise the two pages containing the problematic articles was reasonable given the particular circumstances of this case. These circumstances included the very recent replacement of Stergos by Emerson, who may not have been entirely familiar with Spectrum editorial and production procedures, and the pressure felt by Reynolds to make an immediate decision so that students would not be deprived of the newspaper altogether.

In sum, we cannot reject as unreasonable Principal Reynolds' conclusion that neither the pregnancy article nor the divorce article was suitable for publication in Spectrum. Reynolds could reasonably have concluded that the students who had written and edited these articles had not sufficiently mastered those portions of the Journalism II curriculum that pertained to the treatment of controversial issues and personal attacks, the need to protect the privacy of individuals whose most intimate concerns are to be revealed in the newspaper, and "the legal, moral, and ethical restrictions imposed upon journalists within [a] school community" that includes adolescent subjects and readers. Finally, we conclude that the principal's decision to delete two pages of Spectrum, rather than to delete only the offending articles or to require that they be modified, was reasonable under the circumstances as he understood them. Accordingly, no violation of First Amendment rights occurred....

Notes

1. The Court suggested that it is unnecessary to have specific written regulations covering prepublication controls over school-sponsored publications because doing so could have unduly constrained the ability of teachers to educate. Is this reasonable? Should boards adopt such policies?

2. From an educational viewpoint, were both issues equally as problematic? Would, or should, the result be the same today?

3. In an interesting, albeit non-publication case, a federal trial court in Missouri ruled that a superintendent could prevent a school marching band from playing the song "White Rabbit" because it was used to promote illegal drug use. *McCann v. Fort Zumwalt School Dist.*, 50 F.Supp.2d 918 [136 Educ. L. Rep. 390] (E.D.Mo.1999).

[Case No. 114] Board Liability for Sexual Harassment by School Staff

FRANKLIN v. GWINNETT COUNTY PUBLIC SCHOOLS

Supreme Court of the United States, 1992.
503 U.S. 60, 112 S.Ct. 1028, 117 L.Ed.2d 208 [72 Educ. L. Rep. 32].

Justice White delivered the opinion of the Court.

This case presents the question whether the implied right of action under Title IX of the Education Amendments of 1972, (Title IX), which this Court recognized in *Cannon v. University of Chicago*, supports a claim for monetary damages.

I

Petitioner Christine Franklin was a student at North Gwinnett High School in Gwinnett County, Georgia, between September 1985 and August 1989. Respondent Gwinnett County School District operates the high school and receives federal funds. According to the complaint ... Franklin was subjected to continual sexual harassment beginning in the autumn of her tenth grade year (1986) from Andrew Hill, a sports coach and teacher employed by the district. Among other allegations, Franklin avers that Hill engaged her in sexually oriented conversations in which he asked about her sexual experiences with her boyfriend and whether she would consider having sexual intercourse with an older man, that Hill forcibly kissed her on the mouth in the school parking lot; that he telephoned her at her home and asked if she would meet him socially; and that, on three occasions in her junior year, Hill interrupted a class, requested that the teacher excuse Franklin, and took her to a private office where he subjected her to coercive intercourse. The complaint further alleges that though they became aware of and investigated Hill's sexual harassment of Franklin and other female students, teachers and administrators took no action to halt it and discouraged Franklin from pressing charges against Hill. On April 14, 1988, Hill resigned on the condition that all matters pending against him be dropped. The school thereupon closed its investigation.

In this action, the District Court dismissed the complaint on the ground that Title IX does not authorize an award of damages. The Court of Appeals affirmed....

Because this opinion conflicts with a decision of the Court of Appeals for the Third Circuit, we granted certiorari. We reverse.

II

In *Cannon v. University of Chicago*, the Court held that Title IX is enforceable through an implied right of action. We have no occasion here to reconsider that decision. Rather, in this case we must decide what remedies are available in a suit brought pursuant to this implied right. As we have often stated, the question of what remedies are available under a statute that provides a private right of action is "analytically distinct" from the issue of whether such a right exists in the first place. Thus, although we examine the text and history of a statute to determine whether Congress intended to create a right of action, we presume the availability of all appropriate remedies unless Congress has expressly indicated otherwise. This principle has deep roots in our jurisprudence.

A

"[W]here legal rights have been invaded, and a federal statute provides for a general right to sue for such invasion, federal courts may use any available remedy to make good the wrong done." *Bell v. Hood.* The Court explained this longstanding rule as jurisdictional and upheld the exercise of the federal courts' power to award appropriate relief so long as a cause of action existed under the Constitution or laws of the United States.

The *Bell* Court's reliance on this rule was hardly revolutionary. From the earliest years of the Republic, the Court has recognized the power of the Judiciary to award appropriate remedies to redress injuries actionable in federal court, although it did not always distinguish clearly between a right to bring suit and a remedy available under such a right. In *Marbury v. Madison,* for example, Chief Justice Marshall observed that our Government "has been emphatically termed a government of laws, and not of men. It will certainly cease to deserve this high appellation, if the laws furnish no remedy for the violation of a vested legal right."....

B

Respondents and the United States as *amicus curiae,* however, maintain that whatever the traditional presumption may have been when the Court decided *Bell v. Hood,* it has disappeared in succeeding decades. We do not agree.... That a statute does not authorize the remedy at issue "in so many words is no more significant than the fact that it does not in terms authorize execution to issue on a judgment."....

The United States contends that the traditional presumption in favor of all appropriate relief was abandoned by the Court in *Davis v. Passman,* and that the *Bell v. Hood* rule was limited to actions claiming constitutional violations. The United States quotes language in *Davis* to the effect that "the question of who may enforce a *statutory* right is fundamentally different from the question of who may enforce a right that is protected by the Constitution." The Government's position, however, mirrors the very misunderstanding over the difference between a cause of action and the relief afforded under it that sparked the confusion we attempted to clarify in *Davis*. Whether Congress may limit the class of persons who have a right of action under Title IX is irrelevant to the issue in this lawsuit. To reiterate, "the question whether a litigant has a 'cause of action' is analytically distinct and prior to the question of what relief, if any, a litigant may be entitled to receive." *Davis*, therefore, did nothing to interrupt the long line of cases in which the Court has held that if a right of action exists to enforce a federal right and Congress is silent on the question of remedies, a federal court may order any appropriate relief.

Contrary to arguments by respondents and the United States that *Guardians Ass'n v. Civil Service Comm'n of New York City,* and *Consolidated Rail Corporation v. Darrone,* eroded this traditional presumption, those cases in fact support it. . . . The general rule, therefore, is that absent clear direction to the contrary by Congress, the federal courts have the power to award any appropriate relief in a cognizable cause of action brought pursuant to a federal statute.

III

We now address whether Congress intended to limit application of this general principle in the enforcement of Title IX. Because the cause of action was inferred by the Court in *Cannon,* the usual recourse to statutory text and legislative history in the period prior to that decision necessarily will not enlighten our analysis. Respondents and the United States fundamentally misunderstand the nature of the inquiry, therefore, by needlessly dedicating large portions of their briefs to discussions of how the text and legislative intent behind Title IX are "silent" on the issue of available remedies. Since the Court in *Cannon* concluded that this statute supported no express right of action, it is hardly surprising that Congress also said nothing about the applicable remedies for an implied right of action.

During the period prior to the decision in *Cannon,* the inquiry in any event is *not* " 'basically a matter of statutory construction,' " as the United States asserts. Rather, in determining Congress' intent to limit application of the traditional presumption in favor of all appropriate relief, we evaluate the state of the law when the Legislature passed Title IX. In the years before and after Congress enacted this statute, the Court "follow[ed] a common-law tradition [and] regarded the denial of a remedy as the exception rather than the rule." As we outlined in Part II, this has been the prevailing presumption in our federal courts since at least the early 19th century. In *Cannon,* the majority upheld an implied right of action in part because in the decade immediately preceding enactment of Title IX in 1972, this Court had found implied rights of action in six cases. In three of those cases, the Court had approved a damages remedy. Wholly apart from the wisdom of the *Cannon* holding, therefore, the same contextual approach used to justify an implied right of action more than amply demonstrates the lack of any legislative intent to abandon the traditional presumption in favor of all available remedies.

In the years after the announcement of *Cannon,* on the other hand, a more traditional method of statutory analysis is possible, because Congress was legislating with full cognizance of that decision. Our reading of the two amendments to Title IX enacted after *Cannon* leads us to conclude that Congress did not intend to limit the remedies available in a suit brought under Title IX. In the Rehabilitation Act Amendments of 1986, Congress abrogated the States' Eleventh Amendment immunity under Title IX, Title VI, § 504 of the Rehabilitation Act of 1973, and the Age Discrimination Act of 1975. This statute cannot be read except as a validation of *Cannon*'s holding. A subsection of the 1986 law provides that in a suit against a State, "remedies (including remedies both at law and in equity) are available for such a violation to the same extent as such remedies are available for such a violation in the suit against any public or private entity other than a State." While it is true that this saving clause says nothing about the nature of those other available remedies, absent any contrary indication in the text or history of the statute, we presume Congress enacted this statute with the prevailing traditional rule in mind.

In addition to the Rehabilitation Act Amendments of 1986, Congress also enacted the Civil Rights Restoration Act of 1987. Without in any way altering the existing rights of action and the corresponding remedies permissible under Title IX, Title VI, § 504 of the Rehabilitation Act, and the Age Discrimination Act, Congress broadened the coverage of these antidiscrimination provisions in this legislation.... We cannot say, therefore, that Congress has limited the remedies available to a complainant in a suit brought under Title IX.

IV

Respondents and the United States nevertheless suggest three reasons why we should not apply the traditional presumption in favor of appropriate relief in this case.

A

First, respondents argue that an award of damages violates separation of powers principles because it unduly expands the federal courts' power into a sphere properly reserved to the Executive and Legislative Branches. In making this argument, respondents misconceive the difference between a cause of action and a remedy. Unlike the finding of a cause of action, which authorizes a court to hear a case or controversy, the discretion to award appropriate relief involves no such increase in judicial power. Federal courts cannot reach out to award remedies when the Constitution or laws of the United States do not support a cause of action. Indeed, properly understood, respondents' position invites us to *abdicate* our historic judicial authority to award appropriate relief in cases brought in our court system. It is well to recall that such authority historically has been thought necessary to provide an important safe-guard against abuses of legislative and executive power, as well as to ensure an independent Judiciary. Moreover, selective abdication of the sort advocated here would harm separation of powers principles in another way, by giving judges the power to render inutile causes of action authorized by Congress through a decision that *no* remedy is available.

B

Next, consistent with the Court of Appeals' reasoning, respondents and the United States contend that the normal presumption in favor of all appropriate remedies should not apply because Title IX was enacted pursuant to Congress' Spending Clause power. In *Pennhurst State School and Hospital v. Halderman,* the Court observed that remedies were limited under such Spending Clause statutes when the alleged violation was *unintentional.* Respondents and the United States maintain that this presumption should apply equally to *intentional* violations. We disagree. The point of not permitting monetary damages for an unintentional violation is that the receiving entity of federal funds lacks notice that it will be liable for a monetary award. This notice problem does not arise in a case such as this, in which intentional discrimination is alleged. Unquestionably, Title IX placed on the Gwinnett County Public Schools the duty not to discriminate on the basis of sex, and "when a supervisor sexually harasses a subordinate because of the subordinate's sex, that supervisor 'discriminate[s]' on the basis of sex." We believe the same rule should apply when a teacher sexually harasses and abuses a student. Congress surely did not intend for federal moneys to be expended to support the intentional actions it sought by statute to proscribe. . . .

C

Finally, the United States asserts that the remedies permissible under Title IX should nevertheless be limited to backpay and prospective relief. In addition to diverging from our traditional approach to deciding what remedies are available for violation of a federal right, this position conflicts with sound logic. First, both remedies are equitable in nature, and it is axiomatic that a court should determine the adequacy of a remedy in law before resorting to equitable relief. Under the ordinary convention, the proper inquiry would be whether monetary damages provided an adequate remedy, and if not, whether equitable relief would be appropriate. Moreover, in this case the equitable remedies suggested by respondent and the Federal Government are clearly inadequate. Backpay does nothing for petitioner, because she was a student when the alleged discrimination occurred. Similarly, because Hill—the person she claims subjected her to sexual harassment—no longer teaches at the school and she herself no longer attends a school in the Gwinnett system, prospective relief accords her no remedy at all. The Government's answer that administrative action helps other similarly situated students in effect acknowledges that its approach would leave petitioner remediless.

V

In sum, we conclude that a damages remedy is available for an action brought to enforce Title IX. The judgment of the Court of Appeals, therefore, is reversed, and the case is remanded for further proceedings consistent with this opinion.

So ordered.

Notes

1. There were no dissents in *Franklin*. Even so, Justice Scalia's concurrence was joined by Chief Justice Rehnquist and Justice Thomas.

2. School officials have universally adopted policies against sexual harassment. What specific provisions should policies contain?

[Case No. 115] Board Non–Liability for Sexual Harassment by School Staff

GEBSER v. LAGO VISTA INDEPENDENT SCHOOL DISTRICT

Supreme Court of the United States, 1998.
524 U.S. 274, 118 S.Ct. 1989, 141 L.Ed.2d 277 [125 Educ. L. Rep. 1055].

JUSTICE O'CONNOR delivered the opinion of the Court.

The question in this case is when a school district may be held liable in damages in an implied right of action under Title IX of the Education Amendments of 1972 (Title IX), for the sexual harassment of a student by one of the district's teachers. We conclude that damages may not be recovered in those circumstances unless an official of the school district who at a minimum has authority to institute corrective measures on the district's behalf has actual notice of, and is deliberately indifferent to, the teacher's misconduct.

I

In the spring of 1991, when petitioner Alida Star Gebser was an eighth-grade student at a middle school in respondent Lago Vista Independent School District (Lago Vista), she joined a high school book discussion group led by Frank Waldrop, a teacher at Lago Vista's high school. Lago Vista received federal funds at all pertinent times. During the book discussion sessions, Waldrop often made sexually suggestive comments to the students. Gebser entered high school in the fall and was assigned to classes taught by Waldrop in both semesters. Waldrop continued to make inappropriate remarks to the students, and he began to direct more of his suggestive comments toward Gebser, including during the substantial amount of time that the two were alone in his classroom. He initiated sexual contact with Gebser in the spring, when, while visiting her home ostensibly to give her a book, he kissed and fondled her. The two had sexual intercourse on a number of occasions during the remainder of the school year. Their relationship continued through the summer and into the following school year, and they often had intercourse during class time, although never on school property.

Gebser did not report the relationship to school officials, testifying that while she realized Waldrop's conduct was improper, she was uncertain how to react and she wanted to continue having him as a teacher. In October 1992, the parents of two other students complained to the high school principal about Waldrop's comments in class. The principal arranged a meeting, at which, according to the principal, Waldrop indicated that he did not believe he had made offensive remarks but apologized to the parents and said it would not happen again. The principal also advised Waldrop to be careful about his classroom comments and told the school guidance counselor about the meeting, but he did not report the parents' complaint to Lago Vista's superintendent, who was the district's Title IX coordinator. A couple of months later, in January 1993, a police officer discovered Waldrop and Gebser engaging in sexual intercourse and arrested Waldrop. Lago Vista terminated his employment, and subsequently, the Texas Education Agency revoked his teaching license. During this time, the district had not promulgated or distributed an official grievance procedure for lodging sexual harassment complaints; nor had it issued a formal anti-harassment policy.

Gebser and her mother filed suit against Lago Vista and Waldrop in state court in November 1993, raising claims against the school district under Title IX, 42 U.S.C. § 1983, and state negligence law, and claims against Waldrop primarily under state law. They sought compensatory and punitive damages from both defendants. After the case was removed, the United States District Court for the Western District of Texas granted summary judgment in favor of Lago Vista on all claims, and remanded the allegations against Waldrop to state court.

. . .

Petitioners appealed only on the Title IX claim. The Court of Appeals for the Fifth Circuit affirmed....

... We granted certiorari to address the issue and we now affirm.

II

Title IX provides in pertinent part: "No person . . . shall, on the basis of sex, be excluded from participation in, be denied the benefits of, or be subjected to discrimination under any education program or activity receiving Federal financial assistance." The express statutory means of enforcement is administrative: The statute directs federal agencies that distribute education funding to establish requirements to effectuate the nondiscrimination mandate, and permits the agencies to enforce those requirements through "any . . . means authorized by law," including ultimately the termination of federal funding. The Court held in *Cannon v. University of Chicago* that Title IX is also enforceable through an implied private right of action, a conclusion we do not revisit here. We subsequently established in *Franklin v. Gwinnett County Public Schools* that monetary damages are available in the implied private action.

In *Franklin*, a high school student alleged that a teacher had sexually abused her on repeated occasions and that teachers and school administrators knew about the harassment but took no action, even to the point of dissuading her from initiating charges. The lower courts dismissed Franklin's complaint against the school district on the ground that the implied right of action under Title IX, as a categorical matter, does not encompass recovery in damages. We reversed the lower courts' blanket rule, concluding that Title IX supports a private action for damages, at least "in a case such as this, in which intentional discrimination is alleged." *Franklin* thereby establishes that a school district can be held liable in damages in cases involving a teacher's sexual harassment of a student; the decision, however, does not purport to define the contours of that liability.

We face that issue squarely in this case. Petitioners, joined by the United States as amicus curiae, would invoke standards used by the Courts of Appeals in Title VII cases involving a supervisor's sexual harassment of an employee in the workplace. In support of that approach, they point to a passage in *Franklin* in which we stated: "Unquestionably, Title IX placed on the Gwinnett County Public Schools the duty not to discriminate on the basis of sex, and 'when a supervisor sexually harasses a subordinate because of the subordinate's sex, that supervisor "discriminate[s]" on the basis of sex.' We believe the same rule should apply when a teacher sexually harasses and abuses a student.'" *Meritor Savings Bank, FSB v. Vinson* directs courts to look to common law agency principles when assessing an employer's liability under Title VII for sexual harassment of an employee by a supervisor. Petitioners and the United States submit that, in light of *Franklin's* comparison of teacher-student harassment with supervisor-employee harassment, agency principles should likewise apply in Title IX actions.

Specifically, they advance two possible standards under which Lago Vista would be liable for Waldrop's conduct. First, relying on a 1997 "Policy Guidance" issued by the Department of Education, they would hold a school district liable in damages under Title IX where a teacher is " 'aided in carrying out the sexual harassment of students by his or her position of authority with the institution,' " irrespective of whether school district officials had any knowledge of the harassment and irrespective of their response upon becoming aware. That rule is an expression of respondeat superior liability, i.e., vicarious or imputed liability, under which recovery in damages against a school district would generally follow whenever a teacher's authority over a student facilitates the harassment. Second, petitioners and the United States submit that a school district should at a minimum be liable for damages based on a theory of constructive notice, i.e., where the district knew or "should have known" about harassment but failed to uncover and eliminate it. Both standards would allow a damages recovery in a broader range of situations than the rule adopted by the Court of Appeals, which hinges on actual knowledge by a school official with authority to end the harassment.

Whether educational institutions can be said to violate Title IX based solely on principles of respondeat superior or constructive notice was not resolved by *Franklin's* citation of *Meritor*. That reference to

Meritor was made with regard to the general proposition that sexual harassment can constitute discrimination on the basis of sex under Title IX, an issue not in dispute here. In fact, the school district's liability in *Franklin* did not necessarily turn on principles of imputed liability or constructive notice, as there was evidence that school officials knew about the harassment but took no action to stop it. Moreover, *Meritor's* rationale for concluding that agency principles guide the liability inquiry under Title VII rests on an aspect of that statute not found in Title IX: Title VII, in which the prohibition against employment discrimination runs against "an employer," Title IX contains no comparable reference to an educational institution's "agents," and so does not expressly call for application of agency principles.

In this case, moreover, petitioners seek not just to establish a Title IX violation but to recover damages based on theories of respondeat superior and constructive notice. It is that aspect of their action, in our view, that is most critical to resolving the case. Unlike Title IX, Title VII contains an express cause of action and specifically provides for relief in the form of monetary damages. Congress therefore has directly addressed the subject of damages relief under Title VII and has set out the particular situations in which damages are available as well as the maximum amounts recoverable. With respect to Title IX, however, the private right of action is judicially implied and there is thus no legislative expression of the scope of available remedies, including when it is appropriate to award monetary damages. In addition, although the general presumption that courts can award any appropriate relief in an established cause of action, coupled with Congress' abrogation of the States' Eleventh Amendment immunity under Title IX, led us to conclude in *Franklin* that Title IX recognizes a damages remedy, we did so in response to lower court decisions holding that Title IX does not support damages relief at all. We made no effort in *Franklin* to delimit the circumstances in which a damages remedy should lie.

III

Because the private right of action under Title IX is judicially implied, we have a measure of latitude to shape a sensible remedial scheme that best comports with the statute. That endeavor inherently entails a degree of speculation, since it addresses an issue on which Congress has not specifically spoken. To guide the analysis, we generally examine the relevant statute to ensure that we do not fashion the scope of an implied right in a manner at odds with the statutory structure and purpose.

Those considerations, we think, are pertinent not only to the scope of the implied right, but also to the scope of the available remedies. We suggested as much in *Franklin*, where we recognized "the general rule that all appropriate relief is available in an action brought to vindicate a federal right," but indicated that the rule must be reconciled with congressional purpose. The "general rule," that is, "yields where necessary to carry out the intent of Congress or to avoid frustrating the purposes of the statute involved."

Applying those principles here, we conclude that it would "frustrate the purposes" of Title IX to permit a damages recovery against a school district for a teacher's sexual harassment of a student based on principles of respondeat superior or constructive notice, i.e., without actual notice to a school district official. Because Congress did not expressly create a private right of action under Title IX, the statutory text does not shed light on Congress' intent with respect to the scope of available remedies. Instead, "we attempt to infer how the [1972] Congress would have addressed the issue had the . . . action been included as an express provision in the" statute.

As a general matter, it does not appear that Congress contemplated unlimited recovery in damages against a funding recipient where the recipient is unaware of discrimination in its programs. When Title IX was enacted in 1972, the principal civil rights statutes containing an express right of action did not provide for recovery of monetary damages at all, instead allowing only injunctive and equitable relief. It was not until 1991 that Congress made damages available under Title VII, and even then, Congress carefully limited the amount recoverable in any individual case, calibrating the maximum recovery to the size of the employer. Adopting petitioners' position would amount, then, to allowing unlimited recovery of damages under Title IX where Congress has not spoken on the subject of either the right or the remedy, and in the face of evidence that when Congress expressly considered both in Title VII it restricted the amount of damages available.

Congress enacted Title IX in 1972 with two principal objectives in mind: "[T]o avoid the use of federal resources to support discriminatory practices" and "to provide individual citizens effective protection against those practices." The statute was modeled after Title VI of the Civil Rights Act of 1964 which is parallel to Title IX except that it prohibits race discrimination, not sex discrimination, and applies in all programs receiving federal funds, not only in education programs. The two statutes operate in the same manner, conditioning an offer of federal funding on a promise by the recipient not to discriminate, in what amounts essentially to a contract between the Government and the recipient of funds.

That contractual framework distinguishes Title IX from Title VII, which is framed in terms not of a condition but of an outright prohibition. Title VII applies to all employers without regard to federal funding and aims broadly to "eradicat[e] discrimination throughout the economy." Thus, whereas Title VII aims centrally to compensate victims of discrimination, Title IX focuses more on "protecting" individuals from discriminatory practices carried out by recipients of federal funds. That might explain why, when the Court first recognized the implied right under Title IX in Cannon, the opinion referred to injunctive or equitable relief in a private action, but not to a damages remedy.

Title IX's contractual nature has implications for our construction of the scope of available remedies. When Congress attaches conditions to the award of federal funds under its spending power, as it has in Title IX and Title VI, we examine closely the propriety of private actions holding the recipient liable in monetary damages for noncompliance with the condition.

... If a school district's liability for a teacher's sexual harassment rests on principles of constructive notice or respondeat superior, it will likewise be the case that the recipient of funds was unaware of the discrimination. It is sensible to assume that Congress did not envision a recipient's liability in damages in that situation.

Most significantly, Title IX contains important clues that Congress did not intend to allow recovery in damages where liability rests solely on principles of vicarious liability or constructive notice. Title IX's express means of enforcement—by administrative agencies—operates on an assumption of actual notice to officials of the funding recipient. The statute entitles agencies who disburse education funding to enforce their rules implementing the nondiscrimination mandate through proceedings to suspend or terminate funding or through "other means authorized by law." Significantly, however, an agency may not initiate enforcement proceedings until it "has advised the appropriate person or persons of the failure to comply with the requirement and has determined that compliance cannot be secured by voluntary means." The administrative regulations implement that obligation, requiring resolution of compliance issues "by informal means whenever possible," and prohibiting commencement of enforcement proceedings until the agency has determined that voluntary compliance is unobtainable and "the recipient ... has been notified of its failure to comply and of the action to be taken to effect compliance."

In the event of a violation, a funding recipient may be required to take "such remedial action as [is] deem[ed] necessary to overcome the effects of [the] discrimination." While agencies have conditioned continued funding on providing equitable relief to the victim, the regulations do not appear to contemplate a condition ordering payment of monetary damages, and there is no indication that payment of damages has been demanded as a condition of finding a recipient to be in compliance with the statute. In *Franklin*, for instance, the Department of Education found a violation of Title IX but determined that the school district came into compliance by virtue of the offending teacher's resignation and the district's institution of a grievance procedure for sexual harassment complaints.

Presumably, a central purpose of requiring notice of the violation "of the appropriate person" and an opportunity for voluntary compliance before administrative enforcement proceedings can commence is to avoid diverting education funding from beneficial uses where a recipient was unaware of discrimination in its programs and is willing to institute prompt corrective measures. The scope of private damages relief proposed by petitioners is at odds with that basic objective. When a teacher's sexual harassment is imputed to a school district or when a school district is deemed to have "constructively" known of the teacher's harassment, by assumption the district had no actual knowledge of the teacher's conduct. Nor, of course, did the district have an opportunity to take action to end the harassment or to limit further harassment.

It would be unsound, we think, for a statute's express system of enforcement to require notice to the recipient and an opportunity to come into voluntary compliance while a judicially implied system of enforcement permits substantial liability without regard to the recipient's knowledge or its corrective actions upon receiving notice. Moreover, an award of damages in a particular case might well exceed a recipient's level of federal funding. Where a statute's express enforcement scheme hinges its most severe sanction on notice and unsuccessful efforts to obtain compliance, we cannot attribute to Congress the intention to have implied an enforcement scheme that allows imposition of greater liability without comparable conditions.

IV

Because the express remedial scheme under Title IX is predicated upon notice to an "appropriate person" and an opportunity to rectify any violation, we conclude, in the absence of further direction from Congress, that the implied damages remedy should be fashioned along the same lines. An "appropriate person" under § 1682 is, at a minimum, an official of the recipient entity with authority to take corrective action to end the discrimination. Consequently, in cases like this one that do not involve official policy of the recipient entity, we hold that a damages remedy will not lie under Title IX unless an official who at a minimum has authority to address the alleged discrimination and to institute corrective measures on the recipient's behalf has actual knowledge of discrimination in the recipient's programs and fails adequately to respond.

We think, moreover, that the response must amount to deliberate indifference to discrimination. The administrative enforcement scheme presupposes that an official who is advised of a Title IX violation refuses to take action to bring the recipient into compliance. The premise, in other words, is an official decision by the recipient not to remedy the violation. That framework finds a rough parallel in the standard of deliberate indifference. Under a lower standard, there would be a risk that the recipient would be liable in damages not for its own official decision but instead for its employees' independent actions. Comparable considerations led to our adoption of a deliberate indifference standard for claims under § 1983 alleging that a municipality's actions in failing to prevent a deprivation of federal rights was the cause of the violation.

Applying the framework to this case is fairly straightforward, as petitioners do not contend they can prevail under an actual notice standard. The only official alleged to have had information about Waldrop's misconduct is the high school principal. That information, however, consisted of a complaint from parents of other students charging only that Waldrop had made inappropriate comments during class, which was plainly insufficient to alert the principal to the possibility that Waldrop was involved in a sexual relationship with a student. Lago Vista, moreover, terminated Waldrop's employment upon learning of his relationship with Gebser. Justice Stevens points out in his dissenting opinion that Waldrop of course had knowledge of his own actions. Where a school district's liability rests on actual notice principles, however, the knowledge of the wrongdoer himself is not pertinent to the analysis.

Petitioners focus primarily on Lago Vista's asserted failure to promulgate and publicize an effective policy and grievance procedure for sexual harassment claims. They point to Department of Education regulations requiring each funding recipient to "adopt and publish grievance procedures providing for prompt and equitable resolution" of discrimination complaints, and to notify students and others that "it does not discriminate on the basis of sex in the educational programs or activities which it operates," Lago Vista's alleged failure to comply with the regulations, however, does not establish the requisite actual notice and deliberate indifference. And in any event, the failure to promulgate a grievance procedure does not itself constitute "discrimination" under Title IX. Of course, the Department of Education could enforce the requirement administratively: Agencies generally have authority to promulgate and enforce requirements that effectuate the statute's nondiscrimination mandate, even if those requirements do not purport to represent a definition of discrimination under the statute. We have never held, however, that the implied private right of action under Title IX allows recovery in damages for violation of those sorts of administrative requirements.

V

The number of reported cases involving sexual harassment of students in schools confirms that harassment unfortunately is an all too common aspect of the educational experience. No one questions that a student suffers extraordinary harm when subjected to sexual harassment and abuse by a teacher, and that the teacher's conduct is reprehensible and undermines the basic purposes of the educational system. The issue in this case, however, is whether the independent misconduct of a teacher is attributable to the school district that employs him under a specific federal statute designed primarily to prevent recipients of federal financial assistance from using the funds in a discriminatory manner. Our decision does not affect any right of recovery that an individual may have against a school district as a matter of state law or against the teacher in his individual capacity under state law or under 42 U.S.C. § 1983. Until Congress speaks directly on the subject, however, we will not hold a school district liable in damages under Title IX for a teacher's sexual harassment of a student absent actual notice and deliberate indifference. We therefore affirm the judgment of the Court of Appeals.

It is so ordered.

Notes

1. Do you agree with the outcome in this case?

2. Is there anything that school officials and/or parents could have done to have prevented this kind of situation from occurring?

[Case No. 116]　Peer-to-Peer Sexual Harassment

DAVIS v. MONROE COUNTY BOARD OF EDUCATION

Supreme Court of the United States, 1999.
526 U.S. 629, 119 S.Ct. 1661, 143 L.Ed.2d 839 [134 Educ. L. Rep. 477].

JUSTICE O'CONNOR delivered the opinion of the Court.

Petitioner brought suit against the Monroe County Board of Education and other defendants, alleging that her fifth-grade daughter had been the victim of sexual harassment by another student in her class. Among petitioner's claims was a claim for monetary and injunctive relief under Title IX. . . . The District Court dismissed petitioner's Title IX claim on the ground that "student-on-student," or peer, harassment provides no ground for a private cause of action under the statute. The Court of Appeals for the Eleventh Circuit, sitting en banc, affirmed. We consider here whether a private damages action may lie against the school board in cases of student-on-student harassment. We conclude that it may, but only where the funding recipient acts with deliberate indifference to known acts of harassment in its programs or activities. Moreover, we conclude that such an action will lie only for harassment that is so severe, pervasive, and objectively offensive that it effectively bars the victim's access to an educational opportunity or benefit.

I

A

Petitioner's minor daughter, LaShonda, was allegedly the victim of a prolonged pattern of sexual harassment by one of her fifth-grade classmates at Hubbard Elementary School, a public school in Monroe County, Georgia. According to petitioner's complaint, the harassment began in December 1992, when the classmate, G.F., attempted to touch LaShonda's breasts and genital area and made vulgar statements such as " 'I want to get in bed with you' " and " 'I want to feel your boobs.' " Similar conduct allegedly occurred on or about January 4 and January 20, 1993. LaShonda reported each of these incidents to her mother and to her classroom teacher, Diane Fort. Petitioner, in turn, also contacted Fort, who allegedly assured petitioner that the school principal, Bill Querry, had been informed of the incidents. Petitioner contends that, notwithstanding these reports, no disciplinary action was taken against G.F.

G.F.'s conduct allegedly continued for many months. In early February, G.F. purportedly placed a door stop in his pants and proceeded to act in a sexually suggestive manner toward LaShonda during physical education class. LaShonda reported G.F.'s behavior to her physical education teacher, Whit Maples. Approximately one week later, G.F. again allegedly engaged in harassing behavior, this time while under the supervision of another classroom teacher, Joyce Pippin. Again, LaShonda allegedly reported the incident to the teacher, and again petitioner contacted the teacher to follow up.

Petitioner alleges that G.F. once more directed sexually harassing conduct toward LaShonda in physical education class in early March, and that LaShonda reported the incident to both Maples and Pippen. In mid-April 1993, G.F. allegedly rubbed his body against LaShonda in the school hallway in what LaShonda considered a sexually suggestive manner, and LaShonda again reported the matter to Fort.

The string of incidents finally ended in mid-May, when G.F. was charged with, and pleaded guilty to, sexual battery for his misconduct. The complaint alleges that LaShonda had suffered during the months of harassment, however; specifically, her previously high grades allegedly dropped as she became unable to concentrate on her studies, and, in April 1993, her father discovered that she had written a suicide note. The complaint further alleges that, at one point, LaShonda told petitioner that she " 'didn't know how much longer she could keep [G.F.] off her.' "

Nor was LaShonda G.F.'s only victim; it is alleged that other girls in the class fell prey to G.F.'s conduct. At one point, in fact, a group composed of LaShonda and other female students tried to speak with Principal Querry about G.F.'s behavior. According to the complaint, however, a teacher denied the students' request with the statement, " 'If [Querry] wants you, he'll call you.' "

Petitioner alleges that no disciplinary action was taken in response to G.F.'s behavior toward LaShonda. In addition to her conversations with Fort and Pippen, petitioner alleges that she spoke with Principal Querry in mid-May 1993. When petitioner inquired as to what action the school intended to take against G.F., Querry simply stated, " 'I guess I'll have to threaten him a little bit harder.' " Yet, petitioner alleges, at no point during the many months of his reported misconduct was G.F. disciplined for harassment. Indeed, Querry allegedly asked petitioner why LaShonda " 'was the only one complaining.' "

Nor, according to the complaint, was any effort made to separate G.F. and LaShonda. On the contrary, notwithstanding LaShonda's frequent complaints, only after more than three months of reported harassment was she even permitted to change her classroom seat so that she was no longer seated next to G.F. Moreover, petitioner alleges that, at the time of the events in question, the Monroe County Board of Education (Board) had not instructed its personnel on how to respond to peer sexual harassment and had not established a policy on the issue.

B

On May 4, 1994, petitioner filed suit in the United States District Court for the Middle District of Georgia against the Board, Charles Dumas, the school district's superintendent, and Principal Querry. The complaint alleged that the Board is a recipient of federal funding for purposes of Title IX, that "[t]he persistent sexual advances and harassment by the student G.F. upon [LaShonda] interfered with her ability to attend school and perform her studies and activities," and that "[t]he deliberate indifference by Defendants to the unwelcome sexual advances of a student upon LaShonda created an intimidating, hostile, offensive and abus[ive] school environment in violation of Title IX." The complaint sought compensatory and punitive damages, attorney's fees, and injunctive relief.

The defendants (all respondents here) moved to dismiss petitioner's complaint under Federal Rule of Civil Procedure 12(b)(6) for failure to state a claim upon which relief could be granted, and the District Court granted respondents' motion. With regard to petitioner's claims under Title IX, the court dismissed the claims against individual defendants on the ground that only federally funded educational institutions are subject to liability in private causes of action under Title IX. As for the Board, the court concluded that Title IX provided no basis for liability absent an allegation "that the Board or an employee of the Board had any role in the harassment."

Petitioner appealed the District Court's decision dismissing her Title IX claim against the Board, and a panel of the Court of Appeals for the Eleventh Circuit reversed.... The Eleventh Circuit panel recognized that petitioner sought to state a claim based on school "officials' failure to take action to stop the offensive acts of those over whom the officials exercised control," and the court concluded that petitioner had alleged facts sufficient to support a claim for hostile environment sexual harassment on this theory.

The Eleventh Circuit granted the Board's motion for rehearing en banc and affirmed the District Court's decision to dismiss petitioner's Title IX claim against the Board. The en banc court relied, primarily, on the theory that Title IX was passed pursuant to Congress' legislative authority under the Constitution's Spending Clause and that the statute therefore must provide potential recipients of federal education funding with "unambiguous notice of the conditions they are assuming when they accept" it. Title IX, the court reasoned, provides recipients with notice that they must stop their employees from engaging in discriminatory conduct, but the statute fails to provide a recipient with sufficient notice of a duty to prevent student-on-student harassment.

Writing in dissent, four judges urged that the statute, by declining to identify the perpetrator of discrimination, encompasses misconduct by third parties....

We granted *certiorari*, in order to resolve a conflict in the Circuits over whether, and under what circumstances, a recipient of federal educational funds can be liable in a private damages action arising from student-on-student sexual harassment (citations eliminated).... We now reverse.

II

Title IX provides, with certain exceptions not at issue here, that

"[n]o person in the United States shall, on the basis of sex, be excluded from participation in, be denied the benefits of, or be subjected to discrimination under any education program or activity receiving Federal financial assistance." 20 U.S.C. § 1681(a).

Congress authorized an administrative enforcement scheme for Title IX. Federal departments or agencies with the authority to provide financial assistance are entrusted to promulgate rules, regulations, and orders to enforce the objectives of § 1681, and these departments or agencies may rely on "any ... means authorized by law," including the termination of funding to give effect to the statute's restrictions.

There is no dispute here that the Board is a recipient of federal education funding for Title IX purposes. Nor do respondents support an argument that student-on-student harassment cannot rise to the level of "discrimination" for purposes of Title IX. Rather, at issue here is the question whether a recipient of federal education funding may be liable for damages under Title IX under any circumstances for discrimination in the form of student-on-student sexual harassment.

A

Petitioner urges that Title IX's plain language compels the conclusion that the statute is intended to bar recipients of federal funding from permitting this form of discrimination in their programs or activities. She emphasizes that the statute prohibits a student from being "subjected to discrimination under any education program or activity receiving Federal financial assistance." It is Title IX's "unmistakable focus on the benefited class," rather than the perpetrator, that, in petitioner's view, compels the conclusion that the statute works to protect students from the discriminatory misconduct of their peers.

Here, however, we are asked to do more than define the scope of the behavior that Title IX proscribes. We must determine whether a district's failure to respond to student-on-student harassment in its schools can support a private suit for money damages. This Court has indeed recognized an implied private right of action under Title IX, and we have held that money damages are available in such suits. Because we have repeatedly treated Title IX as legislation enacted pursuant to Congress' authority under the Spending Clause, however, private damages actions are available only where recipients of federal funding had adequate notice that they could be liable for the conduct at issue. When Congress acts pursuant to its spending power, it generates legislation "much in the nature of a contract: in return for federal funds, the States agree to comply with federally imposed conditions." ...

... [R]espondents urge that Title IX provides no notice that recipients of federal educational funds could be liable in damages for harm arising from student-on-student harassment. Respondents contend, specifically, that the statute only proscribes misconduct by grant recipients, not third parties. Respondents argue, moreover, that it would be contrary to the very purpose of Spending Clause legislation to impose liability on a funding recipient for the misconduct of third parties, over whom recipients exercise little control.

We agree with respondents that a recipient of federal funds may be liable in damages under Title IX only for its own misconduct. The recipient itself must "exclud[e] [persons] from participation in, ...

den[y] [persons] the benefits of, or ... subjec[t] [persons] to discrimination under" its "program[s] or activit[ies]" in order to be liable under Title IX. The Government's enforcement power may only be exercised against the funding recipient, and we have not extended damages liability under Title IX to parties outside the scope of this power. . . .

We disagree with respondents' assertion, however, that petitioner seeks to hold the Board liable for G. F.'s actions instead of its own. Here, petitioner attempts to hold the Board liable for its own decision to remain idle in the face of known student-on-student harassment in its schools. In *Gebser*, we concluded that a recipient of federal education funds may be liable in damages under Title IX where it is deliberately indifferent to known acts of sexual harassment by a teacher. In that case, a teacher had entered into a sexual relationship with an eighth-grade student, and the student sought damages under Title IX for the teacher's misconduct. We recognized that the scope of liability in private damages actions under Title IX is circumscribed by *Pennhurst's* requirement that funding recipients have notice of their potential liability. . . . in *Gebser* we once again required "that 'the receiving entity of federal funds [have] notice that it will be liable for a monetary award' " before subjecting it to damages liability. We also recognized, however, that this limitation on private damages actions is not a bar to liability where a funding recipient intentionally violates the statute. In particular, we concluded that *Pennhurst* does not bar a private damages action under Title IX where the funding recipient engages in intentional conduct that violates the clear terms of the statute.

Accordingly, we rejected the use of agency principles to impute liability to the district for the misconduct of its teachers. Likewise, we declined the invitation to impose liability under what amounted to a negligence standard—holding the district liable for its failure to react to teacher-student harassment of which it knew or should have known. Rather, we concluded that the district could be liable for damages only where the district itself intentionally acted in clear violation of Title IX by remaining deliberately indifferent to acts of teacher-student harassment of which it had actual knowledge. Contrary to the dissent's suggestion, the misconduct of the teacher in *Gebser* was not "treated as the grant recipient's actions." Liability arose, rather, from "an official decision by the recipient not to remedy the violation." By employing the "deliberate indifference" theory already used to establish municipal liability ... we concluded in *Gebser* that recipients could be liable in damages only where their own deliberate indifference effectively "cause[d]" the discrimination. The high standard imposed in *Gebser* sought to eliminate any "risk that the recipient would be liable in damages not for its own official decision but instead for its employees' independent actions."

Gebser thus established that a recipient intentionally violates Title IX, and is subject to a private damages action, where the recipient is deliberately indifferent to known acts of teacher-student discrimination. Indeed, whether viewed as "discrimination" or "subject[ing]" students to discrimination, Title IX "[u]nquestionably ... placed on [the Board] the duty not" to permit teacher-student harassment in its schools and recipients violate Title IX's plain terms when they remain deliberately indifferent to this form of misconduct.

We consider here whether the misconduct identified in *Gebser*-deliberate indifference to known acts of harassment—amounts to an intentional violation of Title IX, capable of supporting a private damages action, when the harasser is a student rather than a teacher. We conclude that, in certain limited circumstances, it does. As an initial matter, in *Gebser* we expressly rejected the use of agency principles in the Title IX context, noting the textual differences between Title IX and Title VII. (citations eliminated). Additionally, the regulatory scheme surrounding Title IX has long provided funding recipients with notice that they may be liable for their failure to respond to the discriminatory acts of certain nonagents. The Department of Education requires recipients to monitor third parties for discrimination in specified circumstances and to refrain from particular forms of interaction with outside entities that are known to discriminate.

The common law, too, has put schools on notice that they may be held responsible under state law for their failure to protect students from the tortious acts of third parties. In fact, state courts routinely uphold claims alleging that schools have been negligent in failing to protect their students from the torts of their peers.

This is not to say that the identity of the harasser is irrelevant. On the contrary, both the "deliberate indifference" standard and the language of Title IX narrowly circumscribe the set of parties whose known acts of sexual harassment can trigger some duty to respond on the part of funding recipients. Deliberate indifference makes sense as a theory of direct liability under Title IX only where the funding recipient has some control over the alleged harassment. A recipient cannot be directly liable for its indifference where it lacks the authority to take remedial action.

The language of Title IX itself—particularly when viewed in conjunction with the requirement that the recipient have notice of Title IX's prohibitions to be liable for damages—also cabins the range of misconduct that the statute proscribes. The statute's plain language confines the scope of prohibited conduct based on the recipient's degree of control over the harasser and the environment in which the harassment occurs. If a funding recipient does not engage in harassment directly, it may not be liable for damages unless its deliberate indifference "subject[s]" its students to harassment. That is, the deliberate indifference must, at a minimum, "cause [students] to undergo" harassment or "make them liable or vulnerable" to it. Moreover, because the harassment must occur "under" "the operations of" a funding recipient, the harassment must take place in a context subject to the school district's control.

These factors combine to limit a recipient's damages liability to circumstances wherein the recipient exercises substantial control over both the harasser and the context in which the known harassment occurs. Only then can the recipient be said to "expose" its students to harassment or "cause" them to undergo it "under" the recipient's programs. We agree with the dissent that these conditions are satisfied most easily and most obviously when the offender is an agent of the recipient. We rejected the use of agency analysis in *Gebser*, however, and we disagree that the term "under" somehow imports an agency requirement into Title IX. As noted above, the theory in *Gebser* was that the recipient was directly liable for its deliberate indifference to discrimination. Liability in that case did not arise because the "teacher's actions [were] treated" as those of the funding recipient; the district was directly liable for its own failure to act. The terms "subjec[t]" and "under" impose limits, but nothing about these terms requires the use of agency principles.

Where, as here, the misconduct occurs during school hours and on school grounds—the bulk of G.F.'s misconduct, in fact, took place in the classroom—the misconduct is taking place "under" an "operation" of the funding recipient. In these circumstances, the recipient retains substantial control over the context in which the harassment occurs. More importantly, however, in this setting the Board exercises significant control over the harasser. We have observed, for example, "that the nature of [the State's] power [over public school children] is custodial and tutelary, permitting a degree of supervision and control that could not be exercised over free adults." On more than one occasion, this Court has recognized the importance of school officials' "comprehensive authority . . . , consistent with fundamental constitutional safeguards, to prescribe and control conduct in the schools." The common law, too, recognizes the school's disciplinary authority. We thus conclude that recipients of federal funding may be liable for "subject[ing]" their students to discrimination where the recipient is deliberately indifferent to known acts of student-on-student sexual harassment and the harasser is under the school's disciplinary authority.

At the time of the events in question here, in fact, school attorneys and administrators were being told that student-on-student harassment could trigger liability under Title IX. In March 1993, even as the events alleged in petitioner's complaint were unfolding, the National School Boards Association issued a publication, for use by "school attorneys and administrators in understanding the law regarding sexual harassment of employees and students," which observed that districts could be liable under Title IX for their failure to respond to student-on-student harassment. Drawing on Equal Employment Opportunity Commission guidelines interpreting Title VII, the publication informed districts that, "if [a] school district has constructive notice of severe and repeated acts of sexual harassment by fellow students, that may form the basis of a [T]itle IX claim." The publication even correctly anticipated a form of *Gebser's* actual notice requirement: "It is unlikely that courts will hold a school district liable for sexual harassment by students against students in the absence of actual knowledge or notice to district employees." Although we do not rely on this publication as an "indicium of congressional notice," we do find support for our reading of Title IX in the fact that school attorneys have rendered an analogous interpretation.

Likewise, although they were promulgated too late to contribute to the Board's notice of proscribed misconduct, the Department of Education's Office for Civil Rights (OCR) has recently adopted policy guidelines providing that student-on-student harassment falls within the scope of Title IX's proscriptions. (citations eliminated).

We stress that our conclusion here—that recipients may be liable for their deliberate indifference to known acts of peer sexual harassment—does not mean that recipients can avoid liability only by purging their schools of actionable peer harassment or that administrators must engage in particular disciplinary action. We thus disagree with respondents' contention that, if Title IX provides a cause of action for student-on-student harassment, "nothing short of expulsion of every student accused of misconduct involving sexual overtones would protect school systems from liability or damages." Likewise, the dissent erroneously imagines that victims of peer harassment now have a Title IX right to make particular remedial demands. In fact, as we have previously noted, courts should refrain from second-guessing the disciplinary decisions made by school administrators.

School administrators will continue to enjoy the flexibility they require so long as funding recipients are deemed "deliberately indifferent" to acts of student-on-student harassment only where the recipient's response to the harassment or lack thereof is clearly unreasonable in light of the known circumstances. The dissent consistently mischaracterizes this standard to require funding recipients to "remedy" peer harassment, and to "ensur[e] that ... students conform their conduct to" certain rules. Title IX imposes no such requirements. On the contrary, the recipient must merely respond to known peer harassment in a manner that is not clearly unreasonable. This is not a mere "reasonableness" standard, as the dissent assumes. In an appropriate case, there is no reason why courts, on a motion to dismiss, for summary judgment, or for a directed verdict, could not identify a response as not "clearly unreasonable" as a matter of law.

Like the dissent, we acknowledge that school administrators shoulder substantial burdens as a result of legal constraints on their disciplinary authority. To the extent that these restrictions arise from federal statutes, Congress can review these burdens with attention to the difficult position in which such legislation may place our Nation's schools. We believe, however, that the standard set out here is sufficiently flexible to account both for the level of disciplinary authority available to the school and for the potential liability arising from certain forms of disciplinary action. A university might not, for example, be expected to exercise the same degree of control over its students that a grade school would enjoy, ... and it would be entirely reasonable for a school to refrain from a form of disciplinary action that would expose it to constitutional or statutory claims.

While it remains to be seen whether petitioner can show that the Board's response to reports of G.F.'s misconduct was clearly unreasonable in light of the known circumstances, petitioner may be able to show that the Board "subject[ed]" LaShonda to discrimination by failing to respond in any way over a period of five months to complaints of G.F.'s in-school misconduct from LaShonda and other female students.

B

The requirement that recipients receive adequate notice of Title IX's proscriptions also bears on the proper definition of "discrimination" in the context of a private damages action. We have elsewhere concluded that sexual harassment is a form of discrimination for Title IX purposes and that Title IX proscribes harassment with sufficient clarity to satisfy *Pennhurst's* notice requirement and serve as a basis for a damages action. (citations eliminated). Having previously determined that "sexual harassment" is "discrimination" in the school context under Title IX, we are constrained to conclude that student-on-student sexual harassment, if sufficiently severe, can likewise rise to the level of discrimination actionable under the statute.(citations eliminated). The statute's other prohibitions, moreover, help give content to the term "discrimination" in this context. Students are not only protected from discrimination, but also specifically shielded from being "excluded from participation in" or "denied the benefits of" any "education program or activity receiving Federal financial assistance." § 1681(a). The statute makes clear that, whatever else it prohibits, students must not be denied access to educational benefits and opportunities on the basis of gender. We thus conclude that funding recipients are properly held liable in damages only where they are deliberately indifferent to sexual harassment, of which they have actual knowledge, that is so severe, pervasive, and objectively offensive that it can be said to deprive the victims of access to the educational opportunities or benefits provided by the school.

The most obvious example of student-on-student sexual harassment capable of triggering a damages claim would thus involve the overt, physical deprivation of access to school resources. Consider, for example, a case in which male students physically threaten their female peers every day, successfully preventing the female students from using a particular school resource—an athletic field or a computer lab, for instance. District administrators are well aware of the daily ritual, yet they deliberately ignore requests for aid from the female students wishing to use the resource. The district's knowing refusal to take any action in response to such behavior would fly in the face of Title IX's core principles, and such deliberate indifference may appropriately be subject to claims for monetary damages. It is not necessary, however, to show physical exclusion to demonstrate that students have been deprived by the actions of another student or students of an educational opportunity on the basis of sex. Rather, a plaintiff must establish sexual harassment of students that is so severe, pervasive, and objectively offensive, and that so undermines and detracts from the victims' educational experience, that the victim-students are effectively denied equal access to an institution's resources and opportunities. (citations eliminated).

Whether gender-oriented conduct rises to the level of actionable "harassment" thus "depends on a constellation of surrounding circumstances, expectations, and relationships," including, but not limited to, the ages of the harasser and the victim and the number of individuals involved. Courts, moreover, must bear in mind that schools are unlike the adult workplace and that children may regularly interact in a manner that would be unacceptable among adults. Indeed, at least early on, students are still learning how to interact appropriately with their peers. It is thus understandable that, in the school setting, students often engage in insults, banter, teasing, shoving, pushing, and gender-specific conduct that is upsetting to the students subjected to it. Damages are not available for simple acts of teasing and name-calling among school children, however, even where these comments target differences in gender.

Rather, in the context of student-on-student harassment, damages are available only where the behavior is so severe, pervasive, and objectively offensive that it denies its victims the equal access to education that Title IX is designed to protect.

The dissent fails to appreciate these very real limitations on a funding recipient's liability under Title IX. It is not enough to show, as the dissent would read this opinion to provide, that a student has been "teased," or "called ... offensive names." Comparisons to an "overweight child who skips gym class because the other children tease her about her size," the student who "refuses to wear glasses to avoid the taunts of 'four-eyes,'" and "the child who refuses to go to school because the school bully calls him a 'scaredy-cat' at recess," are inapposite and misleading. Nor do we contemplate, much less hold, that a mere "decline in grades is enough to survive" a motion to dismiss. The dropoff in LaShonda's grades provides necessary evidence of a potential link between her education and G.F.'s misconduct, but petitioner's ability to state a cognizable claim here depends equally on the alleged persistence and severity of G.F.'s actions, not to mention the Board's alleged knowledge and deliberate indifference. We trust that the dissent's characterization of our opinion will not mislead courts to impose more sweeping liability than we read Title IX to require.

Moreover, the provision that the discrimination occur "under any education program or activity" suggests that the behavior be serious enough to have the systemic effect of denying the victim equal access to an educational program or activity. Although, in theory, a single instance of sufficiently severe one-on-one peer harassment could be said to have such an effect, we think it unlikely that Congress would have thought such behavior sufficient to rise to this level in light of the inevitability of student misconduct and the amount of litigation that would be invited by entertaining claims of official indifference to a single instance of one-on-one peer harassment.

By limiting private damages actions to cases having a systemic effect on educational programs or activities, we reconcile the general principle that Title IX prohibits official indifference to known peer sexual harassment with the practical realities of responding to student behavior, realities that Congress could not have meant to be ignored. Even the dissent suggests that Title IX liability may arise when a funding recipient remains indifferent to severe, gender-based mistreatment played out on a "widespread level" among students.

The fact that it was a teacher who engaged in harassment in *Franklin* and *Gebser* is relevant. The relationship between the harasser and the victim necessarily affects the extent to which the misconduct can be said to breach Title IX's guarantee of equal access to educational benefits and to have a systemic effect on a program or activity. Peer harassment, in particular, is less likely to satisfy these requirements than is teacher-student harassment.

C

Applying this standard to the facts at issue here, we conclude that the Eleventh Circuit erred in dismissing petitioner's complaint. Petitioner alleges that her daughter was the victim of repeated acts of sexual harassment by G.F. over a 5-month period, and there are allegations in support of the conclusion that G.F.'s misconduct was severe, pervasive, and objectively offensive. The harassment was not only verbal; it included numerous acts of objectively offensive touching, and, indeed, G.F. ultimately pleaded guilty to criminal sexual misconduct. Moreover, the complaint alleges that there were multiple victims who were sufficiently disturbed by G.F.'s misconduct to seek an audience with the school principal. Further, petitioner contends that the harassment had a concrete, negative effect on her daughter's ability to receive an education. The complaint also suggests that petitioner may be able to show both actual knowledge and deliberate indifference on the part of the Board, which made no effort whatsoever either to investigate or to put an end to the harassment.

On this complaint, we cannot say "beyond doubt that [petitioner] can prove no set of facts in support of [her] claim which would entitle [her] to relief." Accordingly, the judgment of the United States Court of Appeals for the Eleventh Circuit is reversed, and the case is remanded for further proceedings consistent with this opinion.

It is so ordered.

Notes

1. In dissent, Justice Kennedy feared that the Court's ruling would have left school boards susceptible to an avalanche of costly liability. While his concerns have apparently not been borne out, were they well-founded?

2. What can, or should, school officials do to eliminate peer-to-peer sexual harassment?

Chapter 14

STUDENTS WITH DISABILITIES

Introduction[1]

The educational rights of students with disabilities are governed primarily by two[2] federal statutes: Section 504 of the Rehabilitation Act (Section 504),[3] the first federal civil rights law protecting the rights of the disabled, and the Individuals with Disabilities Education Act (IDEA).[4] Prior to the enactment of these laws, many states overlooked the educational needs of children with disabilities.[5]

Two federal class action suits provided a major thrust for the development of the law of special education. In *Pennsylvania Association for Retarded Children v. Pennsylvania (PARC)*,[6] a federal trial court, in a consent decree, enunciated many of the principles that would be included in the IDEA. In *PARC,* the parties agreed that mentally retarded children, or those who were thought to have been mentally retarded, could neither have been denied admission to public schools nor subjected to changes in their educational placements unless their parents received procedural due process and that placements in regular school classrooms were preferable to those in more restrictive settings. The court also ruled both that all children can learn in school settings and that educators had to provide all students who were mentally retarded with placements that afforded them a free appropriate public education and training programs that were appropriate to their individualized needs.

Mills v. Board of Education of the District of Columbia (Mills)[7] addressed the merits of the case in which the parents of seven named

---

1. The initial version of this chapter was adapted with the permission of the publisher, the National Catholic Education Association, from CHARLES J. RUSSO, JOSEPH D. MASSUCCI, ALLAN G. OSBORNE, JR., & GERALD M. CATTARO. CATHOLIC SCHOOLS AND THE LAW OF SPECIAL EDUCATION: A REFERENCE GUIDE (2002). *See also* Charles J. Russo & Allan G. Osborne, Jr. *The Legal Rights of American Students with Disabilities: An Overview.* AUSTRALIA & NEW ZEALAND JOURNAL OF LAW & EDUCATION, VOL. 3, No. 2, 45–60 (1998).

2. A third law, the Americans with Disabilities Act, 42 U.S.C.A. §§ 12101 *et seq.,* which extends similar protections to individuals in the private sector and has limited implications for public schools, is beyond the scope of this chapter.

3. 29 U.S.C.A. § 794(a). This statute is in the appendix.

4. 20 U.S.C.A. §§ 1400 *et seq.* Portions of this statute are in the appendix.

5. For apparently the earliest reported case involving a student with a disability, *see Watson v. City of Cambridge*, 32 N.E. 864 (Mass. 1893) (upholding a student's exclusion from school because he was "weak-minded"). *See also State v. Board of Educ. of City of Antigo*, 172 N.W. 153 (Wis. 1919) (affirming the exclusion of a student whose paralysis caused him to speak hesitatingly and drool uncontrollably even though he had the academic ability to benefit from school because "his physical condition and ailment produce[d] a depressing and nauseating effect upon the teachers and school children.").

6. 334 F.Supp. 1257 (E.D.Pa.1971), 343 F.Supp. 279 (E.D.Pa.1972).

7. 348 F.Supp. 866 (D.D.C.1972).

exceptional children filed suit in the federal trial court in Washington, D.C., on behalf of perhaps as many as 18,000 students with disabilities who were not receiving programs of specialized education. Most of the children, who were also minorities, were classified as having behavioral problems or being mentally retarded, emotionally disturbed, and/or hyperactive. The court rejected the contention of educational officials that the school board lacked resources for all of its students, deciding that it had to spend its funds equitably so that all children would have been educated in a manner consistent with their individualized needs and abilities. The court decreed that the board could not deny services to children with disabilities or exclude them from school without providing them and their parents with due process. At the same time, the court ordered the board to provide due process safeguards before any child was excluded from the public schools, reassigned, or had special education services terminated while outlining elaborate due process procedures that essentially formed the foundation for the due process safeguards that were included in the IDEA.

In light of the developments spurred on by *PARC* and *Mills*, this chapter examines the major elements of Section 504 and the IDEA along with key cases from the large amount of litigation that they have generated.

Section 504 of the Rehabilitation Act of 1973

Section 504 of the Rehabilitation Act of 1973, which traces its origins to the wake of World War I, at which time the United States government sought to provide vocational rehabilitation to injured soldiers, is the oldest federal law addressing the needs of the disabled. According to Section 504, in language that is similar to that in Title VI[8] of the Civil Rights Act of 1964 and Title IX of the Educational Amendments of 1972,[9] "[n]o otherwise qualified individual with a disability in the United States ... shall, solely by reason of her or his disability, be excluded from the participation in, be denied the benefits of, or be subjected to discrimination under any program or activity receiving [f]ederal financial assistance...."[10]

At the outset, there are at least four major differences between Section 504 and the IDEA. First, while Section 504 applies to school systems that receive federal financial assistance, whether in the form of money, books, or free lunches, they do not receive additional funds under its provisions like the boards that serve children who qualify for IDEA services.[11] Second, Section 504 protects individuals under the broader notion of impairment rather than the IDEA's reliance on the statutorily defined concept of disability. Third, Section 504 has no age limitation.

---

8. 42 U.S.C.A. §§ 2000 *et seq.* Portions of this statute are in the appendix.

9. 20 U.S.C.A. § 1681. Portions of this statute are in the appendix.

10. 29 U.S.C.A. § 794(a).

11. In light of the fact that costs associated with special education have long been contentious, the revised IDEA set the goal of achieving its initial 1975 promise of funding 40 percent of the national average of per-pupil spending by 2011. 20 U.S.C.A. §§ 1411(a)(2)(A)(ii), (h)(7)(B)(i).

Fourth, the IDEA includes much more extensive due process provisions than Section 504. Moreover, while Section 504 covers students, employees, and others, including parents, in schools, and the IDEA is limited to students, this discussion focuses on the rights of children.

Section 504 defines an eligible individual as one "who (i) has a physical or mental impairment which substantially limits one or more of such person's major life activities, (ii) has a record of such an impairment, or (iii) is regarded as having such an impairment."[12] In order to have "a record of impairment," one must have a history of, or been identified as having, a mental or physical impairment that substantially limits one or more major life activities,[13] including learning and working.[14] Once a student is identified as having an impairment, school officials must consider whether the child is "otherwise qualified."

In order to be "otherwise qualified," children must be "(i) of an age during which nonhandicapped persons are provided such services, (ii) of any age during which it is mandatory under state law to provide such services to handicapped persons, or (iii) [one] to whom a state is required to provide a free appropriate public education [under the IDEA]."[15] Persons who are "otherwise qualified,"[16] meaning that they are eligible to participate in programs or activities despite the existence of impairments, must be permitted to so do in such activities as long as they can be provided with "reasonable accommodations."[17]

Once officials determine that children are "otherwise qualified" to receive assistance under Section 504, they must decide what accommodations they are willing to provide. Even though Section 504 and its regulations do not explicitly require school officials to develop written agreements that are similar to the Individualized Education Programs that are mandated under the IDEA, it is not uncommon for them to do so. These written agreements, commonly referred to as Section 504 service plans, typically include demographic and other relevant information about children such as their impairments, the names of individuals who participated in developing them, copies of reports and data that

---

12. 29 U.S.C.A. § 706(7)(B). According to Section 504's regulations,

(i) Physical or mental impairment means (A) any physiological disorder or condition, cosmetic disfigurement, or anatomical loss affecting one or more of the following body systems: neurological; musculoskeletal; special sense organs; respiratory, including speech organs; cardiovascular; reproductive, digestive, genito-urinary; hemic and lymphatic; skin; and endocrine; or (B) any mental or psychological disorder, such as mental retardation, organic brain syndrome, emotional or mental illness, and specific learning disabilities. 34 C.F.R. § 104.3(j)(2)(i).

13. 34 C.F.R. § 104.3(j)(2)(iv).

14. 34 C.F.R. § 104.3(j)(2)(i). ("Major life activities means functions such as caring for one's self, performing manual tasks,

walking, seeing, hearing, speaking, breathing, learning, and working.").

15. 34 C.F.R. § 104.3(l)(2).

16. "Otherwise qualified" was enunciated in *Southeastern Community College v. Davis*, 442 U.S. 397, 410, 99 S.Ct. 2361, 60 L.Ed.2d 980 (1979) [Case No. 117] and modified in *Alexander v. Choate*, 469 U.S. 287, 105 S.Ct. 712, 83 L.Ed.2d 661 (1985) to the extent that the Court added that such an individual is capable of participating in a program or activity if a reasonable accommodation is available.

17. For an interesting case, *see Ohio Civil Rights Comm'n v. Case Western Reserve Univ.*, 666 N.E.2d 1376 [110 Educ. L. Rep. 1202] (Ohio 1996) (denying a blind student admission to a medical school on the basis that the accommodations that she sought were not reasonable).

were relied on in putting plans together, a description of the accommodations that school officials are willing to make, and information about how often and where the services are to be provided.

Reasonable accommodations may involve minor adjustments such as permitting a child to be accompanied by a service dog[18] or having a hearing interpreter.[19] Academic modifications might include allowing students more time to complete tests or assignments, having tutors, and/or permitting them to use computers to record answers on examinations. In modifying facilities, officials do not have to make every room and/or area of buildings accessible since it may be enough to bring services to children in areas of schools that have been adapted for their use.

Section 504 also prohibits discrimination by requiring educators to make individualized modifications for students who are "otherwise qualified." To this end, officials must offer benefits, and/or services that are comparable to those available to students who are not disabled. As such, children who are covered by Section 504 must receive comparable materials, teacher quality, length of school term, and daily hours of instruction. These programs should not be separate from those available to students who are not disabled unless segregation is essential for them to be effective. While school officials are not prohibited from offering separate programs for students with disabilities, children cannot be required to attend such classes if it is not possible to serve them adequately in such settings.[20] If programs are offered separately, facilities must be comparable.[21]

Even if children appear to be "otherwise qualified" under Section 504, school officials can rely on one of three defenses to avoid being charged with noncompliance. This represents another major difference between Section 504 and the IDEA since the latter does not recognize any defenses. First, officials can be excused from making accommodations that would result in "a fundamental alteration in the nature of [a] program."[22] The second defense allows officials to avoid making modifications that would impose "undue financial burden[s]"[23] on institutions. The third defense is that "otherwise qualified" students can be excluded from programs if their presence creates a substantial risk of injury to themselves or others.[24] For example, a child with a significant visual impairment could possibly be excluded from a biology laboratory class that involves the use of scalpels for fear of becoming injured. Even so, in order to comply with Section 504, officials would likely have to offer a reasonable accommodation such as providing a computer-assisted pro-

---

18. *Sullivan v. Vallejo City Unified School Dist.*, 731 F.Supp. 947 [59 Educ. L. Rep. 73] (E.D. Cal.1990).

19. *Jones v. Illinois Dep't of Rehab. Servs.*, 689 F.2d 724 [6 Educ. L. Rep. 927] (7th Cir.1982).

20. 34 C.F.R. § 104.4(b)(3).

21. 34 C.F.R. § 104.34(c).

22. *Southeastern Community College v. Davis*, 442 U.S. 397, 410, 99 S.Ct. 2361, 60

L.Ed.2d 980 (1979) [Case No.117]; *Alexander v. Choate*, 469 U.S. 287, 105 S.Ct. 712, 83 L.Ed.2d 661 (1985).

23. *Davis, id.* at 412.

24. *See School Bd. of Nassau County v. Arline*, 480 U.S. 273, 287–88, 107 S.Ct. 1123, 94 L.Ed.2d 307 [37 Educ. L. Rep. 448] (1987). [Case No. 65] gram to meet an instructional goal that is consistent with the one that would have been achieved in the laboratory.

In order to guarantee that an appropriate education is made available to all students, Section 504's regulations include due process requirements for evaluation that are similar to, but are not extensive as, those under the IDEA. Among these requirements, Section 504 directs school board officials to file assurances of compliance that their programs are nondiscriminatory,[25] take voluntary remedial actions if they have violated the law so as to overcome the effects of conditions that resulted in limiting the participation of individuals with disabilities,[26] complete self-evaluations to ensure that they comply with Section 504,[27] designate a staff member as compliance coordinator,[28] and adopt grievance procedures[29] even though neither the law nor an accompanying regulation specify what steps such a process should follow. Section 504 also requires all recipients of federal financial aid to provide notice to students, parents, employees, and others that they do not discriminate on the basis of disability.[30]

A party that is not satisfied with regard to a school system's delivery of services under Section 504[31] can file a complaint with the Office of Civil Rights, which is responsible for enforcing the law, within 180 days[32] of when an alleged infraction occurred. In another difference with the IDEA, nothing in Section 504's regulations require an aggrieved party to exhaust administrative remedies via a due process hearing before filing suit in federal court. In one such case, a federal trial court in New York rejected a school board's motion for summary judgment where there was evidence that officials acted with deliberate indifference to the pervasive, severe disability harassment that a child suffered at the hands of peers.[33]

Individuals with Disabilities Education Act

Generally

Initially enacted in 1975 as the Education for All Handicapped Children Act,[34] the IDEA was revised in 1986, 1990, 1997, and 2004; the 2004 version of the IDEA became fully effective on July 1, 2005.[35] As a condition of receiving federal funds,[36] the IDEA, and its regulations,[37]

25. 34 C.F.R. § 104.5.

26. 34 C.F.R. § 104.6(a)(b).

27. 34 C.F.R. § 104.6(c).

28. 34 C.F.R. § 104.7(a).

29. 34 C.F.R. § 104.7(b).

30. 34 C.F.R. § 104.8.

31. 7 C.F.R. § 2.300(a)(1)(vi).

32. 34 C.F.R. § 100.7(b).

33. *K.M. ex rel. D.G. v. Hyde Park Cent. School Dist.*, 381 F.Supp.2d 343 [201 Educ. L. Rep. 510] (S.D.N.Y. 2005).

34. The IDEA is still sometimes referred to as P.L. 94–142, indicating that it was the one hundred and forty-second piece

of legislation introduced during the Ninety–Fourth Congress. For the sake of consistency, this chapter refers to the IDEA, which incorporated the changes in the Individuals with Disabilities Education Improvement Act, even for cases that were resolved before its 1990 reauthorization and name change.

35. For the sake of consistency, this chapter refers to the most recent re-authorization of the IDEA as the 2004 version of the law.

36. *Fayette County Bd. of Educ. v. M.R.D. ex rel. K.D.*, 158 S.W.3d 195 [197 Educ. L. Rep. 413] (Ky. 2005).

37. As this book heads to press in the Spring of 2006, the final version of the affirmatively direct states, through local educational agencies or school boards, to identify, evaluate, and serve all children with disabilities,[38] including those in private schools,[39] regardless of the severity of their needs.

Insofar as the so-called child-find provisions are included as a related service in the IDEA's regulations, many school systems screen pre-school children[40] to assist in the early identification of students with disabilities.[41] Changes in the 2004 version of the IDEA now require not only that public school officials identify children who attend private schools in the districts where they attend classes, rather than within which they live, but also to provide child-find activities for these students that are comparable to those used in public schools. Public school officials must also report the number of children from private schools who are evaluated, identified as having disabilities, and served to state education agencies.[42]

Another noteworthy change associated with identifying children in need of special education services requires state officials to develop policies and procedures to prevent the over-identification or disproportionate representation of students by race and ethnicity.[43] This provision also directs educators to record the number of students from minority groups who are in special education classes and to provide early-intervention services for children in groups that are deemed to be over-represented.

In order to be covered by the IDEA, children must meet four requirements. First, students must be between the ages of three and twenty-one.[44] Second, children must have specifically identified disabili-

IDEA's regulations have yet to be promulgated. Insofar as there may be changes between the proposed and final versions of the regulations, readers should make certain that they have the most up to date information.

38. *See Carmel Cent. School Dist. v. V.P. ex rel. G.P.*, 373 F.Supp.2d 402 [199 Educ. L. Rep. 666] (S.D.N.Y. 2005) (declaring that only children classified as disabled are entitled to special education services from their public school boards under the IDEA).

39. Proposed regulation 34 C.F.R. § 300.129. This chapter refers to non-public schools as private because this is the term that the IDEA and its regulations apply.

40. 20 U.S.C.A. §§ 1412 (3)(A), 1412(a)(10)(a).

41. *See, e.g., Independent School Dist. No. 709 v. Bonney*, 705 N.W.2d 209 [202 Educ. L. Rep. 828] (Minn. Ct. App. 2005) (affirming that school board officials violat-

ed the IDEA and state law in not providing services for pre-school children with disabilities).

42. 20 U.S.C.A. § 1412(a)(10)(A)(ii).

43. 20 U.S.C.A. §§ 1412 (a)(24), 1418 (d)(1)(A)(B).

44. 20 U.S.C.A. § 1412(a)(1)(A). The IDEA also addresses the needs of a children aged 3 through 9 who are "(i) experiencing developmental delays, as defined by the State and as measured by appropriate diagnostic instruments and procedures, in 1 or more of the following areas: physical development; cognitive development; communication development; social or emotional development; or adaptive development." 20 U.S.C.A. § 1401(3)(B)(i). See *Pardini v. Allegheny Intermediate Unit*, 420 F.3d 181 [201 Educ. L. Rep. 44] (3d Cir. 2005) (applying the stay-put provision to a three-year old child who was covered by an individual family service plan as it transitioned to an IEP).

ties.[45] Third, students must be in need of special education,[46] meaning that they need a free appropriate public education[47] in the least restrictive environments that are directed by the contents of their Individualized Education Programs (IEPs).[48] Fourth, children must be in need of related services.[49]

The IDEA includes extensive due process protections to safeguard the rights of children[50] and their parents.[51] Among these protections, parents must be informed before consenting to any referrals, evaluations, and/or placements of their children[52] and have the right to take part in developing IEPs that direct the education of their children.[53] In such a case, the Fourth Circuit held that parents in South Carolina who chose not to participate in its formulation could not render school officials liable for not having an IEP completed and signed since their failure to do so was caused by their own lack of cooperation.[54] In an important addition in this regard, the IDEA now stipulates that state and local officials are not required to develop IEPs for students if their parents either refuse to consent to the receipt of special education services or fail to respond to requests to provide their consent.[55] This section of the IDEA also establishes that if parents do not consent to initial evaluations or fail to respond to requests to provide consent, local school officials can still pursue initial evaluations by utilizing the procedures described in the IDEA's due process provisions, unless doing so would be inconsistent with state law relating to parental consent.[56]

Once students are placed in special education settings, school officials must notify parents before trying to change their placements.[57] Parents may be entitled to independent evaluations at public expense if they disagree with board evaluations[58] or if school officials fail to evaluate children in timely manners.[59] If parents successfully challenge the assessments of their children, they can be reimbursed for the costs of

45. 20 U.S.C.A. § 1401(3)(A)(i). This section reads that:

The term "child with a disability" means a child—

(i) with mental retardation, hearing impairments (including deafness), speech or language impairments, visual impairments (including blindness), serious emotional disturbance (referred to in this chapter as "emotional disturbance"), orthopedic impairments, autism, traumatic brain injury, other health impairments, or specific learning disabilities....

46. 20 U.S.C.A. § 1401(3)(A)(ii).

47. 20 U.S.C.A. § 1401(9).

48. 20 U.S.C.A. §§ 1401(11), 1414(d).

49. 20 U.S.C.A. § 1401(3)(A)(ii).

50. 20 U.S.C.A. § 1415.

51. The IDEA's expanded definition of parent covers a natural, adoptive, or foster parent, a guardian, and an individual acting in the place of a natural or adoptive parent (including a grandparent, stepparent, or other relative) with whom a child lives, or an individual who is legally responsible for a child's welfare. 20 U.S.C.A. § 1401(23).

52. 20 U.S.C.A. § 1414(a)(1)(D)(I). *Gill v. Columbia 93 School Dist.*, 217 F.3d 1027 [145 Educ. L. Rep. 894] (8th Cir.2000), *reh'g and reh'g en banc denied*.

53. 20 U.S.C.A. §§ 1414(d)(1)(B)(i).

54. *MM ex rel. DM v. School Dist. of Greenville County*, 303 F.3d 523 [169 Educ. L. Rep. 59] (4th Cir.2002).

55. 20 U.S.C.A. § 1414(a)(1)(D)(ii) (II)(III).

56. 20 U.S.C.A. § 1414(a)(1)(D)(ii)(I).

57. 20 U.S.C.A. § 1415(b)(3)(A).

58. 20 U.S.C.A. § 1415(b)(1).

59. *Idea Public Charter School v. District of Columbia*, 374 F.Supp.2d 158 [199 Educ. L. Rep. 754] (D.D.C. 2005). *But see Herbin ex rel. Herbin v. District of Columbia*, 362 F.Supp.2d 254 [197 Educ. L. Rep. 142] (D.D.C. 2005) (rejecting a claim that a four-month delay in evaluating a child was a violation of the IDEA where current evaluations existed and educators were unable to determine why the request was necessary).

doing so.[60] Conversely, if a board's evaluation was appropriate, parents are not entitled to further testing at public expense.[61]

The IDEA also includes directives,[62] supplemented by the Family Education Rights and Privacy Act (FERPA)[63] and its regulations,[64] that protect the confidentiality of all information used in the evaluation, placement, and education of students with disabilities.[65] While FERPA is examined in some detail in Chapter 12, it is worth noting that the IDEA has made an important clarification concerning the transfer of parental rights to students who have achieved the age of majority. Pursuant to this part of the law, when children with disabilities who are not adjudicated incompetent under state law achieve the age of majority, school officials must notify them and their parents that the parental rights of access have been transferred to their children.[66] However, there is a special rule for students who are not adjudicated incompetent but do not have the ability to provide informed consent with respect to their educational programming. In such a situation, school officials must establish procedures for appointing their parents, or if they are not available, another appropriate person, to represent students' educational interests throughout their remaining period of eligibility under the IDEA.[67]

Individualized Education Programs

IEPs must provide students with disabilities with more than trivial advancement.[68] In addition, IEPs must be developed by teams that are identified by various names depending on state law. IEPs must describe students' current levels of educational performance, annual goals and short-term objectives, the specific services that they will receive, the extent to which they can take part in general education, the date services are to begin and how long they will be offered, and criteria to evaluate whether they are achieving their goals.[69] In addition, IEPs must discuss how students' disabilities affect their ability to be involved in and progress in inclusive settings and necessary modifications to allow them to take part in the general curriculum. IEPs must also detail any related services that students need to benefit from their IEPs.[70] A new provision in the 2004 version of the IDEA specifies that IEP teams are no longer required to develop benchmarks and short-term objectives for children

60. *A.S. ex rel. S. v. Norwalk Bd. of Educ.*, 183 F.Supp.2d 534 [161 Educ. L. Rep. 827] (D. Conn.2002).

61. *R.L. ex rel. Mr. L. v. Plainville Bd. of Educ.*, 363 F.Supp.2d 222 [197 Educ. L. Rep. 181] (D. Conn. 2005); *Vasheresse v. Laguna Salada Union School Dist.*, 211 F.Supp.2d 1150 [168 Educ. L. Rep. 228] (N.D.Cal.2001).

62. 20 U.S.C.A. § 1417(c).

63. 29 U.S.C.A. § 1232g.

64. Proposed regulation 34 C.F.R. §§ 300.610 *et seq.*

65. 20 U.S.C.A. § 1417(c).

66. 20 U.S.C.A. § 1415(m)(1).

67. 20 U.S.C.A. § 1415(m)(2).

68. *D.F. ex rel. N.F. v. Ramapo Cent. School Dist.*, 430 F.3d 595 [203 Educ. L. Rep. 500] (2d Cir. 2005).

69. 20 U.S.C.A. § 1414(d)(1)(A). *See also, e.g., Mackey v. Board of Educ. for Arlington Cent. School Dist.*, 373 F.Supp.2d 292 [199 Educ. L. Rep. 655] (S.D.N.Y. 2005) (reiterating the IDEA's general provisions concerning IEPs).

70. 20 U.S.C.A. § 1414(d)(1)(A)(i)(IV).

with disabilities other than for those who take alternate assessments aligned to alternate achievement standards.[71]

Once assessments are completed, and children are identified as being in need of IEPs, school officials must convene IEP meetings within thirty calendar days.[72] Once an IEP is developed, officials must implement it "[a]s soon as possible."[73] IEP team must include a child's parents; at least one of a student's regular education teachers if the child is, or will be participating, in regular education; at least one special education teacher or, if appropriate, one of the child's special education providers; a representative of the school system who is qualified to provide, or supervise, the delivery of special education, knowledgeable about general education, the school system's resources, and evaluation procedures; an individual who can interpret the instructional implications of evaluation results; other individuals, at the discretion of parents or school officials, who are knowledgeable or have special expertise concerning the student; and, when appropriate, the child.[74] If a student attends a private school, then a representative of the school should be present at IEP conferences.[75]

Prior to the enactment of the 2004 version of the IDEA, federal appellate courts reached mixed results over whether regular education teachers should attend IEP meetings. On the one hand, the Ninth Circuit found that a school board in Washington's failure to include a regular education teacher on a child's IEP team would have been a significant violation of the IDEA since he was going to spend time in a regular education setting.[76] On the other hand, the Fourth Circuit[77] did not think it necessary for a school board in North Carolina to have a regular education teacher at an IEP meeting since the child was not being considered for a placement in regular education.[78]

IEPs must be reviewed at least annually[79] and re-evaluated at least once every three years unless parents and local school officials agree that re-evaluations are unnecessary.[80] The 2004 IDEA includes three significant changes with regard to IEPs. First, the IDEA no longer specifies the need for benchmarks and short-term objectives for children with disabili-

---

71. 20 U.S.C.A. § 1414(d)(1)(A)(I).

72. Proposed regulation 34 C.F.R. § 300.323(c)(1).

73. Proposed regulation 34 C.F.R. § 300.323(c)(2).

74. Proposed regulation 34 C.F.R. § 300.321(a).

75. Proposed regulation 34 C.F.R. § 300.325(a)(2).

76. *M.L. v. Federal Way School Dist.*, 394 F.3d 634 [194 Educ. L. Rep. 811] (9th Cir. 2005), *cert. denied*, ___ U.S. ___, 125 S.Ct. 2941, 162 L.Ed.2d 867 (2005). *See also Werner v. Clarksville Cent. School Dist.*, 363 F.Supp.2d 656 [197 Educ. L. Rep. 244] (S.D.N.Y. 2005) (positing that a board failed to comply with the IDEA's procedural requirements by not including a representa-

tive from its recommended therapeutic placement at a child's IEP meeting).

77. *Cone v. Randolph County Schools*, 103 Fed.Appx. 731 (4th Cir. 2004), *cert. denied*, 543 U.S. 1124, 125 S.Ct. 1077, 160 L.Ed.2d 1075 (2005).

78. For a similar result, see *Johnson ex rel. Johnson v. Olathe District Schools Unified School Dist. No. 233, Special Servs. Div.*, 316 F.Supp.2d 960 [188 Educ. L. Rep 307] (D. Kan. 2003) (stating that a board did not violate the IDEA by failing to include a regular education teacher on a child's IEP team since he was not going to spend any time in a regular educational class).

79. 20 U.S.C.A. § 1414(d)(4).

80. 20 U.S.C.A. § 1414(a)(2)(B)(ii).

ties other than those who take alternate assessments aligned to alternate achievement standards.[81] Second, the IDEA allows up to fifteen states to pilot comprehensive multi-year IEPs that do not exceed three years and which are designed to coincide with natural transition points in a child's education.[82] The third change permits minor changes to IEPs to be made by means of conference calls or letters.[83] Moreover, as children near graduation or begin to "age out" of special education, school officials must develop individualized transition services plans to promote their movement to post-school activities.[84]

Two related changes accompany the proposed three-year IEP provision. The first seeks to reduce the significant amount of paperwork associated with the delivery of special education services[85] by permitting up to fifteen states to pilot paperwork-reduction plans to reduce the burden on teachers, administrators, and related service providers.[86] The second compliments the paperwork reduction provisions by directing the Secretary of Education to develop model forms for IEPs, individualized family service plans, the IDEA's procedural safeguards, and its prior written notice provisions no later than when the IDEA's final regulations are promulgated.[87]

Free Appropriate Public Education

Under the IDEA, children are entitled to instruction, at no cost to their parents, that is specially designed to meet their unique needs.[88] If parents have insurance, they can be asked to put in claims to help defray costs.[89] Yet, this does not mean that school officials can refuse to provide services if parents are unwilling, or unable, to bill their insurance carriers.

Inasmuch as neither the IDEA nor its regulations include a definition of "appropriate," it was necessary to seek judicial intervention for an understanding of this term. In *Board of Education of the Hendrick Hudson Central School District v. Rowley (Rowley)*,[90] its first case involving the IDEA, the Supreme Court interpreted "appropriate" as providing a floor of opportunities rather than as a vehicle to maximize a child's potential.

In *Rowley*, parents of a kindergarten student in New York who was hearing impaired challenged their school board's refusal to provide their daughter with a sign-language interpreter. After a hearing officer and lower federal courts agreed that officials had to provide the child with an

---

81. 20 U.S.C.A. § 1414(d)(1)(A)(I).

82. 20 U.S.C.A. § 1414(d)(5)(A).

83. 20 U.S.C.A. § 1414(f).

84. 20 U.S.C.A. § 1414(d)(1)(A)(vii)(II); 20 U.S.C.A. § 1401(30). *Browell v. Lemahieu*, 127 F.Supp.2d 1117 [150 Educ. L. Rep. 732] (D. Hawai'i 2000).

85. 20 U.S.C.A. § 1408(2)(A).

86. 20 U.S.C.A. § 1414(d)(5)(B)(i).

87. 20 U.S.C.A. § 1417(e).

88. 20 U.S.C.A. § 1401(29).

89. Proposed regulation 34 C.F.R. § 300.154(f).

90. 458 U.S. 176, 102 S.Ct. 3034, 73 L.Ed.2d 690 [5 Educ. L. Rep. 34] (1982) [Case No. 118]. *See also Todd v. Duneland School Corp.*, 299 F.3d 899 [168 Educ. L. Rep. 67] (7th Cir.2002).

interpreter on the basis that an appropriate education was one that would have allowed her to achieve at about the same level as her peers who were not disabled, the Court reversed in favor of the board.

The Supreme Court, acknowledging that the child earned passing marks and advanced academically without the sign-language interpreter, reasoned that an "appropriate" education was one that met the IDEA's procedures and was "sufficient to confer some educational benefit"[91] on her by providing "a basic floor of opportunity."[92] In being convinced that the child received "some educational benefit" without the sign-language interpreter, the Court concluded that she was not entitled to one even though she might have achieved at a higher level had officials provided her with such assistance.

Rowley's interpreting the IDEA as having set a minimum level of appropriateness does not prevent states from setting higher standards. To date, courts have upheld higher state requirements in California,[93] Michigan,[94] Missouri,[95] New Jersey,[96] and North Carolina.[97] Some of these courts recognized that the higher state standards replaced the federal requirements since the IDEA expects special education programs to meet "the standards of the state educational agency."[98] Conversely, at least one state, West Virginia, specifies that "no state rule, policy or standard under this article or any county board rule, policy or standard governing special education may exceed the requirements of federal law or regulation."[99]

Courts have interpreted *Rowley's* "some educational benefit" criterion as requiring more than minimal growth,[100] adding that it must be meaningful[101] or appreciable.[102] In this regard, the Eleventh Circuit maintained that in order to meet the *Rowley* criteria, student gains must

91. *Rowley, id* at 200.

92. *Fayette County Bd. of Educ. v. M.R.D. ex rel. K.D.*, 158 S.W.3d 195, 202 [197 Educ. L. Rep. 413] (Ky. 2005) (denying a parental request for reimbursement for a unilateral private school placement), citing to *Rowley, id.*

93. *Pink v. Mt. Diablo Unified School Dist.*, 738 F.Supp. 345 [61 Educ. L. Rep. 120] (N.D.Cal. 1990).

94. *Nelson v. Southfield Pub. Schools*, 384 N.W.2d 423 [31 Educ. L. Rep. 567] (Mich.Ct.App. 1986); *Barwacz v. Michigan Dep't of Educ.*, 681 F.Supp. 427 [46 Educ. L. Rep. 98] (W.D.Mich. 1988).

95. *Lagares v. Camdenton R–III School Dist.*, 68 S.W.3d 518 [162 Educ. L. Rep. 1003] (Mo. Ct.App.2001).

96. *Geis v. Board of Educ. of Parsippany–Troy Hills*, 774 F.2d 575 [27 Educ. L. Rep. 1093] (3d Cir.1985).

97. *Burke County Bd. of Educ. v. Denton*, 895 F.2d 973 [58 Educ. L. Rep. 918] (4th Cir.1990); *CM ex rel. JM v. Board of Educ. of Henderson County*, 85 F.Supp.2d

574 [142 Educ. L. Rep. 299] (W.D.N.C. 1999), *aff'd in part, rev'd and rem'd in part*, 241 F.3d 374 [151 Educ. L. Rep. 157] (4th Cir.2001), *on remand*, 184 F.Supp.2d 466 [162 Educ. L. Rep. 126] (W.D.N.C.2002).

98. 20 U.S.C.A. § 1401(a)(9)(B).

99. W. VA. CODE ANN. § 18–20–5(3).

100. *Hall v. Vance County Bd. of Educ.*, 774 F.2d 629 [27 Educ. L. Rep. 1107] (4th Cir.1985); *Carter v. Florence County School Dist. Four*, 950 F.2d 156 [71 Educ. L. Rep. 633] (4th Cir. 1991), *aff'd on other grounds*, 510 U.S. 7, 114 S.Ct. 361, 126 L.Ed.2d 284 [86 Educ. L. Rep. 41] (1993); *County School Bd. of Henrico County, Va. v. Z.P. ex rel. R.P.*, 399 F.3d 298 [195 Educ L. Rep. 715] (4th Cir. 2005).

101. *Samuel Tyler W. ex rel. Harvey W. v. Northwest Indep. School Dist.*, 202 F.Supp.2d 557 [165 Educ. L. Rep. 572] (N.D. Tex. 2002).

102. *Chris C. v. Gwinnett County School Dist.*, 780 F.Supp. 804 [72 Educ. L. Rep. 146] (N.D. Ga.1991).

be measurable.[103] Regardless of which criteria apply, under the IDEA's so-called "zero-reject" approach, reflected most notably by a seminal case from the First Circuit,[104] all eligible children must be served regardless of the severity of their disabilities.

Requiring school board officials to provide children with disabilities with a "public education" is closely aligned with the fact that it must be free. That is, the IDEA contemplated that "free" means at public expense, even if children are not educated in public schools. This notion is reflected in the ensuing discussions of the continuum of placements and on the rights of students who attend private schools.

Least Restrictive Environment

Students with disabilities must be educated in the least restrictive environment.[105] In carrying out this requirement for children with disabilities, school board officials must provide a continuum of alternative placements from least to most restrictive.[106] The first four options, which are typically in a child's home school, are full inclusion in a regular class, inclusion in a regular class with help such as a teacher's aide,[107] partial inclusion with an aide with some time spent in a resource room, and a self-contained placement in a resource room.[108] The final, more restrictive, options are special day schools, hospital or homebound instruction, or residential placements.[109] In an addition that may ultimately affect where children can be educated, the IDEA now forbids school officials from requiring parents to obtain prescriptions for their children for substances such as Ritalin that are covered by the Controlled Substances Act as a condition of attending school, being evaluated, or receiving special education services.[110]

Two federal appellate courts agreed that educators must review a variety of factors when considering the restrictiveness of the environment within which children are to be educated. In a case from New Jersey, the Third Circuit announced a two-part test for assessing compli-

103. *JSK v. Hendry County School Bd.*, 941 F.2d 1563 [69 Educ. L. Rep. 689] (11th Cir.1991).

104. The seminal case on "zero-reject" is *Timothy W. v. Rochester, N.H., School Dist.*, 875 F.2d 954 [54 Educ. L. Rep.74] (1st Cir.1989), *cert. denied*, 493 U.S. 983, 110 S.Ct. 519, 107 L.Ed.2d 520 (1989). [Case No. 119]

105. 20 U.S.C.A. §§ 1406(b)(2), 1412(a)(5).

106. Proposed regulation 34 C.F.R. § 300.115(a).

107. *A.B. ex rel. D.B. v. Lawson*, 354 F.3d 315 [184 Educ. L. Rep. 37] (4th Cir. 2004).

108. *Lt. T.B. ex rel. N.B. v. Warwick School Comm.*, 361 F.3d 80 [186 Educ. L. Rep. 15] (1st Cir. 2004).

109. Proposed regulation 34 C.F.R. § 300.115(b)(1).

110. 20 U.S.C.A. § 1412(a)(25). For some of the earlier litigation over Ritalin, see, *e.g.*, *De Bord v. Board of Educ. of the Ferguson–Florissant School Dist.*, 126 F.3d 1102 (8th Cir. 1997) and *Davis v. Francis Howell School Dist.*, 138 F.3d 754 [124 Educ. L.Rep. 840] (8th Cir. 1998) (agreeing that school officials did not violate Section 504 or the IDEA in refusing to administer Ritalin to students who were unruly). *See also Valerie J. v. Derry Co-op. School Dist.*, 771 F.Supp. 483 [69 Educ. L. Rep. 1067] (D.N.H. 1991) (indicating that school officials could not require the student to take Ritalin to control his behavior since they failed to comply with a hearing officer's order that it be administered based on a physician's prescription and with parental consent).

ance with the IDEA's least restrictive environment mandate.[111] The first element considers whether education in regular classrooms, with the use of supplementary aids and services, can be achieved satisfactorily. Under the second part of the test, if placements outside of regular classrooms are necessary, educators must consider whether children are mainstreamed, now referred to as full inclusion, as much as possible.[112]

In a dispute from California, the Ninth Circuit expanded the existing criteria, stipulating that IEP teams had to take four factors into account in placing students: the educational benefits of placing children in regular classrooms; the nonacademic benefits of such placements; the effect that the presence of students with disabilities would have on teachers and other children in classes; and the costs of inclusionary placements.[113] In a case dealing with cost, the federal trial court in Utah pointed out that if school officials are considering two different programs, either one of which offers an appropriate education, they can take expense into account when making placement decisions.[114]

The IDEA's goal of full inclusion notwithstanding, not all students with disabilities must be placed in regular education classes.[115] Courts have approved more restrictive placements where students could not function in regular classes, even with supplementary aids and services[116] or inclusion did not succeed.[117]

Private School and Residential Placements

Officials may have to place children in private schools if boards lack appropriate options[118] such as when students have low incidence disabilities and there are not enough other pupils with the same needs in systems to warrant the development of programs.[119] At the same time, courts may order residential placements for students with severe, profound, or multiple disabilities if they need twenty-four hour programming or consistency between school and home.[120] Residential placements

---

111. *Oberti v. Board of Educ. of the Borough of Clementon School Dist.*, 995 F.2d 1204 [83 Educ. L. Rep. 1009] (3d Cir. 1993).

112. This test first appeared in *Daniel R.R. v. State Bd. of Educ.*, 874 F.2d 1036 [53 Educ. L. Rep. 824] (5th Cir.1989). *See also Greer v. Rome City School Dist.*, 967 F.2d 470 [76 Educ. L. Rep. 26] (11th Cir. 1992).

113. *Sacramento City Unified School Dist. Bd. of Educ. v. Rachel H.*, 14 F.3d 1398 [89 Educ. L. Rep. 57] (9th Cir.1994).

114. *L.B. and J.B. v. Nebo School Dist.*, 214 F.Supp.2d 1172 [168 Educ. L. Rep. 771] (D.Utah 2002).

115. *Beth B. v. Van Clay*, 282 F.3d 493 [162 Educ. L. Rep. 47] (7th Cir.2002).

116. *Clyde K. v. Puyallup School Dist. No. 3*, 35 F.3d 1396 [94 Educ. L. Rep. 707] (9th Cir. 1994); *Capistrano Unified School*

Dist. v. Wartenberg, 59 F.3d 884 [101 Educ. L. Rep. 640] (9th Cir.1995).

117. *Beth B. v. Van Clay*, 282 F.3d 493 [162 Educ. L. Rep. 47] (7th Cir.2002); *School Dist. of Wisconsin Dells v. Z.S. ex rel. Littlegeorge*, 295 F.3d 671 [167 Educ. L. Rep. 40] (7th Cir.2002).

118. 20 U.S.C.A. § 1412(a)(10)(B). *See, e.g., Reid ex rel. Reid v. District of Columbia*, 401 F.3d 516 [196 Educ. L. Rep. 402] (D.C. Cir. 2005); *Casey K. ex rel. Norman K. v. St. Anne Community High School Dist. No. 302*, 400 F.3d 508 [196 Educ. L. Rep. 38] (7th Cir. 2005), *cert. denied*, ___ U.S. ___, 126 S.Ct. 354, 163 L.Ed.2d 63 [202 Educ. L. Rep. 29] (2005).

119. *See, e.g., Colin K. v. Schmidt*, 715 F.2d 1 [13 Educ. L. Rep. 221] (1st Cir.1983).

120. *Gladys J. v. Pearland Indep. School Dist.*, 520 F.Supp. 869 (S.D.Tex. 1981).

may also be made if children have significant behavioral disorders[121] or need total immersion in educational environments in order to progress.[122] In such a case, the Fourth Circuit affirmed that a private day school in Virginia with small classes that offered a great deal of individual attention, structure and clinical support, and an experienced staff was an appropriate placement for a child with psychiatric needs.[123] However, a school board is not required to provide a residential placement so that children can reach their full potential.[124]

If children need residential placements for solely educational reasons, school boards must pay for the entire cost.[125] If placements are made because students have, for example, medical[126] or psychological[127] needs, then school systems may only be required to pay for the educational costs of residential placements.[128] The issue of who must pay when parents unilaterally place their children in private schools is discussed below under the heading "Tuition Reimbursement."

Students in Religiously Affiliated Private Schools

As reflected in Chapter 2, there has been a great deal of litigation over the boundaries of state aid to students who attend religiously affiliated private schools. As with so many other areas, the delivery of special education services is no exception.

In *Zobrest v. Catalina Foothills School District,*[129] the Supreme Court was of the opinion that the Establishment Clause did not prevent a school board in Arizona from providing the on-site delivery of the services of a sign-language interpreter for a student who attended a Roman Catholic high school. The Court noted that since the interpreter was essentially a conduit through whom information passed, the on-site delivery of this service was constitutionally acceptable. Four years later, in *Agostini v. Felton,*[130] the Court largely eliminated barriers against the

121. *Chris D. v. Montgomery County Bd. of Educ.,* 743 F.Supp. 1524 [62 Educ. L. Rep. 1001] (M.D. Ala.1990).

122. *Abrahamson v. Hershman,* 701 F.2d 223 [9 Educ. L. Rep. 837] (1st Cir. 1983).

123. *Jennings v. Fairfax County School Bd.,* 39 Fed.Appx. 921 [167 Educ. L. Rep. 688] (4th Cir.2002). *But see Reese v. Board of Educ. of Bismark R–V School Dist.,* 225 F.Supp.2d 1149 [171 Educ. L. Rep. 231] (E.D.Mo.2002).

124. *Johnson ex rel. Johnson v. Olathe Dist. Schools Unified School Dist. No. 233, Special Services Div.,* 316 F.Supp.2d 960 [188 Educ. L. Rep. 307] (D. Kan. 2003).

125. Proposed regulation 34 C.F.R. § 300.104. *Abrahamson v. Hershman,* 701 F.2d 223 [9 Educ. L. Rep. 837] (1st Cir. 1983); *Mrs. B. v. Milford Bd. of Educ.,* 103 F.3d 1114 [115 Educ. L. Rep. 324] (2d Cir. 1997); *Knable ex rel. Knable v. Bexley City School Dist.,* 238 F.3d 755 [150 Educ. L. Rep. 628] (6th Cir.2001), *cert. denied,* 533

U.S. 950, 121 S.Ct. 2593, 150 L.Ed.2d 752 (2001).

126. *Clovis Unified School Dist. v. California Office of Admin. Hearings,* 903 F.2d 635 [60 Educ. L. Rep. 728] (9th Cir.1990).

127. *Gladstone School Dist. v. AM,* 105 F.3d 664 (9th Cir.1996).

128. *But see Lamoine School Comm. v. Ms. Z. ex rel. N.S.,* 353 F.Supp.2d 18 [195 Educ. L. Rep. 511] (D. Me. 2005) (remarking that a school committee could not avoid its responsibility for the costs of a residential placement simply because it addressed a student's physical, emotional, psychological, or behavioral difficulties rather than/or in addition to his educational problems because these problems were intertwined).

129. 509 U.S. 1, 113 S.Ct. 2462, 125 L.Ed.2d 1 [83 Educ. L. Rep. 930] (1993).

130. 521 U.S. 203, 117 S.Ct. 1997, 138 L.Ed.2d 391 [119 Educ. L. Rep. 29] (1997). [Case No. 11]

on-site delivery of services to students who attended religiously affiliated private schools as long as appropriate safeguards were in place. While the 1997 modifications of the IDEA adopted a similar perspective, its regulations placed restrictions on the amount of services that children can receive in their religiously affiliated private schools.

Students whose parents voluntarily enroll them in private schools are entitled to some level of special education services. This means that school board officials must budget only a proportionate share of their federal IDEA funds on children whose parents placed them in private schools.[131] The IDEA gives public school officials, in consultation with representatives from private schools, the authority to select which students from private schools will be served, what services they will receive, and how they will be delivered.[132]

State and local educational agencies can now supplement federal funds in providing special education services to children whose parents have placed them in private schools while public agencies can offer services to these students either directly or by contract with other agencies or organizations as long as local school boards maintain control of all funds and ownership of any equipment or materials purchased with public funds.[133] Of course, public school personnel can continue to conduct diagnostic tests on-site in private schools to evaluate whether children are eligible for services in programs that are supported by public funds.[134]

The IDEA permits, but does not require,[135] public school officials to provide the on-site delivery of special education services for students with disabilities whose parents have placed them in "private, including religious, schools, to the extent consistent with the law,"[136] as long as appropriate safeguards are in place to avoid excessive entanglement with religious institutions. If services are not offered on-site and students must be transported to locations to receive them, boards must provide transportation.[137] Under this provision, the cost of transportation may be included in calculating the minimum amount of federal funds that school boards must spend on students in private schools. School boards need not transport children between their homes and religious schools since they must only do so between sites during the school day.

131. 20 U.S.C.A. § 1412(a)(10)(A)(i).

132. 20 U.S.C.A. § 1412(a)(10)(A)(iii).

133. 20 U.S.C. § 612(a)(10)(A)(I). This represents the rule that federal funds can supplement, not supplant, local funds. *See State of Washington v. United States Dep't of Educ.*, 905 F.2d 274 [60 Educ. L. Rep. 1118] (9th Cir. 1990).

134. *See Meek v. Pittenger*, 421 U.S. 349, 95 S.Ct. 1753, 44 L.Ed.2d 217 (1975); *Wolman v. Walter*, 433 U.S. 229, 97 S.Ct. 2593, 53 L.Ed.2d 714 (1977).

135. *K.R. by M.R. v. Anderson Community School Corp.*, 125 F.3d 1017 [121 Educ.

L. Rep. 490] (7th Cir.1997), *cert. denied*, 523 U.S. 1046, 118 S.Ct. 1360, 140 L.Ed.2d 510 (1998); *Cefalu on Behalf of Cefalu v. East Baton Rouge Parish School Bd.*, 117 F.3d 231 [119 Educ. L. Rep. 338] (5th Cir. 1997); *Russman v. Board of Educ. of City of Watervliet*, 150 F.3d 219 [128 Educ. L. Rep. 576] (2d Cir.1998), *on remand*, 92 F.Supp.2d 95 [143 Educ. L. Rep. 784] (N.D. N.Y.2000), *vacated*, 260 F.3d 114 [156 Educ. L. Rep. 70] (2d Cir.2001).

136. 20 U.S.C.A. § 1412(a)(10)(A)(i)(III).

137. Proposed regulation 34 C.F.R. § 300.139(b).

Students in private schools are entitled to receive services from personnel who meet the same standards as educators in public schools[138] even though they may receive a different amount from their peers in public schools.[139] In fact, since children in private schools have no right to the same amount of aid as if they were enrolled in public schools, they are not entitled to IEPs. Instead of IEPs, officials must develop services plans that describe the aid that they will offer to children in private schools.[140] Services plans must not only meet IEP content requirements but must also be developed, reviewed, and revised in a manner consistent with the IEP process.[141] Moreover, the IDEA's procedural safeguards do not apply to complaints that school boards failed to deliver services to students in private schools.[142]

The IDEA limits the amount of money that school boards must spend to deliver services to students in private schools. The total is restricted to a proportionate amount of the federal funds that boards receive based on the number of students in private schools in relation to the overall number of children in a district.[143] Boards are not prohibited from using state or local funds to offer more than the IDEA requires since the regulation only sets a minimum amount that they must spend on children who attend religiously affiliated private schools. As identified earlier, a change in the IDEA's child-find provision now requires school board officials both to identify children who attend private schools in the districts where they attend classes rather than within which they live and to employ child-find activities for students in private schools that are comparable to those used for their peers in the public schools.[144]

Officials cannot use IDEA funds to help finance existing instructional programs in the private schools that students with disabilities attend.[145] Further, the regulations do allow boards to employ public school personnel in private schools as long as they are not supplanting services that are normally provided by those institutions.[146] Additionally, equipment purchased with IDEA funds can only be used on-site in private schools for the benefit of students with disabilities.[147] The net result is that while children in religious schools are entitled to receive some special education services, funding restrictions limit the amount of services that they can receive.

Extended School Year Programs

Children with disabilities who need educational programming that extends beyond regular school years are entitled to placements at public

138. Proposed regulation 34 C.F.R. § 300.138(a)(1).

139. Proposed regulation 34 C.F.R. § 300.138(a)(2).

140. Proposed regulation 34 C.F.R. § 300.138(b).

141. Proposed regulation 34 C.F.R. § 300.138(b)(2)(ii).

142. Proposed regulation 34 C.F.R. § 300.140(a). *Gary S. v. Manchester School Dist.*, 374 F.3d 15 [189 Educ. L. Rep. 494] (1st Cir. 2004), *cert. denied*, 543 U.S. 988, 125 S.Ct. 505, 160 L.Ed.2d 373 (2004).

143. 20 U.S.C.A. § 1412(a)(10)(A)(i)(I). *Fowler v. Unified School Dist.*, 128 F.3d 1431 [122 Educ. L. Rep. 391] (10th Cir. 1997).

144. 20 U.S.C.A. § 1412(a)(10)(A)(ii).

145. Proposed regulation 34 C.F.R. § 300.141(a).

146. Proposed regulation 34 C.F.R. § 300.142.

147. Proposed regulation 34 C.F.R. § 300.144.

expense.[148] The Fifth[149] and Tenth[150] Circuits interpreted the IDEA as meaning that children are entitled to extended year programs when they regress and the time it takes to regain, often addressed as regression-recoupment, lost skills interferes with their overall progress toward attaining IEP goals and objectives. On the other hand, the Fourth[151] and Seventh[152] Circuits recognized that if regression is minimal, extended school year programs are not required.[153] The Fifth Circuit later decided that a student was not entitled to extended year services in his residential placement.[154] The court was of the view that the child's parents were unable to establish the need for what they sought where school officials developed an appropriate IEP for him in an inclusive setting that offered educational support and assistive-technology adaptations.

Minimum-Competency Tests

Minimum-competency tests may be used either as graduation requirements to assure that students receiving diplomas have acquired specified knowledge bases or to identify children who have not achieved competency in basic skills and may require remedial instruction. Insofar as the IDEA requires students with disabilities to participate in some form of state assessments,[155] the accountability provisions of the No Child Left Behind Act, which requires local school systems to make adequate yearly progress,[156] may have a major impact on the delivery of special education services.

States may require students with disabilities to pass competency tests before earning high school diplomas as long as these examinations satisfy three guidelines. First, tests must be valid, reliable measures of what students have been taught.[157] Second, since educators must afford students with disabilities and their parents sufficient notice that they

---

148. Proposed regulation 34 C.F.R. § 300.106.

149. *Alamo Heights Indep. School Dist. v. State Bd. of Educ.*, 790 F.2d 1153 [32 Educ. L. Rep. 445] (5th Cir.1986). *See also J.W. v. Contoocook Valley School Dist.*, 154 F.Supp.2d 217 [156 Educ. L. Rep. 224] (D.N.H. 2001).

150. *Johnson By and Through Johnson v. Independent School Dist. No. 4 of Bixby, Tulsa County, Okla.*, 921 F.2d 1022 [64 Educ. L. Rep. 1027] (10th Cir.1990), *cert. denied*, 500 U.S. 905, 111 S.Ct. 1685, 114 L.Ed.2d 79 (1991).

151. *MM ex rel. DM v. School Dist. of Greenville County*, 303 F.3d 523 [169 Educ. L. Rep. 59] (4th Cir.2002).

152. *Anderson v. Thompson*, 658 F.2d 1205 (7th Cir.1981); *Todd v. Duneland School Corp.*, 299 F.3d 899 [168 Educ. L. Rep. 67] (7th Cir.2002).

153. *See also Moser v. Bret Harte Union High School Dist.*, 366 F.Supp.2d 944 [198 Educ. L. Rep. 171] (E.D. Cal. 2005) (asserting that under federal law, regression-recoupment is not the standard for the availability of extended year services).

154. *Kenton County School Dist. v. Hunt*, 384 F.3d 269 [192 Educ. L. Rep. 55] (6th Cir. 2004).

155. 20 U.S.C.A. § 1412(a)(16).

156. 20 U.S.C.A. §§ 6301, 6311, 6312, 6316.

157. *Debra P. v. Turlington*, 730 F.2d 1405 [16 Educ. L. Rep. 1120] (11th Cir. 1984); *Anderson v. Banks*, 520 F.Supp. 472 (S.D.Ga.1981), *modified*, 540 F.Supp. 761 [4 Educ. L. Rep. 1127] (S.D.Ga.1982), *appeal dismissed sub. nom. Johnson v. Sikes*, 730 F.2d 644 [16 Educ. L. Rep. 1085] (11th Cir.1984).

must pass competency tests in order to receive diplomas,[158] IEPs should specify areas in need of additional instruction. Third, consistent with the non-discrimination standards in the IDEA's evaluation procedures, tests cannot be racially, linguistically, or ethnically discriminatory.[159]

Parents of children with disabilities are responsible for working with other members of IEP teams in formulating the components of IEPs for their children.[160] Accordingly, school officials should make parents aware of the general content of tests, where and how they are to be administered, and the purposes for which results are to be used.

Related Services

Children with disabilities are entitled to related, or supportive, services to help them to benefit from special education.[161] The term "related services" does not include medical devices that are surgically implanted or their replacements.[162]

Transportation, including such specialized equipment as adapted buses, lifts, and ramps, is probably the most common related service. Even so, an ongoing question concerns where children who are entitled to transportation must be dropped off after school. While the Fifth Circuit explained that a child is entitled to transportation to the home of a caretaker, even if that person lived outside of a district's attendance boundaries,[163] the Eight Circuit reached the opposite result, maintaining that a child was not entitled to be dropped off at a day care center that was outside of his school's attendance area.[164]

Perhaps the most controversial aspect of related services is the distinction between medical and school health services. Procedures that must be performed by licensed physicians are exempted medical services.

---

158. *Debra P., id.* (striking down thirteen-month notice). *But see Anderson v. Banks,* 520 F.Supp. 472 (S.D.Ga.1981), *modified,* 540 F.Supp. 761 [4 Educ. L. Rep. 1127] (S.D.Ga.1982) (finding 24 months to be sufficient).

159. 20 U.S.C.A. § 1414(b)(3).

160. 20 U.S.C.A. § 1414(d)(1)(B)(i).

161. The IDEA defines related services as

(26) Related services

(A) In general

The term "related services" means transportation, and such developmental, corrective, and other supportive services (including speech-language pathology and audiology services, interpreting services, psychological services, physical and occupational therapy, recreation, including therapeutic recreation, social work services, school nurse services designed to enable a child with a disability to receive a free appropriate public education as described in the individualized education program of the child, counseling services, including rehabilitation counseling, orientation and mobility services, and medical services, except that such medical services shall be for diagnostic and evaluation purposes only) as may be required to assist a child with a disability to benefit from special education, and includes the early identification and assessment of disabling conditions in children.

(B) Exception

The term does not include a medical device that is surgically implanted, or the replacement of such device.

20 U.S.C.A. § 1401(26)(A).

162. 20 U.S.C.A. § 1401(26)(B).

163. *Alamo Heights Indep. School Dist. v. State Bd. of Educ.,* 790 F.2d 1153 [32 Educ. L. Rep. 445] (5th Cir. 1986).

164. *Fick ex rel. Fick v. Sioux Falls School Dist. 49–5,* 337 F.3d 968 [179 Educ. L. Rep. 144] (8th Cir. 2003), *reh'g and reh'g en banc denied* (2003).

Evaluating this distinction can be complicated since many students with significant medical needs require twenty-four-hour nursing services that fall somewhere on the continuum between school health services and medical services.

The Supreme Court first addressed the issue of related services in *Irving Independent School District v. Tatro*,[165] observing that procedures such as catheterizations that can be performed by a school nurse or trained layperson are a required related service under the IDEA. The Court extended this rationale in *Cedar Rapids Community School District v. Garret F.*,[166] interpreting the IDEA as requiring a board to provide, and pay for, regardless of cost, a full-time nurse while a student was in school since his medical condition needed constant monitoring.

Assistive Technology

The definitions of assistive technology devices[167] or services,[168] were first included in the IDEA in 1990 and expanded in its 1997 amendments and regulations. Yet, assistive technology is not included in the definitions of special education or related services. Assistive technology fits within the definitions of special education as specially designed instruction and related services as developmental, corrective, or supportive services. Instead of including assistive technology within either of these definitions, Congress made assistive technology a separate category from special education and related services. Accordingly, assistive technology can be considered to be either a special education service, a related service, or a supplementary aid or service. Regardless of which rubric they are covered by, boards must provide students with disabilities with supplementary aids and services that allow them to be educated in the least restrictive environment.[169]

Assistive technology devices are any items, pieces of equipment, or product systems that are used to increase, maintain, or improve the functional capabilities of students with disabilities.[170] These devices may include commercially available, modified, or customized equipment. An assistive technology service includes "selecting, designing, fitting, customizing, adapting, applying, maintaining, repairing, or replacing assistive technology devices."[171]

To the extent that assistive technology is mandatory if it is necessary to provide children with the services identified in their IEPs,[172] teams must consider whether students need these items in order to ensure that their placements are appropriate.[173] Despite this language,

165. 468 U.S. 883, 104 S.Ct. 3371, 82 L.Ed.2d 664 [18 Educ. L. Rep. 138] (1984).

166. 526 U.S. 66, 119 S.Ct. 992, 143 L.Ed.2d 154 [132 Educ. L. Rep. 40] (1999). [Case No. 120]

167. 20 U.S.C.A. § 1401(1).

168. 20 U.S.C.A. § 1401(2).

169. *Oberti v. Board of Educ. of the Borough of Clementon School Dist.*, 995 F.2d 1204 [83 Educ. L. Rep. 1009] (3d Cir. 1993).

170. 20 U.S.C.A. § 1401(1).

171. 20 U.S.C.A. § 1401(2)(c).

172. Proposed regulation 34 C.F.R. § 300.105(a).

173. Proposed regulation 34 C.F.R. § 300.324(a)(2)(v).

the IDEA does not include provisions directing IEP teams to document their discussions of students' assistive technology needs or justify whether they were required. If IEP teams believe that students need school-provided assistive technology devices in their homes, then children are entitled to have them there.[174]

On a particular item, if students with hearing impairments, including deafness, wear hearing aids to school, educators must ensure that they are functioning properly.[175] At the same time, students with disabilities are entitled to access to any general technology that is available to peers who are not disabled. Of course, if students require accommodations in order to use general technology, they must be provided. On the other hand, in a case from New York, the Second Circuit ruled that a student whose learning disability affected his ability in mathematics could not use a more advanced calculator in a class where the evidence demonstrated that he was capable of passing the course with the assistance of a less advanced calculator.[176] The court commented that not permitting the student to use the calculator was consistent with the educational goals of the curriculum for the course and that his own lack of effort contributed to his failing grade.

Discipline

As important, and challenging, as the topic of disciplining students with disabilities is, the IDEA did not address it until 1997. The IDEA now permits school officials to discipline students as long as they follow procedures that do not deprive children of their rights.[177] Early case law determined that while students with disabilities could not be expelled for misconduct that was a manifestation of their disabilities, they could have been excluded if no such relationship was present.[178]

Honig v. Doe (Honig)[179] is the Court's first, and only, case involving discipline and special education. In a dispute over whether school officials in California could exclude two students with disabilities from school, the Court addressed three issues. First, the Court affirmed that the case was moot with regard to one of the two students because he was already over the age of twenty-one. Second, in refusing to write in a dangerousness exception into the statute, the Court affirmed that the IDEA's stay-put provisions prohibit educators from unilaterally excluding students with disabilities from school for dangerous or disruptive actions that are manifestations of their disabilities during the pendency

---

174. Proposed regulation 34 C.F.R. § 300.305(a)(2).

175. Proposed regulation 34 C.F.R. § 300.105(b).

176. *Sherman v. Mamaroneck Union Free School Dist.*, 340 F.3d 87 [179 Educ. L. Rep. 617] (2d Cir. 2003).

177. *LIH ex rel. LH v. New York City Bd. of Educ.*, 103 F.Supp.2d 658 [145 Educ. L. Rep. 1031] (E.D.N.Y.2000).

178. *See, e.g., Stuart v. Nappi,* 443 F.Supp. 1235 (D.Conn.1978); *S–1 v. Turlington,* 635 F.2d 342 (5th Cir.1981), *cert. denied,* 454 U.S. 1030, 102 S.Ct. 566, 70 L.Ed.2d 473 (1981); *School Bd. of Prince William County, Va. v. Malone,* 762 F.2d 1210 [25 Educ. L. Rep. 141] (4th Cir. 1985).

179. 484 U.S. 305, 108 S.Ct. 592, 98 L.Ed.2d 686 [43 Educ. L. Rep. 857] (1988). [Case No. 121]

of review proceedings. The Court added that officials could impose normal, non-placement-changing procedures, including temporary suspensions for up to ten school days for students who posed immediate threats to school safety. The Court recognized that if educators and parents agreed, students could have been given interim placements as proceedings went forward. If this approach failed, the Court acknowledged that officials could have filed suit for injunctive relief to remove children. Third, an equally divided Court affirmed that school officials could be compelled to provide services directly to students with disabilities when local boards failed to do so.[180]

Honig's failure to resolve all of the legal issues surrounding disciplining students with disabilities led to additional litigation and eventual legislative action.[181] Congress thus sought to clarify unanswered questions by creating specific procedures as part of the IDEA's 1997 Amendments.[182] In a major change, the IDEA affords educators the authority to suspend special education students for not more than ten school days as long as similar sanctions apply to children who are not disabled.[183] Under such circumstances, officials must conduct functional behavioral assessments for students if they have not already done so and must address their underlying misconduct.[184]

The IDEA's regulations specify that a series of removals that result in a pattern of exclusions that cumulatively have children with disabilities out of school for more than ten school days may be considered changes in placements.[185] The regulations make it clear that if students are suspended for misbehavior that is substantially similar to past misbehavior that was found to be a manifestation of their disabilities, then this constitutes changes in placements.[186] In making such judgments, the regulations direct school officials to consider the length of each removal, the total amount of time that children have been removed from school, and the proximity of the removals to one another in evaluating whether changes in placements occurred.[187]

Educators can remove students with disabilities from school for separate, but dissimilar, acts of misconduct for more than ten cumulative days in a school year.[188] School officials are not required to continue special education services for students who are removed for up to ten-

---

180. *Doe by Gonzales v. Maher*, 793 F.2d 1470 [33 Educ. L. Rep. 124] (9th Cir. 1986).

181. *Hayes Through Hayes v. Unified School Dist. No. 377*, 877 F.2d 809 [54 Educ. L. Rep. 450] (10th Cir.1989); *Hacienda La Puente Unified School Dist. of Los Angeles v. Honig*, 976 F.2d 487 [77 Educ. L. Rep. 1117] (9th Cir.1992); *Light v. Parkway C–2 School Dist.*, 41 F.3d 1223 [96 Educ. L. Rep. 98] (8th Cir.1994), *reh'g and suggestion for reh'g en banc denied, cert. denied*, 515 U.S. 1132, 115 S.Ct. 2557, 132 L.Ed.2d 811 (1995).

182. 20 U.S.C.A. § § 1415(i)(j)(k)(*l*).

183. 20 U.S.C.A. § 1415(k)(1)(B).

184. 20 U.S.C.A. § 1415(k)(1)(D)(ii).

185. Proposed regulation, 34 C.F.R. § 300.536(b)(1).

186. Proposed regulation 34 C.F.R. § 300.536(b)(2).

187. Proposed regulation 34 C.F.R. § 300.536(b)(3).

188. Proposed regulation 34 C.F.R. § 300.530(b)(1).

days cumulatively unless they are routinely provided to students who are not disabled and who have been removed under similar circumstances.[189]

Officials now have increased authority when dealing with students with disabilities who possess weapons or drugs at school.[190] Under an expanded definition of a dangerous weapon, the IDEA incorporates language from another federal statute such that it now includes instruments, devices, materials, and substances that are capable of inflicting harm in addition to firearms, but does not include small pocket knives.[191] In addition, the IDEA defines illegal drugs as controlled substances but excludes ones that may be legally prescribed by physicians.[192]

Pursuant to these provisions for the immediate removal of students with disabilities, school officials may unilaterally transfer children to interim alternative placements for up to forty-five days for carrying or possessing weapons[193] or for knowing possession, use, sale, or solicitation of drugs[194] on school property or at school functions as long as this sanction applies under similar circumstances for students who are not disabled.[195] In an important addition in the 2004 version of the IDEA, students who have inflicted serious bodily injury on other persons while at school, on school premises, or at a school function can be placed in alternative educational settings.[196] In defining serious bodily harm, the IDEA relies on another federal law which defines "serious bodily injury" as one that involves a substantial risk of death, extreme physical pain, protracted and obvious disfigurement, or protracted loss or impairment of the function of a bodily member, organ, or mental faculty.[197]

When students are moved to alternative placements, educators must conduct functional behavioral assessments and implement behavioral intervention plans if they are not already in place.[198] If plans were in place when children misbehaved, IEP teams must review them and their implementation in order to make any necessary modifications.[199] If parents disagree with alternative placements and request hearings, consistent with the IDEA's stay-put provision, their children must remain in the alternative settings.[200] Once the forty-five day period expires, officials must return students to their former placements even if hearings regarding school board proposals to change their placements are pending unless parents and school officials agree otherwise.[201]

189. Proposed regulation 34 C.F.R. § 300.536(d)(3).

190. 20 U.S.C.A. §§ 1415(k)(7)(A)–(B).

191. 18 U.S.C. § 930(g)(2).

192. 20 U.S.C.A. § 1415(k)(7)(B). For the full categorization of controlled substances, see 21 U.S.C. § 812(c).

193. 20 U.S.C.A. § 1415(k)(1)(G)(i).

194. 20 U.S.C.A. § 1415(k)(1)(G)(ii).

195. 20 U.S.C.A. § 1415(k)(1)(C).

196. 20 U.S.C.A. § 1415(k)(1)(G)(iii).

197. 18 U.S.C.A. § 1365(h)(3).

198. 20 U.S.C.A. § 1415(k)(1)(D)(ii); proposed regulation 34 C.F.R. § 300.530(d)(ii).

199. Proposed regulation 34 C.F.R. § 300.530(f)(1)(ii).

200. 20 U.S.C.A. § 1415(k)(4)(A). *See J.S., ex rel. Duck v. Isle of Wight County School Bd.*, 368 F.Supp.2d 522 [198 Educ. L. Rep. 587] (E.D. Va. 2005) (rejecting a mother's claim that school officials violated her son's rights by suspending him and placing him in an alternative school due to accusations of a sexual nature by a female student).

201. 20 U.S.C.A. § 1415(k)(4)(A).

Under the IDEA's interim alternative placement requirements, school officials must permit students to continue to progress in the general education curriculum where they still receive necessary services that are outlined in their IEPs.[202] Educators must also provide students with services and modifications that are designed to prevent the misbehavior from recurring.[203]

The IDEA now includes definitions and procedures to evaluate whether misconduct is related to students' disabilities.[204] The IDEA defines a manifestation as conduct that was caused by or had a direct and substantial relationship to students' disabilities or was the direct result of the failure of school officials to implement IEPs properly.[205] In reviewing whether placements were inappropriate, IEP teams should use the same standards that applied when they prospectively evaluated whether proposed placements were appropriate. If IEP teams interpret misconduct as either a manifestation of students' disabilities or as a result of inappropriate placements or IEPs, children may not be expelled or suspended for more than ten days and school officials must reconsider their current placements.[206] In making manifestation determinations, IEP teams must consider all relevant information, including evaluations and diagnostic results as well as student observations.[207]

As with other aspects related to special education, manifestation determinations are subject to the IDEA's administrative appeals process. The 2004 amendments state that hearings incident to manifestation determinations are to be expedited, meaning that they must occur within twenty school days of the date on which one was requested and that a hearing officer must render a decision within ten days of the hearing.[208] If parents contest manifestation determinations, then educators must postpone long-term suspensions or expulsions until hearings have been completed, even though students may remain in interim alternative educational settings.[209] In addition to leaving children in their then current, or pendent, placements, hearing officers may issue change in placement orders.[210]

A case from Maine illustrates the principle that if misbehavior is not a manifestation of a child's disability, then a student may be disciplined in the same manner as any peer who is not disabled.[211] The federal trial court held that since the school's pupil evaluation team ascertained that a student with a learning disability's expulsion for violating his school's drug policy was unrelated to his disability, it would not order his reinstatement.

The IDEA clarified whether school officials can discontinue services for children who are properly expelled for misconduct that is not

202. 20 U.S.C.A. § 1415(k)(1)(D)(i).

203. 20 U.S.C.A. § 1415(k)(1)(D)(ii).

204. 20 U.S.C.A. § 1415(k)(4).

205. 20 U.S.C.A. § 1415(k)(1)(E)(i).

206. 20 U.S.C.A. § 1415(k)(1)(C).

207. 20 U.S.C.A. § 1415(k)(1)(E)(i).

208. 20 U.S.C.A. § 1415(k)(4)(B).

209. 20 U.S.C.A. § 1415(k)(4)(A).

210. 20 U.S.C.A. § 1415(k)(3)(B).

211. *Farrin v. Maine School Admin. Dist. No. 59*, 165 F.Supp.2d 37 [157 Educ. L. Rep. 709] (D. Me.2001).

disability-related. In codifying a federal policy that directed school officials to provide services for a student who was excluded for misbehavior that was not disability-related, the IDEA essentially repudiated a case from Virginia wherein the Fourth Circuit rejected the notion that such a requirement existed.[212] The IDEA mandates that an appropriate education must be made available to all students with disabilities including those who have been expelled from school.[213] In other words, even if students have been expelled in accord with the IDEA's provisions for misbehavior that was unrelated to their disabilities, they must be provided with services that will allow them to progress toward achieving their IEP goals.[214]

Prior to the adoption of the statute's 1997 revisions, courts disagreed over the treatment of students who were not yet assessed for special education but claimed to have been covered by the IDEA. Officials must now provide the IDEA's protections to students if they knew that children were disabled before they misbehaved.[215] As reflected by a case from Connecticut, officials are considered to be on notice if parents request an evaluation.[216] Educators may also be considered to be on notice in light of a student's prior behavioral and academic performance, and a teacher's expressed concern about a student's performance.[217] An exception exists if educators already conducted evaluations and concluded that students were not disabled or if parents refused to grant their permission for evaluations or declined offered special education services.[218]

If parents request evaluations during a time when students are subject to disciplinary sanctions, they must be conducted in an expedited manner.[219] Consistent with the IDEA's stay-put provision, until expedited evaluations are completed, students must remain in the placements deemed appropriate by educators.[220] If evaluation teams discern that children are disabled, they must provide students with special education services.[221] In a case reaching what can be described as mixed results, a federal trial court in Mississippi decided that while school officials violated the IDEA by failing to provide a testing procedure to evaluate whether a student who was expelled for bringing a Swiss Army knife to school had a disability, they did not contravene the statute's stay-put provision in excluding the child.[222]

In a final matter, the IDEA's discipline provisions do not prohibit school officials from reporting student crimes to the proper authorities

212. *Commonwealth of Va., Dep't of Educ. v. Riley*, 106 F.3d 559 [116 Educ. L. Rep. 40] (4th Cir.1997).

213. 20 U.S.C.A. §§ 1412(a)(1)(A), 1415(k)(1)(D)(i).

214. Proposed regulation 34 C.F.R. § 300.530(d)(i).

215. 20 U.S.C.A. § 1415(k)(8).

216. *J.C. v. Regional School Dist. No. 10*, 115 F.Supp.2d 297 [147 Educ. L. Rep. 935] (D. Conn.2000), *rev'd on other*

grounds, 278 F.3d 119 [161 Educ. L. Rep. 68] (2d Cir.2002).

217. 20 U.S.C.A. § 1415(k)(5)(B).

218. 20 U.S.C.A. § 1415(k)(5)(C).

219. 20 U.S.C.A. § 1415(k)(5)(D)(ii).

220. 20 U.S.C.A. § 1415(k)(5)(D)(ii).

221. 20 U.S.C.A. § 1415(k)(5)(D)(ii).

222. *Colvin ex rel. Colvin v. Lowndes County, Miss. School Dist.*, 114 F.Supp.2d 504 [147 Educ. L. Rep. 601] (N.D.Miss. 1999).

or impeding law enforcement and judicial authorities from carrying out their responsibilities.[223] If officials do report crimes, they must make copies of students' special education and disciplinary records available to appropriate authorities.[224]

Dispute Resolution

"The IDEA favors prompt resolution of disputes"[225] over the education of children with disabilities because it acknowledged the need to help children who may be at formative stages in their development. Consistent with the previous sentence, in 2004, Congress presented new findings in the IDEA that "[p]arents and schools should be given expanded opportunities to resolve their disagreements in positive and constructive ways," and that "[t]eachers, schools, local educational agencies, and States should be relieved of irrelevant and unnecessary paperwork burdens that do not lead to improved educational outcomes."[226] To this end, parents who disagree with any of the actions of IEP teams or school board officials about the placements of their children may request mediation in lieu of adversarial proceedings.[227] Insofar as mediation is voluntary, it may not be used to deny or delay parental requests for administrative hearings.

Parents may also request due process hearings, which must be presided over by fair and impartial third-party decision makers,[228] if they are not satisfied with any aspect of their child's education[229] such as where school officials refused to assess whether their child had a disability,[230] where they disagreed with the findings and recommendation that school officials offered,[231] and/or where they were dissatisfied with the content or implementation of their child's IEP.[232] Boards may request due process hearings if parents refuse to consent to evaluations of their children.[233]

In an important preliminary matter with regard to dispute resolution, the Supreme Court resolved the split between the circuits in addressing the question of who bears the burden of proof when a party challenges the contents of an IEP in a due process hearing. In *Schaffer*

---

223. 20 U.S.C.A. § 1415(k)(6)(A). *Commonwealth v. Nathaniel N.*, 764 N.E.2d 883 [162 Educ. L. Rep. 951] (Mass. App. Ct.2002) (affirming that a juvenile court proceeding did not constitute a change in placement even when it took place due to a student's misconduct at school).

224. 20 U.S.C.A. § 1415(k)(6)(B).

225. *Sanders v. Santa Fe Pub. Schools*, 383 F.Supp.2d 1305, 1311 [201 Educ. L. Rep. 931] (D.N.M. 2004). *But see Herbin ex rel. Herbin v. District of Columbia*, 362 F.Supp.2d 254 [197 Educ. L. Rep. 142] (D.D.C. 2005) (permitting a four-month delay in responding to a request for a reevaluation).

226. 20 U.S.C.A. §§ 1400(c)(8)–(9).

227. 20 U.S.C.A. § 1415(e).

228. 20 U.S.C.A. § 1414(a)(1)(ii)(I).

229. 20 U.S.C.A. §§ 1415(1)(A).

230. *Hacienda La Puente Unified School Dist. of Los Angeles v. Honig*, 976 F.2d 487 [77 Educ. L. Rep. 1117] (9th Cir. 1992).

231. *Dong v. Board of Educ.*, 197 F.3d 793 [140 Educ. L. Rep. 116] (6th Cir. 1999).

232. *Kuszewski v. Chippewa Valley Schools*, 117 F.Supp.2d 646 [148 Educ. L. Rep. 745] (E.D. Mich. 2000).

233. *Yates v. Charles County Bd. of Educ.*, 212 F.Supp.2d 470 [168 Educ. L. Rep. 238] (D.Md. 2002).

ex rel. Schaffer v. Weast,[234] the Court affirmed the judgment of the Fourth Circuit which placed the burden of proof on the party challenging an IEP. In rejecting the claim that parents who questioned their son's IEP were at a disadvantage due to a lack of knowledge, the Court found that they had significant due process protections available to make sure that this was not the case. The Court emphasized that while the question was not then before it, states could, as several already have, override what it described as the default position and place this burden of proof on school boards.

Depending on state law, either state or local school boards may conduct due process hearings.[235] In states with two-tiered systems, if local boards conduct initial hearings, either party can appeal to the state.[236]

In another important addition, the IDEA now has a two-year limitations period during which a party can request a due process hearing.[237] However, if state law has a different limitations period, that period prevails. Moreover, the IDEA stipulates that the federal statute of limitations is to be stayed if parents can show that school board officials misrepresented that they resolved a disagreement or if they withheld pertinent information from the parents.[238]

A hearing officer, typically selected pursuant to state law, must be impartial, meaning that one cannot be an employee of the state or the school board involved in a student's education or have a personal or professional interest in the outcome.[239] An individual who otherwise qualifies as a hearing officer is not considered an employee of a state or board solely by virtue of being paid by the agency to serve in this capacity.[240] Each public agency is required to keep a list of qualified hearing officers along with an explanation of their qualifications.[241]

Within fifteen days of receiving parental requests for due process hearings, school officials must meet with them in mandatory resolution sessions to discuss their disagreement.[242] If the parties are able to resolve their differences, they must execute a legally binding agreement that is enforceable in any state court of competent jurisdiction or in any federal district court.[243] The parties may void this agreement within three business days of its being executed.[244]

If parents and school officials are unable to resolve their differences within thirty-days, then the due process time lines come into play.[245]

234. ___ U.S. ___, 126 S.Ct. 528, 163 L.Ed.2d 387 [203 Educ. L. Rep. 29] (2005). [Case No. 122]

235. 20 U.S.C.A. § 1415(f)(1)(A).

236. 20 U.S.C.A. § 1415(g).

237. 20 U.S.C.A. § 1415(f)(3)(C).

238. 20 U.S.C.A. § 1415(f)(3)(D).

239. 20 U.S.C.A. § 1415(f)(3)(A). This section also delineates the qualities that hearing officers should possess. Although some states specify that hearing officers

should be attorneys, it is not required under federal law.

240. Proposed regulation 34 C.F.R. § 300.511(c)(2).

241. Proposed regulation 34 C.F.R. § 300.511(c)(3).

242. 20 U.S.C.A. § 1415(f)(1)(B).

243. 20 U.S.C.A. § 1415(f)(1)(B)(iii).

244. 20 U.S.C.A. § 1415(f)(1)(B)(iv).

245. 20 U.S.C.A. § 1415(f)(1)(B)(ii).

Under these provisions, a hearing officer must render a final decision based on the record[246] within forty-five days after the expiration of the thirty-day period.[247] Even so, a hearing officer can grant specific extensions of these time frames at the request of either party.[248] A hearing officer's order is final unless one of the parties appeals.[249] In a state with a two-tiered due process hearing system, officials must ensure that final judgments are reached within thirty days of when requests for reviews are made.[250]

In preparing for hearings, both parties must make full disclosures of all evaluations that have been completed by that date and recommendations that they intend to rely on at least five business days in advance.[251] If a party fails to provide this information, a hearing officer can prevent it from introducing the relevant evaluation or recommendation at the hearing without the consent of the other party.[252]

As quasi-judicial proceedings, the parties to due process hearings have the right to be accompanied and advised by counsel and by individuals with special knowledge or training with respect to the problems of children with disabilities;[253] the right to present evidence and confront, cross-examine, and compel the attendance of witnesses;[254] the right to a written, or, at the option of the parents, electronic verbatim record of such hearing;[255] and the right to written, or, at the option of the parents, electronic findings of fact and final adjudications.[256]

A party that is not pleased by the result of administrative proceedings may appeal to the state or federal courts within ninety days[257] or the appropriate state time limitation[258] but, before doing so, must first exhaust all administrative remedies unless it is futile to do so.[259] As illustrated by a case from the Second Circuit, where school officials failed to notify parents in New York of their procedural rights, they were not required to exhaust administrative remedies.[260] Two years later, the Seventh Circuit reasoned that where a student's alleged injuries for physical and emotional harm were non-educational ones for which the IDEA did not provide remedies, exhaustion was unnecessary.[261] While administrative or judicial actions are pending, the IDEA's stay-put

246. 20 U.S.C.A. § 1415(f)(3)(E)(i)(ii).

247. 20 U.S.C.A. § 1415(i).

248. Proposed regulation 34 C.F.R. § 300.515(c).

249. 20 U.S.C.A. § 1415(i)(1)(A).

250. Proposed regulation 34 C.F.R. § 300.515(b).

251. 20 U.S.C.A. § 1415(f)(2)(A).

252. 20 U.S.C.A. § 1415(f)(2)(B).

253. 20 U.S.C.A. § 1415(h)(1).

254. 20 U.S.C.A. § 1415(h)(2).

255. 20 U.S.C.A. § 1415(h)(3).

256. 20 U.S.C.A. § 1415(h)(4).

257. 20 U.S.C.A. § 1415(i)(2)(A).

258. 20 U.S.C.A. § 1415(i)(2)(B).

259. For cases recognizing exceptions to exhaustion of remedies, *see Blanchard v. Morton School Dist.*, 420 F.3d 918 [201 Educ. L. Rep. 106] (9th Cir. 2005); *Polera v. Board of Educ. of the Newburgh Enlarged City School Dist.*, 288 F.3d 478 [164 Educ. L. Rep. 573] (2d Cir. 2002).

260. *Weixel v. Board of Educ. of the City of N.Y.*, 287 F.3d 138 [163 Educ. L. Rep. 640] (2d Cir. 2002).

261. *McCormick v. Waukegan School Dist. #60*, 374 F.3d 564 [189 Educ. L. Rep. 518] (7th Cir. 2004).

provisions require that unless school officials and parents agree[262] or officials obtain either a hearing officer's order[263] or a judicial decree[264] granting them permission to change their placements, students must remain in their then current settings.[265]

Courts can review the record of administrative proceedings, hear additional evidence,[266] and grant such relief as they deem appropriate based on the preponderance of evidence standard.[267] Still, the Supreme Court has advised judges not to substitute their views of proper educational decision-making for that of school authorities.[268] To this end, in *Rowley* the Court declared that

> We ... have cautioned that courts lack the "specialized knowledge and experience" necessary to resolve "persistent and difficult questions of educational policy." We think that Congress shared that view when it passed the Act.... Congress' intention was not that the Act displace the primacy of States in the field of education, but that States receive funds to assist them in extending their educational systems to the handicapped. Therefore, once a court determines that the requirements of the Act have been met, questions of methodology are for resolution by the States.[269]

As extensive as it is, the IDEA is not the exclusive avenue through which parents can enforce the rights of their children. The IDEA stipulates that none of its provisions can be interpreted as restricting or limiting the rights, procedures, and remedies available under the Federal Constitution, Section 504, or other federal laws protecting the rights of students with disabilities.[270]

Remedies

As indicated above, once parents take school systems to court in disputes over the placements of their children, the judiciary has the power to provide relief that it deems appropriate.[271] Courts can provide monetary damages, tuition reimbursement, compensatory services, and attorney fees.

262. 20 U.S.C.A. § 1415(j).

263. 20 U.S.C.A. § 1415(k)(2).

264. *Honig v. Doe*, 484 U.S. 305, 108 S.Ct. 592, 98 L.Ed.2d 686 [43 Educ. L. Rep. 857] (1988).

265. *Pardini v. Allegheny Intermediate Unit*, 420 F.3d 181 [201 Educ. L. Rep. 44] (3d Cir. 2005) (applying this principle to a three-year old child who was covered by an individual family service plan as it transitioned into an IEP).

266. 20 U.S.C.A. § 1415(i)(2)(C)(i)(ii). *School Bd. of Collier County, Fla. v. K.C.*, 285 F.3d 977 [163 Educ. L. Rep. 111] (11th Cir. 2002); *A.S. v. Trumbull Bd. of Educ.*, 359 F.Supp.2d 102 [196 Educ. L. Rep. 518] (D. Conn. 2005).

267. 20 U.S.C.A. § 1415(i)(2)(C)(iii). For discussion of this standard, *see, e.g.*, *Kruelle v. New Castle County School Dist.*, 642 F.2d 687 (3d Cir. 1981); *Independent School Dist. No. 283 v. S.D. by J.D.*, 88 F.3d 556 [110 Educ. L. Rep. 987] (8th Cir. 1996); *Evanston Community Consol. School Dist. Number 65 v. Michael M.*, 356 F.3d 798 [184 Educ. L. Rep. 692] (7th Cir. 2004); *Lamoine School Comm. v. Ms. Z. ex rel. N.S.*, 353 F.Supp.2d 18 [195 Educ. L. Rep. 511] (D. Me. 2005).

268. *Board of Educ. of Hendrick Hudson Cent. School Dist. v. Rowley*, 458 U.S. 176, 102 S.Ct. 3034, 73 L.Ed.2d 690 [5 Educ. L. Rep. 34] (1982).

269. *Id.* at 208.

270. 20 U.S.C.A. § 1415(*l*).

271. 20 U.S.C.A. § 1415(i)(2)(C)(iii).

Damages

Courts generally have not imposed monetary damages on school officials who failed to provide appropriate educational placements for children with disabilities.[272] While courts do not ordinarily award general damages for "pain and suffering,"[273] recent litigation suggests that this may be changing. As evidence of this possible shift in judicial thinking, courts have written that monetary damages may be available under other statutes, such as Section 504, if parents can show that school officials engaged in intentional discrimination or egregiously disregarded the rights of their children.[274]

Tuition Reimbursement

Parents who disagree with the placements of their children may enroll them in private schools and attempt to recover the costs of tuition.[275] In *Burlington School Committee v. Department of Education, Commonwealth of Massachusetts*,[276] the Supreme Court pointed out that parents are entitled to tuition reimbursement if they can show that officials failed to offer appropriate placements and their chosen placements are appropriate. The Court posited that awarding reimbursement simply requires boards to pay retroactively for costs that they should have absorbed from the beginning. Subsequently, in *Florence County School District Four v. Carter*,[277] the Court noted that parents are entitled to reimbursements even if their chosen placements are not in state-approved facilities as long as they place their children in settings that are otherwise appropriate.

When parents place their children in private schools, they do so at their own financial risk since they are not entitled to reimbursements if board officials can show that they offered, and could provide, appropriate placements. In two separate cases, the First Circuit[278] agreed that parents were not entitled to tuition reimbursement where they did not apprise school officials that they were changing the placements of their children and did not afford them opportunities to re-evaluate the children.[279]

272. *See, e.g., Polera v. Board of Educ. of the Newburgh Enlarged City School Dist.*, 288 F.3d 478 [164 Educ. L. Rep. 573] (2d Cir.2002); *Bradley v. Arkansas Dep't of Educ.*, 301 F.3d 952 [168 Educ. L. Rep. 646] (8th Cir.2002).

273. *See, e.g., Ft. Zumwalt School Dist. v. Missouri State Bd. of Educ.*, 865 F.Supp. 604 [95 Educ. L. Rep. 253] (E.D.Mo.1994).

274. *See, e.g., W.B. v. Matula*, 67 F.3d 484 [104 Educ. L. Rep. 28] (3d Cir.1995); *Whitehead v. School Dist. for Hillsborough County*, 918 F.Supp. 1515 [108 Educ. L. Rep. 239] (M.D. Fla. 1996).

275. 20 U.S.C.A. § 1412(a)(10)(C)(ii).

276. 471 U.S. 359, 105 S.Ct. 1996, 85 L.Ed.2d 385 [23 Educ. L. Rep. 1189] (1985).

277. 510 U.S. 7, 114 S.Ct. 361, 126 L.Ed.2d 284 [86 Educ. L. Rep. 41] (1993).

278. *Greenland School Dist. v. Amy N.*, 358 F.3d 150 [185 Educ. L. Rep. 73] (1st Cir. 2004); *Ms. M. ex rel. K.M. v. Portland School Comm.*, 360 F.3d 267 [185 Educ. L. Rep. 819] (1st Cir. 2004).

279. *See also Werner v. Clarksville Central School Dist.*, 363 F.Supp.2d 656 [197 Educ. L. Rep 244] (S.D.N.Y. 2005).

Compensatory Services

Tuition reimbursement is likely to be of little assistance to parents who cannot place their children in private schools because they cannot afford to pay for tuition. If parents cannot afford to make unilateral placements, their children may remain in inappropriate settings while disputes work their way through administrative and legal proceedings. If this occurs, courts can award extra educational services and prospective relief to compensate parents, and their children, for the loss of appropriate educational services.

The courts observed that compensatory services, like reimbursements, are designed to offer relief for the failure of school board officials to provide children with appropriate educations.[280] The rationale for awards of compensatory services is that appropriate remedies should not be available only to students whose parents can afford to pay for alternate educational placements while litigation is pending. Compensatory services are ordinarily awarded for the time that children were denied services[281] even if they passed the IDEA's age limit.[282]

As with tuition reimbursement, compensatory services can be awarded only if hearing officers or courts agree that school officials failed to provide appropriate placements. In such a case, the Eighth Circuit affirmed that parents in Missouri were entitled to compensatory services for their son after officials improperly ended homebound services and left him without any programming.[283] Conversely, the federal trial court in Massachusetts concluded that since a school committee provided all of the educational programming that a child was entitled to under his IEP, he was not entitled to compensatory services.[284]

Attorney and Expert Witness Fees

It almost goes without saying that litigation can be costly. Often parents who succeeded in court against their school boards had reasonable expectations of being reimbursed for the legal expenses they incurred in safeguarding the educational rights of their children. Parents have argued that they achieved little when they prevailed but were left with significant legal bills. As such, parents are entitled to representa-

280. *Burr by Burr v. Ambach*, 863 F.2d 1071 [50 Educ. L. Rep. 964] (2d Cir.1988), *vacated and remanded sub nom. Sobol v. Burr*, 492 U.S. 902, 109 S.Ct. 3209, 106 L.Ed.2d 560 [54 Educ. L. Rep. 410] (1989), *re-aff'd on remand*, 888 F.2d 258 [56 Educ. L. Rep. 1126] (2d Cir.1989), *cert. denied*, 494 U.S. 1005, 110 S.Ct. 1298, 108 L.Ed.2d 475 (1990); *Blackman v. District of Columbia*, 374 F.Supp.2d 168 [199 Educ. L. Rep. 764] (D.D.C. 2005).

281. *Todd D. by Robert D. v. Andrews*, 933 F.2d 1576 [67 Educ. L. Rep. 1065] (11th Cir.1991); *Birmingham v. Omaha School Dist.*, 298 F.3d 731 [167 Educ. L. Rep. 632] (8th Cir.2002).

282. *Pihl v. Massachusetts Dep't of Educ.*, 9 F.3d 184 [87 Educ. L. Rep. 341] (1st Cir.1993); *Jones v. Schneider*, 896 F.Supp. 488 [103 Educ. L. Rep. 700] (D.V.I. 1995).

283. *Hale ex rel. Hale v. Poplar Bluffs R–I School Dist.*, 280 F.3d 831 [161 Educ. L. Rep. 778] (8th Cir.2002).

284. *Shawsheen Valley Reg'l Vocational Technical School Dist. School Comm. v. Commonwealth of Mass. Bureau of Special Educ. App.*, 367 F.Supp.2d 44 [198 Educ. L. Rep. 217] (D. Mass. 2005).

tion and legal fees, but must be represented by attorneys[285] rather than lay advocates.[286]

In *Smith v. Robinson*,[287] the Supreme Court was of the opinion that parents of children with disabilities could not recover legal expenses from their school boards even if they prevailed. Unhappy with that result, Congress amended the IDEA by passing the Handicapped Children's Protection Act (HCPA).[288] The HCPA grants courts the ability to award attorney fees to prevailing parents[289] in actions or proceedings brought against their school boards pursuant to the IDEA. Awards must be based on a variety of factors,[290] including the prevailing rates in the area in which cases were litigated,[291] and are subject to review to ensure that trial courts did not abuse their discretion.[292]

Courts can deny parents attorney fees if they reject settlement offers and failed to obtain more favorable judicial relief;[293] if they reached settlements without resorting to due process hearings;[294] if they reached settlements pursuant to the IDEA's complaint resolution procedures;[295] if attorney fees were excessive;[296] if the time billed for legal services was excessive;[297] or if they were attorneys representing their own children.[298]

285. 20 U.S.C.A. § 1415(h)(1).

286. *See In re Arons*, 756 A.2d 867 [146 Educ. L. Rep. 763] (Del. 2000), *cert. denied sub nom. Arons v. Office of Disciplinary Counsel of Sup. Ct. of Del.*, 532 U.S. 1065, 121 S.Ct. 2215, 150 L.Ed.2d 208 (2001).

287. 468 U.S. 992, 104 S.Ct. 3457, 82 L.Ed.2d 746 [18 Educ. L. Rep. 148] (1984).

288. 20 U.S.C.A. §§ 1415(i)(3)(B)(C). For limitations on attorney fees, *see* 20 U.S.C.A. §§ 1415(i)(3)(D)–(G).

289. *See, e.g., G.M. ex rel. R.F. v. New Britain Bd. of Educ.*, 173 F.3d 77 [134 Educ. L. Rep. 24] (2d Cir.1999); *Birmingham v. Omaha School Dist.*, 298 F.3d 731 [167 Educ. L. Rep. 632] (8th Cir.2002).

290. For a list of factors that courts take into consideration when setting attorney fees, *see Board of Educ. of Frederick County v. I.S. ex rel. Summers*, 358 F.Supp.2d 462 [196 Educ. L. Rep. 487] (D. Md. 2005).

291. 20 U.S.C.A.§ 1415(i)(3)(B). *Angela L. v. Pasadena Indep. School Dist.*, 918 F.2d 1188 [64 Educ. L. Rep. 350] (5th Cir.1990).

292. *A.R. ex rel. R.V. v. New York City Dep't of Educ.*, 407 F.3d 65 [197 Educ. L. Rep. 525] (2d Cir. 2005).

293. 20 U.S.C.A. § 1415(i)(3)(D)(I). *Mr. L. & Mrs. L. on Behalf of Matthew L. v. Woonsocket Educ. Dep't*, 793 F.Supp. 41 [76 Educ. L. Rep. 398] (D.R.I.1992); *Dell v. Board of Educ.*, 918 F.Supp. 212 [108 Educ. L. Rep. 139] (N.D.Ill.1995).

294. *See, e.g., P.O. ex rel. L.T. v. Greenwich Bd. of Educ.*, 210 F.Supp.2d 76 [167 Educ. L. Rep. 743] (D.Conn.2002).

295. *Vultaggio ex rel. Vultaggio v. Board of Educ., Smithtown Cent. School Dist.*, 216 F.Supp.2d 96 [169 Educ. L. Rep. 155] (E.D.N.Y.2002).

296. *Holmes v. Millcreek Township School Dist.*, 205 F.3d 583 [142 Educ. L. Rep. 667] (3d Cir.2000); *S.W. ex rel. N.W. v. Board of Educ. of City of N.Y. (Dist. Two)*, 257 F.Supp.2d 600 (S.D.N.Y.2003).

297. *Cavanaugh ex rel. Cavanaugh v. Cardinal Local School Dist.*, 409 F.3d 753 [198 Educ. L. Rep. 443] (6th Cir. 2005), *reh'g denied* (2005); *Dale M. ex rel. Alice M. v. Board of Educ. of Bradley–Bourbannais High School Dist. No. 307*, 29 F.Supp.2d 925 [131 Educ. L. Rep. 959] (C.D.Ill.1998); *Sabatini v. Corning–Painted Post Area School Dist.*, 190 F.Supp.2d 509 (W.D.N.Y. 2001).

298. *See, e.g., Rappaport v. Vance*, 812 F.Supp. 609 [81 Educ.L. Rep. 64] (D. Md. 1993), *appeal dismissed*, 14 F.3d 596 (4th Cir. 1994); *Miller v. West Lafayette Community Sch. Corp.*, 665 N.E.2d 905 [110 Educ. L. Rep. 370] (Ind. 1996); *Erickson v. Board of Educ. of Baltimore County*, 162 F.3d 289 [131 Educ. L. Rep. 31] (4th Cir.1998), *opinion amended and superseded*, 165 F.3d 260 [131 Educ. L. Rep. 928] (4th Cir.1998), *cert. denied*, 526 U.S. 1159, 119 S.Ct. 2049, 144 L.Ed.2d 216 (1999); *Doe v. Board of Educ. of Baltimore County*, 165 F.3d 260 [131 Educ. L. Rep. 928] (4th Cir. 1998); *Woodside v. School Dist. of Philadelphia Bd. of*

Yet, not all courts agree that parents who are attorneys are not entitled to fees.[299] On another matter, the Eighth Circuit went so far as to reduce fees to a mother in Minnesota that it identified as "overly litigious."[300]

In what may turn out to be one of the more significant additions in the 2004 version of the IDEA, the law permits school boards to seek reimbursement of their legal expenses when parents file complaints that are later found to be frivolous, unreasonable, or without foundation or when litigation was continued after it clearly became frivolous, unreasonable, or without foundation.[301] This change permits boards to recover costs from attorneys who file suit on behalf of parents if their actions are premised on improper purposes, cause unnecessary delays, or needlessly increase the cost of litigation.[302] A federal trial court in California, relying on the Federal Rules of Civil Procedure, imposed similar sanctions on a school board. The court penalized a board and its attorney for raising frivolous objections, making misstatements, and mischaracterizing facts in violation of the principle that officials cannot continue suits that are clearly frivolous, unreasonable, or without foundation or engage in tactics that unnecessarily prolong litigation or otherwise abuse the process.[303]

The status of attorney fees under the so-called catalyst theory, pursuant to which courts have awarded fees if litigation, or the threat of a suit or administrative actions, motivated school board officials to grant parental requests, is now in doubt.[304] The viability of the catalyst theory is uncertain in light of a non-school case, *Buckhannon Board & Care Home v. West Virginia Department of Health and Human Resources* (*Buckhannon*).[305] In *Buckhannon*, the Supreme Court rejected the catalyst theory in asserting that the prevailing party must succeed in court by obtaining a judgment on the merits or a consent decree. Federal courts have since reached mixed results over this question. On the one hand, the First,[306] Second,[307] and Third[308] Circuits and at least two federal trial courts[309] denied requests for attorney fees based on settle-

---

Educ., 248 F.3d 129 [153 Educ. L. Rep. 525] (3d Cir. 2001).

299. *See Pardini v. Allegheny Intermediate Unit*, 420 F.3d 181 [201 Educ. L. Rep. 44] (3d Cir. 2005); *Matthew V. v. DeKalb County School Sys.*, 244 F.Supp.2d 1331 [174 Educ. L. Rep. 731] (N.D. Ga. 2003).

300. *Independent School Dist. No. 623, Roseville, Minn. v. Digre*, 893 F.2d 987, 992 [58 Educ. L. Rep. 92] (8th Cir.1990).

301. 20 U.S.C.A. § 1415(i)(3)(B)(i)(II).

302. 20 U.S.C.A. § 1415(i)(3)(B)(i)(III).

303. *Moser v. Bret Harte Union High School Dist.*, 366 F.Supp.2d 944 [198 Educ. L. Rep. 171] (E.D. Cal. 2005).

304. *See, e.g., Daniel S. v. Scranton School Dist.*, 230 F.3d 90 [149 Educ. L. Rep. 17] (3d Cir. 2000); *Doucet ex rel. Doucet v. Chilton County Bd. of Educ.*, 65 F.Supp.2d

1249 [139 Educ. L. Rep. 375] (M.D. Ala. 1999).

305. 532 U.S. 598, 121 S.Ct. 1835, 149 L.Ed.2d 855 (2001).

306. *Doe v. Boston Pub. Schools*, 358 F.3d 20 [185 Educ. L. Rep. 62] (1st Cir. 2004).

307. *J.C. v. Regional School Dist. 10, Bd. of Educ.*, 278 F.3d 119 [161 Educ. L. Rep. 68] (2d Cir. 2002).

308. *John T. ex rel. Paul T. v. Delaware County Intermediate Unit*, 318 F.3d 545 [173 Educ. L. Rep. 442] (3d Cir. 2003); *J.O. ex rel. C.O. v. Orange Township Bd. of Educ.*, 287 F.3d 267 [164 Educ. L. Rep. 44] (3d Cir. 2002).

309. *J.S. v. Ramapo Cent. School Dist.*, 165 F.Supp.2d 570 [157 Educ. L. Rep. 728] (S.D.N.Y. 2001); *P.O. ex rel. L.T. v. Green-*

ment agreements. Conversely, since the District of Columbia Circuit[310] and at least three federal trial courts[311] distinguished *Buckhannon*, they continued to grant requests for attorney fees.

Amid a split between the circuits, as this book heads to press, the Supreme Court has agreed to review whether parents may recover fees for expert witnesses under the IDEA. While the Circuit Court for the District of Columbia refused to award such fees to parents,[312] the Second Circuit, in a case of first impression from New York, reached the opposite result.[313] In the case that is headed to the Court, the Second Circuit affirmed a trial court ruling that interpreted the IDEA's fee shifting provision as also covering the costs of expert witnesses who assisted parents in obtaining services for their son.

Financial Considerations

The IDEA explicitly provides federal funding to states that, in turn, pass the monies on to local school board officials to assist in paying for the delivery of special education services. Despite the fact that the federal government has helped to pay for the cost of delivering special education services, since the amount of federal IDEA funds is often inadequate, educators have unsuccessfully challenged the statute as an unfunded federal mandate.[314]

Aware of the need to provide assistance for state and local school officials as they pay for the costs associated with the delivery of special education services, the IDEA has set the goal of achieving its initial 1975 promise of funding 40 percent of the national average of per-pupil spending by 2011.[315] While these provisions are not mandatory, the IDEA has increased the authorized levels for funding the excess costs associated with educating students with disabilities by about $2.3 billion each year.[316]

In a related financial matter, given the high cost of caring for some children, such as those who are medically fragile,[317] the IDEA now authorizes school officials to use IDEA funds to establish and maintain

---

wich Bd. of Educ., 210 F.Supp.2d 76 [167 Educ. L. Rep. 743] (D. Conn. 2002).

310. *Goldring v. District of Columbia*, 416 F.3d 70 [200 Educ. L. Rep. 25] (D.C. Cir.2005) (granting attorney, but not expert witness, fees for an administrative proceeding).

311. *See, e.g., Ostby v. Oxnard Union High*, 209 F.Supp.2d 1035 [167 Educ. L. Rep. 732] (C.D. Cal. 2002); *Johnson v. District of Columbia*, 190 F.Supp.2d 34 [163 Educ. L. Rep. 366] (D.D.C. 2002); *D.M. ex rel. G.M. v. Board of Educ., Center Moriches Union Free School Dist.*, 296 F.Supp.2d 400 [184 Educ. L. Rep. 762] (E.D.N.Y. 2003).

312. *Goldring v. District of Columbia*, 416 F.3d 70 [200 Educ. L. Rep. 25] (D.C. Cir.2005).

313. *Murphy v. Arlington Cent. School Dist. Bd. of Educ.*, 402 F.3d 332 [196 Educ. L. Rep. 415] (2d Cir. 2005), *cert. granted in part*, ___ U.S. ___, 126 S.Ct. 978, 163 L.Ed.2d 721 (2006).

314. *See, e.g., City of Worcester v. The Governor*, 625 N.E.2d 1337 [88 Educ. L. Rep. 227] (Mass. 1994); *Nashua School Dist. v. State*, 667 A.2d 1036 [105 Educ. L. Rep. 578] (N.H. 1995).

315. 20 U.S.C.A. § 1411(a)(2)(A)(ii).

316. For the specific projected amounts of aid, *see* 20 U.S.C.A. § 1411(h)(7)(B)(i).

317. *See, e.g., Timothy W. v. Rochester, N.H., School Dist.*, 875 F.2d 954 [54 Educ. L. Rep.74] (1st Cir.1989), *cert. denied*, 493 U.S. 983, 110 S.Ct. 519, 107 L.Ed.2d 520 (1989). [Case No. 119] "risk pools" to aid local school systems in providing high-cost services or for the unexpected enrollments of students with disabilities.[318] The IDEA also permits school board officials to allocate unused funds to be placed in a pool for the next fiscal year.[319]

[Case No. 117]   Eligibility Under Section 504 of the Rehabilitation Act

SOUTHEASTERN COMMUNITY COLLEGE v. DAVIS

Supreme Court of the United States, 1979.
442 U.S. 397, 99 S.Ct. 2361, 60 L.Ed.2d 980.

JUSTICE POWELL delivered the opinion of the Court.

This case presents a matter of first impression for this Court: Whether § 504 of the Rehabilitation Act of 1973, which prohibits discrimination against an "otherwise qualified handicapped individual" in federally funded programs "solely by reason of his handicap," forbids professional schools from imposing physical qualifications for admission to their clinical training programs.

I

Respondent, who suffers from a serious hearing disability, seeks to be trained as a registered nurse. During the 1973–1974 academic year she was enrolled in the College Parallel program of Southeastern Community College, a state institution that receives federal funds. Respondent hoped to progress to Southeastern's Associate Degree Nursing program, completion of which would make her eligible for state certification as a registered nurse. In the course of her application to the nursing program, she was interviewed by a member of the nursing faculty. It became apparent that respondent had difficulty understanding questions asked, and on inquiry she acknowledged a history of hearing problems and dependence on a hearing aid. She was advised to consult an audiologist.

On the basis of an examination at Duke University Medical Center, respondent was diagnosed as having a "bilateral, sensori-neural hearing loss." A change in her hearing aid was recommended, as a result of which it was expected that she would be able to detect sounds "almost as well as a person would who has normal hearing." But this improvement would not mean that she could discriminate among sounds sufficiently to understand normal spoken speech. Her lipreading skills would remain necessary for effective communication: "While wearing the hearing aid, she is well aware of gross sounds occurring in the listening environment. However, she can only be responsible for speech spoken to her, when the talker gets her attention and allows her to look directly at the talker."

Southeastern next consulted Mary McRee, Executive Director of the North Carolina Board of Nursing. On the basis of the audiologist's report, McRee recommended that respondent not be admitted to the

---

318. 20 U.S.C.A. § 1411(e)(3).   **319.** *Id.*

nursing program. In McRee's view, respondent's hearing disability made it unsafe for her to practice as a nurse. In addition, it would be impossible for respondent to participate safely in the normal clinical training program, and those modifications that would be necessary to enable safe participation would prevent her from realizing the benefits of the program: "To adjust patient learning experiences in keeping with [respondent's] hearing limitations could, in fact, be the same as denying her full learning to meet the objectives of your nursing programs."

After respondent was notified that she was not qualified for nursing study because of her hearing disability, she requested reconsideration of the decision. The entire nursing staff of Southeastern was assembled, and McRee again was consulted. McRee repeated her conclusion that on the basis of the available evidence, respondent "has hearing limitations which could interfere with her safely caring for patients." Upon further deliberation, the staff voted to deny respondent admission.

Respondent then filed suit in the United States District Court for the Eastern District of North Carolina, alleging both a violation of § 504 of the Rehabilitation Act of 1973 and a denial of equal protection and due process. After a bench trial, the District Court entered judgment in favor of Southeastern . . .

. . . the District Court concluded that respondent was not an "otherwise qualified handicapped individual" protected against discrimination by § 504. In its view, "[o]therwise qualified, can only be read to mean otherwise able to function sufficiently in the position sought in spite of the handicap, if proper training and facilities are suitable and available." Because respondent's disability would prevent her from functioning "sufficiently" in Southeastern's nursing program, the court held that the decision to exclude her was not discriminatory within the meaning of § 504.

On appeal, the Court of Appeals for the Fourth Circuit reversed. It did not dispute the District Court's findings of fact, but held that the court had misconstrued § 504. . . . the appellate court believed that § 504 required Southeastern to "reconsider plaintiff's application for admission to the nursing program without regard to her hearing ability." It concluded that the District Court had erred in taking respondent's handicap into account in determining whether she was "otherwise qualified" for the program, rather than confining its inquiry to her "academic and technical qualifications." The Court of Appeals also suggested that § 504 required "affirmative conduct" on the part of Southeastern to modify its program to accommodate the disabilities of applicants, "even when such modifications become expensive."

Because of the importance of this issue to the many institutions covered by § 504, we granted *certiorari*. We now reverse.

II

As previously noted, this is the first case in which this Court has been called upon to interpret § 504. It is elementary that "[t]he starting point in every case involving construction of a statute is the language itself." Section 504 by its terms does not compel educational institutions to disregard the disabilities of handicapped individuals or to make substantial modifications in their programs to allow disabled persons to participate. Instead, it requires only that an "otherwise qualified handicapped individual" not be excluded from participation in a federally funded program "solely by reason of his handicap," indicating only that mere possession of a handicap is not a permissible ground for assuming an inability to function in a particular context.

The court below, however, believed that the "otherwise qualified" persons protected by § 504 include those who would be able to meet the requirements of a particular program in every respect except as to limitations imposed by their handicap. Taken literally, this holding would prevent an institution from taking into account any limitation resulting from the handicap, however disabling. It assumes, in effect, that a person need not meet legitimate physical requirements in order to be "otherwise qualified." We think the understanding of the District Court is closer to the plain meaning of the statutory language. An otherwise qualified person is one who is able to meet all of a program's requirements in spite of his handicap.

The regulations promulgated by the Department of HEW to interpret § 504 reinforce, rather than contradict, this conclusion. According to these regulations, a "[q]ualified handicapped person" is, "[w]ith respect to postsecondary and vocational education services, a handicapped person who meets the academic and technical standards requisite to admission or participation in the [school's] education program or activity...."

A ... note emphasizes that legitimate physical qualifications may be essential to participation in particular programs. We think it clear, therefore, that HEW interprets the "other" qualifications which a handicapped person may be required to meet as including necessary physical qualifications.

III

The remaining question is whether the physical qualifications Southeastern demanded of respondent might not be necessary for participation in its nursing program. It is not open to dispute that, as Southeastern's Associate Degree Nursing program currently is constituted, the ability to understand speech without reliance on lipreading is necessary for patient safety during the clinical phase of the program. As the District Court found, this ability also is indispensable for many of the functions that a registered nurse performs.

Respondent contends nevertheless that § 504, properly interpreted, compels Southeastern to undertake affirmative action that would dispense with the need for effective oral communication. First, it is suggested that respondent can be given individual supervision by faculty members whenever she attends patients directly. Moreover, certain required courses might be dispensed with altogether for respondent. It is not necessary, she argues, that Southeastern train her to undertake all the tasks a registered nurse is licensed to perform. Rather, it is sufficient to make § 504 applicable if respondent might be able to perform satisfactorily some of the duties of a registered nurse or to hold some of the positions available to a registered nurse.

Respondent finds support for this argument in portions of the HEW regulations discussed above. In particular, a provision applicable to postsecondary educational programs requires covered institutions to make "modifications" in their programs to accommodate handicapped persons, and to provide "auxiliary aids" such as sign-language interpreters. Respondent argues that this regulation imposes an obligation to ensure full participation in covered programs by handicapped individuals and, in particular, requires Southeastern to make the kind of adjustments that would be necessary to permit her safe participation in the nursing program.

We note first that on the present record it appears unlikely respondent could benefit from any affirmative action that the regulation reasonably could be interpreted as requiring. [A federal regulation], for example, explicitly excludes "devices or services of a personal nature" from the kinds of auxiliary aids a school must provide a handicapped individual. Yet the only evidence in the record indicates that nothing less than close, individual attention by a nursing instructor would be sufficient to ensure patient safety if respondent took part in the clinical phase of the nursing program. Furthermore, it also is reasonably clear that [the regulation] does not encompass the kind of curricular changes that would be necessary to accommodate respondent in the nursing program. In light of respondent's inability to function in clinical courses without close supervision, Southeastern, with prudence, could allow her to take only academic classes. Whatever benefits respondent might realize from such a course of study, she would not receive even a rough equivalent of the training a nursing program normally gives. Such a fundamental alteration in the nature of a program is far more than the "modification" the regulation requires.

Moreover, an interpretation of the regulations that required the extensive modifications necessary to include respondent in the nursing program would raise grave doubts about their validity. If these regulations were to require substantial adjustments in existing programs beyond those necessary to eliminate discrimination against otherwise qualified individuals, they would do more than clarify the meaning of § 504. Instead, they would constitute an unauthorized extension of the obligations imposed by that statute.

The language and structure of the Rehabilitation Act of 1973 reflect a recognition by Congress of the distinction between the evenhanded treatment of qualified handicapped persons and affirmative efforts to overcome the disabilities caused by handicaps. Section 501(b), governing the employment of handicapped individuals by the Federal Government, requires each federal agency to submit "an affirmative action program plan for the hiring, placement, and advancement of handicapped individuals...." These plans "shall include a description of the extent to which and methods whereby the special needs of handicapped employees are being met." Similarly, § 503(a), governing hiring by federal contractors, requires employers to "take affirmative action to employ and advance in employment qualified handicapped individuals...."

Under § 501(c) of the Act, by contrast, state agencies such as Southeastern are only "encourage[d] ... to adopt and implement such policies and procedures." Section 504 does not refer at all to affirmative action, and except as it applies to federal employers it does not provide for implementation by administrative action. A comparison of these provisions demonstrates that Congress understood accommodation of the needs of handicapped individuals may require affirmative action and knew how to provide for it in those instances where it wished to do so.

Although an agency's interpretation of the statute under which it operates is entitled to some deference, "this deference is constrained by our obligation to honor the clear meaning of a statute, as revealed by its language, purpose, and history." Here, neither the language, purpose, nor history of § 504 reveals an intent to impose an affirmative-action obligation on all recipients of federal funds. Accordingly, we hold that even if HEW has attempted to create such an obligation itself, it lacks the authority to do so.

IV

We do not suggest that the line between a lawful refusal to extend affirmative action and illegal discrimination against handicapped persons always will be clear. It is possible to envision situations where an insistence on continuing past requirements and practices might arbitrarily deprive genuinely qualified handicapped persons of the opportunity to participate in a covered program. Technological advances can be expected to enhance opportunities to rehabilitate the handicapped or otherwise to qualify them for some useful employment. Such advances also may enable attainment of these goals without imposing undue financial and administrative burdens upon a State. Thus, situations may arise where a refusal to modify an existing program might become unreasonable and discriminatory. Identification of those instances where a refusal to accommodate the needs of a disabled person amounts to discrimination against the handicapped continues to be an important responsibility of HEW.

In this case, however, it is clear that Southeastern's unwillingness to make major adjustments in its nursing program does not constitute such discrimination. The uncontroverted testimony of several members of Southeastern's staff and faculty established that the purpose of its program was to train persons who could serve the nursing profession in all customary ways. This type of purpose, far from reflecting any animus against handicapped individuals is shared by many if not most of the institutions that train persons to render professional service. It is undisputed that respondent could not participate in Southeastern's nursing program unless the standards were substantially lowered. Section 504 imposes no requirement upon an educational institution to lower or to effect substantial modifications of standards to accommodate a handicapped person.

Respondent's argument misses the point. Southeastern's program, structured to train persons who will be able to perform all normal roles of a registered nurse, represents a legitimate academic policy, and is accepted by the State. In effect, it seeks to ensure that no graduate will pose a danger to the public in any professional role in which he or she might be cast. Even if the licensing requirements of North Carolina or some other State are less demanding, nothing in the Act requires an educational institution to lower its standards.

One may admire respondent's desire and determination to overcome her handicap, and there well may be various other types of service for which she can qualify. In this case, however, we hold that there was no violation of § 504 when Southeastern concluded that respondent did not qualify for admission to its program. Nothing in the language or history of § 504 reflects an intention to limit the freedom of an educational institution to require reasonable physical qualifications for admission to a clinical training program. Nor has there been any showing in this case that any action short of a substantial change in Southeastern's program would render unreasonable the qualifications it imposed.

V

Accordingly, we reverse the judgment of the court below, and remand for proceedings consistent with this opinion.

So ordered.

Notes

1. An argument can be made that if parents were fully aware of the parameters of Section 504, then schools would have to operate differently. Would this be beneficial?

2. Note that all students who are covered by Section 504 are not necessarily covered by the IDEA's more specific eligibility requirements.

3. As indicated at the start of this chapter, Section 504 applies to anyone in a school building. In one such case, a federal trial court in New York directed school officials to provide a sign language interpreter for deaf parents of normal-hearing students in order to enable them to participate in school-initiated conferences incident to the academic or disciplinary aspects of their education. *Rothschild v. Grottenthaler*, 725 F.Supp. 776 [57 Educ. L. Rep. 832] (S.D.N.Y. 1989).

[Case No. 118]   Interpreting Appropriateness under the IDEA

BOARD OF EDUCATION OF THE HENDRICK HUDSON CENTRAL SCHOOL DISTRICT v. ROWLEY

Supreme Court of the United States, 1982.
458 U.S. 176, 102 S.Ct. 3034, 73 L.Ed.2d 690 [5 Educ. L. Rep. 34].

JUSTICE REHNQUIST delivered the opinion of the Court.

This case presents a question of statutory interpretation. Petitioners contend that the Court of Appeals and the District Court misconstrued the requirements imposed by Congress upon States which receive federal funds under the Education of the Handicapped Act. We agree and reverse the judgment of the Court of Appeals.

I

. . .

The Education of the Handicapped Act (Act) provides federal money to assist state and local agencies in educating handicapped children, and conditions such funding upon a State's compliance with extensive goals and procedures. The Act represents an ambitious federal effort to promote the education of handicapped children, and was passed in response to Congress' perception that a majority of handicapped children in the United States "were either totally excluded from schools or [were] sitting idly in regular classrooms awaiting the time when they were old enough to 'drop out.' " . . .

. . . The Act broadly defines "handicapped children" to include "mentally retarded, hard of hearing, deaf, speech impaired, visually handicapped, seriously emotionally disturbed, orthopedically impaired, [and] other health impaired children, [and] children with specific learning disabilities."

The "free appropriate public education" required by the Act is tailored to the unique needs of the handicapped child by means of an "individualized educational program" (IEP). . . . The IEP, which is prepared at a meeting between a qualified representative of the Local or regional educational agencies must review, and where appropriate revise, each child's IEP at least annually.

. . . although the Act leaves to the States the primary responsibility for developing and executing educational programs for handicapped children, it imposes significant requirements to be followed in the discharge of that responsibility. Compliance is assured by provisions permitting the withholding of federal funds upon determination that a participating state or local agency has failed to satisfy the requirements of the Act, and by the provision for judicial review. . . .

II

This case arose in connection with the education of Amy Rowley, a deaf student at the Furnace Woods School in the Hendrick Hudson

Central School District, Peekskill, N.Y. Amy has minimal residual hearing and is an excellent lipreader. During the year before she began attending Furnace Woods, a meeting between her parents and school administrators resulted in a decision to place her in a regular kindergarten class in order to determine what supplemental services would be necessary to her education. Several members of the school administration prepared for Amy's arrival by attending a course in sign-language interpretation, and a teletype machine was installed in the principal's office to facilitate communication with her parents who are also deaf. At the end of the trial period it was determined that Amy should remain in the kindergarten class, but that she should be provided with an FM hearing aid which would amplify words spoken into a wireless receiver by the teacher or fellow students during certain classroom activities. Amy successfully completed her kindergarten year.

As required by the Act, an IEP was prepared for Amy during the fall of her first-grade year. The IEP provided that Amy should be educated in a regular classroom at Furnace Woods, should continue to use the FM hearing aid, and should receive instruction from a tutor for the deaf for one hour each day and from a speech therapist for three hours each week. The Rowleys agreed with parts of the IEP, but insisted that Amy also be provided a qualified sign-language interpreter in all her academic classes in lieu of the assistance proposed in other parts of the IEP. Such an interpreter had been placed in Amy's kindergarten class for a 2–week experimental period, but the interpreter had reported that Amy did not need his services at that time. The school administrators likewise concluded that Amy did not need such an interpreter in her first-grade classroom. . . .

When their request for an interpreter was denied, the Rowleys demanded and received a hearing before an independent examiner. After receiving evidence from both sides, the examiner agreed with the administrators' determination that an interpreter was not necessary because "Amy was achieving educationally, academically, and socially" without such assistance. The examiner's decision was affirmed on appeal by the New York Commissioner of Education on the basis of substantial evidence in the record. . . . the Rowleys then brought an action in the United States District Court for the Southern District of New York, claiming that the administrators' denial of the sign-language interpreter constituted a denial of the "free appropriate public education" guaranteed by the Act.

The District Court found that Amy "is a remarkably well-adjusted child" who interacts and communicates well with her classmates and has "developed an extraordinary rapport" with her teachers. It also found that "she performs better than the average child in her class and is advancing easily from grade to grade," but "that she understands considerably less of what goes on in class than she could if she were not deaf" and thus "is not learning as much, or performing as well academically, as she would without her handicap," This disparity between Amy's achievement and her potential led the court to decide that she was not receiving a "free appropriate public education," which the court defined as "an opportunity to achieve [her] full potential commensurate with the opportunity provided to other children." According to the District Court, such a standard "requires that the potential of the handicapped child be measured and compared to his or her performance, and that the resulting differential or 'shortfall' be compared to the shortfall experienced by nonhandicapped children" . . .

A divided panel of the United States Court of Appeals for the Second Circuit affirmed . . .

We granted certiorari to review the lower courts' interpretation of the Act. Such review requires us to consider two questions: What is meant by the Act's requirement of a "free appropriate public education"? And what is the role of state and federal courts in exercising the review granted by 20 U.S.C.A. § 1415? We consider these questions separately.

III

A

This is the first case in which this Court has been called upon to interpret any provision of the Act. As noted previously, the District Court and the Court of Appeals concluded that "[t]he Act itself does not define 'appropriate education,'" but leaves "to the courts and the hearing officers" the responsibility of "giv[ing] content to the requirement of an 'appropriate education.'" Petitioners contend that the definition of the phrase "free appropriate public education" used by the courts below overlooks the definition of that phrase actually found in the Act. Respondents agree that the Act defines "free appropriate public education," but contend that the statutory definition is not "functional" and thus "offers judges no guidance in their consideration of controversies involving 'the identification, evaluation, or educational placement of the child or the provision of a free appropriate public education.'" The United States, appearing as amicus curiae on behalf of respondents, states that "[a]lthough the Act includes definitions of a 'free appropriate public education' and other related terms, the statutory definitions do not adequately explain what is meant by 'appropriate.'"

We are loath to conclude that Congress failed to offer any assistance in defining the meaning of the principal substantive phrase used in the Act. It is beyond dispute that, contrary to the conclusions of the courts below, the Act does expressly define "free appropriate public education":

> "The term 'free appropriate public education' means *special education* and *related services* which (A) have been provided at public expense, under public supervision and direction, and without charge, (B) meet the standards of the State educational agency, (C) include an appropriate preschool, elementary, or secondary school education in the State involved, and (D) are provided in conformity with the individualized education program required under section 1414(a)(5) of this title."

"Special education," as referred to in this definition, means "specially designed instruction, at no cost to parents or guardians, to meet the unique needs of a handicapped child, including classroom instruction, instruction in physical education, home instruction, and instruction in hospitals and institutions." "Related services" are defined as "transportation, and such developmental, corrective, and other supportive services ... as may be required to assist a handicapped child to benefit from special education."

Like many statutory definitions, this one tends toward the cryptic rather than the comprehensive, but that is scarcely a reason for abandoning the quest for legislative intent. Whether or not the definition is a "functional" one, as respondents contend it is not, it is the principal tool which Congress has given us for parsing the critical phrase of the Act. We think more must be made of it than either respondents or the United States seems willing to admit.

According to the definitions contained in the Act, a "free appropriate public education" consists of educational instruction specially designed to meet the unique needs of the handicapped child, supported by such services as are necessary to permit the child "to benefit" from the instruction.... the definition also requires that such instruction and services be provided at public expense and under public supervision, meet the State's educational standards, approximate the grade levels used in the State's regular education, and comport with the child's IEP. Thus, if personalized instruction is being provided with sufficient supportive services to permit the child to benefit from the instruction, and the other items on the definitional checklist are satisfied, the child is receiving a "free appropriate public education" as defined by the Act....

Noticeably absent from the language of the statute is any substantive standard prescribing the level of education to be accorded handicapped children. Certainly the language of the statute contains no requirement like the one imposed by the lower courts—that States maximize the potential of handicapped children "commensurate with the opportunity provided to other children." That standard was expounded by the District Court without reference to the statutory definitions or even to the legislative history of the Act. Although we find the statutory definition of "free appropriate public education" to be helpful in our interpretation of the Act, there remains the question of whether the legislative history indicates a congressional intent that such education meet some additional substantive standard. For an answer, we turn to that history.

B

(i)

As suggested in Part I, federal support for education of the handicapped is a fairly recent development. Before passage of the Act some States had passed laws to improve the educational services afforded handicapped children, but many of these children were excluded completely from any form of public education or were left to fend for themselves in classrooms designed for education of their nonhandicapped peers ...

This concern, stressed repeatedly throughout the legislative history, confirms the impression conveyed by the language of the statute: By passing the Act, Congress sought primarily to make public education available to handicapped children. But in seeking to provide such access to public education, Congress did not impose upon the States any greater substantive educational standard than would be necessary to make such access meaningful. Indeed, Congress expressly "recognize[d] that in many instances the process of providing special education and related services to handicapped children is not guaranteed to produce any particular outcome." Thus, the intent of the Act was more to open the door of public education to handicapped children on appropriate terms than to guarantee any particular level of education once inside.

Both the House and the Senate Reports attribute the impetus for the Act and its predecessors to two federal-court judgments rendered in 1971 and 1972.... The first case, (*PARC*), was a suit on behalf of retarded children challenging the constitutionality of a Pennsylvania statute which acted to exclude them from public education and training. The case ended in a consent decree which enjoined the State from "deny[ing] to any mentally retarded child *access* to a free public program of education and training."

PARC was followed by *Mills v. Board of Education of District of Columbia*, a case in which the plaintiff handicapped children had been excluded from the District of Columbia public schools. The court's judgment ... provided that "no [handicapped] child eligible for a publicly supported education in the District of Columbia public schools shall be excluded from a regular school assignment by a Rule, policy, or practice of the Board of Education of the District of Columbia or its agents unless such child is provided (a) adequate alternative educational services suited to the child's needs, which may include special education or tuition grants, and (b) a constitutionally adequate prior hearing and periodic review of the child's status, progress, and the *adequacy* of any educational alternative."

Mills and *PARC* both held that handicapped children must be given access to an adequate, publicly supported education. Neither case purports to require any particular substantive level of education. Rather, like the language of the Act, the cases set forth extensive procedures to be followed in formulating personalized educational programs for handicapped children. The fact that both *PARC* and *Mills* are discussed at length in the legislative Reports suggests that the principles which they established are the principles which, to a significant extent, guided the drafters of the Act. Indeed, immediately after discussing these cases the Senate Report describes the 1974 statute as having "incorporated the major principles of the right to education cases." Those principles in turn became the basis of the Act, which itself was designed to effectuate the purposes of the 1974 statute.

It is evident from the legislative history that the characterization of handicapped children as "served" referred to children who were receiving some form of specialized educational services from the States, and that the characterization of children as "unserved" referred to those who were receiving no specialized educational services....

(ii)

Respondents contend that "the goal of the Act is to provide each handicapped child with an equal educational opportunity." We think, however, that the requirement that a State provide specialized educational services to handicapped children generates no additional requirement that the services so provided be sufficient to maximize each child's potential "commensurate with the opportunity provided other children." Respondents and the United States correctly note that Congress sought "to provide assistance to the States in carrying out their responsibilities under ... the Constitution of the United States to provide equal protection of the laws." But we do not think that such statements imply a congressional intent to achieve strict equality of opportunity or services.

The educational opportunities provided by our public school systems undoubtedly differ from student to student, depending upon a myriad of factors that might affect a particular student's ability to assimilate information presented in the classroom. The requirement that States provide "equal" educational opportunities would thus seem to present an entirely unworkable standard requiring impossible measurements and comparisons. Similarly, furnishing handicapped children with only such services as are available to nonhandicapped children would in all probability fall short of the statutory requirement of "free appropriate public education"; to require, on the other hand, the furnishing of every special service necessary to maximize each handicapped child's potential is, we think, further than Congress intended to go. Thus to speak in terms of "equal" services in one instance gives less than what is required by the Act and in another instance more. The theme of the Act is "free appropriate public education," a phrase which is too complex to be captured by the word "equal" whether one is speaking of opportunities or services.

The legislative conception of the requirements of equal protection was undoubtedly informed by the two District Court decisions referred to above. But cases such as *Mills* and *PARC* held simply that handicapped children may not be excluded entirely from public education ...

... To the extent that Congress might have looked further than these cases which are mentioned in the legislative history, at the time of enactment of the Act this Court had held at least twice that the Equal Protection Clause of the Fourteenth Amendment does not require States to expend equal financial resources on the education of each child.

In explaining the need for federal legislation, the House Report noted that "no congressional legislation has required a precise guarantee for handicapped children, i.e. a basic floor of opportunity that would bring into compliance all school districts with the constitutional right of equal protection with respect to handicapped children." Assuming that the Act was designed to fill the need identified in the House Report—that is, to provide a "basic floor of opportunity" consistent with equal protection—neither the Act nor its history persuasively demonstrates that Congress thought that equal protection required anything more than equal access. Therefore, Congress' desire to provide specialized educational services, even in furtherance of "equality," cannot be read as imposing any particular substantive educational standard upon the States.

The District Court and the Court of Appeals thus erred when they held that the Act requires New York to maximize the potential of each handicapped child commensurate with the opportunity provided nonhandicapped children. Desirable though that goal might be, it is not the standard that Congress imposed upon States which receive funding under the Act. Rather, Congress sought primarily to identify and evaluate handicapped children, and to provide them with access to a free public education.

(iii)

Implicit in the congressional purpose of providing access to a "free appropriate public education" is the requirement that the education to which access is provided be sufficient to confer some educational benefit upon the handicapped child. It would do little good for Congress to spend millions of dollars in providing access to a public education only to have the handicapped child receive no benefit from that education. The statutory definition of "free appropriate public education," in addition to requiring that States provide each child with "specially designed instruction," expressly requires the provision of "such ... supportive services ... as may be required to assist a handicapped child to benefit from special education." We therefore conclude that the "basic floor of opportunity" provided by the Act consists of access to specialized instruction and related services which are individually designed to provide educational benefit to the handicapped child.

The determination of when handicapped children are receiving sufficient educational benefits to satisfy the requirements of the Act presents a more difficult problem. The Act requires participating States to educate a wide spectrum of handicapped children, from the marginally hearing-impaired to the profoundly retarded and palsied. It is clear that the benefits obtainable by children at one end of the spectrum will differ dramatically from those obtainable by children at the other end, with infinite variations in between. One child may have little difficulty competing successfully in an academic setting with nonhandicapped children while another child may encounter great difficulty in acquiring even the most basic of self-maintenance skills. We do not attempt today to establish any one test for determining the adequacy of educational benefits conferred upon all children covered by the Act. Because in this case we are presented with a handicapped child who is receiving substantial specialized instruction and related services, and who is performing above average in the regular classrooms of a public school system, we confine our analysis to that situation.

The Act requires participating States to educate handicapped children with nonhandicapped children whenever possible. When that "mainstreaming" preference of the Act has been met and a child is being educated in the regular classrooms of a public school system, the system itself monitors the educational progress of the child. Regular examinations are administered, grades are awarded, and yearly advancement to higher grade levels is permitted for those children who attain an adequate knowledge of the course material. The grading and advancement system thus constitutes an important factor in determining educational benefit. Children who graduate from our public school systems are considered by our society to have been "educated" at least to the grade level they have completed, and access to an "education" for handicapped children is precisely what Congress sought to provide in the Act.

C

When the language of the Act and its legislative history are considered together, the requirements imposed by Congress become tolerably clear. Insofar as a State is required to provide a handicapped child with a "free appropriate public education," we hold that it satisfies this requirement by providing personalized instruction with sufficient support services to permit the child to benefit educationally from that instruction. Such instruction and services must be provided at public expense, must meet the State's educational standards, must approximate the grade levels used in the State's regular education, and must comport with the child's IEP. In addition, the IEP, and therefore the personalized instruction, should be formulated in accordance with the requirements of the Act and, if the child is being educated in the regular classrooms of the public education system, should be reasonably calculated to enable the child to achieve passing marks and advance from grade to grade.

In defending the decisions of the District Court and the Court of Appeals, respondents and the United States rely upon isolated statements in the legislative history concerning the achievement of maximum potential as support for their contention that Congress intended to impose greater substantive requirements than we have found. These statements, however, are too thin a reed on which to base an interpretation of the Act which disregards both its language and the balance of its legislative history. . . . As already demonstrated, the Act and its history impose no requirements on the States like those imposed by the District Court and the Court of Appeals. A fortiori Congress has not done so unambiguously, as required in the valid exercise of its spending power.

IV

A

As mentioned in Part I, the Act permits "[a]ny party aggrieved by the findings and decision" of the state administrative hearings "to bring a civil action" in "any State court of competent jurisdiction or in a district court of the United States without regard to the amount in controversy." The complaint, and therefore the civil action, may concern "any matter relating to the identification, evaluation, or educational placement of the child, or the provision of a free appropriate public education to such child." In reviewing the complaint, the Act provides that a court "shall receive the record of the [state] administrative proceedings, shall hear additional evidence at the request of a party, and, basing its decision on the preponderance of the evidence, shall grant such relief as the court determines is appropriate."

The parties disagree sharply over the meaning of these provisions, petitioners contending that courts are given only limited authority to review for state compliance with the Act's procedural requirements and no power to review the substance of the state program, and respondents contending that the Act requires courts to exercise de novo review over state educational decisions and policies. We find petitioners' contention unpersuasive, for Congress expressly rejected provisions that would have so severely restricted the role of reviewing courts. In substituting the current language of the statute for language that would have made state administrative findings conclusive if supported by substantial evidence, the Conference Committee explained that courts were to make "independent decision[s] based on a preponderance of the evidence."

But although we find that this grant of authority is broader than claimed by petitioners, we think the fact that it is found in § 1415, which is entitled "Procedural safeguards," is not without significance. When the elaborate and highly specific procedural safeguards embodied in § 1415 are contrasted with the general and somewhat imprecise substantive admonitions contained in the Act, we think that the importance Congress attached to these procedural safeguards cannot be gainsaid. It seems to us no exaggeration to say that Congress placed every bit as much emphasis upon compliance with procedures giving parents and guardians a large measure of participation at every stage of the administrative process as it did upon the measurement of the resulting IEP against a substantive standard. We think that the congressional emphasis upon full participation of concerned parties throughout the development of the IEP, as well as the requirements that state and local plans be submitted to the Secretary for approval, demonstrates the legislative conviction that adequate compliance with the procedures prescribed would in most cases assure much if not all of what Congress wished in the way of substantive content in an IEP.

Thus the provision that a reviewing court base its decision on the "preponderance of the evidence" is by no means an invitation to the courts to substitute their own notions of sound educational policy for those of the school authorities which they review. The very importance which Congress has attached to compliance with certain procedures in the preparation of an IEP would be frustrated if a court were permitted simply to set state decisions at nought. The fact that § 1415(e) requires that the reviewing court "receive the records of the [state] administrative proceedings" carries with it the implied requirement that due weight shall be given to these proceedings. And we find nothing in the Act to suggest that merely because Congress was rather sketchy in

establishing substantive requirements, as opposed to procedural requirements for the preparation of an IEP, it intended that reviewing courts
should have a free hand to impose substantive standards of review which
cannot be derived from the Act itself. In short, the statutory authorization to grant "such relief as the court determines is appropriate" cannot
be read without reference to the obligations, largely procedural in
nature, which are imposed upon recipient States by Congress.

Therefore, a court's inquiry in suits brought under § 1415(e)(2) is
twofold. First, has the State complied with the procedures set forth in
the Act? And second, is the individualized educational program developed through the Act's procedures reasonably calculated to enable the
child to receive educational benefits? If these requirements are met, the
State has complied with the obligations imposed by Congress and the
courts can require no more.

B

In assuring that the requirements of the Act have been met,
courts must be careful to avoid imposing their view of preferable
educational methods upon the States. The primary responsibility for
formulating the education to be accorded a handicapped child, and for
choosing the educational method most suitable to the child's needs,
was left by the Act to state and local educational agencies in cooperation with the parents or guardian of the child. The Act expressly
charges States with the responsibility of "acquiring and disseminating
to teachers and administrators of programs for handicapped children
significant information derived from educational research, demonstration, and similar projects, and [of] adopting, where appropriate, promising educational practices and materials." In the face of such a clear
statutory directive, it seems highly unlikely that Congress intended
courts to overturn a State's choice of appropriate educational theories
in a proceeding conducted pursuant to § 1415(e)(2).

We previously have cautioned that courts lack the "specialized
knowledge and experience" necessary to resolve "persistent and difficult
questions of educational policy." We think that Congress shared that
view when it passed the Act. As already demonstrated, Congress' intention was not that the Act displace the primacy of States in the field of
education, but that States receive funds to assist them in extending their
educational systems to the handicapped. Therefore, once a court determines that the requirements of the Act have been met, questions of
methodology are for resolution by the States.

V

Entrusting a child's education to state and local agencies does not
leave the child without protection. Congress sought to protect individual
children by providing for parental involvement in the development of
state plans and policies and in the formulation of the child's individual
educational program . . . .

VI

Applying these principles to the facts of this case, we conclude that the Court of Appeals erred in affirming the decision of the District Court. Neither the District Court nor the Court of Appeals found that petitioners had failed to comply with the procedures of the Act, and the findings of neither court would support a conclusion that Amy's educational program failed to comply with the substantive requirements of the Act. On the contrary, the District Court found that the "evidence firmly establishes that Amy is receiving an 'adequate' education, since she performs better than the average child in her class and is advancing easily from grade to grade." In light of this finding, and of the fact that Amy was receiving personalized instruction and related services calculated by the Furnace Woods school administrators to meet her educational needs, the lower courts should not have concluded that the Act requires the provision of a sign-language interpreter. Accordingly, the decision of the Court of Appeals is reversed, and the case is remanded for further proceedings consistent with this opinion.

So ordered.

Notes

1. *Rowley* sets a fairly low standard. The dissent interpreted Congressional intent in enacting the IDEA as providing children with disabilities with educational opportunities commensurate with those of their peers who are not disabled. How might such an interpretation have changed the face of special education? Regular education?

2. The Court has been reluctant to re-examine the issues it addressed in *Rowley*. Should the Court reconsider the meaning of an appropriate education? Should Congress?

[Case No. 119] "Zero Reject" for Students with Disabilities

TIMOTHY W. v. ROCHESTER, NEW HAMPSHIRE, SCHOOL DISTRICT

United States Court of Appeals, First Circuit, 1989.
875 F.2d 954 [54 Educ. L. Rep. 74].

BOWNES, CIRCUIT JUDGE.

Plaintiff-appellant Timothy W. appeals an order of the district court which held that under the Education for All Handicapped Children Act, a handicapped child is not eligible for special education if he cannot benefit from that education, and that Timothy W., a severely retarded and multiply handicapped child was not eligible under that standard. We reverse.

I. BACKGROUND

Timothy W. was born two months prematurely on December 8, 1975 with severe respiratory problems, and shortly thereafter experienced an intracranial hemorrhage, subdural effusions, seizures, hydrocephalus, and meningitis. As a result, Timothy is multiply handicapped and profoundly mentally retarded. He suffers from complex developmental disabilities, spastic quadriplegia, cerebral palsy, seizure disorder and cortical blindness. His mother attempted to obtain appropriate services for him, and while he did receive some services from the Rochester Child Development Center, he did not receive any educational program from the Rochester School District when he became of school age.

On February 19, 1980, the Rochester School District convened a meeting to decide if Timothy was considered educationally handicapped under the state and federal statutes. . . . The school district adjourned without making a finding. In a meeting on March 7, 1980, the school district decided that Timothy was not educationally handicapped—that since his handicap was so severe he was not "capable of benefitting" from an education, and therefore was not entitled to one. During 1981 and 1982, the school district did not provide Timothy with any educational program.

In May, 1982, the New Hampshire Department of Education reviewed the Rochester School District's special education programs and made a finding of non-compliance, stating that the school district was not allowed to use "capable of benefitting" as a criterion for eligibility. No action was taken in response to this finding until one year later, on June 20, 1983, when the school district met to discuss Timothy's case. . . . The school district, however, continued its refusal to provide Timothy with any educational program or services.

In response to a letter from Timothy's attorney, on January 17, 1984, the school district's placement team met. . . . The placement team recommended that Timothy be placed at the Child Development Center so that he could be provided with a special education program. The Rochester School Board, however, refused to authorize the placement team's recommendation to provide educational services for Timothy, contending that it still needed more information. . . .

On April 24, 1984, Timothy filed a complaint with the New Hampshire Department of Education requesting that he be placed in an educational program immediately. On October 9, 1984, the Department of Education issued an order requiring the school district to place him, within five days, in an educational program, until the appeals process on the issue of whether Timothy was educationally handicapped was completed. The school district, however, refused to make any such educational placement. On October 31, 1984, the school district filed an appeal of the order. There was also a meeting on November 8, 1984, in which the Rochester School Board reviewed Timothy's case and concluded he was not eligible for special education.

On November 17, 1984, Timothy filed a complaint in the United States District Court, pursuant to 42 U.S.C. § 1983, alleging that his rights under the Education for All Handicapped Children Act the corresponding New Hampshire state law (RSA 186–C), § 504 of the Rehabilitation Act of 1973 and the equal protection and due process clauses of the United States and New Hampshire Constitutions, had been violated by the Rochester School District. The complaint sought preliminary and permanent injunctions directing the school district to provide him with special education, and $175,000 in damages.

A hearing was held in the district court on December 21, 1984.... On January 3, 1985, the district court denied Timothy's motion for a preliminary injunction, and on January 8, stated it would abstain on the damage claim pending exhaustion of the state administrative procedures....

In September, 1986, Timothy again requested a special education program. In October, 1986, the school district continued to refuse to provide him with such a program, claiming it still needed more information....

On May 20, 1987, the district court found that Timothy had not exhausted his state administrative remedies before the New Hampshire Department of Education, and precluded pretrial discovery until this had been done. On September 15, 1987, the hearing officer in the administrative hearings ruled that Timothy's capacity to benefit was not a legally permissible standard for determining his eligibility to receive a public education, and that the Rochester School District must provide him with an education. The Rochester School District, on November 12, 1987, appealed this decision to the United States District Court by filing a counterclaim, and on March 29, 1988, moved for summary judgment. Timothy filed a cross motion for summary judgment....

On July 15, 1988, the district court rendered its opinion entitled "Order on Motion for Judgment on the Pleadings or in the Alternative, Summary Judgment." ... The court made rulings of law and findings of fact. It first ruled that "under EAHCA [the Education for All Handicapped Children Act], an initial determination as to the child's ability to benefit from special education, must be made in order for a handicapped child to qualify for education under the Act." After noting that the New Hampshire statute (RSA) was intended to implement the EAHCA, the court held: "Under New Hampshire law, an initial decision must be made concerning the ability of a handicapped child to benefit from special education before an entitlement to the education can exist." The court then reviewed the materials, reports and testimony and found that "Timothy W. is not capable of benefitting from special education.... As a result, the defendant [school district] is not obligated to provide special education under either EAHCA [the federal statute] or RSA 186–C [the New Hampshire statute]." Timothy W. has appealed this order....

The primary issue is whether the district court erred in its rulings of law. Since we find that it did, we do not review its findings of fact.

II. THE LANGUAGE OF THE ACT

A. The Plain Meaning of the Act Mandates a Public Education for All Handicapped Children

The Education for All Handicapped Children Act, [hereinafter the Act], was enacted in 1975 to ensure that handicapped children receive an education which is appropriate to their unique needs. In assessing the plain meaning of the Act, we first look to its title: The Education for All Handicapped Children Act. The Congressional Findings section of the Act states that there were eight million handicapped children, that more than half of them did not receive appropriate educational services, and that one million were excluded entirely from the public school system. Given these grim statistics, Congress concluded that "State and local educational agencies have a responsibility to provide education for all handicapped children...." In directly addressing the educability of handicapped children, Congress found that "developments in the training of teachers and in diagnostic and instructional procedures and methods have advanced to the point that, given appropriate funding, State and local educational agencies can and will provide effective special education and related services to meet the needs of handicapped children." The Act's stated purpose was "to assure that *all* handicapped children have available to them ... a free appropriate public education which emphasizes special education and related services designed to meet their unique needs, ... [and] to assist states and localities to provide for the education of all handicapped children ..."

The Act's mandatory provisions require that for a state to qualify for financial assistance, it must have "in effect a policy that assures all handicapped children the right to a free appropriate education." The state must "set forth in detail the policies and procedures which the State will undertake ... to assure that—there is established a goal of providing full educational opportunity to *all* handicapped children ..., [and that] a free appropriate public education will be available for *all* handicapped children between the ages of three and eighteen ... not later than September 1, 1978, and for *all* handicapped children between the ages of three and twenty-one ... not later than September 1, 1980...." The state must also assure that "*all* children residing in the State who are handicapped, regardless of the severity of their handicap, and who are in need of special education and related services are identified, located, and evaluated...."

The language of the Act could not be more unequivocal. The statute is permeated with the words "*all* handicapped children" whenever it refers to the target population. It never speaks of any exceptions for severely handicapped children. Indeed, as indicated *supra,* the Act gives priority to the most severely handicapped. Nor is there any language whatsoever which requires as a prerequisite to being covered by the Act, that a handicapped child must demonstrate that he or she will "benefit" from the educational program. Rather, the Act speaks of the state's responsibility to design a special education and related services program that will meet the unique "needs" of all handicapped children. The language of the Act in its entirety makes clear that a "zero-reject" policy is at the core of the Act, and that no child, regardless of the severity of his or her handicap, is to ever again be subjected to the deplorable state of affairs which existed at the time of the Act's passage, in which millions of handicapped children received inadequate education or none at all. In summary, the Act mandates an appropriate public education for all handicapped children, regardless of the level of achievement that such children might attain.

B. Timothy W.: A Handicapped Child Entitled to An Appropriate Education

Given that the Act's language mandates that all handicapped children are entitled to a free appropriate education, we must next inquire if Timothy W. is a handicapped child, and if he is, what constitutes an appropriate education to meet his unique needs.

(1) *Handicapped children:*

. . .

There is no question that Timothy W. fits within the Act's definition of a handicapped child: he is multiply handicapped and profoundly mentally retarded. He has been described as suffering from severe spasticity, cerebral palsy, brain damage, joint contractures, cortical blindness, is not ambulatory, and is quadriplegic.

. . .

The record shows that Timothy W. is a severely handicapped and profoundly retarded child in need of special education and related services. Much of the expert testimony was to the effect that he is aware of his surrounding environment, makes or attempts to make purposeful movements, responds to tactile stimulation, responds to his mother's voice and touch, recognizes familiar voices, responds to noises, and parts his lips when spoon fed. The record contains testimony that Timothy W.'s needs include sensory stimulation, physical therapy, improved head control, socialization, consistency in responding to sound sources, and partial participation in eating. The educational consultants who drafted Timothy's individualized education program recommended that Timothy's special education program should include goals and objectives in the areas of motor control, communication, socialization, daily living skills, and recreation. The special education and related services that have been recommended to meet Timothy W.'s needs fit well within the statutory and regulatory definitions of the Act.

We conclude that the Act's language dictates the holding that Timothy W. is a handicapped child who is in need of special education and related services because of his handicaps. He must, therefore, according to the Act, be provided with such an educational program. There is nothing in the Act's language which even remotely supports the district court's conclusion that "under [the Act], an initial determination as to a child's ability to benefit from special education, must be made in order for a handicapped child to qualify for education under the Act." The language of the Act is directly to the contrary: a school district has a duty to provide an educational program for every handicapped child in the district, regardless of the severity of the handicap.

III.   LEGISLATIVE HISTORY

An examination of the legislative history reveals that Congress intended the Act to provide a public education for all handicapped children, without exception; that the most severely handicapped were in fact to be given priority attention; and that an educational benefit was neither guaranteed nor required as a prerequisite for a child to receive such education. These factors were central, and were repeated over and over again, in the more than three years of congressional hearings and debates, which culminated in passage of the 1975 Act.

A.   Education For All Handicapped Children

The Act was a response to tomes of testimony and evidence that handicapped children were being systematically excluded from education outright, or were receiving grossly inadequate education. The Office of Education provided Congress with a report documenting that there were eight million handicapped children, and that more than four million of them were not receiving an appropriate education, including almost two million who were receiving *no* education at all. . . .

The record is replete with statements by legislators that the Act was in response to this deplorable state of affairs. . . .

Moreover, the legislative history is unambiguous that the primary purpose of the Act was to remedy the then current state of affairs, and provide a public education for *all* handicapped children. . . .

. . . . The Senate Committee recognized "the need for a final date in legislation by which time *all* handicapped children are to be provided a free appropriate public education," and that "the failure to provide a right to education to handicapped children cannot be allowed to continue." . . . .

B.   Priority For The Most Severely Handicapped

Not only did Congress intend that all handicapped children be educated, it expressly indicated its intent that the most severely handicapped be given priority. This resolve was reiterated over and over again in the floor debates and congressional reports, as well as in the final legislation. . . .

. . .

This priority reflected congressional acceptance of the thesis that early educational intervention was very important for severely handicapped children. . . .

If the order of the district court denying Timothy W. the benefits of the Act were to be implemented, he would be classified by the Act as in even greater need for receiving educational services than a severely multi-handicapped child receiving inadequate education. He would be in the *highest priority*—as a child who was not receiving any education at all.

C. Guarantees of Educational Benefit Are Not A Requirement For Child Eligibility

In mandating a public education for all handicapped children, Congress explicitly faced the issue of the possibility of the non-educability of the most severely handicapped. The Senate Report stated, "The Committee recognizes that in many instances the process of providing special education and related services to handicapped children is not guaranteed to produce any particular outcome." The report continued: "The Committee has deleted the language of the bill as introduced which required objective criteria and evaluation procedures by which to assure that the short term instructional goals were met."

Thus, the district court's major holding, that proof of an educational benefit is a prerequisite before a handicapped child is entitled to a public education, is specifically belied, not only by the statutory language, but by the legislative history as well. We have not found in the Act's voluminous legislative history, nor has the school district directed our attention to, a single affirmative averment to support a benefit/eligibility requirement. But there is explicit evidence of a contrary congressional intent, that *no* guarantee of any particular educational outcome is required for a child to be eligible for public education.

We sum up. In the more than three years of legislative history leading to passage of the 1975 Act ... the Congressional intention is unequivocal: Public education is to be provided to all handicapped children, unconditionally and without exception. It encompasses a universal right, and is not predicated upon any type of guarantees that the child will benefit from the special education and services before he or she is considered eligible to receive such education. Congress explicitly recognized the particular plight and special needs of the severely handicapped, and rather than excluding them from the Act's coverage, gave them priority status. The district court's holding is directly contradicted by the Act's legislative history, as well as the statutory language.

D. Subsequent Amendments to the Act

In the 14 years since passage of the Act, it has been amended four times. Congress thus has had ample opportunity to clarify any language originally used, or to make any modifications that it chose. Congress has not only repeatedly reaffirmed the original intent of the Act, to educate all handicapped children regardless of the severity of their handicap, and to give priority attention to the most severely handicapped, it has in fact *expanded* the provisions covering the most severely handicapped children. Most significantly, Congress has never intimated that a benefit/eligibility requirement was to be instituted. ...

In summary, the Congressional reaffirmation of its intent to educate all handicapped children could not be any clearer. It was unequivocal at the time of passage of the Act in 1975, and it has been equally unequivocal during the intervening years. The school district's attempt in the instant case to "roll back" the entire thrust of this legislation completely ignores the overwhelming congressional consensus on this issue.

IV.   CASE LAW

A.   Cases Relied on in the Act

In its deliberations over the Act, Congress relied heavily on two landmark cases, *Pennsylvania Association for Retarded Children v. Commonwealth of Pennsylvania (PARC)*, and *Mills v. Board of Education of the District of Columbia*, which established the principle that exclusion from public education of any handicapped child is unconstitutional.... The Consent Agreement for the case, approved by the court, concluded that "Pennsylvania may not deny any mentally retarded child access to a free public program of education and training." In *Mills*, the court held that denying handicapped children a public education was violative of the constitutional guarantees of equal protection and due process. It ordered that the District of Columbia "shall provide to each child of school age a free and suitable publicly-supported education regardless of the degree of the child's mental, physical or emotional disability or impairment."

B.   All Handicapped Children are Entitled to a Public Education

Subsequent to the enactment of the Act, the courts have continued to embrace the principle that all handicapped children are entitled to a public education, and have consistently interpreted the Act as embodying this principle....

.   .   .

C.   Education is Broadly Defined

The courts have also made it clear that education for the severely handicapped under the Act is to be broadly defined. In Battle, the court stated that under the Act, the concept of education is necessarily broad with respect to severely and profoundly handicapped children, and "[w]here basic self help and social skills such as toilet training, dressing, feeding and communication are lacking, formal education begins at that point." ...

In the instant case, the district court's conclusion that education must be measured by the acquirement of traditional "cognitive skills" has no basis whatsoever in the 14 years of case law since the passage of the Act. All other courts have consistently held that education under the Act encompasses a wide spectrum of training, and that for the severely handicapped it may include the most elemental of life skills.

D.   Proof of Benefit is Not Required

The district court relied heavily on *Board of Education of Hendrick Hudson Central School District v. Rowley* in concluding that as a matter of law a child is not entitled to a public education unless he or she can benefit from it. The district court, however, has misconstrued *Rowley.* . . .

Rowley focused on the *level* of services and the quality of programs that a *state* must provide, not the criteria for *access* to those programs. The Court's use of "benefit" in *Rowley* was a substantive limitation placed on the state's choice of an educational program; it was not a license for the state to exclude certain handicapped children. In ruling that a state was not required to provide the maximum benefit possible, the Court was *not* saying that there must be proof that a child will benefit before the state is obligated to provide any education at all. Indeed, the Court in *Rowley* explicitly acknowledged Congress' intent to ensure public education to all handicapped children without regard to the level of achievement that they might attain. . . .

Rowley simply does not lend support to the district court's finding of a benefit/eligibility standard in the Act. As the Court explained, while the Act does not require a school to maximize a child's potential for learning, it does provide a "basic floor of opportunity" for the handicapped, consisting of "access to specialized instruction and related services." Nowhere does the Court imply that such a "floor" contains a trap door for the severely handicapped. Indeed, *Rowley* explicitly states: "[t]he Act requires special educational services for children 'regardless of the severity of their handicap,'" and "[t]he Act requires participating States to educate a wide spectrum of handicapped children, from the marginally hearing-impaired to the profoundly retarded and palsied."
. . .

And most recently, the Supreme Court, in *Honig v. Doe*, has made it quite clear that it will not rewrite the language of the Act to include exceptions which are not there. The Court, relying on the plain language and legislative history of the Act, ruled that dangerous and disruptive disabled children were not excluded from the requirement of 20 U.S.C.A. § 1415(e)(3), that a child "shall remain in the then current educational placement" pending any proceedings, unless the parents consent to a change. The Court rejected the argument that Congress could not possibly have meant to allow dangerous children to remain in the classroom. The analogous holding by the district court in the instant case—that Congress could not possibly have meant to "legislate futility," i.e. to educate children who could not benefit from it—falls for the reasons stated in *Honig*. The Court concluded that the language and legislative history of the Act was unequivocal in its mandate to educate all handicapped children, with no exceptions. The statute "means what it says," and the Court was "not at liberty to engraft onto the statute an exception Congress chose not to create." As Justice Brennan stated: "We think it clear . . . that Congress very much meant to strip schools of the *unilateral* authority they had traditionally employed to exclude disabled students . . . from school." (emphasis in original). Such a stricture applies with equal force to the case of Timothy W., where the school is attempting to employ its unilateral authority to exclude a disabled student that it deems "uneducable."

The district court in the instant case, is, as far as we know, the only court in the 14 years subsequent to passage of the Act, to hold that a handicapped child was not entitled to a public education under the Act because he could not benefit from the education. This holding is contrary to the language of the Act, its legislative history, and the case law.

V. CONCLUSION

The statutory language of the Act, its legislative history, and the case law construing it, mandate that all handicapped children, regardless of the severity of their handicap, are entitled to a public education. The district court erred in requiring a benefit/eligibility test as a prerequisite to implicating the Act. School districts cannot avoid the provisions of the Act by returning to the practices that were widespread prior to the Act's passage, and which indeed were the impetus for the Act's passage, of unilaterally excluding certain handicapped children from a public education on the ground that they are uneducable.

The law explicitly recognizes that education for the severely handicapped is to be broadly defined, to include not only traditional academic skills, but also basic functional life skills, and that educational methodologies in these areas are not static, but are constantly evolving and improving. It is the school district's responsibility to avail itself of these new approaches in providing an education program geared to each child's individual needs. The only question for the school district to determine, in conjunction with the child's parents, is what constitutes an appropriate individualized education program (IEP) for the handicapped child. We emphasize that the phrase "appropriate individualized education program" cannot be interpreted, as the school district has done, to mean "no educational program."

We agree with the district court that the Special Education Act of New Hampshire, . . . implements the federal statute. . . .

The judgment of the district court is reversed, judgment shall issue for Timothy W. The case is remanded to the district court which shall retain jurisdiction until a suitable IEP for Timothy W. is effectuated by the school district. Timothy W. is entitled to an interim special educational placement until a final IEP is developed and agreed upon by the parties. The district court shall also determine the question of damages.

Costs are assessed against the school district.

Notes

1. The IDEA now authorizes state officials to use IDEA funds to establish and maintain "risk pools" to aid local school systems in providing high-cost services or for the unexpected enrollment of students with disabilities. 20 U.S.C.A. § 1411(e)(3).

2. Should school boards be responsible for all of the costs associated with the placement of children such as Timothy W. even if education makes up only a small component of their IEPs?

[Case No. 120]   Nursing Services Under the IDEA

CEDAR RAPIDS COMMUNITY SCHOOL
DISTRICT v. GARRET F.

Supreme Court of the United States, 1999.
526 U.S. 66, 119 S.Ct. 992, 143 L.Ed.2d 154 [132 Educ. L. Rep. 40].

JUSTICE STEVENS delivered the opinion of the Court.

The Individuals with Disabilities Education Act (IDEA) ... was enacted, in part, "to assure that all children with disabilities have available to them ... a free appropriate public education which emphasizes special education and related services designed to meet their unique needs." Consistent with this purpose, the IDEA authorizes federal financial assistance to States that agree to provide disabled children with special education and "related services." The question presented in this case is whether the definition of "related services" in § 1401(a)(17) requires a public school district in a participating State to provide a ventilator-dependent student with certain nursing services during school hours.

I

Respondent Garret F. is a friendly, creative, and intelligent young man. When Garret was four years old, his spinal column was severed in a motorcycle accident. Though paralyzed from the neck down, his mental capacities were unaffected. He is able to speak, to control his motorized wheelchair through use of a puff and suck straw, and to operate a computer with a device that responds to head movements. Garret is currently a student in the Cedar Rapids Community School District (District), he attends regular classes in a typical school program, and his academic performance has been a success. Garret is, however, ventilator dependent, and therefore requires a responsible individual nearby to attend to certain physical needs while he is in school.

During Garret's early years at school his family provided for his physical care during the school day. When he was in kindergarten, his 18–year-old aunt attended him; in the next four years, his family used settlement proceeds they received after the accident, their insurance, and other resources to employ a licensed practical nurse. In 1993, Garret's mother requested the District to accept financial responsibility for the health care services that Garret requires during the schoolday. The District denied the request, believing that it was not legally obligated to provide continuous one-on-one nursing services.

Relying on both the IDEA and Iowa law, Garret's mother requested a hearing before the Iowa Department of Education. An Administrative Law Judge (ALJ) received extensive evidence concerning Garret's special needs, the District's treatment of other disabled students, and the assistance provided to other ventilator-dependent children in other parts of the country. In his 47–page report, the ALJ found that the District has about 17,500 students, of whom approximately 2,200 need some form of special education or special services. Although Garret is the only ventilator-dependent student in the District, most of the health care services that he needs are already provided for some other students. "The primary difference between Garret's situation and that of other students is his dependency on his ventilator for life support." The ALJ noted that the parties disagreed over the training or licensure required for the care and supervision of such students, and that those providing such care in other parts of the country ranged from nonlicensed personnel to registered nurses. However, the District did not contend that only a licensed physician could provide the services in question.

The ALJ explained that federal law requires that children with a variety of health impairments be provided with "special education and related services" when their disabilities adversely affect their academic performance, and that such children should be educated to the maximum extent appropriate with children who are not disabled. In addition, the ALJ explained that applicable federal regulations distinguish between "school health services," which are provided by a "qualified school nurse or other qualified person," and "medical services," which are provided by a licensed physician. The District must provide the former, but need not provide the latter (except, of course, those "medical services" that are for diagnostic or evaluation purposes). According to the ALJ, the distinction in the regulations does not just depend on "the title of the person providing the service"; instead, the "medical services" exclusion is limited to services that are "in the special training, knowledge, and judgment of a physician to carry out." The ALJ thus concluded that the IDEA required the District to bear financial responsibility for all of the services in dispute, including continuous nursing services.

The District challenged the ALJ's decision in Federal District Court, but that court approved the ALJ's IDEA ruling and granted summary judgment against the District. The Court of Appeals affirmed. It noted that, as a recipient of federal funds under the IDEA, Iowa has a statutory duty to provide all disabled children a "free appropriate public education," which includes "related services." The Court of Appeals read our opinion in *Irving Independent School Dist. v. Tatro*, to provide a two-step analysis of the "related services" definition in § 1401(a)(17)—asking first, whether the requested services are included within the phrase "supportive services"; and second, whether the services are excluded as "medical services." The Court of Appeals succinctly answered both questions in Garret's favor. The Court found the first step plainly satisfied, since Garret cannot attend school unless the requested services are available during the school day. As to the second step, the court reasoned that *Tatro* "established a bright-line test: the services of a physician (other than for diagnostic and evaluation purposes) are subject to the medical services exclusion, but services that can be provided in the school setting by a nurse or qualified layperson are not."

In its petition for *certiorari*, the District challenged only the second step of the Court of Appeals' analysis. The District pointed out that some federal courts have not asked whether the requested health services must be delivered by a physician, but instead have applied a multifactor test that considers, generally speaking, the nature and extent of the services at issue. We granted the District's petition to resolve this conflict.

II

The District contends that § 1401(a)(17) does not require it to provide Garret with "continuous one-on-one nursing services" during the schoolday, even though Garret cannot remain in school without such care. However, the IDEA's definition of "related services," our decision in *Irving Independent School District v. Tatro* and the overall statutory scheme all support the decision of the Court of Appeals.

The text of the "related services" definition broadly encompasses those supportive services that "may be required to assist a child with a disability to benefit from special education." As we have already noted, the District does not challenge the Court of Appeals' conclusion that the in-school services at issue are within the covered category of "supportive services." As a general matter, services that enable a disabled child to remain in school during the day provide the student with "the meaningful access to education that Congress envisioned."

This general definition of "related services" is illuminated by a parenthetical phrase listing examples of particular services that are included within the statute's coverage. "[M]edical services" are enumerated in this list, but such services are limited to those that are "for diagnostic and evaluation purposes." The statute does not contain a more specific definition of the "medical services" that are excepted from the coverage of § 1401(a)(17).

The scope of the "medical services" exclusion is not a matter of first impression in this Court. In *Tatro* we concluded that the Secretary of Education had reasonably determined that the term "medical services" referred only to services that must be performed by a physician, and not to school health services. Accordingly, we held that a specific form of health care (clean intermittent catheterization) that is often, though not always, performed by a nurse is not an excluded medical service. We referenced the likely cost of the services and the competence of school staff as justifications for drawing a line between physician and other services, but our endorsement of that line was unmistakable. It is thus settled that the phrase "medical services" in § 1401(a)(17) does not embrace all forms of care that might loosely be described as "medical" in other contexts, such as a claim for an income tax deduction.

The District does not ask us to define the term so broadly. Indeed, the District does not argue that any of the items of care that Garret needs, considered individually, could be excluded from the scope of 20 U.S.C.A. § 1401(a)(17). It could not make such an argument, considering that one of the services Garret needs (catheterization) was at issue in *Tatro,* and the others may be provided competently by a school nurse or other trained personnel. As the ALJ concluded, most of the requested services are already provided by the District to other students, and the in-school care necessitated by Garret's ventilator dependency does not demand the training, knowledge, and judgment of a licensed physician.While more extensive, the in-school services Garret needs are no more "medical" than was the care sought in *Tatro*.

Instead, the District points to the combined and continuous character of the required care, and proposes a test under which the outcome in any particular case would "depend upon a series of factors, such as [1] whether the care is continuous or intermittent, [2] whether existing school health personnel can provide the service, [3] the cost of the service, and [4] the potential consequences if the service is not properly performed."

The District's multifactor test is not supported by any recognized source of legal authority. The proposed factors can be found in neither the text of the statute nor the regulations that we upheld in *Tatro*. Moreover, the District offers no explanation why these characteristics make one service any more "medical" than another. The continuous character of certain services associated with Garret's ventilator dependency has no apparent relationship to "medical" services, much less a relationship of equivalence. Continuous services may be more costly and may require additional school personnel, but they are not thereby more "medical." Whatever its imperfections, a rule that limits the medical services exemption to physician services is unquestionably a reasonable and generally workable interpretation of the statute. Absent an elaboration of the statutory terms plainly more convincing than that which we reviewed in *Tatro*, there is no good reason to depart from settled law.

Finally, the District raises broader concerns about the financial burden that it must bear to provide the services that Garret needs to stay in school. The problem for the District in providing these services is not that its staff cannot be trained to deliver them; the problem, the District contends, is that the existing school health staff cannot meet all of their responsibilities and provide for Garret at the same time. Through its multifactor test, the District seeks to establish a kind of undue-burden exemption primarily based on the cost of the requested services. The first two factors can be seen as examples of cost-based distinctions: Intermittent care is often less expensive than continuous care, and the use of existing personnel is cheaper than hiring additional employees. The third factor-the cost of the service-would then encompass the first two. The relevance of the fourth factor is likewise related to cost because extra care may be necessary if potential consequences are especially serious.

The District may have legitimate financial concerns, but our role in this dispute is to interpret existing law. Defining "related services" in a manner that *accommodates* the cost concerns Congress may have had is altogether different from using cost *itself* as the definition. Given that § 1401(a)(17) does not employ cost in its definition of "related services" or excluded "medical services," accepting the District's cost-based standard as the sole test for determining the scope of the provision would require us to engage in judicial lawmaking without any guidance from Congress. It would also create some tension with the purposes of the

IDEA. The statute may not require public schools to maximize the potential of disabled students commensurate with the opportunities provided to other children and the potential financial burdens imposed on participating States may be relevant to arriving at a sensible construction of the IDEA. But Congress intended "to open the door of public education" to all qualified children and "require[d] participating States to educate handicapped children with nonhandicapped children whenever possible."

This case is about whether meaningful access to the public schools will be assured, not the level of education that a school must finance once access is attained. It is undisputed that the services at issue must be provided if Garret is to remain in school. Under the statute, our precedent, and the purposes of the IDEA, the District must fund such "related services" in order to help guarantee that students like Garret are integrated into the public schools.

The judgment of the Court of Appeals is accordingly

Affirmed.

Note

The dissent argued that since *Tatro* could not be "squared with the text of IDEA," the Court should not have applied it in *Garret F.* The dissent added that even assuming that the Court was correct in *Tatro*, its unwarranted extension ignored the constitutionally-mandated rules of construction applicable to legislation enacted pursuant to Congress' spending power. Do you agree?

[Case No. 121] Disciplining Students with Disabilities

HONIG v. DOE

Supreme Court of the United States, 1988.
484 U.S. 305, 108 S.Ct. 592, 98 L.Ed.2d 686 [43 Educ. L. Rep. 857].

JUSTICE BRENNAN delivered the opinion of the Court.

As a condition of federal financial assistance, the Education of the Handicapped Act requires States to ensure a "free appropriate public education" for all disabled children within their jurisdictions. In aid of this goal, the Act establishes a comprehensive system of procedural safeguards designed to ensure parental participation in decisions concerning the education of their disabled children and to provide administrative and judicial review of any decisions with which those parents disagree. Among these safeguards is the so-called "stay-put" provision, which directs that a disabled child "shall remain in [his or her] then current educational placement" pending completion of any review proceedings, unless the parents and state or local educational agencies otherwise agree. Today we must decide whether, in the face of this statutory proscription, state or local school authorities may nevertheless unilaterally exclude disabled children from the classroom for dangerous or disruptive conduct growing out of their disabilities. In addition, we are called upon to decide whether a district court may, in the exercise of its equitable powers, order a State to provide educational services directly to a disabled child when the local agency fails to do so.

I

. . .

The present dispute grows out of the efforts of certain officials of the San Francisco Unified School District (SFUSD) to expel two emotionally disturbed children from school indefinitely for violent and disruptive conduct related to their disabilities. In November 1980, respondent John Doe assaulted another student at the Louise Lombard School, a developmental center for disabled children. Doe's April 1980 IEP identified him as a socially and physically awkward 17–year-old who experienced considerable difficulty controlling his impulses and anger. Among the goals set out in his IEP was "[i]mprovement in [his] ability to relate to [his] peers [and to] cope with frustrating situations without resorting to aggressive acts." Frustrating situations, however, were an unfortunately prominent feature of Doe's school career: physical abnormalities, speech difficulties, and poor grooming habits had made him the target of teasing and ridicule as early as the first grade; his 1980 IEP reflected his continuing difficulties with peers, noting that his social skills had deteriorated and that he could tolerate only minor frustration before exploding.

On November 6, 1980, Doe responded to the taunts of a fellow student in precisely the explosive manner anticipated by his IEP: he choked the student with sufficient force to leave abrasions on the child's neck, and kicked out a school window while being escorted to the principal's office afterwards. Doe admitted his misconduct and the school subsequently suspended him for five days. Thereafter, his principal referred the matter to the SFUSD Student Placement Committee (SPC or Committee) with the recommendation that Doe be expelled. On the day the suspension was to end, the SPC notified Doe's mother that it was proposing to exclude her child permanently from SFUSD and was therefore extending his suspension until such time as the expulsion proceedings were completed. The Committee further advised her that she was entitled to attend the November 25 hearing at which it planned to discuss the proposed expulsion.

After unsuccessfully protesting these actions by letter, Doe brought this suit. . . . Alleging that the suspension and proposed expulsion violated the EHA, he sought a temporary restraining order canceling the SPC hearing and requiring school officials to convene an IEP meeting. The District Judge granted the requested injunctive relief and further ordered defendants to provide home tutoring for Doe on an interim basis; shortly thereafter, she issued a preliminary injunction directing defendants to return Doe to his then current educational placement at Louise Lombard School pending completion of the IEP review process. Doe reentered school on December 15, 5 1/2 weeks, and 24 school-days, after his initial suspension.

Respondent Jack Smith was identified as an emotionally disturbed child by the time he entered the second grade in 1976. School records prepared that year indicated that he was unable "to control verbal or physical outburst[s]" and exhibited a "[s]evere disturbance in relationships with peers and adults." Further evaluations subsequently revealed that he had been physically and emotionally abused as an infant and young child and that, despite above average intelligence, he experienced academic and social difficulties as a result of extreme hyperactivity and low self-esteem. Of particular concern was Smith's propensity for verbal hostility; one evaluator noted that the child reacted to stress by "attempt[ing] to cover his feelings of low self worth through aggressive behavior [,] . . . primarily verbal provocations."

Based on these evaluations, SFUSD placed Smith in a learning center for emotionally disturbed children. His grandparents, however, believed that his needs would be better served in the public school setting and, in September 1979, the school district acceded to their requests and enrolled him at A.P. Giannini Middle School. His February 1980 IEP recommended placement in a Learning Disability Group, stressing the need for close supervision and a highly structured environment. Like earlier evaluations, the February 1980 IEP noted that Smith was easily distracted, impulsive, and anxious; it therefore proposed a half-day schedule and suggested that the placement be undertaken on a trial basis.

At the beginning of the next school year, Smith was assigned to a full-day program; almost immediately thereafter he began misbehaving. School officials met twice with his grandparents in October 1980 to discuss returning him to a half-day program; although the grandparents agreed to the reduction, they apparently were never apprised of their right to challenge the decision through EHA procedures. The school officials also warned them that if the child continued his disruptive behavior—which included stealing, extorting money from fellow students, and making sexual comments to female classmates—they would seek to expel him. On November 14, they made good on this threat, suspending Smith for five days after he made further lewd comments. His principal referred the matter to the SPC, which recommended exclusion from SFUSD. As it did in John Doe's case, the Committee scheduled a hearing and extended the suspension indefinitely pending a final disposition in the matter. On November 28, Smith's counsel protested these actions on grounds essentially identical to those raised by Doe, and the SPC agreed to cancel the hearing and to return Smith to a half-day program at A.P. Giannini or to provide home tutoring. Smith's grandparents chose the latter option and the school began home instruction on December 10; on January 6, 1981, an IEP team convened to discuss alternative placements.

After learning of Doe's action, Smith sought and obtained leave to intervene in the suit. The District Court subsequently entered summary judgment in favor of respondents on their EHA claims and issued a permanent injunction. In a series of decisions, the District Judge found that the proposed expulsions and indefinite suspensions of respondents for conduct attributable to their disabilities deprived them of their congressionally mandated right to a free appropriate public education, as well as their right to have that education provided in accordance with the procedures set out in the EHA. The District Judge therefore permanently enjoined ... any disciplinary action other than a 2–or 5–day suspension against any disabled child for disability-related misconduct, or from effecting any other change in the educational placement of any such child without parental consent pending completion of any EHA proceedings. In addition, the judge barred the State from authorizing unilateral placement changes and directed it to establish an EHA compliance-monitoring system or, alternatively, to enact guidelines governing local school responses to disability-related misconduct. Finally, the judge ordered the State to provide services directly to disabled children when, in any individual case, the State determined that the local educational agency was unable or unwilling to do so.

... the Ninth Circuit affirmed the orders with slight modifications. Agreeing with the District Court that an indefinite suspension in aid of expulsion constitutes a prohibited "change in placement" under § 1415(e)(3), the Court of Appeals held that the stay-put provision admitted of no "dangerousness" exception and that the statute therefore rendered invalid those provisions of the California Education Code permitting the indefinite suspension or expulsion of disabled children for misconduct arising out of their disabilities. The court concluded, however, that fixed suspensions of up to 30 schooldays did not fall within the reach of § 1415(e)(3), and therefore upheld recent amendments to the state Education Code authorizing such suspensions. Lastly, the court affirmed that portion of the injunction requiring the State to provide services directly to a disabled child when the local educational agency fails to do so.

Petitioner Bill Honig, California Superintendent of Public Instruction, sought review in this Court, claiming that the Court of Appeals' construction of the stay-put provision conflicted with that of several other Courts of Appeals which had recognized a dangerousness exception and that the direct services ruling placed an intolerable burden on the State. We granted certiorari to resolve these questions and now affirm.

II

At the outset, we address the suggestion, raised for the first time during oral argument, that this case is moot. Under Article III of the Constitution this Court may only adjudicate actual, ongoing controversies. That the dispute between the parties was very much alive when suit was filed, or at the time the Court of Appeals rendered its judgment, cannot substitute for the actual case or controversy that an exercise of this Court's jurisdiction requires. In the present case, we have jurisdiction if there is a reasonable likelihood that respondents will again suffer the deprivation of EHA-mandated rights that gave rise to this suit. We believe that, at least with respect to respondent Smith, such a possibility does in fact exist and that the case therefore remains justiciable.

Respondent John Doe is now 24 years old and, accordingly, is no longer entitled to the protections and benefits of the EHA, which limits eligibility to disabled children between the ages of 3 and 21.... and thus the case is moot as to him. Respondent Jack Smith, however, is currently 20 and has not yet completed high school. Although at present he is not faced with any proposed expulsion or suspension proceedings, and indeed no longer even resides within the SFUSD, he remains a resident of California and is entitled to a "free appropriate public education" within that State. His claims under the EHA, therefore, are not moot if the conduct he originally complained of is " 'capable of repetition, yet evading review.' " Given Smith's continued eligibility for educational services under the EHA, the nature of his disability, and petitioner's insistence that all local school districts retain residual authority to exclude disabled children for dangerous conduct, we have little difficulty concluding that there is a "reasonable expectation," that Smith would once again be subjected to a unilateral "change in placement" for conduct growing out of his disabilities were it not for the statewide injunctive relief issued below.

Our cases reveal that ... we generally have been unwilling to assume that the party seeking relief will repeat the type of misconduct that would once again place him or her at risk of that injury. No such reluctance, however, is warranted here. It is respondent Smith's very inability to conform his conduct to socially acceptable norms that renders him "handicapped" within the meaning of the EHA. As noted above, the record is replete with evidence that Smith is unable to govern his aggressive, impulsive behavior—indeed, his notice of suspension acknowledged that "Jack's actions seem beyond his control." In the absence of any suggestion that respondent has overcome his earlier difficulties, it is certainly reasonable to expect, based on his prior history of behavioral problems, that he will again engage in classroom misconduct. Nor is it reasonable to suppose that Smith's future educational placement will so perfectly suit his emotional and academic needs that further disruptions on his part are improbable....

We think it equally probable that, should he do so, respondent will again be subjected to the same unilateral school action for which he initially sought relief. In this regard, it matters not that Smith no longer resides within the SFUSD. While the actions of SFUSD officials first gave rise to this litigation, the District Judge expressly found that the lack of a state policy governing local school responses to disability-related misconduct had led to, and would continue to result in, EHA violations, and she therefore enjoined the state defendant from authorizing, among other things, unilateral placement changes. She of course also issued injunctions directed at the local defendants, but they did not seek review of those orders in this Court. Only petitioner, the State Superintendent of Public Instruction, has invoked our jurisdiction, and he now urges us to hold that local school districts retain unilateral authority under the EHA to suspend or otherwise remove disabled children for dangerous conduct. Given these representations, we have every reason to believe that were it not for the injunction barring petitioner from authorizing such unilateral action, respondent would be faced with a real and substantial threat of such action in any California school district in which he enrolled. Certainly, if the SFUSD's past practice of unilateral exclusions was at odds with state policy and the practice of local school districts generally, petitioner would not now stand before us seeking to defend the right of all local school districts to engage in such aberrant behavior.

We have previously noted that administrative and judicial review under the EHA is often "ponderous," and this case, which has taken seven years to reach us, amply confirms that observation. For obvious reasons, the misconduct of an emotionally disturbed or otherwise disabled child who has not yet reached adolescence typically will not pose such a serious threat to the well-being of other students that school officials can only ensure classroom safety by excluding the child. Yet, the adolescent student improperly disciplined for misconduct that does pose such a threat will often be finished with school or otherwise ineligible for EHA protections by the time review can be had in this Court. Because we believe that respondent Smith has demonstrated both "a sufficient likelihood that he will again be wronged in a similar way," and that any resulting claim he may have for relief will surely evade our review, we turn to the merits of his case.

III

The language of § 1415(e)(3) is unequivocal. It states plainly that during the pendency of any proceedings initiated under the Act, unless the state or local educational agency and the parents or guardian of a disabled child otherwise agree, "the child *shall* remain in the then current educational placement." (emphasis added). Faced with this clear directive, petitioner asks us to read a "dangerousness" exception into the stay-put provision on the basis of either of two essentially inconsistent assumptions: first, that Congress thought the residual authority of school officials to exclude dangerous students from the classroom too obvious for comment; or second, that Congress inadvertently failed to provide such authority and this Court must therefore remedy the oversight. Because we cannot accept either premise, we decline petitioner's invitation to rewrite the statute.

Petitioner's arguments proceed, he suggests, from a simple, commonsense proposition: Congress could not have intended the stay-put provision to be read literally, for such a construction leads to the clearly unintended, and untenable, result that school districts must return violent or dangerous students to school while the often lengthy EHA proceedings run their course. We think it clear, however, that Congress very much meant to strip schools of the *unilateral* authority they had traditionally employed to exclude disabled students, particularly emotionally disturbed students, from school. In so doing, Congress did not leave school administrators powerless to deal with dangerous students; it did, however, deny school officials their former right to "self-help," and directed that in the future the removal of disabled students could be accomplished only with the permission of the parents or, as a last resort, the courts.

As noted above, Congress passed the EHA after finding that school systems across the country had excluded one out of every eight disabled children from classes. In drafting the law, Congress was largely guided by the recent decisions in *Mills v. Board of Education of District of Columbia* and *PARC*, both of which involved the exclusion of hard-to-handle disabled students. *Mills* in particular demonstrated the extent to which schools used disciplinary measures to bar children from the classroom. . . .

Congress attacked such exclusionary practices in a variety of ways. It required participating States to educate *all* disabled children, regardless of the severity of their disabilities, and included within the definition of "handicapped" those children with serious emotional disturbances. It further provided for meaningful parental participation in all aspects of a child's educational placement, and barred schools, through the stay-put provision, from changing that placement over the parent's objection until all review proceedings were completed. Recognizing that those proceedings might prove long and tedious, the Act's drafters did not intend to operate inflexibly and they therefore allowed for interim placements where parents and school officials are able to agree on one. Conspicuously absent from § 1415(e)(3), however, is any emergency exception for dangerous students. This absence is all the more telling in light of the injunctive decree issued in *PARC*, which permitted school officials unilaterally to remove students in " 'extraordinary circumstances.' " Given the lack of any similar exception in *Mills*, and the close attention Congress devoted to these "landmark" decisions, we can only conclude that the omission was intentional; we are therefore not at liberty to engraft onto the statute an exception Congress chose not to create.

Our conclusion that § 1415(e)(3) means what it says does not leave educators hamstrung. The Department of Education has observed that, "[w]hile the [child's] placement may not be changed [during any complaint proceeding], this does not preclude the agency from using its normal procedures for dealing with children who are endangering themselves or others." Such procedures may include the use of study carrels, timeouts, detention, or the restriction of privileges. More drastically, where a student poses an immediate threat to the safety of others, officials may temporarily suspend him or her for up to 10 schooldays. This authority, which respondent in no way disputes, not only ensures that school administrators can protect the safety of others by promptly removing the most dangerous of students, it also provides a "cooling down" period during which officials can initiate IEP review and seek to persuade the child's parents to agree to an interim placement. And in those cases in which the parents of a truly dangerous child adamantly refuse to permit any change in placement, the 10–day respite gives school officials an opportunity to invoke the aid of the courts under, which empowers courts to grant any appropriate relief.

Petitioner contends, however, that the availability of judicial relief is more illusory than real, because a party seeking review under § 1415(e)(2) must exhaust time-consuming administrative remedies, and because under the Court of Appeals' construction of § 1415(e)(3), courts are as bound by the stay-put provision's "automatic injunction," as are schools. It is true that judicial review is normally not available under § 1415(e)(2) until all administrative proceedings are completed, but as we have previously noted, parents may bypass the administrative process where exhaustion would be futile or inadequate. While many of the EHA's procedural safeguards protect the rights of parents and children, schools can and do seek redress through the administrative review process, and we have no reason to believe that Congress meant to require schools alone to exhaust in all cases, no matter how exigent the circumstances. The burden in such cases, of course, rests with the school to demonstrate the futility or inadequacy of administrative review, but nothing in § 1415(e)(2) suggests that schools are completely barred from attempting to make such a showing. Nor do we think that § 1415(e)(3) operates to limit the equitable powers of district courts such that they cannot, in appropriate cases, temporarily enjoin a dangerous disabled child from attending school. As the EHA's legislative history makes clear, one of the evils Congress sought to remedy was the unilateral exclusion of disabled children by *schools,* not courts, and one of the purposes of § 1415(e)(3), therefore, was "to prevent *school* officials from removing a child from the regular public school classroom over the parents' objection pending completion of the review proceedings." The stay-put provision in no way purports to limit or pre-empt the authority conferred on courts by § 1415(e)(2); indeed, it says nothing whatever about judicial power.

In short, then, we believe that school officials are entitled to seek injunctive relief under § 1415(e)(2) in appropriate cases. In any such action, § 1415(e)(3) effectively creates a presumption in favor of the child's current educational placement which school officials can overcome only by showing that maintaining the child in his or her current placement is substantially likely to result in injury either to himself or herself, or to others. In the present case, we are satisfied that the District Court, in enjoining the state and local defendants from indefinitely suspending respondent or otherwise unilaterally altering his then current placement, properly balanced respondent's interest in receiving a free appropriate public education in accordance with the procedures and requirements of the EHA against the interests of the state and local school officials in maintaining a safe learning environment for all their students.

IV

We believe the courts below properly construed and applied § 1415(e)(3), except insofar as the Court of Appeals held that a suspension in excess of 10 schooldays does not constitute a "change in placement." We therefore affirm the Court of Appeals' judgment on this issue as modified herein. Because we are equally divided on the question whether a court may order a State to provide services directly to a disabled child where the local agency has failed to do so, we affirm the Court of Appeals' judgment on this issue as well.

Affirmed.

Notes

1. Without addressing the merits of the case, the dissent was of the opinion that the entire case should have been rendered moot since neither of the students was in school. Do you agree?

2. What can, or should, school officials do to protect the educational and safety rights of other children when students with disabilities are disruptive in class?

3. Insofar as an equally divided Court affirmed that state officials could have been compelled to provide services directly to students with disabilities when local school boards failed to do so, this part of the case is binding only in the Ninth Circuit. For the earlier judgment, *see Doe by Gonzales v. Maher*, 793 F.2d 1470 [33 Educ. L. Rep. 124] (9th Cir.1986).

[Case No. 122]   Burden of Proof at Due Process Hearings

SCHAFFER EX REL. SCHAFFER v. WEAST

Supreme Court of the United States, 2005.
___ U.S. ___, 126 S.Ct. 528, 163 L.Ed.2d 387 [203 Educ. L. Rep. 29].

JUSTICE O'CONNOR delivered the opinion of the Court.

The Individuals with Disabilities Education Act (IDEA or Act) is a Spending Clause statute that seeks to ensure that "all children with disabilities have available to them a free appropriate public education." Under IDEA, school districts must create an "individualized education program" (IEP) for each disabled child. If parents believe their child's IEP is inappropriate, they may request an "impartial due process hearing." The Act is silent, however, as to which party bears the burden of persuasion at such a hearing. We hold that the burden lies, as it typically does, on the party seeking relief.

I

A

Congress first passed IDEA as part of the Education of the Handicapped Act in 1970 and amended it substantially in the Education for All Handicapped Children Act of 1975 . . . .

IDEA is "frequently described as a model of 'cooperative federalism.'" It "leaves to the States the primary responsibility for developing and executing educational programs for handicapped children, [but] imposes significant requirements to be followed in the discharge of that responsibility. For example, the Act mandates cooperation and reporting between state and federal educational authorities." Participating States must certify to the Secretary of Education that they have "policies and procedures" that will effectively meet the Act's conditions.(Unless otherwise noted, [the Court applied] ... the pre–2004 version of the statute because this is the version that was in effect during the proceedings below. We note, however, that nothing in the recent 2004 amendments appears to materially affect the rule announced here.) State educational agencies, in turn, must ensure that local schools and teachers are meeting the State's educational standards. Local educational agencies (school boards or other administrative bodies) can receive IDEA funds only if they certify to a state educational agency that they are acting in accordance with the State's policies and procedures.

The core of the statute, however, is the cooperative process that it establishes between parents and schools. The central vehicle for this collaboration is the IEP process. State educational authorities must identify and evaluate disabled children, develop an IEP for each one, and review every IEP at least once a year. Each IEP must include an assessment of the child's current educational performance, must articulate measurable educational goals, and must specify the nature of the special services that the school will provide.

Parents and guardians play a significant role in the IEP process. They must be informed about and consent to evaluations of their child under the Act. Parents are included as members of "IEP teams." They have the right to examine any records relating to their child, and to obtain an "independent educational evaluation of the[ir] child." They must be given written prior notice of any changes in an IEP, and be notified in writing of the procedural safeguards available to them under the Act. If parents believe that an IEP is not appropriate, they may seek an administrative "impartial due process hearing." School districts may also seek such hearings, as Congress clarified in the 2004 amendments. They may do so, for example, if they wish to change an existing IEP but the parents do not consent, or if parents refuse to allow their child to be evaluated. As a practical matter, it appears that most hearing requests come from parents rather than schools.

Although state authorities have limited discretion to determine who conducts the hearings, and responsibility generally for establishing fair hearing procedures, Congress has chosen to legislate the central components of due process hearings. It has imposed minimal pleading standards, requiring parties to file complaints setting forth "a description of the nature of the problem" and "a proposed resolution of the problem to the extent known and available at the time." At the hearing, all parties may be accompanied by counsel, and may "present evidence and confront, cross-examine, and compel the attendance of witnesses." After the hearing, any aggrieved party may bring a civil action in state or federal court. Prevailing parents may also recover attorney's fees. Congress has never explicitly stated, however, which party should bear the burden of proof at IDEA hearings.

B

This case concerns the educational services that were due, under IDEA, to petitioner Brian Schaffer. Brian suffers from learning disabilities and speech-language impairments. From prekindergarten through seventh grade he attended a private school and struggled academically. In 1997, school officials informed Brian's mother that he needed a school that could better accommodate his needs. Brian's parents contacted respondent Montgomery County Public Schools System (MCPS) seeking a placement for him for the following school year.

MCPS evaluated Brian and convened an IEP team. The committee generated an initial IEP offering Brian a place in either of two MCPS middle schools. Brian's parents were not satisfied with the arrangement, believing that Brian needed smaller classes and more intensive services. The Schaffers thus enrolled Brian in another private school, and initiated a due process hearing challenging the IEP and seeking compensation for the cost of Brian's subsequent private education.

In Maryland, IEP hearings are conducted by administrative law judges (ALJs). After a 3–day hearing, the ALJ deemed the evidence close, held that the parents bore the burden of persuasion, and ruled in favor of the school district. The parents brought a civil action challenging the result. The United States District Court for the District of Maryland reversed and remanded, after concluding that the burden of persuasion is on the school district. Around the same time, MCPS offered Brian a placement in a high school with a special learning center. Brian's parents accepted, and Brian was educated in that program until he graduated from high school. The suit remained alive, however, because the parents sought compensation for the private school tuition and related expenses.

Respondents appealed to the ... Fourth Circuit. While the appeal was pending, the ALJ reconsidered the case, deemed the evidence truly in "equipoise," and ruled in favor of the parents. The Fourth Circuit vacated and remanded the appeal so that it could consider the burden of proof issue along with the merits on a later appeal. The District Court reaffirmed its ruling that the school district has the burden of proof. On appeal, a divided panel of the Fourth Circuit reversed. Judge Michael, writing for the majority, concluded that petitioners offered no persuasive reason to "depart from the normal rule of allocating the burden to the party seeking relief." We granted *certiorari*, to resolve the following question: At an administrative hearing assessing the appropriateness of an IEP, which party bears the burden of persuasion?

II

A

The term "burden of proof" is one of the "slipperiest member[s] of the family of legal terms." Part of the confusion surrounding the term arises from the fact that historically, the concept encompassed two distinct burdens: the "burden of persuasion," *i.e.,* which party loses if the evidence is closely balanced, and the "burden of production," *i.e.,* which party bears the obligation to come forward with the evidence at different points in the proceeding. We note at the outset that this case concerns only the burden of persuasion, as the parties agree, and when we speak of burden of proof in this opinion, it is this to which we refer.

When we are determining the burden of proof under a statutory cause of action, the touchstone of our inquiry is, of course, the statute. The plain text of IDEA is silent on the allocation of the burden of persuasion. We therefore begin with the ordinary default rule that plaintiffs bear the risk of failing to prove their claims.

Thus, we have usually assumed without comment that plaintiffs bear the burden of persuasion regarding the essential aspects of their claims. For example, Title VII of the Civil Rights Act of 1964, does not directly state that plaintiffs bear the "ultimate" burden of persuasion, but we have so concluded. In numerous other areas, we have presumed or held that the default rule applies. . . .

The ordinary default rule, of course, admits of exceptions. For example, the burden of persuasion as to certain elements of a plaintiff's claim may be shifted to defendants, when such elements can fairly be characterized as affirmative defenses or exemptions. Under some circumstances this Court has even placed the burden of persuasion over an entire claim on the defendant. But while the normal default rule does not solve all cases, it certainly solves most of them. Decisions that place the *entire* burden of persuasion on the opposing party at the *outset* of a proceeding-as petitioners urge us to do here-are extremely rare. Absent some reason to believe that Congress intended otherwise, therefore, we will conclude that the burden of persuasion lies where it usually falls, upon the party seeking relief.

B

Petitioners contend first that a close reading of IDEA's text compels a conclusion in their favor. They urge that we should interpret the statutory words "due process" in light of their constitutional meaning, and apply the balancing test established by *Mathews v. Eldridge*. Even assuming that the Act incorporates constitutional due process doctrine, *Eldridge* is no help to petitioners, because "[o]utside the criminal law area, where special concerns attend, the locus of the burden of persuasion is normally not an issue of federal constitutional moment."

Petitioners next contend that we should take instruction from the lower court opinions of *Mills v. Board of Education* and *Pennsylvania Association for Retarded Children v. Commonwealth* (hereinafter *PARC*). IDEA's drafters were admittedly guided "to a significant extent" by these two landmark cases. As the court below noted, however, the fact that Congress "took a number of the procedural safeguards from *PARC* and *Mills* and wrote them directly into the Act" does not allow us to "conclude that Congress intended to adopt the ideas that it failed to write into the text of the statute."

Petitioners also urge that putting the burden of persuasion on school districts will further IDEA's purposes because it will help ensure that children receive a free appropriate public education. In truth, however, very few cases will be in evidentiary equipoise. Assigning the burden of persuasion to school districts might encourage schools to put more resources into preparing IEPs and presenting their evidence. But

IDEA is silent about whether marginal dollars should be allocated to litigation and administrative expenditures or to educational services. Moreover, there is reason to believe that a great deal is already spent on the administration of the Act. Litigating a due process complaint is an expensive affair, costing schools approximately $8,000–to-$12,000 per hearing. Congress has also repeatedly amended the Act in order to reduce its administrative and litigation-related costs. For example, in 1997 Congress mandated that States offer mediation for IDEA disputes. In 2004, Congress added a mandatory "resolution session" prior to any due process hearing. It also made new findings that "[p]arents and schools should be given expanded opportunities to resolve their disagreements in positive and constructive ways," and that "[t]eachers, schools, local educational agencies, and States should be relieved of irrelevant and unnecessary paperwork burdens that do not lead to improved educational outcomes."

Petitioners in effect ask this Court to assume that every IEP is invalid until the school district demonstrates that it is not. The Act does not support this conclusion. IDEA relies heavily upon the expertise of school districts to meet its goals. It also includes a so-called "stay-put" provision, which requires a child to remain in his or her "then-current educational placement" during the pendency of an IDEA hearing. Congress could have required that a child be given the educational placement that a parent requested during a dispute, but it did no such thing. Congress appears to have presumed instead that, if the Act's procedural requirements are respected, parents will prevail when they have legitimate grievances.

Petitioners' most plausible argument is that "[t]he ordinary rule, based on considerations of fairness, does not place the burden upon a litigant of establishing facts peculiarly within the knowledge of his adversary." But this "rule is far from being universal, and has many qualifications upon its application." School districts have a "natural advantage" in information and expertise, but Congress addressed this when it obliged schools to safeguard the procedural rights of parents and to share information with them. As noted above, parents have the right to review all records that the school possesses in relation to their child. They also have the right to an "independent educational evaluation of the[ir] child." The regulations clarify this entitlement by providing that a "parent has the right to an independent educational evaluation at public expense if the parent disagrees with an evaluation obtained by the public agency." IDEA thus ensures parents access to an expert who can evaluate all the materials that the school must make available, and who can give an independent opinion. They are not left to challenge the government without a realistic opportunity to access the necessary evidence, or without an expert with the firepower to match the opposition.

Additionally, in 2004, Congress added provisions requiring school districts to answer the subject matter of a complaint in writing, and to provide parents with the reasoning behind the disputed action, details about the other options considered and rejected by the IEP team, and a description of all evaluations, reports, and other factors that the school used in coming to its decision. Prior to a hearing, the parties must disclose evaluations and recommendations that they intend to rely upon. IDEA hearings are deliberately informal and intended to give ALJs the flexibility that they need to ensure that each side can fairly present its evidence. IDEA, in fact, requires state authorities to organize hearings in a way that guarantees parents and children the procedural protections of the Act. Finally, and perhaps most importantly, parents may recover attorney's fees if they prevail. These protections ensure that the school bears no unique informational advantage.

III

Finally, respondents and several States urge us to decide that States may, if they wish, override the default rule and put the burden always on the school district. Several States have laws or regulations purporting to do so, at least under some circumstances.... Because no such law or regulation exists in Maryland, we need not decide this issue today. Justice BREYER contends that the allocation of the burden ought to be left *entirely* up to the States. But neither party made this argument before this Court or the courts below. We therefore decline to address it.

We hold no more than we must to resolve the case at hand: The burden of proof in an administrative hearing challenging an IEP is properly placed upon the party seeking relief. In this case, that party is Brian, as represented by his parents. But the rule applies with equal effect to school districts: If they seek to challenge an IEP, they will in turn bear the burden of persuasion before an ALJ. The judgment of the United States Court of Appeals for the Fourth Circuit is, therefore, affirmed.

It is so ordered.

THE CHIEF JUSTICE took no part in the consideration or decision of this case.

Notes

1. Is this decision fair to parents (and their children)?

2. Should individual states be free to set their own burdens of proof?

Chapter 15

SCHOOL DESEGREGATION

Introduction

Brown v. Board of Education, Topeka (Brown I),[1] is arguably the Supreme Court's most important case involving K–12 education, if not of all time. In *Brown I*, the Court struck down de jure segregation, based on law, as opposed to de facto segregation, based on the facts, on the ground that it deprived African American students of the right to equal educational opportunities in violation of the Equal Protection Clause of the Fourteenth Amendment.[2] *Brown I* also served as the catalyst that led to fundamental changes in American society.

Brown v. Board of Education

"Separate but equal" entered the national legal consciousness in *Plessy v. Ferguson*,[3] a case from Louisiana dealing with discrimination in public railway accommodations. The concept traces its origins to a dispute wherein the Supreme Judicial Court of Massachusetts upheld "separate but equal" in denying an African American student the opportunity to attend a school for white children that was closer to her home.[4] The Supreme Court explicitly extended "separate but equal" to K–12 education in *Gong Lum v. Rice*,[5] a dispute from Mississippi in which it upheld the exclusion of a student of Chinese descent from a public school for white children.

By the time *Brown I* reached the Supreme Court, proponents of equal educational opportunities had begun to make judicial headway. In the companion cases of *Sweatt v. Painter*[6] and *McLaurin v. Oklahoma State Regents for Higher Education*,[7] the Court repudiated inter and intra institution segregation, respectively, in higher education. Relying in part on the precedent set in these cases, the National Association for the Advancement of Colored People, led by its chief counsel and future Supreme Court Justice Thurgood Marshall, challenged racial segregation in K–12 schools.

---

1. 347 U.S. 483, 74 S.Ct. 686, 98 L.Ed. 873 (1954). [Case No. 123]

2. On the same day that it announced its judgment in *Brown I*, the Court struck down segregation in the public schools of Washington, D.C., reasoning that the practice violated the Due Process Clause of the Fifth Amendment, which applies to the federal government. *Bolling v. Sharpe*, 347 U.S. 497, 74 S.Ct. 693, 98 L.Ed. 884 (1954).

3. 163 U.S. 537, 16 S.Ct. 1138, 41 L.Ed. 256 (1896).

4. *Roberts v. City of Boston*, 59 Mass. (5 Cush.) 198 (1850).

5. 275 U.S. 78, 48 S.Ct. 91, 72 L.Ed. 172 (1927).

6. 339 U.S. 629, 70 S.Ct. 848, 94 L.Ed. 1114 (1950).

7. 339 U.S. 637, 70 S.Ct. 851, 94 L.Ed. 1149 (1950).

Brown I, a class action suit from Kansas, disputed a state law that permitted the exclusion of African American students from schools attended by white children. *Brown I* also questioned state constitutions and statutes from Delaware, South Carolina, and Virginia that required racially segregated schools.

After being unable to reach a decision during its 1952–53 Term, the Supreme Court reheard oral arguments in December of 1953. The Court handed down its monumental ruling on May 17, 1954. Writing for a unanimous Court, Chief Justice Earl Warren framed the issue as:

> Does segregation of children in public schools solely on the basis of race, even though the physical Facilities and other "tangible" factors may be equal, deprive the children of the minority group of equal educational opportunities?[8]

The Court answered, "[w]e believe that it does."[9] Relying, for perhaps the first time, in part on data from the social sciences, in evidence presented by psychologist Dr. Kenneth B. Clark, who testified about the deleterious effect that segregation had on African American children,[10] the Court held "that in the field of public education the doctrine of 'separate but equal' has no place. Separate educational facilities are inherently unequal."[11]

As important as *Brown I* was, and is, it was limited to ending segregation. Thus, the Court conducted further oral arguments to consider remedies. A year later, in *Brown v. Board of Education, Topeka, II (Brown II)*, the Court directed school officials to act "with all deliberate speed"[12] in implementing its mandate to provide equal educational opportunities for all children regardless of race. While recognizing that additional time might be necessary to bring about change, the Court set the burden of proof on the need for more time on school boards acting in the public interest and consistent with good faith compliance as soon as practicable. In addition, *Brown II* placed primary responsibility on educational officials to take initial steps to desegregate schools while ordering lower courts to retain their jurisdiction and to evaluate whether the actions of school boards constituted good faith implementation of its dictates.

Delineation of the Constitutional Mandate

Brown I and *II* met with less than universal acclaim in many parts of the United States. In *Cooper v. Aaron*,[13] its first post-*Brown* desegregation case, the Court made it clear that a governor and legislature could not refuse to implement its mandate. A year after President Eisenhower dispatched federal troops to Little Rock, Arkansas, to enforce a desegregation order, the local board sought to postpone the effective date of its

---

8. 347 U.S. 483, 493, 74 S.Ct. 686, 98 L.Ed. 873 (1954).

9. *Id.*

10. *Id.* at 495, note 11.

11. *Id.* at 495.

12. 349 U.S. 294, 301, 75 S.Ct. 753, 99 L.Ed. 1083 (1955). [Case No. 124]

13. 358 U.S. 1, 78 S.Ct. 1401, 3 L.Ed.2d 5 (1958).

plan due to turmoil and hostilities, a situation that state officials encouraged. While showing some sympathy for the board, the Court rejected its request for a postponement, reminding officials that constitutional rights "are not to be sacrificed or yielded to the violence and disorder which have followed upon the actions of the Governor and Legislature."[14]

The Supreme Court did not accept another case involving school desegregation until it reviewed a dispute from Knoxville, Tennessee, five years later. In *Goss v. Board of Education*[15] the Court struck down a program that would have permitted students to request transfers back to their original schools when, after re-zoning, they would have been in a racial minority. The Court rejected the plan, which was based solely on racial factors, due to its fear that this approach would have led back to racial segregation.[16]

Ten years after *Brown I*, in *Griffin v. County School Board of Prince Edward County (Griffin)*, the Court declared that "[t]he time for 'mere deliberate speed' had run out."[17] The Court invalidated a plan that would have closed public schools in a county in Virginia while the commonwealth contributed to the support of private segregated white schools. Acknowledging that the plan would have denied African American students the right to equal protection, the Court pointed out that they were entitled to immediate relief.

A year later, in *Rogers v. Paul*,[18] the Court ruled in favor of African American students in Arkansas who challenged a plan that would have desegregated only one grade per year. The Court determined that while full implementation of a desegregation plan was pending, students were entitled to immediate transfers to schools that they were excluded from due to race and had more extensive course offerings available.

In *Green v. County School Board of New Kent County (Green)*[19] the Court considered freedom-of-choice plans for the first time. Realizing that little progress had been made in breaking down a dual (or segregated) system in Virginia since *Brown*, the Court explained that the school board there bore the burden of developing a realistic desegregation plan. Although not expressly striking this plan down, the Court was of the opinion that if other reasonably available remedies such as zoning could have been used to achieve quicker and more effective conversions to unitary status, then freedom-of-choice plans were unacceptable. In its rationale, the Court enunciated the six so-called *Green* factors that continue to be a key measure in evaluating whether a dual system has achieved unitary status. These factors address the composition of a

---

14. 358 U.S. 1, 16, 78 S.Ct. 1401, 1409, 3 L.Ed.2d 5 (1958).

15. 373 U.S. 683, 83 S.Ct. 1405, 10 L.Ed.2d 632 (1963).

16. In the same year, in *McNeese v. Board of Educ., Community Unit School Dist. 187*, 373 U.S. 668, 83 S.Ct. 1433, 10 L.Ed.2d 622 (1963), the Court posited that an aggrieved party did not have to exhaust administrative remedies in state court before turning to the federal courts for relief.

17. 377 U.S. 218, 234, 84 S.Ct. 1226, 12 L.Ed.2d 256 (1964).

18. 382 U.S. 198, 86 S.Ct. 358, 15 L.Ed.2d 265 (1965).

19. 391 U.S. 430, 88 S.Ct. 1689, 20 L.Ed.2d 716 (1968).

student body, faculty, staff, transportation, extracurricular activities, and facilities.

Dissatisfied with the slow pace of implementing desegregation, in *Alexander v. Holmes County Board of Education* (*Alexander*), the first case under recently appointed Chief Justice Warren Burger, the Court discarded the "all deliberate speed" standard for evaluating progress. Instead, the Court asserted that "the obligation of every school district [is] to terminate dual school systems at once and to operate now and hereafter only unitary schools."[20] Reversing judgments that granted time extensions to school boards in Mississippi, the Court found that dual systems immediately had to give way to unitary districts while objections and amendments to court-ordered plans could be heard only after systems achieved unitary status.

Remedies for De Jure Segregation

The immediate impact of the Court's declaration in *Alexander* to, in effect, integrate now and litigate later, led to a myriad of lower court orders for desegregating dual systems. To the extent that the lower courts called for a variety of arrangements, inconsistencies appeared over precisely what was constitutionally required and by what techniques they could be achieved. The Court addressed these issues in *Swann v. Charlotte–Mecklenburg Board of Education* (*Swann*),[21] delineating the responsibilities of school officials in desegregating a dual school system.

Swann is noteworthy for two reasons. First, *Swann* was the Court's last unanimous judgment in a major school desegregation case. Second, *Swann* is the first case in which the Court examined the use of busing to achieve school desegregation. *Swann* involved a federal trial court in North Carolina's approval, and the Fourth Circuit's modification, of a plan creating restructured attendance zones that relied on busing to bring about a greater racial balance in the schools. Conceding that it could not establish rigid guidelines for busing, the Court noted that if assigning children to neighborhood schools did not effectively dismantle segregated schools, then a federal trial court could employ busing to implement an equitable solution.

As part of its analysis in *Swann*, the Court discussed other matters that it had not reviewed extensively. As to school construction, the Court maintained that in devising remedies for de jure segregation, officials and the courts must see to it that future construction and abandonment is not used to perpetuate or re-establish dual systems. Turning to one-race schools, the Court thought that where a proposed plan for conversion from a dual to a unitary system contemplated the continued existence of some schools that were all or predominately of one race, officials must demonstrate that such assignments are genuinely nondiscriminatory. The Court added that while it is not necessary for every

---

20. 396 U.S. 19, 20, 90 S.Ct. 29, 24 L.Ed.2d 19 (1969).

21. 402 U.S. 1, 91 S.Ct. 1267, 28 L.Ed.2d 554 (1971). [Case No. 125]

school in a district to reflect a system's racial composition as a whole, a federal trial court may apply a racial ratio or quota as a starting point in shaping a remedy since so-called "racially neutral" assignment plans are insufficient to counteract the continuing effects of past segregation. Looking to the future, the Court indicated that boards did not have to make annual adjustments in the racial compositions of student bodies once they ended segregation.

The Court handed down two similar judgments on the same day in refusing to permit city school districts to be carved out of segregated county systems since doing so would have slowed down their shifts to unitary status. The difference was that in *Wright v. City Council of Emporia*,[22] the motivation for change came from city officials in Virginia, while in *United States v. Scotland Neck City Board of Education*,[23] the impetus came from the North Carolina legislature.

Another novel question before the Court was the scope and authority of the federal judiciary in remedying de jure segregation. The Court pondered whether adjacent districts that were heavily populated by whites could have been required to participate in remedies where de jure segregated systems contained such high percentages of African American students that meaningful racial mixing could not have taken place. In *Milliken v. Bradley (Milliken I)*,[24] the first major defeat for supporters of school desegregation since *Brown I*, the Court answered that such a remedy was impermissible absent proof that the state or surrounding districts were involved in discriminatory acts.

Milliken I involved a federal trial court's order which called for a multi-district, area-wide desegregation remedy that would have required fifty-three suburban districts to participate in the process of desegregating schools in Detroit, Michigan. The trial court contended that since Detroit's schools were already segregated and proposed remedies would have exacerbated the situation, it had to go beyond district boundaries in crafting a remedy. A closely divided Supreme Court reversed in believing that the inter-district remedy was inappropriate.[25] The Court remarked that absent evidence that they were segregated or that their boundaries were created in order to promote segregation, the suburban boards were not accountable, especially since they did not even have a chance to present their case or to participate in developing the proposed remedy.

On remand in *Milliken I*, a federal trial court's proposed remedy created student assignment and remedial plans for the Detroit schools

---

22. 407 U.S. 451, 92 S.Ct. 2196, 33 L.Ed.2d 51 (1972).

23. 407 U.S. 484, 92 S.Ct. 2214, 33 L.Ed.2d 75 (1972).

24. 418 U.S. 717, 94 S.Ct. 3112, 41 L.Ed.2d 1069 (1974). [Case No. 126]

25. Despite *Milliken I*, later cases permitted inter-district remedies. *See, e.g., Newburg Area Council v. Board of Educ. of Jefferson County, Ky.*, 510 F.2d 1358 (6th Cir.1974), *cert. denied*, 421 U.S. 931, 95 S.Ct. 1658, 44 L.Ed.2d 88 (1975); *United*

States v. Board of School Commr's of the City of Indianapolis, 503 F.2d 68 (7th Cir. 1974), *cert. denied*, 421 U.S. 929, 95 S.Ct. 1655, 44 L.Ed.2d 86 (1975); *Evans v. Buchanan*, 555 F.2d 373 (3d Cir.1977), *cert. denied*, 434 U.S. 880, 98 S.Ct. 235, 54 L.Ed.2d 160 (1977); *Hoots v. Commonwealth of Pa.*, 672 F.2d 1107 [3 Educ. L. Rep. 244] (3d Cir.1982), *cert. denied sub nom. Churchill Area School Dist. v. Hoots*, 459 U.S. 824, 103 S.Ct. 55, 74 L.Ed.2d 60 (1982).

while directing the state to share equally in their cost. In *Milliken v. Bradley II,*[26] the Court affirmed that the remedy was appropriate since the trial court based its judgment on substantial evidence aimed at eradicating the vestiges of de jure segregation. In affording a measure of vindication for supporters of school desegregation, the Court concluded that the lower court acted within its jurisdiction in ordering prospective relief and requiring the state to share fiscal responsibility for implementing the remedy.[27]

The Supreme Court first addressed de facto segregation in *Keyes v. School District No. 1, Denver, Colorado (Keyes).*[28] In *Keyes*, the Court was of the view that the actions of school board officials may have the effect of creating de jure segregation. As such, the case is addressed here rather than under de facto segregation. *Keyes* was also the first case in which the Court specified that another minority group, Mexican American students, should be placed in the same category as African American children since both suffered from the effects of segregated schools.

In *Keyes*, the Court affirmed earlier findings of de jure segregation in one section of Denver that were caused by the school board's establishment of school sites and attendance zones, which created and maintained segregated schools, thereby, in effect, creating a spatial presumption when defining segregation. Put another way, even though the schools were not segregated by law or the state constitution, the Court was convinced that the board's actions led to the creation of a core of inner-city schools that served minority students that were inferior to those educating children in predominately white schools in the rest of the city. Based on its recognition that the board's action gave rise to a prima facie case of intentional discrimination, the Court shifted the burden to school officials to demonstrate that they had not deliberately created segregated schools.

Resolved three years after *Keyes*, *Pasadena City Board of Education v. Spangler*[29] was the Court's first desegregation case from California. The Court stated that once a school district achieved unitary status, its board was not obligated to make annual readjustments in attendance zones to reflect demographic changes in population.

In the subsequent round of litigation the Court examined remedies for de jure segregation, beginning with a dispute over questions of proof and the function of the federal judiciary. The Sixth Circuit, having twice invalidated a remedy as inadequate, upheld an extensive system-wide busing plan for Dayton, Ohio. However, in *Dayton Board of Education v.*

26. 433 U.S. 267, 97 S.Ct. 2749, 53 L.Ed.2d 745 (1977). [Case No. 127]

27. The Court reached a similar result with regard to a state's duty to pay for a remedy in *Missouri v. Jenkins III*, 515 U.S. 70, 115 S.Ct. 2038, 132 L.Ed.2d 63 [100 Educ. L. Rep. 506] (1995), *appeal after remand, Jenkins v. Missouri*, 103 F.3d 731 [115 Educ. L. Rep. 302] (8th Cir.1997). *See also United States v. Board of School Commr's of City of Indianapolis*, 677 F.2d 1185 [4 Educ. L. Rep. 447] (7th Cir.1982), *cert. denied sub nom. Orr v. Board of School Commr's of City of Indianapolis*, 459 U.S. 1086, 103 S.Ct. 568, 74 L.Ed.2d 931 (1982) (placing the entire burden of paying for an inter-district remedy on the state where it was solely responsible for the violations).

28. 413 U.S. 189, 93 S.Ct. 2686, 37 L.Ed.2d 548 (1973). [Case No. 128]

29. 427 U.S. 424, 96 S.Ct. 2697, 49 L.Ed.2d 599 (1976).

Brinkman,[30] the Court vacated and remanded in writing that where the board's actions did not have a system-wide effect, the judicial remedy had to be narrowly tailored to apply only to schools that were adversely impacted by the board's actions. On remand, the Sixth Circuit held that a system-wide remedy was warranted. In *Dayton Board of Education v. Brinkman (Dayton II)*,[31] the Supreme Court affirmed that since board actions at least partially contributed to the district's being segregated, officials had to act to rid the entire system of discrimination.[32]

On the same day that the Court resolved *Dayton II*, it considered a second case from Ohio in which a federal trial court and the Sixth Circuit agreed on a system-wide desegregation remedy. In *Columbus Board of Education v. Penick*,[33] the Court affirmed that since there was long-standing proof of intentional segregation by the local board, a system-wide remedy was appropriate. According to the Court, local school board officials preserved a segregated system by such practices as assigning African American teachers only to schools with predominantly black student bodies, manipulating attendance zones, and making site selections for new schools that had the foreseeable and anticipated effect of preserving racial separation in schools.

In *Missouri v. Jenkins (Jenkins II)*,[34] the Supreme Court examined the financing of desegregation remedies. After lower federal courts essentially agreed that Kansas City and the State of Missouri had to finance a desegregation order, the local board claimed that it was unable to raise its share of the funds without violating state school finance and taxing laws. The Court affirmed that while the federal judiciary cannot impose a tax increase, it can require a board to levy property taxes at a rate adequate to fund a desegregation remedy and can enjoin the operation of statutes that would have prevented the board from complying with its order. The Court relied on the need to enforce the Equal Protection Clause in the United States Constitution and *Griffin* wherein it posited that if public schools were closed in one county to avoid desegregation, courts could require a county legislative body to levy taxes to preserve a desegregated district. *Jenkins II* was the last Supreme Court victory for proponents of school desegregation.

The Court next examined when officials in a formerly unitary system did enough to remedy segregation. In a dispute involving a desegregation decree that had been in effect for more than twenty years, *Board of Education of Oklahoma City Public Schools v. Dowell*,[35] the

30. 433 U.S. 406, 97 S.Ct. 2766, 53 L.Ed.2d 851 (1977).

31. 443 U.S. 526, 99 S.Ct. 2971, 61 L.Ed.2d 720 (1979).

32. The court-ordered remedy for busing in Dayton, the last school system in Ohio operating under such an order, terminated in April 2002. Scott Elliott, *Desegregation Busing Ends; Pact Avoids Court Hearing*, DAYTON DAILY NEWS, April 16, 2002, at A1.

33. 443 U.S. 449, 99 S.Ct. 2941, 61 L.Ed.2d 666 (1979).

34. 495 U.S. 33, 110 S.Ct. 1651, 109 L.Ed.2d 31 [59 Educ. L. Rep. 298] (1990), *subsequent appeal, Jenkins v. Missouri*, 949 F.2d 1052 [71 Educ. L. Rep. 409] (8th Cir. 1991). The Court refused to hear an appeal in an earlier iteration of this case, *cert. denied, Missouri v. Jenkins I*, 484 U.S. 816, 108 S.Ct. 70, 98 L.Ed.2d 34 [42 Educ. L. Rep. 34] (1987).

35. 498 U.S. 237, 111 S.Ct. 630, 112 L.Ed.2d 715 [64 Educ. L. Rep. 628] (1991), *on remand*, 778 F.Supp. 1144 [71 Educ. L. Rep. 741] (W.D.Okla.1991), *aff'd sub nom.*

Court decided that insofar as desegregation orders are not meant to operate in perpetuity, the judiciary had to consider whether a board acted in good faith in eliminating the vestiges of past discrimination as far as practicable.[36] Moreover, the Court acknowledged that in addressing whether a board remedied the vestiges of past discrimination, a court had to take the six *Green* factors into consideration.

A year later, the Court accepted another question of first impression, whether judicial supervision of a desegregation order can be achieved incrementally. In *Freeman v. Pitts*,[37] the Court, relying on a federal trial court in Georgia's application of the *Green* factors, remanded for further consideration. The Court declared that since equity required the adjustment of remedies in a feasible and practical manner that returned control of school districts to regular educational officials, a federal trial court can relinquish its control over a desegregation plan incrementally as long as it is content that a board made a good faith commitment to complying with its order.[38]

In *Missouri v. Jenkins III* (*Jenkins III*),[39] the Court revisited the ongoing litigation in Kansas City, Missouri. This time, the Court decreed that lower federal courts exceeded their discretion in mandating a costly desegregation remedy. The trial court had ordered the state to pay for both across-the-board salary increases for virtually all personnel and quality education programs including the creation of a comprehensive magnet school[40] and a capital improvements plan, at a total cost of more than $1.3 billion dollars, since student achievement was still at or below national norms on many grade levels. The more than decade-long gap since *Jenkins III* is the longest time period within which the Court has not addressed a school desegregation case since *Brown I*, reflecting its disengagement in this important arena.

Dowell v. Board of Educ. of Oklahoma City Pub. Schools, 8 F.3d 1501 [87 Educ. L. Rep. 67] (10th Cir.1993). [Case No. 129]

36. For similar results, *see, e.g., Coalition to Save Our Children v. Board of Educ.*, 90 F.3d 752 [111 Educ. L. Rep. 132] (3d Cir.1996); *Lockett v. Board of Educ. of Muscogee County School Dist.*, 111 F.3d 839 [117 Educ. L. Rep. 487] (11th Cir.1997), *reh'g en banc denied*, 121 F.3d 724 (11th Cir.1997); *Manning v. School Bd. of Hillsborough County*, 244 F.3d 927 [152 Educ. L. Rep. 51], *cert. denied*, 534 U.S. 824, 122 S.Ct. 61, 151 L.Ed.2d 28 (2001); *People Who Care v. Rockford Bd. of Educ. School Dist. No. 205*, 246 F.3d 1073 [152 Educ. L. Rep. 543] (7th Cir. 2001).

37. 503 U.S. 467, 112 S.Ct. 1430, 118 L.Ed.2d 108 [72 Educ. L. Rep. 717] (1992), *on remand*, 979 F.2d 1472 [78 Educ. L. Rep. 696] (11th Cir.1992), *on remand*, 942 F.Supp. 1449 [114 Educ. L. Rep. 178] (N.D.Ga.1996), *aff'd*, 118 F.3d 727 [119 Educ. L. Rep. 844] (11th Cir.1997). [Case No. 130]

38. For cases reaching a similar result, *see Belk v. Charlotte–Mecklenburg Bd. of Educ.*, 269 F.3d 305 [158 Educ. L. Rep. 86] (4th Cir.2001), *cert. denied, sub nom. Capacchione v. Charlotte–Mecklenburg Bd. of Educ.*, 535 U.S. 986, 122 S.Ct. 1537, 152 L.Ed.2d 465 (2002); *Holton v. City of Thomasville School Dist.*, 425 F.3d 1325 [202 Educ. L. Rep. 54] (11th Cir. 2005).

39. 515 U.S. 70, 115 S.Ct. 2038, 132 L.Ed.2d 63 [100 Educ. L. Rep. 506] (1995). [Case No. 131]

40. For another case involving magnet schools, *see Hernandez v. Board of Educ. of Stockton Unified School Dist.*, 25 Cal. Rptr.3d 1 [195 Educ. L. Rep. 919] (Cal. Ct. App. 2004) (affirming that state funding for magnet schools did not violate the state constitutional prohibition against racial discrimination in education for two years where the trial court found that the district achieved unitary status).

Teacher Desegregation

The Supreme Court did not address faculty desegregation until more than a decade after *Brown I*. When the desegregation plan for Richmond, Virginia, failed to contain a provision for faculty assignments, the Fourth Circuit determined that this omission was an insufficient reason to reject the proposed remedy. The court asserted that after it eliminated all direct discrimination in student assignments, it could examine the effect of teacher assignments on the schools. In *Bradley v. School Board, City of Richmond (Bradley)*,[41] the Supreme Court noted that the case should have been remanded for hearings over the claim that racial assignments of staff affected student rights. The Court ascertained that there was no merit to the suggestion that the relationship between faculty allocations on an alleged racial basis and the adequacy of desegregation plans was entirely speculative. In refusing to postpone proposed hearings, the Court reasoned that it had to act since more than a decade passed since it called for the desegregation of public school facilities "with all deliberate speed."

Following *Bradley*, progress in desegregation of school faculties continued at a slower pace than for students. The absence of a clear test to apply made it cumbersome for lower federal courts to formulate specific decrees that could have helped to prevent unconstitutional delays. In one such case, *United States v. Montgomery County Board of Education*,[42] the Court upheld a plan under which the goal for faculty desegregation was that each school in a district in Alabama would have approximately the same ratio of African American and white teachers as existed in the system as a whole.

A year later, the Fifth Circuit, in an appeal of cases from states throughout the Southeast, adopted this ratio concept as a guide for integrating teaching staffs in the so-called *Singleton* criteria.[43] The same court later explained that at the time of its initial judgment, the trial court should have insisted on immediate steps to assure that the composition of the faculty in each school reflected the district-wide racial ratio of faculty members and that all teachers accept reassignment as a condition of continued employment.[44] In the latter case, the trial court accepted the slow pace of faculty change predicated on the board's claim that a more rapid pace would have caused "white flight" among the faculty. The Fifth Circuit retorted that the fear of faculty resistance to desegregation measures, like the fear of community resistance, could not be the basis for failing to adopt the plan most likely to achieve a unitary system.

Other legal problems affecting teachers in the desegregation process arose in connection with non-retention of large numbers of African

---

41. 382 U.S. 103, 86 S.Ct. 224, 15 L.Ed.2d 187 (1965).

42. 395 U.S. 225, 89 S.Ct. 1670, 23 L.Ed.2d 263 (1969).

43. *Singleton v. Jackson Mun. Separate School Dist.*, 419 F.2d 1211 (5th Cir.1969),

cert. denied, 396 U.S. 1032, 90 S.Ct. 612, 24 L.Ed.2d 530 (1970).

44. *United States v. DeSoto Parish School Bd.*, 574 F.2d 804 (5th Cir.1978).

Americans. In states lacking tenure laws, judicial review was the only effective remedy available to teachers. The courts took the long history of racial discrimination and the failure of many public school systems to desegregate into account in light of the suddenly disproportionate reduction in the ranks of African American teachers. This increase gave rise to an inference of discrimination, thereby placing the burden of proof on boards to justify their actions by setting up objective employment standards for hiring and retaining teachers.

In a case from North Carolina in which the Fourth Circuit first enunciated the principle of equal treatment, all white teachers who expressed their desire to be retained were able to keep their jobs while sixteen out of twenty-four African American teachers who worked in the previous year were not rehired.[45] The Fourth Circuit later pointed out that African American teachers who were no longer needed due to a reduction of enrollment by minority students in their schools were entitled to preference for re-employment in the system over new candidates as long as this arrangement was used for white teachers.[46]

Courts in states where de jure segregation was the norm followed the lead of the Fourth Circuit. For example, the Fifth Circuit, in applying the so-called *Singleton* criteria, indicated that the objective and reasonable non-discriminatory standards which applied in cases of dismissal or demotion, had to have been developed prior to a staff reduction.[47] The court was of the opinion that no staff vacancy could have been filled through recruitment of a person of a race, color, or national origin different from that of the individual who was dismissed or demoted until each qualified displaced staff member was offered an opportunity to fill the vacancy. Conversely, the Fifth Circuit thought that the criteria applicable to dismissal or demotion during a staff reduction due to desegregation did not apply to personnel actions which took place when there was no reduction, even if a school system was still in the desegregation process.[48]

The Fifth Circuit, in a series of judgments, added that any reductions invoking the *Singleton* criteria had to have been related to desegregation[49] and that any reductions may have been measured by appropriate subclasses, such as high school teachers and/or principals, rather than by overall figures.[50] As to demotions, insofar as the court was concerned that responsibility is the central value to be protected,[51] individuals could have been considered to have been demoted even though they received salary increases.[52] Yet, where a principal was

45. *Chambers v. Hendersonville City Bd. of Educ.*, 364 F.2d 189 (4th Cir.1966).

46. *North Carolina Teachers Ass'n v. Asheboro City Bd. of Educ.*, 393 F.2d 736 (4th Cir.1968).

47. *Singleton v. Jackson Mun. Separate School Dist.*, 419 F.2d 1211 (5th Cir.1969), *cert. denied*, 396 U.S. 1032, 90 S.Ct. 612, 24 L.Ed.2d 530 (1970).

48. *Wright v. Houston Indep. School Dist.*, 569 F.2d 1383 (5th Cir.1978).

49. *Hardy v. Porter*, 546 F.2d 1165 (5th Cir.1977).

50. *Pickens v. Okolona Mun. Separate School Dist.*, 527 F.2d 358 (5th Cir.1976).

51. *Lee v. Russell County Bd. of Educ.*, 563 F.2d 1159 (5th Cir.1977).

52. *Lee v. Macon County Bd. of Educ.*, 453 F.2d 1104 (5th Cir.1971).

named an administrative assistant to a superintendent, the court did not treat this as a demotion despite the change of title.[53] Finally, where a demotion was at issue, the court observed that the *Singleton* criteria placed the burden of proof on a plaintiff to show that there was, in fact, a demotion.[54]

Cases involving non-retention of individual African American teachers led to important results. In a dispute from North Carolina, a school board chose not to renew the contract of an African American teacher with thirteen years of experience in its schools and a masters degree despite the fact that the African American principal in her all-black school recommended that she be rehired. When the superintendent notified the principal that the allocation of teachers for his school was to be reduced for the next year because, under a newly instituted freedom-of-choice plan, African American pupils transferred to formerly all-white schools, he did not provide instructions on how to reduce staff. Once the teacher was informed that she was not going to retain her position, the superintendent suggested that she apply for a job at other schools in the county. After the female teacher was not hired in any of the schools, a federal trial court deferred to the board's choosing not to rehire the teacher.[55] On appeal, a unanimous en banc panel of the Fourth Circuit reversed in favor of the teacher, maintaining that she was entitled to the opportunity to be considered objectively for re-employment with the burden of justifying a failure to rehire placed on the board.[56]

Clearly, desegregating a teaching staff was an essential element in correcting de jure segregation of students. As such, court orders were premised on the rights of students and were not confined to actions necessary to vindicate the rights of African American teachers. The First Circuit made this point when it upheld a desegregation order in a dispute from Boston.[57] The court wrote that since the school system had not achieved unitary status with regard to hiring faculty and administrative staff, officials had a continuing duty to reach set hiring goals for minority candidates.[58] The Third Circuit agreed in principle in rejecting a suit by four white teachers from Pennsylvania who sought to invalidate a racial ratio for staff assignments in a school district after commonwealth officials released it from a requirement that was imposed as a condition of eligibility for federal funds.[59] A year later, the Sixth Circuit affirmed the continuation of a similar teacher assignment policy, rejecting a challenge from teachers who claimed that it violated equal

---

53. *Lee v. Macon County Bd. of Educ.*, 470 F.2d 958 (5th Cir.1972).

54. *Lee v. Pickens County School Sys.*, 563 F.2d 143 (5th Cir.1977).

55. *Wall v. Stanly County Bd. of Educ.*, 259 F.Supp. 238 (M.D.N.C.1966).

56. *Wall v. Stanly County Bd. of Educ.*, 378 F.2d 275 (4th Cir.1967).

57. *Morgan v. Kerrigan*, 509 F.2d 599 (1st Cir.1975). *See also Morgan v. Kerrigan*, 509 F.2d 580 (1st Cir.1974), *cert. denied*, 421 U.S. 963, 95 S.Ct. 1950, 44 L.Ed.2d 449 (1975).

58. *Morgan v. Burke*, 926 F.2d 86 [65 Educ. L. Rep. 1075] (1st Cir.), *cert. denied sub nom. Boston Teachers Union Local 66 v. Morgan*, 503 U.S. 983, 112 S.Ct. 1664, 118 L.Ed.2d 386 (1992).

59. *Kromnick v. School Dist. of Philadelphia*, 739 F.2d 894 [19 Educ. L. Rep. 52] (3d Cir. 1984), *cert. denied*, 469 U.S. 1107, 105 S.Ct. 782, 83 L.Ed.2d 777 [21 Educ. L. Rep. 1157] (1985).

protection and conflicted with their collective bargaining contract.[60] The court determined that the plan was substantially related to the important governmental objective of achieving a racially integrated faculty throughout the district and did not conflict with the bargaining contract. The court was satisfied that involuntary transfers and denials of requests for voluntary transfers had a race-neutral impact.

The Supreme Court refused to hear an appeal in a case from New York that involved a plan that was approved by the Second Circuit for both preserving elements of a teacher desegregation program that required hiring of minority teachers and considering seniority rights of majority teachers during a period of layoffs due to fiscal problems and declining enrollments.[61] The court rejected arguments that state law or collective bargaining contracts could prevail over the constitutional mandate to eliminate vestiges of de jure segregation from an urban system that were being perpetuated in its teaching staff. The court upheld a percentage layoff plan but invalidated one of its aspects as needlessly harsh in its treatment of recall rights of laid-off probationary and permanent teachers.

In *Wygant v. Jackson Board of Education (Wygant)*,[62] the Supreme Court struck down a plan from Michigan that was reached through collective bargaining to cover layoffs even though there was no discrimination prior to its implementation. Under the provision, the seniority basis for layoffs was to be adjusted so that at no time would there be a greater percent of minority personnel whose contracts were terminated than the current percent of minority staff who were employed when a reduction-in-force (RIF) went into effect. This approach led to layoffs of white teachers who were senior to African Americans who were retained. A plurality of the Court vitiated the plan as violating equal protection. According to the plurality, while layoffs placed the entire burden of achieving racial equality on particular individuals, hiring goals were a less intrusive means of accomplishing similar purposes since the burden that had to be borne by innocent individuals was diffused to a considerable extent among society generally.[63]

The Second Circuit applied *Wygant* in rejecting a RIF plan that would have removed only white teachers in Connecticut.[64] The court emphasized that even though a RIF plan had to have been narrowly tailored, a proportional layoff scheme could have been developed where there was an earlier consent decree that did not address layoffs. Instead, the court held that the bargaining agreement spoke in terms of preserv-

60. *Jacobson v. Cincinnati Bd. of Educ.*, 961 F.2d 100 [74 Educ. L. Rep. 51] (6th Cir.1992), *cert. denied*, 506 U.S. 830, 113 S.Ct. 94, 121 L.Ed.2d 55 (1992).

61. *Arthur v. Nyquist*, 712 F.2d 816 [12 Educ. L. Rep. 663] (2d Cir.1983), *cert. denied*, 467 U.S. 1259, 104 S.Ct. 3555, 82 L.Ed.2d 856 [19 Educ. L. Rep. 23] (1984).

62. *Wygant v. Jackson Bd. of Educ.*, 476 U.S. 267, 106 S.Ct. 1842, 90 L.Ed.2d 260 [32 Educ. L. Rep. 20] (1986), *reh'g denied*,

478 U.S. 1014, 106 S.Ct. 3320, 92 L.Ed.2d 728 [35 Educ. L. Rep. 20] (1986).

63. For another case where a plaintiff prevailed in challenging a race-based affirmative action policy in conjunction with a RIF, *see Cunico v. Pueblo School Dist. No. 60*, 917 F.2d 431 [63 Educ. L. Rep. 713] (10th Cir.1990).

64. *Crumpton v. Bridgeport Educ. Ass'n*, 993 F.2d 1023 [83 Educ. L. Rep. 63] (2d Cir.1993).

ing gains made. The court offered that laying off teachers from only one race in an effort to remedy past injustices was an impermissible means toward reaching a legitimate end. The panel directed the trial court to consider whether there was a strong rationale for ruling that hiring practices contributed to creating a segregated school system before crafting such a remedy.

Another case involving RIF was days away from oral argument before the Supreme Court when the parties reached a settlement.[65] At issue was a dispute from New Jersey wherein a school board, mistakenly acting on its belief that its affirmative action program required it to terminate the contract of a white, rather than an African American, teacher, based solely on race, dismissed the white woman even though the two had virtually identical credentials. An en banc Third Circuit affirmed that since the board's plan, which was adopted to promote racial diversity rather than remedying discrimination or the effects of past discrimination, trammeled the rights of non-minorities, it was unconstitutional.[66]

De Facto Segregation

Definition and Scope

De facto, as opposed to de jure, segregation occurs when, without any governmental action or inaction, a substantial majority of students in a school are of the same racial or ethnic minority. Insofar as *Brown I* and *II* began a line of cases that focused on de jure segregation in public schools, de facto segregation remained ripe for judicial review.

Outside of the South, some local educational officials gerrymandered attendance zones and/or took other steps to contribute to keeping large concentrations of African Americans in segregated schools. Remedying such actions came under *Brown II's* auspices since the segregation in question came about due to governmental action. Thus, although often referred to as de facto, such actions were really covert de jure segregation.

An early leading case of "false de facto" segregation came from New York where the Second Circuit was convinced that a board re-aligned attendance boundaries and, until about ten years earlier, permitted transfers of white, but not African American, students within the area of the school in controversy where more than 90 percent of the student body was black.[67] In light of this situation, the court contended that the purpose and effect of the school board's approach was to produce a

---

65. Mark Walsh, *N.J. District Settles Case on Race Bias: Action Heads off High Court Review*, EDUCATION WEEK, Nov. 26, 1997, at 1, 22.

66. *Taxman v. Board of Educ. of the Township of Piscataway*, 91 F.3d 1547 1547 [111 Educ. L. Rep. 696] (3d Cir.1996), *cert. granted*, 521 U.S. 1117, 117 S.Ct. 2506, 138 L.Ed.2d 1010 [122 Educ. L. Rep. 389] (1997), *cert. dismissed*, 522 U.S. 1010, 118 S.Ct. 595, 139 L.Ed.2d 431 [122 Educ. L. Rep. 570] (1997).

67. *Taylor v. Board of Educ. of City School Dist. of New Rochelle*, 294 F.2d 36 (2d Cir.1961), *cert. denied*, 368 U.S. 940, 82 S.Ct. 382, 7 L.Ed.2d 339 (1961).

substantially segregated school in violation of the Fourteenth Amendment as a form of de jure segregation.

Courts increasingly ruled that "false de facto" segregation had to be corrected. For instance, a federal trial court in California indicated that board action, and inaction, caused a pattern of racial imbalance involving students and staff.[68] The court realized that board officials redrew attendance zone lines from time to time while adhering to policies calling for neighborhood schools and opposing forced cross-town busing as staff-assignment policies created racial imbalances. When ordered to submit a plan to remedy the situation, the board complied and parents unsuccessfully petitioned the Ninth Circuit.[69] When the board tried to be relieved from implementing the plan due to changed circumstances, most notably, alleged "white flight," wherein large numbers of white residents moved away from a district, the Ninth Circuit again denied relief.[70]

In a similar case from Michigan, the Sixth Circuit recognized that school officials purposefully segregated African American students over a lengthy period of time.[71] Even though officials had taken some steps to alleviate racial imbalances, since the court discerned that they were inadequate, it approved a medial plan that included busing to cure the effects of years of purposeful segregation. When, on appeal, the board's attorney argued that the plan would have required it to expend large sums of money that might not have been available, the court turned a deaf ear to its plea. In upholding the remedial plan, the court asserted that failing to implement the plan would have done no more than reaffirm the previous inadequate policies. A year earlier, the Seventh Circuit became the first court to call for busing as a partial remedy in a school desegregation case; the dispute involved inequities in school zoning, student transfers, and transportation in Illinois.[72]

The Supreme Court finally addressed de facto segregation in *Keyes v. School District No. 1, Denver, Colorado*,[73] discussed earlier, although it conceded that the actions of school board officials may have the effect of creating de jure segregation. In a more recent, multifaceted case from Illinois involving minority and limited English proficient students, a federal trial court rejected a school board's motion to dismiss a class action suit claiming that it denied them the right to equal educational opportunities.[74] The court commented that the plaintiffs' allegations that the local board evidenced a discriminatory intent in implementing its redistricting plan that closed neighborhood schools in minority areas and

68. *Spangler v. Pasadena City Bd. of Educ.*, 311 F.Supp. 501 (C.D.Cal.1970).

69. *Spangler v. Pasadena City Bd. of Educ.*, 427 F.2d 1352 (9th Cir.1970), *cert. denied*, 402 U.S. 943, 91 S.Ct. 1607, 29 L.Ed.2d 111 (1971).

70. *Spangler v. Pasadena City Bd. of Educ.*, 519 F.2d 430 (9th Cir.1975).

71. *Davis v. School Dist. of City of Pontiac*, 443 F.2d 573 (6th Cir.1971), *cert. denied*, 404 U.S. 913, 92 S.Ct. 233, 30 L.Ed.2d 186 (1971).

72. *United States v. School Dist. 151 of Cook County, Ill.*, 432 F.2d 1147 (7th Cir. 1970), *cert. denied*, 402 U.S. 943, 91 S.Ct. 1610, 29 L.Ed.2d 111 (1971).

73. 413 U.S. 189, 93 S.Ct. 2686, 37 L.Ed.2d 548 (1973). [Case No. 128]

74. *Leslie v. Board of Educ. for Ill. School Dist. U–46*, 379 F.Supp.2d 952 [201 Educ. L. Rep. 151] (N.D. Ill. 2005).

that the plan had racially disparate effects, including undue transportation burdens and insufficient services and educational opportunities for students of limited English proficiency, were sufficient to state a claim that educators violated their rights to equal protection.

Duty to Correct

A basic question relevant to de facto segregation is whether educators had to act to correct racial imbalances that developed through housing patterns and the uniform application of school zoning and student-transfer policies.[75] While five circuit courts responded that boards were not required to do so,[76] this did not mean that unequal facilities, programs, and/or staffs were permitted to remain in predominantly minority schools. Faced with such situations, tangible school deficiencies required school boards to enact positive corrective measures, not on the ground of racial balance per se, but on the basis of general equality of educational opportunity. The judicial attitude in this regard seemed to have been to remedy reasonably correctable educational inequalities but not to have required racial mixing per se.[77]

One of the lengthiest and most comprehensive cases in the history of urban school desegregation arose in Washington, D.C., where the federal trial court ordered extensive changes ranging from school zoning patterns and teacher segregation to tracking while targeting financial inequities as an underlying cause in denying equal educational opportunities to all students.[78] In a noteworthy aspect of this case, the court struck down the tracking system of ability grouping based primarily on the facts that educators placed students by relying on questionable early-testing procedures and that it was exceedingly difficult to change tracks.[79] When the board chose not to appeal and refused to allow the superintendent to do so, he resigned, and, joined by a member of the board, challenged the trial court's order as a form of judicial interference in the administration of the schools. The District of Columbia Circuit Court affirmed most of the trial court's substantive points, including its abolition of tracking.[80] However, rather than affirm the entire decree,

---

75. For the latest iteration in long term litigation involving housing inequities in the context of school desegregation, *see United States v. Yonkers Board of Educ.*, 30 F.Supp.2d 650 [131 Educ. L. Rep. 990] (S.D.N.Y.1998).

76. *See Bell v. School City of Gary, Ind.*, 324 F.2d 209 (7th Cir.1963), *cert. denied*, 377 U.S. 924, 84 S.Ct. 1223, 12 L.Ed.2d 216 (1964); *Downs v. Board of Educ.*, 336 F.2d 988 (10th Cir.1964), *cert. denied*, 380 U.S. 914, 85 S.Ct. 898, 13 L.Ed.2d 800 (1965); *Springfield School Comm. v. Barksdale*, 348 F.2d 261 (1st Cir.1965); *Offerman v. Nitkowski*, 378 F.2d 22 (2d Cir. 1967); *Deal v. Cincinnati Bd. of Educ.*, 369 F.2d 55 (6th Cir.1966), *cert. denied*, 389 U.S. 847, 88 S.Ct. 39, 19 L.Ed.2d 114 (1967).

77. *Deal v. Cincinnati Bd. of Educ.*, 369 F.2d 55 (6th Cir.1966), *cert. denied*, 389 U.S. 847, 88 S.Ct. 39, 19 L.Ed.2d 114 (1967).

78. *Hobson v. Hansen*, 269 F.Supp. 401 (D.D.C.1967).

79. A federal trial court, on remand in a long-running case, ruled that since vestiges of segregation remained in a district with regard to academic tracking, special education, and programs for students who have limited English proficiency, the state would have to assist in helping to implement remedies. *United States v. Yonkers Branch–NAACP*, 123 F.Supp.2d 694 [149 Educ. L. Rep. 721] (S.D.N.Y.2000).

80. *Smuck v. Hobson*, 408 F.2d 175 (D.C.Cir.1969).

1054 SCHOOL DESEGREGATION Ch. 15

the court remanded so that a newly elected board, replacing the appointed one, would not have been unduly restricted in creating new programs.

In a case from New Jersey, the federal trial court rejected a claim that state educational officials failed to do more to remedy racial imbalances in the schools.[81] The court decreed that since the degeneration of the state's unitary system of public education to extreme racial imbalance was beyond the scope of its jurisdiction, the complaint failed to present a claim for which relief could have been granted. On further review in *Spencer v. Kugler*,[82] the Court upheld a plan that, although not segregative in intent, resulted in de facto segregation.

The Supreme Court of California found that school boards had a state constitutional duty to enact reasonably feasible steps to alleviate segregation regardless of whether it was de jure or de facto.[83] The court reasoned that the judiciary's function is to evaluate whether a board initiated a course of action to alleviate the effects of segregation and had made reasonable progress toward that goal. The court ascertained that if such were not the case, then judicial intervention was warranted to protect the rights of minority children. The court indicated that each school in a district need not reflect the racial composition of a system as a whole since its duty was to eliminate imbalances in those schools in which the minority enrollment was so disproportionate as to isolate the children in them from integrated educational experiences.

In a later iteration of the same case from California, voters approved a state constitutional amendment prohibiting state courts from ordering mandatory pupil assignments or transportation unless the federal judiciary would have done so to remedy a federal constitutional violation. When this amendment was subjected to an equal protection challenge in *Crawford v. Board of Education of the City of Los Angeles*,[84] the Supreme Court rejected the claim that once a state chooses to do more than the Fourteenth Amendment requires, it may never recede. The Court declared that the Fourteenth Amendment did not embody a racial classification and neither declared nor implied that persons be treated differently on account of race. The Court explained that it only forbade state courts from ordering pupil school assignments or transportation plans absent a Fourteenth Amendment violation, adding that a discriminatory motive could not be imputed to the almost 69 percent of the electorate that voted for the amendment.

The Seventh Circuit rejected the argument that a school board's failure to comply with a statute from Illinois that it eliminate de facto segregation created a conclusive presumption of segregative intent.[85] The court stated that the board's failure to correct de facto segregation was insufficient to establish segregative intent, especially where the law

---

81. *Spencer v. Kugler*, 326 F.Supp. 1235 (D.N.J.1971).

82. 404 U.S. 1027, 92 S.Ct. 707, 30 L.Ed.2d 723 (1972).

83. *Crawford v. Board of Educ. of City of Los Angeles*, 551 P.2d 28 (Cal.1976).

84. 458 U.S. 527, 102 S.Ct. 3211, 73 L.Ed.2d 948 [5 Educ. L. Rep. 82] (1982).

85. *Coates v. Illinois State Bd. of Educ.*, 559 F.2d 445 (7th Cir.1977).

provided that a board could, under some conditions, think that existing attendance boundaries need not be revised.

Power to Correct

Another basic question was whether school officials could have taken steps to correct racial imbalances that developed due to housing patterns coupled with the uniform application of school zoning and student transfer policies. Courts responded that officials had a duty to remedy such imbalances. The Supreme Court included dicta to this effect in *Swann* and endorsed it in *Washington v. Seattle School District No. 1.*[86] The main challenges in these cases came from individuals who argued that race could not have been considered for any purpose and that the United States Constitution was colorblind for all purposes, a contention that has been rejected in its absolute form. Constitutionality depends on the purpose of looking at race as a factor since the courts interpret the Constitution as preventing the invidious use of race to disadvantage persons or racial groups. To ignore race would not only have made it virtually impossible to dismantle dual school systems but would also have defeated *Brown's* mandate by precluding attempts to prevent or correct de facto segregation.

As discussed in Chapter 12, courts have largely upheld state legislation requiring local school boards to take race into account in pupil assignment policies,[87] supporting state[88] and local[89] educational officials who sought to correct racial imbalances. Even so, courts cautioned educators who made decisions with regard to admissions and transfers where race is a factor to take equal protection concerns into consideration.[90]

The Supreme Court of Washington discussed many of the arguments against busing to achieve better racial balances in schools that experienced de facto segregation.[91] Residents in Seattle who opposed mandatory busing enjoined the board from implementing its plan for a year. The court dissolved the injunction in acknowledging that a system of volun-

86. 458 U.S. 457, 102 S.Ct. 3187, 73 L.Ed.2d 896 [5 Educ. L. Rep. 58] (1982).

87. *School Comm. of Boston v. Board of Educ.*, 227 N.E.2d 729 (Mass.1967), *appeal dismissed*, 389 U.S. 572, 88 S.Ct. 692, 19 L.Ed.2d 778 (1968); *Tometz v. Board of Educ.*, 237 N.E.2d 498 (Ill.1968).

88. *Vetere v. Allen*, 258 N.Y.S.2d 77 (N.Y.1965); *Jenkins v. Township of Morris School Dist.*, 279 A.2d 619 (N.J.1971).

89. *Balaban v. Rubin*, 250 N.Y.S.2d 281 (N.Y.1964).

90. *See, e.g., Eisenberg v. Montgomery County Pub. Schools*, 197 F.3d 123 [140 Educ. L. Rep. 88] (4th Cir.1999), *cert. denied*, 529 U.S. 1019, 120 S.Ct. 1420, 146 L.Ed.2d 312 (2000) (insisting on the need for a compelling interest in applying a di-

versity profile with regard to student transfers into a magnet school). *But see In re Boston's Children First*, 244 F.3d 164 [153 Educ. L. Rep. 20] (1st Cir.2001) (rejecting a challenge to an assignment scheme that took race into consideration); *Belk v. Charlotte–Mecklenburg Bd. of Educ.*, 269 F.3d 305 [158 Educ. L. Rep. 86] (4th Cir.2001), *cert. denied sub nom. Capacchione v. Charlotte–Mecklenburg Bd. of Educ.*, 535 U.S. 986, 122 S.Ct. 1537, 152 L.Ed.2d 465 (2002) (dissolving an injunction which would have required a school board to refrain from race based lotteries and other mechanisms since nothing in the record suggested that it would use race in an unconstitutional manner).

91. *Citizens Against Mandatory Bussing v. Palmason*, 495 P.2d 657 (Wash.1972).

tary student transfers had not accomplished the altogether proper objective of creating desegregated schools. The court specified that the board developed the plan with the help of experts and laymen who conducted hearings where all were urged to express their opinions. Interestingly, the plaintiffs who sought the delay had not submitted a plan. The court rejected the contention that a referendum should have taken place, dismissing the notion that students have had the right to attend the schools closest to their homes in pointing out that in a city of the size of Seattle, the confines of a neighborhood were not much observed in day-to-day life. The court thus refused to invalidate the board's plan for equalizing educational opportunities for all students because some parents feared that their children would have been disadvantaged by attending schools outside of their immediate neighborhoods. The court also rejected the theory that parents had the right to select public school for their children. As discussed below, in *Washington v. Seattle School District No. 1*,[92] the Supreme Court struck the initiative down as unconstitutional.

White parents filed most of the suits challenging local school board policies that were designed to correct racial imbalances. Yet, African American parents filed early suits claiming that they were forced to absorb all or most of the inconveniences of reassignments. In such a dispute from California, a federal trial court struck down a board's plan as unconstitutional when it closed an apparently suitable school for African American students and transferred them to schools where the majority of students were white.[93] The court invalidated the plan in observing that since it was neither absolutely nor reasonably necessary, it had to consider the fairly obvious fact that it placed the burden of desegregation entirely on one racial group, namely African American students.

On the other hand, the Second Circuit determined that a school board in Connecticut did not deny African American and Puerto Rican children equal protection under the law by busing them to white neighborhood schools without concurrently operating African American neighborhood schools and cross-busing white children.[94] The court was satisfied that inasmuch as the board voluntarily adopted the plan absent a history of de jure segregation, officials had no duty to act. The court noted not only that the board's good faith attempt to improve education of children in some neighborhoods by transferring them to other schools did not infringe any rights but also that all neighborhoods had to be treated the same unless distinctions emerged due to improper purposes.

Legislatures have created state-level commissions to deal with issues of discrimination and human relations. The ability of such commissions to order corrective measures to remedy de facto segregation in school systems depended on their enabling statutes. For example, the Supreme

92. 458 U.S. 457, 102 S.Ct. 3187, 73 L.Ed.2d 896 [5 Educ. L. Rep. 58] (1982).

93. *Brice v. Landis*, 314 F.Supp. 974 (N.D.Cal.1969).

94. *Norwalk Core v. Norwalk Bd. of Educ.*, 423 F.2d 121 (2d Cir.1970).

Court of Pennsylvania maintained that a commission had the authority to order local school boards to end discriminatory practices and draw up plans for eliminating de facto segregation in some schools.[95] The court added that the commission did not have to find that a board intentionally fostered and maintained segregation before invoking its authority as it only had to determine whether there was an imbalance. The court later conceded that the commission could have adopted a mathematical definition of de facto segregation.[96] Conversely, the Supreme Court of Kansas pointed out that a state commission was not empowered to order a local board to reassign teachers in order to produce a better racial balance on its staff.[97]

Power to Prevent Correction

Federal courts in New York and Michigan struck down state legislation aimed at preventing correction of de facto segregation while it was given an innocuous meaning in an attempt to preserve its constitutionality in California prior to the Supreme Court's doing so. After the legislature in New York enacted a law prohibiting student assignments for balancing purposes except by elected school boards, a federal trial court struck it down.[98] The court asserted that the statute was unconstitutional because it created a single exception to the broad supervisory powers that the state commissioner of education exercised over local school boards. The court concluded that since the statute established a purely racial classification by treating educational matters involving race differently from other issues involving schooling and it made dealing with racial imbalances in the public schools more difficult, it was unconstitutional.

When the school board in Detroit voluntarily adopted a plan to provide a better balance between African American and white students in twelve high schools, the state legislature attempted to counteract this by enacting an open-enrollment policy which granted preference to students living near each school. The legislation was limited to "first class" school districts, of which Detroit was the only one. The Sixth Circuit invalidated the act as unconstitutional because it obstructed lawful steps to protect Fourteenth Amendment rights.[99] Even in expressing no opinion as to whether the board was obligated to adopt all or any part of its plan, the court distinguished this case from one of its earlier judgments[100] on the basis that this board acted on its own while in the previous action the plaintiffs sought to force it to act. In a second case from Michigan that reached the Sixth Circuit, after a board adopted a

95. *Pennsylvania Human Relations Comm'n v. Chester School Dist.*, 233 A.2d 290 (Pa.1967).

96. *Pennsylvania Human Relations Comm'n v. Uniontown Area School Dist.*, 313 A.2d 156 (Pa.1973).

97. *Londerholm v. Unified School Dist. No. 500*, 430 P.2d 188 (Kan.1967).

98. *Lee v. Nyquist*, 318 F.Supp. 710 (W.D.N.Y.1970), *aff'd*, 402 U.S. 944, 91 S.Ct. 1618, 29 L.Ed.2d 112 (1971).

99. *Bradley v. Milliken*, 433 F.2d 897 (6th Cir.1970).

100. *Deal v. Cincinnati Bd. of Educ.*, 369 F.2d 55 (6th Cir.1966), *cert. denied*, 389 U.S. 847, 88 S.Ct. 39, 19 L.Ed.2d 114 (1967).

plan to correct de facto segregation, voters recalled all of the members who voted for the plan. The plaintiffs subsequently challenged the new board's stated intention of rescinding the plan at the end of the school year. The Sixth Circuit affirmed an injunction that prevented the new board from rescinding the plan since doing so would have had the effect of reassigning students to their previously segregated schools.[101]

In California, plaintiffs challenged a statute that prevented school boards from requiring students to be transported for any reason without written parental permission. The state's highest court, upholding the law, treated it as not interfering with a board's power to assign students to schools in order to improve racial balances.[102] The court interpreted the law in light of its literal meaning that students were not required to use any school transportation. The court feared that any other interpretation would have rendered the statute unconstitutional since it could not have been upheld to the extent that it conferred governmental support on a system of de facto segregation.

After unsuccessful attempts to block busing to remedy de facto segregation in Seattle, voters endorsed a measure that would have prevented local boards from requiring students to attend schools other than one of the two closest to their homes and from utilizing any of a number of assignment methods such as redefining attendance zones and pairing schools. Expressly accepting the analytical approach of a federal trial court, in *Washington v. Seattle School District No. 1*,[103] the Supreme Court vitiated the initiative as unconstitutional. The Court was of the view that since the voter initiative impermissibly classified individuals based on race and sought to end busing to achieve racial integration, it violated the equal protection rights of minority students. The Court posited that although state level officials could have made all student assignments, they could not have delegated the matter to local boards with race-conscious strings attached.

Proof of Intent to Discriminate

Whether a governmental action, which had a disproportionately adverse effect on African Americans, singly or as a class, was racially motivated was the crux of constitutional litigation because, depending on the answer, courts applied the law of de jure or de facto segregation. In the pre-*Brown* South, district-wide segregation was based on codified state law. As such, since the question of intent was academic, courts relied on district-wide remedies for de jure segregation. On the other hand, outside of the South, since segregation was typically de facto rather than de jure, plaintiffs had to prove segregative intent before the federal courts would intervene, with the scope of remedies depending on the extent of the violations.

101. *National Ass'n for the Advancement of Colored People, Lansing Branch v. Lansing Bd. of Educ.*, 485 F.2d 569 (6th Cir.1973).

102. *San Francisco Unified School Dist. v. Johnson*, 479 P.2d 669 (Cal.1971).

103. 458 U.S. 457, 102 S.Ct. 3187, 73 L.Ed.2d 896 [5 Educ. L. Rep. 58] (1982).

The essential Supreme Court case with regard to judicially uncovered segregative intent is *Keyes*. Even so, in litigation in other fields, the Court offered guidelines that clarified what evidence may have been probative as to discriminatory intent. The Court's most extensive elaboration of this principle was in *Village of Arlington Heights v. Metropolitan Housing Development Corporation (Arlington Heights)*,[104] a non-school case wherein it upheld a zoning ordinance dealing with low-cost housing. Although conceding that the elements were not exhaustive, the Court enunciated six factors for assessing whether official action had a discriminatory intent. These factors address an action's impact, its historical background, the sequence of events leading up to it, departures from normal procedural sequences, departures from the weighting usually given operative factors, and its legislative or administrative history.

Amid the cases that cited *Arlington Heights*, some courts treated discriminatory intent as a ground for imposing liability in school settings.[105] If a plaintiff establishes a prima facie case of purposeful segregation by relying on factors such as those enunciated in *Arlington Heights*, a board can rebut the presumption by offering evidence that its actions or inactions were consistent with racially neutral policies that were reasonably associated with acceptable educational practices. In order to support a claim of a constitutional violation, a plaintiff must show more than disparate impact. In such a case, the Supreme Court ruled that a plaintiff must provide evidence that a decision-maker "selected or reaffirmed a particular course of action at least in part 'because of,' not merely 'in spite of,' its adverse effects."[106] In a footnote, the Court explained that "[t]his is not to say that the inevitability or foreseeability of consequences of a neutral rule has no bearing upon the existence of discriminatory intent."[107]

[Case No. 123] Eliminating Racial Segregation in Public Schools

BROWN v. BOARD OF EDUCATION OF TOPEKA (I)

Supreme Court of the United States, 1954
347 U.S. 483, 74 S.Ct. 686, 98 L.Ed. 873

MR. CHIEF JUSTICE WARREN delivered the opinion of the Court.

These cases come to us from the States of Kansas, South Carolina, Virginia, and Delaware. They are premised on different facts and different local conditions, but a common legal question justifies their consideration together in this consolidated opinion.

In each of the cases, minors of the Negro race, through their legal representatives, seek the aid of the courts in obtaining admission to the

---

104. 429 U.S. 252, 97 S.Ct. 555, 50 L.Ed.2d 450 (1977).

105. *See, e.g., Arthur v. Nyquist*, 573 F.2d 134 (2d Cir.1978), *cert. denied*, 439 U.S. 860, 99 S.Ct. 179, 58 L.Ed.2d 169 (1978); *United States v. Texas Educ. Agency*, 564 F.2d 162 (5th Cir. 1977); *National Ass'n for the Advancement of Colored Peo-*

ple *v. Lansing Bd. of Educ.*, 559 F.2d 1042 (6th Cir.1977), *cert. denied*, 434 U.S. 997, 98 S.Ct. 635, 54 L.Ed.2d 491 (1977).

106. *Personnel Adm'r of Mass. v. Feeney*, 442 U.S. 256, 99 S.Ct. 2282, 60 L.Ed.2d 870 (1979).

107. *Id.* at 279, note 25.

public schools of their community on a nonsegregated basis. In each instance, they have been denied admission to schools attended by white children under laws requiring or permitting segregation according to race. This segregation was alleged to deprive the plaintiffs of the equal protection of the laws under the Fourteenth Amendment. In each of the cases other than the Delaware case, a three-judge federal district court denied relief to the plaintiffs on the so-called "separate but equal" doctrine announced by this Court in *Plessy v. Ferguson*. Under that doctrine, equality of treatment is accorded when the races are provided substantially equal facilities, even though these facilities be separate. In the Delaware case, the Supreme Court of Delaware adhered to that doctrine, but ordered that the plaintiffs be admitted to the white schools because of their superiority to the Negro schools.

The plaintiffs contend that segregated public schools are not "equal" and cannot be made "equal," and that hence they are deprived of the equal protection of the laws. Because of the obvious importance of the question presented, the Court took jurisdiction. Argument was heard in the 1952 Term, and reargument was heard this Term on certain questions propounded by the Court....

In the first cases in this Court constructing the Fourteenth Amendment, decided shortly after its adoption, the Court interpreted it as proscribing all state-imposed discriminations against the Negro race. The doctrine of "separate but equal" did not make its appearance in this Court until 1896 in the case of *Plessy v. Ferguson*, involving not education but transportation. American courts have since labored with the doctrine for over half a century. In this Court, there have been six cases involving the "separate but equal" doctrine in the field of public education. In *Cumming v. Board of Education of Richmond County*, and *Gong Lum v. Rice*, the validity of the doctrine itself was not challenged. In more recent cases, all on the graduate school level, inequality was found in that specific benefits enjoyed by white students were denied to Negro students of the same educational qualifications. (*State of Missouri ex rel. Gaines v. Canada*; *Sipuel v. Board of Regents of University of Oklahoma*; *Sweatt v. Painter*; *McLaurin v. Oklahoma State Regents*). In none of these cases was it necessary to re-examine the doctrine to grant relief to the Negro plaintiff. And in *Sweatt v. Painter*, the Court expressly reserved decision on the question whether *Plessy v. Ferguson* should be held inapplicable to public education.

In the instant cases, that question is directly presented. Here, unlike *Sweatt v. Painter*, there are findings below that the Negro and white schools involved have been equalized, or are being equalized, with respect to buildings, curricula, qualifications and salaries of teachers, and other "tangible" factors. Our decision, therefore, cannot turn on merely a comparison of these tangible factors in the Negro and white schools involved in each of the cases. We must look instead to the effect of segregation itself on public education.

In approaching this problem, we cannot turn the clock back to 1868 when the Amendment was adopted, or even to 1896 when *Plessy v.*

Ferguson was written. We must consider public education in the light of its full development and its present place in American life throughout the Nation. Only in this way can it be determined if segregation in public schools deprives these plaintiffs of the equal protection of the laws.

Today, education is perhaps the most important function of state and local governments. Compulsory school attendance laws and the great expenditures for education both demonstrate our recognition of the importance of education to our democratic society. It is required in the performance of our most basic public responsibilities, even service in the armed forces. It is the very foundation of good citizenship. Today it is a principal instrument in awakening the child to cultural values, in preparing him for later professional training, and in helping him to adjust normally to his environment. In these days, it is doubtful that any child may reasonably be expected to succeed in life if he is denied the opportunity of an education. Such an opportunity, where the state has undertaken to provide it, is a right which must be made available to all on equal terms.

We come then to the question presented: Does segregation of children in public schools solely on the basis of race, even though the physical facilities and other "tangible" factors may be equal, deprive the children of the minority group of equal educational opportunities? We believe that it does.

In *Sweatt v. Painter*, in finding that a segregated law school for Negroes could not provide them equal educational opportunities, this Court relied in large part on "those qualities which are incapable of objective measurement but which make for greatness in a law school." In *McLaurin v. Oklahoma State Regents*, the Court, in requiring that a Negro admitted to a white graduate school be treated like all other students, again resorted to intangible considerations: ". . . his ability to study, to engage in discussions and exchange views with other students, and, in general, to learn his profession." Such considerations apply with added force to children in grade and high schools. To separate them from others of similar age and qualifications solely because of their race generates a feeling of inferiority as to their status in the community that may affect their hearts and minds in a way unlikely ever to be undone. The effect of this separation on their educational opportunities was well stated by a finding in the Kansas case by a court which nevertheless felt compelled to rule against the Negro plaintiffs:

> "Segregation of white and colored children in public schools has a detrimental effect upon the colored children. The impact is greater when it has the sanction of the law; for the policy of separating the races is usually interpreted as denoting the inferiority of the Negro group. A sense of inferiority affects the motivation of a child to learn. Segregation with the sanction of law, therefore, has a tendency to [retard] the educational and mental development of Negro children and to deprive them of some of the benefits they would receive in a racial[ly] integrated school system."

Whatever may have been the extent of psychological knowledge at the time of *Plessy v. Ferguson*, this finding is amply supported by modern authority. Any language in *Plessy v. Ferguson* contrary to this finding is rejected.

We conclude that in the field of public education the doctrine of "separate but equal" has no place. Separate educational facilities are inherently unequal. Therefore, we hold that the plaintiffs and others similarly situated for whom the actions have been brought are, by reason of the segregation complained of, deprived of the equal protection of the laws guaranteed by the Fourteenth Amendment. This disposition makes unnecessary any discussion whether such segregation also violates the Due Process Clause of the Fourteenth Amendment.

Because these are class actions, because of the wide applicability of this decision, and because of the great variety of local conditions, the formulation of decrees in these cases presents problems of considerable complexity. On reargument, the consideration of appropriate relief was necessarily subordinated to the primary question—the constitutionality of segregation in public education. We have now announced that such segregation is a denial of the equal protection of the laws. In order that we may have the full assistance of the parties in formulating decrees, the cases will be restored to the docket, and the parties are requested to present further argument on Questions 4 and 5 previously propounded by the Court for the reargument this Term. The Attorney General of the United States is again invited to participate. The Attorneys General of the states requiring or permitting segregation in public education will also be permitted to appear as *amici curiae* upon request to do so by September 15, 1954, and submission of briefs by October 1, 1954.

It is so ordered.

Notes

1. In *Cumming v. Board of Educ. of Richmond County*, 175 U.S. 528, 20 S.Ct. 197, 44 L.Ed. 262 (1899), the Supreme Court refused to enjoin a board in Georgia from operating a high school for white children when officials claimed that a lack of funds prevented them from having one for African American children. The Court thought that granting the injunction would have disadvantaged the white children without providing any advantage to the African American students. The opinion was written by Justice Harlan, the sole dissenter in *Plessy* three years earlier.

2. In *Sweatt v. Painter*, 339 U.S. 629, 70 S.Ct. 848, 94 L.Ed. 1114 (1950), and *McLaurin v. Oklahoma State Regents for Higher Educ.*, 339 U.S. 637, 70 S.Ct. 851, 94 L.Ed. 1149 (1950), the Court emphasized the importance of "intangible factors" in connection with equal educational opportunity for the first time. Even so, the Court did not focus on purely psychological considerations until *Brown I*.

3. The Supreme Court does not often render unanimous judgments in cases dealing with significant matters of social policy. Clearly, the Justices were aware of the importance of a single statement in this situation. Would an 8–1 ruling have had the same impact?

4. The Court called for an end to segregated schooling in *Brown I* and its progeny. Yet, the Court never affirmatively ordered school systems to integrate. What do you think about this distinction?

[Case No. 124]   Remedies for Segregation

BROWN v. BOARD OF EDUCATION OF TOPEKA (II)

Supreme Court of the United States, 1955.
349 U.S. 294, 75 S.Ct. 753, 99 L.Ed. 1083.

Mr. Chief Justice Warren delivered the opinion of the Court.

These cases were decided on May 17, 1954. The opinions of that date, declaring the fundamental principle that racial discrimination in public education is unconstitutional, are incorporated herein by reference. All provisions of federal, state, or local law requiring or permitting such discrimination must yield to this principle. There remains for consideration the manner in which relief is to be accorded.

Because these cases arose under different local conditions and their disposition will involve a variety of local problems, we requested further argument on the question of relief. In view of the nationwide importance of the decision, we invited the Attorney General of the United States and the Attorneys General of all states requiring or permitting racial discrimination in public education to present their views on that question. The parties, the United States, and the States of Florida, North Carolina, Arkansas, Oklahoma, Maryland, and Texas filed briefs and participated in the oral argument.

These presentations were informative and helpful to the Court in its consideration of the complexities arising from the transition to a system of public education freed of racial discrimination. The presentations also demonstrated that substantial steps to eliminate racial discrimination in public schools have already been taken, not only in some of the communities in which these cases arose, but in some of the states appearing as *amici curiae,* and in other states as well. Substantial progress has been made in the District of Columbia, and in the communities in Kansas and Delaware involved in this litigation. The defendants in the cases coming to us from South Carolina and Virginia are awaiting the decision of this Court concerning relief.

Full implementation of these constitutional principles may require solution of varied local school problems. School authorities have the primary responsibility for elucidating, assessing, and solving these problems; courts will have to consider whether the action of school authorities constitutes good faith implementation of the governing constitutional principles. Because of their proximity to local conditions and the possible need for further hearings, the courts which originally heard these cases can best perform this judicial appraisal. Accordingly, we believe it appropriate to remand the cases to those courts.

In fashioning and effectuating the decrees, the courts will be guided by equitable principles. Traditionally, equity has been characterized by a practical flexibility in shaping its remedies and by a facility for adjusting and reconciling public and private needs. These cases call for the exercise of these traditional attributes of equity power. At stake is the personal interest of the plaintiffs in admission to public schools as soon as practicable on a nondiscriminatory basis. To effectuate this interest may call for elimination of a variety of obstacles in making the transition to school systems operated in accordance with the constitutional principles set forth in our May 17, 1954, decision. Courts of equity may properly take into account the public interest in the elimination of such obstacles in a systematic and effective manner. But it should go without saying that the vitality of these constitutional principles cannot be allowed to yield simply because of disagreement with them.

While giving weight to these public and private considerations, the courts will require that the defendants make a prompt and reasonable start toward full compliance with our May 17, 1954, ruling. Once such a start has been made, the courts may find that additional time is necessary to carry out the ruling in an effective manner. The burden rests upon the defendants to establish that such time is necessary in the public interest and is consistent with good faith compliance at the earliest practicable date. To that end, the courts may consider problems related to administration, arising from the physical condition of the school plant, the school transportation system, personnel, revision of school districts and attendance areas into compact units to achieve a system of determining admission to the public schools on a nonracial basis, and revision of local laws and regulations which may be necessary in solving the foregoing problems. They will also consider the adequacy of any plans the defendants may propose to meet these problems and to effectuate a transition to a racially nondiscriminatory school system. During this period of transition, the courts will retain jurisdiction of these cases.

The judgments below, except that in the Delaware case, are accordingly reversed and remanded to the District Courts to take such proceedings and enter such orders and decrees consistent with this opinion as are necessary and proper to admit to public schools on a racially nondiscriminatory basis with all deliberate speed the parties to these cases. The judgment in the Delaware case—ordering the immediate admission of the plaintiffs to schools previously attended only by white children—is affirmed on the basis of the principles stated in our May 17, 1954, opinion, but the case is remanded to the Supreme Court of Delaware for such further proceedings as that court may deem necessary in the light of this opinion.

It is so ordered.

Notes

1. Was the Court's use of the phrase "with all deliberate speed" a mistake? Considering the realities of the situation existing in the South at that time, did the Court have alternatives?

2. Was it realistic for the Court to expect locally-elected school boards to be effective in eliminating racial segregation?

3. The Court placed the burden of establishing time frames for compliance on local boards acting under judicial supervision. Insofar as education is a state function, can you think of reasons why the Court did not place the responsibility on state officials?

[Case No. 125]   Guidelines for Eliminating Racial Segregation

SWANN v. CHARLOTTE–MECKLENBURG BOARD OF EDUCATION

Supreme Court of the United States, 1971.
402 U.S. 1, 91 S.Ct. 1267, 28 L.Ed.2d 554.

MR. CHIEF JUSTICE BURGER delivered the opinion of the Court.

We granted certiorari in this case to review important issues as to the duties of school authorities and the scope of powers of federal courts under this Court's mandates to eliminate racially separate public schools established and maintained by state action. *Brown v. Board of Education* (*Brown I*).

This case and those argued with it arose in states having a long history of maintaining two sets of schools in a single school system deliberately operated to carry out a governmental policy to separate pupils in schools solely on the basis of race. That was what *Brown v. Board of Education* was all about. These cases present us with the problem of defining in more precise terms than heretofore the scope of the duty of school authorities and district courts in implementing *Brown I* and the mandate to eliminate dual systems and establish unitary systems at once. . . .

I

The Charlotte–Mecklenburg school system, the 43d largest in the Nation, encompasses the city of Charlotte and surrounding Mecklenburg County, North Carolina. The area is large—550 square miles—spanning roughly 22 miles east-west and 36 miles north-south. During the 1968–1969 school year the system served more than 84,000 pupils in 107 schools. Approximately 71% of the pupils were found to be white and 29% Negro. As of June 1969 there were approximately 24,000 Negro students in the system, of whom 21,000 attended schools within the city of Charlotte. Two-thirds of those 21,000—approximately 14,000 Negro students—attended 21 schools which were either totally Negro or more than 99% Negro. . . .

II

Nearly 17 years ago this Court held, in explicit terms, that state-imposed segregation by race in public schools denies equal protection of the laws. At no time has the Court deviated in the slightest degree from that holding or its constitutional underpinnings. . . .

Over the 16 years since *Brown II,* many difficulties were encountered in implementation of the basic constitutional requirement that the State not discriminate between public school children on the basis of their race. Nothing in our national experience prior to 1955 prepared anyone for dealing with changes and adjustments of the magnitude and complexity encountered since then. Deliberate resistance of some to the Court's mandates has impeded the good-faith efforts of others to bring school systems into compliance. The detail and nature of these dilatory tactics have been noted frequently by this Court and other courts.

By the time the Court considered *Green v. County School Board* in 1968, very little progress had been made in many areas where dual school systems had historically been maintained by operation of state laws. In *Green,* the Court was confronted with a record of a freedom-of-choice program that the District Court had found to operate in fact to preserve a dual system more than a decade after *Brown II.* While acknowledging that a freedom-of-choice concept could be a valid remedial measure in some circumstances, its failure to be effective in *Green* required that

> The burden on a school board today is to come forward with a plan that promises realistically to work *now* ... until it is clear that state-imposed segregation has been completely removed.

This was plain language, yet the 1969 Term of Court brought fresh evidence of the dilatory tactics of many school authorities. *Alexander v. Holmes County Bd. of Educ.* restated the basic obligation asserted in *Griffin v. County School Board* and *Green,* that the remedy must be implemented *forthwith.*

The problems encountered by the district courts and courts of appeals make plain that we should now try to amplify guidelines, however incomplete and imperfect, for the assistance of school authorities and courts. The failure of local authorities to meet their constitutional obligations aggravated the massive problem of converting from the state-enforced discrimination of racially separate school systems....

III

The objective today remains to eliminate from the public schools all vestiges of state-imposed segregation....

If school authorities fail in their affirmative obligations under these holdings, judicial authority may be invoked. Once a right and a violation have been shown, the scope of a district court's equitable powers to remedy past wrongs is broad, for breadth and flexibility are inherent in equitable remedies....

School authorities are traditionally charged with broad power to formulate and implement educational policy and might well conclude, for example, that in order to prepare students to live in a pluralistic society each school should have a prescribed ratio of Negro to white students reflecting the proportion for the district as a whole. To do this as an educational policy is within the broad discretionary powers of school authorities; absent a finding of a constitutional violation, however, that would not be within the authority of a federal court. As with any equity case, the nature of the violation determines the scope of the remedy. In default by the school authorities of their obligation to proffer acceptable remedies, a district court has broad power to fashion a remedy that will assure a unitary school system.

The school authorities argue that the equity powers of federal district courts have been limited by Title IV of the Civil Rights Act of 1964. The language and the history of Title IV shows that it was not enacted to limit but to define the role of the Federal Government in the implementation of the *Brown I* decision. It authorizes the Commissioner of Education to provide technical assistance to local boards in the preparation of desegregation plans, to arrange "training institutes" for school personnel involved in desegregation efforts, and to make grants directly to schools to ease the transition to unitary systems. It also authorizes the Attorney General, in specified circumstances, to initiate federal desegregation suits. Section 2000c(b) defines "desegregation" as it is used in Title IV:

> " 'Desegregation' means the assignment of students to public schools and within such schools without regard to their race, color, religion, or national origin, but 'desegregation' shall not mean the assignment of students to public schools in order to overcome racial imbalance."

Section 2000c–6, authorizing the Attorney General to institute federal suits, contains the following proviso:

> "nothing herein shall empower any official or court of the United States to issue any order seeking to achieve a racial balance in any school by requiring the transportation of pupils or students from one school to another or one school district to another in order to achieve such racial balance, or otherwise enlarge the existing power of the court to insure compliance with constitutional standards."

On their face, the sections quoted support only to insure that the provisions of Title IV of the Civil Rights Act of 1964 will not be read as granting new powers. The proviso in § 2000c–6 is in terms designed to foreclose any interpretation of the Act as expanding the *existing* powers of federal courts to enforce the Equal Protection Clause. There is no suggestion of an intention to restrict those powers or withdraw from courts their historic equitable remedial powers. The legislative history of Title IV indicates that Congress was concerned that the Act might be read as creating a right of action under the Fourteenth Amendment in the situation of so-called "de facto segregation," where racial imbalance exists in the schools but with no showing that this was brought about by discriminatory action of state authorities. In short, there is nothing in the Act which provides us material assistance in answering the question of remedy for state-imposed segregation in violation of *Brown I*. The basis of our decision must be the prohibition of the Fourteenth Amendment that no State shall "deny to any person within its jurisdiction the equal protection of the laws."

IV

We turn now to the problem of defining with more particularity the responsibilities of school authorities in desegregating a state-enforced dual school system in light of the Equal Protection Clause. Although the several related cases before us are primarily concerned with problems of student assignment, it may be helpful to begin with a brief discussion of other aspects of the process.

In *Green,* we pointed out that existing policy and practice with regard to faculty, staff, transportation, extracurricular activities, and facilities were among the most important indicia of a segregated system. Independent of student assignment, where it is possible to identify a "white school" or a "Negro school" simply by reference to the racial composition of teachers and staff, the quality of school buildings and equipment, or the organization of sports activities, a *prima facie* case of violation of substantive constitutional rights under the Equal Protection Clause is shown.

When a system has been dual in these respects, the first remedial responsibility of school authorities is to eliminate invidious racial distinctions. With respect to such matters as transportation, supporting personnel, and extracurricular activities, no more than this may be necessary. Similar corrective action must be taken with regard to the maintenance of buildings and the distribution of equipment. In these areas, normal administrative practice should produce schools of like quality, facilities, and staffs. Something more must be said, however, as to faculty assignment and new school construction.

In the companion *Davis* case, the Mobile school board has argued that the Constitution requires that teachers be assigned on a "color blind" basis. It also argues that the Constitution prohibits district courts from using their equity power to order assignment of teachers to achieve a particular degree of faculty desegregation. We reject that contention.

. . .

The construction of new schools and the closing of old ones is one of the most important functions of local school authorities and also one of the most complex. They must decide questions of location and capacity in light of population growth, finances, land values, site availability, through an almost endless list of factors to be considered. The result of this will be a decision which when combined with one technique or another of student assignment, will determine the racial composition of the student body in each school in the system. Over the long run, the consequences of the choices will be far reaching. People gravitate toward school facilities, just as schools are located in response to the needs of people. The location of schools may thus influence the patterns of residential development of a metropolitan area and have important impact on composition of inner city neighborhoods.

In the past, choices in this respect have been used as a potent weapon for creating or maintaining a state-segregated school system. In addition to the classic pattern of building schools specifically intended for Negro or white students, school authorities have sometimes, since *Brown,* closed schools which appeared likely to become racially mixed through changes in neighborhood residential patterns. This was sometimes accompanied by building new schools in the areas of white suburban expansion farthest from Negro population centers in order to maintain the separation of the races with a minimum departure from the formal principles of "neighborhood zoning." Such a policy does more than simply influence the short-run composition of the student body of a new school. It may well promote segregated residential patterns which, when combined with "neighborhood zoning," further lock the school system into the mold of separation of the races. Upon a proper showing a district court may consider this in fashioning a remedy. . . .

V

The central issue in this case is that of student assignment, and there are essentially four problem areas:

    (1) to what extent racial balance or racial quotas may be used as an implement in a remedial order to correct a previously segregated system;

    (2) whether every all-Negro and all-white school must be eliminated as an indispensable part of a remedial process of desegregation;

    (3) what are the limits, if any, on the rearrangement of school districts and attendance zones, as a remedial measure; and

    (4) what are the limits, if any, on the use of transportation facilities to correct state-enforced racial school segregation.

(1) Racial Balances or Racial Quotas.

. . .

We are concerned in these cases with the elimination of the discrimination inherent in the dual school systems, not with myriad factors of human existence which can cause discrimination in a multitude of ways on racial, religious, or ethnic grounds. The target of the cases from *Brown I* to the present was the dual school system. The elimination of racial discrimination in public schools is a large task and one that should not be retarded by efforts to achieve broader purposes lying beyond the jurisdiction of school authorities. One vehicle can carry only a limited amount of baggage. It would not serve the important objective of *Brown I* to seek to use school desegregation cases for purposes beyond their scope, although desegregation of schools ultimately will have impact on other forms of discrimination. We do not reach in this case the question whether a showing that school segregation is a consequence of other types of state action, without any discriminatory action by the school authorities, is a constitutional violation requiring remedial action by a school desegregation decree. This case does not present that question and we therefore do not decide it.

Our objective in dealing with the issues presented by these cases is to see that school authorities exclude no pupil of a racial minority from any school, directly or indirectly, on account of race; it does not and cannot embrace all the problems of racial prejudice, even when those problems contribute to disproportionate racial concentrations in some schools. . . .

. . . If we were to read the holding of the District Court to require, as a matter of substantive constitutional right, any particular degree of racial balance or mixing, that approach would be disapproved and we would be obliged to reverse. The constitutional command to desegregate schools does not mean that every school in every community must always reflect the racial composition of the school system as a whole. . . .

We see therefore that the use made of mathematical ratios was no more than a starting point in the process of shaping a remedy, rather than an inflexible requirement. From that starting point the District Court proceeded to frame a decree that was within its discretionary powers, an equitable remedy for the particular circumstances. As we said in *Green,* a school authority's remedial plan or a district court's remedial decree is to be judged by its effectiveness. Awareness of the racial composition of the whole school system is likely to be a useful starting point in shaping a remedy to correct past constitutional violations. In sum, the very limited use made of mathematical ratios was within the equitable remedial discretion of the District Court.

(2) One–Race Schools.

The record in this case reveals the familiar phenomenon that in metropolitan areas minority groups are often found concentrated in one part of the city. In some circumstances certain schools may remain all or largely of one race until new schools can be provided or neighborhood patterns change. Schools all or predominantly of one race in a district of mixed population will require close scrutiny to determine that school assignments are not part of state-enforced segregation.

In light of the above, it should be clear that the existence of some small number of one-race, or virtually one-race, schools within a district is not in and of itself the mark of a system which still practices segregation by law. The district judge or school authorities should make every effort to achieve the greatest possible degree of actual desegregation and will thus necessarily be concerned with the elimination of one-race schools. No *per se* rule can adequately embrace all the difficulties of reconciling the competing interests involved; but in a system with a history of segregation the need for remedial criteria of sufficient specificity to assure a school authority's compliance with its constitutional duty warrants a presumption against schools that are substantially disproportionate in their racial composition. Where the school authority's proposed plan for conversion from a dual to a unitary system contemplates the continued existence of some schools that are all or predominately of one race, they have the burden of showing that such school assignments are genuinely nondiscriminatory. The court should scrutinize such schools, and the burden upon the school authorities will be to satisfy the court that their racial composition is not the result of present or past discriminatory action. . . .

(3) **Remedial Altering of Attendance Zones.**

The maps submitted in these cases graphically demonstrate that one of the principal tools employed by school planners and by courts to break up the dual school system has been a frank—and sometimes drastic—gerrymandering of school districts and attendance zones. An additional step was pairing, "clustering," or "grouping" of schools with attendance assignments made deliberately to accomplish the transfer of Negro students out of formerly segregated Negro schools and transfer of white students to formerly all-Negro schools. More often than not, these zones are neither compact nor contiguous; indeed they may be on opposite ends of the city. As an interim corrective measure, this cannot be said to be beyond the broad remedial powers of a court....

No fixed or even substantially fixed guidelines can be established as to how far a court can go, but it must be recognized that there are limits. The objective is to dismantle the dual school system. "Racially neutral" assignment plans proposed by school authorities to a district court may be inadequate; such plans may fail to counteract the continuing effects of past school segregation resulting from discriminatory location of school sites or distortion of school size in order to achieve or maintain an artificial racial separation. When school authorities present a district court with a "loaded game board," affirmative action in the form of remedial altering of attendance zones is proper to achieve truly nondiscriminatory assignments. In short, an assignment plan is not acceptable simply because it appears to be neutral.

In this area, we must of necessity rely to a large extent, as this Court has for more than 16 years, on the informed judgment of the district courts in the first instance and on courts of appeals.

We hold that the pairing and grouping of non-contiguous school zones is a permissible tool and such action is to be considered in light of the objectives sought....

(4) **Transportation of Students.**

The scope of permissible transportation of students as an implement of a remedial decree has never been defined by this Court and by the very nature of the problem it cannot be defined with precision. No rigid guidelines as to student transportation can be given for application to the infinite variety of problems presented in thousands of situations. Bus transportation has been an integral part of the public education system for years, and was perhaps the single most important factor in the transition from the one-room schoolhouse to the consolidated school. Eighteen million of the nation's public school children, approximately 39% were transported to their schools by bus in 1969–1970 in all parts of the country.

The importance of bus transportation as a normal and accepted tool of educational policy is readily discernible in this and the companion case. The Charlotte school authorities did not purport to assign students on the basis of geographically drawn zones until 1965 and then they allowed almost unlimited transfer privileges. The District Court's conclusion that assignment of children to the school nearest their home serving their grade would not produce an effective dismantling of the dual system is supported by the record.

Thus the remedial techniques used in the District Court's order were within that court's power to provide equitable relief; implementation of the decree is well within the capacity of the school authority.

The decree provided that the buses used to implement the plan would operate on direct routes. Students would be picked up at schools near their homes and transported to the schools they were to attend. The trips for elementary school pupils average about seven miles and the District Court found that they would take "not over 35 minutes at the most." This system compares favorably with the transportation plan previously operated in Charlotte under which each day 23,600 students on all grade levels were transported an average of 15 miles one way for an average trip requiring over an hour. In these circumstances, we find no basis for holding that the local school authorities may not be required to employ bus transportation as one tool of school desegregation. Desegregation plans cannot be limited to the walk-in school.

An objection to transportation of students may have validity when the time or distance of travel is so great as to risk either the health of the children or significantly impinge on the educational process....

VI

The Court of Appeals, searching for a term to define the equitable remedial power of the district courts, used the term "reasonableness." In *Green,* this Court used the term "feasible" and by implication, "workable," "effective," and "realistic" in the mandate to develop "a plan that promises realistically to work, and ... to work *now.*" On the facts of this case, we are unable to conclude that the order of the District Court is not reasonable, feasible and workable. However, in seeking to define the scope of remedial power or the limits on remedial power of courts in an area as sensitive as we deal with here, words are poor instruments to convey the sense of basic fairness inherent in equity. Substance, not semantics, must govern, and we have sought to suggest the nature of limitations without frustrating the appropriate scope of equity.

At some point, these school authorities and others like them should have achieved full compliance with this Court's decision in *Brown I.* The systems will then be "unitary" in the sense required by our decisions in *Green* and *Alexander.*

It does not follow that the communities served by such systems will remain demographically stable, for in a growing, mobile society, few will do so. Neither school authorities nor district courts are constitutionally required to make year-by-year adjustments of the racial composition of student bodies once the affirmative duty to desegregate has been accomplished and racial discrimination through official action is eliminated from the system. This does not mean that federal courts are without power to deal with future problems; but in the absence of a showing that either the school authorities or some other agency of the State has deliberately attempted to fix or alter demographic patterns to affect the racial composition of the schools, further intervention by a district court should not be necessary. . . .

Notes

1. What do you think about the Court's discussion of "racial quotas" and the desirability, and/or necessity of the judiciary's using them to fashion remedies to correct de jure segregation?

2. In a companion case decided the same day, the Court reversed a judgment from the Supreme Court of Georgia in holding that the latter erroneously interpreted the busing provisions in the Civil Rights Act of 1964. *McDaniel v. Barresi*, 402 U.S. 39, 91 S.Ct. 1287, 28 L.Ed.2d 582 (1971). In another, the Court partially reversed an order of a federal trial court in Alabama on the basis that it gave inadequate consideration to the possible use of bus transportation and split zoning to remedy segregation. *Davis v. Board of School Commr's of Mobile County*, 402 U.S. 33, 91 S.Ct. 1289, 28 L.Ed.2d 577 (1971).

3. The Fourth Circuit, in *Belk v. Charlotte–Mecklenburg Bd. of Educ.*, 269 F.3d 305 [158 Educ. L. Rep. 86] (4th Cir.2001), *cert. denied sub nom. Capacchione v. Charlotte–Mecklenburg Bd. of Educ.*, 535 U.S. 986, 122 S.Ct. 1537, 152 L.Ed.2d 465 (2002), ended judicial oversight in Charlotte–Mecklenburg when it was satisfied that the district achieved unitary status because it met all of the *Green* factors.

[Case No. 126]   The Status of Inter-district Desegregation Remedies

MILLIKEN v. BRADLEY (I)

Supreme Court of the United States, 1974.
418 U.S. 717, 94 S.Ct. 3112, 41 L.Ed.2d 1069.

MR. CHIEF JUSTICE BURGER delivered the opinion of the Court.

We granted certiorari in these consolidated cases to determine whether a federal court may impose a multidistrict, areawide remedy to a single district *de jure* segregation problem absent any finding that the other included school districts have failed to operate unitary school systems within their districts, absent any claim or finding that the boundary lines of any affected school district were established with the purpose of fostering racial segregation in public schools, absent any finding that the included districts committed acts which effected segregation within the other districts, and absent a meaningful opportunity for the included neighboring school districts to present evidence or be heard on the propriety of a multidistrict remedy or on the question of constitutional violations by those neighboring districts.

I

. . .

The District Court found that the Detroit Board of Education created and maintained optional attendance zones within Detroit neighborhoods undergoing racial transition and between high school attendance areas of opposite predominant racial compositions. These zones, the court found, had the "natural, probable, foreseeable and actual effect" of allowing White pupils to escape identifiably Negro schools. Similarly, the District Court found that Detroit school attendance zones had been drawn along north-south boundary lines despite the Detroit Board's awareness that drawing boundary lines in an east-west direction would result in significantly greater desegregation. . . .

The District Court found that in the operation of its school transportation program, which was designed to relieve overcrowding, the Detroit Board had admittedly bused Negro Detroit pupils to predominantly Negro schools which were beyond or away from closer White schools with available space. This practice was found to have continued in recent years despite the Detroit Board's avowed policy, adopted in 1967, of utilizing transportation to increase desegregation. . . .

With respect to the Detroit Board of Education's practices in school construction, the District Court found that Detroit school construction generally tended to have segregative effect with the great majority of schools being built in either overwhelmingly all-Negro or all-white neighborhoods so that the new schools opened as predominantly one race schools. . . .

The District Court also found that the State of Michigan had committed several constitutional violations with respect to the exercise of its general responsibility for, and supervision of, public education. The State, for example, was found to have failed, until the 1971 Session of the Michigan Legislature, to provide authorization or funds for the transportation of pupils within Detroit regardless of their poverty or distance from the school to which they were assigned; during this same period the State provided many neighboring, mostly White, suburban districts the full range of state supported transportation. . . .

Turning to the question of an appropriate remedy for these several constitutional violations, the District Court . . . proceeded to order the Detroit Board of Education to submit desegregation plans limited to the segregation problems found to be existing within the city of Detroit. At the same time, however, the state defendants were directed to submit desegregation plans encompassing the three-county metropolitan area despite the fact that the school districts of these three counties were not parties to the action and despite the fact that there had been no claim that these outlying counties, encompassing some 85 separate school districts, had committed constitutional violations. . . .

. . . [Eventually] the court designated 53 of the 85 suburban school districts plus Detroit as the "desegregation area" and appointed a panel to prepare and submit "an effective desegregation plan" for the Detroit schools [276,000 students] that would encompass the entire desegregation area [503,000 additional students]. . . .

The Court of Appeals . . . agreed with the District Court that "any less comprehensive a solution than a metropolitan area plan would result in an all black school system immediately surrounded by practically all white suburban school systems, with an overwhelming white majority population in the total metropolitan area." The court went on to state that it could "[not] see how such segregation can be any less harmful to the minority students than if the same result were accomplished within one school district."

Accordingly, the Court of Appeals concluded that "the only feasible desegregation plan involves the crossing of the boundary lines between the Detroit School District and adjacent or nearby school districts for the limited purpose of providing an effective desegregation plan." It reasoned that such a plan would be appropriate because of the State's violations, and could be implemented because of the State's authority to control local school districts....

II

Proceeding from these basic principles [from prior desegregation cases], we first note that in the District Court the complainants sought a remedy aimed at the *condition* alleged to offend the Constitution—the segregation within the Detroit City School District.... Thereafter, however, the District Court abruptly rejected the proposed Detroit-only plans on the ground that "while it would provide a racial mix more in keeping with the Black–White proportions of the student population, [it] would accentuate the racial identifiability of the [Detroit] district as a Black school system, and would not accomplish desegregation." ... Consequently, the court reasoned, it was imperative to "look beyond the limits of the Detroit school district for a solution to the problem of segregation in the Detroit schools ..." since "[s]chool district lines are simply matters of political convenience and may not be used to deny constitutional rights." Accordingly, the District Court proceeded to redefine the relevant area to include areas of predominantly White pupil population in order to ensure that "upon implementation, no school, grade or classroom [would be] substantially disproportionate to the overall racial composition" of the entire metropolitan area....

Viewing the record as a whole, it seems clear that the District Court and the Court of Appeals shifted the primary focus from a Detroit remedy to the metropolitan area only because of their conclusion that total desegregation of Detroit would not produce the racial balance which they perceived as desirable. Both courts proceeded on an assumption that the Detroit schools could not be truly desegregated—in their view of what constituted desegregation—unless the racial composition of the student body of each school substantially reflected the racial composition of the population of the metropolitan area as a whole. The metropolitan area was then defined as Detroit plus 53 of the outlying school districts....

Here the District Court's approach to what constituted "actual desegregation" raises the fundamental question ... as to the circumstances in which a federal court may order desegregation relief that embraces more than a single school district. The court's analytical starting point was its conclusion that school district lines are no more than arbitrary lines on a map "drawn for political convenience." Boundary lines may be bridged where there has been a constitutional violation calling for interdistrict relief, but, the notion that school district lines may be casually ignored or treated as a mere administrative convenience is contrary to the history of public education in our country. No single tradition in public education is more deeply rooted than local control over the operation of schools; local autonomy has long been thought essential both to the maintenance of community concern and support for public schools and to quality of the educational process....

The Michigan educational structure involved in this case, in common with most States, provides for a large measure of local control and a review of the scope and character of these local powers indicates the extent to which the inter-district remedy approved by the two courts could disrupt and alter the structure of public education in Michigan. The metropolitan remedy would require, in effect, consolidation of 54 independent school districts historically administered as separate units into a vast new super school district.... Entirely apart from the logistical and other serious problems attending large-scale transportation of students, the consolidation would give rise to an array of other problems in financing and operating this new school system. Some of the more obvious questions would be: What would be the status and authority of the present popularly elected school boards? Would the children of Detroit be within the jurisdiction and operating control of a school board elected by the parents and residents of other districts? What board or boards would levy taxes for school operations in these 54 districts constituting the consolidated metropolitan area? What provisions could be made for assuring substantial equality in tax levies among the 54 districts, if this were deemed requisite? What provisions would be made for financing? Would the validity of long-term bonds be jeopardized unless approved by all of the component districts as well as the State? What body would determine that portion of the curricula now left to the discretion of local school boards? Who would establish attendance zones, purchase school equipment, locate and construct new schools, and indeed attend to all the myriad day-to-day decisions that are necessary to school operations affecting potentially more than three quarters of a million pupils? ...

It may be suggested that all of these vital operational problems are yet to be resolved by the District Court.... But it is obvious from the scope of the inter-district remedy itself that absent a complete restructuring of the laws of Michigan relating to school districts the District Court will become first, a *de facto* "legislative authority" to resolve these complex questions, and then the "school superintendent" for the entire area. This is a task which few, if any, judges are qualified to perform and one which would deprive the people of control of schools through their elected representatives.

Of course, no state law is above the Constitution. School district lines and the present laws with respect to local control, are not sacrosanct and if they conflict with the Fourteenth Amendment federal courts have a duty to prescribe appropriate remedies.... But our prior holdings have been confined to violations and remedies within a single school district. We therefore turn to address, for the first time, the validity of a remedy mandating cross-district or inter-district consolidation to remedy a condition of segregation found to exist in only one district.

The controlling principle consistently expounded in our holdings is that the scope of the remedy is determined by the nature and extent of the constitutional violation. Before the boundaries of separate and autonomous school districts may be set aside by consolidating the separate units for remedial purposes or by imposing a cross-district remedy, it must first be shown that there has been a constitutional violation within one district that produces a significant segregative effect in another district. Specifically it must be shown that racially discriminatory acts of the state or local school districts, or of a single school district have been a substantial cause of inter-district segregation. Thus an inter-district remedy might be in order where the racially discriminatory acts of one or more school districts caused racial segregation in an adjacent district, or where district lines have been deliberately drawn on the basis of race. In such circumstances an inter-district remedy would be appropriate to eliminate the inter-district segregation directly caused by the constitutional violation. Conversely, without an inter-district violation and inter-district effect, there is no constitutional wrong calling for an inter-district remedy.

The record before us, voluminous as it is, contains evidence of *de jure* segregated conditions only in the Detroit schools; indeed, that was the theory on which the litigation was initially based and on which the District Court took evidence....

The constitutional right of the Negro respondents residing in Detroit is to attend a unitary school system in that district. Unless petitioners drew the district lines in a discriminatory fashion, or arranged for White students residing in the Detroit district to attend schools in Oakland and Macomb Counties, they were under no constitutional duty to make provisions for Negro students to do so....

III

We recognize that the six-volume record presently under consideration contains language and some specific incidental findings thought by the District Court to afford a basis for interdistrict relief. However, these comparatively isolated findings and brief comments concern only one possible inter-district violation and are found in the context of a proceeding that, as the District Court conceded, included no proofs of segregation practiced by any of the 85 suburban school districts surrounding Detroit....

IV

. . .

We conclude that the relief ordered by the District Court and affirmed by the Court of Appeals was based upon an erroneous standard and was unsupported by record evidence that acts of the outlying districts affected the discrimination found to exist in the schools of Detroit. Accordingly, the judgment of the Court of Appeals is reversed and the case is remanded for further proceedings consistent with this opinion leading to prompt formulation of a decree directed to eliminating the segregation found to exist in Detroit city schools, a remedy which has been delayed since 1970. . . .

Notes

1. In *Haney v. County Bd. of Educ. of Sevier County*, 429 F.2d 364 (8th Cir.1970), the Eighth Circuit ordered consolidation of single racial school districts in Arkansas that remained in existence following *Brown*. Would this order have stood under *Milliken I*?

2. The Court emphasized the need for local control in education. The dissent believed that since the state is responsible for education, officials had the duty to use all available resources to correct segregation regardless of where it occurred. What, if any, is the relationship between control of the schools and segregation?

3. What do you think about the Court's emphases on the lack of evidence of segregation outside of Detroit, coupled with the fact that the other school systems were not allowed to be heard on the appropriateness of the proposed multi-district remedy?

[Case No. 127]　The Federal Courts and Intra–District Remedies for Segregation

MILLIKEN v. BRADLEY (II)

Supreme Court of the United States, 1977.
433 U.S. 267, 97 S.Ct. 2749, 53 L.Ed.2d 745.

MR. CHIEF JUSTICE BURGER delivered the opinion of the Court.

We granted certiorari in this case to consider two questions concerning the remedial powers of federal district courts in school desegregation cases, namely, whether a District Court can, as part of a desegregation decree, order compensatory or remedial educational programs for schoolchildren who have been subjected to past acts of *de jure* segregation, and whether, consistent with the Eleventh Amendment, a federal court can require state officials found responsible for constitutional violations to bear part of the costs of those programs.

Due to the intervening death of Judge Stephen J. Roth, who had presided over the litigation from the outset, the case on remand was reassigned to Judge Robert E. DeMascio [who] promptly ordered respondent Bradley and the Detroit Board to submit desegregation plans limited to the Detroit school system. On April 1, 1975, both parties submitted their proposed plans. . . .

In addition to student reassignments, the Board's plan called for implementation of 13 remedial or compensatory programs, referred to in the record as "educational components." These compensatory programs, which were proposed in addition to the plan's provisions for magnet schools and vocational high schools, included three of the four components at issue in this case—in-service training for teachers and administrators, guidance and counseling programs, and revised testing procedures. Pursuant to the District Court's direction, the State Department of Education on April 21, 1975, submitted a critique of the Detroit Board's desegregation plan; in its report, the Department opined that, although "[i]t is possible that none of the thirteen 'quality education' components is essential ... to correct the constitutional violation ...", eight of the 13 proposed programs nonetheless deserved special consideration in the desegregation setting. Of particular relevance here, the State Board said:

> "Within the context of effectuating a pupil desegregation plan, the in-service training [and] guidance and counseling ... components appear to deserve special emphasis."

After receiving the State Board's critique, the District Court conducted extensive hearings on the two plans over a two-month period. Substantial testimony was adduced with respect to the proposed educational components, including testimony by petitioners' expert witnesses. Based on this evidence and on reports of court-appointed experts, the District Court on August 11, 1975, approved, in principle, the Detroit Board's inclusion of remedial and compensatory educational components in the desegregation plan....

The District Court expressly found that the two components of testing and counseling, as then administered in Detroit's schools, were infected with the discriminatory bias of a segregated school system.... The District Court also found that, to make desegregation work, it was necessary to include remedial reading programs and in-service training for teachers and administrators....

Having established these general principles, the District Court formulated several "remedial guidelines" to govern the Detroit Board's development of a final plan. Declining "to substitute its authority for the authority of elected state and local officials to decide which educational components are beneficial to the school community," the District Judge laid down the following guidelines with respect to each of the four educational components at issue here:

(a) *Reading.* Concluding that "[t]here is no educational component more directly associated with the process of desegregation than reading," the District Court directed the General Superintendent of Detroit's schools to institute a remedial reading and communications skills program "[t]o eradicate the effects of past discrimination...." The content of the required program was not prescribed by the court; rather, formulation and implementation of the program was left to the Superintendent and to a committee to be selected by him.

(b) *In-Service Training.* The court also directed the Detroit Board to formulate a comprehensive in-service teacher training program, an element "essential to a system undergoing desegregation." In the District Court's view, an in-service training program for teachers and administrators, to train professional and instructional personnel to cope with the desegregation process in Detroit, would tend to ensure that all students in a desegregated system would be treated equally by teachers and administrators able, by virtue of special training, to cope with special problems presented by desegregation, and thereby facilitate Detroit's conversion to a unitary system.

(c) *Testing.* Because it found, based on record evidence, that Negro children "are especially affected by biased testing procedures," the District Court determined that, frequently, minority students in Detroit were adversely affected by discriminatory testing procedures. Unless the school system's tests were administered in a way "free from racial, ethnic and cultural bias," the District Court concluded that Negro children in Detroit might thereafter be impeded in their educational growth. Accordingly, the court directed the Detroit Board and the State Department of Education to institute a testing program along the lines proposed by the local school board in its original desegregation plan.

(d) *Counseling and Career Guidance.* Finally, the District Court addressed what expert witnesses had described as psychological pressures on Detroit's students in a system undergoing desegregation. Counselors were required, the court concluded, both to deal with the numerous problems and tensions arising in the change from Detroit's dual system, and, more concretely, to counsel students concerning the new vocational and technical school programs available under the plan through the cooperation of state and local officials.

Nine months later, on May 11, 1976, the District Court entered its final order. Emphasizing that it had "been careful to order only what is essential for a school district undergoing desegregation," the court ordered the Detroit Board and the state defendants to institute comprehensive programs as to the four educational components by the start of the September 1976 school term. The cost of these four programs, the court concluded, was to be equally borne by the Detroit School Board and the State. To carry out this cost-sharing, the court directed the local board to calculate its highest budget allocation in any prior year for the several educational programs and, from that base, any excess cost attributable to the desegregation plan was to be paid equally by the two groups of defendants responsible for prior constitutional violations, *i.e.*, the Detroit Board and the state defendants. . . .

This Court has not previously addressed directly the question whether federal courts can order remedial education programs as part of a school desegregation decree. However, the general principles governing our resolution of this issue are well settled by the prior decisions of this Court. In the first case concerning federal courts' remedial powers in eliminating *de jure* school segregation, the Court laid down the basic rule which governs to this day: "In fashioning and effectuating the [desegregation] decrees, the courts will be guided by equitable principles." *Brown v. Board of Education (II).*

Application of those "equitable principles," we have held, requires federal courts to focus upon three factors. In the first place, like other equitable remedies, the nature of the desegregation remedy is to be determined by the nature and scope of the constitutional violation. The remedy must therefore be related to "the *condition* alleged to offend the

Constitution. . . ." *Milliken I.* Second, the decree must indeed be *remedial* in nature, that is, it must be designed as nearly as possible "to restore the victims of discriminatory conduct to the position they would have occupied in the absence of such conduct." Third, the federal courts in devising a remedy must take into account the interests of state and local authorities in managing their own affairs, consistent with the Constitution. In *Brown II* the Court squarely held that "[s]chool authorities have the *primary* responsibility for elucidating, assessing, and solving these problems. . . ." If, however, "school authorities fail in their affirmative obligations . . . judicial authority may be invoked." Once invoked, "the scope of a district court's equitable powers to remedy past wrongs is broad, for breadth and flexibility are inherent in equitable remedies."

In challenging the order before us, petitioners do not specifically question that the District Court's mandated programs are designed, as nearly as practicable, to restore the schoolchildren of Detroit to a position they would have enjoyed absent constitutional violations by state and local officials. And, petitioners do not contend, nor could they, that the prerogatives of the Detroit School Board have been abrogated by the decree, since of course the Detroit School Board itself proposed incorporation of these programs in the first place. Petitioners' sole contention is that, under *Swann,* the District Court's order exceeds the scope of the constitutional violation. Invoking our holding in *Milliken I* petitioners claim that, since the constitutional violation found by the District Court was the unlawful segregation of students on the basis of race, the court's decree must be limited to remedying unlawful pupil assignments. This contention misconceives the principle petitioners seek to invoke, and we reject their argument.

The well-settled principle that the nature and scope of the remedy are to be determined by the violation means simply that federal court decrees must directly address and relate to the constitutional violation itself. Because of this inherent limitation upon federal judicial authority, federal court decrees exceed appropriate limits if they are aimed at eliminating a condition that does not violate the Constitution or does not flow from such a violation, or if they are imposed upon governmental units that were neither involved in nor affected by the constitutional violation, as in *Milliken I.* But where, as here, a constitutional violation has been found, the remedy does not "exceed" the violation if the remedy is tailored to cure the "*condition* that offends the Constitution."

The "condition" offending the Constitution is Detroit's *de jure* segregated school system, which was so pervasively and persistently segregated that the District Court found that the need for the educational components flowed directly from constitutional violations by both state and local officials. These specific educational remedies, although normally left to the discretion of the elected school board and professional educators, were deemed necessary to restore the victims of discriminatory conduct to the position they would have enjoyed in terms of education had these four components been provided in a nondiscriminatory manner in a school system free from pervasive *de jure* racial segregation.

In the first case invalidating a *de jure* system, a unanimous Court, speaking through Chief Justice Warren, held in *Brown I:* "Separate educational facilities are inherently unequal." And in *United States v. Montgomery County Board of Education*, the Court concerned itself not with pupil assignment, but with the desegregation of faculty and staff as part of the process of dismantling a dual system.....

Montgomery County therefore stands firmly for the proposition that matters other than pupil assignment must on occasion be addressed by federal courts to eliminate the effects of prior segregation. Similarly, in *Swann* we reaffirmed the principle that "existing policy and practice with regard to faculty, staff, transportation, extracurricular activities, and facilities were among the most important indicia of a segregated system." In a word, discriminatory student assignment policies can themselves manifest and breed other inequalities built into a dual system founded on racial discrimination. Federal courts need not, and cannot, close their eyes to inequalities, shown by the record, which flow from a longstanding segregated system.

In light of the mandate of *Brown I* and *Brown II,* federal courts have, over the years, often required the inclusion of remedial programs in desegregation plans to overcome the inequalities inherent in dual school systems.....

... On this record ... we are bound to conclude that the decree before us was aptly tailored to remedy the consequences of the constitutional violation. Children who have been thus educationally and culturally set apart from the larger community will inevitably acquire habits of speech, conduct, and attitudes reflecting their cultural isolation. They are likely to acquire speech habits, for example, which vary from the environment in which they must ultimately function and compete, if they are to enter and be a part of that community. This is not peculiar to race; in this setting, it can affect any children who, as a group, are isolated by force of law from the mainstream.

Pupil assignment alone does not automatically remedy the impact of previous, unlawful educational isolation; the consequences linger and can be dealt with only by independent measures.....

Petitioners also contend that the District Court's order, even if otherwise proper, violates the Eleventh Amendment.....

The decree to share the future costs of educational components in this case fits squarely within the prospective-compliance exception.... That exception ... permits federal courts to enjoin state officials to conform their conduct to requirements of federal law, notwithstanding a direct and substantial impact on the state treasury. The order challenged here does no more than that. The decree requires state officials, held responsible for unconstitutional conduct, in findings which are not challenged, to eliminate a *de jure* segregated school system. More precisely, the burden of state officials is that set forth in *Swann*-to take the necessary steps "to eliminate from the public schools all vestiges of state-imposed segregation." The educational components, which the District Court ordered into effect *prospectively,* are plainly designed to wipe out continuing conditions of inequality produced by the inherently unequal dual school system long maintained by Detroit.

... We ... hold that such prospective relief is not barred by the Eleventh Amendment....

Notes

1.   Lower federal courts frequently ordered specific remedies other than busing or different student assignment techniques in attempting to correct the effects of de jure segregation. This was the first time the Court considered remedies other than student or teacher reassignments.

2.   Do you agree with the guidelines set forth by the trial court? To what extent, if at all, did the trial court, despite its disclaimer, substitute its authority for that of state and local education officials in deciding which programs were beneficial to the school community?

[Case No. 128]   Standards Applicable to Segregation Not Imposed by Law

KEYES v. SCHOOL DISTRICT NO. 1, DENVER, COLORADO

Supreme Court of the United States, 1973.
413 U.S. 189, 93 S.Ct. 2686, 37 L.Ed.2d 548.

MR. JUSTICE BRENNAN delivered the opinion of the Court.

This school desegregation case concerns the Denver, Colorado, school system. That system has never been operated under a constitutional or statutory provision that mandated or permitted racial segregation in public education. Rather, the gravamen of this action ... is that respondent School Board alone, by use of various techniques such as the manipulation of student attendance zones, schoolsite selection and a neighborhood school policy, created or maintained racially or ethnically (or both racially and ethnically) segregated schools throughout the school district, entitling petitioners to a decree directing desegregation of the entire school district....

I

Before turning to the primary question we decide today, a word must be said about the ... method of defining a "segregated" school. Denver is a tri-ethnic, as distinguished from a bi-racial, community. The over-all racial and ethnic composition of the Denver public schools is 66% Anglo, 14% Negro, and 20% Hispano.... What is or is not a segregated school will necessarily depend on the facts of each particular case. In addition to the racial and ethnic composition of a school's student body, other factors, such as the racial and ethnic composition of faculty and staff and the community and administration attitudes toward the school must be taken into consideration....

... [T]hough of different origins Negroes and Hispanos in Denver suffer identical discrimination in treatment when compared with the treatment afforded Anglo students. In that circumstance, we think petitioners are entitled to have schools with a combined predominance of Negroes and Hispanos included in the category of "segregated" schools.

II

... Petitioners proved that for almost a decade after 1960 respondent School Board had engaged in an unconstitutional policy of deliberate racial segregation in the Park Hill schools. Indeed, the District Court found that "[b]etween 1960 and 1969 the Board's policies with respect to these northeast Denver schools show an undeviating purpose to isolate Negro students" in segregated schools "while preserving the Anglo character of [other] schools." This finding did not relate to an insubstantial or trivial fragment of the school system. On the contrary, respondent School Board was found guilty of following a deliberate segregation policy at schools attended, in 1969, by 37.69% of Denver's total Negro school population, including one-fourth of the Negro elementary pupils, over two-thirds of the Negro junior high pupils, and over two-fifths of the Negro high school pupils. In addition, there was uncontroverted evidence that teachers and staff had for years been assigned on the basis of a minority teacher to a minority school throughout the school system. Respondent argues, however, that a finding of state-imposed segregation as to a substantial portion of the school system can be viewed in isolation from the rest of the district, and that even if state-imposed segregation does exist in a substantial part of the Denver school system, it does not follow that the District Court could predicate on that fact a finding that the entire school system is a dual system. We do not agree. We have never suggested that plaintiffs in school desegregation cases must bear the burden of proving the elements of *de jure* segregation as to each and every school or each and every student within the school system. Rather, we have held that where plaintiffs prove that a current condition of segregated schooling exists within a school district where a dual system was compelled or authorized by statute at the time of our decision in *Brown I,* the State automatically assumes an affirmative duty "to effectuate a transition to a racially nondiscriminatory school system," that is, to eliminate from the public schools within their school system "all vestiges of state-imposed segregation."

This is not a case, however, where a statutory dual system has ever existed. Nevertheless, where plaintiffs prove that the school authorities have carried out a systematic program of segregation affecting a substantial portion of the students, schools, teachers, and facilities within the school system, it is only common sense to conclude that there exists a predicate for a finding of the existence of a dual school system. Several considerations support this conclusion. First, it is obvious that a practice of concentrating Negroes in certain schools by structuring attendance zones or designating "feeder" schools on the basis of race has the reciprocal effect of keeping other nearby schools predominantly white. Similarly, the practice of building a school—such as the Barrett Elementary School in this case—to a certain size and in a certain location, "with conscious knowledge that it would be a segregated school," has a substantial reciprocal effect on the racial composition of other nearby schools. So also, the use of mobile classrooms, the drafting of student transfer policies, the transportation of students, and the assignment of faculty and staff, on racially identifiable bases, have the clear effect of earmarking schools according to their racial composition, and this, in turn, together with the elements of student assignment and school construction, may have a profound reciprocal effect on the racial composition of residential neighborhoods within a metropolitan area, thereby causing further racial concentration within the schools. . . .

In short, common sense dictates the conclusion that racially inspired school board actions have an impact beyond the particular schools that are the subjects of those actions. This is not to say, of course, that there can never be a case in which the geographical structure of, or the natural boundaries within, a school district may have the effect of dividing the district into separate, identifiable and unrelated units. Such a determination is essentially a question of fact to be resolved by the trial court in the first instance, but such cases must be rare. In the absence of such a determination, proof of state-imposed segregation in a substantial portion of the district will suffice to support a finding by the trial court of the existence of a dual system. Of course, where that finding is made, as in cases involving statutory dual systems, the school authorities have an affirmative duty "to effectuate a transition to a racially nondiscriminatory school system."

III

. . .

On the question of segregative intent, petitioners presented evidence tending to show that the Board, through its actions over a period of years, intentionally created and maintained the segregated character of the core city schools. Respondents countered this evidence by arguing that the segregation in these schools is the result of a racially neutral "neighborhood school policy" and that the acts of which petitioners complain are explicable within the bounds of that policy. . . .

. . . Plainly, a finding of intentional segregation as to a portion of a school system is not devoid of probative value in assessing the school authorities' intent with respect to other parts of the same school system. On the contrary where, as here, the case involves one school board, a finding of intentional segregation on its part in one portion of a school system is highly relevant to the issue of the board's intent with respect to the other segregated schools in the system. This is merely an application of the well-settled evidentiary principle that "the prior doing of other similar acts, whether clearly a part of a scheme or not, is useful as reducing the possibility that the act in question was done with innocent intent." . . .

. . . [W]e hold that a finding of intentionally segregative school board actions in a meaningful portion of a school system, as in this case, creates a presumption that other segregated schooling within the system is not adventitious. It establishes, in other words, a prima facie case of unlawful segregative design on the part of school authorities, and shifts to those authorities the burden of proving that other segregated schools within the system are not also the result of intentionally segregative actions. This is true even if it is determined that different areas of the school district should be viewed independently of each other because, even in that situation, there is high probability that where school authorities have effectuated an intentionally segregative policy in a meaningful portion of the school system, similar impermissible considerations have motivated their actions in other areas of the system. We emphasize that the differentiating factor between *de jure* segregation and so-called *de facto* segregation ... is *purpose* or *intent* to segregate. Where school authorities have been found to have practiced purposeful segregation in part of a school system, they may be expected to oppose system-wide desegregation, as did the respondents in this case, on the ground that their purposefully segregative actions were isolated and individual events, thus leaving plaintiffs with the burden of proving otherwise. But at that point where an intentionally segregative policy is practiced in a meaningful or significant segment of a school system, as in this case, the school authorities cannot be heard to argue that plaintiffs have proved only "isolated and individual" unlawfully segregative actions. In that circumstance, it is both fair and reasonable to require that the school authorities bear the burden of showing that their actions as to other segregated schools within the system were not also motivated by segregative intent....

Thus, respondent School Board having been found to have practiced deliberate racial segregation in schools attended by over one-third of the Negro school population, that crucial finding establishes a prima facie case of intentional segregation in the core city schools. In such case, respondent's neighborhood school policy is not to be determinative "simply because it appears to be neutral."

IV

In summary, the District Court on remand, *first,* will afford respondent School Board the opportunity to prove its contention that the Park Hill area is a separate, identifiable and unrelated section of the school district that should be treated as isolated from the rest of the district. If respondent School Board fails to prove that contention, the District Court, *second,* will determine whether respondent School Board's conduct over almost a decade after 1960 in carrying out a policy of deliberate racial segregation in the Park Hill schools constitutes the entire school system a dual school system. If the District Court determines that the Denver school system is a dual school system, respondent School Board has the affirmative duty to desegregate the entire system "root and branch." If the District Court determines, however, that the Denver school system is not a dual school system by reason of the Board's actions in Park Hill, the court, *third,* will afford respondent School Board the opportunity to rebut petitioners' prima facie case of intentional segregation in the core city schools raised by the finding of intentional segregation in the Park Hill schools. There, the Board's burden is to show that its policies and practices with respect to schoolsite location, school size, school renovations and additions, student-attendance zones, student assignment and transfer options, mobile class-room units, transportation of students, assignment of faculty and staff, etc., considered together and premised on the Board's so-called "neighborhood school" concept, either were not taken in effectuation of a policy to create or maintain segregation in the core city schools, or, if unsuccessful in that effort, were not factors in causing the existing condition of segregation in these schools. Considerations of "fairness" and "policy" demand no less in light of the Board's intentionally segregative actions. If respondent Board fails to rebut petitioners' prima facie case, the District Court must, as in the case of Park Hill, decree all-out desegregation of the core city schools....

Notes

1.　Note the indicia in the last paragraph for determining what makes a school segregated.

2.　Denver did not achieve unitary status until twenty-two-years later. *Keyes v. Congress of Hispanic Educators*, 902 F.Supp. 1274 [104 Educ. L. Rep. 1067] (D.Colo.1995), *appeal dismissed sub nom. Keyes v. School Dist. No. 1, Denver, Colo.*, 119 F.3d 1437 [120 Educ. L. Rep. 158] (10th Cir.1997).

[Case No. 129]　Desegregation Orders Not Meant to Operate in Perpetuity

BOARD OF EDUCATION OF OKLAHOMA CITY PUBLIC SCHOOLS, INDEPENDENT SCHOOL DISTRICT NO. 89, OKLAHOMA COUNTY, OKLAHOMA v. DOWELL

Supreme Court of the United States, 1991.
498 U.S. 237, 111 S.Ct. 630, 112 L.Ed.2d 715 [64 Educ. L. Rep. 628].

CHIEF JUSTICE REHNQUIST delivered the opinion of the Court.

Petitioner Board of Education of Oklahoma City sought dissolution of a decree entered by the District Court imposing a school desegregation plan. The District Court granted relief over the objection of respondents Robert L. Dowell, black students and their parents. The Court of Appeals for the Tenth Circuit reversed, holding that the Board would be entitled to such relief only upon " '[n]othing less than a clear showing of grievous wrong evoked by new and unforeseen conditions....' " We hold that the Court of Appeals' test is more stringent than is required either by our cases dealing with injunctions or by the Equal Protection Clause....

I

This school desegregation litigation began almost 30 years ago. In 1961, respondents, black students and their parents, sued petitioners, the Board of Education of Oklahoma City (Board), to end *de jure* segregation in the public schools. In 1963, the District Court found that Oklahoma City had intentionally segregated both schools and housing in the past, and that Oklahoma City was operating a "dual" school system—one that was intentionally segregated by race. In 1965, the District Court found that the School Board's attempt to desegregate by using neighborhood zoning failed to remedy past segregation because residential segregation resulted in one-race schools. Residential segregation had once been state imposed, and it lingered due to discrimination by some realtors and financial institutions. The District Court found that school segregation had caused some housing segregation. In 1972, finding that previous efforts had not been successful at eliminating state imposed segregation, the District Court ordered the Board to adopt the "Finger Plan," under which kindergarteners would be assigned to neighborhood schools unless their parents opted otherwise; children in grades 1–4 would attend formerly all white schools, and thus black children would be bused to those schools; children in grade 5 would attend formerly all black schools, and thus white children would be bused to those schools; students in the upper grades would be bused to various areas in order to maintain integrated schools; and in integrated neighborhoods there would be stand-alone schools for all grades.

In 1977, after complying with the desegregation decree for five years, the Board made a "Motion to Close Case." The District Court held that "... Jurisdiction in this case is terminated ipso facto subject only to final disposition of any case now pending on appeal." This unpublished order was not appealed.

In 1984, the School Board faced demographic changes that led to greater burdens on young black children. As more and more neighborhoods became integrated, more stand-alone schools were established, and young black students had to be bused farther from their inner-city homes to outlying white areas. In an effort to alleviate this burden and to increase parental involvement, the Board adopted the Student Reassignment Plan (SRP), which relied on neighborhood assignments for students in grades K–4 beginning in the 1985–1986 school year. Busing continued for students in grades 5–12. Any student could transfer from a school where he or she was in the majority to a school where he or she would be in the minority. Faculty and staff integration was retained, and an "equity officer" was appointed.

In 1985, respondents filed a "Motion to Reopen the Case," contending that the School District had not achieved "unitary" status and that the SRP was a return to segregation. Under the SRP, 11 of 64 elementary schools would be greater than 90% black, 22 would be greater than 90% white plus other minorities, and 31 would be racially mixed. The District Court refused to reopen the case, holding that its 1977 finding of unitariness was *res judicata* as to those who were then parties to the action, and that the district remained unitary. The District Court found that the School Board, administration, faculty, support staff, and student body were integrated, and transportation, extracurricular activities and facilities within the district were equal and nondiscriminatory. Because unitariness had been achieved, the District Court concluded that court-ordered desegregation must end.

The Court of Appeals for the Tenth Circuit reversed. . . .

On remand, the District Court found that demographic changes made the Finger Plan unworkable, that the Board had done nothing for 25 years to promote residential segregation, and that the school district had bused students for more than a decade in good-faith compliance with the court's orders. The District Court found that present residential segregation was the result of private decisionmaking and economics, and that it was too attenuated to be a vestige of former school segregation. It also found that the district had maintained its unitary status, and that the neighborhood assignment plan was not designed with discriminatory intent. The court concluded that the previous injunctive decree should be vacated and the school district returned to local control.

The Court of Appeals again reversed, holding that " 'an injunction takes on a life of its own and becomes an edict quite independent of the law it is meant to effectuate.' " ... it held that a desegregation decree remains in effect until a school district can show "grievous wrong evoked by new and unforseen conditions" and "dramatic changes in conditions unforseen at the time of the decree that ... impose extreme and unexpectedly oppressive hardships on the obligor." Given that a number of schools would return to being primarily one-race schools under the SRP, circumstances in Oklahoma City had not changed enough to justify modification of the decree. The Court of Appeals held that, despite the unitary finding, the Board had the " 'affirmative duty ... not to take any action that would impede the process of disestablishing the dual system and its effects.' "

We granted the Board's petition for certiorari to resolve a conflict between the standard laid down by the Court of Appeals in this case and that laid down in *Spangler v. Pasadena City Board of Education* and *Riddick v. School Bd. of City of Norfolk*. We now reverse the Court of Appeals.

II

We must first consider whether respondents may contest the District Court's 1987 order dissolving the injunction which had imposed the desegregation decree. Respondents did not appeal from the District Court's 1977 order finding that the school system had achieved unitary status, and petitioner contends that the 1977 order bars respondents from contesting the 1987 order. We disagree, for the 1977 order did not dissolve the desegregation decree, and the District Court's unitariness finding was too ambiguous to bar respondents from challenging later action by the Board.

The lower courts have been inconsistent in their use of the term "unitary." Some have used it to identify a school district that has completely remedied all vestiges of past discrimination. Under that interpretation of the word, a unitary school district is one that has met the mandate of *Brown v. Board of Education*. Other courts, however, have used "unitary" to describe any school district that has currently desegregated student assignments, whether or not that status is solely the result of a court-imposed desegregation plan. In other words, such a school district could be called unitary and nevertheless still contain vestiges of past discrimination. That there is such confusion is evident in *Georgia State Conference of Branches of NAACP v. Georgia*, where the Court of Appeals drew a distinction between a "unitary school district" and a district that has achieved "unitary status." The court explained that a school district that has not operated segregated schools ... "for a period of several years" is unitary, but that a school district cannot be said to have achieved "unitary status" unless it "has eliminated the vestiges of its prior discrimination and has been adjudicated as such through the proper judicial procedures."

We think it is a mistake to treat words such as "dual" and "unitary" as if they were actually found in the Constitution. The constitutional command of the Fourteenth Amendment is that "[n]o State shall ... deny to any person ... the equal protection of the laws." Courts have used the terms "dual" to denote a school system which has engaged in intentional segregation of students by race, and "unitary" to describe a school system which has been brought into compliance with the command of the Constitution. We are not sure how useful it is to define these terms more precisely, or to create subclasses within them. But there is no doubt that the differences in usage described above do exist. The District Court's 1977 order is unclear with respect to what it meant by unitary and the necessary result of that finding. We therefore decline to overturn the conclusion of the Court of Appeals that while the 1977 order of the District Court did bind the parties as to the unitary character of the district, it did not finally terminate the Oklahoma City school litigation. In *Pasadena City Board of Education v. Spangler*, we held that a school board is entitled to a rather precise statement of its obligations under a desegregation decree. If such a decree is to be terminated or dissolved, respondents as well as the school board are entitled to a like statement from the court.

III

The Court of Appeals relied upon language from this Court's decision in *United States v. Swift and Co.*, for the proposition that a desegregation decree could not be lifted or modified absent a showing of "grievous wrong evoked by new and unforeseen conditions." It also held that "compliance alone cannot become the basis for modifying or dissolving an injunction." We hold that its reliance was mistaken.

In *Swift*, several large meat-packing companies entered into a consent decree whereby they agreed to refrain forever from entering into the grocery business. The decree was by its terms effective in perpetuity. The defendant meatpackers and their allies had over a period of a decade attempted, often with success in the lower courts, to frustrate operation of the decree. It was in this context that the language relied upon by the Court of Appeals in this case was used.

United States v. United Shoe Machinery Corp. explained that the language used in *Swift* must be read in the context of the continuing danger of unlawful restraints on trade which the Court had found still existed.... In the present case, a finding by the District Court that the Oklahoma City School District was being operated in compliance with the commands of the Equal Protection Clause of the Fourteenth Amendment, and that it was unlikely that the school board would return to its former ways, would be a finding that the purposes of the desegregation litigation had been fully achieved. No additional showing of "grievous wrong evoked by new and unforeseen conditions" is required of the school board.

In *Milliken v. Bradley [II]*, we said:

"[F]ederal-court decrees must directly address and relate to the constitutional violation itself. Because of this inherent limitation upon federal judicial authority, federal-court decrees exceed appropriate limits if they are aimed at eliminating a condition that does not violate the Constitution or does not flow from such a violation. . . ."

From the very first, federal supervision of local school systems was intended as a temporary measure to remedy past discrimination. *Brown* considered the "complexities arising from the transition to a system of public education freed of racial discrimination" in holding that the implementation of desegregation was to proceed "with all deliberate speed." *Green* also spoke of the "transition to a unitary, nonracial system of public education."

Considerations based on the allocation of powers within our federal system, we think, support our view that quoted language from *Swift* does not provide the proper standard to apply to injunctions entered in school desegregation cases. Such decrees, unlike the one in *Swift*, are not intended to operate in perpetuity. Local control over the education of children allows citizens to participate in decisionmaking, and allows innovation so that school programs can fit local needs. The legal justification for displacement of local authority by an injunctive decree in a school desegregation case is a violation of the Constitution by the local authorities. Dissolving a desegregation decree after the local authorities have operated in compliance with it for a reasonable period of time properly recognizes that "necessary concern for the important values of local control of public school systems dictates that a federal court's regulatory control of such systems not extend beyond the time required to remedy the effects of past intentional discrimination."

The Court of Appeals, as noted, relied for its statement that "compliance alone cannot become the basis for modifying or dissolving an injunction" on our decision in *United States v. W.T. Grant Co.* That case, however, did not involve the dissolution of an injunction, but the question of whether an injunction should be issued in the first place. This Court observed that a promise to comply with the law on the part of a wrongdoer did not divest a district court of its power to enjoin the wrongful conduct in which the defendant had previously engaged.

A district court need not accept at face value the profession of a school board which has intentionally discriminated that it will cease to do so in the future. But in deciding whether to modify or dissolve a desegregation decree, a school board's compliance with previous court orders is obviously relevant. In this case the original finding of *de jure* segregation was entered in 1961, the injunctive decree from which the Board seeks relief was entered in 1972, and the Board complied with the decree in good faith until 1985. Not only do the personnel of school boards change over time, but the same passage of time enables the District Court to observe the good faith of the school board in complying with the decree. The test espoused by the Court of Appeals would condemn a school district, once governed by a board which intentionally discriminated, to judicial tutelage for the indefinite future. Neither the principles governing the entry and dissolution of injunctive decrees, nor the commands of the Equal Protection Clause of the Fourteenth Amendment, require any such Draconian result.

Petitioner urges that we reinstate the decision of the District Court terminating the injunction, but we think that the preferable course is to remand the case to that court so that it may decide, in accordance with this opinion, whether the Board made a sufficient showing of constitutional compliance as of 1985, when the SRP was adopted, to allow the injunction to be dissolved. The District Court should address itself to whether the Board had complied in good faith with the desegregation decree since it was entered, and whether the vestiges of past discrimination had been eliminated to the extent practicable.

In considering whether the vestiges of *de jure* segregation had been eliminated as far as practicable, the District Court should look not only at student assignments, but "to every facet of school operations—faculty, staff, transportation, extra-curricular activities and facilities."

After the District Court decides whether the Board was entitled to have the decree terminated, it should proceed to decide respondent's challenge to the SRP. A school district which has been released from an injunction imposing a desegregation plan no longer requires court authorization for the promulgation of policies and rules regulating matters such as assignment of students and the like, but it of course remains subject to the mandate of the Equal Protection Clause of the Fourteenth Amendment. If the Board was entitled to have the decree terminated as of 1985, the District Court should then evaluate the Board's decision to implement the SRP under appropriate equal protection principles.

The judgment of the Court of Appeals is reversed, and the case is remanded to the District Court for further proceedings consistent with this opinion.

It is so ordered.

Note

Many school desegregation cases experienced multiple rounds of litigation. Inasmuch as this is the case, do you think that the Court was signaling that it was no longer concerned with school desegregation? If so, what should the role of the federal judiciary be in school desegregation cases?

[Case No. 130]   Incremental Termination of Judicial Oversight of Desegregation Plans

FREEMAN v. PITTS

Supreme Court of the United States, 1992.
503 U.S. 467, 112 S.Ct. 1430, 118 L.Ed.2d 108 [72 Educ. L. Rep. 717].

JUSTICE KENNEDY delivered the opinion of the Court.

DeKalb County, Georgia, is a major suburban area of Atlanta. This case involves a court-ordered desegregation decree for the DeKalb County School System (DCSS). DCSS now serves some 73,000 students in kindergarten through high school and is the 32nd largest elementary and secondary school system in the Nation.

DCSS has been subject to the supervision and jurisdiction of the United States District Court for the Northern District of Georgia since 1969, when it was ordered to dismantle its dual school system. In 1986, petitioners filed a motion for final dismissal.... We now [hold] that a district court is permitted to withdraw judicial supervision with respect to discrete categories in which the school district has achieved compliance with a court-ordered desegregation plan. A district court need not retain active control over every aspect of school administration until a school district has demonstrated unitary status in all facets of its system.

I

A

For decades before our decision in *Brown v. Board of Education* (*Brown I*) and our mandate in *Brown v. Board of Education* (*Brown II*), which ordered school districts to desegregate with "all deliberate speed," DCSS was segregated by law. DCSS's initial response to the mandate of *Brown II* was an all too familiar one. Interpreting "all deliberate speed" as giving latitude to delay steps to desegregate, DCSS took no positive action toward desegregation until the 1966–1967 school year, when it did nothing more than adopt a freedom of choice transfer plan. Some black students chose to attend former *de jure* white schools, but the plan had no significant effect on the former *de jure* black schools.

In 1968 we decided *Green v. New Kent County School Bd.* We held that adoption of a freedom of choice plan does not, by itself, satisfy a school district's mandatory responsibility to eliminate all vestiges of a dual system. *Green* was a turning point in our law in a further respect.... We said that the obligation of school districts once segregated by law was to come forward with a plan that "promises realistically to work, and promises realistically to work *now*." The case before us requires an understanding and assessment of how DCSS responded to the directives set forth in *Green.*

Within two months of our ruling in *Green,* respondents, who are black school children and their parents, instituted this class action in the United States District Court for the Northern District of Georgia. After the suit was filed, DCSS voluntarily began working with the Department of Health, Education and Welfare to devise a comprehensive and final plan of desegregation. The District Court in June 1969 entered a consent order approving the proposed plan, which was to be implemented in the 1969–1970 school year. The order abolished the freedom of choice plan and adopted a neighborhood school attendance plan that had been proposed by the DCSS and accepted by the Department of Health, Education and Welfare subject to a minor modification. Under the plan all of the former *de jure* black schools were closed and their students were reassigned among the remaining neighborhood schools. The District Court retained jurisdiction.

Between 1969 and 1986 respondents sought only infrequent and limited judicial intervention into the affairs of DCSS....

In 1986 petitioners filed a motion for final dismissal of the litigation. They sought a declaration that DCSS had satisfied its duty to eliminate the dual education system, that is to say a declaration that the school system had achieved unitary status. The District Court approached the question whether DCSS had achieved unitary status by asking whether DCSS was unitary with respect to each of the factors identified in *Green*. The court considered an additional factor that is not named in *Green*: the quality of education being offered to the white and black student populations.

The District Court found DCSS to be "an innovative school system that has travelled the often long road to unitary status almost to its end," noting that "the court has continually been impressed by the successes of the DCSS and its dedication to providing a quality education for all students within that system." It found that DCSS is a unitary system with regard to student assignments, transportation, physical facilities, and extracurricular activities, and ruled that it would order no further relief in those areas. The District Court stopped short of dismissing the case, however, because it found that DCSS was not unitary in every respect. The court said that vestiges of the dual system remain in the areas of teacher and principal assignments, resource allocation, and quality of education. DCSS was ordered to take measures to address the remaining problems.

B

Proper resolution of any desegregation case turns on a careful assessment of its facts. Here, as in most cases where the issue is the degree of compliance with a school desegregation decree, a critical beginning point is the degree of racial imbalance in the school district, that is to say a comparison of the proportion of majority to minority students in individual schools with the proportions of the races in the district as a whole. This inquiry is fundamental, for under the former *de jure* regimes racial exclusion was both the means and the end of a policy motivated by disparagement of or hostility towards the disfavored race. In accord with this principle, the District Court began its analysis with an assessment of the current racial mix in the schools throughout DCSS and the explanation for the racial imbalance it found....

In the extensive record that comprises this case, one fact predominates: remarkable changes in the racial composition of the county presented DCSS and the District Court with a student population in 1986 far different from the one they set out to integrate in 1969. Between 1950 and 1985, DeKalb County grew from 70,000 to 450,000 in total population, but most of the gross increase in student enrollment had occurred by 1969, the relevant starting date for our purposes. Although the public school population experienced only modest changes between 1969 and 1986 (remaining in the low 70,000's), a striking change occurred in the racial proportions of the student population. The school system that the District Court ordered desegregated in 1969 had 5.6% black students; by 1986 the percentage of black students was 47%.

To compound the difficulty of working with these radical demographic changes, the northern and southern parts of the county experienced much different growth patterns. The District Court found that "[a]s the result of these demographic shifts, the population of the northern half of DeKalb County is now predominantly white and the southern half of DeKalb County is predominantly black." In 1970, there were 7,615 nonwhites living in the northern part of DeKalb County and 11,508 nonwhites in the southern part of the county. By 1980, there were 15,365 nonwhites living in the northern part of the county, and 87,583 nonwhites in the southern part. Most of the growth in the nonwhite population in the southern portion of the county was due to the migration of black persons from the city of Atlanta. Between 1975 and 1980 alone, approximately 64,000 black citizens moved into southern DeKalb County, most of them coming from Atlanta. During the same period, approximately 37,000 white citizens moved out of southern DeKalb County to the surrounding counties.

. . .

The demographic changes that occurred during the course of the desegregation order are an essential foundation for the District Court's analysis of the current racial mix of DCSS. As the District Court observed, the demographic shifts have had "an immense effect on the racial compositions of the DeKalb County schools." From 1976 to 1986, enrollment in elementary schools declined overall by 15%, while black enrollment in elementary schools increased by 86%. During the same period, overall high school enrollment declined by 16%, while black enrollment in high school increased by 119%. These effects were even more pronounced in the southern portion of DeKalb County....

Respondents argued in the District Court that this racial imbalance in student assignment was a vestige of the dual system, rather than a product of independent demographic forces. In addition to the statistical evidence that the ratio of black students to white students in individual schools varied to a significant degree from the system-wide average, respondents contended that DCSS had not used all available desegregative tools in order to achieve racial balancing....

Although the District Court found that DCSS was desegregated for at least a short period under the court-ordered plan of 1969, it did not base its finding that DCSS had achieved unitary status with respect to student assignment on that circumstance alone. Recognizing that "[t]he achievement of unitary status in the area of student assignment cannot be hedged on the attainment of such status for a brief moment," the District Court examined the interaction between DCSS policy and demographic shifts in DeKalb County.

The District Court noted that DCSS had taken specific steps to combat the effects of demographics on the racial mix of the schools. Under the 1969 order, a biracial committee had reviewed all proposed changes in the boundary lines of school attendance zones. Since the original desegregation order, there had been about 170 such changes. It was found that only three had a partial segregative effect....

The District Court also noted that DCSS, on its own initiative, ... [had taken some steps to promote more balanced student assignments]....

Having found no constitutional violation with respect to student assignment, the District Court next considered the other *Green* factors, beginning with faculty and staff assignments.... [It ordered more to be done to integrate teachers and to disperse black administrators throughout the system.] ...

Addressing the more ineffable category of quality of education, the District Court rejected most of respondents' contentions that there was racial disparity in the provision of certain educational resources (e.g., teachers with advanced degrees, teachers with more experience, library books), contentions made to show that black students were not being given equal educational opportunity. The District Court went further, however, and examined the evidence concerning achievement of black students in DCSS. It cited expert testimony praising the overall educational program in the district, as well as objective evidence of black achievement....

Despite its finding that there was no intentional violation, the District Court found that DCSS had not achieved unitary status with respect to quality of education because teachers in schools with disproportionately high percentages of white students tended to be better educated and have more experience than their counterparts in schools with disproportionately high percentages of black students, and because per pupil expenditures in majority white schools exceeded per pupil expenditures in majority black schools. From these findings, the District Court ordered DCSS to equalize spending and remedy the other problems.

The final *Green* factors considered by the District Court were: (1) physical facilities, (2) transportation, and (3) extracurricular activities....

In accordance with its factfinding, the District Court held that it would order no further relief in the areas of student assignment, transportation, physical facilities and extracurricular activities. The District Court, however, did order DCSS to establish a system to balance teacher and principal assignments and to equalize per pupil expenditures throughout DCSS. Having found that blacks were represented on the school board and throughout DCSS administration, the District Court abolished the biracial committee as no longer necessary.

Both parties appealed to the United States Court of Appeals for the Eleventh Circuit.... [which held that the board had to satisfy all six *Green* factors at the same time in order to achieve unitary status].

II

Two principal questions are presented. The first is whether a district court may relinquish its supervision and control over those aspects of a school system in which there has been compliance with a desegregation decree if other aspects of the system remain in noncompliance. As we answer this question in the affirmative, the second question is whether the Court of Appeals erred in reversing the District Court's order providing for incremental withdrawal of supervision in all the circumstances of this case.

A

The duty and responsibility of a school district once segregated by law is to take all steps necessary to eliminate the vestiges of the unconstitutional *de jure* system. This is required in order to insure that the principal wrong of the *de jure* system, the injuries and stigma inflicted upon the race disfavored by the violation, is no longer present....

The concept of unitariness has been a helpful one in defining the scope of the district courts' authority, for it conveys the central idea that a school district that was once a dual system must be examined in all of its facets, both when a remedy is ordered and in the later phases of desegregation when the question is whether the district courts' remedial control ought to be modified, lessened, or withdrawn. But, as we explained last term in *Board of Education of Oklahoma City v. Dowell,* the term "unitary" is not a precise concept:

> "[I]t is a mistake to treat words such as 'dual' and 'unitary' as if they were actually found in the Constitution.... Courts have used the term 'dual' to denote a school system which has engaged in intentional segregation of students by race, and 'unitary' to describe a school system which has been brought into compliance with the command of the Constitution. We are not sure how useful it is to define these terms more precisely, or to create subclasses within them."

It follows that we must be cautious not to attribute to the term a utility it does not have. The term "unitary" does not confine the discretion and authority of the District Court in a way that departs from traditional equitable principles.

That the term "unitary" does not have fixed meaning or content is not inconsistent with the principles that control the exercise of equitable power. The essence of a court's equity power lies in its inherent capacity to adjust remedies in a feasible and practical way to eliminate the conditions or redress the injuries caused by unlawful action. Equitable remedies must be flexible if these underlying principles are to be enforced with fairness and precision. . . .

. . . A federal court in a school desegregation case has the discretion to order an incremental or partial withdrawal of its supervision and control. This discretion derives both from the constitutional authority which justified its intervention in the first instance and its ultimate objectives in formulating the decree. The authority of the court is invoked at the outset to remedy particular constitutional violations. In construing the remedial authority of the district courts, we have been guided by the principles that "judicial powers may be exercised only on the basis of a constitutional violation," and that "the nature of the violation determines the scope of the remedy." A remedy is justifiable only insofar as it advances the ultimate objective of alleviating the initial constitutional violation.

We have said that the court's end purpose must be to remedy the violation and in addition to restore state and local authorities to the control of a school system that is operating in compliance with the Constitution. . . . Partial relinquishment of judicial control, where justified by the facts of the case, can be an important and significant step in fulfilling the district court's duty to return the operations and control of schools to local authorities. . . .

We hold that, in the course of supervising desegregation plans, federal courts have the authority to relinquish supervision and control of school districts in incremental stages, before full compliance has been achieved in every area of school operations. While retaining jurisdiction over the case, the court may determine that it will not order further remedies in areas where the school district is in compliance with the decree. That is to say, upon a finding that a school system subject to a court-supervised desegregation plan is in compliance in some but not all areas, the court in appropriate cases may return control to the school system in those areas where compliance has been achieved, limiting further judicial supervision to operations that are not yet in full compliance with the court decree. In particular, the district court may determine that it will not order further remedies in the area of student assignments where racial imbalance is not traceable, in a proximate way, to constitutional violations.

A court's discretion to order the incremental withdrawal of its supervision in a school desegregation case must be exercised in a manner consistent with the purposes and objectives of its equitable power. Among the factors which must inform the sound discretion of the court in ordering partial withdrawal are the following: whether there has been full and satisfactory compliance with the decree in those aspects of the system where supervision is to be withdrawn; whether retention of judicial control is necessary or practicable to achieve compliance with the decree in other facets of the school system; and whether the school district has demonstrated, to the public and to the parents and students of the once disfavored race, its good faith commitment to the whole of the court's decree and to those provisions of the law and the Constitution that were the predicate for judicial intervention in the first instance.

In considering these factors a court should give particular attention to the school system's record of compliance. A school system is better positioned to demonstrate its good-faith commitment to a constitutional course of action when its policies form a consistent pattern of lawful conduct directed to eliminating earlier violations. . . .

B

We reach now the question whether the Court of Appeals erred in prohibiting the District Court from returning to DCSS partial control over some of its affairs. We decide that the Court of Appeals did err in holding that, as a matter of law, the District Court had no discretion to permit DCSS to regain control over student assignment, transportation, physical facilities, and extracurricular activities, while retaining court supervision over the areas of faculty and administrative assignments and the quality of education, where full compliance had not been demonstrated.

It was an appropriate exercise of its discretion for the District Court to address the elements of a unitary system discussed in *Green,* to inquire whether other elements ought to be identified, and to determine whether minority students were being disadvantaged in ways that required the formulation of new and further remedies to insure full compliance with the court's decree. Both parties agreed that quality of education was a legitimate inquiry in determining DCSS' compliance with the desegregation decree, and the trial court found it workable to consider the point in connection with its findings on resource allocation. . . . The District Court's approach illustrates that the *Green* factors need not be a rigid framework. . . .

That there was racial imbalance in student attendance zones was not tantamount to a showing that the school district was in noncompliance with the decree or with its duties under the law. Racial balance is not to be achieved for its own sake. It is to be pursued when racial imbalance has been caused by a constitutional violation. Once the racial imbalance due to the *de jure* violation has been remedied, the school district is under no duty to remedy imbalance that is caused by demographic factors. . . . If the unlawful *de jure* policy of a school system has been the cause of the racial imbalance in student attendance, that condition must be remedied. The school district bears the burden of showing that any current imbalance is not traceable, in a proximate way, to the prior violation.

The findings of the District Court that the population changes which occurred in DeKalb County were not caused by the policies of the school district, but rather by independent factors, are consistent with the mobility that is a distinct characteristic of our society. . . .

The requirement that the school district show its good faith commitment to the entirety of a desegregation plan so that parents, students and the public have assurance against further injuries or stigma also should be a subject for more specific findings. We stated in [*Board of Educ. of Oklahoma City v.*] *Dowell* that the good faith compliance of the district with the court order over a reasonable period of time is a factor to be considered in deciding whether or not jurisdiction could be relinquished. A history of good-faith compliance is evidence that any current racial imbalance is not the product of a new *de jure* violation, and enables the district court to accept the school board's representation that it has accepted the principle of racial equality and will not suffer intentional discrimination in the future. . . .

Notes

1. Consider the Court's emphasis in the first paragraph under I B. Also observe its repeated emphasis on the element of good-faith compliance.

2. The Court placed the burden of showing that any current imbalance in student attendance patterns is not the result of earlier de jure segregation on local school boards. Was this fair? Was it appropriate?

3. What do you think of this case? Can a school system truly be desegregated if elements of segregation remain?

[Case No. 131]   Limits on Judicial Authority in School Desegregation Litigation

MISSOURI v. JENKINS (III)

Supreme Court of the United States, 1995.
515 U.S. 70, 115 S.Ct. 2038, 132 L.Ed.2d 63 [100 Educ. L. Rep. 506].

CHIEF JUSTICE REHNQUIST delivered the opinion of the Court.

As this school desegregation litigation enters its 18th year, we are called upon again to review the decisions of the lower courts. In this case, the State of Missouri has challenged the District Court's order of salary increases for virtually all instructional and noninstructional staff within the Kansas City, Missouri, School District (KCMSD) and the District Court's order requiring the State to continue to fund remedial "quality education" programs because student achievement levels were still "at or below national norms at many grade levels."

I

A general overview of this litigation is necessary for proper resolution of the issues upon which we granted certiorari. This case has been before the same United States District Judge since 1977. . . . Plaintiffs alleged that the State, the surrounding suburban school districts (SSD's), and various federal agencies had caused and perpetuated a system of racial segregation in the schools of the Kansas City metropolitan area. The District Court realigned the KCMSD as a nominal defendant and certified as a class, present and future KCMSD students. The KCMSD brought a cross-claim against the State for its failure to eliminate the vestiges of its prior dual school system.

After a trial that lasted 7 1/2 months, the District Court dismissed the case against the federal defendants and the SSD's, but determined that the State and the KCMSD were liable for an intradistrict violation, i.e., they had operated a segregated school system within the KCMSD. The District Court determined that prior to 1954 "Missouri mandated segregated schools for black and white children." Furthermore, the KCMSD and the State had failed in their affirmative obligations to eliminate the vestiges of the State's dual school system within the KCMSD.

In June 1985, the District Court issued its first remedial order and established as its goal the "elimination of all vestiges of state imposed segregation." The District Court determined that "[s]egregation ha[d] caused a system wide reduction in student achievement in the schools of the KCMSD." The District Court made no particularized findings regarding the extent that student achievement had been reduced or what portion of that reduction was attributable to segregation....

The District Court, pursuant to plans submitted by the KCMSD and the State, ordered a wide range of quality education programs for all students attending the KCMSD....

The KCMSD was awarded an AAA rating in the 1987–1988 school year, and there is no dispute that since that time it has " 'maintained and greatly exceeded AAA requirements.' " The total cost for these quality education programs has exceeded $220 million.

The District Court also set out to desegregate the KCMSD but believed that "[t]o accomplish desegregation within the boundary lines of a school district whose enrollment remains 68.3% black is a difficult task." Because it had found no interdistrict violation, the District Court could not order mandatory interdistrict redistribution of students between the KCMSD and the surrounding SSD's. The District Court refused to order additional mandatory student reassignments because they would "increase the instability of the KCMSD and reduce the potential for desegregation." ...

In November 1986, the District Court approved a comprehensive magnet school and capital improvements plan and held the State and the KCMSD jointly and severally liable for its funding. Under the District Court's plan, every senior high school, every middle school, and one-half of the elementary schools were converted into magnet schools. The District Court adopted the magnet-school program to "provide a greater educational opportunity to all KCMSD students" and because it believed "that the proposed magnet plan [was] so attractive that it would draw non-minority students from the private schools who have abandoned or avoided the KCMSD, and draw in additional non-minority students from the suburbs...." Since its inception, the magnet-school program has operated at a cost, including magnet transportation, in excess of $448 million ...

In June 1985, the District Court ordered substantial capital improvements to combat the deterioration of the KCMSD's facilities.... [it] dismissed as "irrelevant" the "State's argument that the present condition of the facilities [was] not traceable to unlawful segregation." Instead, the District Court focused on its responsibility to "remed[y] the vestiges of segregation" and to "implemen[t] a desegregation plan which w[ould] maintain and attract non-minority enrollment." The initial phase of the capital-improvements plan cost $37 million. The District Court also required the KCMSD to present further capital-improvements proposals "in order to bring its facilities to a point comparable with the facilities in neighboring suburban school districts." In November 1986, the District Court approved further capital improvements in order to remove the vestiges of racial segregation and "to ... attract non-minority students back to the KCMSD."

In September 1987, the District Court adopted, for the most part, KCMSD's long-range capital-improvements plan at a cost in excess of $187 million. The plan called for the renovation of approximately 55 schools, the closure of 18 facilities, and the construction of 17 new schools.... As of 1990, the District Court had ordered $260 million in capital improvements. Since then, the total cost of capital improvements ordered has soared to over $540 million.

As part of its desegregation plan, the District Court has ordered salary assistance ... only for teachers within the KCMSD. Since that time, however, the District Court has ordered salary assistance to all but three of the approximately 5,000 KCMSD employees. The total cost of this component of the desegregation remedy since 1987 is over $200 million.

The District Court's desegregation plan has been described as the most ambitious and expensive remedial program in the history of school desegregation. The annual cost per pupil at the KCMSD far exceeds that of the neighboring SSD's or of any school district in Missouri. Nevertheless, the KCMSD, which has pursued a "friendly adversary" relationship with the plaintiffs, has continued to propose ever more expensive programs. As a result, the desegregation costs have escalated and now are approaching an annual cost of $200 million. These massive expenditures have financed high schools in which every classroom will have air conditioning, an alarm system, and 15 microcomputers; a 2,000–square-foot planetarium; green houses and vivariums; a 25–acre farm with an air-conditioned meeting room for 104 people; a Model United Nations wired for language translation; broadcast capable radio and television studios with an editing and animation lab; a temperature controlled art gallery; movie editing and screening rooms; a 3,500–square-foot dust-free diesel mechanics room; 1,875–square-foot elementary school animal rooms for use in a zoo project; swimming pools; and numerous other facilities. Not surprisingly, the cost of this remedial plan has "far exceeded KCMSD's budget, or for that matter, its authority to tax." The State ... has borne the brunt of these costs.

II

With this background, we turn to the present controversy. First, the State has challenged the District Court's requirement that it fund salary increases for KCMSD instructional and noninstructional staff. The State claimed that funding for salaries was beyond the scope of the District Court's remedial authority. Second, the State has challenged the District Court's order requiring it to continue to fund the remedial quality education programs for the 1992–1993 school year.

The District Court rejected the State's arguments. . . .

The Court of Appeals for the Eighth Circuit affirmed. . . . [and later] denied rehearing en banc, with five judges dissenting. . . .

Because of the importance of the issues, we granted certiorari to consider the following: (1) whether the District Court exceeded its constitutional authority when it granted salary increases to virtually all instructional and noninstructional employees of the KCMSD, and (2) whether the District Court properly relied upon the fact that student achievement test scores had failed to rise to some unspecified level when it declined to find that the State had achieved partial unitary status as to the quality education programs.

III

Respondents argue that the State may no longer challenge the District Court's remedy, and in any event, the propriety of the remedy is not before the Court. We disagree on both counts. In *Jenkins II*, we granted certiorari to review the manner in which the District Court had funded this desegregation remedy. Because we had denied *certiorari* on the State's challenge to review the scope of the remedial order, we resisted the State's efforts to challenge the scope of the remedy. Thus, we neither "approv[ed]" nor "disapprov[ed] the Court of Appeals' conclusion that the District Court's remedy was proper."

Here, however, the State has challenged the District Court's approval of across-the-board salary increases for instructional and noninstructional employees as an action beyond its remedial authority. An analysis of the permissible scope of the District Court's remedial authority is necessary for a proper determination of whether the order of salary increases is beyond the District Court's remedial authority and thus, it is an issue subsidiary to our ultimate inquiry. Given that the District Court's basis for its salary order was grounded in "improving the desegregative attractiveness of the KCMSD" we must consider the propriety of that reliance in order to resolve properly the State's challenge to that order. We conclude that a challenge to the scope of the District Court's remedy is fairly included in the question presented.

. . .

In short, the State has challenged the scope of the District Court's remedial authority. . . . there is no unfairness or imprudence in deciding issues that have been passed upon below, are properly before us, and have been briefed by the parties. We turn to the questions presented.

Almost 25 years ago, in *Swann v. Charlotte–Mecklenburg Board of Education* we dealt with the authority of a district court to fashion remedies for a school district that had been segregated in law in violation of the Equal Protection Clause of the Fourteenth Amendment.... we also recognized the limits on such remedial power....

Three years later, in *Milliken I* we held that a District Court had exceeded its authority in fashioning interdistrict relief where the surrounding school districts had not themselves been guilty of any constitutional violation. We said that a desegregation remedy "is necessarily designed, as all remedies are, to restore the victims of discriminatory conduct to the position they would have occupied in the absence of such conduct." ...

Three years later, in *Milliken v. Bradley (Milliken II)*, we articulated a three-part framework derived from our prior cases to guide district courts in the exercise of their remedial authority.

In the first place, like other equitable remedies, the nature of the desegregation remedy is to be determined by the nature and scope of the constitutional violation. *Swann v. Charlotte–Mecklenburg Board of Education*. The remedy must therefore be related to "the condition alleged to offend the Constitution...." Second, the decree must indeed be remedial in nature, that is, it must be designed as nearly as possible "to restore the victims of discriminatory conduct to the position they would have occupied in the absence of such conduct." Third, the federal courts in devising a remedy must take into account the interests of state and local authorities in managing their own affairs, consistent with the Constitution.

We added that the "principle that the nature and scope of the remedy are to be determined by the violation means simply that federal-court decrees must directly address and relate to the constitutional violation itself." In applying these principles, we have identified "student assignments, ... 'faculty, staff, transportation, extracurricular activities and facilities'" as the most important indicia of a racially segregated school system.

Because "federal supervision of local school systems was intended as a temporary measure to remedy past discrimination" we also have considered the showing that must be made by a school district operating under a desegregation order for complete or partial relief from that order. In Freeman, we stated that

> [a]mong the factors which must inform the sound discretion of the court in ordering partial withdrawal are the following: [1] whether there has been full and satisfactory compliance with the decree in those aspects of the system where supervision is to be withdrawn; [2] whether retention of judicial control is necessary or practicable to achieve compliance with the decree in other facets of the school system; and [3] whether the school district has demonstrated, to the public and to the parents and students of the once disfavored race, its good-faith commitment to the whole of the courts' decree and to those provisions of the law and the Constitution that were the predicate for judicial intervention in the first instance.

The ultimate inquiry is " 'whether the [constitutional violator] ha[s] complied in good faith with the desegregation decree since it was entered, and whether the vestiges of past discrimination ha[ve] been eliminated to the extent practicable.' "

Proper analysis of the District Court's orders challenged here, then, must rest upon their serving as proper means to the end of restoring the victims of discriminatory conduct to the position they would have occupied in the absence of that conduct and their eventual restoration of "state and local authorities to the control of a school system that is operating in compliance with the Constitution."

The State argues that the order approving salary increases is beyond the District Court's authority because it was crafted to serve an "interdistrict goal," in spite of the fact that the constitutional violation in this case is "intradistrict" in nature. "[T]he nature of the desegregation remedy is to be determined by the nature and scope of the constitutional violation." The proper response to an intradistrict violation is an intradistrict remedy that serves to eliminate the racial identity of the schools within the affected school district by eliminating, as far as practicable, the vestiges of de jure segregation in all facets of their operations.

. . . this case involved no interdistrict constitutional violation that would support interdistrict relief. Thus, the proper response by the District Court should have been to eliminate to the extent practicable the vestiges of prior de jure segregation within the KCMSD: a system-wide reduction in student achievement and the existence of 25 racially identifiable schools with a population of over 90% black students.

The District Court and Court of Appeals, however, have felt that because the KCMSD's enrollment remained 68.3% black, a purely intradistrict remedy would be insufficient. But, as noted in Milliken I we have rejected the suggestion "that schools which have a majority of Negro students are not 'desegregated' whatever the racial makeup of the school district's population and however neutrally the district lines have been drawn and administered."

Instead of seeking to remove the racial identity of the various schools within the KCMSD, the District Court has set out on a program to create a school district that was equal to or superior to the surrounding SSD's. Its remedy has focused on "desegregative attractiveness," coupled with "suburban comparability. . . ."

The purpose of desegregative attractiveness has been not only to remedy the system-wide reduction in student achievement, but also to attract nonminority students not presently enrolled in the KCMSD. This remedy has included an elaborate program of capital improvements, course enrichment, and extracurricular enhancement not simply in the formerly identifiable black schools, but in schools throughout the district. The District Court's remedial orders have converted every senior high school, every middle school, and one-half of the elementary schools in the KCMSD into "magnet" schools. The District Court's remedial order has all but made the KCMSD itself into a magnet district.

. . .

The District Court's remedial plan in this case, however, is not designed solely to redistribute the students within the KCMSD in order to eliminate racially identifiable schools within the KCMSD. Instead, its purpose is to attract nonminority students from outside the KCMSD schools. But this interdistrict goal is beyond the scope of the intradistrict violation identified by the District Court. In effect, the District Court has devised a remedy to accomplish indirectly what it admittedly lacks the remedial authority to mandate directly: the interdistrict transfer of students.

In *Milliken I* we determined that a desegregation remedy that would require mandatory interdistrict reassignment of students throughout the Detroit metropolitan area was an impermissible interdistrict response to the intradistrict violation identified.... We held that before a district court could order an interdistrict remedy, there must be a showing that "racially discriminatory acts of the state or local school districts, or of a single school district have been a substantial cause of interdistrict segregation."

. . .

What we meant in *Milliken I* by an interdistrict violation was a violation that caused segregation between adjoining districts. Nothing in *Milliken I* suggests that the District Court in that case could have circumvented the limits on its remedial authority by requiring the State of Michigan, a constitutional violator, to implement a magnet program designed to achieve the same interdistrict transfer of students that we held was beyond its remedial authority. Here, the District Court has done just that: created a magnet district of the KCMSD in order to serve the interdistrict goal of attracting nonminority students from the surrounding SSD's and distributing them within the KCMSD. The District Court's pursuit of "desegregative attractiveness" is beyond the scope of its broad remedial authority.

Respondents argue that the District Court's reliance upon desegregative attractiveness is justified in light of the District Court's statement that segregation has "led to 'white flight' from the KCMSD to suburban districts." The lower courts' "findings" as to "white flight" are both inconsistent internally and inconsistent with the typical supposition, bolstered here by the record evidence, that "white flight" may result from desegregation, not de jure segregation. The United States, as amicus curiae, argues that the District Court's finding that "de jure segregation in the KCMSD caused white students to leave the system ... is not inconsistent with the district court's earlier conclusion that the suburban districts did nothing to cause this 'white flight' and therefore could not be included in a mandatory interdistrict remedy." But the District Court's earlier findings, affirmed by the Court of Appeals, were not so limited....

In *Freeman*, we stated that "[t]he vestiges of segregation that are the concern of the law in a school case may be subtle and intangible but nonetheless they must be so real that they have a causal link to the de jure violation being remedied." The record here does not support the District Court's reliance on "white flight" as a justification for a permissible expansion of its intradistrict remedial authority through its pursuit of desegregative attractiveness.

. . .

The District Court's pursuit of "desegregative attractiveness" cannot be reconciled with our cases placing limitations on a district court's remedial authority. It is certainly theoretically possible that the greater the expenditure per pupil within the KCMSD, the more likely it is that some unknowable number of nonminority students not presently attending schools in the KCMSD will choose to enroll in those schools. Under this reasoning, however, every increased expenditure, whether it be for teachers, noninstructional employees, books, or buildings, will make the KCMSD in some way more attractive, and thereby perhaps induce nonminority students to enroll in its schools. But this rationale is not susceptible to any objective limitation. This case provides numerous examples demonstrating the limitless authority of the District Court operating under this rationale. In short, desegregative attractiveness has been used "as the hook on which to hang numerous policy choices about improving the quality of education in general within the KCMSD."

Nor are there limits to the duration of the District Court's involvement. The expenditures per pupil in the KCMSD currently far exceed those in the neighboring SSD's. Sixteen years after this litigation began, the District Court recognized that the KCMSD has yet to offer a viable method of financing the "wonderful school system being built." Each additional program ordered by the District Court—and financed by the State—to increase the "desegregative attractiveness" of the school district makes the KCMSD more and more dependent on additional funding from the State; in turn, the greater the KCMSD's dependence on state funding, the greater its reliance on continued supervision by the District Court. But our cases recognize that local autonomy of school districts is a vital national tradition and that a district court must strive to restore state and local authorities to the control of a school system operating in compliance with the Constitution.

The District Court's pursuit of the goal of "desegregative attractiveness" results in so many imponderables and is so far removed from the task of eliminating the racial identifiability of the schools within the KCMSD that we believe it is beyond the admittedly broad discretion of the District Court. In this posture, we conclude that the District Court's order of salary increases, which was "grounded in remedying the vestiges of segregation by improving the desegregative attractiveness of the KCMSD" is simply too far removed from an acceptable implementation of a permissible means to remedy previous legally mandated segregation.

Similar considerations lead us to conclude that the District Court's order requiring the State to continue to fund the quality education programs because student achievement levels were still "at or below national norms at many grade levels" cannot be sustained. The State does not seek from this Court a declaration of partial unitary status with respect to the quality education programs. It challenges the requirement of indefinite funding of a quality education program until national norms are met, based on the assumption that while a mandate for significant educational improvement, both in teaching and in facilities, may have been justified originally, its indefinite extension is not.

Our review in this respect is needlessly complicated because the District Court made no findings in its order approving continued funding of the quality education programs. Although the Court of Appeals later recognized that a determination of partial unitary status requires "careful fact finding and detailed articulation of findings" it declined to remand to the District Court. Instead it attempted to assemble an adequate record from the District Court's statements from the bench and subsequent orders. In one such order relied upon by the Court of Appeals, the District Court stated that the KCMSD had not reached anywhere close to its "maximum potential because the District is still at or below national norms at many grade levels."

But this clearly is not the appropriate test to be applied in deciding whether a previously segregated district has achieved partially unitary status. The basic task of the District Court is to decide whether the reduction in achievement by minority students attributable to prior de jure segregation has been remedied to the extent practicable. Under our precedents, the State and the KCMSD are "entitled to a rather precise statement of [their] obligations under a desegregation decree." Although the District Court has determined that "[s]egregation has caused a system wide reduction in achievement in the schools of the KCMSD" it never has identified the incremental effect that segregation has had on minority student achievement or the specific goals of the quality education programs.

In reconsidering this order, the District Court should apply our three-part test from *Freeman v. Pitts*. The District Court should consider that the State's role with respect to the quality education programs has been limited to the funding, not the implementation, of those programs. As all the parties agree that improved achievement on test scores is not necessarily required for the State to achieve partial unitary status as to the quality education programs, the District Court should sharply limit, if not dispense with, its reliance on this factor. Just as demographic changes independent of de jure segregation will affect the racial composition of student assignments, so too will numerous external factors beyond the control of the KCMSD and the State affect minority student achievement. So long as these external factors are not the result of segregation, they do not figure in the remedial calculus. Insistence upon academic goals unrelated to the effects of legal segregation unwarrantably postpones the day when the KCMSD will be able to operate on its own.

The District Court also should consider that many goals of its quality education plan already have been attained: the KCMSD now is equipped with "facilities and opportunities not available anywhere else in the country." KCMSD schools received an AAA rating eight years ago, and the present remedial programs have been in place for seven years. It may be that in education, just as it may be in economics, a "rising tide lifts all boats," but the remedial quality education program should be tailored to remedy the injuries suffered by the victims of prior de jure segregation. . . .

On remand, the District Court must bear in mind that its end purpose is not only "to remedy the violation" to the extent practicable, but also "to restore state and local authorities to the control of a school system that is operating in compliance with the Constitution."

The judgment of the Court of Appeals is reversed.

It is so ordered.

Notes

1. Note how the composition of the Court can influence the outcome of cases. The four dissenters in *Jenkins II*, Chief Justice Rehnquist and Justices Kennedy, O'Connor, and Scalia, were joined by Justice Thomas who was not on the bench in 1990, in creating the majority in this case.

2. The Court was clearly concerned with the cost of implementing the desegregation order in this case. Is such a concern justified?

*

APPENDIX

SELECTED PROVISIONS OF THE UNITED STATES CONSTITUTION

Article I

Section 1. All legislative Powers herein granted shall be vested in a Congress of the United States....

Section 8. The Congress shall have Power To.... provide for the ... general Welfare of the United States;....

Section 10. No State shall ... pass any ... law impairing the obligation of contracts....

Article II

Section 1. The executive Power shall be vested in a President of the United States of America.

Article III

Section 1. The judicial Power of the United States shall be vested in one supreme Court and in such inferior Courts as the Congress may from time to time ordain and establish.

Article VI

Section 2: This Constitution, and the Laws of the United States which shall be made in Pursuance thereof; and all Treaties made, or which shall be made, under the Authority of the United States, shall be the supreme Law of the Land; and the Judges in every State shall be bound thereby, any Thing in the Constitution or Laws of any State to the Contrary notwithstanding.

Amendment 1

Congress shall make no law respecting an establishment of religion, or prohibiting the free exercise thereof; or abridging the freedom of speech, or of the press; or the right of the people peaceably to assemble, and to petition the Government for a redress of grievances.

Amendment 4

The right of the people to be secure in their persons, houses, papers, and effects, against unreasonable searches and seizures, shall not be violated, and no warrants shall issue, but upon probable cause, supported by oath or affirmation, and particularly describing the place to be searched, and the persons or things to be seized.

Amendment 5

No person ... shall be compelled in any criminal case to be a witness against himself, nor be deprived of life, liberty, or property, without due process of law; nor shall private property be taken for public use, without just compensation.

Amendment 8

Excessive bail shall not be required, nor excessive fines imposed, nor cruel and unusual punishments inflicted.

Amendment 10

The powers not delegated to the United States by the Constitution, nor prohibited by it to the States, are reserved to the States respectively, or to the people.

Amendment 11

The judicial power of the United States shall not be construed to extend to any suit in law or equity, commenced or prosecuted against one of the United States by citizens of another State, or by citizens or subjects of any foreign State.

Amendment 14

Section 1. All persons born or naturalized in the United States, and subject to the jurisdiction thereof, are citizens of the United States and of the State wherein they reside. No State shall make or enforce any law which shall abridge the privileges or immunities of citizens of the United States; nor shall any State deprive any person of life, liberty, or property, without due process of law; nor deny to any person within its jurisdiction the equal protection of the laws.

SELECTED FEDERAL STATUTORY PROVISIONS APPLICABLE TO SCHOOLS

Family Educational Rights and Privacy Act

20 U.S.C.A. § 1232g

(a) Conditions for availability of funds to educational agencies or institutions; inspection and review of education records; specific information to be made available; procedure for access to education records; reasonableness of time for such access; hearings; written explanations by parents; definitions

(1)(A) No funds shall be made available under any applicable program to any educational agency or institution which has a policy of denying, or which effectively prevents, the parents of students who are or have been in attendance at a school of such agency or at such institution, as the case may be, the right to inspect and review the education records of their children. If any material or document in the education record of a student includes information on more than one student, the parents of one of such students shall have the right to inspect and review only such part of such material or document as relates to such student or to be informed of the specific information contained in such part of such material. Each educational agency or institution shall establish appropriate procedures for the granting of a request by parents for access to the education records of their children within a reasonable period of time, but in no case more than forty-five days after the request has been made.

(B) No funds under any applicable program shall be made available to any State educational agency (whether or not that agency is an educational agency or institution under this section) that has a policy of denying, or effectively prevents, the parents of students the right to inspect and review the education records maintained by the State educational agency on their children who are or have been in attendance at any school of an educational agency or institution that is subject to the provisions of this section.

(C) The first sentence of subparagraph (A) shall not operate to make available to students in institutions of postsecondary education the following materials:

(i) financial records of the parents of the student or any information contained therein;

(ii) confidential letters and statements of recommendation, which were placed in the education records prior to January 1, 1975, if such letters or statements are not used for purposes other than those for which they were specifically intended;

(iii) if the student has signed a waiver of the student's right of access under this subsection in accordance with subparagraph (D), confidential recommendations—

(I) respecting admission to any educational agency or institution,

(II) respecting an application for employment, and

(III) respecting the receipt of an honor or honorary recognition.

(D) A student or a person applying for admission may waive his right of access to confidential statements described in clause (iii) of subparagraph (C), except that such waiver shall apply to recommendations only if (i) the student is, upon request, notified of the names of all persons making confidential recommendations and (ii) such recommendations are used solely for the purpose for which they were specifically intended. Such waivers may not be required as a condition for admission to, receipt of financial aid from, or receipt of any other services or benefits from such agency or institution.

(2) No funds shall be made available under any applicable program to any educational agency or institution unless the parents of students who are or have been in attendance at a school of such agency or at such institution are provided an opportunity for a hearing by such agency or institution, in accordance with regulations of the Secretary, to challenge the content of such student's education records, in order to insure that the records are not inaccurate, misleading, or otherwise in violation of the privacy rights of students, and to provide an opportunity for the correction or deletion of any such inaccurate, misleading or otherwise inappropriate data contained therein and to insert into such records a written explanation of the parents respecting the content of such records.

(3) For the purposes of this section the term "educational agency or institution" means any public or private agency or institution which is the recipient of funds under any applicable program.

(4)(A) For the purposes of this section, the term "education records" means, except as may be provided otherwise in subparagraph (B), those records, files, documents, and other materials which—

(i) contain information directly related to a student; and

(ii) are maintained by an educational agency or institution or by a person acting for such agency or institution.

(B) The term "education records" does not include—

(i) records of instructional, supervisory, and administrative personnel and educational personnel ancillary thereto which are in the sole possession of the maker thereof and which are not accessible or revealed to any other person except a substitute;

(ii) records maintained by a law enforcement unit of the educational agency or institution that were created by that law enforcement unit for the purpose of law enforcement;

(iii) in the case of persons who are employed by an educational agency or institution but who are not in attendance at such agency or institution, records made and maintained in the normal course of business which relate exclusively to such person in that person's capacity as an employee and are not available for use for any other purpose; or

(iv) records on a student who is eighteen years of age or older, or is attending an institution of postsecondary education, which are made or maintained by a physician, psychiatrist, psychologist, or other recognized professional or paraprofessional acting in his professional or paraprofessional capacity, or assisting in that capacity, and which are made, maintained, or used only in connection with the provision of treatment to the student, and are not available to anyone other than persons providing such treatment, except that such records can be personally reviewed by a physician or other appropriate professional of the student's choice.

(5)(A) For the purposes of this section the term "directory information" relating to a student includes the following: the student's name, address, telephone listing, date and place of birth, major field of study, participation in officially recognized activities and sports, weight and height of members of athletic teams, dates of attendance, degrees and awards received, and the most recent previous educational agency or institution attended by the student.

(B) Any educational agency or institution making public directory information shall give public notice of the categories of information which it has designated as such information with respect to each student attending the institution or agency and shall allow a reasonable period of time after such notice has been given for a parent to inform the institution or agency that any or all of the information designated should not be released without the parent's prior consent.

(6) For the purposes of this section, the term "student" includes any person with respect to whom an educational agency or institution maintains education records or personally identifiable information, but does not include a person who has not been in attendance at such agency or institution.

(b) Release of education records; parental consent requirement; exceptions; compliance with judicial orders and subpoenas; audit and evaluation of federally-supported education programs; recordkeeping

(1) No funds shall be made available under any applicable program to any educational agency or institution which has a policy or practice of permitting the release of education records (or personally identifiable information contained therein other than directory information, as defined in paragraph (5) of subsection (a) of this section) of students without the written consent of their parents to any individual, agency, or organization, other than to the following—

(A) other school officials, including teachers within the educational institution or local educational agency, who have been determined by such agency or institution to have legitimate educational interests, including the educational interests of the child for whom consent would otherwise be required;

(B) officials of other schools or school systems in which the student seeks or intends to enroll, upon condition that the student's parents be notified of the transfer, receive a copy of the record if desired, and have an opportunity for a hearing to challenge the content of the record;

(C)(i) authorized representatives of (I) the Comptroller General of the United States, (II) the Secretary, or (III) State educational authorities, under the conditions set forth in paragraph (3), or (ii) authorized representatives of the Attorney General for law enforcement purposes under the same conditions as apply to the Secretary under paragraph (3);

(D) in connection with a student's application for, or receipt of, financial aid;

(E) State and local officials or authorities to whom such information is specifically allowed to be reported or disclosed pursuant to State statute adopted—

(i) before November 19, 1974 . . .

(ii) after November 19, 1974, if—
(I) the allowed reporting or disclosure concerns the juvenile justice system and such system's ability to effectively serve, prior to adjudication, the student whose records are released; and
(II) the officials and authorities to whom such information is disclosed certify in writing to the educational agency or institution that the information will not be disclosed to any other party except as provided under State law without the prior written consent of the parent of the student.

(F) organizations conducting studies for, or on behalf of, educational agencies or institutions for the purpose of developing, validating, or administering predictive tests, administering student aid programs, and improving instruction, if such studies are conducted in such a manner as will not permit the personal identification of students and their parents by persons other than representatives of such organizations and such information will be destroyed when no longer needed for the purpose for which it is conducted;

(G) accrediting organizations in order to carry out their accrediting functions;

(H) parents of a dependent student of such parents, as defined in section 152 of Title 26;

(I) subject to regulations of the Secretary, in connection with an emergency, appropriate persons if the knowledge of such information is necessary to protect the health or safety of the student or other persons; and

(J)(i) the entity or persons designated in a Federal grand jury subpoena, in which case the court shall order, for good cause shown, the educational agency or institution (and any officer, director, employee, agent, or attorney for such agency or institution) on which the subpoena is served, to not disclose to any person the existence or contents of the subpoena or any information furnished to the grand jury in response to the subpoena; and

(ii) the entity or persons designated in any other subpoena issued for a law enforcement purpose, in which case the court or other issuing agency may order, for good cause shown, the educational agency or institution (and any officer, director, employee, agent, or attorney for such agency or institution) on which the subpoena is served, to not disclose to any person the existence or contents of the subpoena or any information furnished in response to the subpoena. . . .

Individuals with Disabilities Education Act

20 U.S.C.A. §§ 1400 *et seq.*

§ 1401   Definitions

Except as otherwise provided, in this chapter:

(3) Child with a disability

(A) In general

The term "child with a disability" means a child—

(i) with mental retardation, hearing impairments (including deafness), speech or language impairments, visual impairments (including blindness), serious emotional disturbance (referred to in this chapter as "emotional disturbance"), orthopedic impairments, autism, traumatic brain injury, other health impairments, or specific learning disabilities; and

(ii) who, by reason thereof, needs special education and related services.

(B) Child aged 3 through 9

The term "child with a disability" for a child aged 3 through 9 (or any subset of that age range, including ages 3 through 5), may, at the discretion of the State and the local educational agency, include a child—

(i) experiencing developmental delays, as defined by the State and as measured by appropriate diagnostic instruments and procedures, in 1 or more of the following areas: physical development; cognitive development; communication development; social or emotional development; or adaptive development; and

(ii) who, by reason thereof, needs special education and related services.

(9) Free appropriate public education

The term "free appropriate public education" means special education and related services that—

(A) have been provided at public expense, under public supervision and direction, and without charge;

(B) meet the standards of the State educational agency;

(C) include an appropriate preschool, elementary school, or secondary school education in the State involved; and

(D) are provided in conformity with the individualized education program required under section 1414(d) of this title.

(10) Highly qualified

(A) In general

For any special education teacher, the term "highly qualified" has the meaning given the term in section 9101 of the Elementary and Secondary Education Act of 1965 [20 U.S.C.A. § 7801], except that such term also—

(i) includes the requirements described in subparagraph (B); and

(ii) includes the option for teachers to meet the requirements of section 9101 of such Act by meeting the requirements of subparagraph (C) or (D).

(B) Requirements for special education teachers

When used with respect to any public elementary school or secondary school special education teacher teaching in a State, such term means that—

(i) the teacher has obtained full State certification as a special education teacher (including certification obtained through alternative routes to certification), or passed the State special education teacher licensing examination, and holds a license to teach in the State as a special education teacher, except that when used with respect to any teacher teaching in a public charter school, the term means that the teacher meets the requirements set forth in the State's public charter school law;

(ii) the teacher has not had special education certification or licensure requirements waived on an emergency, temporary, or provisional basis; and

(iii) the teacher holds at least a bachelor's degree.

(C) Special education teachers teaching to alternate achievement standards

When used with respect to a special education teacher who teaches core academic subjects exclusively to children who are assessed against alternate achievement standards established under the regulations promulgated under section 1111(b)(1) of the Elementary and

Secondary Education Act of 1965 [20 U.S.C.A. § 6311(b)(1)], such term means the teacher, whether new or not new to the profession, may either—

(i) meet the applicable requirements of section 9101 of such Act for any elementary, middle, or secondary school teacher who is new or not new to the profession; or

(ii) meet the requirements of subparagraph (B) or (C) of section 9101(23) of such Act as applied to an elementary school teacher, or, in the case of instruction above the elementary level, has subject matter knowledge appropriate to the level of instruction being provided, as determined by the State, needed to effectively teach to those standards.

(D) Special education teachers teaching multiple subjects

When used with respect to a special education teacher who teaches 2 or more core academic subjects exclusively to children with disabilities, such term means that the teacher may either—

(i) meet the applicable requirements of section 9101 of the Elementary and Secondary Education Act of 1965 [20 U.S.C.A. § 7801] for any elementary, middle, or secondary school teacher who is new or not new to the profession;

(ii) in the case of a teacher who is not new to the profession, demonstrate competence in all the core academic subjects in which the teacher teaches in the same manner as is required for an elementary, middle, or secondary school teacher who is not new to the profession under section 9101(23)(C)(ii) of such Act [20 U.S.C.A. § 7801(23)(C)(ii)], which may include a single, high objective uniform State standard of evaluation covering multiple subjects; or

(iii) in the case of a new special education teacher who teaches multiple subjects and who is highly qualified in mathematics, language arts, or science, demonstrate competence in the other core academic subjects in which the teacher teaches in the same manner as is required for an elementary, middle, or secondary school teacher under section 9101(23)(C)(ii) of such Act [20 U.S.C.A. § 7801(23)(C)(ii)], which may include a single, high objective uniform State standard of evaluation covering multiple subjects, not later than 2 years after the date of employment.

(E) Rule of construction

Notwithstanding any other individual right of action that a parent or student may maintain under this subchapter, nothing in this section or subchapter shall be construed to create a right of action on behalf of an individual student or class of students for the failure of a particular State educational agency or local educational agency employee to be highly qualified.

(F) Definition for purposes of the ESEA

A teacher who is highly qualified under this paragraph shall be considered highly qualified for purposes of the Elementary and Secondary Education Act of 1965 [20 U.S.C.A. § 6301 et seq.].

(14) Individualized education program; IEP

The term "individualized education program" or "IEP" means a written statement for each child with a disability that is developed, reviewed, and revised in accordance with section 1414(d) of this title.

(23) Parent

The term "parent" means—

(A) a natural, adoptive, or foster parent of a child (unless a foster parent is prohibited by State law from serving as a parent);

(B) a guardian (but not the State if the child is a ward of the State);

(C) an individual acting in the place of a natural or adoptive parent (including a grandparent, stepparent, or other relative) with whom the child lives, or an individual who is legally responsible for the child's welfare; or

(D) except as used in sections 1415(b)(2) of this title and 1439(a)(5) of this title, an individual assigned under either of those sections to be a surrogate parent.

(26) Related services

(A) In general

The term "related services" means transportation, and such developmental, corrective, and other supportive services (including speech-language pathology and audiology services, interpreting services, psychological services, physical and occupational therapy, recreation, including therapeutic recreation, social work services, school nurse services designed to enable a child with a disability to receive a free appropriate public education as described in the individualized education program of the child, counseling services, including rehabilitation counseling, orientation and mobility services, and medical services, except that such medical services shall be for diagnostic and evaluation purposes only) as may be required to assist a child with a disability to benefit from special education, and includes the early identification and assessment of disabling conditions in children.

(B) Exception

The term does not include a medical device that is surgically implanted, or the replacement of such device.

(29) Special education

The term "special education" means specially designed instruction, at no cost to parents, to meet the unique needs of a child with a disability, including—

(A) instruction conducted in the classroom, in the home, in hospitals and institutions, and in other settings; and

(B) instruction in physical education.

(30) Specific learning disability

(A) In general

The term "specific learning disability" means a disorder in 1 or more of the basic psychological processes involved in understanding or in using language, spoken or written, which disorder may manifest itself in the imperfect ability to listen, think, speak, read, write, spell, or do mathematical calculations.

(B) Disorders included

Such term includes such conditions as perceptual disabilities, brain injury, minimal brain dysfunction, dyslexia, and developmental aphasia.

(C) Disorders not included

Such term does not include a learning problem that is primarily the result of visual, hearing, or motor disabilities, of mental retardation, of emotional disturbance, or of environmental, cultural, or economic disadvantage.

Title IX of Education Amendments of 1972

20 U.S.C.A. § 1681

(a) Prohibition against discrimination; exceptions

No person in the United States shall, on the basis of sex, be excluded from participation in, be denied the benefits of, or be subjected to discrimination under any education program or activity receiving Federal financial assistance, except that:

(1) Classes of educational institutions subject to prohibition

in regard to admissions to educational institutions, this section shall apply only to institutions of vocational education, professional education, and graduate higher education, and to public institutions of undergraduate higher education;

(2) Educational institutions commencing planned change in admissions

in regard to admissions to educational institutions, this section shall not apply (A) for one year from June 23, 1972, nor for six years after June 23, 1972, in the case of an educational institution which has begun the process of changing from being an institution which admits only students of one sex to being an institution which admits students of both sexes, but only if it is carrying out a plan for such a change which is approved by the Secretary of Education or (B) for seven years from the date an educational institution begins the process of changing from being an institution which admits only students of only one sex to being an institution which admits students of both sexes, but only if it is carrying out a plan for such a change which is approved by the Secretary of Education, whichever is the later;

(3) Educational institutions of religious organizations with contrary religious tenets

this section shall not apply to an educational institution which is controlled by a religious organization if the application of this subsection would not be consistent with the religious tenets of such organization;

(4) Educational institutions training individuals for military services or merchant marine

this section shall not apply to an educational institution whose primary purpose is the training of individuals for the military services of the United States, or the merchant marine;

(5) Public educational institutions with traditional and continuing admissions policy

in regard to admissions this section shall not apply to any public institution of undergraduate higher education which is an institution that traditionally and continually from its establishment has had a policy of admitting only students of one sex;

(6) Social fraternities or sororities; voluntary youth service organizations

this section shall not apply to membership practices—

(A) of a social fraternity or social sorority which is exempt from taxation under section 501(a) of Title 26, the active membership of which consists primarily of students in attendance at an institution of higher education, or

(B) of the Young Men's Christian Association, Young Women's Christian Association, Girl Scouts, Boy Scouts, Camp Fire Girls, and voluntary youth service organizations which are so exempt, the membership of which has traditionally been limited to persons of one sex and principally to persons of less than nineteen years of age;

(7) Boy or Girl conferences

this section shall not apply to—

(A) any program or activity of the American Legion undertaken in connection with the organization or operation of any Boys State conference, Boys Nation conference, Girls State conference, or Girls Nation conference; or

(B) any program or activity of any secondary school or educational institution specifically for—

(i) the promotion of any Boys State conference, Boys Nation conference, Girls State conference, or Girls Nation conference; or

(ii) the selection of students to attend any such conference;

(8) Father-son or mother-daughter activities at educational institutions

this section shall not preclude father-son or mother-daughter activities at an educational institution, but if such activities are provided for students of one sex, opportunities for reasonably comparable activities shall be provided for students of the other sex; and

(9) Institution of higher education scholarship awards in "beauty" pageants

this section shall not apply with respect to any scholarship or other financial assistance awarded by an institution of higher education to any individual because such individual has received such award in any pageant in which the attainment of such award is based upon a combination of factors related to the personal appearance, poise, and talent of such individual and in which participation is limited to individuals of one sex only, so long as such pageant is in compliance with other nondiscrimination provisions of Federal law.

(b) Preferential or disparate treatment because of imbalance in participation or receipt of Federal benefits; statistical evidence of imbalance

Nothing contained in subsection (a) of this section shall be interpreted to require any educational institution to grant preferential or disparate treatment to the members of one sex on account of an imbalance which may exist with respect to the total number or percentage of persons of that sex participating in or receiving the benefits of any federally supported program or activity, in comparison with the total number or percentage of persons of that sex in any community, State, section, or other area: Provided, That this subsection shall not be construed to prevent the consideration in any hearing or proceeding under this chapter of statistical evidence tending to show that such an imbalance exists with respect to the participation in, or receipt of the benefits of, any such program or activity by the members of one sex.

(c) "Educational institution" defined

For purposes of this chapter an educational institution means any public or private preschool, elementary, or secondary school, or any institution of vocational, professional, or higher education, except that in the case of an educational institution composed of more than one school, college, or department which are administratively separate units, such term means each such school, college, or department.

Equal Access Act

20 U.S.C.A. § 4071

Denial of equal access prohibited

(a) Restriction of limited open forum on basis of religious, political, philosophical, or other speech content prohibited

It shall be unlawful for any public secondary school which receives Federal financial assistance and which has a limited open forum to deny equal access or a fair opportunity to, or discriminate against, any students who wish to conduct a meeting within that limited open forum on the basis of the religious, political, philosophical, or other content of the speech at such meetings.

(b) "Limited open forum" defined

A public secondary school has a limited open forum whenever such school grants an offering to or opportunity for one or more noncurriculum related student groups to meet on school premises during noninstructional time.

(c) Fair opportunity criteria

Schools shall be deemed to offer a fair opportunity to students who wish to conduct a meeting within its limited open forum if such school uniformly provides that—

(1) the meeting is voluntary and student-initiated;

(2) there is no sponsorship of the meeting by the school, the government, or its agents or employees;

(3) employees or agents of the school or government are present at religious meetings only in a nonparticipatory capacity;

(4) the meeting does not materially and substantially interfere with the orderly conduct of educational activities within the school; and

(5) nonschool persons may not direct, conduct, control, or regularly attend activities of student groups.

(d) Construction of subchapter with respect to certain rights

Nothing in this subchapter shall be construed to authorize the United States or any State or political subdivision thereof—

(1) to influence the form or content of any prayer or other religious activity;

(2) to require any person to participate in prayer or other religious activity;

(3) to expend public funds beyond the incidental cost of providing the space for student-initiated meetings;

(4) to compel any school agent or employee to attend a school meeting if the content of the speech at the meeting is contrary to the beliefs of the agent or employee;

(5) to sanction meetings that are otherwise unlawful;

(6) to limit the rights of groups of students which are not of a specified numerical size; or

(7) to abridge the constitutional rights of any person.

(e) Federal financial assistance to schools unaffected

Notwithstanding the availability of any other remedy under the Constitution or the laws of the United States, nothing in this subchapter shall be construed to authorize the United States to deny or withhold Federal financial assistance to any school.

(f) Authority of schools with respect to order, discipline, well-being, and attendance concerns

> Nothing in this subchapter shall be construed to limit the authority of the school, its agents or employees, to maintain order and discipline on school premises, to protect the well-being of students and faculty, and to assure that attendance of students at meetings is voluntary.

No Child Left Behind Act

20 U.S.C.A. § 6301

Strengthening and Improvement of Elementary and Secondary Schools

Subchapter I. Improving The Academic Achievement of the Disadvantaged

Statement of purpose

The purpose of this subchapter is to ensure that all children have a fair, equal, and significant opportunity to obtain a high-quality education and reach, at a minimum, proficiency on challenging state academic achievement standards and state academic assessments. This purpose can be accomplished by

> (1) ensuring that high-quality academic assessments, accountability systems, teacher preparation and training, curriculum, and instructional materials are aligned with challenging State academic standards so that students, teachers, parents, and administrators can measure progress against common expectations for student academic achievement;

> (2) meeting the educational needs of low-achieving children in our Nation's highest-poverty schools, limited English proficient children, migratory children, children with disabilities, Indian children, neglected or delinquent children, and young children in need of reading assistance;

> (3) Closing the achievement gap between high and low-performing children, especially the achievement gaps between minority and nonminority students, and between disadvantaged children and their more advantaged peers;

> (4) holding schools, local educational agencies, and States accountable for improving the academic achievement of all students, and identifying and turning around low-performing schools that have failed to provide a high-quality education to their students, while providing alternatives to students in such schools to enable the students to receive a high-quality education;

> (5) distributing and targeting resources sufficiently to make a difference to local educational agencies and schools where needs are greatest;

> (6) improving and strengthening accountability, teaching, and learning by using State assessment systems designed to ensure that

students are meeting challenging State academic achievement and content standards and increasing achievement overall, but especially for the disadvantaged;

(7) providing greater decisionmaking authority and flexibility to schools and teachers in exchange for greater responsibility for student performance;

(8) providing children an enriched and accelerated educational program, including the use of schoolwide programs or additional services that increase the amount and quality of instructional time;

(9) promoting schoolwide reform and ensuring the access of children to effective, scientifically based instructional strategies and challenging academic content;

(10) significantly elevating the quality of instruction by providing staff in participating schools with substantial opportunities for professional development;

(11) coordinating services under all parts of this title with each other, with other educational services, and, to the extent feasible, with other agencies providing services to youth, children, and families; and

(12) affording parents substantial and meaningful opportunities to participate in the education of their children.

20 U.S.C.A. § 7801

(19) Exemplary teacher

The term "exemplary teacher" means a teacher who—

(A) is a highly qualified teacher such as a master teacher;

(B) has been teaching for at least 5 years in a public or private school or institution of higher education;

(C) is recommended to be an exemplary teacher by administrators and other teachers who are knowledgeable about the individual's performance;

(D) is currently teaching and based in a public school; and

(E) assists other teachers in improving instructional strategies, improves the skills of other teachers, performs teacher mentoring, develops curricula, and offers other professional development.

(23) Highly qualified

The term "highly qualified"—

(A) when used with respect to any public elementary school or secondary school teacher teaching in a State, means that—

(i) the teacher has obtained full State certification as a teacher (including certification obtained through alternative routes to certification) or passed the State teacher licensing examination, and holds a license to teach in such State, except that when used with respect to any teacher teaching in a public charter school, the term means that the teacher meets the requirements set forth in the State's public charter school law; and

(ii) the teacher has not had certification or licensure requirements waived on an emergency, temporary, or provisional basis;

(B) when used with respect to—

(i) an elementary school teacher who is new to the profession, means that the teacher—

(I) holds at least a bachelor's degree; and

(II) has demonstrated, by passing a rigorous State test, subject knowledge and teaching skills in reading, writing, mathematics, and other areas of the basic elementary school curriculum (which may consist of passing a State-required certification or licensing test or tests in reading, writing, mathematics, and other areas of the basic elementary school curriculum); or

(ii) a middle or secondary school teacher who is new to the profession, means that the teacher holds at least a bachelor's degree and has demonstrated a high level of competency in each of the academic subjects in which the teacher teaches by—

(I) passing a rigorous State academic subject test in each of the academic subjects in which the teacher teaches (which may consist of a passing level of performance on a State-required certification or licensing test or tests in each of the academic subjects in which the teacher teaches); or

(II) successful completion, in each of the academic subjects in which the teacher teaches, of an academic major, a graduate degree, coursework equivalent to an undergraduate academic major, or advanced certification or credentialing; and

(C) when used with respect to an elementary, middle, or secondary school teacher who is not new to the profession, means that the teacher holds at least a bachelor's degree and—

(i) has met the applicable standard in clause (i) or (ii) of subparagraph (B), which includes an option for a test; or

(ii) demonstrates competence in all the academic subjects in which the teacher teaches based on a high objective uniform State standard of evaluation that—

(I) is set by the State for both grade appropriate academic subject matter knowledge and teaching skills;

(II) is aligned with challenging State academic content and student academic achievement standards and developed in consultation with core content specialists, teachers, principals, and school administrators;

(III) provides objective, coherent information about the teacher's attainment of core content knowledge in the academic subjects in which a teacher teaches;

(IV) is applied uniformly to all teachers in the same academic subject and the same grade level throughout the State;

(V) takes into consideration, but not be based primarily on, the time the teacher has been teaching in the academic subject;

(VI) is made available to the public upon request; and

(VII) may involve multiple, objective measures of teacher competency.

Age Discrimination in Employment Act

29 U.S.C.A. § 623

Prohibition of age discrimination

(a) Employer practices

It shall be unlawful for an employer—

(1) to fail or refuse to hire or to discharge any individual or otherwise discriminate against any individual with respect to his compensation, terms, conditions, or privileges of employment, because of such individual's age;

(2) to limit, segregate, or classify his employees in any way which would deprive or tend to deprive any individual of employment opportunities or otherwise adversely affect his status as an employee, because of such individual's age; or

(3) to reduce the wage rate of any employee in order to comply with this chapter.

(c) Labor organization practices

It shall be unlawful for a labor organization—

(1) to exclude or to expel from its membership, or otherwise to discriminate against, any individual because of his age;

(2) to limit, segregate, or classify its membership, or to classify or fail or refuse to refer for employment any individual, in any way which would deprive or tend to deprive any individual of employment opportunities, or would limit such employment opportunities or otherwise adversely affect his status as an employee or as an applicant for employment, because of such individual's age;

(3) to cause or attempt to cause an employer to discriminate against an individual in violation of this section.

(f) Lawful practices; age an occupational qualification; other reasonable factors; laws of foreign workplace; seniority system; employee benefit plans; discharge or discipline for good cause

It shall not be unlawful for an employer, employment agency, or labor organization—

(1) to take any action otherwise prohibited under subsections (a), (b), (c), or (e) of this section where age is a bona fide occupational qualification reasonably necessary to the normal operation of the particular business, or where the differentiation is based on reasonable factors other than age, or where such practices involve an employee in a workplace in a foreign country, and compliance with such subsections would cause such employer, or a corporation controlled by such employer, to violate the laws of the country in which such workplace is located;

(2) to take any action otherwise prohibited under subsection (a), (b), (c), or (e) of this section—

> (A) to observe the terms of a bona fide seniority system that is not intended to evade the purposes of this chapter, except that no such seniority system shall require or permit the involuntary retirement of any individual specified by section 631(a) of this title because of the age of such individual; or

> (B) to observe the terms of a bona fide employee benefit plan—

>> (i) where, for each benefit or benefit package, the actual amount of payment made or cost incurred on behalf of an older worker is no less than that made or incurred on behalf of a younger worker, as permissible under section 1625.10, title 29, Code of Federal Regulations (as in effect on June 22, 1989); or

>> (ii) that is a voluntary early retirement incentive plan consistent with the relevant purpose or purposes of this chapter.

>> Notwithstanding clause (i) or (ii) of subparagraph (B), no such employee benefit plan or voluntary early retirement incentive plan shall excuse the failure to hire any individual, and no such employee benefit plan shall require or permit the involuntary retirement of any individual specified by section 631(a) of this title, because of the age of such individual. An employer, employment agency, or labor organization acting under subparagraph (A), or under clause (i) or (ii) of subparagraph (B), shall have the burden of proving that such actions are lawful in any civil enforcement proceeding brought under this chapter; or

(3) to discharge or otherwise discipline an individual for good cause.

Section 504 of the Rehabilitation Act

29 U.S.C.A. § 794(a)

No otherwise qualified individual with a disability in the United States, as defined in section 705(20) of this title, shall, solely by reason of her or his disability, be excluded from the participation in, be denied the benefits of, or be subjected to discrimination under any program or activity receiving Federal financial assistance or under any program or activity conducted by any Executive agency or by the United States Postal Service. The head of each such agency shall promulgate such regulations as may be necessary to carry out the amendments to this section made by the Rehabilitation, Comprehensive Services, and Developmental Disabilities Act of 1978. Copies of any proposed regulation shall be submitted to appropriate authorizing committees of the Congress, and such regulation may take effect no earlier than the thirtieth day after the date on which such regulation is so submitted to such committees.

Section 1981 (Civil Rights Act of 1866)

42 U.S.C.A. § 1981

§ 1981. Equal rights under the law

(a) Statement of equal rights

All persons within the jurisdiction of the United States shall have the same right in every State and Territory to make and enforce contracts, to sue, be parties, give evidence, and to the full and equal benefit of all laws and proceedings for the security of persons and property as is enjoyed by white citizens, and shall be subject to like punishment, pains, penalties, taxes, licenses, and exactions of every kind, and to no other.

(b) "Make and enforce contracts" defined

For purposes of this section, the term "make and enforce contracts" includes the making, performance, modification, and termination of contracts, and the enjoyment of all benefits, privileges, terms, and conditions of the contractual relationship.

(c) Protection against impairment

The rights protected by this section are protected against impairment by nongovernmental discrimination and impairment under color of State law.

Section 1983 (Civil Rights Act of 1871)

42 U.S.C.A. § 1983

Every person who, under color of any statute, ordinance, regulation, custom, or usage, of any State or Territory or the District of Columbia, subjects, or causes to be subjected, any citizen of the United States or other person within the jurisdiction thereof to the deprivation of any rights, privileges, or immunities secured by the Constitution and laws, shall be liable to the party injured in an action at law, suit in equity, or other proper proceeding for redress, except that in any action brought against a judicial officer for an act or omission taken in such officer's judicial capacity, injunctive relief shall not be granted unless a declaratory decree was violated or declaratory relief was unavailable. For the purposes of this section, any Act of Congress applicable exclusively to the District of Columbia shall be considered to be a statute of the District of Columbia.

Title VI of Civil Rights Act of 1964

42 U.S.C.A. § 2000d

No person in the United States shall, on the ground of race, color or national origin, be excluded from participation in, be denied the benefits of, or be subjected to discrimination under any program or activity receiving Federal financial assistance.

Title VII of Civil Rights Act of 1964

42 U.S.C.A. § 2000e–2(a)

(a) Employer practices

It shall be an unlawful employment practice for an employer—

(1) to fail or refuse to hire or to discharge any individual, or otherwise to discriminate against any individual with respect to his compensation, terms, conditions, or privileges of employment, because of such individual's race, color, religion, sex, or national origin; or

(2) to limit, segregate, or classify his employees or applicants for employment in any way which would deprive or tend to deprive any individual of employment opportunities or otherwise adversely affect his status as an employee, because of such individual's race, color, religion, sex, or national origin.

(c) Labor organization practices

It shall be an unlawful employment practice for a labor organization—

(1) to exclude or to expel from its membership, or otherwise to discriminate against, any individual because of his race, color, religion, sex, or national origin;

(2) to limit, segregate, or classify its membership or applicants for membership, or to classify or fail or refuse to refer for employment any individual, in any way which would deprive or tend to deprive any individual of employment opportunities, or would limit such employment opportunities or otherwise adversely affect his status as an employee or as an applicant for employment, because of such individual's race, color, religion, sex, or national origin; or

(3) to cause or attempt to cause an employer to discriminate against an individual in violation of this section.

* * *

(m) Impermissible consideration of race, color, religion, sex, or national origin in employment practices

Except as otherwise provided in this subchapter, an unlawful employment practice is established when the complaining party demonstrates that race, color, religion, sex, or national origin was a motivating factor for any employment practice, even though other factors also motivated the practice.

*

GLOSSARY

Action. A lawsuit.

Ad litem. Literally, for the suit. For the purposes of a particular suit.

Ad valorem. According to value. Refers to a tax imposed on the value of property.

Affidavit. A written statement made under oath.

Agent. One authorized to act in behalf of another.

Amicus curiae. Literally, friend of the court. Refers to a brief submitted by one that is not a party to a suit.

Appellant. Party bringing an action in a higher court.

Appellee. Party against whom an action is brought in a higher court.

Arguendo. Literally, in arguing. For the sake of argument something is assumed to be true.

Assault. A threat or attempt to inflict bodily injury where a victim has reason to believe that an injury may be inflicted.

Battery. Unlawful physical touching.

Bequest. Gift of personal property by a will.

Bona fide. Literally, in good faith.

Case at bar. The case presently being decided by a court.

Caveat. Literally, let one beware; a warning.

Certiorari. Literally, to be informed of. A proceeding in which a higher court reviews a decision of an inferior court.

Class action. A suit brought by one or more persons on behalf of all persons similarly situated as to their complaint and proposed remedy.

Collateral. Indirect; not directly connected to the matter at hand.

Color of law. Acting as if one has the appearance of a legal right.

Complainant. One initiating a suit; a plaintiff.

Consent decree. A judgment that is agreed on by the parties to a suit and approved by a court. Insofar as a consent decree it is not the result of a judicial determination, but is subject to continued judicial supervision, it is of limited precedential value.

Cy pres. Literally, as near as possible. This doctrine can be invoked by a court when the purpose of a charitable trust cannot be fulfilled literally.

Damages. A monetary award to a party which has been injured by the wrongful act of another. Damages are usually compensatory, or legal, as those which are actually demonstrated or reasonably estimated, to redress a wrong and place an injured party in the position that she or he would have been in but for the injury. Equitable damages, as reflected in an injunction or mandamus, direct a party to do, or refrain from doing, a specified act. Under limited circumstances, damages can be punitive or exemplary to punish a wrongdoer and to serve as a deterrent.

Declaratory judgment. A judgment establishing the rights of the parties or deciding a point of law without an order for any action.

De facto. Literally, in fact; in reality.

Defendant. The party against whom an action is brought.

De jure. Literally, by action of law.

De minimi. Literally, concerning something minimal. Something so insignificant as to be unworthy of judicial attention.

Demurrer. Allegation to the effect that, even if facts asserted by plaintiff are true, there is no cause of action.

De novo. Literally, concerning the new thing; a judicial proceeding at which all that transpired at prior proceedings is ignored.

Deposition. Statement of a witness under oath, obtained before trial, in oral question and answer format with cross-examination as if it were offered in court.

Devise. Gift of real estate by a will.

Dicta, short for obiter dictum. Literally, a remark by the way. A gratuitous statement in a judicial opinion that is not necessary to a cases's resolution. Dicta is persuasive precedent.

Directory. Involving no invalidating consequence if disregarded.

Dolens volans. Literally, whether willing or unwilling.

Duress. Unlawful pressure to do what one ordinarily would not do.

En banc. Literally, in the bench. A judgment by all of the judges of a court.

Enjoin. To direct a party to maintain the status quo either by doing or refraining from doing a specific act; the writ is called an injunction.

Equity. Concept of fairness or justice whereby a court is empowered to remedy a situation where rights are being violated but existing law does not cover the situation.

Estoppel. A bar precluding one from making an assertion because of a prior act.

Et alia, et al. Literally, and others.

Et sequitur, et seq. Literally, and those following.

Executory. Not completed; dependent on the occurrence of a future act.

Ex officio. Literally, by authority of the office.

Ex parte. Literally, on one side. A proceeding at which only one party appears.

Express. Directly set forth in words.

Expunge. Obliterate; physically remove, as from a record.

Ex relations, ex rel. Literally, out of the elation. A proceeding initiated, typically by the state, on behalf of one who provides the information.

Face. What the words alone mean, without amplification or specific application; usually expressed as "on its face."

Guilty. Legally responsible in a criminal matter.

Holding. A court's ruling or decision on a question at bar.

Infra. Literally, below; following.

Injunction. See "enjoin."

In loco parentis. Literally, in place of the parent; having some of the rights and duties of a parent.

Instant case. The case presently before a court.

Inter alia. Literally, among other things.

Interrogatory. A written examination before trial, usually in question and answer format.

Ipso facto. Literally, in and of itself.

Judgment. Final determination by a court.

Laches. Unreasonable delay in bringing a legal action to assert a right and which may result in prejudice to party.

Liable. Legally responsible in a civil matter.

Libel. Written defamation.

Malfeasance. Acting with an unlawful or evil intent.

Malice. Improper motive; intentionally committing a wrongful act without justification or excuse.

Mandamus. Literally, we command. A judicial writ directing a public official to execute a non-discretionary duty.

Material. Important.

Merits. The factual issues raised, as distinguished from procedural issues; the substance of a case rather than procedural matters.

Ministerial. Not involving discretion as to whether or how an act is to be performed; this is an administrative, rather than a policy-making, function.

Misfeasance. Improperly committing a lawful act.

Mitigation. Diminution of a penalty imposed by law, as with damages for breach of contract which are reduced in amount by circumstances not barring a cause of action but only affecting the extent of an injury.

Modus operandi. Literally, method of operating.

Moot case. No longer a live case or controversy; a case in which a judgment would be abstract with no practical effect.

Nexus. Connection.

Nonfeasance. Failing to perform a duty.

Novation. Substitution of a new obligation for an old one.

Nunc pro tunc. Literally, now for then. Acts permitted to be done after the time that they should have been done and given retroactive effect.

Opinion. Reasoning that explains a court's judgment. The opinion of the court is the reasoning accepted by a majority of participating judges; it authoritatively enunciates the law of a case. Views of individual judges who agree with the court's judgment, but not its full rationale, may appear in concurring opinions; views of judges who disagree are in dissenting opinions.

Parens patriae. Literally, parent of the country. Concept of the state's guardianship over persons, such as minors, who are unable to direct their own affairs.

Pari materia. Literally, of the same matter.

Parol Evidence. Verbal evidence.

Pendent jurisdiction. Doctrine whereby federal courts under limited conditions can decide matters of state law as well as federal matters involved in a single suit.

Per curiam. Literally, by the court; an opinion with no identification of the author.

Per se. Literally, in and of itself.

Petitioner. Party bringing a case before a court; the appellant in an appellate case.

Plaintiff. The party instituting a legal action.

Plenary. Full power or authority.

Police power. The inherent power of government to impose restrictions in order to provide for health, safety, and welfare of its constituents.

Prayer. A request for relief.

Preempt. Take control of; preclude actions by others.

Prima facie. Literally, on the first appearance, on its face; evidence supporting a conclusion unless it is rebutted.

Pro forma. Literally, as a matter of form; not carefully considered.

Pro Se. Literally, for the self, a suit wherein one acts as one's own attorney.

Quantum meruit. Literally, as much as its deserved; reasonable value of goods furnished or services rendered.

Quasi. Literally, as if; almost.

Quid pro quo. Literally, this for that; something done in exchange for an act of another.

Quo warranto. Literally, by what authority; a writ to test a claim to a public office.

Ratio decidendi. Literally, the reason for a decision; the opposite of dicta, it sets forth a court's rational

Reductio ad absurdum. Literally, reduction to the absurd. An interpretation which would lead to results clearly illogical or not intended.

Remand. To send a case back to the court from which it was appealed for further action by the lower court.

Res judicata. Literally, a thing decided; the final outcome in a case.

Respondent. Party against whom a legal action is brought; the appellee in an appellate case.

Reverter. A provision whereby one who transfers property retains the right to reclaim the property under specific conditions.

Scienter. Literally, knowingly. Knowledge of a set of facts.

Slander. Oral defamation.

Stare decisis. Literally, to abide by. The doctrine of precedents whereby prior judicial decisions are followed under similar facts.

Status quo. Literally, state in which. The positions and relationships existing at a particular point in time.

Sua sponte. Literally, of one's own will. Voluntarily; without necessity or prompting.

Sub judice. Literally, under or before a judge or court. A matter being considered by a court.

Summary. Immediate; without a full proceeding.

Supra. Literally, above; preceding.

Tort. A civil wrong not involving contracts.

Ultra vires. Literally, beyond the powers. Outside the legal power of an individual or body.

Vacate. To annul.

Vel non. Literally, or not.

Vested. Fixed; accrued; not subject to any contingency.

Void. Having no legal force or effect.

Waiver. Voluntary and intentional relinquishment of a known right.

*

INDEX

References are to Pages.

†